# CITIZEN EMPEROR

*Napoleon: The Path to Power, 1769–1799*

*Talleyrand*

*Theatres of Violence: Massacre, Mass Killing and
Atrocity throughout History* (co-editor)

*Napoleon and his Empire: Europe 1804–1814* (co-editor)

*The French Revolution and Napoleon: A Sourcebook* (co-editor)

*Napoleon and Europe* (editor)

*Modern Prussian History, 1830–1947* (editor)

*The Rise of Prussia, 1700–1830* (editor)

# CITIZEN EMPEROR

## NAPOLEON IN POWER

PHILIP DWYER

Yale UNIVERSITY PRESS   NEW HAVEN & LONDON

Published with assistance from the Annie Burr Lewis Fund.

First published 2013 in the United States by Yale University Press and in Great Britain by
Bloomsbury Publishing Plc.

Yale University Press books may be purchased in quantity for educational, business, or
promotional use. For information, please e-mail sales.press@yale.edu (U.S. office) or
sales@yaleup.co.uk (U.K. office).

Maps by ML Design.
Typeset by Hewer Text UK Ltd, Edinburgh.
Printed in the United States of America.

Library of Congress Control Number: 2013950572
ISBN 978-0-300-16243-1 (hardcover: alk. paper)

A catalogue record for this book is available from the British Library.

This paper meets the requirements of ANSI/NISO Z39.48-1992 (Permanence of Paper).

10 9 8 7 6 5 4 3 2 1

For my mother,
Pat Dwyer

Victory is a Goddess greedy for death; her laurel is a branch dripping blood and soaked in tears.

Maurice de Tascher, *Notes de Campagne*

# CONTENTS

# CONQUEST, 1805–1807

# CRUCIBLE, 1808–1811

## THE ADVENTURER, 1813–1814

# REGENERATION, 1799–1802

# I

# The Invention of a Saviour

## 'Neither Excitement nor Enthusiasm'

It was still dark, the early hours of the morning of 11 November 1799. Bonaparte's carriage stopped before a modest house in the rue de la Victoire where Josephine was waiting for him in bed in a state of nervous anxiety. They stayed up talking for a while, going over the events of the previous day. He learnt that his mother and one of his sisters, Pauline, had come to the house. They had been at the theatre when they heard the rumour that Bonaparte had just escaped an assassination attempt.[1] Pauline apparently had been unable to stop crying until news arrived that all was well. The strain the conspirators must have suffered over the last two days would have been enormous. Bonaparte appears to have taken it in his stride, with the exception of that little incident that had taken place amid the Council of Five Hundred at Saint-Cloud when the epithet 'Outlaw' was hurled at him by a number of deputies, furious to see a soldier enter the chamber where they were deliberating. He had nearly fainted. A little later that morning, when Bonaparte dismissed his secretary Bourrienne, he supposedly said as an aside, 'By the way, we will sleep tomorrow at the Luxembourg [Palace].'[2]

Bonaparte was just thirty years old. He still cut a relatively svelte figure although over the years he would become portly, if not obese. His dark-brown hair was beginning to recede. He had a scar on his leg where an English bayonet had once pierced him. His skin was sallow, and his eyes grey. He was five feet six inches tall with a slight build. He did not have any children, but he would eventually sire four or five, only one of them legitimate, and none of them with his first wife Josephine. By any standards, his had been a meteoric rise. Less than three years before, he had been a nonentity on the political and military scene. Now he was one of the major political contenders, and in time would become one of the most recognized men in European history, with a hat and a pose – that is, his right hand in his vest or his hands folded behind his back – that would become iconic.[3] No one yet knew, however, what he was truly capable of.

Newspaper accounts of the previous evening's events had already appeared by the time Bonaparte awoke after a few hours' sleep. It was 20 Brumaire in the Year VIII (11 November 1799), a *décadi*, a rest day in the revolutionary calendar. At the Château de Saint-Cloud on the western outskirts of Paris, where the coup unfolded in the night of 10–11 November, the conspirators had formed a new provisional government – dubbed the Consulate because headed by three consuls, Emmanuel Joseph Sieyès, Roger Ducos and Bonaparte. The trip from Josephine's house in the rue de la Victoire to the Luxembourg Palace, where Bonaparte was to meet with the other two provisional consuls, was a short one. On his way, he would have seen people going about their daily business, taking a stroll on what turned out to be a mild, rainy day, gazing at the troops that had been positioned at strategic points throughout the city. Some stopped to read the proclamations posted on the walls of Paris explaining what had taken place, possibly relieved to discover that Bonaparte had escaped an assassination attempt against him, smiling perhaps at the story of the defenestration of the Five Hundred. The minister of police, Joseph Fouché, was doing his best to spread that one around the cafés and the theatres.

From a reading of the official explanations, plus the accounts given in some of the newspapers, it would have been apparent even to the most heedless observer that the coup had been Bonaparte's, or that he was at least the central figure, and that therefore he was now nominally holding the reins of government. That is why reaction to the coup varied according to what one thought of Bonaparte, or conversely according to how much one detested the ousted regime that had been in power since the fall of Robespierre, the Directory. In Paris, Christine Reinhard talked of how the people were jubilant, and of how, even a week later, the enthusiasm for the new regime had not waned – 'you would think that we had returned to the first days of liberty'.[4] Given that her husband was minister for foreign affairs, she may have portrayed things in a somewhat rosier light than they actually were. Paris, by other accounts, appears to have been relatively indifferent. A curious police report stated that the coup was met with 'neither excitement nor enthusiasm' (*ni l'exaltation ni l'enthousiasme*).[5] This was portrayed as a positive thing. 'It is at the bottom of people's hearts that this contentment resides.'

Paris was not France, and for the moment nothing was certain. The Brumairians, as the conspirators were called (named after the month of Brumaire in the revolutionary calendar, the month in which the coup took place), did not know how the rest of the country was going to react, and that included the army.[6] More than sixty generals had been involved in the coup,[7] but the troops belonged to the garrison of Paris, were personally loyal to Bonaparte and had been well prepared in advance. It was normal that they should publish a declaration of support in the newspaper the *Moniteur universel*, but reactions within the rest of the army were far from uniform.[8] General André Masséna, for example, at the head of about 35,000 demoralized troops in Italy, wrote that opinion was generally not favourable, while some divisions and a number of officers were openly opposed to it.[9] Officers in the Army of the North (based in Holland) expressed some reservations, as did the commanding general of Marseilles.[10] One cannot assume that because Bonaparte was a renowned general the army was completely swayed by him. On the contrary, the army was home to enough oppositional elements to make it a potentially dangerous institution.[11] Eventually, the officer corps was purged, but that would come later.[12]

The reactions in the administration were mixed too. A number of local authorities took the initiative and sent messages of adherence to the new authorities – this was the case in the north and east of the country, that is, those areas under direct threat from invasion[13] – but at Toulouse there was talk of a Jacobin uprising. At Grenoble the National Guard refused to swear an oath of loyalty to the new regime. At Metz the commander of the town had to establish order by force and impose martial law in several surrounding areas. In 1789, the revolutionaries had divided France into eighty-nine departments. One week after the coup, the regime could count on the adhesion of only thirteen departments. The departmental administration of the Jura, for example, characterized Bonaparte as a 'usurping tyrant'.[14]

This is why, ten days after the coup, the consuls decided to send one delegate to each military division (there were twenty-six in all), to carry the 'good news' and to nip in the bud any signs of resistance to the changeover. The delegates, all officers, had far-reaching powers to suspend or replace public functionaries, to close political clubs and to post proclamations. Three weeks later, however, twenty departments had still not sent in congratulations. Even then, the letters received did little more than mirror the propaganda the new regime had already sent to the provinces. It has to be said, though, that most officials in the departments appear to have welcomed the coup, happier to be rid of the Directory than to see Bonaparte's arrival on the political scene. Few were downright hostile.[15] Even those individuals who had opposed the coup eventually had to face the political reality and come round to the new regime.[16]

In view of the rapid turnover of political personalities since 1789, many people did not expect the new regime to last very long. In the last ten years, there had been five governments – the National Assembly (1789), the National Constituent Assembly (1789–91), the Legislative Assembly (1791–2), the National Convention (1792–5) and the Directory (1795–9) – and the country had swung from absolute monarchy to a republic when the king, Louis XVI, was executed in 1793. After that, the Revolution lurched to the left as increasingly radical factions vied for power, culminating in the ascendancy within the Convention of a group known as the Jacobins and the formation of an executive, the Committee of Public Safety, dominated by one of the leading members of the Jacobins, Maximilien Robespierre.[17] During the reign of the Convention, more than 16,000 people were guillotined, another 25,000 were summarily executed by one means or another, and hundreds of thousands died as a result of a bloody civil war. This was the Terror, which was brought to an end only when Robespierre was over-thrown in 1794, meeting the same fate as his victims. The Directory that ruled France from 1795 to 1799 did a reasonably good job in the face of war and civil unrest, but was characterized by corruption, scandal, an egregious flouting of the electoral system, and a parliamentary coup.

For Bonaparte and his collaborators, the best way to overcome the impres-sion that his government was transitory, one more in a long line of governments, was to make sure he was seen to act, quickly and decisively. Three days after the coup, Bonaparte made a dramatic gesture towards political reconciliation by repealing the Law of Hostages. The Law, passed in June 1799, was consid-ered to be one of the most odious edicts promulgated by the Directory and called for local authorities to round up people who were then held as political hostages. It was a means of keeping rebellious regions quiet.[18] Bonaparte personally went to the Temple Prison in Paris to release the hostages, and from there went on to other prisons, demanding the list of inmates, reportedly saying: 'It was an unjust law that deprived you of your freedom and it was my first duty to restore liberty to you.'[19]

It was a media coup; the police reports noted how much of a favourable impact it had had on the public.[20] Bonaparte's personal involvement in the release of prisoners had nothing to do with his humanity. It was also telling of the kind of regime now in place, and the kind of man heading it. The ration-alization of the Penal Code in 1791 had completely eliminated the possibility of a head of state interfering in the legal process to grant pardons; it was consid-ered a remnant of the *ancien régime*, at odds with the Revolution's notion of equality of all before the law. Bonaparte, however (though probably inadvert-ently), was reclaiming the right to patrimonial justice, to the historic prerogative of the executive pardon, years before it was institutionalized in the imperial Constitution. In short, he was already acting if not quite yet as a monarch, then as though everything already devolved from his person.

A series of conciliatory measures designed to help heal the social and polit-ical rifts affecting France followed this dramatic first gesture, many of them directed towards royalists: Bonaparte freed refractory priests who had been detained on the islands of Ré and Oléron off the Atlantic coast; he began talks with the rebels in the Vendée and concluded a truce; in Calais, he freed émigré prisoners who were about to be executed; the very day the new Constitution was adopted (25 December), the law against émigrés was repealed, and those deported after the coup of Fructidor (September 1797) were allowed to return; more than 50,000 émigrés were removed from the list of the proscribed (a general amnesty followed in 1802); Sunday mass was restored; the oath of loyalty that priests had been required to take was done away with; a ceremony was held in honour of Pope Pius VI, who had died at Valence in August 1799;

and the festival of 21 January, the anniversary of Louis XVI's execution – which the revolutionaries dubbed 'the festival of the just punishment of the last king of the French'[21] – was abolished, as was the oath of hatred for royalty. A decision was made to keep only two national feast days as state celebrations: the festival of 14 July and the commemoration of 10 August 1792, the days on which the monarchy was overthrown and the Republic was founded. No other revolutionary government had dared offer such generous conciliatory gestures, obviously calculated, but which nevertheless marked the determination of Bonaparte to bring civil strife to an end.

Like most government bodies, however, the left hand did not necessarily know what the right was doing. Much of the moral capital Bonaparte won through these acts of clemency was almost squandered by Joseph Fouché's repressive machinery that went into action in the days after the coup. On 12 November, as a result of the first meeting between the provisional consuls and probably on the insistence of Sieyès, a mandate was issued for the arrest of about seventy former terrorists, Jacobins and various notorious Parisian *sans-culottes*. It may have been a reflex action based on precedent.[22] Fouché was ordered to draw up a list of suspects that was, deliberately it seems, incoherent. Among the names one could find the hideous drunkard Gabriel Mamin who, in 1792, had bragged about having killed the Princess de Lamballe during the September Massacres and of having ripped out her heart. But one could also find the victor of the battle of Fleurus in June 1794, General Jean-Baptiste Jourdan, as well as a number of deputies who had made themselves conspicuous at Saint-Cloud by their hostility towards Bonaparte. They were joined by deputies who had not even been at Saint-Cloud but who were nevertheless suspected of being hostile to the regime. Thirty-seven individuals were deported to Guiana (commonly referred to as the dry guillotine, because death was slow but certain to come), while twenty-two others were confined to the islands of Ré and Oléron where survival rates were as low as in Guiana. All the newspapers, with the exception of the royalist press, protested against measures that were obviously meant to eliminate what was left of the Jacobin faction.[23] The outcry, not least from people who had supported the coup, made the provisional consuls realize they had made a mistake. They could not play at being above factions, law-abiding and non-violent if they immediately struck at the Jacobins.

Two weeks later, Bonaparte rescinded the deportation decree on the grounds that 'The [Jacobin] faction that would have wished to form a state within the state no longer exists . . . To conserve public tranquillity, we no longer need to do anything but maintain a strict surveillance over those same individuals.'[24] Bonaparte made sure that Sieyès was blamed for the mistake, distancing himself politically from any perceived wrongdoing, weakening his rival in the process.[25] This kind of measure enabled the Brumairians to differentiate their coup from all those that had preceded them (previous coups had always ended in arrests, executions and deportations). Nevertheless, a warning shot had been fired across the bow of Jacobin dissidents.[26]

### 'Despair of Relying on Yourselves and Rely Only on Me'

The problems facing the new regime were enormous: civil war raged in the west, brigandage, which could entail anything from highway robbery to assaults on towns by armed bands, was rife in many areas of France[27] – some historians speak of a banditry psychosis[28] – the treasury was empty, and the threat of an allied coalition, the second against France, loomed large. The coalition had formed while Bonaparte was in Egypt and consisted largely of Austria and Russia with British backing. By the end of 1799, it had succeeded in clawing back all the territory Bonaparte had won in northern Italy in 1796–7. The new rulers would have to work hard to win the support of a disillusioned public that had lost faith in both politicians and the democratic process. The Brumairians, therefore, not only had to make sure the army was either onside or neutralized, but they also had to convince the local administrations throughout the country to continue their work. Most importantly of all, however, they had to convince the public that the change in regime was warranted and for the good of France. Their success in all of this was by no means an easy or an assured thing. It was a gradual and uneven process that was to prove much more difficult than the actual seizure of power.

Bonaparte emerged during this process as the undisputed head of the French state. Given his character, his ascendancy might appear a foregone conclusion, but in the days and weeks after Brumaire that was by no means the case. The coup had enabled him to become involved in the decision-making process at the highest levels, but the guiding light behind the coup had been and still was Emmanuel Joseph Sieyès. Like the regime's gradual consolidation of power, Bonaparte's domination of the executive took place slowly, and has to be understood from two different perspectives. The first was bureaucratic. In this process, as we shall see, Bonaparte was able to outmanoeuvre his opponents strategically and, with the support of a number of key figures among the Brumairians, focus power on his person.

The second was political, was much more subtle and went hand in hand with the regime's consolidation of power. It consisted of giving the country an overarching narrative the French could believe in. The narrative too was centred on Bonaparte's person. At the end of their first meeting at the Luxembourg Palace, the provisional consuls adopted a proclamation to the French people that perpetuated the myth of the Directorial government about to collapse into general chaos and the arrival of a new government that was to bring everything back to order.[29] A few days later, Bonaparte declared in the

*Moniteur*, 'I refused to be the man of one faction.'[30] He thus portrayed himself as outside the circle of conspirators; they had come to him as a man above the political infighting, a theme Bonaparte had exploited ever since his days in Italy in 1796–7 and which he would constantly hammer home over the coming weeks and months. The formula used to express this – 'neither red bonnets nor red heels' (*ni bonnet rouge, ni talon rouge*)[31] – epitomized the Brumairians' desire to be done once and for all with the bloody power struggles that had characterized the Revolution. At the time, this approach was referred to as the 'fusion between different parties'.[32] Bonaparte was thus portrayed as the man who could restore order after chaos.[33]

This was smart politics, although it was not the first time a revolutionary government had attempted to steer a middle course between royalism and Jacobinism. It had been the approach adopted after the fall of Robespierre, but

Anonymous, *La France avant le 18 Brumaire de l'an VIII* (France before 18 Brumaire in the Year VIII), 1800. The caption reads: 'Grieving, destitute of everything, driven by despair and discord, France is revived by hope and delivered by Bonaparte into the hands of peace. Time traces that happy day into the annals of history.'

the then government failed to find a balance. The Brumairians represented too narrow a base upon which to construct a new regime and therefore had to appeal to wider sections of French society. Bonaparte was able to do this because he was prepared to work with anybody, no matter what their past, as long as they were willing to support the regime, a radical departure from previous revolutionary governments.[34] In the process, he weakened the Jacobin and royalist factions from whence these people came.[35] In reality, there were very few regicides and few declared royalists among Bonaparte's collaborators, but one should not dismiss his willingness to work with all-comers as political opportunism. Behind the rhetoric was a real desire to carry out social and political reforms that would heal the rifts brought about by the Revolution, and to attract to him men whose political opinions had a short time before made them enemies of the state.[36]

It is clear what Bonaparte was doing in the weeks after Brumaire, and he appears to have been fully aware of it at the time. He was sending a message – the new regime was different. It was prepared to go a long way to heal the rifts, but at the same time it would no longer tolerate political extremes. In doing so, Bonaparte was saying to the French political elite, 'despair of relying on yourselves and rely only on me'.[37] There were to be no more factions, Jacobins, terrorists or moderates. There were only Frenchmen.[38] Bonaparte's political programme was outlined in a newspaper article, which he probably wrote himself, and which appeared in the *Ami des Lois* on 6 December 1799. Relying on 'liberal ideas', he intended embellishing the Republic, fixing mistakes, relying on political and religious tolerance and overlooking past insults.[39]

'Do You Want to be King?'

Sieyès was aware that by bringing Bonaparte into the conspiracy he risked losing control. It had been a risk he was prepared to run. The struggle for supremacy had begun almost as soon as the two men met, and could end only with one being victorious and the other eliminated as a political force.[40] Over the coming weeks, power became centred on Bonaparte who, by the strength of his character, gained ground little by little. In the course of the meeting in the Luxembourg Palace between the three provisional consuls the morning after the coup, Bonaparte managed to get himself nominated as president of the provisional Consulate. We do not know exactly how this happened; only much later did Napoleon claim he simply took over the presidency, but one cannot place too much store in that assertion.[41] Accounts have the third provisional consul, Roger Ducos, who had been Sieyès' man up to this point, recognize Bonaparte's ascendancy by declaring, 'General, it is pointless voting on the presidency, it belongs to you by right.'[42] Sieyès apparently made a grimace but was obliged to concede. In an astute move, however, Bonaparte suggested that each preside for twenty-four hours at a time under the title of 'Consul of the day' (*Consul du jour*).[43] Since Bonaparte was first in alphabetical order, his name appeared before the other two consuls on the orders issued that day.

Whatever happened, in the struggle between Sieyès and Bonaparte for preeminence Bonaparte won the first round. Rotating the presidency was a feint that signalled his determination to be seen as humble, as someone upon whom power had been thrust, as a reluctant leader who assumed the mantle of office only because of the grave dangers confronting France.[44] Besides, there were a number of advantages in being president that first day. His signature appeared foremost on the proclamations issued that very evening, giving the impression that he was in charge. More importantly, he presided over the meeting that decided on the new ministers.[45] Despite the image one may have of a Bonaparte presiding alone over the reforming period that was the Consulate, he was in fact surrounded by talented men without whom neither the nature nor the extent of his reforms would have been as impressive.

The most pressing issue was a new constitution. When the conspirators had become involved in the coup, many believed Sieyès already had one in his pocket. Antoine Boulay de la Meurthe, another prominent Brumairian, claimed that when he approached Sieyès the morning after the coup and said to him, 'I have reason to believe, and it is the general opinion, that you have a constitution all ready,' Sieyès replied, 'I have a few ideas in my mind, but nothing is written, and I have neither the time nor the patience to write one.'[46] As the self-flaunted expert on constitutions he was nevertheless expected to produce one. Sieyès set to work over the coming days, dictating his ideas to Boulay de la Meurthe.[47] In one of his drafts, there was a Senate, a Tribunate and a Legislative Corps, as well as two consuls, one for domestic and one for foreign affairs, over which a Grand Elector would preside, a pet idea that he had been harbouring since 1795. The Grand Elector, a position earmarked for Bonaparte, was meant to oversee the executive branch but without real power; he would intervene only if a conflict arose within the executive. When Bonaparte was presented with this plan in what proved to be a stormy meeting on 1 December, he turned to Sieyès and said, 'Have I heard you correctly? Are you proposing a position where I will name those who are given something to do, while I am allowed to do nothing?'[48] For practical as well as personal reasons, Bonaparte rejected the whole idea, calling the Grand Elector 'a pig fattened by a few millions', a reference to the wealth the Elector was meant to avail himself of as representative of the nation.[49] Sieyès is supposed to have shot back at Bonaparte, 'Do you want to be king, then?'[50] The quip was more prescient than Sieyès could ever have imagined.

'Blood will Flow Up to your Knees'

Bonaparte naturally wanted a strong executive. Sieyès was very wary of giving him one. We can pass over the turgid details of their struggle around the Constitution,[51] except to say that the meetings that took place over this two-week period were a learning process for Bonaparte in which he observed and studied those about him. On balance, he was in a world with which he was not familiar and in which he was still ill at ease. He was pitting himself against men more politically experienced and more articulate than he.

We have a number of different but not incompatible accounts of Bonaparte's behaviour during this period. According to one, when people resisted his idea of a strong executive, he got angry, stamped his feet and even accused the legislators of wanting to start a civil war. 'Blood will flow up to your knees!' he is supposed to have said.[52] This sort of bullying tactic was in keeping with Bonaparte's character, although he was for the moment restrained, especially in comparison with later years. When he did lose his temper, however, he would almost immediately manage to control himself and become more conciliatory.[53] Another depiction has him listening at meetings without saying much, expressing his frustration and boredom either by vandalizing the arm of his chair with a pocketknife or doodling on pieces of paper that he would scrunch up and throw away.[54] Another portrayal has him wearing down Sieyès and his faction by drawing things out. What Bonaparte could not win through force of argument and logic, he won through physical stamina. After several nights' discussion, the fifty commissioners who had been assembled to debate the Constitution would succumb to tiredness in the face of a young, determined and indefatigable Bonaparte.

These discussions culminated in a meeting on 12 December in Bonaparte's apartments at the Luxembourg Palace, during which the final draft was read out and adopted. Many of the principles embodied in Sieyès' draft Constitution were approved. The Constitution of the Year VIII, as it was called, divided the French legislature into three bodies – the Tribunate (100 members), the Legislative Corps (300 members) and the Senate (80 members), to be housed in the Luxembourg Palace. There were no elections; deputies were simply appointed from the existing Council of Five Hundred and Council of Elders. There was a conscious effort to take the people out of the political process so that the 'ignorant classes' could no longer exercise any influence.[55] The Tribunate was meant to be a forum in which bills, referred to it by a Council of State (an advisory body that more or less filled the same role as the Royal Council), were discussed but not voted on. It was the task of the Legislative Corps to vote on the bills, but without discussion. The Senate acted as a kind of Supreme Court and nominated the members of the two lower houses, a third force, controlling the other two legislative bodies.[56] Anyone familiar with Roman history could see the parallels, and certainly some did not believe Bonaparte would be content for long with the role of consul.[57]

That same day, the election of the executive took place. Three new consuls were to reign for a period of ten years, but one would have more power than the other two. The story goes that a large urn was placed on a table and slips of paper were given to each of the fifty commissioners who wrote down the names of their choice. During the vote, Bonaparte leant against a fireplace for warmth. The counting was just about to begin when Bonaparte approached the table, turned towards Sieyès and said: 'Instead of counting them, let us give a new testimony of gratitude to Citizen Sieyès by giving him the right to designate the three first public officers of the Republic, and agree that those he designates would have been the same as those we have just nominated.'[58]

It was an incredible development. Bonaparte probably did not fear the surprises a secret ballot may have hidden. The public expected him to become First Consul, and nothing suggests that the commissioners would have voted otherwise.[59] Possibly a number of commissioners had intended, as a form of protest, to direct their votes for Third Consul to a liberal by the name of Pierre Daunou. Bonaparte, on the other hand, wanted a show of unanimity and offered Sieyès the semblance of political primacy by allowing him to nominate the three consuls. Sieyès consequently declared that Bonaparte should be First Consul, and that Jean-Jacques Régis de Cambacérès and Charles-François Lebrun, both Bonaparte's choices, should be Second and Third.[60] Bonaparte had consulted widely that day about the choice of Second and Third Consuls and had settled on these two men, the first a revolutionary who had voted for the death of the king and the second a representative of the *ancien régime*.[61] At eleven o'clock that evening, he tossed the unopened voting slips into the fireplace.[62]

The choice of the other two consuls falls within Bonaparte's desire to appear above factions. The most important was the forty-seven-year-old minister of justice, Cambacérès, a small man who stammered and made 'singular' movements of his head when talking,[63] a charismatic lawyer with a revolutionary past who can be seen with his chin jutting out bearing the hand of justice in Jacques-Louis David's later painting of Napoleon's coronation as emperor. He was, however, one of those loyal bureaucrats upon whom the Empire would later be founded, widely respected for his competence and hard work, and for his knowledge of judicial matters. As a member of the National Convention, he had voted for the execution of Louis XVI in 1793 and was, consequently, one of the rare regicides to occupy high office in the Consulate, eventually becoming arch-chancellor and the second most important person in the Empire. The appointment of someone with such a strong revolutionary past was a concession to the republicans, but Bonaparte also considered him a 'consummate businessman' full of experience and moderation.[64] Cambacérès, greatly neglected by history, was going to play a considerable role in consolidating Bonaparte's hold on power.[65]

The choice of the Third Consul was a little more difficult. After talking to a number of people, Bonaparte decided on the sixty-year-old Lebrun, a specialist in finance whose reputation predated the Revolution. As a member of the Estates General in 1789, he had been a constitutional monarchist. What Cambacérès was to the republicans, Lebrun was to the royalists. 'A grand and noble old man' was how one contemporary described him, with 'abundant thick white hair artistically curled, a pale, uniform complexion, a long face, obstinate, eyes sunken and covered, a false expression'.[66] Like Cambacérès, he was an efficient bureaucrat, discreet and honest, who played an important role in the financial recovery of France under the Consulate.

### A Regime of 'Servitude and Silence'

Two weeks later, on Christmas Eve, the provisional consuls held their last meeting, and the three new consuls were officially recognized. The situation had radically changed for Bonaparte over the last month. As First Consul, he now had extensive powers. He could propose laws, direct finances and undertake the necessary measures to protect the state if it were threatened, and he was in charge of foreign affairs and the army. No deliberation with the other two consuls was necessary. He could name and dismiss his ministers, something which he took advantage of immediately.

He made his brother Lucien minister of the interior, a reward for playing a key role during the coup. Lazare Carnot, dubbed the Organizer of Victory during the early years of the revolutionary wars, was named minister of war. Charles-Maurice de Talleyrand, apostate bishop, nicknamed the *diable boiteux* ('lame devil') because of a clubfoot, and the man most responsible for the nationalization of Church lands during the Revolution, was put in charge of foreign affairs, a post he had held during the Directory. The other ministers were maintained in office, but entirely subordinated to the will of the First Consul, something Lucien would learn painfully over the coming months. If Bonaparte was the military genius, Lucien saw himself as the civilian genius. The problem was, however, that while not without talent and a certain charm he had an inflated sense of self-importance and lacked a consistency in his views and his approach that quickly made him a liability to his brother.

Almost immediately the legislature had been formed, a clash of wills occurred between Bonaparte and a clique within the Tribunate, alarmed at the amount of power he had managed to acquire.[67] The first session of the Tribunate, held at the Palais Royal on 1 January 1800, is interesting for what it tells us about the men who had been chosen to fill the positions. The Palais Royal had once belonged to Louis XVI's cousin, the Duc d'Orléans, and had been a site of political agitation in the early days of the Revolution, the place from which the

crowds marched on the Bastille. In those surroundings, a deputy by the name
of Honoré Duveyrier evoked the memory of the revolutionary journalist and
politician Camille Desmoulins, warning Bonaparte that 'If people talk of a
fifteen-day idol, we should not forget that we have overthrown idols that have
lasted fifteen centuries [a reference to the Bourbon monarchy].'[68] Similarly, a
few days later, the first bill presented to the legislature regulating the procedures by which laws were to be passed created alarm among some of the
deputies. The deputy, thinker and writer Benjamin Constant, for example,
who already had a reputation for liberal ideas, was worried by the time limits
that had been set the Tribunate to discuss laws and declared, 'Without the
independence of the Tribunate, there will be no harmony, no constitution,
there will be nothing but servitude and silence; a silence that the whole of
Europe will hear and judge.'[69]

This kind of criticism found little echo either within the legislature or
among the public. On the contrary, the day after Constant's speech, a number
of tribunes rose to defend the structure of the legislature. The rest of the country, carried on the swell of mounting popular support for Bonaparte, appeared
outraged by the opposition. There was a social and political movement, characterized by an anti-democratic current, in favour of a strong executive. After
all, Brumaire had been a conservative coup made up of politicians who were
sympathetic to the idea.[70] This includes the members of the Senate, where a
much more vigorous voice in opposition could have developed, perhaps even
an independent power capable of standing up to Bonaparte. As we shall see,
however, the Senate was to become complicit in the personalization of Bonaparte's power.

A normal politician would have been content with majority support in the
Tribunate and the press, but not Bonaparte. He had none of the skills traditionally associated with modern political leaders – parliamentary manoeuvring,
a talent for oratory, a willingness to work behind the scenes – and was less than
patient with the minority opposition. In the context of war abroad, and the
social and political divisions brought about by the Revolution, there was no
tolerance for politicians who did not rally. Bonaparte counter-attacked. Newspapers favourable to the government were used to print articles condemning
the chambers and went so far as to suggest that the troublemakers be dismissed.[71]

Not all the newspapers, however, were in favour of either Bonaparte or the
new regime. On the contrary. That problem was easily solved. Two months
after Brumaire, on 17 January 1800, a decree was published that suppressed
sixty of the seventy-three Paris newspapers.[72] The motive given – some of
them were 'instruments in the hands of the enemies of the Republic'[73] – was
not an exaggeration; forty of the suppressed newspapers passed for royalist,
but the republican press was also eliminated, with the exception of the

*Moniteur universel*, which became the official organ of the state. Over the next few months, a further three newspapers disappeared. Between 1800 and 1804, two more papers would be silenced. By the end of 1811, only four newspapers would be left in Paris with a run of around 34,000 copies, their content strictly controlled. In the provinces, the number would be reduced to one newspaper per department, a measure that led to the creation of a good number of news-papers in departments that did not have them.[74]

The suppression of newspapers in France was little short of spectacular, another kind of coup, except that instead of getting rid of the journalists, the regime got rid of the newspapers they wrote for.[75] The press was to present a uniform façade so that anything that might contradict the image propagated by the authorities, such as resistance to conscription and news of suicides, was eliminated from its columns. It is easy to interpret this attack on the press as an attack on freedom of speech, but it elicited little or no public protest, which leads one to suggest that either the public was indifferent or it approved of the measure. In part, this was a return to the system employed by *ancien régime* governments to control the press and public opinion. The monarchy had a monopoly over political news, and newspapers had to pay to get access to it. Moreover, there was never more than one newspaper in each major town. But the desire to restrict press freedom was also a reaction to the excesses experi-enced during the Revolution when anything and everything had been permitted, from the incitement to massacre in 1792 to rabid populist newspa-pers such as *L'Ami du peuple* (The Friend of the People) and *Le Père Duchesne* (The Father Duchesne), in which sentences were punctuated with the word *foutre* (an approximation of the English word 'fuck').[76] This freedom, moder-ates believed, had been in part responsible for the radicalization of the Revolution and had enabled factions to flourish. That is the reason why the press suffered a number of restrictions after the fall of Robespierre when forty-odd newspapers were banned.[77] Total freedom of the press was again introduced after the fall of Robespierre, but within a short time the Directory found itself assailed by an orgy of invective from neo-Jacobin as well as royalist newspa-pers. Bonaparte's decision to shut down so many newspapers was about controlling the flow of information, but it was also about national reconcilia-tion as touted by the Brumairians. Journalists, contemporaries believed, had usurped the role of the elected authorities, had sustained the factionalism that had riven French society and had become inimical to 'public order'.[78]

Newspapers then did not serve the same purpose as we have come to expect of the press today. Eighteenth-century French newspapers were outlets of particular political viewpoints.[79] The press as an instrument of radical politics, something contemporaries were all too familiar with from the Revolution, inspired fear and was therefore considered dangerous.[80] Bonaparte was unwill-ing to see a repeat of the revolutionary years and believed that freedom of the press would lead to a proliferation of both Jacobin and royalist views.[81] The Consulate was above all about restoring order. To do that, the control of the press was considered essential to put an end to the political upheavals that had plagued France.

Press censorship in Napoleonic France was less harsh than in the three absolutist eastern European powers – Austria, Prussia and Russia – although by no means as liberal as in Britain. True, there was now far more censorship than there had been in pre-revolutionary France, but Bonaparte's measures were the continuation of a trend; censorship had become increasingly more rigorous in France towards the end of the century, and he had inherited from the Directory censorship laws empowering the police to suppress newspapers. However, despite what some historians have asserted, the press under Napoleon was not entirely docile.[82] Between 1800 and 1804, Bonaparte used the tensions between different newspapers to his advantage.[83] An opposition journalism existed and persisted throughout the Consulate and into the Empire.[84] Debate was certainly restricted, and authors might have been unable to find a publisher for their work when they touched on issues the government preferred to avoid, but opposition pamphlets and songs continued to circulate in Paris.[85]

### The Vessel of State Arrives in Port

With the government in place, Bonaparte and his conspirators now had to convince the French people they were legitimate, and in the process come up with some sort of programme. This was slowly formulated over the coming weeks and months, but in the initial stages a number of texts were produced that vaguely define the political concepts with which Bonaparte (and his colleagues) wanted to be associated. The first is a proclamation to the French people announcing the Consular regime on 15 December 1799 – order, justice, stability, force and above all moderation were some of the key words emphasized in the text, in which it was clearly stated that 'the Revolution is fixed on the principles with which it began. It is finished.'[86] That word 'Consular' was meant to assure the political elite, well versed in ancient history, that the Republic would continue and would be consolidated vaguely following a Roman model.[87]

Everything that emanated from Paris from that time on deliberately promoted the image of a unifying government. At the same time, the regime disseminated an image of a Directorial France left in ruin, its roads and ports in a poor state, law and order a shambles, and public confidence in the institutions of government destroyed. One pamphlet that caused quite a stir when it appeared was written by the editor of one of Bonaparte's Italian newspapers, Marc-Antoine Jullien (although published anonymously). It took the form of a dialogue between two people identified as 'A' and 'B', the latter immediately recognized as Bonaparte. Jullien lays the groundwork by lamenting the deplorable state of affairs in France before Bonaparte came on the scene:

> There was no national representation, no government, no constitution. Our conquests lost, our laurels tarnished, peace impossible except on dishonourable terms, our armies destroyed, the French name reviled by both enemies and allies, the republic fallen into the utmost debasement and misery, the aims of the revolution miscarried, the fruits of our labours, sacrifices and victories annihilated, the dregs of faction agitating and disputing with foreigners over the shreds of our country – that is what struck the observer.[88]

And that is only the beginning of a long list of complaints, many of them either false or grossly exaggerated, perpetuated in the press of the day.[89] The point was to show just how bad things were so that Bonaparte looked as though he had dragged France from the edge of the abyss. It is a theme commonly found in some paintings, often using allegories, depicting Brumaire in the months and years after the coup.

In Antoine-François Callet's *Tableau allégorique du 18 Brumaire* (Allegorical painting of 18 Brumaire), for example, the forces of light drive away the forces of darkness.[90] At the bottom of the painting, one can see a boat that is meant to be, according to the description in the catalogue of the Salon for that year, 'the vessel of State' arriving in port. This was a reference to the plebiscite of February 1800, which legitimated Brumaire (see below). On board the vessel one can see a number of the best-known pieces of art pillaged from Italy – the Horses of St Mark, the *Laocoön*, the *Apollo of Belvedere*, the *Transfiguration* by Raphael – next to which are piles of enemy flags. France is represented by a woman holding an olive branch and supported by fifteen *Renommées* (figures of Renown) that represent the armies of the Republic. Especially prominent is a figure in Egyptian headdress standing in for the Army of Egypt (which Bonaparte had commanded in 1798–9). One art historian has suggested that these two combined figures represent Bonaparte. It is possible; peace and the army are together, so to speak. One should not forget that on the eve of Brumaire – an allusion to which can be seen in the sign of Sagittarius depicted in the sky – Bonaparte declared, 'I alone am the representative of the people.' In other words, Bonaparte and the people are one, and the government, embodied in the Hercules-like figure in the foreground holding a *fasces* – representing the departments of France – resting on a rock, is below France/Bonaparte. Beneath the foot of Hercules/the government are the enemies of peace and order, including a leopard symbolizing Great Britain. The people and democracy are thus portrayed in an inferior position to Bonaparte.[91]

Antoine-François Callet, *Tableau allégorique du 18 Brumaire an VIII ou La France sauvée* (Allegorical painting of 18 Brumaire year VIII or France is saved), 1800. The painting was executed in the weeks following Brumaire, and then presented in a larger format at the Salon of 1801.

Given the effort the new regime put into convincing people that France had been on the brink of collapse, it is hardly surprising that it became the dominant interpretation. 'Those who have not lived through the epoch of which I speak', wrote the Duc de Broglie many years later of the period before Brumaire, 'can form no idea of the profound misery into which France fell. We were plunging back under full sail into the abyss of the Terror without a gleam of consolation or hope.'[92] People came to assume that Bonaparte alone had pulled France out of the morass into which the Revolution and especially the Directory had plunged the country.

'The End of our Suffering'
Article 95 of the new Constitution indicated that a plebiscite would take place, in keeping with the practice adopted by the revolutionaries in 1793 and again in 1795. Bonaparte insisted on implementing the measure, against the advice of Sieyès, and justified his decision by citing the pre-revolutionary philosopher

Rousseau: any law that was not ratified by the people was null and void. The plebiscite was a genuine attempt to consult the people, but it was also a political strategy to cut the ground from under the feet of the opposition.[93]

Any male over the age of twenty-five could vote. The polling took place from the end of December 1799 to the end of January 1800. It was the first time since the beginning of the Revolution that individuals had been able to vote directly, without having to go through primary and secondary assemblies.[94] Every man could register his vote in writing, and if he chose to do so explain his reasons, followed by a signature. The procedure was meant to avoid fraud, but it was designed to put pressure on citizens to vote for the regime. It took a certain amount of courage to vote no. The registers were to be burnt after the votes had been counted, but fortunately for historians they were kept. Some of the comments that people made in voting, limited in number it is true, are revealing of what people thought of the new regime, the Constitution and Bonaparte. In Paris, for example, one voter wrote, 'I can at last see the end of our suffering.' He considered the new Constitution to be a 'social act' that would inevitably lead to the 'happiness of France'.[95] In the Aube, on the other hand, some thought they were voting not for Bonaparte but simply for a new constitution.[96] In the Var, another voter accepted the new Constitution on the grounds that it would be the 'grave of factions' and that it would lead to 'order, peace, and respect for people and property'. It is evident that peace, and the desire to put the Revolution to bed once and for all, were the overwhelming preoccupations expressed by those sympathetic towards the coup.

The results were not as good as the regime either expected or publicly asserted. Many thought Brumaire was just another political upheaval brought about by the same people responsible for past upheavals. The presence of Bonaparte did not change that view.[97] Given the short time in which it was organized, however, the lack of information that circulated and the unusually cold weather for that time of year, the plebiscite was still a resounding success for the regime. True, only about 25 to 30 per cent of the electorate turned out, or about 1.5 million real 'yes' votes.[98] That was not unusual, nor was the result dishonourable. In the previous ten years, the turnout had ranged from 60 per cent during the heady days of the first election of the Revolution (1789 and 1790), to between less than 10 and 30 per cent, depending on the department, for the election to the Legislative Assembly (1791), and between 4 and 27 per cent for the election to the Convention (1792). As for the previous two plebiscites (1793 and 1795), their rate of participation was, respectively, around 50 per cent (1.8 million votes), and between 14 and 17 per cent (1 million votes).[99]

The voting numbers were, therefore, consistent with the low participation rate of the electorate, and consistent with the general indifference to national politics that had resulted from war, economic upheaval and religious persecution. But that was not good enough for Lucien Bonaparte, who 'corrected' the results by systematically exaggerating the figures, and by counting the army – 500,000 votes – as a whole.[100] We simply do not know the extent to which Bonaparte was involved, or if not, whether he was aware of the manipulation. By presenting the results of the plebiscite as an overwhelming endorsement of the coup, the country's new political rulers were legitimized.


Repression and Reconciliation

The Brumairians, however, did not wait for the results to enforce the Constitution and assert their power. One of the most important and difficult problems facing the Consulate, and therefore high on Bonaparte's agenda, was the civil war in the west of France, a conflict that had raged since 1793 and had cost hundreds of thousands of lives. The rebels, variously described as Chouans or Vendéens, often with royalist or counter-revolutionary leanings, were relatively well organized and received wide support among the local populations. It was necessary, for the sake of the future stability of the government, as well as for Bonaparte's image as the man above factions, to bring the civil war to a speedy conclusion. There were two ways Bonaparte went about this. The first was by meeting counter-revolutionary and royalist leaders. On 26 December 1799, for example, he met the Chouan leader Baron Hyde de Neuville.[101] He was accompanied by the commandant of the Vendéens in the region of Angers, Fortuné d'Andigné. In the course of the interview, Bonaparte is supposed to have urged them to rally to his banner: 'my government will be the government of youth and talent'. At the same time, and with a smile on his lips, he threatened to exterminate all who did not come over to him.[102]

Two days after that meeting, Bonaparte issued a 'Letter to the inhabitants of the departments of the west' in which he promised a pardon to rebels willing to repent, as well as undertaking, as we have seen, a number of measures that would help appease opponents of the regime.[103] This was followed, however, by a second proclamation: anyone taken with arms in hand, or found inciting rebellion, would be summarily executed.[104] This was no idle threat. The violent and often brutal repression against rebels practised by the revolutionary governments was continued under the new Consular regime.[105]

To drive the point home, examples were made of a number of individuals. The first was a young man by the name of Henri de Toustain, in Paris to visit his brother in the Temple by virtue of the armistice. He was nevertheless arrested, dragged before a military commission and, despite no evidence being brought to bear against him other than a few white cockades (symbols of the Bourbons) found in his hotel room, condemned to death. He was shot on the Plaine de Grenelle on 25 January 1800. On another occasion, Bonaparte promised the Chouan leader Louis de Frotté a personal amnesty, but when Frotté gave himself up he was summarily executed without so much as a trial.[106] The news was announced to the Legislative Corps by a member of the Council of State and fellow conspirator, Pierre-Louis Roederer, who in a melodramatic gesture also presented the deputies with the counter-revolutionary items that had been taken with the capture of Frotté's general staff: crosses of St Louis, fleurs de lys and the daggers emblematic of every eighteenth-century conspirator.[107] Bonaparte liked to set examples – 'Every day we shoot here five or six Chouans,' he wrote to General Brune, the commander of the Army of the West[108] – and was capable of doing so at the expense of human life. After years of political upheaval and social unrest, the French appeared to be far less interested in the preservation of 'liberty' than in a return to law and order.[109] The restrictions on the press meant that the repression was not widely reported, but there was a great deal of local support for these repressive measures.

If the politics of reconciliation was sometimes little more than rhetoric, the repression of unrest in France, whether counter-revolutionary or plain criminal, was ruthless. Bonaparte ordered General Brune to clean up the Vendée, and to 'let the rebels of Morbihan begin to feel the whole weight and the horrors of war'.[110] Brune's tactics were brutal. On 25 January, republican troops took control of Pont-du-Loch, killed 500–600 rebels and were then unleashed on the surrounding villages.[111] It was enough to decide an already flagging, dispirited resistance to abandon the royalist cause, for the moment, and begin to surrender. Bonaparte specified in a letter to one of his generals fighting in the west that any rebels caught should be 'exterminated'.[112] It was a word he had used before.[113] Those under his command knew what was expected of them. Any town or village that harboured brigands would be burnt and reduced to cinders.[114] Suspects were arrested, interrogated (that is, tortured) and secretly imprisoned, not only in the west of France, but in any region that resisted the centralizing, modernizing impulse from revolutionary Paris.

The violence in the west of France was by far the worst, but in at least ten other departments brigandage and assassinations (political or otherwise) continued through the months of March and April 1800, with varying degrees of intensity. In the south-east of France, for example, Catholic and royalist brigands were particularly active between 1796 and 1802, bringing the region to the verge of anarchy.[115] The response from the Consular regime was to use repressive tactics similar to those that had been used by other revolutionary governments. Seven flying columns were formed – four in the Midi, three in Brittany – made up of gendarmes, National Guard and regular troops, attached to which were military commissions, whose task it was to arrest, try and execute any brigands caught.[116] Thousands were arrested, and hundreds were executed by firing squad.

In Brittany, between September 1800 and February 1801, in the first six months of their existence the military commissions tried more than 1,200 people, a third of whom were condemned to death, mostly for criminal offences like armed robbery.[117] Another 150 were killed while 'resisting arrest'. The trials and executions were widely publicized and often occurred on powerful local sites of memory, places where counter-revolutionaries had committed atrocities. The regime was making a point. Violence against the state and its citizens would no longer be tolerated. While the number of executions between 1800 and 1802 was around 2,300, it is an exaggeration to assert that Bonaparte unleashed a veritable 'Consular Terror'.[118] By comparison, at the height of the Terror in 1793, some 1,900 people were executed in Lyons for participating in a revolt against Paris.[119] The repression of 'banditry' under Bonaparte was harsh, but entirely in keeping with *ancien régime* notions of the rule of order.

One cannot underestimate the success of this mixture of repression and reconciliation in consolidating the new regime.[120] Bonaparte succeeded where other revolutionary governments did not because he deployed larger numbers of regular troops to quash resistance, and he consistently used an apparatus of repression (flying columns, military commissions and the regular imposition of a state of siege on hundreds of towns and villages). The royalist cause was going to be weakened even further when Bonaparte concluded peace with Britain in 1802. By then, his policies had started to pay off; counter-revolution and banditry in the departments where they had once been rife were under control. The politics of reconciliation coupled with extraordinarily brutal measures was a winning combination that brought the regime acceptance and, more importantly, followers. Bonaparte knew how to take the credit for all these successes.

# 2

# 'Perfect Glory and Solid Peace'

## The Seat of Power

The day after the results of the plebiscite were announced (19 February 1800), Bonaparte vacated the Luxembourg for the Tuileries Palace, redubbed the Palace of the Government (*Palais du gouvernement*). The transfer of the executive to the palace of a former king, a king executed by the 'nation', was the occasion for the first large-scale public manifestation of the new regime.[1] One police report referred exaggeratedly to the 'rejoicing' (*allégresse*) of the people and the acclamations from the crowds lining the streets to watch the procession.[2] The repossession of the former royal palace was supposed to respect republican forms. There was nothing remarkable about the procession of carriages that drove that day through the streets of Paris from the Luxembourg to the Tuileries: the servants were dressed in hand-me-downs from the Directory, and there was as yet no return of powdered hair or livery.[3] And yet the procession took on the appearance of a royal entry.[4] Cavalry headed the procession, followed by the Council of State in carriages that looked a little worse for wear, as did the horses drawing them. Then fifty musicians preceded the general staff of Paris, followed by ministers in various carriages, the guides brought over from Egypt, transformed into the Chasseurs de la garde, the aides-de-camp and, finally, the carriage with the three consuls, drawn by six white horses, a gift from the Holy Roman Emperor. The procession closed with the horse guard.[5]

The procession, whose pomp was muted, was something entirely new, and was all about a display of power to the public and the world. It was also in stark contrast to the way in which European monarchs generally behaved in the eighteenth century. Most other European sovereigns would not have dared be so brazen in their display of power. The Holy Roman Emperor, Francis II, for example, preferred 'domestic obscurity', and went about in a carriage drawn by two not six horses, and no guards.[6] Remarkable too was the mixture of representatives of both the civilian administration and the military. The military were present not just as an escort to the civilian authorities, and not just as an integral part of the parade. They were placed at the head of the procession, signifying that they were now the premier corps in the state.[7] It was also a subtle reminder to the army that Bonaparte was in command and that it was to serve him, as well as a reminder to the public that he was master of the army.

'The crowds had not gathered in any magnificence along the route,' wrote one observer, 'but there were enough people there. A few were surprised that the move was such a great affair; it is certain that that little representation was a test of [public] opinion.'[8] Cries of 'Vive Bonaparte!' and 'Vive la République!' could be heard in the crowd – during the Consulate it was not uncommon for the two to be paired together[9] – but the procession also drove past a barrier made of wood upon which an inscription was mounted that read, 'Royalty has been abolished in France, and it will never return.'[10] That remained to be seen, but the procession allowed the crowd to identify with the new government, as well as with the army.

The Tuileries Palace no longer exists; fire gutted it during the civil war in 1870 and it was later razed. One can imagine where the palace once was, though, between the wings of the Louvre, the garden of the Tuileries on one side and the courtyard presently containing the glass pyramids on the other. The kings of France had resided there, if only rarely, since the seventeenth century, so the palace was important to the people of Paris.[11] Taking possession of the former domicile of the kings of France was marking a change in regime, underlining

Edouard Baldus, *Le Louvre et les Tuileries vus de la cour Napoléon* (The Louvre and the Tuileries seen from the Napoleon Courtyard), c. 1860. This photograph was taken before the fire of 1870 from the so-called Napoleon Courtyard, where today the glass pyramids are to be found. The work on the courtyard had only just been completed; the trees were newly planted. The triumphal arch of the Carrousel, built between 1806 and 1808 to commemorate Napoleon's victories, is still in its original place. The troop reviews (about which more below) took place between the iron grille, barely discernible in the background and behind the arch, and the palace.

Bonaparte's power. As a former royal residence, it had more than just symbolic significance. 'The idea that prevailed over him [Bonaparte]', wrote Cambacérès, 'was to give the government the character of seniority [*ancienneté*] that it lacked.' He would have liked to make disappear all the governments that had existed since 1792, so that Consular power appeared to be the heir of the monarchy.[12]

Once Bonaparte had taken over the reins of power, he was conscious of the need to introduce an element of continuity, even if it was only symbolic, between his regime and those of the past. The Tuileries was a symbol not only of the monarchy, but also of the state. The fact that the other two consuls, Cambacérès and Lebrun, did not move to the Tuileries – they chose as their residences, respectively, the Hôtel d'Elbeuf and the Hôtel de Flore (abandoned in 1802 for the Hôtel de Noailles) – meant also that Bonaparte was from that moment on the only consul at the centre of power. The Tuileries was where Bonaparte received the ministers, as well as foreign visitors and foreign ambassadors, many of whom were struck by his febrile activity. It reinforced the distinction between the First Consul and the other two, and lent a certain regal character to Bonaparte and the regime.

Two days after Bonaparte had moved into the Tuileries, France was given a new, highly centralized administrative structure known as the prefectural system, part of a reorganization wanted by Bonaparte, but which Lucien as minister of the interior largely carried out. In charge of each department was a prefect. Power emanated from the centre, that is, Bonaparte, and was to reach down the line to prefects, sub-prefects and the local mayor.[13] Bonaparte was not yet in a position personally to name the ninety-eight prefects who had to be found to govern each department. For the moment, he relied on his close advisers for suggestions. Nor was the reform without controversy; some in the Tribunate believed that a form of tyranny – people were already using the word in connection with Bonaparte – was being introduced.

In those first weeks in power, Bonaparte made a number of important symbolic gestures. He had dug up the 'trees of liberty' that had been planted in the courtyard of the Tuileries during the Revolution, on the pretext that they were creating too much shade. Similarly, he had the Phrygian bonnets that had been painted on the walls of the palace removed, although he made sure that some connection with the revolutionary past was maintained. The façade of the Tuileries, damaged by cannon shot when it was stormed by the mob on 10 August 1792, was restored, but the words 'tenth August' were painted around the indentations made by the shot.[14] Then, almost as soon as Bonaparte had moved into the Tuileries, a new form of etiquette was introduced, leading to a formalization of the relations of power, tentative at first but increasingly complex as the Consulate evolved.[15] Finally, Bonaparte instituted a ceremonial review of troops in the courtyard of the palace. Sometimes on foot, sometimes

on horseback, he went through the ranks stopping to talk with both officers
and rank and file.

The review became a regular feature of life at the Tuileries when Bonaparte was in Paris, and would be held every ten or twenty days, after which
the officers would be invited to a banquet. Bonaparte fell into the habit of
reviewing the troops whenever he thought necessary, even when on campaign.
This was no vain parade, but an occasion for him to reveal to the people of
Paris his army, the source of his glory, 'and to exert on all the souls of that
empire, an irresistible ascendancy of power, of force, of genius, and of fortune
joined together in one man'. [16] Troops were encouraged to shout 'Vive Bonaparte!' In the process, the First Consul strengthened the bonds between
himself and his men, reinforcing the image of Bonaparte (and later Napoleon) as father figure.[17]

These reviews or parades could be gruelling exercises that sometimes went
on for seven or eight hours.[18] However, by listening to and addressing the
men's complaints, by appearing to care about the welfare of his troops, by
coming into contact with them, questioning and joking with his men – Bonaparte still allowed a degree of familiarity – remembering them from previous
campaigns (often with a little help from his aides) and asking about their families, he deliberately cultivated a closer relationship with his troops than any
other contemporary head of state. Anecdotes about Bonaparte's friendliness
with his troops became the stuff of legend. Memoirs, letters and journals are
replete with examples of individual soldiers' encounters with him, sometimes
in formalized settings such as the reviews, sometimes as he walked through
campsites while on campaign, repeated in publications such as newspapers and
pamphlets.[19]

The parades were also political theatre, providing a dazzling display of
Bonaparte's position as both military and political leader.[20] All his public
appearances were strictly choreographed and announced well in advance to
give those who wanted to see him the chance to take up positions where
they could. The windows of the apartments of the palace that commanded a
view of the courtyard would be occupied hours beforehand.[21] At the same
time, Bonaparte was creating a cult of honour in which individuals would
publicly receive recognition for their valour on behalf of the nation.[22] In
turn, the nation was meant to be proud of what it had achieved, while any
foreigners present were intended to respect and fear what it was capable of.
The presence of military uniforms on the streets of Paris was noted by visitors to the capital in later years, as were the monthly parades. This did not
always give the impression it was meant to. For English tourists like
Abraham Raimbach, hardly sympathetic to the First Consul or the French,
the 'universal appearance' of the military at every public occasion was the
visible sign of 'an oppressive power'.[23]

### The Search for Peace

Military parades might appear incongruous for a man who made a point of portraying himself as the 'hero of peace', but this kind of public performance was as much about consolidating Bonaparte's power and authority, of legitimating it, as it was about underlining the role of the military in the new regime. Bonaparte's image was undergoing a transformation in the first years of his rule.[24] We see a merging of all the different images that had till now been used in the press – the victorious general, the man of science, the orientalist, the hero – into one, that of Bonaparte as General of Peace.

The first inkling came with a spectacular propaganda coup. On Christmas Day 1799, Bonaparte wrote to the crowned heads of England and Austria expressing his wish for a prompt reconciliation.[25] The letters marked a rupture with the aggressive behaviour of the Directory. Although historians have speculated that the offer was never serious – Bonaparte needed to consolidate his position at home by a resounding military victory against the Austrians[26] – evidence suggests that he would have accepted at least a truce before launching a war with Austria.[27]

Bonaparte was a conundrum to the British, a character who had come to their attention through his conquests of Italy and Egypt where the 'poisoning incident'* was to colour British views of him for the rest of his life.[28] With the coup, the British were unsure what to expect, and unsure where to place Bonaparte on the French political spectrum. Was he another rabid Jacobin, an 'ambitious Corsican',[29] or someone bent on founding his own dynasty? A debate about Bonaparte even took place in parliament.[30] British views of him were, it would appear, hopelessly muddled.[31] Only much later, after the resumption of war in 1803, did the British government launch an anti-Bonaparte propaganda campaign.[32]

George III did not reply to Bonaparte's letter. Indeed, it was unusual, although not wholly inadmissible, for Bonaparte to have bypassed the prime minister to address the king personally, and could therefore be considered a violation of normal diplomatic procedure.[33] If done out of ignorance, it demonstrated a lack of familiarity with British procedure; the cabinet and not the king discussed and decided questions of foreign policy. Since Bonaparte apparently took this step against the advice of Talleyrand,[34] we can surmise that he knew what he was doing, and that it was therefore deliberately calculated, a theatrical gesture that would make him look good in the eyes of the French public. This does not mean that Bonaparte was insincere – some diplomatic back-channels were used, to no avail, to get negotiations going *before* the public letter to the king[35] – but rather that he thought Britain would remain intractable.

---

* On the retreat from St John of Acre in 1799, Bonaparte had ordered lethal doses of opium to be administered to troops in Jaffa dying of the plague.

Anonymous, *The Corsican Crocodile dissolving the Council of Frogs*, 1799. A popular British caricature of Bonaparte's coup. Metamorphosed into a crocodile, having come straight from Egypt, he is holding in each hand a deputy-frog. Two elements of the black legend are already present: Bonaparte wearing a crown and therefore as usurper of legitimate power; and as a monster devouring his own people. Bonaparte, and later Napoleon, became the first major European figure in the history of satire.

Prime Minister William Pitt decided there should be no official answer, and indeed led a personal attack against the First Consul in the Commons on 3 February 1800, condemning Bonaparte, the French Revolution and the Republic.[36] He insisted that Britain could make peace with France only if the Bourbon monarchy were restored. He was, under the circumstances, a little short-sighted; the British cabinet had placed far too much faith in their allies and had grossly underestimated Bonaparte's position. The British foreign secretary, Lord Grenville, one of many Britons convinced that France was still Jacobin, wrote to Talleyrand (and not Bonaparte) to say that if France truly wished peace, it had to recall its legitimate dynasty forthwith.[37]

The reply from the Austrian minister of foreign affairs, Johann Amadeus Baron von Thugut, was a little less haughty but no less discouraging.[38] In fact, Britain and Austria made the same mistake as in 1792 and 1793, when they went to war against France under the misguided impression that the country was far weaker than it really was. Admittedly, Austria, like Britain, was speaking from a position of strength – it dominated most of northern Italy at this stage, having won back Bonaparte's hard-fought gains from his first campaign – and wanted to negotiate on that basis. Bonaparte, on the other hand, wanted to negotiate on the basis of the Treaty of Campo Formio of 1797.[39] He was effectively asking Austria to give up all its gains in northern Italy and to hand them back to the French. This was a less than sincere offer on the part of Bonaparte, one that Austria naturally rejected. The traditional explanation for Austria's behaviour – that it had territorial ambitions in Italy which only a successful war could bring about – is valid, but the real reason was Austria's desire to remain a great power.[40]

One could hardly blame the European powers for not warmly embracing Bonaparte's peace overtures. He was a relatively unknown factor, and doubts about the regime's stability and viability predominated in the courts of Europe. In view of the rapid turnover of political personalities in France since 1789, it would have been rash to make any predictions about the durability of the new regime; many people did not expect Bonaparte to last very long. In February 1800, for example, the royalist Hyde de Neuville was told by one of his collaborators that Bonaparte's fall was both imminent and certain.[41]

Most historians have assumed that in writing these letters to the kings of Britain and Austria Bonaparte was looking for a propaganda coup, that it was an attempt to portray himself as the champion of peace rather than earnestly looking for a settlement through negotiations. There is an element of this; even he later admitted that he needed the war, that the Republic would have been 'lost' without it, and that it was necessary to continue the momentum sparked by Brumaire in order to end the Revolution.[42] Bonaparte's true intentions are revealed in a proclamation to the army issued the same day he sent his peace overtures. He stated that now it was a question not of defending the borders of France, but of invading the states of the enemy. When the time came, he promised, he would be among his troops.[43] The same day too he sent a letter to the minister of war, Louis-Alexandre Berthier, advising him that he intended to form what he dubbed the 'Army of Reserve', made up of recruits and troops freed up after the cessation of hostilities in the west of France as well as units from the Rhine.[44] Officially, the army was placed under the command of Berthier; the new Constitution forbade a consul from taking command of any army. Bonaparte got around this by serving in the coming campaign in an unofficial, advisory capacity.

Given the attitude of the European courts towards France and the fact that, militarily speaking, Bonaparte was on the back foot, a negotiated settlement was highly unlikely at this stage. A military solution was the only option left to him in 1800. To prepare public opinion for the coming campaign, the French press published the British (and Austrian) rebuffs thereby bolstering

Bonaparte's position, underlining the extent to which his desire for peace had been sincere. In the face of the rejection of peace, his preparations for war were justified.[45] The stratagem worked; the peace initiative made the First Consul popular not only inside France but in much of Europe, while the replies received from London and Vienna made those powers appear to be bent on continuing the war.[46] Soon after the rebuff from Britain, a proclamation was issued to the people of France in which Bonaparte clearly blamed England for the continuation of the war and promised them peace through victory.[47] According to the police reports, the public was worried about the resumption of fighting.[48] The hope for peace was still very much alive, as it had been throughout the final years of the Directory.

## Preparations for War

Bonaparte had a number of armies at his disposal: in Holland there was General Charles-Pierre Augereau at the head of 20,000 men whose job was to prevent an eventual English invasion of that coast; in Germany General Jean-Victor Moreau commanded 100,000 men; in Switzerland, General Etienne-Jacques Macdonald was in charge of 14,000 men; then in Italy, where the French position was precarious to say the least, there was an army around 40,000 strong under the orders of General Masséna. The formation of the Army of Reserve was meant to bring another 56,000–60,000 men into campaign. By the end of 1799, almost all of Italy had been evacuated by the French while Russian and Austrian troops had occupied Milan. Masséna held on in the last French stronghold in Italy, Genoa, in what was to become one of the most horrific sieges of the revolutionary period; more than 30,000 people died there of starvation and disease.[49]

The problems facing Bonaparte were formidable. The French army was not in very good shape in 1800. Reports from the Army of the Rhine asserted that 'The soldier is naked . . . most corps have not been paid in six, eight, ten *décadis*' (that is, for sixty, eighty, one hundred days), and that the troops were 'neither armed, nor clothed; their needs are enormous'. In Switzerland, the troops lived from hand to mouth.[50] Not only did the army suffer from considerable material shortages, but many of the officers, it was claimed, were 'apathetic'; the non-commissioned officers were even worse. 'The majority is ignorant, pretentious and slack,' noted a report from the inspector general.[51] Reorganization was badly needed, and that is what Bonaparte embarked upon. He now had complete control over the direction of the army and could thus reform it and co-ordinate the coming campaign as he saw fit.

Possibly the most significant reform was the adoption of the *corps d'armée* (army corps of anywhere between 20,000 and 30,000 men, and 5,000 cavalry) at the beginning of March 1800. These were units with integrated cavalry and

artillery, allowing them to manoeuvre independently of each other until it was
time to unite a number of corps in battle. The army corps was a system Bonaparte inherited rather than introduced, but he nevertheless systematically
formalized it.[52] He also continued the practice of having his armies live off the
countryside, something that had been adopted during the revolutionary wars
in response to the enormous logistical problems in supplying hundreds of
thousands of volunteers. In addition, the conscription system was streamlined,
although it was a number of years before it was perfected.[53]

On 25 January, the order came for the Army of Reserve to gather at Dijon,
halfway between the Rhine and Italy.[54] In this way, Bonaparte hoped to keep
the Austrians guessing about the army's final destination, since from there it
could strike anywhere between Mainz in Germany and Genoa in Italy. He
does not yet appear to have made up his mind about where the main theatre of
operations would be, although everything points to Germany.[55] That made
sense. As Moreau, commander of the Army of the Rhine, aptly pointed out in
a letter to the First Consul, it was much easier to march on Munich than on
Verona, and Austria was much more likely to sue for peace once the French
had occupied Bavaria than if they occupied northern Italy.[56] In other words, at
this stage of Bonaparte's thinking, Italy was to be a secondary theatre of operations, subordinated to Germany and its army. He tried, therefore, to work
with Moreau, and sent his aide-de-camp, Michel Duroc, to get an exact idea of
the situation on the ground.[57]

Moreau was described by a German visitor to Paris as an 'excellent man', open,
honest and pleasant. He had a dark complexion, a full oval face, dark eyes that
were clear and looked straight ahead, a strong, virile nose, somewhat sensual
lips, a round but well-formed chin, and a deep, well-modulated voice. He was
of medium height, but solid and vigorous, always calm and poised.[58] When he
first met Bonaparte at the Luxembourg Palace after the latter's return from
Egypt in October 1799, he had already earned a reputation as a competent
general. He had volunteered in 1791 and two years later had fought at the
battle of Neerwinden (which was a severe defeat for the French forces). Under
the wing of General Jean Pichegru, Moreau rose through the ranks to take
command of the Army of the North by the age of twenty-eight, despite not
having any formal military training.

Approached by the conspirators before Brumaire, Moreau had actually
declined to play an active part in the coup, thereby paving the way for Bonaparte. In fact, it was Moreau who recommended Bonaparte to them. Once in
power, Bonaparte offered him the Army of the Rhine. Moreau appears as a
consequence genuinely to have co-operated with Bonaparte, at least for the
first few months after Brumaire. Relations between the two men were tested
when the supplies Moreau badly needed for his army did not eventuate, or at

least not quickly enough, when his troops were depleted to strengthen the
Army of the Reserve, and when Bonaparte began directly interfering in the
Army of the Rhine.[59] The real sticking point came over the forthcoming
campaign plan and the command of the Army of the Rhine. Rumour had it
that Bonaparte intended taking command himself, something that he was
indeed considering. That kind of rumour offended Moreau, resentful that it
meant he would have to play a secondary role. Worse, however, since Moreau
was a much more conservative commander, he rejected Bonaparte's plan of
campaign. Instead, in March 1800, he sent his own plans, along with his chief
of staff, Jean-Joseph Dessolles, to Paris to explain the details. Dessolles was
also to tell Bonaparte that if he persisted in his ideas then he should name
someone else commander-in-chief of the Army of the Rhine.[60]

After three days of arguing with Dessolles, Bonaparte let Moreau have his way.
It was perhaps the only time in his career that Bonaparte allowed himself to be
contradicted, supposedly retorting that what Moreau was not capable of doing in
Germany he would do in Italy.[61] Only months after Brumaire, he was more
inclined to be conciliatory, especially with someone who had supported the coup,
and he certainly wanted to avoid an ugly rupture with such a prominent
commander. Both men, it has to be said, went to some trouble to plaster over the
cracks and to suggest publicly that all was well.[62] A convention was eventually
signed between the two on 16 April 1800 (the Convention of Basle) – a sign that
Bonaparte was almost dealing with a separate entity within the army – in which
Moreau agreed to begin the attack by 20 April at the latest and, after having pushed
the Austrians back to the city of Ulm, to send a fifth of his men (25,000 men led
by the able General Claude-Jacques Lecourbe) to join the Army of Italy.[63]

## 'Like a Thunderbolt'

It was only after the decision to leave Moreau in charge of Germany that
Bonaparte resolved to make Italy the main area of operations. It was a lucky
choice. Without Bonaparte knowing, the Austrians had also decided to make
Italy their main theatre of operations and began reinforcing the army there
under General Michael von Melas,[64] at seventy-one the oldest general on staff,
a Dutchman in the service of the Austrian army.

Bonaparte left Paris on 6 May at two o'clock in the morning, after having
spent the evening at the Opera. He had received two messages. The first was
that Moreau had won a victory on the Rhine the previous day, at Stockach,
north of Lake Constance, after a bloody thirteen-hour battle that ended at nine
in the evening. (Between 3 May and 19 June, Moreau had occupied Bavaria and
inflicted a number of defeats on the Austrians.) It was more or less the news
Bonaparte was waiting for; now his flank would be secure while he fought in
Italy. The second was a secret message from Masséna, which he had managed

to smuggle out of Genoa where the Austrians were besieging him. It stated that he could not hope to hold out for longer than fifteen days.

Bonaparte handed over power to Cambacérès, who for the next two months effectively and efficiently ran the country in his absence. There was a bit of a commotion when news of the First Consul's sudden departure became known in Paris: his detractors saw it as a chance to wrest power from him; his supporters, anticipating a successful outcome to the campaign, were already talking about reinforcing his personal powers.[65] Travelling in his berline (covered carriage), alone with his secretary Bourrienne, Bonaparte made rapid progress, reaching Dijon on the morning of 7 May. Starting from Dijon on his way to Italy gave him the opportunity to see what impact Brumaire had had on the French population, but he also used the occasion to make himself personally known to a large number of the French outside Paris. The reaction, if a letter from a witness by the name of Emmanuel Jober can be believed, was quite remarkable. Jober saw Bonaparte at Morez in the Jura where he arrived in the evening of 8 May:

> All the windows were illuminated. The mayor, Perrad, told him: 'Citizen First Consul, be kind enough to show yourself to us.' He appeared at the door. He stopped for half an hour. We cried out: 'Bonaparte, show yourself to the good citizens of the Jura! Is it really you? Are you going to give us peace?' He replied in a faltering voice, 'Yes, yes . . .' He seemed happy. A smile remained on his lips, but his great pallor and the traces of tiredness and work imprinted on his forehead overwhelmed us with tenderness and brought tears to our eyes . . . You will not be able to imagine the profound effect this scene had on our spirits. We will still be talking of it with feeling to our children's children.[66]

The emotion seems utterly out of proportion to the encounter, but Bonaparte was a celebrity, and his fame was growing. Eventually, that celebrity would transform itself into something deeper until a cult would develop around him.

When he arrived in Geneva the next day, he would have noticed as he drove through one of the city gates an arch erected in haste by the Prefect Eymard, with the inscription, 'To Bonaparte and the Armies', and, 'To Victory and Peace'.[67] Bonaparte spent the next three days in Geneva organizing the coming offensive. The army was to march from Geneva into Piedmont and Lombardy as fast as possible by passing through either the Saint-Bernard or the Simplon Pass. On 24 April, Bonaparte was still hesitating between the two options. It was not until late in the day, on 27 April, that he decided on the Saint-Bernard. The plan to cross the Alps may not even have come from him; it may have been the brainchild of another general, Paul Thiébault.[68] The decision was kept secret for two weeks – only a few superior officers were in the know – for it could work only if there were no resistance from the Austrians.

*    *    *

In order to outflank the enemy Bonaparte had decided on a feat that was difficult to accomplish. Other generals and their armies had crossed the Alps since
Hannibal's achievement during the Second Punic War in 218 BC: Charlemagne
did so in 773 in order to attack the kingdom of the Lombards, while the French
king, Francis I, did so on two occasions, in 1515 and again in 1524, in order to
attack Italy.[69] One of the more recent crossings was by the Russian commander
Alexander Suvorov, who went over the St Gotthard Pass in September 1798,
although his 23,000 men did not pass at a point as high as the Saint-Bernard,
and the weather was more clement. Lecourbe – nicknamed 'General Fish' by
the Austrians because of the ease with which he forded rivers – gave battle
around St Gotthard in August 1799, while six months after Bonaparte's feat,
and in the continuing campaign against the Austrians in Italy, General Jacques
Macdonald received the order to cross the Splügen, a narrow mountain pass
2,000 metres high, in a snow storm in December 1800 with the loss of more
than a hundred men to avalanches.[70] If Bonaparte's crossing resonated with the
public to a degree that others did not, it was in large part due to the propaganda campaign that followed. The Saint-Bernard consequently took on
symbolic meaning not associated with previous military feats (other than
Hannibal's), denoting a victory of the new over the old.[71] The mountain, the
ice and the snow represented the obstacles against which the revolutionaries
had to struggle. Overcoming those obstacles would lead to a new beginning, a
new order.

In this as in so many things, Bonaparte was lucky. Between 15 and 21 May,
the week in which the passage took place, the weather could not have been
better,[72] despite what he declared in a letter to his fellow consuls: 'We are fighting against the ice, the snow, tempests and avalanches.'[73] That was to dramatize
the feat for public consumption, making it seem a good deal more dangerous
than it was; the letter was sent from Martigny where Bonaparte had set up
headquarters, and was written before he had even attempted to cross the pass
himself. The weather did not stop him from complaining to Josephine, 'I have
been here for three days, in the middle of the Valais and the Alps, in a Bernardine convent. One never sees the sun; judge for yourself if we are comfortable.'[74]

That week, across the Great Saint-Bernard Pass, almost 2,500 metres in alti-
tude, could be seen a long line of soldiers and cavalry leading their horses by
their bridles. The army was strung out over forty kilometres. The route was
dangerous – narrow, winding roads on precipices – but it was also the shortest
route across the Alps. Getting the artillery across presented a number of logistical difficulties; after experimenting with several methods, General Auguste
Marmont, in command of the artillery, placed the guns in hollowed-out tree
trunks that were then dragged through the snow, a task that took two days.
The caissons (chests containing ammunition) posed even greater problems.[75]
On 16 May, General Jean Lannes crossed with the advance guard and occupied

the town of Aosta after making short shrift of a Croatian detachment guarding the town. The rest of the army took three days to cross, held up for a while at Fort Bard, which stood across a single road leading out of the Alps. Bonaparte's commanders were enterprising enough to bypass the position. The infantry could do that by following mule tracks; the artillery, however, had to pass right under the fort, and succeeded in getting only half a dozen pieces through over several nights. The rest of the artillery were tied down trying to reduce the fort (which they did not succeed in doing until early June).

Incognito and accompanied only by Bourrienne, Bonaparte made the crossing in the wake of the bulk of the army. On his arrival on 20 May 1800 at Bourg-Saint-Pierre in Switzerland on the other side of the Alps, more than 35,000 troops had already crossed. In all, around 45,000 men and 6,000 cavalry, as poorly equipped as the Army of Italy of 1796, were to take this narrow, badly kept road. Half were raw conscripts who received their training along the way. Desertion rates and sickness were probably on a par with most of the other campaigns of the revolutionary wars: the 43rd Demi-Brigade lost 180 to desertion and another 77 to sickness.[76] The organization of the campaign was, moreover, chaotic. Some divisions managed to forget their cannon in the depots in France, while it generally proved difficult if not impossible to supply the troops with basic provisions.[77]

Ten days after the crossing began, on 26 May, Lannes took the village of Ivrea at the southern foot of the Alps. The way was now clear into the plains of Piedmont. This extraordinarily rapid movement across the highest natural barrier in Europe gave Bonaparte complete strategic surprise. 'We have fallen like a thunderbolt,' he wrote to his elder brother Joseph. 'The enemy did not expect us and still seems scarcely able to believe it.'[78] He spent a few days at Ivrea regrouping and awaiting reinforcements, leaving on 30 May. On the eve of his departure, he wrote another letter to Josephine: 'I am in bed. In an hour's time I leave for Vercelli . . . The enemy is completely baffled and still cannot guess what we are at. Within the next ten days I hope to be back in the arms of my Josephine, who is always good, when she isn't crying and playing the *civetta* [coquette].'[79] He was to prove himself right, but he first had to press on to Milan, where he hoped to pick up badly needed matériel.

When he got there two days later, on 2 June, at six-thirty in the evening in the rain, he received a less enthusiastic welcome than he had four years earlier. The planned grand entrance in a gilt-leafed coach drawn by six white horses was a washout; the locals, either taken by surprise or possibly expecting a return of the Austrians, were indifferent.[80] Bonaparte was put out.[81] It was not until a performance at La Scala opera house two nights later that he received a warm reception. His entry into Milan was meant to be a detour in an attempt to find cannon in the enemy's arsenals, because most of the French artillery had been bottled up in the mountains, caught in the fighting around Fort Bard. As a result, he had to

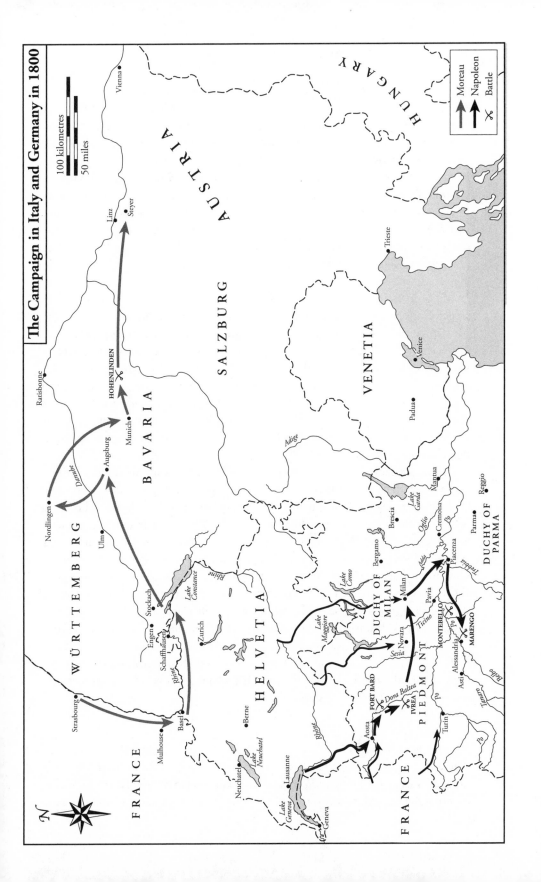

The Campaign in Italy and Germany in 1800

100 kilometres
50 miles

Moreau
Napoleon
Battle

FRANCE
WÜRTTEMBERG
Strasbourg
Nordlingen
Ulm
Ratisbonne
Vienna
AUSTRIA
Linz
Steyer
HOHENLINDEN
Munich
Augsburg
Danube
BAVARIA
Mulhouse
Basel
Engen
Schaffhausen
Stockach
Zurich
Rhine
Lake Constance
SALZBURG
HELVETIA
Neuchatel
Lake Neuchatel
Berne
Rhône
Lausanne
Lake Geneva
Geneva
FRANCE
Aosta
FORT BARD
Dora Baltea
IVREA
PIEDMONT
Turin
Po
Asti
Tanaro
Alessandria
MONTEBELLO
MARENGO
Bormida
Po
Novara
Sesia
Ticino
Pavia
DUCHY OF MILAN
Milan
Lake Maggiore
Lake Como
Bergamo
Adda
Oglio
Brescia
Lake Garda
Mincio
Cremona
Mantua
Piacenza
Trebbia
DUCHY OF PARMA
Parma
Reggio
VENETIA
Padua
Venice
Trieste
HUNGARY
Adige

change his plans. His intention had been to descend into north Italy through Aosta to take the main Austrian army under General Melas from behind, thus trapping the Austrians between Masséna in Genoa and his own forces. At Milan, however, Bonaparte learnt from captured Austrian dispatches of Masséna's capitulation at Genoa (on 4 June). At first, he did not believe it.[82] Although he had given permission to Masséna to surrender, he had nevertheless hoped he would hold on and help him attack Melas in a pincer movement. Melas was now free to manoeuvre as he saw fit. Bonaparte decided to attack as soon as he could; he left Milan on 9 June to move on Alessandria. In the Order of the Day issued to the army, he predicted that the outcome of the fighting would be 'a perfect glory and a solid peace' (*gloire sans nuage et paix solide*).[83]

In Milan, in fact at La Scala, Bonaparte again ran into the twenty-seven-year-old singer Giuseppina Grassini, considered to have one of the finest voices in Italy. He slept with her that same night (Berthier found him the next morning at breakfast with her).[84] Four years earlier, when Grassini had sung for Bonaparte at Mombello during the first Italian campaign, she offered herself to him but he rejected her out of love for Josephine. Now, he began a liaison, later taking her back to Paris and buying her a little house in the rue Chanteraine, the very same street where Josephine had once lived. That and the fact that Giuseppina is Italian for Josephine makes one wonder whether Bonaparte's fling was not wrapped in nostalgia.

Bonaparte had not lost all interest in Josephine; it was simply that his ardour had cooled, to be supplanted by another, more powerful aphrodisiac – power.[85] As he had during the first Italian campaign, he wrote to Josephine on a regular basis, but the passion that had characterized his previous letters had gone. 'I am at Geneva, my dear friend,' he wrote on 9 May. 'I will leave here this night . . . I love you very much. I wish you to write to me often and to remain convinced that my Josephine is very dear to me. A thousand lovable things to the little cousin; tell her to behave, do you hear?'[86] Bonaparte was not referring to a relative of Josephine's. The letters were still warm and affectionate, but much more restrained, the tone a far cry from the heady days of the earlier campaign. Josephine was no longer going to inspire him in the coming battles. In fact, the relationship changed dramatically over this period so that the roles were reversed, with Josephine the jealous partner, crying, sulking, orchestrating scenes over Bonaparte's peccadilloes.

### 'Calm on a Fiery Horse'
The crossing of the Alps has been immortalized in David's portrait, executed after the successful completion of the campaign. Bonaparte refused to sit for the painting but a true likeness was never the objective of Napoleonic portraiture.

The Art Archive/Malmaison Museé du Château/Gianni Dagli Orti

Jacques-Louis David, *Le Premier Consul franchissant les Alpes au col du Grand Saint-Bernard* (The First Consul crossing the Alps at the summit of the Grand Saint-Bernard), 1801.

When David proposed painting him with a sword in his hand Bonaparte replied that battles were no longer won with swords. He wished to be portrayed 'calm on a fiery horse'.[87] David complied with Bonaparte's request – it was a question of representing the heroic nature of the feat – and we see him on a rearing horse pointing to some distant summit, spurring his men on to victory, the wind pushing him forward as his cloak swirls around him. In fact, there is not one but five versions of the painting.[88] The original, completed in four months between September 1800 and January 1801, has Bonaparte wearing an orange cloak riding a bay horse. David realized later that the portrait had neither Bonaparte's eyes nor his mouth, which he rectified in the version commissioned by the King of Spain.[89] Later versions though have Bonaparte looking sterner and less serene. One copy could be seen in St Petersburg in 1802 for the entry price of a rouble.[90] The horse is white, brown or speckled depending on the version painted by David's students, one of whom, François Jean-Baptiste Topino-Lebrun, along with the sculptor Giuseppe Ceracchi, was later executed for conspiring to take Bonaparte's life. The one most often used as an illustration has Bonaparte wearing a red cloak on a black and white horse. Bonaparte particularly liked the painting, which was endlessly repeated in cheap popular engravings, as well as on medals, tobacco boxes, fans and other household objects.

The painting is an idealization – indeed it came under criticism from some quarters for being too theatrical[91] – in the tradition of sovereigns on horseback that had existed since Titian's portrait of *The Emperor Charles V on Horseback*. David's painting also bears a remarkable resemblance to Jean-Baptiste François Carteaux's portrait of Louis XVI done in 1791.[92] David's work is certainly more dramatic than Carteaux's. Movement is captured in the flowing cape in a way that makes Carteaux's painting look like a still life. This type of iconography was habitually used in portraits of kings. Bonaparte was now appropriating a monarchical topos, putting himself on the same level as the European monarchs.

At the centre of the painting is Bonaparte in heroic pose, pointing towards some unseen goal. The painting does not focus on the Alpine crossing itself, even though the onlooker is reminded of previous crossings – the names of two other figures who performed the same feat, Hannibal and Charlemagne (Karolus Magnus), are carved into rock in the bottom left-hand corner, along with Bonaparte's, making the parallels all too obvious. The painting is, therefore, about both Bonaparte as hero and Bonaparte as statesman. The wide-eyed horse over which the First Consul has complete control, judging by the expression of composure on his face, symbolizes the French state, and perhaps the Revolution itself,[93] a metaphor that would have been obvious to observers at the time. The mane and tail of the rearing horse are both swept forward in the same direction as Bonaparte's hair. Man and animal, or Bonaparte and the state, are driving forward.[94] The bayonets barely visible in the distance represent in some respects the Revolution marching forward, but now significantly relegated to the background.

When news of the crossing reached Paris on 5 June, 'it electrified all the good citizens at the same time as it disconcerted dissidents of all parties'.[95] The police report for that day showed that two individuals who had spoken out against Bonaparte were thrown into the ponds in the Tuileries gardens. But the euphoria did not last long. Eight days later, news arrived that Genoa had fallen to the Austrians. The mood in Paris changed dramatically. The First Consul bore the brunt of the blame, at least in the cafés, clubs and literary societies. Bonaparte was jealous of Masséna, Jacobins claimed, which is why he had not come to his aid. Public confidence was badly affected; peace seemed even further away.[96] The crossing of the Alps had been of enormous strategic importance because it enabled Bonaparte to attack the Austrians in the rear at Marengo. A preliminary battle was fought at Montebello on 9 June. After that, no further news reached Paris, increasing anxiety about the outcome of the campaign. All eyes were turned towards Italy. A police report pointed out that the 'unique object' of people's concern was whether Bonaparte was dead or alive.[97]

# 3

# Italy and the Consolidation of Power

### 'In God's Name, Return if You Can'

A story about the military planning that predated the second Italian campaign has Bonaparte lying on the floor of his study in the Tuileries, stretched full length over a map of Italy, sticking coloured pins into it, before announcing, 'I will engage him [Melas] here – on the plain of Scrivia [not far from Alessandria].'[1] The anecdote is almost certainly apocryphal and was meant, like much of the propaganda surrounding Bonaparte's military prowess, to demonstrate his genius at predicting where to strike the enemy, entirely in keeping with the image of invincible general that he was still in the process of constructing.

The decision to march on the fortified city of Alessandria was made at the last minute, only after Bonaparte had reached Milan and learnt of the capitulation of Genoa. As the French approached the village of Marengo, Melas withdrew his forces into Alessandria.[2] It was an unexpected thing to do. Although the forces in question were roughly equal – around 31,500 French troops compared to about 34,000 Austrian – the Austrians enjoyed superiority in both cannon and cavalry, both of which could be put to devastating use on the plain around Marengo. It led Bonaparte to conclude, mistakenly, that Melas must have been contemplating a withdrawal before the troops liberated by the ending of the siege of Genoa had been able to join him. He was possibly encouraged to think along those lines by an Austrian spy.[3]

Bonaparte also accepted at face value the assertions of a staff officer that the Austrians had pulled up their pontoon bridges across the River Bormida, between Marengo and Alessandria. This reinforced the idea that Melas was indeed withdrawing. If Bonaparte had made effective use of his light cavalry to reconnoitre the area he would have discovered that this was not true. As a result, Bonaparte, convinced that Melas would have to head either north to cross the Po or south towards Genoa, sent out two divisions to block the Austrian retreat in those directions: General Desaix, at the head of General Boudet's division, with around 5,300 men, was to head south and block the road to Genoa; while General Lapoype, with around 3,400 men, was sent north towards Valenza on the Po. This reduced the French forces now facing the 34,000-strong Austrian army, with over a hundred cannon, to about 24,000 men and only fourteen cannon.[4]

Melas had not been thinking of withdrawing at all. Instead, he had already decided he would attack Bonaparte early on 14 June across the three pontoon bridges, and along a sixteen-kilometre front.[5] It took Bonaparte some time to realize what was actually happening. Uncharacteristically, he dismissed reports of the Austrians attacking one of his generals, Claude-Victor Perrin (known as Victor), as a rearguard action designed to disguise the main army's retreat. He did not appreciate the extent of the Austrian attack, and hence his own mistakes, until late in the morning. It was only then that he sent off messages to Desaix and Lapoype in desperate tones to join the battle. 'I thought to attack the enemy,' he scribbled to Desaix. 'He has attacked me first. In God's name, return if you can.'[6] If there is some doubt about the actual wording, the tenor of the message was clear. A note reached Desaix about one in the afternoon when he was about twelve kilometres from the field of battle. The troops under his command marched, ran, marched again till they reached the battlefield about five o'clock in the evening.

They arrived in the nick of time. Bonaparte had managed to check the Austrian advance on the right flank, but in order to do so he had had to commit all his reserves as well as the Consular Guard, a formation of elite troops that had been created in November 1799 to protect the executive (it would be transformed into the Imperial Guard in May 1804). On the left flank, things were much worse. Victor's troops, who had been fighting for over six hours and had run out of ammunition, had begun pulling back in some disorder, despite attempts by Bonaparte, riding about in the middle of the ranks, to rally the troops. At four o'clock in the afternoon, the ageing Melas (he was seventy-one), slightly wounded and exhausted by the day's fighting, received a round of applause from his officers and returned to Alessandria to rest.[7] He thought his presence for what he assumed would be a mopping-up operation was no longer necessary and he handed over command to the chief of staff, General Anton Zach, who paused to organize a column of 6,000 men before launching it through Marengo. At this point, the battle *had* been lost by Bonaparte; with no reserves left and diminishing ammunition, he would have been unable to withstand the onslaught.

It was then that Desaix's men arrived behind Victor's troops. Even now the Austrians should have won the day, but for a lucky coincidence. Desaix, at the head of his troops, urged the left flank forward. At that precise moment, a French cannon shot caused a number of Austrian ammunition wagons to explode. The Austrian grenadiers faltered while two quick-thinking French officers took advantage of the situation: General Kellermann (the son of the victor of Valmy in 1792) led a 500-man cavalry charge against the Austrian flank; and General Marmont rushed to the front lines with eight cannon and began to fire canister shot into the Austrian lines. Desaix was shot dead at the beginning of the French counter-attack, but the damage to the Austrians was already done. Galvanized by the arrival of reinforcements, the French counter-attacked along the line, and by six o'clock the Austrians were in full retreat.

*     *     *

The defeat of the Austrian army was anything but decisive, although many historians have a tendency to write as though it were. The Austrians retreated in good order; the 5,600 men lost during the battle (reports vary), as well as the 2,900 men taken prisoner,[8] represented a significant number of the troops engaged in battle that day but only a small proportion of the men Melas had at his disposal in northern Italy – at least another 100,000. Melas, however, was discouraged by the turn of events. Rather than continue the fight, he sent General Skal to French headquarters to propose a suspension of arms. Bonaparte, surprised and under the impression that the Austrians would regroup and attack the next day, immediately accepted.[9] In the armistice that followed, Austrian troops abandoned Piedmont, Lombardy and Genoa and withdrew behind the River Mincio. In the words of the Prussian military theorist Heinrich Dietrich von Bülow, Bonaparte did not seize success; Melas threw it away.[10]

It was just as well. The French were in a much worse condition than the Austrians suspected. The French losses amounted to at least 4,700 killed and wounded.[11] Moreover, the survivors were utterly exhausted and could not pursue the enemy or hammer home their advantage. This is where Bonaparte put the lessons learnt in Italy during the first campaign into practice. Over the coming weeks, months and even years, he modified his account so that he was able to represent the battle and the campaign in a more favourable light: his behaviour during the campaign was calculated, everything went according to his plans. The fact that he kept coming back to this particular battle in order to rewrite its history, more than any other battle of his career, is indicative of just how much it preoccupied him.[12]

Marengo was not a decisive victory. On the contrary, the manner in which Bonaparte had conducted the battle was foolhardy. He had dispersed his forces looking for the enemy and had been forced into fighting a battle with inferior numbers. In the official reports, however, the mistakes were glossed over and the reality distorted. As with the battles of Lodi and Arcola in Italy in 1796, over time Bonaparte's role grew in the telling of the tale, as did his system of tactics.[13] The battle he described in later years was an idealized account that he was running in his head, a preview of what was going to happen at Austerlitz when he deliberately retreated in order to lure the enemy into a disadvantageous position. And as with the first Italian campaign, the Austrian generals were credited with more talent than they deserved. In reality, Melas did not consult with his generals, none of whom knew what was expected of them, or even what roads they were supposed to follow.[14]

'If I Die, It Would be a Misfortune'
When Bonaparte crossed the Alps, nobody knew what awaited him and nobody could predict with certainty that he would carry off a victory and consolidate his

power. He might have been killed, as had happened to so many other republican generals, or he might not have been able to give a repeat performance of his first campaign in Italy. If the campaign had been a fiasco, and if he had been killed, a power vacuum would have been created. Even before Marengo, some of the leading Brumairians, worried about what would happen to the newly created political edifice if its mainstay were to die in battle, reached an agreement over Bonaparte's possible replacement. If the details of this episode remain obscure – many of the memoirs from the period are silent about it – there is little doubt that the Brumairians, possibly fearing a return of the Bourbons, acted to fill the potential void.[15] One account has Joseph as the ringleader, but this is unlikely.[16] Joseph is supposed to have announced that if his brother ever vacated power, he would support Cambacérès.[17] Another witness has Sieyès at the centre of intrigue.[18] Even though Lucien, arrogant and ambitious, considered himself a kind of regent in the absence of his brother – he had refused to work with the Second Consul, Cambacérès, on the pretext that he received orders only from the First Consul – he was prevented from playing a greater role during this period by the sudden death of his pregnant wife, Christine Boyer, as a result of pulmonary disease. The death profoundly affected him.[19]

In any event, people much preferred the more modest Joseph, who was also the first to bring up the subject of a successor, on 5 May, a few days before Bonaparte left Paris to join the army in Italy. He had asked Bonaparte for a letter designating him his successor, failing which he would retire from public life.[20] After all, he was the nominal head of the family, and he was not so much soliciting a favour as reclaiming his right. Bonaparte did not reply, but the problem was exacerbated by rumours of a French defeat in Italy, and indeed of the death of Bonaparte. A meeting was held in Auteuil attended by a number of deputies where those present discussed who would be most suitable to replace Bonaparte in the event of his death. After deliberating over the hero of the American Revolution Gilbert du Motier, Marquis de Lafayette, Carnot, the very young Duc d'Enghien, the Duc d'Orléans, Joseph's brother-in-law General Jean-Baptiste Bernadotte and Moreau – Joseph's name was not even put forward – they anointed Lazare Carnot, whom Bonaparte had just recalled from exile and named minister of war.[21] Carnot was allegedly sounded out and accepted.[22]

None of this represented a real threat to Bonaparte's power. It is, however, revealing of a number of issues that preoccupied the political elite, not the least of which was how to establish the new government on more solid foundations. The news of victory at Marengo, which reached Paris on 22 June, put a halt to their intrigues, rallied those in the army who may have had reservations and silenced the opposition, for the moment at least. There was, of course, a reckoning when Bonaparte returned to Paris, a scene at the Tuileries, although just how sincerely angry he was is difficult to gauge.[23] Those who had been involved in the meetings were marginalized – Carnot was eventually eased out of his portfolio as minister for war, and Lucien appears to have been relegated to the outer circles from this time on[25] – while those who had remained steadfastly loyal to Bonaparte were rewarded. Cambacérès remained in high esteem until the collapse of the Empire.

Two interesting insights can be gleaned from these political intrigues. The first is that the struggle for power in the highest echelons of government had not yet played itself out. For Bonaparte, this was a situation of his own making; by centring all power in his person he had created a state of affairs in which, if ever he were to disappear, a political tussle for power would ensue. There were still enough men around capable of assuming power, or at least men who thought they were capable of doing so. The second is that the question of a successor was being openly discussed less than a year into the new regime.

Roederer, the Brumairian, had raised the question of a successor on a number of occasions, but Bonaparte always avoided giving a definitive answer. On one of those occasions, Roederer received the famous reply, 'My natural heir is the French people. There is my child.'[26] It was meant for public consumption, or at least for those republicans willing to listen, and played to the image of Bonaparte as 'good son of the Revolution'.[27] The problem for the First Consul was that he could not think who could replace him. 'The French', he admitted to Roederer, 'can be governed only by me. I am persuaded that no one other than me, be it Louis XVIII, be it Louis XIV, could govern France at the moment. If I die, it would be a misfortune.'[28] This conceit is shocking but hardly surprising. It was to declare publicly that the sovereignty of the people resided in him.[29]

It was not until the military bulletin of 15 June that Bonaparte announced the outcome of Marengo. He managed to highlight the important events in the battle with theatrical flair: 'Four times during the battle we retreated, and four times we advanced. More than sixty cannon were taken and retaken at different points and at different times, by both sides. There were twelve cavalry charges, with varying success.' The bulletin also contained the stirring lines, 'Children, remember that it is my custom to sleep on the field of battle. – Long live the Republic! Long live the First Consul!'[30]

The bulletin reached Paris on 22 June. The consuls immediately ordered salvoes of cannon to be fired in celebration; the bulletin was hastily printed and posted all over Paris but especially in the working-class districts. The populace exploded with joy, as though, according to one newspaper report, 'struck by an electric spark'.[31] The centre of celebrations was the Faubourg Saint-Antoine.[32] Shopkeepers closed their doors and headed for the Tuileries, where a large crowd had gathered.[33] That evening saw the 'first spontaneous illumination that has taken place in nine years. Work was suspended for the whole day.'[34] One contemporary entering Paris that evening through the customs barrier at the Place du Trône (today the Place de la Nation) passed more than 200 fires around which people were dancing and celebrating as he drove through to where the Bastille had once been.[35] A Te Deum was improvised in the Church of Saint-Gervais (near the town hall, the Hôtel de Ville), attracting so many people that the congregation spilled out on to the street.[36] That was nothing compared to the Te Deum organized in Notre Dame on 24 June, which môre than 60,000 people attended.[37] Bonaparte had, to paraphrase Fouché, conquered not so much Italy as France.[38]

The victory was celebrated not only in Paris but throughout France.[39] Between Milan and Lyons, the route Bonaparte took to return to Paris was lined with people who turned out to see the victor; Lyons and Dijon reserved a welcome for him as warm as on his return from Egypt.[40] The exhilaration can in part be explained not only because Marengo was the victory of the army but because, to many, it was unimaginable that the enemy coalition would now survive for long. After Marengo even Bonaparte thought peace was inevitable.[41]

## The Hero Returns

Bonaparte's decision to return to Paris shortly after the battle is significant. News of 'intrigues' in Paris had reached his ears and, because he thought a plot against him was afoot, he resolved to return to the seat of power. He left Masséna in charge of the army. From Lyons, he wrote to his brother Lucien: 'I will arrive in Paris without warning. My intention is to have neither triumphal arches nor any other kind of ceremony. I have too good an opinion of myself to have any respect for such trinkets. I know of no other triumph than public satisfaction.'[42] Was this an affectation of simplicity, or an instinctive dislike of the theatricality of a grand entrance? It was probably a mixture of both of these things, although whatever reservations he may have had about grand displays did not prevent him, as in Italy, from comparing himself to a force of nature.[43] In that vein, he wanted to impress by the speed with which he travelled; he would arrive in Paris when people thought that he was still in Milan. When he stopped in Lyons on the way, his hotel was mobbed by a crowd anxious to catch a glimpse of him.[44] At two o'clock in the morning of 2 July he arrived in the Tuileries accompanied by his aide-de-camp Duroc and his secretary Bourrienne.

The next day, Paris witnessed something it had not seen in a long time: workers from the *faubourgs* descended on the palace to greet the First Consul. 'An immense crowd filled the terraces and the courtyards of the Tuileries. Never have we seen shine more universally an air of joy, contentment and gratitude on [people's] faces. This evening, all of Paris is here.'[45] The crowds were still in the streets at midnight, even though there was no music and no dancing.[46] One of the principal reasons Bonaparte was so easily accepted at the outset of his regime was that he was seen as the general who could bring about peace.[47] It was a recurring theme in the regime's propaganda, at least in the early years.[48] The campaign of 1800 was supported because of its potential to bring the war to an end. 'It is to have peace,' wrote a journalist in the *Décade philosophique*, 'to obtain a just and honourable one, to repress ambition, and especially to guarantee its independence, that it is permissible to support the war.'[49]

One can only speculate about the extent to which Bonaparte associated military victory and political legitimacy, in both the first and second Italian campaigns, but, as we shall see, the idea would become an obsession with him. He incorrectly associated his popularity with victory and assumed that in order to stay in power he would have to continue to generate military successes. The regime, however, was not contingent on the continuation of good 'fortune' on the battlefield. It was dependent on peace in Europe. Talleyrand was one of the first to see this, and also, as we shall see, one of the first to try to dissociate himself from a man unable to overcome his need to win battles.

## The Festival of the Concord

The fate of the battle of Marengo was immediately linked to Bonaparte's personal destiny: the outcome had been favourable because it was preordained that he would rise to greater things. The illusion was immediate and universal. The royalist agent Hyde de Neuville wrote that Marengo was the baptism of Bonaparte's personal power. It consolidated his reputation as a military leader and consequently his position as a political leader, a sentiment echoed by historians.[50] In some respects, Bonaparte anchored the Revolution through this victory, guaranteeing its reforms, and assuring the Revolution's supporters that peace within France would soon follow. He could reconcile the French around this victory.

Only twelve days after the return of Bonaparte from Italy, the victory was connected to the celebration of 14 July, which since 1790 had been known as the Festival of the Federation.[51] Although it coincided with the anniversary of the storming of the Bastille, the Festival of the Federation was, in its first years, much more about bringing the nation together around the throne, and then around the Republic.[52] Bonaparte appropriated the celebrations, dubbing them the Festival of the Concord, and used the occasion to glorify the coup that had brought the regime to power, as well as to commemorate the death of Desaix.[53] The celebrations were meant to weaken what little hold radical revolutionaries still had over the Revolution. The Republic was being founded on a new basis – peace, concord, humanity, happiness, the *patrie*.[54]

Bonaparte had thought about the programme weeks before.[55] When in Milan, he had engaged two Italian singers – Francesco Bianchi and Giuseppina Grassini – to sing a duet celebrating the 'deliverance' of the Cisalpine Republic, a sister state in the north of Italy created by Bonaparte in July 1797. He wanted something new which at the same time gave Paris back the spectacles that were part and parcel of the monarchy of the *ancien régime*.[56] There were to be no more revolutionary parades, no more allegorical or mythological processions, although the flamboyant Lucien, who helped plan the proceedings, proposed a chariot race around the Champ de Mars.[57] Bonaparte had reservations, but the race nevertheless went ahead.

The festival began on the eve of the public holiday. Theatres were opened to the public for free, but with plays that had been determined in advance by the government, and the Quai Desaix was inaugurated in memory of the general's death.[58] The next day, at five in the morning, a twenty-one-gun salute announced the official ceremonies.[59] Festivities filled the whole day, beginning with a ceremony at the Place de la Revolution (Concorde) when the first stone was laid for a column dedicated to the memory of soldiers who had died for the Republic.[60] Lucien gave a speech for the occasion, and with an intellectual sleight of hand drew a parallel between the Revolution and the coup by declaring that '18 Brumaire has completed the work of 14 July.'[61]

A conscious effort was made throughout the festivities to draw a parallel between the two events. This was echoed in a number of government-inspired pamphlets, such as the *Adresse aux français sur le Quatorze juillet* (Address to the French on the Fourteenth of July): 'It appears to us that the 14 July is separated only by the stormy night of 18 Brumaire, which was, so to speak, the following day.'[62] The difference was that since the new government had come to power, 'France has reconquered all the benefits of 14 July, acquired in Europe more consideration than the monarchy ever had, and increased its territory to the boundaries that nature has allocated it.'[63]

The contentment with the new regime and with Bonaparte, who was still a curiosity among the Parisian crowds at this early stage of his rule, was palpable. The crowds would run to try and catch a glimpse of the man, yelling 'Vive Bonaparte!'[64] As he was riding from the Concorde to the Invalides, someone broke through the crowds to kiss his saddle cover.[65] We are already beginning to see the type of adulation that would later lead to the cult of Napoleon. For some at least this was a public manifestation of the end of the Revolution. 'If we had still feared', wrote one journalist, 'that the Revolution was not over, today there remained no doubt in that regard.'[66] While the reaction of the Parisian population varies according to the sources,[67] Cambacérès claimed that it was the first popular and spontaneous manifestation of joy in over nine years, that is, since the Festival of the Federation of July 1790. All the other celebrations of 14 July gave the impression of being forced.[68]

The Festival of the Concord coincided with a funeral ceremony, the first of many, held in the Temple of Mars (the Invalides) to commemorate the death of

Desaix. It too was widely reported in the press.[69] The flags captured from the enemy in Italy were suspended from the dome, and a statue of Liberty was erected, at the foot of which the three consuls were seated. To their right was a cenotaph in honour of Desaix. The ceremony was much more about Bonaparte (living) than about Desaix (dead), and it was to set the pattern for all the ceremonies that followed. It transformed Desaix into a hero, but it conferred on Bonaparte an almost sacred character.[70]

Publicly honouring dead generals, not all of whom had fallen on the field of battle, was a relatively new phenomenon. Between 1797 and 1803 generals such as Lazare Hoche, Jean Baptiste Kléber and Bonaparte's brother-in-law, Charles Leclerc, succumbed either to sickness, to assassination or to death in battle.[71] The deaths of these generals were used by the state as part of the heroicization of the public figure, a sort of cult of the revolutionary martyr. Statues were consequently built not only to remind the public of popular heroes who had died for the *patrie*, but often to link them to either Bonaparte or one of his campaigns. In the case of Desaix and Kléber, for example, their statues were given an Egyptian flavour, stirring memories of the campaign in Egypt, helping thus to promote Bonaparte's own legend.

Between the victory at Marengo and the Festival of the Republic on 23 September 1800, at least a dozen separate civil celebrations were held in Paris, not counting the religious celebrations, to honour the heroes who had died at Marengo.[72] On the last of these, the Festival of the Republic, Bonaparte laid the first stone of a statue in honour of Desaix in the Place des Victoires.[73] Here too, as with the funeral ceremony, much was made of the occasion. The consuls were accompanied by their ministers and by an important military escort, speeches were made, music was played, songs were sung.

## 'Why am I Not Permitted to Weep?'

The battle of Marengo had been a disaster in many respects and had come close to defeat for Bonaparte, largely as a result of his mistakes. One eyewitness account has him, for a moment, sitting on the levee of a ditch on the main road to Alessandria, holding his horse by the bridle, flicking pebbles with his riding crop, apparently lost in thought and oblivious to what was going on around him.[74]

Marengo, as we have seen, was really won by Generals Kellermann and Desaix,[75] but Bonaparte exploited it to the full. The celebration of 'Maringo', as it was first called by the newspapers, was centred on the First Consul; the army was barely mentioned. Marengo helped consolidate his hold on power, placing him at the heart of the state,[76] and reinforcing his status as hero of the Republic, perhaps more so than that other key moment in the early part of

© BnF, Dist. RMN-Grand Palais/image BnF

Claude Dejoux's *Monument du Général Desaix tel qu'il a été projeté, composé et exécuté en modèle pour la Place des Victoires en 1806* (Monument to General Desaix as it was designed, composed and performed as a model for the Place des Victoires in 1806), no date. The base of the monument measured 6 metres by 3.25. The statue itself, made of bronze, was more than five metres high. When it was finished and erected in August 1810, Desaix's nudity was criticized. Hidden by scaffolding less than two months later, under the pretext of a flaw in the pouring of the bronze, the scaffolding remained in place until 1814, when the statue was finally taken down.

his reign, the Peace of Amiens (about which more later).[77] If Marengo has gone down in history as one of Bonaparte's victories – indeed, one historian has called it 'arguably the most important battle of his career'[78] – it is largely because it became the object of an intense propaganda campaign, both written and iconographic.[79] But, as with the first campaign in Italy, Marengo was quickly reclaimed and interpreted by lesser-known writers and artists. Within days of news reaching Paris, plays were being performed to celebrate the victory, written by enterprising playwrights taking advantage of public sentiment: *Bataille de Marengo, ou la Conquête d'Italie* (The battle of

Marengo, or the conquest of Italy) played at the Cité-Variétés (27 June 1800); *La Nouvelle inattendue, ou la Reprise de l'Italie* (The unexpected news, or the retaking of Italy) played twice in one hour at the Théâtre des Troubadours on 1 July 1800. Cambacérès arrived in time to see the audience cry out, 'The play! The play! A second representation of the piece!' The actors willingly obliged.[80]

Even the military who had lived through the battle reacted with a kind of heroic reflex, recounting anecdotes that could not possibly have happened, glorifying their generals, but especially their commander-in-chief. Thus, *chef de bataillon* Gruyer wrote in a letter dated 18 June that 'The All-mighty Bonaparte arrived on the battlefield with his friend Desaix. Then, the brave general Desaix fell dead from a ball next to the First Consul who exclaimed, "Melas will be defeated!"'[81] As for Bonaparte, the smoke had hardly cleared when he dictated the bulletin of 15 June to Bourrienne that was issued the following day and distributed throughout France (and later Europe).[82] Bourrienne had been in constant contact with Joseph-Jean Lagarde, the general secretary of the consuls, sending him almost daily bulletins dictated by Bonaparte.[83] If they were not an entirely new means of sending out information from the battlefield – military bulletins had existed for some decades now – Bonaparte exploited their use like no other. They continued where his dispatches from the first Italian campaign had left off, inundating France (and later Europe) with an often distorted account of what had taken place, perpetuating the image of a supernatural warrior chief. We can thus read of Bonaparte descending the Saint-Bernard, 'picking himself up from the snow, crossing precipices and sliding over torrents'.[84] The bulletin written after Marengo contains a relatively accurate description of the engagement, although even here, in this first draft of the account of the battle, Bonaparte places himself at the centre of the action, as 'riding the whirlwind and directing the storm'.[85] Interestingly, the battle is represented as a victory for the French soldiers' irresistible élan inspired by the commander's charisma and not by feelings of patriotism.

Accompanying the glory, however, was also a touch of pathos. Bonaparte had learnt as early as the first campaign in Italy that revealing the soft side of his nature made good press. He therefore unabashedly exploited the death of Desaix for as much political advantage as he could. What his aide-de-camp Muiron had been for the first Italian campaign,[86] Desaix became for the second – that is, a loyal lieutenant willing to lay down his life for his commander (and the Republic), although he was celebrated this time round with the help of the machinery of state.[87] The bulletin described how Desaix, dying in the arms of his aide-de-camp, Anne-Charles Lebrun, the son of the Third Consul, said, 'Go and tell the First Consul that I die regretting not to have done enough to live on in the memory of posterity.'[88] Of course, these words were never uttered, but they echo the dying words of earlier faithful royal servants to their kings.[89] Bonaparte was being portrayed as the figurehead of the nation, the symbol around which the country could unify. It also put the onus of anointing Desaix on Bonaparte. Immortality emanated, so to speak, from the First Consul.[90]

The autopsy carried out in Milan showed that Desaix had died instantly by a bullet to the heart; this was almost as soon as the French counter-attack began.[91] Moreover, since he was not wearing his general's uniform at the time, his death went perfectly unnoticed and his body, almost naked after being stripped by marauders, was not retrieved until two days later by one of his aides-de-camp, Anne-Jean-Marie-René Savary, and was embalmed two days after that in Milan.[92] It is even possible that he was shot by friendly fire as he turned around to harangue his own troops. Bonaparte insisted that the bulletin record his own words, supposedly uttered on hearing of the death of Desaix: 'Why am I not permitted to weep?'[93] It is an interesting question, even if rhetorical. In an age when men readily cried in public,[94] there are no accounts of Bonaparte ever openly weeping. This does not mean that he was not affected by Desaix's death, but we do not know with certainty whether he even liked the general or considered him a friend.[95] If he lavished praise on him, it was because he was dead and could not therefore pose a threat to his own reputation. Others who knew Desaix certainly did weep openly.[96] The following day Bonaparte wrote to his fellow consuls telling them that he was 'plunged in grief' for a man whom he had 'loved and esteemed'.[97] These words and the paintings that captured the moment of Desaix's death displayed at the Salon of 1806 were meant as political commentary, a kind of civic sermon that would serve to inspire others, and were recognized as 'true' because enveloped in a documentary style.[98]

A good tale is worth telling time and again, and if told often enough it eventually becomes difficult to see the difference between the reality and fiction. In 1804, shortly before the proclamation of the Empire, Berthier, who had done so much to promote Bonaparte's name in Italy and Egypt by the publication of exaggerated accounts of those campaigns, added to the First Consul's aura by publishing a narrative of the battle of Marengo, placing the responsibility for the victory squarely at his feet.[99] The *Relation de la bataille de Marengo* conveniently forgot the role played by Desaix and even Kellermann, and presented the retreat the French were forced into towards the end of the day as part of Bonaparte's overall plan, so that he was portrayed as having perfect control of the situation from beginning to end.[100] During the Consulate, Marengo was to become a point of reference for future Napoleonic battles, and was re-enacted on a number of occasions (at Marly in 1800, and again in 1805 when Napoleon was en route to Milan to be crowned king of Italy). It is possible that Bonaparte's conscience was pricked by this (mis)use of a comrade's body, but if so he never talked about it. General Kellermann believed that 'Of all the victories carried off by Bonaparte, Marengo is the one from which he obtained the greatest profit for the least

Jean Broc, *Mort du général Desaix à la bataille de Marengo le 14 juin 1800* (Death of General Desaix at the battle of Marengo on 14 June 1800), 1806.

personal glory. He was tormented by it; he was weak enough to want to appropriate it all the more since it belonged to him the least. It explains the contradictory and untruthful accounts, which he told and retold again and again.'[101]

### 'If I am a Traitor, Become Brutus'

Bonaparte left for the army in the costume of the French Institute (what is called the *habit vert*, dark-blue vest and trousers with green brocade in the form of olive leaves worn by the learned members of the Institut de France or the French Academy). On his return he was dressed in a military uniform, and it was in that uniform that he was now mostly (but not yet always) to appear in public, including when he presided over the Council of State. Not that this was unusual. Most European monarchs appeared in public in military uniform; so too did presidents like George Washington. Bonaparte, on the other hand, had until then studiously avoided doing so in order not to alienate the intellectuals associated with Brumaire. After Marengo, his uniform was a sure sign that he seemed not to care any longer about what they thought, and that the military was now at the forefront of political life.

Some took this as a sign that the Republic was dead; Bonaparte was already being called a tyrant in 1800, in the sense given to the word by Plutarch – that is, an absolute ruler. Republicans publicly demonstrated their disapproval, and were to do so throughout the Consulate. One young officer was seen 'kissing with transport a bust of Marcus Brutus'.[102] That was not as extreme, however, as the young man who shot himself in the head in front of a statue of Liberty, shortly after Bonaparte came to power.[103] Of course, the implication was that Bonaparte was a despot like Julius Caesar and that another Brutus had to be found to do away with him. Another wrote that almost all the generals in the army were enemies of Bonaparte.[104] There were even members of the Consular Guard who were supposed to have been heard speaking out against him.[105] It is true that some of them whinged about the discipline and the dress code imposed on them, and some officers railed against what they considered to be the 'atrocious despotism' (*despotisme affreux*) that weighed on France, but they were probably the exception.[106]

After his victory at Marengo, radical elements within the royalist and Jacobin movements seemed more determined than ever to eliminate Bonaparte. The number of assassination attempts made against Bonaparte (and later Napoleon) is not known with any certainty, but somewhere between twenty and thirty plots were hatched in the course of his reign.[107] To put this into perspective, plots against the life of the king during the eighteenth century were not rare. Between 1680 and 1750, about fifty assassination plots were uncovered against French kings.[108] Between the years 600 and 1800, a total of 219 European kings were murdered, while another 338 met a violent end.[109] During the Consulate, both republicans and royalists sought to put an end to Bonaparte's reign through assassination. But then those dubbed the 'exclusives' or 'anarchists' by the Bonapartists – that is, those bent on overthrowing the government – did not have any other means at their disposal. Since insurrection in the *faubourgs* was a thing of the past, no longer possible after its leaders had, for the most part, been guillotined during the Terror, and since there was no longer the possibility of a parliamentary opposition within the complex system that had been established by the Constitution of the Year VIII, the only means of acting against Bonaparte's supposed tyranny was through conspiracy or individual attacks. There was, moreover, a certain tradition, an expectation created since the Revolution, that the true defenders of liberty would stand up to those who threatened it. In 1790 a 'Brutus Legion' and in 1792 the 'volunteers of tyrannicide' were created to assassinate the sovereigns of Europe.[110] The killing of a man considered to have illegitimately appropriated the government, namely Bonaparte, was portrayed by the opposition as tyrannicide.

The theme of tyrannicide was taken up in a republican pamphlet written by Bernard Metge entitled *Le Turc et le militaire français* (The Turk and the French soldier). The pamphlet begins with an indictment of Bonaparte for the crimes which he was allegedly responsible for, notably spilling French blood, the murder of inhabitants of Egypt and taking public money.[111] It goes on to accuse him of abandoning the army in Egypt, and concludes that in 'my country a general who had committed the thousandth part of the crimes that your Bonaparte has sullied himself with would have paid with his head'. In essence, the pamphlet was a call for Bonaparte's murder. Another pamphlet, the *Code des tyrannicides* (Code of the tyrannicides), expressed the same sort of sentiment. It went so far as to quote Bonaparte himself – 'If I am a traitor, become Brutus' – as a justification for his elimination.[112] The same reasoning persisted in the royalist camp; newspaper articles and pamphlets along those lines, funded or supported by the British government and written by émigrés, began to reach France.[113]

Most of the assassination attempts were nevertheless badly organized. What is considered to be the last 'Jacobin plot' (11 October 1800), known as the 'Conspiracy of the Opera', or the 'Conspiracy of the Knives', included the Corsican malcontent Joseph Aréna (brother of the Corsican deputy Barthélemy Aréna, who was accused of wanting to stab Bonaparte during the coup of Brumaire), an Italian refugee by the name of Diana, the sculptor Giuseppe Ceracchi, who had modelled a bust of Bonaparte at Montebello in Italy, the painter Topino-Lebrun, a former pupil of David's, who designed the daggers with which they intended to assassinate the First Consul, and a former employee of the Committee of Public Safety, Dominique Demerville.[114] They were arrested in the crowd waiting for Bonaparte to come out of the Opera.[115] The group was infiltrated and indeed manipulated by the police, with the knowledge of Bonaparte, who wanted to profit from the public sympathy that would come his way after the plot was dramatically uncovered.[116] The public, however, was never to know the extent to which the police had controlled the conspirators: they were simply told that Bonaparte had miraculously escaped a trap organized by 'terrorists' – read Jacobins or the far left. They were subsequently executed, while Bonaparte used the presence of Italians among the conspirators as a pretext to expel from France Italian revolutionaries whose opinions were a little too radical for his liking.[117]

A couple of weeks later, a slightly more serious affair led to the arrest of Bernard Metge and a dozen or so other conspirators.[118] It was Metge, the police discovered, who had written *Le Turc et le militaire français*, in which he called for the birth of 'a thousand Brutuses' to assassinate the tyrant Bonaparte. This group planned to throw what were known as 'red eggs' or 'incendiary eggs' (*oeufs rouges* or *oeufs incendiaires*), a kind of hand grenade that would explode like a Molotov cocktail, into Bonaparte's carriage as it passed by, but they too were arrested before the plan could be put into effect. One of the conspirators arrested was Thomas Desforges, who had been a friend of Josephine's before her marriage with Bonaparte. Metge was later executed.

These plots did a great deal to enhance the popularity of Bonaparte. Laure, Duchesse d'Abrantès, the wife of General Junot, recalled the overwhelming feelings Bonaparte inspired in people in the winter of 1800: 'Confidence returned; everyone saw General Bonaparte with the same eyes and at that time those eyes looked on him with love . . . How he was loved then! Yes, he was loved, he was loved everywhere, and even when there was no love there was admiration and confidence in his character.'[119] No doubt, but then Laure may have been the dupe of propaganda after Marengo that made Bonaparte out to be a humane leader, beloved by his troops. If both royalists and terrorists were attempting to assassinate him, it meant that Bonaparte was both revolutionary and an enemy of Jacobin excesses. The idea appealed to a country that aspired to peace after ten years of internal strife.[120] After the uncovering of these conspiracies, Bonaparte was cheered by the crowds whenever he appeared in public. Indeed, the month of October 1800 led to an outpouring of public assurances of affection for the First Consul.[121]

It also provided an excellent opportunity for what some in Bonaparte's entourage had been considering, namely, bestowing on Bonaparte the Consulate for life, and giving him the powers to name a successor. To lend support to this argument, a pamphlet by Lucien appeared at the end of October, probably written with the help of the journalist and founder of the *Mercure de France* Louis Fontanes, possibly at the instigation of Bonaparte himself, entitled *Parallèle entre César, Cromwell, Monck et Bonaparte*.[122] Whoever the author was, he deliberately cast back to the time of the Merovingians and Carolingians to compare Bonaparte with Charles Martel[123] and Charlemagne. He also harked back to ancient Rome when Caesar, as consul, had become dictator for life and was then proclaimed king, only to be assassinated by Brutus (among others) on the Ides of March.[124] Ten years of civil war followed before Augustus triumphed and proclaimed the Empire. The author preferred this option, minus the assassination, and suggested that in order to avoid further civil unrest in France, it was best to confer a hereditary dignity on the First Consul, or at least to enable him to name his successor. The last few paragraphs in particular raised the need for a hereditary office without, however, ever mentioning the word 'hereditary'. 'If all of a sudden the *patrie* were to lose Bonaparte, where are his heirs, where are the institutions which could maintain his example and perpetuate his genius? The fate of thirty million men is linked to the life of one man!'

Coming less than one month after the assassination attempt against Bonaparte by Aréna and Ceracchi, the pamphlet reinforced rumours surrounding Bonaparte's political ambitions, and led people to believe that it was nothing less than a government manoeuvre.[125] As such, the reaction was less than favourable. Prefects from all over the country sent in complaints.[126] Moreau let Bonaparte know personally that the impact the pamphlet had produced on the Army of the Rhine was deplorable.[127] In short, the debate about an heir had come too soon. Bonaparte may have been testing the waters by allowing his brother to publish the text – Bourrienne, who cannot be trusted, asserts that he had seen an annotated version of it in Bonaparte's office before it was published[128] – but it is more likely that the initiative came from those in his entourage. A month or so later, Bonaparte admitted to Roederer that he had 'given the idea [for the pamphlet], in order to respond to English calumnies', but that 'the last two pages are madness; heredity has never been instituted; it instituted itself. It is too absurd to be accepted as law.'[129] If the pamphlet had been designed to test the waters on the question of allowing a hereditary succession based on the Bonaparte family, the response was a resounding no.[130]

As a result, Lucien was made the fall guy. The standard account of this event has Lucien being called to Paris by Bonaparte to explain himself.[131] Fouché was present at the meeting. Lucien could not deny that the pamphlet had been sent by his office and on his orders, but in his defence he claimed that Fontanes had written the piece and that he had overstepped his orders. That was, to put it mildly, an equivocation. In the scene that followed, Fouché and Lucien threw insults at each other with verve. Fouché made it personal by listing the number of mistresses that Lucien had accrued – although this would hardly have discredited him in the eyes of his brother. Lucien's counter-accusations were much more to the point: Fouché was charged with taking some of the gaming taxes (which was true). Bonaparte had to intervene and did so in support of Fouché, his minister of police. Beside himself, Lucien threw his minister's portfolio on to his brother's desk and stormed out of the Tuileries.

Public opinion had turned against Lucien not only because his name was associated with the pamphlet, but also because he gained the unfortunate reputation of being a spendthrift.[132] Moreover, as minister of the interior he had been difficult. He had simply refused to work with the other two consuls and had exasperated them with his lack of discipline. Fouché was ordered to seize the remaining copies of the *Parallèle*. A thousand of them were burnt in front of the Invalides to appease the army.[133] Tensions within the Bonaparte family were exacerbated when, during an encounter at the Tuileries, the matriarch Letizia took sides with Lucien; Joseph attempted to mediate between his two brothers; and their sister Elisa, who had become close to Lucien during his period of mourning, was reduced to tears.[134] Talleyrand solved the problem by suggesting that Lucien be shunted off to Madrid as ambassador. The very next day,

8 November, Lucien left Paris to enter a kind of gilded exile; the man who had helped bring his brother to power was now effectively marginalized. Josephine and her daughter, Hortense, both of whom detested Lucien, were delighted.[135]

The balance of power had dramatically shifted in Bonaparte's entourage. With Lucien out of the way, and Carnot having resigned, Fouché's influence was more pronounced than ever. This worried the more moderate elements in Bonaparte's circle.[136] Fouché's hands were covered in blood; he had been responsible for one of the worst massacres committed during the Revolution, in Lyons in 1793. More than 1,800 people had been killed during the repression of a revolt in the city.[137] The moderates in Bonaparte's circle were now on the lookout for an opportunity to diminish if not eliminate Fouché altogether. As for the crisis sparked by the pamphlet, it was short-lived, largely because Bonaparte had acted so swiftly to distance himself from his brother that people were inclined to believe Lucien had been acting on his own. Bonaparte emerged from the fray if not squeaky clean, then absolved from accusations of excessive ambition. What lingered in the air though was the question of a successor. It was brought to a head by an attempt on Bonaparte's life that very nearly succeeded.

# 4

# Peace

On Christmas Eve 1800, little more than a year after Brumaire, Bonaparte and his party left the Tuileries on their way to the Opera.[1] A new piece by Joseph Haydn was being performed, *The Creation*, and the boxes had been rented within twenty-four hours of its opening. All Paris had turned out.[2] The orchestra had started playing the introduction, the 'Representation of Chaos', when the audience heard an explosion in the distance. Jacques Marquet de Montbreton de Norvins, who had managed to get a box, emerged into the theatre to see a pale and out-of-breath Hugues-Bernard Maret, one of Bonaparte's secretaries, talking animatedly to a friend; he had just learnt that there had been an assassination attempt against the First Consul. Within moments the whole theatre was abuzz with the news. When Bonaparte appeared, all eyes turned to him.[3] The applause was so loud and energetic that the auditorium shook. Bonaparte, visibly moved, got up several times to thank the public until, on his signal, the opera recommenced.

Bonaparte had not wanted to go to the Opera that evening; he was tired and he much preferred tragedy to opera. It was his daughter-in-law, Hortense, who insisted. When the Consular party was about to enter the carriage, Bonaparte commented on the shawl Josephine was wearing, so she went off to get another. The incident made them leave the Tuileries a little late, and possibly saved their lives. Josephine's carriage, which carried her daughter and her pregnant sister-in-law Caroline Bonaparte, would normally have followed immediately behind the First Consul. Now it was at some distance. The First Consul's carriage reached the nearby rue Saint-Nicaise shortly before eight o'clock. Bonaparte's coachman, who had had a little too much to drink, managed to avoid the merchant's cart that partially blocked the street, and then continued on his way. A few seconds later, a deafening blast rocked the coach and threw most of the mounted grenadiers accompanying Bonaparte to the ground. Josephine's carriage, which had not yet reached the cart, was lifted off the ground, the windows broken and Hortense lightly wounded.[4] The cart had exploded, leaving a number of people dead – the figures range between four and ten[5] – twenty-odd people wounded and a dozen or so houses damaged. Some of the popular prints that followed centred on the destruction caused by the explosion. Among the dead was a fifteen-year-old girl by the name of Peusol who had been asked by the would-be assassins to hold the horse harnessed to the

Anonymous, *Explosion de la machine infernale de la rue Nicaise, après le passage de la voiture du premier Consul* (Explosion of the infernal machine in rue Nicaise, after the passage of the First Consul's carriage), no date. The accent in this engraving is on Bonaparte escaping death by a hair's breadth. This was part of the narrative constructed around the assassination attempt: a few seconds earlier, and the 'genius of liberty', the Saviour of France, would have been killed.[6] The conclusion people were meant to draw was that providence was at work to protect Bonaparte.

cart. She was found in a gutter, in the middle of the rue Saint-Nicaise. The blast had ripped off her clothes, and both arms, which were found on either side of the street. Her mother, a widow, a street vendor who sold buns, reclaimed the body two days later.

Bonaparte escaped without so much as a scratch. In fact, he had been asleep, dreaming that he was at Arcola, crossing the Tagliamento river under the Austrian bombardment. When the bomb went off – later dubbed the *machine infernale* – he is supposed to have woken up with the cry, 'We are undermined!', or so goes the legend.[7] Bonaparte showed remarkable composure under the circumstances, at least in public at the Opera. Once back in the Tuileries, however, he began ranting against those whom he assumed were responsible for the assassination attempt – the Jacobins. The *machine infernale* was the first of its kind, a precursor of the improvised explosive device, designed to cause as much damage and to kill as many as possible. Over the coming days, Bonaparte more or less bullied the Council of State and the

Tribunate into adopting extraordinary measures (rather than using the existing judicial structures) to deal with the Jacobins.[8]

Things came to a head on 1 January 1801. The Council of State proposed reviving the infamous revolutionary tribunals, which had expedited the delivery of the victims of the Terror to the guillotine and were again under consideration as a means of dealing with brigandage in the provinces. But Bonaparte wanted blood and he wanted it right away. 'The tribunals you talk of would be too slow in action. More drastic vengeance is needed, something as rapid as gunfire. *Blood must flow!* As many culprits must be shot as there were victims.'[9] Bonaparte insisted that a further 150–200 former 'terrorists' be deported without trial. If there was no proof against them for the *machine infernale*, they had committed all sorts of crimes during the Revolution and had gone unpunished; they were now getting their just deserts. A member of the Council of State, Antoine-Clair Thibaudeau, present during this rant, summed up the argument nicely: 'It is no longer a question of *judging* according to existing laws or according to laws that have yet to be passed, but of *deporting* and *shooting* as a measure of public safety.'[10]

The investigation that followed the explosion, however, came up with an entirely different set of culprits. A number of anecdotes recount just how the police managed to track down the perpetrators, but all agree that this is one of the first examples of modern forensic investigation. Not much of the horse that had drawn the explosive contraption remained. Some maintain that the head, others a newly shod leg, was taken and shown to the blacksmiths of Paris until one recognized it; others that a description of the horse and the cart was posted around Paris. Whatever the means, the police were able to find the merchant who had sold the cart and horse to the 'terrorists' and got a description from him.[11] Using his police files, Fouché began rounding up suspects and learnt in the course of his investigations that royalists were behind the plot.[12] But when he reported the results of his investigation in the presence of Bonaparte, the minister of the interior and the Council of State, Bonaparte simply retorted that 'anarchists' and *septembriseurs* (a reference to those who had committed the massacres in Paris of September 1792) were to blame. 'I will not be misled,' he declared. 'There are no nobles, Chouans or priests in any of this. It is the work of *septembriseurs*, scoundrels covered in crime who are in permanent conspiracy, in open rebellion . . . against each succeeding government.'[13]

Fouché was instructed to draw up a list of 'anarchists' even as he was completing his investigations into the suspected royalist perpetrators. He complied, probably afraid that if he did not obey he would simply be dismissed from office.[14] No amount of proof could persuade Bonaparte to change his mind; he refused to rescind the orders against the Jacobins. To do so would weaken not only his own authority, but also that of the Senate.[15] The list was ready by 4 January. As a result, 130 men, accused of no specific crime, not even that of being involved in the assassination attempt, and without appearing before a judge, were condemned. The arrests caused quite a bit of consternation in the working-class districts like the Faubourg Saint-Antoine.[16] As the accused were taken through Paris on their way to their final destinations, some people looking on gave vent to their hostility towards them, but most were indifferent.[17] Of the 104 who were actually deported, over half died in exile. Some were simply kept on the island of Oléron or the Île de Ré off the Atlantic coast, but most were shipped to Guiana, or to the Seychelles (considered even worse than Guiana). A few of them made their way back to France in 1809 after an Anglo-Portuguese-Brazilian operation against Guiana, but they were rearrested and imprisoned in 1813. Those sent to the Seychelles fared the worst. Of the seventy sent there, thirty-eight had died by the end of 1807, nine had escaped and only twenty-three survived. When they petitioned Napoleon for clemency in January 1807, he ignored their pleas.[18]

A man who was later to become a prefect during the Empire, the Baron de Barante, referred to Bonaparte's decision to arrest, condemn and deport these men as 'an act of absolute power', in the course of which the Senate lost all backbone and became his docile tool.[19] It is true that throughout their ordeal no one protested or attempted to defend those on the list. Even after two royalists had been executed for the assassination attempt – a domestic servant by the name of Carbon and a former naval officer by the name of Saint-Réjant – no one thought of rescinding the decree against the Jacobins. But it is an exaggeration to claim that the Senate had become Bonaparte's docile tool. On the contrary, most of the political elite were complicit in the process, out of a desire on the part of the conservative establishment to see radical Jacobins eliminated once and for all.

Of more interest is what this tells us about Bonaparte, and why he so relentlessly pursued the Jacobins. His desire for blood, the demand for vengeance, shows the extent to which he was personally affected by the explosion. It is a little glib to suppose that it brought out the Corsican in him, but it certainly brought to the fore his authoritarian tendencies.[20] As for his willingness to blame the Jacobins, in some respects it was an easy enough conclusion to jump to: a Jacobin by the name of Chevalier, a former employee in the armaments workshop of the Committee of Public Safety, had been arrested only a few weeks previously after having experimented with and detonated a contraption similar to the *machine infernale* (he was later executed).[21] Moreover, Fouché's spies had kept the First Consul well informed of the Jacobins' talk of wanting to kill him or blow him up, although they were mostly empty threats muttered under the influence of alcohol. When the assassination attempt took place, therefore, Bonaparte and others were only too willing to believe that the Jacobins were the authors and that it was time to purge France of these 'criminal elements'. The fact that the prefect of police, Louis-Nicolas Dubois, who came in for a drubbing from Bonaparte on the night of the assassination attempt, went about arresting a number of 'fanatical demagogues' only lent credence to the general belief that Jacobins must have been behind the plot.[22]

That attitude can be seen in letters sent to Paris by supporters of the regime who expressed outrage at the assassination attempt.[23] To that extent, if Bonaparte's initial reaction was emotive, the actions that followed are best understood in the light of cold politics. Little did it matter that Bonaparte himself had been a Jacobin in his youth; of utmost importance now was to send a very clear message to anyone thinking of plotting against his life – they would be swiftly and ruthlessly dealt with. For this reason, all opposition was stigmatized by using a particular vocabulary – its disparate members were called 'terrorists', 'exclusives', 'enragés' and 'anarchists'.[24] Napoleon later justified his willingness to eliminate all opponents when he instructed Joseph, by then King of Spain, to shoot rebels or send them to the galleys. 'I obtained tranquillity in France only after arresting 200 firebrands, bandits and September murderers, whom I then sent to the colonies. Since then, the mood in the capital has changed as if a whistle had suddenly blown.'[25]

## Hohenlinden

In some respects, the *machine infernale* was a sign that the politics of national reconciliation pursued by the Brumairians had not succeeded, at least not in relation to Bonaparte. The peace that was soon to be concluded, however, would allow the Brumairians to make considerable progress down that path.

From a military perspective, this is a curious phase in Bonaparte's career. He did not take to the field again once hostilities with Austria were resumed at the end of autumn 1800, preferring instead to leave the campaign to Moreau, conferring on him command of the armies in Germany.[26] It is not as if he had to. His position had been considerably strengthened by Marengo, although after the intrigues at Auteuil he may still have felt a little unsure of his power-base. Of course, Moreau's position in the Army of the Rhine was still very strong. This is one of the reasons Bonaparte left Germany to Moreau. Whatever his reasons, while France was at war the First Consul was never away from the capital for any length of time. The period between his return to Paris from the second Italian campaign in July 1800 and his departure for the campaign that would culminate in Austerlitz in September 1805 (with short trips to various parts of the French Empire) was the longest during which he stayed in and around Paris.

After Marengo, Bonaparte again wrote to the King of Austria suing for peace.[27] It was unfortunate timing; the court of Vienna had just signed an agreement with London promising that, in return for subsidies, Austria would continue the war until February 1801. Vienna nevertheless sent a diplomat by the name of General Francis Count Saint Julien to Paris, not so much to conclude peace as to win time so that the Austrian army could organize itself before launching another campaign. Saint Julien arrived in Paris in July 1800. He was an inexperienced although ambitious diplomat; Bonaparte and Talleyrand quickly bamboozled him into signing peace preliminaries based on the Treaty of Campo Formio. In fact, Saint Julien, believing that he was doing the right thing and that he would be greeted on his return to Vienna as a hero, had no authorization to sign a peace treaty and had on the contrary received instructions to 'do nothing'.[28] When he returned to Vienna, he was thrown into prison for overstepping his instructions. The Austrian government thereby disavowed its envoy and showed its real intentions to the world.

A week prior to his arrival, one of Moreau's commanders, General Lecourbe, had won a victory at Feldkirch (13 July) against the Austrian General Kray, as a result of which Moreau signed an armistice (as far as the fighting in Germany was concerned), at Parsdorf not far from Munich. With Vienna yet again under threat from the Army of the Rhine the armistice was greeted with relief by Austrians. Francis II decided to send his new foreign minister, Count Louis Cobenzl, to Lunéville, a town in Lorraine about thirty kilometres south-east of Nancy, where negotiations were meant to take place between the two countries. Cobenzl arrived there in November, but was invited to Paris by Bonaparte. There the First Consul locked himself away with Cobenzl in his office for an entire night, discussing the possibility of an arrangement with Austria. Talleyrand gives an account of the scene between the two men, at nine o'clock in the evening, with Bonaparte having arranged the lighting and furniture – no chairs except the one Bonaparte was sitting on and only one lamp – in order to intimidate his interlocutor.[29] But it was to negligible effect; Cobenzl went back to Lunéville without having budged an inch. With the failure of negotiations, Bonaparte had little choice but to announce that hostilities would resume on 22 November 1800.

In making the announcement, Bonaparte gave the Austrians advance warning, and they acted quickly. On 27 November, an army of 100,000 men under the (nominal) command of Francis's brother Archduke John crossed the River Inn and took the offensive in Bavaria, outflanking Moreau. Moreau was nonetheless able to regroup and fought a pitched battle at Hohenlinden, about thirty-five kilometres outside Munich, where on 3 December 1800, despite being badly outgunned, he inflicted a crushing defeat on the Austrian forces.[30] Moreau was Bonaparte's military equal in some respects, but not as decisive in action. Even though the road to Vienna now lay wide open, he hesitated a few days about what to do before finally lumbering on towards the Austrian capital. It took him another twenty-five days to march 300 kilometres, a leisurely pace by anyone's standards. When he was within sixty-five kilometres of

Vienna, another of Francis's brothers, the Archduke Charles, asked for and obtained an armistice from the French.

Bonaparte had just returned from the theatre when Bourrienne handed him a dispatch announcing the victory; immediately understanding its implications, the First Consul is supposed to have jumped for joy.[31] Moreau's campaign in Germany had been more successful, in political terms at least, than Bonaparte's second campaign in Italy. It was the general's victory at Hohenlinden, rather than Bonaparte's victory at Marengo, which sealed Austria's fate in the war and forced it to conclude peace. It was Hohenlinden, much more than Marengo, which consolidated Bonaparte's hold on power.[32]

One could be forgiven then for thinking that Bonaparte was slightly jealous. He did not send a letter of congratulations to Moreau, and not much was made of the victory in the press; a letter recounting the victory was published in the *Moniteur*,[33] and mention was made of a delegation sent by the Tribunate to Bonaparte to propose that 3 December become a national feast day.[34] The most Bonaparte conceded was a letter to the Legislative Corps in which he referred to the 'victory of Hohenlinden resounding throughout Europe', but Moreau's name, interestingly, was never once mentioned.[35] In fact, the battle was almost never cited in the press in conjunction with the name of Moreau and was never celebrated in painting the way other Bonapartist victories were commemorated.[36] This was ungenerous to say the least and demonstrates how much Bonaparte may have felt threatened by Moreau's success.

Contemporaries believed that Bonaparte now saw Moreau as a dangerous rival.[37] The general was annoyed by Bonaparte's lack of acknowledgement, and some would have it that he too was jealous of the First Consul's ascendancy.[38] Slights received by his wife at Josephine's summer residence west of Paris, the Château de Malmaison – on one occasion, Bonaparte did not ask her how her husband was doing, on another Josephine kept her waiting before receiving her – did not help matters.[39] When, a month after the battle, Bonaparte finally did write to Moreau, it was a very brief response to a letter he had received about the re-establishment of the Kingdom of Poland, and only then did he refer indirectly to the campaign in which the general had 'surpassed' himself.[40]

France was not big enough for two heroes. Moreau's victories were never allowed to outshine that of Marengo. Two articles appeared in the *Moniteur* that suggested Moreau had not paid the Army of the Rhine in seven or eight months, and that it was going to be paid from the Public Treasury.[41] The story was entirely incorrect; Bonaparte may have had these little bits of information inserted in order to discredit Moreau. The general had in effect paid his men through contributions that had been imposed on the German population, to the tune of forty-four million francs. The suggestion, vague in nature but clear to contemporaries, was that either Moreau was a drain on the public coffers, or he had pocketed the money for himself. Given that the state controlled the press, Moreau was unable to reply to these accusations. Instead, he had a response published at his own expense.[42]


## 'We Blessed the Name of Bonaparte'

While various offensives and counter-offensives were being undertaken in Switzerland, the Tyrol and northern Italy, the peace negotiations with Austria continued at a sluggish pace.[43] Joseph had been sent by his brother to represent France; he entertained the Austrian envoy, Count Cobenzl, at Mortefontaine, his house north of Paris, in a series of dinners, balls, theatre outings and excursions to neighbouring sites.[44] Joseph was not without some diplomatic experience; he had been ambassador to Rome during the Directory and had negotiated peace with the United States earlier in the year, but if Bonaparte sent his brother to Lunéville it was not because of his negotiating skills. He wanted rather to maintain control over foreign policy. Bonaparte, through Talleyrand, controlled Joseph tightly, corresponding with him every day, placing by his side trusted, experienced aides who could help him out.[45]

Talks did not start in earnest until December, after the French victory at Hohenlinden. Vienna now found itself fighting virtually alone; Russia had to all intents and purposes left the Second Coalition and no further help (financial or otherwise) could be expected from Britain. Paul I of Russia was so keen for Austria to make peace with France that he took the extraordinary step of moving a Russian army to the Austrian border as a threat.[46] The court of Vienna, on the other hand, was divided about what to do and what kind of peace it wanted.[47]

The diplomats nevertheless reached an agreement on 9 February 1801, based on the Treaty of Campo Formio.[48] Austria recognized France's annexation of the left bank of the Rhine, the annexation of Belgium and the 'independence' of Holland, Helvetia and the Cisalpine and Ligurian Republics (which were reconstituted and expanded).[49] The former Grand Duke of Tuscany was to be compensated in Germany. France retained Venice and the Venetian possessions in the Adriatic. A new kingdom was established – Etruria – and given to a member of the Spanish House of Bourbon, Luis, whose capital was Florence.

Germany also underwent some dramatic modifications, although not for the last time. Francis II acted in his capacity as ruler of the Habsburg monarchy and the Holy Roman Empire. An Imperial Diet was convened to look at the question of compensating the German princes affected by the French annexations, but it was understood (although never put in writing) that compensation would be achieved through the secularization of the German ecclesiastical states. The German Diet, which sat at Regensburg, would be the scene of two years of negotiating, bribing, persuading and general diplomacy that kept the smaller German princes and some of the more powerful European courts extremely busy. The Holy Roman Empire became to all intents and purposes defunct, central Europe fell under French rather than Austrian influence, while northern Italy, Switzerland, Belgium and the territories on the left bank of the Rhine now fell firmly within the French orbit.

Austrian politicians complained from the start of the harshness of the terms of Lunéville. 'Here is this wretched treaty that I have been sadly obliged to sign. It is dreadful,' wrote Cobenzl, 'both in its form and in its substance.'[50] Historians since have reiterated how severe were the clauses of the treaty, and argue that the seeds of future conflict were to be found within them.[51] This is to take the complaints of Austrian diplomats at face value when Austria really had nothing to complain about. It had gone to war and lost. The treaty signed at Lunéville was not all that different to Campo Formio. In fact, the court of Vienna, much like other European courts at the time, was not acting in good faith. Vienna had dragged its feet at the negotiating table and, when it realized it had to come to terms, did so grudgingly, bitterly resenting having to give up territory in Italy. Bonaparte and the French did not understand the depth of Austria's resentment and hatred at having lost the war and at having its great-power status damaged as a result.

No matter how conciliatory the French may have been, resentment would have festered until the Austrians found an excuse to go to war against France at some time in the future, in the hope of clawing back whatever territories they had lost. However, the treaty and the annexations did not diverge in any way from the policies of other revolutionary governments. All Bonaparte did was adopt and carry through somewhat more successfully policies that had been the mainstay of French governments, royalist or republican, for many decades. It was the culmination of a Continental policy that France had striven after ever since the government of Richelieu in the seventeenth century – that is, the diminution of Austrian power, the French domination of northern Italy, an alliance with Spain, and the exclusion of Britain from Continental affairs. At this stage of his rule, then, Bonaparte's policies did not differ from traditional French foreign political interests.

The reaction among the French people on hearing the news of the signing of peace with Austria in February 1801 was elation. 'What a magnificent peace! What a start to the century,' wrote the *Journal des Débats*.[52] Many years later, an artillery officer, Jean-Nicolas-Auguste Noël, reminisced that 'The Peace [of Lunéville] was welcomed everywhere with rapture, and everywhere, I can assert, the name of Bonaparte was blessed.'[53] A telling sign of Bonaparte's popularity is that the price of his image in popular engravings doubled, tripled in the space of a few days.[54] Celebrations in Paris were orchestrated by the regime for 21 March, when the peace treaty was published and made officially public: entry to theatres was free of charge; the palace and the Tuileries gardens were illuminated; the prefect of police, Dubois, ordered the façades of all households to be illuminated.[55]

Letters of congratulation came pouring in from all over the country, mostly written by officials. Their declamations of joy – 'Oh, immortal glory to the illustrious and beneficent genius who gave the land peace and France happiness'[56] – may therefore be a little suspect, but this should not devalue the outbursts of authentic jubilation with which the news was greeted around the country. The curé of Saint-Colombe, in Castillon, a village in Provence, wrote to say, 'It is through you, O Bonaparte, that the heavens fill today with joy, the Church and the state of France. What joy in the hearts of all faithful Christians and good French citizens! Europe and the whole universe admire you.'[57] A few letters even came from countries outside France, such as Holland, Italy and Prussia. A certain Pieter Pypers from Amsterdam wrote, 'All the inhabitants of the earth owe you their respect: You are their liberator . . . their father.'[58]

The months leading up to the signing of the treaty had built up expectations that there would be a general European peace, expectations that continued for some time. The festivities celebrating the declaration of peace with Austria lasted a whole month, in both Paris and the provinces, and regained momentum when the treaty was ratified by Austria in March 1801. In Germany, the poet Johann Christian Friedrich Hölderlin wrote the 'Friedensfeier' (Peace celebration) and what was in hindsight a somewhat rash letter to his friend Christian Lanauer asserting that with Bonaparte's proclamation of the end of the Revolution and the signing of peace the spirit of conquest in Europe would be eclipsed.[59] Hölderlin reflected a certain optimism among most texts published on Lunéville.[60] In southern Germany in particular, the theatre of war for the last decade, the peace of Lunéville was enthusiastically welcomed and was attributed to the genius of Bonaparte.[61]

### 'The August Pacifier of the World'

Over the coming months, Bonaparte consolidated his position on the international scene, and attempted to isolate Britain, France's only remaining enemy. First, he carried off a diplomatic coup by persuading Spain, as an ally, to invade Portugal.[62] The treaty that resulted from the short-lived War of the Oranges, a non-event in military terms, saw Portugal close its ports to British trade. Although the treaty was not entirely to Bonaparte's liking – his brother Lucien signed an agreement, the Treaty of Badajoz, which sent Bonaparte into a rage and which he at first refused to ratify[63] – France's only remaining enemy was isolated even further with the formation of a League of Armed Neutrality in northern Europe. Made up of neutral Russia, Prussia, Denmark and Sweden, the league was exasperated by British incursions on shipping and the interference with trade that resulted. The British maintained their right to search and confiscate any ship carrying what they loosely termed contraband – that is, any goods that might assist the French in their war effort. Between 1796 and February 1801, the British navy captured over 600 fishing boats and merchant ships.[64] Although France played no direct role in the formation of the league, Bonaparte certainly encouraged it, and it helped bring about a rapprochement with Paul I of Russia. Paul sent Stepan A. Kolychev to Paris, the first ambassador since Catherine the Great withdrew her representative in 1792. Kolychev was welcomed by a detachment of troops at the French border and escorted all the way to Paris.[65] It was a strange choice by a tsar who purportedly wanted to heal relations between the two countries. Kolychev was staunchly Francophobe, and behaved in such a way that both Bonaparte and Talleyrand soon came to the conclusion that he did not represent the views of the Tsar.[66] Finally, France brought the Quasi-War – an undeclared war with the United States (1798–1800) fought mostly at sea – to an end (the Treaty of Mortefontaine), thereby eliminating the possibility of another ally for the British.[67]

Britain was now the only power left at war with France. After peace had been signed with Austria, Bonaparte, giving in to Talleyrand's repeated urgings, once again made peace overtures to Britain in March 1801. In fact, Talleyrand had not waited for Bonaparte to come around to his way of thinking and had already put out feelers by sending an envoy, Casimir, Comte de Montrond, to London in January 1801. Montrond, who spoke English well after having spent time in London as an émigré and was a popular figure there, was to discover whether public opinion in England would be favourable to negotiations with the new regime. He learnt that the new prime minister, Henry Addington, and the new secretary of state for foreign affairs, Lord Hawkesbury, were both eager to begin discussions. With Bonaparte's permission, negotiations were formally begun and continued over a period of six months.

This was possible largely because the man who most opposed revolutionary France in Britain, at least in the government, William Pitt, had fallen from grace after seventeen years in power. The sore point had, ostensibly, been Catholic Emancipation – Pitt had promised it to the Irish as the price for union with Britain, but George III had rejected the notion and refused to compromise – but really a combination of factors led to Pitt resigning in February 1801, including disagreements over how and whether to pursue the war, and his own ill-health.[68] Addington, the speaker of the House of Commons, replaced Pitt. The 'Ministry of All Talents', as the new British government became known, felt the need for peace.[69] Addington did not see much point in continuing, alone, a war that had been going on since 1793. Apart from the fact that there was trouble brewing in Ireland,[70] Britain had incurred a vast national debt – of the order of £537 million – and did not have the means to attack the French. Furthermore, poor harvests and the disruption to overseas trade had led to dramatic rises in the price of food within Britain and to enough social unrest to justify fears of revolution.[71] The new foreign secretary, Lord Hawkesbury, a man so nervous he was referred to as the 'grand figitatis', decided that talks with Bonaparte were called for, and wrote to the French ambassador in London, Louis-Guillaume Otto, to say he was ready to parley.[72]

It was the beginning of a long, tortuous and complicated negotiation, full of tricks, deceit, complaints, prevarication and what the French call *mauvais foi* (bad faith), in which each side tried to gain a territorial advantage before finally signing preliminaries on 1 October 1801. It was easier to agree on the principles than to spell out the details.[73] Paris exploded with joy; shops and boutiques closed while crowds gathered in the streets and gardens; others ran through the Tuileries garden shouting 'Vive la République! Vive le Premier Consul!'[74] The same reaction occurred in England the day the preliminaries were announced in the *London Gazette*; the people of London celebrated for days.[75] 'The world are delighted with the Peace being heartily tired of the War,' wrote Lord Braybrooke, 'and none of the people have as yet thought a moment of the terms.'[76] A crowd gathered at Otto's house where he had the word 'Concord' illuminated, but it was mistaken by an illiterate mob for the word 'Conquered' and caused a disturbance. Otto replaced it with the word 'Amity'.[77] Mail coaches were decorated with laurels and signs reading 'Peace with France'. The windows on the house of the English pamphleteer and journalist William Cobbett were broken by the crowd because he refused to illuminate them. Similar reactions occurred in other parts of the country. In Durham, a statue of Britannia was crowned with a Phrygian bonnet and a placard announcing 'No Income Tax'. That, in effect, is how most people interpreted the positive benefits of peace – no troops, no taxes, lower prices.[78] When the French envoy, General Lauriston, arrived in London ten days later with his government's ratification of the preliminaries, and the crowd mistook him for Bonaparte's brother, they unhitched the horses from his carriage and pulled him along in triumph through the streets from Oxford Road, down the Mall, a street that was exclusively reserved for the royal family, to the residence of the French ambassador in Hertford Street.[79]

The preliminaries were meant to serve as a guideline and were to be consolidated by talks involving most of the countries that had taken part in the War of the Second Coalition (France, England, Spain, Holland, Portugal and the Ottoman Empire). Both sides expected the details to be worked out quickly, but they dragged on for another six months, during which time the British would be pushed to the brink of war. Indeed, what little goodwill there was among the British public appears to have been exhausted by January 1802 in the face of prolonged negotiations. By that stage, the Cabinet had decided that, if they were not concluded soon, Britain would have to resume war.[80]

The city of Amiens, a provincial capital of around 40,000 inhabitants, was chosen as the town in which the negotiations were to take place because it was reasonably close to both London and Paris (about 320 kilometres from London and 130 kilometres from Paris). Lord Cornwallis, the same defeated at York-town during the American Revolution in 1781, represented the British at Amiens. Halfway through the negotiations, Bonaparte started to interfere, as he had done with Lunéville, sending Joseph to negotiate on his behalf. Corn-wallis described Joseph as 'a well meaning, although not a very able, man'.[81] Joseph's relative inexperience, and Bonaparte's meddling, probably dragged things on longer than necessary. Cornwallis, on the other hand, sixty-four years of age and therefore Joseph's senior by three decades, had years of admin-istration, as well as his service in the military, behind him.[82] Even so, he was not helped in this task by a number of people in the British delegation who come across as insufferable snobs. Colonel Nightingall, for example, considered all Frenchmen he came into contact with to be 'rogues'. He described Joseph, although 'rather the best among them', as not at all having the 'manners of a gentleman', even if he meant well and was civil. Joseph's wife, Julie, was described as a 'very short, very thin, very ugly, and very vulgar little woman'.[83] The prefect of the department, whom the colonel's servant insisted on calling the 'Perfect', was described as a 'very ill-looking scoundrel'. Joseph and the French were much more discreet. We don't really know what Joseph thought of the English, although he was at pains to portray Cornwallis in his memoirs as a hale and hearty fellow who wanted to do away with etiquette and negoti-ate frankly and in good faith.[84] The negotiations nevertheless progressed in an atmosphere of mutual distrust and some disdain, and in conditions that were less than ideal.

We can forgo the tedious details surrounding the prolonged negotiations.[85] Of more interest is the final treaty as well as the reaction to the announcement of the peace preliminaries. By the Peace of Amiens the British government was, effectively, recognizing French hegemony on the Continent, and this did not sit well with a largely Francophobe English political elite. The peace terms were thus universally condemned in Britain. Much of the venom was directed at Henry Addington, and British historians since then have attacked the government as largely weak and ineffective, often citing as proof the fact that the French capitulation in Egypt arrived in London one day after the signing of the preliminaries. There was, in fact, a general willingness on the part of many members of parliament to continue the war and the capitulation in Egypt would have given them the excuse needed to do so. Hawkesbury was relieved that the news arrived when it did, too late to influence the outcome of the negotiations.[86] Some, such as Lord Auckland, claimed to have been ashamed of the terms, while former government ministers like William Windham exaggeratedly called the preliminaries 'the death-blow to the country'.[87] Lord Grenville disapproved on the grounds that the government of France 'knew no bounds, either moral or civil', and was 'ruled by no principles', and that under the circumstances to argue that Bonaparte's ambition had been circumscribed was 'criminal nonsense'.[88] Lord Malmesbury 'disapproved' of the treaty and thought that it would not last long.[89] Lord Minto wrote that, among the educated, 'dissatisfaction with the peace is the prevailing sentiment'.[90] George III referred to it as an 'experimental peace'.[91] Admittedly, most of these men were 'ultra' royalists who hated Addington and who saw the clash with France in terms of ideology.[92] But even members of the Whig opposition, in favour of peace with France, found the terms unacceptable. Politicians, however, do not always represent the views of the people.

If Britain had given up everything, nothing it gave up had belonged to it in the first place. Besides, Britain was, realistically, in no position to continue the struggle alone. Its only allies – Portugal, Naples and the Ottoman Empire – were ineffectual. Bonaparte had ordered Spanish troops into Portugal to block the ports there to British shipping, a foretaste of his Iberian policy in years to come. An added impetus to concluding peace was given by the condition of the British economy (exacerbated by crop failures in 1799 and 1800, and the ban on British exports imposed by the League of Armed Neutrality), the state of the country's finances and the rioting that was taking place at home as a result of high food prices. To some, this looked like the French Revolution all over again.[93]

As with Lunéville, news of peace with Britain resulted in an outpouring of affection for Bonaparte. The populations of Paris and the northern departments, not to mention the large commercial ports that had suffered considerably during the war, were elated.[94] Celebrations took place in Bordeaux and Rouen.[95] This time, however, the affection was not merely official. People from all walks of life felt the need to write to Bonaparte to express their gratitude and admiration.[96] Admittedly, some of these letters were self-interested, like that from an octogenarian officer, former general of a division. He wrote to add his congratulations 'to those of all good Frenchmen on the occasion of the definitive peace, due to your great spirit, and that is the greatest achievement of your immortal glory', but then he went on to ask Bonaparte to help his family.[97] Most, however, were completely altruistic, such as the letter from a commissary in Bordeaux, who wrote, 'To the well deserved title of victor and magnanimous conqueror is joined that of universal peacemaker. Blessed be the titulary God of France who in his goodness gave us in your person such a rare gift.'[98] One gets the impression reading these letters that people expected peace to be permanent, which is why they were so ecstatic. One cannot underestimate the impact Amiens made on the people of France.

Talleyrand conceded, 'One can say without the slightest exaggeration that at the time of the Peace of Amiens, France enjoyed, in foreign relations, a power, a glory, and an influence beyond any the most ambitious mind could have desired for her. And what rendered this situation even more wonderful was the rapidity with which it had been accomplished.'[99] In effect, in the space of about two and a half years, between November 1799 when Bonaparte came to power and June 1802 when the Consular regime signed a peace treaty with the Ottoman Empire, France ensured that it was not at war with anyone for the first time since April 1792. Bonaparte was consequently referred to as the 'august pacifier of the world'.[100] To bring the point home, the festivities celebrating Amiens were timed to coincide with the second anniversary of the coup of Brumaire, confirming the trust that many people placed in Bonaparte; he had ushered in a period of peace in which the peoples of Europe were now 'united in one single family'.[101] Some contemporaries at least believed Amiens to be not only the end of the war, but also the end of the Revolution.[102]

On 8 November 1801, Paris was awoken by salvoes of artillery; the city had been decked out for celebration. Balls, receptions and fireworks punctuated the official ceremonies. A hot-air balloon with the different flags of the European powers floated over the city. A flotilla of rowing boats with musicians and actors in the national dress of the main European powers floated down the Seine from the Concorde to the Théâtre du Commerce. The peoples of Europe were represented, dancing to the music of Méhul, Gossec and Haydn, announcing a peace built on friendship and understanding. The revolutionaries had dared dream of a universal peace; Bonaparte seemed on the verge of accomplishing that dream.

On 9 November, on the Place de la Concorde, a mock battle was organized in which cannon roared, drums were beaten and trumpets sounded to military tunes, and towns made of cardboard were stormed. At the beginning of this huge theatrical performance, the doors of the Temple of Peace were closed and an actor dressed as Discord and accompanied by 'infernal divinities' rode around the square in a chariot drawn by black horses. He was soon chased from the scene so that peace was restored.[103] Much later, when Bonaparte visited Amiens in 1803, he was received with an enthusiasm 'impossible to describe'.[104] The horses were unharnessed and the crowds pulled his coach along, triumphal arches were constructed in his honour and everywhere he was greeted and portrayed as the restorer of France.

Before Bonaparte came to power, none of the military victories in Italy made as much of an impact as the announcements of peace at Leoben and Campo Formio. The same can be said of the French public after he came to power. It was peace, just as much as victory (of course they are two sides of the same coin), that enhanced Bonaparte's prestige. Public sentiment found an outlet in the newspapers acceptable to the regime where any number of odes and panegyrics were to be found.[105] To give but one example, a piece in the *Journal des arts* described Bonaparte as 'A great being, who in the century of the Caesars would have been elevated to the level of the gods', who could have continued to make war, but who instead hastened to make peace.[106] This falls within the 'rhetoric of praise' used in the eighteenth century, although it would in other circumstances have applied to a sovereign, not to the head of a republican state.

## Bonaparte's Paris

With peace, Paris became *une grande auberge* for foreigners. A tourist entering the city in 1802 or 1803 would have encountered what was still essentially a medieval town with streets so narrow and dirty that 'not a ray of sunshine can

Pierre Adrien Le Beau, *Traité de Paix signé à Amiens le 24 [25] Mars, An 10* (Treaty of Peace signed at Amiens on 24 [25] March in the Year 10), 1803. Bonaparte, in the centre of the picture, is surrounded by Europe's monarchs, dressed in their regalia, in contrast to the simple uniform he is wearing. All of them have come to offer homage to him.[107] The caption reads, 'Bonaparte pacificateur de l'Europe unit les puissances qui jurent la paix sur l'autel de la bonne foi' (Bonaparte, pacifier of Europe, unites the powers, which swear peace on the altar of good faith). Note the King of England who is a little to one side of the other group of monarchs (to the right of Bonaparte). Minerva is to the left, fighting off the dark forces; Abundance to the right.

penetrate the whole year round'.[108] It took about four and a half hours to walk around the walls of Paris.[109] As for the broader streets, they were covered in jet-black dirt, quite 'troublesome' when it rained. The vicinity of the Tuileries Palace was marred by a collection of small slum dwellings, many of which were cleared after the assassination attempt against Bonaparte in the rue Saint-Nicaise. The city was, in effect, growing so quickly – an English tourist guide compared Paris to 'the root of a monstrous tree, which, watered by a stream, and, planted in a happy climate, has shot forth enormous branches both in height and width'[110] – and there was so little room to put the population that people tended to crowd together in areas designated by the geographical origins of the migrants: masons from the Corrèze gathered around the Place de Grève; labourers from Lorraine and the west of France chose the Marais; water carriers came from the Cantal, the Puy-de-Dôme or Aveyron and clustered around the Place Vendôme.[111] Then of course there was the smell, of dirt, of human waste, and the hordes of beggars that tourists would have to fend off. The walls were covered in posters of all shapes, sizes and colours advertising everything from plays at the theatre to balls, concerts, restaurants, hotels, tailors, doctors, schools, fencing masters, charlatans selling universal cures and rewards for lost pets.[112]

Much of the daily commerce took place on the streets, bridges and quays of Paris where hawkers peddled their wares using expressions that only the servants could make sense of. 'Here is the mackerel which isn't dead; it's coming, it's coming.' 'Herrings on ice, new herrings!' 'By the boat, by the boat, the oyster seller!' 'Baked apples!' For cold cakes, 'They're burning, they're burning, they're burning!' For almond biscuits, 'Here is the delight of the ladies, here is the delight!' For oranges, 'Portugal, Portugal!' On top of this came the cries, the confused clamour of second-hand clothes dealers, wandering glaziers, sellers of parasols, of old iron, water carriers, all in a perpetual din of barking and yelling. Worst of all were the ink sellers: 'It's me, here I am, it's him, here I am. Like that, madam, no one has ever seen anything like it, mia, mia, mia, mia, mia, mia, never, never, anything like it.'[113] When they all came together at a busy intersection, the noise was indescribable. People on the whole were polite, although one English visitor to Paris complained of the 'somewhat abrupt and familiar manners' of the lower classes.[114] Even the manners of the upper classes were not exactly refined; it was customary for example to spit indoors, something done 'to excess'.[115]

Fashionable young men and women were to be found strolling in the gardens of Paris,[116] or eating at restaurants, a by-product of the Revolution, such as Véry, no longer the first restaurant in Paris since the arrival of Naudet on the scene, or the Rocher de Cancale and the Trois Frères Provençaux, which became famous for Chicken Marengo, or at the gambling houses and cafés at the Palais Royal.[117] There were over 3,000 restaurants to choose from, and more than 4,000 cafés.[118]

At some, one could get a fixed-price menu for between thirty-six and forty sous, for which one received soup, a *bouilli*, two entrées, an entremets, as much bread as one could eat, a dessert and half a bottle of good wine.[119] If dining alone, it was possible to choose from an à la carte menu. Dinner was served between four and seven, supper as late as two in the morning.[120]

French social life seems to have resumed with a vengeance. The Duchesse d'Abrantès estimated that in the course of the winter of 1801–2, in Paris alone, there were as many as 8,000–10,000 balls and hundreds of dinner parties.[121] Even taking into account some exaggeration, it was clear that the winter of that year was 'brilliant' compared to those that had preceded it. Salons were encouraged to open their doors again, in the knowledge that a revival of high society was bound to be good for the economy as well as reclaiming Paris's place as a centre of European elegance, intellect and pleasure.[122] The salons were made to serve the state by shoring up the legitimacy of the new regime.[123] They were also a means of keeping an eye on what was being said. The opening of the salons was a sign that things were starting to return to normal, that relations between the elites and the new regime were beginning to improve. The regime worked hard to bring them around by its astute use of the politics of reconciliation it had been pursuing since coming to power.[124]

### 'No One Dares Now Talk Politics'

In Britain after Amiens, everything French was back in fashion. English ladies and gentlemen of the upper classes flocked to Paris to catch up with the latest fashions, while businessmen and merchants renewed their contacts. But they all came to catch a glimpse, if they could, of the First Consul in person. In the face of so many tourists wanting to visit the country – possibly as many as 10,000, including two-thirds of the House of Lords[125] – there was a fear on the part of some British politicians and writers that the English tourists would somehow succumb to radical ideas and return as proselytizing Jacobins.[126] There was no need to worry; the vast majority of these tourists were people of means who travelled with large baggage trains. Lord Mount Cashell, for example, travelled with his wife, her companion, two daughters, three sons, a tutor, a governess and four servants.[127]

Calais, an ugly town according to one English tourist, was often the first port of call, after a five- to ten-hour journey across the Channel.[128] Francis William Blagdon arrived there on 16 October 1801; he claimed to be the first non-official Englishman to have reached the Continent. It was another fifty hours by coach to Paris across 197 English miles of poor roads and dirty inns.[129] Once there, tourists had to register with the police, but they then moved about as they pleased, renting furnished apartments or staying in fashionable (or not so fashionable) hotels near the Palais Royal in the rue de

Richelieu – there were more than 3,000 in Paris at the beginning of the Consulate[130] – where they were sometimes 'skinned alive'.

The accounts English tourists later wrote of their travels are revealing of what they thought of post-revolutionary France. Henry Redhead Yorke, a Francophile, published one of the most famous travelogues of this period. He had initially, like many educated Britons, been in favour of the Revolution, and had visited in its early days in 1792. Ten years later, his description of the country and its people reflects his own ideas about the Revolution and Bonaparte, whom he referred to even then as the 'tyrant'. Yorke was at pains to portray the new regime as one with police spies prowling around in every coffee house, where 'no one dares now talk politics'.[131] English tourists came away with the impression that this was indeed a military regime, that Bonaparte needed the military to stay in power, and that the political situation was still deeply unstable.[132]

Tourists in Paris in the eighteenth century, ably led by one of the first English tourist guides of the city, a *Practical Guide During a Journey from London to Paris*, did what they do today: they headed for the Louvre where, for the first time and mingling with the 'people', they were able to see the treasures looted from Italy by Bonaparte's army. Alternatively they went and pestered the artist David.[133]

Above all, however, the object of English curiosity was Bonaparte. Visitors were always keen either to get an introduction or to catch a glimpse of the man. Bonaparte, or his reputation, made an impression on many who saw him.[134] Lord Aberdeen, William Pitt's ward, was given the unusual honour of dining with him at Malmaison.[135] Joseph Farington caught a glimpse of the First Consul at the monthly review of troops, Place du Carrousel, and described him as 'of a higher style than any picture or bust of him' that he had seen.[136] Samuel Romilly, who would become solicitor general a few years later, saw Bonaparte in public in conversation with one of the Montgolfier brothers (French balloonists, Joseph-Michel and Jacques-Etienne Montgolfier). He was pleasantly surprised. 'He has a mildness, a serenity in his countenance which is very prepossessing; and none of that sternness which is to be found in his pictures.'[137] Others, however, remained steadfastly unmoved. The poet Samuel Rogers thought him nothing more than a 'little Italian'.[138]

Nor was Charles James Fox, the leading opposition figure in the British House of Commons, an admirer. He went to France accompanied by a large party that included, among others, Lord Holland, an influential Whig politician, and his wife.[139] Fox hesitated over paying his respects to Bonaparte while in Paris; it was clearly in Bonaparte's interests to be seen with Fox, a man who had pursued peace for some time, but it was not altogether in Fox's interests to be seen with Bonaparte, for fear of being branded an apologist. In the end, he succumbed and was introduced to Bonaparte at a *lever* on a hot summer's day, at which most of the diplomatic corps were present, as well as a number of other prominent English personalities. Bonaparte heaped praise upon Fox, calling him 'the greatest man of one of the greatest countries in the world'. Fox, however, had always had trouble with public acclamation, indeed treated it with contempt, to the point where he could be positively rude to those who flattered him. Bonaparte was no exception. Before Amiens, Fox had always been against the war with France, but he seems to have come away with the impression that liberty was 'asleep'.[140] He took exception to the French army remaining on a war footing even after the signing of peace – Bonaparte was 'startled, surprised and displeased' by Fox's reaction[141] – but was especially disappointed by what he saw as the First Consul's intellectual failings, 'very deficient upon every subject, no powers or extent of mind – the predominance of Bonaparte [is] the greatest imposition that was ever practised upon the whole world'.[142] More worrying perhaps, Fox believed that Bonaparte was acting virtually as king, and presciently predicted that he would be elevated to emperor.[143] Fox was not the only one to be disenchanted. Lord Holland, who was later to criticize the British government for its decision to send Napoleon to St Helena, described him aptly as 'impatient of contradiction, to a degree not only amounting to a blemish in his moral character, but to weakness in his understanding'.[144]

# 5

# The Politics of Fusion

## The Return of the Emigrés

When François-René, Vicomte de Chateaubriand, returned to Paris from self-imposed exile on Holy Friday in the spring of 1800, he entered the city on foot by the Barrière de l'Etoile, part of the customs wall around Paris, walked down the Champs-Elysées, and then across the Place de la Revolution. He had fled the Revolution after seeing his family château in Brittany burnt down by peasants. His mother was arrested and died in prison; other members of his family were guillotined during the Terror. He walked not far from the spot where they were executed, afraid, he said with some embellishment, 'of putting my foot in blood, of which there remained no trace. I found it impossible to take my eyes away from that place where the instrument of death had been raised. I thought I saw before me in their shirts, bound near the bloody machine, my brother and my sister-in-law; there had fallen the head of Louis XVI.'[1] The sentiments were exaggerated, but Chateaubriand was nevertheless one of the many aristocrats to rally to the new regime during the months that followed Brumaire. He was ready to offer his services and had solicited the protection of Bonaparte's sister, Elisa Bacciochi, to facilitate his return.[2]

Chateaubriand's walk into Paris shows the extent to which people hoped the Consulate would reconcile the opposing factions in France to create a semblance of political harmony. 'The government no longer wants,' wrote Lucien, as minister of the interior, 'no longer recognizes factions and only sees in France Frenchmen.'[3] Beneath the façade of harmony deep divisions still existed, but enormous progress had been made towards healing the rifts in French society created by the Revolution. And that, in many respects, was what the Consulate was all about: a strong executive, national reconciliation and peace through military conquest. One of the most remarkable steps along the path to political reconciliation and social appeasement was the abolition of all penalties against émigrés and an invitation for them to return to France.

During the Revolution, somewhere between 180,000 and 200,000 people had fled France; not all of them appeared on the official list of émigrés, which was made up of about 100,000 names.[4] As well as members of the nobility, they included domestics, priests, labourers and peasants as well as members of the bourgeoisie.[5] Between October 1800 and October 1801, almost 3,500 people had been crossed off the list of émigrés, thus allowing them to return to France.[6] In April 1802, a general amnesty was granted that saw thousands more come back. Even before that, émigrés like Fontanes and Chateaubriand had been secretly returning to France, something the authorities had been turning a blind eye to. All of this was perfectly in keeping with Bonaparte's policy of reconciliation, and was part of a larger strategy of pacification.[7] This was not some vain impulse to surround himself with the cream of *ancien régime* society; it was a political calculation that, at best, became an uneasy alliance. Once again, however, Bonaparte had to overcome the resistance of staunch republicans for whom a return of the émigrés was unthinkable.

At first, Bonaparte actually opposed the idea of recalling them.[8] He had fought against them when royalists had rebelled at Toulon in 1793 and they had been in the ranks of the Austrian army in Italy. In Syria, it had been an émigré, Phéllipeaux, who had contributed to his defeat before the walls of St John of Acre. The idea put to him by Fouché that they might be brought back in large numbers appeared dangerous. Fouché, on the other hand, considered them more dangerous outside the country than under surveillance within. The first measures allowing émigrés to re-enter the country introduced in the first half of 1800 were accompanied by a number of newspaper articles written by Fouché, designed to appease republicans. Thus, in *Le Diplomate* in January 1800, the minister of police declared that the doors were irrevocably closed to 'traitors and parricides'.[9] By the end of 1801, however, inundated with requests from émigrés, he was pushing for a general amnesty. The alternative was to have individual émigrés appear before a court of law, something Fouché feared might encourage some of them to reclaim their lost property. A simple pardon from the state, on the other hand, would not bring into question the usurpation of their property during the Revolution.[10]

With his hold on power increasing, Bonaparte came around to the idea. Now that war had been brought to an end, there was no reason for émigrés to continue fighting France in foreign or émigré armies, and in any event they would be demobilized. On 11 April 1802, the Council of State accepted a law granting amnesty to émigrés; a *senatus consultum* – an act voted on by the Senate that had the force of law – followed on 26 April. The amnesty was accorded to all individuals who availed themselves of it before 23 September and who were prepared to take an oath of loyalty to the Constitution. Only those who had been the leaders of rebel bands or enemy armies were excluded (as well as a few other categories such as princes of the House of Bourbon, or deputies who had been declared guilty of treason – in all fewer than 1,000 people).[11] To those who accepted the offer, the state agreed to restore whatever property had been seized during the Revolution, but which had not yet been sold. This lure, coupled with the nostalgia for France felt by many émigrés, had an immediate and overwhelming effect – over 40,000 émigré families crossed the Channel and the Rhine to return home.[12] 'The fashion was to return', one émigré lamented, 'just as it once was to leave.'[13] What few realized, however, was that the return was swaddled in police surveillance – up to one-third of police personnel were involved in watching returned émigrés – and that Fouché arrested dozens of them and had them imprisoned without trial.[14]

Emigrés had been attacked for years, held responsible for everything from inflation to famine.[15] One can imagine then how much the introduction of an amnesty was a topic of general conversation.[16] From police reports we know that republicans were offended and that even officers in the Consular Guard were wary that émigrés would be imposed on them. Most people, however, seem to have approved of the measure and considered it a sign of the government's strength.[17] As for officers who had emigrated and even fought in the royalist Army of Condé against France, it was now a question of deciding whether they could serve Bonaparte. The choice would have been difficult for many, but it appears that a number of former royalist officers did indeed opt for Bonaparte, some for financial reasons, others because they wanted to serve France.[18] Their integration was facilitated by the fact that they kept their former ranks. This was then a pragmatic decision for some but that does not mean they necessarily hid their royalist sentiments. As we shall see, a number of them were to welcome the return of the Bourbons in 1814 and betray Napoleon in the process.

According to one police report, there were two types of returning émigrés: those who were young and found the decision on the part of Bonaparte magnanimous; and those who were 'encrusted' in the ways of the *ancien régime* and awaited the return of their 'legitimate' sovereign.[19] It was no doubt a simplistic appraisal of a complex situation, but there is some evidence to suggest that a number of returning nobles ensconced themselves in their old neighbourhoods and formed a sort of royalist colony, living an alternative life with their own salons, balls and receptions.[20] Moreover, some returning émigrés were convinced that their lands, confiscated and sold off during the Revolution, would be returned to them. This resulted in enormous friction between returning nobles and those who had acquired their land, which some-times led to violence. In Normandy, for example, a number of returned émigrés were murdered, their throats cut.[21] Nevertheless, the émigrés were now here to stay. They too had become part and parcel of Bonaparte's politics of fusion. The only people not to rally were a royalist fringe living either on the margins or attached to the court of Louis XVIII in exile.

## A Vaccine against Religion

One week after the amnesty of émigrés, on 18 April 1802, Easter Sunday according to the old Gregorian calendar, a mass and then a Te Deum were celebrated in Notre Dame to mark both the signing of peace with Great Britain and the Concordat with the Catholic Church.[22] The aisles of the cathedral had been decked out with Gobelin tapestries, while two canopies of crimson and gold had been erected, crowned with plumes of white feathers.[23] Under one canopy sat the consuls, and under the other the papal legate, Cardinal Gian Batista Caprara. The Te Deum was, according to one English witness, 'the grandest thing I ever heard'. Mixing the two ceremonies was meant to placate public elements hostile to the Concordat – a treaty reconciling the French state with the Church – but really the ceremony was about the religious, not the diplomatic peace, and it was the former that was the subject of conversations in the cafés of Paris.[24]

The First Consul and his entourage left the Tuileries at about eleven o'clock to weave their way through the streets to the cathedral – described by an English visitor as a 'dirty place, and miserable'[25] – escorted by cavalry and announced by a sixty-gun salute and the pealing of the cathedral bells. It was the first time in ten years that the people of Paris had heard the bells ring out over their city and it brought tears to the eyes of those who lived close by.[26] It was also the first time in many years that the crowds saw livery in the official procession to the cathedral, while old royal carriages were dragged out of storage and spruced up for use by the dignitaries. According to one English observer, on seeing the livery the crowds exclaimed how delighted they were to see a bit of colour again.[27] Bonaparte's carriage was drawn by eight horses, the number once reserved for the king. The soldiers forming the guard of honour along the route certainly let it be known what they thought of it all – not much – while old royalists muttered at the sight of Bonaparte's carriage. There were grumblings in some of the cafés the next day, but that was probably not the sentiment of the vast majority of people; workers thought that the restoration of the churches would see them employed.[28] Cambacérès later claimed that a large number of people, 'expressing their joy by continuous acclamations', followed the consuls from the Tuileries to Notre Dame.[29] It was not so much the pomp, by now an increasingly familiar sight, that impressed the crowds as the fact that Catholicism was now being officially recognized by the regime, and could now be openly practised by the faithful.

At about one o'clock, the dignitaries of the regime filed into the cathedral, Bonaparte at their head, followed by the other two consuls, then the various members of the Council of State, the Senate, the legislature, the army and only then, tellingly, by the Church hierarchy. Contemporaries were not unaware how strange it was to see men like Talleyrand and Fouché – the former a defrocked priest, the latter a priest who never took his final vows – make the sign of the cross.[30] A point was being made. The Church was now subordinated to the state and was to remain that way.[31] Many of those present were decidedly unimpressed by the amount of gold braid, purple and carmine cloth. The military in particular were present against their will – they had been co-opted for the occasion by Berthier, the minister of war – disgusted by any arrangements with a Church that had betrayed the Revolution and against which they had fought so hard. They let the whole world know just what they thought of the ceremony.

Masséna was one of them. He disliked Bonaparte intensely and referred to him in private as 'that bugger there' (*ce bougre-là*).[32] From his house in Reuil he was known to have stood on a hill overlooking Malmaison and said to the great amusement of his friends, 'From here, I can piss on him whenever I want.'[33] When Masséna and about sixty other generals entered the cathedral, they discovered that no seats had been reserved for them. 'Go and fuck yourself' was Masséna's response to the assistant master of ceremonies; the generals simply manhandled some priests and took over their seats.[34] They calmed down after Bonaparte, annoyed by the disturbance, turned and glared at them.[35] Jean-François Boulart, a colonel in the artillery, was sickened by the spectacle. He later recalled that 'There was in me a profound aversion and disgust aroused by the lies, and all I saw was lies and hypocrisy.'[36] He nevertheless came away with the feeling that there was much to look forward to. 'Who [are] they trying to fool?' remarked another disgruntled republican.[37] Certain generals, such as Jourdan, Augereau, Brune and Lannes, were considered too republican and were given various missions away from Paris during the celebrations.

Moreau's mother-in-law, Mme Hulot, and his wife, Eugénie, took seats reserved for the Bonaparte family; no one dared say anything to them.[38] At one stage Bonaparte had thought of having the army's flags blessed by the Archbishop of Paris but probably in the face of objections from the military abandoned the idea.[39] Opposition to the Concordat was expressed that evening during a reception held at the Tuileries to celebrate the event. General Delmas was heard replying to a question from Bonaparte that he had thought the ceremony at Notre Dame 'a wonderful mummery [*une belle capucinade*]. It is a shame that the million or so men who got themselves killed destroying what you have re-established were not there.'[40] Such frank talk was not appreciated; Delmas was exiled from Paris for his effrontery and was not reinstated in the army until the Empire had its back to the wall in 1813.[41]

Moreau too had come out against the Concordat and, although invited to attend the ceremony at Notre Dame, decided instead to go for a walk in the Tuileries gardens, publicly distancing himself from the event.[42] He was becoming, possibly in spite of himself, the centre of an opposition movement, and was emulating Bonaparte's earlier tactics. After his victories in Bavaria, and his return to Paris in December 1802, for example, he attended a dinner at the ministry of war not in military uniform but in civilian dress – a simple brown morning coat, knee-length breeches and silk stockings.[43] He may very well have been making a statement, ridiculing the elaborate uniforms that were already starting to appear at the Consular court, attempting to give Bonaparte an object lesson in modesty.

*　　*　　*

Bonaparte's attitude towards the Church had never been as radical as the Jacobins'. Unlike the revolutionary governments that had preceded him, he entirely understood the role of religion in society, and realized that for religion to cease being such a divisive issue bridges had to be mended with the Church.[44] This was above all a practical and not a spiritual process, part of the politics of fusion and reconciliation.[45] Revolutionaries for the most part accepted the measures in favour of the Church, as did the vast majority of the French people, who wanted a restoration of the Catholic religion. Some newspapers, such as the conservative *Mercure de France*, had been campaigning, albeit discreetly, in favour of the Catholic Church.[46] In July 1800, a further nail was hammered into the anti-clerical coffin when Bonaparte allowed people to choose between Sunday and the *décadi* of the revolutionary calendar as their day off (admittedly, the *décadi* was still observed only in a few towns).[47]

It is nevertheless significant that the first public manifestation of Bonaparte's decision to initiate a reconciliation with the Catholic Church had taken place outside France, in Italy. On 5 June 1800, Bonaparte gathered the ecclesiastical hierarchy of Milan for a Te Deum. It was the first time that an official of the French Republic had been seen at a Catholic ceremony since the early days of the Revolution, and Bonaparte made sure that all France and Europe knew of it.[48] During the Te Deum, he made a speech in which he declared that a rapprochement between the French government and the papacy was now possible.[49] On 25 June, he had a conversation with Cardinal Martiniana at the town of Vercelli, about seventy kilometres from Turin, during which the idea of a treaty or Concordat with the Church was discussed. Bonaparte had taken the first step, and in doing so had signalled his desire to tackle head on the religious question.

Not that Bonaparte was religious. His attitude has always been depicted as strictly utilitarian, but one should not forget that he was born and raised a Catholic and that if he was not what one might call a true believer, nor was he an atheist.[50] 'Without religion', he wrote, 'there is no happiness and no possible future.'[51] It seems that he had lost his faith and begun to question the purpose of the Church around the age of thirteen, but religion nevertheless continued to play an important part in his life. Bonaparte's religious beliefs aside, he was perfectly aware that religion was necessary for the stability of the state, and he sensed that the public mood in France had swung in favour of religion, a mood which his government could harness for political purposes.[52]

However, Bonaparte does not appear to have appreciated the enormous problems that had to be overcome, which involved questions of what to do with a Church whose property had been nationalized and that had been rent in two by the revolutionaries with the introduction of an oath of loyalty to the Civil Constitution of the Clergy.[53] Only about half of parish priests and a few bishops took the oath; the rest were deemed 'refractory'. It obliged all

Catholics to choose between the Revolution and Rome. Bonaparte naively thought that an arrangement could be forced through in a short space of time. In much the same way that he had negotiated treaties with defeated powers, Bonaparte believed he was negotiating from a position of strength – an army in Tuscany threatened to invade the Papal States if the Church did not toe the line – and believed that he could obtain what he wanted without conceding anything. That was Bonaparte's way of negotiating – place a knife to your opponent's throat and then tell him what he is about to concede. But this was to ignore the fact that the spiritual power and influence of the Church had not been diminished by ten years of Revolution and the material losses that went with it.

After weeks of fruitless negotiations, Bonaparte called the Holy See's envoy, Monsignor Spina, to Malmaison and threatened to convert to Lutherism or Calvinism if he did not get his way.[54] It was, of course, an empty threat, one among many, and we should not be taken in by his blustering. He sensed how far he could push an opponent in order to gain concessions. This approach was part of what one historian has dubbed the 'frontiers of manoeuvre'.[55] One of the stumbling blocks had been Talleyrand. A bishop during the *ancien régime*, he had walked away from the Church during the Revolution and was one of the men responsible for the nationalization of Church property in France. He did not want a Concordat that would prevent a defrocked priest from marrying; he had his sights set on a certain Mme Grand, considered one of the most beautiful women in Europe, even if she was lacking somewhat in *esprit* (Bonaparte described her rather ungraciously as a 'stupid old tart').

It was only with the arrival of Cardinal Ercole Consalvi in Paris, and a sudden bout of 'rheumatism' that obliged Talleyrand to take the waters, that progress was made.[56] A number of drafts and counter-drafts were exchanged in the space of a few days; Bonaparte threw the eighth draft into the fire. Consalvi, the papal secretary of state, was invited to Malmaison for a meeting with Bonaparte in June 1801;[57] Joseph was appointed to assist Bonaparte's principal negotiator, Etienne-Alexandre Bernier (who in turn worked under Talleyrand), in the hope that everything could be concluded by 14 July. A meeting was held at Joseph's house at Mortefontaine on the 13th that lasted twenty hours. Progress was made, but not enough for an accord. On the evening of the 14th, Consalvi attended a gala dinner during which the negotiations continued. It was on this occasion that Bonaparte told him that Rome would 'shed tears of blood' if he did not sign.[58] It was perhaps enough to give the final impetus to talks; an accord was signed the next day after another marathon twelve-hour session.

During the night of 15–16 July 1801, Cardinal Consalvi signed the Concordat of seventeen articles in Joseph's residence. As a preamble, the French government recognized the Roman Catholic religion as being that of the 'great majority of the French people'. The implication was that there were other faiths, and that the state would now remain neutral in questions of religion.[59] One of the terms of the Concordat was formal recognition of Bonaparte's government, something that the First Consul insisted upon because he rightly assumed it would be a blow against royalism; it undermined one of their objections to the Revolution. It was not the end of the process, however. The treaty was signed in secret – it was not made public until Easter Sunday on 8 April 1802 – and still had to be passed by the legislative bodies, something that was by no means assured.[60] The Concordat was ratified in Rome on 15 August and in Paris on 8 September 1801. Meanwhile Bonaparte, at the suggestion of Talleyrand and without consulting the pope, Pius VII, inserted the infamous addendum referred to as the 'Organic Articles',[61] which were published at the same time as the Concordat in 1802 in order to give the impression that Rome had agreed to them. Introduced at the last minute in an attempt to appease anti-clericals within the assemblies, the Organic Articles imposed a much more 'caesaro-papist formula' on Church–state relations: they denied the pope authority to intervene in many areas of the French Church; they strengthened the First Consul's power to do so; they formalized the loss of Church property during the Revolution; and they brought all papal communications with the French clergy under the strict control of the government.[62]

At the end of the negotiations, Bonaparte is supposed to have said to a senator by the name of Pierre-Jean-Georges Cabanis, 'Do you know what is this Concordat I have just signed? It is a vaccine against religion: in fifty years, there will be no religion in France.'[63] It was a rather glib prognostication. Rather than the end of all religious problems in France – the Concordat is after all highlighted as one of the main achievements of Bonaparte's early reign – it was really the start of a new set of problems that would quickly deteriorate into a bitter and protracted struggle between the Church and the French state, the likes of which had not been seen since the Middle Ages.[64] Little was resolved by the Concordat. Certainly, the pope had conceded a great deal. In order to maintain the right to invest bishops, he was obliged to recognize the Republic, to accept the existence of a French Church that was subordinate to the state, to submit to the nationalization of Church lands, to see Catholicism reduced to *a* religion rather than *the* religion of France, and to agree to the collective resignation of all bishops, something that Bonaparte insisted on so that he could then recompose the whole French episcopacy according to his own likes and dislikes. The negotiations around the naming of bishops had been, moreover, long and bitter. Indeed, both the Church in Rome and the negotiators in Paris were surprised at just how bitter and protracted affairs became.[65] Of the ninety-four bishops holding sees before the Concordat, fifty-five had to resign while the remaining thirty-seven formally opposed the measure and formed a small schismatic Church, dubbed the 'Petite Eglise', hostile to both Bonaparte and the Concordat.

The Concordat, coming on top of Lunéville and Amiens, was nevertheless to give a tremendous boost to Bonaparte's reputation in ways we might find difficult to grasp today. He had realized that the only way to resolve the religious question in France, without recourse to constant repression, was to defuse the schism that had been precipitated by the Constitutional Oath of the Clergy during the Revolution.[66] However, much like the revolutionaries who had precipitated the conflict in the first place, he was determined that the state should remain in control of the Church. With the Church now seemingly onside, Bonaparte took a considerable step towards the further consolidation of his regime.

'The Head of Medusa Should Show Itself No More!'

Opposition to the Concordat came from all quarters, but the most important within the assemblies were the Ideologues – *philosophes* with moderate republican convictions.[67] Outspoken anti-clericals, republicans still locked in a revolutionary mind-set, were to be found in the Council of State, in the Legislative Corps and in the Tribunate where they were to cause trouble when the first drafts of the Concordat were presented to them in October 1801. For these men of the Revolution, any compromise with the Church was seen as a concession to 'religious fanaticism', the type that had produced the schism in the Church and had inspired counter-revolution in the Vendée.

Those who opposed the Concordat waited until the legislature reconvened after a lengthy vacation in November 1801. Among them was the constitutional bishop Henri Grégoire, a former revolutionary who had fought for an independent Gallican Church.[68] The opponents of the rapprochement with Rome expected Bonaparte to present the Concordat for approval early on, at which time they planned to flex their collective muscle by vigorously opposing it.[69] However, the tension flaring between Bonaparte and his opponents came to a head not over the Concordat itself, but over the ratification of a peace treaty with Russia. When the treaty was brought before the Tribunate for approval in December 1801, a storm erupted over the use of the word 'subject' in the phrase 'the subjects of the two powers'.[70] A former Jacobin in the Tribunate objected that Frenchmen were citizens, and not subjects. Even though the session was held in secret – the gallery was cleared so that dissent could not be heard in public – and even though the Tribunate eventually passed the treaty by sixty-five votes to thirteen, Bonaparte was taken aback. In an audience with the tribune Stanislas de Girardin, the First Consul is supposed to have said, 'You know that I am always ready to give each of you the explanations you might want on any of the bills. My kindness does not go so far, however, as to want to enter into a discussion with those *curs* [*chiens*], because you would have to be a *cur* to risk the resumption of war for the sake of one word.'[71]

The 'war' that Bonaparte was referring to was probably the rivalry between political factions that had radicalized the Revolution. If such a trivial matter as the use of the word 'subject' could be the cause of dispute, one could only imagine what would happen when something as controversial as the Concordat was debated. Bonaparte could not afford to lose that vote; it was something in which he had personally invested a great deal in the face of vehement opposition from republicans. To risk a showdown over the Concordat at this stage was to risk a possible defeat at the hands of the legislative bodies.[72] In order to test their loyalty, therefore, Bonaparte submitted the Civil Code instead.

Bonaparte's name is linked to the uniform body of laws that was the Civil Code – he later claimed that it was his greatest achievement – but in reality he neither inspired nor wrote those laws.[73] It was something that had been envisaged both by the monarchy and by the revolutionaries.[74] After Brumaire, Bonaparte set up a commission of four people to work on a draft text. It was finished in January 1801, and was then handed over to the Council of State for discussion and modification. Ever since, historians have debated the extent to which he influenced the Code.[75]

Why did Bonaparte succeed where the revolutionaries failed?[76] Was he really the driving force behind it, or was it that the Code could be brought to fruition only in a period of political stability? This is one of those occasions in which his dynamism came to the fore. We know that he took part in a little over half the sessions of the Council of State dedicated to discussing the Code over a three-year period, but, like any body of law, the Code was the result of a collective effort, reflecting the needs of an emerging elite.[77] According to Bonaparte's own account, he listened and generally let the members of the committee get on with the job.[78] He does not seem, according to some witnesses, to have had much impact on the proceedings. His almoner, the Duc de Broglie, recalled that he would often ask questions and listen patiently, but when things went on too long he would interrupt, and then talk at length without much coherence.[79] He may have pushed the debates in certain directions they may not have otherwise taken, but it is certainly an exaggeration to think that the Code would not have seen the light of day without him.[80] The minutes of the sessions at which he assisted, published during the Empire, appear to have given him a larger role than he actually had.[81]

Where Bonaparte did facilitate the completion of the Code is in allowing specialists to advise him, and by getting jurists onside (in much the same way as he had used scientists on the expedition to Egypt). And, as we shall shortly see, he got it passed into law.[82] The whole point of the Code was to establish a peaceful society based on the notions of patriarchy and private property.[83] Doing so was a means of disarming the counter-revolution, for only through a uniform set of laws could the Brumairians hope to build a harmonious society.[84] What

Bonaparte was attempting to do over and above the codification of laws, however, was to impose a powerful image of himself as father of the nation.[85] Thus the newly codified legal system emphasized duty and structure, while the Revolution's egalitarian inheritance laws were abandoned in favour of more paternalistic legislation in which the authority of the father was paramount.[86]

When Bonaparte submitted the Civil Code to the Legislative Corps and the Tribunate, things did not go smoothly. Both institutions criticized the articles severely, asserting that the Republic was being enslaved, that the Legislative Corps had to be put before those who had the power to execute the law (that is, Bonaparte),[87] and overwhelmingly voted to reject the first bill.[88] The public's reaction to the rejection was not favourable, and was seen for what it was – a clash, unwelcome from the public's point of view, between Bonaparte and the legislative bodies.[89] When the second bill was rejected in the Tribunate at the beginning of 1802, Bonaparte announced that he was withdrawing any laws being considered by the chambers, regretting that he would have to put them off for another time.[90] He effectively sent the legislative bodies to Coventry; for the next two and a half months, they were starved of laws so that in effect they could not function.

Supporters of Bonaparte scratched their heads trying to figure out why both the Tribunate and the Legislative Corps had rejected the Civil Code with such vehemence. Different reasons were put forward, none of them convincing: the deputies disliked Bonaparte; they were jealous of the role of the Council of State; it was the fault of the émigrés; it was the Jacobins in the assemblies; it was Sieyès.[91] The most likely explanation is that, offended that just about everybody other than the legislative assemblies had been consulted in the drafting of the Code, the deputies were sending a message to Bonaparte, warning him to take them more seriously.[92]

Bonaparte's ire against the legislative assemblies had been brewing for some time, ever since the *machine infernale*. In a newspaper article in the *Journal de Paris*, he complained of the 'twelve or fifteen obscure metaphysicians' who 'believed themselves a party' and who made 'long speeches they think perfidious but which are only ridiculous'.[93] Part of the explanation has to do with Bonaparte's character. He was incapable of tolerating criticism, because any criticism was perceived as a direct attack on his person. Those who did not agree with him were tongue-lashed, almost always in public, in an attempt to humiliate them into submission. We will come across this overblown response time and again, whenever he met with resistance.

Part of the explanation, however, was also political and had to do, somewhat perversely, with what Bonaparte saw as an ideal form of government. He simply could not fathom how such a body could be so obstructionist, possibly fearing what had happened to Louis XVI in the face of a difficult assembly. It was the type of factionalism that had led to the worst excesses of the

Revolution and therefore could not be tolerated. Such was the obsession with factions, such was the demand for unity, that any opposition was considered a threat to the government. In private, Bonaparte was calling the deputies 'vermin that I have on my clothes', characterizing opposition as an 'intolerable insolence'.[94] The state's representatives were expected to keep their mouths shut, or suffer the ultimate penalty – dismissal – from what was, after all, a lucrative sinecure. There was no lack of men ready to fill vacant posts.[95] Besides, the vast majority of the political elite were compliant, even when they disliked or disagreed with the bills that were before their consideration. No one, for example, resigned from the Senate in protest against a measure they might have disagreed with.[96]

Bonaparte did not come away from this experience thinking that he had to improve parliamentary strategizing, something he certainly could have been better at, or that he should make do with having his bills passed by a majority vote. No, Bonaparte came away resenting the opposition, and thinking he had to have a polity completely subservient to his will. He used the same argument once used by the revolutionaries, namely, that his government represented the sovereign will of the people, and the will of the people could not be opposed.[97] It was 'the nation's will', he wrote, 'that they [the members of the Tribunate] should in no way obstruct the government, and that the head of Medusa should show itself no more either among our Tribunes or in our assemblies'.[98]

In private, Bonaparte considered the possibility of another coup against these obstructive parliamentary bodies,[99] but Cambacérès came up with an alternative solution. The Constitution stipulated that one-fifth of deputies in each chamber – twenty tribunes and sixty legislators – should be renewed every year, which would normally be effected by the drawing of lots. Instead, Cambacérès suggested that the Senate compile a list of those who would be excluded.[100] In effect, Cambacérès used existing parliamentary regulations to eliminate those who were considered too critical or who had demonstrated an independence of mind that displeased the First Consul.

In this manner, Bonaparte succeeded in purging the chambers of the most recalcitrant elements, and replacing them with more malleable characters. With the purge came a change in procedures in the Tribunate so that all bills were now sent for preliminary examination to one of three new committees – finance, interior and legislation. Lucien, who had returned from Madrid ostensibly reconciled with his brother, was one of the newly appointed members to the Tribunate. On 1 April, he was elected president of the committee that reviewed the Concordat. There was no question of the Concordat not passing now; the agreement was adopted on 3 April 1802, only a week after the Peace of Amiens was signed. When it came to the vote in the Tribunate, only seven members (out of eighty-five) voted against. Similar figures occurred in the Legislative Corps – 228 for and 21 against.[101] The Concordat had, however, taken nine months to pass through the legislative bodies.

The purge did not entirely eliminate opposition to Bonaparte, which continued, but it was timid and limited. After a while, those who stood on principle usually gave up trying and retired from public life. Cabanis is an example.[102] He was one of the Ideologues who had supported Brumaire and a strong executive as the best means of assuring democracy, and who had been given a position in the Senate as a reward. But increasingly he became disillusioned with the way in which Bonaparte co-opted power. Every now and then he would dare to criticize the First Consul, indeed he was one of the few who did, and occasionally he would cast a negative vote in the Senate. But that is as far as his opposition went. He eventually turned away from public life to pursue private scholarship, giving vent now and then in private to his feelings against Bonaparte and later Napoleon.[103]

Bonaparte faced grumblings from staunch republicans and the Ideologues over the Concordat, but he also had to face refractory elements within the clergy – as we have seen, thirty-seven bishops refused to resign from their sees as they were required to by the treaty – and within the army.[104] Despite this, the Concordat was an overwhelming success in garnering support for the regime. The treaty and many of the religious institutions put in place under Bonaparte had but one objective – for the state to regain control over the religious question and to heal the social rift that had occurred during the Revolution. Bonaparte would now have at his disposal a corps of 'prefects in purple' who could help him extend his power over the French, but no more so, it has to be said, than the former kings of France.[105] If Bonaparte was able to write to his uncle, Cardinal Fesch, 'The Concordat is not the triumph of any one party, but the reconciliation of all,'[106] it was because the agreement with the Church deprived royalists and the counter-revolutionaries of their most powerful ammunition. Religion had been a fundamental factor in the revolts in the Vendée and in the Midi; the Concordat solidly placed the Church on the side of Bonaparte and the Consulate.

The Concordat was by no means perfect, nor indeed had the whole of French society been reconciled to the regime and to Bonaparte. For the moment, however, it enabled Catholics to rally to a 'monarchical plebiscitary republic'. Leading ecclesiastics helped this process by depicting Bonaparte as a providential man, placed by God at the head of France, in the same way Cyrus, Constantine and Clovis had once been placed by God at the head of their people.[107] Religion was to become one of the foundations of the new regime and of Bonaparte's political legitimacy. In signing the treaty with Pope Pius VII, he assumed the same rights and prerogatives towards the Catholic Church as the former kings of France.[108] In the eyes of the pope, therefore, he held his power from God. The state, Bonaparte and religion were increasingly intermixed. According to article 8 of the Concordat, for example, mass was to end with the following prayer: 'O Lord, save the Republic; O Lord, save the consuls' (*Domine, salvam fac rempublicam; domine, salvos fac consules*).[109] It wasn't long before the word 'consuls' was replaced with 'consul'.

## Portraying Bonaparte

The peace treaties and the Concordat were fully exploited by the regime, and reinforced the reputation gained by Bonaparte in Italy as a warrior who despised war and who offered peace to vanquished enemies.[110] The religious and military peace enabled Bonaparte to conquer areas of public opinion that had not yet come over to the regime.[111] Much of what we see in the press during this period is about France returning to the 'European family', while the artistic representations of Bonaparte during this period also played to this

Anonymous, *Allégorie du Concordat* (Allegory of the Concordat), 1802. Bonaparte appears to be parting the darkness in order to reveal religion, bathed in light, to France. This painting was probably the result of a competition that was held in 1802.

theme. For example, a competition was organized under the auspices of Lucien's successor as minister of the interior, Jean-Antoine Chaptal, calling on artists to celebrate the Peace of Amiens and the re-establishment of religious cults.[112]

The results were mediocre. The director of the Central Museum of the Arts, Dominique Vivant Denon, was so disappointed by the absence of submissions from the great artists, and by the pedestrian quality of those paintings submitted, that he recommended the regime abandon altogether the use of competitions for art works.[113] The government consequently thought through the manner in which the regime interacted with artists. From the beginning of 1803, artistic competitions were mostly replaced by the commissioning of works of art from chosen artists.[114] This gave the regime a great deal more control over what was portrayed, but it also provided Bonaparte with much greater say in how he and his accomplishments were represented: he ordered at least ten portraits in 1803 alone from artists who included Jean-Antoine Gros, Jean-Baptiste Greuze and Jean-Auguste-Dominique Ingres.

A typical example of a Bonaparte portrait for this period, replete with the symbols that allowed the onlooker to interpret the painting's political message, is Gros' *Bonaparte, Premier Consul* (Portrait of the First Consul). Bonaparte ordered four copies for presentation to a number of important towns.[115] Indeed, the regime was behind a concerted effort to place his image in public buildings where for the last ten years only allegories of Liberty or the Republic had been on display.[116] The symbolism in the painting was evident to contemporaries. On a table covered with a brocaded cloth lie a number of parchments, one of which listed the treaties that had been signed by Bonaparte. Bonaparte is pointing to the word 'Lunéville', underlining the point that it was a precondition of the Peace of Amiens, but also that he had defeated the Second Coalition.[117] In this manner, he is being presented as an energetic and decisive leader, but more importantly as the bearer of peace, in stark contrast to the inept regimes that had preceded him.[118] Gros' painting became the prototype of the official portrait of Bonaparte – in half-civilian, half-military costume – but it also falls within the French tradition of portraying monarchs in what might be called a 'royal posture' of the king as bearer of peace, which had been present from Louis XIII through to Louis XVI.[119] Gros' painting thus linked Bonaparte to past monarchs. The only difference at this stage is the absence of the attributes of power, such as a globe or the hand of justice. The best sculptors were likewise engaged by the state to carve representations of Bonaparte. Two of the best-known busts are by Antonio Canova and Antoine-Denis Chaudet, both commissioned in 1802, both done in a Greco-Roman style, with hundreds if not thousands of cheap copies made in plaster of Paris that could be found on 'every gingerbread stall' in Paris.[120] Even at this early stage, enterprising entrepreneurs cashed in on the mania around Bonaparte by producing his image on just about anything they could get away with, including barley sugar in the form of Bonaparte's head.

Peter Willi/SuperStock

Antoine Gros, *Bonaparte, Premier Consul* (Bonaparte, First Consul), 1802. Bonaparte's face is a copy of the Arcola portrait.

This helps us understand the point towards which we are now heading – the foundation of the Empire. A number of Bonaparte's portraits are modelled on monarchical representations of *ancien régime* kings, minus the glitz and glamour. His portraits are more austere – he was ruling a republic after all – and there is certainly nothing pretentious about them, but they are nevertheless monarchical for all that, containing many of the qualities of princely portraits. This will naturally become more pronounced with the onset of the Empire, as Bonaparte made a concerted effort to distance himself from the Revolution and to develop links with the Catholic monarchies of Europe. But for the moment there is a disarming, almost Spartan simplicity about them, more in keeping with revolutionary than later imperial iconography.[121]

It is their simplicity that contributed towards forging, as well as populariz-
ing, Bonaparte's image. That image was nothing more than an artificial creation
meant to enhance both his reputation and his career. But here is the rub: Bonaparte at first identified with the image, and then began to assume and believe in
it so that eventually the artificial creation took over and became the character.
As for the reception of his portraits, it necessarily differed depending on where
the onlooker's political tendencies lay, or whether the onlooker was a Frenchman or a foreigner.[122] Two things can be said with a degree of confidence.
Within a year of the coup, through newspapers and popular prints, Bonaparte
and the Consulate became one. Bonaparte, although perceived differently by
different people, became at one and the same time the victorious general, the
man of providence, the Saviour of the Revolution and the man of peace.[123] The
perception was more than the result of a successful propaganda campaign; it
was based on the real accomplishments of Bonaparte and his collaborators,
reinforced by the manner in which those achievements were portrayed.

If the iconography depicting Bonaparte before he came to power had a
limited audience, after Brumaire he was able to reach out to many more people.
One way of doing this was through the Paris Salon. The Salon had been initiated in Paris in 1725 and was held in the Grand Salon or the Salon Carré of the
Louvre.[124] Artists were invited to exhibit their work, and were thus seen to be
in favour with the king. Once a jury and prizes were introduced in the middle
of the eighteenth century, it became *the* major event of Parisian artistic life and
one of the most effective ways for artists to earn a reputation. From 1804, the
Salon took place every two years, and was judged by a jury of six artists named
by the government. For the regime, however, the Salon was much more than an
artistic exercise. It was a means of getting a particular message across to a wide
audience. The Salons were popular – they attracted up to 100,000 visitors – and
since they were free one could encounter a cross-section of Parisian society.[125]

More often than not the themes that were treated in the Salon were no
longer current. Unlike popular engravings, which were often spontaneous,
immediate reactions to an event, the works displayed at the Salon usually took
a number of years to complete. Catalogues accompanied the exhibition and
sometimes gave detailed descriptions of the paintings, especially for historical
subjects. The descriptions were sometimes so detailed that they constituted
history lessons in themselves. It is easier to understand Gros' painting in that
context, as part of a concerted effort to overcome Bonaparte's two-dimen-
sional figure as military hero and victorious general and to create an image
more in keeping with his new role. Bonaparte himself had always understood
that power was above all civilian.[126] After Brumaire, and within a short space
of time, the victorious, young, republican hero virtually disappeared and was
replaced by a far more reflective, more mature (gone is the long hair of his
youth), more meditative image of the responsible statesman, legislator rather

than warrior. Bonaparte was now portrayed presenting treaties, giving a constitution, establishing the Concordat, preparing the Civil Code or installing himself in the Tuileries. As we shall see, he even managed to appropriate the role of the enlightened legislator.[127] This does not mean, however, that military exploits were no longer celebrated. On the contrary, battle paintings continued to be produced at an ever-greater rate. One of the strengths of Napoleonic iconography was its ability to touch people's hearts in a simple manner; the emphasis was on realism. At the Salon of 1802, the largest crowds gathered around paintings of Marengo.

The Art Archive/Malmaison Musée du Château/Gianni Dagli Orti

Antoine-Jean Gros, *Portrait équestre de Bonaparte, Premier consul, à Marengo* (Equestrian portrait of Bonaparte, First Consul, at Marengo), 1803. Bonaparte is seen here giving out a sword of honour to the grenadiers of the Consular Guard after the battle of Marengo. It is a tellingly different image of Bonaparte, despite the face being recycled from Gros' painting of Arcola, for he is looking down on his soldiers from atop a horse. Gone are any egalitarian trappings.[128]

# EMPIRE, 1802–1804

# 6

## The Conservative Turn

### 'The Men of the Revolution Have Nothing to Fear'

The reverberations of the Peace of Amiens were to have profound consequences for the direction politics would take. A number of people in Bonaparte's entourage – Lucien and Talleyrand among others – wished to see the First Consul's powers extended, although we do not know who came up with the idea of prolonging them indefinitely. We know that Bonaparte too was thinking along these lines, although he would not say so publicly. Rather than officially ask for anything for himself, he was in the habit of working behind the scenes to have honours 'offered' to him. Even though a number of discussions had taken place between him and the other two consuls, as well as with a number of tribunes and senators,[1] it is likely that he and his entourage only ever insinuated, never clearly stated, what they had in mind. There was, moreover, some discussion of these issues in the press. Roederer published a thin pamphlet entitled *Un citoyen à un sénateur* (A citizen to a senator), in which one could find a plea for giving Bonaparte the time necessary to accomplish his great oeuvre.[2] These manoeuvrings no doubt resulted in the vague idea, which began to circulate in the spring of 1802, that the legislature should offer some sort of recompense to Bonaparte for his achievements.

On 6 May, Cambacérès sent for the president of the Tribunate, Georges-Antoine Chabot de l'Allier, and informed him that it would be appropriate if the Tribunate used its powers to 'express a wish that would be agreeable to the First Consul'.[3] Just what that wish should be was left to the Tribune's imagination. Chabot de l'Allier went away thinking of a modest recompense like the title 'Pacificator' or 'Father of the People',[4] and seems not even to have thought of granting Bonaparte the consulship for life. When Chabot spoke before the Tribunate that same day, he asked that the First Consul be given a 'grand recompense', and urged the Tribunate to express the will of the people by proposing that Bonaparte be accorded 'a dazzling sign of the Nation's gratitude'.[5] The Tribunate adopted the proposal unanimously, but the phrase was so ambiguous that it has been interpreted as a blatant evasion, proof that the Tribunate was determined not to extend Bonaparte's already extensive powers.[6] It was left to the Senate to do so. On 8 May, Bernard-Germain de Lacépède, a slavish follower of Bonaparte,[7] proposed that the First Consul's tenure be extended for another ten years. The proposal was debated and eventually carried, sixty votes to one. Men like Fouché, Grégoire and Sieyès, united in their dislike of Bonaparte, had been working behind the scenes to persuade the senators against the idea of giving Bonaparte more than an extension of ten years and had won the day.[8]

General François-Joseph Lefebvre, the former commandant of Paris who had played an important role during the coup of Brumaire, brought the news of the Senate's decision to Bonaparte thinking he would be pleased with the outcome. He was not.[9] Cambacérès had to calm him down, and that evening, along with Joseph and Lucien who had joined their brother in his office, Cambacérès proposed another expedient – to overlook the Senate's decision by appealing directly to the people. In a reply to the Senate, through Cambacérès, Bonaparte maintained that 'The vote of the people invested me with the supreme Magistracy. I could not feel myself assured of their confidence unless the act that kept me in office was yet again sanctioned by its vote.'[10] This veiled threat was read the next day to a delegation of senators who had come to congratulate Bonaparte on his extension of power for another ten years. That same day Bonaparte departed for Malmaison; he had decided to leave the political manoeuvring to Cambacérès.

Before holding another plebiscite, however, Bonaparte wanted to know the opinion of the Council of State; he hoped to obtain the approbation of this institution and use it in his struggle with the Senate. An extraordinary session was held on 10 May with Cambacérès, Lebrun and all the ministers (except Fouché) present. Thibaudeau, without whom the role of the Council of State in this whole affair would have remained obscure, described the session.[11] During the meeting, one of the architects of the Civil Code, Félix-Julien-Jean Bigot de Préameneu, briefed beforehand by the Second Consul, argued that 'the people had to be consulted in the forms established for all elections', and that therefore the vote of the nation could not be restricted to the ten years suggested by the Senate. The Council of State was obliged to ask the people of France whether or not the First Consul should be elected for life.[12] The underlying argument was that they had to give the government stability and this could not be done by an extension of another ten years. We know that at this meeting Cambacérès declared that if a perpetual extension of Bonaparte's powers was necessary, then it was up to the people to decide the constitutional changes that would result. In other words, Cambacérès established the principle of a plebiscite. It remained to be decided what question would be asked. A few hours later, everything had been arranged and two questions formulated: 'Should Napoleon Bonaparte be made Consul for Life?' (it was the first time his Christian name had appeared in public), and 'Should he have the right to designate his successor?' When Cambacérès asked if anyone had anything to add, no one responded. It was then put to the vote. Five members of the Council abstained, but most voted for it, though with little joy or enthusiasm.[13]

Dedicated republicans were beginning to be worried, but not enough to do anything. Théophile Berlier, for example, a republican and a member of the

Council of State, pointed out that 'It was difficult for me not to see retrograde tendencies [in all this], which grieved me all the more since I was sincerely attached to the First Consul.' Berlier was still convinced, as no doubt were many others, that Bonaparte was the man sent by providence to consolidate 'our republican institutions and to make them respected by all of Europe'.[14] The word 'Republic' still remained, and that seems to have been enough to placate those who may have had reservations about Bonaparte's intentions. But just as importantly, for men like Berlier, Boulay de la Meurthe, Thibaudeau and others, Bonaparte was the best guarantee of the Revolution. The refrain – 'The men of the Revolution have nothing to fear; I am their best guarantee' – was constantly repeated both by Bonaparte and by his supporters.[15]

This was in essence another successful parliamentary coup. Bonaparte was supposed to have been kept in the dark, and he even left the room in which they deliberated the plebiscite on 10 May, but that was nothing more than pretence. Nevertheless, even for him this was moving faster than he thought prudent. He rejected the second question relating to heredity, although Cambacérès attempted to persuade him to keep it.[16] Not that Bonaparte wanted the power to name a successor; as he intimated to Cambacérès, informing the public of his successor was next to worthless. Rather he was playing a game of moderation. Now that the Council of State, the rival institution of the Senate, had offered him more than he had ostensibly desired, he appeared more modest by rejecting part of their offer.[17] Moreover, he thought it would no doubt engender a debate that he preferred to avoid at this stage, fearful that his opponents could rally round the question. Who could oppose, on the other hand, the indefinite prolongation of his powers?

One senator, Jean-Denis Lanjuinais, is reported to have said, 'They want us to give France a Master. What is to be done? Any resistance from now on would be pointless, whole armies would be needed to oppose it. The only thing to be done is to keep quiet; it is the course of action I have taken.'[18] In fact, the Senate was not as meek as has been made out. Under the circumstances, it did the only thing it could do: it prevaricated by naming a commission to consider the question. The commission eventually handed down a finding that stated, 'there is, at present, no action to be taken in relation to the messages in question'. This was a reference to the notes sent by Bonaparte and the two consuls informing the Senate that they would be consulting with the people. In other words, impotent before the turn of events, the Senate nevertheless found a way to reject the call for a plebiscite.[19] It was not much of an act of defiance. On 11 May, the members of the Senate, along with those belonging to the Tribunate and the Legislative Corps, went to the Tuileries to congratulate the First Consul. The deputies handed Bonaparte their independence on a silver platter.

### The Imagination of the French People

So another plebiscite was prepared, paying lip-service to the revolutionary notion of the sovereignty of the people. The plebiscite of 1802, however, was concerned with Bonaparte's powers and title. As with the plebiscite of 1800, registers were opened at the communal level. Voters were meant to pronounce publicly in writing whether they were for or against the life consulship (the other two consuls were implicitly included in the plebiscite). The groundwork was laid by the regime through the media of the day,[20] by the local administration and also this time by the Church; it could hardly refuse anything to a man who had just given its members the freedom to practise. The Bishop of Metz, for example, came out officially for a 'yes' vote.[21]

Unlike the plebiscite of 1800, the results of 1802 did not need to be inflated. About 3.6 million 'yes' votes were recorded, a reflection of the general acceptance of Bonaparte as head of state as well as of the Consular regime that had brought stability to France's political landscape. In fact, the number of real 'yes' votes had doubled since 1800. These figures mean two things: that only two out of five Frenchmen eligible to vote had done so, a proportion which nevertheless represents the summit of popular adherence to the man and his system; and that, despite the acceptance of Bonaparte, the regime could not capitalize on it in the way it had done in 1800 when the results were falsified.[22] Once again, the 'no' vote was negligible, although many of the negative votes came from the army, disappointed republicans who did not wish for a life Consulate; the strongest opposition came from the Army of the West, commanded by General Bernadotte, and from the Army of Italy.[23] That some within the army were displeased by the idea of a Consulate for life may have had nothing to do with Bonaparte – there is some indication that discontent over lack of pay motivated some to vote 'no' – but most would have voted 'no' on ideological grounds.[24]

The results of the plebiscite were announced around two in the afternoon on 3 August. The Senate arrived at the Tuileries in grand costume accompanied by a cavalry escort. Bonaparte was in the middle of an audience with foreign ambassadors; it was suspended. The new president of the Senate, François Barthélemy, addressed the First Consul in terms that made it seem the Senate were in perfect accord with the will of the people. Indeed, the phrase pronounced was 'The French people names and the Senate proclaims Napoleon Bonaparte, First Consul for Life.'[25] In a break with tradition, both monarchical and revolutionary, and in spite of Bonaparte's refusal of the offer, he was granted the power to name his successor, a right that not even the kings of France had enjoyed. For the senators, it was a humiliating position to be in. They had opposed the Consulate for life and were in effect now consecrating their own downfall in front of the representatives of the monarchs of Europe. Bonaparte replied in a set speech that was, according to an Irish witness, concealed in the crown of his hat.[26]

In a remarkable declaration that contains equal doses of vanity and hubris, he claimed that the 'prosperity of France shall be secured against the caprices of fate and the uncertainties of the future', by his efforts and those of government officials. While he did not take all the credit for restoring France, its people had nevertheless summoned him to 'restore universal justice, order and equality'.[27] 'I am from this moment on a level with other sovereigns, for ultimately they are, like me, rulers for their lifetime only. They and their Ministers will have more respect for me now. The power of a man who turns all the business of Europe round his fingers should not be, or seem to be, based on a precarious foundation.'[28] This argument, that Bonaparte was now on a par with other European heads of state, would be invoked again as a justification during the weeks leading up to the Empire, but it is one that says much more about Bonaparte than about European political conditions. Nothing had prevented the monarchs of Europe from having diplomatic relations with France before the Consulship for life. This was a question not of France being treated as an equal, but rather of Bonaparte's self-esteem, or lack of it.

Two weeks later, on 15 August, which also happened to be Bonaparte's birthday, the Consulship for life was marked by a reception at the Tuileries for various members of the legislative bodies and foreign ambassadors, followed by a concert given by 300 instrumentalists playing the music of Cherubini, Méhul and Rameau. In the afternoon a Te Deum was celebrated at Notre Dame, as well as in all the other churches in Paris. That evening, a nine-metre star was erected high above one of the towers of Notre Dame, in the centre of which was depicted the sign of the Zodiac under which Bonaparte was born – Leo. The façade of the Hôtel de Ville was illuminated in much the same way as it had been during festivities under the *ancien régime*. A firework display with over 12,000 rockets was set off – although the crowds were apparently unimpressed – and a thirteen-metre-high statue of Peace was erected on the Pont Neuf, placed on a globe of the world, so that the whole was thirty-two metres high.[29] It was meant to bear witness to the gratitude of the nation. The street celebrations lasted till one in the morning.

From this time on, Bonaparte used to say that his power was founded on the imagination of the French people – that is, that it was founded not on a realistic assessment of his achievements, but rather on an idealized version.[30] Members of his entourage disputed that interpretation, but there was nevertheless an increasing belief that Bonaparte was vital to the proper functioning of the state. Everything was being brought back to that one question – the indispensability of the First Consul. It led to a debate, of sorts, around the desirability of the establishment of heredity.[31] Depending on the source, we can read that Bonaparte was either for or against the idea of hereditary power, which is to say that his attitude was ambivalent to say the least. If in August 1802 he was reported as having said, 'heredity alone can prevent the counter-revolution',[32] he rejected the idea during a meeting of the Council of State: 'Heredity is absurd, not in the sense that it does not ensure the stability of the state, but because it is impossible in France . . . How can one reconcile the heredity of the first magistrate with the first principle of sovereignty of the people?'[33]

Bonaparte's thinking may have evolved to reflect a change in popular attitudes, a move away from republican virtue towards monarchical principles. Not only were his intimate advisers already urging Bonaparte to re-establish some form of monarchy, but so too were some of his royalist opponents, persuaded that 'once the monarchy had been re-established in France, they would only have to drive away the parvenu monarch, or, if he could not be overthrown, to await his death in order to give back to its former owners the throne he had raised up'.[34] They were not, as things turned out, far off the mark, since constitutional monarchy was the type of government the revolutionaries of 1789 had wanted to implement. People were now starting to talk about it once more.

The Consulship for life was important not only for how Bonaparte was perceived by the people of France but also for how the state was now perceived.[35] Bonaparte increasingly came to embody the head of the Church in France, the executive and the head of the army. He was thus breaking with the revolutionary tradition by combining the military and the government in his person, which put him at a distinct advantage over any other European head of state, a position the world had not seen since Frederick the Great. Alexander I of Russia (successor of Paul I, who had been assassinated in March 1801) and Frederick William III of Prussia may have been nominally head of their respective armies, but they left the effective command to competent generals. Not so Bonaparte. France's army was also his army. He not only appeared at its head, he not only shared the hardships of the troops on the ground, but he was also personally responsible for both victory and defeat. 'Bonaparte', reflected the novelist, essayist and opponent Germaine de Staël, 'ably took hold of the enthusiasm of the French for military glory, and associated their self-love with his victories as well as his defeats. He gradually took the place of the Revolution in everyone's mind, and attached to his name alone all the national sentiment that had raised France in the eyes of foreigners.'[36]

The state was increasingly embodied in Bonaparte's person. It was one way in which the state was given sense and meaning in the aftermath of ten years of revolutionary upheaval. However, this meant that any opposition to the regime centred on his person as well. He thus became, from the time he assumed power, the unique object of all the conspiracies directed against the state.[37] As his power increased, so too did the number of his enemies, most of whom were persuaded that it was simply a question of striking a blow against one man for the whole edifice to come tumbling down.[38] The knives were being sharpened in the shadows.

## Pots of Butter and Malcontent Republicans

The combination of the Concordat and the Consulship for life was bound to exasperate republicans. A good deal of that exasperation came from the army. A police report showed the extent to which its upper echelons were angry at what they considered to be Bonaparte's flouting of republican principles, afraid that it would somehow lead to a restoration of the monarchy.[39] And there were a lot of generals and superior officers in Paris with little or nothing to do. At the beginning of the Consulate, between 6,000 and 7,000 officers were sidelined or were put on half-pay while the army was either purged or reorganized to fit Bonaparte's vision.[40] These officers complained loudly of their treatment and vented their anger and frustration on the person whom they held responsible for their plight.[41] They went around causing trouble, or at least speaking their minds, which to Bonaparte meant the same thing, getting involved in factional politics, speaking out against reconciliation with the Church and publicly insulting members of the government.[42]

Bonaparte had been aware from the start that the army would oppose negotiations with the Catholic Church, but he knew that he had to press ahead regardless.[43] The people needed religion, and the government had to control that religion.[44] For the moment, republican opposition within the army was limited to a series of rather ineffectual public gestures reminiscent of badly behaved adolescents. There was no attempt at a concerted political opposition.[45] Oppositional elements within the military and administration did not know how to express their discontent, or were so cut off from mainstream society that they were unable to do so. Republican exasperation with Bonaparte seems to have reached a peak in 1802.[46] Certain generals, out of political conviction or personal enmity towards the First Consul, began conspiring against him. Their opposition has sometimes been referred to rather melodramatically as the 'Generals' Plot', but it was never really more than a half-baked conspiracy among a group of high-ranking officers, Jacobins, that posed no real threat to either the regime or Bonaparte's life.[47] They did little more than vent their feelings against Bonaparte. Meetings were supposed to have been held in Paris, at Rueil, in which a plan was sketched out that would have divided France into twelve provinces, each led by a general. Paris was to go to Bonaparte. Masséna was supposed to bring him a declaration outlining the decision – he appears to have become the centre of attraction for some of these officers – but he refused, and that was the end of it.[48] Indeed, most of the republican military opposition to Bonaparte, while it may have been pervasive in some sections of the army, was uncoordinated and dispersed. Throughout the Consulate and the Empire, the police now and then arrested individuals, but none of them ever posed a serious threat to the regime.[49]

One of the more notorious conspiracies involved the production and distribution of pamphlets denouncing Bonaparte as a tyrant. Rennes was the centre

of the 'conspiracy' where Bernadotte's chief of staff and close friend General
Edouard François Simon was charged with printing and distributing anti-
government leaflets that were meant to prepare the army for a coup. Two
leaflets were printed,[50] and were supposed to be distributed throughout the
country in stoneware pots used in the manufacture of butter. One of them,
*Appel aux armées françaises par leurs camarades* (A call to the French armies by
their comrades), declared, 'Soldiers, you no longer have a fatherland, the
Republic no longer exists and your glory is tarnished. Your name has faded and
is without honour. A *tyrant* has seized power, and who is that tyrant? *Bonaparte!*'[51] Thousands of copies were distributed. Some of them eventually fell
into the hands of the local authorities, who traced them back to Bernadotte's
entourage. It was so swiftly nipped in the bud – Fouché contacted the prefects
who then inspected the post office in their localities – that the public never
heard about the so-called 'Conspiracy of Pamphlets' (*conspiration des libelles*).[52]

Simon was arrested (and eventually released in June 1804), as were at least
nineteen superior officers, who were discharged or exiled, including one of
Moreau's aides-de-camp.[53] Consequently, Fouché interrogated Moreau, but
the general laughed off the suggestion of any involvement, calling it a 'conspiracy of pots of butter' (*conspiration des pots de beurre*). Bernadotte was
implicated in the affair, although it is unlikely that he was aware of what was
going on. What could he hope to achieve from such an amateurish attempt at
overthrowing Bonaparte?[54] Bernadotte was, by all accounts, jealous of Bonaparte – he had opposed Brumaire, and had insisted that Bonaparte appear
before a court martial and even that he be shot for having abandoned his army
in Egypt – and had since frequently met with senators hostile to the First
Consul, so it was easy for Bonaparte to assume he was involved in the plot.


## 'An Aura of Fear'

During the Consulship for life, Bonaparte eliminated everything that reminded
people of the Revolution, right down to the manner in which people conducted
themselves in his presence. Very quickly a change occurred in the way people
dressed at the Tuileries. At the beginning of 1801, a member of the Tribunate,
André-François Miot, Comte de Mélito, noted how trousers, sabres and cockades had already been replaced by silk stockings, shoe buckles, ceremonial
swords and hats placed under the arm.[55] Most people were unaccustomed to
these new social norms, and there were apparently some interesting mixtures
of dress that invited a certain amount of ridicule from those who knew better.
Miot de Mélito cites the case of a man who turned up at the palace superbly
dressed in a purple velvet frock coat, white stockings, a sword, and buckles on
his shoes, but who combined it with a black cravat, considered a very serious
breach of the dress code. The old aristocracy could not help but compare their

own manners with those who did not know how to behave, or who could not perform simple tasks like walking on a waxed floor properly.[56]

By introducing social forms that had been part and parcel of court life during the *ancien régime*, Bonaparte was at one and the same time asserting the regime's social as well as political legitimacy. In doing so, he obliged the old aristocracy and the new elites to mix and to behave in the same manner. The politics of social fusion was central to the regime's success. That was only one aspect. Etiquette was as much about how people perceived Bonaparte as about creating an artificial barrier between himself and his entourage, thereby conveying a sense of power.[57] This was observed by a contemporary writer and social commentator, Louis-Sébastien Mercier: 'Etiquette, a prince will say, is a puerile thing about which I would be the first to laugh, but it is the only bulwark that separates me from other men. Remove it, I am nothing more than a gentleman.'[58] It was a method Bonaparte had employed in Italy, creating 'an aura of fear' (*une auréole de crainte*) around his person that prevented familiarity of any kind.[59] Bonaparte's court, in other words, is also revealing of the man. The fact that it was excessively formal, even by the standards of the day, lends weight to the idea that he strove to erect barriers between his intimate self and his surrounds. Access to Bonaparte, and later more so to Napoleon, was strictly controlled; precedence was introduced so that, depending on a person's rank and function, he could enter only certain rooms in the Tuileries Palace.[60] According to one British witness, the rooms leading to the First Consul's personal apartments were each reserved. 'On the days of the grand parade, the first room is destined for officers as low as the rank of captain, and persons admitted with tickets; the second, for field-officers; the third, for generals; and the fourth, for counsellors of state, and the diplomatic corps.'[61] It would seem that fear equalled respect in Bonaparte's mind.

To carry through the introduction of a new etiquette, Bonaparte and his would-be courtiers, most of whom came from the provincial bourgeoisie and were utterly unaccustomed to the ways of pre-revolutionary aristocratic society, had to learn everything anew.[62] They were obliged to rely on books, and on those who could remember what it had been like: old valets were interrogated, nobles who had lived at the courts of Louis XV and Louis XVI were consulted. There were of course few former members of the French court to consult; emigration had hit the *noblesse de robe* hardest. Two, however, were found: Mme de Montesson and Mme de Campan. Mme de Campan had been Marie-Antoinette's *femme de chambre* and had run a finishing school for girls in Saint-Germain-en-Laye (both Caroline and Hortense had gone to school there), so she knew a thing or two about etiquette, as did Mme de Montesson, the wife of Louis Philippe, Duc d'Orléans (the father of Philippe-Egalité, whose son would become king in 1840), who had befriended Josephine during the Revolution.

Josephine was to play an important role in this social legitimizing, holding informal breakfasts at the Tuileries and at Malmaison for between five and fifteen young women at a time, so that they could become acquainted with the customs of good society without feeling intimidated.[63] Bonaparte wanted *ancien régime* court traditions to continue because they represented an exercise in the display of power, but he also, like the Bourbon monarchs before him, wanted to create a social centre of power that would become uncontested, and in the process marginalize all others. Naturally, not everyone was happy with the outcome. Certain officers complained that it was now difficult to get to see Bonaparte, and that monarchical forms had replaced military camaraderie.[64]

## A Republic in Uniform

The introduction of etiquette was a gradual process but not an entirely successful one if some of the contemporary accounts are to be believed. The Tuileries was run with military precision, while the rules governing relations between people would eventually become excessively formal, to the point where conversation and friendships were stifled and boredom became the rule.[65] People would nevertheless attend because to do so was to be at the centre of power. Etiquette was strictly regulated by Bonaparte, right down to the number of gun salutes or the duration of church-bell ringing during inspection tours. So too was the official hierarchy; it gave precedence to civilians over the military. However, in order to reinforce that precedence, and give all French officials, right down to the local mayor, an exterior symbol of their power, they were now required to wear a uniform – including high-school students.[66] Indeed, every member of court from the highest to the lowest was now told what to wear and when to wear it. Bonaparte too wore civilian dress in the weeks and months after Brumaire, but on his return from Marengo he stopped wearing the Consular uniform on a regular basis and started wearing the green and white uniform of a colonel of the Chasseurs à cheval, at least on weekdays.[67] At weekends he would wear the blue and white uniform of a colonel of the Grenadiers à pied. It would appear that he rarely donned civilian dress after that – he did so during the signing of the Treaty of Amiens in March 1802 and at the Te Deum for the Concordat the following month for example. That was not the case for the rest of the court, the luxury of which soon became the object of much gossip and rumour.[68] Bonaparte thus deliberately juxtaposed his simple dress with that of the elaborate dress found at court and among the high-ranking military.[69] In this way, he became the link between the people and the court,[70] dressing down even as he gave strict orders to everyone else to dress up. He was not the only French monarch to have used this controlling technique: Henry III and Henry IV had consciously and successfully done the same, while Bonaparte's predecessor, Louis XVI, had also preferred simple dress to elaborate court costume. 'The right to dress simply', Bonaparte is supposed to have said, 'does not belong to everyone.'[71]

In the realm of diplomacy, too, there was a return to more formalized styles. The revolutionaries had made a conscious effort to break with *ancien régime* diplomatic norms, tainted by association with the aristocracy.[72] Their approach had hardly been successful, and did a good deal to scandalize, shock and alienate the courts of Europe. Soon enough, political expediency triumphed over ideological commitments, and traditional diplomatic conventions were reintroduced during the Directory. Bonaparte, however, went a step further. In 1800, Pierre Bénézech, a former minister of the interior and member of the Council of Five Hundred, now a member of the Council of State, was given the job of receiving foreign ambassadors, and acted as a kind of master of the ceremonies. In November 1801, a key post was given to Bonaparte's friend Michel Duroc – he was made governor of the Tuileries, with a colossal salary of 24,000 francs per year. From 1802 on, the First Consul started to hold audiences in a manner reminiscent of the former kings of France. It was important at the early stages of his reign, however, not to shock republicans and revolutionaries too much, which is why, as a sop to them, he used as many people as possible who had risen through the ranks during the Revolution.

Etiquette was not simply a personal display of power. Bonaparte was giving himself, as head of state, a certain prestige, but he was also attempting to efface the egalitarianism that had been one of the primary values of the Revolution. In the process, he could banish from his entourage elements he considered undesirable. The flipside to that coin was that he could confide important functions to members of the former nobility in order to facilitate their reintegration into the state. All of this was codified in the *Etiquette du Palais Impérial*, which first appeared in print in 1805, and which was a clearer guide to the power structure of the state than the redundant Constitution. It is an extraordinary document for understanding the nature of the Napoleonic Empire, how court life was regulated and who could have access to the Emperor.[73] The *lever* and the *coucher*, ceremonies surrounding the act of getting up in the morning and going to bed in the evening, which had fallen into disuse under Louis XVI, were revived during the Consulate and were now codified.[74] Bonaparte greatly simplified the practice: the bedroom receded into the domain of the private and was no longer the central focus of the *lever* or the *coucher*, as it had been; he simply 'received' in a salon before going to bed or on getting up. There were two further distinctions: admittance to the court was based on military rank or official position rather than, as at the court of Versailles, social status or lineage; and anyone in an official capacity, as we have seen, was now obliged to wear a uniform. As under the former kings of France, etiquette and uniforms were a means of controlling and dominating those in Napoleon's entourage.[75] Uniform became an important part of court life and was a return in many respects to the *ancien régime* courts where a coat, knee-breeches and silk stockings were obligatory. For a society now built around the idea of meritocracy, but not equality or egalitarianism, this was also a way of making a clear distinction between those with power and influence and those without.[76] It was also a sign of the increasing regimentation, if not militarization, of French society. In July 1804, a decree was issued regulating the official costume of the Empire, designed by Jean-Baptiste Isabey.[77]

The court came to dominate French society and politics in a way that it had never done before, even during the time of Louis XIV.[78] Napoleon's court, with more than 2,700 officials and over 100 chamberlains, was much larger than anything that had preceded it – the Houses of the Emperor and Empress were four times larger than those of the royals during the *ancien régime* – and was the largest in Europe.[79] If all the households belonging to his relatives were included, the number probably rose to over 4,000.

### 'Weeping Tears of Blood'

In keeping with this new attitude of creating artificial barriers, Bonaparte rarely acted with any warmth at court; he never shook hands, for example. There were, however, a few notable exceptions to the rule, occasions during which Bonaparte lost his sangfroid and displayed emotion, as when he gave foreign diplomats a dressing down. One of those occasions involved the British ambassador to Paris, Charles Whitworth.

The choice of Lord Whitworth as ambassador is an indication of what the British government thought of the French and the Treaty of Amiens. Whitworth was a zealous anti-revolutionary, was directly involved in the plot to assassinate the Tsar Paul I and was a close friend of Lord Grenville, who had opposed peace with France. Whitworth's dispatches portrayed Bonaparte as a deranged tyrant of the same ilk as Paul I.[80] In one letter written in April 1803, he described the actions taken by the First Consul as exhibiting 'a picture of despotism, violence, and cruelty, at the contemplation of which humanity sickens'.[81] As charming as Bonaparte could be at times, he failed to melt Whitworth's cold exterior. Paris could not help but interpret Whitworth's uncompromising stance as being determined by the British government.[82] In many respects it was.

Things came to a head during a reception of the diplomatic corps in the Tuileries on 13 March 1803.[83] Josephine, attended for the first time by maids of honour, was holding an audience in one of the drawing rooms, at which the foreign ambassadors were present.[84] Bonaparte was not expected – he had just held another audience in one of his own rooms – but he nevertheless decided to pay a visit. At first, he seems to have been in good spirits, doing the rounds, exchanging banter with the foreign diplomats present, including Whitworth. But then he came back to Whitworth and demanded to know why the conditions of Amiens had not yet been fulfilled. He was referring to the requirement that Britain should withdraw from Malta. Whitworth is supposed to have replied that Egypt had been evacuated and that Malta would be as soon as the other conditions of the treaty were filled. Whitworth then had to face a two-hour monologue at the end of which Bonaparte delivered an ultimatum – give up Malta or go to war.

Whitworth's version of events in his reports caused a little storm in London.[85] He chose to underline Bonaparte's 'agitation', and his own imperturbability. There is one other available British eyewitness account, that by the Reverend John Sanford, who happened to be present in Josephine's drawing room, which emphatically denies that Bonaparte raised his voice.[86] 'The impropriety consisted in the unfitness of the place for such a subject.' The Russian plenipotentiary, Arkady Morkov, another Francophobe, wrote of Bonaparte addressing the assembly in a 'loud voice: *Malta or war, and a curse on those who violate treaties!*'[87] It is possible (although there is nothing to support this view) that Whitworth and Morkov consulted each other in the days that followed, and perhaps even worked each other up into a bit of a lather.

Much has been made of this incident, as though it were a turning point in the history of relations between the two countries, but really the scene is indicative of a general malaise between France and the great powers rather than of a deterioration in diplomatic relations. We know that Bonaparte was in the habit of losing his temper, but on this occasion his outburst was not egregious. His behaviour can in part be explained by naivety. In matters of foreign policy and even diplomatic etiquette, he was an inexperienced amateur, credulous enough to think that he could act and speak on the international scene in the same way that he spoke to his soldiers, and that he could do so without consequence. However, his behaviour has also to be seen within a broader context. The French were masters of the Continent, they considered themselves to be the epitome of European civilization,[88] and most French generals, not to mention the political elite, agreed with the policies Bonaparte had adopted. The attitude of the British was insufferable and inflexible; they were meddling in Continental affairs and they had failed to fulfil their treaty obligations.

Neither side was about to give ground, so that by the time Whitworth had arrived in Paris, war between the two countries was inevitable.[89] It was simply a question of timing. The reasons why can be rattled off, although it is much more difficult to understand why the British acted at that particular moment.[90] The French would appear to be responsible for the rupture. The British objected to France intervening in a civil war that was raging in Switzerland in October 1801, imposing a new constitution and a new treaty, the Act of Mediation that enabled France to control the Alpine passes[91]; to keeping Holland occupied by French troops;[92] to annexing Piedmont in

September 1802; but most of all to continuing French designs on Egypt.[93]
None of the concerns raised by the British breached the Treaty of Amiens.
The French intervention in Switzerland, for example, was consistent with
French meddling in that country going back more than sixty years.[94] French
behaviour was aggressive and worrying, and generated suspicion about
whether Bonaparte could be trusted. But the British did breach the Treaty of
Amiens by failing to give up Malta, and they did so on the pretext of French
policy in Piedmont and Switzerland.[95] The real reason was that they needed
Malta, key to the naval domination of the western Mediterranean, to prevent
what they feared most, a second French attempt to conquer Egypt and the
consequent threat to India.

One can add to the mix the virulent anti-French/anti-Bonaparte campaign
in the English press that consisted of a series of articles and caricatures attacking both Bonaparte and his family, which by all accounts irritated and possibly
even hurt him.[96] He had his secretary, Bourrienne, read out the British papers
during his morning ablutions.[97] The *Morning Post*, for example, described him
as a 'Mediterranean mulatto'.[98] It is true that Addington asked newspapers,
unofficially, not to publish defamatory articles against Bonaparte, but this
could hardly have the desired impact.[99] A leading émigré journalist, Jean-
Gabriel Peltier, was prosecuted for criminal libel as a sop to Bonaparte, but
that was the extent of it.[100] The foreign secretary Lord Hawkesbury tried to
reassure the First Consul that the British government would deport royalists
involved in distributing anti-Bonaparte propaganda, but this was never done.[101]
Instead, the government paid lip-service to freedom of speech, and protested
its impotence regarding the expulsion of émigré journalists, claiming that it
lacked the authority to do so. In contrast, pro-French journalists were expelled
from Britain using the Alien Act without so much as the pretence of a trial.[102]
The French consequently perceived London's position as hypocritical. Bonaparte responded by waging a campaign to silence the hostile press in England
by trying to bribe émigré journalists – with some notable successes – and by
putting diplomatic pressure on governments to pursue journalists hostile to
the Consulate. If the British government did little to placate Bonaparte, it is
because it did not want to, exacerbating an already tense situation and creating
a climate in which compromise was impossible.[103]

Neither side had peace at heart. The French–British disagreement had its
root in deep-seated cultural antipathies exacerbated by years of war and an
unwillingness to come to an understanding.[104] When Whitworth delivered an
oral ultimatum to Talleyrand on 26 April – evacuate Holland within a month
and agree to a temporary British occupation of Malta (for a period of ten years)
– Talleyrand asked for it to be submitted in writing. Whitworth declined,
saying that he was unauthorized to do so; Talleyrand did not even bother passing on the ultimatum to Bonaparte (Whitworth repeated the ultimatum to

Joseph later that same day).[105] Talleyrand quite possibly did not take Whit-worth's threats very seriously, since he was getting upbeat reports from his ambassador General Antoine-François Andréossy in London, suggesting that the talks to prevent a rupture were progressing.[106] As for Whitworth, not submitting the ultimatum in writing seems a strange thing to do at such a crit-ical juncture. Either the ultimatum was bluff, therefore, something that he used to prod the French into compromise, or he had determined to precipitate a rupture. The latter seems more likely since two days later he asked for pass-ports for himself and his family to be delivered on 2 May.

It was obvious to all that war was going to resume sooner rather than later. On 1 May 1803, after a *lever* at the Palace, Bonaparte addressed a number of senators and councillors of state alluding to the likelihood of war. 'England will finish by weeping tears of blood,' he is supposed to have exclaimed; 'the war, it has begun.'[107] It may have been bluster, but he appears to have been genuinely upset by the manner in which Britain had delivered the ultimatum. In Paris, the certainty of war had been on everyone's lips for the past weeks and months.[108] The British, too, had been preparing for war, at least since March 1803, when most of the navy had been manned and supplied.

Britain officially declared war on 18 May 1803. Two days before the decla-ration, the British seized 1,200 French and Dutch merchant ships and more than £200 million-worth of merchandise. Bonaparte responded on 22 May by ordering the arrest of all British subjects and the seizure of all British ships and merchandise in France and the Italian Republic (the name of the Cisalpine Republic was changed in January 1802).[109] The increased political tensions and the likelihood of war had already decided many tourists to leave and they had been doing so in a steady stream since March, some returning home, others moving on to neighbouring countries. 'Flight was the order of the day,' accord-ing to one English tourist, Bertie Greatheed, 'and the most judicious prepared immediately for their departure.'[110] Surprisingly, Bertie was not one of them; when he went to get his passport on 23 May, he was informed that he was a prisoner of war. As a result of Bonaparte's decree, unusual in that there was no precedent for the internment of foreign nationals on the outbreak of war, just about every British man, woman and child who could be got hold of was arrested and held, in some instances until the end of the conflict. They were at first kept in Paris and then progressively dispersed to a number of provincial towns, the most important of which was Verdun, where they were held in the local fortress. The French claimed that 7,500 were arrested, but this seems to be a grossly inflated figure and it is more likely that 700–800 were detained.[111] How many of these people escaped in the course of the conflict is difficult to know.

The peace had lasted fourteen months. The war was going to last another twelve years.

'Six Centuries of Outrage to Avenge'[112]
The arrest of British nationals was accompanied by a campaign in the French press against Britain that was reminiscent of language directed against the Revolution's enemies at the height of the Terror; it called for the extermination of perfidious Albion.[113] Before the peace, Britain had been portrayed as the new Carthage, a tyrant on the high seas, with an immense and insatiable ambition, countered by a French government that fought only 'for peace and the Happiness of the world'.[114] In September 1803, Bonaparte enlisted the help of Bertrand Barère de Vieuzac, renowned for having called for the extermination of all rebels in the Vendée in 1793, and asked him to direct his talents at the English.[115] He did so with a newspaper whose sole purpose was to underline the perfidy of the English government, the despotism of its commerce and the problems the country faced.[116] 'There is no piracy, no brigandage, no crime, no cowardice in Europe of which it [the British government] is not the instigator, the agent or the accomplice.'[117] The person most responsible for everything from piracy to espionage, to assassinations and counterfeiting was that 'degenerate child' Pitt.[118]

The newspaper was hardly a roaring success, but it was playing a tune most French people were familiar with. Some of the more extreme examples of Anglophobia could be found in the popular pamphlets of the day.[119] This propaganda campaign was one of the reasons why the French, although by no means welcoming it, believed war justified, especially when, as we shall see, a plot to kill Bonaparte was tied to the British government. Bonaparte capably portrayed himself during this period as the victim, and not as the aggressor, as someone whom Britain despised and hired assassins to murder. If he had to draw his sword once more to defend the *patrie* it was because perfidious Albion, the term most commonly associated with Britain,[120] obliged him to do so. It was a theme that the regime played on throughout the Empire. It was able to do so successfully because of the longstanding and traditional hatred between the two countries.

George III, as well as most of the military and political elite, remained supremely confident that the French would fail in their attempt to cross the Channel.[121] The English public, on the other hand, was a good deal more anxious.[122] The *Morning Post* reported in the first week of October that the invasion was to take place 'immediately', after strong gales had dispersed the British fleet.[123] In some regions, rumours about an impending invasion caused a panic that has been dubbed the Great Terror. The Reverend Thomas Twining left Colchester, because he was 'afraid to stay in it'.[124] To meet this threat there was, apart from the Royal Navy, a militia of around 110,000 men – whose fighting quality was dubious, but who might have been used in guerrilla actions – and about 129,000 regular army troops.[125] Admiral Nelson suggested that Charles-François Dumouriez, a French general who had defected to the Austrians in 1793, be brought to London to draw up plans on how to meet an invasion.[126] It led to schemes for a scorched-earth policy and the creation of a vast network of coastal defences.[127] Seventy-four Martello towers were constructed along the coast.[128] A telegraph system – consisting of wooden cabins with frames containing shutters – was set up to communicate between the coast and the roof of the Admiralty in London.[129] But some hare-brained schemes were also born of the moment, which, in hindsight, appear to have been an overreaction. They included the construction of the Royal Military Canal behind the Romney Marshes in the south-east of England – nineteen metres wide, and almost three metres deep – which was somehow meant to impede the advancing French, and the construction of dams built to flood the Lea Valley outside London.[130] Much of this was offset by satire. *The Times* published a piece loosely based on the Hamlet soliloquy in which Bonaparte is heard to repeat the lines, 'T'invade or not t'invade – that is the question.'[131]

# 7

# The End of the Revolution

## The Plot to Kill Bonaparte

Victory in war was not the only means of eliminating Bonaparte from the scene.

On 23 August 1803, an English ship brought Georges Cadoudal and a number of other royalist agents to the French coast where they disembarked on the beaches of Biville-sur-Mer, not far from Dieppe in Normandy. Cadoudal was a big, corpulent, blond man, who had been dubbed 'Gideon' during the Chouan struggle against the Revolution.* Described as having 'a short, squashed nose, blue eyes, a small mouth, a round dimpled chin, a flat face, hair à la Titus,† and thin sideburns',[1] Cadoudal was intelligent, completely devoted to the royalist cause, audacious and untiring, and he hated Bonaparte with a passion.[2] His best friend and his brother had both been killed in the struggle against the revolutionary state. He had left France in 1800 after the offensive launched by Bonaparte against the counter-revolution. Before Cadoudal left, Pitt, informed of what the group was up to, asked him to bring back Bonaparte alive – there were thoughts even at this stage of exiling him to St Helena – but whether he really believed that Bonaparte would be captured and not killed is another matter. It was not the first time that the British government had been involved in eliminating a European sovereign whose foreign policy they found to be an impediment. It had been, after all, deeply implicated in the assassination of Paul I of Russia in 1801.

When Cadoudal and his small band landed, they made their way to Paris in stages, arriving on 30 August. During the five months he was there, Cadoudal would change his place of residence as often as he could so as not to get caught, on one occasion living only a few hundred metres from the prefecture of police. His plan was to stop Bonaparte on the road to Saint-Cloud or Malmaison, occasions when the First Consul moved around with only a weak escort. Even then, however, it was obvious that a fight would be necessary, and Cadoudal would have to gather a sufficient number of men,[3] as well as weapons and horses, to overwhelm Bonaparte's guard; this necessarily carried the

---

* Gideon means 'destroyer' or 'mighty warrior'.
† Hair à la Titus had different meanings at different periods of the Revolution. In the aftermath of the Terror, it was a very short and uneven cut, echoing the cropped hair of victims of the guillotine. It later took on softer tones, and was modelled on classical busts of the Emperor Titus.

risk of someone leaking the plan, inadvertently or deliberately. One response was to kill anyone who got in the way; in the second half of December 1803, a dozen executions were carried out against denunciators and government functionaries. Louis XVI's brother, the Comte d'Artois, is meant to have assured Cadoudal before the royalist left Britain that he would appear on French soil to launch a general insurrection as soon as he received news of Bonaparte's kidnapping. It was impractical madness, based on the notion that it was enough to eliminate one man for the whole system to crumble. The fact that the émigré press had been focusing its attacks on the head of the French state probably contributed to that illusion.[4] And yet Cadoudal was convinced he could pull it off.

General Charles Pichegru lent his support (he had escaped from Guiana where he had been exiled after Fructidor in 1797), and was also transported on a British vessel to France where he landed on 16 January 1804. His role was to convince Moreau to take part in the conspiracy, to overthrow the government and assume provisional control while awaiting the return of the Comte d'Artois.[5] The plan was puerile in its conception, not to mention the fact that the police were on the plotters' tails from the moment they entered Paris.[6] We know that Pichegru met with Moreau at the beginning of 1804. One of the conspirators, General Frédéric-Michel de Lajolais, turned up at Moreau's house announcing the arrival of Pichegru and asking for an interview.[7] Moreau refused, but Pichegru took advantage of a reception being held on 1 February to introduce himself into Moreau's house. Moreau, wary of getting involved, simply declared that he did not want to participate in the restoration of the Bourbons and told him to flee to Germany. Some historians, more sympathetic towards Bonaparte, find in Moreau a small-minded, vain man who bore a grudge against Bonaparte because he considered that his own military victories had not received due attention. This was true, but personal motives do not make for sound politics, and were in any event a poor excuse to plot against a head of state. Moreau himself perhaps understood this, or perhaps had greater political ambitions than the conspirators realized; he rejected the royalist solution but seemed prepared to discuss the plot with the conspirators. In February, another meeting between Pichegru and Moreau took place, this time with Cadoudal present; several other meetings between the two generals followed.

This was imprudent, given the counter-intelligence networks that were in place. Over a period of several weeks the police cast their net wide; houses were raided and anyone slightly suspect was brought in for questioning, and more often than not thrown in jail. Those with powerful protectors could get out within a day or so; others were imprisoned for weeks on end.[8] At the beginning of February, Cadoudal's servant, Louis Picot, was arrested and revealed the presence of Cadoudal and Pichegru in Paris.[9] On 9 February, another conspirator was arrested, Bouvet de Lozier.[10] After a failed suicide attempt – he tried to hang himself in his cell but a jailer cut the cord in time – he revealed the name of another accomplice: Moreau. 'Monsieur [that is, the Comte d'Artois] was to arrive in France and put himself at the head of the royalist party, Moreau promised to join the Bourbon cause.' Bonaparte was in the middle of being shaved by his valet, Constant, when the minister of justice and grand judge, Claude-Ambroise Régnier, who had personally questioned the prisoner, came to tell him the news. Bonaparte, nevertheless, acted with some caution.[11]

There was nothing shocking about Pichegru being implicated in a plot against Bonaparte; he had been involved with royalist plots before and was known to the authorities. Moreau was another story. What was Bonaparte supposed to do with the victor of Hohenlinden? Were other generals involved? Bonaparte must have been feeling paranoid at this point, although we have no idea what he actually thought since he never revealed himself, at least not on a level that would satisfy the curious biographer. He spoke about this event on St Helena a number of times, but without really assuming responsibility for his acts and always hiding behind the façade of 'reasons of state'.[12]

The conspirators hoped to get Moreau onside and, through him, part of the army he commanded, more loyal to its commander-in-chief than to the government. Moreau's reputation was such that many reformed officers (officers on half-pay) considered him an alternative to Bonaparte.[13] During an emergency meeting of the Council of State, the First Consul read out Bouvet de Lozier's confession. Talleyrand and Fouché did not see any proof of guilt but it was enough for Bonaparte. Ignoring their advice, he had an order for Moreau's arrest issued. Moreau was taken on the morning of 15 February 1804, his carriage surrounded by elite gendarmes as he was crossing the bridge at Charenton, coming into Paris.[14]

One should not underestimate the ruthlessness of Bonaparte. At the same time that Moreau was taken into custody, 356 other arrests were made, some of them of ultra-republican and royalist generals.[15] It was an opportune moment to purge the army once and for all of elements that opposed the regime. Nevertheless, news of Moreau's arrest caused a tremendous stir in Paris.[16] The police reports from this period are witness to how much the public disapproved of it.[17] He was popular, and was assumed to be a republican, at least in army circles. 'Everyone here praises and extols you,' wrote Moreau's brother.[18] For those in the army, Hohenlinden was considered a great victory; Moreau, regarded as the 'son of the Revolution', was idolized by republicans. Rather than see in his arrest proof that he had been involved in a plot against the government, people suspected Bonaparte of trying to eliminate a rival on his route to absolute power.[19] Officers who had served with Moreau considered his disgrace to have been prompted by jealousy on the part of the First

Consul.[20] A delegation from the Tribunate even went to Bonaparte to plead Moreau's case.[21] If the people of Paris had not exactly been shaken as if by an earthquake, as one diplomat put it, many were taken aback.[22]

Almost two weeks later, sold out by a supposed friend, Cadoudal was arrested after a chase through the streets of Paris that ended in one police officer being killed and another wounded. His description had been posted on the walls of Paris, as well as in the *Moniteur*, so it was only a matter of time before he was caught. Shortly afterwards, on 28 February 1804, Pichegru was arrested, also denounced by a 'friend'.[23] The whole conspiracy was unravelling. Imprisoned in the Temple, where only a few short years before the royal family had been held, Cadoudal willingly admitted to wanting to 'attack the First Consul with violence [*vive force*]', although he denied that he had ever met Moreau. Under torture, the conspirators admitted that a Bourbon prince was expected in France.

## The Kidnapping and Execution of the Duc d'Enghien

The arrest of Georges Cadoudal was a great coup for the regime; people no longer questioned whether there had been a plot to kill Bonaparte, and it led to people doubting Moreau's innocence. If a plot really existed, and so many people had been arrested, then Moreau could not have been arrested without reason.[24] In the meantime, everyone was scratching their heads trying to figure out who was the 'prince' Cadoudal referred to. Certainly, the Comte d'Artois came to mind and was the prince most people were talking about in the cafés in Paris. There had been, months before Cadoudal's arrest, rumours that Artois was about to land in France.[25] Bonaparte took them seriously enough to send General Savary, whom we met when he was Desaix's aide-de-camp, in person to the cliffs of Biville-sur-Mer to watch out for his arrival. A vessel did approach the coast and Savary tried to lure it in further by lighting signal fires, but the ship sailed away.

The government was persuaded that Artois was the prince in question, but he was inaccessible, safely tucked away in England. The only Bourbon prince anywhere near French territory was the Duc d'Enghien, in Ettenheim, a small village on the Rhine in Baden about forty kilometres south of Strasbourg, where he lived 'in great simplicity', attending to his garden with the few friends that had remained with him.[26] The only reason why Enghien, tenth in line to the throne, was living in Ettenheim in the first place was to be with the Princess Charlotte de Rohan, with whom he was in love. Rumour had it, entirely false as far as we know, that Enghien sometimes visited Strasbourg, then on French territory.[27] The prince, although not involved in the plot, was in the pay of the English and was believed to be working towards an invasion of France and the restoration of the Bourbon monarchy. It was for that reason that Bonaparte ordered that he be kidnapped and brought back to Paris.

Rarely did Bonaparte make important decisions without first consulting his ministers and closest advisers. This is what occurred on 10 March at the Tuileries. We do not have any details about what was actually said during this meeting, and most of what we have was written by those present years after the fall of the Empire, at a time when the Bourbons were back on the throne. Their accounts were therefore an attempt to play down their involvement in the killing of a prince of the blood, and cannot be considered particularly accurate. The two other consuls supposedly raised objections, Lebrun arguing that it would make a 'terrible noise', and Cambacérès that public opinion would be even more worked up against them, coming as it did on top of the arrest of Moreau.[28] Cambacérès was reprimanded for his trouble by Bonaparte along the lines of 'It becomes you well [*il vous sied bien*] to be so scrupulous, to be so sparing of the blood of kings, you who voted for the death of Louis XVI.'[29] We do have a document from Talleyrand, who let his views be known a couple of days before. This was, he wrote, an occasion to resolve any concerns about the stability of the government. Bonaparte had the right to defend himself. 'If justice must punish rigorously, it must also punish without exceptions.'[30] Talleyrand's suggestion is clear – in order to allay any fears that there might be a return of the former royal House, an example had to be set. Two days after the meeting, Bonaparte was at Malmaison. It was from there that he ordered Enghien kidnapped, and held in the Château de Vincennes, on the outskirts of Paris, and not in the Temple, where state prisoners were usually kept. It is difficult to know whether Bonaparte, as some claim, hesitated a good deal before ordering Enghien's arrest,[31] but once the decision was made it seems likely that there was every intent to execute him.[32]

Everything was quickly put into place. On 15 March, a squad of several hundred troops and gendarmes, under the command of General Michel Ordener, penetrated the neutral territory of Baden in a commando-style raid and captured Enghien in Ettenheim.[33] It was indicative of the arrogance of the French, born of military superiority, that Bonaparte did not even bother to ask the Elector of Baden for approval to enter his territory. If he had done so, it is highly unlikely the Elector would have been able to refuse. Not doing so, however, caused a diplomatic storm, and a good deal of ill-will. Before being kidnapped, Enghien was going about his life, untroubled, despite a number of signs that should have put him on his guard. According to one source, he received a messenger from Paris at the beginning of March warning him that he had been discussed at the highest political levels. He at first refused to believe that he could be the subject of a kidnap, and then when he was brought around to the idea, severely underestimated the extent of the force that would be deployed against him.[34]

After being held in a prison in Strasbourg, Enghien was brought to Paris where he arrived in the evening of 20 March. The only thing that he had with him was his pug, Mohiloff, and only then because the pug had chased after its master all the way from Ettenheim, even swimming across the Rhine, before being allowed to get into the carriage used to escort the Duc. At the Château de Vincennes, Enghien was interrogated around midnight before appearing before a military tribunal. At the last minute, Bonaparte, who was possibly having second thoughts, sent the prefect of police, Pierre-François Réal, to interrogate the prisoner further. He arrived too late. At two o'clock in the morning, the tribunal condemned Enghien to death, a sentence that was carried out immediately. His grave had already been dug in the moat of the château, next to what is known as the Queen's Tower, and a firing squad had been made up of elite gendarmes. At three in the morning, by the light of a lantern, Enghien fell under a hail of musket shot, his dog by his side. Before doing so, his last words were supposed to have been 'How awful it is to die this way and at the hands of Frenchmen.'[35] We are not too sure what happened next, but when his body was exhumed in 1816, it was discovered that his skull had been crushed with a rock. The pug stayed over its master's grave howling for several days until the wife of the commander of the château adopted it.

Bonaparte intended making a very simple political statement – that his blood was as precious as that of any other head of state, and that there was nothing sacred about the Bourbons.[36] He knew perfectly well therefore what he was doing; the moment the Duc was kidnapped at Ettenheim, his death was a foregone conclusion. His execution is in fact revealing of Bonaparte's style of government. If one compares it with the trial and execution of Louis XVI, the king at least had a defence lawyer; the revolutionaries observed legal procedure. The murder of Enghien, on the other hand, was carried out with no regard for legal procedure, in front of a kangaroo court, in the dead of night. The only plausible explanation for Bonaparte's deciding Enghien should not receive a trial, apart from the fact that his abduction was less than legal, was because he felt he might get off. There was no concrete proof of his involvement in a plot against Bonaparte's life. This is, of course, something that Bonaparte must have been aware of even while the abduction was taking place.

At St Helena, Napoleon assumed responsibility for Enghien's death, almost. He argued that it had been an act of self-protection, a question of 'me or them', although he rewrote history to say that if he had known Enghien had asked to see him, he would have pardoned him.[37] On this, as on so many other points, Napoleon cannot be believed. It is unlikely that Savary would have precipitated matters without the prior consent of his master.[38] And yet the memoirs of the period (all written after the collapse of the Empire, it must be stressed) recall the news of the Duc's execution as a great shock. Armand de Caulaincourt, later Napoleon's master of the horse, who was part of the commando raid that crossed into Baden, is supposed to have cried, angry that he might have been made use of by Bonaparte in the crime;[39] Bonaparte's brother-in-law, Joachim Murat, is said to have burst into tears;[40] Josephine's son Eugène de Beauharnais was 'upset' because it had sullied Bonaparte's glory;[41] there had already been a scene between Josephine and Bonaparte on the night of the execution in which she supposedly knelt before him imploring him to spare Enghien, and when Eugène arrived at Malmaison the next day he found her in tears, directing the 'strongest criticisms' at Bonaparte, who listened in silence;[42] Talleyrand said he disapproved and is often quoted as quipping, 'It is worse than a crime, it is a blunder,' although this is probably apocryphal and has also been attributed to Fouché.[43] At the time, though, people who may have disapproved remained silent. When Bonaparte was informed of the death of Enghien, he supposedly murmured a passage from Voltaire's play *Alzira*:

> Of the Gods that we worship the difference see:
> To avenge and to kill is enjoined unto thee;
> But mine, when I fall 'neath thy murderous blow,
> Only bids me feel pity and pardon bestow.[44]

That too smacks of literary embellishment. In any event, Bonaparte was observed by one contemporary receiving news of the execution when he was described as 'troubled, preoccupied, sunk in thought . . . walking up and down his apartment, his hands at his back, his head bent down'.[45]

Despite the secrecy surrounding the execution, rumours raced immediately around Paris, spread by what the authorities called 'Chouans and émigrés'. Apart from a few foreign diplomats who were shocked by the news, Paris remained relatively indifferent.[46] But then newspapers were unable to state what they thought of the execution, so there could be no public debate on the subject. On the whole the French people were hardly moved by the death of a Bourbon, one moreover they had never heard of. Enghien's execution was seen as part of the Consular process of suppressing the political extremism that had torn France apart during the Revolution. The judgment of the military tribunal that tried Enghien, along with a number of other documents, was quickly printed and distributed. It is believed that more than 50,000 copies were sold in two days, a bestseller even by today's standards, and which leads one to suspect that if public opinion did not approve outright of the act, it was at the very least curious to find out about it.[47]

This was not the case for the rest of Europe.[48] Historians often point to the reaction among the courts of Europe and the extent to which Enghien's execution was supposed to be considered one of the most infamous public crimes of the era. It is true that Enghien's execution heightened the mistrust that existed in Berlin, Vienna and Petersburg, but relations between these courts and Paris were already strained – in the case of Russia and Austria, to breaking point.

The execution did not, therefore, have as great an impact as some historians have contended.[49] News of the execution in Petersburg came on a Saturday; the next day the Tsar ordered his court to go into mourning. After mass that Sunday, as the Tsar and Tsarina passed through the room in which the diplomatic corps was in attendance, they made a point of ignoring the French ambassador.[50] Admittedly, the execution of Enghien did not directly affect Russia, but the court of Petersburg, and Russian educated opinion, was nevertheless horrified.[51] One should, however, take this show of outrage, this public rebuke, with a grain of salt. The court would not have gone into mourning in normal circumstances – that is, if Enghien had died while a Bourbon was on the throne. It was not entirely cold calculation on Alexander's part but was nevertheless a convenient pretext for acting against France.[52]

In practical terms Russia responded with little more than a strongly worded letter sent to Bonaparte by the Tsar. He could hardly take the moral high ground. Not only had Alexander's father, Paul I, been assassinated in a palace plot only a few years before, but Alexander himself seems to have been involved in the affair. Bonaparte publicly baited Alexander on that possibility by publishing an article in the *Moniteur* in which he defended his actions, asking whether the Tsar would not have acted to seize the English involved in the killing of his father, Paul I, if he had found them no more than a league from the frontier.[53] Alexander was duly infuriated by the newspaper article. The execution of Enghien hardened Russian attitudes towards France and Bonaparte; most of the Russian gentry now came to see the First Consul as a despot – to show his contempt, one nobleman named his dogs 'Napoleoshka' and 'Josephinka' – even if attitudes were to remain profoundly ambivalent.[54]

In Prussia, Frederick William III was shocked by news of the execution, but was determined to hold fast to his policy of neutrality. Even when his wife, Luise, suggested imitating the Russian court by going into mourning, a number of leading ministers at court did their best to dissuade the royal couple from such an action, fearful that it might incur the wrath of Bonaparte.[55] And that was the norm: those most directly touched, the Bourbons of Naples, Florence and Madrid, said very little and thought it prudent not to act. So too the court of Vienna, which kept tellingly quiet, and Pope Pius VII, who is reported to have wept copiously at the news; the King of Sweden was indignant.[56] A sense of powerless outrage gripped the courts of Europe.

It has often been argued that the readiness of Europe's political elite to come to some sort of arrangement with Bonaparte disappeared in 1804, largely as a result of the execution of Enghien (and later with the proclamation of the Empire).[57] The execution may have been carried out for reasons of state, but it dealt a moral blow to the regime. Some nobles who had rallied to Bonaparte now turned their backs on him. Chateaubriand is a case in point. Convinced

that Brumaire represented a turning point in French political affairs, he had
become so accepting of the regime that he dedicated the second edition of his
book *Le Génie du christianisme* (The genius of Christianity) to Bonaparte
with the following words: 'One cannot help but recognize in your destiny the
hand of Providence who marked you from afar for the accomplishment of his
prodigious designs. The people look upon you. France, extended by its victories, has placed in you its hopes.'[58] He even went so far as to write to Bonaparte's
sister, Elisa, 'You know my deep admiration and my absolute devotion to this
extraordinary man.'[59] But once Enghien had been executed, Chateaubriand
completely repudiated the man and his regime; to him Bonaparte's methods
smacked of the Jacobin terrorist.

Six days after the execution of Enghien, echoes of a resumption of monarchical forms began to be heard.[60]

## Bonaparte Becomes Napoleon

The possibility of introducing an empire was raised and openly discussed for the
first time in a Council meeting at Saint-Cloud on 13 April 1804.[61] By that stage,
the groundwork had been laid. We have seen how Bonaparte's entourage began
to take on the appearances of an *ancien régime* court, displacing the few republican attitudes that had survived. The Prussian ambassador, the Marquis de
Lucchesini, remarked on this, as did the English chargé d'affaires, Anthony
Merry, who wrote home in May 1802 that Bonaparte would be 'Caesar or nothing', 'provided he does not go towards it with too much precipitation', while the
Russian ambassador was speaking of Bonaparte having revived the 'empire of
the Gauls'.[62] Bonaparte's profile was readily available on coin by that time. That
same year, the secretary of the German legation in Paris was openly referring to
Bonaparte as 'der Fürst', or the Prince.[63] The Swedish ambassador, Jean-François,
Baron de Bourgoing, received at the Tuileries in 1801, gave a speech in which he
pointed out that the difference between his own country's monarchical Constitution and the Consular Constitution was nominal.[64]

Contemporaries were well aware then that a political transition was taking
place. It fuelled talk about the possibility of bringing back some sort of
monarchy. That does not mean the transition was seamless. Opinions were
divided, with certain former revolutionaries against Bonaparte increasing his
power any further,[65] while others were keen to see his position enhanced.
According to the Marquis de Lucchesini, two factions formed over this issue.
On the one hand were what he called the 'Constitutionals', in favour of any
measures that supported a restoration of monarchical structures.[66] The Constitutionals were purposefully seeking to cement the Brumaire settlement with a
hereditary succession, and they led a campaign in the press between March and
June 1802 in that vein.[67] As we have seen, they had tried to slip the question of

heredity into the plebiscite over the Consulship for life, without Bonaparte's knowledge.[68] On the other hand were what Lucchesini dubbed the 'Conventionals', who considered the move towards a Consulate for life a violation of the agreement that had been concluded among the Brumairians.[69] The idea of a return to monarchical forms was repulsive to them. Fouché boasted to foreign diplomats in Paris that if Bonaparte tried to have himself crowned, he would be stabbed to death before the day was out.[70]

A struggle then had been taking place in Bonaparte's entourage over the future political direction of the country. By the beginning of 1804, the proponents of a monarchical system had become the dominant faction and they had succeeded in getting Bonaparte to come around to the idea. It is erroneous to think he was pushing for an empire out of bald ambition; there were a considerable number of influential people in his entourage who thought along similar lines, namely, that a type of constitutional hereditary monarchy was the best political system available. Bonaparte, nevertheless, wanted the matter discussed with absolute candour in the Council of State – he even absented himself from the deliberations to make them feel at ease – as long it did not become a public debate.

Michel Regnaud de Saint-Jean d'Angély took the initiative to propose that the Council move towards a hereditary dynasty. He argued that it was 'the only means of preserving France from the rifts associated with the changes and the election of the first magistrate'.[71] But when another member of the Council, Antoine-François de Fourcroy, proposed that they go on record to approve the principle of a hereditary empire, silence followed. It was broken by Théophile Berlier, a regicide and committed republican, who expressed his reservations about sacrificing that for which so many had died – the Republic. Berlier had also opposed the Consulate for life, and was not about to give ground on this issue.[72]

The debate that followed, and it appears to have been vigorous since it lasted over four sessions, was about whether, at a time when things seemed to be going so well, such a change was necessary. In the end, twenty members voted in favour of hereditary rule while seven voted to postpone the transformation.[73] When those seven members refused to sign the address to Bonaparte on the grounds that they could not sign something that had been against their wishes, the First Consul insisted that individual opinions were to be submitted and signed by each councillor of state. He was worried that if the dissenters signed a separate counter-address, it might somehow become public knowledge.[74] Anything less than a unanimous façade at this stage would be an embarrassment. In other words, by inviting each councillor of state to write down his objections the opposition was fobbed off.[75] This is what happened; nothing came of their opposition and no sanctions were imposed against the seven members who had expressed reservations; they played by Bonaparte's rules and kept their views in-house.

The question was also debated in the Tribunate. Speeches from the Tribunate were often printed in the *Moniteur*. Dissenting voices here, therefore, were likely to be heard in public. Admittedly, the more difficult tribunes had been purged in 1802, but there was still enough life left in the institution to cause a potential upset. Here the motion was put that Bonaparte 'be named Emperor and in that quality charged with the government of the Republic'.[76] An obscure tribune by the name of Jean François Curée, a former Jacobin, member of the Convention and a regicide to boot, but one who had supported Brumaire, was given the opportunity to introduce the proposition (the result of weeks of manoeuvring). On 28 April, he gave a long speech to his colleagues in which he posed the question whether the First Consul should be declared emperor and whether the imperial dignity – imperiality as it was called at the time[77] – should be declared hereditary in his family. Curée argued for a new dynasty that would act as a barrier against a return of 'factions and of that house that we proscribed in 1792' – that is, the House of Bourbon.[78] The argument repeated by almost all of the tribunes who followed was that France's political stability could be founded only on the institution of hereditary power. The insistence with which tribune after tribune got up and argued in favour of the principles of 1789 as the rationale for a return to monarchical forms ought to give pause for reflection.

The vast majority of those who spoke expressed their gratitude towards Bonaparte. Only five or six members of the Tribunate (out of forty-nine present) expressed their opposition. Nevertheless, there was one prominent voice of dissent – Lazare Carnot. He had been named to the Tribunate in March 1802, and had stubbornly opposed the slow decline of the principle of elective government. He got up and made a number of critical observations. He pointed to the United States as an example of a working republic.[79] He declared that he would not vote for the re-establishment of the monarchy, but he watered down his oppositional stance by stating that if the Empire were adopted by the French people, he would adhere to it. Carnot's association with the Committee of Public Safety and with the Directory took a lot of shine from his moral aura, however. Besides, given the number of tribunes who scrambled to undo his message by extolling the virtues of Bonaparte, it probably did not make much of an impact.

It was the Senate, however, that had the power to sanction the transformation to Empire. It had, in any event, initiated the whole movement in the first place when it underlined the desirability of making Bonaparte's achievements permanent in March 1804.[80] It was more than ready then to endorse any proposals to implement a hereditary monarchy. How could it have been otherwise? Bonaparte had 'bought' the Senate shortly after the Consulate for life when he created special dignities called 'senatories'. There were thirty-one in all, each covering an area of three or four departments. The nominated senator was to keep watch over this region with the obligation of touring it once a year. In exchange, he received a generous gift of property, and an added income of 20,000 livres per year.[81] This does not explain why senators voted for the Empire, but it does allow us to understand the element of self-interest in all of this.

The Senate, nevertheless, voted in the belief that certain conditions would be met – the independence of the institutions of the state; the right to vote on taxation; the guarantee of property; individual freedom; freedom of the press; elections; the responsibility of ministers; and the inviolability of the Constitution – so that the 'social pact', as they called it, would remain intact.[82] For many, it was a question of getting back to what the Revolution of 1789 had been all about before it started to go badly wrong. In some respects, so the argument went, the proclamation of a hereditary empire was simply returning to what the revolutionaries of 1789 had wanted all along – uniting 'hereditary power to a representative government'.[83] This is what the senators seemed to have opted for, a type of constitutional monarchy, a 'third way' between a republic and absolute monarchy. One senator pointed out that 'the Senate, as a body, did nothing more than sanction measures which it had no means of opposing, even [with] the appearance of resistance'.[84] Many historians have assumed as a result that the Senate was a weak institution that rubber-stamped Bonaparte's unbridled ambition.

On 18 May 1804, Bernard-Germain de Lacépède appeared before the Senate to read the findings of a commission that had been established to review the Constitution in the light of a declaration of the Empire.[85] In the debate that followed, the only dissenting voice to be heard was that of the Abbé Grégoire, who had moreover opposed the Consulate. When it came to a vote, the *senatus consultum* was overwhelmingly approved with three votes against and two abstentions. The *senatus consultum* suggested that Bonaparte be recognized, not as 'Emperor of France', which would have recalled the appellation of the French kings, but as 'Emperor of the French'. This meant that Bonaparte's rule extended to the people of France but that he did not own the territory.[86] That same day, Bonaparte used his surname for the last time. From then on he would always sign his name 'Napoleon'.*

The day the Empire was proclaimed, the Senate came as a body to Saint-Cloud to deliver the news of the proclamation. They were acting a little precipitately since the change in the Constitution had yet to be confirmed through a plebiscite, but everybody considered it a foregone conclusion. The setting of the scene in the official accounts of the period has the ring of a stage drama.

---

* Interestingly, the acute accent was immediately added so that the name became Frenchified into 'Napoléon'. Napoleon, however, never wrote his name with an accent, and he was never referred to in public as 'Napoleon' before that date, but always simply as 'Bonaparte'.

Bonaparte is supposed to have declared: 'You have judged the heredity of the supreme office necessary in order to shelter the French people from the plots of our enemies and the unrest that would arise from rival ambitions . . . I invite you then to share with me all your thoughts.'[87] Cambacérès replied that they had come to offer the title 'emperor' to Bonaparte, 'for the glory as well as the happiness of the Republic'.

For the first time, Bonaparte was addressed as 'Sire' and 'Majesty'. It would take time for some of the revolutionaries, even if they supported the Empire, to get used to a term not heard in Paris for over ten years. After the ceremony, when Napoleon spoke to a number of those present, a few were able to address him as 'Sire' without any difficulty, whereas others stumbled over the right formula, commencing their sentences with 'Citizen First Consul' or 'General', before remembering that 'Sire' and 'Majesty' were now de rigueur.[88] The new Emperor was to be surrounded with imperial dignitaries: Joseph was named grand elector; Cambacérès arch-chancellor of the Empire; Eugène arch-chancellor of state; Lebrun arch-treasurer; Louis connétable, or constable, a military distinction; and Murat grand admiral. One of the most notable nominations among the civil dignitaries was that of Talleyrand as grand chamberlain, who thereby eclipsed Duroc as marshal of the palace, Ségur as grand master of ceremonies and Caulaincourt as grand écuyer. In addition, eighteen marshals were named, although several of them, not least Bernadotte, had hardly been the most loyal of generals.

## 'Sea of Dreams, Empire of Reality'

The title 'emperor' was more than a change of form; it carried a number of implications that had been rejected by the Revolution. The power of transmitting the title to an heir was given to Bonaparte by plebiscite, something the kings of France never enjoyed. The plebiscite was the basis of the legitimacy of Napoleon's regime – supporters of the Empire could always argue that no other 'nation has exercised so fully the right of sovereignty; never has it delegated more freely to a head of state the power to reign over it; never has a prince, in ascending the throne, rallied to him a suffrage that was more unanimous and more solemn'.[89] Napoleon, nevertheless, had to convince the French public that the transition to Empire was not only fitting but also desirable. He ordered one of his propagandists, Joseph Fiévée, to conduct a campaign in the press emphasizing the advantages of a monarchy.[90] The *Journal des Débats*, for example, underlined how much the previous monarchy had deserved to lose the throne – it had shown itself to be unworthy – all the while carefully pointing out that the institution was in itself perfectly desirable; it was the monarch who had been abandoned through an excess of weakness and incapacity.[91] In short, the argument was that the Bourbons had lost the throne, and that the

French people had deposed them because of their inability to rule.[92] From
there it follows that if one dynasty was incapable of ruling then, as had occurred
throughout the history of France, it would be replaced by another, in the same
way that Clovis and Charlemagne came to the throne.[93]

The notion of empire was part and parcel of the French elite's intellectual
and cultural baggage, although the connotations associated with the word
were very different from the meaning it later assumed when the French dominated the Continent.[94] Nor was the idea of empire incompatible with the idea
of a republic. On the contrary, unlike a monarchy, which was associated with
divine right, an empire was acquired by merit.[95] And yet it was a vague enough
term for Napoleon and his supporters to use in the creation of a new political
model.[96] It is perhaps one of the reasons why 'empire' was chosen over 'monarchy': it helped draw a clear distinction between the new regime and that of the
Bourbons.[97] The concept of empire should not, however, be confused with that
of hereditary monarchy; they are two distinct notions (although this is invariably overlooked in accounts of the transformation of the French Republic in
which 'empire' and 'hereditary monarchy' become synonymous). What Napoleon and the political elite instituted in May 1804 was in effect a constitutional
monarchy, which is what conservative and moderate political thinkers had
wanted since the beginning of the Revolution in 1789. 'The time has come',
Duvidal de Montferrier proclaimed in the Tribunate, 'to leave the sea of dreams
and to approach the empire of reality . . . The crown of Charlemagne is the just
heritage for one who has known how to imitate him.'[98]

If the peace and stability Bonaparte was able to impose on France and Europe
were rewarded with the Consulate for life, the attempt to kill him in 1804 was
the excuse to introduce a type of monarchy. It was then that he thought, once
again, of consolidating his power around a more imposing title that would
render his person inviolable.[99] Up to then, he had dealt with the problem of
naming a successor by telling people what they wanted to hear. He would tell
staunch republicans, like Thibaudeau, that the Revolution had put an end to the
concept of hereditary succession once and for all. Then he would tell Fouché,
'People in Paris believe I am going to make myself emperor. I am not going to
do anything of the sort. For the last three years enough great things have been
done under the title consul. We have to keep it. I do not believe that *we need a
new name for a new empire*.'[100] At most, Bonaparte claimed, he would accept
the title of 'Grand Consul'. On another occasion though, he is supposed to
have told Fouché that opposition to putting a crown on his head would be very
weak.[101] He was obviously caught in a bind and did not want to think particularly either about his own death or about naming a successor with all the
political problems which that would entail. Things came to a head, however,
with the Cadoudel assassination plot. Part of the reasoning was that since all the
assassination attempts were directed against his person, if a hereditary successor

were designated, then the survival of the government and of the system put in place would not be jeopardized if he were to disappear.

Thus heredity, and the Empire that came with it, was about constructing a durable political system, rather than a sop to Bonaparte's vanity and ambition, one that placed France on an equal footing with every other court in Europe.[102] In one outburst against his brother Joseph leading up to the coronation, he is supposed to have exclaimed, 'Does he believe that I have brought about these changes for me? That I value the titles he seems to disdain?'[103] He argued that he was adopting the imperial title only so that he would now be on a par with the sovereigns of Europe. That was pretext. One cannot help but feel that behind the practical reason was a deep, obsessive need not only to be recognized by his peers, but also to dominate them.

If we take our gaze away from Bonaparte for a moment and look at what some in the French political elite were urging, we get a very different picture to the one often presented by historians when they talk about the founding of the Empire. A clue is to be found in a letter written by Talleyrand to Napoleon in July 1804, a short while after the proclamation of the Empire. 'Your Majesty knows, and I have pleasure in repeating it, that weary, disgusted by the political systems that have aroused the passion and caused the misfortune of the French over the last ten years, it is only by you and for you that I hold with the institutions you have founded.'[104]

Two elements are at play here: Talleyrand had confidence in the man and in the institutions that he had helped put in place after ten years of political unrest and was, therefore, willing to hitch his star to Napoleon's. But Talleyrand also believed that a hereditary, constitutional monarchy was the political system that held the most promise for stability.[105] Or at least this was the line adopted by those who supported the Empire, and which was faithfully repeated long after it had disappeared.[106] By taking part in Brumaire, by encouraging a shift away from radical political structures to ultimately conservative and, one could argue, counter-revolutionary political structures, the supporters of empire were in some respects representative of the reconciliation finally taking place between the Revolution and the *ancien régime*.

Most European powers were prepared to recognize Napoleon and his new title. The exceptions were Britain, at war with France (Pitt was re-elected prime minister on 10 May 1804), Sweden and Russia, about to enter another coalition.[107] Alexander's minister for foreign affairs, Adam Czartoryski, believed the Empire gave the Revolution a façade of legitimacy. He feared, therefore, that it marked not the end of the Revolution but its ominous continuation by other means.[108] This view was typical of conservatives of the day. The German publicist Friedrich von Gentz, for example, working for the Austrian Chancellery, also believed that to recognize Napoleon was to 'sanction the Revolution and all its doctrines'.[109] Russia consequently attempted to persuade the other powers that the title would 'serve as a pretext for [Napoleon's] unbounded ambition to extend his domination still further'.[110]

It succeeded with some, such as the Porte (the government of the Ottoman Empire), but not others. In Vienna, Napoleon's adoption of the imperial title was disliked and posed particular problems for Francis as titular head of the Holy Roman Empire.[111] The Austrians were alarmed, with good reason, that Napoleon was re-establishing the Empire of Charlemagne – in part because so much was made of Charlemagne in France at the time[112] – and that he would extend his influence over the Holy Roman Empire.[113] Vienna was fearful that George III would feel obliged to proclaim himself 'Emperor of Great Britain' or that the Tsar would insist on parity with Austria. Nevertheless, the Austrian chancellor argued that the re-establishment of monarchical government, which is how he referred to the Empire, was 'necessary for the tranquillity of all governments'.[114] The main reason, however, why Austria decided to recognize the French Empire was in order not to offend Napoleon and thereby risk war; it also wanted to maintain diplomatic parity with France.[115] That is why Cobenzl recommended that Austria, at the same time, adopt its own imperial title.[116]

This was a question of prestige. If the Holy Roman Empire collapsed, then Francis would be left with lesser-sounding titles – King of Bohemia and Hungary, and Grand Duke of Austria. Till then, the Austrian 'Roman Emperor' had enjoyed precedence over every other European monarch, including the Russian Tsar, largely because he supposedly represented a direct line to the ancient Roman emperors. He was therefore at the head of the only 'genuinely imperial' state in Europe, against which all others had to define themselves.[117] By brushing aside the Holy Roman Empire, Napoleon had also brushed to one side the title and the claim, and at the same time assumed the western imperial mantle. Francis, therefore, agreed to recognize Napoleon's title in return for Napoleon's recognizing Francis as 'Emperor of Austria'.[118]

## A Troublesome Family

The reaction of the sovereign heads of Europe to the proclamation of the Empire was the least of Napoleon's problems. He had a much more difficult task dealing with his family and relatives. The family was a permanent centre of criticism, cabals and intrigues that he quite rightly perceived as a danger, but it was one which, given the structure of Corsican family ties, he would never overcome. He seemed to delight in stirring it up and in pitting one member against another. The family, on the other hand, believed it had every right to share in the benefits of Napoleon's power, regardless of how little its members had contributed to his success.

Let us deal with the brothers first. Relations between Napoleon and Joseph had been difficult ever since Joseph declined the presidency of the Italian Republic in 1802, on the pretext that the Republic would be too dependent on France.[119] Relations were made worse by the resumption of war with Britain (Joseph was against the war), by his involvement in the marriage of Lucien with Alexandrine Jouberthon (about which more below), and more particularly by the question of the succession. On 2 April 1804, Bonaparte had a meeting with his elder brother. He told Joseph that he planned to adopt the son of Louis and Hortense with the aim of making him his heir. It was a rude shock to Joseph who had obviously given no thought to Napoleon fathering or adopting a son.[120] It was also a clumsy manoeuvre on the part of Bonaparte since he had not consulted with either Louis or Hortense on the matter. Joseph immediately ran to Louis, warned him of Bonaparte's intentions and persuaded him to oppose the adoption.

It cannot have been too hard a task; Louis was not terribly well disposed towards his brother after being obliged to marry Josephine's daughter, Hortense, in January 1802. It was a misjudged attempt on the part of Josephine to cement relations between the two families. The marriage was disastrous, but produced children. One of them was Napoleon-Charles, but Louis was hardly going to allow Napoleon to adopt him, the more so since rumour had it that Napoleon-Charles was Napoleon's biological son (there are no grounds for believing this to be the case).[121] If Louis was furious, Joseph was also beside himself at the suggestion – he is supposed to have said that it would be better for his family and France if his brother were dead[122] – and he also attacked Bonaparte for suggesting a hereditary system that would, as he saw it, exclude him and his children from any future succession. He urged Napoleon to leave Josephine for what he called 'political reasons'.[123] Tension between the two brothers became so bad that Napoleon decided to send Joseph to the camp of Boulogne, 'so that he could have his part of the glory'.[124]

If relations with Joseph were tense, relations with Lucien were brought to breaking point. Lucien, we know, was the hothead of the family, an uncontrollable free spirit who could not tolerate, even less than Napoleon could, any form of constraint.[125] As minister of the interior, he had jurisdiction over the theatres. It is possible that he took advantage of his position to 'seduce' a number of actresses. Rumour was that it was not safe for a young woman to enter his office.[126] In the summer of 1802, Lucien met a divorcée by the name of Alexandrine Jouberthon, considered a remarkable beauty. In May 1803, they were secretly married in a religious ceremony, the same day that Alexandrine gave birth to a baby boy (they would go on to have ten children). Bonaparte did not know of this, although rumours of their marriage had been circulating in the months leading up to it. Bonaparte had been thinking of arranging some sort of political alliance with his brother through marriage with Marie-Louise, Queen of Etruria, who had only recently become a widow herself. When Bonaparte brought up the subject at a family dinner a few days after the marriage, Lucien made light of it. But after Bonaparte had left he confessed to Joseph that he was already married. Joseph, although he did not say so then, thought it was one of the greatest calamities that could have happened. In a conversation at Mortefontaine in the presence of Miot de Mélito, he is said to have exclaimed, 'In truth, it seems that fate blinds us and wants, through our own faults, to return France to its former masters.'[127] Bonaparte was told eventually, but he considered the marriage null and void. He sent Joseph, Murat and Cambacérès to talk with Lucien, but no amount of negotiating could make Lucien change his mind or persuade him to agree not to let his new wife carry the Bonaparte name.[128] When Lucien consequently refused to divorce her, he was stripped of his senatorial rank and removed from the line of succession, and he had no input into the foundation of the Empire. He moved to Rome with his wife. In 1810, when Napoleon annexed the Papal States, Lucien decided to leave Europe once and for all, and set sail for the United States. The British intercepted his vessel and Lucien was taken to England where he spent the rest of the war as a prisoner – at Thorngrove in Worcestershire – until the collapse of the Empire in 1814.

Jérôme faced a similar dilemma to his brother, but reacted very differently. On Christmas Eve 1803, he married an American woman, a rich shipowner's daughter from Baltimore, Elizabeth Patterson.[129] Jérôme was nineteen at the time, had left the naval vessel on which he was serving to take in the United States and had met and quickly married Elizabeth even though, according to French law, he was not legally of age (the Civil Code stated that in order to marry one had to be twenty-five or else have the permission of one's parents). Like Lucien, Jérôme married without his brother's knowledge. When he learnt of it through a dispatch from the French consul general in America, Bonaparte simply refused to recognize the marriage and obliged his mother to sign a statement in front of a notary declaring that she had not given her consent to the marriage (a little rich coming from a man who had married a woman the family disapproved of).[130]

When Jérôme brought his wife back to Europe from the United States in April 1805 (they landed in Portugal), Napoleon ordered him to travel overland to Italy (through Spain and southern France), and insisted that Elizabeth not leave the ship. If they tried to head for Paris, he instructed Fouché to arrest Jérôme and to send packing Mlle Patterson, as he persisted in calling her, back to America.[131] Jérôme left Elizabeth, pregnant, in Lisbon, no doubt convinced at this stage that he could persuade his brother to change his mind. He did not. Jérôme may have loved Elizabeth – he certainly wrote to her saying that he loved her as much as life itself[132] – and he may have said that he would rather kill his own children than declare them illegitimate,[133] but at some stage he gave in to his brother's pressing demands. If he had been wilful as a youth, always refusing to toe the line, it now seems he was incapable of bucking his brother, at least on this issue. Napoleon was probably dangling before him the prospect of a kingdom if he did as he was told. It took all of ten days for Jérôme to change his mind.

Napoleon was 'generous' in victory. 'My brother,' he wrote adopting an imperial tone, 'there is no fault that sincere remorse cannot efface in my eyes.'[134] He then promised a pension to Elizabeth of 60,000 francs a year. What that reveals of Jérôme's character – a certain opportunism, a lack of resolve, an inability to live independently outside the family circle (unlike Louis) – is academic, but it does not say much. When faced with the choice between love and ambition, he was crass enough to choose ambition. One contemporary at least thought him the most proud, the most impolite, the most ignorant and the most ambitious young man he had ever encountered.[135] Jérôme saw Elizabeth only one more time, in 1822 when they ran into each other in a museum in Florence. They did not stop to talk; Jérôme was with a new wife. The declarations one can find in his earlier letters to her – 'you have a place in my affections which no power, no political expediency can take away' – had been long forgotten.[136]

At the dinner reserved for members of the family after the proclamation of the Empire, the marshal of the palace, Michel Duroc, arrived to inform everyone about the new protocols. Their brother would have to be referred to as 'sire'. Joseph and Louis were accorded the title 'prince', while their respective wives – Julie and Hortense – were to be called 'princess'. It is possible that Joseph at first refused the title, but he soon came round.[137] Caroline, twenty-two years of age and now married to Murat, could not bring herself to call the daughter of a soap merchant (Julie, the wife of Joseph), as well as Josephine's daughter, 'princess', especially since she herself would be officially known only as 'Mme la Maréchal'. Elisa Bacciochi, five years older than her sister, described as 'haughty, nervous, passionate, dissolute, devoured by the double hiccough of love and ambition', felt the same way.[138] Her title, since she was married to Colonel Bacciochi, would simply be 'colonelle'. When Napoleon finally arrived for dinner, he could see they were visibly upset.[139] Rather than placate them, he just rubbed it in their faces, deliberately addressing Julie and Hortense as 'princess' as often as he could. Caroline's rage eventually transformed itself into tears; she had to gulp down large glasses of water in an effort to get a hold of herself, but tears kept coming back. During this ordeal, according to one witness, Napoleon 'smiled rather maliciously'.[140]

The next day, the three siblings – Napoleon, Caroline and Elisa – had a violent quarrel in Josephine's salon, resorting now and then to their Corsican patois to insult each other. Caroline complained to Napoleon that he had condemned them to 'obscurity, to scorn', while others were being covered in honours and distinctions. It was probably on this occasion (or the preceding evening, we are not sure) that Napoleon replied, 'Really, if one listened to my sisters, one would believe that I had robbed my family of the heritage of the late king, our father,' an epigram repeated all over Paris it was thought so witty.[141] By this stage, Caroline, to bring home her point, managed to faint right there on the floor, while Elisa let out piercing cries. Caroline seems to have known that a little histrionics went a long way with her brother. The very next day (20 May), an article appeared in the *Moniteur* announcing that Caroline, Elisa and Pauline were also being given the title of 'princess'. (It was at this time that Pauline, who was in Italy when she learnt of the title, changed her name from Paulette, as till then she had been commonly known.) To add to the burlesque, their husbands were not elevated to the rank, at least not yet.

As for Letizia, in Rome, she decided that she would not attend the planned coronation. Part of her disapproved of the whole thing, possibly out of fear that her son was getting a little too big for his boots – she had nightmares about some fanatical republican assassinating him[142] – but part of her seems to have been upset over the lack of distinctions and the lack of money coming her way. Napoleon's uncle, Letizia's half-brother Cardinal Fesch, wrote to him on the subject in July 1804.[143] If the daughters had become Imperial Highnesses, was it appropriate that the mother of all these princes and princesses be considered a simple subject? Besides, her entourage were already unofficially referring to her as 'Majesté'.

Napoleon was put on the spot, and he now had to find a title for his mother. After consulting with the experts and looking at books on protocol and etiquette, no easy thing since this was setting a precedent, Letizia was given the title 'Madame'. However, during the *ancien régime* 'Madame' had been a title used to designate the daughters of the king. In case Napoleon one day had a daughter, therefore, the words, 'mother of His Majesty the Emperor' were tacked on to the end of 'Madame'. It was, admittedly, a little long and was never really used; Napoleon always referred to her as 'Madame'. The title 'Madame Mère' (Madam Mother) that eventually came into use was never official.[144] Nor was it something that pleased Letizia very much. In fact, she was mortified by its spectacular lack of brilliance, and was not afraid to let her son know how displeased she was. But then she was a hard woman to please at the best of times; even a monthly pension of 25,000 francs did not put a smile on her disgruntled countenance.

A constitutional monarchy of sorts, even if it did contain the germ of an autocratic system, had at last been reached; the Revolution had been consolidated; the counter-revolution had been dealt a hefty blow not only through the founding of the Empire, but particularly through an accord with the Catholic Church; a certain number of revolutionary principles had been put into

practice such as equality before the law and freedom of religion; the sale of
nationalized Church lands (*biens nationaux*) had been guaranteed; and a new
legal system codifying and consolidating the gains of the Revolution had been
introduced.[145] Napoleon was thus seen as the person most responsible for
steering the 'vessel of the Republic' into safe harbour, 'sheltered from all
storms'.[146] The democratic experiment that had been the Revolution had
reached its limits; it was time to replace the political anarchy that had reigned
over the last ten years with a durable authority.[147] That authority should reside
in one person, with enough force to bring about a 'social pact' and to

*Dix-huit Brumaire* (18 Brumaire). Frontispiece to Louis Dubroca, *Les quatre fondateurs des
dynasties françaises, ou Histoire de l'établissement de la monarchie française, par
Clovis . . . Pépin et Hugues Capet; et . . . Napoléon-le-Grand . . .* (The four founders of the
French dynasties, or The history of the establishment of the French monarchy), Paris, 1806.
Note the broken tablets at the bottom of the frame representing the three previous dynasties
– Merovingian, Carolingian and Capetian. The message is simple but clear: Napoleon, the
successor to these dynasties, is helping France get back on its feet.

consolidate the country's institutions on solid foundations.[148] 'It is the product of his genius, and at the same time a just reward for his work.'[149] What other system, one pamphleteer asked, offered such stability and such hope?[150] The Empire was therefore proposed as a more efficient alternative to both monarchy and democracy, and Napoleon presented as a vehicle of hope, a force that would create a better world.[151]

It was not the fall of Robespierre in 1795 that brought the Revolution to an end, nor did it end in 1799 with the coup of Brumaire, even if one of the first things Bonaparte did was to declare it over. Nor did it end in 1802 with the Peace of Amiens. The Revolution came to an end in 1804 with the proclamation of the Empire, and more powerfully and symbolically, in December of that year during the coronation ceremony at the Cathedral of Notre Dame. At that moment, when Napoleon crowned himself emperor, the political principles of 1789 were finally realized.[152]

# 8

# 'The First Throne of the Universe'

## The Trial of General Moreau

Ten days after the proclamation of the Empire, on 28 May 1804, the trial of Moreau and Cadoudal, along with forty-five others accused of plotting to kill Napoleon, opened at ten in the morning. Pichegru was not present: he had been found dead in his cell. A black silk cravat and a little baton were found around his neck; he had garrotted himself.[1] Napoleon immediately ordered a public inquest. There is no evidence that Pichegru was murdered, or that Napoleon could even have benefited from his murder, but that did not stop some from believing his death had been ordered by the Emperor.[2]

The terrain had been prepared by the publication of a number of pamphlets, as well as articles in the press. One anonymous pamphlet portrayed Cadoudal in a less than flattering light, as someone who had accepted money and support from England, and who had pursued a 'system of assassination' against those who had thrown their support behind the Consulate.[3] In addition, a list of 'brigands' charged by Britain with the task of assassinating Napoleon was posted on walls throughout France, Moreau's name at the top.[4] Moreau's interrogation and the proceedings of the trial were also published in an attempt to convince the public of his guilt, but to no avail.[5] The strategy backfired on Napoleon, in part because of Moreau's reputation. Moreau and his supporters also used the press in an attempt to clear his name.[6] As we have seen, the general's innocence was not as clear-cut after the arrest of Pichegru and the execution of Enghien. The regime attempted to associate his name with the royalists, while putting him on trial with people like Pichegru made him appear guilty by association. Despite their best efforts, however, the Emperor's men did not succeed in tarnishing Moreau's name.

That is why the trial caused a stir in fashionable circles. The trial of celebrities always seems to find an echo in a populace avid for scandal. Moreau's friends gathered at the Palais de Justice in the hope of turning the crowd against the regime.[7] A considerable number of Moreau's supporters congregated outside the court, unable to get in. The court itself was packed with military men. Long gone were the days, however, when the crowds of Paris could determine the course of national politics; impressive security measures had been taken to make sure nothing of the sort would happen. Six thousand troops were stationed in and around the court to keep order. Just to make sure the odds were on the government's side, a *senatus consultum* did away with the jury the defendants would normally have been allowed. The possibility of an acquittal was not being risked. The president of the panel of judges (there were ten in all), a man by the name of Hémart, who had earned a reputation during the Terror, was ordered by the prefect of police, Réal, to find the accused guilty and to sentence them to death.[8] Things nevertheless did not go terribly well for the prosecution: portraits of the accused were sold outside the Palais de Justice; Cadoudal passionately defended his cause; while public opinion in general seems to have been with Moreau. Mme de Staël, Mme Récamier, numerous officers, even the gendarmes meant to guard him displayed a marked sympathy for the general. At theatres throughout Paris, every time there was an allusion to the conflict between Napoleon and Moreau, the public demonstrated its preference for Moreau.[9] One diplomat reported that the 'army and its generals spoke against the Emperor with a freedom that makes one fear anything'.[10]

At four o'clock in the morning of 10 June, the verdict was read out in an overcrowded room. Moreau got off lightly – two years in prison – but even this was considered harsh by those present. In the brouhaha that followed, the room was evacuated, the convicted man taken back to the Temple, and the area around the Palais de Justice cleared by the troops. There had been no riot, just a few republicans expressing their discontent. Twenty other defendants were not as lucky as Moreau; they were condemned to death, including the Marquis de Rivière, Armand de Polignac and Cadoudal (although eight were pardoned).[11] Three carts each containing four prisoners and four priests were conducted from the Conciergerie to the Place de Grève, in front of the Hôtel de Ville, where in a scene reminiscent of the days of the Terror the condemned men were executed in front of a large crowd. Windows along the way had been rented out so that people could get a better look at what had become an unusual sight. Cadoudal was offered a pardon but he rejected it and preferred to go to his death with the men who had followed him, arguing with the others at the foot of the scaffold about who was to go first. Cadoudal won. Legend has it that shortly before his execution he said, 'We wanted a king, we have made an emperor.'[12]

The retraction of evidence during the trial by two witnesses, who now claimed never to have seen Pichegru and Moreau together, Cadoudal's silence and the death of Pichegru combined to 'save' Moreau. Napoleon in person intervened, writing to Cambacérès asking him to intercede and to get the judges to review their initial finding.[13] The Emperor is supposed to have said to Bourrienne after hearing the verdict, 'They asserted that he was guilty and here they are treating him like a pickpocket! What am I supposed to do with him now?'[14] He was perhaps that much more exasperated by the verdict since it went against the orders he had given the judges. Nevertheless, when the wife of Moreau asked permission for her husband to be allowed to leave for America, Napoleon assented. Moreau returned to Europe in 1813 in the service of the Tsar, only to be killed on the battlefield of Dresden by a cannon ball that struck his right leg, went through the horse he was riding and then shattered his left leg. He died after days of terrible suffering.


## 'The Most Perfect of Men'

Once Napoleon had eagerly accepted the idea of hereditary power, representatives of the state and the army were mobilized to show their support. General Nicolas Jean-de-Dieu Soult, commander of two large military camps at Montreuil and Saint-Omer, was asked to provide information about how the army would react to the idea of Napoleon's becoming hereditary ruler.[15] On 10 April, only weeks before the official proclamation, Soult wrote a letter to Napoleon indicating that the army 'desired and demanded that you be proclaimed Emperor of the Gauls' and that heredity be established in his family.[16]

It was shortly after this that the official petitions in favour of heredity were supported by declarations from the army. This aspect of the public relations campaign appears to have been orchestrated by the minister for war, Berthier, who first ordered that a report written by the minister of justice, Claude-Ambroise Régnier, on the Cadoudal–Pichegru plot be read to the troops,[17] but it is also possible that Napoleon's brothers, Joseph and Lucien, were behind the initiative.[18] Many commanders understood what was expected of them. This was a top-down process. We know, for example, that some commanders circulated model petitions to their troops,[19] and that a number of the top military brass petitioned Napoleon to adopt the 'title of Emperor that Charlemagne carried'. 'Does it not belong by right to the man who reminds us of it as a legislator and warrior?'[20] Some historians have interpreted these expressions as an attempt to intimidate the legislature.[21] However, there is nothing to suggest that the army as an institution was behaving any differently from other institutions in its demand for an emperor.

A similar process took place in the administration, much of it orchestrated by Fouché.[22] In March and April 1804, in the wake of the Cadoudal–Pichegru plot, dozens of letters from individual prefects, judges, mayors, towns and electoral colleges were published in the *Moniteur*. Most of these petitions lamented the dangers facing the First Consul, confounded the good of the nation with his personal wellbeing, and offered him their thanks, support and sometimes love.[23] They expressed solidarity with Bonaparte, often portrayed him as 'saviour' and hero, but most of all expressed a desire to exact vengeance on those held responsible for the assassination attempt – that is, the British. 'Do they ignore the fact', wrote the sub-prefect of the department of the Aisne, 'that heaven protects our *patrie* and that the vastness of faithful citizens forms an impenetrable rampart around the First Consul against the attacks of perfidy?'[24] In a letter to Bonaparte from François Louis Marguet, who described himself as a 'simple citizen' from Besançon, the outrage against 'perfidious England' is palpable. He declared that Bonaparte's death 'would be a public calamity. The fatal day that takes you from the French people will be the last day of their liberty and their happiness.'[25] This particular aspect of the petitions can be seen as an attempt on the part of the Consular regime to garner support for the coming war with Britain and, indirectly, to consolidate Bonaparte's personal hold on power. The rhetoric used was based on two sentiments: overwhelming enthusiasm for Bonaparte and for the apparent gains that had been made in French society since his coming to power; and fear of losing those gains if he were to disappear.[26]

At first there was no mention of heredity or empire in any of the petitions from the country's most important institutions.[27] The only time the word 'empire' was mentioned, in a petition from the president of the electoral college of Sésia in Italy, was a general reference to the 'vast empire' that Bonaparte governed.[28] One can find, however, a vague reference in the petition from the department of the Roër to Bonaparte receiving, in the country of Charlemagne, 'the just tribute of love, respect and recognition' which was his due, and which points to the possibility of a higher office. But that is the extent of it. Not until Jean-François Curée gave the lead in the Tribunate, his speech being published in the *Moniteur* on 1 May, demanding that Bonaparte be named emperor, was the process officially set in motion.[29] This was the first time that someone in an official capacity had openly spoken out in favour of the title. Shortly after that, petitions started to appear demanding that heredity and the executive power be united. As we now know, the prompting for Curée's declaration came from Bonaparte himself, but that does not diminish the fact that from this time on the floodgates were opened and that what followed cannot be discounted as a propaganda coup organized by a few behind the scenes.

After the declaration of the Empire, a number of these letters played on the same themes that we have already encountered among the political elite – that is, that France had been 'lost' since the convocation of the Estates General in 1789 because of 'ambitious innovators'. In one letter, the commercial tribunal for the town of Soissons was convinced 'by its own experience' that a hereditary leader 'can alone assure their [the French people's] happiness in consolidating the power of the nation'.[30] Some professed to having been 'always for the government of one man', but up until then that opinion had been fatal and they had not been able to do anything to win acceptance for the idea.[31]

Among ordinary citizens, one can find an open adherence to empire that cuts across socio-economic categories, and that took on emotional dimensions rarely discussed by historians.[32] Once the Empire was declared, thousands of private individuals wrote to express support not so much for the idea of empire as for the idea of Napoleon – 'the greatest of conquerors, the most perfect of men' – as emperor.[33] Some of these documents are collective petitions containing a brief letter of support and congratulations, followed by a list of signatures that may or may not have been entirely voluntary.[34] Some are letters from individuals attempting to curry favour with the regime.[35] The vast majority, however, are marked by an affective bond that appears to escape rationalization.

In a letter to Napoleon from a woman in Avignon named Carrié, for example, one can find the following sentence: 'The supreme being has fulfilled my prayer, God who can do all grant that the good and perfect health of our Emperor, who is closer to a Divinity than a man, be everlasting.' Napoleon was often compared to a divinity, as in this letter from the 'woman Garnier', from Ober-Ingelheim (near Mainz), who declared that 'Your Majesty was in my eyes, and in those with tender hearts, a tutelary God actually your empire by the grace of God [sic].'[36] In addition, dozens of poems, sometimes printed, often handwritten, are dedicated to Napoleon's ascension.[37] Much of this material traces the life of the Emperor in flattering terms as well as presaging his rise to power. These documents of support for him were also a spontaneous political response to the predicament facing the French nation – the threat of war with Britain and the possibility of losing through assassination the man many now considered to be the Saviour of the Revolution.

Here too we find material that rejects the Revolution as a democratic experiment and supports, if not the idea of monarchy, then at least the notion of a strong executive centred on one man. 'Fourteen centuries of monarchy,' declares a pamphlet by General Jean Sarrazin, 'even if often feebly administered, speak more eloquently in favour of the throne than fourteen years of misfortune and setbacks for the republican state.'[38] General Henry, writing from Nantes, argued that he was 'convinced by experience that under the Republic, the supreme power remained too long divided between the hands of many', which had resulted in constant anarchy and disorder, and that the centralization of power was best suited to empire.[39] The desire to see order restored was a constant; a surrogate to the tribunal of first instance at Versailles wrote that even if the Consulate was able to 'dissipate the deep darkness of night' certain souls remained troubled. 'It is time', he continued, 'to revive the social order, [and it is time] that sovereign power is reunited in the hands of one man.'[40] There is, moreover, a prevailing sentiment among many of these letters that Napoleon deserved the throne through his actions.[41]

There are so many letters – one of them includes a helpful remedy against poison[42] – that it seems the movement towards empire revived monarchical tendencies that had lain dormant during the Republic. The sentiments expressed often fall within the logic of what might be called a monarchical reflex – that is, a resurgence of belief in the sacred nature of the monarchy, and not just any monarchy, but one founded in the person of Napoleon.[43] This is not the same, however, as the notion of sacrality that existed in *ancien régime* France; it had now taken on a new form, founded on notions of individual destiny (Napoleon's), as well as on the sovereignty of the people. Hence the constant references to 'providence' or the 'hand of God' having placed Napoleon on the throne or of having saved him from assassination attempts so that he could continue his work,[44] or to the title 'emperor' as a reward for his services to the state (often with the assertion that he had saved France from ruin),[45] or to the idea that France could be saved from domestic and foreign enemies only when hereditary power resided in one family.[46] There are, moreover, references to Napoleon as father of the people,[47] remarkably similar to the kinds of patriarchal discourse found prior to 1789. Consequently, one cannot but conclude that the letters embodied a set of beliefs and values that were profoundly rooted in the cultural practices of the day, notwithstanding the creation of a republic and the execution of the king in 1792.[48] The person of Napoleon came to symbolize all that French

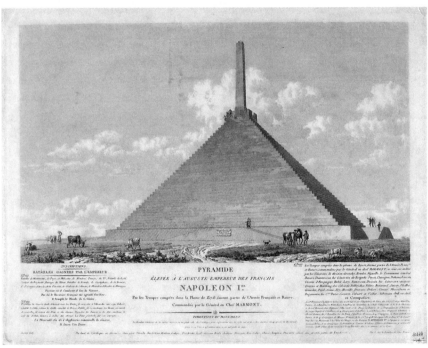

Anonymous, *Pyramide élevé à l'Auguste empereur des Français, Napoléon 1er* (Pyramid erected to the August Emperor of the French, Napoleon I), no date. On his own initiative, General Marmont built this imposing pyramid in the space of a month at the Camp of Utrecht. Forty-five metres tall, it was surmounted by an eighteen-metre obelisk.[49] Today dubbed the Pyramid of Austerlitz, it can still be seen outside the city of Utrecht in Holland. Each face was marked with an inscription, one of which contained the declaration that the pyramid was built as a testimony to the army's 'admiration and love' for Napoleon.

politics and society had been striving for since 1789 – the embodiment of the ideals of the Revolution, as well as the principle of constitutional monarchy.

In spite of this public outpouring, support for the Empire was by no means unanimous. There was never a concerted intellectual or political opposition to it, but resistance to it can be found throughout its existence.[50] Most of it came either from republican elements in the military,[51] from former Jacobins or from royalists. General Verdier, for example, a friend of the defunct General Kléber, was at Leghorn when news of the proclamation reached the army through the *Moniteur*. He was so angry that he tore up the newspaper in front of several other officers (he was denounced and disgraced for three years).[52] At Toulon, opinions were divided; pamphlets and caricatures were being circulated against Napoleon. At Clermont-Ferrand, he was publicly insulted, enough for the police to take note.[53] At Nîmes, during the night of 7–8 August, a group of opponents calling themselves the 'Implacables' posted insults against Napoleon in the public squares of the town.[54] At the camp of Bolougne, where the gathered army was predominantly republican, the proclamation of the Empire represented for many a return to old monarchical structures. Despite this, few officers refused to sign the petitions in favour of empire and some that did refuse were relieved of their commands.[55] Even some who admired Napoleon were a little worried about the extent of his ambition. 'He only wanted supreme power', wrote one officer, 'to break all the chains that, as First Consul, he still encountered . . . Why did we have a bloody revolution to return [to the monarchy] so quickly?'[56]

## Plebiscitary Leadership

The matter of heredity was taken to the people of France. Another plebiscite was held, this time during the month of June 1804. There was no mention of the imperial title, and the people were not asked to approve or disapprove of the Empire. They were simply asked to ratify what had already taken place.

The official results, revealed in August, were almost the same as those of the plebiscite of 1802 – over 3.5 million had voted 'yes' and only 2,569 had voted 'no' – but in reality the overall turnout had fallen, in some regions dramatically, so that there were 300,000 fewer votes than in 1802.[57] One has to take into account that by this stage France was actually larger than it had been in 1802 – several new departments had been added – and that the results for the army and navy were grossly exaggerated.[58] In some departments, the local prefects simply doubled the number of 'yes' votes received from their subordinates, and at the same time slightly reduced the number of negative votes.[59] This kind of fraud appears to have been common. It tells us at the very least that some local administrators were keen to produce strong positive returns so that their administration looked well in Paris. Corruption was built into the imperial system at the lowest levels, and was indicative of a hierarchy dependent on the approval of one man.

About 35 per cent of the electorate turned out to vote (the regime boasted that it was 40 per cent), which in itself was a better turnout than previous elections and plebiscites had achieved. It is also interesting to note that while some departments returned a higher 'yes' vote, many more – including Brittany, the east, the centre, the south-west and Languedoc – returned a much lower 'yes' vote than in 1802, sometimes up to 40 and even 50 per cent lower. This has been interpreted to mean that popular support for Napoleon was starting to wane,[60] but it is more likely there were real concerns about the nature of a hereditary regime and about the future of the representative system. 'I would vote affirmatively', wrote one voter in the Aube, 'if the history of all peoples did not teach me that the granting of supreme power for life, even in the hands of the most honest man, has very often changed the attitude of the individual in question. Such an accretion of power has frequently been dangerous for public and personal liberties.'[61] Nevertheless, the vote was still a resounding vote of confidence in the person of Napoleon.[62] Given the figures and in the face of a reasonably high turnout, it would appear that his policy of national reconciliation was finally starting to bear fruit. But the real victory came from the manner in which the plebiscite was used by the regime to promote Napoleon as someone who had been called to the throne by the people of France, and that it was his personal merits that had led him there.

## Trinkets and Baubles

In the six months between the declaration of the Empire in May and the coronation ceremony in December, an entirely new, original iconography had to be invented. Just as former and indeed future monarchs created symbols to assert and strengthen a claim to the throne, so too did Napoleon and his entourage have to devise symbols that had their roots in both the Roman and Carolingian Empires, as well as reconnecting with French national history.[63] Napoleon appears to have temporized. Prior to the Revolution, enormous importance had been placed in the body of the king as representative of the monarchy. After the execution of Louis XVI in 1792, the sacred character of the king's body had been defiled, so to speak, and it would have been difficult to turn back the clock. As a consequence, the importance of kingship began to be displaced on to the trappings of rule, in this case on to the new symbols and insignia that were created to represent Napoleon's new status as emperor.[64]

One of the most important decisions concerned the icons that would represent the new dynasty, for that was in effect what Napoleon was founding. The architects Charles Percier and Pierre-François-Léonard Fontaine suggested a lion resting its paw on a glaive or spear.[65] After discussing a number of possibilities – the eagle, the owl, the elephant (very fashionable at the time), the lion, the cock and even the fleur de lys – Napoleon favoured the lion.[66] This was

eventually rejected around July 1804 in favour of the eagle, on the urging of
Vivant Denon. The eagle not only evoked Charlemagne, but inspired the imagination of contemporaries, and placed Napoleon's reign firmly within the
tradition of the universal empires of the past.[67]

That was not to be the only symbol, however. In June 1804, when the coat
of arms was being designed, Cambacérès proposed the bee. In ancient times,
the bee was a symbol of immortality and resurrection, but people also remembered that metal jewellery in the form of bees had been discovered in the tomb
of the father of Clovis, Childeric I (440–81), at Tournai in 1653, during the
reign of Louis XIV.[68] It is more likely that what was discovered were cicadas or
crickets, and they were not emblems but votive objects placed on the royal
clothes: insects enabled the soul of the departed to fly more easily towards
heaven.[69] The bee was nevertheless a symbol that drew on the past, even if
contemporaries had incorrectly interpreted its historical significance. It was
also meant to be a metaphor for France: the beehive was the Republic, with its
leader a hard worker. And perhaps it was hoped that the French would be as
submissive as drones working for the queen. The bee enabled the regime to
draw a link between the furthest reaches of French history – the Merovingian
dynasty founded by Childeric – and the present.

On 15 July 1804, Their Majesties put on a display for the people. Napoleon
arrived at the Church of the Invalides in the uniform of a colonel of the Guard,
riding a horse covered in gold, his boots resting in stirrups of solid gold.
Josephine was in a carriage drawn by eight horses, bedecked in diamonds. They
assisted at a mass by Cardinal Caprara, the papal legate – Napoleon was sitting on
a throne during the proceedings – after which the Emperor personally awarded
the first civilian Legion of Honour. Julie Talma, the wife of the well-known actor
François-Joseph Talma, called the ceremony the 'distribution of the trinkets'.[70]

The Legion of Honour had been established by decree in May 1802, in the face
of strong opposition. Two years of bitter political battles followed before the
award was realized in the form of a medal in July 1804.[71] More deputies opposed
the Legion of Honour than opposed the reintroduction of slavery in 1802.[72] They
feared Bonaparte was returning to the principles of the *ancien régime*, while
others feared the creation of a class of notables, a type of (military) aristocracy,
that would become exclusively loyal to him. Bonaparte had gone against the
revolutionary grain by introducing this system of awards, but it reflects his
personal preferences. In Italy in 1796, he had begun to invent new awards for his
soldiers, usually in the form of swords of honour, in order to create an affective
bond with his men.[73] Moreover, the Legion was designed to reward those who
had rendered services to the state – merit was the defining condition of entry –
thereby creating a kind of elite that would remain loyal to the state, that is,
Bonaparte, and on which he could count. It was also designed to recompense

those who had fought to establish the Revolution and those who had helped bring about Brumaire.[74] More than that, however, it was based on a conception of 'social amelioration' – people could strive to get ahead in the service of the state.[75]

The Legion also has to be seen as one among many attempts to rally the elite to the regime, and not only within France. It was, therefore, a form of political control, or at least of political persuasion, in which the holders of the medal were expected not only to remain loyal to the state, but in some respects to become propagandists for the regime. Along with a pension, the person received a medal with Napoleon's image on one side, and the imperial eagle on the other, with the inscription *Honneur et Patrie*. Republican virtues and national honour were meant to inspire Frenchmen to serve the *patrie*, one of the reasons many republicans hated the idea; the concept of 'honour' not only smacked of the old monarchy, but was also associated with the nobility.[76] Napoleon was, in some respects, creating a civil society modelled on the army, a strictly hierarchical order of merit.[77]

As a result of opposition to the introduction of the Legion, Bonaparte was forced to push the matter through the Council of State, but even then ten out of fourteen voted against the law. In part, their reaction was one of revenge for the defeats they had suffered in the course of 1802. It then went to the Legislative Corps where, after one of the most open and heated debates, the measure was finally endorsed, but only by 166 to 110 votes. Such a margin was unheard of before and was particularly noticeable given that its members had only recently been purged. The Tribunate saw similar scenes, but there too it passed by 56 votes to 38. Former revolutionaries were particularly vociferous; they feared the introduction of an 'order' (although the word was never used) that would lead to the abandonment of the principle of equality. Even those who normally supported Napoleon in the Tribunate spoke against it.[78]

If former revolutionaries criticized the new project, the military were not particularly keen either. The idea of being associated with a medal that would also be awarded to civilians was distasteful.[79] Moreau publicly ridiculed the idea by making his cook a 'knight of the pot' (*chevalier de la casserole*).[80] Students at the Ecole Polytechnique denigrated the Legion of Honour as a reward for charlatanism and not merit.[81] And yet Bonaparte's reaction to all this was quite moderate; he tried to get a number of generals who had resisted the idea of empire on side by promoting them to his Guard.[82] And once the medal was distributed, it soon became accepted if not coveted.

## Boulogne

The Legion of Honour was taken to the army. Ever since the declaration of war, Bonaparte had been gathering troops along the northern shorelines in preparation for an invasion of England. Between June 1803 and September 1805, some 170,000 men were assembled along the coast between Montreuil in the north of France and Utrecht in Holland, possibly the largest number of men in history brought together for a single campaign.[83] The central point of this concentration was the port town of Boulogne.

One day after Napoleon's thirty-fifth birthday, on 16 August 1804, a grand ceremony took place near Boulogne, on the cliffs overlooking the English Channel, with the French fleet sailing off the coast, in what has been described as one of the 'most elaborate military festivals of the Napoleonic period'.[84] Over 100,000 men were drawn up in a semicircle around a raised platform, forming a sort of natural amphitheatre, on top of which was the bronze throne of Dagobert, the Merovingian king who helped unify the Franks in the seventh century.[85] A salvo of artillery and 2,000 beating drums announced the arrival of Napoleon, easily recognizable on his grey horse and by the clothes he wore. He dismounted, walked up the steps to the enormous stage, to the music of Jean-François Le Sueur, composed for the occasion, keeping the rhythm of the music in his step. The music would be used again during the coronation. The Emperor took his place on the throne. Behind him were over 200 captured enemy flags. To the left was a helmet supposed to have belonged to Bertrand du Guesclin, Constable of France during the Hundred Years' War. To the right, a breastplate of the Chevalier Bayard, hero of the Italian Wars of the late fifteenth and early sixteenth centuries, and the shield of the French Renaissance king Francis I, who conducted a series of wars in Italy at the beginning of the sixteenth century; two further shields contained the 2,000 medals of the Legion of Honour that were about to be distributed.[86]

Very few people would have appreciated the significance of these artefacts – not even, it would appear, the artist Philippe-August Hennequin, who accompanied Vivant Denon to Boulogne. In his memoirs, he was more concerned with describing how the weather seems to have been subject to Napoleon's will. There had been an overcast stormy sky, he wrote, until the moment Napoleon sat on the throne, when 'the clouds divided and let a ray of light escape that fell on the trophy behind the emperor'.[87] Nevertheless, the fact that ancient symbols of royal power were used as a central prop during a ceremony to celebrate the distribution of the controversial Legion meant that notions of royalism, republicanism and even imperialism were combined on stage for the first time.[88]

Once on stage, the grand chancellor of the Legion of Honour, Bernard-Germain de Lacépède, asked Napoleon to swear the oath of the Legion of Honour. Not many people would have heard him in the wind but, on cue, hundreds of thousands of voices rang out with 'Vivat!' when the oath was taken. Napoleon also asked the troops to swear an oath of loyalty to him. 'And you, soldiers, do you swear to defend, at the peril of your life, the honour of the French name, your *patrie* and your Emperor?'[89] This ceremony, which harks back to the ancient Roman tradition of the troops swearing an oath of loyalty to the emperor, was one means used by Napoleon to invest the Empire with

Detail from Philippe Auguste Hennequin, *Napoléon Ier distribue les croix de la légion d'honneur au camp de Boulogne le 16 août 1804* (Napoleon distributing the Cross of the Legion of Honour at the camp of Boulogne on 16 August 1804), 1806. The painting appeared in the Salon of 1806. Today, an obelisk marks the spot where the throne of Dagobert was placed for the ceremony.

princely forms of traditional obedience, as well as legitimating the transformation of the Republic into an empire. According to one eyewitness, those present were 'electrified', although whether this was the case for everyone is questionable.[90] The ceremony was, in any event, a blatant attempt to seduce the army and to garner support for Napoleon, especially in the context of the recent trial of General Moreau. That, along with the Concordat and the proclamation of the Empire, had disaffected a good number of republicans among the military.

## Charlemagne, Not Caesar (or Alexander)

Legitimating what contemporaries began to call the 'fourth dynasty' took place on another level as well.[91] In order to be accepted as a sovereign by the other European monarchs, and in order to impose his dynasty, Napoleon had to invent a past, or rather legitimate the transformation of power by making a link between his own regime and those of the past.[92] He therefore actively encouraged the comparison not only with Charlemagne but also with Alexander, Caesar and Hannibal, as well as with a number of other historical figures, in the press as well as in paintings, engravings and medals. Caesar was an obvious reference point since he was not only the head of a dictatorship of public safety, so to speak, but sought to legitimate and perpetuate his power through a hereditary succession.[93] Many of the institutions created during the early years of Napoleon's reign were modelled, very loosely, on this period of Roman history: the consuls held executive power; the tribunes shared legislative power with the senators, and so on. The French Republic was thus subtly assimilated with the Roman Republic. The proclamation of the Empire in 1804 seemed, in many respects, the logical outcome of these Roman Republican institutions. It was important though that Napoleon was associated not only with a French but also with a European heritage.[94]

Central to that heritage was the Emperor Charlemagne (742–814), who ruled over much of western Europe, and who is regarded as the founder of both the French and German monarchies.[95] Napoleon and his propagandists never tired of making the comparison.[96] For example, an item in the *Journal de Paris* states that there is only one hand in all of Europe capable of wearing the sword of Charlemagne, that of 'Bonaparte the Great'.[97] It is no coincidence, therefore, to see in the painting by David of Bonaparte crossing the Alps the names of Hannibal, 'Karolus Magnus' (Charlemagne) and Bonaparte carved into the rock in the bottom left-hand corner (see p. 39). Napoleon understood the extraordinary potential of the myth of Charlemagne, a myth moreover that had been reworked and revamped in the years preceding the outbreak of Revolution in France, and which had become closely linked to debates throughout the eighteenth century on absolutism and the nature of the monarchy. Charlemagne came

Jean Bertrand Andrieu, *Alliance avec la Saxe* (Alliance with Saxony), 1806. The medal shows the profiles of the Emperors Napoleon and Charlemagne.

© RMN-Grand Palais (Sèvres, Cité de la Céramique/Martina Beck-Coppola)

to represent the human face of absolutism, a legislator who had redressed the nation and had established a constitution. This is why he represented such an ideal historical type for the regime; like Charlemagne, Napoleon wanted to unite the nation around his person. Moreover, contemporaries looked on Charlemagne as a king who had restored order after a period of chaos, and who had occupied a throne left morally vacant by the previous Merovingian dynasty.

The idea of Charlemagne was pressed home in a newspaper campaign that took place shortly before the proclamation of the Empire,[98] but it had been present almost as soon as Bonaparte became a public figure.[99] Admittedly, the output of pamphlets and books was not impressive – and it does not seem to have inspired the popular imagination – but the message was clear, especially since the idea of Charlemagne was meant to be flexible enough to appeal to both republicans and royalists.[100] Some of the material, therefore, was written with republicans in mind. In these writings, Napoleon represented the republican ideal, a meritocratic system in which anyone could become anything. According to the official line, the title of emperor was to serve the interests, the wellbeing and the glory of the nation, and had nothing to do with the personal interests of Napoleon.[101] It was, once again, a question of 'curbing all factions, bringing together all parties and erasing even the memory of the former divisions'.[102]


'The Restorer of the Roman Empire'
Bonaparte had been thinking of Augustus.[103] The idea of officially associating Napoleon with the reign of Charlemagne belonged to Louis Fontanes. In September 1804, in order to make the association clearer, Napoleon paid a visit to Aachen, the city in which Charlemagne was crowned in the year 800, and where his memory was still very much alive.[104] Officially, Napoleon's visit was to be a tour of the four departments of the Rhine, but he was also to receive the homage of a number of Germanic princes. While there, he took part in a procession in which what were believed to be the relics of Charlemagne (the skull and an arm) were ceremoniously carried to the cathedral, where he stood before what contemporaries believed to be Charlemagne's resting place.[105]

We now know the relics were bogus, but the gesture was nevertheless pregnant with symbolic meaning. Aachen was a kind of pilgrimage, a nod in the direction of a national hero, once emperor of the western world. But Napoleon was also testing the waters. Meeting with the Germanic princes was a way of measuring princely opinion (Charlemagne had also received the German princes at Mainz on his way to Rome to be crowned emperor). Napoleon went on to visit a dozen or so other cities as he wound his way down the Rhine to Mainz, a sort of *Via triumphalis*, as his new subjects turned out to greet the imperial couple; crowds got bigger the closer they got to Mainz. At a reception in Mainz on 21 September, he held court (for the first time outside Paris), and more or less received homage from most of the German princes while he did his best to charm them.[106] This was designed partly to counteract the effects of the Enghien affair, and partly to bring the German princes onside in the lead-up to another war. The German princes may have made a choice based on Realpolitik, but German intellectuals and republicans were far more circumspect, if not disillusioned by Napoleon's decision to adopt the imperial mantle.[107] He had betrayed his revolutionary roots; for *ancien régime* nobles, he could never be anything more than an upstart.

## The Thaumaturge King

In keeping with the drive to portray Napoleon as monarch, artists were also enlisted. The highlight of the Salon of 1804, measuring five metres by seven, was Gros' *Bonaparte Visiting the Plague Victims of Jaffa*.[108] The painting's public and critical reception at the Salon that year was enthusiastic. A secret police bulletin reported that all classes of society had been 'moved' by the painting.[109] It was helped by the fact that the memory of the expedition to Egypt was still fresh in people's minds. The artist, Antoine-Jean Gros, later recounted that when the doors of the studio in which the painting was executed, the former Jeu de Paume in Versailles, were closed shortly before its transfer to the Louvre, a crowd of workers gathered outside and begged him, money in hand, to be allowed to see it.[110] One witness recalled that 'the sincere admiration which this composition excited was so general that painters from all the respected schools united to carry to the Louvre a great laurel wreath to hang above Gros's picture'.[111] The press described it as the greatest success of the Salon.[112]

Two aspects of the paintings are worth dwelling on. The first is that it portrays the French army in defeat, or at least decimated by the plague. The scene is one of dire misery in which the arrival of the saviour – Bonaparte – appropriately recognized by the light cast on him in contrast to the dark shadows that engulf the dying, illuminates the whole and brings the promise of healing. The real subject of the painting is, after all, not so much the army as Bonaparte as active hero who extends his hand in a Christ-like gesture to heal a victim of the plague, as if in the royal tradition his touch could heal the sick. At the same time, both Arab and French medical personnel are busy around him trying to stem the tide of death. The contrast between light and darkness is meant as a metaphor to highlight Bonaparte's supernatural qualities. Bonaparte gives life, an image mirrored in a poem that appeared a year later in the *Mercure de France*, 'L'Hospice de Jaffa' (The hospital at Jaffa), in which Napoleon appears on a chariot accompanied by both Glory and Humanity to bring light and life.[113] The failure of the Syrian expedition was thus transformed through Bonaparte's glamorous gesture into a victory, of sorts.[114]

This painting is not only another element in the construction of the Napoleonic legend, it was meant to provide an alternative vision to the rumours about Bonaparte's order to poison plague victims at Jaffa.[115] This rumour reached France through the returning army,[116] as well as appearing in the clandestine publications that circulated. In 1802, for example, Robert Wilson published an account of the Egyptian and Syrian campaigns that accused Bonaparte of having massacred the prisoners at Jaffa and of having poisoned sick French troops.[117] It seems to have gained wide currency, even if it was dismissed by most supporters of the regime as simply British propaganda.[118]

Placed between Bonaparte and the plague victim whose arm is raised so that his bubo can be examined is Nicolas René Desgenettes, the very man whose criticism of Bonaparte's policies towards the plague helped fan the rumours about poisoning in the first place. His inclusion was a clear attempt to negate those rumours by associating him with Bonaparte's gesture.[119] A man who might be Berthier has his arm around Bonaparte's waist as if to hold him back from the victim, while pressing a handkerchief against his face. The gesture is repeated by General Jean-Baptiste Bessières, who was with Bonaparte in Egypt, hardly discernible in the shadows behind Berthier. Bonaparte's face, on the other hand, is uncovered, as though he were immune to the stench. The Turk, a local Christian, who is kneeling to cut a bubo is based on an actual character: he was almost always drunk but was considered to be a local specialist in the disease. Desgenettes often saw him dragged from an alcohol-induced sleep and led, or sometimes driven by a baton, into the hospital where, without any precaution, he would incise the buboes, wipe his bistoury or surgical knife and then replace it between his forehead and his turban. The doctor who has succumbed to the plague in the right-hand corner is probably a man by the name of Saint-Ours who did die at Jaffa. He represents the many medical personnel who died of the plague during the Syrian campaign. Finally, just above Saint-Ours is a man suffering from what was commonly referred to as ophthalmia (a general term used to describe several kinds of conjunctivitis), who is trying to grope his way towards Bonaparte, an image inspired no doubt by the biblical gesture of the blind man at Jericho.

If the painting is clearly meant to counter the poison rumours, it can also be interpreted as part of the tradition of the thaumaturge king.[120] The anointed kings of France would appear outside the cathedral at Rheims and demonstrate the miraculous character of their office – the king's body being rendered sacred by the anointing ceremony – by laying hands on the sufferers of scrofula. It meant that people were allowed to touch the king's mantle, or at least its hem. The practice was discontinued under Louis XV, but was revived under Louis XVI.[121] Napoleon could not renew this practice, but we see the idea of the king's sacred body reintroduced in Gros' painting, albeit elliptically, so that for the first time the dignity of the citizen and that of the monarch are combined to form a new amalgam, the dignity of the citizen-monarch.

Detail of Antoine-Jean Gros, *Bonaparte visitant les pestiférés de Jaffa* (Bonaparte visiting the plague victims at Jaffa), 1804. It is an image, as one historian has put it, of 'Christ in a republican uniform'.[122]

That interpretation is contested, but it certainly shows Napoleon as the 'caring father', in the tradition of the clement ruler (about which more below).[123] Moreover, the painting's political message is ambiguous.[124] An alternative interpretation is the use of illness as a metaphor to describe the sickly French body politic.[125] Gros quite possibly thought in terms of metaphor – Bonaparte arriving as saviour to heal a sick, faction-ridden France. Moreover, the plague was often associated with political upheaval, an expression of anarchy, literally a 'pest'.[126] Gros' painting, therefore, represents the ravaged body politic, portrayed by French soldiers languishing in various postures. An alternative to chaos and death is presented to the onlooker – the uniformed soldier, in the form of Bonaparte and his generals. The logical conclusion is that allegiance to Napoleon was the only alternative to the dissent and factionalism that had riven French society.

### Rendering Napoleon Sacred

And that was the message driven home time and again by the regime: namely, just as Brumaire was necessary to bring all Frenchmen together, so too was the Empire designed to heal the festering social and political wounds of the Revolution. The crowning moment of this campaign was to be a religious ceremony in the Cathedral of Notre Dame designed to impress the people of Europe and at the same time lend weight to Napoleon's claim to the throne.

Once again, Louis Fontanes seems to have had the idea for a religious coronation, although it did not go down well with everyone.[127] Comte Jean-Baptiste Treilhard in the Council of State, for example, questioned the need for it. He was among a number of politicians who preferred a civil ceremony on the Champ de Mars, to be put off till the following year.[128] For most in the Emperor's entourage, however, the political symbolism of a religious ceremony was understood. Fontanes, for example, suggested that Napoleon adopt the pomp traditionally associated with the kings of France, urging him not to neglect the religious elements of the *sacre* (consecration).[129] As Jean-Etienne-Marie Portalis, later to become director of religious affairs, pointed out to Napoleon, 'anything that renders sacred the person who governs is a good thing'.[130] Contemporaries were well aware, in other words, that the ceremony was about constructing an appearance of legitimacy through the use of tradition, costume and symbolism.

The choice of Notre Dame for the ceremony is itself an interesting one. Napoleon at first proposed that the coronation should not take place in Paris, which obliged the councillors of state to debate alternatives, each one eliminated in turn so that Paris soon became the obvious choice.[131] Rheims, the cathedral where every French king except two (Louis VI and Henry IV) had been crowned, was for that reason eliminated: it was too closely associated with the former monarchy. Aachen, where not only Charlemagne but thirty-four other emperors and ten empresses had been crowned, was ruled out by the pope on the grounds that he did not want to visit the region because it contained too many Lutherans.[132] The clergy of Orleans proposed that city's cathedral, but the offer does not appear to have been seriously considered.

That left Paris, but Napoleon nevertheless hesitated. Since the Moreau affair, public approval of the regime had been tepid, and the capital remained a hotbed of republicanism.[133] In June, Napoleon suggested that the Champ de Mars would be an appropriate place for a coronation, and at first the members of the Council of State agreed.[134] He revisited the question a couple of weeks later, having had second thoughts in the meantime. He had decided that the people were to be excluded from the event. If an altar was placed in the middle of the Champ de Mars, he declared, it would become a populist ceremony. It was important that Paris should not think of itself as the nation. This was no longer the Revolution, when the people of Paris had intervened directly in the political process.[135] Besides, there was always the risk of bad weather; it would not look dignified if the imperial family were exposed to the rain and the mud, as had been the case during the Festival of the Federation in 1790.[136]

The Church of Saint-Louis at the Invalides was considered as an alternative location – it had been the site of a number of civil and military ceremonies during the Revolution and the Consulate – but Fontanes thought the church inadequate for such a grand occasion and recommended instead Notre Dame.[137] Napoleon agreed. Notre Dame had undergone a number of transformations during the Revolution, from a cathedral to a Temple of Reason, to a Temple of the Supreme Being, to the principal church of the Theophilanthropists, before finally reverting to the Catholic faith in April 1802. It was transformed once again for the coronation. The gothic interior of Notre Dame was hidden behind decorations of red and blue silk designed by Charles Percier and François-Léonard Fontaine, who thereby converted it into a vast theatre, a neo-Greek temple. Buildings around the cathedral were demolished to make room – the space in front of the building was cleared, resulting in the square that we see today – while triumphal arches along the route leading to the cathedral were erected.

A member of the Council of State, Portalis, suggested the idea of having the pope confer on Napoleon a blessing that would transform the Empire into a Christian monarchy, and Napoleon into a legitimate monarch.[138] Bringing the pope to Paris, however, was no easy thing. In the past, the pope had travelled to crown the king of France on only two occasions: when Stephen II (III) crowned Pepin (the Short) King of the Franks in 754; and when Stephen IV (V) crowned Louis the Pious emperor in 816 at Rheims, almost a thousand years before. All other kings and emperors anointed by the pontiff had gone to Rome, including Charlemagne. Napoleon, however, wanted the pope to come to him, thereby asserting the power of the French Church,[139] and the power of the Emperor over the pope. The presence of the pope, moreover, would help cut the religious base from under the counter-revolution, and bring about the national reconciliation Napoleon was aiming at. This is not to say that there was no opposition to the pope's presence, but Napoleon's wishes prevailed. It was in that respect an attempt to recreate, at least on the surface, the coalition between throne and altar that had existed before the Revolution, as well as challenging Francis as Holy Roman Emperor for the domination of Germany.[140]

Negotiations with the Vatican began in May, very tentatively at first.[141] Napoleon told the papal legate in Paris, Cardinal Caprara, of his wish to be consecrated by the pope, but added that he did not yet want to make a formal request for fear of its being rejected.[142] The pope at first baulked, arguing that there would have to be a serious religious motive for him to leave Rome. The Curia pointed to the illegitimacy of the monarch, the pope's poor health, the fear that he would not be respected in revolutionary France, and the policy of freedom of religion practised under Napoleon. If the negotiations took several months to conclude, it was because Rome had every advantage in drawing things out: it would leave a better impression with the courts of Europe (a too hasty agreement would look bad); and it hoped to receive from Napoleon as many changes in its favour as possible (the pope was looking to alter the situation that had developed ever since Napoleon imposed the Organic Articles on the Church). Eventually, however, the pope had to concede on almost every point, but the process was exhausting and made him very anxious and in the end quite sick.[143]

Accompanied by an imposing entourage of ecclesiastics and servants – 108 people divided into four convoys, though it was not as imposing as Napoleon had hoped – the pope did not leave Rome until 2 November. Fêted along the route in Italy, he took at least two weeks to reach Paris. At Lyons (19 November), in spite of torrential rain, 80,000 people turned out to see him.[144] Napoleon sent his uncle, Cardinal Fesch, to hurry things along, while Cardinal Cambacérès, Archbishop of Rouen and the arch-chancellor's brother, was also sent to greet the convoy.[145] The date of the coronation kept having to be put back – from 9 to 25, to 26, then to 29 November and finally to 2 December. The pope would have preferred Christmas Day, the day on which Charlemagne had been crowned in 800, and was no doubt dallying in order to get his way.

When the pope's convoy reached the forest of Fontainebleau on 25 November, Napoleon met him according to a prearranged plan, as though he had come across the pontiff by chance while out hunting, to avoid having to genuflect before him.[146] Then, in what has to be one of the strangest meetings of any two heads of state before or since, he waited until the pope had got out of his carriage before he dismounted and went to meet him on foot. Before they could get too close, however, the imperial carriage came between them: Napoleon got in on the right side (the place of honour), while the pope got in on the left. They then drove to Fontainebleau together, accompanied by a fittingly pagan escort of Mamelukes. The Château de Fontainebleau, which had not been used since the beginning of the Revolution, had been prepared to receive both entourages. Forty apartments, 200 lesser lodgings and stables for 400 horses had to be made ready. Preparations were still not quite complete when the pope arrived. He was left standing at the top of the main staircase where Napoleon had accompanied him. A quip about the event was soon circulating in Paris – *Le Pape Pie sans lit* (Pope Pius without a bed).[147]

This first encounter was to decide the etiquette for the remainder of the pontiff's visit. Napoleon and the pope entered the city at around 7.30 on a dark winter's evening. It is impossible to know how to read this, and whether Napoleon wanted the pope's arrival in Paris to go unnoticed. Word got out, though, and a large crowd gathered at the Barrière d'Italie, in spite of the cold and the darkness, to await the arrival of His Holiness. As soon as the carriages appeared, cries of 'Long live the Emperor!' and 'Long live His Holiness!' rang out.[148] It was only the next day that the rest of Paris, assisted by a pealing of church bells, found out that the pope was at the Tuileries. Crowds of people flocked to the palace where they would call out for him to appear, and would then kneel to receive his blessings. In the course of 29 November, he did so twenty times.[149] Indeed, he was becoming so popular that, according to some, Napoleon was starting to get jealous.[150]

From the moment of Pius VII's arrival, it was obvious that Napoleon intended to make the pontiff subordinate to him. Everything was organized in such a way that the spiritual power of the Church was subjected to the temporal power of the French state.[151] Pius was, for example, obliged to walk and sit on Napoleon's left (rather than on his right), he was obliged to wait for an hour and a half in Notre Dame on the day of the coronation before Napoleon arrived,[152] and was, if eyewitness reports are anything to go by, entirely dominated by Napoleon's personality. The pope, on the other hand, felt 'a mixture of admiration and fear, of paternal tenderness and pious gratitude' towards Napoleon.[153]

The Art Archive/Musée de Château de Versailles/Gianni Dagli Orti

Jacques-Louis David, *Portrait du Pape Pius VII* (Pope Pius VII), 1805. Pius VII was sixty-two years of age, and was according to contemporaries a 'good man', diffident, without ambition, but sharp and subtle. The modesty of his appearance and something of that goodness seems to come through the canvas of David's portrait. One of the reasons he agreed to come to Paris was his belief that he could influence Napoleon and even bring him around to his way of thinking – to convert him, so to speak.

## A Vexed Question

Then Josephine dropped a bombshell. Every member of the Bonaparte family hated Josephine, and continually intrigued to diminish her influence.[154] Conscious of her precarious position, and in an attempt to shore it up, she took the initiative and asked for a secret audience with the pope to reveal that she and Napoleon had not been married in a religious ceremony. The pope refused to carry out the coronation unless the union was immediately consecrated. Josephine had not informed Napoleon of her intentions. It was an astute move on her part; a religious ceremony made divorce not impossible but at least more difficult.[155] Napoleon had been outmanoeuvred. The coronation was worth a mass. At around four in the afternoon on the eve of the coronation, Cardinal Fesch conducted the wedding ceremony, assisted by the curé of Saint-Germain l'Auxerrois.

The Art Archive/Musée de Louvre/SuperStock

Detail of Pierre Paul Prud'hon, *Portrait de Joséphine de Beauharnais* (The Empress Josephine), 1805. Josephine, portrayed here in dress typical of the era, was said to have had a significant influence on feminine fashion. A few weeks before the coronation, one of her ladies-in-waiting, Elisabeth de Vaudey, described her as pretty and witty. There had, however, been talk of Napoleon's divorcing Josephine and marrying a princess from the Margrave of Baden.

When it came to the coronation ceremony then, one can imagine the tensions and petty jealousies simmering under the surface of the Bonaparte family. At a meeting at Saint-Cloud on 17 November, a terrible scene occurred between Joseph and Napoleon about the ceremonial rules. Napoleon's sisters and sisters-in-law refused to carry the Empress's train during the ceremony, as etiquette required.[156] 'Do I have to be there to swell his wife's court?' Pauline is supposed to have complained. 'Oh, honourable indeed, Bonapartes in the suite of Beauharnais. Truly, my sisters make me sick with their submission.'[157] Elisa, Pauline and Caroline saw in the gesture an insult for which they would never forgive Josephine. Joseph protested on their behalf. The fundamental issue really was that the Bonaparte family objected to seeing Josephine crowned empress.[158] Napoleon's reaction was predictable: he hurled abuse at his brother. When the meeting was adjourned, the argument continued between the two brothers in private and became more and more heated, to the point where Joseph offered to resign the imperial dignity and retire to Germany. Eventually, the princesses agreed to submit after the description of their role in the official proceedings was changed from 'carrying the train' (porter la queue) to 'holding the mantle' (soutenir le manteau).[159]

Less than a week later, Napoleon had another meeting with Joseph and gave him three choices: to resign and withdraw from public affairs; to continue to enjoy the rank of prince all the while opposing Napoleon's 'system'; or to unite with Napoleon and become his 'first subject'.[160] Nevertheless, the Emperor warned, if Joseph refused to come to the coronation ceremony and to fulfil the role that had been assigned to him, he would be from that moment on Napoleon's enemy. It is a remarkable confrontation – the elder brother harangued by the younger, forcing him to toe the line. Faced with these options, Joseph rallied to his brother, although perhaps not as wholeheartedly as Napoleon would have liked. Joseph's reaction was, however, going to stick in Napoleon's craw. A measure of Napoleon's hurt can be seen in the rather strange analogy he later used to describe the experience: he likened it to a man telling another that he was screwing his lover, only to tell him the next day that he had been joking. The damage had been done.

# 9

# Citizen Emperor

## The Coronation

On 1 December 1804, the day before the coronation, the Emperor received the Senate at the Tuileries, seated on his throne, as they brought him the official results of the plebiscite on the Empire. The president of the Senate, François de Neufchâteau, poet and revolutionary, gave a speech that lasted three-quarters of an hour in which Napoleon was congratulated for having 'steered the vessel of the Republic into port'. Napoleon, like a wonder of God, had set the limits of the Revolution and had founded the first monarchy that did not control the freedom of its subjects. The Emperor replied using for the first time the expression 'my people'. Miot de Mélito noticed that it did not go down terribly well, but that no one voiced an objection.[1]

It snowed all that night until about eight in the morning.[2] Parisians woke to find their city covered, the noises typical of a big city dulled by a white blanket. Workers had to be quickly mobilized to shovel the snow away and to lay sand along the route the procession was going to take. If the workers had risen early, the hairstylists had not yet gone to bed. Some of them had started as early as two in the morning. Mme Campan had her hair done at 4 a.m.; Mlle Avrillon, the Empress's lady-in-waiting, at 5.[3] Once the stylists had done their job, rather than go to bed and risk messing their hair, some women preferred to sleep upright in a chair, waiting until the time had come to get dressed.[4] Between the foundation of the Empire in May 1804 and the coronation ceremony six months later, a whole new courtly attire had to be designed, fabricated and adopted. It required so much work that artisans of the fashion industry had to be brought to Paris from Lyons to make all the costumes in time for the ceremony.[5] If the ceremony itself was forgotten, the fashions were not; they would set the trend in Europe for decades to come.

In spite of the overcast sky and the cold weather, Parisians, 'more curious than eager', turned out in great numbers to witness the event,[6] especially in the square before Notre Dame, but also along the route the procession was to take, where soldiers in their brand-new uniforms formed a guard of honour. According to the playwright Charles Brifaut, Parisians at first 'refused' to take the ceremony seriously, but within a month France was on its knees before the Emperor.[7] Windows and balconies along the route of the procession were rented at exorbitant prices, three to four hundred francs for a balcony that could barely hold five or six people, the equivalent of anything from a quarter- to a half-year's wage for a worker.[8]

The doors of the cathedral were thrown open at six o'clock in the morning; many of the 20,000 guests, impatient or wanting to get seated early, started arriving, handing over their invitations to the master of ceremonies.[9] Accommodation in Paris had to be found for the thousands of people invited to the ceremony, who often arrived with members of their family. Many of the troops brought in for the occasion had to be billeted on the people. The prefecture of police calculated that 700 carriages brought guests to their destination; they had to be parked somewhere during the ceremony and that could only be done by the police requisitioning stables and private courtyards in the surrounding streets.[10] The presence of these early arrivals, however, only interfered with the workers completing their last-minute preparations.[11]

Pius VII's procession, made up of ten carriages, left the Tuileries at about nine in the morning. It was delayed because the French were unaware of the custom that called for the pope to be preceded by the apostolic nuncio, in this case a man by the name of Speroni, on a mule holding a cross; they had to run about finding a suitable mount at the last minute.[12] When Speroni passed down the street of Saint-Denis, in what was essentially a working-class district, the crowds laughed so much that the pope could not prevent himself from joining in.[13] Speroni too was good-natured enough to laugh too.

The procession took about an hour and a half to make the journey to the cathedral. There had already been some discussion about how the pope was to enter Notre Dame. He should have been carried into the cathedral on his portable throne, the *sedia gestatoria*, but we now know that Napoleon had opposed the traditional entry for fear that it would look more grandiose than his own. Other, more practical reasons were given though: the gallery through which the throne had to pass was too narrow; a similar gesture had been made during the Revolution when the radical journalist and politician Jean-Paul Marat had had himself carried into Notre Dame on a chair.[14] The chamberlain of the palace, Auxonne de Thiard, has left us with a description of Napoleon barefoot, half-clad, wearing a dressing gown, less than an hour before he was due to leave.[15] The imperial couple left the Tuileries between ten and eleven o'clock and travelled through the streets to the cathedral in a procession made up of twenty-five carriages, drawn by 152 horses, escorted by six cavalry regiments. The order of the procession said a good deal about where real power in the Empire lay: the twenty-two 'grand officers' of the Legion of Honour, all generals, were at the head of the parade, closely followed by the commanders of the military divisions and the generals of division.[16] Only then did the civilian authorities follow – judges, court officials, civic and religious leaders.

Mass attendance at public festivities is not necessarily the same thing as public acceptance of the existing (or in this case new) social and political order.[17] As it turned out, the crowd waiting for the procession was a good deal more reserved than had been hoped, despite the massive and costly build-up over the two months leading up to the ceremony. But then people had to wait around all day in a cold that was bound to dampen the spirits of even the most ardent supporters. Descriptions of the mood of the crowd depend on the political leanings of the author, their position along the path of the procession and the time of day. Jean-Nicolas-August Noël, lined up with his detachment along the route, believed that 'little enthusiasm was shown', despite what was written in the official reports, and that only a few of the public and the urchins who ran alongside the procession cried out 'Vive l'Empereur'.[18] Noël was a republican at heart who disliked the whole affair, but others agreed with him. One onlooker, no great admirer of Napoleon, wrote to tell his sister that he saw the procession drive past while he was standing on the corner of the Place du Carrousel: 'There was a small crowd, extremely calm.'[19] Miot de Mélito asserted that acclamations were rare and uttered without enthusiasm.[20] Other reports were less categorical. Hortense de Beauharnais spoke of the large crowds but described their applause as the 'customary cheering' – that is, they applauded because that was the thing to do.[21] 'Acclamations did not lack along the route,' wrote one of Josephine's ladies-in-waiting, Claire Elisabeth de Rémusat. She gives the impression, however, that the crowds were there out of curiosity more than anything else and that they 'did not have that enthusiastic elan that a sovereign jealous of receiving the testimony of love for these subjects might have desired, but they could not satisfy the vanity of a master proud and not in the least sensitive'.[22]

The only people in fact to claim that the crowds were enthusiastic were the police and some of the troops present. The police reports ring overly positive, praising the good mood of the people and the 'concert of praise and blessings'. The report written by the prefect of police, Dubois, smacks of the toadying that inevitably accompanies power.[23] As for the troops, they were specifically chosen for the occasion.[24] Elie Krettly, a fervent supporter of the imperial regime, remarked on the 'universal joy' among the crowds that lined the route, although this was after the ceremony.[25] (The return procession through the popular quarters, like the rue Saint-Martin, was much more enthusiastic.[26] An indication that the people of Paris were willing participants lies in the number of houses illuminated along the return route of the procession. By the time the imperial couple reached the Tuileries two hours later, through an alley that had been illuminated by 500 torches, it was already half past six in the evening.)[27]

Enthusiastic or not, Paris was obliged to put on its best face for the occasion. A fountain thirteen metres high had been constructed on the Esplanade des Invalides; three bridges had been built over the River Seine to facilitate the traffic, one of which, the Pont des Arts, had only recently been inaugurated; houses had been destroyed to help circulation, especially around the cathedral on the Île de la Cité; the rue de Rivoli, the Place du Carrousel and the Quai

Bonaparte were completely paved (a rare thing in Paris); and footpaths had been installed in as many of the principal streets as possible, a first in France.[28] In fact, the coronation marks the beginning of the modernization of the city of Paris.[29] Workers had been active day and night, seven days a week, in order to complete everything in time.

The weather nevertheless threatened to spoil the event, but, as the faithful reported, the skies cleared to reveal a blue sky as Napoleon's carriage, drawn by eight white horses, drew up in front of the cathedral, or more precisely in front of the huge, round, tent-like vestibule that been especially constructed by Percier and Fontaine. There, the imperial couple donned the robes they were to wear for the coronation, mantles of crimson velvet, embroidered with gold bees and eagles. Napoleon entered the cathedral wearing a laurel of gold oak and olive leaves that were meant to represent victory, peace and civic virtue. The painter Jean-Baptiste Isabey had done Josephine's make-up.[30] They entered the cathedral to the acclamations of the assembled spectators. 'In my whole life,' declared one witness, 'I have never seen or heard anything like it.'[31]

A little after midday, Napoleon and Josephine proceeded down the centre of the cathedral, accompanied by the music of Le Sueur, played by 500 musicians. According to some, Napoleon looked a little grotesque in his imperial regalia, but to others he offered an imposing spectacle.[32] The cardinal legate, Caprara, and the Archbishop of Paris, Monsignor Belloy, ninety-five years old, along with twenty-four other bishops led the couple into the cathedral where they took their place on their respective thrones just in front of the altar.[33] A mass was then said during which the bishops took an oath to obey the government, but also to reveal anything that might be organized against the state in their dioceses (they thereby became informants). Caprara had optimistically announced to Consalvi, the papal secretary of state, that Napoleon would take Holy Communion, but he did not. It had been a sticking point in the weeks leading up to the ceremony, but Caprara insisted that the Holy See bend to Napoleon's will on this count too.[34]

It was a long ceremony, three hours and more. Some had been there since six o'clock, so guests had to go in and out of the cathedral, to relieve themselves, to buy food and drink. Guests brought back with them bread, brioches, sausages and chocolate and munched away; no one was the slightest bit offended.[35] Others chatted, and could not have been more bored. The sermon, given by Monsignor Boisgelin, who had spoken at the coronation of Louis XVI, was a long homily. There was so much talking and laughing going on that he was drowned out.

Napoleon and Josephine sat facing the high altar. All the symbols of the Carolingian Empire on the altar were blessed individually by the pope, including a set of spurs, what was supposed to be Charlemagne's sword, the sceptre of

Charles V adorned with a statuette of Charlemagne, and a replica of Charlemagne's crown made especially for the occasion. According to contemporary accounts, Napoleon was calm but very pale and visibly moved.[36] Did he realize the enormity of what he was about to do? Surely he did, and yet he managed a yawn once or twice, possibly deliberately in order to show the republicans present that he did not really care for the ceremony but was obliged for reasons of state to go along with it.

The act of anointment was designed specifically for the ceremony; it was Napoleon who gave the order to proceed, so that he could speak of an act of 'self-unction'. It is interesting to note that Napoleon did not, as was the tradition in coronation ceremonies, expose parts of his upper body while the anointing was being carried out. Instead, the pope anointed only his head and hands after he had stripped down to a satin tunic.[37] It was only after the objects had been blessed that Napoleon received the ring, the sword, the coat of golden bees, the hand of justice and the sceptre. He then climbed the steps of the altar. The gesture that followed has since become symbolic of Napoleonic power. As the pope appeared to crown him, Napoleon took the laurel from the pope's hands and (re)placed it on his own head. There was no gasp from the assembled dignitaries à la Hollywood's *Désirée*. This part of the proceedings had been discussed and planned beforehand, in fact suggested by Cambacérès.[38] According to one witness, this was the moment everyone had been waiting for. A profound silence reigned over the cathedral. After the crown had been placed on Napoleon's head, everyone in the cathedral stood up spontaneously, the men waving their feathered hats.[39]

This was not the first time a sovereign had crowned himself.[40] Napoleon's excuse was that he did not want any arguments among the court elite about who would presume to hand him the crown in the name of the people.[41] As we have seen, he had entered the cathedral with the crown of laurels already on his head, and carrying the sceptre, which he then placed on the altar before both were blessed by the pope. This gesture turned the ceremony on its head. If Napoleon was already symbolically wearing a crown and if he intended placing Charlemagne's crown on his head in the course of the ceremony, then what was the point of having the pope come all that way?[42] Of course the self-crowning was a matter of Napoleon asserting his political independence, underlining how much he owed his elevation not to the pope but to himself and himself alone. In the age-old conflict between the spiritual and the temporal, Napoleon was vigorously asserting the supremacy of the temporal. This sent not only a political but also a personal message.

Then it was Josephine's turn. As she advanced, her train, which weighed around forty kilograms, was grudgingly carried by the five Bonaparte princesses, a duty they performed so badly that at one point Josephine was unable to move forward.[43] She knelt at Napoleon's feet – a gesture that signified her subordinance to him – and appeared, at least to some in the audience, to be praying to Napoleon rather than to God; tears ran down her cheeks on to her joined hands.[44] Napoleon then took the imperial diadem and placed it, as planned, on his wife's head, although he had trouble making it stay there. There was nothing terribly unusual about a sovereign crowning his wife: the kings of Spain traditionally did so; Frederick I of Prussia had crowned his wife in 1701; and the tsars of Russia, after placing the crown on their own head, took it off and touched their empresses' forehead with it.[45]

In France, however, the coronation of a queen was a rare event – Josephine was the only queen to be crowned and anointed other than Marie de Médicis in 1610 – and this was the first time that an empress had been anointed and crowned, and the first time in French history that a queen had been crowned at the same time as her male counterpart. It raises the question why, if there was no historical precedent for both being crowned at the same time, Napoleon felt it necessary to make the gesture. One Napoleonic scholar has called it a 'caprice'.[46] Napoleon, however, insisted because Josephine thereby came to embody the aspirations of the nation.[47]

Then came the second phase of the ceremony. When the mass was over, Napoleon ascended the 'grand throne' erected on a high platform at the west end of the cathedral, with the crown still on his head. There, with one hand on the Bible, he swore an oath to 'maintain the integrity of the territory of the Republic: to respect and to cause to be respected the laws of the Concordat and of freedom of worship, of political and civil liberty, and the sale of nationalized lands; to raise no taxes except by virtue of the law; to maintain the institution of the Legion of Honour; to govern only in view of the interests, the wellbeing and the glory of the French people'.[48] This was not simply a sop to republicans; it was a social pact, a contract between the French people and their sovereign. If Napoleon broke that contract, then the people would have the right to depose him.[49] It is also the political culmination of the Revolution. Power was conferred on Napoleon not by God but through a secular contract with the French people. Napoleon thus became the first among equals (*primus inter pares*).

The imperial party then returned to the Tuileries by a circuitous route so that the people of Paris could catch a glimpse of their new Emperor. That evening, the imperial couple dined alone, with a skeleton staff. In order to respect the tradition that the symbol of royal power had to be maintained for the whole day, Josephine was required to keep the crown on.[50]

The coronation ceremony was an important step on the path to legitimizing the Empire. On 27 December, at the opening of the Legislative Corps, the minister of the interior, Jean-Baptiste de Nompère de Champagny, explained the legitimacy of the new Empire: it had been called into existence by a *senatus consultum* and a plebiscite. It was from that moment that Napoleon received the title

'Emperor of the French'. No other act was necessary to consecrate his authority. The pomp surrounding the ceremony was subsidiary. What mattered most was the 'immutable oath that ensures the integrity of the Empire, the stability of property, the perpetuity of institutions, respect for the law and the happiness of the nation'.[51] Champagny's speech demonstrates the complexity of the question surrounding Napoleon's legitimacy. Was he emperor simply because he was a victorious general? Did he represent the people or the nation? Was his a monarchy by divine right? Napoleon's rule was based on a number of inherent contradictions, as can be seen in his official title – 'Emperor of the Republic' – as well as in the official coinage that would now circulate throughout the Empire. On the one side were the words 'Napoleon Empereur', and on the other was 'République française'. The word 'Republic' would not disappear until September 1807, even if the coins would remain in circulation for some time.

And yet, in spite of the acceptance of the notion of popular sovereignty, the coronation ceremony harked back to *ancien régime* traditions in which the Church imbued the new sovereign with divine power. Napoleon, although it was never explicitly stated, was using the traditions of the French monarchy to acquire the sacred power that was the foundation of his kingship. The invitations to the coronation pointed out that 'divine providence' had called Napoleon to the throne, a sentiment that can also be found in the media of the day, although in somewhat subtler terms. In short, the idea of divine right is curiously mixed with the notion that Napoleon had been called upon by the French people to adopt the title 'emperor'. The traditional notion of divine right and the revolutionary notion of the sovereignty of the people were thus in precarious balance, and it is perhaps why Napoleon received the appellation of 'Citizen Emperor' at the beginning of his reign.[52]

## Representing the Empire

Jacques-Louis David was a witness to the coronation, although he got to the box originally reserved for him only after a punch-up with the grand master of ceremonies, Louis Philippe, Comte de Ségur.[53] Ségur did not have much respect for David the regicide – as a member of the Convention the artist had voted for the death of the king in 1792 – but he was probably also under a great deal of strain, responsible as he was for the smooth running of the ceremony. David was present because he had been given a commission for four official paintings to celebrate the new dynasty.[54] Only two were ever completed: *Sacre de l'empereur Napoléon et couronnement de l'impératrice Joséphine* (The consecration of Napoleon and the coronation of Josephine), a commentary on the power of Napoleon, and the *Serment de l'armée fait à l'empereur après la Distribution des Aigles au Champ de Mars* (The Distribution of the Eagles). The *Arrivée de Napoléon Ier à l'Hôtel de Ville* (The arrival at the Hôtel de

Ville) never got beyond the drawing stage, while the misleadingly entitled *L'intronisation* (The enthronement), which was meant to portray Napoleon swearing an oath to uphold the Constitution before the representatives of the Senate, the Legislative Corps and the Tribunate, did not even get that far. The commission was intended to represent the four ceremonies that took place over a four-day period and that were meant to celebrate the four components upon which the regime was founded – the sacred, the civic, the municipal and the military.[55]

David initially wanted to paint Napoleon crowning himself. We know he changed his mind before May 1807, supposedly because, after making a number of sketches, he could not find a convincing enough pose.[56] It is more likely that he was persuaded by fellow artists, including a former pupil,

The Art Archive/Musée de Château de Versailles/Collection Dagli Orti

Detail of David's painting, *Sacre de l'empereur Napoléon et couronnement de l'impératrice Joséphine* (The consecration of Napoleon and the coronation of Josephine), 1807. The size of the painting was monumental, even by the standards of the day. At the bottom of the painting were the words *Napoleonis, Francorum Imperatoris, primarus pictor* (Napoleon, Emperor of France, by the first painter), taken off during the Restoration. The painting, in other words, was meant to be more than a historical document. The spectator understood that it was full of political meaning.

François Gérard, to abandon what would have looked like arrogant posturing, and instead settled on Napoleon crowning Josephine.[57] However, the claim that Josephine connived with David to alter the subject matter of the painting is hardly credible, especially since we know just how controlling Napoleon could be. It is more likely that he knew of everything beforehand.[58]

The actual moment captured is that of Napoleon paying tribute to his wife, a banal husband in, as one art critic has put it, a bourgeois comedy of devotion.[59] At the same time, Napoleon was publicly recognizing Josephine; through this 'ritual of legitimation' she was now placed at the summit of the state, a gesture that paradoxically underlined her political insignificance, since she was completely subordinated to Napoleon and excluded from the political decision-making process.[60] Pius VII, on the other hand, at Napoleon's insistence, was given a passive role, doing little more than bless the couple.[61]

The choice of this particular moment in the ceremony may have been inspired by other works of art, such as the *Couronnement de Marie de Médicis* by Rubens, which was at the Luxembourg Palace (now at the Louvre), or Gabriel-François Doyen's *Louis XVI reçoit l'hommage des chevaliers de l'ordre du Saint-Esprit à Reims* (Louis XVI receiving the homage of the Knights of the Order of St Esprit at Rheims), or again Leonard Gautier's *Henry IV*, or even the illuminated medieval manuscripts of the *History of St Louis*.[62] Marie de Médicis was Henry IV's second wife, so it is interesting to note that not only was David emulating a Bourbon ceremony, he was also indirectly referring to the only Bourbon king with whom Napoleon allowed a comparison to be drawn.

Be that as it may, it is Josephine and not Napoleon who is the centre of this work of art, and hence the subject of the coronation. Josephine is seen kneeling before her imperial master, the husband, head bowed, submissive, waiting to receive the crown, while everyone else looks on passively. The moment was designed to promote the myth of the unified family. The message of the painting was further reinforced by the presence of Madame Mère, who was never reconciled to the fact that Napoleon had married Josephine, and who did not take part in the ceremony (she was in Rome at the time). In the painting, she is forced to bear witness to their union, included in the painting at her son's insistence in order to reinforce the idea of imperial rule as dynastic. Napoleon's sisters, who had sulked at having to carry Josephine's train, are standing behind her, serene and demure. David portrayed Josephine in flattering terms as young – one of his daughters posed for the portrait – in order to demonstrate she was still of childbearing age, though she was forty-one.[63]

The painting was finally finished in November 1807, but it was not until 4 January 1808 that Napoleon (he had been away in Italy), accompanied by a large entourage, paid David a visit in his studio in the abandoned Cluny church on the Boulevard Saint-Germain. He walked up and down the length of the

painting for half an hour, which was a very long time for Napoleon, admiring
the result and no doubt trying to identify certain characters. Given that there
were some 150 people portrayed in the painting it is not surprising he took so
long before pronouncing, 'It is very beautiful! What truth! It is not a painting;
one walks into this picture.'[64] The act of obliging the artist as well as the
courtiers to wait before declaring in favour of the painting smacks of a theatrical gesture. He then, somewhat presumptuously, congratulated David on
guessing his 'thoughts' by portraying him as a French 'chevalier' or knight,
probably a reference to the *chevaleresque*, which had been for some years an
important term in the new 'national' history that Napoleon wanted to identify
with.[65] The compliments soon gave way to a few suggestions for changes to be
made. The pope was to be shown in a more active role, so that he appeared to
give the proceedings his blessing, and the cardinal legate was to carry the
Empress's ring. One can imagine David biting his tongue and having to come
up with a tactful answer, however much it must have galled. What did Napoleon really know about art? Even then, David depicted a pontiff whose blessing
hand was limp and lacking energy.[66]

The following month, after three years of work, the painting was ready to
be exhibited in the Louvre (although David took it with him to Brussels in
1816 and continued to work on it there), where it can be viewed today and
where some visitors invariably spend time trying to identify the participants
with the help of a Lucite attached to the painting's frame, just as the public did
in 1808 using a line engraving that was for sale. The painting was, according to
one description, a book in which history could be read.[67] The most important
characters were pointed out in a schematic diagram on the lower part of the
frame of the painting when it was first made public in 1808. In this sense the
painting is a work of journalism, a Who's Who of the imperial court.

On the whole, the painting was well received; some even felt compelled to
cry out, 'Vive l'Empereur!'[68] According to the newspaper accounts, crowds
were always found gathering before the painting.[69] It was as close as the people
could get to the actual ceremony itself, especially since it gave some the illusion
that they were somehow there.[70] The police reports, which Napoleon read
daily, provide a reasonably accurate account of what people were saying
about the painting, and hence about the regime. Since the subject of the painting was Josephine, and even though she appears a great deal younger than she
actually was, it appears to have exacerbated rumours about divorce, and about
the permanence of the new dynasty.[71] If Napoleon did not have any children,
it was said the new dynasty would not outlive him. There were few criticisms
directed at the painting itself, although they existed. As one contemporary
critic observed, tongue in cheek, it was not the type of painting to lend
itself to a critique.[72] The main criticism seems to have been aimed at the
gallery of portraits that dominates the background and some of the

foreground. They were only sketched, it was said, and not adequately finished. Moreover, they were looking into space or at nothing at all.[73]

But the painting was displayed for only one month; it was taken down in March 1808 so that a copy could be made for the Gobelins factory, a project that like many other imperial commissions never materialized. It is not a question, therefore, of how much of an impact this painting would have made on the thousands who queued to see it during the Salon of 1808; the impact would have been relatively limited – to the people of Paris and its environs. The vast majority of the French, if they were to see any representations of the coronation at all, were more likely to see woodcut prints or engravings based on David's work. One of the most popular was a woodcut engraving entitled *Représentation du sacre [et] du couronnement* in which the principal events that took place during the ceremony – the papal anointment, the self-coronation and the crowning of Josephine – are all portrayed.

Well before the completion of David's painting a number of portraits of Napoleon in coronation robes were commissioned. François Gérard's *Napoléon Ier en costume du sacre* was ordered in 1805 (and later copied in tapestries by the Gobelins). The official, unashamedly regal portrait pleased Napoleon so much that it was reproduced and given to relations, allies, courtiers and every French mission abroad, which is why there are so many

*Représentation du sacre [et] du couronnement de Napoleon I, Empereur des Français* (Representation of the consecration [and] coronation of Napoleon I, Emperor of the French), no date, but probably 1804. A popular woodcut print of the main stages of the coronation. The few engravings that represent Napoleon kneeling before the pope were destined for a Catholic audience, and were meant to underscore Napoleon as first son of the Church.

© The Art Archive/Musée Carnavalet Paris/Gianni Dagli Orti

Joseph Siffred Duplessis, *Portrait officiel du roi Louis XVI, roi de France (1754–1793), en grand manteau royal* (Official portrait of Louis XVI, King of France, in grand royal mantle), 1777.

copies of the painting in existence today. In many respects, it has its roots in the *ancien régime* portraits of the French kings, and is comparable to Joseph Siffred Duplessis' *Louis XVI en grand manteau royal*.

However stiff Duplessis' painting looks, it was in fact in keeping with the convention of informality that had first been instituted by the portrait of Louis XIV in his coronation robes by Hyacinthe Rigaud. In that painting, the crown was placed on a cushion, instead of on the king's head.[74] In the portraits of all three monarchs – Louis XIV, Louis XVI and Napoleon – they can be seen leaning on their sceptres in about as relaxed a manner as a sovereign was allowed. In Duplessis' portrait, Louis XVI is not wearing a crown. However, in Gérard's painting, Napoleon is wearing his crown, or at least a laurel wreath. He is also carrying a sceptre that is as big as a spear.[75] A degree of formality is thus introduced that not even the Bourbon monarchs either before or after Napoleon used. This is an affirmation of Napoleon's monarchical status.

Very different was Jean-Auguste Dominique Ingres' painting of *Napoléon Ier sur le trône impérial*, a symbol of Napoleon's imperial power.[76] The stiffly formalistic neo-classical style belies a more radical symbolism. First, Napoleon

Palace of Versailles/Peter Willi/SuperStock

Baron François Gérard, *Napoléon Ier en costume du sacre* (Napoleon I in his imperial robes), 1806. Napoleon is wearing the coronation garments: the embroidered white silk tunic; the white gloves, also embroidered; and the mantle of purple velvet lined with ermine. On his head is a golden laurel wreath. In his right hand, which is wearing the emerald ring, he is carrying the sceptre. On the cushion on the stool to his right is the hand of justice and the globe. These last two were destroyed during the Restoration.

is seated, something that was rare in portraits of monarchs. He stares at the onlooker, holding in his right hand the sceptre of the Emperor Charles V, while in his left he holds the hand of justice. The face is the only exposed part of his body (the feet and hands are covered), and even then it is very stylized. What was meant to be the sword of Charlemagne, but which in fact was a contemporary fantasy, hangs by his left leg. There is even the suggestion of a halo identifying Napoleon with God.[77] The Emperor is thereby transformed into a 'terrifying deity', in the same vein as the painting of Zeus carried out by Phidias.[78] The face is like a cameo of the first Emperor of Rome, Augustus, but it was meant to be likened to Jupiter. Indeed, Ingres proposed this analogy since Napoleon's posture is similar to Ingres' own painting *Jupiter et Thétis*. The end result, however, was more imperial than even the imperial regime could stomach.[79]

The Art Archive/DeA Picture Library

Jean-Auguste-Dominique Ingres, *Napoléon Ier sur le trône impérial ou Sa Majesté l'Empereur des Français sur son trône* (Napoleon I on the imperial throne), 1806.

The painting was purchased by the Legislative Corps, despite an unfavourable secret report to the minister of the interior by Jean-François-Léonor Mérimée, an adjunct secretary at the Ecole des Beaux-Arts, who visited Ingres' studio at the end of August, a couple of weeks before the opening of the 1806 Salon.[80] Mérimée's impressions of the painting – he described it as 'Gothic' and 'barbarous' – corresponded completely with the almost universal adverse public reaction that was to follow.[81] Even a fellow artist, François Gérard, invited to Ingres' studio, was supposedly shocked by what he saw.[82] The portrait had a negative effect on just about everyone who saw it (including Ingres' teacher David, who found the painting incomprehensible),[83] both art critics and the crowds that streamed past to view it during the Salon. A play on words with the artist's name dubbed the painting *mal-Ingres* (sickly), no doubt repeated from the types of quips that could be found in the pamphlets of the time: *Vous avez fait votre empereur mal, Ingres* (You have made your Emperor sickly, Ingres), or again, *Vous avez fait mal Ingres, le portrait de Sa Majesté* (Ingres, you have badly made the portrait of His Majesty).[84]

One critic suggested that Ingres had single-handedly retrogressed art four centuries since it was nothing less than gothic, a term that had not often been used till then.[85] The criticisms were aesthetic, but also in part political.[86] A former Jacobin by the name of Chaussard who had, like many other Jacobins, accepted Napoleon largely because he had portrayed himself as a simple man of the people, objected to Ingres' work precisely because it was too lavish, too elaborate and too retrograde. It somehow did not sit well with the image of the young, victorious and largely republican military hero that Bonaparte had cultivated in the past. Royalist critics, on the other hand, were not impressed by this blatant attempt to legitimize the Empire through a return to monarchical symbols.[87] Criticism came not only from those hostile to the regime but from those, on the contrary, who supported it, outraged that Ingres seemed to herald a return to Bourbon traditions. The painting somehow took away the heroic from Napoleon's character.[88] Ingres was hurt by the reaction. He had had every reason to believe that his painting would be a success.

## The Distribution of the Eagles

Three days after the coronation, the Distribution of the Eagles took place on the Champ de Mars in front of the Ecole Militaire where Napoleon graduated in 1785. At eleven o'clock in the morning, the imperial couple and their respective households, accompanied by detachments of chasseurs, Mamelukes, grenadiers and gendarmes, proceeded to the Ecole Militaire, which had been transformed for the occasion by Percier and Fontaine into a covered gallery which one approached by climbing forty steps. The event was in some respects a tribute to the importance of the army in the new imperial regime.[89] The entire edifice was covered in velvet.

Regimental commanders from both the regular army and the National Guard, in the pouring rain – Fontaine speaks of 'the most disastrous day of the whole winter'[90] – with few or no spectators, took an oath of loyalty to the Emperor to defend their standards to the death. Josephine and most of the court ladies retired to warmer spots. Only Caroline remained with her brother and followed the ceremony to the end. 'Soldiers,' Napoleon shouted, 'here are your standards, these eagles will always be your rallying point; they will go everywhere the Emperor deems it necessary for the defence of his throne and his people. Do you swear to sacrifice your lives in their defence and to maintain them constantly on the road to victory? Do you swear it?' Those present are supposed to have shouted out as one voice, 'We swear it.' Several salvoes of artillery were then fired, and the troops marched past.

This was the first time that troops had been obliged to swear an oath to defend their eagles, which were in deliberate imitation of the standards employed by Roman legions, and which had replaced the flags and standards

Jean-Baptiste Isabey, from *Le livre du sacre*. The *Livre du sacre* was a sort of official record book of designs and prints of highlights of both the coronation and the ceremonies that followed, as well as the uniforms worn. Although begun in 1804, it was not completed and published until 1815, during the Hundred Days.[91] Here we see the façade of the Ecole Militaire, looking on to the Champ de Mars, redecorated for the occasion.

used during the revolutionary wars.[92] The eagles, made of wood and gold and mounted on poles, became associated with the Empire. Just as importantly, the troops were also given the tricolour, thus marrying two symbols, one representing the Empire, the other the Republic. Though the ceremony did not make that much of an impression on those gathered, we know how highly prized the eagles became in the regiments. Any number of accounts of the extremes to which soldiers went to protect them in the course of battle are testimony to the value placed on them by the men assigned to protect them.[93] A great deal of splendour was on display in these ceremonies to encourage the bonding of the officers of the army to its commander-in-chief. In later years, the ceremony for newly promoted officers would take place in the Salle du Trône at the Tuileries (when Napoleon was in Paris), while Hugues-Bernard Maret, director of Napoleon's cabinet, read out the oath.[94] Napoleon had done this kind of thing before, but on a smaller scale, almost as dress rehearsals for what took place on the Champ de Mars. During the festivals of 14 July, in 1797, 1801 and again in 1802, for example, he had distributed flags to different units and had them swear an oath: 'You will always need to rally to this flag;

swear that it will never fall into the hands of the enemies of the republic, and that you will all perish, if necessary, to defend it.'[95] On this occasion, the ceremony was over in a very short time, and the whole thing ended in utter confusion. Soldiers milled about in the middle of the plain, which had turned to mud, their uniforms soaked through, their hats deformed by the rain, all of them freezing cold and none of them sure what to do next.[96] The only incident of any note was the appearance of a young man who approached the steps to the throne shouting, 'No Emperor! Liberty or death!' He was immediately arrested. A medical student by the name of Faure, he was incarcerated in Charenton, a hospital for the insane, where he was to stay until he was 'cured'.

David's painting of the *Distribution des Aigles*, a kind of Napoleonic version of his *Serment des Horaces* (Oath of the Horatii), was not completed until

Jacques-Louis David, *Serment de l'armée fait à l'Empereur après la distribution des Aigles au Champ de Mars* (Oath of the army made to the Emperor after the Distribution of the Eagles on the Champ de Mars), 1810. Napoleonic theatre at its best, even though it reaches absurd proportions. Note the general in the front of the group, inspired by Giovanni da Bologna's figure of *Mercury*, standing on tiptoe on one leg. The viewer is floating in mid-air so to speak, at the top of the extraordinary, temporary flight of stairs constructed for the occasion by Percier and Fontaine, all the better to see the action and read the banners.[97]

1810. The artist had to overcome a number of difficulties, including the fact that Josephine was no longer Napoleon's wife, so she, along with her ladies-in-waiting, had to be painted out of the original picture.[98] We are used to that kind of thing happening in modern dictatorships, but this is the first time that history had been deliberately altered by a modern European head of state. One can see where Josephine should have been; the space is emphasized by Eugène de Beauharnais' out-thrust leg. One art historian has suggested a subversive element to the painting: Napoleon is lost in the crowd of courtiers, confronting an unruly army over which he has no control.[99] It is a sign that, by the time the painting was completed, people had tired of the man and his regime, perhaps no better illustrated than by a detail, another subversive element, in the painting that is generally overlooked.[100] In the bottom right-hand corner a soldier, with his back to the onlooker, is walking away with a folded flag marked 'La République'.

The theme of patriotic sacrifice that was at the core of this ceremony was hardly new. The difference now was that those who were prepared to lay down their lives did so for the sake of one man rather than for an ideal. Napoleon was confounding, perhaps deliberately, the type of patriotic self-sacrifice people had become accustomed to during the Revolution with sacrifice to his person, as he now came to represent the nation, the *patrie*, dressed in imperial gold and velvet. It was a perception that troops would sometimes have and even admit to – that is, 'we confused the love we had for the sovereign with that which we had for the *patrie*'.[101]

In Napoleon's own mind, the Empire, the nation and his person eventually became one. 'The throne of France was vacant,' he is supposed to have told the Austrian ambassador to Paris, Klemens von Metternich, 'the king overthrown . . . The old throne of France is buried under its rubble; I had to found a new one . . . I am like the Empire; there is therefore a perfect homogeneity between myself and the Empire.'[102] During the *ancien régime*, the king's body was considered sacred, containing within it a 'corporeal mystique'. The execution of the king in 1792 had symbolically brought that mystique to an end, and in effect transferred it to another abstract concept – the nation. The nation then had replaced the idea of the sovereign.[103] Part of the desacralization, the desecration, of the monarchy was the accompanying vandalism that destroyed its images and symbols – anything from the fleur de lys to statues of past kings had to disappear. A political culture emerged that defined the new state and its members – now called citizens, not subjects – and situated every individual's place in the nation. The king, the monarchy and its heroes were no longer celebrated but rather the Republic, the nation and its heroes were. In some respects, then, the ceremonies held to celebrate the foundation of the Empire were about writing a new national narrative.

Eventually it would appear that the idea of the nation was displaced on to the person of the Emperor and that, as the kings of France before him represented paternal authority, so now Napoleon represented a father figure. Just as the kings of France had embodied the nation, so did the Emperor. From May 1804, the revolutionary term 'citizen' was replaced by the terms 'monsieur' and 'subject', without the outcry that accompanied the use of the latter word in 1801 (see p. 87).[104] Service to Napoleon was embodied in the notion of service to the state. This should be seen as the end result of a long political struggle to personify a particular vision of the national community, which had raged since 1789. One could easily apply the adage of the seventeenth-century theologian Jacques-Bénigne Bossuet, 'The whole state is in the person of the prince.'[105] It also meant that increasingly the state revolved around the will of one man so that he could appoint and dismiss at will, as well as ignore the law. Here Napoleon's character merged with the political rhetoric that he had adopted at the beginning of his reign to justify the coup and his hold on power, namely, that he was above factions, although gradually he interpreted this to mean that he was above the law.

The popular visual representations of Napoleon as emperor – paintings, engravings, cheap woodprints, busts and medallions[106] – reinforce the message of Napoleon as father of the nation. Anointed by the Church, he was not only to be venerated, he was to set an example by his clemency and goodwill towards the less fortunate. He did so on the occasion of the coronation, as he had done at the very beginning of the Consulate, by freeing 'a great number of prisoners' from the Temple and the Abbey Saint-Germain.[107] Louis XVI had done the same thing shortly before his coronation at Rheims in 1775.

## The People's Empire

For two weeks after the coronation, Paris and the Empire celebrated the foundation of the new dynasty in a series of festivities, receptions, banquets, balls, fireworks and solemn audiences either at the Tuileries or at the Hôtel de Ville. During that time, no dignitary was allowed to appear at court dressed in anything but the costume worn on the day of the coronation. It was customary for the municipality of Paris to offer a sumptuous reception to new sovereigns. This had been done in 1514 on the occasion of the marriage of Mary of England to Louis XII, in 1687 for the marriage of Louis XIV, in 1739 and 1745 when Louis XV's children were married, and of course for the marriage of Louis XVI and Marie-Antoinette.[108]

Some of the events were quite unexpected; for example, a balloon constructed by the famous aeronaut André-Jacques Garnerin was to lift into the air a crown twenty times larger than life. The crown, made of coloured glass in imitation of the actual crown, actually succeeded in taking off . . . and floating away. It landed almost two days later in Lake Bracciano near Rome. Napoleon wrote to the pope the following extraordinary missive: 'The balloon which has so providentially arrived in Rome . . . should, it seems to me, be devotedly conserved in memory of this extraordinary event [the coronation]. I wish that Your Holiness should have it put in a particular place where foreigners can see it in passing with an inscription that states that, in so many hours, it arrived in Rome.'[109]

More spectacular were the fireworks. The principal display took place on the banks of the River Seine between the Tuileries and the Hôtel de Ville, but it was the signal for twelve other displays to be set off in Paris. Things did not quite work out the way they were supposed to, however. Instead of lasting fifty-five minutes, the fireworks lasted only fifteen.[110] The centrepiece of the display was Napoleon's crossing of the Saint-Bernard. It was almost a symbol of the trajectory that the Emperor had taken to reach the summit that was the coronation, the symbol of the 'radiance of their victories [those of Napoleon and his men]'.[111] Fireworks were traditionally considered a symbol of transformation, perhaps signifying an end to the wars that had led to the Empire combined with the fires of regeneration.

Dance halls were erected on the Place de la Concorde, the Place de la Bastille, the Place Vendôme and the Place des Vosges, locations emblematic of the city but also sites of the Revolution; Montgolfier balloons were used to transport and drop off eagles throughout the city. For the people, wine literally flowed from the city's fountains.[112] Similar celebrations were held in cities throughout the Empire.[113] Towns were illuminated to show their approval of the proceedings (except in Angoulême where a certain General Malet, whom we shall come across again, refused to celebrate the event. He was relieved of his command). The festivities put the city of Paris in debt for many years to come.[114]

## The Jacobin Emperor

Large crowds do not bonds of loyalty make. Whether Napoleon actually succeeded in the objective of the public festivities is another question. Nor did the role of the pope lend as much prestige as the Emperor had hoped. Anti-clerical republicans among the people of Paris, still quite numerous, were appalled to see the return of the Church in force. Though they had accepted the Concordat as a necessary evil, though they could see the advantages of having the pope in Paris to lend a certain amount of prestige, they were unhappy with the warm reception the faithful had reserved for the holy pontiff. There were consequently numerous pamphlets and protests against the ceremony based on those reasons alone, and quite a number of jokes about Napoleon.[115] Not all of them came from republicans. The English had a field day with the coronation; caricaturists like James Gillray made fun of the imperial procession, in images that were confiscated as soon as they reached French territory.[116] Like all political satires directed at Napoleon, they were designed to contest the political system he had constructed, and to undermine his authority by questioning his legitimacy.

Napoleon was aware that different sections of the French elite were unhappy with the proclamation of the Empire. The ceremony itself was supposed to have taken the various political and religious tendencies into consideration, but it was so complex as to remain unintelligible to the vast majority of onlookers. Republicans disliked the presence of the pope and the return to a ceremony used during the *ancien régime*. The Catholic faithful reproached Napoleon for his treatment of Pius VII, for not having taken Holy Communion and for having crowned himself. Royalists rejected the coronation outright. Throughout France over the coming months, anti-Napoleonic placards were posted on the walls of towns as important as Paris and as far away as the Corrèze, a department in the south of France, where one could read, 'Long Live Louis XVIII! Down with Napoleon and his whole clique!'[117] Napoleon represented everything royalists despised, especially the principle of meritocracy. The participation of the pope at the coronation, and in particular the anointment, was nothing short of a scandalous farce, a second death for Louis XVI, an insult to the memory of those who had died defending the monarchy.[118]

Many of the European monarchies were also circumspect about the coronation: the only princes to attend were from the German vassal states (Baden, Hesse-Darmstadt, Hesse-Homburg, Solms-Lich, Nassau-Weilburg, Isenburg, Löwenstein, Löwenstein-Wertheim). The Austrian ambassador excused himself while the other courts of Europe (apart from England) sent either an ambassador or a minister. One should not read too much into this; it was not customary for great-power sovereigns to travel to their fellow sovereigns' coronation ceremonies. Francis recognized the elevation of Napoleon to the imperial dignity but, as we have seen, he sugarcoated the pill by declaring himself Francis I, Emperor of Austria. Nevertheless, the French Empire was not universally accepted in Vienna and was perceived in some circles as a humiliation: Napoleon had after all crowned himself with the putative crown of Charlemagne, traditionally associated with the Habsburg monarchy, and had essentially taken Austria's role in central Europe without consulting it.

If Napoleon had thought that by becoming a monarch he would ensure that French political institutions were 'a little more in harmony with theirs [that is, with other monarchies]', he was sadly mistaken. For him, it may have been a question of being able to take tea with other European monarchs on an equal footing, but other European sovereigns, monarchs by divine right, would never accept him as an equal. Napoleon himself seems to have doubted the importance of the coronation as a legitimizing ritual; the lack of public enthusiasm for the event as well as the tepid manner in which the elites responded seems to have made an impact on him.[119] The *Moniteur* did not even give an official account of the coronation ceremony; the festivities that followed were reported on much more.[120] Indeed, the imperial regime was reluctant to use it as a setpiece in its political propaganda. The Abbé de Pradt, Napoleon's chaplain, declared that 'in various parts of France where his travels and his functions had enabled him to observe, he had found no favourable trace left by this act'.[121] The anniversary of the coronation was celebrated every year on the first Sunday of December – a perfectly normal thing for a monarch to do – but more often than not public opinion confused the date with the battle of Austerlitz.

# CONQUEST, 1805–1807

# IO

# 'The Rage of Conquest and Ambition'

## King of All Italy

Napoleon seemed to possess an extraordinary ability to antagonize his European neighbours although mostly he did so inadvertently. His assumption of the title 'King of Italy', however, was considered one of the most provocative steps, and gave the impression that he was bent on the domination of the whole Italian peninsula.

Bonaparte had effectively ruled over northern Italy for the previous two years. After drawing up a constitution for the Italian Republic, which gave its president quasi-absolute powers, he summoned a congress – a *consulta* – of 500 Italian notables to Lyons, halfway between Milan and Paris, at the end of 1801.[1] The congress was meant to discuss, but really simply to approve, the Constitution and choose a president (it was the first time the title had been used in monarchical Europe). Its members elected, after a somewhat circuitous route, and not surprisingly, Bonaparte. However, as soon as there was talk of transforming the French Republic into a monarchy, it was inevitable that the Italian Republic would follow suit. The only question was who was going to govern the Italian kingdom. As early as 3 March 1804, among the many letters published in the *Moniteur* urging Bonaparte to adopt the imperial crown, an Italian general by the name of Pino wrote to suggest that he should also become King of Italy.[2] On 7 May, only days before the Empire was proclaimed, Bonaparte had a conversation with the foreign minister of the Italian Republic, Ferdinando Marescalchi, about the future of Italy. The country was, suggested Bonaparte, too weak to be independent and too strong to be annexed.[3] It would be better, he went on, if it were transformed into a monarchy. Marescalchi got the message. He reported back to the vice-president of the Italian Republic, Melzi d'Eril, who immediately called a *consulta*, and voted for the transformation of the Republic into a hereditary monarchy under Napoleon and his descendants (28 May). In that way, it appeared as though the request came from the Italian Republic and not from Napoleon. There is no room here to go into the complex negotiations that took place between Napoleon and Melzi but, as ever determined to have his way, the Emperor rejected any attempt to negotiate conditions, and even threatened to annex Italy outright (a complete contradiction of his earlier statement).

This was probably an empty threat. The annexation of the Italian Republic would have aroused Austria to action, and Napoleon knew it. His priority at this time was the invasion of England. In an attempt to placate Austria, Talleyrand suggested he offer the crown to his brother, Joseph. Joseph at first agreed and the affair seemed to have been concluded by 31 December 1804. There is no reason to doubt Napoleon's sincerity in offering the throne to his brother, despite what some historians have said.[4] In doing so, he appeared less threatening to Austria. He even sent a letter to Francis II announcing that his brother would be adopting the Italian mantle.[5] However, when Joseph was informed that he would have to renounce his rights to the French throne, he baulked. Several meetings between the two brothers and their representatives were unable to overcome this stand-off.[6] It is possible that Joseph declined not so much out of a desire to remain next in line as over the impossibility of reigning in Italy given the likelihood of Napoleon's regular interference. Napoleon then asked his brother Louis (again) whether he could adopt his newborn son – Napoleon Louis Bonaparte – with the intention of making him King of Italy. Louis, however, refused and was so aggressively against the plan that Napoleon physically threw him out of his office.[7] The Emperor even wrote to Lucien asking him to renounce Mme Jouberthon in favour of a throne.[8] He received no reply. Napoleon then turned to his adopted son, Eugène de Beauharnais, and named him viceroy of Italy, but this only happened on 7 June. As far as one can tell, Eugène was simply informed about this, not consulted. The appointment left him cold; he was only twenty-three, more interested in having a good time, but in Paris, not Milan, which he did not much like. Suddenly jerked out of a life of pleasure and thrown into the political deep end where he was expected to govern in Napoleon's name, he had to deal with finances, the administration, justice, religion, the Civil Code and everything involved with governing a country as diverse and heterogeneous as the Kingdom of Italy.[9] Eugène, as it turned out, proved a very competent ruler, but his step-father was very hands-on, controlling the smallest details even while he was away on campaign, virtually running the kingdom by proxy.[10]

The behaviour of Joseph and Louis under these circumstances, as we saw in the lead-up to the proclamation of the Empire, was not only impolitic but downright disastrous for French foreign policy. Neither of them was capable of thinking beyond his own personal interests. Napoleon's adoption of the title of 'King of Italy', not particularly welcomed by Italian public opinion,[11] considerably worsened relations between France and other European powers, particularly Russia and Austria, even though Napoleon attempted to placate Francis with a letter explaining that his intention was to 'take from myself the crown of Italy and to separate it from the crown of France'.[12] Considering that almost in the same breath Napoleon annexed Genoa and Liguria in June 1805 – thus creating three new departments that were added to the six already carved out of the former Kingdom of Piedmont – and that at the same time he created the Principality of Lucca and Piombino, which he then gave to his sister Elisa, his actions were hardly likely to appease Austria.[13]

*   *   *

Napoleon left Paris at the end of March 1805 and travelled to Milan across the Mont Cénis pass. He stopped at Marengo along the way to commemorate the battle and to inaugurate a monument to the dead. He arrived in Milan on 8 May for a ceremony that was to see him crowned King of Italy two weeks later. He was, according to some contemporary accounts, greeted with an enthusiasm that bordered on the hysterical.[14] Women and children cried with joy, and some even threw themselves on their stomachs on the street over which his carriage was to pass, an act which was interpreted by the French as a desire to be crushed by its wheels after having had the pleasure of seeing the Emperor.

Just as Charlemagne was crowned King of Lombardy in 774, Napoleon was crowned King of Italy in the Duomo of Milan on 26 May 1805. It followed the same ceremony as in Notre Dame but was officiated instead by Cardinal Caprara, who though still papal legate to France had become Archbishop of Milan. The pope refused to attend, having since understood that Napoleon was using the Church for his own ends. Italian nobles, unimpressed by the creation of the kingdom, expressed their disapproval by staying away, often pleading poverty as an excuse.[15] Again Napoleon crowned himself, using the Iron Crown of Lombardy (it was made of gold but supposedly contained a thin band of iron from the Cross). On this occasion he proclaimed, 'Iddio me l'ha data, guai a chi la toccherà' (God gave it to me, woe to anyone who touches it), the words traditionally spoken by all those who received the Lombard crown (and which have since become a common saying in Italy). The legend on his insignia read *Rex totius Italiae* (King of all Italy). This, as it turned out, was to have important repercussions, to the extent that one has to wonder whether Napoleon was entirely aware of what he was doing. Northern Italy was one of the regions where Austria and France had conflicting interests. Indeed, the area had been a bone of contention dating back to Francis I in the sixteenth century, and would remain so until the Austrian army's ultimate defeat in Italy by the forces of Napoleon III in 1859.

Austria grudgingly accepted an Italian republic, and would even have accepted an Italian monarchy. It might have accepted Napoleon as King of Italy too. What it could not accept, however, was seeing him claim the Iron Crown of Lombardy.[16] Napoleon's incorporation of northern Italy into the French Empire was a violation of the Treaty of Lunéville, which clearly stated that Italy would remain independent of France.[17] It was plain, therefore, that Napoleon had no regard for treaties and broke them whenever it suited him (yet he always complained when other powers did not uphold their treaty obligations). When Austria remonstrated with a diplomatically worded note pointing out its concerns – namely, that it would accept the transformation of the Italian Republic into a monarchy as long as it remained independent – it was criticized for sticking its nose in Italian affairs.

The foundation of the Empire, the merger of the French and Italian thrones and the increasing influence of the French in Germany all made the court of Vienna exceedingly apprehensive about its own future. Austria had been directly challenged in what were traditionally considered its geopolitical spheres of influence.[18] Not only was Italian independence compromised, but there were rumours of an offensive–defensive alliance between France and Bavaria directed against Austria.[19] As early as January 1805, Vienna began to mobilize troops on the Bavarian border on the pretext of setting up a cordon sanitaire against an outbreak of yellow fever. At the same time, a second army started taking up positions on the frontier with Italy, in the Tyrol. This activity was bound to be noticed in Paris, where Talleyrand made it known to his Austrian counterpart that the situation could hardly be tolerated. Although Napoleon did not believe that Austria wanted to go to war, he did the only thing he knew how – he opposed force with force.[20]

© RMN-Grand Palais (musées de l'Île d'Aix)/Gérard Blot

Andrea Appiani the Elder, *Napoleon I, roi d'Italie* (Napoleon I, King of Italy), 1805.

## The Rebirth of the Coalition

It was Russia, and not Austria or Britain, at the centre of the new coalition against France, the third since the beginning of the revolutionary wars in 1792.[21]

The Tsar of Russia, Alexander I, had come to power in 1801 after the assassination of his father Paul. An idealist who was not always in touch with the harsh reality of Russian or European politics, Alexander spent the first few years of his reign consolidating his hold on power and attempting to reform the Russian state. It is traditionally argued that he turned his attention to foreign affairs only once his domestic policies had faltered and then collapsed, but it now seems clear that he was involved in forming a coalition against France well before those reforms were implemented.[22]

At first, Alexander, like a number of other European statesmen, admired the First Consul for putting an end to the Revolution, but, ironically considering that the Tsar was an absolutist monarch, doubts began to trouble him when Bonaparte declared himself Consul for life in 1802.[23] The Tsar's adviser Adam Czartoryski believed that 'reason' would eventually prevail and that Europe or Russia would be able to persuade Bonaparte to adopt more moderate and just principles.[24] Czartoryski may very well have been one of the few in Europe to believe that Bonaparte would eventually moderate his ambition. Other Russian politicians, like Count Alexander Vorontsov, chancellor between 1802 and 1804, wrote of the need to stop 'the perpetual encroachments of the French government whose views tend towards nothing less than destroying all other governments or of making them into allies and vassals'.[25] Russia was, however, in much the same manner as Prussia and to a lesser extent Austria, prepared to accept Bonaparte, despite any reservations it may have had, and deal with France as practically as possible. That is why Alexander worked behind the scenes, for a while, to find some sort of solution between France and the other European powers for a general peace settlement.[26] He was already thinking of a kind of European federation that would help construct a new European order. Secret negotiations took place between Russia and Britain that would enable Alexander to make a peace offer to Bonaparte that included the British giving up Malta. This would place the allies on the moral high ground. Britain, however, had no intention of giving up Malta and Alexander's plans fell through. He was left with a poor opinion of Britain's motives for continuing the war against France.[27] But his opinion of Napoleon also deteriorated to the point where the Tsar began to consider him 'one of the most famous tyrants that history has produced'.[28] In June 1804, a few months after the execution of the Duc d'Enghien, Alexander sent an ultimatum to Napoleon demanding that he withdraw from northern Germany and Naples. Napoleon naturally rejected the ultimatum,[29] which led to Alexander breaking off relations with France in September. As with much foreign policy during the period, it was a question of Napoleon acting and the other powers reacting.

Alexander was nevertheless hesitant about going to war. 'The idea of a war weighs on him and torments him,' wrote Czartoryski.[30] The court of Petersburg around this time was divided into (at least) two factions: one, backed by the British and including a number of prominent men who may even have been on their payroll,[31] was pushing hard for war; and a non-interventionist group wanted nothing to do with the West. By the end of 1803, the pro-war faction appears to have prevailed. Alexander sent diplomats to Vienna, Berlin and London to sound them out about the possibility of a renewed coalition. London eventually agreed to subsidize Russia to the tune of £1.2 million or the equivalent of fielding an army of about 100,000 men. Other alliance treaties were signed with Austria (November 1804), Sweden (January 1805), Naples (September 1805), the Ottoman Empire (September 1805) and Prussia (November 1805), although the latter was purely defensive.[32] Russia was, therefore, the principal agent in a new European concert against France.

Napoleon too was looking for support on the Continent, and he was helped by the fact that Britain was not exactly popular in many European courts.[33] He had already secured French influence in southern Germany by concluding treaties with Bavaria, Baden and Württemberg (although the latter two only after the war had begun).[34] His objective was to make sure that his rear was safe while he attacked Britain, but he also had thereby a passage through to Austria if the occasion arose. The southern German powers, combined with Holland, Spain and northern Italy, meant that Napoleon proved better at forming an effective coalition than the allies, not because their combined power was stronger but because the southern German states gave him an easy and secure route into the heart of Austria.[35] Or so goes the argument. As we shall see, southern Germany, as it had so many times before, became the battleground over which the war was fought. For the moment, Napoleon's diplomatic efforts were combined with a public relations exercise. As in 1800, he wrote to the various kings of Europe in an apparent attempt to find a peaceful solution to the problem, but, as in 1800, these initiatives cannot be taken too seriously.[36] The journey on the road to Austerlitz had begun.

## The Army of England

The threat of invasion provoked nightmares among the people of England.[37] The French camp at Boulogne could be seen 'quite distinctly' from some parts of the English coast. In France, however, Napoleon used the war with England to unify the nation around his person, possibly to greater effect than the coronation. There was no real enthusiasm for the war despite the long-held hatred of the French for the English; the French people needed convincing both that it was the right thing to do and that an invasion of England was in the realms of the possible.[38] That is why the planned invasion was the object of a propaganda campaign. Several songs for the invasion were ordered, as were several comic plays.[39] A series of medallions representing those who had successfully invaded England – Caesar, Septimius Severus, William the Conqueror, Henry VII – was struck.[40] A statue of William the Conqueror and a square named after him were considered for Saint-Germain near Paris.[41] At the camp at Boulogne, a number of ancient Roman arms were coincidentally uncovered, as well as coins of William the Conqueror, precisely where Bonaparte's tent was pitched.[42] It was an omen of things to come. Just as Charlemagne had been disinterred and used by the regime, so too was William the Conqueror, not to justify the impending invasion of England but to demonstrate that there was a historical precedent and that therefore an invasion was possible. At one stage, Vivant Denon even came up with the hare-brained idea of burying a statue of William the Conqueror in the Seine and then uncovering it as if by chance; the statue was then to be hauled upriver to Paris in a barge, once again as an omen of the impending invasion of England.[43] Fortunately, Bonaparte did not buy into the scheme. On the other hand, the Bayeux tapestry was brought from Calvados to Paris and exhibited at the Louvre at the beginning of 1803, announcing the French victory that was about to take place;[44] hundreds of copies of the exhibition catalogue were distributed to the army. Whether any of this had an impact on public opinion is doubtful. On 23 September 1805, Napoleon appeared before the Senate and gave a speech explaining that he was about to leave the capital and rejoin the army at Boulogne.[45] As he left the Senate, driving through Paris to Saint-Cloud, he noticed that the mood of the crowds had 'cooled, and he was greeted with less alacrity than usual'.[46] Their reaction hurt him, but then crowds rarely, if ever, cheer the outbreak of war.

One determining factor would have allowed Napoleon to invade England: he had to control the Channel for several days while the French flotilla sailed across in convoys of 200 boats.[47] His plan was somehow to convince the British that he was going to cross the Channel without the protection of the French fleet. He succeeded to such an extent that many diplomats of the time, some military figures such as the Archduke Charles and even members of the British government and senior officers in the Royal Navy were persuaded that the whole idea of an invasion was a confidence trick. In the meantime, Napoleon was trying to combine the scattered French navy and manoeuvre them away from Europe, in the hope that the British fleet would give chase. The French could then turn around and unite in the Channel long enough to give them naval superiority.[48]

Given the size of the fleet that was assembled (more than forty ships of the line, twenty frigates, fourteen corvettes and twenty-five brigs, more if the Spanish fleet is taken into account), as well as the thousands of landing craft that were purpose built, and the millions of francs that were spent in preparations, it is clear that Napoleon was serious about an invasion of England. Any suggestion that he was not, that he was putting on a show of force in the hope of obliging London to negotiate, or indeed that the camp at Boulogne was a front to 'facilitate the assembling of troops for a Continental war', can be discounted.[49] Speculation about Napoleon's intentions existed at the time. The Prussian ambassador reported back to Berlin in May 1804 that Bonaparte's 'secret wish' was for war on the Continent.[50] Doubts about Napoleon's real plans were further inflamed by an alleged admission to Metternich in 1810 that he never meant to invade England and that the army gathered at Boulogne was 'always an army against Austria'.[51] This is, however, little more than an indication of Napoleon's inability to admit defeat – in this case, the aborted invasion – and his tendency to rewrite the past to conform to his idealized views of it. At the time, he was so confident that the invasion would be successful that dies were prepared for a commemorative medal to celebrate the victory. On one side is a profile of Napoleon crowned with laurels, and on the other an image of Hercules strangling Antaeus.[52] Beneath is the optimistic inscription 'Struck in London, 1804'. All the evidence suggests, therefore, that Napoleon planned to invade England, but that he also realized there was a possibility of war with the Eastern powers, rumours of which abounded in the summer of 1804.[53]

John Fairburn, *A View of the French raft, as seen afloat at St. Maloes in February 1798*, 13 February 1798. Rumours of an impending invasion inspired English caricaturists to imagine the most outlandish plans to cross the Channel. This print shows a raft, 180 metres long, bristling with 500 cannon, capable of transporting 15,000 troops. Others showed floating fortresses that would transport men and matériel by balloon, and even a cross-Channel tunnel. There was talk of steamboats, submarines, torpedoes and blockading British ports with mines, all aspects of modern naval warfare which, at the beginning of the nineteenth century, were far from practical.[54]

Bonaparte's initial orders were for landing craft to be ready by December 1803, only six months after the formation of the army, but the timeframe was unrealistic and over the coming months the number and type of craft ordered were to change dramatically.[55]

The projected invasion of England, ambitious in its breadth and scope, was certainly much better planned and prepared than the expedition to Egypt.[56] Nevertheless, despite the enormous effort put into its organization, any chance of success depended on luck. In one exercise conducted in July 1805, Marshal Ney's entire corps, including horses and equipment, were embarked on barges at Etaples (twenty-five kilometres south of Boulogne) in forty-nine minutes.[57] However, an exercise held in bad weather on 20 July 1804 at Napoleon's insistence demonstrated just how unsuitable the flat-bottomed boats were for the rough Channel seas. To his credit, Admiral Bruix, in command of the flotilla at Boulogne, refused to obey the order to put to sea; it was clear to all that a storm was brewing. Bruix and Napoleon almost came to blows over the matter, Napoleon threatening to strike the admiral with his riding crop, Bruix placing his hand on the hilt of his sword as those in the Emperor's entourage stood around dumbfounded. Napoleon got his way, as a result of which twelve boats and barges sank with the loss of between 200 and 400 men.[58] At one stage, Napoleon got into a boat and ordered the crew to row him out to help others, but to little effect. In a letter to Josephine the following day, he referred to the incident in romantic terms. 'The soul was between eternity, the ocean and the night.' He went to bed at five in the morning with the impression that he had lived through some sort of 'romantic or epic dream'.[59]

The Royal Navy did not stand idly by and watch the French amass an invasion fleet. They attacked and harassed whenever and wherever they could, in spite of the coastal defences erected to protect the fleet. In 1804, the Royal Navy lost twenty-one ships blockading the French ports.[60] Every now and then they would bombard one of the ports in lightning raids that could sometimes have devastating effects. On other occasions, these attacks were easily beaten off. Many believed as a result of the British efforts that an invasion was impossible, but Napoleon insisted preparations go ahead.

## The Battle of Cadiz

The minister of the navy, Rear-Admiral Denis Decrès, was an experienced sailor who had engaged the British in a number of different theatres, but he was no match for Napoleon, who attempted to control the everyday workings of the navy during this period. Besides, Decrès was far from convinced of the potential success of an invasion. His lack of faith in the ability of his own fleet was a continual drawback.[61] Letter after letter addressed to Napoleon rated as negligible the chances of gaining the necessary naval superiority in the Channel.[62]

There was a momentary setback when Vice-Admiral Latouche-Tréville, in command of the Mediterranean fleet at Toulon and whom many considered to be the best naval officer in France, died suddenly in August 1804, after an illness he had contracted while at Saint-Domingue.[63] As a consequence, plans for the invasion were more or less put on hold; Napoleon even temporarily gave up the idea, at least for the immediate future.[64] However, alternative plans had been developed by the spring of 1805.[65] A replacement was found in the person of Vice-Admiral Pierre-Charles Villeneuve, but he was not Latouche-Tréville. On the contrary, Villeneuve appears to have been traumatized by his experience during the battle of the Nile, which saw Nelson obliterate the French fleet off Aboukir. Villeneuve escaped that battle with his life, but developed as a consequence a morbid dread of Nelson. He was not, therefore, the kind of commander who could lead by daring example.[66] He at first refused the command, but was persuaded against his better judgement to accept. At the end of September 1804, he was briefed on a new strategy in which the invasion of England was only one part of a much larger plan to attack Britain in the rest of the world, including Africa, South America, the Caribbean and Ireland.[67] In the event, the strategy was never put into effect, but it provides us with an insight into Napoleon's mind-set, the extent of his ambition and his determination to strike at England wherever he could. A definitive invasion plan was not decided on until the middle of April 1805. It was the seventh and probably least nonsensical in a line of impracticable plans. Before that, Napoleon had constantly changed his mind about what he wanted and what he expected from his subordinates. Even once the definitive plan had been adopted, he had no realistic conception of the limits and possibilities of naval warfare, and did not take into account the fact that the French vessels were manned by inexperienced sailors.

The plan was reasonable enough. It required Vice-Admiral Honoré-Joseph Ganteaume, the man who had brought Bonaparte back from Egypt and who was now blockaded in Brest, to break out and head for Martinique. At the same time, Villeneuve was to break out of Toulon, meet up with the Spanish fleet at Cadiz and then rendezvous with Ganteaume in the Caribbean. Once there, they were to conquer some English islands and reinforce the garrisons on Saint-Domingue, Guadaloupe and Martinique. They were then to return to Europe and help free the Spanish and French vessels in the port of El Ferrol, thus giving them a combined strength of thirty-four or thirty-five ships. This is more or less what Villeneuve did (but not Ganteaume, who refused to move from Brest). Villeneuve broke out of Toulon at the end of March and sailed for the Caribbean; favourable winds and the absence of British frigates allowed him to do so. His squadron of nineteen ships reached Martinique on

16 May. For almost two weeks, after dropping anchor in the harbour of Fort de France, Villeneuve did nothing until, on 30 May, new orders from Napoleon arrived instructing him to capture nearby British possessions. This he set out to do in a rather lacklustre manner,[68] but soon learnt that Nelson had arrived in Barbados. Rather than confront him, he decided to return to Europe.

As Villeneuve approached the European mainland on 22 July, he encountered a British squadron off the coast of Cape Finisterre (Cabo Fisterra) in Galicia.[69] There was a brief encounter in fog in which the English, under Admiral Sir Robert Calder, seem to have got the better of the French, but neither Calder nor Villeneuve, 'timid and irresolute', persisted and the engagement was broken off. According to one story, when one of the captains of a French vessel, Rear-Admiral Magon de Médine, saw the signal to break off, he went into such a rage that he stormed up and down his ship shouting abuse, and threw his spyglass and wig at Villeneuve as he passed by.[70] Napoleon at first accepted Villeneuve's self-serving reports of the encounter, which portrayed himself in a glowing and the Spanish in a poor light, even though they, and not the French, had borne the brunt of the fighting.[71] Part of the problem with the French navy's lacklustre performance was that Villeneuve appears to have been depressed, and may even have been on the verge of a nervous breakdown.[72] He eventually took refuge in the Bay of Biscay in the north-west of Spain (2 August). Eight days later, he weighed anchor, but rather than head north to Boulogne where the army was waiting, he headed south for Cadiz.[73] By that stage, an invasion was out of the question (about which more below) and new orders were sent to Villeneuve to head for the Mediterranean and to disembark the troops at Naples.[74]

Villeneuve did not receive those instructions until 28 September, and it was not until 18 and 19 October that he finally set sail from Cadiz.[75] He was intercepted by Nelson off Cape Trafalgar in what has been described as the 'greatest sea-fight of the century'.[76] The losses were catastrophic for the French naval effort against Britain. Of the thirty-three ships of the line in the combined Franco-Spanish fleet, twenty-two were destroyed or captured. Admiral Villeneuve, no match for the genius of a Nelson, was taken prisoner and escorted to England. He was released in April 1806, but without a command and in disgrace; a few days after his release he committed suicide in a hotel in Rennes, aptly named the Hôtel de la Patrie. His body was found naked from the waist up; he is supposed to have plunged a knife into his breast, near his heart, six times.[77] The sixth struck home. Even in death, he was hesitant and inept. The note he left behind gives an indication of the man's state of mind: 'Alone, reviled by the Emperor, rejected by a minister who was my friend, having an immense responsibility for a disaster I am blamed for and for which inevitably I am brought here, I must be the object of horror for everyone, and must die.'[78]

At the time, Trafalgar was referred to as the battle of Cadiz. When

Napoleon received news of the defeat he went into a rage against Villeneuve, although he may very well have been relieved to have someone to blame for the failed invasion.[79] There is some evidence that he was beginning to doubt whether the scheme would succeed, and that he was getting ready to call off the invasion even before he moved against Austria.[80] This is possibly why he never attempted an invasion again, even after gaining a hold over the Continent. For the English, on the other hand, Trafalgar, in spite of the death of Nelson, represented the triumph of the chosen Protestant nation against a country that had 'offended God', the instrument of His avenging hand.[81]

## Seven Torrents Descend on Germany

Let us go back a little to before the battle of Trafalgar. It was not until July 1805 that Napoleon suspected that a newly formed coalition was moving against him. He then realized that two Russian armies were massing on the Polish border, while Austrian troops were concentrating on the Bavarian border, in Venetia and in the Tyrol.

This is why Napoleon dictated a letter to his arch-chancellor in August which states his position in blunt terms: 'The fact is that this power [Austria] is arming itself; I wish to disarm it; if it does not, I will go there with 200,000 men to pay it a good visit that it will remember for a long time.'[82] From that time on, Napoleon instructed the French ambassador in Vienna, Alexandre-François de La Rochefoucauld, to demand explanations about Austrian troop movements. By the middle of August, the French, through Talleyrand, had virtually delivered an ultimatum.[83] If Vienna were intimidated by these threats and backed down, then Napoleon would have assured his rear while going ahead with plans to invade England. If the threats came to naught, then he had at least laid the diplomatic groundwork for an attack against Austria at a later stage.

On 22 August, Napoleon urged Villeneuve to leave Brest – Villeneuve had said that he might be sailing for Brest or Cadiz, but between 10 and 21 August no one knew where he was – without losing a moment: 'England is ours. We are all ready, everything is embarked. Appear within twenty-four hours and it's all over.'[84] The very next day, however, he decided that if Villeneuve were not able to make the rendezvous, he would postpone the invasion for a year.[85] It is from that moment that one can date the decision to abandon the Channel crossing, even if Napoleon had been thinking about the possibility of a Continental war for some months. The idea of turning around the Army of England, rebaptized the Grand Army (Grande Armée) on 13 August, and launching an attack on Austria, as well as possibly Prussia and Russia, had been considered as early as the end of 1804, and into the summer of 1805.[86] There is some indication, however, that Napoleon remained convinced there was no threat to him from either Russia or Austria, at least until about July 1805, months after those two countries had started planning for war.[87] There was an evident reluctance on Napoleon's part to believe that the eastern European monarchs had hostile intentions towards him. Thus when news of an increase in Austrian garrison strengths on the Italian border reached him, he issued a strongly worded letter to Francis and moved troops to the region, but seemed easily appeased by the explanation he received from the Austrian Emperor that they were not aimed at France.[88] Napoleon's willingness to accept Francis's word at face value was not simply a matter of good faith. He believed, wrongly, that Austria, and for that matter Russia, would not be swayed by British offers of a new coalition.[89]

The Austrians and Russians, on the other hand, had been planning an offensive against France since February, although they did not start to mobilize troops, for fear of arousing Napoleon's suspicions, until September–October.[90] Napoleon's spies, in that respect, had let him down; he was blithely unaware of just how advanced their plans were or indeed of the true intentions of Francis and Alexander. When Murat attempted to warn Napoleon that a treaty had been concluded – he appears to have got wind of it from his own intelligence sources – Napoleon reprimanded him, insisting that the rumours were false and fabricated.[91] Napoleon even attempted to bend reality to his own will by instructing Fouché to fabricate letters from Petersburg to show just how well the French and Russians got on.[92] He finally acted in August by sending a letter to Francis through their respective foreign ministers.[93] It was a belated attempt to argue Austria out of an alliance with Russia but it was also warning of what would happen if a Continental war obliged him to turn his forces from the Channel coast to Italy and Germany. A few days later, however, he received a letter from the court of Vienna – a response to his demands to disarm – that was hardly likely to reassure him.[94] A power that breaks a treaty, and refuses all claims concerning it, the letter declared, was just as guilty of committing an aggression as if it had attacked another unjustly. It was in part a pointed lesson on how to behave as a great power and as head of state, and in part justification for Austria's mobilizing of its troops. It had been obliged to do so, gradually, in response to the French mobilization, and because of a lack of conciliatory approaches. Napoleon, not surprisingly, did not see things the same way. In his mind, France was being forced into a war by Austrian aggression; at least that was the official line.[95]

Napoleon's decision to turn on his adversaries has been clouded in myth and is often referred to as the 'Boulogne dictation' (dictée de Boulogne). According to this legend, Napoleon dictated in one draft the plan of the forthcoming campaign to one of his councillors of state, Comte Pierre Antoine Daru. The exaggeration has been pointed out many times before,[96] but it is worth underlining that Napoleon would have had to consult with many people – other generals, intendants and administrators – and would have had to think through numerous options, before deciding on the final draft, which is what the dictation appears to be. The main idea was simple: prevent the Russians from joining up with the Austrians in Germany. Moreover, although Napoleon had ordered his troops to gather on the Rhine, he did not decide on a plan of attack until the end of September, when he realized what the Austrian dispositions were likely to be.[97] Underlying the simplicity of his objectives, however, was a complexity in operational planning that was to revolutionize warfare for the next century and more.[98]

The army, divided into seven corps or seven 'torrents' as Napoleon referred to them,[99] set out on 29 August 1805. The time these men had spent in camp at Boulogne in part explains why he was so successful in the campaigns fought between 1805 and 1809.[100] The army and its officers had been constantly exercised between 1803 and 1805 in every aspect of drill and tactics. This was a new army – only about 12 per cent of the troops were veterans of the revolutionary wars – that literally drilled seven days a week in their battalions or divisions, and held army corps manoeuvres twice a month when they practised live musket and cannon fire.[101] Or at least most of them did. There are memoirs from this period that paint a less flattering portrait of the army in training and that describe it as far less disciplined than has been made out.[102] Nevertheless, the training and discipline were drilled into most, so that they were superbly fit, which is why they were able to march from early morning till nightfall, covering about 390 kilometres, an average of fifty-five kilometres a day, in seven days.[103]

This is not to say that the forced marches did not take their toll. The march to the Rhine was fraught with difficulties, not the least being the precarious supply situation. Once again, the French believed that a combination of foraging and relying on supply depots would solve any provisioning problems. The only trouble was there were virtually no supply depots, despite orders being sent out to prepare them in advance.[104] As a consequence of both the rapidity of the march and the lack of supplies, commanding officers had neither the time nor the means to feed their men, so the troops were authorized to pillage for food. Villages would be completely stripped bare.[105] Bad weather and a constant lack of food meant that not only did the army go hungry but it was often in disarray.[106] Although it is impossible to give any exact figures for the numbers of men who fell by the wayside, deserted or simply died of exhaustion, it seems that of the 210,000 men who started out from Boulogne, less than half were present at Austerlitz.[107]

But advance they did, and very quickly, on a 120-kilometre front between Stuttgart and Würzburg. This was in some respects a new way of waging warfare, the first time that Napoleon deployed the bulk of his troops at one central point with the objective of inflicting a knockout blow against the enemy.[108] The Austrian commander, General Mack, made the decision to concentrate his scattered forces in a line from Ulm to Ingolstadt. Mack's plans were possibly influenced by rumours that the British had landed at Boulogne and that Napoleon was retreating.[109] He was convinced that Ulm was the key to any allied plan of attack and wrote to the Russian commander, Mikhail Kutuzov, whose vanguard had started to arrive in Braunau, some 250 kilometres further east, to join him to strike a blow against Napoleon. Kutuzov was wary, and thought that Mack would be better off getting out of Ulm to join him.[110]


'Fighting England in Germany'

Kutuzov was right. Baron Karl Mack, ambitious but ill equipped for the operations he was about to face, was appointed quartermaster general of the army, largely at the insistence of the foreign minister, Count Franz Colloredo-Waldsee, in April 1805 when it was obvious that war with France was inevitable. Mack has borne the brunt of the blame for the failure at Ulm, but in some respects he was a scapegoat for the political failings of the Austrian monarchy. He was possibly singled out for this role not only for the defeat he endured but also because he was one of the very few commoners who had risen to achieve such a high rank – *Feldmarschalleutnant*, the equivalent of a major-general. Mack was by no means as stupid as some historians have made him out to be, and inspired the likes of Archduke Charles, who later almost defeated Napoleon at Wagram.

The Grande Armée arrived before Ulm on 15 October. It had taken seventeen days to march 210,000 men some 250 kilometres from the Rhine to the outskirts of Ulm.[111] Mack was trapped inside the city with the bulk of his army. The next day, the town was bombarded. Mack refused to admit reality and persisted, for a while, in believing that the army before the walls of Ulm was nothing more than a feint. There is an eyewitness report that has the old man, 'a night cap under his hat, wearing a blue coat, being supported under the arm by his valet, dragging his feet along the ramparts, assuring everyone that it was nothing more than a feint and that the enemy was in full retreat'.[112] He ordered his officers not to speak of surrender – 'triumph or die' was the term he used[113] – and seems, initially at least, to have been determined to resist, declaring that in the event of a prolonged siege he would be the first to eat horse flesh.[114] It never came to that. Napoleon sent an emissary asking for Mack's surrender, and even though he rejected Napoleon's demand, the senior officers present in Ulm insisted that he save the army and accept.[115] Mack restored some lost face by negotiating a somewhat unconventional arrangement: the Austrian army would be allowed to surrender with full military honours – on 25 October. If before that date a Russian relief force arrived, the Austrians would be expected to fight. If none were forthcoming, they would be taken prisoner. Napoleon, better informed about where the Russians were than the Austrians, allowed the delay in the knowledge that they were still several hundred kilometres away. In fact, Mack surrendered five days later when he realized the Russians would not arrive in time. Twenty-five thousand men filed into captivity past Napoleon – who happened to be suffering from a cold[116] – bringing to 50,000 the number of Austrians who had been captured since the start of the campaign. Mack too went to prison with his men but was soon released. In Vienna, news of the capitulation left everyone 'chop-fallen', although it was hardly spoken about in public.[117] Mack was later condemned to death by a court martial, but had his sentence commuted to two years in prison. He was released in 1808 and lived the rest of his life in obscurity.

In Paris, news of the capitulation of Ulm was announced before a performance of Racine's *Iphigénie* on 24 October at the Comédie Française. When the actor playing Agamemnon uttered the following lines:

> Mais qui peut dans sa course arrêter ce torrent?
> Achille va combattre et triomphe en courant.
> (But who can halt this torrent in its course?
> Achilles leaps into the fray and triumphs as he runs.)

the audience burst into applause, expressing its support for Napoleon, the regime and his victory.[118]

Napoleon asked for an armistice after Ulm, but it was probably only to lull the allies into a false sense of security.[119] He pushed ahead and by 24 October he was entering Munich. As with everywhere he now went, throngs of people flocked to catch a glimpse of the 'man of destiny', people illuminated their homes, church bells rang out and cannon roared in salute. The enthusiasm of the people of Munich for Napoleon appears to have been sincere.[120] We have no idea what kind of impact this type of adulation, typical of his experience now in France but increasingly common also outside the Empire, was having on his psyche. He never mentions the impression it might have made on him in any of his letters or latterday reminiscences. It would be safe to assume, however, that no one can come away untouched by this sort of acclaim. Part of the crowd reaction stems from Napoleon's posing as the protector of the smaller German states against Austrian territorial ambitions. The Elector of Bavaria, Max Joseph, was not there to greet him; he had fled to Würzburg at the beginning of September in the face of the Austrian advance.[121] Described by contemporaries as a 'big brewer of beer', 'a good, jolly, farmer-like looking fellow', Max Joseph had hestitated before entering into an alliance with Napoleon, almost paralysed before the enormity of the decision he was facing.[122]

That Austria decided to invade Bavaria in a pre-emptive strike did not help. Faced with French pressure, Austrian arrogance and the ambition of his chief minister, Maximilian Montgelas, Max Joseph succumbed at the end of August and threw in his lot with Napoleon.

As a consequence of Ulm and the entry of the French into Munich, Francis decided to evacuate the Austrian capital. It would be the first time in 320 years that Vienna had been occupied by a foreign army. Napoleon tried on at least two occasions to persuade the Austrian Emperor to sign a separate peace with France, but Francis would have none of it.[123]

By 11 November, Murat, with the advance troops, was within sight of Vienna; he entered two days later. Napoleon, however, was furious with Murat (and possibly piqued) for getting sidetracked instead of vigorously pursuing the Russian army; he sent him a blistering letter.[124] He realized from afar what Murat close up did not, namely, that he had diverted the army for no good reason. The glory of entering the imperial capital had blinded Murat to his real task, which was to pursue and destroy the Russian army. Thus he allowed the Russians to cross the Danube, unmolested, possibly in the mistaken belief that they were withdrawing completely from the campaign and heading home. In Murat's defence, we should acknowledge that Napoleon had intimated to him when they were in Linz at the beginning of November that the seizure of Vienna would put him in a position to negotiate.[125] If we take Murat's logic into account, the decision to invest Vienna was the right one. By doing so, it was hoped the war would be brought to a speedy end. The reality, however, was that the failure to destroy the Russian army prolonged the war considerably.

Napoleon made his entry into Vienna on 14 November, and set up residence at the Schönbrunn Palace. Although Vienna had been threatened with occupation by Bonaparte during the first Italian campaign, this was the first major foreign capital to be occupied by the French since the beginning of the revolutionary wars, and it was therefore the object of some national pride.[126] When news of the entry reached Paris on 26 November, whatever reservations the public may have had about going to war so shortly after the Empire had been founded were entirely dissipated.[127] The joy was all the greater since it replaced a feeling of anxiety over the fate of Napoleon and the army, about which no news had been received since Ulm.[128] The four most recent issues of the military bulletin sold so quickly that demand outstripped supply.[129]

Vienna, considered beautiful by most observers of the time, was an international capital of music, with a multi-ethnic population of more than 200,000, covered with unpaved roads that sometimes blew up clouds of dust, and surrounded by two rings of fortification in between which were trees and fields. Outside the city walls, however, the *faubourg* extended well beyond. One English tourist complained that there was no intellectual life,

# The Campaigns in Central Europe, 1805–1813

DENMARK

*Baltic Sea*

Lübeck
Hamburg
*Elbe*
*Weser*
Hannover
Stettin
PRUSSIA
Danzig
Königsberg
Tilsit
EYLAU FRIEDLAND
ALLENSTEIN

BRANDENBURG
Berlin
*Vistula*
PULTUSK
GROSS BEEREN
Magdeburg
DENNEWITZ
Poznan
*Warta*
Warsaw
CONFEDERATION
WARTENBURG
LEIPZIG
AUERSTEDT
*Oder*
DUCHY OF
WARSAW
LUTZEN
JENA
KATZBACH
BAUTZEN
DRESDEN
Breslau
Erfurt
Weimar
KULM
SILESIA
Kosel
Cracow
GALICIA
Prague
Nürnberg
BOHEMIA
*Vltava*
MORAVIA
Brünn
AUSTERLITZ
OF THE RHINE
ECKMÜHL
*Danube*
ABENSBURG
ULM
LANDSHUT
AUSTRIAN
Munich
Linz
WAGRAM
HOHENLINDEN
Vienna
ASPERN/ESSLING
Salzburg
Pressburg
*Danube*
SALZBURG
Leoben
Buda Pest
*Tisza*
HUNGARY

Trento
VENETIA
Ljubljana
*Drava*
EMPIRE
Mantua
Zagreb
SLAVONIA
Neusatz
Bologna
ITALY
ILLYRIA
Belgrade
*Danube*
Florence
SAN MARINO
BOSNIA
SERBIA
TUSCANY
Zadar
Bosna-Saray
*Adriatic Sea*
MONTENEGRO
PAPAL
STATES
Ragusa
Rome
Kotor

Napoleon's Campaigns
→ 1805
→ 1806–07
→ 1809
→ 1813
✕ Battle

250 kilometres

150 miles

NAPLES

and that 'vice, ignorance, and vanity stalk about the streets'.[130] That was an exaggeration no doubt: even in the depths of winter, theatres and the opera were open every night, and in the summer there was the Prater, a large public park in which one could find 'music, dancing . . . drinking and carousing, in almost every part'. There was no time for any of that, however. After a few days, Napoleon was on the road again, heading for Znaïm (today Znojmo in the Czech Republic), about ninety kilometres north-west of Vienna. On the way, he received a letter from Admiral Decrès informing him of the outcome of the battle of Trafalgar.

## The 'Bloodiest [Battle] Ever Recorded'

Despite initial maulings at the hands of the French earlier in the campaign (at Ulm and again at Dürnstein on the Danube, about seventy-three kilometres from Vienna), the Russians had retreated in good order, and the allies were now slowly converging on Olmütz (present-day Olomouc, in the Czech Republic) in the Austrian region of Moravia. There, Alexander and Francis had to decide what to do next. They were essentially reduced to two options: withdraw further east and await the arrival of Austrian and Russian reinforcements; or engage with the enemy towards the south-west, near Brünn (present-day Brno), as soon as possible. The choice was between adopting a defensive strategy until the allies had gathered overwhelming forces and could engage Napoleon in a decisive battle – it seems likely that this is what they were originally intent on doing, as allied troops were arriving from every direction and Prussian troops were threatening Napoleon's badly outstretched flank – and taking the offensive.[131] Kutuzov favoured a withdrawal east, as did most of the senior Russian and Austrian generals, those experienced in war at least, wary of engaging Napoleon. Alexander, surrounded by young, inexperienced subordinates, all of whom were eager to do battle with the French, chose to act.

Napoleon arrived at the village of Brünn on the morning of 20 November, and spent the next day reconnoitring the area. Not far from the village of Austerlitz (Slavkov u Brna), he came across a plateau known as the Pratzen Heights, supposedly saying to one of his aides-de-camp, 'Young people, study this terrain well, we are going to do battle here.'[132] Napoleon occupied the heights and was able to familiarize himself with the terrain over the next week or so, during which time his plan of operations took shape.[133] The Austrians too were familiar with the terrain. Their army had conducted manoeuvres there in 1803 and again in 1804.[134] On 30 November 1805, however, Napoleon decided to withdraw his troops from the heights, taking up positions in front of them. It is likely he did so thinking that if the allies arrived and saw the French on top of the heights, they might be reluctant to engage in battle. When the combined Austro-Russian army did arrive on 1 December, it looked as though Napoleon had committed a grave tactical error. The Austro-Russian forces numbered about 86,000 men, supported by 278 cannon. The French numbered about 73,000 men with 139 cannon. Napoleon, in other words, was slightly outnumbered and significantly outgunned. Some have seen in the decision to withdraw from the heights an ability on Napoleon's part to devise an overall plan of operations well before the battle had commenced, so that, like a military Mozart, he saw the whole thing play out in his mind before it happened. It is possible but unlikely.[135]

Napoleon's plan was simple, but it rested on two assumptions, neither of which were inevitable: that the allies would leave the Pratzen Heights to attack; and that Marshal Louis-Nicolas Davout would arrive during the day to reinforce his right wing. To arrive, Davout had to force his men to march from Vienna, about 140 kilometres away, in forty-eight hours.[136] Indeed, so much was dependent on those assumptions that Napoleon did not even bother making contingency plans. It is true that Major-General Franz von Weyrother a senior commander in the Austrian army, was given leeway to devise a plan that saw the allied left flank and centre descend from the heights to join up with the right wing in a kind of pincer movement that aimed to take Napoleon's army from the rear. Napoleon guessed that this is what the allies might do, but he could not know it. He was therefore taking an awful gamble by evacuating the heights in the hope that the allies would behave as he predicted.

A scene is described in Tolstoy's *War and Peace* in which General Weyrother presented his plan of battle to the assembled commanders, among whom was Kutuzov, asleep. If the scene ever took place, Kutuzov would have known about the plan before it was presented, so the nap, given that he had been marginalized from the decision-making process, may have been nothing more than a silent protest at its inadequacies.[137] It proved to be an egotistical gesture; if he had spoken up, it might well have encouraged other officers, Russian or Austrian, to raise objections or point to its flaws. None did, no doubt believing it inappropriate to speak out in the face of the commanding officer's silence. It would have been better if the allies had remained firmly entrenched on the heights in a secure position to await the French onslaught. That they decided against this may have something to do with their desire to save face and to make up for losses incurred in the early stages of the campaign.

On the eve of battle, Napoleon decided to reconnoitre the enemy positions by the light of their bivouac fires, and ventured into the area between the lines. On returning to camp, one of the grenadiers accompanying him decided to make a makeshift torch of burning straw to light his way. He was soon recognized and followed or preceded by many more soldiers with many more torches. As they held them aloft, they began crying out 'Vive l'Empereur!' It is said that there was so much light generated by these thousands of torches that the allied camp believed the French had decided either on a night attack or to break camp.[138] Many of his troops would have been aware it was the anniversary of Napoleon's coronation and would have found a release for the tension typical of the night before a great battle, so that there was soon a 'general conflagration, a movement of enthusiasm', that may even have taken Napoleon by surprise.[139] By all accounts he was visibly touched; when he retired later that night, he is supposed to have said that it was the finest evening of his life.[140]

In the depths of the night, the torch. The scene has been described so many times that it has become an obligatory anecdote in any account of the battle. There is obviously some truth in the claim that Napoleon had condescended to come down to the level of the common soldier to partake of his bread (or potato as the case may be), since it is mentioned by a number of people.[141] But it was also meant as a kind of living allegory in which Napoleon, wandering through the camp, became the light-filled centre who threw back the darkness of the night and unified the troops around his person.

The sun rose that morning over a scene covered in fog. It was to help, rather than hinder, Napoleon's plans: the French right wing was to feign retreat and to hold the bulk of the allied army, which would descend from the Pratzen Heights in order to attack the retreating French. At the right moment, the French centre and left wing would attack the heights, thereby catching the allies in a pincer movement. By mid-afternoon, this is exactly what happened; the French had occupied the heights and were firing on the enemy below. An attempt by the Russian–Austrian army to extricate itself from the trap turned into a rout. Some of the Russian troops tried to escape across an icy lake. A French officer by the name of Jean-Baptiste Barrès took part in the manoeuvre, throwing the Russians on to the frozen lake.[142] According to him, 12,000–15,000 men ran across so that they all broke through the ice at the same time.

Napoleon's account of this retreat across the ice was grossly exaggerated in the 30th Bulletin, giving the impression that 20,000 Russians drowned after he gave the order for his artillery to fire shells to break up the ice.[143] In fact, the marshes were far too shallow for that many to have drowned; possibly only a hundred men died that way.[144] Fewer than 2,000 out of 10,000 troops in the 1st Column were listed missing in action by the Russians, many of whom would have been lost before reaching the marshes. As in some of the battles in Italy, Napoleon greatly inflated the number of enemy dead and wounded (at least 15,000 dead in the bulletin when in reality it was closer to 4,000), while minimizing the number of French dead and wounded.[145] More interesting is the question why he would want to highlight the drownings on the Satschen marshes, an episode that must have appeared harsh, even to contemporaries used to the brutalities of war. It is possible that the episode was meant to remind people of two similar events in history: one of biblical proportions, the drowning of the Pharaoh's army in the Red Sea; the other more recent, the defeat of the Russians by the Teutonic Knights on the frozen surface of Lake Peipus in 1242. Probably no other event in the battle struck imaginations so deeply, so that it was accepted, repeated and exaggerated in the telling by veterans for years afterwards.

Alexander was isolated from the army on the Pratzen Heights quite early in the day, the rest of which he spent in the rear with his surgeon, two Cossacks and a couple of servants, with no contact and ignorant of how the battle was unfolding. After the battle was over, he was seen riding away with his small entourage, overcome by despair. At one stage, he got off his horse, sat on the wet ground at the foot of a tree, covered his face with a handkerchief and burst into tears. Major Carl Friedrich von Toll, a witness to the scene, attempted to offer a few words of consolation.[146] Alexander was not weeping about the carnage, but about the personal humiliation he had just suffered. His English doctor, James Wylie, did what any respectable nineteenth-century doctor would do under the circumstances – he gave the Tsar a few drops of opium in some wine to calm his nerves.[147] We have no idea how Francis reacted to the defeat, although he must have been discouraged. When he met Alexander some time during the morning of the next day,[148] he informed him that he wished to open negotiations with Napoleon. This kind of surrender was typical on the part of the Austrians. The allies could have continued to fight – a sizeable portion of the army remained intact and reinforcements were on their way – but there was a general lack of will to carry on. The collapse of the Third Coalition was as much about lack of trust and indecision on the part of the Eastern powers (certainly on the part of Prussia's Frederick William and then, once defeated at Austerlitz, on the part of Alexander), exacerbated by a lack of communication, as it was about Napoleon's mastery on the field and bullying off. Alexander lacked the determination that he would later gain after seeing the Grande Armée ravage his country in 1812. After Austerlitz, he was hesitant about war, probably overwhelmed by the enormity of the decisions before him.[149]

Francis was more than ready to agree to an armistice. He met with Napoleon two days after the battle, on 4 December, at a mill between Zaroschitz and Nasedlowitz, but since the mill had been completely ransacked the meeting took place in the open.[150] He was, like his Prussian counterpart, not really made to be king. He had the 'the most pale complexion possible', always wore the same uniform of white coat, red trousers and black boots, appeared shy and embarrassed when he spoke, and resembled more a member of the bourgeoisie than a king.[151] He nevertheless plucked up enough gumption to put all the blame on the English for what had just transpired, those 'merchants of human flesh' as he called them. Napoleon was conciliatory. His initial offer to

Francis was reasonably moderate; he did not threaten to take any territories away from Austria at this stage. In the immediate aftermath of the battle, he was still unsure where he stood – that is, whether the war would continue. The Prussians could have yet joined the fray, Archduke Charles had reached the Danube, and the Russian army was still largely intact. That is why Napoleon agreed to an armistice so readily. He did not know that Alexander had given up the fight and had decided to return home. He was, moreover, in a rather precarious position that a more ruthless wartime opponent would have exploited: his troops were overextended, exhausted and without any further reserves. If the allies had done their sums, they would have seen that they could still outnumber Napoleon.

Austerlitz helped obliterate the defeat at Trafalgar, which is why news of that battle, which had taken place six weeks previously on 21 October, was not released until after Ulm and Austerlitz.[152] Of more significance, Austerlitz was the first imperial victory of any note (more so than Ulm) and the regime made much of it. Over time, it became more than a military victory, part of the Napoleonic legend, even in the Emperor's lifetime, galvanizing future soldiers, even placating French public opinion anxious about the war and the directions it was taking. Contemporaries, especially those who had fought at Austerlitz, immediately recognized that they had lived through something extraordinary. 'What a battle,' exclaimed Commandant Salmon to his wife. 'Since the world was made nothing like it has happened.'[153] As news trickled through to the rest of Europe, Napoleon's propaganda hit home so that the defeat appeared much worse than it was. The conservative political commentator Joseph de Maistre, writing to King Victor Emmanuel I of Sardinia, described Austerlitz as the 'bloodiest [battle] ever recorded in modern history'.[154] The expressions he used were 'rivers of blood' and 'piles of bodies', and he spoke of 'Horror and indignation'. Worse was to occur in later years, but it is significant that the reaction among Europe's political elite was laden with foreboding. 'Roll up the map of Europe,' Pitt is reputed to have said, 'it will not be wanted these ten years.'[155]

And yet, paradoxically, news of the battle, which trickled into Paris on 10 December, does not appear to have produced as great a reaction as the French entry into Vienna.[156] There was an attempt to involve the people in victory celebrations – in Paris, for example, the theatres were opened to the public, while in the province some prefects decided to distribute bread and wood to the poor[157] – but Paris crowds were notoriously unpredictable. One should not read too much into the simple presence of a crowd, especially if it involved obtaining something for free; a crowd did not necessarily mean overwhelming support for either Napoleon or the regime.[158] The Paris prefect of police was obliged to 'invite' the inhabitants of that imperial city to illuminate their dwellings.[159] When a festival was organized to transfer the numerous enemy flags Napoleon had captured and sent to Paris – this took place on 1 January 1806 – the reaction of the onlookers seems to have been muted. It was obvious to one witness at least that some in the crowd had been paid to attend and to cheer.[160]

If the sentiments of the war-weary were not as enthusiastic as supporters of the regime might have expected, the fawning of the elite was very much in evidence, especially among Church prelates. In a Te Deum to celebrate the victory, the vicar of the Church of Saint-Merri in Paris declared that the French people, 'whom God cherishes, is saved, the Lord himself has fought amid the ranks of our valiant warriors'.[161] And he went on to describe Napoleon in the most flattering light: 'He seems, this Hero, similar to the morning star, all the more brilliant because it succeeds the long nights and announces serene days.' Cardinal Belloy, the Archbishop of Paris, wrote privately to Napoleon to say that he was great in the eyes of the world because his aptitude for the art of war had determined the destiny of Europe, but he was even greater in the eyes of religion because of the homage he had paid God.[162] A number of poems, some published in pamphlet form (sometimes in Latin), and even plays, were sent to Napoleon celebrating the victory of Austerlitz.[163]

'Peace is an Empty Word'

One year after the foundation of the Empire, Charles de Rémusat, a former noble who had rallied to Bonaparte, believed that its success was not yet assured.[164] The news of the battle of Austerlitz did not change that, but it undoubtedly lent a certain splendour or éclat to Napoleon's reign. The brilliant military campaign consolidated his position and reinforced the aura of invincibility that he had been cultivating since the first Italian campaign.

In many respects, Austerlitz completed the transformation of Bonaparte into Napoleon. Before that, contemporaries could be forgiven for thinking that he was just another competent French general, if somewhat better than most. There was nothing particularly novel about his campaigns in either Italy or Egypt that could have led contemporary military observers to think that they were dealing with a genius on the field. The Italian campaign of 1796–7 was marked by the rapidity of his successes, as well as their political exploitation, but there was no one battle as decisive as the knockout blow that was Austerlitz. The Egyptian campaign had very mixed results, but was easily exploited by Bonaparte in an aura-building exercise. The battle of Marengo, as we know, he almost lost. Moreover, the campaign was only won six months later with the victory of Moreau at Hohenlinden. Austerlitz was different; it was the first decisive battle – the war was effectively over in three months – a feat that was to be successfully repeated at Jena-Auerstädt and Friedland.[165] But it also changed the way in which Napoleon approached campaigning. He believed he had developed a new approach and that he could repeat the performance each time he went to war.[166] Part of the reason for this was that the characteristics of Napoleonic warfare – the speed with which marches were carried out, the mutual support derived from corps formations, and the maintenance of large reserves in the rear ready for the decisive blow – were not yet so readily documented or discussed as to have become generally recognized.[167]

Austerlitz is often seen too as a watershed in the development of Napoleon's character. We do not know what he thought about his victory or what may have gone through his mind when he defeated Francis and Alexander, but it must have had an impact on him. From that time he is supposed to have assumed an increasingly imperious tone. This, however, is based on the mistaken assumption that he was something other than imperious from the start. There is enough evidence to suggest that since the first campaign in Italy he had been growing in arrogance and conceit. Take, for example, his aside to Cambacérès in August 1805, months before Austerlitz. After dictating a letter to Talleyrand ordering him to inform French envoys throughout Europe that he was being forced to go to war with Austria, Napoleon turned to his archchancellor and remarked, 'Anyone would have to be totally mad to make war against me.'[168]

In October, in a memorandum written from Strasbourg, Talleyrand had argued that France would be much better off with Austria as its ally rather than its inveterate enemy. He recommended a 'lenient peace' with Austria, one that would even lead to an Austro-French defensive alliance.[169] This could be done, he argued, by setting up what today would be called buffer states between Austria and France in Germany. It was an intelligent enough approach, although scholars have pointed to its flaws, namely, that it excluded Austria from any direct control in Italy and Germany and thus set the foundations for future conflict.[170] Napoleon appears to have been persuaded by his foreign minister's arguments – until after Austerlitz, when his attitude hardened overnight. In victory, he became less generous. He imposed a demanding treaty on Austria not so much as a result of the victory, but because Austria quickly became isolated on the diplomatic scene, after being abandoned by both Prussia and Russia. What he was now looking for was not peace – a word he thought empty[171] – but rather a 'glorious peace'; any negotiation had to be conducted from a position of strength.

It was. On 26 December, Austria signed the Treaty of Pressburg, incurring a considerable number of territorial losses: Venice, Dalmatia and Istria were ceded to the Kingdom of Italy; Brixen, Trent, Vorarlberg and the Tyrol were ceded to Bavaria.[172] In addition, Vienna was saddled with a war indemnity of forty million francs. It was in part a result of Napoleon's belief that Austria was his main Continental enemy – a belief engendered by his experiences in Italy during the first and second Italian campaigns: he was therefore trying to hobble the country so that it could no longer do any harm.[173] Although it makes no sense from either a foreign-political or even a personal perspective, Napoleon felt he had been duped by Austria. If it had appeared willing to negotiate with him before the outbreak of war, that was (in his mind) a ruse allowing it time to mobilize for battle.[174]

   This is possible, but another explanation can be offered. The defeat of Austria and Russia presented Napoleon with an opportunity that had not existed before the battle. He was now in a position to reshape all of southern, northern and central Europe, to transform the Grand Nation into the Grand Empire.[175] Over the next few months, he installed Joseph as King of Naples, and Louis as King of Holland (Eugène, it will be recalled, had already been installed as viceroy of Italy). In Germany, the Holy Roman Empire was abolished and replaced by a Confederation of the Rhine under French influence. The Electors of Bavaria and Württemberg were made kings, while Charles, Duke of Baden had his duchy transformed into a Grand Duchy. As with previous treaties hammered out by Napoleon, such as Leoben, Lunéville and Amiens, the seeds of further unrest were very much present. Francis always hated the peace that had been imposed on him at Pressburg, and he began to look around for allies to undo it almost immediately the guns had fallen silent. And as with other treaties signed by Napoleon, he reneged on them within months.

# The Grand Empire

## Napoleon the Great, Napoleon the Saint

Napoleon returned to Paris in the first flush of victory on the evening of 26 January 1806. In the weeks and months following the battle of Austerlitz, one can discern an attempt not only to exploit the victory to the fullest, but also to establish a cult centred on Napoleon. In an issue of the *Moniteur* in 1806, the minister of the interior Chaptal published an 'Ode sur les victoires de Napoléon le Grand' (Ode to the victories of Napoleon the Great), in which a Frenchman wakes up Homer to ask him to come back to sing the glory of a hero who by his actions had effaced the names of the great heroes of antiquity.[1] References to Napoleon as 'Great' were in evidence even before the coronation in December 1804, but they were uttered in private.[2] Now there was public acknowledgement of the epithet as the Senate passed a vote to construct a monument to 'Napoleon the Great'.

Propaganda was not a word employed by contemporaries. Instead, people spoke of the 'management of opinion' (*direction de l'opinion*).[3] That is why Napoleon insisted on having men who were 'attached' to him at the head of the newspapers, and who had the 'good sense' not to publish material that was damaging to the nation.[4] There was a punitive as well as a constructive tradition involved in cultivating his image. The punitive tradition was common to eighteenth-century absolutist states and involved removing those who tarnished Napoleon's image. Journalists and newspapers were censored or closed down, and in extreme circumstances journalists were executed.

The constructive tradition involved grafting Napoleon's image on to existing popular culture.[5] To this end the Emperor tolerated and even encouraged traditions, such as religious festivals and other public celebrations, that dated back to the pre-revolutionary era, and that he could use to promote his image. Thus the Festival of the Federation on the anniversary of 14 July was first relegated to a public holiday in 1803 and 1804, and was no longer celebrated at all after 1805. Instead, Napoleon created his own festivals with a military aura. The translation of the remains of Marshal Henri de La Tour d'Auvergne, Vicomte de Turenne, to the Invalides in 1801, the construction of triumphal arches, the Distribution of the Eagles, the celebration of victories, and the translation of Frederick the Great's sword to the Invalides in 1807 fall into that pattern. The army often took centre stage in Napoleonic festivities to create a 'culture of war' that united citizens and conscripts around the flag.[6] The most

Napoleonic of festivals was the creation of the anniversary of St Napoleon. But the regime went even further by attempting to instil a degree of sacrality that had not been seen since before the Revolution: an imperial catechism was introduced that made a direct link between God and Napoleon; and 15 August, which happened to coincide with both the Assumption and Napoleon's birthday, was declared a national holiday to celebrate the founding of a new saint – St Napoleon.

In the Catholic calendar, 15 August was the Feast of the Assumption. Under the Empire, however, the Virgin Mary was conveniently forgotten and effectively replaced by a St Napoleon invented to fit the regime's agenda. Napoleon's birthday became a sort of 'personal canonization by decree'.[7] A number of dates were toyed with, including Easter and Corpus Christi, both of which

Antoine-François Callet, *Allégorie à la victoire d'Austerlitz, 2 décembre 1805* (Allegory of the victory of Austerlitz, 2 December 1805), 1806. A series of twelve paintings was commissioned to decorate the gallery of the Diane Palace at the Tuileries. One of the most interesting is this allegorical painting by Callet in which Napoleon is represented as the god Mars driving before him the two imperial eagles of Russia and Austria.

were rejected by Napoleon; even he was not so conceited as to want to associate himself directly with Christ.

It was (and is) customary in France to celebrate the feast day of one's name-sake, but Napoleon's feast day became a pretext to celebrate the birth of Napoleon,[8] almost as though it would have been improper simply to declare his birthday a national day of celebration.[9] Nevertheless, the introduction of a new saint and a new feast day did not occur overnight. The Feast of St Napoleon was first mentioned in the *Almanach national de la France* (National almanac) in 1802, details of which were published the following year.[10] In the literature of the day, Bonaparte was referred to as the *Pacificateur des Nations* (Peacemaker of nations) and as the *Régénérateur de la France* (Regenerator of France), as the person around whom everyone could rally, the person able to stifle discord, themes that had been touted even before his ascension to power in 1799.[11] The festivities celebrating his nomination as Consul for life were held on 15 August.[12] The feast day was mentioned again at the camp of Boulogne when Napoleon was handing out Legions of Honour (16 August 1804). In 1805, the canons of Nice asked Napoleon for permission to dedicate an altar to a (non-existent) St Napoleon.[13] All of this seems to have been designed to prepare public opinion leading up to the first official celebration of the feast day in 1806.

Once again, the prefects were enlisted to make sure that everyone understood exactly what was expected of them. Letters were sent to the mayors of the towns and villages throughout France instructing them that this was the occasion to 'express their appreciation and gratitude', and to 'take all appropriate measures to give this festival the greatest solemnity'.[14] It was meant to celebrate 'the memory of our internal regeneration', and to encourage local communities to celebrate the state and the head of state. It was then as much an exercise in state building as it was an exercise in the cult of the personality.[15] The creation of a feast day of St Napoleon combined the religious obedience of Napoleon's subjects with his own heroic cult.

The Feast of St Napoleon was celebrated every year till the end of the regime, and always followed the same pattern – a religious ceremony at Notre Dame, public games, bunting, illuminations. The celebrations were low-key; the most outlandish public display occurred during the inaugural official celebration in Paris when an illuminated star nine metres in diameter was hoisted from the towers of Notre Dame, but even that was tame by the standards of the day.[16] This modesty is possibly why they do not appear to have generated much enthusiasm,[17] and why the day was usually set aside for laying the first stones of public works and monuments.[18] Plays, poems and pamphlets – homages to Napoleon – all lent weight to the idea that this was a national feast day to honour the man responsible for dragging France back from the political abyss that was the Revolution.[19] 'The season of tears is past,' declared one

St. Napoleon Officier romain, Martyr

Anonymous, *Saint Napoléon Officier romain, Martyr* (St Napoleon, Roman officer, martyr), no date. One of the few iconographic pieces from the Empire depicting St Napoleon. On the left-hand side is a frame containing an image of the martyr in prison.

pamphlet, 'the Angels, protectors of this nation, have made a clear sky shine over it; they have dissipated, for ever, those horrible clouds that contained death within them; they have turned off the thunder, closed the tombs, and have delivered peace and happiness to France.'[20] It would not be the last time that an author drew a parallel between the heavens and Napoleon, but this does not mean to say that it had much of an impact on the imaginations of those who were called on to celebrate it. On the contrary, the invention of a St Napoleon exasperated rather than pleased Catholics in the Empire outside France, and its substitution for the Assumption was to prove a two-edged sword. When relations between the imperial state and the Church were good – and they were for a short while – then things played in Napoleon's favour. When relations turned sour, priests often used the occasion if not to preach against Napoleon, then to preach instead about the Virgin Mary.[21] In Belgium and in Italy, some clergy sidelined the new festival and continued discreetly to celebrate the Assumption.[22] It was a risky business; priests who openly flouted imperial edicts could be arrested and could have their churches closed.

## 'He is the One God Created'

Napoleon went a step further, using religion to lay the basis for what would become a personal cult. In 1806, he decided to introduce an imperial catechism, which was meant to render religious instruction uniform throughout the Empire, and which children were required to recite at Sunday schools from May 1806; it was never approved by the pope. Napoleon rewrote parts of the old catechism, and included the following remarkable clauses:

> Q. – Are there not particular reasons that should attach us more strongly to Napoleon I, our Emperor?
>
> A. – Yes, for he is the one God created in difficult circumstances in order to re-establish public worship and the holy religion of our fathers, and in order to become its protector. He has restored and preserved public order, by his profound and active wisdom; he defends the State by his powerful arm; he has become the anointed of the Lord, by the consecration he received from the Sovereign Pontiff, head of the universal Church.
>
> Q. – What should we think of those who fail in their duty towards our Emperor?
>
> A. – According to the apostle, St Paul, they would be resisting the order established by God Himself, and would render themselves worthy of eternal damnation.[23]

The Imperial Catechism was an attempt by Napoleon to define a subject's duties by placing himself within the tradition of European monarchs anointed by God. As such, it represents a radical shift away from the secular nature of the French polity towards a more traditional notion of rule by divine right. Those who now failed in their duty towards Napoleon would find themselves facing 'eternal damnation'.

However, not all Catholics were going to heed these imperatives. There was a good deal of passive resistance to the adoption of the Catechism both among the Church hierarchy and among the faithful.[24] In Belgium, in the annexed Rhine departments and in Italy, its introduction in 1806 met with strong resistance, to the point where it had to be abandoned.[25] Over time, a number of 'Catechisms' sprang up in reaction to the Imperial Catechism. In Spain, for example, a *Catecismo civil* (Citizens' catechism) was published in 1808, distributed in hundreds of thousands of copies, and translated into almost every

European language.[26] Not long afterwards, the Prussian poet and playwright Heinrich von Kleist wrote a strongly anti-Napoleonic *Katechismus der Deutschen* (Germans' catechism).[27]

> Q. – Where do I find it, this Germany of which you speak, and where does it lie?
> A. – Here, my father. – Do not confuse me.
> Q. – Where?
> A. – On the map.
> Q. – Yes, on the map! – This map is from the year 1805. – Don't you know what happened in the year 1805 when the Treaty of Pressburg was concluded?
> A. – After the treaty, Napoleon, the Corsican Emperor, laid waste to it through an act of violence.
> Q. – Well? And yet it exists all the same?

## The Bonapartes in Europe

At the end of December 1805, while Napoleon was in Munich awaiting the ratification of peace with Austria, he sent a missive to Joseph that was clearly meant as an order. He intended, he informed his brother, to take over the Kingdom of Naples and Joseph was being named commander-in-chief of the Army of Naples. On receiving the letter, Joseph had forty-eight hours to leave Paris for Rome.[28] He himself could not be there in person, Napoleon wrote, because affairs in Paris would keep him occupied. The directive surprised Joseph; there was a good deal of conjecture in Paris at the time about whether his departure for Italy was to be seen as a disgrace or a promotion.[29] Certainly, there were rumours that he was going to be crowned king – this was about the time Napoleon was negotiating with Holland to have Louis installed as its king – but given that he had refused the Italian throne, the Neapolitan throne would have had little attraction for Joseph. For the moment it was a military posting; Joseph was promoted to the rank of general for the occasion and given the unusual title of 'Lieutenant of the Emperor'.[30] Joseph was meant to win his kingdom at the head of an army.

The Kingdom of Naples was ruled by King Ferdinand IV, married to Maria Carolina, daughter of the Empress Maria Theresa.[31] She hated the French for what they had done to her younger sister, Marie-Antoinette, and vowed to crush anything that smacked of revolution. Tensions between the French Republic and the Neapolitan House of Bourbon, in other words, went back some way. While Napoleon was engaged in campaigning against Austria and Russia, Ferdinand reluctantly signed a treaty in which he agreed to remain neutral. That promise was fleeting. Under the influence of his prime minister, the English-born Sir John Acton, and no doubt with a little prodding from Maria Carolina, Ferdinand allowed an Anglo-Russian expeditionary force to land in the Bay of Naples in November 1805.[32] As a result of what Napoleon considered a betrayal, he decided to intervene. This was not, it should be underlined, the first time the French had tried to control the kingdom. In 1799, the Neapolitan Bourbons were chased from their home and a short-lived (from January to June of that year) Parthenopean Republic was set up that, if it was not under French control, was entirely dependent on a French armed presence for its existence.[33] The Republic was overthrown by a counter-revolution and those who had supported it were brutally murdered.

Napoleon used the breach of neutrality as an excuse to invade and conquer.[34] Contemporaries like Nelson had predicted it years before; Napoleon had been thinking about such an invasion for some time; northern and central Italy were already firmly under French control; by occupying Naples he would have the whole peninsula. The advantages that would ensue were enormous: he would be able to eliminate Naples as a centre of French émigré activity; and he would be able to exclude the British from Italy and use the ports to help rebuild his navy. Besides, he had not entirely given up on his plans to dominate the Mediterranean and to invade Egypt again. There was the illusion too that Naples was rich since it was one of the largest cities in Europe with a population of over 550,000 people. In reality, it was socially and economically backward. It has been calculated, for example, that there were more than 100,000 ecclesiastics living in the kingdom, approximately one for every fifty inhabitants.[35]

The temptation, then, to drag Naples into the modern era and to unlock its wealth was too great. Days before Napoleon informed Joseph that he was being sent to Naples, even before French troops had marched south, he issued a proclamation from Vienna's Schönbrunn Palace declaring that the 'dynasty of Naples has ceased to reign'.[36] The expedition to Naples, with Joseph nominally in charge, was meant to oust the Bourbons and replace them with a prince of his own House. 'You,' he told Joseph, 'if that suits; another if it does not at all suit.'[37] Napoleon, in other words, does not seem to have cared whether Joseph took up the offer or not. Joseph accepted. We do not know why; there is nothing in his letters or memoirs that indicate what he was thinking, and his biographers are surprisingly silent on this point. We can assume that discussions of a kind went on behind the scenes between the two brothers, especially around the sticking point that decided Joseph to renounce the throne of Italy in 1805, namely, his right to the French succession. But there are no records of those negotiations. It is possible that Napoleon simply confronted Joseph with an ultimatum: accept the Neapolitan throne or lose everything.[38] At the end of March 1806, Napoleon conferred on him the title of 'King of Naples and Sicily'; he retained the

Château de Fontainebleu, Seine-et-Marne/Giraudon/The Bridgeman Art Library

François Pascal Simon, Baron Gérard, *Portrait de Joseph Bonaparte, roi d'Espagne* (Joseph Bonaparte, King of Spain), after 1808.

French title 'Grand Elector' and his rights of succession.[39] It was a watershed moment in the creation of a 'Grand Empire', a phrase that was used for the first time in Joseph's succession.[40]

Joseph was not the only member of the Bonaparte family to benefit from the creation of the Empire. In May 1806, rumours were flying around Paris and Amsterdam that Louis would be made King of Holland. This did indeed occur the following month, but not without intense and public political discussions in Holland about the transformation of the two-centuries-old Republic into a monarchy, a good deal more intense than what had occurred in France in 1804.[41] If Napoleon offered Louis the Dutch throne it was in part because no other member of his family could fill the post. Lucien was out of favour and would not re-enter the family fold; Jérôme was only twenty-one years of age, too young and too inexperienced to take up a position of such responsibility;

Joseph was already ensconced in Italy, as was Napoleon's stepson, Eugène. The only male member of the family not yet to have an important post, Murat, was soon to become Grand Duke of Cleves and Berg, but he could hardly take precedence over Napoleon's brother. Louis too hesitated before accepting the position, but he gave way in the end to Napoleon's insistence, not however without a public humiliation.

A witness tells of a curious family scene that took place at Saint-Cloud on 6 June 1806, the day after the official ceremony proclaiming Louis king.[42] Louis' son, Napoleon Charles, nicknamed the *Petit-Chou* (little darling), who would die the following year of croup, had learnt a fable that he performed before Napoleon and his guests seated at table for lunch. The fable in question was Aesop's 'The Frogs Who Desired a King'. Napoleon thought the story was hilarious, and in doing so revealed a great deal about what he really thought of his brother. Frogs were traditionally used to caricature the Dutch, but in this fable they demanded a king of Jupiter, who sent them instead a piece of wood. When they complained, he sent them a crane, which proceeded to eat them all. The allusion was clear, at least to Napoleon: the Dutch were stupid and they were about to get a king who would do his bidding. As for Louis, Napoleon did not appear to set much store by him. 'Everyone knows', he wrote shortly before annexing Holland in 1810, 'that without me, you are nothing.'[43]

Louis had traits in common with his elder brother – he was rather a dreamer, a bit melancholic and maladroit – but he was by no means as dynamic. He had a reputation for being lazy (not entirely deserved), was a hypochondriac and had a love of sumptuousness that he shared with some of his other siblings (but not Napoleon). Napoleon had a sincere fondness for him, while Louis admired, even imitated, Napoleon in just about everything he did, including his physique (much like Napoleon, Louis was becoming flabby and overweight). For a while, Louis attempted to maintain his brother's work rhythm – getting up at five in the morning, holding audiences from seven to nine, Council of State from nine to twelve and so on – but he had to abandon that schedule after a year as his health deteriorated. Louis, in other words, took to heart his functions as King of Holland and worked (sometimes) selflessly for his new subjects, attempting to fit in with the Dutch as much as possible, trying to win them over after a cool reception on his arrival in 1806. He had a tough job of it, not least because he was in a sort of constitutional limbo, having been declared king while the Dutch republican constitution was left largely unchanged, and also because of the demands placed on him by his brother.[44] Napoleon tried to control Louis' life in much the same way that he tried to control the lives of all his siblings as well as those in his close entourage. It was only once he became king that Louis began to stand up for himself, to grow into his role, to take on his brother, to

© RMN-Grand Palais (Château de Fontainebleu)/Jean-Pierre Lagiewski

Charles Howard Hodges, *Louis Napoleon, King of Holland from 1808–1810*, 1809.

argue with him, even to reply to his letters in a sarcastic tone. This newfound independence irritated Napoleon greatly and from that moment things began to sour.

When Napoleon rebuked his brothers and sisters, which was often, he did not generally hold back. 'I am angry,' he would write, or 'you understand nothing about the administration' or again, 'You are going about this like a scatterbrain [*un étourdi*].'[45] Within a short time of Joseph's arriving in Naples, Napoleon was already accusing him of being too soft, insisting on more vigour in his dealings with the people of Naples, and suggesting that he was a 'do-nothing king' (*roi fainéant*), an evident and not particularly flattering allusion to the Merovingian kings of the Middle Ages.[46] The same tone can be seen in his letters to Louis, whom he dubbed a 'prefect king' (*roi préfet*).[47] One of the first pieces of advice Napoleon offered his brother was not to be kind. 'A prince who in the first year of his reign is considered to be kind, is a prince who is mocked in his second year.'[48] Even when his siblings did carry out his orders to the letter, Napoleon's reactions were often ungracious.

Napoleon's brothers and sisters responded in different ways to these verbal assaults. Joseph attempted to flatter his younger brother to bring him onside or simply ignored him. Lucien left the clan and never returned. Louis became recalcitrant, arguing that by devoting himself to the wellbeing of his people, he would make himself worthy of his brother's name.[49] Jérôme became defensive; Joachim and Caroline Murat were to become more and more distant. Only Eugène, Pauline and Elisa kept on good terms with Napoleon, although Pauline's libertine behaviour can be interpreted as a form of revolt. The key to understanding his 'system' – a word used by Napoleon himself to describe the family alliances within the Empire – is straightforward: Napoleon wanted his siblings to be extensions of him. He almost never gave them enough autonomy to rule in their own right – although they sometimes ignored his demands and ruled as they saw fit – and he always expected them to obey him unswervingly, to impose enormous sacrifices on their own peoples for the sake of the glory of France and Napoleon.

Napoleon used his family in his dynastic politics. He pressured, cajoled and bullied his relatives into accepting marriages with the sovereign houses of Europe for the sake of political alliances that would cement his dynasty, mobilizing any family member who was of marriageable age.[50] This was quite typical of French and European dynasties. Both Louis XIV and Louis XV had installed members of their family on the thrones of Spain, Naples and Parma (which Napoleon set about undoing). In January 1806, Eugène was married to the daughter of the King of Bavaria, Augusta Amelia (one of the rare couples in the grand scheme of things who formed a lasting, loving bond). The marriage was celebrated in great pomp in Munich. In April 1806, Josephine's cousin Stéphanie de Beauharnais, with whom Napoleon was a little in love, was married to the Crown Prince Karl, Grand Duke of Baden. The family was thereby allied to two powerful southern German states that had been enlarged and transformed into kingdoms by Napoleon in the territorial reconfiguration that followed Austerlitz. To consolidate the German bonds, Jérôme, whose marriage to Elizabeth Patterson was annulled by the Archbishop of Paris, was married off to Catherine, the daughter of King Frederick of Württemberg (they too seem to have formed a loving couple, although it did not prevent Jérôme from playing the field).[51] In 1808, one of Murat's nieces, Marie-Antoinette Murat, was married to a prince of Hohenzollern-Sigmaringen, while another of Josephine's cousins, Stéphanie Tascher de La Pagerie, married the Prince of Arenberg. In 1810, her brother, Louis Tascher de La Pagerie, married the daughter of the Prince Regent of Leyen. Not all these marriages were happy, but the stakes were high and the feelings of Napoleon's relatives counted for little.

Napoleon had been thinking of creating a federal system, a 'league' as he called it, to replace the sister republics of the revolutionary era before Austerlitz, but his victory gave a certain impetus to the idea of a political system based on bloodline, and made it more difficult for the minor princes of central

Europe to say no to his requests. The fundamental problem with this system of alliances was that most of the personalities in place, despite being close relatives, were hardly well disposed towards either the system or its creator. Like an autocratic head of family, Napoleon knew best, and he treated most of his siblings with barely concealed contempt. They were disinclined to adhere strictly to his economic blockade of Britain (see below). It was contrary to the economic interests of their own subjects, and they sometimes surrounded themselves with ministers and advisers who were openly Francophobe and Anglophile. This was the case, for example, with Louis, who often went to take the waters, and who left in charge ministers who were interested in maintaining good commercial relations with Britain.[52]

## 'Breathing a Desire for Revenge'

The 'system' required Napoleon to maintain the Continent on a constant war footing against Britain. There was once again, however, the possibility of peace when, in January 1806, Pitt the Younger died, exhausted, gout ridden, possibly alcoholic, depressed by the fiasco that was the Third Coalition.[53] He left behind a country divided between those who wanted to continue the war and those who wanted peace. George III was obliged to offer the office of prime minister to Lord Grenville, and the foreign office to a man he detested, Charles James Fox. Along with Henry Addington, they formed a coalition that became known as the 'Ministry of All the Talents'.[54] In the face of the failure of the Third Coalition and the prospect of going it alone in what would have been an expensive and protracted war, the 'bloodhounds', as members of the war party referred to themselves, felt that they had little choice but to join the peace party and urge George III to come to terms with France.

In March 1806, therefore, Fox wrote to Talleyrand informing him that he had had a meeting with a man named Guillet de La Gevrillière, who had come to him admitting a plot to assassinate Napoleon. By English law they could not hold him, and he was writing to warn the French of a potential danger.[55] Talleyrand replied and saw this for what it was, a diplomatic opening. Several letters were exchanged between them and in April Talleyrand suggested that their plenipotentiaries meet at Lille to discuss the possibility of peace.[56] Talleyrand then was instrumental in initiating and pursuing peace negotiations with England in the winter of 1805–6. He brought Napoleon around to the idea little by little, and he kept the hope of a successful outcome burning by always promising more than he had the right to in his informal correspondence with the English representative. He acknowledged the principle of maintaining their respective conquests, gave London to understand that Napoleon would be agreeable to restoring the Electorate of Hanover, and promised that he would do everything so that Malta would remain an English possession (which was not exactly promising much at all as the island was already in English hands and they were hardly likely to give it up). We will pass over the rather strange negotiations that followed, which involved Lord Yarmouth, an unscrupulous rake who was probably in Talleyrand's pocket, and any discussion about whether Napoleon took the negotiations seriously.[57] The peace negotiations with Britain are of interest only for what follows, namely, war with Prussia.

The outbreak of war between France and Prussia in 1806 was the result of years of mistrust. When Prussia withdrew from the First Coalition in 1795, it created a zone of neutrality in the north of Germany that comprised other states, including Hanover and Saxony, as well as the Hanseatic cities Hamburg, Lübeck and Bremen. But the neutrality zone was essentially hollow. Caught between two powerful states – France in the west and Russia in the east – the Prussian king had limited room for manoeuvre, and Frederick William III had neither the political will nor the military nous to impose himself on northern Germany.[58] Instead, he let Napoleon trample over Prussia's neutrality on a number of occasions. In May 1803, Bonaparte ordered French troops to occupy the Electorate of Hanover. In October 1804, French troops kidnapped the British envoy to Hamburg, Sir George Rumbold, resulting in a storm of protest from Berlin (Rumbold was accredited to the court of Berlin).[59] The protests must have made an impact on Napoleon because he released Rumbold; it was possibly the only time that he publicly backed down, although this was not much. What he had really been after were the papers in Rumbold's possession, convinced as he was that the British ambassador was involved in some sort of spy ring. It was nonsense, but coming after the Cadoudal plot this episode was an indication of the depth of Napoleon's paranoia regarding the British.

A more serious violation of Prussian neutrality occurred in October 1805, when Napoleon ordered Marshal Bernadotte and his troops to march through the Prussian territory of Ansbach and Bayreuth on their way south to join up with forces in Bavaria.[60] Just what he was thinking by ordering French troops through Prussian territory at a time when he had a special envoy in Berlin trying to coax their king into an alliance with France is difficult to say. The official explanation offered to Frederick William – that France had crossed Prussian territory before, during the revolutionary wars, and believed it could do so again – may be as straightforward an explanation for Napoleon's arrogant behaviour as one can find.[61] As a result of the violation, public sentiment against France reached new heights. One young French officer sent to Berlin with dispatches noted how people he once knew no longer spoke to him, and how officers of the Prussian Noble Guard, in a public display of warlike contempt, whetted their swords on the steps of the French embassy.[62] It was a wonderfully melodramatic gesture, born of a conceit that could no longer be justified. Prussia had soundly defeated France during the Seven Years' War, had occupied Holland in the space of a few weeks in 1787, and during the War of the First Coalition had held its own against the French. But the gesture belies the divisions that existed within the army about the advisability of going to war. The Prussian army was about to discover that it was no longer a match for Napoleon.

Frederick William, normally reserved and even timid, was furious when news of the violation reached Berlin. He signed a secret alliance with Russia (the Treaty of Potsdam), and sent his foreign minister, Count Christian von Haugwitz, to deliver an ultimatum to Napoleon. However, by the time Haugwitz caught up with Napoleon at Schönbrunn outside Vienna, the situation had radically changed: Napoleon had defeated the allies at Austerlitz.[63] Faced with an irate Napoleon, and knowing that Austria was negotiating a separate peace, the Prussian envoy signed a treaty of alliance with France on 15 December 1805 that obliged his country to occupy the Electorate of Hanover – the possession of the King of England – and to close the North Sea ports to British goods. Prussia thus went from being a member of the coalition and an enemy of France to becoming an ally of Napoleon nominally at war with Britain.[64] The volte-face was not without controversy in high political circles in Berlin, but as one prominent Prussian personality put it, 'France is all-powerful and Napoleon is the man of the century; what have we to fear if united with him?'[65]

A lot, as it turned out. The strange series of events was no doubt one of the reasons why Frederick William overreacted when rumours of Napoleon handing back Hanover to Britain reached Berlin; they pushed the Prussian elite over the edge. The real issue was Napoleon's continued interference in northern Germany. For Berlin, this was intolerable; it represented a mortal threat to the very existence of Prussia as a great power. Napoleon therefore had to be resisted at all costs. In the months of June and July 1806 Frederick William and his cabinet decided on war with France.[66] It was a bold if not foolhardy move considering that Prussia was almost alone. Almost, but not quite. Feelers had been put out to Russia to join Prussia in the coming struggle. Alexander, who had all this time been negotiating with France, went to Berlin in November 1805, and was received with more than usual pomp by a Frederick William desperate to impress.[67] He went so far as to rebaptize St George Square, east of the city, Alexanderplatz. A treaty was signed between Russia and Prussia that committed Russian troops to a new, fourth coalition against France. The problem was timing. Prussia was keen to launch an offensive against France as soon as possible and did not wait for Russian troops to arrive. The Prussians did so in part because they no more trusted their Russian allies than they did their French foe, and in part because they needed to show their allies they were determined.[68]

In September 1806, when Napoleon heard that Prussia was mobilizing against him, he could hardly believe it. By then, Prussia was the only Eastern great power against which he had not tested his mettle. It was also one he mistrusted: he had not forgotten its rapprochement with the allies in the spring of 1805. 'The memory of the harm the Prussian armies . . . could have done . . . is still alive, festering, breathing a desire for revenge.'[69] It is perhaps why, consciously or otherwise, he set about provoking Prussia into a showdown.

Napoleon in all of this, as was his wont, saw himself not as aggressor but as victim. While he had done just about everything in his power to antagonize both Russia and Britain, and had precipitated a conflict with Prussia, he was still able to write to Talleyrand to say, 'I have no interest in disturbing the peace on the Continent.'[70] He had the impression that he was alone, and that there was no possibility of an 'alliance with any great European power'. What he referred to as his 'system of peace' was in effect a system of conquest and occupation.[71] True, there was little or no chance of coming to any agreement with Prussia. His attitude towards Berlin was dictated by what he considered to be its despicable behaviour on the international scene, behaviour that was not worthy of the country of Frederick the Great.[72]

Avenging Rossbach

Countries sometimes go to war expecting to lose, and do so because fighting and losing is better than not fighting at all.[73] Frederick William's decision to go to war could not have come at a worse time. Austria was still reeling from its defeat the previous year and it was probably not averse to seeing Prussia take a hiding from Napoleon; Pitt had died and the new government in London had entered into tentative negotiations with France; Britain and Sweden had declared war against Prussia, and Britain was not in any case prepared to consider Prussia's demands for money until it had withdrawn from Hanover, something that would have placed Prussia in a strategically weakened position; while the Confederation of the Rhine enabled Napoleon to dispose of even more troops.[74] On top of all that there was the strategic blunder represented by the Prussian ultimatum at this particular point in time. It was bad enough that the Russians were still far away and would take months to march enough troops into the field of operations, but Prussia had acted too soon. French troops were still stationed in the south of Germany from the campaign the previous year. Declaring war while the French were still in Germany enabled Napoleon quickly to launch an offensive, to march directly north, to pass the Prussian army and then to turn west against it, pushing it ever further away from Berlin and potential Russian reinforcements.[75]

Charles William Ferdinand, Duke of Brunswick, against his own better judgement, reluctantly took on the role of Prussia's commander-in-chief, and yet his own state remained neutral. This was the man who had lost the battle of Valmy in 1792, a defeat admittedly inflicted by a larger French army, but his reputation, despite his advanced age – he was seventy-one – remained intact. Brunswick was typical of the Prussian officer corps; of its 142 generals, half were over sixty, thirteen over seventy, and another four over eighty.[76] In this particular instance, as we shall see, youth and energy were going to run rings around old age and experience. According to one Prussian officer, Friedrich von Müffling, Brunswick took over in order to avoid war.[77] Apart from Gebhard Leberecht von Blücher, none of the Prussian generals, who correctly assessed the comparative strengths of the Prussian and French armies, were terribly confident of victory.[78] The king was so pessimistic that he predicted a catastrophe that would make people forget Austerlitz.[79] Despite this, the political elite in Berlin made the decision to go to war, or rather, once the decision had been made it was difficult to back down.

If the Prussian high command was racked with self-doubt, the troops were confident of success. They should not have been. They had not fought a war in over ten years. Moreover, there were two very different conceptions about how to wage war. Napoleon set out to achieve a decisive blow, concentrating all his troops in the process; the Prussians on the other hand prepared for a war of 'moderate intensity' and did not therefore see the necessity of concentrating forces quickly or in one place.[80] In a mirror image of Valmy at the beginning of the revolutionary wars, the French army was going to interpose itself between the Prussian army and Berlin so that their fronts were reversed.

Napoleon left Saint-Cloud on 25 September 1806 and reached Bamberg on 6 October, Kronach on the 8th. He often travelled at night in order to avoid the congestion on the roads, caused by his own troops. He rode into Jena on the afternoon of 13 October, past French units that were already looting the town.[81] There was little he could do. The German philosopher Georg Hegel was living in Jena at the time, putting the finishing touches to his *Phenomenology of Spirit*. He saw Napoleon ride out of town later in the afternoon to inspect the French positions, and described him as the 'soul of the world' (*Weltseele*). 'It is truly a remarkable sensation to see such an individual on horseback, raising his arm over the world and ruling it . . . It is only from heaven, that is, from the will of the French Emperor, that matters can be set in motion.'[82] This was Napoleon as autonomous force, as world force, as wave of destiny that swept all before him, supremely confident on the eve of battle. He sent off a letter to Talleyrand asserting that everything, everything had gone according to plan, and that 'interesting things' would happen in two or three days.[83] He was convinced the Prussians did not stand a chance and that their generals were imbeciles. In fact, he was mistaken in one respect; he did not find himself confronting the main Prussian army, but rather a secondary army under Prince Hohenlohe.

When Napoleon gave the order to attack at about five o'clock on the morning of 14 October, a thick layer of fog masked the landscape so that visibility, at least for a few hours, was limited to about ten paces.[84] As the sun rose, however, it turned into a clear, beautiful autumn day. The Comte de Chamans was woken from a bad sleep by the sound of cannon; he and his corps marched through a forest that had hidden them the previous day and soon engaged with the Prussians on the left flank.[85] Despite his belief that he was engaging the main Prussian army, Napoleon was facing Hohenlohe's corps of about 40,000 against whom he could bring 55,600 men, with another 40,000 troops expected during the course of the day. Hohenlohe should have fought a rearguard action, trying to join up with the bulk of the Prussian forces further north. Instead, he counter-attacked, taking the village of Jena, and then just stood there in open formation as the French skirmishers and artillery weighed into his hapless troops. Hohenlohe was expecting reinforcements from General Rüchel, about ten kilometres away. Rüchel was of the old school; it took him five hours to get his men to travel that distance, marching them in step and in line as though they were on a parade ground instead of hurrying to the scene of the battle. By the time he got there, it was too late.

It was Davout who ran into the bulk of the Prussian forces east of the town of Auerstädt in what has been described as one of the most extraordinary feats of the Napoleonic wars.[86] Approximately 27,000 French troops and 44 cannon faced 63,000 Prussians supported by 230 guns.[87] Things went very badly very quickly for the Prussians. Their commander, the Duke of Brunswick, was shot in the eye early in the battle and later died, Marshal von Möllendorf, a senior military adviser, was captured, Prince Henry mortally wounded, and Prince William seriously wounded. When informed that Brunswick had been wounded, Frederick William took over as commander, but he was soon out of his depth. By noon, his troops were caught in a murderous crossfire from the French who occupied high ground on both flanks. Later than afternoon, the king broke off the battle – even before news had come in of what was taking place to the south, at Jena – though he still possessed strong reserves. The retreat towards Weimar that evening took place in good order until they came across the fleeing army of Hohenlohe. Only then did chaos take over the main army, made worse by the large number of camp followers who blocked the roads and inhibited an orderly retreat.[88] A better-integrated, better-led French army defeated a poorly integrated, poorly led Prussian army. It would be years before the Prussians fully learnt the lessons of defeat.

Davout should have been supported by Bernadotte, who commanded a corps of 20,000 men; he was near by and heard the sound of the guns. Bernadotte had, moreover, received orders from Berthier that morning to join Davout. He simply chose to ignore them, as well as Davout's repeated pleas for assistance.[89] Instead, he followed to the letter Napoleon's earlier orders to join him at Apolda, although he was so slow in getting there that it took him all day to cover the twelve kilometres that separated them. He did not reach Jena until after the battle was over.[90] Why Bernadotte was not severely punished, as the army expected, is difficult to say.[91] Napoleon later admitted that he had signed an order for Bernadotte's court martial but that he later tore it up.[92] Was he thinking of his first love, Désirée, now the marshal's wife, or did he believe that Bernadotte would try to atone for his conduct by recognizing that he had performed disgracefully?[93] If so, he appears to have judged the man well; Bernadotte ruthlessly pursued the retreating Prussians over the coming weeks.

Napoleon did not find out what had happened until later in the evening when he got back to Jena. Waiting in front of an inn where he planned to spend the night was an officer from Davout's staff who explained that Davout had fought and defeated the main body of the Prussian army forty kilometres away at Auerstädt. Napoleon at first refused to believe it but soon had to face the reality of the situation, paying tribute to Davout in the next day's bulletin.[94] But that was all the praise Davout was to receive. As had happened in the past – think of Moreau and Hohenlinden – Davout's victory was completely sidelined. In contemporary reports, the two separate battles were reduced to one – Jena – with Auerstädt becoming the right wing of a larger battle. Indeed, from his very first bulletin, Napoleon only ever spoke of Jena.[95] Even at the height of his power, he was jealous of others' successes and, despite getting on well with Davout, was not about to let one of his lieutenants outshine him. This is not to say that he did not richly reward Davout for his services – he was later made Duc d'Auerstaedt – but his praise remained private.[96] Auerstädt was never to play a large role in the regime's propaganda and was more or less forgotten (there is no Pont d'Auerstädt in Paris, there is no monument of any kind, and no paintings were commissioned). As we shall see, the defeat of Prussia was to be represented in different ways.

A few days later, on 18 October, on his way to Berlin, Napoleon stopped to visit the nearby battlefield of Rossbach. Rossbach was a defeat inflicted on the French by Prussia in November 1757 during the Seven Years' War, and it had profoundly marked French popular memory to the point that there were constant calls throughout the second half of the eighteenth century to have the blight washed away. That Napoleon was finally able to do this was a considerable achievement; he ordered that the memorial to the Prussian victory be dismantled and transported back to Paris.[97] This too was a deliberate attempt on his part to draw a comparison between himself and Frederick the Great, and was to become a prominent theme in Napoleonic propaganda over the coming years.[98]

Pierre Antoine Vafflard, *L'Armée française renverse la colonne commémorative de Rossbach, le 18 octobre 1806* (The French army topples the commemorative column of Rossbach, 18 October 1806), Salon of 1810.

## A Triumphant Napoleon . . .

About ten days after the collapse of the Prussian army, on 24 October 1806, the French made their entry into Berlin.[99] Napoleon arrived three days later – he gave Davout the honour of leading his corps through the city first – on a glorious autumn day, church bells ringing, guns resounding, receiving the keys of the city from Prince Hatzfeld (arrested shortly afterwards for spying). Unlike his treatment of Vienna after the victory of Austerlitz, Napoleon made a point of making a triumphal entry into Berlin, underlining Prussia's defeat with a humiliating military parade through the Brandenburg Gate (on top of which was the Quadriga – a set of bronze statues of four horses representing peace – but not for much longer), and riding down Unter den Linden.[100] It was about three in the afternoon; a large crowd – 'the whole population of Berlin', according to one witness[101] – drawn by a mixture of sorrow, admiration and curiosity, had turned out to see the successor of Frederick the Great, looking a little heavier than he had just a few years before.[102] The humiliation was made worse by the fact that only a week

Charles Meynier, *Entrée de Napoléon Ier entouré de son Etat major dans Berlin, 27 octobre 1806, il passe par la porte de Brandebourg* (Entry of Napoleon I into Berlin surrounded by his chiefs of staff, 27 October 1806, he passes by the Brandenburg Gate), 1810. The citizens of Berlin are portrayed greeting Napoleon with an enthusiasm that is belied by contemporary reports that depict a mournful crowd.[103]

previously a rumour had reached Berlin that Napoleon had been destroyed at Jena. The city was rudely brought back to reality.

Berlin was considered one of the most beautiful European cities of its day, with the old quarter, Friedrichstadt, made up of large streets lined with beautiful houses and imposing buildings, including the royal palace.[104] The town was also renowned for the Tiergarten where even during the week the inhabitants gathered, especially in the cafés that surrounded the park. One could find women drinking coffee and working on their needlepoint, and men drinking beer and smoking pipes. The population of Berlin had tripled over the past hundred years, with more than 150,000 inhabitants when it was occupied by the French. At the time, Berlin was a mixture of old and new, the new being the private residences one could find along the Friedrichstrasse and Unter den Linden, most of which were built under Frederick the Great, while the old quarters were overcrowded and dirty. A constant complaint of visitors was the smell emanating from the stagnant waters of the streams and fouling the new quarters.[105] When the French arrived, however, the streets were deserted, at least according to some accounts.[106] Thousands had fled the enemy's arrival at the signal given by the court, which decamped to Memel, then no more than a small seaport on the Baltic near the Russian border on the outer limits of the kingdom.

At Potsdam, where Napoleon spent several days, he went to visit the tomb of Frederick the Great, in the Garnison Kirche.[107] According to witnesses, Napoleon stood before it, silent, alone with a select few from his entourage, in contemplation for about ten minutes.[108] The imperial propaganda machine made much of this scene. Images of Napoleon deep in thought before the tomb were produced in the months and years that followed. It was both a mark of respect for Frederick as general and sovereign and a means of enhancing Napoleon's own reputation by obliging people to compare him to Frederick, one of the greatest generals of the eighteenth century. This is how Napoleon preferred to portray his defeat of Prussia, by capturing the moment he stood before Frederick's tomb. It is a moment that says two things: that Prussia's former

Marie Nicolas Ponce-Camus, *Napoléon Ier méditant devant le cercueil de Frédéric II de Prusse dans la crypte de la Garnisonskirche de Potsdam, 25 octobre 1806* (Napoleon I meditating before the tomb of Frederick II of Prussia in the crypt of the Garnison Kirche in Potsdam, 25 October 1806), 1808. The painting was meant to portray Napoleon in marked contrast with the portraits of the kings of Europe, simple in his dress, which made him the son of the Revolution.

greatness was dependent on one man, just as France's present glory was dependent on Napoleon; and that Napoleon was the more brilliant of the two.[109]


## ... Encounters an Obdurate Frederick William

At the beginning of the campaign against Prussia there were signs that public opinion in France was tiring of the incessant wars.[110] Napoleon had, after all, promised peace. If Austerlitz was greeted with muted enthusiasm, news of Jena received an even cooler reception.[111] The authorities did not even bother organizing a public celebration for the victory at Jena-Auerstädt. Napoleon had to instruct the prefect of the Seine, Frochot, to 'facilitate the explosion of enthusiasm'.[112] Police reports made it plain that, in some centres at least, the populace was sick of the war, and this before any military defeats or reverses had taken the shine off Napoleon's aura. Some believed the victory over Prussia would serve only to make the Emperor ever more intractable and that peace would be postponed even further. One officer later argued that after the Prussian campaign educated officers in the army realized that Napoleon's promises were empty and that they no longer fought for peace but to satisfy his unbounded ambition.[113] This individual may have been writing with hindsight, but there is enough to indicate that people were becoming wary of what they saw as Napoleon's expansionist designs.

Just how widespread this feeling may have been is impossible to judge, and in any event usually consisted of little more than disgruntled individuals venting their frustrations.[114] It is, however, possibly one of the reasons why the Senate sent a delegation to Berlin in November 1806 to petition Napoleon not to continue the war in the east, urging him to make peace.[115] Napoleon's response was to present the delegation with Frederick the Great's sword, which he reportedly said he would rather have than twenty million francs. Napoleon did not tell anyone that he intended taking the sword, along with a few other decorative objects; he simply took them and had them transferred to the Invalides in Paris.[116] If it was his way of allaying any fears the Senate might have had, it was an odd way of doing so.[117]

Much was made of the transfer of Frederick's sword to the chapel of the Hôtel des Invalides in May 1807.[118] It was then a retirement home for invalid veterans, about 900 of whom had fought during the Seven Years' War; Napoleon dedicated the sword to them.[119] Present too were the members of the Senate, the Tribunate, the Legislative Corps and the Council of State, as well as a number of military officials. After the coronation, and the marriage with the Emperor Francis's daughter Marie-Louise some years later, it is considered to have been the biggest ceremony in Napoleonic France.[120] Napoleon himself was away fighting in the east, but his empty throne was the centrepiece of the decorations and was there to remind everyone that the ceremony was really about him. In effect, what was meant to be a celebration of the soldiers of the Grande Armée, as well as veterans of the Seven Years' War, was about Napoleon's innate genius. Like Frederick the Great, Napoleon had succeeded in creating a powerful country – Frederick out of nothing, Napoleon out of a country in chaos.[121]

The celebrations culminated in a selection of paintings taken from the royal collection in Berlin exhibited at the Musée Napoleon (what is now the Louvre).[122] As with the French occupation of northern Italy in the late 1790s, so too the French occupation of northern Germany in 1806 and 1807 was accompanied by a systematic plundering of the private collections of the German princes.[123] Between 1806 and 1807, the French absconded with a number of important artworks – 50 statues, 80 busts, 193 bronze objects, 32 drawings and 367 paintings, including some by Rembrandt, Raphael, Titian and Van Dyck, not to mention a number of rare manuscripts and books.

Peace was not going to come right away, although that it did not do so was not entirely Napoleon's fault. He stayed in Berlin for one month (from 28 October to 24 November), offering Frederick William peace terms that, under the circumstances, were not unreasonable. Prussia was 'only' to give up its territories west of the Elbe. Frederick William, unwisely as it turned out, refused. Faced with the option of continuing the struggle or concluding peace, he wanted to continue the struggle, hoping that the Russians would help turn the military situation around. At a council held on 21 November 1806, he decided to fight on. The decision has been described as 'one of the great turning points in the history of the Prussian monarchy'.[124]

Frederick William III suffered from what contemporaries referred to as 'melancholia'. In other words, he was a depressive, a condition probably made worse by the fact that he was steeped in the Prussian Pietist tradition, an evangelical religious movement, a German form of ascetic Protestantism that incited its members to lead vigorously Christian, pious lives.[125] It also meant he was more likely to dwell on his own personal failings. Combined with a hesitant nature, this did not make for a good prince in time of war. Nevertheless, faced with limited options, Frederick William did not capitulate; before the arrival of the French, he fled his capital to the easternmost corner of his kingdom, along with the state treasure, saved in the nick of time.[126]

Frederick William was prepared to hold out, but this was not the case for his army. Napoleon's forces were in an extremely strong position; they met little resistance as they advanced east across Prussia, one fortress after another surrendering within the space of a few months, often without a struggle, and often when in a position to hold out, if only the will to do so were present. The Prussian army capitulated, ignominiously for some, realistically for others. One explanation for its total disintegration was the collapse of morale, similar to the defeat of the French army in the face of the German invasion in 1940. In part, this may have been due to the quality of the Prussian officer corps.[127] A declaration by the king that any commander who surrendered for no good reason would be 'shot without mercy' made little impact.[128] In the face of the resounding defeat, and the overwhelming impression that the army was in no condition to launch a counter-attack, there seemed little strategic point in holding out.

By the middle of autumn, 96 per cent of the Prussian army had been taken prisoner by the French. More than 140,000 troops and over 2,000 cannon were captured. In some places, Stettin for example, a garrison of 5,000 men, with ample supplies, surrendered to 800 French troops. Erfurt with a garrison of 12,000 troops did not make a stand; the city negotiated its surrender the very same day the French arrived before its gates. Küstrin surrendered only days after the Prussian king had left the town on his voyage eastwards.[129] When Marshal Ney turned up in front of Magdeburg, the city's commander, Franz Kasimir von Kleist, had little choice but to surrender in the face of overwhelming pressure from its inhabitants.[130] Others held out longer, partly in the expectation that the Russian alliance would inevitably come good, and partly because it took so long for the French to transport siege material. The siege of Neiss in Silesia is a case in point. General Vandamme encircled the town at the end of February 1807; the siege was broken off for a while in March and was then resumed with the arrival of siege guns in the middle of April. However, the governor of Neiss refused to surrender until an armistice was signed at the end of May 1807, allowing him to hand over the fort in the middle of June, if the Russians did not arrive before then.[131] Breslau held out almost three months. Kolberg on the Baltic coast, under the command of Major August Neidhardt von Gneisenau, who would become one of the key figures of the Prussian reform movement, surrendered in July 1807. Kolberg was not the only fortress to hold out for any length of time, but it was transformed into a struggle that would later take on mythic proportions, made much of by the Nazis in the last stages of the Second World War.[132] The subjugation of Silesia, it has to be said, took eight months, from October 1806 to July 1807.

After dealing with the Prussian army, Napoleon still had to contend with two Russian armies lumbering their way westwards. One, under Levin August von Bennigsen, consisted of about 64,000 men, and entered Poland at the beginning of November 1806. The other, under Friedrich von Buxhöwden, was made up of about 46,000 men. Napoleon could muster about 80,000 men, although many more had been called up and were on their way.

Before setting off, Napoleon attempted to bring the war to Britain by issuing what was referred to as the Berlin Decree (and later, in November 1807, in the Milan Decree). These decrees extended the trade war throughout Europe by prohibiting the import of any British goods into the Continent, and the confiscation of any vessels (neutral or otherwise) that so much as put into a British port. Since Napoleon could not engage with Britain directly, he was attempting to cripple its economy, something he regarded as a 'mathematical certainty', by creating an economic cordon around Europe that excluded Britain, what became known as the Continental System.[133] Thousands of customs men would be posted all along the coasts and rivers of Europe in an effort to keep out British goods. It was an impossible task – smuggling became rife – but it marked a turning point in Napoleon's imperial expansion as he extended it across northern and southern Europe in the pursuit of victory against Britain, but ultimately at the expense of his own Empire.[134] The British responded by imposing a counter-blockade of Europe (the Orders in Council in 1807) – the 'Continental Blockade' – enforced by the Royal Navy. Napoleon's economic cordon would eventually become the cornerstone of his system, one that, when it crumbled, would help bring the whole edifice crashing down.

That was some years away yet. Napoleon was necessarily oblivious to what was to come, confident that he could deal with the Russians, and with what was left of the Prussian army. He left Berlin on 25 November, and entered Warsaw on the night of 19 December 1806, somewhat discreetly under the circumstances. The preparations made to receive him in the city – he was meant to drive through a triumphal arch on which was inscribed 'Long Live Napoleon, the Saviour of Poland. He was Sent to us Straight from Heaven' – were frustrated by his late arrival.[135] Four days later was the start of what is referred to as the Polish campaign. A couple of smaller battles were fought in pursuit of the Russians – at Pułtusk the day after Christmas in 1806 and again at Gołymin twenty kilometres further north on the same day – but the main Russian army continued to elude the French and to withdraw further east.

## Walewska

While the troops were, for the most part, lodged in the countryside, headquarters were in Warsaw, and the French, by all accounts, had a delightful time of it. 'With the exception of theatres,' wrote Savary, 'the city presented all the gaieties of Paris.'[136] Warsaw, with a population of around 85,000 people (about 18 per cent were Jewish), was situated on a huge plain on the Vistula, with an imposing castle that was once the residence of the kings of Poland.[137] According to the legend, it was here, on New Year's Day 1807, at an inn near Błonie, that Napoleon first laid eyes on Maria Walewska. She approached Napoleon's marshal of the palace, Michel Duroc, and asked to be presented to him in the street. She obviously made an impression on the Emperor, exciting him no doubt with the prospect of an easy conquest. Duroc, who often played the palace pimp, was afterwards sent to look for her, but was unsuccessful. So too was the chief of the Warsaw police, a man by the name of Bielinski. It was Prince Joseph Poniatowski, governor of Warsaw, who identified her.

So much for the legend. Everything about their first meeting remains obscure, including where and when it may have taken place. They may have met at Błonie, but then it would have been 18 December 1806; Duroc was not by Napoleon's side, he had been wounded the preceding day; Napoleon was probably not, as is often asserted, riding in a carriage but on horseback, as the mud was too thick for a carriage. An alternative version is that Murat, or possibly Talleyrand, was sent to find Napoleon a woman for the night, a Polish conquest of sorts.[138] We do know that Maria and Napoleon met (again) on the night of 17 January during a ball given by Talleyrand. Napoleon must have been smitten; he sent numerous invitations for her to visit him at the royal palace, which she just as persistently refused, until others, Polish patriots, interceded. As for Walewska, from an old noble family, married off at the age of eighteen to a man fifty years her senior, Athanasius Colonna-Walewski, she was persuaded to seduce Napoleon, or at least approach him, by Polish patriots who hoped that she would then be able to influence him to restore Poland. That, in any event, is the way she preferred to present things in her memoirs.[139]

However they may have met, the outcome is better known; Napoleon decided to have an affair with Maria. It was not the first time he had dallied with other women, but despite his discretion – apart from a few people in his entourage, the public remained unaware of his liaison with Maria until the publication of the memoirs of his valet, Constant, in 1830 – Josephine must have suspected something. She wrote to him repeatedly asking for permission to join him in Warsaw. Napoleon fobbed her off with excuses – she was needed in Paris, the roads were bad, the weather was terrible, the distances too great – but the more he did so the more suspicious she became, no doubt aware that the end of their relationship was close.[140] At one point he even declared how humiliated he was to think that his wife did not trust him. He forbade her to cry any more; 'it is very ugly'.[141] At Josephine's hints that he was having an affair, Napoleon's responses were a mixture of feigned surprise – 'I don't know what you mean by ladies'; hypocrisy – 'I love only my little Josephine, good, sulky and capricious'; and condescending reproach – 'she is ever lovable, apart from the times when she is jealous'.[142] The tenderness he felt for Josephine was still there – when on campaign he often reproved her for not writing enough while he wrote two or three times a week – but the passion was definitively gone.[143] If Napoleon's letters to Josephine were reserved, this was not the case for the little notes that he was passing to Maria. 'I see only you, I admire only you, I want only you.' Or again, 'Oh, come! come! All your hopes will be fulfilled,' he promised.[144] 'Whenever I have thought a thing impossible or difficult to obtain, I have desired it all the more.' It said as much about his attitude towards women as about his desire to get his way in all things. But now, as Emperor, propriety was thrown to the wind.

Maria was hardly in a position to resist. When she finally went to him he may very well have forced himself upon her. His valet talks of a woman 'overcome by events', who constantly cried, and who left about two in the morning (still crying).[145] But she returned, several times, whether out of duty, fear or misguided love, and spent a few weeks with him at the Finckenstein Palace, living together as husband and wife (he called her his 'wife'). Between 1 April and 6 June, when he finally took the field again in pursuit of the Russians, Napoleon virtually transferred the centre of power to the palace. He was in love, and in love there was a newfound energy the likes of which he had not seen in years. In the two months he was at Finckenstein, from the beginning of April till the end of May 1807, he dictated and wrote something like 775 letters on everything from the reorganization of the army to the Opera in Paris, the education of young girls and the creation of a chair in history at the College of France.[146]

François Pascal Simon, Baron Gérard, *Marie Laczinska (1786–1817), comtesse Waleska, puis comtesse d'Ornano* (Maria Laczinska (1786–1817), Countess Walewska, then Countess Ornano), 1810.

# 12

# Zenith

## The Great Debacle

Morale in the army was not good. During the campaign in Poland, the French had to face three enemies: the mud, the cold and the Russians. The joy they felt at having conquered Prussia in less than two months soon gave way to despondency at having to pursue the enemy into a country that could not adequately supply them, where the roads were bad or consisted of dirt tracks that turned to mud when it rained. Conditions on the road to Pułtusk were so bad, wrote Captain Coignet, that 'We were obliged to tie our shoes around our ankles with cord, and when we pulled our legs out of the soft sand, our shoes would stick in the wet mud. Sometimes we had to take hold of one leg, pull it out like a carrot, lift it forwards, and then go back for the other, take hold of it with both hands, and make it take a step forwards also . . . the older men began to lose heart; some of them committed suicide rather than face such privations any longer.'[1]

The country was so poor that, unable to loot, soldiers were reduced to begging for small sums of money – the men had not been paid in months – and articles of clothing.[2] The troops were living like refugees rather than conquerors, and the further east they went the worse it got. The lack of supplies led to an incredible breakdown in discipline the likes of which had not been seen since the worst days of the revolutionary wars. Sergeant Lavaux complained that the troops had not eaten anything other than potatoes for three weeks, with the result that many came down with diarrhoea and were incapable of walking more than a couple of kilometres without rest.[3] The troops were unhappy with Napoleon for continuing the war, especially in such harsh conditions – it was during this period that the term *grognard* (grumbler) was coined to describe the Old Guard – and they were not afraid to show it. Some questioned why they were fighting there at all. 'That we fight in and for a good country, well and good, but the blood that has flowed to ensure the possession of such a kingdom, which I would not want for anything, is pointless.'[4] Eventually, Napoleon decided to abandon the pursuit and to take winter quarters north of Warsaw.

The Poles greeted the French as liberators. Their country had been partitioned out of existence in 1795 between the three eastern European powers (Austria, Russia and Prussia), and the Prussians, who had claimed the land around Warsaw, had practised a policy of cultural assimilation; everything had to be done in German. So when the Prussians were defeated at Jena, and news of the French approach reached Warsaw, the city's youth filled the restaurants to clink glasses, sing patriotic songs and shout for their liberators and brothers.[5] The retreating Prussians were hooted out of the city. When the French arrived, on 21 November 1806, the city was illuminated, tables were laid out in the streets and squares to celebrate, and the people of Warsaw supposedly vied with each other to house the troops.

Napoleon had meant to stay put all winter, spending his time in Warsaw encouraging Russia's traditional enemies, the Porte and the Shah of Persia, to open secondary fronts.[6] But fighting broke out in north Poland that soon had troops on both sides mobilized and heading towards what looked like a major clash. Napoleon used the fighting as a pretext to try and deliver a knockout blow to the Russians around the village of Jonkendorf (present-day Jonkowo). However, the Russian commander, Bennigsen, learnt of Napoleon's plans through dispatches captured by Cossacks and managed to avoid the trap that was being set. A short battle was fought on 3 February 1807 at Jonkendorf, but the French took time to get everything into place. It was not till three in the afternoon that the cannonade started in earnest; by four or five o'clock it was already dark. It meant the action had to be broken off for the night. However, as day broke the next day, it revealed an empty field; Bennigsen had retreated north towards Landsberg.

The French went in pursuit. They caught up with Bennigsen eighty kilometres to the north, on the evening of 5 February, near a small town called Preussisch-Eylau. There Bennigsen turned and faced the French. It took another two days for the French forces to gather, the first substantial body of troops not arriving till the early afternoon of 7 February.[7] Fighting took place in the streets of the town that same day, although there does not appear to have been a plan by Napoleon to seize the town before nightfall, and what started as a skirmish escalated into heavy fighting.[8] By the beginning of the next day, between 63,000 and 90,000 French troops were lined up against 60,000–90,000 Russians.[9] If those figures are uncertain, what is not is that the Russians considerably outgunned the French – 460 Russian against 200 French cannon. At Eylau, Napoleon witnessed the devastating impact massed Russian guns could have. The Russian army traditionally carried more cannon than any other European army, and used them in support of its troops to deadly effect. At this particular battle, the Russian army had six cannon to every 1,000 men. The French in contrast had two cannon for the same number.[10] Napoleon would attempt to increase that ratio over the next few years to five in 1,000, but he never succeeded in getting much more than half that of the Russian army.[11] After Eylau, he changed tactics and almost invariably undertook a massed artillery assault before launching an infantry attack.[12]

The battle that followed on that overcast, cold winter's day, some of it conducted in the thick of a snowstorm, was a scene of butchery. At one point,

Augereau's advancing troops came under fire from both Russian and French guns; of the 1,500 men in his corps, 1,200 were killed and 300 were wounded. One can still walk over the fields where they were slaughtered, about 700 metres east of the town cemetery. The battle itself was complete chaos, littered with mistakes, misunderstandings and close calls. By mid-morning, the situation had deteriorated badly for Napoleon. The Russians had gained the upper hand and it looked as though they would pierce the French centre and drive them off. Russian troops stormed into Eylau and came close to taking Napoleon, who was using the church steeple as a lookout. It was only because his personal escort sacrificed itself that Napoleon was not killed or captured. He was saved at two other decisive moments in the battle, first by Murat whose cavalry charge into the Russian centre forced them to retreat, and again later in the day by Ney, who did not reach the battlefield until seven in the evening. By ten o'clock that night, after fourteen hours of battle, fighting came to a standstill. After a rowdy council of war, Bennigsen decided to withdraw during the night. The story goes, undoubtedly apocryphal, that as Napoleon prepared to pull back, Davout put his ear to the ground and heard the sounds of the Russian retreat.[13]

Pierre-François Percy, the chief surgeon in Napoleon's army, lamented after the battle that 'everywhere, you saw corpses and dead horses. Carriages passed over them. The artillery chopped them up and crushed their skulls and limbs.'[14] On the second day of the battle Percy rode around and later described what he saw: 'Never had such a small space been covered with so many bodies. The snow was stained everywhere by blood . . . The noise of the artillery, the smoke from the fires, the smell of powder, the cries of the wounded being operated on, all that I saw and heard will never leave my memory.' The next morning the Comte de Saint-Chamans went to find Napoleon to deliver a message from Soult. He found him in a 'kind of little farm' in the village of Eylau, lying fully dressed on a mattress in the corner next to a stove. He looked tired, worried and demoralized. When Saint-Chamans delivered Soult's message, that the Russians had retreated, Napoleon's physiognomy changed completely; his face became radiant.[15]

'Quel massacre,' Ney is supposed to have remarked, 'and for nothing.'[16] Later that morning (9 February), Napoleon toured the battlefield, unshaven and still covered in mud. It is a moment that has gone down in Napoleonic legend, when he was touched if not shocked by what he saw, an episode memorialized by the painting by Gros. Some veterans describe Napoleon as being 'broken hearted'; officers and soldiers whose limbs were being amputated cried out 'Vive l'Empereur' just before dying.[17] It seems improbable, although not impossible, so deep ran the affection of some of his troops. It was not, however, the sentiment of most of the survivors. If before Eylau they had grumbled, now they were in a mutinous mood. During a review of his troops,

Saint-Chamans recalled that 'Amid cries of "Vive l'Empereur!" I heard many soldiers shouting: "Long live Peace!" Others: "Long live Peace and France!", Others again shouted: "Bread and Peace!" This was the first time I saw the morale of the French army a little shaken, but it had suffered so much only to arrive at the slaughter of Eylau that this could not be otherwise.'[18] One regiment flew a black cloth in mourning for the dead rather than the imperial eagle. The army was in a grim mood. 'The fatigues of a winter campaign in a devastated country, the absolute lack of food and forage, the excessive cold, the active service demanded by the outposts had put men and horses on their knees. Every day our ranks were thinned.'[19] The expectation persisted. One of the Tsar's envoys, Lieutenant-General Prince Dimitrii Lobanov-Rostovsky, recounted that during the negotiations at Tilsit, Napoleon was greeted with shouts of 'Vive la Paix!' from the French troops.[20]

Eylau was the bloodiest battle fought in Europe up to that time. Losses on both sides were horrific. A conservative estimate puts the French losses at around 12,000 killed and wounded but goes as high as 30,000. The Russians lost anywhere between 12,000 and 15,000 men killed and as many wounded.[21] It is impossible to calculate the number of casualties because of the subsequent efforts on the part of the imperial authorities to hide the extent of the carnage. According to some estimates, French casualties at Eylau were greater than those at Austerlitz, Jena and Auerstädt combined.[22] And, uniquely in the annals of the Napoleonic wars, Napoleon himself remained on the battlefield for eight days in order to help bury the dead and look after the wounded.

The outcome of the battle could have gone either way, and for the French to have described it as a victory was nothing more than propaganda. Napoleon was contemplating a retreat when the Russians decided to move first. Those who had survived realized that the losses had been massive – how could they not? – and some at least wrote home, so that news of the scale of the carnage began to filter back to France, leaving Paris 'stupefied', in a state of desolation.[23] The potential consequences for Napoleon were serious. Eylau could undermine his reputation, and hence both his authority and his legitimacy.[24] He consequently attempted to counter the rumours about the butchery that had taken place.[25] Privately, he wrote to people in his entourage; publicly, he ordered Cambacérès to organize celebrations,[26] telling him to write up an account of 'one of the most memorable' battles of the war in the *Moniteur*, and asking others to 'spread the . . . news . . . in an unofficial way'.[27]

Napoleon's desire to hide the extent of the carnage is one of the key themes in his letters back to Paris during the weeks after the battle.[28] Since it was impossible to overcome the negative impression Eylau had left on public opinion, Cambacérès suggested an alternative approach – an account of the aftermath of the battle. Napoleon was thus to be presented to the public not as a victorious general, but as a man appalled by the losses. The official story was circulated throughout France via the famous 58th Bulletin of the Grande Armée, in which the French losses were reduced to 1,900 killed and 5,700 wounded, while 7,000 Russians were reported dead, although we can notice two words that had never appeared in a bulletin before that date (and that did not do so again) – 'horror' and 'massacre' – both used to describe the aftermath of battle.[29]

For the first time, the reader was being asked to imagine the result of a battle: nine or ten thousand bodies, four or five thousand dead horses, the debris of muskets, sabres, cannon balls, munitions and cannon next to which their gunners lay dead, and the whole scene depicted against a background of snow. Napoleon went one step further, personally dictating to General Henri-Gatien Bertrand a supposed eyewitness account of the battle attesting to the exploits of the French. His *Relation de la bataille d'Eylau par un témoin oculaire* (Account of the battle of Eylau by an eyewitness), presented as a translation from the German, was simultaneously published in Berlin and Paris.[30] In it, the battle was portrayed as a victory. Consequently, individual losses or acts of sacrifice were highlighted, such as the supposed last words of a dying officer, absurd and tasteless: 'I die happy since victory is ours, and I expire on the bed of honour.'[31]

It is with some justification that historians have seen in this nothing more than a cynical exercise in damage control, an attempt by Napoleon to displace concern over the French dead and wounded on to the enemy dead and wounded.[32] Before making a judgement, it is worth recalling that Napoleon was probably shocked by this loss of life, as was every other witness who wrote about it, either shortly afterwards or indeed many years later. In his memoirs, François-Frédéric Billon, assistant to the surgeon-in-chief Dominique Jean Larrey, left us with an account of Napoleon's visit to the battlefield: 'I was standing on a stone bench against the wall when he passed near me. The emperor was doing his best to prevent his horse trampling on so many human remains; unable to do so, he gave up the reins, and that is when I saw him cry.'[33]

Billon wrote up the account decades later. Did he really see Napoleon crying or was he simply reporting what he had read about this episode, thus playing into the hands of the propagandist? This gruesome description of the trampling of Napoleon's horse over body parts is meant to elicit a feeling of pathos for the Emperor, one aspect of how carnage can be used to counter the negative fallout from a battle, but there is nevertheless no denying that Napoleon was affected – up to a point. The day after the battle, he wrote to Maria Walewska asking whether she suffered as much as he from the separation.[34] His letter to Josephine about a week later was of a somewhat different tenor. 'The countryside is covered with the dead and dying,' he wrote. 'It is not the the [sic] best part of war. One suffers and the soul is oppressed to see so many victims. Nevertheless, I am doing very well.'[35] It is the written stammer that makes one think that, yes, the aftermath may have disturbed Napoleon, despite what might appear to the modern reader as the thoughtlessness of 'I am doing very well.' That, however, falls within the logic of a regime that was built around the person of one man. If the Emperor was well, the state was well. His concern, in other words, did not run particularly deep and certainly not deeply enough for him actually to do anything for the wounded. While the French wounded were treated relatively well, most of the Russian wounded died in appalling conditions.[36] Helping them may never have crossed his mind. The Russian wounded were left on the battlefield, and more often than not froze to death. Those Russian troops capable of reaching their own hospital at Grodno were more than likely to starve to death.[37] According to one account of his visit, Napoleon got off his horse and started to walk across the battlefield; then, after prodding one of the corpses with his foot, he turned to his generals and declared: 'This is so much small change.'[38]

And yet, despite the mauling, the Russians still refused to give up. One French officer, Fantin des Odoards, considered the Russians' reluctance to surrender the result of their 'semi-civilized' state, incapable of accepting the generosity of the victors.[39] Napoleon, on the other hand, was desperate for peace, for in an unprecedented move, six days after Eylau, he wrote to Frederick William offering to restore all his former lands in return for a renewal of the Franco-Prussian alliance.[40] Frederick William replied on 21 April, suggesting a general peace congress that would be held in then neutral Copenhagen. Napoleon urged Prussia not to wait. He was, in other words, recommending Prussia to enter into a separate arrangement with France, leaving Russia in the lurch. Nothing came of this.

## 'One More Victory'

Napoleon spent the months of March and April 1807 considerably reinforcing the army, possibly realizing that if the Russians had beaten him at Eylau, he would have had few reserves and would therefore have had difficulty fending off attacks in Germany.[41] A new army of 100,000 men was raised. It marks a turning point in the composition of the Grande Armée. Increasingly, from this time, more and more foreign contingents would make up the numbers. In the new corps commanded by Marshal Lefebvre, for example, only 10,000 out of the 30,000 men were French. The rest were Poles, Italians and Germans.

Napoleon took to the field with this new Grande Armée. The Russians under Bennigsen attacked first. On 5 June they moved through the town of Heilsberg (present-day Lidzbark Warmiński). Napoleon marched north to try and counter them. A battle of sorts took place on 10 June during which the French lost over 10,000 men for little or no gain (the Russians lost around 8,000). Once again, the Russians held their ground. It looked as though the fighting was going to continue the next day – the Russians began with a heavy bombardment in the morning – but threatened by a flanking movement they decided to retreat during the night of 11–12 June, abandoning their supplies and wounded.

The pursuit continued. Napoleon surmised that Bennigsen would attempt to cross the River Alle – in order to get to Königsberg – at the town of Friedland (today Pravdinsk in Russia) on the left bank about forty-eight kilometres south-west of Königsberg. Napoleon made the error of splitting his force in two, sending 60,000 men under Murat, Soult and Davout to try and capture Königsberg, while he sent Lannes with around 10,000 men to try and take the bridgeheads at Friedland. Lannes and Bennigsen reached Friedland at around the same time during the night of 13–14 June, from opposite banks of the river.[42] The next morning, the French found themselves facing 45,000 Russians. Bennigsen saw a chance and crossed the river in the belief that he would easily be able to defeat the advance guard, then make off before Napoleon and the bulk of the French army arrived. He was mistaken; more and more Russian troops got caught up trying to defeat the French so that by mid-morning the whole Russian army had crossed the river. By then, they had lost the advantage of numerical superiority; by late morning the two sides were more or less equal. Bennigsen had let slip an opportunity to destroy Lannes completely. Not only that, but he was no longer able to use the river as a defensive barrier; he now had it, and the town of Friedland with its narrow streets, at his back (and he was in no position to retreat; it had taken him five hours to get his army across the river over a few bridges and pontoons).

Napoleon arrived a little after midday and took over command of the fighting, but he did not launch a full-scale attack until 5.30 that evening, by which time the French had almost 80,000 men available. Napoleon, 'radiating joy', convinced he was about to destroy the Russian force, galloped past his troops reminding them that it was the anniversary of Marengo. Attack and counter-attack followed, but each time the Russian assaults were successfully stymied so that they were pushed back into an ever-diminishing area within the town where they fought until the streets were heaped with dead and wounded.[43] The Russians were slaughtered where they stood.[44] At one point, General Victor brought up thirty guns to fire into the Russian infantry, gradually reduced their range from about 1.4 kilometres to within sixty paces and poured case shot into their ranks, inflicting devastating casualties. The French should have annihilated the Russians, but for some inexplicable reason Napoleon held back troops that had not engaged till then. Things were bad enough as they were: the Russians suffered anywhere between 18,000 and 20,000 casualties – about 30 per cent of the army – for 8,000 French. Bennigsen was able to extricate the remaining troops, but the Russian army was no longer in any position to fight. 'My dear,' Napoleon wrote to Josephine the next day, 'I write you only a line for I am very tired.'[45] There was not much humanity shown for the dead and the dying. The battle finished around eleven in the evening, just as light was fading. Fantin des Odoards was obliged to spend the night where he found himself, trying to get some sleep on a blood-soaked field, with a dead horse for a pillow.

> I was overwhelmed with sleep and fatigue, but I could not sleep ... I waited for dawn, going over the events in my head, and thinking of the friends which they had deprived me of. Only a deaf person or someone deprived of all sensitivity would have been able to sleep amid the deplorable noise made around us by the unfortunate wounded whose moaning was carried afar by the wind in the silence of the night.[46]

In the heat of the moment, wrote Fantin des Odoards, the individual was capable of being transformed into a brutal killer, but in the cold light of day, when one could see the consequences of the killing on the field of battle, 'he cursed the war and its authors and, without daring to admit it, felt remorse at being among the passive instruments of such horrors'.[47]

This second major defeat in two years was as traumatic for Alexander as the battle of Austerlitz.[48] Bennigsen wrote a letter to the Tsar (15 June) asking him to put an end to the fighting. Most of the Russian generals in Alexander's entourage agreed that there was little point in continuing the war: the army was so depleted and Prussia so crushed that the path to Russia lay completely open. There were others though, such as his new foreign minister, Count Andrei Budberg, 'wound up to a pitch of fury against Bonaparte',[49] who still insisted on Russia's potential to win a war of attrition.[50] Napoleon was in no better shape; the burden of the war in terms of casualties was beginning to take its toll.[51] He too had been thinking of putting an end to the conflict, and of offering Alexander an alliance.[52] It is what a number of politicians in France were also hoping for. On 18 June, shortly after the battle of Friedland, Talleyrand sent off a missive to Napoleon stating that he hoped it was the last victory he would be obliged to win because, 'wonderful though it is, I have to admit that it would lose in my eyes more than I can say if Your Majesty were to march to new battles and expose himself to new dangers ... because I know how much Your Majesty despises them'.[53] In 'court speak', Talleyrand was suggesting that he believed Napoleon was driven by some vague and indiscriminate desire to dominate, invade and conquer, and that it was time to stop. A similar sentiment was expressed by the Archbishop of Paris, Cardinal Jean-Siffrein Maury; when writing to Napoleon to congratulate him on his victory he insinuated that enough was enough. 'The war is hence exhausted through its own exploits. Enough victories, enough triumphs, enough wonders.'[54] It was the first time the elite had expressed reservations about where Napoleon was leading them, but he did not, probably could not, heed the warning.

As a result of Napoleon's outstretched hand, Alexander's mood was transformed overnight from despondency to excitement. He had lost tremendous personal and political prestige through two major defeats in as many years, so Napoleon was offering him in some respects a way out. He could save face by concluding a treaty which not only was profitable to Russia but would be the harbinger of international peace.

## The Partition of the World
Tilsit (today Sovetsk) was then a small town on the left bank of the River Niemen that marked the boundary between Prussia and Russia. The river was also the official demarcation line between the opposing forces; troops were lined up on either side of the river facing each other, so Napoleon came up with the idea of building a raft and meeting in the middle. If it had taken place elsewhere, rather than on a raft, the meeting would quickly have raised concerns about etiquette, prestige and status.[55] On this elaborate raft, about four by six metres, stood a small central salon with two antechambers on either side; the salon was made of wood and painted white to resemble a tent. On one side was painted an 'N' and on the other an 'A'. Everything was ready by about 12.30 in the afternoon on 25 June 1807, and timed so that the two emperors, each accompanied by a small entourage, would leave their respective shores simultaneously and arrive at the raft at the same time, the first meeting of two European monarchs since 1532.[56] It must have been a strange sight. Alexander, tall, Napoleon shortish; Alexander speaking fluent French, Napoleon speaking it with a heavy accent.[57] If Napoleon was driven, Alexander was vain, full of *esprit*, the expression of the day and, according to one close observer, not quite all there.[58] But neither was showing his true colours. The meeting, which took place in the salon that was constructed on the raft, lasted two hours, unburdened in some respects by court etiquette and the eyes of courtiers – there are no contemporary accounts. Once the initial encounter was over, and for the next two weeks, they spent a good deal of time together reviewing troops, exchanging presents and decorations, attending the theatre, dinners, parades and balls together. The Imperial Guard, on Napoleon's orders, held a banquet for their Russian counterparts.[59] The festivities were designed not only to flatter Alexander, but also to portray an idealized relationship between the two rulers. The last evening they spent talking at great length, although we know nothing of what was said between the two men.[60]

This was staged diplomacy at its best. Napoleon and Alexander were playing conciliatory roles, both expressing ideas that they thought the other wanted to hear, and both came away seemingly infatuated with the other. But one has to wonder to what extent those sentiments were sincere. Alexander is supposed to have said something like, 'If only I had seen him [Napoleon] sooner! The veil is torn asunder and the time of error is passed.'[61] For his part, Napoleon wrote to Josephine to say that Alexander was a 'very handsome and good but young emperor'.[62] We know, however, that in private Alexander considered Napoleon a parvenu. Behind the scenes he was assuring those in his entourage that 'We shall see his fall with calmness', or he made references to the 'true moment' when they would strike against Napoleon.[63] One should consequently treat with some scepticism the assertion that Alexander was charmed by Napoleon (and vice versa). The problem with Napoleon is that, more so than Alexander, he took the diplomatic discourse at face value. In the grander scheme of things, he was disadvantaged. Alexander was surrounded by advisers, not to mention the aristocracy and the diplomatic corps, who hated Napoleon and the French.

The whole spectacle at Tilsit was meant to place Napoleon and Alexander on the same level; they were now portrayed as royal allies, as equal brothers. In his correspondence, Napoleon addressed Alexander (as he did other sovereigns of Europe) as 'my cousin', as though they were members of the same family. (After his marriage to the Austrian princess Marie-Louise, Napoleon would refer to Louis XVI as his 'poor uncle'.)[64] Even the act of embracing, which Napoleon did to Francis after Austerlitz and to Alexander at Tilsit, was meant to put him on an equal footing. Tilsit was, therefore, quite a diplomatic coup for Napoleon. Until then, Alexander had refused to recognize his status as emperor, but now not only was he obliged to do so in a public manner, he had to agree to treat Napoleon as an equal in the treaty stipulations that followed.

Tilsit was in effect made up of three treaties, two agreed by France with Russia and one with Prussia. The Russian alliance was, in some respects, breaking with recent tradition; France had played the Austrian card to the exclusion of the Russians for decades. There were people in Napoleon's entourage who still thought that this was the best option for France. Armand de Caulaincourt, sent to Petersburg as ambassador after Tilsit, warned Napoleon that French behaviour was having an adverse impact on European public opinion.[65] Russia had not been crushed, as had Austria and Prussia, and so did not have to come to the negotiating table, except that it was tired of the war. It meant that Russia came away with more territory than before it entered the war – a sizeable chunk of Prussia and the annexation of Finland (which had belonged to Sweden, at war with France), in return for a promise to close Russian ports to English goods. There was talk of an eventual partition of the Ottoman Empire, but as we shall see this was an ever-moving feast with Napoleon, who could agree to it one day and change his mind the next, and the issue was probably raised at the conference table as a sort of lure to get Alexander more interested

Adolphe Roehn, *Entrevue de Napoléon Ier et du tsar Alexandre Ier de Russie sur le Niémen le 25 juin 1807* (Meeting of Napoleon I and Tsar Alexander of Russia on the Niemen, 25 June 1807), 1807. The raft was decorated with garlands and wreaths, the letters 'A' and 'N', and French and Russian flags. There was no sign of the Prussian flag, despite being on Prussian territory. The threatening clouds unwittingly evoke troubles that lay ahead. The Niemen symbolized for the next five years the demarcation point between East and West. Interestingly, in this painting, and unlike the highly choreographed meeting that saw the two emperors approach and board the raft simultaneously, Napoleon is depicted waiting for Alexander's arrival, placing him in a position of ascendancy.

in an alliance. Napoleon also gained from the alliance, although only in terms of prestige. His title and his Empire were now recognized by Russia. Tilsit was, on the surface, a partition of the Continent between the two emperors, France dominating western and central Europe, while Russia dominated the east. This was not a particularly new idea and recognized what already existed. As early as 1801, political commentators had remarked that mainland Europe was divided between the two powers, so that the idea of a bi-hegemony had become quite current.[66]

With Russia on his side, Napoleon was hoping for a free hand in central Europe. It was not that he did not already have one, but Prussia and Austria were less likely to cause problems knowing that Russia was not going to ally with them. More than that, though, Napoleon was hoping that Russia would make Britain think twice about continuing the war against France.[67] The former stratagem was unnecessary and the latter proved unfruitful.[68] Alexander, on the other hand, was obliged finally to recognize both the French annexations and Napoleon's imperial title, as well as the royal titles of his three brothers. But he also believed that peace would now reign over Europe,[69] that the treaty would benefit his people by allowing him to continue to reform Russian society, and that he would be given free rein to expand eastwards towards Constantinople.[70]

The second treaty was signed two days later, and concerned Prussia. Once peace was decided, it was simply a question of agreeing on the price. Alexander was faced with a moral dilemma of sorts; he did not want to appear to abandon his ally Frederick William, but he had no real choice.[71] Prussia was in no position to continue the campaign, and Russia was not prepared to continue the struggle alone (nor was it able to at this stage), all the more so since Napoleon had been getting cosy with the Ottoman Empire. Frederick William was present at Tilsit, but was not invited to take part in the negotiations. While the

© BnF, Dist. RMN-Grand Palais/image BnF

Anonymous, *Diné donné par Sa Majesté Napoléon I.er . . . à Leurs Majestés Alexandre I.er . . . Frédéric [Guillaume] III . . . Grand Duc de Berg* (Dinner offered by His Majesty Napoleon I . . . to Their Majesties Alexander I . . . Frederick [William] III . . . and the Grand Duke of Berg), 1807. In this engraving, Napoleon is the equal of his eastern European counterparts, Alexander I and Frederick William IIII, dining together in an intimate setting, as though they were friends. Such a dinner never occurred, and the scene belies the hostility that Frederick William and to a lesser extent Alexander felt towards Napoleon.

two emperors were meeting on the raft, the King of Prussia, on whose land this meeting was taking place, was obliged to wait on the bank of the river, wrapped in a Russian overcoat, to learn the outcome of the discussions.[72] After two hours, the Tsar came ashore to inform him that Napoleon would see him, but only on the following day.

The next day, Frederick William was invited by Napoleon to board the raft for an audience, but he was treated little better than an envoy, and was made to wait in an antechamber while Napoleon and Alexander saw to some unfinished paperwork. When the two finally met, there was no dialogue, no discussions or negotiations. Instead, Napoleon badgered Frederick William about the mistakes he and his generals had made during the campaign. He did not even deign to inform the king what he had decided. A week later, in a desperate and rather pathetic gesture, Frederick William sent his wife, Queen Luise, 'to save Prussia', to intervene, to plead with Napoleon not to annex territories that had been with the kingdom for centuries.[73] The queen used all the charm and coquettishness that she was capable of, and in her own words 'cried for the love of humanity', but to little effect. Napoleon was careful not to say anything that could later be used to wrest concessions from him.

Luise and her husband suffered one humiliation after another; whenever the three monarchs rode in public, Frederick William trotted behind Napoleon and Alexander, as though he were a minor German prince. The Prussian royal couple were put up in a flour mill, one still being used by French troops to grind grain and housing the mules of the miller. 'It was a competition to see who could make the most noise to interrupt the sleep of the poor King and his beautiful queen.'[74] Prussia was reduced to a size on a par with Bavaria, losing half its territory and its population, so that it became little more than a buffer state between the French and Russian empires. Former Prussian territory in the west was incorporated into the newly created Kingdom of Westphalia, with a population of about two million people, while most of the Polish lands in the east went to create the Duchy of Warsaw.

Not only did Napoleon partition the Prussian state, but it had to endure two years of occupation during which the French extorted about 1.4 billion francs, more than sixteen times the Prussian state's annual revenue.[75] And this is not counting the depredations of the troops. Prussia was despoiled in ways that no other French-occupied country had been till then, with a degree of vengeance that lacked humanity. East Prussia in particular suffered from having to feed an army of 350,000 men. Whole villages were destroyed, estates burnt to the ground, livestock decimated and harvests confiscated and often wasted through misuse. The figures are mind-boggling. Between August 1807 and December 1808, more than 100,000 horses were taken from Berlin, and more than 760,000 from the province of Brandenburg. Just about all the livestock was taken; in East Prussia, only 2 to 5 per cent of the pre-war totals were left. The enormous hardships this kind of destruction and exploitation caused cannot be underestimated. Lack of food led to the weakening of people's immune systems so that the inevitable outbreaks of dysentery, cholera and typhoid resulted in high death tolls. Berlin's infant mortality rate rose to about 75 per cent in 1807–8.[76] Suicide rates went up to six to ten per week in Berlin and Potsdam; unemployment and 'melancholy' were the usual motives.

Napoleon's treatment of Prussia and Frederick William is puzzling. In a letter to Josephine written shortly before Jena, he said that he felt sorry for Frederick William because he was 'good'.[77] Now, however, his behaviour was downright vindictive. Napoleon had considered an alternative – demanding the abdication of Frederick William III in exchange for territorial benefits that he hoped would have brought about the complete loyalty of a new monarch.[78] German historians generally argue that Napoleon even considered eliminating the House of Hohenzollern and giving the Prussian throne to his brother Jérôme, but under some pressure from Alexander he agreed to let the kingdom continue to exist.[79] Certainly, it would not have been the first time Napoleon had overthrown a ruling house; recall the Bourbon dynasty in Naples being ousted and replaced by Joseph in 1806 (and we will soon see the example of Spain). There is nothing, however, that allows us to draw the conclusion that Napoleon was bent on the destruction of Prussia.[80]

## 'Everybody Hated the French'

Many contemporaries believed that the alliance between the two great powers, France and Russia, could not last. The Austrian ambassador to Paris, Metternich, may have been a little more prescient than most, but he was also convinced that the two emperors would inevitably fall out.[81] Given the reaction in Russia to the treaty it is not surprising. If the initial response to the end of the war was one of relief, the Russian political elite was less than impressed by Alexander's performance on the battlefield.[82] As the extent of the alliance began to be revealed in the latter part of 1807, Alexander's popularity dwindled further. The Russian people, moreover, had trouble coming to terms with the fact that the Tsar had signed a treaty with a man who had been stigmatized as the Antichrist by the Orthodox Church. Rumours were going around that God had punished Alexander for being a parricide.[83] The opinions of the ordinary Russian peasant might not have counted for much, but those of the elite did; they were so unhappy that there was talk of plots against Alexander throughout 1807 and 1808, although no serious attempts against his life were made.[84] Much of this discontent would have been fanned by French émigrés in Petersburg,[85] but it did not take much to convince the conservative political elite that an alliance with France was a bad idea.

Although he was well received by Alexander, when General Savary arrived in Petersburg as the new French ambassador he discovered that a large proportion of the court was in open opposition towards the Tsar's policies – he reported that France had only two friends in Russia, the Tsar and his foreign minister, Count Nikolai Petrovich Rumiantsev[86] – to the extent that, thinking his task futile, Savary asked to be recalled to Paris.[87] Savary was a poor choice in the first place. Not only was he a particularly difficult character – as undiplomatic as only a soldier who had spent his whole life campaigning could be – and especially disdainful of Russian ways, he had also been involved in the abduction and murder of the Duc d'Enghien. It would appear to be either a deliberate insult – in the same manner as the appointment of the Francophobe Count Peter Alexandrovich Tolstoy as Paris ambassador at the end of 1807 – or at least an indication of just how unthinking Napoleon could be. Admittedly Savary was recalled and replaced by General Armand de Caulaincourt after only a short time – Caulaincourt was more or less forced into going[88] – but the situation remained just as awkward. Although more acceptable to the nobility at Petersburg as an *ancien régime* noble who had been brought up at the court of Versailles, Caulaincourt was nevertheless shunned at first by Russian society, and was never invited to their balls, while attention was lavished on the Prussian ambassador (thus making it perfectly clear where their feelings lay). Alexander, it would appear, was completely isolated in his pro-French stance, so that the English faction, which included the Empress-Mother, Mariia Federovna, predominated at court.[89] The Russian military in particular, shocked by the defeats suffered at Austerlitz and Friedland, chafed at the bit and desired nothing more than a chance to get their own back. That first winter, the Tsar tried to appease public opinion by hosting an inordinate number of balls, but not even this could alter the nobility's animosity towards France.[90] When the Prussian royal couple visited in 1809, Petersburg society showed their contempt of the French representative by ostentatiously lavishing attention on them.

In a conversation with the Westphalian ambassador at the court of St Petersburg, Baron Bussche, the American ambassador, John Quincy Adams, reported his saying that 'everybody hated the French, he [Bussche] partook of that hatred, as being connected with them, though he hated them as much as anybody. I said it did appear as if many people here did not love the French. 'Tis universal, said he. There is the Emperor and Romanzoff on one side, and the whole people on the other.'[91] It is no coincidence that Francophobia in Europe often coincided with the rise of romantic nationalism.[92] This was also the case in Russia where there was a debate about Gallomania, where plays now began to appear that mocked what was deemed the excessive occidentalization of dress, and where literature began to be critical, if not of the Tsar's foreign policy, then of Napoleon.[93] Where once the Russian elite had made a point of appearing as French as possible – in manners, language and clothes – there was now a conscious desire, at least in certain circles, to embrace Russian culture and history, and to reject any reforms as being too pro-Western. Alexander, therefore, had to contend with opposition at home, and the difficulties involved in reforming a system that did not want to be reformed.[94]


'The Heavens Gave Birth to Bonaparte for Victory'

Tilsit was the culmination of ten months of bitter war that had cost tens of thousands of lives, both civilian and military. Napoleon badly needed to redeem his image as a man of peace, especially after the fallout surrounding Eylau, and Tilsit was the type of glorious peace that he could offer the French public.[95] News of the treaty in France was greeted with joy; the people accepted the military conquests and victories as the necessary corollary of peace.[96] In Rouen in 1807, officials were overwhelmed by the reaction of the crowds when people spontaneously broke into dancing in the streets.[97] Colonel Noël, returning to his home province of Lorraine in 1807, was struck by how enthusiastically Napoleon was acclaimed in the belief that a definitive peace was at hand.[98] And not only in France. As Napoleon toured through Saxony on his way to meet its newly appointed king, he was greeted everywhere he went with loud cheers.[99] Inscriptions decorated houses with the word *Friedensbringer* ('Bearer of Peace') in big capital letters.

When Napoleon returned home after an absence of ten months, he did not go straight to Paris, but rather to his château at Saint-Cloud. He was thirty-eight years of age and had been in power for seven years, and he was, to all intents and purposes, master of Europe. The Franco-Russian accord looked to many as though it was the dawn of a new era that would bring peace to Europe. This moment, perhaps more than any other, represented the height of Napoleon's popularity with the people of France. He had in that time defeated Austria (twice), defeated Russia, and reduced Prussia to a middle-sized German state, one among many.[100] He had dissolved the Holy Roman Empire and replaced it with a Confederation that he controlled. He had created a string of sister monarchies, most of which were ruled by his siblings. To contemporaries, he appeared unstoppable, his power and his ambition disproportionate.

It was not until two weeks later that he went to the capital, where his first public appearance took place on the morning of his birthday. Celebrations were held not only for Napoleon's birthday but also to celebrate Jena and Tilsit. The prefects were ordered to organize celebrations right down to village level. In the larger towns, parades, fireworks, public speeches and Te Deums were arranged alongside public banquets and dances that went on into the night.[101] In Paris, at least, the crowds turned out in great numbers in what would appear to be a genuine manifestation of enthusiasm, a desire to celebrate the man and his reign. Fouché wrote a report that very evening addressed to Napoleon in which he stressed that the people had turned out to celebrate not only the hero, but also the monarch.[102] There was a procession, which deliberately recalled the triumphal processions of ancient Rome, of about 10,000 soldiers of the Imperial Guard that went from the Arc de Triomphe (a temporary arch at this stage) down the Champs-Elysées to the Tuileries Palace and the Arc du Carrousel, which had been completed during their absence in central Europe.[103] 'All the windows, all the roofs of the houses in the Faubourg Saint-Martin and boulevards were lined with the curious.'[104] Speeches (and pamphlets) glorifying the army (and thereby indirectly Napoleon) were made.[105] The Guard was then led back to the Champs-Elysées where a huge banquet had been laid out on tables set up along the length of the avenue. Placards indicated where each of the regiments were to sit; a tent for the general staff was set up at the Rond Point; toasts were made to the Emperor, the city of Paris and the Grande Armée. Poems distributed in the Imperial Guard's honour compared them to the 'ten thousand immortals'.[106] When the rest of the Grande Armée entered Paris through the Porte de la Villette, Marshal Bessières at its head, through a triumphal arch that had been especially built but not yet completed for the occasion, large numbers of people turned out.[107] In Paris, the celebrations were crowned with gigantic firework displays. The festivities continued over the next few days and included balloon flights, wine flowing freely from the fountain at the Marché des Innocents, orchestral music and more fireworks.[108]

Napoleon became the object of innumerable eulogies, outlandish flattery[109] and biographical portraits, some bordering on the ridiculous ('He sometimes pats dogs, more for their faithfulness, which he admires in them, than for the pleasure he derives from it').[110] His birth was now associated with the appearance of a comet in the skies, as though the heavens had conspired to announce the greatness that destiny had in store for him.[111] It was only normal that the gods Jupiter and Mars had taken France under their protection.[112] The Civil Code was about to be changed to the Code Napoleon. This acclaim is similar to what happened after Austerlitz, but was perhaps even more intense. Theatres took up the refrain, quickly producing plays to mark the moment, such as *Les bateliers du Niémen* (The boatmen of the Niemen), a comedy in one act. 'Here's an epoch that will hold its place in history,' exclaims one of the protagonists. Indeed, everyone was conscious of just how significant an event Tilsit was.

Peace was also projected on to Napoleon by some of the religious elite. The Bishop of Cambrai described him as the lieutenant of God who was charged with executing the 'great work of Heaven' in order to procure 'a stable and solid peace for his people'.[113] The Abbé Lemoyne wrote in the same vein but also declared that 'the Heavens gave birth to Bonaparte for victory'.[114] They did so not because it was expected of them or out of some sort of reflex that automatically drew an association with their king/emperor and the Bible; they did so because they believed in him, and in his mission.[115] That is why the bishops of France, of their own accord, decided to call Napoleon the new Cyrus, after the biblical figure who delivered the Jews from captivity in Babylon, in the hope that he would restore the Church and defeat France's enemies.[116]

## The Limits of Despotism

On Napoleon's return from Tilsit, a number of contemporaries remarked on the change that seemed to have come over him. Physically, he had grown more portly, his eyes had lost their vivacity; mentally, he seemed more preoccupied and withdrawn.[117] Was he exhausted from the campaign or did he realize that the alliance with Alexander could not last and that war was again inevitable? Had he been marred by the brutality of the campaign and the senseless slaughter of troops? Did he see, after his love affair with Maria Walewska, that his marriage with Josephine could not go on? It is of course impossible to tell – he never expressed any misgivings either in writing or to those in his entourage – but there is little doubt that the campaign in the East had changed him both mentally and physically.

Historians often point to 1807 as a decisive year on the road towards a hardening in Napoleon's attitudes, and an increase in his 'despotic' behaviour.[118] Since the Tribunate had been discreetly purged in 1802, relations between it and the Emperor had been cordial if not downright self-serving. This did not save it, however, from extinction. It had largely outlived its purpose, and been unable to secure the complete co-operation of the Legislative Corps when bills were passed.[119] The story went around that Napoleon simply went one morning to the hall where the Tribunate deliberated, locked the door and put the key in his pocket.[120] The judiciary was also purged; more than 160 magistrates lost their jobs, some for incompetence, others because of their political opposition to the Empire, despite the fact that they had been appointed for life.[121]

For all that, legal boundaries to Napoleon's power were not entirely removed. He still had to contend with the Senate and the Legislative Corps where men spoke out against bills if they did not agree with them. Napoleon, however, was not listening and found it objectionable that a small opposition continued in existence. In many respects, 1807 marks the parting of the ways for some in Napoleon's entourage who did not agree with the tenor and colour of the Empire. Talleyrand, for example, disillusioned with the direction that foreign policy was taking, offered his resignation in August 1807, and quite possibly expected it to be refused. It was not. He was replaced by Jean-Baptiste de Nompère de Champagny, a relative nonentity, devoted to Napoleon, minister of the interior for a while, but who had no experience in foreign affairs. He was exactly the kind of foreign minister Napoleon desired, someone who would do his bidding without nagging about alternative approaches or the consequences of his actions. Increasingly, the legislative bodies were marginalized so that by 1811 the deputies sat for only five weeks, and not at all after that for another eighteen months.

The hardening of Napoleon's outlook was also reflected in the regime's attitude towards public opinion and the press, and towards any form of opposition. Criticisms were taken very personally by Napoleon. Thus, in late 1807, he used an unflattering comparison between himself and Nero made by Chateaubriand as a pretext to close down the newspaper *Mercure de France*.[122] That year, the number of political newspapers in Paris was reduced to four: the *Moniteur*, the *Journal de l'Empire*, the *Gazette de France* and the *Journal de Paris*. Increasingly the government was interested in controlling the content of articles before they appeared in the press.[123] This was another stage on the road to despotism. Almost as soon as Bonaparte was in power, his enemies castigated him as a tyrant, a despot and a usurper.[124] Napoleon certainly worked against the revolutionary principle of elected assemblies and the notion of popular sovereignty, of the power residing in the people, by increasing the power of the executive (and hence of the imperial administration).[125]

But was he for all that a 'despot'? If one examines Bonaparte's political beliefs as a revolutionary, it is quite clear he leant towards a strong executive and a strong leader. In 1797, for example, at a time when Robespierre was considered a 'monster' by many, Bonaparte praised him as leading the only strong government in France since the origins of the Revolution.[126] As ruler, there can be no doubt that Napoleon was authoritarian – he applied the rules of a military camp to running the state – but he was also a populist, and a nationalist. What we see then is the evolution of his reign towards what has been dubbed 'democratic absolutism', which consisted of Napoleon moving away from revolutionary concepts like the sovereignty of the people and advancing gradually towards the notion of absolutism by divine right, all the while maintaining a footing in popular sovereignty.[127] The years from 1804 to 1807 witnessed the evolution between these two phases. Any association of Napoleon's regime with the words 'authoritarianism' or 'totalitarianism' is anachronistic. He was not a precursor of the twentieth-century totalitarian dictators.[128] Rather than look forward, we should look to the past. If Napoleon is to be compared with anyone, a closer approximation would be Louis XIV. Napoleon was an absolutist monarch, the last of the enlightened despots.[129]

This raises the question of whether Napoleon was himself looking back or forward, in an attempt to create new political structures. He was doing both. He paid lip-service to the French Revolution by maintaining certain revolutionary principles – equality before the law, freedom of religion, the protection of property. Yet, at the same time, and more and more as his regime progressed,

he adopted *ancien régime*-style trappings at court. Many of these developments had the approval of the French political elite. Direct democracy as it was
known during the Revolution had already been on the wane during the
Directory.[130] There was also a decline in the direct vote, something of which
the elite approved. One of the best ways of obtaining strong and stable government, they argued, was to distance the people from politics by placing severe
restrictions on their voting rights.[131]

Napoleon's attitudes, like those of the elite, were rooted in his own experiences during the Revolution, and as a result he had a profound conviction that
elected assemblies were useless.[132] As institutions they had already been abased
during the Directory. The rest was a face-saving exercise designed not to worry
diehard republicans and democrats, a façade motivated by a concern not to
appear to break abruptly with the Revolution. 'I alone am the representative of
the people,' he liked to say, intimating that he had been chosen by them.[133]

# 13
# 'The Devil's Business'

## The Lion and the Lamb

What might have happened, what could have been, had Napoleon been less driven, more complacent, or more determined to pursue peace rather than conquest? What if he had paid heed to the words of Fontanes: 'Woe to a sovereign who is only great at the head of his army'?[1] But that would be to argue against Napoleon's very nature. He possessed a 'drive to glory', an innate desire to control and to dominate.[2] Anyone who stood in his way was brushed aside, any who resisted were crushed and eliminated. Over the next few years, three things were to stand in the way of his complete domination of the Continent; Alexander, England and Pius VII. Napoleon's conflict with the pope, as we shall see, was to evolve into a prolonged and bitter struggle between the secular power of the French state and the spiritual power of the Church.

After the coronation, Pius VII stayed for several months in Paris, in the hope of obtaining something concrete for the effort he had put into the voyage. After all, Cardinal Fesch had held out to him the possibility of a normalization of relations between the Church in Italy and France and the new imperial state. Each time Pius attempted to meet with Napoleon to discuss the issue of returning the papal territories that had been annexed in the course of 1802, he was brushed off.[3] The showdown really came, though, when the Civil Code was introduced into the Kingdom of Italy in January 1806. The Code brought two things that were anathema to the Church: divorce, and the primacy of civil over religious marriage. Pius reacted in the only way he could, by not approving the investiture of four new bishops in the kingdom. He did not refuse outright so as not to infuriate Napoleon; he simply adjourned the investitures.

There were other occasions for increased tensions between the two. In October 1805, Marshal Laurent Gouvion Saint-Cyr occupied the port town of Ancona on the Adriatic, part of the Papal States, supposedly in order to avert the danger of an Anglo-Russian landing. Similarly, Civita Vecchia, not far from Rome, was occupied in May 1806. In both cases, the French did not even bother to inform the papacy of their intentions and simply walked in, in violation of the pope's neutrality. At the same time as writing a letter to Napoleon in which he virtually threatened to break off relations, the pope also instructed the papal administrators in occupied territory not to co-operate with the French. Rather than see this for what it was, namely, the head of a territorial state unnerved by a seemingly unwarranted French incursion, Napoleon

suspected that the papacy was about to change sides, and spat out the prover-
bial dummy. This was on the eve of Austerlitz, so Napoleon was no doubt
anxious about his southern flank. That is why he wrote to the pope asking for
assurances that he would remain loyal in the face of the enemies of the Empire.[4]

Napoleon considered Italy, all of Italy, his by right of conquest, and said so in
a letter to the pope. 'If I leave sovereigns in Italy,' he continued, 'it is not so that
they favour my enemies and give me issues to worry about.'[5] The bottom line is
that the Papal States could not remain independent of or neutral towards the
Empire. They were expected to integrate into the Continental System, and cease
all contact and commerce with England. This was, moreover, the advice that
Cardinal Consalvi gave to Pius.[6] Napoleon was prepared to pull out all the stops
and go over the head of the pope to hold a Council to discuss the religious future
of Italy and Germany.[7] This blustering and bullying worked, for a while. The
pope invited Napoleon to Rome to negotiate an accord, something Napoleon
would never have contemplated. In the end, after much toing and froing, Cardinal de Lattier de Bayane was sent to Paris to try to smooth things over.

The cardinal did not succeed. Diplomatic relations were broken off at the end
of 1807 with the recall of the papal envoy to Paris, Monsignor della Genga; in
diplomatic terms, it was a kind of declaration of war. At the beginning of 1808,
Eugène received orders to prepare to march on Rome.[8] Napoleon had for a
short time envisaged an Italian confederation that would bring together the
Kingdom of Italy, Naples and the Papal States. In order to put some pressure
on the pope, Napoleon tried to isolate him, sending a number of cardinals back
to their dioceses. It was not until 20 April that the pope confirmed his refusal
to adhere to Napoleon's geopolitical plan for Italy. The refusal resulted in
Napoleon annexing a number of papal territories (Urbino, Macerata, Ancona
and Camerino) to the Kingdom of Italy. The French ambassador in Rome,
Jean-Marie Alquier, was warned only three weeks later so as not to fritter away
the advantage of surprise (not that there would have been much armed resistance anyway). Alquier was nevertheless to attempt to negotiate one more time,
and to make sure that the pope knew what the consequences would be if an
agreement were not reached.

In fact, the order to occupy Rome had already gone out. The last-minute
negotiations attempted by Alquier may have been nothing more than a smoke-
screen, or an attempt to lull the Vatican into a false sense of security. Besides,
Alquier was not really trusted in Paris; he came across as too conciliatory.[9]
Napoleon had been holding back from outright annexation for about two
years, no doubt afraid of the reaction from both the pope – excommunication
was a possibility – and Catholics in general.[10] He ordered French troops under
General Sextius Alexandre de Miollis to march on Rome. Miollis entered the
Eternal City on 2 February 1808, took possession of the Castel Sant'Angelo,

marched up to the doors of the pope's residence, the Quirinal, and aimed eight cannon directly at it. It was going a little overboard; the pope, surrounded by his cardinals, was praying in the Pauline Chapel. The occupation of Rome had taken a few hours and met with little resistance. The French arrested any English visitors and those Neapolitans who had remained loyal to Ferdinand IV found loitering in the city.

The next day, General Miollis was granted an audience with the pope, who declared that he considered himself a prisoner. If you think that the pope is a 'simple, sweet, easy' man, warned the French ambassador, then you would be mistaken. Pius VII was physically frail, but he boasted to the ambassador that if his predecessor had lived like a lion and died like a lamb, he, who had lived like a lamb, would die like a lion.[11] This was not mere rhetoric. The pope was just as determined – or intractable, depending on one's point of view – as Napoleon. He boasted to Alquier that he would rather be hacked to pieces, or skinned alive, than enter into Napoleon's system.

Once again we see how Napoleon's mind operated in this affair. By invading the Papal States he had in fact acted rashly. Not only was it now impossible for him to evacuate the pope's territories without some sort of arrangement, but he had no idea what he was going to do next (we will see this behaviour repeated when he occupied Moscow). He was of course persuaded that Pius VII would come to see reason once French troops were living on his doorstep, but this was to underestimate the pope's determination. Two motives govern Napoleon's diplomatic behaviour: impatience, and an inability to make the least concession to his adversary. As a result, he always opted for force as a solution to his problems. He presented Pius VII with an ultimatum – join the Empire or suffer annexation – that necessarily had to be rejected. His actions from then on were even more heavy-handed than usual. By annexing outright the Papal States, he had in one stroke undone everything he had achieved through the Concordat – namely, religious peace – and now risked putting not only the ecclesiastical hierarchy offside, but also Catholics throughout the Empire.[12]

His dealings with the pope show a lack of understanding that is stunningly obtuse, born of an inability to see his opponent's point of view. This would point to a lack of intelligence on the part of any other head of state, but how does one explain this ingrained inability in Napoleon to come to workable arrangements with his interlocutors? The answer is simple – he was an inveterate bully who could have no equals, only vassals, and who could not understand the pope's spiritual strength and determination. In his own mind, Napoleon's temporal power was bound to win out over the pope's spiritual authority. He approached his differences with the Church in much the same way he would approach a battlefield, determined to subdue his opponent. He was never to understand the depth of this misconception.

*　　*　　*

A *consulta* had been meeting throughout the first half of 1809 – it was convoked when the French occupied Rome – and was to deliver its findings on what to do with the Eternal City on 1 January 1810. Annexation, it would appear, was the only solution left open to Napoleon. If he restored the pope to his temporal states, relations between the Catholic Church and France would be back to square one.[13] He still had to decide how the Papal States were going to be integrated into the Empire. He could either give them to one of his relatives, or incorporate them within the Kingdom of Italy or the Kingdom of Naples. In the end, he decided to annex them outright and transform them into French departments. This was not going to happen without repercussions on Catholic opinion, even in France. The terrain had to be prepared by a propaganda campaign that was aimed at convincing the French that the popes had always been the enemies of France and that direct French intervention in Italy had not been without historical precedent.[14]

### The Famine March

The same can be said of Napoleon's intervention in the Iberian Peninsula. A number of traditional views explain why Napoleon got involved in Portugal, and then Spain.[15] The most obvious one has already been mentioned – his unrestrained ambition, his need to conquer, his need for fresh triumphs, so that others would continue to fear him. That kind of explanation belies the complexity of the problems facing him and is a somewhat pat response: Napoleon did what he did, because he was Napoleon.[16]

The most obvious alternative explanation, one with which most historians would agree, is that the invasion of the Peninsula was born of the need to eliminate any country that was aiding and abetting France's enemies, especially Britain. Napoleon himself admitted that all his wars of conquest were designed to gain control of the coasts of Europe.[17] Conquest and expansion were simply a means of getting at the British by extending a blockade that would bring the 'nation of shopkeepers' to its knees through economic strangulation.[18] To that extent, Napoleon simply implemented an economic policy that had begun during the Convention and the Directory, and which he continued to implement after coming to power. France signed a number of preferential economic treaties with other states (Naples, Spain, Portugal and Russia in 1801, the Ottoman Empire in 1802, Spain again in 1803, the Kingdom of Italy in 1803 and again in 1806) that excluded British goods from those states' ports.[19] Of course, for the blockade to work, it had to become universal, and France had to control the ports of all of Europe. There is a disarming simplicity to this logic, one that is difficult to fault, namely, that the implementation of economic measures to defeat Britain led to the expansion of the Empire. All Napoleon's conquests and annexations after 1802, his whole foreign policy – including the invasion of Russia in 1812 – can be explained from this perspective.

So, too, can the invasion of Portugal. To simplify, relations between Lisbon and Paris had been tense for some time, largely because the Portuguese, despite signing the Treaty of Badajoz in June 1801, had not entirely closed their ports to English trade. Moreover, the British often used Lisbon to refit and supply their ships in the Mediterranean. French diplomatic efforts to exclude the British came to naught, provoking a frustrated and angry reaction from Napoleon.[20] If we are to allow the logic of Napoleon's economic system against Britain, there was little choice but armed intervention, with all the complications and uncertainties which that brought with it. But one should also keep in mind that Napoleon was doing little more than continuing a policy adopted by the Directory, which had also considered an invasion of Portugal as a means of striking at Britain, but which it had never been able to carry through.[21]

Napoleon delivered an ultimatum to the Prince Regent, Dom João of Portugal: close the country's ports to the British by 1 September, or face a declaration of war.[22] He threatened the Portuguese ambassador, Lourenço Lima, that if his court did not comply, 'in two months the House of Braganza would cease to reign in Europe'.[23] Napoleon was in the habit of dictating to smaller powers and expected that his orders would be obeyed. In any event, Portugal was hardly in a position to resist, and it did not. In reply, Dom João declared war on Britain – although he did not arrest British subjects as Napoleon had requested – closed ports to British shipping, closed off Britain's naval bases in the Atlantic and its access to the Mediterranean, and offered his nine-year-old son in marriage to Napoleon's niece. João believed that Napoleon would be flattered to form an alliance with one of Europe's oldest monarchies. He was mistaken; Napoleon rejected the offer.[24] In fact, Portugal was playing a double game. The chief minister, António de Azevedo, was at the same time reassuring London that any measures against it were show, and secretly requested Britain's assistance. Portugal had, after all, been allied to Britain since 1703. Clearly, it had absolutely no intention of breaking off relations with Britain.

Napoleon was no dupe; he was perfectly aware of what the Portuguese were up to. It is possible that he was contemplating overthrowing the House of Braganza, and putting one of his relatives in its place, as early as 1804.[25] The other alternative was to partition Portugal between the King of Spain, Carlos IV, the Queen of Etruria, Maria Luisa, regent for her young son Charles Louis, and the Spanish favourite, Don Manuel Godoy, the Prince of Peace.[26] The partition was even formalized in a treaty at Fontainebleau in October 1807. That plan never materialized because of the rupture between France and Spain. That same month, Napoleon ordered General Junot through Spain – that the Spanish king allowed this was without precedent in the country's history – to arrive in Lisbon by forced marches.[27] The invasion took place in terrible conditions, in heavy rain, with limited shelter and in a country so poor that there was little in the way of food to pillage.[28] Junot pushed his men so hard – covering around 1,000 kilometres in four weeks, an average of about thirty-four kilometres a day – that only 1,500 of the original 25,000 troops managed to drag themselves that far.[29] One general dubbed it the 'famine march' and esti-mated that between 1,700 and 1,800 men died of hunger, exhaustion, drowning and rock falls. The expedition was meant to strong-arm Portugal into submis-sion. In other words, Napoleon again used force as a tool in his diplomatic armoury, ignoring what the French consul general in Lisbon, France Hermann, had been warning would happen. Junot arrived in Lisbon only to find that Dom João, along with thousands of courtiers, had boarded ship and fled, sail-ing for Brazil, persuaded in part by a British threat to bombard Lisbon if they did not (Copenhagen had been bombed for three days only a few months before). It was an embarrassment for Napoleon, gazumped by the English just as his troops were in reach of their goal – the Portuguese fleet.[30]

## A Despised Family

If the reasons for Napoleon intervening in Portugal appear reasonably straight-forward, the same cannot be said for Spain. The fact that he was thinking of partitioning Portugal and handing over suzerainty to the King of Spain should put paid to any assertion that he was always bent on eliminating the House of Bourbon in Europe. There was very little long-term thinking in his foreign policy choices, most of which were short-term responses to specific develop-ments, even if that development was the consequence of his own actions.[31] What happened then in the six months between the Treaty of Fontainebleau at the end of October 1807 and April 1808 when Napoleon deposed the ruling house of Spain and put his brother on the throne?

Political intrigue and a family dispute that got out of hand is the short answer. The Spanish royal family was possibly the most dysfunctional of all the dysfunctional royal families in Europe. The queen, Maria Luisa, granddaugh-ter of Louis XV, an empty-headed, vain, ardent, unpredictable woman who meddled in politics and dabbled in love affairs – she was accused by contem-poraries of being a modern-day Messalina, promiscuous wife of the Emperor Claudius – inflicted her 'odd tastes' and 'scabrous fantasies' on the rest of the country.[32] An unflattering portrait by the Russian ambassador to Madrid has her completely withered at the age of thirty-eight; she had lost all her teeth by then and wore a set of ill-fitting dentures.[33] The king, a 'hale, good-humoured, obliging man', often remarked, albeit jokingly, that she was ugly and getting old, and this was at least fourteen years before Napoleon invaded Spain.[34] The royal couple had virtually handed over power to Godoy, who had ruled over

Spain for fifteen years. Godoy was one of those *favoritos* (royal favourites) littered across Spanish history. Rumour had it that he slept with the queen, though little but gossip supports the assertion.[35]

The king's son, Fernando, Prince of Asturias, a spiteful, stupid boy with 'an ugly face, a tubby figure, round knees and legs', hated his mother and her favourite, Godoy, and had designs on the throne.[36] At the end of October 1807, on the same day the Treaty of Fontainebleau was ratified, Carlos uncovered a plot to overthrow Godoy. Fernando was directly implicated, as a result of which he was confined to a cell in the Escurial, a monastery near the Sierra de Guadarrama, about fifty kilometres north-east of Madrid. The plot revealed the hostility of two competing factions at court, one around the king, Charles IV, and led by Godoy, the other an aristocratic party centred on the Prince of Asturias and some prominent courtly aristocrats. The two factions were in basic political agreement, especially in their desire to ally with France, and fought only for power.[37] Increasingly, however, the Spanish came to see Fernando as the martyr and the king and queen, as well as Godoy, as the problem. It was a view encouraged by Napoleon, who told his foreign minister to organize a campaign in the Spanish press against Godoy.[38]

Napoleon's attitude towards Godoy was in part shaped by what he had discovered when he was in Berlin in 1806; he was shown correspondence that proved that Spain, which was meant to be an ally, had conspired against him.[39] Convinced that Prussia would defeat France, Godoy had put out feelers for a triple alliance with Russia and Britain, and was foolish enough to publish a manifesto that designated Napoleon as their principal enemy, calling the Spanish to arms. Napoleon did nothing for the moment, but he no doubt filed it at the back of his mind, ready to use when the opportunity arose. We know just how vindictive he could be, so he may have built up resentment against Spain for flirting with the coalition, or at the very least now considered it an untrustworthy ally.

Though Napoleon's troops entered Spain unopposed – the Emperor did have, after all, the acquiescence of the king by the Treaty of Fontainebleau – the French presence caused anger among both the people and the political elite, an anger directed against Godoy, who was blamed for letting the French in. During the night of 17 March, supporters of Fernando, and a mob stirred up and recruited from among the people of Madrid, laid siege to the royal palace.[40] The *motìn* (or popular riot) of Aranjuez, as the incident is known (named after a town about forty-eight kilometres south of the capital, where the royal family was in residence), resulted in Carlos abdicating in favour of his son, who then became Fernando VII. We now think that Napoleon encouraged Fernando in his intrigues and then, as we shall shortly see, used him to take possession of the Spanish throne.[41] It is from this time on as well that we can see a radical turn in Spanish attitudes toward the French. For the moment, incidents involving the murder of French soldiers remained isolated, but generally speaking relations between French troops and the Spanish deteriorated dramatically from this point.[42]

We can pass over the complicated fallout from this palace coup. Joachim Murat, appointed the Emperor's lieutenant to the army in Spain,[43] was only a few kilometres away from Madrid when news of Carlos's overthrow reached him. He was visibly shaken by the event, predicting in a letter to Napoleon that blood was going to flow, and that Europe would blame France for it.[44] Murat urged Napoleon to come to Madrid to sort out the mess, but by this stage Napoleon had already decided that the Spanish House of Bourbon would soon cease to exist.[45] On 1 April, he wrote to Murat to say that the Guard had already been sent towards Madrid, something that did not bode well for the Spanish royal house.

Napoleon's thinking on Spain evolved over time and went from what one could call its instrumentalization as part of an overall strategic goal – excluding the British from the Continent – to incorporating it within his Empire.[46] This is a turning point, what one historian has referred to as a 'foreign-political slide', into what is commonly dubbed the Spanish quagmire, and which would result in his first military and political defeat.[47] It is worth, however, dwelling on the reasons why Napoleon decided to intervene in the first place and the methods he used to achieve his goals. This is no easy task for, as with most things surrounding Napoleon, there are no clear-cut policies; he often contradicted himself, left his options open, chose one that suited the moment, and justified his actions *a posteriori*.

Over the preceding months, Napoleon had hesitated between several solutions: he could invade Spain and oblige the Spanish royal house to flee to South America (just as the House of Braganza had); he could leave Carlos IV on the throne, an unlikely option unless he also removed Godoy from the political scene; he could replace Carlos with Fernando, compliant and well liked by the people, but there was no guarantee that Fernando would be any more capable of ruling Spain than Carlos;[48] he could join the two dynasties by marriage with a French princess;[49] he could take the northern provinces and leave Fernando to reign over the rest of the country; or he could overthrow the Bourbons and replace them with someone from his own family. Napoleon was no doubt thinking of Louis XIV, who had done just that during the War of the Spanish Succession (1701–14).

A marriage alliance with the Spanish Bourbons appears to have been a possibility as late as January 1808.[50] Napoleon met with his brother Lucien in Mantua in December 1807, in the hope of persuading him to marry off his daughter Charlotte, who was only thirteen years old, to Fernando of Spain, but Lucien would not hear of it (which is interesting, considering that he had tried to marry off Napoleon himself to one of Carlos IV's daughters). It is impossible to tell whether Napoleon was serious or whether this was simply a ploy to get Lucien to divorce his wife. At any rate, Napoleon wrote to say that he loved him 'as he loved above all else his family', and that he had no fault other than being emperor and powerful. He was sure, however, to explain the situation in which he found himself, both in Europe and vis-à-vis his family. 'But placed as he is, he does not want to be wrong, he does not want that which interferes with his established system of which he alone is the source and creator.'[51] In other words, Napoleon made a distinction between himself as Emperor and himself as brother.

The question is when did Napoleon decide to overthrow the Spanish Bourbons? The riot of Aranjuez and the carryings-on of the Spanish royal family must have prompted him to act decisively. In March 1808, he offered Louis the Spanish throne; 'the climate of Holland does not suit you', Louis was glibly informed. He was not persuaded. 'I am not the governor of a province. By what right could I ask an oath of loyalty from another people, if I do not remain loyal to the one that I gave Holland when I ascended the throne?'[52] Napoleon then turned to Joseph, much to the chagrin of Murat, who was hoping this time to obtain a crown.[53] Although he reiterated that nothing was certain, Napoleon decided to intervene militarily by the end of the month of March. A week after Carlos and Fernando had both abdicated (see below), he informed Joseph that he had made him King of Spain.[54] 'In Madrid you are in France; Naples is at the end of the world. I wish that immediately after having received this letter you leave the regency with whomever you want... and that you leave on 20 [May] and that you are here on 1 June.' Murat would eventually be given Joseph's throne in Naples.

Just as he had accepted Naples from his brother's hands, so too did Joseph accept Spain, without on the surface objecting to this new development. He liked Naples so it was with great regret that he left.[55] The thing that irked him the most was having to hand Naples over to Murat.[56] By this stage, countries, their rulers and their people had become pawns on the chequerboard of Napoleon's strategic games. His decisions were utterly devoid of thought for the people involved, and the consequences for them. Joseph was not consulted, he was told. One could look at the offer of Spain as a reward of sorts for the manner in which Joseph had conducted himself in Naples; but then he had little choice.[57] Napoleon must have considered that he would be acceptable both to Spanish liberals in favour of a French intervention and to the Spanish people. Joseph, moreover, had experience in dealing with a region in revolt (Calabria), so he could bring some knowledge to bear in the pacification of the country. What he thought of all this, however, remains unknown.

So too are Napoleon's thoughts, although he was pouring troops into Spain, and seizing control of a number of strategic points, like the fortresses of Pamplona and Barcelona (which aroused suspicions about the reason for the

French military presence). The ease with which Junot had marched into Portugal, virtually unopposed, and the fact that his troops were able to take up positions in Spain in the midst of the political turmoil that was disturbing Madrid, must have made an impression on Napoleon.[58] In December 1807, around 25,000 troops were stationed between Burgos and Vitoria. By April 1808, more than 120,000 men had crossed the Pyrenees and were now garrisoned in the Peninsula.[..]

Napoleon was naive or foolish enough to believe the flattering reports he was receiving from his special envoys in Madrid, such as Lannes, Berthier, Murat and Savary, as well as the new ambassador to Spain, Josephine's brother-in-law François de Beauharnais. Beauharnais, a mediocre diplomat, presented Napoleon with inaccurate reports about what was happening in the Spanish capital, and grossly exaggerated the welcome the Emperor would receive from the Spanish.[59] These men were not lying, but they too had little knowledge of the country themselves and frequented only pro-French aristocratic circles in Madrid, the *afrancesados*, which gave them a distorted conception of what Spain was about. On the other hand, Napoleon received reports of the changes that had taken place in Spain and the potential of the Spanish to commit 'great excesses',[60] but he chose to ignore them. He preferred instead to believe that he was popular in Spain, and that the Spanish monarchy was not.[61] The fact that Murat wrote shortly after arriving in Madrid to say that Napoleon was awaited as if he were the Messiah probably did not help.[62]

Worse, Napoleon, imbued with a number of cultural clichés about the Spanish, had only a distorted idea of Spain and its people. He echoed sentiments commonly held at the time when he wrote that the Spanish were 'vile and cowardly, about the same as I found the Arabs to be'.[63] His low opinion of both the Portuguese and the Spanish may have had something to do with his decision to intervene in the Peninsula.[64] However, he had never set foot there and had never read a book about either country. In looking at Spain it suited him to see a dilapidated monarchy in a backward country; it blinded him to the reality of the situation – the profoundly religious nature of its people, their attachment to traditions, their fiercely independent nature, the regionalist sentiments that pervaded the provinces.[65] Napoleon certainly seems to have underestimated the resources needed to control Spain. If the Abbé de Pradt is to be believed, he spoke of needing no more than 12,000 men in all.[66] 'It is child's play,' he is supposed to have said. 'Those people do not know what French troops are. Believe me, it will be over quickly. When my great political chariot is launched, it has to pass; woe to those who find themselves under its wheels.'[67] To his mind, because Spain was dominated by the Church and the Inquisition, and as a consequence was 'superstitious', it was backward by French standards.

One pre-eminent scholar believes that Napoleon acted alone in deciding to invade Spain.[68] It is a view that ignores a number of factors, not least that Napoleon was in the habit of making important decisions only after consulting others. There was, moreover, what might be called an 'interventionist faction' at the imperial court, which included people like Talleyrand, Murat and Champagny, all in favour of a military solution to Spain's dynastic woes.[69] It is possible that Talleyrand saw intervention in Spain as a means of forcing Britain to concede defeat.[70] Champagny, the foreign minister, fearful that the political crisis in Spain could be used to Britain's advantage, recommended that a prince, a friend of France, assume the Spanish throne.[71]

The invasion of the Peninsula has to be seen within a wider, international context: it was also about control of Latin America, as well as about a future partition of the Ottoman Empire.[72] Napoleon annexed Tuscany, Parma, Lucca and other central Italian states in March 1807, and he annexed the Kingdom of Etruria in March 1808 as a way of controlling the ports of Taranto and Brindisi, all with a view to organizing an expedition to the Mediterranean.[73] We know this is what he had in mind when he ordered Rear-Admiral Decrès to concentrate the fleet at Taranto with the aim of transporting 30,000 men in October 1808 to (possibly) Tunis, Algiers or Egypt.[74] In the winter of 1807–8, Napoleon also made plans to invade Sicily, but suddenly cancelled them in favour of an expedition to reinforce the garrison at Corfu.[75] Corfu was a good point from which to launch a naval invasion of Egypt.

And for that the navies of Portugal and Spain were important. One of the secret articles of the Treaty of Tilsit called for the uniting of all European fleets in a concerted attack against the Royal Navy. It is an indication that Napoleon was still thinking in terms of defeating Britain, or at least of contesting its domination of the high seas. In July 1807, a combination of the French, Russian, Danish, Swedish, Spanish and Portuguese fleets would have given the French numerical superiority in ships of the line.[76] But in the erratic environment that was early nineteenth-century European diplomacy, circumstances could change very rapidly. In September 1807, the British again attacked Copenhagen and captured seventeen Danish ships of the line along with eleven frigates; a small number were deemed unseaworthy and burnt, but it added greatly to the British naval arsenal.[77] In 1805, Sweden entered into an alliance with Britain, adding an extra twelve ships of the line, which then proceeded to blockade the Russian port of Kronstadt, disabling a further twenty Russian ships of the line.[78] And as we have seen, General Junot, sent to seize the Portuguese fleet at the end of 1807, did not arrive in time; a further twenty ships (ten Russian, ten Portuguese) were lost as they either sailed for Brazil or were blocked up in Portuguese ports. Another thirty ships were lost with the invasion of Spain (including some French ships that had found harbour in Cadiz after Trafalgar), seized by the British.

In all then, nearly one hundred ships of the line were lost to Napoleon before he could get his hands on them, a figure that makes Trafalgar pale in comparison. In order to make up the losses, he launched an ambitious ship-building programme. The goal was 150 ships of the line, a figure he was well under way to achieving by the time he invaded Russia in 1812 and which would have given him something close to a 50 per cent numerical superiority over the British.[79] Britain was never able to have more than 113 ships of the line at sea at any one time, and even then they were often badly under-manned. One could be forgiven for thinking that the French ships were poorer in quality than the British, but that was not always the case. Although reluctant to fight, because they were unable to escape the British blockades often enough to put to sea for exercise, more than a few French captains knew how to manoeuvre.[80]

## 'A Pitiful Intrigue'

Rather than travel to Madrid, Napoleon expected the Spanish royal family to come to him, or at least to meet him halfway, on French territory, at Bayonne (a stone's throw from Biarritz and the Spanish border). Fernando had to appear before Napoleon as a means of letting him know who was boss, a tactic the Emperor had used on previous occasions. General Savary, a sort of Mr Fix-it, who often did Napoleon's dirty work, was sent to Madrid to persuade Carlos IV and now Fernando VII to accept Napoleon's 'mediation', and to lure Fernando to a meeting outside France.[81] Savary told Fernando that if he wanted to be recognized by France, he had to meet the Emperor. To sweeten the pill, and at the suggestion of Savary, Napoleon wrote to Fernando saying that he was prepared to recognize him as the legitimate King of Spain, if his father had not abdicated under duress, and that he should come to Bayonne so that they could discuss the matter.[82] On 10 April 1808, much to the disappointment of the Madrilenian crowds, Fernando set out to meet Napoleon, leaving behind a *junta* (council) to govern in his absence; Carlos and Maria Luisa set out a few days later.

Napoleon was already there, having arrived on 14 April after a tour through France from Bordeaux; he was still popular if the size of the crowds that turned out to see and greet him are anything to go by.[83] At Bayonne, he took up residence in the Château de Marracq – 'very cramped and very unpleasant'[84] – about a league from Bayonne. It was summer, but it rained a good deal and the flies were a pest; 'one couldn't yawn without swallowing one', noted Josephine's lady-in-waiting. When Fernando arrived six days later, after travelling through a country in which French troops were already very present, he was received with all the pomp due his rank. If Napoleon's public show of affection were anything to go by, Fernando could be forgiven for thinking that the warnings about his character were exaggerated. Very quickly, however, Napoleon let it be known (through Savary) that he had decided the Bourbons would no longer reign in Spain.[85] One can only imagine the stupefaction with which Fernando must have greeted this announcement. Over the next week, his advisers attempted to convince Napoleon not only of the injustice of such an act, but also of how politically inept it would be. 'The war in Spain', warned one of Fernando's advisors, 'will be an indestructible hydra, which . . . may in time cause the destruction of your house.'[86] The negotiations, carried out between Fernando's representatives and Napoleon,[87] stalled until the arrival of the former's parents on 30 April, received with all the honours due a royal couple.

The next phase of this tragi-comic farce involved Napoleon putting Fernando in the same room as his father so that a confrontation could take place. The first family reunion, on 1 May, was stormy to say the least. Carlos went so far as to hit his son during an argument while his mother demanded of Napoleon that Fernando be hung.[88] When Napoleon organized another family reunion on 5 May, after receiving news of the uprising against the French in Madrid, Carlos told Fernando that he was responsible for the blood that had flowed in Madrid and that if he did not give up his right to the throne, he would be treated as a traitor. Carlos was playing into Napoleon's hands. Rather than reconcile father and son, Napoleon insisted that Fernando abdicate in favour of his father. He did this by deploying the usual range of emotions he had developed to bully people into submission: first persuasion and entreaties, followed by threats and more threats, and then when that did not work the abandoning of all semblance of reason as he worked himself into a rage. At one point he is supposed to have told Fernando, 'It is necessary to choose between abdication and death.'[89] Eventually, Fernando acceded to the pressure and abdicated, handing back the throne to Carlos. Napoleon then insisted that Carlos abdicate, something that was much easier to accomplish, in favour of himself. Napoleon in turn gave the crown to his brother. The royal couple were placed under virtual house arrest, first at Talleyrand's domain, the Château de Valençay, about sixty kilometres south of Blois, where Talleyrand was obliged to entertain them – Napoleon even suggested that Mme de Talleyrand could bring five or six women with her in the hope that Ferdinand would form a liaison with one of them[90] – then at the Château de Compiègne, then at Mazargues near Marseilles, and finally at the Barberini Palace in Rome. Fernando stayed at Valençay, where he was to spend the rest of the war.

It had unfolded like a family melodrama worthy of a twentieth-century soap opera.[91] Murat was given the lieutenancy of the kingdom while the crisis was being sorted out. In other words, Napoleon considered himself to be above Carlos, and that he had every right to intervene in the country's domestic problems.[92]

## 'Glorious Insurrection'

Napoleon's intervention in Spain has been almost universally condemned, whether by contemporaries who lived through it or by historians writing about it. It is considered to be the reef upon which the Napoleonic vessel foundered.[93] Napoleon believed he knew how the Spanish would react to French intervention in the dispute. In most other countries the French had entered where there was a threat of political instability and unrest. In Switzerland, Italy, Holland and parts of Germany, the French presence had been, if not welcomed, then tolerated by the local elites as it guaranteed law and order. There was no reason to think Spain would act any differently, especially since Napoleon had been a reasonably popular figure among the Spanish elites before 1808.[94] The Emperor expected Spain to behave, therefore, like the other 'great' powers and for the whole campaign to be a walkover.[95] That image was to change within a few weeks.

French troops were able to occupy the key cities in the country without any armed opposition, while the *junta* in Madrid pledged loyalty to Napoleon and his brother Joseph. If there was one thing that nobody expected – and historians have used much ink writing about it – it was the uprising of the people against their new masters. The bloody insurrection now known as the Second of May (Dos de Mayo) had been more or less planned in advance, orchestrated by sections of the Anglophile, pro-Fernando Spanish nobility, although many of the events on the day were spontaneous, supposedly triggered by an attempt to prevent the son and daughter of Carlos IV from leaving Madrid. It is also possible that the French provoked an uprising in order to 'set an example' by crushing the insurgents.[96] As many women took part in the uprising as men. In the battles that were fought in the Puerta del Sol and the Puerta de Toledo, women from the popular districts were reportedly seen running into the French cavalry with knives and scissors in order to stab the horses' bellies.[97]

The uprising in Madrid on 2 May was the trigger for a general insurrection throughout Spain in late May and early June.[98] In the days and weeks that followed, uprisings occurred in most of the major urban centres. The French response was merciless. On his own initiative, Murat ordered all prisoners taken with arms to be shot, any person owning a weapon to be arrested and shot, any assembly of eight or more people to be dispersed by gunfire, any person distributing seditious pamphlets or literature to be looked upon as an English agent and shot, and any village in which a French soldier had been killed to be burnt to the ground.[99] In Madrid, the French ordered 5,000 locals, anyone they could grab, to be shot. They found a convenient place for the executions at the Prado (just outside the present Hotel Ritz), at the Church of Buen Suceso and on the Príncipe Pió hill. We can see the executioners at work in Goya's *The Third of May*, considered by some to be one of his greatest paintings, even though it was probably not done until six years after the event. It is, nevertheless, a wonderful representation of human brutality and the suffering of its victims. If Murat's troops are portrayed as faceless automatons, lined up ready to fire, the victims are caught in different poses awaiting their deaths: a monk is praying, another man covers his eyes, a defiant man in a white shirt opens his arms like Christ on the cross as if to say, 'Here is my chest, shoot me.'

The number of deaths resulting from the insurrection and the subsequent repression is difficult to determine. We know that somewhere between 150 and 200 French soldiers were killed by the *madrileños*, and that the likely number of Spanish dead was around 1,000.[100] The French ran through the streets killing anyone they found armed.[101] Those who resisted the French were bakers, locksmiths, shoemakers, coachmen, students, glassblowers and muleteers, according to the lists of the dead compiled afterwards, and now held at the Municipal Archive of Madrid.[102] At first the *Moniteur*, which reported that 'cool-headed observers', French and Spanish, could see trouble coming, spoke of 'several thousand of the country's worst subjects' killed during the repression, but later, in order to scotch any rumours about the extent of the savagery employed, the newspaper published an article claiming that those killed were 'all rebel insurgents and common people who had rioted; not one peaceful man died, and the loss of Spaniards is not as great as it had been previously thought'.[103]

The insurrection in Madrid served Napoleon's purposes: the rebellion was integrated into a narrative surrounding the overthrow of the Spanish monarchy. The pretext used by Napoleon to justify the overthrow was that the nation was in ruins, and that this had been in part brought about by Godoy and the internal intrigues wrought by Fernando. It was a theme Napoleon played to over the coming months and years.[104] Spain, which had once ruled the world, which had once had great kings, no longer did so because its 'government had been passed into the hands of the weak'.[105] As with France and the overthrow of the Directory at Brumaire, as with the overthrow of the Bourbons in Naples, so too had Napoleon rescued Spain from the abyss. He had no other interest in intervening in Spanish affairs than 'those of all kings and all fathers'. The argument was hardly likely to convince. Later, because of the reaction of the courts of Europe to these machinations, not to mention the reaction of the people of France – just about everyone was aghast[106] – those involved in the fall of the Spanish House of Bourbon later attempted to distance themselves from it. Talleyrand, for one, whose role was not insignificant even if he was not there in person, later blamed Napoleon and referred to Bayonne as a 'pitiful intrigue' (*intrigue pitoyable*).[107]

The overthrow of the Spanish monarchy not only shocked the vast majority of European royal houses, because it went against the core of their political philosophy – the principle of legitimate monarchy – but also appalled many who had remained steadfastly loyal to Napoleon till then. It tarnished Napoleon's reputation; there was a general feeling that he had done something 'unworthy', 'odious', 'atrocious', all words that one can find in commentaries of the time.[108] Much was made of this by contemporaries who opposed Napoleon. From the start the early histories of the reign described his intervention as unjust and accused him of having deliberately provoked a crisis so that he could then step in.[109] The statesmen of Europe did not understand why Napoleon should go to the trouble of overthrowing a ruling house that was already completely subservient to him.[110]

### 'A Barbarous and Inhospitable Land'

And nor did the French, who universally condemned the war in the Peninsula. Public opinion in France, already tired of the incessant warring, did not take kindly to the way in which France had become embroiled in Spain. Secret police bulletins through the summer of 1808 and from various towns and regions in France underline the degree to which public opinion was hostile to French intervention in Spain.[111] This was even more the case for the military called on to fight in the Peninsula. General Hulot, who accompanied Junot into Portugal, complained that he had to fight 'for the ambition and the pride of one family, with no benefit for France, with no glory for us!'[112] Colonel Noël wrote of the 'indignation' aroused by the events at Bayonne and believed that Napoleon was imposing a war on France out of pride and ambition.[113] There is enough material in the letters and diaries of the day to indicate a general malaise or discontent with the French involvement in Spain.[114] This appeared to be a war started for the Emperor's personal gain and was thus fought with reluctance by the officers and troops.[115]

The French entered Spain in the belief that it was already 'a barbarous and inhospitable land'.[116] Their experiences were only going to reinforce that prejudice. They had been brought up on this idea since well before the Revolution. It was the remarkable brutality of the French, the wanton destruction, the ruthless butchery that turned many Spaniards, even those who had at first sympathized with the invader, against them. It was the viciousness of the Spanish, the excessive zeal and the seeming delight with which they slaughtered the invader that marked Spain as the worst field of operations a Frenchman could be posted to. Francisco Goya's etchings and paintings of the disasters of war are damning indictments of human cruelty, even though we are not sure whether he was actually witness to any of these events. General Saint-Laurent, who commanded at Vitoria, wrote to a friend: 'We have the whole country against us. As the Army has been without pay for a very long time, and the phrase "distribution of food" has disappeared from the dictionary, one would think we were among Vandals. Nothing is respected; the war, which has continued for

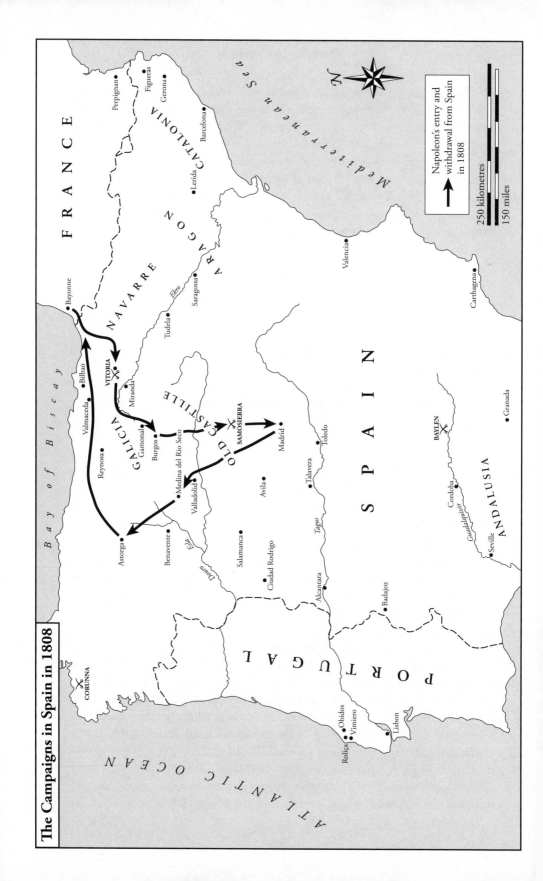

# The Campaigns in Spain in 1808

FRANCE

SPAIN

PORTUGAL

ATLANTIC OCEAN

Bay of Biscay

Mediterranean Sea

CATALONIA

ARAGON

NAVARRE

GALICIA

OLD CASTILLE

ANDALUSIA

Perpignan

Figueras

Gerona

Barcelona

Lerida

Valencia

Carthagena

Bayonne

Ebro

Saragossa

Tudela

Bilbao

VITORIA

Miranda

Granada

Valmaceda

Reynosa

Gamonal

Burgos

Medina del Rio Seco

SAMOSIERRA

Madrid

Toledo

BAYLEN

Cordoba

Guadalquivir

Seville

Benavente

Valladolid

Avila

Talavera

Tagus

Astorga

Esla

Salamanca

Ciudad Rodrigo

Alcantara

Badajoz

Douro

CORUNNA

Rolica

Obidos

Vimiero

Lisbon

Napoleon's entry and withdrawal from Spain in 1808

250 kilometres

150 miles

too long, kills morale; it is a question of who plunders the best . . . It is enough
to make one blow one's brains out.'[117] All Spaniards, according to Sergeant-
Major Rattier of the Imperial Guard, hated the French.[118] Maurice de Tascher, a
twenty-one-year-old officer and cousin to Jospehine, wrote of the fanaticism of
the Spanish, including their women. While in the town of Écija, between Seville
and Granada, young girls of twelve to fifteen years of age would pass him in the
street making a stabbing gesture to the throat. Another young girl told him that
his head would make a nice ornament in front of her door.[119]

This is not the place to go into the war in Spain and in particular the guerrilla
war, treated in some recent works, nor to explore the extreme violence that
underlined the struggle between the Spanish and the French, except to say that,
while popular resistance to the French invasion was widespread and deep, lasting from 1808 till the French were ousted in 1814, support for the war among
the Spanish was anything but enthusiastic. The impact of the guerrilla war is
now thought to have been much less impressive than has traditionally been
made out.[120] One also has to point out that Spain was, in comparison to the rest
of Europe, already a very violent country. In the 1830s for example, its crime
rate was one of the highest in Europe.[121] But there were other difficulties facing
the French, not the least of which was the absence of Napoleon from the field.
Despite his rank, General Savary was placed in overall control of military operations, something that the marshals subordinated to him could not tolerate.
This was indeed one of the reasons why the French were never able to gain
complete control over the country – competing interests, petty rivalries and a
good deal of pride impeded the French efforts to repress what quickly became
a generalized revolt. Savary, moreover, did not go about things with a light
hand. He behaved like any other French general – he ordered those under his
command to crush the revolt with unflinching brutality. The slightest provoca-
tion, the least bit of resistance, was met with the harshest repression. To cite but
two among a never-ending list of atrocities, when some of the inhabitants of the
town of Torquemada, halfway between Burgos and Valladolid, burnt an effigy
of Napoleon on 6 June 1808, Marshal Bessières had the town razed. When the
town of Córdoba was stormed by the French that same month, it was sacked
without mercy.[122] The French ambassasor to Madrid, the Comte Laforest, was
embarrassed to 'repeat all the excesses' committed by French generals.[123]

Napoleon had an inkling of what was going on – he later referred to Spain
as the 'devil's business' that was costing him dearly[124] – but he never really
appreciated either the difficulties or the complexities of the Spanish theatre.
He simply ordered the revolt to be put down, and was not averse to instructing
some of his generals to make examples of recalcitrant populations. He returned
to Paris on 14 August, suffering from what one historian has described as a
kind of 'personal euphoria'.[125] One can cite the victories at Austerlitz and Jena
as turning points, moments when Napoleon became even more imbued with a

sense of destiny than he already was, when he believed himself invincible. Bayonne too seems to have contributed to that feeling of self-grandiosity.

## Bailén

It is easy to look on the Spanish uprising with the benefit of hindsight, but nothing in contemporary European experience could have anticipated its depth and extent. There was every reason to believe that the generals on the ground would eventually be able to get the upper hand and suppress any resistance to French authority. Napoleon was certainly more optimistic, oblivious of the loyalty the people of Spain felt towards their royal family. He wrote to Cambacérès that 'opinion in Spain is taking the direction I wish. Law and order is everywhere restored, and it is nowhere troubled.'[126] He was quickly disillusioned. The first efforts to suppress the revolt by sending in five flying columns ended in failure, so that by the end of June Napoleon had to rethink his initial strategy. There were some initial successes when the road to Madrid was opened, which allowed Joseph to travel to the capital to assume the throne.

Joseph set out for Madrid at the beginning of July, accompanied by a few collaborators who had served him well in Naples. Based on his experiences there, he had every intention of using Spanish notables to help him run his kingdom. He brought with him a constitution, the first in Spanish history, which was a mixture of French and Spanish traditions. Even before he arrived, though, a vibrant and abundant pamphlet literature was being directed against both him and the French: Joseph was portrayed as a drunkard and nicknamed *Pepe Botella* (Joseph the Bottle); the French were depicted as 'Jews, heretics and sorcerers'.[127] Pamphlets called for liberty and independence, and portrayed Napoleon as a new Attila the Hun.[128] The *afrancesados* countered with their own propaganda, but it was of little use.[129] When Joseph entered the capital on 20 July 1809, he was greeted with indifference. The bells may have rung out, the streets and some of the windows along the way may have been decorated, commemorative medallions may even have been struck, but the people remained silent.[130] The new king organized a *corrida* to celebrate his arrival; almost no one turned out.[131] He wrote to his brother in an attempt to open his eyes to what lay before them. Napoleon curtly replied, 'I will find the columns of Hercules in Spain, but not the limits to my power.'[132]

Then came news of the disastrous military defeat at Bailén. It was not of itself a significant battle. About 21,000 French troops engaged about 27,000 Spanish regulars commanded by General Castaños on a plain covered with olive groves. The fighting took place all day in temperatures of 40 degrees Celsius, resulting in a number of men dying of heat exhaustion. General Pierre Dupont, who led the French forces badly, surrendered, in part because another general,

Dominique Vedel, refused to come to his aid. Dupont was able to negotiate the repatriation of the officers, as well as their baggage, which included art works and treasures looted from Andalusia, but not of their men. When news of the surrender reached Napoleon in Bordeaux on 2 August, he was furious. Anger turned to despair and, in the middle of the night, 'plaintive cries involuntarily came from his breast'.[133] He considered Dupont's surrender an act of cowardice – it was the first time since 1801 that a Napoleonic army had laid down its arms[134] – and decided that the responsible officers should be tried for treason. When Dupont was repatriated along with five other officers, they were arrested.

The fate of the men captured at Bailén was horrendous.[135] The terms of surrender stipulated that the French were to be escorted to the nearest port and transported to France. Apart from a few senior officers who were allowed to return home, the Spanish ignored the agreement. The men were robbed and indiscriminately murdered by the Spanish crowds along the way to Cadiz.[136] Those who survived the ordeal starved on prison hulks in Cadiz harbour, although some British naval officers did intervene now and then on humanitarian grounds. The survivors were transferred to Cabrera in the Balearic Islands, where they were left to fend for themselves.[137] In 1812, four years after they had been captured, Marshal Suchet offered to exchange 2,000 Spanish regulars for the worst cases, but Arthur Wellesley, later Duke of Wellington, disgracefully refused the offer. When the survivors finally returned home in 1814, out of the initial 18,000 men only about 1,800 remained alive.

The French public, however, learnt little or nothing of the defeat at Bailén. The newspapers of the day did not report it, and were not allowed to.[138] Militarily this was not a particularly great setback, even if it obliged Napoleon to take the head of a concerted military campaign against Spain, something that he had not counted on when he first intervened. Just as important was the impact this defeat had on the peoples of Europe. It created a dent in the myth of French (but not yet Napoleon's) invincibility. The Prussians took heart from the defeat and its military strategists began to think in terms of a national uprising (which never eventuated);[139] in Russia, public opinion was sympathetic to the guerrilla cause and some saw in it a model that could be applied if France were ever to invade;[140] the war party in Vienna gained the ascendancy and convinced the Austrian Emperor it was time to rearm. The court of Vienna, moreover, refused to recognize Joseph's new title. Napoleon confronted Metternich during a diplomatic reception and asked him outright if Austria wanted war. One cannot be sure what kind of answer Napoleon was expecting, other than perhaps to put Metternich on the spot; the Austrian ambassador obfuscated by replying that their measures were purely defensive.[141] And in Spain, '*the whole nation*', wrote Joseph to his brother, 'is exasperated and has decided to support, arms in hand, the party they have embraced'.[142]

On 31 July, after being there for only ten days, Joseph decided to abandon

Madrid in a panic reaction brought about by Bailén. His flight left a vacuum in the capital that was immediately filled by the rebels. At the same time, Junot, who had managed to hold on to Portugal with his small force, was forced to withdraw in the face of an English army led by Arthur Wellesley, who proceeded to inflict a series of checks and defeats on the badly dispersed French. Junot was defeated near Vimeiro (21 August) and as a result signed the so-called Convention of Cintra, which virtually handed over Portugal to the English but allowed for his men to be repatriated.

Napoleon learnt of the somewhat precipitate withdrawal of his brother from Madrid some time in the second half of August 1808. He was furious, grabbed the hapless General Mathieu Dumas, who had brought him Joseph's dispatch, by the lapels and shook him violently before replying, 'I see that I must go there myself and wind up the machine.'[143] Before that, however, Napoleon had to do two things. First, in September 1808, he transferred 200,000 veteran troops from Germany to Spain, where they joined the 100,000 men already there, to make up for the losses the French had incurred. The second thing was get diplomatic assurances from his ally, Alexander, so that he could be free to act in Spain without having to worry about Germany.

# CRUCIBLE, 1808–1811

# 14

# The Desolate Father

## Erfurt, the German Princes and a Russian Bear

A meeting with the Tsar was proposed before Napoleon knew about Bailén, at the end of July 1808 (he had been in fact been thinking of suggesting this since early in the year). After Bailén, and with Austria now making threatening noises, it became more urgent. Ostensibly, the meeting was to reaffirm the Franco-Russian alliance, but it was really about making sure central Europe was calm, that Austria was 'worried and contained', so that Napoleon could have a free hand in Spain.[1] In a letter to his brother Jérôme, Napoleon expressed a somewhat more ambitious goal, 'to confer on the situation of European affairs, the means to end the troubles of the world and to restore general tranquillity'.[2] To meet with Alexander to discuss the future of Europe was also to send a signal that the Emperor and the Tsar enjoyed a personal relationship. It was moreover a way of showing the world that, although nominally equal, in reality the Tsar was subordinated to the Emperor.

Talleyrand, rather than the foreign minister Champagny, was to accompany Napoleon to Erfurt, even though he was in disgrace.[3] When he returned to Paris from Valençay, Napoleon gave Talleyrand the Russian diplomatic correspondence. Talleyrand was meant to beguile the other princes at Erfurt, but he was also possibly the only person in Napoleon's entourage who could advise him on how to stand up to Alexander. No one knew the Emperor's own thoughts better. Napoleon still believed Talleyrand to be a faithful, if recalcitrant, servant. However, even before he had arrived in Erfurt, Talleyrand had made up his mind to work against Napoleon. What followed was a complicated game of intrigue by Talleyrand, who enlisted the aid of an unsuspecting Caulaincourt, and Alexander, already used to playing a double game when it came to France (recall the Russian attitude during the lead-up to war with Prussia in 1806). If the memoirs of the Baron de Vitrolles are to be believed, Talleyrand went so far as to dictate to Alexander, through the intermediary of the Princess of Thurn and Taxis, what he should say to Napoleon.[4] The image is attractive, but probably exaggerated, although there is no doubt that Talleyrand influenced Alexander's attitude at Erfurt.[5]

Erfurt was also organized to remind the German princes that Napoleon was still very much in control.[6] The Emperor's displays of power, theatrical to say the least, were always designed to demonstrate his overwhelming military and political superiority. The very fact that every prince and king in central Europe felt obliged to attend the meeting speaks volumes about his power and their submission to him, as does the manner in which the German princes behaved – fawning, servile, 'embarrassing', according to one witness.[7] Admittedly, they did not all go willingly. Many felt that it was a further sign of Napoleon's despotic power, while some, including people in the Tsar's entourage, were fearful, quite irrationally under the circumstances, that the same fate awaited them as had befallen Carlos IV and his son at Bayonne only a few months earlier.[8] The only two central European sovereigns not to attend were Frederick William of Prussia and Francis of Austria, but then neither was invited, Francis in particular, so convinced was Napoleon that he was preparing for war.[9]

Erfurt, halfway between the Rhine and the Elbe, was Alexander's suggested location.[10] The town, once an important trading centre, now part of the Kingdom of Westphalia, was given a makeover for the occasion. Buildings were renovated, streets relaid, triumphal arches erected, the main streets and squares illuminated with lanterns. Every decent house in the town had been commandeered for a sovereign and his suite. The twenty or so inns were full, mostly with tourists and hangers-on to the various courts.[11] The house in which Napoleon was to stay was furnished with carpets from the Gobelins, porcelain, bronze figures, candelabras, chandeliers, and furniture that had been manufactured especially in Gotha, so that the building was transformed into a fashionable house in the Empire style.

On 27 September 1808, on the road to Weimar, a few kilometres outside the city, at a village called Münchenholzen, Napoleon met Alexander, and from there they rode into Erfurt together.[12] They spent the next two weeks in each other's company. Napoleon did everything he could to seduce Alexander, entertaining him with numerous balls and concerts, the classics played by the best actors brought from Paris, some of whom were beautiful women he tried introducing into Alexander's bed.[13] Nothing was left to chance, including the selection of plays that were to be performed, always at the very heart of Napoleon's political thinking.[14] For the benefit of the French and German public, Alexander made an effort to get on well with Napoleon. It was, however, a façade. Public opinion back home was against the meeting. Alexander's mother, Mariia Federovna, staunchly conservative, narrow-minded and, despite her German background and poor Russian, the centre of a 'patriot' faction at court, implored him not to go, not 'voluntarily to bow your forehead . . . before the idol of fortune, an idol accursed of present and future humanity; step back from the edge of the precipice!'[15] The Tsar's sister similarly wrote to say that 'In my whole life, I will never get used to the idea of knowing you spent your days with Bonaparte; it has the air of a bad joke when one says it, but does not seem possible.'[16]

The festivities were gloss; the two emperors got to work almost immediately after the Tsar's arrival. The first meeting, in Talleyrand's presence, was
cordial and Napoleon still appears to have been enamoured of Alexander – in
a letter to Josephine he declared that if Alexander were a woman he would
make him his mistress.[17] They met almost every afternoon for a few hours
after that, but the negotiations soon ran into difficulties, over Prussia,
Austria, Spain and in particular over Russian ambitions in the Middle East.[18]
Prussia had turned to Alexander for help in an attempt to diminish the
burden of the French occupation. In that respect, Alexander succeeded at
least in having Prussia's war indemnity slightly reduced. In return for his
adhesion to the Continental System, he hoped to obtain French support for
his plans to partition what was already perceived to be a degenerate, crumbling empire, but in this he was to be sadly disappointed. Napoleon had no
consistent policy towards the Ottoman Empire; at times he wanted to be its
ally, at other times he thought of grand plans for its partition. At the Treaty
of Tilsit, there had indeed been a general consensus between Alexander and
Napoleon along those lines. It was one of the fundamentals of their agreement, and was perhaps *the* factor that persuaded Alexander to hitch his star
to Napoleon's. We can spare the reader the vagaries of Napoleon's history of
broken promises, backflips and unlikely plans for expeditions to Constantinople, and from there on to the Euphrates and India (now with Russian, now
with Austrian troops), except to say that nothing practical ever came of these
military musings, and Alexander felt betrayed.[19]

Negotiations over the Ottoman Empire went on throughout 1808, but
without getting anywhere. Napoleon was preoccupied with Spain. In
September that year, however, at Erfurt, Napoleon agreed to the Russian
demands for the Ottoman provinces of Wallachia and Moldavia (now incorporated into present-day Romania) in return for which Russia promised to
support Napoleon if he were attacked by Austria (something Alexander had
already promised at Tilsit, and which he failed to do when the time came).
The partition of the Ottoman Empire was just another chapter in the book
of possibilities, an opportunity Napoleon might take, one day, when circumstances were different, after Spain had been resolved. As we saw, part of the
reason Spain and Naples were occupied in the first place was to seize control
of their navies, and to use their ports for possible springboards into North
Africa. But here too, as with most things Napoleonic, the attitude of France
towards the Ottoman Empire has to be seen in a longer French foreign-
political context: it had been a point of contention in the relationship between
France and Russia for the preceding hundred years, and looked again like
souring relations between Alexander and Napoleon (along with the question
of Poland, which we will treat elsewhere).[20]

*         *         *

After that first meeting, as Talleyrand escorted the Tsar back to his carriage, Alexander repeated to him several times in a low voice: 'Nous nous verrons' (We will meet). On reaching his own apartments, Talleyrand found a note from the Princess of Thurn and Taxis, the Queen of Prussia's sister, informing him of her arrival. Talleyrand went to her immediately, and was joined a short while later by the Tsar. 'He was most amiable and communicative,' Talleyrand later wrote, 'and asked the princess for some tea, telling her that she should give us some every evening after the theatre.'[21] It was on this occasion that Talleyrand said to Alexander: 'Why are you here? . . . The French people are civilized, their sovereign is not. It is up to the sovereign of Russia then to be the ally of the French people.' The lines, often cited, are probably apocryphal and are to be found only in later editions of Metternich's memoirs.[22] These few sentences nevertheless contain the germ of the allies' political thinking. If not Talleyrand, then the European political elite was now starting to make a fundamental distinction between Napoleon on the one hand and the French people on the other, one that would not be forgotten by the Tsar. The implication was clear: Napoleon was not France, and he was acting like a despot. Those who served him, therefore, were not obliged to follow. In some respects, those few sentences were also the culmination of a long history of political thinking on the subject.[23] It was the justification used by Talleyrand to work against Napoleon, and it gave someone like the Tsar a moral pretext to back out of the Treaty of Tilsit and to think about a rapprochement with Austria.

And so it was arranged that the Tsar and Talleyrand would meet in the Princess of Thurn and Taxis's drawing room every day to discuss the meetings between Napoleon and Alexander. It was there that Talleyrand asked Alexander to save Europe by standing up to Napoleon. It was there that Talleyrand schooled Alexander in how to negotiate with Napoleon (Alexander would sometimes take notes while Talleyrand dictated). And it was there that he eventually convinced Alexander, and perhaps Metternich, that France was not Napoleon, and that Austria and Russia should form a bulwark against Napoleon's insatiable ambition.[24]

Standing up to Napoleon had its consequences. At one stage Napoleon was so frustrated with Alexander's obstinacy that, working himself into a melodramatic rage, he threw his hat on to the ground and stamped on it (that is possibly why he got through 160–170 hats in the course of his career).[25] In the face of this outburst, Alexander is supposed to have kept his cool, and replied to Napoleon, 'When you become violent I just become stubborn. With me anger is of no avail. Let us discuss, and be reasonable, or I will go.' It belied his real intentions. Alexander was not terribly interested in an accommodation of any description with Napoleon. In fact, he was playing for time, hoping not to alienate his powerful ally, and trying to keep his own domestic opposition in check. Even before he had arrived in Erfurt, Alexander wrote to his sister Catherine that 'Bonaparte thinks that I am nothing but an idiot. *They laugh longest who laugh last!* and I put all my hope in God.'[26] In the same vein, Alexander wrote to his mother that it was necessary to 'enter for some time into his [Napoleon's] views and to prove to him that he could trust his [Alexander's] intentions and plans'.[27]

On 7 October 1808, on the anniversary of Napoleon's victory at Jena, a hunt was organized on the battlefield itself (about fifty kilometres from Erfurt). The hunt was a pretext. Really, Napoleon wanted to take Alexander on a personal tour, giving him a dramatic account of the battle of Jena from a knoll that overlooked the field. The Tsar played along. He knew how to hide his real sentiments when he had to. Only a few days before, at a performance of Voltaire's play *Oedipus*, when the line 'The friendship of a great man is a gift of the gods' was pronounced, Alexander stood up and, in a flamboyant gesture, took Napoleon's hand, while the whole audience applauded.[28] What was Napoleon thinking then by showing Alexander the site of another victory? Was it a veiled warning, a reminder that any resistance would meet the same fate as the King of Prussia had met? Quite apart from the humiliation that Alexander must have felt at being given a lesson by the man who had so resoundingly trounced him at Austerlitz, it was a tactless thing to do, the action of a man who was profoundly insecure, at least in this relationship. The same night as Voltaire's play and Alexander's public profession of friendship, Napoleon's valet Constant heard his master cry out and went to wake him. He found the Emperor 'extended across his bed in a convulsive posture, his sheets and his blankets thrown some distance, and his whole person in a frightful state of nervous tension. His opened mouth let escape inarticulate sounds, his chest seemed greatly weighed down, and he had one of his hands pressed, clenched, in the pit of his stomach.'[29] Napoleon was obliged to change his nightshirt; it was soaked through with sweat. He had had a nightmare and had dreamt that a bear had opened his chest and was devouring his heart.

One cannot, with any degree of certainty, translate a dream of this nature, but a possible interpretation is that Napoleon must have realized, if only unconsciously, that Russia (and Alexander) represented danger. Something at the back of his mind must have been ringing alarm bells. When Erfurt was over, leaving Alexander on the road to Moscow and returning in his carriage to Erfurt, Napoleon was in a pensive mood.[30] Erfurt had been a failure, and he realized it even though he was unaware of Talleyrand working against him behind the scenes. He ended up with a treaty that was different from Tilsit, but was not what he had in mind. Alexander had been considerably less accessible than at Tilsit and had assiduously avoided committing himself to a war with Austria. Napoleon believed that things had gone wrong because the Tsar wanted to treat him as an equal,[31] something he would not tolerate. He expected Alexander to behave as a subordinate and that was that. Alexander had no choice but to behave defiantly.

A convention was nevertheless signed between the two countries (12 October 1808), leaving Russia with Moldavia and Wallachia, as well as Finland. In return, Napoleon was supposedly able to count on Russian assistance in the event of war with Austria. In other words, Alexander came away with concrete territorial gains; Napoleon came away with a promise.

'When Will the Blood Cease to Flow?'

Pierre Corneille's seventeenth-century masterpiece *Cinna*, a favourite of Napoleon's, was one of the plays performed at Erfurt by actors from the Théâtre-Français. There is a line in Act III when one of the characters, Emilie, cries out, 'Treachery is noble when aimed at tyranny' (*la perfidie est noble envers la tyrannie*). Talleyrand may have felt a certain sense of satisfaction on hearing it. Once he had returned to Paris, he continued to play the spy. Alexander decided to maintain two ambassadors at the Tuileries. One, Prince Kurakin, was an eccentric whose idiosyncrasies caused a great deal of amusement at court. The other, Count Karl von Nesselrode, was a thirty-year-old Westphalian nobleman who had entered Russian service during the revolutionary wars. He was sent to Paris ostensibly as an adviser to the Russian ambassador, Kurakin, but was actually Alexander's personal liaison with Talleyrand.[32] Although Talleyrand no longer had as much access to Napoleon's person as in the past, he was still reasonably well informed of his intentions and plans and did not hesitate to communicate them to Nesselrode. Talleyrand knew, for example, that war with Russia was approaching but did not expect it until April 1812 (which turned out to be an exact estimate). In the meantime, he offered Alexander some sound advice: to assume a defensive position, to use the time to prepare and to resume relations with Britain.[33]

Talleyrand was not yet actively working for Napoleon's overthrow, but rather was encouraging Austria and Russia to form a united block against him by insisting that they should not readily sacrifice their own strategic interests. At every opportunity after Erfurt, Talleyrand would publicly criticize the government in the severest terms, and thereby encourage others to do the same.[34] Aimée de Coigny, an ardent royalist and one of Talleyrand's friends, remarked that 'all Paris' was visiting him in secret. The memoirs of the period give the strong impression that Talleyrand was involved in some sort of conspiracy. This was not the case; rather, he acted as a kind of magnet around which oppositional elements gathered.[35] As for his motives, it is possible Talleyrand thought that if he managed to present a strong front, public opinion would force the Emperor to moderate his ambitions; Talleyrand, of course, knew that any remarks he made criticizing Napoleon would be reported directly back. At the same time, however, by voicing his opposition he was publicly seen to be an opponent of the government's policies; if ever there were a change in regime he could always say that he had opposed Napoleon and there would be people aplenty to confirm this.

In many respects, Talleyrand's stance conforms to the general opposition towards war and the desire for peace prevalent in French society during the latter stages of the Empire.[36] This attitude began to find an echo with a minority of individuals – prominent members of the imperial government, the administration and even the army – opposed to further conquests, or who at least believed that their fortunes were being endangered by the lack of political stability on the Continent.[37] Self-interest and self-preservation were probably as great a motivation, if not greater, in opposing Napoleon as the desire to see stability in France and Europe. In Talleyrand's case, however, it should also be seen as typical of *ancien régime* aristocratic behaviour, when it was quite common for nobles to form an alliance with other court nobles or members of the royal family in order to oppose the king's policies.

The clergy too began to speak out against Napoleon and it is here one can possibly find a more accurate reflection of the malaise that started to take hold of the population as the wars dragged on with no end in sight. The Church had become increasingly disillusioned with Napoleon after 1807, but especially after the arrest of the pope in July 1809 (see below). Not all were anti-Napoleon, but even those who had supported the regime, such as the Bishop of Troyes, Etienne Antoine de Boulogne, were starting to wonder where it would all end. In 1809 the bishop publicly expressed the hope that Napoleon would soon conclude his conquests to 'sanctify the war', to work towards 'closing all the wounds opened by it, to root out all the disorders it has borne, and to dry all the tears that it has caused to shed'.[38] It is fair to say that the Bishop of Clermont reflected a general concern among the notables about the war in asking publicly, 'When will the blood cease to flow?'[39]

The masterstroke in this oppositional policy was Talleyrand's reconciliation with his old enemy, Joseph Fouché, the minister of police. The antipathy between the two was almost a given in the French political landscape. They had publicly attacked each other for years in the bitterest of terms. The reconciliation, engineered by Talleyrand's former secretary and number two at the ministry of foreign affairs, Comte Alexandre d'Hauterive, was revealed in dramatic fashion.[40] At a reception in 1809 at the rue de Varenne, Talleyrand's Paris residence, and after all the guests had arrived, the major-domo announced in a loud voice the minister of police. The councillor of state Etienne-Denis Pasquier recounts how a silence immediately fell upon the assembly and every head turned towards the entrance into the salon. The only sound that could be heard was Talleyrand limping across the room to greet the new arrival. Then, linking arms – the scene elicited the famous quip from Chateaubriand, 'vice leaning on the arm of crime' – the two men moved from room to room, theatrically absorbed in a whispered conversation.[41]

This may have been the first time they had met in full view of everyone – it was therefore a very public demonstration of their intentions – but they had been meeting secretly for some time at Hauterive's house in Bagneux, on the outskirts of Paris, and at Suresnes at the house of the Princess de Vaudémont, a former mistress of Paul Barras, one-time putative head of the Directory.[42] Although we have no idea what was discussed, an accord of sorts seems to have been reached around the question of what to do if Napoleon were killed while away on campaign in Spain.

The question was one that had lingered since the early days of the Consulate when the false news reached Paris that Napoleon had been killed at the battle of Marengo. As we saw, a number of men in the political elite were ready to succeed Bonaparte in the event of his untimely demise.[43] Eight years later, the problem of Napoleon's potential sudden death and the succession were still unresolved. The general opinion among contemporaries was, therefore, that Talleyrand and Fouché were working not for the overthrow of Napoleon, but for the consolidation of his regime through the establishment of a lasting peace and the founding of a dynasty.[44] In case of Napoleon's death, Talleyrand had a secret plan to have either Joseph or Murat recognized as Emperor and French troops withdrawn behind the Rhine.[45] It appears that Murat was not only aware of the plotting, but was prepared to take part in it.[46] In this vein, both Talleyrand and Fouché had wanted Napoleon to divorce Josephine, and to marry into one of Europe's legitimate dynasties to produce an heir. At this stage of proceedings men like Talleyrand and Fouché had more to gain from a reformed Napoleonic regime than from Napoleon's overthrow, which would mean either the restoration of the Bourbon dynasty or a new republican government.

### The Consolatory Gaze

War was the fundamental cause of opposition to Napoleon and the fundamental cause of popular discontent. His popularity had taken a beating since the battle of Eylau and efforts had been made to remedy the situation. Two months after the battle, for example, a decision was taken to organize a painting competition with a prize of 16,000 francs.[47] It was the first time that a competition had been announced since the rather lacklustre response to the Peace of Amiens and the Concordat. Painters were invited to submit sketches based on specifications that were supplied by Vivant Denon. The winner was to receive the commission for the full painting. The painting was meant to depict the day after the battle, when Napoleon visited the field, with emphasis on his treatment of the wounded. The instructions to the competitors were very explicit, to an extent unusual for a commissioned painting, and much more detailed than the official description of the winning entry that is usually cited. The costumes of the principal figures were carefully described, as was the weather, the position of the secondary figures, and the landscape. Vivant Denon had actually witnessed the battle and made ink sketches of the topography as well as the positions of all the principal figures (he drew everything he saw and had assembled an impressive archive of sketches of every Napoleonic battle).⁴⁸ Twenty-six sketches were submitted for the competition.⁴⁹ Jean-Antoine Gros, nagged by Denon, reluctantly submitted an entry, and won.⁵⁰

The opening of the Salon of 1808 displaying Gros' painting was supposed to coincide with the second anniversary of the battle of Jena.⁵¹ A series of paintings had been ordered to portray the most important scenes from the battlefields of 1806 and 1807, including Napoleon's entry into Berlin and the dismantling of the monument at Rossbach.⁵² Gros' painting, on the other hand, is one of a number of paintings that portrayed Napoleon as clement ruler, 'stopping in front of the wounded, having them questioned in their language, having them consoled and helped in front of his eyes'.⁵³ This was a generous conqueror. Surprised, the vanquished prostrate themselves before him, holding out their arms as a sign of recognition. Napoleon was thus transformed from bloody tyrant into a Christ-like saviour who had come upon the battlefield to bring help to the dying and wounded. In the painting, a wounded enemy soldier, his arm in a sling and on bended knee before Napoleon's horse, is touching the Emperor's holy body, but there is also a chasseur 'who during his dressing forgets his pain, to show his gratitude and devotion to the victor'.⁵⁴ Gros is once again conferring on Napoleon the aura of the sacred: the Emperor's hand is raised, almost as though he is blessing the survivors or the battlefield.⁵⁵

The competition was an attempt to quell the rumours that had spread about the extent of the carnage at Eylau. Like the portrait of Bonaparte at Jaffa, Gros' portrait of Napoleon as 'healing king' helping the wounded and dying was meant to counter the accusations that he had uselessly squandered the lives of thousands of men.⁵⁶ When it was displayed at the Salon of 1808, it met with enormous success.⁵⁷ Unlike Ingres or David, more concerned with the trappings of power in their portraits, Gros attempts to get at Napoleon's character. *Jaffa* and *Eylau* are in some respects psychological portraits, stressing the complex inner nature of the subject.⁵⁸ Nevertheless, as was the case with *Jaffa*, the *Eylau* painting is one of the most graphic portrayals of pain and death yet depicted. In *Jaffa*, however, the suffering was confined to the shadows on the margins of the painting. In *Eylau*, the suffering is centre stage, or at least in the foreground, and therefore quite unmistakable. Gros is meeting head-on the damaging rumours about the carnage. By showing that Napoleon abhorred the suffering, indeed by giving him a Christ-like quality

Antoine-Jean Gros, *Napoléon Ier sur le champ de bataille d'Eylau (9 février 1807)*
(Napoleon on the battlefield of Eylau (9 February 1807)), 1808. Napoleon's chief surgeon,
Pierre-François Percy, is depicted to the left, helping up a Lithuanian who is saluting the
Emperor.

with, seemingly, powers to heal, the artist is declaring that Napoleon could
not be held responsible for the suffering.[59]

Napoleon's upturned gaze can be interpreted in any number of ways: as a
Christ-like supplication to the Almighty; as looking towards his star now
hidden by the clouds;[60] as a paradoxical gaze of blindness ('looking heaven-
ward, Napoleon is "blind" in the sense of looking beyond the field of action',
as if God were absent).[61] Whichever way one looks at it, Napoleon evades
responsibility for the carnage. It is the detail that intrigues. Here is a Napoleon,
dressed in a pelisse of grey satin lined with fur, a killer of men, but who is
portrayed as a saint. What can it possibly mean to offer a blessing to the victims
of the battle?[62] Napoleon is meant to console, to help the wounded. His face
now takes on the expression of 'heroic humanity'.[63] He thus appears to be even
more heroic.[64] The contrast between the snow and Napoleon's entourage, who
are painted in darker colours than the Emperor, and the pallor of his face are all
used to create the perception that we are looking at a sublime character. Moreover, despite the fact that Napoleon was driven by military conquest – indeed his
whole being existed to conquer – he knew that he could not simply rely on
brutal military glory to maintain or justify his power. He needed respect, and
for that he had to be seen to engage in acts that were worthy of emulation.

## The Clemency of His Majesty

The theme of Napoleon as a clement ruler was something he had been at pains to emphasize since first coming to power. Propaganda after Marengo, for example, focused on Bonaparte as a humane leader, beloved by his troops, a typology that dates back to the first Italian campaign. Paintings from the earliest years of his reign began to portray Bonaparte not only as the victorious general, but also as a general who cared for his men. The Salon of 1801 displayed two such examples by Nicolas-Antoine Taunay, *Passage des Alpes par le général Bonaparte* (The crossing of the Alps by General Bonaparte), in which Bonaparte is encouraging a tired soldier to lift a cannon wheel, and the *Attaque du Fort de Bard* (Attack on Fort Bard), in which soldiers contemplate a sleeping Bonaparte 'with the most tender sensitivity'.[65] In this respect, the image of a caring and even Christian (because pardoning) Bonaparte was in stark contrast to the systematic elimination of all opposition in France, which as we have seen sometimes resulted in executions, just as it was in contrast to the conditions in which the troops actually lived and died on the battlefields and in the hospitals. The newspapers made sure to mention any act that reinforced Bonaparte's compassionate character. In the days leading up to the coronation, for example, he pardoned a 'large number' of prisoners, because they were fathers often locked away for debt.[66] In 1804, before the proclamation of the Empire, it was incumbent upon the soon-to-be-crowned 'father of the people' to help fathers of families. After the foundation of the Empire, stories about Napoleon's clemency continued to circulate – one comes across them in the newspapers, pamphlets, memoirs and letters of the day[67] – but they were also present in artistic representations of Napoleon, as well as in literature, the theatre and opera.[68] The idea is especially prevalent in the later paintings of the Empire, and coincides in part with the resurrection of monarchical notions of divine right – we can thus see Napoleon granting clemency to his defeated enemies but also extending French civilization to barbarian cultures – and in part with the rising toll of dead and wounded across Europe.[69] In order to counter the anti-Napoleonic propaganda that depicted him as warmonger and butcher, government-inspired art increasingly focused on the idea of Napoleon as merciful ruler.

An example is the case of the Prussian Prince Hatzfeld, arrested in Berlin in 1806 on suspicion of spying. Sent to present Napoleon with the keys of the city, as the troops were filing past he counted them and sent off his findings to Prince Hohenlohe, in command of what was left of the Prussian army. The evidence against him was circumstantial, so it is quite possible that after the pleas of his wife, who was eight months pregnant and who supposedly fainted a number of times in the course of a reading of the indictment, Napoleon, 'touched' by this show of feelings,[70] used this occasion as an overt demonstration of his clemency. If any artists were looking for a subject to paint, this was one that was

ready-made. A number approached Vivant Denon with proposals for works on
the subject.[71] Paintings and engravings of Mme de Hatzfeld kneeling, crying,
supplicating Napoleon abounded after 1806.[72] That Napoleon was according an
act of mercy to a woman was not without significance. It was possibly seen as
more acceptable to accord clemency to a woman, since she is in a position of
submission, than to a male conspirator, for example. Napoleon was not, however,
averse to forcing the king's Noble Guard, the very same who had sharpened
their blades on the steps of the French embassy at the outbreak of war, to march
past the embassy as prisoners between two rows of soldiers, a gesture that might
be considered a little spiteful but was approved of by some Berliners who blamed
the Guard for pushing the king into war.

In 1806, Jean-François Dunant painted the *Trait de générosité française*
(Gesture of French generosity), in which Napoleon is seen distributing money

akg-images/Laurent Lecat

Marguerite Gérard, *La clémence de Napoléon Ier: Napoléon et la princesse de Hatzfeld*
(The clemency of Napoleon I: Napoleon and the Princess of Hatzfeld), 1806. In this
painting, later bought by Josephine, Napoleon points to the fire, indicating where Mme
Hatzfeld should throw the letter of accusation against her husband. It was the final act, so
to speak, in the melodrama. The gesture in the painting is, in any event, one of *clementia*
– clemency.[73]

to Austrian prisoners (very similar, it has to be said, to Philibert-Louis Debu-court's 1785 painting *Le trait d'humanité de Louis XVI*, in which he is portrayed distributing alms to a family of poor peasants). The year 1806 also saw Jean-Baptiste Debret's *Napoléon Ier saluant un convoi de blessés autri-chiens* (Napoleon salutes a convoy of wounded Austrians). Debret was inspired by a piece of official propaganda, a bulletin that was reprinted in the *Journal de Paris* shortly after the battle of Ulm. It described Napoleon's benevolence, based on an eyewitness account, when, seeing a line of Austrian wounded file past him, he took off his hat, made all the other officers in his entourage do the same and said aloud, 'Honour to courageous misfortune' (*Honneur au courage malheureux*).[74] Since there are no other accounts of this particular anecdote, it may be entirely fictive. The point being made, however, was that Napoleon was not only a victorious general, but also a benevolent, generous and kind ruler. This type of painting had the added advantage of taking away the focus from scenes of battle and the French casualties that ensued.[75] Napoleon's compassion for others goes so far as to encompass the enemy.

It was really after Eylau and the intervention in Spain that the clemency theme was emphasized in a desperate attempt to portray Napoleon in a better light to the people of France. There may have been some parallels with the ancient Roman tradition of depicting leaders in certain poses – Napoleon addressing his men, or entering a conquered city – but these paintings were meant to hide their opposite reality, that of the brutality of war.[76] At the Salon

akg-images/VISIOARS

Jean-Baptiste Debret, *Napoléon Ier saluant un convoi de blessés autrichiens et rendant hommage au courage malheureux, octobre 1805* (Napoleon salutes a convoy of wounded Austrians, and renders homage to courageous misfortune, October 1805), 1806.

of 1808, there were a number of pardon scenes, including Pierre-Narcisse Guérin's *Bonaparte fait grâce aux révoltés du Caire* (Bonaparte pardoning the rebels in Cairo).[77]

Commissioned in 1806, the painting depicts a scene that took place shortly after the Revolt of Cairo in October 1798 when Bonaparte made a public display of pardoning the rebels on El-Bekir Square. The whole point of paintings like this was to reinforce the paternal nature of the ruler over the ruled. Napoleon is slightly elevated, looking down at the supplicants who look back with a mixture of expressions ranging from fear, humiliation and resignation to what seems to be anger and defiance. It some respects, it is an allegory of the French as both conquerors and liberators. While French guards surround the group of rebels, one of them in the foreground releases a prisoner from his shackles, highlighting not only French moral superiority but also the promise of liberation to those who obey and submit.

Ironically, since some of the worst French massacres were committed there, Egypt was also the subject of at least four paintings touching on Napoleon's clemency. In Guillaume François Colson's *Trait de clémence du général Bonaparte* (Gesture of clemency from General Bonaparte) of 1812,

Pierre-Narcisse Guérin, *Bonaparte fait grâce aux révoltés du Caire, le 30 octobre 1798* (Bonaparte pardoning the rebels in Cairo, 30 October 1798), 1806–8. Bonaparte offered an amnesty, but only after brutally putting down the revolt. Hundreds were arrested and executed in the days that followed.[78]

*akg-images/Jean-Claude Varga*

Guillaume François Colson, *Trait de clémence du général Bonaparte envers une famille arabe lors de l'entrée de l'armée française à Alexandrie le 3 juillet 1798* (Gesture of clemency from General Bonaparte towards an Arab family during the entry of the French army into Alexandria on 3 July 1798), 1812. Napoleon holds out his hand in an act that calls a halt to the killing. Ten years on, he was still getting mileage out of Egypt.

an Arab mother and her child can be seen adopting a similar position to that of the wounded Lithuanian in Gros' painting of Eylau, kneeling near Napoleon's horse, hand outstretched to touch the saddle or the horse: 'Caesar, you want me to live, well, heal me and I will serve you faithfully as I served Alexander.'[79]

## 'A War of Cannibals'

The concerted effort to transform Napoleon's image was a reaction to a crisis in public opinion, not only among the people, but also in the army, that would persist and grow as military reverses took the shine off Napoleon's reputation. Spain significantly contributed to that crisis.

After Erfurt, Napoleon prepared to intervene directly in Spain. In fact, with the exception of the invasion of Russia, he paid more attention to preparing public opinion in France about what was happening in Spain than he did about any other campaign.[80] He had decided to intervene personally in August or

September, after the military disasters of Bailén (19 July 1808) and Vimeiro (21 August). In the campaign that followed, over three months from November 1808 to January 1809, he was able to redress the situation.

By 6 November 1808, Napoleon was in Vitoria ready to assume command of more than 240,000 men.[81] His plan was quite simple: take Madrid so that Joseph could govern with whatever means were at his disposal. There was little between Bayonne and Madrid that would prevent him from doing so. Under his command was not the army of raw recruits that had been mishandled by the Spanish until now. It was battle hardened and led by some of the best generals the French had, although it has to be said that their performance at certain stages of the campaign was going to be sadly wanting. Be that as it may, Napoleon's presence in Spain made victory possible, but it also highlighted the deficiencies of a system built around one man. When present, Napoleon demanded and received reports on every aspect of the campaign – civil and military – several times a day. In his absence, with no central command, the French invasion was characterized by inefficiency, exacerbated by the petty rivalries between various military and civilian leaders, none of whom wanted to obey others they considered to be of lesser rank.

'It is a war of cannibals,' complained Ney. Atrocities were committed on both sides. As the French moved into territory previously occupied but abandoned, they committed some horrendous depredations – villages were burnt to the ground, 'rebels', 'terrorists' as the French liked to call them, were hung to set an example, churches were ransacked.[82] In a deeply Catholic country, that was a certain way to alienate the locals. Napoleon expected any rebels caught to be hung and, it is said, all prisoners to be shot, especially if civilians were caught with weapons in hand. The action was designed to strike fear into the population.[83] At least one memoirist asserted that he received the order but was horrified by it.[84] He realized that 'to have the prisoners shot was a useless barbarity, for it served only to excite the hatred the Spanish felt towards us'.[85]

Under Napoleon's direction, the French inflicted a number of rapid defeats on the Anglo-Spanish armies. General Soult took Burgos on 10 November; the town was pillaged terribly.[86] Even the cemetery was ransacked in the vain hope of finding valuables in the coffins, with decomposing and skeletal bodies being abandoned along the footpath.[87] An officer by the name of Castellane saved a woman from being raped by fifty men, but many others were subjected to the same atrocity.[88] Napoleon entered the city the next day (and Joseph the day after that), disgusted by the stench of rotting bodies from those killed during the fighting. Napoleon stayed in Burgos all of ten days as the bulk of the army marched through, trying to beat his undisciplined army into shape, drawing up

notes for Joseph on the government of Spain.[89] General Victor defeated the
retreating Anglo-Spanish army at Espinosa de Los Monteros after a battle that
lasted twenty hours. Soult took Reinosa, Ney Soria, while Lannes fought and
won at Tudela. In every case, the poorly trained Spanish were outnumbered by
the French troops. After those encounters, the road to Madrid was wide open.
Advance troops approached the northern suburbs of Madrid on 1 December.
Napoleon arrived the next day, the anniversary of Austerlitz. He would have
preferred to enter the city without a fight, so that Joseph could re-enter the
capital on a sound footing. But the *junta* haughtily rejected Napoleon's offer,
delaring that the 'people of Madrid were resolved to bury themselves under
the ruins of their houses rather than permit the French to enter the city'.[90] It
was foolish. Napoleon ordered an assault on the capital to begin at dawn on 3
December. It lasted but a few hours and was all over by eleven o'clock that
same morning. When Napoleon dispatched another offer to 'pardon' the city,
the *junta* sent a delegation to negotiate. They were treated to one of Napoleon's famous scenes of rage; he let loose a storm of abuse and threatened that
if the city had not surrendered by six the following morning, he would put to
the sword every man taken arms in hand.[91]

At the beginning of the nineteenth century, Madrid was about the same size as
Berlin with a population around 235,000. Despite the religiosity of the Spanish, the city was an Enlightenment city par excellence, probably better designed
and equipped than any the French troops had yet seen. The streets were paved,
which was not often the case for Paris, and there were pavements along wide
avenues planted with trees.[92] The grand buildings that were the monarchy's
façade hid a large working-class population that had played a significant role
in the uprising.[93] Napoleon entered on 4 December. We can discount the official reports according to which he was greeted with 'an extreme pleasure'.[94] He
was to remain there for a little over two weeks, not in the royal palace, which
he wanted to leave vacant for his brother, but on the outskirts of the city in a
house at Chamartín, working incessantly to put in place the administrative
structures that would consolidate his hold on the country and to bring Spain
into line with the rest of the Empire: he abolished feudal rights, internal
customs barriers and the Inquisition; a third of all Church lands were confiscated;[95] and as was now the norm, the French grabbed whatever they could
from the Spanish art collections.[96] The confiscation of Church lands simply
confirmed Spaniards in their belief that Napoleon was an atheist. At least some
of the pillage was carried out by superior officers for their own personal gain,
unable to overcome the temptation of taking 'two or three small paintings',
hoping that they would go unnoticed.[97] We will pass over the rapine certain
generals and marshals became notorious for, but they included Pierre Dupont,
Junot, Marmont, Masséna, Lannes and Soult.[98]

If the occupation of the city was orderly, the political repression that followed was severe. In flagrant contravention of the agreement Napoleon had signed with the *junta* only a few days before, he ordered the arrest of a long list of people declared traitors, including the Council of the Inquisition. Any officers who remained in the city were declared prisoners of war. The Duc de Saint-Simon was a French émigré who had chosen to fight against the French army at the siege of Madrid in May 1808, and was thus guilty of treason. Captured, he was condemned to be shot, an expression of Napoleon's frustration at seeing French émigrés continue to fight against the Empire, despite the politics of reconciliation he had adopted early in his reign.[99] Saint-Simon's daughter, desperate to gain an audience with Napoleon in order to plead for her father's life, eventually found him in the middle of military manoeuvres where she threw herself at his feet. Napoleon granted clemency in a display of public compassion. It was grandstanding at its most spectacular.

akg-images/VISIOARS

Antoine Charles Horace Vernet, *Napoléon Ier devant Madrid, l'Empereur recevant une députation de la ville, 3 décembre 1808* (Napoleon I before Madrid, the Emperor receiving a deputation from the city, 3 December 1808), 1810. Again we are presented with the image of merciful statesman pardoning those who had revolted against him. It contrasts with the brutal reality of Napoleon's occupation of Madrid. On the left, a deputation from the city of Madrid implores the Emperor to accept their surrender. Gros exhibited a similar painting in 1810.

Napoleon was still in Madrid at the end of December when he received news that the British under Sir John Moore had clashed with elements of Soult's cavalry at Sahagún, almost 300 kilometres north of Madrid. His forces set out from Madrid on 20 December. Ney led the advance party and on the evening of the 21st reached the Sierra de Guadarrama, a mountain range that lay across the road to Madrid, a natural obstacle that could be crossed fairly easily through the Guadarrama pass. The next day, the weather conditions worsened and the troops accompanying Napoleon found it difficult to follow. Napoleon never let anything as trivial as the weather get in his way. He insisted, despite snowdrifts and high winds, that the pass be negotiated. The Dragoons of the Guard were ordered over first. They got a quarter of the way up the road and then turned back, reporting that it was impossible to go any further. Napoleon nevertheless pushed his troops ahead. Some recalled that the crossing of the Sierra de Guadarrama was far worse than that of Saint-Bernard, and that the wind was so strong that the troops could hardly make any headway.[100] A number of men died in the course of the day, either of cold or falling from precipices, so that Napoleon, even though he was there, in the thick of it, was openly threatened. Soldiers from the Lapisse Division goaded each other to shoot him first, accusing each other of cowardice for not doing so. Napoleon heard it all, but seemed to take it in his stride.[101] In any event, his persistence paid off; they got across by the end of 23 December, although many would later recall the crossing with horror.

The pursuit proved fruitless. Moore managed to evade the French, although Napoleon's interpretation of the British retreat was slightly out of touch with the reality. He wrote to Josephine to say that they were 'fleeing in a terrified fashion'.[102] It is true that Moore was hard pressed, and that the condition of his troops did not allow him to turn and fight a battle at any point during the retreat, but they were able to withdraw, in good order, all the way to Coruña, where he was evacuated by the Royal Navy. When Napoleon realized this was going to happen, he reduced the size of his force and handed it over to Soult.

## The Courtier's Mask . . .

Napoleon had decided to leave Spain, without having fought a standing battle. As in Egypt, and as in Russia only two years later, he informed only a few people in his entourage that he was going home. He told Joseph that he would be in Paris for twenty days or so and that he would be back around the end of February. The same day he changed his mind and wrote that it would be the end of October 1809.[103]

The news he received from France was not the most encouraging. He was getting alarming reports about a 'conspiracy' that was forming in Paris (a reference to the Talleyrand–Fouché alliance).[104] It was also increasingly obvious that

Austria was mobilizing its army against France. There was, therefore, good reason to return, but Napoleon also seems to have been influenced in his decision by an unrealistic assessment of the situation on the ground in Spain. He fully believed his job there was over; he had broken the back of Spanish resistance, and had thrown the Anglo-Spanish army out of Spain through Coruña.[105] 'The Spanish affair is done with,' he wrote to Jérôme, and that appears to be the extent of his thinking on the matter.[106] He left instructions with a number of his commanders to crush what resistance remained, and advised Joseph on the best way to control Madrid – a few good hangings would do the trick.[107]

After giving the orders to have everything prepared for a dash to Paris, and writing to Joseph to spread the rumour that he would be back within a month,[108] Napoleon left Valladolid on 17 January 1809, and travelled the first 120 kilometres in five hours. The news that he was leaving did not impress those left behind; nobody wanted to be in Spain.[109] Paul Thiébault, who was travelling from Valladolid to Burgos, was passed by Napoleon and his aide-de-camp, galloping so fast that the rest of his retinue and his guard were a minute or two behind.[110] Napoleon reached the capital on 23 January, having travelled over 1,100 kilometres in six days. He had been in Spain all of three months, but had learnt nothing. He did not come away with a better appreciation of the difficulties of occupying the country, and he appears to have been convinced that whatever resistance the French met was temporary. However, his hold over Spain in 1809 was precarious. He did not control Portugal, which would subsequently be used as an entry point by the British to introduce troops, and he had not won the hearts and minds of the Spanish people by implementing reforms. On the contrary, the Spanish resented having their traditions overturned. The instructions Napoleon left on the manner of concluding the campaign reveal how much he treated Spain as though it were another conventional war, and show the extent to which he simply did not understand what was happening on the ground.

Napoleon's sudden return to Paris did not go down well. There was all sorts of conjecture about his motives: that things were going badly in Spain and that he was abandoning its conquest; that war with Austria was inevitable; that relations with Russia had deteriorated; and that those close to him were plotting.[111] There is a grain of truth to all of these suppositions. One of the first people Napoleon saw on his return was Cambacérès. That evening he berated him for not warning him of the rapprochement between Talleyrand and Fouché.[112] It was not until five days later, however, on the afternoon of Saturday 28 January, during a meeting of the Council of State that there was a scene.[113] The Comte de Montesquiou, recently admitted to the Council and about to be sworn in, was the only person to commit the scene to paper. Napoleon started off in a reasonable enough tone, critical of those who had intrigued behind his back without naming any names. When he saw that Talleyrand remained entirely passive, he increasingly lost his temper. The dressing down that followed lasted between thirty minutes and two hours.[114] Napoleon started by complaining that they had interpreted as unfortunate a campaign that was marked by success and that they had been acting as if the succession were open. Interestingly, the minister of finance, Nicolas-François Mollien, suggests that the opinions Napoleon attributed to Fouché and Talleyrand were those to be found among the general public, and that it was this more than anything else that had made an impression on Napoleon.

During this outburst Napoleon supposedly shouted at Talleyrand the now famous phrase: 'You are nothing but shit in silk stockings.' It is a wonderful line, although undoubtedly apocryphal.[115] It is clear though that Napoleon thought it, and probably uttered something similar to Caulaincourt years later. Throughout the ordeal, Talleyrand maintained an imperturbable façade, limiting himself when it was all over to the mildest of reactions by remarking to someone standing near by, 'What a pity that such a great man should be so ill bred.' Two days later, in evident disgrace, Talleyrand lost his position of grand chamberlain, although even that did not prevent him from attending court as though nothing had happened. For Talleyrand was not disgraced, or not entirely. He kept the title of 'Vice Grand Elector', a purely honorific position with no responsibilities. He was never again admitted to a private audience with Napoleon, who never again asked him his opinion, but he was always kept within reach. Fouché, surprisingly, retained his job, for the moment. He was dismissed from office in June 1810, supposedly for having secretly entered into peace negotiations with Britain.

Talleyrand, from a profoundly aristocratic family with an abundance of 'good taste' – a studied elegance, simple manners, complete self-control – cultivated a polite exterior, and one that was so deeply embedded it would never crack, even in the face of extreme adversity.[116] This is about a polite façade that gave nothing away, an important element of court politics. Court society was a society of masks, a society in which one learnt to dissimulate one's thoughts and feelings.[117] Talleyrand's inscrutable face was born of the need to protect himself from the gaze of the Other. Louis XVI, for example, would never give way to impulse or testify to feelings by some sort of physical expression. Reactions that revealed true feeling rather than calculated behaviour gave rivals a trump card that could then be used to harm or discredit.

## . . . and Napoleon's Bad Behaviour

Napoleon's insulting behaviour, on the other hand, was a blatant sign of disrespect after which it was permissible, even justifiable, for Talleyrand to sever or manipulate the relationship with him as he saw fit.[118] One suspects that

Talleyrand never forgave Napoleon for what was a very public humiliation. As a result of this and other slights he was to suffer over the coming years, the love and admiration he had once felt for Napoleon were gradually transformed into hatred.[119]

In this particular instance, Napoleon's verbal onslaught revealed a sense of betrayal by someone who had professed such deep affection for him on so many occasions. It is entirely possible that he knew, consciously or not, that Talleyrand had undermined his efforts at Erfurt. It is even possible that a Janus-faced Fouché had informed Napoleon of this.[120] But that is only part of the story. Of petty noble origin, a rough and ready soldier without tact and with little self-control, Napoleon almost never refrained from violent outbursts, even in front of foreign dignitaries. There are innumerable examples of him insulting, abusing and even assaulting courtiers, both men and women (although admittedly he never laid a hand on any woman), almost as though he took a distinct pleasure in humiliating those beneath him.[121] We know that he could lose control and lash out, sometimes using a riding crop to thrash his poor interlocutor across the head and shoulders. He did this to his secretary (when he was in Syria), and cut his groom with his whip (when in Poland). The groom had been helping him mount his horse and did so a little too vigorously, sending his imperial master flying over the other side.[122]

Napoleon did not reserve his violence for his servants; high-ranking men came in for thrashings too. The Comte de Volney, a writer and member of the Senate, was kicked in the stomach during a 'discussion' about the Concordat in 1802. Napoleon then rang for someone to come and pick him up and coldly ordered him to his carriage.[123] Volney sent in his resignation as senator the next day, though Bonaparte did not accept it. Napoleon once hit the minister of the interior, Chaptal, with a roll of papers, like a master hitting his dog; and he is said to have pushed the minister of justice (Régnier, not Molé) on to a sofa and laid into him with his fists. During the campaign in Germany in 1813 he struck a general across the face. Diplomats too came in for verbal drubbings – recall the scene with Whitworth, but he also verbally attacked the Austrian envoy in 1808, the Russian envoy in 1811 and a deputy from Hamburg in 1813 – as did monarchs. We saw what happened with Alexander in Erfurt in 1808. Some historians believe, echoing Napoleon's own assertion, that these scenes were carefully prepared and were intended to strike fear into his opponents so that they would become compliant.[124] It is possible that he did so in a few instances, but on other occasions it is evident that the outburst was spontaneous, and violent.

Napoleon referred to these episodes as his 'outbursts' (the word in French is *transports*, which can also mean 'rapture'). Essentially he was an egalitarian; he treated everybody the same; no one was exempt from his rage. He lacked the dignity, the courtesy and the serenity that was meant to characterize a monarch, and his behaviour is in sharp contrast to the way in which he was customarily depicted in paintings of the day – dignified and calm. Napoleon, however, was by no means the only eighteenth-century sovereign to behave appallingly. The King of Württemberg, Frederick I, was known for hitting his ministers and staff officers with a baton.[125] Alexander of Russia had a terrible temper and was capable of threatening and insulting with the best of them.

In the army, it was not uncommon for French officers, in pre-revolutionary times at least, to hit their men, either punching them, whipping them with their riding crops or hitting them with the flat of their swords (this was not limited to the French; corporal punishment in the Prussian army was notorious even by eighteenth-century standards). These were the times: physical abuse was common and a reasonably acceptable mode of behaviour. Power is often a question of force, something Napoleon used as an instrument of government, rather than refined manners. There is, however, the flipside to this coin – there are witnesses who insist that they never saw Napoleon lose his temper and that he was very attentive to others.[126] It shows the extent to which no historical evidence can be taken at face value.

# 15
# The Tide Turns

## 'For the Love of the Fatherland'

'There can no longer be any question what Napoleon wants,' Archduke
Charles wrote to the Austrian Emperor, Francis. 'He wants everything.'[1]
Napoleon's behaviour in Spain left the courts of Europe with the impression
that his ambition knew no bounds. By that stage, Austria had already decided
to go to war. The head of the war faction was the minister for foreign affairs,
Johann-Philipp von Stadion. A professional diplomat who had served as
ambassador at the courts of Berlin and St Petersburg, he had been in charge of
foreign affairs since the end of 1805. Over the course of December 1808 and
January 1809, he was able to convince the four important groupings at court
– the military, the bureaucracy, the diplomatic corps and the imperial family –
that it was in Austria's best interests to resume war against France.[2] The war
faction, encouraged by the difficulties the French were encountering in Spain,
also comprised two of the Emperor's own brothers – Grand Duke Ferdinand
of Würzburg and Archduke John – as well as a number of other senior military
and administrative figures, and the Emperor's (third) wife, Maria Ludovica.
Genuinely disturbed by the reports floating around Vienna of French atrocities in Spain, and inspired by the resistance of the Spanish people, Maria
Ludovica began urging her husband to make a stand against Napoleon. Given
that Francis was terribly in love with her, scholars generally agree that her
influence over him was decisive.[3]

Spain was an important factor, but the Austrian ambassador to Paris, the
young, brilliant, if slightly delusional, and staunchly conservative aristocrat
Klemens von Metternich, also had a part to play. His dispatches from Paris
since the beginning of his mission in 1806 created a number of mistaken
impressions: that war with France was inevitable; that Napoleon's ultimate
objective was the partition of the Habsburg monarchy; and that France was
exhausted and tired of Napoleon's ambitious projects.[4] Metternich reported
that opposition to Napoleon was beginning to form at the highest political
levels, and that the only people prepared to support another war were a small
section of the army – that is, that Napoleon had lost the support of the French
nation, whose greatest desire was peace.[5] As 1809 progressed, Metternich
insisted that there could be no peace with a 'revolutionary system', and that
Napoleon had declared 'eternal war' against the European powers.[6] Spain
simply reinforced the view already held by Metternich, namely, that Napoleon

was truly bent on universal domination. Talleyrand, who is reported to have told Metternich that Napoleon 'hated [Austria] to death', gave those views a little impetus.[7] Metternich had been a long-time advocate of conciliation with France, so his reports may have been that much more powerful.

When Stadion recalled Metternich to Vienna for political consultations between November 1808 and January 1809 (Napoleon was away in Spain), the ambassador spoke personally with the Austrian Emperor on a number of occasions, and later submitted three memoranda on the situation, urging that Austria take advantage of Napoleon's absence in Spain to launch an attack against him.[8] Stadion, too, delivered a memorandum in which he reminded Francis that Napoleon had boasted in 1806 that he would make his dynasty the oldest in Europe.[9] It simply reinforced the notion that no monarchy was safe. It did not take much for Stadion to convince Francis that with the House of Bourbon now virtually eliminated from Europe, the Habsburgs were next on Napoleon's hit list. The fact that Napoleon had made threatening noises against Austria the previous year while he was at Erfurt, openly suggesting that he was in a position to dismember the Austrian monarchy if he wanted to, only reinforced the perceived threat.[10] Appeasement was no longer possible under those conditions. At most, it would delay the inevitable destruction of the Habsburg monarchy. Even the Archduke Charles had to concur, and suggested that Austria start making preparations for a war, even though he did not hold out much hope of success.[11]

Charles was right about Austria's chances of success, and he ought to have known. He was considered one of the ablest generals of his time, and he had been placed in charge of reforming the Austrian army after the last resounding defeat in 1805. That was three years before, during which time a gigantic effort had been made to mobilize almost 450,000 men, and another 150,000 had been organized into a national militia known as the Landwehr,[12] while the army had been restructured with the formation of independent army corps and the reorganization of the field artillery. The last two reforms, however, were problematic since, introduced only at the beginning of 1809, they had not yet become firmly established. Corps commanders, for example, had little or no practical experience, unlike their French counterparts who were all battle hardened.[13]

Charles had, in effect, attempted to transpose the French Revolution's 'nation in arms' – the idea that the entire population was at the disposal of the country's war machine – on to Austria, believing naively that when war broke out the people of Germany would rally behind the Austrian throne in much the same way that the Spanish people had rallied behind their monarchy. Vienna had been inspired by the Spanish example – reports about Spain regularly appeared in the *Wiener Zeitung*[14] – but some in the Austrian political elite mistakenly believed they could somehow replicate the people's uprising from the top. There was a concerted effort to mobilize public support for the war through newspapers, pamphlets, poems, sermons from church pulpits and official proclamations: Francis II appealed to all Austrian men to join either the army or the militia 'for the love of the fatherland'.[15] Patriotic journals attempted to whip up support among the people, especially since many of those inspired in this way were conscripted for the first time. It was necessary to convince them that the war was meaningful, to instil particular ideas about the 'fatherland' and 'national honour', and to convince them that dying for the fatherland was the highest form of manly behaviour.[16] It was expecting too much. That kind of nationalist fervour was still in its incipient stages; Austria in 1809 was not France in 1792.

## Eckmühl

Charles got off to a bad start.[17] The original plan was to march from Bohemia to the River Main in the hope of inspiring northern Germany to rise up, but then Charles changed his mind and ordered the army to concentrate in Bavaria. In doing so, he threw everyone and everything into disarray. Both supplies and troops had to be redirected, losing ten precious days in the process, and allowing the French time to concentrate their forces. Worse, once in Bavaria the Austrians proved lethargic and failed to crush the Bavarian army.

Napoleon, accompanied by Josephine this time, left Paris early in the morning of 13 April 1809. Seven hundred kilometres and four days later, they reached Donauwörth, about one hundred kilometres north-west of Munich. It was there that Napoleon learnt that the enemy was trying to break through at Regensburg (Ratisbon) further to the east. He therefore ordered his forces to concentrate at that town. Five days of fighting followed while Napoleon, complacent, unable to take seriously an army he had defeated many times before, tried to direct operations from a distance, without being fully apprised of the situation in a number of areas of operations. He was, therefore, basing his calculations on inaccurate information and on conjecture. It was not until 20 April when he arrived before Abensberg (not far from Regensburg) that he was able personally to direct operations. The battle that followed south of Regensburg at Eckmühl (or Eggmühl) on 22 April was indecisive and did no more than maul the main Austrian army.[18]

There followed the storming of Regensburg during which Napoleon was wounded slightly in the heel (23 April). News of the incident quickly ran through the ranks, which is exactly why, despite the pain – 'it hardly scratched the Achilles tendon', he reassured Josephine – he immediately got back on his horse and rode among the ranks, bestowing decorations on soldiers he passed.[19] The upshot was that Napoleon failed to deliver a knockout blow and the Archduke Charles made good his escape across the Danube. The campaign

Pierre Gautherot, *Napoléon Ier, blessé au pied devant Ratisbonne, est soigné par le chirurgien Yvan, 23 avril 1809* (Napoleon I, wounded in the foot at Ratisbon, is treated by the surgeon Yvan, 23 April 1809), 1810. An idealized vision of Napoleon's wounding. Gautherot was a student of David.

was really only just beginning. Charles, however, was made so despondent by the mauling he had received at Eckmühl that he was already prepared to throw in the towel and advised his brother to make peace.[20]

The road to Vienna was now open again. This time, unlike in 1805, the city was to be defended. Preparations for its defence, however, began far too late, not until 5 May.[21] By then, most of the city's 200,000 inhabitants had fled the approach of the French. There was some cursory resistance when the French finally arrived at the gates of the capital on 13 May – the French bombarded some of the outlying suburbs – but the city's garrison withdrew to the northern bank of the Danube, destroying all four bridges across the river in their retreat.[22] In the days leading up to the French occupation, public opinion in Vienna had turned from support for the war to relief that it would soon be over. An inhabitant of Vienna reported that the city's women rushed to greet the French soldiers with such alacrity that it reminded him of 'Sodom and Gomorrah'.[23]

It was no doubt a slight exaggeration, even if the city held a certain number of delights. The writer Stendhal saw 'a pretty woman at every step', heard excellent music and went to see some Italian ballets.[24] The city would normally have offered a variety of theatres that were always well attended, and there were public balls every Sunday evening. Like most cities of its day, only a few streets had pavements, and these were lined with elegant mansions. The two most famous were the Herren Gasse and the Kohlgraben. There were too a number of imposing imperial buildings, fine squares and museums. And if one could not find any amusements in the city, then a ride to one of the parks surrounding the city, such as the Prater, the Augarten or the Lusthaus, held 'pleasing scenery' and 'extensive and romantic views'.

Napoleon occupied Vienna and took up residence at the Schönbrunn Palace on the outskirts of the city. Occupying a capital, as he had discovered with Prussia (and would again discover with Russia) did not mean the end of the war. Despite Charles's pleadings, Francis decided to fight on. Charles subsequently took up position on the northern bank of the Danube so that there was a river between his forces and the French in Vienna. He had managed to bring together about 115,000 men. Napoleon, on the other hand, had only about 82,000 men and did not yet realize the strength of the Austrian army facing him.

## 'So the Man is Mad'

The battle took place in a difficult context.[25] Napoleon may have taken Vienna, but the war was going badly for the French on other fronts. In Italy, Eugène, after some initial successes, was defeated by Archduke John at Sacile (16 April 1809). The Tyrol rose in revolt, a revolt that had been carefully prepared by a local named Andreas Hofer.[26] There were uprisings in Prussia led by Major von Schill and in Hesse led by Colonel Dernburg.[27] In northern Germany, opposition to the French began to radicalize, disguised within organizations like the League of Virtue (Tugendbund) or gymnastic associations that practised 'shooting and reading', but which were fronts for German nationalism.[28] Censorship did its best to control the flow of news, and Napoleon could shoot journalists that overstepped the mark (as happened to Johann Philipp Palm in 1806), but he could not stem the tide of ideas. In the Iberian Peninsula, Soult had been obliged to retreat from Portugal. In Holland, a British expeditionary force landed at Walcheren.[29] In Italy, relations with the pope were at breaking point. And on top of all that there was an economic crisis both in the Empire and in France proper brought about by bad harvests and the consequences of Britain's Continental Blockade.[30]

The precariousness of the Empire was never more evident than during this conjuncture when, once again, it seemed as though its future existence hinged on the outcome of one battle. To come to grips with Archduke Charles, though, Napoleon had to cross the Danube. Since the bridges had been burnt, Lobau, an island in the river east of the city, was chosen as the place most suitable for building a temporary crossing. The river was wider and slower here than at other parts, and the water shallower. French sappers began to construct the pontoons needed to span the 750 metres between the banks of the Danube and the island on 19 May. The bridge was completed and the troops started to cross at around midday on 20 May, but a large hulk floated down the river by the Austrians broke the bridge so that no more troops could get across that night.[31] Napoleon was still not aware at this stage that he was facing the bulk of the Austrian army. Clearly, the French scouting parties sent across to reconnoitre had not done their job.

The French repaired the bridge overnight so that there was a steady stream of troops marching across the next morning. It was then that Charles decided to bring up his army and launch an attack across a ten-kilometre front, centring on the villages of Aspern and Essling, only a short distance from the Austrian capital. The Viennese gathered in the Prater to watch, or climbed what roofs and church towers they could to get a glimpse of the battle unfolding before them, but were unable to see much for the thick pall of smoke that lay over the field.[32] Charles caught the French completely by surprise. Aspern changed hands six or seven times in the course of the day but the French managed to hang on there, and did so at Essling too with a good deal more ease. The bridge was again broken during the day with the result that after midday the flow of troops to the island was interrupted. When Napoleon realized the extent of the Austrian forces he was facing, he briefly considered calling off the whole operation, but once Charles began to attack he had to persist.[33]

The outcome of the next day's battle would depend on whether the French could keep open the bridge in order to maintain the flow of troops. The first day's fighting saw 31,000 French facing over 100,000 Austrians. By the beginning of the second day of the battle, with troops crossing during the night, the French were still considerably outnumbered and outgunned, 62,000 men and 144 guns compared to over 100,000 men and 260 guns. Napoleon nevertheless went on the offensive, ordering Lannes to push through the centre. Lannes did as instructed, and it looked as though victory was in sight when an Austrian counter-attack led personally by Charles restored the situation. After the bridge had been broken again at eight o'clock, and again, following repairs, after midday by a floating mill that had been set on fire, Napoleon had no choice but to call off the battle. He had crossed the bridge earlier in the day and was even engaged in siting cannon when news arrived around four in the afternoon that Lannes had been wounded. Napoleon ordered a retreat back on to the island of Lobau. It was a defeat of sorts: 15,000–19,000 French killed and wounded (although the bulletin reported only 4,100 French casualties) compared to around 20,000–22,000 Austrian killed and wounded. Napoleon's adversaries were learning how to make war.[34] If in military terms this was by no means a major setback, it hurt Napoleon politically. It was the first time that, if not defeated, his army had been contained, at least in Europe (contemporaries had a tendency to forget about Syria).

By all accounts, Napoleon was shocked by Lannes' wounding.[35] When he saw him being carried by two carabiniers he rushed over, weeping according to some, and had to be pulled away by Duroc. Napoleon saw Lannes later that day in what was reported to be a heartrending meeting after Larrey, the surgeon-in-chief, had amputated both legs. He visited Lannes once or twice a day for the next week. Lannes had been with him since the first Italian campaign and was a passionate adherent of the Emperor. It looked for a while as though he might recover, but nine days after the battle, on 31 May, after passing in and out of delirium, he died of gangrene.[36] The death of Lannes appears to have affected Napoleon deeply. Did Napoleon kiss Lannes' forehead and bathe it in his tears?[37] It is unlikely, though he did mourn, but that too was a political gesture. The imperial propaganda machine exploited Napoleon's personal sorrow, portraying him not as warrior, but rather as father figure who hated war and deplored the loss of one of his cherished children.

Albert-Paul Bourgeois, *Le Maréchal Lannes mortellement blessé près d'Essling le 22 mai 1809* (Marshal Lannes mortally wounded after the battle of Essling, 22 May 1809), 1810. The focus is not so much on Lannes dying as on Napoleon as grieving father, who occupies the centre of the painting. The emphasis increasingly in the latter part of the Empire is on the person of Napoleon, and not on his military conquests.

The mistakes Napoleon had made were in retrospect obvious: he should have built more than one bridge across the Danube; and he should have assembled as many troops as possible on Lobau before crossing. More remarkable though is the lack of initiative on the part of Archduke Charles. He did not have a killer instinct; he should have bombarded Lobau mercilessly, especially since Napoleon seems to have been overcome with inertia – exhausted, depressed – for the next thirty-six hours. But Charles did not press home his advantage, motivated by a desire to keep the Austrian army intact, and by what he saw as an opponent that was as threatening as Napoleon – Russia. He consequently gave Napoleon all the time in the world to evacuate Lobau.

In Buda, where the Austrian court had fled, a young princess by the name of Marie-Louise heard of the victory, and confided to a friend, 'It is the first time that Napoleon himself has been defeated, and we must thank God for it . . . but we must not be too puffed up with pride . . . and I must confess that I am so accustomed to disappointments that I dare not hope for too much.'[38] Certainly, the court of Vienna hoped – believed – that the battle would encourage Berlin and Petersburg to join the fray. That did not happen. The hawks at the court of Berlin pushed for intervention, on the side of the coalition needless to say.[39] Prussia even made an offer to join, but that was dependent on two conditions: Austria accepting Prussian hegemony in northern Germany, and Russia giving its approval. Alexander, on the other hand, was more interested in conquering Finland and the Danubian principalities than in coming to Vienna's aid.[40] Admittedly, Alexander was caught in a bind – officially tied to France, he was sympathetic to the Austrian cause – but Austria had certainly been working under the mistaken assumption that he would not only come out fully on its side, but would bring Prussia with him. It is little wonder then that Napoleon complained to Savary, 'They have all given themselves rendezvous over my tomb, but none of them wants to be the first to arrive.'[41]

For some, it was not Spain but rather the battle of Essling that marks a turning point in Napoleon's popularity.[42] We know that news of the costliness of the battle troubled Parisian opinion; it was the first time that the Emperor's reputation as a military genius was tarnished, to the point that some were now toying with the idea that he had gone mad.[43] It is the first time the term was used to describe Napoleon, and even though it was not yet used very seriously, the idea would continue to grow. It was, moreover, a sort of justification for opposition to the regime; one is not being disloyal if the man at the helm no longer has the respect of those he is leading and is now suspected of being 'mad'. Over the next few years, people would come back to that idea. Jérôme's wife, Catherine of Württemberg, for example, during Napoleon's tour of Belgium and the northern coasts in 1810, when it looked as though he was again contemplating an invasion of England, wrote in her diary that 'I would say to myself that man is crazy, it is cruel to destroy because of a difference of opinion! and why cannot they [the Bonapartes] enjoy quietly, peacefully, the infinite blessings that Providence has lavished on them!'[44] The Comtesse de Boigne, admittedly a monarchist so her testimony has to be treated with caution, pointed to the sheer indifference with which the sound of the cannon announcing another victory was greeted by the Parisian population at large. They had had their fill of victories; another battle won meant more men had to be conscripted; another town conquered meant that further towns had to be occupied.[45]

### The Battle of the Cannon

Austria was in a relatively good position to continue the fighting and emerge victorious. Its troops had taken Warsaw, Dresden and Bayreuth, and the Tyrol was in revolt. What was lacking, perhaps above all else, was political determination. Charles, despite his near victory, still wanted to negotiate with Napoleon, while Stadion was insistent that the struggle continue. These two opposing views split the administration and the army into two camps, one supporting war, the other supporting peace, and in some respects prevented the Austrian army from taking the offensive. What Charles did instead was wait for Napoleon to attack.

Napoleon had to regroup and prepare for the next offensive. This time, he prepared well and did so over the next six weeks.[46] Units were brought closer to Vienna so that almost 160,000 troops were positioned in and around the city by the end of June, military stores were built up, and the artillery was given a badly needed boost with the incorporation of Austrian as well as extra French cannon so that there were around 500 guns available by the time hostilities resumed. Five good bridges were built across the Danube while Lobau was turned into a fortified area with 129 guns. Skirmishes and artillery barrages had taken place in the days leading up to the morning of 4 July, when about one hundred French artillery pieces opened up, covering the crossing of the Danube, further south than the previous month. This time, there were no incidents, and the bridges built by the sappers were more solid. Moreover, barques and boats were also used to assist thousands of troops to cross over.

The next day, the two armies faced each other, formidable in size, for what was later dubbed the battle of Wagram, and once again it was avidly watched from the roofs, bell towers and church steeples of Vienna.[47] Napoleon commanded 190,000 men and disposed of 500 artillery pieces, while this time Charles had considerably fewer – 140,000 men and about 450 artillery pieces, all spread out along a twenty-two-kilometre front.[48] Charles was hoping for another 30,000 men to arrive under his brother Archduke John, who had been engaged in Italy, but he was still too far away. John's arrival would probably not have made all that much difference to the outcome of the battle in any event; Napoleon was aware that he was moving towards the battlefield and had placed four divisions in reserve to meet him.

The first day (5 July) went well for Napoleon; he managed to get all his men across the Danube without incident, attack the Austrian formations and secure a central position. A number of crises during the day were staved off, on both sides. At one point, the French appeared to be on the point of breaking through the centre when Archduke Charles appeared with reinforcements to shore up his faltering lines. Later, panic set in among the Italian troops under Macdonald's command; they turned tail and fled in a way that had never been seen before among Napoleon's troops, and were stopped only by the bayonets of the Imperial Guard.[49] By that stage, late in the day, the impetus the French had initially gained began to fade with the light. No ground or real strategic advantage had been obtained by either side at the end of the first day's fighting, although things had not gone too badly for Napoleon. He was still in a position to deliver a decisive blow the next day. That night he slept sheltered by a pile of drums, dozing in between interviews with officers who came up for orders.

The troops did not sleep many hours that night. Fighting was resumed the next day (6 July) as soon as light broke, around four in the morning. The Austrian Emperor was able to watch the battle unfold from the Bisamberg heights; by his side was Metternich who had come from Paris at the end of May. It was far less like an eighteenth-century battle and much more like a modern-day battle in which artillery played a pivotal role. At one stage, Napoleon assembled, with great difficulty, about 100 cannon to pound the Austrian centre, before launching an attack of 15,000 men to break through. They were stopped; Napoleon was obliged to throw in his reserves. By three o'clock that afternoon, the battle had been won – Napoleon took a few moments' nap on the ground – even though fighting continued till nightfall. The Austrians, much to their credit, retreated in good order – Charles's reputation, at least as commander, remained intact – while the French cavalry was too exhausted to pursue them.

Wagram was dubbed the 'battle of the cannon'. The French estimated that they had expended around 100,000 rounds over two days, while the Austrians fired a similar number. Napoleon may have won the field, but he lost almost as many men as the Austrians – probably around 39,000 killed, wounded or taken prisoner, one-quarter of effectives on the field of battle (regardless of the grossly under-reported casualty figures in the bulletins).[50] Estimates are as high as 66,000 men killed and wounded.[51] The casualties included forty generals and more than 1,800 junior officers. The Austrian figures were comparable. Charles reported that around 37,000 troops had been killed, wounded or taken prisoner, about one-quarter of effectives (although it is possible the real figure was higher).[52] The battle was, consequently, far from decisive and did not strike a mortal blow at the enemy. The Austrians had performed well and had extricated themselves in good order as soon as Charles realized that the battle was likely to be lost. His troops exhausted, Napoleon was obliged to give them a night's sleep before pursuing the enemy.

Marmont and Masséna caught up with them a few days later (10 July) at Znaim, and although the Austrians engaged and held off the French, a completely demoralized Charles asked for an armistice. Hugues-Bernard Maret, now foreign minister, and Duroc were against any suspension of hostilities; they wanted to push ahead and destroy the enemy. It was Napoleon, with some help from Berthier, who reined in his generals. He no doubt realized that his men were exhausted and that the troops of 1809 were not those of 1805. The troops were not the only ones exhausted. This campaign began to show the flaws in Napoleon's own condition. By the end of it, after being on the road for more than three months, he was physically and quite possibly mentally drained. The armistice was signed at two in the morning of 12 July. Napoleon returned to Schönbrunn the next day.

It was the end of Charles's career. On 18 July, his brother Francis removed him from his post as commander-in-chief of the Austrian army. The only man who up until now had proved a match for Napoleon, and who was still considered one of the most able Austrian generals, was never to lead men into battle again.[53]

The campaign and the loss of men that resulted should have given Napoleon pause for thought. It did not. Wagram was one of the largest land battles that had ever been fought up till then, involving 300,000 troops along a twenty-kilometre front, and is often considered a turning point not only in the Napoleonic wars but in modern warfare in general. It says a great deal about the rapidly changing nature of warfare under Napoleon. In Italy in 1796 the major battles pitched around 50,000 men against each other in engagements that at most lasted a day. Now, the major battles involved hundreds of thousands of men and thousands of cannon fighting for two or three days.[54] Wagram also foreshadowed a change in the way battles were fought: cavalry was rendered less effective, the artillery took centre-stage, and campaigns were less about knockout blows than a war of attrition.

Until this point in time, Napoleon's military flair had been extraordinary, but he had made a good deal more out of his victories, politically, through propaganda, than the reality warranted. Egypt, as we know, was a half-success, although one would not know it from reading contemporary accounts of it; Marengo was a battle almost lost, through lack of foresight on Bonaparte's part if you will, or bad luck, won only by the timely intervention of others; Austerlitz was a brilliant victory but had become so steeped in legend, playing into his own myth of manifest destiny, that it became easy for Napoleon to believe he had planned everything, foreseen everything, well beforehand; Jena was a battle won, but it was Davout who defeated the bulk of the Prussian army at Auerstädt; Eylau had been a bloodbath and was really a draw.

This was the first time Napoleon had encountered an enemy who had his measure. Charles had learnt from his past encounters with the French. Napoleon had won the campaign but at a cost, and this was telling because it was the only time he did not attempt to exploit his victories for political purposes. There were few attempts to exploit the battle as a great victory.[55] The artistic focus, as we have seen, was on the death of Lannes, and Napoleon in mourning. There were only ever popular representations of the battle, attempts by enterprising individuals to cash in on the event.[56] When Napoleon returned to Paris, there were no celebrations, and the attempt by a fawning Institute to bestow on him the title 'Augustus' and 'Germanicus' fell flat. Napoleon replied that there was nothing 'to envy in what we know of the Roman emperors'.[57]

More than anything, the campaign in Austria brought Napoleon to the realization that he could no longer count on Alexander. He had personally asked the Tsar to intervene on a number of occasions, but the Russians took an eternity to reach the theatre of operations, and when they arrived, entering Galicia on 3 June 1809, they did everything in their power to avoid confronting the Austrians.[58] In fact, Alexander had already secretly informed Austria that he would not attack them. His behaviour was indicative of how onerous he found the French alliance, but it also made a profound impression on Napoleon, to the point where, 'wounded', he no longer believed in his Russian ally.[59] Relations between the two nevertheless had to appear normal even if behind the scenes mistrust and suspicion were the rule. Napoleon wondered what concessions he might make in order to get him back onside, grudgingly giving Russia part of Austrian Galicia as a 'reward' for its part in the campaign.

## Schönbrunn

In the negotiations with Austria that followed, Napoleon did not entirely have the upper hand. The Austrians were still capable, it was thought, of putting another 250,000 men in the field (even if that proved not to be the case; the Austrian army was depleted and morale was low, to say the least). Before Wagram, Napoleon had toyed with the idea of breaking up the Austrian Empire by promoting a Hungarian national revolution: Francis would be forced to abdicate and the Empire would then be divided between the archdukes into three kingdoms – Austria, Hungary and Bohemia.[60] The other option was to force Francis to abdicate in favour of his brother, the Grand Duke Ferdinand. Davout for one was pushing him towards partition; thousands of proclamations in French, German and Hungarian were distributed, calling on the Magyars to revolt and promising them an independent state.[61]

But Napoleon never vigorously pursued these ideas. Instead, through the ineffectual Champagny, he presented Austria with an ultimatum: either Francis would have to abdicate if Austria were to maintain its territorial integrity; or Austria would have to lose territory if Francis were to remain.[62] Napoleon wanted a victor's treaty that would impress upon Europe the extent of the victory of Wagram, and for that to happen Austria was going to have to sacrifice as many subjects again as at Pressburg, the treaty that had concluded the campaign of 1805. Since Francis did not abdicate, Austria had to give up control over its territories in the Confederation of the Rhine, Galicia (returned to the Duchy of Warsaw) and the Adriatic ports of Trieste and Fiume (the Illyrian Provinces), making Austria landlocked and bringing it into line with Napoleon's attempt to exclude Britain from the Continent. In the process, it lost 3.5 million souls. Moreover, it had to pay an indemnity of 200 million francs (Vienna was forced to confiscate all silver in private hands in an attempt to meet the indemnity),[63] and reduce its army to 150,000 men.

The reaction of the Austrian people to the peace – the Treaty of Schönbrunn – was similar in some respects to that of the German people in 1919. There was relief the war was over, but also a feeling that somehow the Austrian people had been not so much defeated as betrayed by the diplomats at the negotiating table.[64] Contemporaries condemned the conditions – Stadion commented that the treaty may have avoided Austria's complete destruction, but it would nonetheless effect a slow strangulation.[65] Similarly, most historians describe this as a harsh treaty, one going so far as to call it 'vicious', but it certainly was not in comparison to Prussia's treatment a few years earlier – there was no army of occupation as in Prussia that bled the country dry – and it was certainly not as severe as Napoleon's Bavarian ally would have liked it to have been.[66]

Two days before the conclusion of peace with Austria, on 12 October 1809, Napoleon was reviewing the army at Schönbrunn when an eighteen-year-old by the name of Friedrich Stapps, the son of a Lutheran minister, approached him as though he were about to present a petition.[67] When he drew close, however, he tried to pull out a dagger, but was caught by Napoleon's aide-de-camp, General Jean Rapp. Napoleon interrogated the young man at length, trying to find out what had motivated him. As a gesture of magnanimity, he offered to pardon Stapps in return for an apology, but the youth refused. 'I want no pardon,' he is supposed to have said. 'I only regret having failed in my attempt.' Napoleon, according to Rapp, had never been so confounded. Stapps's replies and his determination to both kill Napoleon and die for a cause astonished the Emperor.

Napoleon had faced assassination attempts before, when French republicans used the example of Brutus as inspiration. Here too we are dealing with a sort of German Brutus. Stapps appears to have been quite clear about what he was doing and what his objective was: to bring about peace on the Continent through the death of the man he most held responsible for war. Inspired by Schill's rebellion in Westphalia, Stapps's gesture was deeply patriotic and self-less, if not misguided. It was important, therefore, to paint him as insane; he in turn could not serve as an inspiration to others. He was accused of espionage, declared mad and condemned by a military tribunal on 15 October. He was shot the next day at seven in the morning. His last words were 'Long Live Liberty! Long Live Germany! Death to the Tyrant!'


'I am Charlemagne'

While Napoleon was fighting it out on the island of Lobau, tensions between him and Pius VII came to a head. On 10 June 1809, before a population rubbing its eyes in disbelief, French troops raised the tricolour over the Castel Sant'Angelo.[68] Pius, looking on behind a curtain from his window in the Quirinal, pronounced 'Consummatum est' (It is finished), an echo of the words spoken by Christ on the Cross. It signalled the end of the pope, even if only temporarily, as a secular head of state.

Relations between Napoleon and the pope had been strained ever since the French had occupied Rome in 1808. Pius responded by refusing to invest any bishops nominated by Napoleon. For his part, Napoleon refused any compromise, largely because he now believed, unlike in the days of the Concordat, that his power was well established and that there was no reason for conciliation.[69] He had always had difficulty in according the Church a particular status within his political system, but he now more than ever identified with Charlemagne. As his successor, Napoleon expected the Church to bend to his will and would get angry whenever the ecclesiastical hierarchy showed signs of independence. In a letter to the Vatican in 1806, for example, he declared, 'I am Charlemagne, for like Charlemagne I join the crown of France with the crown of the Lombards . . . I shall make no outward changes if [the pope] behaves well. Otherwise, I shall reduce him to the status of bishop of Rome.'[70] A little later that same year he wrote to Cardinal Fesch to complain about the pope's behaviour: 'My eyes are wide open, and I am not deceived unless I want to be . . . I am Charlemagne, the sword of the Church, their Emperor, and . . . I must be treated as such.'[71] On another occasion, he railed at members of the French hierarchy of the Church for over an hour for not sorting out relations with the papacy more quickly. According to Talleyrand he kept on repeating the phrase, 'you want to treat me like Louis the Pious. Do not confuse the son with the father. You see in me Charlemagne . . . I am Charlemagne . . . yes, I am Charlemagne.'[72]

Napoleon was determined to bend Rome to his will; the future of his political system depended on it. Spanish bishops had refused to recognize Joseph, and the same thing was happening in Naples with Murat: Italian bishops had been instructed not to recognize him. Throughout Italy, bishops were receiving secret instructions from Rome and were preaching against Napoleon and the Empire from the pulpit. It was a cold war that the pope was leading against Napoleon. It was no doubt the reason why Napoleon decided, while he was in Vienna, to annex the Papal States outright. He did so in the name of his 'predecessor' Charlemagne, and in the name of separating the 'ridiculous temporal power' of the pope from the spiritual.[73]

Napoleon, however, went one step further. He not only annexed the Roman states outright, he made sure the symbols of the pontiff – his ring, his seals, his tiara, the ornaments he wore during ceremonies – were brought to Paris. He seriously began to think about transferring the Holy See to Paris, or at least out of Rome, as he tried to move the direction of spiritual affairs away from Rome to his capital.[74] As outrageous as Napoleon's behaviour might appear, it was nevertheless consistent with revolutionary policy: the revolutionaries too had held the previous pope, Pius VI, captive at Valence (he died in captivity in August 1799); they too had attempted to subordinate the interests of the Church to the state; they too had attempted to bring the Church into line with the reforms that had been carried out in France. In that vein, hundreds of Roman convents were dissolved and thousands of clerics found themselves on the street.[75]

The Concordat was in tatters. The rhetoric used to justify the annexation was curious – it was time for the imperial eagles to retake possession of their ancient territories; Charlemagne's domains would be left in the hands of a worthy heir; Rome belonged to the Emperor.[76]

The pope's only recourse was a papal bull – the *Quum memoranda* – that detailed what the papacy had had to endure from the French over the previous few years. On 10 June 1809, shortly after the tricolour flag had been raised over the city, Pius excommunicated and anathematized those responsible for the outrage against the Church. Napoleon was not directly named, or even designated as a *vitandus* (someone who was to be avoided), but it was clear who the bull was aimed at. Napoleon could no longer receive communion, and his soul was condemned to eternal damnation.

The damage was incalculable.[77] It was not the first time that the papacy had used its spiritual powers in the struggle against domineering secular heads of state, although one had to go back a long time to meet the last sovereign excommunicated by the Church, Henry IV of Navarre in the sixteenth century. Napoleon's excommunication was bound to have a nefarious effect on Catholic views of him throughout Europe and undid much of the goodwill that had been gained through the Concordat. Catholics, according to one Bavarian officer, were now prepared to unite with Protestants against Napoleon.[78]

Officially, the Gallican Church never recognized the authority of the pope to excommunicate. Napoleon adopted the same attitude, writing to the minister of religion, Félix-Julien-Jean Bigot de Préameneu, that it was so ridiculous it was not even worth a response.[79] In private, however, Napoleon referred to the pope as 'raving mad' (*fou furieux*), and ordered Murat to imprison Cardinal Bartolomeo Pacca, pro-secretary of state, and other supporters of the pope.[80] In another letter he wrote, 'you must arrest, even in the pope's house, all those who plot against public tranquillity and the safety of my soldiers'.[81] A rather ambitious French general by the name of Etienne Radet interpreted this as meaning they were authorized to arrest the pope if necessary, largely because in another letter Napoleon urged them to treat him as if he were just another bishop.

This is what they did on 6 July, at two o'clock in the morning. The French stormed the papal residence, the Quirinal Palace. They had to break down thirteen doors in order to get to Pius. Radet eventually found himself before the pontiff, hatchet in hand, possibly looking a little dishevelled after all the chopping and hacking. The pope was sitting calmly at his desk, waiting with a dozen or so people. Radet had been swept away in the moment until face to face with the pope, and now hesitated over what to do next, suddenly realizing the enormity of the act.[82] Pius VII was asked to accompany him to a berline. He blessed the French troops before being escorted away. They headed for Genoa, then Grenoble, where he stayed for a few weeks, and where crowds converged on the gates of the prefecture in which he was being held to obtain his blessing, before he was finally sent back to Savona, a small port town on the Italian Riviera. On the way, at Nice, a crowd of 16,000 people gathered to greet him. He would stay at Savona until May 1812.

Napoleon's reaction was one of anger and embarrassment, calling the act a 'great madness' (*une grande folie*).[83] He wrote to Cambacérès that the arrest had been carried out without his orders, but then he was inclined to blame subordinates for his mistakes.[84] Those orders, as already mentioned, had been ambiguous to say the least. 'An operation of this magnitude should not have been carried out without my having been warned, and without my deciding the place where it would be conducted' – which leads one to think that the whole affair suited him. 'What is done is done. I am not for all that unhappy with your zeal,' he wrote to General Miollis, in charge of troops in Rome. 'The pope will never return to Rome.'[85] If he had wanted, he could easily have given orders to release the pope. He did not. Instead, to use a modern euphemism, he went into damage control, to limit, as best he could, the news of his excommunication from spreading – an impossibility – or at least to try and diminish the impact such an event was bound to have on the attitude of Catholics throughout the Empire and Europe. Rumours of the pope's abduction were doing the rounds in Paris as early as 20 July, less than a week after the event. The situation looked as if it was going to revert to the days when the Church and the Revolution were locked in struggle for the control of the people of

France. Back then, the people had to choose between the Revolution and their faith. Now, Catholics throughout the Empire were put in the same predicament, obliged to choose between Napoleon and their Church.

At one stage in September, Napoleon even envisaged bringing the pope to live near Paris.[86] A lot of effort was put into persuading him to move from Savona, but Pius simply declared that wherever he went he would be a prisoner.[87] (In the end, he was brought by force to Fontainebleau in June 1812.) Little by little, though, from 1809 on, the administration of the Holy See was brought to Paris. Hundreds of carriages laden with archives of one sort or another wound their way from Rome, and were deposited in the Hôtel de Soubise (today the French National Archives). Hundreds more came from the rest of the Empire: Holland, Germany, Spain, even Austria. With them came some of the most important personalities in the Church after the pope, including the secretary of the congregation, and the two apostolic tribunals, the Datery and the Penitentiary.

'Politics Has No Heart'
Relations between the pope and Napoleon were made worse, if that were possible, by the Emperor's decision to divorce Josephine. While he was in Vienna in 1809, he ordered the passage between his apartments and Josephine's at Fontainebleau to be boarded up.[88] It was symptomatic of his attitude towards her. He had by now mentally and emotionally cut himself off from her. At one stage he admitted to her that he loved her still, but that 'politics has no heart'.[89] Years later, on St Helena, he would admit that though he still loved her, he had lost all respect for her. She was too much of a liar, too ready to deceive or hide things from him, even concealing how much she owed her debtors. And she constantly owed money. It has been calculated that on clothes alone Josephine spent around 1.1 million francs a year, more than the much-criticized Marie-Antoinette.[90] She owned between three and four hundred shawls, over nine hundred dresses and thousands of pairs of gloves. Napoleon tolerated her lavish spending in ways he would not have tolerated in others, as a means perhaps of buying peace of mind.[91]

Her extravagance was not the main problem, however: that was Napoleon's infidelities. Ironically, rather than drawing Napoleon and Josephine closer together, the coronation and the marriage pulled them further apart since court etiquette now required that they sleep in different bedrooms. It made Napoleon's dalliances easier and they became more frequent. The Empress's ladies-in-waiting were almost like a seraglio for Napoleon. Part of the problem was that many in his close entourage, including his family, were only too happy to provide willing women. Napoleon's sister Caroline and her husband, Murat, appear to be have been on the lookout for a woman who could replace Josephine and thought they had found her in Marie-Antoinette Adèle Duchâtel, one of Josephine's ladies-in-waiting, a black-haired, blue-eyed beauty with a large mouth. Napoleon took up with her only weeks after an affair with a certain Elisabeth de Vaudey. Here too followed a tremendous scene between him and Josephine – plates and vases were thrown and smashed – but he would not back down. He continued to see Mme Duchâtel for a few more years, although he always saw her concurrently with other women, until he realized she was incredibly ambitious, at which point he asked Josephine for advice on how to get rid of her.[92] Napoleon had taken a number of women to his bed from 1800, twenty-five that we know of before he remarried, all of them much younger than Josephine.[93] Some of them were supplied by his sisters. In December 1806, a son was born to nineteen-year-old Eléonore Denuelle de La Plaigne, reader to Caroline Murat, who had encouraged if not arranged the liaison behind Josephine's back, an indication of just how much the family hated her. Eléonore called her son Léon (after Napo-leon). Most historians agree that it was from about the time of the birth of his first illegitimate son that the idea of divorce took firm root; it proved that he was fertile and that Josephine was not.[94] In 1808 and 1809, he enjoyed a liaison with one of the women in Pauline's suite, a beautiful Italian by the name of Christine de Mathis; Pauline played the part of the procuress.[95] Divorce was given added impetus by the birth of another son, Alexandre, to Maria Walewska, on 4 May 1810.

Josephine's inability to procreate and the need to ensure the succession were only the ostensible reasons for divorce. In fact, Napoleon had a fitting heir, Eugène de Beauharnais, whom he had formally adopted in 1806. Far more competent as both ruler and general than any of Napoleon's brothers, he was the preferred successor. Why then, given the example of Caesar and Augustus, both of whom had adoptive sons, was Napoleon not content with Eugène? Was this really about Napoleon's ego, as one contemporary suggested, or about geopolitics?[96] In public, Napoleon asserted that 'adopted children are not satisfactory for founding new dynasties',[97] but that is patently not the case. Lots of kings in Napoleon's own day did not have male heirs and their dynasties survived. When Napoleon married Josephine in front of the pope and crowned her empress in 1804, he must have realized that she was not going to bear him any children; they had already been together for seven years. It is true that the Bonapartes might not have accepted Eugène, as Josephine's progeny, as heir to the throne, but that was hardly a consideration. It is more likely, therefore, that Napoleon wanted a son, and in keeping with his increasingly conservative turn, a son to a princess of royal blood, so that through the boy's mother he would legitimately belong to one of the reigning houses of Europe. Divorce and remarriage then were about consolidating his rule through an established reigning house, and, as far as that went, the more prestigious the better.

© RMN-Grand Palais (musée des châteaux de Malmaison et de Bois-Préau/Daniel Arnaudet/Jean Schormans

Andrea Appiani, *Portrait du prince Eugène de Beauharnais, vice roi d'Italie* (Portrait of Prince Eugène de Beauharnais, viceroy of Italy), 1810.

Divorce had crossed Napoleon's mind before: in 1799 when he returned from Egypt; in 1804 shortly after the proclamation of the Empire, when Josephine caused a scandal over Napoleon's relations with Marie-Antoinette Duchâtel; and again during his stay at Fontainebleau in the autumn of 1807.[98] It is a little ironic then that he considered divorce more seriously about the same time as David's painting of the coronation appeared at the Salon of 1808. By that stage, rumours of divorce had been circulating for quite some time, no doubt fed by knowledge that Napoleon had put out feelers to Alexander at Erfurt about the possibility of marrying one of his sisters.[99] People contemplating David's painting in the Louvre speculated about Josephine and Napoleon's desire to obtain an heir. The liberation of the divorce laws during the Revolution led to a widespread acceptance of divorce, even if the total numbers of dissolutions remained quite low.[100]

Napoleon still cared for Josephine and was putting off the inevitable in order not to hurt her. Whenever he was unfaithful he seems to have done what many a cheating husband does – take out his guilt and frustration on his wife. In a letter to a confidante, Josephine complained of Napoleon's bad moods and the scenes he was making; she discovered that the cause of all the unhappiness was a visit to Paris of the singer La Grassini.[101] In 1808, at the Château de Marracq where Napoleon stayed when dealing with the Spanish royal house at Bayonne, Josephine arrived with two women, Mlles Gazzani and Guillebault, with the intention of handing them over to her husband.[102] It is possible that she thought if Napoleon was going to continue to be unfaithful, then better to choose his lovers herself. He confided later to General Bertrand that the thing he disliked most about Josephine was that she was willing to go to any lengths to keep him attached to her.

Bonaparte had been a romantic through and through, a romanticism that had in part been bruised by Josephine's own infidelity. She had thereby unwittingly helped to create a cynic and complete his disillusionment with the world. From about the time of Egypt onwards, Bonaparte's attitude towards women became more callous.[103] When he became head of state, the women he did have serious relations with can be counted on the fingers of one hand – Marie-Antoinette Duchâtel, Carlotta Gazzani, Christine de Mathis, one of Pauline's ladies-in-waiting, and Marguerite-Joséphine George.[104] But there was something peculiar in his romantic conquests, and that was his need to boast about them.[105] Not only was he capable of recounting in the most intimate detail all that went on in the bedchamber, he was also perfectly relaxed talking to Josephine about them. For the most part they were conquests; Napoleon did not love women. He denied them his time – he was notoriously as quick in bed as he was at the dinner table – and consequently he denied them any intimacy whatsoever. There were, however, two women who managed again to touch that romantic core. Both were Maries – Maria Walewska and Marie-Louise.

The showdown between Napoleon and Josephine took place at the Tuileries on 30 November 1809, a scene that is now part of the legend.[106] Napoleon had returned from Fontainebleau a few days before, and was distracted enough for the prefect of the palace, the Baron de Bausset, to notice. Dinners were held in silence. After one of those dinners with Josephine, and after having dismissed everyone from the room, Napoleon announced that he had decided to divorce her. We do not know what he said but Josephine responded with violent sobs. Bausset, sitting in the salon outside and realizing what was happening, prevented an usher from entering the room and going to her aid. It was Napoleon who opened the door and allowed Bausset to enter, whereupon he found Josephine prostrate on a rug on the floor, emitting what he referred to as 'heartbreaking cries and lamentations'. It was what contemporaries called 'an attack of nerves', the end result of months of anxiety. In any event, it added a melodramatic touch to the end of a relationship that had lasted almost fifteen years. Napoleon asked Bausset, a largish man, to carry her to her apartments while Josephine pretended to faint. Napoleon led the way with a lamp, until they had to descend a narrow staircase leading to Josephine's bedroom, where-upon the Emperor called over a palace servant to take the lamp; he seized

Josephine's feet while Bausset held her under her arms so that her back was pressed up against his chest and her head resting on his right shoulder. It was at that point that she is supposed to have whispered, 'You're holding me too tight.' Napoleon too played his part as they shed tears together that evening. No doubt there was sorrow and regret on the part of Josephine – she was losing everything after all, although Napoleon would look after her material comfort – and a tinge of regret on his part.

To divorce Josephine, much like other monarchs in other centuries, Napoleon had to obtain the dissolution of the marriage from the pope, and given that he was being held prisoner it was unlikely that he would co-operate.[107] Besides, the precedent had not been very encouraging: Napoleon had in the past unsuccessfully attempted to get the pope to annul the marriage of Jérôme to Elizabeth Patterson. Instead, Napoleon turned to the Parisian ecclesiastical hierarchy, which in January 1810 declared his marriage annulled.

The Bonaparte family must have been delighted. They had never hidden their dislike of Josephine, and had been pushing for divorce for some years.[108] There were others at court, including Fouché, who had also lobbied in favour of divorce, possibly in the knowledge that public opinion believed the Empire would not outlive Napoleon if there were no direct heir.[109] There were, however, those who did not favour divorce. Cardinal Fesch, who took his role seriously, was not convinced by the juridical arguments and insisted that everything had been in order when the pair had married in 1804. It was Cambacérès, a former lawyer, who came to the rescue and found a loophole in the law.[110] He argued that since the religious marriage (which was celebrated shortly before the coronation) did not take place in the presence of witnesses it was clandestine and therefore irregular.

The divorce was not made public right away. We know that Josephine was seen at a ball on 4 December at the Hôtel de Ville looking downcast. On 14 or 15 December, she was obliged to appear before the Council of State, in the presence of Napoleon and the grand officers of the Empire, to declare that she consented to divorce. All the family dignitaries were present, including Letizia, the Emperor's brothers Joseph, Louis and Jérôme and their wives, Caroline and Murat, Eugène, and Pauline. During this 'family meeting' Napoleon took a sheet of paper and read from it. It was when he came to the words 'She has graced my life for fifteen years' that he allowed some emotion to come through. Then Josephine in turn read from a sheet of paper but was unable to continue as she was crying so much. Regnaud de Saint-Jean d'Angély, counsellor of state, and secretary of state to the imperial family, had to finish for her.[111] It was a moving occasion, at least for those who liked the Empress.[112] Before she left the Tuileries, Napoleon spent a few hours with her in a tête-à-tête and, according to one account, sobbed on bended knee before her.[113] However, he was in a situation of his own making. He was not obliged to divorce her. This was not about great-power politics or geostrategic necessity. It was about personal ambition. Josephine was sacrificed not at the altar of international relations, but at the altar of Napoleon's ego. To shed tears, as he did on this occasion, was to suggest that he was the victim, thereby absolving himself from responsibility for his actions.[114] Contemporaries were hardly likely to oblige. The streets of Paris were not pleased by the divorce.[115] In the army, many felt Josephine had been hard done by. 'He shouldn't have left the old woman; she brought him luck and us too.'[116]

Two days later, Jospehine left the Tuileries in the pouring rain, never to return. Nothing was sadder, as one contemporary put it, than to see the Tuileries widowed by an empress loved by the people.[117] Napoleon spent the next fortnight at the Trianon, a residence in Versailles, dining with her for the last time on 17 December, writing a dozen notes to her before the month was out, attempting to assuage his guilty conscience by a last spurt of affection. Nostalgia perhaps.[118]

# 16

# Bourgeois Emperor, Universal Emperor

## 'I am Marrying a Womb'

Once the divorce had been decided on, there was the question of a suitable bride. This was going to be the scene of intensive lobbying between various political factions at court.[1] On 26 January 1810, the limits of the problem were laid out by Napoleon at a private council at the Tuileries. A French noble was out of the question; French monarchs invariably married foreign brides. So too was a minor German princess. Napoleon had his sights set much higher. It came down to choosing between a Russian, an Austrian and a Saxon princess.[2] In this he was following the same principle he had laid down for his own relatives: strengthening the dynasty by a policy of alliances through strategic marriage.

Those in favour of a Russian alliance suggested one of the Tsar's sisters.[3] They were for the most part opposed to an Austrian marriage; it reminded them a little too much of Marie-Antoinette, while Austria had traditionally been an implacable enemy of France. Fouché was able to produce a report on the mood of the Parisian populace that warned against any Austrian connection.[4] Much stronger, however, was the Austrian lobby, which advocated an alliance with Emperor Francis's daughter, Marie-Louise, eighteen years of age. For Fontanes, who had been a supporter of the return to monarchical forms in France, a marriage with an Austrian princess, after having executed one only sixteen years previously, was a symbolic act of expiation.[5] The lobby supporting the Austrian solution did so with such vigour, however, that Cambacérès suspected Napoleon had organized the whole thing.[6]

In fact, Napoleon preferred the Russian option. At Erfurt, he had asked Talleyrand to approach Alexander about marrying one of his two unmarried sisters.[7] The elder was Grand Duchess Ekaterina Pavlovna, who was twenty in 1808, and was considered witty, intelligent and charming. The younger was the Grand Duchess Anna, who was only fifteen years old. Alexander's estranged wife, Elisaveta Alekseevna, wrote of Ekaterina that she had 'a tone that would not be suitable for a woman of forty', much less for a woman of twenty.[8] There was no doubt a touch of bitterness in that remark: Ekaterina was well liked among the Francophobe faction at court and was considered a possible replacement for the Tsar.[9] Indeed, she was considered the mirror image of her grandmother, Catherine II, who had overthrown her husband, Peter III, to reach the throne.[10]

It was their mother though, the Empress Dowager, Mariia Federovna, the former wife of Paul I, who had absolute control over whom they could marry, and she hated Napoleon. Nevertheless, the Russian court was under the mistaken belief at the end of 1807 that a marriage alliance between Napoleon and the Grand Duchess Ekaterina was probable.[11] Shortly after Alexander's return from Erfurt, perhaps alarmed at Napoleon's intentions, the Empress Dowager married off Ekaterina to a distant cousin, Prince George of Holstein-Oldenburg.[12] This did not seem to bother Napoleon very much, largely because he had set his sights on the younger of the two sisters, Anna. He pushed home the point as relations between the two countries worsened, no doubt in the hope of repairing the cracks.

At the end of November 1809 – that is, before the divorce had been finalized – Napoleon instructed Caulaincourt, the French ambassador in Petersburg, to approach Alexander formally with a request for his sister's hand in marriage. 'It will be a proof to me', he wrote to Caulaincourt, 'that Alexander is an ally. It [the divorce] would be a real sacrifice for me. I love Josephine. I will never be happier with anyone else, but my family . . . and all the politicians insist on it in the name of France.'[13] Yes, well, the sacrifice was possibly all on the Russian side. Alexander stalled for as long as he could – he used his mother as an excuse, saying that she felt Anna was too young, that she had lost two daughters through early childbirths and did not want to see another married before she was eighteen – so that by the beginning of 1810 Napoleon was still waiting for an answer. The Empress Dowager, although she had nothing but contempt for the French, may nevertheless have been playing to public opinion, perhaps for her own ends. She had briefly attempted to govern in the place of her murdered husband before handing over the reins of power to her son, but over the years she had managed to gather around her all those discontented with the regime's pro-French stance.[14]

By this time Napoleon realized what Alexander's lack of enthusiasm meant, and he decided on pre-empting the humiliation that would inevitably come with a refusal by turning to Austria. Three days after receiving a courier from Petersburg, on 6 February 1810, he withdrew his offer of marriage while Eugène officially asked the Austrian ambassador, Prince Schwarzenberg, for the hand of Marie-Louise. Napoleon had already sounded out the Austrian court so Schwarzenberg was authorized well in advance to accept such an offer. That same day, Napoleon had a marriage contract drawn up, a duplicate of that which had been prepared for Louis and Marie-Antoinette in 1770. The marriage then was at the political level a public relations coup.[15] In diplomatic terms, this was to turn his back on Russia. It was a deliberate choice; Napoleon knew that relations with Russia were less than perfect. In fact, the choice of an Austrian princess made matters worse.

*    *    *

News of the forthcoming marriage was accompanied by a concerted effort in the press to prepare for the arrival of (another) Austrian princess. Poets, musicians, writers, painters were all enlisted.[16] Plays with the marriage as a background to the plot were quickly written and performed, although it is impossible to tell whether audiences looked on all this with amusement or cynicism. On the other hand, if Comte Otto, now the French ambassador to Vienna, is to be believed – but, then, what else could he say? – the announcement of marriage was greeted favourably by all classes of Viennese society,[17] even if Viennese aristocracy considered the alliance undignified.[18] This was not the case in those parts of the Empire, such as the Rhineland, where pro-Austrian sentiment was strong.[19] In those regions, news of the marriage made a deep impression, reinforcing the belief that Napoleon and the Empire were here to stay. The regime was being given a degree of legitimacy that it had lacked in royalist eyes till then.[20] Even Joseph de Maistre wrote to the King of Sardinia that from this time on Napoleon would have to be treated like any other sovereign.[21]

When Alexander learnt of the forthcoming marriage he, quite unreasonably under the circumstances, was miffed, believing that Napoleon had been playing a double game – and this despite having sent a letter effectively refusing Napoleon's request on the grounds that Anna's mother felt there could be no marriage for at least two more years. Russian public opinion was just as offended.[22] Moreover, the Tsar considered the marriage alliance between Austria and France a real danger. It brought the two countries closer together, even if only on paper, appeared to be a potential strategic threat to Russia and made him look a fool to his own people.[23] The fact is that Vienna had taken a much more active interest in a marriage alliance with Napoleon and had approached the French with a marriage proposal in 1809 almost as soon as the guns were stilled.[24]

The alliance represented a shift in thinking for Napoleon, away from Russia towards Austria. Admittedly, the Austria of 1810 was not at its peak – it had been greatly reduced in size since the start of the wars and had been defeated four times by France – but the arguments put forward by Talleyrand in favour of an Austrian alliance were persuasive (though somewhat specious). They consisted largely of a belief that Russia was politically too unstable and that its foreign policy was too closely linked to the person of the Tsar; a change in ruler would invariably lead to a change in policy, as had occurred with the death of Paul I. Austria, on the other hand, was more deeply embedded in a foreign political system that did not rely on the character of one emperor or another.[25] Austria was, in fact, no more consistent in its foreign policy choices than any other great power during this period.

Vienna calculated that having a princess of its own at the French court would disarm Napoleon, and make him less mistrustful towards Austria,

while Marie-Louise would be working inside to promote Austrian interests.[26] Certainly the marriage alliance gave Austria a few years' peace during
which it could heal its wounds after the defeat of 1809, but if Metternich,
now Austria's foreign minister, hoped to exploit the favourable atmosphere
to gain diplomatic concessions, he was to be disappointed.[27] Napoleon was
not mollified and did not want to change the treaty of 1809. In real terms,
Austria gained little tangible from the alliance.[28] One should not think,
however, that the alliance was all to Napoleon's benefit. The court of Vienna
got what it wanted: it prevented France and Russia from drawing closer
together, and bolstered the faltering prestige of Francis. Four wars and four
defeats had done enormous harm to the Austrian monarchy's reputation.
The alliance with Napoleon, even if it was a complete backflip to what it had
practised over the last ten years,[29] strengthened the Austrian throne just as
much as the Austrian monarchy's ancient lineage bolstered Napoleon's
legitimacy.[30] Francis may not have been overjoyed by the prospect of having
Napoleon as a son-in-law,[31] but we know that the announcement of the
marriage in Vienna was well received. Even the streets of Vienna seemed to
welcome the news. Most believed an alliance would force Britain to make
peace and bring about stability on the Continent.[32] As for the political elite,
they were delighted, or at least some of them were, including Metternich,
who believed that he had carried out a great diplomatic coup that had
allowed Austria to resume its place among the great powers only months
after suffering a humiliating defeat.

For Napoleon, the marriage made political sense too. Not only was Austria
(still) a power to be contended with on the Continent, militarily and in terms
of population, but as an ally it would also lend stability to the centre of Europe.
Moreover, French diplomats were able to point out that if Louis XIV and
Louis XV had been able to wage war successfully against Britain, it was in part
due to the Austrian alliance. Finally, the marriage served to appease Napoleon's main bugbear, legitimacy, by injecting Austrian Bourbon blood into the
succession (Marie-Louise was also descended from Charles Quint and Louis
XIV).[33] This worked, up to a point. The number of *ancien régime* nobles who
rallied to the court after 1810 is impressive, even if their adherence was to be
short-lived.[34] Talleyrand was hoping for some kind of European reconciliation, as if the marriage alliance was going to expiate the Revolution's crime of
executing a king. Napoleon tried to make political mileage out of the marriage
alliance by distributing the modern equivalent of a statement to French diplomats abroad. England, he argued, had always claimed that he was out to
destroy Europe's monarchies.[35]

Before the Revolution French courts had functioned like vast families in
which those admitted were given a privileged place. The European monarchies
in particular were tightly bound by blood links, constituting a veritable

'society of princes' whose relations were strictly codified.[36] The mistake that Napoleon made was in thinking that, through marriage, he would be admitted into this family. He was not. He was the relative that everyone tolerates but whom no one likes. And he was disliked in part because he did not behave like a prince. Indeed, he may not even have been entirely aware of the strict rules codifying princely behaviour. He believed that rigorous court etiquette was enough, that to appear princely would position him among the sovereigns of Europe. It could never, however, replace the bonds of blood that linked other crown princes.[37] Etiquette at Napoleon's court became even more rigid after his marriage to Marie-Louise, as if its rigid application was one more proof of the legitimacy of the regime.

## Marie-Louise

Marie-Louise, one of thirteen children, had been her father's favourite and had been brought up to refer to Napoleon as the 'cannibal', the 'usurper' or 'Attila'. As a child she had a doll called 'Bonaparte' that she delighted in torturing.[38] She had even referred to her future husband as the 'Antichrist' and the 'Corsican' in some of her letters, and made the sign of the cross when she heard his name.[39] She had had to flee the capital twice in her lifetime as Napoleon and his troops approached. In short, she was raised to believe that he was a bloodthirsty, cold-hearted killer and to cultivate a deep aversion.[40]

Now, she had to overturn those prejudices and prepare herself, like the dutiful daughter of the Emperor she was, for marriage with a man whom she had learnt to detest. Like her great-aunt Marie-Antoinette, she had received little or no formal education at court. The primary purpose of an Austrian princess was to produce sons to help continue whatever dynasty she was eventually married into. Nevertheless, she was distraught on learning in the newspapers at the beginning of 1810 that Napoleon had divorced Josephine, aware that she would now be considered a potential wife. She wrote to her father reminding him that he had promised he would never force her to marry. But there was something else; she had met and fallen in love with Archduke Francis of Modena, her stepmother's brother.[41] Her father never replied to her letter. And yet she persisted for some time in her naive belief that he would never force her to marry against her will and that his feelings for her would take precedence over dynastic considerations. When she was made aware of the negotiations, she pleaded with him to be spared. To no avail. Francis could do little else but offer her up, regardless of whether she was his favourite or not. As an Austrian princess, as the daughter of the Emperor, Marie-Louise was prepared to make this ultimate sacrifice.[42]

akg-images/Erich Lessing

François Pascal Simon, Baron Gérard, *L'impératrice Marie-Louise* (The Empress Marie-Louise), 1810.

Berthier arrived in Vienna on 8 March 1810, and in a ceremony that took place at the Hofburg Palace, officially asked of Francis, clad in his white uniform, the hand of Marie-Louise. Three days later, a marriage by proxy took place, as was the tradition for unions between reigning houses.[43] Berthier stood in for Napoleon. Archduke Charles represented his father, Francis I, escorting Marie-Louise down the aisle. When Marie-Louise entered France it was to meet a husband she had never laid eyes on. The married couple became acquainted through an exchange of letters. Napoleon knew how to be gallant – 'we set ourselves the constant task of pleasing you in every way'. Marie-Louise knew how to reciprocate – 'I consider it an obligation to acquire the qualities that would make me agreeable to your person.'[44]

She crossed the border near Braunau (the village in which Hitler was to be born seventy-nine years later) on 16 March, following a ceremony that was an exact replica of that which Marie-Antoinette had had to endure in 1770.[45] A neo-classical building spanning the border had been thrown up by French engineers, and divided into three connecting rooms, one facing east which was the Austrian room, one in the middle, a sort of neutral no man's land, and one facing west, the French room. Symbolically, she was meant to enter the

Austrian room as an archduchess, and leave the French room as a French princess.[46] In the process, she was divested of anything resembling or associated with her Austrian past, including her governess, with whom she had been since she was a little girl, her clothes and her pets.[47] After a *toilette* that lasted two hours in which she was bedecked in French perfume, French clothes and a French hairstyle, Caroline met her on the other side, and accompanied her all the way to Compiègne.[48] The presence of Caroline was the only false note: she had, after all, replaced another Caroline, a Bourbon queen and daughter of Francis, on the throne of Naples. Fêted along the way, Marie-Louise did not arrive in Compiègne until 27 March.

On 20 March, Napoleon left Paris, arriving in Compiègne that evening. While waiting, he prepared himself, taking dance lessons with Princess Stéphanie and Hortense, having new clothes made, trying to make himself more fashionable and less serious, less severe, something he thought would please a young woman.[49] One week later, he was to meet her in the forest between Soissons and Compiègne, where a tent had been set up which was to serve the same purpose as the wooden lodges at Braunau, as a sort of passage between two worlds. According to a strict and elaborate protocol ten pages long invented by the imperial regime, Marie-Louise was to advance towards the Emperor, kneel before him – something Napoleon appears to have insisted on, possibly as a form of domination, though queens of France did not kneel but rather bowed – and utter a set speech, which she was to learn along the way. Napoleon, wearing a costume designed by Pauline, was to help her up and embrace her. The couple could then be on their way.[50]

So much for etiquette; Napoleon, who made up the rules, broke them at will. He was so impatient to see his new bride that he ignored the weeks of planning and went to meet her, under a sky that was pouring rain, in front of the church in the town of Courcelles, wearing the same grey coat he had worn at Wagram. Mind you, he had whiled away his time at Compiègne with Christine de Mathis.[51] Napoleon had only seen a portrait of Marie-Louise at that point, one not particularly flattering and which left him with lingering doubts. He had, moreover, been told she was plain if not ugly.[52] He is supposed to have remarked to Murat, 'Obviously my wife is hideous as not one of these young rips has dared say the contrary . . . After all, it is a womb that I am marrying.'[53] He had to be reassured by Berthier that 'The more I know the Empress . . . the more I am certain that, although she cannot be considered a pretty woman, she has all that it takes to make Your Majesty happy.'[54] She has been described as having an oval face, with hair that was somewhere between light brown and blonde, beautiful blue eyes and clear skin, although intellectually she was far from that which she could become.[55] A less gracious portrait would have her as plump, plain and quiet. We have no idea what Napoleon thought of his new Empress the first time he set eyes on her; he may have been pleasantly surprised.

They arrived at Compiègne around ten in the evening on the 27th, when she was introduced to the gathered Bonaparte and Beauharnais family members. She also found waiting for her, to her great surprise, her dog, her birds and an unfinished tapestry Napoleon had had brought to Compiègne against protocol and without her knowledge. After the couple had dined alone with Caroline, it was time for bed. In order to overcome any scruples his young bride might have had about not yet being formally married, Napoleon remarked to Cardinal Fesch in the presence of the new Empress, 'Is it not true that we are married?' 'Yes, Sire,' Fesch supposedly replied, 'after the civil laws.' Decorum required Napoleon to wait for the religious ceremony to be conducted in Paris before taking Marie-Louise to bed – a proxy marriage was symbolic and not legally binding – but patience was not his strong suit, and her virtue was manhandled that same evening as the Corsican upstart of petty noble origins deflowered a princess from one of the oldest reigning houses in

The Art Archive/Musée du Château de Versailles/Gianni Dagli Orti

Pauline Auzou, née Desmarquets, *Arrivée de l'impératrice Marie-Louise à Compiègne le 28 mars 1810 (Marie-Louise recevant les compliments et les fleurs d'un groupe de jeunes filles dans la Galerie du chartrain à Compiègne à 9h du soir)* (Arrival of the Empress Marie-Louise at Compiègne, 28 March 1810 (Marie-Louise receiving compliments and flowers from a group of young women in the Galerie du chartrain at Compiègne at 9 in the evening), 1810.

Europe. One author suggests that Napoleon went about it more as rapist than as lover, an overly harsh judgement.[56] Marie-Louise seems to have become quickly attached to her husband. 'I find that he gains a lot when you get to know him more closely: there is something very engaging and very eager about him that it is almost impossible to resist.'[57]

Ceremonial Paris

The imperial couple arrived in Saint-Cloud on 30 March. What followed were some of the most elaborate political events staged since Napoleon's coronation. There was a rich and detailed round of ceremonies that included a civil wedding on 1 April (which, since the Revolution, had to take place *before* the religious ceremony); a State Entry into Paris which involved more than forty carriages;[58] a religious wedding at the Chapel of the Louvre, celebrated with a good deal more 'order, dignity and contemplation' than that of the coronation;[59] a state banquet at the Tuileries; a public appearance on the palace balcony; fireworks that evening, plus illumination of the Tuileries gardens; receptions held by the Senate, ministers and senior officials of the Empire; a distribution of gold and silver coins to the crowds in the garden outside. The imperial union was also meant to be celebrated in each locality by the marriage of a young girl 'of pure heart' to a returned soldier on leave.[60] Napoleon was very much involved with the organization of the festivities. Every monument and bridge in the capital was illuminated; there was a pagan touch to it all when a Greek temple to the goddess Hymen was erected between the two towers of Notre Dame;[61] festivities were arranged by the Paris municipality including a pantomime – *The Union of Mars and Flora* – on the Champs-Elysées that saw more than 150 people on stage; and there was free distribution of bread and meat. Once again, as with the coronation five and a half years before, it is difficult to know exactly what the people of Paris thought of all this. Witness accounts vary, but most agree that the crowds showed little enthusiasm and that there were few acclamations; they took part in the festivities out of curiosity.[62]

There were two incidents that marred the ceremonies. The first was the refusal of thirteen of the twenty-seven Italian cardinals present in Paris to turn up to the wedding, having decided, finally, to protest against Napoleon's behaviour towards the pope.[63] Their pretext was that the Holy See had not recognized the divorce between Napoleon and Josephine and they did not wish to lend any weight to the marriage by their presence. Thirteen seats remained conspicuously empty therefore around the altar during the ceremony at the Louvre. Napoleon had been forewarned but, typically, did not believe they would have the gall to go through with it. If he entered the Salon Carré all smiles, he came back out furious.[64] His first reaction was to have the cardinals taken out and shot.[65] Reason saw the light of day. They were, however, arrested, sent into exile to various parts of eastern France where they were placed under house arrest, and they had their cardinalates and pensions taken from them. They were, furthermore, forbidden to wear purple, which is why they were commonly referred to as the 'black cardinals'.[66] This was fairly typical behaviour of course. We have seen in the past how Napoleon would eliminate anybody in any position of power who did not fully co-operate with his plans.

The second incident involved the same kind of petty squabbling that had occurred before the coronation, again with Napoleon's sisters and sisters-in-law refusing to carry the Empress's train – tears, simulated fainting, categorical refusals.[67] Napoleon, angry, insulted them and in the end had to deliver an imperial 'I order it.' The Prince Karl von Clary-Aldringen has left an amusing account of the women involved – the Grand Duchess of Tuscany, the Princess of Borghesa, the Queens of Spain and Westphalia – entering the chapel holding Marie-Louise's train, the first grimacing, the second holding a bottle of perfume under her nose as if she were about to faint and the third simply letting go of it in mid-course.[68] The most stubborn was that 'goose' Catherine from Westphalia. The only person to carry it with good grace was Hortense.

One other aspect of these ceremonies is worth dwelling on, if only for what it tells us about the relationship between Napoleon's Empire and *ancien régime* monarchical rituals, namely, the formal 'Entry' into Paris.[69] Gone now was any pretence of Napoleon being a 'republican emperor' as he adopted wholesale the external trappings of monarchy. He had made formal entries into cities before, in order to take symbolic and in many cases actual possession of them. Formal entries were made, for example, into Milan in 1800, Munich in 1805, Berlin in 1806, Danzig in 1807 and Warsaw in 1809. As a plebiscitary dictator, Napoleon was attuned to public opinion and he understood the importance of being seen by his subjects. That is why he insisted on a formal entry into Paris, and why the procession entered through the Arc de Triomphe; it was meant to be a triumphal entry, one in which he would show off his new conquest – Marie-Louise – and thereby help create an affective bond between the imperial couple and the people.[70] In some respects, the entry was the highlight of the ceremony, a sort of public inauguration of the new queen.

Although only the foundations had been laid of the monument that was meant to celebrate Austerlitz, Napoleon ordered the construction of a life-size model made of wood, plaster and cloth. Carpenters were working non-stop for over a month to complete the task in time and although there was, to use a modern-day euphemism, some industrial unrest when the carpenters struck for higher wages, that was soon nipped in the bud. The prefect of police, Dubois, threatened them with imprisonment if they did not return to work immediately and work at the conventional rates. Napoleon and his new bride were thus able to drive through the Arc, or at least a wooden facsimile of it.

The marriage was a turning point in the nature of the Empire, a period of transition, a period in which the question of dynastic succession and continuity were reformulated. An institution that had been specifically French now became ever more 'Germanic'. Greater reliance was laid on Roman and Carolingian traditions, while the court took on an increasingly pan-European flavour.[71] Between 1809 and 1815, some 26 per cent of the senior household officials were non-French, while slightly over a third of those presented at court were also not French.[72] As we have seen, etiquette became much more stringent from this time on; 634 articles regulating court etiquette were modified and introduced in 1811 drawing on *ancien régime* texts that went as far back as 1710.[73] There was too an increasing reliance on the former aristocracy both for diplomatic posts and for appointment as prefects. The number of former nobles in diplomatic missions doubled from around 30 to 60 per cent between 1800 and 1812–13. Similarly, the number of prefects who were of noble birth almost doubled to 41 per cent in that same period.[74] There was even some talk of moving the court back to Versailles.[75] The Trianon was restored and refurbished for Napoleon's mother and sisters after 1805, and soft furnishings were ordered in 1811–12 for the château itself, which underwent repair work throughout the Empire. Extraneous events were to interfere before that could happen, but it is clear that the movement towards monarchy and away from the Republic had come full circle.

Men are 'Insufferable'
The imperial couple left Saint-Cloud on 5 April for Compiègne – the whole court followed them – where they stayed for most of the month of April, and where Napoleon spent the closest thing to a honeymoon that his constitution allowed him.[76] By all accounts he was smitten, and behaved like a lovesick puppy, devoted to his new bride,[77] never leaving her alone for more than two hours at a time, showering her with expensive gifts almost every day.[78] For her part, she was not insensitive to the attention she received and began to reciprocate, calling Napoleon by pet names such as 'Po-Po' or 'Nana'.[79]

The relationship was not entirely idyllic though, for she soon discovered what it was like to be married to a man who ruled an empire. When they left on a tour of Belgium at the end of April, visiting many of the port towns along the coast – particularly significant for a region that was once attached to the Austrian Empire – Marie-Louise, unaccustomed to travelling with a man as energetic as Napoleon, who often woke at four in the morning in order to be on the road at five, complained as only a spoilt princess could of the little inconveniences she had to put up with.[80] He may have been emperor of most of Western Europe but in private he was just a married man, and was therefore involved in the spats and squabbles that occur between couples as they work their way through life together. He was used to ordering people about and to getting his own way; she was an eighteen-year-old girl away from home for the first time who kept candles alight in her room because she was afraid of ghosts.[81] She hated the mediocre lodgings they were often put up in, the bad roads, the bad smells, the fatigue of travelling for five weeks. She liked the bedroom unheated at night, he preferred it heated. She liked to travel in the carriage with the window up, he liked to have it down, 'just to annoy me', she wrote in her diary. She was hungry and wanted to stop for lunch, he thought that a woman 'didn't need to eat'.[82] When he got angry and started to yell, she just sulked. Besides, he had some annoying habits, like pinching Marie-Louise's nose, which must have become very tiring very quickly. Men, she thought, were 'insufferable' and if she ever returned to this world she vowed never to marry again.[83] Their time in Belgium was not a particularly happy one for either of them.

Court life at the Tuileries was not particularly gay either. Metternich found the Tuileries 'impossibly pretentious'.[84] Several weeks of receptions were marred by a tragic incident that occurred during a ball offered by the Austrian ambassador to Paris at his embassy, and to which more than 700 people were invited (1 July). A fire broke out fuelled by the turpentine that had been used to help paint the ceilings.[85] The next morning, several burnt bodies were discovered, including the ambassador's sister-in-law Princess Schwarzenberg (four months pregnant) and Princess Leyen (one of Josephine's cousins). Several others died of their burns in the days that followed.[86] The street compared it to Louis XVI's disastrous wedding celebrations when hundreds of people were crushed to death during a fireworks display on the Place Louis XV.[87] It was almost as though it were an omen of things to come, for people could not help but draw unfortunate comparisons between the Napoleonic and Bourbon regimes.

## The King of Rome

Marie-Louise went into labour at around seven in the evening and was still laid up when, at five o'clock the next morning, 20 March 1811, the Grand Marshal of the Empire came out of her chamber to announce that the pains had ceased and that the Empress had fallen asleep. Many went home to rest, while others simply curled up wherever they could. Napoleon, who had been with Marie-Louise throughout the night, went to take a bath – his way of relaxing – but had hardly stepped into it when Dr Antoine Dubois, the First Obstetrician of the Empire, came to say that the pains had started again, and that there were complications.

The birth of an empress's baby is an event surrounded by ceremony. If Marie-Antoinette had to give birth in front of the court as well as, according to tradition, two fishwives from Paris, Marie-Louise's labour was also a public event. The imperial family, the grand dignitaries of the court, the ministers and members of the administrative and clerical elite were gathered in uniform or evening wear for the men, and in what was called *grande toilette* for the women. In all, twenty-two people were present to witness the birth. When Napoleon returned to the bedchamber and was told that there were complications – he was informed by Dubois that the baby was in the breech position – and that in the circumstances it was rare for both mother and child to survive, he did not react as a dynastic ruler but rather as a husband, insisting that everything had to be done to save the mother, somewhat contradicting his earlier assertion that he had merely married a womb.[88]

Dubois managed to turn the baby, so that it emerged, feet first, at around eight or nine in the morning, and at first appeared to be stillborn. It was laid to one side while everyone crowded around the Empress, whose life seemed to be in danger. It was the first physician at court, Dr Jean-Nicolas Corvisart, who picked up the baby, gave it a few drops of liquor, wrapped it in some warm cloth and began to tap its back. The tapping worked; it came to life seven minutes later. Napoleon took the baby in his arms and burst into the adjoining room to announce, 'His Majesty, the King of Rome!'[89] The title 'King of Rome' was traditionally given to the first male child of the Austrian sovereign, as heir to the Holy Roman Empire. Francis effectively ceded this title to Napoleon's son when, during the marriage celebrations, the Austrian foreign minister, Metternich, stood up during a banquet and proposed a toast to the 'King of Rome'. He thus expressed the hope that Napoleon would produce a male heir and that the old imperial title would pass to the new dynasty.

When his daughter-in-law, Queen Hortense, came up to congratulate Napoleon, he replied, 'Ah, I cannot feel happy – the poor woman has suffered so much!'[90] He no doubt meant it. As we have seen, he had developed a genuine fondness for Marie-Louise, and she for him, although he never loved her as much as he had once loved Josephine. It was, nevertheless, the beginning of a new experience that made him feel, or so he confided in Metternich, that 'only now did his life really start'.[91] As for Marie-Louise, with her son's birth, and the tenderness that Napoleon had shown, she began to really love him. 'My affection for my husband', she wrote to her father, 'has increased with the birth of my son. And the devotion and attachment he has shown me throughout this time; I have only to think of it and it brings tears to my eyes.'[92]

The guns announcing the birth rang out over Paris. As soon as the first shot was fired, people in the streets stopped what they were doing and began to count them. Stendhal was still in bed and was woken by the firing. Twenty-two was the magic number; it meant that a boy had been born (because there were only twenty-one for a girl, and 101 for a boy) and it led, according to the police reports, to spontaneous outbursts of acclamations: 'Vive l'Empereur! Vive l'Impératrice! Vive le roi de Rome!'[93] It seems true for once; Henri Beyle, better known as Stendhal, remarked on people in the rue Saint-Honoré applauding as though a 'favourite actor' had appeared.[94] Savary, who had been appointed minister of police in June 1810, recounts an anecdote in his police report from that day about two *portefaix* or peasants arguing in the markets. They were going to fight, but when 'the first cannon shot was heard, they suspended their quarrel to count the shots and on the twenty-second shot, they embraced'.[95] Even royalists seem to have been moved by the event, as Mme de Boigne remarked that there was a loud cry of joy throughout the city that went off like an electric spark.[96] At half-past ten in the morning, Mme Blanchard left the Champs de Mars in a Montgolfier balloon and threw papers into the air announcing the birth of Napoleon's heir. The joy elicited by the birth of a son probably had more to do with people's feeling for Napoleon than with a longing for a stable regime, in which nobody really believed.[97]

That evening there were firework displays and official registers at the Tuileries Palace in which Parisians could congratulate the imperial couple. The *guingettes* – popular drinking places located in the suburbs outside Paris – were full of people of all classes celebrating, and some bosses even gave their

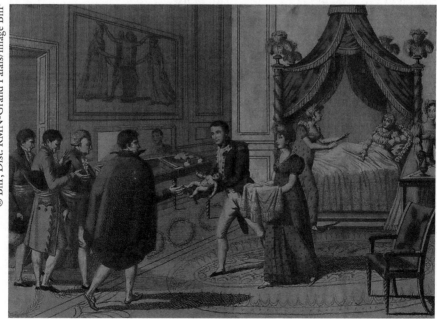

Anonymous, *Accouchement de Marie-Louise, Impératrice des Français* (The confinement of Marie-Louise, Empress of the French), 1811.

workers the day off and a few francs to go and drink.[98] Houses were decorated with improvised inscriptions. Church bells rang out throughout France to announce the birth of Napoleon's son, and in Paris Jews sang prayers of joy on the occasion in the Synagogue.[99] Poems and plays were soon being composed to mark the occasion.[100] If the police reports have to be treated with circumspection – the usual language is used, namely, 'never has a demonstration of sentiment been more lively and more general' – prefects' reports clearly show that the vast majority of the French people seem to have welcomed the occasion, although particular towns, such as Marseilles and Toulon, increasingly hostile to Napoleon, remained indifferent, and annexed cities, like Hamburg, were cool.[101] As in the rest of the Empire, balls, firework displays and popular dances were organized, but while people gladly attended this free entertainment, there is little evidence that it provoked any warm feelings for either Napoleon or his regime. True, a certain number of letters of congratulations were sent to the imperial couple from individuals throughout the Empire,[102] and dozens if not hundreds of eulogies were published,[103] but the further one got away from Paris the colder the reception was likely to be until one reached Rome, where the response from the general population was at best lukewarm, and from the Church downright hostile.[104] That was not surprising, considering the revolutionary-style campaign that Napoleon had been conducting against priests who did not swear an oath of loyalty to him. Dozens of priests simply refused to say any official prayers for the health of Their Majesties, as was required of them.[105]

The public displays were repeated on the day of the boy's baptism in the transept at Notre Dame on 9 June 1811.[106] Pauline became the godmother. Other than that, only Jérôme and Joseph bothered to make the effort to come to Paris. Louis had chosen the path of self-exile after being thrown off the throne of Holland (see below). Caroline, who was invited to become the godmother, stayed away on the pretext of poor health.[107] In fact, she was upset with her brother for the way he had treated her husband, Murat, and because of the rumours that were going around that the Kingdom of Naples might be incorporated into the Empire. Elisa also stayed in Italy, even though after having lost a child less than a year old she had felt like coming to Paris for a change of air.[108] Napoleon refused her permission, possibly because he did not want his son to come into contact with a woman who could bring him bad luck. The ceremony, which although religious also has to be seen in a political context, took place at the end of the day and concluded with a supper held at the Tuileries, which Napoleon and his wife attended in full regalia, crowns on their heads.[109] It was followed by a concert and then a ball. On the Champs-Elysées, *guingettes*, temporary ballrooms and music kiosks had been set up where the people could attend for free. The costly celebrations were frowned upon at a time when there was high unemployment, an economic crisis and uncertainty about the future.

### The Father of the People

The birth of a son – François-Charles-Joseph-Napoléon – would, many thought, transform Napoleon into a less belligerent ruler. A new dynasty was at last in place. Napoleon the Great would eventually give way to Napoleon II, and the rest of Europe would accept the dynasty as legitimate. 'People sincerely anticipated', wrote Savary, 'a period of profound peace; the idea of war and occupations of that sort were no longer entertained as being realistic.'[110] The King of Rome, in other words, was meant to be the guarantor of political stability. Napoleon felt much the same way, believing that with the birth of his son there was a future for his dynasty. 'Empires are created by the sword', he told one diplomat, 'and conserved by heredity.'[111]

The arrival of his son saw a concerted effort to present Napoleon as a devoted family man in order to counter the damage done by the constant warring and loss of life (not to mention the numbers of wounded and mutilated who returned home). Napoleon began to refer to himself as the father of his people, at least since Eylau after which he was heard to say in public: 'A father who loses his children cannot enjoy the charm of victory. When the heart speaks, even glory has no illusions.'[112] The image of the 'father' was evoked in the bulletins and proclamations of the Grande Armée, in which Napoleon portrayed himself as a general (and later a monarch) who shared the hardships of his men, who cared for and looked after them, who was moderate and magnanimous, who spared the lives of his soldiers, who aspired to peace, and who wept at the loss of men close to him.[113] This was never more than a line or two – Napoleon had not taken off his boots in a week, he was soaking wet, he was covered in mud, and so on.[114]

The idea of Napoleon as 'father' had its roots in the traditional association during the *ancien régime* of the monarch with the role of father of his children.[115] The revolutionaries overturned the notion of paternal authority and replaced it with a different idea – 'fraternity' and 'equality' – so Napoleon's attempt to recuperate the former kings' paternal authority can be seen as an attempt to consolidate his own political influence. Over the course of time, the notion among the military of Napoleon as father figure became deeply ingrained.[116] And this went equally for his professed love of peace and his distaste for war. In his letters and public utterances there are an endless number of expressions of peace – 'I desire peace with all Europe, with England even, but I fear war with no one.'[117] The textual image went hand in hand with a visual transformation of his image after 1810. Considering the toll in men inflicted by the wars, it was no longer appropriate to focus on Napoleon as a

Alexandre Menjaud, *Marie-Louise portant le roi de Rome à Napoléon Ier pendant le repas de l'Empereur* (Marie-Louise bringing the King of Rome to Napoleon during the Emperor's dinner), 1812. There is a sentimentality present in paintings of Napoleon as family man that is entirely lacking in previous portraits of him.

military conqueror, as had been the case at the beginning of his rise to power.

It is only a short step from being called 'father of the people' to being described as 'father of the nation [*patrie*]'.[118] The two notions were in fact developed concurrently. During public festivals commemorating the regime, for example the festival of 14 July, co-opted by Bonaparte and transformed into the Festival of the Concord, the person of the First Consul and the Republic became indistinguishable in the political rhetoric of the day. Local prefects, falling in with the notion propagated by the Brumairians that Bonaparte was the Saviour of the Revolution, associated his name with the Republic in official speeches made during public festivities. It is why supporters of the regime were able to cry out 'Vive la République' and 'Vive Bonaparte' in the same breath. Speeches from officials constantly reminded the French public how much they owed Bonaparte so that he quickly came to incarnate the nation.[119] Any number of songs composed during the Consulate and the early years of the Empire depicted Bonaparte/Napoleon as a caring father figure who would provide for his people/children.[120]

Napoleon increasingly portrayed himself and the nation as one and the same,

to the point where, in December 1813, when the Legislative Corps dared criticize him for not pursuing peace actively enough, he retorted, 'To attack me is to
attack the nation.'[121] Again, on New Year's Day, in the Salle du Trône in the
Tuileries, in another scorching attack on the Legislative Corps, he remarked, 'I
alone am the Representative of the People,' a phrase that he repeated often. He
went on to state that 'All authority is in the throne,' and that he was the throne.[122]

There is no better visual example of Napoleon as paternalistic ruler than
David's portrait *Napoléon dans son cabinet de travail* (Napoleon in his study),
first exhibited in the Salon of 1812.[123] This painting was meant to provide an
intimate glimpse into the statesman at work, still in his office late at night while
the rest of the world, his subjects, are sound asleep. This 'fiction of the modern

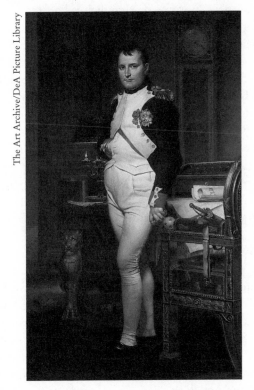

The Art Archive/DeA Picture Library

Jacques-Louis David, *Napoléon dans son cabinet de travail* (Napoleon in his study), 1812.
The painting was commissioned by a Scottish admirer, Lord Alexander Douglas. In other
words, it was not a piece of propaganda, but rather a private commission. It was only briefly
exhibited before being sent to Scotland. In a letter to Douglas, David declared that 'no one
until now has ever made a better likeness in a portrait, not only through the physical features
of the face, but also through this look of kindness, of composure and of penetration that
never left him'.[126]

ruler', as father of the people working late into the night for the benefit of his people, was an image already used by Louis XIV.[124] The glamorous, victorious general has been replaced by an amalgamation of the citizen, an almost bourgeois-like figure, and the royal. We would not even know we are looking at an emperor were it not for the bees on the throne-like chair. In some respects it is a return to the period of portrait painting of Bonaparte as First Consul, when Bonaparte had not yet become the imperial despot.

As always, the devil is in the detail: sheets from the Code Napoleon can be seen on the chair next to him; and his sword is lying to one side, as though he were putting his military role away for the moment to look after the administrative side of his duties. The map, the feather pen and a copy of Plutarch's *Hominus illustri* all point in that direction. Some have preferred to see in David's painting a 'profoundly ambivalent' portrait that implicitly lionizes Napoleon as First Consul while being critical of him as emperor.[125] Note the candles sputtering as the clock shows that it is almost a quarter past four in the morning.

Napoleon deliberately left the candles in his study at the Tuileries alight all night in order to give the impression that he worked at all hours, which was in part true. He did have a habit of getting up at two or three o'clock and working through to six or seven, when he would go back to bed for an hour or two.[127] The newspapers disseminated the image of a ruler who worked tirelessly for his people; the reports gave contemporaries the impression they were dealing with a superior being who ate and slept little. 'Never had a head of state ruled so much by himself.'[128] Jean-Antoine Chaptal, who resigned from the administration in 1804 when Bonaparte became emperor, wrote of how Napoleon was capable of working twenty hours a day without ever appearing tired.[129]

This was not without taking its toll. Napoleon was forty-two when his son was born. His work habits and his demeanour, at least at court, began to change with the arrival of a new family in his life. His routine was not as intensive as it had been at the beginning of his reign, and more time was spent socializing at hunts, dinners and balls. He started turning up late to the meetings of the Council of State. He even seems to have lingered longer at table, encouraged by Marie-Louise who was fond of food. Roederer remarked on it and commented, 'General, you have become less expeditious [*expeditif*] at table,' to which the Emperor cleverly replied, 'It is already the corruption of power.'[130] Physically he was starting to undergo a transformation that has often been remarked upon. His was no longer the slim figure that had conquered Italy and Egypt. He had started to fill out and to develop a paunch. Some contemporaries believed it was a sign of decline.[131] Contact with Napoleon no longer automatically induced awe. On the contrary, some observers were disappointed by what they saw. Thus the writer Charles-Paul de Kock, in Paris in 1811, sneaked into the Tuileries Palace pretending to be part of an orchestra in order to catch a glimpse of him. He found Napoleon 'yellow, obese, puffy, and his head pushed into his shoulders. I was expecting a God, I saw only a fat man.'[132]

## Towards the Universal Monarchy

Would Napoleon then ever have been contented with his family, with living the life of a bourgeois monarch? To answer that question is to understand Napoleon, to fathom the vastness of his ambition, to get a glimpse of how others saw him, and what drove him to do what he did.

In Napoleon's time a number of terms were used interchangeably – 'universal monarchy', 'universal empire', 'universal domination', 'world domination', the empire of Rome or Charlemagne – to characterize his towering ambition. In the late eighteenth and early nineteenth centuries, however, these terms were all expressions of a growing fear, relatively widespread, that Napoleon's victories and his seemingly unlimited ambition

© RMN-Grand Palais (musée des châteaux de Malmaison et de Bois-Préau)/Gérard Blot

Antoine Aubert, *Napoléon le Grand* (Napoleon the Great), 1812. The caption reads: 'Brilliant, immense star, he enlightens, he renders fruitful, and alone creates all the destinies of the world at will.'

would translate into something more than simple hegemony on the Continent. The term 'universal empire' was, moreover, almost always used pejoratively (as it generally had been since the sixteenth century).[133] In 1802, the Russian ambassador to Paris reported that Napoleon had spoken to him about proclaiming the 'empire of the Gauls'.[134] Indeed, Russian statesmen drew a comparison between France and the Roman Empire and the wars that led other states to be either annihilated or made into allies or vassal states. 'Europe', warned the Russian chancellor, Vorontsov, in 1803, 'has always been considered a republic or large society in which perhaps three or four [powers] had influence, but never one master.'[135]

Europe's political elite suspected Napoleon of harbouring ambitions to create a universal monarchy. The Prussian king, Frederick William III, spoke of his 'inordinate ambition' (*ambition démesurée*), while the Prussian ambassador to Paris, Girolamo Lucchesini, believed that Napoleon was going to 'recreate Charlemagne'.[136] The Prussian foreign minister Karl August von Hardenberg, writing to Metternich in 1804, thought that that 'fool' Napoleon was 'aiming for world domination; he wishes to accustom us all to regard ourselves as his subjects who must accommodate his every whim'.[137] Russia's political elite was also under the impression that Napoleon was attempting to create a universal monarchy. They devised a number of measures to counter the possibility.[138] Alexander I's Polish adviser Prince Adam Czartoryski believed that the proclamation of the Empire brought Napoleon a step closer to the idea of 'universal domination', and came to understand that the adoption of the imperial title in 1804 made him think he might be able to realize the 'old dream of universal monarchy'.[139] Napoleon's assumption of the throne of the newly created Kingdom of Italy in May 1805, and his annexation of the Republic of Genoa the following month, was grist for the mill and reinforced the belief that he was aspiring to a '*monarchie universelle*'.[140] The impression grew with every Napoleonic victory.

Two other developments reinforced the notion. The first was the annexation of Holland and the Papal States into the Empire in 1810. Rumours about the proclamation of a universal monarchy had been circulating for weeks. When Armand de Caulaincourt confronted Napoleon on the matter, his response was appropriately enigmatic: 'This business is a dream, and I am wide awake.'[141] Second, when Napoleon invaded Russia in 1812, rumours were rife that once he had dealt with Alexander, he would march on Constantinople, China or India and deal a blow to the British. 'There is talk of going to India,' wrote Boniface de Castellane on 5 October 1812. 'We have such confidence that we do not even think about whether such an enterprise might be successful, but only about the number of months' march that would be necessary and the time it would take letters to come from France.'[142] The suggestion is, of course, that he would set out from Moscow not only to deal a blow to Britain, but also to conquer the East. One French historian recently gave the claim a fillip when he asserted that coronation gear was found in the French baggage train during the retreat from Moscow and concludes, somewhat speculatively, that Napoleon had moved from the idea of a 'universal republic' towards that of a 'universal empire' and that, after defeating Russia, he planned to have himself crowned in the Kremlin.[143]

There are a number of occasions when Napoleon is supposed to have asserted that his goal was to rule the world. Miot de Mélito reported a conversation between Napoleon and his brother Joseph during the Consulate in which the First Consul asserted that they would be masters of the world within two years.[144] That was in July 1800. There is the noted quip in a letter from Napoleon to Vice-Admiral Latouche-Tréville concerning the plans to invade England in 1804: 'Let us be masters of the straits for six hours and we shall be masters of the world.'[145] On one occasion, he is supposed to have said to his notorious minister of police, Joseph Fouché, 'I must make all the people of Europe one people, and Paris the capital of the world.'[146] Again, he reportedly said to Fouché shortly before leaving for the Russian campaign, 'How can I help it if a surfeit of power draws me towards dictatorship of the world?'[147] Even if Fouché is to be believed, one can easily dismiss much of what Napoleon said as hyperbole. Nevertheless, the rhetoric was there often enough for those in his entourage to suspect him of wanting to dominate or unite, depending on one's point of view, all of Europe. He declared to the Austrian General Vincent, on 22 July 1806, that he would not be able to take the title 'Emperor of the West' until he had defeated a fourth coalition.[148] In 1811, he told the French diplomat Dominique Dufour de Pradt, 'In five years, I will be master of the world. Only Russia is left, and I will crush it.'[149] That same year he said to the Bavarian General Wrede, 'In three years I will be master of the universe.'[150] After his return from Elba, in April 1815, he admitted in a conversation with the political theorist Benjamin Constant that he had 'wanted to rule the world', and that in order to do it he needed 'unlimited power . . . The world begged me to govern it; sovereigns and nations vied with one another in throwing themselves under my sceptre.'[151] Now *that* is hubris. The idea of a universal monarchy was given further impetus on St Helena. One of the evangelists of the Napoleonic cult, Emmanuel de Las Cases, who perpetuated Napoleon's heroic identity through the publication of the *Memorial of St Helena*, noted the fallen Emperor's utterances throughout his stay on the island. According to his view, Napoleon tamed the Revolution and marched at its head in a struggle to the death against Europe. In the process he became, in some respects, a universal monarch.[152]

That is not much to go on, and some of these assertions have to be treated with a degree of scepticism. Napoleon was in the habit of waxing lyrical, of indulging in exaggeration, of sounding out ideas by expressing them in front of an audience. He may not have taken his own musings on world domination seriously. Moreover, he was heard denying that he had any such ambitions. Well, sort of. In an interview with the papal nuncio to Russia, Monsignor d'Arezzo, in Berlin in November 1806, he complained of the nuncio at Vienna, who had supposedly put it about that Napoleon wanted to make himself 'Emperor of the West'. 'I have never had that idea,' he insisted, although he could not help but add, 'I won't say that it will never happen, but I wasn't thinking about it at the time.'[153] Finally, none of the comments is first hand; all are reported snippets from conversations with Napoleon, some from people who cannot be entirely trusted. Fouché, for example, was intent on portraying himself in a positive light and his former master in a negative one when he wrote his memoirs many years after these conversations took place.

These statements are useful not so much for their accuracy as for the impression they give of what others believed Napoleon's intentions to be, or believed him to be capable of. There is no doubt that Napoleon and the French had hegemonic pretensions on the Continent, but the question that intrigues and is more difficult to answer is whether it went beyond that. There is enough evidence to indicate that Napoleon was pushing the boundaries, seeing how far he could actually go, seeing how much he could emulate Alexander the Great, by at least contemplating, if not pursuing (and in a very haphazard fashion), the extension of French power outside Europe. In his mind, he was the tool of destiny; he felt he was driven towards a goal that he did not know, but that it involved changing the face of the world.[154] And only once his task was finished would all come to an end, as he imagined it, through a fever, a fall from a horse during the hunt, or a cannon ball. Until that time, 'all human effort against me is but naught'.[155]

Where does that leave Napoleon's so-called aspirations for universal monarchy? Two points have to be kept in mind. The first is that Napoleon was a schemer, a dreamer who considered all his options before finally committing to the most practical though not always most 'realistic' plan (think of the Egyptian or Russian expeditions). The second point to keep in mind is that, as some historians have convincingly maintained, his foreign policy was continually renewed and dictated entirely by circumstances and their immediate needs.[156] Napoleon had in fact no coherent imperial foreign policy. Some historians have insisted that he conquered for the sake of conquering, with no defining goals and no overriding, consistent or specific long-term strategic objectives.[157] Since each campaign created new enemies, the wars were continuous and could stop only with the defeat of Napoleon. If he were truly intent on constructing a universal monarchy, then he never did so in any systematic way. Otherwise, he would have incorporated into the Empire most of Germany, including Prussia, defeated in 1806, and he would either have incorporated or partitioned the Habsburg Empire, defeated in four separate wars. Napoleon may have had an aggressive expansionist foreign policy, he may have wanted to dominate and control most of Europe, he may have fantasized about dominating the world's colonial empires, but he could never become 'Emperor of the Universe'.

# 17

# 'A Very Stormy Year'

## Napoleon Reaches Out

Napoleon and Marie-Louise were inseparable for the first twenty-seven months, an experience he had not had with Josephine. The new marriage was, however, only a momentary reprieve from that ambition which gnawed at his soul like a canker. Members of his entourage noticed how much he had changed, notwithstanding the domestic happiness he was meant to be enjoying. He became preoccupied, and fell into periods of meditation, which were in fact a depression. The prefect Prosper de Barante, who was able to observe Napoleon closely during this period, noticed that 'these thoughts were troubling him; his nights were ruined by long periods of insomnia; he would spend hours on a sofa, given over to reflection. Finally he would succumb and fall into a fitful sleep.'[1] He had plenty to worry about. Things had not gone as smoothly in Spain as he had expected, the Germans were groaning under the weight of occupation and exploitation, and the French were desperate for peace. Change, however, was in the nature of the beast. Napoleon was as incapable of resting on his laurels as Alexander the Great had been. Not content with having drawn his own dynasty closer to the established monarchies of Europe, he was now intent on a radical overhaul of the Empire, centred on his person and the consolidation of his power.

Napoleon had created a number of satellite kingdoms in order to rule over Europe more effectively – Joseph in Naples and then in Spain; Louis in Holland; Jérôme in Westphalia; Murat in the Grand Duchy of Berg and then, with Caroline, in Naples; Eugène in Italy; Elisa and her husband, Prince Bacciochi, were given the Kingdom of Etruria (incorporating part of modern Tuscany). It was indeed a system remarkably similar to the Carolingian model in which the brothers and sisters reigned over the far reaches of the Empire. Though these satellite kingdoms were 'given' to his brothers and sisters, Napoleon could just as easily take back what he gave, generally ignoring the domestic interests of the states concerned. The most egregious example of this was Holland. By November 1809, Napoleon had made the decision to annex the kingdom and to attach it to the Empire, undoing the little popularity Louis had managed to build up and increasing Dutch dislike, if not hatred, of the French.[2] Louis was virtually kept under house arrest in Paris for five months from the beginning of December 1809, before he was allowed to return to Holland. While in Paris, he sent a letter ordering Holland to be defended by flooding it, and especially to resist an occupation of Amsterdam. Napoleon was furious when he found out; over the coming weeks and months Louis eventually gave in to his demands. When Louis was finally allowed to leave for Holland at the end of April, a king in name only, and faced with a looming French occupation of his capital, there was a final act of defiance. He actually convoked a council of war to debate whether he should resist, but was wisely dissuaded from acting rashly. On the night of 1–2 July 1810, Louis abdicated in favour of his son (Napoleon Louis), left behind a proclamation and ordered his carriage.[3] Not being possessed of a particularly gracious physique, he fell into a ditch as he was walking to his carriage. Wet and covered in mud, he then disappeared into exile.[4] For a couple of weeks no one knew where he had gone; he travelled in the company of his aide-de-camp and his captain of the Guard, as well as his dog, Tiel, first to Teplitz and then to Graz in Bohemia under the pseudonym the Comte de Saint-Leu. In spite of Napoleon's summonses, Louis refused to return to France. On the contrary, in 1813 he took up residence in Switzerland, seeing a chance to regain his old throne, and wrote to the magistrates of Amsterdam offering his services.

We do not know what Napoleon's siblings may have thought of the annexation of Holland but it obviously did not bode well for their own thrones nor did it enhance the impression Europeans may have formed of the Bonaparte family. In a letter Joseph addressed to his brother, the first in a long time, he lamented 'the dispersion of a family once so united, the change that has come about in the heart of my brother, [and] the gradual weakening of such an immense glory'.[5] It was a thinly veiled jibe. Napoleon had to have total control over the affairs of his relatives' governments. He constantly harassed and criticized his brothers and sisters in letters that were sent to the capitals, Amsterdam, Madrid, Naples, Milan, Florence and Kassel. Murat, as King of Naples, received missive after missive that was scornful, bitter or likely to hurt his pride, depending on the circumstances.[6] And yet he had done a relatively good job in difficult circumstances, managing to consolidate his control over Naples, eliminate resistance in Calabria and defeat an Anglo-Sicilian offensive under General John Stuart, all the while introducing a number of reforms. But Napoleon was unable to recognize the real accomplishments made and refused to allow Murat any semblance of independence.[7]

The situation was similar for Napoleon's other relatives. Jérôme too was deeply upset at the way in which his brother treated him. In August 1810, only a few weeks after the departure of Louis from Holland, Napoleon decided to annex outright the northern coastal regions along the North Sea and the Baltic. Part of this coastal region fell under the rule of Jérôme; he was to lose about 600,000 souls and some of the richest areas in his kingdom. Napoleon informed his brother of his decision by a brief note, which simply stated that it was necessary to place these territories in French hands.[8] Jérôme was furious; it was with great difficulty that the French ambassador in Kassel, Charles-Frédéric Reinhard, persuaded him not to go to Paris to demand compensation. Instead, he sent a letter demanding several territorial indemnities. The letter's tone seemed to amuse Napoleon, who supposedly said on reading it that if Jérôme had an army of 300,000 men, he would invade France.[9] Nor did it alter Napoleon's behaviour towards his brother in any way: the annexations went ahead. Napoleon did not even bother to inform Jérôme of his decision to annex the northern coastal regions; he learnt of the fate of his kingdom through his ambassador to Paris.

To treat his younger brothers this way was one thing, to treat Joseph with the same condescension was another. In the same way that Napoleon had no time for Joseph's complaints when he was King of Naples, so too did he ignore the real difficulties Joseph faced when King of Spain. Joseph did not always like being told what to do by his younger brother, and sometimes complained publicly about him (which always got back to Paris).[10] In fact, Napoleon's behaviour towards his brothers was typical of the way he behaved towards everyone – that is, he hid his true intentions. Joseph would be 'of no consequence' (*peu de chose*), he said, if he were not the Emperor's brother.[11] By the beginning of 1810, Joseph was king in name only. Napoleon had essentially taken direct power out of his hands and given it to a number of military governors, placed in charge of provinces, who were answerable to Napoleon alone. On top of that, Andalusia was given to Marshal Soult as viceroy. Joseph was essentially at the mercy of a group of generals, most of whom despised him.

The summer of 1810 was the height of Napoleon's territorial reach: he ruled directly or indirectly over about 40 per cent of the total European population. The Empire contained forty-four million subjects, all under the same administrative and judicial systems (the Code Napoleon was in principle applied all over the Empire).[2] In addition, the vassal states that fell under Napoleon's sway – the Kingdom of Italy, the Confederation of the Rhine, the Kingdoms of Naples and Westphalia, and the Duchy of Warsaw – comprised another 33–35 million subjects. Here too the Code Napoleon was applied, although often in a watered-down version. The nature of the Empire changed during the decade that it endured. At first it was to be a federated empire.[13] When this arrangement did not work, Napoleon moved towards a unitary empire with a uniform law code.

The birth of his son could potentially have changed all that; it would no longer be necessary to leave those thrones in the hands of his relatives. Eventually they could all be transferred into the hands of his son, thus creating a unified empire. By the summer of 1810 Napoleon was already contemplating dissolving the satellite kingdoms and replacing them with a European government modelled on imperial Rome.[14] A *senatus consultum* passed in February

1810 made Rome the second capital of the Empire, and stipulated that all future emperors would be crowned first at Notre Dame in Paris, and then at St Peter's in Rome (before the tenth year of their reign).[15] It was an evident echo of the Carolingian Empire.[16] With this in mind, preparations were undertaken in Rome to receive Napoleon for a second coronation, which was supposed to take place in either 1813 or 1814. Gardens were planted on the Pincian Hill and dubbed the Gardens of Caesar the Great. The Quirinal Palace was rearranged to accommodate the Emperor, the Empress and the King of Rome. A medal was even struck to commemorate the (forthcoming) occasion with the device: 'The imperial eagle returns to the Capitol'.

## The Phantom Alliance

'Napoleon tyrannized kings', asserted one critic, 'in the same way Robespierre tyrannized the people.'[17] His attitude towards Alexander is a case in point. Relations between France and Russia had deteriorated almost as soon as the ink on the Treaty of Tilsit had dried, to the point where Napoleon now referred to Tilsit as the 'phantom alliance', and he believed that a new war in the east seemed likely.[18] The Russian elite, as we have seen, had never accepted the alliance. The new Russian ambassador to Paris in 1807, for example, Count Peter Alexandrovich Tolstoy, was hostile to both France and Napoleon: he was against the alliance, and against the proposed marriage to one of the Tsar's sisters.[19] When Napoleon complained about Tolstoy, he was replaced by Prince Kurakin, whose attitude was just as inflexible. In 1808, the Tsar's adviser Adam Czartoryski wrote a confidential note to Alexander in which he aired his concerns: 'Napoleon seeks only to establish his supremacy; Prussia served him, he destroyed it; Spain served him, he is going to invade it after dethroning the king, his ally.' Czartoryski believed that Austria would be partitioned and that Russia would be the sole remaining power in Europe until Napoleon sought a passage through Russia to India; that he would re-establish Poland and so on. The only response to the French threat was secretly to arm in alliance with England, Austria and Sweden.[20] Relations between the two countries became more strained after Erfurt, despite the very public displays of harmony between the two men. In fact, Alexander was carefully manoeuvring between public opinion at home, which was hostile to the French alliance (and which reflected Alexander's true feelings) and keeping his French ally placated. The manoeuvre did not work. At home, Alexander was excoriated for the alliance – rumours of a coup abounded – while Napoleon was less than impressed by his ally's evident lack of enthusiasm manifested in the absence of concrete military support during the campaign against Austria in 1809.[21]

At the beginning of 1810, Napoleon appears to have been prepared to take into consideration Russian sensitivities about the one thing that upset

Alexander (and the Russians) the most, Poland. It was the major bone of contention between the two countries.[22] Napoleon did nothing to help his own cause. At the Tsar's behest, he authorized Caulaincourt to enter into negotiations with the Russian foreign minister, Nikolai Petrovich Rumiantsev, so that all four powers concerned – France, Russia, Prussia and Austria – could come to some sort of binding agreement over Poland. A draft agreement was drawn up in January 1810, but Napoleon rejected it on the grounds that he could not undertake to prevent an event that might happen as a result of conditions beyond his control. This kind of sophistry was not only not appreciated in St Petersburg, but caused consternation. Caulaincourt did his best to try to persuade Napoleon to change his mind, arguing that his stance was doing tremendous damage to the relationship, but to no avail.[23] Alexander, who was insisting on these terms – that is, that Napoleon guarantee that there would be no resurrection of the Kingdom of Poland – went so far as to suggest that if Napoleon did not acquiesce he might find it hard to continue the blockade against Britain. Napoleon was understandably outraged, and declared in a letter to Caulaincourt in July 1810 that if Alexander was going to start blackmailing him, and using the Polish question as an excuse for a rapprochement with Britain – for this is what it seemed like in Paris – then there would be war.[24] From that time on, relations between the two countries went into a nosedive, and both sides starting preparing for war.

Napoleon was playing a number of cards at the same time: he wanted to maintain the myth that the Polish kingdom would one day be resurrected, but at the same time he was exploring alternative foreign policy directions.[25] One was a closer alliance with Austria, while the other was to help place Bernadotte on the Swedish throne, a country Russia considered to be within its sphere of influence. The offer of the Swedish throne to a relatively marginal French marshal is one of the stranger stories to come out of the Napoleonic wars.[26] Relations with Bernadotte had always been strained, a relationship made worse by Bernadotte's opposition to Bonaparte's power, and by his poor performance in the field, notably at Wagram. In 1810, he was about to be sent to Rome as its new governor when he was 'elected' heir to the Swedish King Charles XIII, who was childless and in poor health. The proposal was made on the initiative of a member of the Swedish Diet, Baron Karl Otto Mörner, who acted entirely on his own initiative. In fact, the Swedes were so dumbfounded that Mörner was arrested. It took some time for their government to warm to the idea, but they eventually came around to it. When Bernadotte told Napoleon of the offer, he agreed on condition that Bernadotte sign a document saying that he would never take up arms against France. Bernadotte refused, arguing that he could not accept 'foreign vassalage'. In the end, Napoleon relented and did not oppose Bernadotte's election as crown prince, thinking that either the king, Charles XIII, would be around for a while longer yet, or that Sweden was an insignificant player. He may have been glad to be rid of a troublesome marshal. Nor did Napoleon think at all about how this would be seen in St Petersburg. The creation of the Grand Duchy of Warsaw, the recent marriage alliance with Austria and now the election of a French marshal as the Crown Prince of Sweden all gave Russia the impression that it was being encircled.

Relations between the two countries got worse as the year progressed. The sticking point for Napoleon was the Continental System. The Baltic became the principal region through which the system was most breached, and through which English goods were distributed to the rest of mainland Europe.[27] As many as 5,000 merchant ships entered and left the Baltic in 1810. Around the end of October and the beginning of November 1810, Napoleon concluded that the anti-English aspects of the Tilsit agreement were dead.[28] His response, the only one he was capable of, was to make the Baltic more watertight by annexing a number of territories, such as Hamburg, Lübeck, Bremen and, in December 1810, the Duchy of Oldenburg, a territory of some size in north-west Germany. The latter in particular was a thoughtless move. The integrity of the duchy had been guaranteed by the Treaty of Tilsit, but what made matters worse was that Peter, the Duke of Oldenburg, was Alexander I's uncle, while one of Peter's sons, George, was, as we have seen, married to Alexander's sister, the Grand Duchess Ekaterina.[29] The Russian connection was close then, which is no doubt why Napoleon hesitated before acting, and why Alexander reacted the way he did.

Alexander moved troops towards the Polish border, and sent a letter to all the crowned heads of Europe protesting that the annexation was an illegal act.[30] The troop movements were little more than sabre rattling, but were accompanied by a refusal on the part of the Tsar to see Caulaincourt for more than two weeks. More serious was a *ukase*, or edict, issued on 31 December 1810 that allowed neutral merchant ships to enter Russian ports and, moreover, forbade French goods from entering Russian soil (except wine and silk; Alexander was still anxious not to upset the Russian ruling classes). It was a virtual declaration of economic war on France. The Russian minister for foreign affairs, Rumiant-sev, attempted to patch things up by suggesting that the Duke of Oldenburg could be compensated by territory equal in size in the Duchy of Warsaw, something that would have quelled Russian fears about Napoleon's intentions in Poland,[31] but the negotiations led nowhere and Napoleon's repeated suggestions that Alexander send an envoy to Paris to talk over the difficulties between the two countries were spurned. Napoleon simply could not understand what impact his actions were having on attitudes inside Russia.

Napoleon had known for years that public opinion in Russia was decidedly against the French alliance; his emissaries in Petersburg kept him well informed of Russian discontent. The Russian nobility had considered him a despot ever since the assassination of the Duc d'Enghien in 1804 and were on the whole hostile towards the French. The French Empire was perceived, by some at least, to be little more than 'a sort of slavery under which the rest of Europe groaned'. Russia, on the other hand, was the only power that could act as a 'barrier to this devastating torrent, for which nothing is sacred'.[32] As early as 1811, then, some in Alexander's entourage were recommending war. The Tsar had been thinking about it even earlier than that. When Frederick William III's aide-de-camp, Major Friedrich Heinrich Ernst Count von Wrangel, was sent to Petersburg in July 1810 to announce the death of Queen Luise (she died of an unidentified illness that month), Alexander was so upset that he is reported to have said, 'I swear to you to avenge her death, and her murderer [a reference to Napoleon] is to pay for it.' He then told Wrangel in the strictest confidence that he was arming and that he would be ready to attack Napoleon by 1814.[33] Alexander was thinking, at the end of 1810 and the beginning of 1811, of an offensive on Polish territory.[34]

It has to be said that Russian attitudes towards the French – and this also applies to Alexander – were profoundly ambivalent. If they hated what the French Revolution represented – the overthrow of the existing social order – some nobles both admired Napoleon for his brilliance and hated him as 'an enemy of mankind', thinking that war against him was a sacred duty.[35] In previous campaigns, though, the regime had refused to mobilize the nobility's often blustering patriotism and quashed public discussion for fear it might turn against the regime. Moreover, hatred of revolutionary France, resentment of the interruption of commerce with Britain and the ascendancy of the Anglo-phile party at the court of St Petersburg did not necessarily translate into a desire for war.[36] On the contrary, the fear that Napoleon might incite the Russian peasants to rise up against their noble lords convinced many that it was probably best to avoid war at all costs.

'Two Blustering Braggarts'

Both Napoleon and Alexander publicly professed that they did not want war, and yet both sides were drawn into a situation that made war inevitable. At the beginning of 1811, Napoleon told Davout that 'I do not want war with Russia, but I want to take an offensive position.'[37] During an interview at Saint-Cloud in May 1811, he told Alexander's aide-de-camp, General Count Pavel Andreyevich Shuvalov, who had been sent to Paris with a dispatch, 'I am always ready to do what I can to maintain peace, but I will never let my honour be attacked, and who in Europe would believe the part Emperor Alexander has taken over the duchy of Oldenburg, it is a pretext.' And again in the same interview: 'I have no wish to make war on Russia. It would be a crime on my part, for I would be making war without a purpose, and I have not yet, thank

God, lost my head. I am not mad.'[38] In the same vein, he asserted to another of Alexander's aides-de-camp, Colonel Aleksandr Ivanovich Chernyshev, sent a number of times to Paris with personal letters, that he had no intention of re-establishing the Kingdom of Poland.[39] Similarly, Alexander was telling everyone that he would not be the first to draw the sword, and that he had no wish to be saddled with the responsibility of the bloodshed that would inevitably follow war between the two countries.[40] Both Napoleon and Alexander appear to have been genuine enough, but then it was the same old story – neither was prepared to make the sacrifices necessary to reach a compromise. And when Napoleon at last came to the realization of what was actually needed to avoid war, it was already too late. He aptly summed up the situation in a letter to Alexander in April 1811. 'The effect of my military preparations will make Your Majesty increase his own; when news of his actions reaches me here, it will force me to raise more troops: and all this over nothing!'[41] On St Helena, he later admitted that they were like 'two blustering braggarts' who had no desire to fight each other but who sought to frighten each other.[42] Contemporaries, even those hostile to Napoleon, were in no doubt who was responsible for the coming catastrophe. According to Metternich, it was Russia's 'unpardonable manner'.[43]

Caulaincourt was recalled from Petersburg in May 1811. When he arrived in Paris on 5 June, he was immediately ushered into the presence of Napoleon (then at Saint-Cloud), and they spent the next five hours in conversation. Caulaincourt wrote down an account of the interview, and if it is to be treated as at all reliable, it seems clear that Napoleon's ideas on the subject were relatively set, that he discounted any opinions on the matter that contradicted his own, and that he was convinced he was the victim – Russia was trying to humiliate him – rather than the aggressor.[44] Caulaincourt advised against going to war with Russia, urging Napoleon to abandon Poland for the sake of the Russian alliance. His advice would not have made much difference at this late stage.[45] Most people in Napoleon's entourage advised against going to war with Russia, including Captain Leclerc, in charge of preparing a demographic and statistical analysis of Russia and who warned that any French army that penetrated into the Russian interior risked being annihilated like that of Charles XII of Sweden in 1709.[46]

Napoleon, however, had his supporters at court, so that there were two factions, both scoffing at and denouncing the other. At the Hôtel de Galliffet, for example, the new minister for foreign affairs, Hugues-Bernard Maret, now Duc de Bassano (he took over from Champagny in April 1811), worked towards garnering support for the invasion among the Paris elite. His wife organized puppet shows that publicly mocked both Talleyrand and Caulaincourt for their peaceful views.[47] And they were by no means alone. Most of the military believed in the inevitability of victory; they had only to think of Russia's performance at Austerlitz and Friedland to be convinced of the outcome of war.[48] Napoleon himself was likewise convinced that Russia would succumb to his military might and told Alexander's aide-de-camp, Count Shuvalov, as much: 'I can assemble my troops faster . . . you will find before you the double of your forces. I know war, I have been doing it for a long time, I know how one wins and how one loses battles.'[49] Of course he did, but he was underestimating the enemy before him.

By the summer of 1811, then, it seems likely, despite professions to the contrary, that Napoleon had well and truly decided on war.[50] Comte Jacques Claude Beugnot, the man charged with organizing the new Kingdom of West-phalia on behalf of Jérôme, related how during this period Napoleon was tormented by Spain and that he wanted to 'deliver a great blow' against Russia in order to end the conflict with Britain.[51] The Empire, he suggested, even though it stretched from Rome in the south to Hamburg in the north, was still too small for him. Napoleon was persuaded, according to this account, that with Russia on its knees, Spain would fall and the fate of Britain would be settled once and for all. In short, the crisis was fabricated in order to resolve other problems.

In the lead-up to the campaign, the diplomatic preparations, which should have been extensive and which could have benefited France considerably, were utterly woeful. Napoleon's attempts were an exercise less in persuasion than in coercion. A case in point is his relations with the pope; they broke down completely. One of the most vexed questions between Napoleon and the Catholic Church was the investiture of bishops. By 1811, a number of sees had fallen vacant and every name Napoleon put forward as a possible replacement was simply rejected by the pope. Without going into all the details, by the beginning of 1812, Napoleon had informed the pope that since no agreement had been reached he considered the Concordat null and void.[52] In an attempt to get the pope to abdicate (an unreasonable expectation at best), he had him brought to Fontainebleau in the greatest secrecy.[53] The pope's voyage began in the middle of the night of 9 June 1812. Accompanied by a colonel of the Gendarmes by the name of Lagorsse, he was even obliged to wear a black robe over his pontifical clothes to hide his identity. He arrived at Fontainebleau on 19 June in a weakened state.[54] Napoleon had overstepped the mark. While it is an exaggeration to say that this error, as much as any other, contributed to his downfall,[55] it did leave a very poor impression of the man and his regime, especially among the Catholics of Europe.

In more practical, military terms, Napoleon ordered troops to be called up, often imposing unreasonable demands in the process. For example, he notified Frederick William III that he expected full co-operation, and that if he did not get it

Prussia would cease to exist. Not much argument there; Prussia became a virtual client state with the signing of a new Franco-Prussian alliance in February 1812. For some strange reason, especially considering the past strained relations between the two men, Napoleon simply assumed that Bernadotte would remain loyal to France. He threw any possibility of that away when, at the beginning of January 1812, he ordered Davout to occupy Swedish Pomerania.[56] What exactly he was hoping to achieve remains a mystery. If he thought he was somehow going to force Bernadotte's hand he was grossly mistaken.[57] Public opinion in Sweden was understandably outraged. Admittedly, Austria was on board but this was largely due to Metternich's initiative and had less to do with Napoleon. Metternich saw that war was coming and believed that it was in the best interests of Austria to ally with France. He did not believe Russia was capable of withstanding the French onslaught; rather, he thought that it would be destroyed.[58] Three weeks after the Prussians had entered into an alliance with France, therefore, Austria entered into a similar arrangement but with more advantageous conditions.[59] Austria willingly supplied twice as many men as Napoleon had demanded, and Metternich was able to stipulate that they should not be used in Spain or against the English. Moreover, in the event that Russia was defeated, Austria was to receive territorial compensation for its trouble.

This did not prevent Austria from maintaining secret contacts with the court of Petersburg. Even though official relations were broken off, and the Russian representative, Gustav Ernst von Stackelberg, left Vienna, he did not leave Austria. Rather he laid low in Graz, the whole time corresponding with Metternich.[60] The secrecy was in part motivated by a desire to keep a close watch on Russia, and to make sure that Alexander and Napoleon did not conclude a separate peace at the expense of Austria. Francis informed Alexander that, even though he had signed a treaty with France, Austrian troops would do their best to avoid combat with Russian troops in the coming war.[61]

There was also, at the same time as these rather poor diplomatic preparations, a belated attempt to prepare the French public for what was coming. In this Napoleon had an enormous difficulty. Admittedly, rumours of a war with Russia had been rife since 1811, so the general expectation was already there, but no one seems to have been terribly convinced of its necessity.[62] This, combined with what was happening in Spain, as well as adverse economic conditions in France, ensured that Napoleon's popularity was starting seriously to wane.[63] Between 1805 and 1810, Napoleon had lost 9,000 men killed and wounded at Austerlitz; 12,000 at Jena-Auerstädt; 12,000 at Eylau; 12,000 at Friedland; 10,000 at Bailén; 6,000 at Eckmühl; 15,000–19,000 at Aspern; and 39,000 at Wagram.[64] As the wars dragged on the losses got higher, not counting Spain, which was draining the Empire of manpower – over 350,000 men had been sent there by 1811, of whom only 27,000 were withdrawn for the invasion of Russia. The losses came on top of an economic crisis, unemployment and rising grain prices that doubled between 1810 and 1812. There was rioting in Caen in March 1812, when a mill was sacked and burnt down by people demonstrating, unemployed with nothing to eat. Napoleon was so worried by this development that 4,000 troops from the Imperial Guard were sent to the region to quell any further unrest.[65]

Some effort was, nevertheless, made to portray the war as a crusade, something that had been seen once before, in the run-up to Austerlitz.[66] Napoleon had, like most of the French, considered the Russian people barbaric and on the margins of European civilization. The struggle against Russia was, therefore, to an extent, a struggle to the death between two different conceptions of Europe.[67] The point was driven home in works on Russia reprinted or translated into French, such as the English travelogue by Edward Daniel Clarke, *Travels in Various Countries of Europe, Asia and Africa*, which had gone through a number of editions since its first appearance in 1810. There one can find descriptions of the Russian, whether noble or peasant, as 'ignorant, superstitious, cunning, brutal, barbarous, dirty, [and] mean'.[68] Before that, Napoleon had commissioned a series of articles, through the ministry of foreign affairs, ensuring that the few newspapers left in the Empire were able to portray Russians in the most unflattering light, highlighting everything from their 'thick brown skin' to their eyes 'without expression', their weak, lazy, ungrateful character, their 'absolute submissiveness' (read 'slaves', read 'need to be freed'). In short, Russians were portrayed as 'savages', and as 'desolators of society', as 'barbarian hordes . . . who vandalized the civilized world and exterminated peaceful men'.[69] The French Empire contained forty-four million people who enjoyed personal liberty and were among the most civilized in the world. The Russian belonged to a 'half-civilized' people, who were going to be delivered by the soldiers of the Grande Armée.[70] The propaganda campaign continued even as the Grande Armée occupied Moscow. In October 1812, a book appeared by Charles-Louis Lesur, which included a fabricated 'Testament of Peter the Great' designed to demonstrate that Russia was bent on European domination.[71] That accusation was now levelled at Alexander I.[72]

## The Army of the Gauls and the Twenty Nations[73]

On 13 December 1811, Napoleon ordered his librarian, Antoine-Alexandre Barbier, to send him books on Russia and the history of the invasion of Charles XII at the beginning of the eighteenth century.[74] It was a sure sign that he was about to launch a new campaign. According to one of his aides-de-camp, the name of the Swedish king was constantly on his lips.[75] On the 16th, he ordered the recall of the Imperial Guard from Spain.[76] We do not know whether what he read played on his decision, but it is possible. These works portrayed Russia as an ethnically diverse and hence weak conglomerate of peoples, and possibly led to the impression that Russia would be easy to invade and conquer.[77]

Napoleon had begun to regroup his forces in Prussia, Poland and Germany
at the beginning of 1811, in order to strengthen his lines of defence against a
possible Russian attack. During this time, the troops received intensive training; officers were kept busy from five in the morning till six in the evening.[78]
By the beginning of 1812, Napoleon decided to field an army large enough to
intimidate Alexander into submission. 'An army like that of Xerxes, and which
will perform spectacularly like that of Alexander.'[79] That, at least, was the
belief among some of the troops when they realized the extent of the forces
being gathered. Most in the military, however, from the highest-ranking officer
to the lowliest footsoldier, appear to have been against the war.[80] True, there
were some, like Fantin des Odoards, who were looking forward to another
campaign, but they seem to be in a distinct minority.[81] The end result was a
conglomeration of nationalities from all over the Empire, including Napoleon's vassal states and allies. Apart from the French, there were Belgians, Dutch,
Italians, Swiss, Austrians, Prussians, Poles, Bavarians, Badenese, Saxons, Würt-
tembergers, Westphalians, Spaniards, Portuguese and Croats. There were more
Germans than Frenchmen in this army, if one includes those contingents from
the annexed regions of the Rhine.[82] One French officer remarked that the army
resembled the Tower of Babel and that it was impossible to approach a bivouac
without hearing a different language.[83] Only about one in three soldiers who
marched into Russia were French – that is, from what we would today consider
to be France – and most of those were inexperienced. For the vast majority,
this was their first campaign. This was a far cry from the 'nation in arms' that
had galvanized the revolutionary armies. Napoleon's Grande Armée had no
single national identity; it had many identities and was composed of people
who hated the French and Napoleon, and who had even fought against them
in previous wars.[84]

Prussia, along with Saxony, was obliged to quarter and supply the Grande
Armée massed in preparation for the invasion, including delivering all fortresses
and ammunition supplies to the French. Frederick William was required to
leave Berlin, now placed in charge of a French general, and assume residence at
Potsdam.[85] Napoleon continued to humiliate Prussia and its king, insisting on
a new defensive alliance at the beginning of 1812 by which Prussia was made
to furnish a contingent of 20,000 men – this was about half the army that Prussia was allowed – to be placed at Napoleon's disposal. It meant that Napoleon
could in principle deploy them when and where he saw fit. The formal arrangements were worked out in a treaty signed on 5 March. Frederick William and
Hardenberg, who was now chancellor, had little choice but to accept these
humiliating terms. Napoleon had given the Prussian ambassador, Friedrich
von Krusemarck, the choice of having the Grande Armée march on to Prussian
soil as either friend or foe. Prussia, in effect, was treated no differently to an

enemy state, notwithstanding the alliance. It led to one-quarter of the Prussian officer corps leaving the service in protest.[86]

The impact of the Grande Armée on Prussia was even more devastating, if some witnesses are to be believed, than it had been during the occupation of 1807–8. A few figures will give an impression of the enormous amounts Prussia was obliged to hand over. It included more than 30,000 tonnes of flour, two million bottles of beer and another two million of brandy, more than 50,000 tonnes of hay and straw, 15,000 horses, 44,000 oxen and 3,600 carts (with carters).[87] Napoleon in fact ordered the army to live off the land in the weeks leading up to the invasion so as not to eat into the stockpiles of supplies.[88] 'The inhabitants', wrote one Dutch general stationed around Wismar and Greifswald, 'were not kind to us; in good conscience, I could not blame them, for we had acted towards them in bad faith worthy of the Carthaginians, and often I was revolted by the orders I had to carry out.'[89] One Prussian bureaucrat observed that the entire Polish frontier region had been completely devastated.[90] The Grande Armée pillaged the meagre resources available, committing the worst possible depredations in the process.[91] 'The soldiers spread through the countryside in search of food, beating peasants, chasing them from their homes, which they looted from top to bottom, taking their cattle, and engaging in . . . the most reprehensible excesses.'[92] Worse, a conscript wrote of seeing terrible waste along on the road to Poznań (Posen) and Toruń (Thorn), with sacks of wheat left to rot, barrels of alcohol in the gutter, and supplies left in broken-down wagons. The troops were forbidden to help themselves as they passed by.[93] Napoleon should have known better; the army was obviously larger than the inhabitants could realistically be expected to supply, especially since Poland was experiencing serious drought and failed harvests. But he did not seem to care.

### The Imperial Progress

The social season was particularly brilliant that winter in Paris, like a 'candle that flares up brightly just before its final flicker'.[94] When it was over and Napoleon left Saint-Cloud on Saturday 9 May with Marie-Louise, a sizeable proportion of the court was at his side, almost as though they were setting out on a pleasure trip,[95] amid great displays of public loyalty. In Germany, he stopped along the way to receive homage from various princes – the Grand Duke of Hesse-Darmstadt, the Prince of Anhalt-Cöthen, the King of Württemberg and the Grand Duke of Baden.

The imperial progress was heading for Dresden, the capital of the Kingdom of Saxony, and it was designed to impress. Napoleon had summoned his allies in an attempt to instil in them some enthusiasm for his grandiose but hazardous plan to invade Russia. This act of political theatre was meant, once again, to establish a hierarchical relationship between Napoleon and the German princes, and as a consequence to dissuade them from thinking they could betray him while he was away on campaign.[96] Dresden was, in some respects, the mirror image of Erfurt, only this time with Francis II in the role of Alexander. The meeting was meant to overawe the German princes, but it was also intended to present a united front to Alexander, to pressure him into a compromise arrangement,[97] and to intimidate all those who might doubt Napoleon's decisiveness and the loyalty of his allies.

King Frederick Augustus I and Queen Amalie of Saxony met Napoleon on the outskirts of their capital before together making an entry into Dresden by the light of torches as the cannon thundered and church bells pealed.[98] Frederick Augustus had been obliged to vacate the best rooms in the Marcolini Palace, now occupied by Napoleon and his suite. In 1812, Dresden was a town of around 30,000 inhabitants spread over both sides of the River Elbe, the old town on one side and the new on the other.[99] The Saxon king was almost bankrupted entertaining the visiting dignitaries with extravagant balls, banquets, operas, theatre performances and hunting parties. At nine every morning, Napoleon would hold his *lever*, attended not only by the lesser German princes, but also by the kings of Saxony and Prussia, as well as the Emperor of Austria.[100] At first Frederick William of Prussia had no intention of going but was persuaded to do so.[101] Napoleon considered him to be little more than a 'drill sergeant', a 'blockhead', but he was by all accounts prepared to charm the Prussian king at Dresden, to subordinate his true feelings to the interests of the moment, and his need for troops.[102] It must have been a tremendous humiliation for all the German princes concerned, but especially for Francis and his young wife, Maria Ludovica, whose father had lost the throne of Modena to the French many years before. She detested Napoleon for it and no doubt felt bitter resentment and frustration at having to attend these ceremonies. From his own *lever*, Napoleon would lead the princes to observe the *toilette* of Marie-Louise.

While in Dresden, Napoleon made one last attempt to reach Alexander. He sent one of his aides-de-camp, Louis de Narbonne, an old courtier under Louis XVI, to Vilnius where Alexander had set up his headquarters. Narbonne arrived there on 18 May. Alexander is supposed to have asked, 'What does Napoleon want? To subject me to his interests, to force me to measures which ruin my people and, because I refuse, he intends to make war on me, in the belief that after two or three battles and the occupation of a few provinces, perhaps even a capital, I will be obliged to ask for peace whose conditions he will dictate. He is deluding himself!' Then, with a map spread before him, he more or less explained the strategy the Russians would implement over the coming campaign: 'Space is a barrier. If after a few defeats I retreat, sweeping along the population, if I leave it to time, to the wilderness, to the climate to defend me, I may yet have the last word.'[103]

Narbonne reported back his conversation with Alexander.[104] As soon as he had returned to Dresden (on the afternoon of 26 May), he was shown into Napoleon's presence, still covered in the dust from the journey. Alexander had given him a message – 'Tell the Emperor that I will not be the aggressor. He can cross the Niemen, but I will never sign a peace dictated on Russian territory.'[105] Narbonne is supposed to have recommended that Napoleon reconstitute Poland, which he could use as a buffer, but that he should never cross the Niemen.[106] Napoleon, however, was utterly convinced that he would succeed. 'Never has an expedition against them [the Russians] been more certain of success,' he told one of his secretaries, Baron Agathon Jean François Fain. 'Never again will such a favourable concourse of circumstance present itself; I feel it drawing me in, and if the Emperor Alexander persists in refusing my proposals, I shall cross the Niemen.'[107] He thought the whole thing would be over in two months and that a blow to the heart of the Russian Empire, at Moscow, the great, the holy, would shatter any resistance.[108] This not only underestimated Alexander's determination to see the war through to victory, but was an entirely erroneous idea. It might have been apt if someone had remembered that the fall of a major city or a capital – Berlin in 1806, Vienna in 1809, Lisbon or Madrid in 1808 – did not invariably lead to victory. More than likely, however, Napoleon had the Vienna of 1797 and 1805 uppermost in his mind when, the capital being threatened with occupation, the Austrian court sued for peace.

Napoleon was also making the same tactical mistake he had made when venturing out of Egypt into Syria in 1798. Rather than wait for the enemy to cross vast distances, thereby weakening it in the process, he preferred to attack first. Patience was not one of his virtues. His enthusiasm, or self-belief, was enough to persuade some in his entourage that he must be right. Berthier wrote in June 1812 to Soult, in the thick of campaigning in Seville, that 'In one month, we will be at it. A good battle won will decide the question, in January [1813], we will be able to give you a helping hand to finish with the English so that we can get back to our wives.'[109] The problem though was that Napoleon had no real objectives. In May 1812 he told the Austrian foreign minister, Metternich, that the campaign 'will end at Smolensk and Minsk. That is where I shall stop.' He would then establish winter headquarters at Vilnius, from where he would 'organize' Lithuania.[110] He was telling his ambassador in Warsaw, however, that 'I will perhaps go to Moscow.'[111] Not only did he not have an established plan, he changed his mind and hesitated constantly. Historians have concluded that Napoleon's initial intention was, as it had been with every campaign, to seek out one or more decisive battles and to bring the enemy to the negotiating table.[112] There is some indication that he realized just how difficult the task before him was,[113] and that Russia was likely to take a little more time to subdue than other European powers. That is why the troops were to be supplied with twenty-four days' rations, much more than was normally the case, although given the difficulties the supply wagons had in keeping up with the advancing army, this provision soon proved illusory.[114]

One of the great events of the year was the appearance of what was known as the Great Comet of 1811, which remained visible to the naked eye for nine months, a record it held until the appearance of the Great Comet of 1997. The last time the comet was seen by humans was in the time of Ramses II, in about 1254 BC. This time around, it was first seen at Viviers in France on 26 March 1811, and was last seen in southern Russia at Neu Tscherkask on 17 August 1812. In August 1811, the tail divided into two streams, at right angles to one another. By the middle of October that year, William Herschel, who discovered the planet Uranus, estimated that the comet's tail was 160 million kilometres in length. It was variously interpreted as either a good or a bad omen for Napoleon. He was personally convinced that the comet boded well for the coming campaign.

Napoleon remained almost two weeks in Dresden, hoping that Alexander would break down and that, isolated in the face of such power, he would come to the negotiating table. Many people at the time thought he would. When he did not, Napoleon set out on 29 May 1812 to join his troops at their launching positions. The night before the crossing, starting out from the Prince of Eckmühl's headquarters, about a league from Kaunas (Kovno) and the Niemen, he carried out a reconnaissance of the river looking for a place to cross. It was then that, as he was galloping through a wheat field, a hare startled his horse so that he fell. He was almost immediately back on his feet, but it was enough to cast a gloomy pall over Napoleon himself and over those who witnessed the incident, all of them superstitious, thinking it a bad omen.[115] In that moment the comet was forgotten; Napoleon's fall quickly did the rounds of the army.

Only a few hours after he had left Marie-Louise at Dresden, Napoleon was writing to her. His letters to her during the first months of the Russian campaign are different in tenor to those he once wrote to Josephine during his first campaign in Italy. They are less erotic, less passionate, and much more paternal, but they nevertheless demonstrate the depth of his love for her, the love of an older man for a younger woman. They provide us with an insight into his thinking. 'All the promises I made will be kept, so that our separation will last only a short time.' Napoleon hoped that the campaign would last no more than two or three months.[116]

# HUBRIS, 1812

# 18

# The Second Polish War

## The Tempest Breaks

He was likened to a modern Darius, watching part of the army cross from a hill, standing in front of his tent, humming an old folk song, 'Marlborough Has Left for the War', while playing with his riding crop.[1] He was in his element, which is why he was happy.

When Second Lieutenant Ducque arrived on the banks of the Niemen on 23 June 1812, not far from Kaunas, he bivouacked on the hills along the river. There was nothing but troops as far as the eye could see.[2] It must have been an impressive sight and left many men with feelings of 'joy, pride and satisfaction'.[3] Some of them had been marching for four months and it was only now that they were about to set foot on enemy territory.[4] The army started to cross around two in the morning. Pontoon bridges had been constructed over the river, about 180 metres wide at this spot. Since the banks were so steep in parts, the troops found themselves sliding down on their backsides, breaking their speedy descent by grabbing hold of whatever they could. 'It was like a noisy cataract, a cascade of living men.'[5]

Napoleon had already encountered serious supply problems. In Toruń, in the Duchy of Warsaw, he had raged, furious that Pierre Daru, head of the commissariat, and General Mathieu Dumas, intendant general, had not carried out his orders.[6] The problem was transport; it simply could not keep up with the army, nor adequately deliver supplies on time.[7] The French army had not always lived off the land – in 1800 and again in 1807 large supply depots had been organized – and Napoleon had ordered massive supply magazines to be arranged in Prussia and Poland before the start of the campaign. The problem was getting supplies to the front quickly enough. The supply train consisted of more than 25,000 wagons, which included ammunition caissons, portable ovens for baking bread and even portable mills for grinding grain, drawn by something like 90,000 animals, but the roads were so bad that they could not keep up with an army on foot. Even when supplies already existed in the larger towns, such as Toruń, they were often in poor condition. Around 100,000 head of cattle were supposed to follow the army into Russia in order to provide the troops with fresh meat, but one witness who saw a herd of cattle that had originated in Poitou on the way to Toruń described them as skeletons no longer in a state to walk.[8] Jakob Walter, who belonged to the Württemberg corps, described the salted meat they were given to cook (which they suspected had been there since the last campaign in 1807), as 'bluish-black and . . . salty as herrings. It was already tender enough to eat, and we boiled it a few times only to draw off the muriatic acid; and then the broth, not being useful for soup, had to be thrown out.'[9] The supply situation was so bad that recruits fell ill and died in large numbers before they even reached the Russian border. Even the Young Guard, chosen from among the best recruits, was having trouble keeping up.[10]

There was already a sort of conspiracy to hide the truth from Napoleon, even if it was tacit, and had its origins, according to one general of the Young Guard, in self-interest.[11] General Pierre Berthezène gave the example of the Guard, always written up as 50,000-strong, when in reality it almost never exceeded 25,000. It is not that the men in Napoleon's entourage were made up of toadies and flatterers. On the contrary, many frankly spoke their mind. The problem was that Napoleon often either ignored their advice – believing that they did not know enough about the matter or did not possess an overview of the whole – or he got angry when provided with dwindling figures. Rather than face his ire, most preferred to lie.[12] Although the Grande Armée that marched into Russia was about 450,000 men, only about 235,000 crossed the Niemen on that day in a first wave (the rest followed in the days and weeks to come). Russian figures, often dismissed by historians as inaccurately low, actually support this. On the other hand, the number of civilians accompanying the army – wives, prostitutes, servants, victuallers of one kind or another – at a conservative estimate numbered around 50,000.[13] It appeared that every staff officer brought several servants as well as several barouches and calashes carrying their personal effects, not to mention their victuals of wine, pâtés, cheeses, hams and so on.[14] Whatever the true figure, the reason traditionally offered for gathering such a large army in the first place is that either Napoleon was seeking an overwhelming superiority in numbers in order to carry out a crushing blow, or he was expecting a protracted war.[15] It was more likely the former than the latter.

There is some indication too that Napoleon believed the campaign would be over in a matter of weeks or months.[16] He may have been hoping to intimidate Alexander into submission by the sheer size of his force. A number of historians assert that, based on Napoleon's previous campaigns, he was looking for a decisive knockout blow that would be delivered in one or two battles, that he planned to have the campaign over in twenty days, and that he had no intention of being drawn into the vast Russian interior.[17] The Russians themselves believed that this was exactly what he was looking for. If this were the case, then, in hindsight at least, it made little strategic sense to gather such an imposing army that was likely to prevent any sensible Russian general from giving battle. Nor does there seem to be an explanation why Napoleon entered Russia at this particular point and headed for Moscow, rather than going through the more densely populated northern regions towards the capital, St Petersburg, unless it is because he believed that Moscow was the 'veritable' capital of the Russian Empire, the centre of Russian power.[18]

In a proclamation to his troops, Napoleon referred to this campaign as the 'Second Polish War'.[19] The first had finished at Tilsit, he stated, a not so subtle indication that this war too would be 'glorious' like the first. Russia's behaviour, he declared, 'places us between dishonour and war'. He was referring to himself, not France. It was probably the most uninspiring proclamation he ever made. If war was reduced to a dispute between two sovereigns, there was little in the way of justification and little to motivate men to sacrifice themselves. The other problem was that, on crossing the Niemen, Napoleon declared to his troops that they were setting foot on Russian soil. In fact, they were in Lithuania, which meant that the invading army treated the inhabitants, ironically if not tragically, considering that there was no love lost between Lithuanians and Russians, as if they were the enemy.[20]

## The Tsar Dances, the Emperor Fumes

The Russian troops had been at the frontier for months, and Alexander had been at Vilnius for the past two. 'While we were waiting,' reminisced Alexander's aide-de-camp Count Aleksandr Khristoforovich von Benckendorff, 'we gave balls and parties, and our prolonged stay at Vilnius was more like a pleasant trip than preparation for war.'[21] The Tsar and his entourage appear to have spent most of their time socializing, the Lithuanian aristocracy going out of its way to fête him. There were no councils of war and no plans had been drawn up to meet the onslaught. News arrived that the Grande Armée had crossed the Niemen on 24 June.

It came as no surprise; Russian intelligence was well informed of the build-up. Russian military leaders had come to the conclusion, based on past experience, that Napoleon would be looking for a knockout blow. They consequently decided to withdraw behind the River Dvina, about 320 kilometres east of the Niemen. There is some evidence that the Russians had been thinking of doing so since at least the summer of 1811. In March 1810, the Russian minister of war, Michael Barclay de Tolly, submitted a memorandum on the defence of the western region of Russia in which he concluded that the army should withdraw across Belorussia and Lithuania, laying the country waste in the process, until it reached the defensive line of the Dvina and Dnieper rivers.[22] Then they would attack Napoleon's flank. In May 1811, Alexander wrote to Frederick William to say that he would avoid big battles and organize a long retreat.[23] A couple of months later, Alexander told the Austrian envoy to Petersburg, Count Saint Julien, that if attacked he would retreat into his Empire, laying waste the areas he abandoned.[24] This does not mean that the

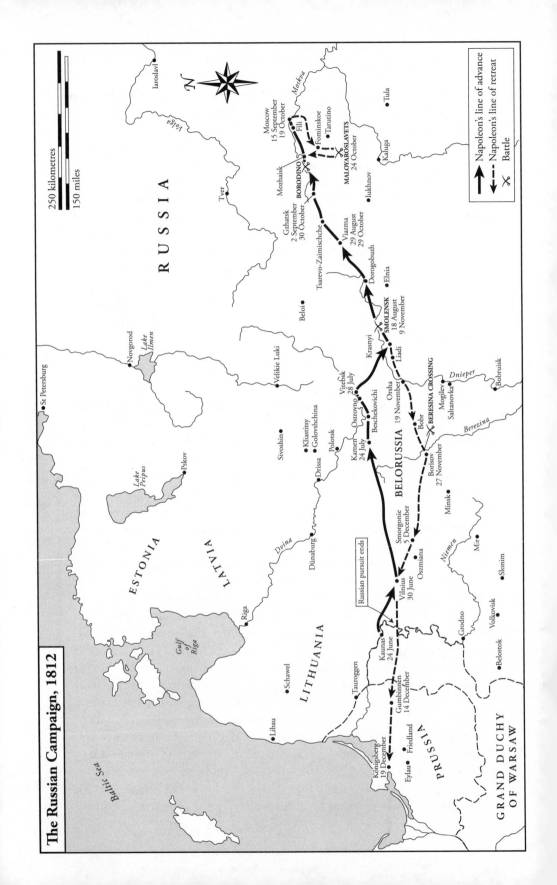

# The Russian Campaign, 1812

**RUSSIA**

**BELORUSSIA**

**ESTONIA**

**LATVIA**

**LITHUANIA**

**PRUSSIA**

**GRAND DUCHY OF WARSAW**

Napoleon's line of advance
Napoleon's line of retreat
Battle

Baltic Sea

Gulf of Riga

Lake Peipus

Lake Ilmen

Volga

Moskva

Dvina

Dnieper

Berezina

Niemen

Iaroslavl

St Petersburg

Novgorod

Pskov

Libau

Riga

Schawel

Tauroggen

Sivoshin

Kliastitsy
Golovshchina

Polotsk

Drissa

Dünaburg

Velikie Luki

Beloi

Tver

Tula

Kaluga

Iukhnov

Moscow
15 September
19 October

Fili

Fominskoe

Tarutino

**MALOYAROSLAVETS**
24 October

Mozhaisk

**BORODINO**
7 September

Gzhatsk
2 September
30 October

Viazma
29 August
29 October

Tsarevo-Zaimischche

Dorogobuzh

Elnia

**SMOLENSK**
18 August
9 November

Krasnyi

Liadi

Vitebsk
28 July

Ostrovno

Beschekovichi

Orsha
19 November

**BERESINA CROSSING**

Bobr

Mogilev

Saltanovka

Bobruisk

Minsk

Borisov
27 November

Kamen
24 July

Smorgonie
5 December

Oszmiana

Vilnius
30 June

Russian pursuit ends

Kaunas
24 June

Gumbinnen
14 December

Grodno

Mir

Slonim

Volkovisk

Belostok

Königsberg
19 December

Eylau

Friedland

defensive strategy was the obvious solution to the Russian problem – there was a debate about the advisability of an offensive strategy over the two years between 1810 and 1812 – but for the moment Alexander decided on an immediate withdrawal, and then decided to accept Napoleon's offer to negotiate – General Aleksandr Balashev was sent – on condition that Napoleon withdraw behind the Niemen.[25] It is unlikely the offer was anything more than a political manoeuvre to show the rest of the world that Alexander was not the aggressor and that he preferred peace to war.

Alexander is often portrayed as leaving Vilnius in a less than dignified manner on hearing of rumours that a French advance guard had been seen.[26] When news of his departure got around, a panic ensued as the staff officers, courtiers and hangers-on all tried to leave at the same time. Only Barclay kept his cool; what stores could not be taken away were set on fire, although more could have been saved if the local officials had not dithered in requisitioning local carts, many of which later fell into Napoleon's hands. This smacks of incompetence and lack of organization, but it was largely the fault of the Tsar. The massive stores had been painstakingly built up over the previous months. They were still burning when, on the afternoon of 28 June, Napoleon rode into Vilnius, a town of about 30,000 inhabitants, big enough for a traveller to find everything to 'whet the appetite'.[27] It had taken all of four days for Napoleon to travel the 200 or so kilometres from the Niemen to Vilnius. Reports on how the French were greeted on arriving in the city are contradictory, some recalling that the inhabitants of Vilnius 'cried with joy on seeing the national flags that were at last unfurled', while others again asserted that the town 'seemed deserted. A few Jews and inhabitants of the lowest classes were the only people to be found in this so-called friendly town,' which the troops treated as though it were enemy territory.[28] Even though Napoleon's entry was made public, the inhabitants did not exhibit the slightest interest in the conqueror of the world. 'Everything was gloomy.'

The Russians did not make a stand at Drissa on the banks of the River Dvina, even though it had been the subject of fortifications for the two years leading up to the invasion. When Barclay arrived with the First Army on 10–11 July, he immediately saw how easy it would be to outflank the fortifications, as did most other generals in his entourage.[29] Another town was chosen as the place to make a stand, Vitebsk, 160 kilometres further south-east. At this point, a number of people in Alexander's entourage persuaded him that he was better off at home attempting to arouse public support for the war than at the front.[30] To his credit, he took the advice, and before leaving he told his commanders that since they were opposed by a greater force not to risk everything in one battle on one day. 'Our entire goal', he wrote to General Pyotr Ivanovich

Bagration, 'must be directed towards gaining time and drawing out the war as long as possible.'[31]

On 1 July, Napoleon summoned Balashev to an interview (he had been waiting to be received for five days), at the same hotel Alexander had stayed in. Napoleon was in a foul mood; he had believed that the Russians would stand and fight for Vilnius. That they did not seems truly to have astonished him; Caulaincourt calls the deception of his Emperor 'heart-breaking'.[32] Napoleon took his disappointment out on poor Balashev, who came in for a drubbing. As he ranted about throwing the barbarians back into their icy wastes, Balashev could hardly get a word in.[33] One can easily dismiss this type of behaviour, typical of Napoleon, but it is worth dwelling on the language used in an attempt to understand his thought processes. He blamed Alexander, and argued that the war had been started by Russia with its demands to evacuate Prussia; Alexander was surrounded by people who had advised him badly. Napoleon boasted that he had gathered an army three times the size of the Russian forces, and that he had conquered a province, Lithuania, without firing a shot. All this points to his increasing inability to assume responsibility for his actions. In fact, he was at a loss. 'I'm already in Vilnius,' he is reported as saying, 'and I still don't know what we are fighting over.'[34] At one stage in the tirade, as he was pacing up and down the room, a small window he had just closed blew open again; in a rage, he tore it off its hinges and threw the window into the courtyard below. No one had wanted this war, he continued, but now that it had started it would end in another triumph; Russia was finished as a great power, he fumed. The blustering went on during the dinner to which the unfortunate Balashev was invited.

His behaviour is in stark contrast to the tone of the letter he gave to Balashev for Alexander in which he professed continued friendship, his peaceful intentions and a desire to talk. In other words, in spite of having marched into Russian territory, Napoleon was astonishingly still hoping to patch things up with Alexander. His assessment of the Tsar's behaviour is intriguing. 'He has rushed into this war', he wrote, 'either because he has been badly advised, or because he is driven by his destiny.'[35] If anyone was being driven by destiny, it was Napoleon.

### 'Like a Ship without a Compass'

Shortly after Vilnius, the hot days and cold nights the troops had to endure were made worse by torrential downpours.[36] The rain not only increased the rates of sickness, but also turned the roads into mud, and resulted in the deaths during one cold stormy night of approximately 8,000 horses.[37] According to one testimony, more than 5,000 horses were lost between Kaunas and Vilnius, a distance of about 120 kilometres.[38] Napoleon wrote to the minister of war,

Henri Clarke, not to bother raising new cavalry regiments since there were not enough horses in all of France and Germany to meet his needs.[39] He entered Russia with around 70,000 cavalry. By the beginning of September more than half of the horses had been lost so that only around 30,000 remained.[40]

We will not dwell at length on the atrocious behaviour of this invading army, unleashed on the unsuspecting inhabitants of Poland, Lithuania and Russia. There are many accounts of pillage, rape and murder, of whole villages being left deprived of absolutely everything. One account from the period reported the story of two eleven-year-old girls who were violated by invading soldiers and subsequently died.[41] One of the girls was supposedly raped on the altar of a church. In a letter written by the Tsar's wife, Empress Elisaveta Alekseevna, in November 1812, she repeated the rumours of French soldiers dragging nuns into churches in Moscow to rape them on the altar. It is impossible to say whether these types of stories were true or whether they were simply lurid tales that brought together two of the greatest Russian fears in the face of invasion – sexual violence and the desecration of churches. There is no doubt that rape was common, however. It features prominently in oral histories of the period collected in Russia between 1864 and 1884. Nor should one doubt the list of complaints about churches being desecrated: soldiers did get drunk, vandalized churches, used them for stables and generally behaved in ways that were seen as brutish by a religious population.

Often, officers would choose a few men from each company to go and get supplies. It was these soldiers who committed the worst excesses, returning after a day's work with a few sacks of flour, or a little cart with provisions pulled by a goat, or a cow, when they were lucky enough not to run into a company of the Imperial Guard who would confiscate their booty for their own use.[42] But we have seen this before and the reader is by now familiar with the litany of complaints that invariably followed in the wake of an advancing army. This behaviour was partly brought about by necessity – the troops desperately lacked supplies and were forced to steal and pillage in order to get by[43] – and was partly the result of arrogance. After Vilnius, things went from bad to worse. One Bavarian officer noted that his troops received absolutely nothing between the Vistula and Moscow.[44]

Napoleon attempted to curb the excesses: a military commission and mobile columns of gendarmes were created in order summarily to execute those caught.[45] Executions of pillagers took place at Vilnius and in the surrounding areas. Some were forced to dig their own graves before being shot.[46] Other troops mutinied and refused to march any further. Captain Coignet recounts how he was shot at by a band of Spanish deserters, most of whom were later arrested; sixty-two were shot in front of firing squads as an example.[47] On one occasion, Napoleon is even said to have attacked some looters he had come across with his riding crop, yelling obscenities at them in the process.[48] But no amount of cruelty invented to deter men from pillaging seemed to have had an effect.

Part of the problem was desertion. Rates were high; as many as 90,000 men were roaming the countryside, attacking, raping and pillaging at will.[49] It has been estimated that after just three weeks and only 320 kilometres, the army had lost more than 100,000 men through sickness and straggling.[50] It would have taken an army to round up these men and enforce military law. Conditions were appalling, even for armies at the time, since they had to sleep outdoors after they had crossed the Niemen. In other campaigns – Italy, Germany, Spain – there was always the possibility of being billeted in villages and of spending the night under a roof. That was not always the case in eastern Europe, not only because of the vast expanses that had to be covered between villages – troops could march seven or eight hours over immense plains without coming across any[51] – but also because of their utterly deplorable state: 'Villages are rare, the houses, built of wood and covered in straw, present the most disagreeable aspect ever seen; the interior is humid and dirty.'[52] As one soldier put it, 'we sighed after towns, like we sighed after a battle'.[53] When the memoirs do make mention of finding shelter, the buildings in question were usually convents of one kind or another.[54] Caulaincourt lamented that there were 'no inhabitants to be found, no prisoners to be taken, not a single straggler to be picked up. There were no spies . . . if I may be permitted the comparison, we were like a ship without a compass in the middle of a vast ocean, knowing nothing of what was happening around us.'[55] The psychological burden of marching across vast distances also began to take its toll. The anxiety this caused was noted by some of the more literate in the army. There were the habitual suicides, hundreds according to one witness. 'Each day we would hear isolated shots in the woods near the road.'[56] Many were overcome by what contemporaries called 'nostalgia', a profound melancholy produced by the constant marching across seemingly endless plains.

Some of the 'deserters' were high ranking. Jérôme fell out with Marshal Davout early in the piece. Feeling slighted that Napoleon had given Davout command over the Westphalian troops, Jérôme suddenly decided to leave the army, informing his brother of the decision on 14 July.[57] The difficult conditions of the campaign and the volley of reproaches Napoleon had fired at him seem to have resulted in a depression and he thought his only way out was to flee. Napoleon attempted to backpedal a little when he learnt of his brother's decision, writing to say that Davout's command was temporary, and pointing out how inexperienced he was compared to the marshal, and ordered him to stay at his post.[58] Jérôme ignored him, and left for Kassel.

Once the army had penetrated some distance into Russia, the villages they did come across were devastated, pillaged, burnt to the ground by retreating Russian troops or indeed by advance parties of the Grande Armée.[59] 'One would have had to witness it to be aware of all the barbarity and the horror of the spectacle.'[60] By the time the army had reached Viasma, some 160 kilometres from Smolensk – what some in the Grande Armée referred to as 'Schnapps town' (*ville au schnapps*)[61] – at the end of August and the beginning of September, most had been forced to sleep in the open and on the ground for at least a month.[62] On balmy summer nights around a campfire, this could be a pleasant enough experience, even if the nights were very short in the northern hemisphere at that time of the year, lasting only a few hours.[63] Even on those nights, it was difficult enough sleeping after an exhausting day's march, but when the weather turned bad, when it rained, which it seems to have done regularly in September,[64] or, as we shall see on the army's return, when it snowed for lengthy periods, the impact on the men was debilitating, even fatal. It is difficult to make fires and dry off when the rains do not let up for days on end, with all the consequences for men's health. Their physical condition was worsened by the lack of food, the heat of the day followed by often bitterly cold nights, even at that time of the year.[65] Much has been written about the retreat from Moscow, but often to the neglect of the long, hot difficult march that preceded the entry into that city, not to mention the sickness caused by the autumn rains.[66] Men literally died of the heat, thirst and hunger, especially since the villages, the only places to contain wells, were few and far between, and even then retreating Russians often threw bodies into them to poison the water.[67] For those not at the head of the army, and who followed in its wake, the sight of roads covered with dead men and horses could hardly have been good for morale.[68]

These are the kinds of things the survivors remembered many years later – the hot sun, men reduced to drinking filthy water, the few provisions available, the lack of wine and meat, and the consuming nature of constant pain, fatigue, thirst and hunger.[69] Some of those who had campaigned in Egypt or Spain claimed that the heat was more oppressive in Russia.[70] Since the roads were made of sand, clouds of dust, like thick fog, were kicked up as soon as the troops set off, eyes, ears, nostrils quickly filling. Some had trouble breathing, while others could not see further than two paces in front of them, and it became impossible to distinguish the colour of uniforms.[71] One way around this was to have the drummers beat at the head of the column so that men did not lose their way.[72] Some were reduced to drinking horses' urine from ruts in the road in an attempt to quench their thirst.[73] Under those conditions – where dehydration and malnutrition were prevalent – it was only a question of time before illnesses like dysentery and diarrhoea started to make inroads.[74]

Napoleon's later campaigns, when compared with his first impressive entry on to the military scene in Italy in 1796, have often been criticized for their lack of flair. This was never more the case than in Russia. Part of the explanation may

have to do with age. At forty-three, he could not sustain the same intensity as
he had managed in his younger years. Moreover, he was now a profoundly
political animal and much of his time was taken up with administrative matters
that had not burdened him in his early career. From 28 June 1812, for example,
he spent eighteen days in Vilnius sorting out correspondence and reorganizing
the army, a necessary thing, but he thereby lost what little initiative he had.[75] It
has been described by one military theorist as one of the worst mistakes of his
career.[76]

Nevertheless, by the time he reached Vitebsk on 27 July, he assumed that
the Russians camped before him would, this time, give battle.[77] He awoke the
next morning, however, only to find that they had once again slipped away.
During the night, Cossacks had kept the campfires burning to give the impression that the army was still there.[78] The Russians had retired in such good
order that, according to some at least, a general feeling of unease began to grip
the French officers who witnessed the skill of troops who retreated without
leaving a single cannon, a single weapon or a single man behind. For the first
but not the last time, Napoleon considered going no further. He had already
lost one-third of his army without so much as engaging the enemy in a battle,
and without having yet reached Russia proper. This is not what he had
expected, and what to do next obviously preoccupied him to the point where
some witnesses recall a perplexed, somewhat indecisive Napoleon. On returning to headquarters (28 July), inside his tents, he is supposed to have taken off
his sword and thrown it on a table covered in maps, exclaiming, 'I am going to
stop here, I want to take stock, to rally, to rest my Army and organize Poland.
The 1812 campaign is over. That of 1813 will do the rest.'[79] According to his
valet, he slept particularly poorly during his stay at Vitebsk, while Caulaincourt claimed that he had never seen Napoleon 'in such a state of irritability'.[80]

It would have been a good idea to stay put. Most of his generals thought it
was time to stop and consolidate.[81] Berthier is supposed to have pleaded with
tears in his eyes; Murat and possibly Davout seem to have been the only generals eager to push on. This was at least a sign that Napoleon was surrounded by
men who were not afraid to speak their minds. How realistic an option stopping was (it was after all only July), or whether their views were born of
frustration, exhaustion, depression and the realization that the Russian landscape was like nothing they had ever encountered before, is difficult to tell.
Marching ten, twelve, fourteen hours a day, the proximity of a village, a creek
or a muddy pond determined where they would halt for the night.[82] Evenings
and nights, however, were spent scouring the countryside for food and water.
The army's strength was nevertheless still reasonably good at this stage. Knowing the supply situation to be disastrous and that the men had suffered as a
result, in an astounding piece of theatre Napoleon berated the supply commissioners in front of the men at one parade. It was a show to remind the men how

much their Emperor cared for them, and by all accounts it worked.[83] Once rested – the following two weeks were spent putting the army back in order, allowing stragglers to catch up and supplying his troops[84] – Napoleon seems to have taken on a more positive, even brash tone. But he remained agitated nevertheless and unsure how to proceed. He had never before faced an enemy that refused to stand ground and fight. What seems to have made up his mind was news that the Russian army had halted at Smolensk, and that Bagration's Second Army had also arrived there in early August. He called a council of war in the first week of August and declared that he was determined to end the war that year. The decisive battle he sought looked as if it was in reach, at Smolensk, and even if the Russians failed to give battle there, he was sure they would do so before Moscow. What he needed was a major victory so that he could, as one general caustically put it, 'hide so many sacrifices under a heap of laurels'.[85]

This was a new development. Moscow had only ever been vaguely talked about before but it was now given expression by Napoleon. Some of those present at the war council expressed concern about this change of attitude. Objections about supply issues were raised but brushed aside. Berthier went so far as to bring the head of the commissariat, Pierre Daru, to Napoleon to hammer home the seriousness of the supply situation, which he warned would probably grow worse as the army continued to march east. With the various detachments that had been posted in garrison towns to protect supply lines along the way, the army was reduced to less than half the original size of the invading army.[86] However, faced with the choice of bedding down in Vitebsk or returning to the Vistula, more or less an admission of defeat if only in his own mind, Napoleon decided that the only realistic option was to push on, at least to Smolensk where there was the possibility of a battle and victory.


'The Corpse of a Dead Enemy Always Smells Good'
Smolensk was surrounded by a crenellated brick wall about eighteen metres high and was cut in two by the River Dnieper (the wall can still be seen today). It was not, for all that, a strong defensive position since the city could be easily outflanked. Despite that, Barclay was coming under strong pressure not only from his own generals but also from Alexander to make a stand.[87] At a council of war on 6 August, he was therefore forced to go over to the offensive despite strong personal doubts about the wisdom of such a move; he was still convinced that the best approach was not yet to risk the destruction of the First and Second Russian armies.

Napoleon's army arrived before the walls of Smolensk on 15 August facing a force of probably no more than 15,000 men.[88] Rather than take the city, however, as he probably could have the next morning, he dithered. By the morning of 17 August, Barclay's army of 30,000 men was entrenched in the city, with another 170,000 occupying the hills on the other side of the Dnieper under Bagration. Napoleon and his troops could clearly see the enemy as they took up position. His decision to attack the defences head on, rather than attempt a flanking manoeuvre, forcing Barclay to abandon the city, appears in retrospect to have been a mistake, but seems to have been made out of a desire to engage with the enemy immediately, so that the Russians could not once again avoid battle. Besides, scouts sent out to find a point at which the Dnieper could be crossed returned with conflicting reports.[89]

The first day of the assault was bloody – 9,000 killed and wounded in the Grande Armée to 11,000 Russian losses – but the city held despite the French mortar shells setting many of the city's wooden houses on fire. It was Barclay, for reasons that are not entirely clear and in the face of vigorous and vociferous opposition from generals and senior officers, who decided to abandon the city to its fate. Here too Napoleon let the Russian army slip out of his grasp by not taking an active enough part in the battle. On 19 August, he retired to Smolensk at five in the evening, thinking he had engaged only the Russian rearguard.

On 18 August, the French entered a town on fire or still smoking. 'Soldiers who had wanted to escape [the fire] had fallen into the streets, suffocated by the flames, and had been burnt. Many no longer resembled men: they were shapeless masses of grilled and charred flesh, that only the iron of a musket, a sword or a few shreds of clothing found beside them made recognizable as corpses.'[90] At around two o'clock that night, when Napoleon was still near his tent near the château of Ivanovskaya, in the company of Berthier, Bessières and Caulaincourt, they were all contemplating the city on fire, which lit up the horizon. 'An eruption of Vesuvius!' Napoleon said to Caulaincourt, according to the latter's *Memoirs*. '"Is not that a fine sight . . . !" "Horrible, Sire." "Bah!", rejoined the Emperor. "Remember, gentlemen, what one of the Roman emperors said, the corpse of a dead enemy always smells good!"'[91] His officers were shocked by the remark, but did no more than look at each other in that meaningful way people do when they share the same thoughts. It was obvious to them then that Napoleon would not remain at Smolensk but that he would push on. Many of those who experienced Smolensk considered it the worst battle they had faced, including Austerlitz, Eylau and Wagram.[92] Others began to wonder what it was all for, and openly to question the direction of the campaign, even those generals who had admired Napoleon.[93]

In fact, Napoleon seems to have been at a loss what to do next. The same choices facing him at Vitebsk now faced him at Smolensk: he could march on to Moscow or St Petersburg, head south into the Ukraine and Kiev, or bring the campaign to a halt and consolidate his gains.[94] It would have made sense to halt and consolidate, given the state of discipline and morale among his forces, and the fact that his communication lines were now stretched to about a thousand kilometres. That, however, was not without its own problems. Lithuania and Belorussia would have found it difficult to feed an army of considerable size for any length of time, something that would have been exacerbated by the onset of winter. Uppermost in Napoleon's mind was that, if he did push on to Moscow, the army would be in a better position to live off the land. He was, after all, only 450 kilometres from Moscow – that is, about two weeks' march – with a couple of months of good campaign weather ahead in the midst of a harvest season in the region around Moscow that would have enabled him to feed his men and horses, and in the face of an enemy army that did not appear capable of resisting the invasion.

There were other considerations, strategic and political.[95] To cease now, in the middle of summer, would give the Russians at least six months to regroup and redeploy troops that were presently tied up in Moldavia, Finland and the Caucasus. A strategic withdrawal would also allow Russia and its allies, Britain and Sweden, to claim a victory, even if it were not one, and thus do damage to Napoleon's reputation. All of these and other factors had to be weighed. Napoleon may have said shortly after the battle that they would be in Moscow in less than a month and would have peace in six weeks, but in actuality he appears to have been plagued by doubts. According to one witness, on the eve of the battle of Smolensk, he did consider setting up winter headquarters at Vitebsk, to consolidate his gains. 'We will drive them a little further back, to ensure that we are left undisturbed. I will fortify my positions. We will rest the troops, and from this base we shall organize the country and see how Alexander likes that . . . I will establish my headquarters at Vitebsk. I will raise Poland in arms, and later on I will choose, if necessary, between Petersburg and Moscow.'[96] Much of this was just wishful thinking, although many (but not all) in his entourage – Berthier, Duroc, Rapp, Caulaincourt and Narbonne – believed that the conquest of Poland had been achieved and that it was time to call a halt to the campaign.[97]

If Napoleon sounded them out it was to get an idea of how they were feeling, of how committed they were to the campaign, and of what morale was like.[98] The more he was drawn into Russia, however, the more he found himself in a bind. He could not stop where he was for any length of time. He could not retreat; it would be an avowal of defeat. His only choice was to continue to advance. And the more he advanced the more anxious he became about what he was doing. If one day Napoleon considered calling a halt, the next he was thinking about pushing on. This could happen when reports came in of Russian troop movements that led him to believe another battle and another victory were possible. In those moments, the prospect of overtaking the enemy, of pressing ahead quickly so that the enemy could not escape, somehow forced him, obliged him almost against his will, to press on.[99] Smolensk certainly gave Napoleon food for thought, especially since there were indications that the Russians themselves might have set the town alight.[100] The inevitability of war and campaigning – that is, the pursuit of the enemy until victory – eventually won out over any practical considerations. Peace was the word most uttered in conjunction with Moscow, according to Baron Fain. He believed that reaching that city would ultimately bring the campaign to an end.[101]

## Borodino

After Smolensk, it had become impossible for Alexander to continue to ignore the complaints about the poor state of the army, its profound demoralization and its disorganization. In addition, many Russian generals felt that it was shameful to retreat in the face of the enemy and their ire was directed, irrationally, against Barclay and Bagration as 'foreigners' (they were both of German descent). Alexander decided, therefore, to appoint Mikhail Ilarionovich Golenischev-Kutuzov commander-in-chief with both Barclay and Bagration under him. Alexander did not like Kutuzov, especially since the debacle at Austerlitz where, against Kutuzov's advice, he had given battle, but it would have been difficult now for him to contradict the advice given to him by all of his senior military advisers. Moreover, public opinion in Petersburg at the time was very much in favour of Kutuzov.[102] Under the circumstances, with a foreign army now deep in Russian territory, Alexander may very well have thought it dangerous to ignore public opinion.[103] While it is an exaggeration to say that he might have faced a palace coup if he did not stand and fight, there is no doubt that grumblings at court were making themselves heard and may have been worrying him.[104]

Kutuzov was sixty-five years old, overweight, mostly blind and badly disfigured (a musket ball had penetrated one of his temples and passed right through his head, leaving him scarred and blind in one eye). He rode badly (he often preferred to ride in a carriage), and often fell asleep in the middle of meetings. Indolent, slovenly and mistrustful of everyone in his entourage, he was nevertheless considered intelligent and cunning and was loved by his troops. His qualities as a commander, however, are questionable and he was certainly mistrusted by the senior officers under his command. He is supposed to have advised Alexander as early as April, well before the Grande Armée had crossed the Niemen, to draw the war out and to avoid giving battle; Napoleon would be defeated in that way much as Charles XII had been defeated.[105] But pressure to give battle made Alexander face the enemy.

That is why a decision was made to stand and defend Moscow, at Borodino.

A fine but cold rain accompanied an autumn wind on the night of 6 September. Add the agitation that habitually accompanies the eve of a great battle, and one can easily understand how tired most of the men must have been, especially after a long day's march. Napoleon does not appear to have had more than a few hours' sleep before getting up with his entourage and touring the lines at dawn the next day.[106] The morning was fine but cold, with patches of fog here and there that lifted at about ten o'clock. To some, it appeared a repeat of conditions at Austerlitz. That same morning, Napoleon received a portrait of the King of Rome about which he was very excited – 'an emotion he could hardly contain'[107] – and which he was keen to show everyone. On the eve of a battle, even the most intrepid warrior is subject to feelings over which he has little control.[108]

At six o'clock in the morning, a French cannon shot gave the signal for the commencement of battle. After a short silence, more than a thousand cannon fired at each other so that it sounded like a continual rolling of thunder, 'producing an artificial earthquake'.[109] 'Everything seemed to announce less a battle than a general extermination.'[110] The initial plan was sound.[111] Napoleon had seen the apparent weakness of Kutuzov's left wing and intended to exploit it by sending Davout and Ney to attack the right while he sent Poniatowski to turn the Russian left flank. All three generals were then meant to push the Russians north up against the Moskva River and annihilate them. Davout proposed taking 40,000 men and marching overnight in a flanking movement that would come behind the enemy's left wing, but Napoleon denied the request on the grounds that it would have deprived the army of a large body of men for much of the opening battle, and that marching at night through heavily wooded terrain was 'too dangerous a manoeuvre'.[112]

By the time the largest army in the world had reached the banks of the Moskva after more than ten weeks of marching, it had been reduced to between 103,000 and 135,000 men (depending on the sources), perhaps fewer given the tendency of commanders to inflate the numbers under their command. The French were, in fact, outnumbered, at least on paper, facing around 155,000 Russians. However, around 30,000 of those were militia who took no part in the fighting; they were used to carry away the wounded (a task that front-line troops would normally perform, often not to return), as well as forming a cordon behind the lines that prevented deserters, including officers, from fleeing.[113] What's more, the Russian cavalry was made up of 8,600 Cossacks, of no use against regular cavalry in a set battle. The Grande Armée deployed 587 cannon, while the Russians had slightly more at 640, though they had many more twelve-pounders than the French, behind defensive positions that were not, however, as strong as some French descriptions have made them out to be.[114] The opposing forces were then roughly equal in strength and quality, although the Russian troops were no doubt more motivated by a desire to defend their homeland. The only thing that could possibly have motivated the multi-national force under Napoleon's command, a point he made in the order of the day, was that a victory would bring them 'abundance, good winter quarters and a rapid return' to their homelands.[115] Finally, the Russian troops were probably in slightly better condition than those of the Grande Armée. A supply line from Moscow had been set up to keep the troops fed, while Napoleon's troops had had to resort to foraging (many had not eaten properly in days); his men were sick, tired, badly clothed (some even went into battle barefoot); and his cavalry was in such an appalling state it was incapable of actually charging.

Napoleon has been criticized for adopting an unimaginative frontal assault rather than attempting an outflanking manoeuvre, the result of a lethargy he seems to have been unable to shake.[116] In his defence it has to be said that, as at Smolensk, he was anxious to give battle, and was concerned that if the Russians got whiff of a flanking movement they would decamp. So he decided to slog it out, although he may have come to regret his decision in the course of the day. When, around ten o'clock in the morning, Murat, Ney and Davout finally managed to batter a hole in the Russian centre, effectively splitting the Russian line in two, and sent messages, all three of them, back to Napoleon requesting that he commit the Guard, Napoleon at first decided to do so, then changed his mind. Part of the Guard was actually on the move when he ordered it to halt. As many have pointed out, a younger Napoleon would have been on his horse riding up to see the situation for himself, but now he stayed in the same position, leaving the Shevardino redoubt over a kilometre behind the front only once in the course of the battle, at about three in the afternoon.[117] From there, it was impossible to see what was actually going on. It was obvious even to contemporaries that Napoleon lacked the energy and enthusiasm with which he normally conducted a battle, riding to points that were particularly difficult in order to galvanize the troops.[118] General Augustin Belliard described him as 'suffering and dejected, his features sunken, the look bleak'.[119] It led Ney to exclaim, 'If he [Napoleon] is no longer a general . . . then he should go back to the Tuileries and let us be generals for him.'[120]

The remark is perhaps a little unfair. Napoleon had sent the commander of the Guard Cavalry, Marshal Jean-Baptiste Bessières, to reconnoitre, and he reported that the Russians were still resisting, the implication being that the Russians might be strong enough to continue to fight the next day. It was Berthier and Murat who argued that it would be pointless sending in the Guard and, as it was the only corps that remained intact, it was necessary to keep it for a later date.[121] Moreover, at about the same time that these requests were coming through, worrying news was filtering in from his left flank. The Guard was told to prepare for a possible march north. Napoleon can be blamed for excessive caution here; the cavalry sighted in the north was easily contained, and it would certainly appear as a result that he missed his chance to crush the Russian army. It is more than likely that if he had committed the Guard, the battle would have been a decisive victory, thereby seriously damaging Russian morale, but it has also been pointed out that the rest of the Russian army would still have retreated down the New Smolensk Road, thus rendering void the strategic outcome.[122]

Historians usually point to Napoleon's state of health to explain his lack-lustre performance during the battle. Shortly before he left for the campaign he was described as having 'put on a good deal of weight'.[123] It has been suggested that this sudden onset of obesity may have been a result of Fröhlich's Syndrome, a rare condition brought on by a pituitary tumour or a damaged hypothalamus that can affect hormone levels.[124] Others have hinted at a form of venereal disease, which may explain the strange behaviour that was remarked upon by some contemporaries. However, there is no hard evidence for either of these diagnoses. It is more likely that he was suffering from dysury, an infection of the bladder that made it difficult to urinate. When he did, it came out in drops, was thick with sediment and caused enormous pain. Moreover, his leg was swollen, he had fits of shivering and had complained of feeling sick, was suffer-ing from a terrible migraine, a persistent dry cough, an irregular pulse and, probably, some sort of psoriasis.[125] None of these symptoms was particularly serious, but they help explain why, no longer a young man, he could not sustain the types of exertion he had once submitted himself to.

This is as good an explanation as any for the lack of initiative he demon-strated throughout the day, barely moving from his seat on the Shevardino redoubt and hardly reacting to the news that was coming in from various parts of the battlefield. As a result, Napoleon kissed goodbye an opportunity, ironi-cally since this was exactly what he had been looking for, to inflict a crushing defeat on the enemy, a knockout blow that would bring the war to an end. The result was the prolongation of the war.

When the French awoke the next day, it came as a surprise to some that the Russians had abandoned the field of battle.[126] Kutuzov had done so after real-izing just how great his losses were, and in particular how many good commanders were out of action. A retreat was ordered, but for the first time since the campaign began, the rearguard performed poorly, largely because it was under the command of the relatively incompetent Cossack general Matvei Platov. Also for the first time, thousands of Russian wounded were left on the field of battle.

Between 60,000 and 90,000 rounds from 587 cannon were fired from the French side that day, and possibly as many again by the Russians.[127] Between 1.4 and 2 million cartridges or 'cartouches' were fired by the French forces. One cannon ball could have a devastating effect, taking off a limb or a head or a large part of a torso before continuing on to maim or kill other people.[128] When the Russians were finally able to clear the battlefield in 1813, they buried or burnt 67,000 bodies and 36,000 horse carcasses.[129] It was the highest loss in any European engagement in a single day's fighting since Hannibal's defeat of the Romans at Cannae in 216 BC, and it was not to be surpassed until the battle of the Somme.[130] Russian losses were devastating: anywhere between 40,000 and 50,000 men killed and wounded, that is, a third of their forces.[131] The casualties of the Grande Armée were fewer – about 30,000–35,000 men killed and wounded, or about 22 per cent of their forces – but just as devastating, especially given the distance from their supply sources.

As was his custom, Napoleon toured the battlefield where lay tens of thousands of dead and wounded, surveying the carnage of what one general referred to as the most disgusting sight he had ever seen – 'Mountains of dead on both sides'.[132] It was raining and the wind was cold. Napoleon was not always able to avoid stepping on a body or a wounded soldier with his horse, so many lay on the ground. General Philippe-Paul, Comte de Ségur (the son of Louis Philippe, Comte de Ségur), noticed that although his expression was impenetrable, he was paler than usual, until, having accidentally stepped on another wounded soldier, he yelled at those in his entourage to go and help them.[133]

A letter to Marie-Louise described the numbers of killed and wounded that Napoleon attempted to but could not really hide.[134] There would be no painting competition this time around to give them some sense of meaning. The Emperor remained at Mozhaisk, thirteen kilometres from Borodino, for three days, locked in his room, gripped with a high fever, probably brought on by work and anxiety.[135] He had also, apparently, become mute, unable to speak above a whisper, forced to write summaries of his dispatches for his secretaries and explaining himself by sign language. This then is a crisis point in Napoleon's life; he knew that all was failing around him but was unable to do anything about it. When Bessières came to read out the list of senior officers wounded during the battle – forty-seven generals and more than one hundred colonels – Napoleon managed to find his voice to interrupt him, only to say, somewhat brusquely, 'Eight days in Moscow and all will be as good as gold.'[136]

# 19
## 'The Struggle of Obstinacy'

### Moscow

The traveller arriving in Moscow on the road from Smolensk passed through a forest at the end of which was a hill, the Poklonnaya Gora (literally the Hill of Worshipful Submission), from where one could get an overview of the entire city. From there the troops would have discovered a city 'more Asiatic than European, standing at the end of a deserted and barren plain'.[1] The rounded church steeples, gilded in gold and silver and reflecting the sunlight, resembled 'luminous globes', Montgolfier aerostats floating in the air.[2] 'Whenever we reached the top of a hill, our eyes tired of looking for our goal [Moscow] through swirls of smoke and dust that . . . obscured the horizon. Then suddenly a cry rang out from the columns up ahead. We squash together, we hurry on, and then a multitude of voices begin to cry out, Moscow! Moscow!'[3] For these westerners setting eyes on Moscow for the first time, it appeared like something out of *One Thousand and One Nights*, a fantastical creation whose architecture and monuments were completely unfamiliar to them. In that 'magical' moment, all the suffering they had endured over the past weeks and months disappeared and gave way to the thought of the pleasure that awaited them.[4]

It was a beautiful day, 14 September, the sun reflecting on the golden domes of the hundreds of churches, over 240 of them, all of which had five domes.[5] With a population of around 275,000, Moscow was the largest city in Russia and the fourth largest in Europe (after London, Paris and Naples).[6] Aristocratic society was dominated by a few incredibly wealthy families and was to that extent more clan-based than, say, St Petersburg. Aristocrats tended to live insular lives, never mixing with people below their class: they worshipped in their own private churches, while very wealthy nobles had their own theatres and troupes. Of the fifteen theatres in Moscow, fourteen were in private residences (theatre was an activity considered sinful and disgraceful by the common people). Most aristocrats spoke French exceedingly well but could not speak or write in Russian.[7] When they did go out they invited each other to balls. It was not for all that a particularly cosmopolitan city; it boasted no more than fourteen coffee houses.[8] More than one French officer remarked on the enormous palaces that were the homes of the Russian aristocracy in Moscow. 'Of an inconceivable luxury,' wrote one Polish count to his wife, 'stucco, colonnades, architecturally delightful. The inside of these beautiful buildings is decorated with taste.'[9] The middle classes, for want of a better term to describe merchants, artisans, minor state officials and so on, totalled about 40,000 people.[10] The vast majority of the population (around 168,000) was made up of the lower classes, that is, house serfs and peasants.

Kutuzov decided to abandon the city during a war council that met at Fili, outside Moscow, on 13 September 1812.[11] He was not, in other words, prepared to make the decision by himself. It was evident that the terrain before Moscow was unsuitable for a defensive battle, and if the battle were lost it would be difficult to retreat through the streets of Moscow quickly and in good order.

A contingent of French troops entered the city about two o'clock on the afternoon of 14 September. Unlike other major European cities that had been occupied by the French, in Moscow the vast majority of the inhabitants simply fled. Some of the 6,200-odd inhabitants remaining (plus another 22,500 wounded Russian soldiers that had been left behind), convinced of the wild rumours flying around about the imminent arrival of allied troops, mistook the French for British and came out to greet them with food.[12] Most of the troops of the Grande Armée thought that the war had come to an end, so they did not bother with the stragglers from the Russian army roaming the streets, as many as 10,000 according to Ségur.[13] The appearance of the Grande Armée before Moscow led everyone to believe that peace would be signed. Even the Russians were convinced of this; Cossacks approached the advance guard with gifts of vodka, while Russian officers speaking fluent French conversed and traded with their French counterparts.[14]

Nothing that happened in Russia, though, was like any other campaign Napoleon had fought. Not only had it taken months for the enemy to stand and fight after being pursued hundreds of kilometres, but they abandoned Moscow – Napoleon called them 'barbarians' for it – and still did not consider themselves to be defeated. Napoleon entered the city on 14 September followed by his Imperial Guard in full parade uniform and with the regimental bands blasting out their music.[15] Few people were there to greet them, and the only cheering that occurred came from his own troops or Russian onlookers who were forced to cheer.[16] Officers in Napoleon's entourage threw silver coins to those Russians who were there, but according to one witness, as soon as the entourage had passed the soldiers robbed them.

For the French, any feelings of joy felt on seeing Moscow – 'the fever of happiness' as one soldier put it – soon gave way to a wave of anxiety.[17] The impression one finds in some of the memoirs is of a Moscow completely deserted and eerily silent as the troops marched in: 'No one in the streets, no one in the houses, no one in the temples. Everything is dead . . . Only occasionally did we glimpse one of these men from the Russian populace who remained among us to get a part of the booty. Covered in rags, their long beards in disorder, they wander alone through the streets like phantoms, and at the approach of a Frenchman, afraid of being robbed, they fade away as if an apparition.'[18] No official deputation came out to greet Napoleon to hand over the keys of the city; no representative of the Tsar came forward to discuss the peace terms. Napoleon waited two hours before the gates of Moscow in the vain hope that some deputation or another would appear. It is understandable then that, in the face of this Russian passivity, he was at a loss to know what to do. When he realized that the city was almost deserted he became 'deeply impressed' and 'greatly disturbed'.[19]

About 100,000 men entered Moscow with Napoleon. Many tens of thousands of others were to be found with corps commanders, or had been placed in strategic centres along the way to keep open the lines of communication with central Europe.[20] After months on the road, some since January,[21] the troops would have been incredibly dirty. Lieutenant Ducque recalled that in the first well-built house he entered he saw his reflection in a mirror, covered in dust and growing a one-month-old beard.[22] It is likely that some had not washed since first setting foot on Russian soil. The filthy, hungry mob that invaded the city was in stark contrast to the traditional image of France held by the educated Russian.[23] When Frédéric List entered Moscow and found a bivouac, it was the first time he had slept under a roof in four months, or sat down at a table on a chair to eat off plates.[24] Letters sent home give an indication of the state of French morale. Captain Richard wrote on 22 September, well before the cold set in, that it was 'one of the most arduous wars we have fought to date'.[25] General Baraguay d'Hilliers wrote to his wife that there was not 'a soldier in the army who does not sigh for the end of the war. The officers sigh even more.'[26] Jean-François Boulart, talking of a fellow officer who had had part of his upper thigh carried away by cannon shot, wrote: 'I wish that I had as much, so that I could consecrate the rest of my days to you and my children . . . The devil take me if the wish I make is not sincere. This profession is too hard for anyone to be able to do it long.'[27]

## 'The Irresponsible Act of a Deranged Asiatic'

Mme de Staël met with the military governor of Moscow, Count Rostopchin, as she passed through the city around the middle of August. In typical French style, she asserted that no other civilized nation resembled savages as much as the Russian people.[28] Rostopchin had assured the people of Moscow that the French would not enter the city, and he had done as much as he possibly could to arouse the ire of the Russian people against the French before and during the invasion, whipping up xenophobic passions while trying to prevent foreigners from being lynched by enraged mobs.[29] Anyone suspected of pro-French sympathies was publicly punished, and foreigners – there were probably about 3,000 working in Moscow at the time – were often abused.[30]

On the whole, there were no strong anti-French feelings among the people of Moscow before the invasion.[31] When they learnt, on 22 June, that Napoleon had entered Russian territory they were 'stupefied', or at least those educated enough to care.[32] Throughout the weeks during the invasion and before the entry of the Grande Armée into Moscow, Rostopchin had assailed the population with inflammatory declarations. At his behest, all sorts of patriotic gestures were made: French snuff was emptied out ostentatiously in the salons of the elite; French pamphlets were burnt; many Muscovites refused to drink French wine; anti-Napoleonic posters were displayed; and the upper classes renounced speaking French. The talk was of a 'national war'. In some respects, this was a way for the authorities to deflect anger that might otherwise be directed against them for failing to defend the country.[33] In one instance in early August, Rostopchin's Belgian cook was denounced for having claimed that Napoleon was coming to liberate the people of Russia: Rostopchin had him publicly flogged and deported to Siberia.[34] The governor also publicly ridiculed French residents before deporting them from Moscow. Fyodor Nikolaevich Glinka had his French books burnt and drove around Moscow in his carriage appealing to Muscovites to give up French wines and drink the national drink, vodka.[35] The atmosphere in Moscow in 1812 was similar, in some respects, to the patriotic fervour whipped up by the revolutionaries in Paris in 1793–4, which led to horrific acts of violence as well as acts of patriotic altruism.[36]

Rostopchin had evacuated the treasures of the Kremlin well before the battle of Borodino and had spoken as early as May about setting the town alight if it fell into the hands of the French; he reiterated the threat many times after that. When Kutuzov decided to abandon the city, it was natural that some Muscovites should seek to revenge themselves on Rostopchin. They surrounded his palace and would have lynched him had he not callously handed over a young man accused of being a French spy.[37] While the mob butchered the unfortunate young man, Rostopchin slipped away.[38] There does not appear to have been any premeditated plan to abandon Moscow; it was simply a reaction to the circumstances.[39] Indeed, it would appear that no one believed the French would actually get to Moscow, and certainly not without the army doing battle before its walls. It is one of the reasons why the population appears to have been so nonchalant, and why news of the arrival of the French exploded like a bombshell.

This was also the case at Petersburg. 'One can hardly depict the general surprise, and especially that of the sovereign, when it was declared . . . that the French were in Moscow, and that nothing had been done to defend it. The sovereign had received no news directly either from Kutuzov or from Rostopchin.'[40] The last time Kutuzov saw Alexander, he had promised that he would rather die than abandon Moscow.[41] Kutuzov had, moreover, claimed to have held Napoleon in check at Borodino, stating that 'despite their superior forces, nowhere had the enemy gained a single yard of land'.[42] The shock of the defeat and the abandonment of Moscow was then all the greater; the atmosphere in Petersburg was tense. Rumours started flying of peasant riots; Alexander's life was feared for. Some observers believed that they were about to witness the fall of another dynasty. 'One can kill the sovereign,' wrote Joseph de Maistre, 'but one cannot contradict him.'[43] On 27 September, the anniversary of Alexander's coronation, the imperial entourage travelled to Kazan cathedral to mark the occasion, although the Tsar was persuaded not to ride on horseback, but to shelter in the carriage of the Empress. It was probably a good decision; people in his entourage were struck by the deathly silence that greeted them as they rode through the city.[44] Immediately after the ceremony, Alexander left for the island of Kamennyi Ostrov in one of the branches of the River Neva, where he now spent most of his time. It would appear that it was after this event that he discovered religion.

Rostopchin left behind the police chief, Voronenko, with orders to set fire to everything he could. By the evening of 15 September, large parts of Petersburg were ablaze. Voronenko was aided by criminal elements (the prisons had been emptied) who went about looting (as did numbers of lower-class Russians) and setting fire to houses. Careless troops belonging to the Grande Armée also looted and sometimes accidentally set fire to houses, and a strong wind fanned the flames.[45] At first, Napoleon refused to believe that the fire could have been started deliberately, until two Russians, caught red-handed, were brought to him; the interrogation took place in his presence.[46]

Napoleon contemplated the fire from the Ivan Tower in the Kremlin, where he had set up residence, then slowly descended the steps, followed by a few officers. Colonel Boulart speaks of the uncertainty that seemed to possess him about whether he should stay or go.[47] In the end, the fire got so bad that Napoleon was forced to evacuate. He took up residence in an imperial palace in the country a few kilometres outside Moscow before the fire died down enough for him to re-enter the city.[48] The park of Peterskoi, frequented by Moscow high society, became the bivouac of the Guard. From there, the light thrown by the fire in Moscow was so bright they could easily read at night.[49] Napoleon, watching the city burn, is supposed to have said, 'What a horrible sight! To do it themselves! All those palaces! What extraordinary resolution! Why, they are Scythians!'[50] It was of course typical of the 'barbaric' behaviour of the Russian people.

There is no doubt that the Russians were to blame for this needless destruction of their city, despite their attempts to rewrite history and Rostopchin's blatant denial of the order he had given in an account he wrote years afterwards.[51] Rostopchin had already set the example by putting his own estate to the torch at Vornovo, south-west of Moscow, a gesture that had a profound impact on the French. After he had learnt that Kutuzov was prepared to abandon Moscow without a fight he had a group of men place inflammable materials in a number of houses in the city, men who were probably directed by officers of the police force.[52] We know too that Cossack detachments, in keeping with the scorched-earth policy that had been practised, set fire to the stores that were left behind.[53] Napoleon blamed Rostopchin, dismissing the fire as 'the irresponsible act of a deranged Asiatic'. In a letter to Alexander he made it clear who had started the fire, but what he failed to understand is that the rest of Russia, and indeed the rest of the world, would not see things that way.

If there was some division of opinion, among educated Russians at least, about who was to blame, this was not the case for the Russian peasants. Their attitude to the fire may have been dominated by a certain fatalism – 'The inhabitants saw their homes burn with an equanimity that only belief in fatalism can give . . . God wanted it that way'[54] – but they blamed the French for the disaster and this greatly increased the discontent among the general population towards Napoleon.[55] The burning city acted as a bright symbol that united Russia around its Tsar. If there was hesitation about what to do with Napoleon before he entered Moscow, the struggle, already evolving towards a brutal drawn-out conflict, had now been transformed into a fight to the death.[56] Alexander learnt of the abandonment and burning of the city from his sister according to some, from one of Kutuzov's aides-de-camp according to others. In any event, he was said to have broken down in tears.[57] For him, there was no question of peace now; 'Only a rogue could now pronounce the word peace.'[58]

The fires began to wane after three days and Napoleon moved back into the city on 18 September, although it does not look as though it was entirely under control until three days after that.[59] An enormous change had come over the city: the streets were no longer recognizable, burnt cadavers, mostly of peasants and wounded soldiers, were intermingled with the remains of horses, dogs, cows. Now and then one would come across men, incendiaries, who had been shot by firing squad and their bodies strung up. The survivors took all that in their stride, indifferent to the devastation and loss of life.[60] The conflagration destroyed about two-thirds of the city, but even though it might have been demoralizing for the occupying army, it was far from being a strategic disaster. Accounts vary, but it is possible that given the supplies left behind in the city Napoleon could have stayed quartered in Moscow for the coming winter if he had so chosen,[61] but his communication lines with Smolensk and then Paris would inevitably have been cut by 'partisans' and Cossack raiding parties.[62] It is erroneous to think, as did some contemporaries, that the Russians, by burning the city, were forcing Napoleon into a precipitate retreat.[63] On the contrary, there is enough anecdotal evidence to suggest that those who were billeted in Moscow, despite the fire, lived reasonably well, and enjoyed an abundance of food, at least for a while.[64] While they may not have been lolling about on precious furs, smoking opulent pipes with tobacco perfumed with roses from India and drinking punch made of Jamaican rum as they were entertained by exotic women – *pace* Sergeant Bourgogne's idyllic reminiscences of their life in Moscow – they at least had shelter and food.[65] The fire may have destroyed most of the city, but there were still enough buildings made of stone that survived.[66]

However, the longer Napoleon stayed in Moscow the more problematic became his situation. Once the neighbouring villages had been exhausted, the army was obliged to look ever further afield for food and fodder.[67] The further afield they were forced to look, the more exhausted became the horses. Lack of fodder meant, naturally, no cavalry, no artillery and no communications with France; the weaker Napoleon became the stronger Kutuzov became. Kutuzov was reinforcing his army of 80,000 men at Tarutino, within easy striking distance of Moscow, as new recruits and soldiers from other fronts arrived over the coming weeks. During that time, the Cossacks constantly harassed Napoleon's supply lines to the point where the verb *cosaquer* was invented to describe their attacks.

### 'I Want Peace, I Need Peace, I Must Have Peace!'

This was hardly an unprecedented situation for Napoleon. There had been other occasions when enemies had failed to submit in the face of defeat – recall Prussia and Spain – but never had an enemy ignored the normal rules of war and continued the struggle in the face of repeated requests to negotiate. It was as much a clash of cultures as a clash of arms, one in which neither side really comprehended the other. Napoleon for one could not hide his disappointment at the way in which the Russians were behaving, or rather were not behaving.[68] He had to decide whether to stay, find winter quarters elsewhere or march on to Petersburg. Some officers, including Eugène, thought that Petersburg was the next obvious phase in the campaign. Ney, on the other hand, suggested resting in Moscow a week and then retreating to Smolensk.[69]

It was also the kind of thing that became the object of conversation among the troops. One soldier, irritated by the Russians' persistent refusal to negotiate, asked of his brother, 'How is one supposed to deal with such cannibals?'[70] Napoleon was probably asking himself the same thing. He had never intended staying in Moscow for any length of time, and now that most of it had been burnt to the ground, it was no longer an appropriate political space for eventual or potential negotiations with Russian authorities. But he was unsure what to do next and procrastinated. Rumours of a departure from Moscow could be heard one day only to be contradicted the next.[71] Napoleon fell back on the hope that Alexander would negotiate; it was the logical thing to do. He desperately looked about Moscow for potential intermediaries, but they were few and far between. One of the few who had not fled Moscow was Alekseyevich Yakovlev, the brother of a Russian diplomatic agent in Germany. He was dragged before Napoleon, who started the interview by berating the poor man, as if he were somehow responsible for the war. In any event, Yakovlev and his family were given safe conduct out of Moscow in order to deliver a letter to Alexander, in which Napoleon stated that 'a single note from him would put an end to hostilities'.[72]

About a week or so later, still without a reply, Napoleon wanted to send Caulaincourt to St Petersburg, but Caulaincourt argued his way out of the mission by insisting, probably correctly, that Alexander would not receive him. Instead, Napoleon sent General Lauriston. 'I want peace, I need peace, I must have peace! Just save my honour!' Napoleon is supposed to have told him.[73] The problem, of course, was that the more he clamoured for peace, the more desperate he looked. He realized this, and yet he still kept sending Alexander new messages.[74] Caulaincourt believes that it revealed an extraordinarily blind faith in his star.[75] How could Napoleon have entertained such illusions, knowing full well that his position in Moscow was tenuous, and that any reverses would transform the Austrian and Prussian troops guarding his rear into his worst enemies? Possibly because 'his enthusiasm was such, and so eager was he to nurture his own illusions, that he nursed the hope of receiving a reply from the Tsar, or at least negotiations for an armistice with Kutusov, which would lead to further results'.[76] Napoleon by now thought his enemies so weak that he could not conceive of any other outcome than victory and a treaty. He was behaving like a jilted lover, begging his partner, who had left him and who had no intention of coming back, to kiss and make up. He seems not to have realized the extent of the rupture. Moreover, the Russians were only too happy to drag things out in what now looks like a deliberate ploy to keep Napoleon in Moscow as long as possible.[77]

This had dire consequences for the occupation and the army. Napoleon was in a relatively strong position strategically, but, for reasons that cannot fully be comprehended, he refused to organize the regions he occupied in the way he had done in previous campaigns. Six weeks after the battle of Smolensk, for example, the streets had still not been cleared of the dead. Bands of brigands made up of deserters had established themselves in various regions. As early as August, the region between Vilnius and Smolensk was 'covered in vagabond soldiers'.[78] Desertion rates were high. Nobody capable had been placed in charge of the areas behind the lines. In Moscow, and most of the other cities the troops had occupied, the Russian administration had absconded and nothing had filled the void. The wounded were totally neglected, and were dying not only from lack of treatment, but from starvation and dehydration; Napoleon did not even bother issuing orders to evacuate them westwards.

Another side to Napoleon was revealed; he dug in his heels and made as though he were not going to move from Moscow until Alexander came to the table. It is what Ségur called a 'struggle of obstinacy', Alexander holding out and Napoleon deferring the day when he would have to call a retreat.[79] Orders had been sent to bring fresh troops to Moscow; there was talk of bringing the Comédie Française to entertain the troops.[80] Napoleon later argued that he had declared his intention of passing the winter in Moscow in the hope that the enemy would be more disposed to negotiate a settlement, although this declaration cannot be taken at face value.[81]

In the meantime, the troops made the best of a bad situation. Since the majority of Russians had fled the city, and two-thirds of it had burnt down, there was not all that much to do. There were some grumblings in the army about staying so long, especially since the lack of supplies began to be felt.[82] Others, like General Dessolle and the Comte de Valence, had asked to be transferred back to France, usually on the pretext, sometimes justified, of ill-health. Some complained of the conditions in which they found themselves – 'badly lodged, no sheets, no shirts, no clothes, no boots, badly fed'[83] – although they were far better off than those living off the land around Moscow, where provisions were a good deal harder to come by, and where troops had been obliged to sleep in the open for weeks. They generally came to Moscow to pillage.[84] Napoleon on the other hand seems to have been living in a world protected from the harsh realities of the troops, and dismissed reports coming in from Murat in the vicinity of Tarutino about the difficulties he was facing.

He was just hanging on in the vain hope that something would come along to put things right. Caulaincourt noted that Napoleon 'could not admit to himself that fortune, which had so often smiled upon him, had quite abandoned his cause just when he required miracles of her'.[85] This is why the Emperor lingered longer in Moscow than he should have, with the consequences that we shall shortly see. He had gone from being an active agent of his own destiny to a passive agent, a state in which the belief in his star assumed fatalist proportions. The delusion went so far that he dismissed suggestions that the Russian winter was harsh, or that the army should be provided with suitable clothing.[86] Admittedly, he was not alone in being lulled into a false sense of security by the exceptionally mild weather they had experienced in October. 'The weather began to turn bad this morning,' General Mouton wrote to his wife, 'but the previous days it was as beautiful and as mild as Brussels, we were all enchanted by the kindness of the heavens.'[87] Even so, it started to snow in the middle of October, which should have forewarned Napoleon of the difficulties ahead. The Russians interpreted this change in the weather as a good omen.[88]

## 'A Cadaver of a Capital'

At the beginning of October, Napoleon instructed his corps commanders to be ready to leave Moscow at short notice.[89] He had had a conversation with Caulaincourt about whether Alexander would respond to new peace overtures; Caulaincourt did not think so. He repeated what he had said so many times, namely, that as the season progressed and winter arrived, the position of the Russians became ever stronger.[90]

Napoleon did not want to hear this. He urged Caulaincourt to leave for Petersburg where he could talk directly with the Tsar. At the same time, however, he was issuing orders to fortify the Kremlin and build redoubts on the Moskva.[91] His behaviour during this period has been described as 'moody and taciturn' but it is a portrayal that fits with his demeanour throughout the campaign, during which he would swing between periods of intense activity – rare but nevertheless testified to by the correspondence that came out of Moscow where he could spend three nights going over the details of the new regulations for the Comédie Française – and stretches when he would while away his time on a sofa, reading novels.[92] It is possible that Napoleon sensed he was on the verge of defeat, which is one reason he put off withdrawing from Moscow for so long, to delay the inevitable.[93] It is only in hindsight, however, that we can say that the decision to stay six weeks in Moscow was fatal. During that time, Kutuzov was reinforced by twenty-six regiments of Don Cossacks, around 15,000 light, irregular cavalry that were to play havoc with Napoleon's retreating army. During that same time, Napoleon's own cavalry was considerably weakened through lack of fodder. If he had stayed only two weeks and had rested his men, one historian has asserted, then the army would have had plenty of time to retreat in good order before both the onset of winter and the arrival of the Don Cossacks in great numbers.[94]

The choices before him were: to march on St Petersburg some 640 kilometres away – the threat was real enough for Alexander's court to start packing[95] – an option that was quickly ruled out as impractical from a supply perspective;[96] to move to Velikiye-Luki, about 160 kilometres north-east of Vitebsk, where he would join with his other two corps commanders, Oudinot and Gouvion Saint-Cyr and go into winter quarters, an option also dropped for supply reasons;[97] to stay in Moscow for the winter with the danger of being cut off from the rest of the Empire; or to head for the Ukraine, which was what Davout was urging (there were rumours to that effect as early as September).[98] Napoleon seems to have been reluctant to engage Kutuzov once again, almost as though he doubted his own abilities or had been dealt a blow to his self-confidence by Borodino.[99] A number of senior military figures in Napoleon's entourage had been urging a withdrawal from Moscow to an area closer to the Empire. They wanted peace, although they do not appear to have confronted Napoleon openly; they included Ney, Murat, Davout, Caulaincourt and Berthier.[100] Some time towards the end of the first week in October he must have made up his mind. He ordered the war booty from the Kremlin packed on 9 October, and the wounded evacuated on 10 October.[101] On 14 October, orders were issued not to bring any further cavalry or artillery forward to Moscow.[102] The treasure and the sick and wounded, an estimated 12,000 men, left on 15, 16 and 17 October.[103]

When Napoleon woke on the morning of 13 October, the ruins of Moscow were covered with a thin, white blanket of snow.[104] It was the first real fall; snow had fallen as early as 27 September, but it had melted almost immediately.[105] This is when it appears he made the decision to take the only other option available to him, to retreat to Smolensk (but not to the Russian border because to do so would give the appearance of a military defeat). But not only the weather played on his mind. The previous day, an incident occurred which demonstrated only too clearly just how precarious was the situation. A courier who had been sent from Moscow to Paris was captured by Cossacks at the same time as a courier from Paris en route to Moscow. Napoleon's line of communications in other words had become tenuous, and he could not tolerate a situation in which he was cut off from Paris. That left only the question of which route to take: he opted to go back the way he had come, though it was problematic to say the least, since the road had been devastated during the advance and the army would find little succour. It was, however, the best road to Smolensk and the most direct route. He could attempt to find a route parallel to but south of the Moscow–Smolensk road, likely to be a source of more supplies than would be available to the north of that road. He could head south for Kaluga on the Oka River 150 kilometres south-west of Moscow, inflict a defeat on Kutuzov – considered an indispensable preliminary move for any retreat to take place[106] – and then head east on a relatively good road to Smolensk. He had left it a bit late but things were by no means dire. Smolensk was ten to twelve days' march from Moscow, and after that Minsk was another ten, Vilnius another fifteen. All of these cities were well stocked and would be able to supply his army with everything it needed. From there, he could draw on reinforcements that were gathering in Prussia and Poland and in the spring march on Petersburg.[107]

When a French delegation returned to Moscow on 17 October after failing to get to St Petersburg, there was no longer any doubt in Napoleon's mind. The next day, he issued orders to retreat through a southern route, to begin two days later.[108] The lack of orders to prepare men for the coming winter, however, bordered on the criminal. It is possible, but highly unlikely, that

Napoleon assumed corps or divisional commanders would take charge of these details. Most of them did not, although a few officers had the foresight to prepare for the bitter winter ahead by finding fur coats, and by making sure they themselves were well provided for.[109] Others were less fortunate, unable to pay the inflated prices for winter clothing in the bazaars erected by enterprising troops.[110] Few officers, Colonel Marbot was one of them, had the foresight to order their men to acquire winter clothing.

The same day Napoleon issued the order to evacuate Moscow, Kutuzov, under tremendous pressure from his more aggressive generals, decided to approve a plan of attack against Murat and his cavalry situated in the vicinity of Tarutino, some hundred kilometres south-west of Moscow. The battle of Vinkovo, as it is called, is of itself of no importance. Murat and his subordinates were caught napping but managed to extricate themselves in the face of overwhelming odds, although they lost about 5,000 men in the process. What is more important is Napoleon's reaction. When he heard of it, for some reason he appears to have lost his nerve and ordered that the departure from Moscow be speeded up by twenty-four hours.

The army started marching out of Moscow on 19 October. Sergeant Bourgogne's regiment started off in the afternoon but it was almost night before they were out of the city.[111] He soon found himself amid a great number of carriages driven by men of different nationalities, all swearing in their mother tongue when their carriages broke down, creating 'such a din as to make your head burst. The turmoil in Moscow at the news of the departure is impossible to describe. One could hardly walk through the streets. Horses, wagon crews, artillery, everything was pell-mell. One cannot imagine what that city contained. The road was covered with wagons for seven or eight leagues.'[112] It would appear that many officers had stolen carriages in which they placed booty they were attempting to take with them.[113] There was a long line of calashes and small carts around which each company was grouped. 'Everyone deposited their individual reserves of food and clothing and believed that they would be able to conserve them throughout the retreat.'[114]

One witness described the hordes leaving Moscow with their plunder as a carnival.[115] Most seem to have been in good spirits and to have recuperated from their long march after spending a number of weeks in Moscow doing little but eating and drinking.[116] The number of civilians who decided to leave with the army could have been as high as 50,000.[117] These were a mixture of men and women who had followed the army into Russia, plus a number of French residents of Moscow, plus female camp followers who had met troops during their stay there, not to mention the prostitutes who decided they were better off following the army than remaining behind, as well as Muscovites employed as domestic servants.[118] As a result, the number of non-military vehicles that accompanied the army, anywhere between 15,000 and 40,000 wagons, caused an enormous traffic jam trying to get out of the city.[119] The column leaving Moscow was three and four carriages wide and between thirty and fifty kilometres long.[120] In one account, the retreating mass covered a width of a few kilometres either side of the road they were following; burning villages indicated the route they had taken.[121] Every now and then an explosion was heard as munitions wagons were abandoned by their crews and then set alight. The further they advanced the more frequent became the explosions.[122] Often the wounded had to be abandoned with horses dying along the way.

Most of the carriages seem not to have been carrying essential supplies, but rather personal loot, anything from clothing to china to furniture and linen.[123] All these things would have been items that one would have found in privileged households, and thus were valuable objects, especially for the common soldier. Almost all the officers of the general staff had 'dressed in the Russian manner'.[124] One group of French women who left Moscow with the army for fear of reprisals were dressed as though they were Parisian bourgeoisie going to a dinner on the lawns of Vincennes or Romainville. Mlle Eléonore, for example, 'who was sitting next to me in a carriage, had a rose-coloured hat, a white dress trimmed with lace, and finally white satin shoes'.[125] One cavalry officer made sure that he was well stocked with provisions, carrying with him rice, flour, sugar, coffee and three big pots of jam.[126] The camps that were set up those first nights did not resemble an army so much as a large fair, in which soldiers were metamorphosed into merchants selling the most precious objects at bargain-basement prices.[127] Soldiers ate off porcelain and drank out of silver vases.

The consequences are easy to foresee in hindsight. Less space was given to vital provisions and the progress of the army was considerably slowed.[128] 'The road was so encumbered with wagons that we sometimes took three hours to do half a league . . . From first light to evening, and into the night, we had been marching and we had hardly gone four leagues . . .'[129] Napoleon knew about the excess baggage carried by the army – during the return journey he stopped on two occasions to watch the army pass by and saw for himself the loot taken from Moscow – but appears to have been unable or unwilling to do anything about it.[130] It was an apparent abundance that masked a real misery; there was little bread or meat after only days from Moscow.[131] What began as a masquerade would end in a massive funeral procession in which the participants would succumb to starvation, disease, the cold and Cossacks.[132]

Indecision seems to have marked Napoleon's thinking during the weeks leading up to the order to retreat, but in addition there does not seem to have been a great deal of certainty about just where he was going to retreat to, or how. He decided to move south, towards Kaluga, as though he were going to give battle to Kutuzov, dug in at Tarutino. Prince Eugène was sent ahead with an advance

party. But two days out of Moscow, on 21 October, Napoleon seems to have
had a change of heart and moved abruptly west towards Fominskoie, ordering
Eugène to take the town of Maloyaroslavets.

It was then too that he sent orders to Marshal Edouard Mortier, who had
been left behind in Moscow with the seriously wounded and 5,000 surviving
members of the Young Guard, to abandon the city. The months of supplies
that had been stocked there were burnt. Mortier was also ordered to blow up
the Kremlin, which is what he set about doing. It was a vengeful, destructive
act devoid of all military or strategic purpose. It shows too that Napoleon had
no intention of returning. The orders were carried out by Generals Noury and
Berthezène, who placed over 90,000 kilos of charges in the cellars of the Kremlin palaces. Fortunately, many of the fuses, soaked from the rain that poured
down on 22 October, failed to ignite, but those that did explode were heard
forty kilometres away.[133]

## Maloyaroslavets

At Maloyaroslavets, a town of about 10,000 people, 120 kilometres south-west
of Moscow, Eugène ran into about 12,000 men under General Dmitry
Sergeyevich Dokhturov, sent by Kutuzov under the mistaken impression that
Eugène's troops were a foraging party – Kutuzov had no idea yet that the
French had abandoned Moscow – no doubt hoping to repeat his victory against
Murat. When Dokhturov realized what was happening, he dug in and waited
for reinforcements to arrive. If Napoleon wanted to push ahead and take
Kaluga, he would have to attack. Kutuzov arrived later in the morning but
decided to withdraw rather than face the brunt of the Grande Armée. He did
so about midday, when he saw that he could no longer hold the town, pulling
back to a defensive position on a ridge that dominated the road along which
Napoleon would have to march. Napoleon arrived at about 1 p.m. with the
bulk of the army, not sure whether he should engage. The French were able to
take the town, but at the cost of between 4,000 and 10,000 men killed and
wounded. Another victory like that, and Napoleon would not have much of
an army left.

Napoleon reconnoitred the next morning, but was again undecided what to
do. He had a chance of defeating Kutuzov, again, but he would still have to fall
back on Smolensk. Moreover, the battle would no doubt be bloody. If he
retreated towards Smolensk, on the other hand, he would have a Russian army
intact on his tail the whole way. He discussed his position further with his
entourage but without coming to a decision.[134] At one stage during the morning, he was almost captured by Cossacks. Berthier and Caulaincourt remained
with Napoleon, swords drawn, while a contingent under Rapp went off to deal
with the Cossacks.[135] We do not know what kind of impression the incident

made on Napoleon, but it is possible that he was shaken, having been attacked within such a short distance of his headquarters. That, along with the costly victory at Maloyaroslavets, seems to have undermined his confidence.

A meeting took place that evening (25 October) in Napoleon's quarters, a little cabin in the village of Gorodnia, during which he consulted his marshals as well as his aides-de-camp about the options before them.[136] Most, it seems, were for turning around and going back up the road towards Mozhaisk and then along the highway to Smolensk, the way they had come. It was the shortest route. Davout was one of the few who preferred heading south through Kaluga, and then finding a new road to the Niemen. Napoleon, undecided, asked Mouton for his opinion, and Mouton also suggested the shorter route to the Niemen. There was a third option that does not appear to have been considered, namely, to turn west to Iukhov and then on to Smolensk along smaller country roads. As a result of the meeting Napoleon elected to turn about and head for Smolensk. It was the first time that he had opted not to give battle when he was in a position to do so. It speaks volumes about his state of mind and his situation. The decision to return to Mozhaisk has been described as one of the worst Napoleon ever made.[137] Not only did his forces lose time retracing their steps – it had taken them nine days to get this far – but they avoided countryside that might have allowed them to replenish supplies in the course of their retreat. Heading back along a route that had already been devastated twice, once by the retreating Russian army and again by the advancing imperial army, deprived them of any possibility of living off the land. Napoleon seems to have been cowed. This decision, like so many of the mistakes made by him during this campaign, was based upon faulty reconnaissance. If he had bothered to send out proper scouting parties to find out what exactly the enemy was up to he would have discovered that Kutuzov was retreating south along the road to Kaluga.[138]

## 'The Empire of Death'
Morale had been high on the way from Moscow to Maloyaroslavets. But the retreat back towards Mozhaisk changed all that. Discipline, which had probably not been very good up till then, began to break down altogether. It is almost as though the troops sensed that they no longer had a leader, or that they could not count on him to get them out. Small bands began to break away, thinking they would have a better chance of survival than with the army (they were wrong). Part of the problem appears to have been the speed at which Napoleon travelled, possibly motivated by a fear that the army would run out of provisions. One historian has calculated that an army of around 120,000 men and 40,000 horses required 850 carts to carry just one day's food and

forage.[139] To feed the French army for any length of time would have required, therefore, many thousands of carts.

On the road to Mozhaisk (27 October), Napoleon had a meeting with General Ferdinand Wintzingerode, a Württemberger in Russian service. He was captured by a patrol as he rode into Moscow to check whether reports about the Grande Armée's withdrawal were true. One of the most angry scenes Napoleon's entourage had ever seen followed as he accused Russia, quite irrationally, of being in the pay of the English, and of having taken part in all the plots against him.[140] It is not known why he got so upset, but angry he was, to the point where after the encounter he ordered a fine large country house near by to be torched along with every village the army passed through on the way to Smolensk.[141] This behaviour is reminiscent of the retreat of the French army from St John of Acre through Palestine, except this time there was an army hard on its heels.[142] Countermanding the order a short time later hardly made any difference. Hundreds of towns and villages were destroyed. 'Under the ashes that were still hot', wrote one witness, 'and which the wind blew towards us, were the bodies of several soldiers or peasants. There were also slain children, and young girls massacred in the same place where they had been raped.'[143]

In the early hours of 29 October, unable to sleep, Napoleon woke and called for Caulaincourt to come into his room, close the door behind him and sit on the bed.[144] It was not Napoleon's habit to allow a member of his staff into close proximity, so it is interesting for what it reveals of his state of mind. At this stage, he was still thinking of winter quarters at Vitebsk, in the belief that the expected arrival of anywhere between 1,500 and 2,000 Polish Cossacks would entirely reverse the situation by fending off the Russian Cossacks, guarding the army and allowing it to rest and feed itself. Whether he was deluding himself or had been misled, or whether he announced this measure in the hope of maintaining morale is impossible to say. In any event, the Polish Cossacks never arrived. Caulaincourt tried to open his eyes to the real state of the army, but his message does not appear to have sunk in. Napoleon took an hour to come around to the thrust of the conversation, which was that he was already thinking of abandoning the army and returning to Paris.

That day, the leading elements of the column crossed the battlefield of Borodino, 'a field of desolation that was still pulsating with horror'.[145] The field was littered with the tell-tale remnants of battle – damaged cannon, broken wagons, helmets, cuirasses, muskets, uniforms in shreds. Thirty thousand dead lay across the field unburied, an 'empire of death' as one witness put it,[146] who had been lying there for the previous fifty days, while hastily dug mass graves had begun to uncover. Many of the bodies had preserved what might be called a physiognomy; all of them had their eyes wide open, their skin the colour of brick red and Prussian blue.[147] According to some accounts, not entirely reliable but which obviously repeated a rumour that was doing the rounds, at least one wounded soldier of the Grande Armée was discovered alive, having lived off horse and human flesh and drunk from a little river filled with cadavers.[148] Other wounded Russians had dragged themselves to the road leading to Moscow and had lived off whatever passers-by gave them to eat.[149] One can imagine the stench and the psychological impact it must have made on the column of men marching through this open cemetery.

Shortly afterwards the first wave of real cold hit (this was around 26 October), so that wherever wood could be found it was burnt, including the barns and houses used by commanding officers for shelter, while men stood around, looking like ghosts, not moving all night in front of those immense fires.[150] 'It is difficult to describe the effect of the first cold snaps on the army,' wrote Lieutenant Ducque.[151] With the onset of winter, the army quickly started to fall apart, and the officers lost control over their men. The cold played a part, combined with the same difficulties they had faced on the way to Moscow, but one should not exaggerate its impact at this stage of the retreat.[152] The Emperor was still with the army; his presence was enough to reassure those present and to prevent a complete breakdown of discipline. Some, however, began to doubt. They were no longer marching as conquerors, but with 'reserve and hesitation', surrounded by Cossacks and hostile peasants, and they lacked everything.[153] Conditions were grim. Most marched from six in the morning till about seven in the evening, some of that in the dark because of the time of the year.[154] The hardest thing seems to have been the lack of sleep for those who had equipment or carriages to prepare. If the troops marched till six or seven, they would try to warm themselves and eat; they might get to sleep around ten, and would then have to wake up at two or three in the morning to get ready to leave. One officer complained that since leaving Moscow he had averaged about four hours' sleep a night.[155] To make matters worse, Cossacks would come skulking round the stragglers like crows.[156]

By 28 October, the road was 'cluttered with a multitude of footsoldiers, some armed, others without arms, the wounded in large numbers, servants, women, and an unprecedented congestion of horses and wagons. There were also among that number fugitives, French families who were fleeing Moscow after having lived there for many years before our arrival.'[157] The wounded were loaded on to carts, but the attempt to help them soon turned sour. 'They fell into the hands of coarse drivers, insolent servants, brutal sutlers, women enriched and arrogant, brothers-in-arms without pity, and all the sequel [a colloquial term of contempt] of wagon drivers. All these people had only one idea: get rid of their wounded.'[158] It was not uncommon for wagon drivers deliberately to drive their horses at speed over rough ground so that a jolt would free them of their charges. When the wounded fell, if they were unable to get up they were driven over by the carriages following whose drivers would fear stopping and thus losing their place in line.[159]

To make matters worse, Russian prisoners marched with the retreating army, guarded by a regiment made up of French, Spanish and Portuguese troops. As they fell by the wayside through sickness or lack of food they were killed by a blow to the head with the butt of a musket, or a shot to the back of the neck.[160] The same order was given to a regiment of grenadiers from Baden, to shoot any prisoners who fell by the wayside too weak to continue.[161] The order supposedly came from Napoleon himself, although it is impossible to verify and may very well be part of the black legend. We know of several massacres of prisoners, including one in which 1,200 Russians were shot in the head by their Portuguese guards.[162] One account has 3,000 Russian prisoners taken out of Moscow and 'parked like sheep' whenever the army stopped. They slept on the ice and snow and were not given any food, as a result of which they resorted to cannibalism.[163]

What did Napoleon think of all this? Did he understand how decimated the army was by the cold and hunger? We know that at one stage he is said to have told Rapp, 'Those poor soldiers make my heart bleed, but there is nothing I can do about it.'[164] But this kind of statement, written many years after the event, was an attempt to portray Napoleon as someone who cared for his men. Some scepticism is called for, especially since there are no contemporary accounts of how he felt. One can argue that as emperor and military leader, he could not give way to 'outpourings of grief or remorse',[165] but the lack of public posturing should not have prevented him from expressing his feelings in private. As far as one can tell, despite the fact that he had the opportunity to take in the full extent of the army's suffering,[166] he does not appear to have cared terribly much, or it did not register.

Napoleon reached Mikhailovska, three days out from Smolensk, on the afternoon of 6 November where he found a courier from Paris informing him of the Malet affair.

In Paris, during the night of 22–23 October, at four o'clock in the morning, an officer calling himself General Lamotte, accompanied by his aide-de-camp, appeared before the door of the Popincourt barracks in east Paris, declaring that the Emperor had died under the walls of Moscow. The Senate, the general declared, had abolished the imperial regime and formed a new, provisional government. The officer in question was General Malet, who had just escaped from prison where he had been incarcerated for plotting to overthrow the regime in 1808.[167] For another twenty-four hours, the conspirators, disorganized though they were, were able to hold Paris by taking charge of the main ministries. The state structures that controlled and directed the Empire remained inert. It was only the cool-headedness of the commander of Paris, General Pierre-Augustin Hulin, that saved the day, but the Council of State remained inactive, as did the Senate. Nor were there any demonstrations in favour of the Empire among the people. The plot was never a serious threat to the regime, but what it demonstrated was that people's loyalties remained with Napoleon, not with the Empire – that is, it had apparently not occurred to anyone that Napoleon's son, the King of Rome, was waiting to take his place.[168]

By the time Napoleon received news of the affair, on 6 November, Malet and his accomplices had been stood against a wall and shot. They were the only generals to be executed during the Consulate and the Empire.[169] Napoleon could not tell from the reports that he was sent whether this was the work of one man or whether it was a widespread conspiracy. The minister of war, Clarke, was saying the latter while his minister of police, Savary, was saying the former.[170] The doubt floating around Paris would soon bring Napoleon to make a decision about his presence with the army.

# 20

# Destiny Forsaken

## 'A Starving Multitude'

To some, the sight of the walls of Smolensk, given that the snow hid the disastrous consequences of the fire, caused as much pleasure as if it were home.[1] The lead columns reached the city on 9 November; it had taken twenty days of uninterrupted marching to get this far. The accounts of the retreat up to that point vary enormously, depending on who is writing them. People lived through different experiences and in different conditions. Some wrote that they arrived 'exhausted with fatigue', and that in twenty years of service they had never been through such a tough campaign.[2] Larrey, the surgeon-in-chief, agreed; on reaching Smolensk he wrote to his wife to say that he had never suffered as much, and he had campaigned in Egypt and Spain.[3] Others wrote that they had not 'suffered too much' before arriving at Smolensk, and that if bread was lacking, there was horsemeat, and even cats in abundance.[4] A sapper by the name of Laurencin (who was to die at Frankfurt-am-Oder in February 1813) had enough money to buy bread, and had with him seven or eight pounds of rice which he would cook in a bit of fat or in water with sugar, so that he was able to continue on his way without too much trouble. Others again were more tongue in cheek, proving that, for some, their sense of humour had survived. Stendhal, ironized, for example, 'that he had just been on a charming trip; three or four times a day I would go from extreme boredom to extreme pleasure', the pleasure triggered by such events as finding a few potatoes.[5] Another quipped about the lovely weather and the lovely camp fires, and about how much he prayed to God for it to start all over again.[6]

Smolensk should have been the end of their suffering. Instead, those organizing the supplies there could not cope with the unruly hordes pressing to get something into their bellies. There was such confusion that just getting into the town through the main gates took hours.[7] Once inside, there were enormous difficulties finding shelter and food.[8] Stores were apparently lower than expected, but there was certainly enough to supply the men for about two weeks. No arrangements were made, however, either to guard or to distribute the provisions. The end result was that they were looted within days. Those who arrived in Smolensk a little later went without. The town, nevertheless, gave the men a few days' rest, as well as food, and even oats for their horses, and the opportunity to prepare for the march ahead.[9] Most naively thought that the worst was behind them and even looked forward to the march to

Vilnius.[10] Those who had survived the leg from Moscow now knew what to expect, so they clothed and outfitted themselves more or less appropriately, replaced old boots with new, and abandoned anything that was not of use to them, including much of the precious booty they had dragged from Moscow.[11] Some, however, could continue no longer. One officer, who had made it to Smolensk with one leg, took a pistol and attempted to shoot himself in the head. His first attempt failed. He dragged himself along the ground until he could find another cartouche. He succeeded the second time around.[12] This had happened often enough during the retreat; men preferred to shoot themselves rather than prolong the suffering.

Napoleon himself arrived at Smolensk on 9 November and began setting up headquarters. The full extent of the disaster had not yet sunk in. He believed Smolensk was the pinnacle of the army's suffering and that he would be able to start reorganizing what remained of it. Indeed, he began dictating a stream of orders to non-existent regiments.[13] It did not take long though for the reality to take root. For most of the march towards Smolensk he had been at the head of his army. Now, at Smolensk, he could see his emaciated army marching into the city, and there was not much of it left. Estimates vary, but at this stage of the retreat there were probably still about 40,000–50,000 men under colours, as well as, remarkably, 220 cannon and as many as 20,000 camp followers. That means that something like 60,000 men had been lost (died, wandered off, killed) in less than three weeks.[14] But this does not take into account the number of men that had been picked up along the way at various outposts and towns, such as at Viazma. Junot had been stationed at Borodino with several thousand men. Joachim-Joseph Delmarche, who had been wounded early in the campaign, joined the retreating army with a friend, both of them walking with makeshift crutches, without any food and without any hope of finding any, except for the horse carcasses littering the way.[15]

At the beginning of November the weather started to get colder – temperatures varied from minus 5 degrees Celsius to minus 12. Lots of snow fell during the night of 2–3 November. In an army that was well prepared and well supplied, these temperatures should not have been a problem. But the retreat from Moscow was so badly organized that the weather had a disastrous impact on the army.[16] By the first week of November, not only were the men suffering from a lack of food and warm clothing, but so much snow had fallen that walking had become difficult.[17] What made matters worse was the lack of preparations for a winter campaign; no gloves, no stockings, no woollen vests or bonnets. The cold of course affected both sides, to the point where the Russians too had to break contact with the fleeing enemy in order to deal with the conditions. Horses died in their droves from this point, unable to cope with the lack of fodder and the fatigue.[18]

This was the turning point; it was the beginning of a six-week period in which the remains of the Grande Armée would be devastated. Provisions were so scarce that even generals were reduced to eating horsemeat,[19] but the colder it got and the further the army advanced, the fewer horses there were and the more difficult it became to cut into the carcasses. Men were reduced to cutting bits of flesh off live horses as they walked alongside them. According to one witness, 'the poor beasts did not show the slightest sign of pain', probably because it was so cold – temperatures soon reached minus 28 degrees Celsius.[20] Thus it was that horses walked on with pieces missing from them for a few days before succumbing. Other soldiers lucky enough to possess a small casserole would walk beside a horse, insert a knife and capture the blood that flowed, which they would then cook to make a primitive blood sausage.[21] More than one officer, believing that he was leading his horse by its reins, turned to find the reins had been cut and the horse gone.[22] As soon as a horse fell to the ground, it was laid upon by groups of starving men cutting away at its flesh.[23] By the beginning of November, the army was no longer an army, but a hungry multitude of individuals whose only objective in life was survival.[24] Most thought the idea of eating horse repugnant,[25] but as the routes were paved with dead carcasses it was the easiest way of gaining some protein. This started to happen a few days into the retreat.[26] At the end of a day's march, one simply chose a carcass and cut off a piece with a knife or sabre, grilled it over a fire and ate. For want of salt, some preferred to season the meat with a little gunpowder.[27] Others preferred to cut open a horse that had just fallen in the hope of getting more choice morsels – liver, heart.[28]

From about the middle of November, men started to fall down along the roads through inanition and fatigue. It was so cold that soldiers could no longer hold their muskets without freezing their hands, even though they had taken the precaution of wrapping them in cloth. As a consequence, many threw away their weapons, even members of the Guard, and those that did not were often too weak to be able to use them.[29] Others were suffering from frostbite of the nose, ears, toes or fingers.[30] Some well-disciplined units managed to keep together, largely as a result of their officers. As the retreat continued, and units broke down, soldiers tended to group according to nationality so that one would find Frenchmen, Germans, Poles or Italians huddled around camp fires or marching together. The Poles seem to have been better prepared than most, no doubt because they were used to the winters. Individuals who were young and in good health had a better chance of surviving. A surgeon named Lagneau, aged thirty-two, used to walking, unlike most who rode, was able to 'endure everything without any untoward consequences'.[31] His only fear was of being wounded and then left to die on the side of the road.

## Napoleon's Despair

With news of the Malet affair, Napoleon gave up the idea of staying in Smolensk over winter and instead hoped to fall back to Orsha, about 160 kilometres away, or possibly to hold the line along the River Berezina while setting up winter quarters in Minsk. After only four days' rest in Smolensk, the army set out again on 12 November – Mortier and the Young Guard first, followed by the Old Guard, Prince Eugène, Davout and Ney at one-day intervals. At Korytnia, where he had stopped for the night, Napoleon called Caulaincourt to his bedside and talked about getting back to Paris as soon as possible. He was in fact so worried about being taken – the encounter with Cossacks at Maloyaroslavets had unnerved him – that he ordered his physician, Dr Yvan, to prepare a sachet of poison that between now and his fall in 1814 he kept with him at all times.[32] Despair had set in, and was not really to leave him until his fall from power, even if there were fits of enthusiasm and hope.

The next day (15 November) Napoleon found the Russians blocking his path, and was obliged to fight his way through to Krasnyi, between Orsha and Smolensk (near the present-day Belorussian border), where he waited for the rest of the army to catch up. The Russians, however, under General Mikhail Miloradovich, often referred to as the Russian Murat, simply blocked the road again so that each section of the army coming up would have to fight its way through. They had to do so in temperatures of between minus 15 degrees Celsius and minus 25. The toll in lives was significant, as many as 10,000 dead and wounded, with around 200 cannon lost, and over 20,000 men taken prisoner, most of whom were so badly treated by the Russians that they would never see their homes again.[33] After Eugène had fought his way through, Napoleon had to decide whether to wait for the others to catch up, in case they had trouble breaking through Miloradovich's roadblock, or to forge on. The situation was made precarious by Kutuzov, who had turned up a few kilometres south of Krasnyi and threatened to cut the road to Orsha.

So Napoleon decided to take the field. In a gesture that either showed a death wish or was born of his irrational sense of invincibility, or perhaps was simply a sign of the utter desperation in which the army found itself, he led his grenadiers into battle. He even gave them a rousing speech in which he drew his sword and supposedly urged his men to swear to die fighting rather than not see France again.[34] They were utterly outnumbered but this did not seem to faze him, and he stood his ground calmly while Russian shells and cannon balls struck all around him. It impressed not only his own men, but the Russians as well, to the point that Miloradovich moved away from the road and left it open for Davout to get through. Even then, Kutuzov could easily have encircled Napoleon – indeed his entourage begged him to – but he stubbornly refused to go head to head with Napoleon.[35] Napoleon's orders spoke of non-existent corps, divisions and regiments, as though they were fully operational units; the missives were being captured by the Russians, giving the mistaken impression that the Grande Armée was much stronger than it actually was. Kutuzov was being very cautious, overly cautious in retrospect, but one has to keep in mind that he was still dealing with Napoleon, considered the greatest general of his day by all concerned. If Kutuzov had been a more hands-on general, or if he had trusted some of his more able subordinates, things would have been very different.

Napoleon did the same thing the next day – that is, he marched at the head of his grenadiers, with shells bursting all around him, as they trudged on to Liady where, that afternoon, he slid into town on his bottom. The approach was so steep and so covered in ice that he and his Old Guard had no other choice. It was perhaps no coincidence that it was only then that Napoleon admitted the army was disintegrating before his eyes. At Dubrovna the next day (19 November), he addressed the Old Guard and told them just that, exhorting them to maintain a strict discipline in order to survive and even inciting them, according to one officer, to punish deserters themselves by stoning.[36] Mind you, there were not many in the Old Guard who did desert or who would have considered it. Napoleon's aura was so great for these men that they responded to his exhortations by raising their bearskins and caps on their bayonets and shouting 'Vive l'Empereur!'[37]

Orsha was reached later that day. The city was reasonably well stocked and Napoleon was under the impression that with a few days' rest here he would be able to rally the army. Also, Victor and Oudinot, in better shape no doubt than the men who had retreated from Moscow, were not far away. What's more, on the evening of 21 November Ney, who was commanding the rearguard and who was thought lost, arrived at Orsha. He had managed to get through with just 900 men, plus four or five thousand stragglers and refugees.[38] In the past week, Napoleon had lost a further 20,000 men, as well as thousands of civilians. At Orsha the order was given to get rid of any excess baggage – incredible to think that it had taken all this time for the order to be given – by burning the carriages and wagons, largely in order to recuperate the horses.

Vengeance

The cold was not the only problem facing the retreating troops. Russian peasants attacked anyone who came to their villages looking for food, or set upon convoys of the sick and wounded, killing anyone they could find.[39] In part this was because they had been called upon to do so by leading generals – Barclay had appealed to all Russians in the occupied areas to 'make sure that not a single enemy soldier can hide himself from our vengeance'[40] – and in part it was simply a knee-jerk reaction to protect life, limb and property. Sir Robert Wilson, an English liaison officer with the Russian army, saw a group of peasants beating out the brains of a line of prisoners in time with a song.[41] One witness is supposed to have seen a French prisoner sold to some Russian peasants for twenty roubles; he was 'baptized' with a cauldron of boiling water and then impaled alive with an iron pike. Prisoners and marauders were hacked to death by women with hatchets, or buried alive.[42] These accounts of torture and atrocity might be considered exaggerated if they were not confirmed by Russian sources.[43] The zeal with which the Russian peasantry took to massacring members of the Grande Armée surprised even hardened veterans of the Iberian Peninsula. In one account, after Russian peasants had harassed French troops marauding around Moscow, Napoleon ordered a large number of peasants to be rounded up and executed as a warning.[44]

Russian soldiers were known to exact their vengeance on prisoners as well.[45] Somewhere between 90,000 and 100,000 prisoners were taken by the Russians. Of those, around 53,000 died in captivity, and 39,000 survived.[46] Although the figures are impossible to verify, we know that the prisoners, made up of all nationalities, also included women (usually wives) and children. They were often stripped naked and killed or left to die, or were marched back to detention camps without being given any sustenance along the way. Stripping victims naked, regardless of their sex, and leaving them to wander in the snow was a common practice among the Cossacks.[47] The Cossacks did so not only because the clothes their victims were wearing were valuable or badly needed, but also because it was a way of humiliating the invader. Often Cossacks sold prisoners, or simply handed them over to local peasants who then played with them at their leisure, inflicting the worst kinds of torture.[48] Alexander's brother, the Grand Duke Constantine, was personally seen executing a French prisoner. We do not know how many were killed in this way but it must have been in the thousands, and it is likely that no more than one in five soldiers captured by either marauding Cossacks or regular Russian troops survived the ordeal. There were also instances of humanity. A canteen lady who was pregnant and near term, and who had been captured by Cossacks and stripped naked while they searched her for money, was left in that condition in the snow. She was picked up by some peasants who took pity on her and welcomed her into their village where she gave birth.[49] A poor midwife in Orel is supposed to have taken five prisoners of war into her home, and even when she had spent all her own money on food went begging on their behalf.[50]

The reaction of the Russian peasant was largely in response to the exactions carried out by troops of the Grande Armée, who pillaged, raped and also massacred Russian prisoners, especially in the closing weeks of the retreat. The Russian peasants armed themselves with muskets taken from the dead and dying along the roads, or from marauders who had been captured and killed. For, in spite of the dangers and the exhaustion, men were forced to leave the main roads in the hope of finding food in villages that had been neither pillaged nor burnt on their way to

Moscow.[51] The further troops moved away from the main body, the less discipline ruled, the more likely they were to carry out excesses against the local populations, assuming of course they could be found. As a result, Russian peasants formed little bands of guerrillas and harassed the retreating army, creating one of the enduring myths of the war of 1812, namely, that it was a people's war.[52]

## The Berezina

On 22 November, Napoleon learnt that Minsk had been taken by Admiral Pavel Chichagov (in fact, it had fallen six days before). It meant that the supplies he had been counting on were lost (along with 5,000 wounded imperial troops), and that he would now have to push on to Vilnius, if not cross the Niemen. Knowing that, Napoleon focused on the town of Borisov, the only place on the Berezina River where there was a bridge that could be crossed. What was going to prove even more of a problem, and one which Napoleon was not yet aware of, was that Chichagov had moved on to the town of Borisov and that in the skirmish which ensued between the Russian forces and Oudinot's advance corps, which managed to take the town, the Russians retreated to the western bank and burnt the wooden bridge across the river in the process. Chichagov then deployed his men along the western bank from opposite Studienka in the north to Usha in the south, waiting for Napoleon to arrive.

Napoleon heard of the skirmish two days later, on 24 November, and it created a change in the man. Rather than become discouraged, he at last found some of the energy that had characterized former campaigns.[53] An officer by the name of Drujon de Beaulieu, guided by local peasants, found a better place to ford the river about twenty kilometres north of Borisov, near Studienka, where the river was only about two metres deep and eighty-seven metres wide.[54] Drujon de Beaulieu convinced Napoleon to direct his attention there. Diversionary efforts made south of Borisov worked; Chichagov sent his whole force south, as a result of which an opportunity was lost to destroy the French army completely (something for which Chichagov would not be forgiven).[55] As soon as the Russians had left Studienka, the sappers got to work. Mostly Dutch sappers under Captain Benthien worked on building a trestle bridge from eight o'clock on the evening of 25 November right through the night and throughout the next morning. The observatory at Vilnius recorded minus 20 degrees Celsius on 24 November, and minus 40 degrees on 26 and 27 November.[56] Even though the sappers were not allowed in the icy waters for more than fifteen minutes at a time, every now and then one would succumb to hypothermia or lose his footing and be swept away. What motivated these men to risk their lives? They were offered a bonus of fifty francs per man, but that was hardly compensation and was not in any event what drove them on. It was unlikely that love of their Emperor motivated them – they were mostly Dutch after all – but rather a sense of duty, knowing that the fate of the army depended on them. There are conflicting reports about whether Napoleon retained the love of his men or whether he was now hated. Caulaincourt maintained that even as soldiers were dying by the roadside, he never heard a single one grumble. Others reported that he was openly heckled.[57]

While the bridge was being built, Napoleon stood on the banks of the Berezina, surrounded by a few other generals such as Oudinot and Murat. Some observers tried to guess what was going on inside his head.[58] He may have thought himself in an impossible situation, caught between two armies, and for that reason ordered the eagles to be burnt.[59] According to one witness, he addressed the dozen or so officers that formed a circle around him and said something along the lines of "'It pains me to see my Old Guard remain behind; their comrades have to do them justice, and hit them." He repeated again, "hit them" [les claquer]. "I am relying on my Old Guard; it has to count on me, on the success of my projects." He repeated the same words several times, looking at us with a sad, broken-down face.'[60]

At one hundred metres long and four metres wide, the bridge was a remarkable achievement, even if it was not the sturdiest of constructions.[61] A second bridge was built fifty metres downstream, for the artillery and the luggage. A third was planned, but not enough materials, most of which were taken from

François Fournier-Sarlovèze, *Passage de la Bérésina par l'armée française, le 28 novembre 1812* (The crossing of the Berezina by the French army, 28 November 1812), drawn around 1812.

the dismantled village of Studienka, could be found. Oudinot crossed first to consolidate the bridgehead on the other bank, then the Guard, then Napoleon. Gendarmes guarded the approaches to the bridges, allowing only active units to cross. Any stragglers and even the wounded being transported in carriages, not to mention the civilians, were pushed to one side, cluttering up the approaches. At one point, panic set in when part of the larger bridge collapsed and plunged into the river where many of the men it took with it would have drowned.[62] Thinking that the narrower bridge would not last long, there was a stampede. Order, however, was slowly restored. Every now and then sections of the bridge would collapse or the trestles would subside into the muddy riverbed, obliging the sappers to wade back into the waters to repair them. In places the bridge sank so that the men's feet were in water.

Victor's corps, holding off the Russian commander General Ludwig Adolf von Wittgenstein, remained on the eastern bank. When most of the army had got across in relative order – despite fights breaking out now and then and the problems caused by dying horses blocking the way – others were allowed to cross. But by this time it was nightfall and most, seeing that they were being defended by Victor whose men had taken up position around the bridge, felt secure enough to remain on the eastern bank for the night. General Jean Baptiste Eblé did his best to try and persuade them to cross but with little success (Eblé survived the retreat only to die at Königsberg).

Battles ensued with Oudinot's troops having to fend off Chichagov on the western bank – he had finally realized that he had been trumped – and Victor's troops fighting off Wittgenstein's 30,000 troops coming from the east. On the second day, after Oudinot had been wounded and forced to retire, Ney stepped into the breach and narrowly avoided a rout. Napoleon ordered what was left of his heavy cavalry into the fray and managed to inflict such serious losses (around 2,000 men) that Chichagov decided to disengage, at least for the day. Things were not going so well for Victor though. Wittgenstein succeeded in an outflanking manoeuvre so that he was able to place his artillery within firing range of the bridges. When he started bombarding the stragglers – thousands of people forming a mass 400 metres wide and a kilometre in length – panic set in and people made a mad rush for the bridges.[63] A few were able to pass in time but others were less fortunate. There are numerous accounts of the crossing, all telling of the harrowing, traumatic circumstances of thousands pushing towards the single bridge that would allow them to safety. They often tell of men trampling on those who had lost their footing, of women and children crushed, of the exhaustion of having to fight for two or three hours even to get to the bridge let alone to cross it, of the terror of that mass of humanity afraid for its life, as though on the banks of the River Styx waiting for that fatal barque to take them across.[64] A few managed to get across on their horses. Some tried to cross the ice but it had not yet set and they fell through it, victims to the cold of the river, although one veteran asserts that in one place a narrow stretch of ice allowed them to cross that way.[65]

Napoleon was able to restore some order only when he managed to get a battery of guns to fire on the Russian positions. By that time, though, the advance guard of Kutuzov's army, under General Miloradovich, had finally caught up and joined Wittgenstein so that the Russians now held numerical superiority of about five to one. Victor nevertheless managed to hold off till nightfall. He was finally given the order to cross to the western bank, under cover of darkness, around 9 p.m., a move that was completed at about one o'clock the next morning. Once again, it appears that those stragglers left on the eastern bank, despite the best efforts of General Eblé, preferred to remain huddled around their camp fires rather than cross during the night. As soon as daylight broke, however, Eblé had no choice but to torch the bridges to prevent the approaching Russians from crossing, leaving thousands on the other side.[66] The sight of the burning bridges, however, did not prevent a final fatal panic. Many of the starving, freezing survivors grew crazed and ran on to the bridges. Other are supposed to have thrown themselves into the river, including women with children, in order to avoid capture by the Russians.[67] Those that were not incinerated, drowned or trampled, faced capture and death.

Estimates of the losses over that three-day period vary enormously, but most historians agree that about 15,000–20,000 troops, as many as a third to one-half of whom were killed in action, and as many as 10,000–30,000 civilians were killed. Russian losses were around 15,000.[68] After the crossing, Napoleon was left with no more than 40,000 soldiers and, once again remarkably under the circumstances, 200 guns. The huge crowd of civilians had been reduced to about 10,000–15,000 people. Some 10,000 people – stragglers, camp followers, refugees – were left behind on the other side of the river.[69] Of those who managed to escape, more than half were to die over the next few weeks.[70]

Despite the losses, the crossing was a remarkable tactical achievement. The Russians had missed an opportunity to annihilate the invading army. Alexander laid the blame for this squarely at Kutuzov's feet. Kutuzov did not reach his objective until two days after Napoleon's army had already crossed, giving the impression that the advance of the bulk of the Russian army was sluggish if not incompetent.[71] The criticism is perhaps harsh, for while the Russians were operating in more favourable circumstances – better clothed, better fed and probably more used to the weather – they had still suffered considerable losses along the way from Moscow. Indeed, in the month or so that the Russians had been tailing Napoleon since Maloyaroslavets, about one-third of their army had succumbed to battle, desertion and fatigue so that by the time it reached Tarutino in October it had been reduced to about 28,000 men.[72] It is possible of course that Kutuzov, unlike the Tsar, had a better sense of the full import of the struggle, and wanted not to destroy Napoleon but merely to drive him from Russian soil. To destroy Napoleon would be of no benefit to Russia, but only to Russia's traditional enemies, Britain and Austria. It was a view shared by others in the army and at court, and would cause some debate over the next year or so as the allies attempted to agree on some sort of strategy for dealing with France and Napoleon.

### 'A Vast and Lugubrious Taciturnity'

If things had been bad for the Grande Armée up to now, they were, if at all possible, about to get worse. The passage from the Berezina to Vilnius, which took about twelve days to complete, was the period in which the army suffered most.[73] Although the men who had survived the crossing basked in their feat and believed, or wanted to believe, that everything would get better, a cold snap hit the retreating troops on 3 December. Unless one has experienced what it is to live outdoors in extremely cold temperatures, it is difficult to imagine just how horrendous it must have been. The only sound that could be heard was that of snow being crunched underfoot as the men trudged along. The worst thing the men could have done in these circumstances was to huddle close to fires at night. If they did not burn themselves or fall asleep around a fire that went out overnight, the contrast between the heat and the cold could often be fatal.[74] Even those who had more or less kept discipline until then were transformed during this period into men indifferent to everyone and everything except their own survival.[75]

As the 'procession' – the name that the survivors gave to the retreating army passing along the main road[76] – continued, acts of brutality and egoism increased as discipline declined. Men who lay down on the road were stripped bare or searched for valuables before they had even expired.[77] One veteran remarked that the route and the places where they bivouacked looked like the aftermath of a field of battle, with bodies, horses and equipment strewn everywhere.[78] Reports of cannibalism are more difficult to verify.[79] They usually involve Russian prisoners who had to resort to this extreme because they were given nothing to eat, and sometimes to behaviour among non-French survivors of the Grande Armée.[80] There are no references to French survivors resorting to cannibalism, which does not mean that French troops did not practise it, but that they did not admit to it, preferring to portray themselves as a little more civilized than the mass of humanity that made up the residue of the Grande Armée. There were reports, even more difficult to verify, of autophagy or self-mutilation in order to eat.[81]

Convoys of food and mail reached the retreating army on 3 and 4 December, but although this was no doubt of some help, it could not prevent the continued disintegration. Fights broke out and murder was committed over food and shelter.[82] The men were essentially left to fend for themselves. A few lucky infantry regiments followed either cavalry or artillery regiments as best they could in order to feed off the dead and dying horses they left behind each morning. Stragglers formed into groups that attempted to stay ahead of the main army in order better to plunder the few standing villages along the way or to steal horses and valuables from encampments during the night.[83] Stealing in order to survive was not all that uncommon.[84] After a while, one could tell exactly when a man was going to fall and die: he would begin to totter, then walk as though drunk, then fall. A few drops of blood might trickle from the nose, and then the limbs would go stiff.[85] 'I noticed three men around a dead horse,' remembered Sergeant Bourgogne:

> two of the men were standing and appeared drunk, they were reeling so much. The third, who was a German, lay on the horse. The poor wretch, dying of hunger and unable to cut into it, was trying to bite it. He ended up dying in that position of cold and hunger. The other two, Hussars, had their mouths and hands covered in blood. We spoke to them but were unable to obtain any response; they looked at us laughing in a frightening manner and, holding on to each other, they sat next to the man who had just died where, probably, they ended up falling into a fatal sleep.[86]

Attributed to François Fournier-Sarlovèze, *Coup d'oeil de la route de Moscou depuis la Bérézina jusqu'au Niémen, 1812* (A look at the route from Moscow from the Berezina to the Niemen, 1812), around 1812.

There were nevertheless isolated acts of heroism in all of this, men going out of their way to save comrades and friends, and sometimes strangers, but increasingly they became the exception to the rule.[87]


## Napoleon Decamps

Not everybody blamed Napoleon for this catastrophe. His aura was so great that many officers, no matter what their nationality, believed that as long as he was with the army everything would be all right.[88] Napoleon himself realized that if the army did not get at least one week's rest at Vilnius, then it was doomed. Serious too were the political consequences of the disintegration of the army. Reports were coming out of Petersburg about the French being defeated, so Napoleon had to act to counter these rumours. He did so in his usual fashion, by exaggerating the achievement at the Berezina. He ordered one of Berthier's aides-de-camp, Anatole de Montesquiou, to travel to Paris with a report stating that over 6,000 prisoners had been taken. Along the way, he was to stop in major towns and spread the news.

This was nothing less than damage control. The most Napoleon could count on was around 40,000 men, all that remained of the once impressive Grande Armée, although there were another 20,000 fresh troops garrisoned at Vilnius. With these men, rested and under competent command, it was reasonable to expect them to hold Vilnius. One should not forget, moreover, that the Russian army was suffering as much from the hardships brought by the cold as the soldiers of the Grande Armée.[89] And once Napoleon had slipped through Kutuzov's fingers at the Berezina, Kutuzov was not inclined to push the pace in pursuit of Napoleon. At this stage, the Russians were hardly in a position to mount a determined attack against Vilnius. If, on the other hand, Napoleon could not hold Vilnius, there was nothing to stop the Russians from moving into Poland and Prussia.

The 29th Bulletin was written on 3 December from Molodechno, about seventy-two kilometres south-east of Vilnius. It blamed the weather for the condition of the army, without however mentioning the horrendous losses it had suffered, except for the horses. It was easy enough for people to read between the lines. Despite mentioning the 'victory' at the Berezina, it would have been clear to all that this was a defeat. One hundred and sixty-four days had gone by since the army crossed the Niemen. About a day's march out of Vilnius, on 5 December, at a small country house outside Smorgonie, Napoleon called his commanders together and told them of his decision to leave for Paris. The fact that he had, once again, almost been captured by Cossacks on the night of 3 December no doubt contributed to his decision to leave. All Russian corps commanders had received the order to try and capture Napoleon, along with a description of him: 'thick waist, hair black, short and flat, strong black beard, shaved to the top of the ear, eyebrows very arched, but deep into the nose, a passionate but irascible look, aquiline nose with continuous traces of tobacco, the chin very prominent'.[90] A hardly flattering but nevertheless reasonably accurate portrait.

Under the circumstances, Napoleon's entourage considered his immediate return to Paris the correct decision to make. This, the Emperor believed, would allow him to keep in line his unreliable German allies, Prussia and Austria, and raise a new army while in France. He was, as we shall see, able to recruit the soldiers, but the assumption that he could keep a firm grasp over Austria and Prussia was mistaken, and the repercussions of his departure on the morale and discipline of the army were much worse than he could have anticipated. The Malet affair may also have played on his mind. He had, after all, been away from the imperial capital for over seven months. His returning home now, comparable in some respects to what had happened in Egypt thirteen years previously – though then he had left the army in a somewhat better condition – may also have been about giving the impression of taking the initiative.[91] 'I am leaving you,' he declared to the army, 'but it is to find three hundred thousand soldiers.'[92] It was a political decision, possibly an apt one at the time, but one that was going to have devastating consequences for the remainder of the Grande Armée. There is no doubt they would have been better served by Napoleon's continued presence.

Napoleon left with a few confidants – Caulaincourt and Duroc among others – on the evening of 5 December in three carriages escorted by a squadron of chasseurs and a squadron of Polish Light Horse of the Old Guard. Officers who still had horses were selected to make up a 'sacred squadron' (*escadron sacrée*) to accompany the Emperor, but the horses were so wretched and the officers so hungry it was dissolved after a few days.[93] Berthier begged, tearfully, to be taken with him but the request was declined.[94] Napoleon travelled incognito, as Caulaincourt's secretary, Reyneval. Most senior officers understood his departure as a political decision, even though many in the lower ranks reproached him and a few insults were heard.[95] As to whether it was accepted by the army, reports vary. Some maintained that very few people openly criticized Napoleon's decision to abandon them to return to Paris.[96] Before he left, however, he consulted with his marshals and generals about who should replace him as commander-in-chief. There were two possibilities: his brother-in-law Murat, or his stepson Eugène. Neither of them was really up to the job militarily – Davout or Ney would have been a better choice – but Napoleon believed that only a member of the imperial family would be able to keep at bay the petty feuding and jealousies bound to spring up between his marshals and generals once he had gone.[97] Besides, Murat was a king and outranked the other marshals. At least that was his reasoning, but he should have known better. The appointment of Joseph as commander-in-chief in

Spain certainly had not stopped the bickering between Napoleon's generals. Since Murat was a king and Eugène only a prince, the mantle fell on to Murat's shoulders.[98]

It was a mistake. Almost as soon as Napoleon had left, his marshals were at each other's throats. Philippe de Ségur recalled, albeit with a good deal of hindsight, the misgivings he felt over Murat's appointment: 'In the empty space left by his [Napoleon's] departure, Murat was hardly visible. We realized then – and only too well – that a great man cannot be replaced.'[99] Part of the problem was that the marshals were far too proud to take orders from one of their own, and Napoleon had made sure that he was surrounded by able lieutenants, not leaders.[100] On 8 December, Berthier wrote to say that the army was in complete disarray.[101]

Murat had been unable to impose his views on those under his command so that the councils of war, which he was supposed to chair, often ended up as shouting matches.[102] Moreover, he demonstrated an extraordinary lethargy by failing to respond to letters from commanders in the field, thereby creating a leadership vacuum. He had, in fact, fallen into a deep funk, and asked permission of Napoleon to leave.[103] Napoleon forbade him to do so. Murat then raged against his brother-in-law, at one point calling him 'mad' (insensé), although he was supposedly put in his place by Davout for having done so.[104] No longer able to continue in the role, Murat summoned Eugène to his headquarters in Poznań. He claimed that he was ill, and that as a result he was leaving the army and going back to Italy where he was going to negotiate with Austria and Britain to keep his throne. In effect, he was abandoning his command and was asking Eugène to take over. It was not yet every man for himself in the face of a crumbling empire, but some of the rats were deserting the imperial ship. On 18 January 1813, Berthier followed Murat, as did most of the marshals, leaving Eugène no choice but to take over. After Murat's departure, Eugène took stock of the situation. Murat 'has left me this great mess', he complained to his wife.[105] Napoleon's response to Murat was cutting: 'You are a good soldier on the battlefield, but off it, you have neither vigour nor character.'[106] Even Napoleon admitted he had made a mistake in appointing Murat.[107] Eugène's appointment was greeted with great relief in the army.[108] It would not have been until he wrote to Napoleon towards the end of January, after Murat had left the army, that the Emperor received a clearer picture of what was going on.[109]

Vilnius should have been a haven for the retreating army; there were enough supplies stocked there to feed 100,000 men for three months, as well as clothes, boots and muskets. A series of events, however, conspired to transform the town into a nightmare, while all the fresh divisions sent out to cover the retreat quickly disintegrated in the cold – most of them were young and inexperienced and knew nothing about how to cope in the extremely harsh conditions that awaited them.[110]

For those who arrived at the gates of Vilnius in the first weeks of December 1812, the reports vary from individual to individual. Some recall that the thought of arriving in a large town kept driving them on, but that within sight of the town one could see nothing but confusion.[111] Others remembered that the depots were full of supplies but that the distribution was non-existent so that the magazines were looted and pillaged. General Hogendorp, governor of the city, who had initially undertaken measures to welcome the troops by setting up notices directing regiments to various places where they could find food, was accused of having abandoned his post once he saw the bulk of the army arrive on 9 December. (It is not at all clear that he did, but if he remained at his post his command was ineffectual.) Louis Joseph Vionnet de Maringoné, an officer in the Grenadiers of the Guard, managed to buy some wine but his stomach had shrunk so much that he had to drink it as though it were medicine, one spoonful every hour.[112] Once inside, Sergeant Bourgogne remembered the curious effect an inhabited house made on him; he had not seen one in almost two months. When the Old Guard arrived, they found a mob of stragglers obstructing the gates: 'in order to enter, they pushed them out of the way, they walked all over them, trampled them underfoot'.[113]

## In a Sleigh with the Emperor

We are obliged to leave the army struggling on to Vilnius and follow Napoleon and his entourage back to Paris. At Gragow, they left the other carriages and the escort behind in order to forge rapidly ahead, passing through Warsaw, Dresden, Weimar, Leipzig, Erfurt, Mainz, Verdun and Château-Thierry, then Paris. At each stage of the return voyage Napoleon stopped to reassure his allies that he had everything under control. From the sublime to the ridiculous there is but one step. He believed he could still beat the enemy, and in effect he had beaten him in open battle whenever the two armies engaged, but what he did not understand was the consequences of the demands he had placed on so many of his allies over the past years. The first part of the passage, between Vilnius and Kaunas, the coldest according to Caulaincourt, was spent simply huddled together, Napoleon 'dressed in thick wool and covered with a good rug, with his legs in fur boots and then in a bag made of bearskin'.[114] Even that was not enough to keep him warm; Caulaincourt had to share half his own bearskin rug. It was so cold that the cloth work in the carriage froze, while small icicles formed under their noses, around the eyebrows and on the eyelids. It was only after leaving Mariampol that the voyage was comfortable enough for the two men to communicate. Nothing of note happened as Napoleon made his way to Paris, except for one intriguing little incident, mentioned only in passing by Napoleon's Mameluke servant, Roustam Raza, who wrote his memoirs many years after the event. When Napoleon stopped off at an inn in a little town outside Kaunas on 6 December 1812, and took the time to have a wash and change his clothes, the discarded shirt and stockings were immediately seized on by 'everyone' and divided into pieces.[115] 'Holy relics' to be preserved? The cult, it would appear, had penetrated even the outer reaches of the Empire.

Caulaincourt's recollections of that ride back to Paris are one of the most intimate and interesting accounts of Napoleon we have. When they halted each evening between five and nine so that Napoleon could rest and the party could dine, and the Emperor dozed off on a chair in front of a fire or on a couch, Caulaincourt would take the time quickly to note down the conversations of that day, or at least what he considered to be important. Alone with him for almost two weeks, sharing the hardships of the road, changing carriages when they either broke down or transferred to a sleigh, stopping at the postmasters' stations along the way for the evening meal, Napoleon opened up to him, and talked of everything from the state of France, of Spain, Prussia, and his brothers through to Russia and England.[116] For Napoleon, talking assuaged his fears, and made the long trip more bearable. Caulaincourt was the sounding board, but whenever he contradicted his imperial master, he invariably received the reply, 'You are young,' or 'You don't understand affairs.' Imagine a reader sympathetic to Napoleon who, with the benefit of hindsight, went back in time to persuade him to moderate his foreign policy in the hope of getting him to change direction. It will give one an idea of the tone of the conversations between the two men. It was, as it turned out, a futile endeavour on the part of Caulaincourt. Whenever he got too close to the bone – that is, when he attacked the Emperor's seemingly unbridled ambition or his passion for war – Napoleon would smile, joke or try to pinch Caulaincourt's ear, a typical gesture on his part, although he probably had some difficulty finding his interlocutor's ear under the fur bonnet he was wearing.[117]

Once the reader cuts through the traditional exculpatory explanations – if it was not for Britain he would have stayed at home; he was tricked by the climate and defeated by winter – the most significant observation worth noting is that he did not, possibly was unable to, recognize the extent of his losses. He was under the illusion that the army would halt at Vilnius for the winter, and that his return to Paris would restore his political ascendancy and would somehow make up for the disasters the army had incurred. It is possible that Napoleon was lost in the past and that he believed, as with his return from Egypt after a very mixed campaign, that his return would simply put everything right again.

Hubris, arrogance and an utter inability to admit his mistakes, which he avoided confronting by expounding on how the enemy could have fought better, were the hallmarks of his monologues. The only mistake he appears capable of acknowledging was to have stayed too long at Moscow. It was not invading Russia in the first place, adopting a Continental System that obliged him to pursue the phantom of economic dominance, fighting a war on two fronts, or being drawn deep into Russia in spite of himself. All those strategic errors he could argue his way out of, as though it were simply a matter of putting up a good argument, rather than dealing with a reality that touched the lives of millions of people. They were abstract ideas in which Napoleon imagined positive outcomes that had little to do with the harsh reality with which he was confronted. Thus the war in Spain, 'only a matter of guerrilla contests', would be resolved in a month or two, once the English had been driven out; 'I can change the face of affairs when I please.'[118] Possibly, but he had to get there, and that was unlikely in the immediate future. It was ironic given that even he was aware that 'in war men could lose in a day what they had spent years in building up'.[119]

## Aftermath

The retreat lasted from about 18 October to 23 December, when advance elements of the Guard entered Königsberg. Even to get to Königsberg, however, was a feat; the remnants of the army were pursued by Cossacks all the way into Prussia. Once there, though, after three months of incredible hardship and deprivation, the survivors could at last rest, eat, sleep, take a bath, change their clothes, tend to their wounds and attempt to come to grips psychologically with the horrors they had lived through. Fantin des Odoards was haunted by the retreat for months afterwards, plagued with black thoughts and nightmares, and confronted with 'an ocean of ice that he could not lose from sight'.[120]

At Königsberg, the inhabitants were so angry with the French that violent confrontations took place.[121] For, after weeks of rumour, news of the destruction of the invasion army reached western Europe with a devastating impact. The reaction wherever the French were hated was the same, one of hope. In London, the city went 'crazy' in the expectation of what the disaster might bring.[122] In Vienna, Napoleon's defeat elicited general joy, toasts were drunk to the health of the victors, and the 'Russian faction' gained increasing ascendancy at court.[123] This is not, however, what Metternich had been expecting and it threw him into some confusion. He did not particularly relish the thought of a Russian army marching into central Europe. The 29th Bulletin was published in Paris on 16 December (two days before Napoleon arrived). For the people of France, it was the first indication that things had not gone well. News of the disaster started to trickle in towards the end of the month. The general reaction was revealing. Some spoke of the 'horror' and 'consternation' into which the people of France were thrown, although there was also a good deal of indignation at the loss of so many men.[124] When news of the calamity reached David, he was heard to remark in a brilliant piece of understatement, 'Ah! ah! That's not quite what we wanted.'[125] In the rest of the country, general indignation is probably the best way to describe how people felt about the fiasco that was Russia, exacerbated by reports coming in from Spain. Soon enough, people hostile to Napoleon felt emboldened by the defeat to express their ire, not only in Paris, but in various towns and regions of France.[126] The people had not yet turned away from their Emperor, but that they were less inclined to support him in times of trouble is clear.

Almost immediately, in the first days and weeks of 1813, anti-Napoleonic pamphlets, newspaper articles and caricatures began to appear, galvanizing public opinion against Napoleon.[127] The Russians had been at work on this for some time already, printing their own bulletins that were distributed to the army and, more importantly, printing calls to revolt in the main languages of the Grande Armée, aimed at both troops and officers.[128] Napoleon was personally held responsible for the suffering that had befallen Europe. Poems published as pamphlets informed people about the French disasters, and explained that Moscow had burnt.[129] Moreover, proclamations issued by both Alexander and Kutuzov – Kutuzov issued a proclamation in January 1813 to his 'children': 'We will make Europe exclaim with astonishment. The Russian army is invincible'[130] – did the rounds of just about every inn in Europe.[131]

It is obvious that people reacted differently to the news in different parts of Europe but what seems clear is that Napoleon's setback helped fuel the hatred of those suffering under French occupation. The conclusion people drew from all this was that, if there were ever to be peace on the Continent, Napoleon would first have to go. In the north of Germany, in the Hanseatic ports where the Continental Blockade had done so much to ruin their commercial life, Napoleon and the French were particularly hated. News of the defeat in Russia, which had occurred so suddenly and so unpredictably, seemed like a miracle to those who opposed the French. Rumour exaggerated, if that were possible, the extent of the defeat and filled the opponents of the Empire with hope: the army had been completely destroyed (more or less true); Napoleon had fled by himself or disguised as a peasant; Prussia and Austria had joined forces with Russia (not yet true); the whole of Germany had risen in revolt (some regions would eventually do so, but not all). The rumours, no matter how absurd, were enough to cause a 'general ferment'.

None of this, however, prepared the people of Prussia for the sight that greeted them as the remnants of the Grande Armée marched back through their territory – the pestilential stench, the rotting flesh in the rotting uniforms. 'Their clothing consisted of rags, straw mats, old women's clothing, sheepskins, or whatever else they could lay their hands on. None had the proper headgear; instead they bound their heads with old cloths or pieces of shirt;

instead of shoes and leggings, their feet were wrapped with straw, fur or rags.'[132] The French subsequently felt the full hatred of the Prussian people who no longer bothered to hide their contempt. 'The ass's kick', as one soldier put it.[133] Rumours of the difficulties the French army had been facing had been filtering back to Prussia since October. When, on 12 November, there were newspaper reports that Napoleon had retreated from Moscow people assumed he had been defeated and openly vented their rage in street riots.[134] The Westphalian legation secretary in Berlin wrote that never had he seen 'such intense hatred'.[135] When the 29th Bulletin was published in Berlin on 14 December, there could no longer be any doubt – Napoleon was defeated. The remnants of the army were greeted with insulting songs,[136] and, much worse than this, armed groups of peasants began attacking stragglers.[137]

As with the figures surrounding the number of men who entered Russia, the figures for those who survived are just as varied. It is thought that about 75,000 troops crossed the Niemen in late 1812, half of whom were Austrian or Prussian and would therefore never fight for Napoleon again, while most of the rest were in so pitiful a state they could not fight, at least not in the immediate future.[138] When one takes into account the Russian military losses – according to one estimate, as many as 300,000 dead[139] – one can reasonably assert that up to one million people died between the end of June 1812, when the expedition into Russia was launched, and February 1813, with the remnants of the army continuing to die from wounds, disease, malnutrition and exhaustion. Of the 27,000 Italian troops only 1,000 made it back.[140] Of the 25,500 Saxon soldiers that went into Russia, 6,000 came back alive.[141] Looking at figures for individual regiments sometimes tells an even bleaker story. Raymond de Montesquiou-Fezensac had 3,000 men under his command. Of those 200 came back with him and another 100 were eventually returned from prison – that is, nine-tenths of his effectives were dead or missing.[142] Similarly, a Sergeant François, writing from Magdeburg on 1 March 1813, described how he had lived off horsemeat for the last six weeks and that only twenty-six men from his battalion of 1,000 men had survived.[143] Of the 28,000 Westphalian troops, those abandoned by Jérôme early in the campaign, about 250 made it back alive. Some 1,700 soldiers left Mecklenburg-Schwerin; only 118 survived the ordeal.[144] For Württemberg, only 500 men of the 15,800 initial contingent returned home.[145] The Poles did not fare any better. Of the 118,000 men who began the campaign, about 90,000 were killed, wounded, made prisoner or went missing.[146]

There was the problem of dealing with the thousands of cadavers, both men and horses, left behind. Somewhere between 160,000 and 200,000 horses were lost during the campaign.[147] The carnage in Moscow was such that reportedly it could be smelt for miles around.[148] The Russians were obliged to organize special teams to follow in the wake of Napoleon in order to bury the dead. We

know from a report of a spy working for Louis Le Lorgne d'Ideville, who
served Napoleon as a secretary-interpreter, that the Russians burnt 253,000
bodies in the districts of Moscow, Vitebsk and Mogilev, most belonging to the
Grande Armée, and another 53,000 in the region of Vilnius.[149] A report from
the Russian ministry of police calculated that 430,707 men had been buried in
this way. Naturally, many others would have been buried by their own men,
while the special teams may have mistaken Napoleon's troops for their own on
occasion, but it gives an idea of the size of the loss and devastation.[150] Around
12,000 bodies, many of which may have been those of wounded Russian
soldiers too sick to move during the evacuation and caught up in the flames at
the beginning of the occupation, were discovered in Moscow when the Russian
army recaptured the city in October 1812.[151] A third of the Russian soldiers
ordered to remove the rotting bodies fell ill themselves. It is not unreasonable
to assume then that Napoleon's army incurred a loss of around 85 per cent in
dead, wounded, deserters and prisoners.[152] Figures cited do not always take
account of the numbers who deserted in the early weeks of the war and who
may have made it out of Russia, possibly as many as 50,000.[153] Nor do they
take into account the number of men who settled in the western provinces of
Russia in the closing stages of the campaign. We know that prisoners were
sometimes given to local landowners as cheap labour and never returned home,
and that others agreed to take service in the Tsar's army, swearing an oath of
loyalty and settling into a new life. Admittedly, this did not happen all that
often. There were nevertheless over 9,000 men in a Russian German Legion
formed out of German prisoners. Most German prisoners, however, remained
loyal to Napoleon, and refused to fight for the Tsar.[154] We know too that a
Russian census carried out in 1837 noted 3,299 Frenchmen, former prisoners,
who had stayed on in the region of Moscow.[155] In what is now Lithuania we
know that a number of men remained there and assimilated with the local
population.[156] During an archaeological dig in 2001 in which 3,269 skeletons
(fifteen female) were uncovered in the centre of the town of Vilnius, and which
turned out to be a mass grave of soldiers from the Grande Armée, a number of
people approached the French cultural centre in town to say that the family
had always said that they were descended from a soldier in Napoleon's army.[157]

When the Russians reached the Niemen in the wake of the remnants of the
Grande Armée, they had to decide whether to pursue Napoleon or leave him
be. They had, after all, achieved their objective by defeating their enemy and
ejecting him from their country. In doing so, their army was exhausted and
many officers had little in mind but rest. It was a crucial decision, one on
which, in some respects, the fate of Napoleon and Europe hinged.[158] If Alexander had decided not to pursue Napoleon, any number of alternative paths
might have opened, but one thing is certain: it would have left Napoleon in

control of central Europe and therefore with his Empire intact. It is not that Alexander or Russia alone were responsible for 'liberating' Europe, but that without Russia's involvement Napoleon would not have been overthrown.

There were conflicting views among the Russians not only on the nature of the war – that is, about whether a war that had been in defence of the fatherland should be transformed into a campaign to destroy Napoleon – but also on whether Russia should pursue the French into central Europe.[159] A number of people in Alexander's entourage, probably the majority – they might be called the isolationists and included Kutuzov, the minister of war, General Count Aleksei Arakcheev, the foreign minister Rumiantsev and the minister of the interior, Admiral Aleksandr Shishkov – did not want to carry the war into Europe and would have been satisfied with taking a few territorial possessions in the west, or with extending Russia's western boundary to the Vistula.[160] Not only was the Russian army in poor shape – at this stage only about 100,000 troops were in any condition to advance beyond Russia – but generals like Kutuzov, hardly a match for Napoleon in open battle, were extremely wary of having to face him on the German plains, and (as we have seen) were worried that his destruction would benefit only Britain.[161] Shishkov was of the same opinion. He would have preferred to see Russia send an auxiliary corps to help Austria, and believed that the bulk of the Russian army should stay behind.[162]

Alexander and a number of younger men in his entourage, among them Karl von Nesselrode, his chief diplomatic adviser who would virtually take over from the foreign minister, and some young officers who would later be drawn to the Decembrist movement – a secret society that led an unsuccessful revolt in St Petersburg in December 1825 – were keen to push on and eventually overthrow Napoleon. Indeed, Alexander had long made up his mind, writing to London in 1812 that he planned on 'liberating Europe from the French yoke'.[163] There is every indication that he had prepared himself for the 'ultimate conflict' with France ever since Erfurt (perhaps earlier),[164] and that he was keen to carry the war into Germany, if not for territorial gains then at least in the role of 'Saviour' or 'Liberator of Europe'.[165] It is said that, in the second half of 1812, Alexander had undergone a sort of religious conversion, so that he believed himself to be God's Chosen One, called upon to bring Christian enlightenment to the world.[166] The fire of Moscow supposedly 'lit up' his soul and filled his heart with a 'warmth and faith' that he had never felt before.[167] He had always had religious convictions, but with the French invasion he increasingly turned to the Bible for inspiration, and especially to the eleventh chapter of the Book of Daniel, in which the King of the North (read Alexander) defeats the King of the South (read Napoleon).[168] Napoleon's defeat became, in his mind, synonymous with God's will, and hence Alexander became His instrument. The Tsar got his way. The Russian army was ordered to pursue the French into Germany.

# THE ADVENTURER, 1813–1814

# 2 1

# 'The Enemy of the Human Race'

## The Limits of Attachment

Napoleon arrived in Paris on 18 December 1812 at the Tuileries Palace just as the clock struck fifteen minutes to midnight.[1] Marie-Louise was genuinely pleased to see her husband and they warmly embraced one another. We have no idea, however, what happened next between them, how much, if at all, Napoleon opened up to her, and what was said after seven months of absence. Regardless of what happened in Russia, the court had a life of its own, so the *lever* took place as usual the next morning at around eleven o'clock. There too Napoleon said nothing about Russia or his predicament, as though it were just another day at the palace. There are, however, conflicting reports about how he behaved during this period. According to Caulaincourt, there was 'no look of the defeated man about him'; he worked all that first day until one in the morning, issuing orders to all and sundry.[2] According to others, he was never the same after his return from Russia; he had neither the ideas nor the force of character to carry them through, nor the same aptitude for work.[3] He also appears to have been in poor health, suffering from a chronic dermatitis that made him scratch to the point of bleeding, and from violent stomach pains. If Paris consoled him – he was back in familiar surroundings, and he immediately fell into his old work habits – inwardly the extent of the defeat must have had an impact on his psyche.

Outwardly, however, Napoleon's confidence does not seem to have been terribly damaged by his setback in Russia. When the Senate and the Council of State paid him a visit the next day, 20 December, he bluntly reminded them that they had not followed protocol in proclaiming his son emperor on hearing of his alleged death. If structurally his regime was relatively secure, its survival beyond Napoleon himself does not appear to have entered into the political elite's consciousness. This is not entirely surprising. Napoleon may have resolved most of the domestic difficulties threatening political stability, unlike the Directory and other earlier revolutionary regimes, but he had largely negated those gains through constant warring. There seems little doubt that the French political elite had grown tired of him, something exacerbated by two developments: the economic crisis of 1810–12 as a result of which the French suffered terribly from crop failures and rising prices;[4] and the introduction of the Guard of Honour (Gardes d'honneur), a scheme designed to 'rally' throughout the Empire (including Italy, Belgium and Holland) the bourgeoisie, who had until then largely managed to avoid conscription by buying replacements – that is, paying people to take their place, although admittedly the number of replacements was always only some 4 per cent.[5] The scheme obliged the sons of the well off to furnish their own horses and equipment,[6] a desperate attempt to make up for the loss of cavalry, and to rally the elite to his regime. The one damaged Napoleon's economic credibility – the economic crisis played a crucial role in undermining support for the regime – while the other hit home where it hurt the elite the most, within their families, and alienated many bourgeois from the regime.

As long as Napoleon had been able to convey an image of himself as the saviour, as an instrument of the public good, he had been assured of power. The political elite ostensibly still submitted to him. When he opened the Legislative Corps on 14 February 1813, he explained the defeat in Russia as a consequence of the weather, and the vast majority of deputies accepted a war budget for the coming year of more than one trillion francs.[7] In the face of military defeat, however, the elites were beginning to lose faith. It is the fate of a charismatic ruler: since everything revolved around his person, Napoleon became responsible for everything, good and bad. Now everybody blamed him, criticized him, denounced him.[8] He was no doubt aware of these sentiments, and believed that the only way of redressing the situation, of bolstering faltering morale, was to launch another campaign and pull off another series of victories through which he might possibly obtain peace.

He wanted to take the offensive in the coming spring, convincing himself that he had learnt the lessons of the Russian fiasco. Letter after letter went out organizing the army for what he knew would end in a campaign in Germany the following year.[9] He wrote to Francis I, explaining the military situation, and asking for another 30,000 men.[10] There was some justification for Napoleon's optimism, even after what had happened in Russia and even after the allies had advanced deep into Germany by the beginning of 1813. At the end of 1812, he was still in a powerful position; he still controlled all of western Europe up to the Oder. Tens of thousands of troops called up as early as September 1812 to replace the losses in Russia were marching to the front by the beginning of 1813.[11] By March 1813, Eugène in Berlin was in command of over 110,000 men and 185 guns. Another 140,000 men with 320 guns were gathering between the Rhine and the Elbe.[12] In all, more than one million men were called up; the class of 1813 but also the classes between 1809 and 1812 were recalled to arms, obliging notables who had managed to keep their sons out of the army by buying replacements to do so again.

Napoleon was not about to take the decision to go to war again alone. A Council meeting was held at the beginning of January 1813, at which people expressed their views. Talleyrand, Caulaincourt, Cambacérès and Decrès all advised peace, moderation and the mediation of Austria.[13] In fact, this type of council was for show. Napoleon had no intention of negotiating peace terms, for to him it would be seen as an avowal of weakness that would make Russia and Austria more demanding. Besides, he had already decided to continue the war. Any hope or expectation by some of his generals that the retreat would prove a useful lesson and cool his warlike ardour was misplaced.[14] He was arming for peace, he told the Austrian ambassador to Paris, Prince Schwarzenberg, and he expected Austria to raise some 200,000 men to threaten the Russians.[15]

The winter of 1812–13 thus passed with Napoleon in Paris trying to reorganize his Empire. There was, to quote Caulaincourt, 'mourning in every family but hope in every heart'.[16] The war with Russia had generally been regarded as unnecessary, and the war in Spain had created a good deal of discontent.[17] At the beginning of the Empire there had been an ideological consensus in favour of conquest and expansion – France was, after all, extending an 'empire of liberty' throughout Europe – when military victory was considered to be the necessary prerequisite for peace. Now, this was no longer accepted. Political consensus, built upon quite fragile foundations, began to waver with the First Polish War, and certainly with the invasion of Spain. It became definitely hostile over Russia. The image of Napoleon and the regime had been indelibly tarnished by the continuing wars.

Hostility varied from region to region, depending on the extent to which war had touched people's lives.[18] Fouché believed that the people and what were called the 'intermediary classes', that is the bourgeoisie, were no longer favourable towards Napoleon even though they were not yet openly hostile.[19] In December 1812, as a result of the Russian defeat, the minister of the interior, the Comte de Montalivet, requested confidential letters from prefects about the mood of the people in the departments. These letters were summarized in reports for the Emperor. For the most part they were reassuring and probably influenced Napoleon in setting his course, especially since it was clear that he would be able to solve the conscription problem.[20] But the letters also made it clear that the French desperately longed for peace. Public declarations of support may have been made by municipal councillors and prefects, but they were largely conforming to imperial expectations.[21] One of Napoleon's failings is that he could think only in terms of triumph and defeat. The fear of defeat made further triumphs always necessary. Moreover, the feelings of grandeur that grew with every triumph rendered it increasingly intolerable that anybody, or any nation, should not recognize his greatness.

The French people wanted nothing more than to enjoy the benefits of a stable peace, and had wanted it now for years.[22] The public was tired of war even before Austerlitz and was unable to arouse any enthusiasm for most of Napoleon's victories. Police reports throughout 1807 made it plain that the populace was sick of war, especially in those regions, like Brittany, that had never entirely accepted either the Republic or the Empire.[23] As the Empire progressed the news of victories fell on a population increasingly indifferent and increasingly war-weary. There was probably no better indication of the extent of disaffection with the regime than the response to conscription. If there had been a gradual diminution in the number of draft dodgers between 1800 and 1810, down from 28 per cent to 13 per cent, the number shot up after 1810 to more than 45 per cent in some departments. That is, almost half of those called up, especially in certain departments in Belgium, in the west and the south-west of France and in Italy, refused to answer the call.[24] Five call-ups, as well as the extraordinary call-ups that had been made to meet the shortfall in men, meant that in 1813 Napoleon conscripted more men than in the previous six years.[25] The numbers of foreign troops continued to increase so that they went from 14 per cent of the Grande Armée in 1808 to 24 per cent in 1813.[26] All males between the ages of twenty and twenty-five were in principle eligible, although only a proportion were ever called up, usually around a third (in 1813–14 the figure climbed to two-thirds, on paper at least).[27] In September 1813, for example, the prefect from the Ariège complained that so many young men were being taken that there would be no one left to procreate.[28] It was no doubt an exaggeration, but it was an indication that the call-up for the year 1813 was considered the most onerous and was going to contribute to the legend of Napoleon as the 'Corsican Ogre'. The Emperor was reduced to trawling all previous classes that had been called up going back as far as 1803 – that is, including men who were now thirty.

## The Germans Strike Back

At the sight of so many bedraggled, wounded and unarmed men straggling through Germany at the beginning of 1813, people quickly reached the conclusion, rightly or wrongly, that the French Empire was on the verge of collapse.[29] Rumours of the Russian seizure of Königsberg, not to mention of the death of Napoleon at Moscow, had reached north Germany by the middle of January.[30] By that stage, some young men, as was the case in Minden, sixty kilometres east of Osnabrück, expressed their opposition to the Empire by running through the streets at night crying 'Vive l'Empereur Alexandre!'[31] By the middle of February, many north Germans were eagerly awaiting the arrival of Russian Cossacks.[32] The more that rumours about the Russians became prevalent, the more tensions increased between the local populations and their French overlords. On 23 February, the tension came to a head in Hamburg where the arrest of some smugglers outside the city gates was the occasion for rioting throughout the city.[33] In Lübeck, French police reported 'a decided effrontery, in the inhabitants' words and deeds, and especially in their relations with the French'.[34] In Leiden, a crowd of peasants forced open the gates of the city, possibly with the intention of hoisting the Orange flag – representing the House of Orange, which ruled Holland until 1795 – but the riot was quickly put down by regular troops.[35] In Oldenburg, the revolts were especially violent after frustrations simmering under the surface finally erupted.[36] The symbols of French imperialism were attacked, the hated customs houses and post office were sacked, and French officials were forced to flee. In some instances – in Hamburg, for example – French troops opened fire on the crowds, killing and wounding dozens.[37] In the departments of the Rhine that had been annexed to France, and in the Grand Duchy of Berg, the first revolts broke out in January 1813; it took French troops two months to suppress them.[38]

Two things are worth noting about these revolts. First, they were the direct consequence of the economic cost of occupation. The Empire had brought heavy burdens of war requisitions and conscription even during the campaign in Russia. In many instances, this had been going on for years. Second, the revolts involved the working and lower-middle classes. The elites, or at least property-owning families, almost invariably sided with the French, out of fear of the lower classes and lawlessness. In other words, the riots were the expression of people's frustration with economic deprivation; there was little or nothing political about them. The obligation to supply Napoleon's armies with men and matériel had been an overwhelming burden the consequences of which would be felt for decades. We have seen how the Grande Armée laid waste to Prussia, but to give two other examples, the town of Nuremberg, with a population of 25,000 people, was obliged to feed and house 350,000 men from August 1813 to June 1814. The town of Erlangen, with a population of 8,000, had to feed and house 34,000 men in 1814.[39] The French were hated because they destroyed livelihoods and reduced countless working- and lower-middle-class lives to poverty.[40] When the French were able to retaliate, however, the local elites always co-operated with them. Reprisals were typically harsh. Special military courts were established in Hamburg. Dozens were arrested, tried and executed on the same day.

If Alexander was determined to pursue Napoleon,[41] this was certainly not the case for either Austria or Prussia. At first, it would appear that Prussia had every intention of staying in the alliance with France. At the end of December 1812, Frederick William wrote to Napoleon to assure him of his 'constant attachment'.[42] He then sent an envoy to Paris in January 1813 to try to come to some agreement with Napoleon in return for his continued loyalty. His demands were quite reasonable under the circumstances: the payment of ninety million francs already owed to Prussia for supplies taken by France, and a few territorial concessions in return for which he would enter into an active alliance against Russia. The alliance was to be sealed with a marriage between a Prussian prince and a Bonaparte. Despite two further alliance proposals made in February 1813, Napoleon's only answer was to continue with requisitions in a manner that was bound to alienate Prussia even further.[43] Moreover, he ordered Eugène to burn any village 'at the least insult', even Berlin if it 'behaved badly'.[44] It may have been a conscious attempt on the part of Napoleon to push Prussia into the arms of Russia, so that he would have an excuse to wage war against the Hohenzollerns, defeat them and finally eliminate the monarchy altogether.[45] He no doubt believed that any future campaign against a Russo-Prussian alliance would be a replay of 1806–7, but given the pyrrhic victory of Eylau this was hubris.

In typical Prussian style, though, at the same time as the Prussians were negotiating with Napoleon, the chancellor, Karl August von Hardenberg, attempted to get Metternich to side with Prussia and Russia against France, and when that did not work to create a central European neutral block that would oblige Napoleon and Alexander to come to terms.[46] Thus, after Napoleon's refusal to negotiate, and against the king's better judgement, Frederick William III issued a proclamation known as *An mein Volk* (To my people) on 17 March 1813, calling on north Germans to rise in a war against Napoleon. It was a patriotic Christian appeal which presented the war against France as both a 'holy war' and a 'people's war'.[47] In nineteenth-century Prussian-German history much was made of this proclamation and the so-called *Erhebung* or uprising against France. As uprisings go, however, it was not much of one, and as proclamations go, Frederick William was playing catch-up. A similar proclamation had been issued by the Prussian assembly of the estates one month previously, on 13 February,[48] after Alexander had crossed the Niemen in pursuit of the remains of the Grande Armée, and more than two months after the Prussian contingent under the command of General Hans David Ludwig von Yorck withdrew and signed a convention with the Russians at Tauroggen (30 December 1812). Yorck's action was at first disowned by Frederick William, fearful of French reprisals.[49] There was a sizeable presence of French troops in the region of Berlin, and some concern that the king might be kidnapped. Frederick William, though, was being overtaken by events: he had already lost control of two-thirds of his army, as well as the provinces of East and West Prussia. Revolution was something he feared even more than Napoleon or the Russians.[50] He had only reluctantly decided to come out publicly against France.

The king's appeal met with a limited popular response: 1,400 men joined the Hanseatic Legion as infantry and another 200 as cavalry in the first days of liberation, often supplying their own equipment, although arms were also eventually supplied by Britain. The numbers increased in the following weeks, so that by April 1813 over 3,600 men had enlisted. Moreover, in what appears to be a German variant of the French National Guard, more than 6,000 men between the ages of eighteen and forty-five joined the Citizens' Militia (*Bürgergarde*), equipped by a re-established Senate in Hamburg. It has to be said, however, that even if the Citizens' Militia represented a break in Hamburg's political culture, it does not seem to have been taken very seriously by the people of Hamburg; few followed training with the dedication that was expected of them.[51] Poorly led, badly trained and badly equipped, they would be no match for regular soldiers once the French returned.

Similar scenes were played out in Berlin, although an appeal to patriotic sentiment was probably unnecessary.[52] Prussian conscription was able to tap into proportionately higher numbers of troops than any other great power – 6 per cent of the population was under arms.[53] (In comparison, the French were conscripting in 1813 about 2.1 per cent of the population, and that was the highest it ever reached for the revolutionary and Napoleonic eras, about the same percentage of men mobilized during the wars of Louis XIV.) The Landwehr units on the other hand were poorly trained and poorly equipped, often lacking in the rudiments of uniforms, shoes and weapons. About 30,000 men volunteered to serve against France, representing about 10 per cent of the overall number of Prussian effectives.[54] Compared to the French *levée en masse* in 1792, this was not a particularly impressive turnout and says a great deal about the structure of Prussian-German society. As for the Free Corps (*Freikorps*) units commanded by Baron Ludwig Adolf Wilhelm von Lützow, they were authorized immediately after the declaration of war by Frederick William in an attempt to recruit young men outside Prussia. By the middle of 1813, they had managed to attract only 3,891, almost half of whom were Prussian.[55]

The sentiments expressed by this small but highly articulate group of men came to define latterday German patriotism. The poet Theodor Körner, for example, whose death in August 1813 and whose writings came to symbolize the patriotism of German middle-class youth, spoke about the 'self-willed heroism of a natural elite, whose sacrifice would inspire God to save the nation'.[56] Certainly, 'patriotism', defined as a love of one's (sometimes adopted) country, was beginning to take hold among people in central Europe at the beginning of the nineteenth century, but it needs to be remembered that the vast majority of troops fighting in the so-called Wars of Liberation were conscripts, among whom few such sentiments could be found. Patriotism as it later came to be defined by nineteenth-century German historians was not to play a decisive role in the coming wars, even if it was present in an incipient form among some of the volunteers.[57] The types of patriotic propaganda that were likely to be most influential were regional rather than national, and the motive inspiring these men was more likely to be revenge or even religion than anything else.[58]

Women also played an important role in mobilizing civil society in Germany for war, encouraging men to enrol, sometimes chastising them for a lack of patriotic fervour, donating time and money to form associations throughout the German-speaking lands, meeting to knit socks and stockings, make shirts and bandages, sewing flags, donating money and jewellery and sometimes publishing patriotic pamphlets, poems and songs.[59] A true measure of 'patriotism' was people's readiness to donate hard cash. In Hamburg, female domestic servants donated over 10,000 marks to help fit out the Hanseatic Legion.[60] In the Austrian Empire, women's associations met to organize war relief and medical care.[61] Metternich's daughter Marie, along with other 'patriots', made dressings for the wounded out of old linen sheets (despite the fact that Austria was still meant to be an ally of France).[62] But there was not the same desire to go to war in Austria in July 1813 as there had been in 1809. On the contrary, despite the general revulsion against Napoleon's conquests, and despite the importance of anti-Napoleonic propaganda, Austrians believed his powers to be so extraordinary that any undertaking against him would be pointless.[63]

This was not the case in Prussia, where there was an intensive propaganda campaign to promote valour and (in a number of pamphlets) 'manly' virtues that encouraged a warlike spirit against France among men and women. The rigours of occupation and the consequent hardships associated with economic decline fuelled the desire to be rid of the French. At the centre of this effort was the notion that to die for the fatherland was the greatest honour.[64] There were also instances of cross-dressing in which women, wearing men's uniforms, would fight alongside men. Some of the more notable examples were Eleonore Prochaska and Anna Lühring who fought with the Lützow Freikorps, even after their gender was discovered.[65] Lühring was the first woman to receive the Iron Cross (even though she was not Prussian).

The Beast of the Apocalypse
It is worth dwelling on the type of imagery used to demonize Napoleon in a bid to galvanize the peoples of Europe.[66] Much of that imagery was religious in nature as were, one could argue, the wars against France.[67] There was a good deal of vitriol, both written and oral, directed against Napoleon by the conquered peoples of Europe, which began to find an outlet in the media of the day only after 1812. It was common enough to portray Napoleon as a blood-thirsty tyrant, 'the enemy of the human race', well before that time.[68] To depict him as 'tyrant' is also to underline the illegitimacy, the evilness, of his reign. It

The Art Archive/Kharbine-Tapabor

Anonymous, *Le petit homme rouge berçant son fils* (The little red man rocking his son), no date but probably 1813–15. A varation on a theme. Instead of the Virgin Mary nursing the infant Jesus, we see a proud devil nursing a baby Napoleon, born in hell. The swaddling is bound with tricolour ribbon, while the devil is holding the Legion of Honour. The caption reads, 'Here is my beloved son, who has given me so much satisfaction,' a quotation from St Mark. Variations of this caricature appeared in Germany in 1813 and 1814.

was the first stage in portraying him as Antichrist. Satan, Lucifer, the Great Horned Serpent or the Devil was an image that flourished not only in most parts of Europe, but as far afield as the United States and Guatemala, regardless of religious affiliations. It appears to have been part of the millenarian movement at the end of the eighteenth century.[69] The description may have had its origins in the innumerable odes, sermons, poems and pamphlets that looked upon the struggle with Napoleon and France as a struggle between good and evil, between the powers of light and darkness.[70]

The onslaught of atheist republican governments against the Catholic Church, in France and abroad, did not do anything to appease the anti-Catholic Francophobia that dominated much of the British pamphlet and broadside literature of the day. On the contrary, there had been a tendency to displace the popular association of the Antichrist with Rome on to republican France.[71] It did not take much of a leap, once this pattern had been established, to project the image of the Antichrist on to Napoleon. One prolific British pamphleteer, Lewis Mayer, counted the number of emperors, popes and heads of state 'alluded to by the horns of St John's first Beast, Rev. 13' and came to the conclusion that there had to date been 665 – Napoleon was the 666th.[72] The British, in short, sought to identify Napoleon, or at least Napoleonic France, with the Beast of the Book of Revelation. All references to 'the angel of the bottomless pit, the king of the locusts, the beast with two horns and the head of the Antichristian powers' were specific biblical allusions to Napoleon. Another millenarian and friend of Samuel Johnson, Hester Lynch Thrale, collected contemporary English anecdotes that led her to conclude the French Revolution had been the harbinger of Napoleon as Antichrist, noting that some women in Wales had told her that his titles added up to 666. Napoleon's conquest of Rome and his arrest of the pope led some British millenarians to conclude that he was the instrument of a Jewish Restoration that would bring on the Christian millennium.[73] Napoleon or 'Boney' was also demonized in popular culture so that nursery rhymes were used to scare children into submission (that continued for a good part of the nineteenth century).

> Baby, baby, naughty baby,
> Hush! you squalling thing, I say;
> Peace this instant! Peace! or maybe
> Bonaparte will pass this way.
>
> Baby, baby, he's a giant,
> Black and tall as Rouen's steeple,
> Sups and dines and lives reliant
> Every day on naughty people.
>
> Baby, baby, if he hears you
> As he gallops past the house,
> Limb from limb at once he'll tear you
> Just as pussy tears a mouse.
>
> And he'll beat you, beat you, beat you,
> And he'll beat you all to pap:
> And he'll eat you, eat you, eat you,
> Gobble you, gobble you, snap! snap! snap![74]

In Russia, Napoleon was referred to in the press during the War of the Third Coalition as 'the son of Satan' or the 'abominable hypocrite'.[75] Alexander called on the Orthodox Church to assist him in the struggle against France.[76] In response the Holy Synod first explained to the faithful the cosmological significance of the struggle against Napoleon: he had taken part in the idolatrous festivals of the French Revolution; he had preached Islam in Egypt; he had restored the Jewish Sanhedrin (a reference to Napoleon calling an assembly of rabbis and Jewish laymen in 1807 to discuss the means of better assimilating Jews); and now he was bent on overthrowing Christianity – with the help of the Jews – and of declaring himself the Messiah. Notable is the Synod's appeal to anti-Semitism in garnering popular support for their campaign. The Synod went on to describe Napoleon as the Antichrist, something that was then accepted by the Russian peasantry as a truism.[77]

In the wake of Tilsit, both the state and the Church were subsequently put in the somewhat difficult position of explaining to the Russian people why the Tsar had signed a treaty with the devil. A rumour doing the rounds in Russian villages claimed that Alexander met Napoleon in the middle of a river in order to wash away his sins.[78] The Synod's initial proclamation condemning Napoleon was banned, as were any sermons based on it, but it had become obvious to those who took scripture a little too literally that if Napoleon was the Antichrist and he had defeated Alexander, then Russia's defeat would usher in the new millennium. Tilsit was interpreted in just that way. The anti-Napoleonic trend in the Russian press continued despite the Treaty of Tilsit and despite Erfurt, so that when war broke out in 1812 Napoleon was already considered the Antichrist by many if not most Russians.[79] The thing that sets the Russian literature apart from its European equivalents is that the Tsar was portrayed as the tool of God, chosen to defeat Napoleon.[80] The more inevitable an invasion came to appear, the more Napoleon was associated with the Antichrist. He was variously referred to in contemporary Russian texts as the 'false Messiah', the 'Gallic Beast' and the 'son of Satan'.[81] (In contrast, and from about 1813 on, Alexander became a divine figure and was closely associated in Russia with the 'divine victory' over Napoleon.)[82] The educated inhabitants of Moscow had a more nuanced view of Napoleon tinged with a mixture of awe and curiosity.[83] The vast majority of Russian peasants, on the other hand, perceived the struggle against Napoleon and the French in religious terms that were deeply rooted in the past.[84]

In Spain, the demonization of Napoleon extended to his family and even to Godoy. Although there does not seem to have been an extensive use of Satanic imagery in that country, there were texts that were reasonably widespread.[85] The Spanish Catechism, published in 1808, associated Napoleon with the devil and considered the French to be heretics.[86] 'Who is the enemy of our happiness? – The Emperor of the French. Who is this man? – A villain, ambitious, the source of all evil and so on.'[87] It is impossible to know what impact this sort of primitive propaganda had on the people of Spain.

Bibliothèque nationale de France

E. T. A. Hoffmann, *Die Exorcisten* (The exorcists), no date but probably late 1813 or early 1814. Napoleon as the devil. In this engraving an Austrian, a Prussian, a Saxon and a Russian soldier (on the left with a knout) help exorcize France, represented by a woman, of Napoleon, portrayed as a little winged devil. An English soldier is taking her pulse. In the background, one can just make out Imperial Grenadiers fleeing, represented as pigs, wearing the traditional bearskin hat.

In Germany, popular engravings portrayed Napoleon as the Devil, or the son of the Devil. The essential characterization of Napoleon, not only among Germans but among other European peoples, was as a tyrant, impious, blood-thirsty, criminal, hypocritical and – possibly what worried Napoleon the most – illegitimate.[88] In 1811, the German poet Ernst Moritz Arndt wrote the following lines in his 'Song of Revenge':

> Denn der Satan is gekommen
> Er hat sich Fleisch und Bein genommen
> Und will der Herr der Erde sein.
> (For Satan has come
> He has taken on flesh and bone
> And wants to be lord of the Earth.)[89]

The Prussian statesman Heinrich Friedrich Karl Freiherr vom Stein ranted about the 'obscene, shameless and dissolute' race that was the French, and declared that Paris should be razed to the ground. Ernst Moritz Arndt confessed, 'I hate all Frenchmen without exception. In the name of God and my people, I teach my son this hatred. I will work all my life towards ensuring that hatred and contempt for this people finds deep roots in German hearts.'[90] Francophobia was rampant in the north of Germany and apparent in the pamphlet literature of the day.[91] Napoleon could not control the negative press in those countries beyond his reach, but even his own subjects considered that his immense appetite and ambition were leading to his destruction. The devastating consequences of his foreign policy in terms of human life undid any positive image Napoleonic propaganda may have created over the previous ten to fifteen years. In the words of Fontaine, 'Blind ambition was his only guide.'[92]

## 'A Policy of Illusion'

About the time the Prussians declared war against France – that is, at the end of March and the beginning of April 1813 – Napoleon was putting the final touches to the new campaign he was about to embark upon. This time, he had set up a Regency Council – the lesson learnt from the Malet affair – to take charge of France in his absence. In order to do so, he had rapidly to bring about a change in the Constitution, pushed through the Senate at the beginning of February, so that a regency under Marie-Louise – aided by a council made up of Cambacérès, Joseph, Louis, Eugène, Murat, Talleyrand and Berthier – could rule if anything were to happen to him.[93] But he also worked long hours trying to put everything in order within the country, preparing his allies and getting the army ready for the campaign ahead.[94] It was a question of reasserting his hold on power before he went off campaigning again, but naming Marie-Louise regent was also a way of flattering Austria, of emphasizing the bond of blood that now existed between the two houses.[95] For a short time he seriously considered having a coronation ceremony for his wife, one that was initially fixed for 3 March and then postponed. The pope put paid to that idea. Napoleon arranged a meeting with him at Fontainebleau in the hope of mending broken bridges.[96] It did not go well. Pius, mentally and physically exhausted, initially signed a provisional agreement that was intended to serve as the basis of a future concordat, but then almost immediately retracted it. An opportunity to placate the Church and Catholics of the Empire had been missed.

Napoleon acted to shore up support at home. All military and civil functionaries were obliged to swear a new oath of loyalty to the King of Rome as heir to the Empire (the ceremony took place on 20 March). Marie-Louise was meant to play a prominent role; Napoleon made a great show of having her by his side in the months after his return and before his departure, attending meetings of the

Council of State and all official functions. She always looked bored, and much like her aunt before her, Marie-Antoinette, was incapable of arousing much affection among the people of Paris. She officially took the title of 'Regent' on 30 March and swore an oath at the Elysée Palace. Marie-Louise was not, at this young age, able to stand up to much older, more experienced men – she was only twenty-two – but she performed her tasks in Napoleon's absence well. However, she could never be anything more than a figurehead, who would ultimately have been subjected to the will of a dominant member of court.

Shortly before Napoleon left for Germany, he had an interview with the Austrian ambassador, Schwarzenberg. Schwarzenberg described Napoleon as someone who was less self-assured than he had been and afraid of losing his position; he even doubted whether he was the same man.[97] During the interview, Napoleon asked the ambassador for a corps of 100,000 men to fight alongside him. If Napoleon had any doubts at this stage about Austria's loyalty, they were not expressed. He simply assumed that Austria would increase its army and co-ordinate its efforts with him. The French ambassador in Vienna transmitted Napoleon's demand on 7 April. The response said to have come from Metternich, if true, is telling. He told the Prussian chancellor, Hardenberg, that the request was proof Napoleon was 'committed to a policy of illusion'.[98] In fact, Napoleon entered the campaign with three illusions: that the Russo-Prussian alliance would disintegrate under a crushing blow; that he would be able to negotiate a separate peace with Russia; and that he could rely on Austria.[99]

The Austrians had not at this stage decided to fight Napoleon, but they had certainly decided to allow the Russian army, now advancing towards the Elbe, free passage into Galicia and Bohemia. There is some reason to believe that given the state of public opinion in Vienna at the time, and the depth of the Austrian people's hatred for Napoleon, it would have been difficult if not impossible for Metternich to side with France. When a rumour did the rounds in Vienna at the beginning of 1813 that Metternich had just signed an alliance with France to commit 300,000 men, it caused a stir the likes of which had not been seen since 1809.[100] Moreover, there were a number of Austrian officers who wanted to force the hand of their royal master in much the same way that the Prussian military had with Frederick William. Archduke John, for one, was working behind the scenes until, at the beginning of March 1813, the leaders of a conspiracy to assassinate Metternich were arrested by the Austrian secret police.[101]

Napoleon finally left Saint-Cloud on 15 April at four in the morning to take charge of the army in the field. There is disagreement about just how effective a fighting force was the Grande Armée of 1813 – one historian asserts that the training of reserve troops was much better in the Russian than in the French army[102] – but it was certainly not the Grande Armée of 1805, let alone that of 1812.[103] What are commonly referred to as the 'Marie-Louise' boys from the class of 1813, 1814 and even 1815 were recognizable, according to General Marmont, by the fact that they were badly trained and lacked complete uniforms.[104] They do not appear to have been able to move as fast as recruits in previous years, as a result of which marches were kept short.[105] Orders were given to spare them so that they marched no more than sixteen kilometres a day.[106] This meant that Napoleon could no longer out-march or vigorously pursue the enemy. Nor were his troops well equipped.[107] By the time he left Paris, though, he had managed to bring together over 200,000 troops, on paper at least, including contingents from the Confederation of the Rhine, and between 450 and 600 cannon.[108] What he lacked, however, was cavalry, which meant that he could not reconnoitre and consequently could not know the enemy's strength or movements with any certainty. At Erfurt ten days after leaving Paris, Napoleon looked worried by these developments.[109] But he did enjoy two slight advantages – unity of command and numerical superiority in troops.

Despite most central European monarchs holding their cards close to their chests, the Confederation of the Rhine was still a precious resource in men, money and matériel. During the Empire, an estimated 80,000 men from the Rhineland served in the French armies.[110] The call-up of men in Germany caused some unrest, and was notable too for the number of desertions.[111] Revolts were put down here and there. The closer the Russians got to the states of the Confederation, the more the loyalty of the German states seemed to waver.[112]

## Lützen and Bautzen
Napoleon took the field in the area of Dresden from where he planned to drive north into Prussia, and relieve the garrison holed up along the Oder and Vistula rivers.[113] On 30 April 1813, he led 120,000 men in the direction of Leipzig where he hoped to confront an allied army under General Wittgenstein. Napoleon arrived two days later to find that Ney was already engaged with Wittgenstein near a farming village called Lützen, twenty kilometres south-west of Leipzig.

The battlefield of Lützen is much as it was 200 years ago. Here, on 2 May, the two armies clashed.[114] It was not a planned battle, but one that developed as each side threw more and more troops into it. Napoleon, on his way to Leipzig, turned back surprised by the amount of cannon fire coming from Lützen, and was able to take control of the situation. He rallied the troops at some risk to his own personal safety,[115] and effectively carried out a flanking movement against the allied commander, Wittgenstein. The French won but were unable to carry through their victory for lack of cavalry. By the end of the day, the losses on both sides were higher than was normal for this kind of battle: around 20,000–22,000 French casualties and between 11,500 and 20,000 for the allies.[116] It was not much of a victory. The allies had learnt a few things over the years and were now much more formidable. Then Napoleon made an operational mistake, the first of many. He split his forces in two, sending 84,000 men north towards Berlin, while keeping the main army under his command.[117]

The allied retreat from the battlefield of Lützen was poorly carried out, but, far worse, the defeat was a heavy blow to morale, already low before the battle,[118] and the Russians and Prussians started throwing recriminations and insults at each other.[119] Things were not much better on the French side. After Lützen, soldiers were just waiting for an opportunity to leave their corps, to get admitted to a hospital or get as far away from any danger as they could. One witness reports that troops were beaten for the slightest misdemeanour, and that even those who fell sick were badly treated.[120] There were complaints too about how badly supplied the army was so that three-quarters of the time men received no meat, which obliged officers to send off marauding parties.[121] Desertion rates mounted as disgust with the army and the war increased. Thousands of soldiers presented with wounds to their hands that were more than suspect.[122] In the ten days following Lützen, with the French pursuing the allies, more than 42,000 French troops deserted.[123]

The allies made a stand at Bautzen, about fifty kilometres east of Dresden, where, over two days on 20–21 May, Napoleon pulled off another pyrrhic victory. On the first day of battle, he enjoyed a slight numerical superiority – around 115,000 men facing 96,000 Russians and Prussians. The next day, however, another 85,000 men under Ney arrived to threaten the allied flank and rear. Under the circumstances, the allies fought remarkably well, but were forced to retreat. Once again figures vary, but the allies suffered 11,000–20,000 casualties compared to around 20,000 French, figures that hide the horror of battle. 'The spectacle I had just witnessed', wrote one survivor, 'made a most painful impression on me.'[124] Napoleon's inability to inflict a crushing blow was in part due to Ney's bungling of affairs.[125] Napoleon realized that an opportunity had been missed. And yet, given the depleted state of the Russian army, if he had had the cavalry to pursue his enemy he might have crushed the Russians and brought the war to an end. Neither the Russian army, which still suffered from the interference of Alexander, nor the Prussian, which had not yet become an effective fighting machine, appeared capable of successfully concluding the war.

*      *      *

One of Napoleon's closest companions in arms, Michel Duroc, was fatally wounded at Bautzen, his stomach ripped open by a cannon ball. Duroc had been with Napoleon since the beginning, in Toulon, and had followed him every step of the way, from Italy to Egypt, through Brumaire to the Tuileries. He was present at every battle, and was one of the few men in Napoleon's entourage who addressed him with the familiar 'tu'. If someone wanted to see Napoleon, they had to go through Duroc. 'He loves me like a dog loves its master,' Napoleon is reported to have once said.[126] Duroc had, however, begun to tire of the constant campaigning and is reported to have confided to Marmont shortly before his death, perhaps foreseeing that the end was close, that Napoleon's desire for battle was insatiable and that they would all be killed as a consequence.[127] Now, dying, he was taken to the nearby house of a German pastor. The Guard was ordered to halt and set up camp.[128] Napoleon spent some time sitting on a stool in front of his tent, his head down and his hands folded. His staff stood a few paces away, watching and waiting in mournful silence.[129] Napoleon went to Duroc that evening; the conversation they supposedly had was reported in the *Moniteur*. It is entirely fabricated. Even though Napoleon was visibly upset – one witness describes Napoleon sobbing[130] – he did not hesitate to use the deathbed scene to render a more humane portrait of himself. One account has Duroc counselling Napoleon to make peace, and then, tiring of him, saying, 'In the name of God, go away and let me die in peace.'[131] When Napoleon returned to his own camp he paced up and down in front of his tent, reflective, sombre.

That night, thousands of fires seemed to light the plain as soldiers bivouacked and prepared what food they had; the moon rose slowly over the horizon; two neighbouring villages were ablaze; men no doubt thought about the bloody day that had just passed. Duroc died in the night.

## The Allies Devise a Plan

Until the battles of Lützen and Bautzen in May 1813, it looked as though the eastern powers were going to fall into the same old patterns that had done them so much harm in previous campaigns. Napoleon was able to fend off the combined Russo-Prussian armies with a number of victories, at least up to June, while the allies were busy arguing among themselves. Despite a façade of unity, there had been intense bickering not only between allied powers but also among individual allied commanders. At the beginning of June, for example, as a result of the drubbing they had received over the preceding weeks, the Russians agreed to an armistice with France – the armistice of Pläswitz – without, however, first consulting with their allies. When the Prussians found out they were furious.[132] The implication was that if Russia could sign an armistice, then it could also sign a separate peace.

On 2 June, Napoleon agreed to the armistice, under some pressure from Caulaincourt and Berthier, at first for thirty-six hours, then two days later for seven weeks (until 20 July). But he almost immediately regretted it. Napoleon's military instincts were right; it was an enormous strategic error, the worst of the campaign, and according to the Emperor himself the 'dumbest decision' of his life. Moreover, he had not realized that the allies were so divided; he could easily have pushed on to the Oder.[133] The armistice gave the allies time to regroup, but then it allowed Napoleon to do so too.[134] The French army was, after all, largely made up of raw recruits who had performed extraordinarily well under the circumstances, but time was needed to gather the stragglers, continue to train them and attempt to strengthen the cavalry.[135] Besides, the suggestion for an armistice came from Austria and Napoleon could ill afford to displease his unwilling ally at this stage. Nevertheless, at that moment he lost the initiative, and he would never again recover it.

This could have been a repeat of the Third Coalition in which a couple of decisive battles – in that instance, Ulm and Austerlitz – undermined the confidence of the commanders, including Francis and Alexander. This time, though, the allies reacted to their tactical military losses in ways they had not done previously: they did not sue for peace, they did not collapse nor fall out. They regrouped in order to fight on. The defeats were now seen for what they were, as setbacks, and not as decisive routs that risked the existence of the Russian and Austrian armies. If Austria lost the war in 1809 it was largely because Archduke Charles was not prepared to risk all for victory. This was no longer the case. Now, there was a determination to carry the war through to the end, a resolve to defeat Napoleon once and for all. It is for this reason that, on the allied side, we now start to hear stories of heroism and feats of bravery in battle that were noticeably absent from previous campaigns.

More importantly, after the battles of Lützen and Bautzen, the allies modified their tactics by deciding not to engage Napoleon, if he could at all be avoided. Instead, they engaged his subordinates where possible.[136] This strategy, referred to as the Trachenberg Plan (sometimes as the Compact of Trachenberg, after the village in Silesia in which it was devised), was decided on at a meeting on 10–12 July 1813 between the Russians, Prussians and Swedes (Sweden entered the war on 7 July) in an atmosphere, according to the official version of the meeting, of 'harmony, confidence and mutual satisfaction'.[137] The atmosphere was anything but. As we shall see, huge disagreements existed among the allies. Nevertheless, the Trachenberg Plan was the eastern powers' first attempt at formulating a common tactical doctrine and it proved to be of tremendous importance.

The architect of the plan has been hotly disputed by historians, particularly in light of its subsequent success, some suggesting that it was Major Carl Friedrich von Toll, others Feldmarschall Josef Wenceslaus Radetzky. It would appear that elements from two different plans were merged. It was, in any event, elegantly simple: wherever Napoleon appeared, the allies would not give battle. Wherever one of his commanders appeared, the allies would attack, and preferably with superior numbers. The aim was to wear down Napoleon, so that he would have to march back and forth against one allied army or another, and then to push him into a corner where they could confront him with overwhelming forces. This would happen, as we shall see, at Leipzig.[138]

## 'Excessive Ambition and Greed'

On 26 June 1813, Metternich was finally able to meet with Napoleon at Dresden where he was staying at the palace of Count Marcolini, grand chamberlain of the King of Saxony. There, he presented Napoleon with the allies' conditions for a preliminary peace.[139] There are only two witnesses to what happened, Metternich and Napoleon, neither terribly reliable. The other accounts we have of this meeting are third hand. In a marathon nine-hour discussion, which saw the Emperor oscillate between rage, harangue and polite conversation, and which at one point saw him accuse Metternich of having accepted a bribe from England,[140] Napoleon rejected the conditions, despite Metternich's insistence that Austria needed and wanted a durable peace. The demands were: the dissolution of the Duchy of Warsaw; the restoration of Prussia to its pre-1806 borders; the return of Illyria to Austria (lost to France after the war of 1809); and the evacuation of the Hanseatic cities and the north of Germany.[141]

The peace conditions were hardly onerous, but having occupied Dresden and Breslau, Napoleon was in a reasonably strong position and found them unacceptable. Most historians have been critical of his decision not to negotiate a settlement. The problem is, even if Napoleon had settled on the conditions presented to him, it is highly unlikely Prussia and Russia would have accepted them; they were now bent on an independent Germany, or at least one not dominated by France. Metternich portrayed Austrian mediation, and his own actions, many years later as a pretext to gain time so that Austria could gather its forces before the final assault.[142] Those assertions should not be taken too seriously. Like any good diplomat, Metternich was more than likely playing both sides to see which would gain Austria the better deal. Austria had far more to gain by procrastinating and appearing to mediate between Napoleon and the allies than in declaring itself either for or against Napoleon.

Napoleon did not trust or believe Metternich. He believed Austria was somehow setting a trap for him. This was not quite the case, but to Metternich's proposals he simply responded, 'Stop lying and tell me what you really want!'[143] He must have had an inkling that Austria was going to go over to the allies. He had been receiving reports from the French ambassador in Vienna, who depicted the mood there as decidedly hostile towards France, both among the people and, especially, in the army.[144] And yet Napoleon does not appear to have taken heed, writing to General Lebrun in Holland that there was nothing to worry about,[145] deluded by what he considered to be the solidity of a marriage alliance, which his father-in-law, and Metternich, now had little time for. Francis was acting as a head of state, not as a doting father, even if he took a good deal of persuading to go over to the allies. The very day after the meeting with Metternich, on 27 June 1813, Austria signed the Treaty of Reichenbach by which it agreed to join the coalition if Napoleon rejected the peace terms offered (above). If France failed to accept peace by 20 July, Metternich warned Napoleon that Austria would join the allies. Metternich, both wary of Napoleon's strategic genius and concerned about what a victorious Russia would mean for Europe, nevertheless kept on trying to come to some sort of arrangement with Napoleon over the coming weeks.[146]

The Reichenbach proposals put to Napoleon were meaningless.[147] The allies were asking Napoleon to withdraw behind the Rhine as the basis for future negotiations, but there was no guarantee that future negotiations would take place. In other words, nothing was said about what Russia and Prussia would do if Napoleon accepted their demands. It is obvious that, given Napoleon's personal identification with the Confederation of the Rhine, any withdrawal from Germany at this stage was impossible. Not only would it be an admission of weakness, but it would also be giving away an enormous strategic advantage by abandoning his German allies, territories the allies would subsequently be able to exploit fully. His response to Austrian peace overtures was almost provocative. He declared 'inalienable' all the territories that France had annexed up to then; this included most of Italy, all of Belgium and Holland, much of western and northern Germany, most of Dalmatia. He constantly boasted of his power and his victories. No one, not even his minister of police, Savary, was allowed to speak to him of France's own need and desire for peace.[148]

And yet Napoleon's situation was becoming more precarious. On 1 July, while in Dresden, he received news of the rout of the French army in Spain. On 21 June, reinforced by troops from Britain, Wellington was able to outmanoeuvre and defeat Jourdan at Vitoria. (Just as Beethoven once dedicated a symphony to Napoleon, he now dedicated one to Wellington – the 'Battle Symphony', often called 'Wellington's Victory'.) To be fair to those generals fighting in Spain, Napoleon had deprived them of some of their best troops, desperately needed to reinforce the newly conscripted armies destined for Germany. He ordered Joseph to hand over the command of the army to Marshal Suchet and to go into retirement behind the Ebro – that is, to hold the north-east of the Peninsula.[149] Even that proved impossible.

※    ※    ※

We can pass over the details of the farce that was the Congress at Prague, the negotiations that took place while the armistice was in operation. No one took the Congress seriously and nothing of any importance came of it. Prussia and Russia sent diplomats of the second order, respectively, Alexander von Humboldt, who was pro-war, and Count Jean Anstett, a relatively unknown French émigré who hated Napoleon. Humboldt whiled away the time working on a translation of Aeschylus' *Agamemnon*; Metternich spent most of his time pining for a woman with whom he was having an affair, Wilhelmina von Sagan, but who took little interest in him, distracted as she was by another lover. Metternich's letters to her remind one of Bonaparte's letters to Josephine during the first Italian campaign.[150] Caulaincourt arrived three weeks late without full powers, with instructions to stall the negotiations for as long as he could, and had informal talks with Metternich.[151] Napoleon was using the Congress to seek a tactical advantage, hoping to prolong the armistice indefinitely, possibly to drive a wedge between the allies.[152] It is obvious, however, that neither Alexander nor Frederick William wanted peace. When, for example, the British representative at Prague, Lord Cathcart, received instructions from the foreign secretary, Lord Castlereagh, to the effect that Britain would be prepared to accept Austrian mediation, Alexander asked him not to inform Metternich. He was worried that peace could be brokered, in which case he would no longer be able to present himself as the saviour of Europe.[153]

Napoleon, on the other hand, was working under the mistaken impression that Austria was bluffing and would not declare war against France. He was intent on trying to outmanoeuvre the allies diplomatically rather than come to some kind of accommodation. It was a foolish thing to risk under the circumstances. When he realized it was a mistake to dither and not accept the conditions the allies were demanding, it was already too late. He sent off a courier at the last minute instructing Caulaincourt to make peace at any price, but the courier did not arrive until two days after the expiry of the armistice.

At the stroke of midnight on the evening of 10 August, Metternich declared to the company gathered at his palace that Austria was at war with France. When Austria's declaration of war was received by Napoleon he wrote to Marie-Louise that her father had 'wanted war out of ambition and disproportionate greed'.[154] This was a bit rich coming from a man who was accused of the same thing by every statesman in Europe. We do not know what Marie-Louise thought about this or whether she was shaken by it. The French people, on the other hand, were kept in the dark. No mention of the declaration of war reached the newspapers, nor was an official announcement made. Napoleon now found against him the largest allied coalition that France had ever had to face. For the first time since the beginning of the revolutionary wars in 1792, not only were all the great powers united against France, but they also had a minimum programme of conditions from which they could negotiate a general peace. This did not automatically ensure an allied victory, or guarantee allied unity, but it made success more likely than at any stage in the last twenty years.

# 22

# The Deliverance of Europe

## 'A Weak, Rotten, Poorly Designed Structure'

The face-off was still roughly equal at this stage but the advantage was swinging towards the allies.[1] On the one side, Napoleon still controlled about 420,000 troops in central Europe (two-thirds of whom were French), 1,284 cannon and about 40,000 cavalry. In addition, another 250,000 troops were tied up in fortresses along the Elbe and in Poland, in northern Italy and in Bavaria. On the other side, now that Austria had entered the war, the allies had about 550,000 troops divided into several armies: 110,000 in the Army of the North, commanded by Bernadotte around the Berlin region; 110,000 in the Army of Silesia commanded by the Prussian general Gebhard von Blücher; an Army of Bohemia made up of Austro-Russian troops about 230,000 strong under the Austrian Field Marshal, Prince Karl Philip von Schwarzenberg, and Barclay. Another 60,000 Russian troops under Bennigsen were in Poland and 30,000 Austrian troops were about to enter Bavaria. The allies had a cavalry of about 60,000 men and 1,380 guns. There were, however, another 350,000 troops in reserve that could be called upon if necessary. The allies, in other words, now had one great advantage – depth of resources. While Napoleon was scraping the barrel to re-establish a respectable army, and could not easily replace the men he lost, the allies were constantly replenishing their ranks and their supplies. That factor was to decide the fate of Napoleon and his Empire.

Austria was the key to Napoleon's defeat. It provided most of the troops, and as a result was consequently able to manoeuvre two key figures into important positions and thereby (largely) shape the campaign to come. They were Schwarzenberg, who became allied commander-in-chief, and his exceptional chief of staff, Feldmarschall Count Radetzky, perhaps two of the most underrated and forgotten personalities in the allied effort to defeat Napoleon. Schwarzenberg was a diplomat capable of harmonizing the conflicting interests of the three eastern European sovereigns (in this respect, he has been likened to General Eisenhower).[2] While Schwarzenberg imposed a semblance of unity on the allied powers, Radetzky dealt with the strategic dispositions.[3]

They both had their jobs cut out for them. The Austrian army had never been immune to political interference and this was the case in 1813. Now, however, Schwarzenberg had not only to contend with the meddling of his own Emperor, Francis I, but also with interference from Alexander I and Frederick William III, all of whom seemed more prepared to listen to their own courtiers and armchair generals than to the advice of the supreme commander in the field.[4] Politics and military affairs were so closely intertwined that it was difficult to distinguish between them. The biggest problem facing Schwarzenberg was Alexander who, at times and in Metternich's words, could be 'silly'; he not only challenged Schwarzenberg's position when he arrived in Prague in August 1813, convinced that he should be in overall charge, but he often issued orders on the battlefield and maintained a correspondence with the Prussian general, Blücher, without the supreme commander's knowledge.[5] Alexander reserved the right to maintain command over the Russian contingents in one of the armies (the Bohemian) and over the reserve troops.[6] Apart from that problem, Russian commanders who received orders that they did not agree with would simply ignore them and issue their own orders.[7] Nor did the nominal command of the armies by Schwarzenberg overcome the bickering that took place between commanders in the field, not only within individual armies, but also between commanders of different nationalities. Blücher's chief of staff, August Neidhardt von Gneisenau, who once wrote that Napoleon could be defeated only by 'war, war and more war', constantly challenged Radetzky's plans.[8] Frederick William III had enormous difficulty reining in some of his more radical officers like Gneisenau, Blücher, who continually disobeyed orders and never saw eye to eye with Gneisenau, and Karl Wilhelm Georg von Grolman, who had led a corps of volunteers against the French in Spain. Alexander's insistence on appointing Peter Wittgenstein to replace Kutuzov, who died suddenly after a brief illness in April 1813,[9] led to a refusal on the part of some Russian army commanders, notably Generals Mikhail Miloradovich and Alexander Tormasov, to follow their new commander-in-chief. Alexander consequently split the army into two, one part under his direct orders and a smaller part under Wittgenstein's.[10] When Wittgenstein resigned after the battles of Lützen and Bautzen in May he was replaced by Barclay, who immediately fell out with Blücher. While Metternich, Frederick William and Alexander eventually attempted to come to some sort of political arrangement with Napoleon, the Prussian military were steeped in and largely motivated by fantasies of revenge that took on the form of a crusade. At Blücher's headquarters, for example, one could find the presence of mystical demagogues and publicists like Ernst Moritz Arndt, Joseph Görres and Friedrich Ludwig Jahn, for whom this was the final battle in the struggle against the Antichrist.[11] The British diplomats at allied headquarters in Germany, Lord Aberdeen, Lord Cathcart and Sir Charles Stewart, did not get on with their Austrian counterparts let alone with each other. Metternich's assistant during these months, Friedrich von Gentz, described the coalition as 'a weak, rotten, poorly designed structure in which hardly two pieces fitted together'.[12] Aberdeen noted on his arrival at allied headquarters in September 1813 that the three allied armies were 'full of mutual discontent and recriminations'.[13]

## Dresden

When Napoleon received news that Blücher was advancing west from Silesia and that a new Russian army under Bennigsen was also advancing towards Silesia, he decided to try and smash Blücher before the arrival of the Russian army. He would have been able to do this on any other occasion, but Blücher, one of the most volatile of the allied commanders who had to fight his own personal demons of depression, venereal disease and alcoholism, was nevertheless disciplined enough to keep to the Trachenberg Plan and avoid contact with Napoleon. At the same time, Schwarzenberg came up through Bohemia, much faster than Napoleon imagined he could, to threaten Dresden where Napoleon had left a corps of about 20,000 men under Gouvion Saint-Cyr. Since Dresden was being threatened, Napoleon decided to break off with Blücher. His initial plan was to march behind the enemy and either destroy it from the rear or at least destroy its supply base. It was a sound plan that, had he been able to carry it through, would have virtually put an end to the allies' war effort in Germany.[14] The assumption was that Gouvion Saint-Cyr could hold out in Dresden for a few days while Napoleon carried out the manoeuvre. However, on 25 August, as Napoleon arrived at Stolpen, some twenty-six kilometres to the east, he was told by Gourgaud and Murat that Saint-Cyr could not possibly hold out unless he was immediately reinforced by Napoleon. Gourgaud and Murat were wrong. Napoleon's first mistake was to listen to them. The second mistake he made was to hole up inside Dresden, rather than staying in the field to attack the allies in the rear.

Napoleon's appearance before Dresden threw the eastern European monarchs into a panic.[15] He again set up headquarters at the Marcolini Palace and even had the actors from the Théâtre-Français come to Dresden so that he could construct a little court around himself. The battle of Dresden pitched about 170,000 allied troops against 120,000 French troops. Some of these, raw conscripts, had marched 190 kilometres in four days – a remarkable feat by any standards – to be on site for the battle, which took place in appalling conditions over two days (26–27 August). We can pass over the details of the battle. It rained so hard that 'no one could make use of their weapons, it was impossible to fire a single shot, as the rain fell without interruption'.[16] The rain turned the countryside into a morass, making it difficult to manoeuvre.

After two days of fighting, Napoleon managed to put the allied army to flight. He was aided in this by Alexander, his own worst enemy, who insisted on getting involved in the battle, ordering troops about without any reference to allied command, wreaking havoc and confusion. It was, nevertheless, a remarkable victory for Napoleon that showed he was still capable of great feats. The French lacked cavalry and were outnumbered. Despite that, for the loss of about 10,000 men (killed and wounded), Napoleon managed to inflict severe casualties on the allies: between 27,000 and 40,000 killed and wounded with another 20,000 (mostly Austrian) troops taken prisoner. The battle could have seen the war brought to an end when the three emperors were almost captured by French troops who had come within metres of their observation post. Schwarzenberg was obliged personally to help fend off the French, sword in hand. On another occasion, General Moreau, who had returned from exile in America to join the Tsar's army as an adviser, was struck in the leg by a cannon ball that went right through the horse, and shattered his other leg. Both legs were amputated and he died a week later. What spooked the allied leaders was that Moreau was only half a horse's length in front of Alexander when he was struck. If Alexander had been hit, the throne would have gone to his brother, Grand Duke Constantine, who did not share Alexander's commitment to defeat Napoleon and who may very well have decided on a dramatic change in policy.[17] Upon such incidents can hinge the fate of empires.

Then, just as Napoleon had achieved victory, he was taken violently ill, vomiting and suffering from a severe case of diarrhoea. He was forced to go back to Dresden where he rested, and by 30 August he had recuperated enough to return. He was not in any position to pursue the retreating allies and perhaps was not aware of the difficult position in which Schwarzenberg now found himself.[18] He ordered Vandamme and Gouvion Saint-Cyr to pursue the retreating enemy; they might have succeeded in inflicting serious damage on the allies, but unexpectedly Napoleon recalled Gouvion Saint-Cyr to Dresden and left Vandamme ill equipped to deal an effective blow. As it turned out, Vandamme was surrounded by a combined allied force and obliged to surrender at Kulm with two-thirds of his army, around 30,000 men (29 and 30 August).

The allied defeat was, in other words, quickly offset by a number of smaller allied victories as they reverted to the Trachenberg Plan.[19] In the two-week period from the middle of August to the beginning of September 1813, the French lost 120,000–150,000 men (killed, wounded, taken prisoner, sick) along with around 200 cannon. And they had nothing to show for it. Their Russian captors, moreover, regularly massacred French prisoners.[20] Napoleon's talents as a general were effectively being stymied, the French were being outmanoeuvred for the first time, and their position in Germany considerably weakened, not strengthened, by continuing to fight. The allies on the other hand had lost around 85,000 men and fifty cannon.[21] But while Napoleon could not readily replace the men he had lost, recruits were pouring into the allied ranks. Within two months of the battle of Dresden, not only had all the allied losses been replaced, but many of the recruits were better trained and better equipped than the French.

Napoleon's communication and supply lines were also being threatened by Cossack and allied cavalry. Even when supply trains were given an escort, there was no guarantee they would get through. On 11 September, for example, a convoy with an escort of 4,000 infantry and 1,500 cavalry was attacked and defeated by an allied force west of Leipzig.[22] Worse, the allies were striking deep into 'French territory'. On the morning of 29 September, Prince Aleksandr Chernyshev attacked Jérôme's capital, Kassel, with five Cossack regiments and six squadrons of regular cavalry. Jérôme, deeply unpopular among the local population, but also no general, decided to flee rather than fight, abandoning his capital.[23] It was a spectacular raid with no apparent strategic value, but it did underline just how vulnerable and tenuous was Napoleon's hold on Germany.

Napoleon was able to hold back the allied advance by showing up on the field wherever his presence was required. But since the allies refused to fight when he appeared, only to do so as soon as he left one field for another, his actions could do no more than delay the inevitable. On 10 October, he took up residence in a moated castle at Bad Düben on the River Mulde, about thirty-three kilometres north-east of Leipzig. It was there that he learnt of the defection of Bavaria. Metternich had reached an agreement with Bavaria through the Treaty of Ried on 8 October.[24] Along with other mid-sized European states, Bavaria had been obliged to provide Napoleon with both men and money, but had always been a reluctant ally whose loyalty was questionable, despite supplying more troops than were actually required, and despite a political elite much more in tune with France than with the eastern powers.[25] The stand-off at Dresden made it clear to a number of German states that Napoleon's strategy in Germany could not work. We do not know how Napoleon reacted to this news. During the few days he was at Bad Düben he dictated almost sixty letters, but was, by all accounts, bored with waiting. A Saxon officer by the name of Major Ernst Otto von Odeleben was able to observe him during this period. He wrote that Napoleon was 'completely at a loose end, seated on a sofa in his room, in front of a large table on which lay a sheet of white paper that he covered with big letters'.[26] The Emperor's inertia was rare enough to deserve mention. Eventually he learnt that various allied armies were converging on his positions from both the north and the south. The obvious decision would have been to strike out quickly at one or the other army, but the Trachenberg Plan put paid to that. Napoleon waited four days before acting. By that time it was too late. What should have been the battle of Castiglione all over again became the battle of Leipzig.

## The Battle of the Nations

Many of the places over which the battle of Leipzig was fought are now obscured by the city, although some of the old road patterns remain, and the fields to the east and south-east of the city are largely still there. At the time, Leipzig, 'redolent of commerce, prosperity, and riches', had about 40,000 inhabitants. Two rivers ran through the city, the Pleisse and the Elster.[27] Despite the Trachenberg Plan, Schwarzenberg was under intense pressure from the Tsar and certain elements within the Prussian military to attack Napoleon. The allies began with a slight numerical advantage – 200,000 troops and 900 cannon compared to 180,000 troops and 700 cannon – and basically had Napoleon pinned down in Leipzig: Blücher was to the north and Schwarzenberg to the south-east. There were, however, another 100,000 fresh allied troops making their way to Leipzig so that Napoleon would quickly lose near-parity after the first day's battle.

During the first day's fighting (16 October), Napoleon took the offensive and managed to inflict serious losses on the allies. The combined losses in men, probably around 60,000 killed and wounded, were the highest suffered in a single day since the beginning of the wars. The fighting stopped when night fell, and the men, exhausted, did their best to bivouac where they were. Often no food and water were provided – they had to fend for themselves – and they made fires with whatever wood they could find (broken musket stocks and wagon wheels). One Hessian soldier noted that in order to cook they had to use water from puddles, since it had rained throughout the day, in which lay the blood of men and horses.[28] Napoleon had committed the bulk of his forces in the hope of breaking through before allied reinforcements arrived. In other words, he had gambled and lost. It meant that he would now have to go on the defensive.

The second day was relatively quiet. Napoleon decided to stay put and rest his troops rather than continue with an offensive, which was in any case no longer possible. The French were almost out of ammunition, and considerable reinforcements on the allied side arrived – over 100,000 in all with hundreds of cannon. Napoleon was aware of this and had already decided on a retreat. However, it appears that he wanted to give the allies a bloody nose before withdrawing in good order. As at Dresden a few weeks earlier, Leipzig offered the possibility of adopting a defensive position while inflicting a defeat on the enemy. Certainly, the odds stacked against Napoleon were far greater this time around, and he could expect no reinforcements, but he was still in a position to exploit allied weaknesses. That day, 17 October, 'The weather was awful and cold rain fell in torrents.'[29]

The inaction, indeed passivity, of Napoleon on the 17th has been remarked upon by a number of historians.[30] He spent the day in his tent, as though in a stupor. That afternoon he had an interview with the Austrian general Maximilian von Merfeldt (sometimes spelt Merveldt), captured the previous day, during which he outlined a peace proposal.[31] In return for the French colonies captured by the British, Napoleon would withdraw from Germany, Holland, Spain and perhaps Italy. Most historians see this for what it was: an attempt to split the allies and to dissolve the coalition through peace overtures. Napoleon still controlled Italy and the Low Countries, however, and there is nothing to indicate that he seriously considered giving them up.

But by the third day of the battle, 18 October, the weather had cleared to reveal between 268,000 and 430,000 allied troops (once again, figures vary enormously), with 1,360 guns formed in a huge semi-circle around Leipzig. On the French side, between 135,000 and 190,000 men were dug in with around 700 guns. In the artillery duel that ensued, more than 95,000 cannon shot were fired on that day alone.[32] Present were men from just about every nationality in Europe. The 'Battle of Nations' as contemporaries dubbed it – the *Völkerschlacht* – was at the time the largest land battle in history. Europe was not to see the likes of it again for another hundred years. Napoleon's troops held on well for the whole day (the battle began at 7 a.m.), until two Saxon brigades, around 3,000 men, as well as about 500 Württemberg cavalry, unexpectedly defected to the allies, a defection that was probably worked out in advance with Bernadotte. The desertion of a few thousand men had no impact on the overall outcome of a battle that involved more than 470,000 troops, although it may have had a greater effect on French morale. Those in close proximity to Napoleon were able to observe 'symptoms of discouragement on his face', although he gave little away.[33] Despite their numerical superiority, the allies could not yet claim a victory.

It was not till the early hours of the morning of 19 October that Napoleon began quietly to pull his troops back into the city, leaving campfires burning in order to fool the allies into thinking they had maintained their positions. As soon as the allies realized what was happening, they attacked. About 30,000 troops under Reynier, Poniatowski and Macdonald held off eight or nine times that number in bitter and vicious street fighting that lasted around six hours, while the rest of the imperial army crossed the only bridge over the Elster River on the road to Erfurt (all the other bridges had been blown before the commencement of the battle). The fighting was so bad in places that the Pleisse River running through Leipzig, admittedly not very wide at this point, was choked with the bodies of dead men and horses, to the point where it is said that men were able to walk across them to get to the other side.[34]

The bulk of the French army managed to get across by about one in the afternoon when the bridge was blown while most of the rearguard was still in the city. Napoleon was apparently taking a nap at Lindenau and was woken by the explosion. This mistake falls on a certain Colonel Montfort who, instead of staying put to oversee the demolition, had gone to Lindenau (not disgracefully fled as soon as allied troops began to appear on the other bank as some historians write) to find out which corps was supposed to be the last across.[35] Montfort was unable to get back quickly enough, with the roads being jammed with troops leaving in the opposite direction. He had left a hapless corporal in charge who, coming under fire from Russian skirmishers drawing near, decided to blow the bridge – he had after all been ordered to do so when the enemy approached – despite the fact that there were still French troops on it.[36] Hundreds managed to swim across, many more drowned, but some 15,000 men were captured as a result. As one recent historian of the wars has pointed out, it is wrong to lay all the blame on a hapless officer (or corporal) when the commander-in-chief did not have the foresight to build extra bridges across the Elster.[37]

It was this, more than any other event, that has led to the battle being depicted as an allied victory, but it was not much of one in retrospect. True, the Grande Armée lost 38,000 dead and wounded, but the allied casualties were about 50 per cent more, around 54,000 men, half of whom were Russian.[38] The figures are telling. Leipzig was the biggest battle of the wars and also one of the bloodiest. Humboldt, who walked over the battlefield the next day, wrote to his sister to say that a large number of dead still lay on the field, many with their arms flung across their faces.[39] It was the first time that Humboldt, a diplomat, had seen the aftermath of battle and, as with most people, it was the little things that stuck in his mind – on this occasion a dog looking for its master, and which could not be coaxed away. The British ambassador to Vienna, Lord Aberdeen, following the Austrian Emperor on campaign, similarly rode over the battlefield and was devastated by what he saw. In a letter to his sister-in-law, he remarked, 'For three or four miles the ground is covered with bodies of men and horses, many not dead. Wretches wounded unable to crawl, crying for water amidst heaps of putrefying bodies. Their screams are heard at an immense distance and still ring in my ears.'[40] The dying and the dead were eventually stripped bare by the local peasantry desperate no doubt for anything that might replace the goods and chattels the troops had taken from them. The following spring, as farmers tilled the fields for the first time since the battle, their ploughs unearthed half-decayed corpses that had been hastily buried in shallow graves during the battle.[41]

The allies pursued Napoleon but failed to catch up with and destroy him. A force of 43,000 men under the Bavarian General Karl von Wrede (the man responsible for taking Bavaria over to Napoleon's enemies) tried to cut Napoleon off in the last days of October at Hanau, not far from Frankfurt, but he was quickly and easily brushed aside.[42] The retreat was, for all that, horrendous. Hudson Lowe, the man who would soon be appointed Napoleon's jailer, served as a liaison officer with the Prussians and was part of the pursuing Army of Silesia. 'For an extent of nearly fifty English miles [eighty kilometres]', he wrote, 'from Eisenach to Fulda the carcasses of dead and dying horses, dead bodies of men who had been shot or perished through hunger, sickness or fatigue, lying on the roads or cast into the ditches, prisoners brought in by Cossacks or light troops, blown-up or destroyed ammunition and baggage wagons in such numbers as absolutely to obstruct the road, sufficiently attested the sufferings of the enemy, whilst pillaged and burning towns and villages marked at the same time the ferocity with which he had conducted himself.'[43] Similarly, Lady Burghersh, who was the wife of a British military commissioner in the Austrian army, was witness to the devastation wrought by the French in retreat. One month after they had passed she reported, 'Every bridge blown up, every village burnt or pulled down, fields completely devastated, orchards all turned up, and we traced their bivouaques all along by every horror you can conceive. None of the country people will bury them or their horses, so there they remain lying all over the fields and roads, with millions of crows feasting – we passed quantities, bones of all kinds, hats, shoes, epaulettes, a surprising quantity of rags and linen – every kind of horror.'[44]

Napoleon tried to hide the defeat by sending twenty enemy flags captured at Leipzig to Paris, as was customary when a victory had been won. The gesture was surrounded in great pomp and ceremony. But this was hardly likely to do either the regime or Napoleon's reputation any good. Leipzig was for Napoleon what Blenheim was for Louis XIV during the War of the Spanish Succession, or what Stalingrad was for the German army on the Eastern Front during the Second World War, a turning point beyond which there could be no victory. No amount of propaganda could hide how widely Leipzig was seen as a personal defeat for Napoleon. It had a huge psychological impact not only on the people of France but also on the statesmen of Europe. When the Prussian reformer Baron vom Stein heard the news of Napoleon's defeat at Leipzig, he wrote to his wife, 'The shame in which he [Napoleon] covered us has been washed away by torrents of French blood.'[45] Hyperbole aside, the sentiment was common enough. Aberdeen wrote to Castlereagh to take the credit for the outcome of the battle on behalf of Englishmen everywhere and declared, 'The deliverance of Europe appears to be at hand.'[46]

The faithful stayed in the ranks, but they were never enough to make up the loss in numbers. On learning of the defeat at Leipzig, an artillery officer in the Guard by the name of Marin, stationed in France, was heard to say, 'I am leaving for the army; I am going to get myself killed for the Emperor.'[47] Captain Burnot, who was in Neuss near Düsseldorf, wrote to his father on 11 November 1813: 'Under the circumstances, and despite what I have suffered during this campaign, nothing could persude me to retire; with all my troubles, and even with a leg missing I can assure you that I will not leave the service. All Frenchmen should do the same. We have to take revenge on those Bavarian and Saxon dogs that are the cause of all our problems and the loss of so many brave men.'[48] It was almost prophetic. Burnot was wounded and had a leg amputated while fighting in France. He died of his wounds on 20 March 1814.

Men like Burnot were increasingly in the minority. Nothing better demonstrates the desperate situation in which Napoleon found himself than the response to a massive call-up he instigated after Leipzig. Between October 1813 and January 1814, he attempted to put more than 930,000 men under arms.[49] Anybody who was reasonably fit and could bear arms – the National Guard, policemen, forest rangers, customs officers, boys under eighteen – was enlisted. The response, however, was less than enthusiastic. As a result of a number of problems, including the short duration of the campaign, the disarray into which the imperial administration seems to have fallen, the lack of supplies and the desertion rates, only one-third of that number answered the call, and of them only about 120,000 actually saw combat.[50] War-weariness is often the reason given for the lack of response in the face of invasion, but we simply do not know how many men actually received the call to arms.[51] Desertion rates were high, between one-third and one-half, and even higher in the German departments.[52] The relative failure of conscription on this occasion seems indicative of the lack of support for both Napoleon and the Empire.[53] There appears to have been a relative indifference to the fate of both. This was not 1792, when the French government was able to garner massive popular support in defence of the Revolution. Another way of looking at things is to say that the Empire was not efficient or ruthless enough to enforce conscription quotas. That does not mean that enthusiasm for Napoleon had hitherto been entirely superficial, but as with every charismatic leader the moment he fails to live up to the reputation he himself has created, support begins to wane.

Given the superiority in allied numbers, Napoleon had performed remarkably well at Leipzig, almost winning the battle on the first day. It is easy enough to argue that it would have been better to withdraw then, before allied reinforcements arrived, but those kinds of judgements can only be reached in hindsight. Napoleon was dispirited, depressed by the turn of events, but it took some time before he could admit to himself that the battle for Germany was over. When he reached Erfurt on 23 October, he still had about 70,000 troops under arms, with another 30,000 stragglers following behind. He could probably muster about 150,000 in all, although he may have lost as many as 100,000 men during and in the days after the battle; considerable numbers of troops belonging to the Confederation deserted between Leipzig and Erfurt.[54] In addition, 325 cannon, 900 ammunition wagons and large quantities of military stores were left behind.[55] Napoleon planned to use Erfurt to refit his men, but these plans came to a crashing halt with the news that Württemberg had defected to the allies. In effect, the battle of Leipzig persuaded those German powers whose loyalty might have been wavering to declare finally for the allies, and caused the rest of the Empire virtually to collapse overnight. In Holland, for example, waves of political agitation shook the country as a direct result of the news of the destruction of Napoleon's army, culminating in a massive riot in Amsterdam (15 November 1813) that saw the governor and former Third Consul Charles-François Lebrun flee and France lose its hold on the country. Authority fell away 'like dead flesh from a skeleton'.[56]

In those circumstances, Napoleon had little choice but to retreat behind the Rhine with the allies hard on his heels.

The coalition faced problems of its own. It had risked falling apart on a number of occasions, but never more so than after victory at Leipzig. Between Leipzig and the Treaty of Chaumont in March 1814, for a period of a little over four months, the allies were divided about their objectives and how to achieve them, sometimes to the point where the whole coalition almost dissolved. They differed over the question of the treatment of the occupied German territories – Alexander refused to stipulate what his territorial claims might be, thus creating friction with Metternich and Austria – and whether or not to push across the Rhine into France.[57] Invasion was a policy favoured by most of the leading allied politicians at this stage: Alexander, Czartoryski and Grand Duchess Catherine on the Russian side, despite opposition from many of the Tsar's ministers and generals;[58] Gneisenau and Blücher among the Prussians; Schwarzenberg among the Austrians. However, Francis I as well as Frederick William III and a number of Austrian and Prussian generals were unwilling at this stage to carry the campaign into France, still wary of Napoleon's military prowess and of the potential for the French people to rise against an invading force.[59] The Prussians in particular had 'little heart for the pursuit'.[60] For these men, there was little to be gained from a prolonged struggle now that Napoleon had been ousted from central Europe. Frederick William appears to have been the staunchest opponent of continuing the war. In the aftermath of Leipzig, allied forces were depleted. The Prussian 1st Regiment of the Foot Guards, for example, had lost a third of its strength since August 1813.[61] A veteran of the battle of Valmy in 1792, having experienced defeat and occupation from 1806 to very recently, the Prussian king could not see the logic of crossing the Rhine and marching on Paris. He much preferred a peace settlement.[62] Bernadotte too opposed the crossing, not wanting to engage French troops on French soil, or to commit his men so far from home.[63] Besides, he was pursuing his own interests, more intent on a campaign against Denmark than against Napoleon.[64] That the coalition did not fall apart is testament to Metternich's perseverance and foresight.

Entwined with the question of whether the allies should push on across the Rhine was that of the future of Napoleon, which presented a complex problem. At the beginning of 1814, the allies, with the possible exception of Alexander, had no intention of overthrowing him.[65] The British did not have his overthrow as a central tenet of their policy; Castlereagh believed that the allies should not 'excite or originate' a change of government.[66] Austria had given the question of France's political future little or no thought. The allies were not about to impose a new regime on France, believing that the French had the right to determine their own government. If the French remained loyal to Napoleon, then it would be difficult for the allies to bring about peace in Europe. What alternative then to Napoleon? There were rumours of Alexander pushing for Bernadotte to assume the throne, possibly influenced by Germaine de Staël and Benjamin Constant, although no one seems to have taken the idea very seriously.[67] When Alexander and Bernadotte met after Leipzig, according to Bernadotte, Alexander urged him to aim for the French throne, but he declined. In any event, Frederick William, Castlereagh and Metternich rejected the suggestion for fear that Bernadotte would become Alexander's puppet. As for a Bourbon restoration, Alexander had little respect for the Comte de Provence (the future Louis XVIII) whom he knew from his time in exile in Russia,[68] and did not believe that he would be able to respect the gains of the Revolution, including representative institutions. He looked for alternatives to the Bourbons, but few were viable.

## Self-Destruction

The War of Liberation was over; the Napoleonic Empire in Germany had ceased to exist. The battle for France was about to begin. Troops jokingly remarked that they had been all the way to Moscow to fetch the Russians to bring them back to France.[69]

On 2 November 1813, Napoleon arrived at Mainz where he set up headquarters. Along the way, he would have seen thousands of stragglers and sometimes small groups of organized men, making their way towards the bridge that could get them across the Rhine and into France at Mainz. Those men no longer looked upon him the way they used to. It was, after all, the second disaster to have befallen him in a year. He was deprived of that infallibility, as a result of which men felt 'more on the same level with him'.[70] Napoleon, on the other hand, was obliged to maintain the same regal façade, even if he came across as 'gloomy and silent' in private; he admitted that the situation was 'unfortunate', but always tried to talk things up.[71] The reality was starker than he was prepared to admit. By the time he reached the Rhine, he had sustained combined losses, through the campaigns of 1812 and 1813, of about 700,000 men.[72] Not all of these were dead or wounded. Many had deserted or gone over to the enemy. On top of the losses in Russia, combined with the drain on manpower that had been Spain, it is evident that any chance now of holding off a combined coalition army was getting bleaker by the day. Only about 40,000–60,000 men remained in any condition to fight, but, worse, troops that could have been used, perhaps as many as 190,000 men, were pointlessly holed up in fortresses across northern Germany. They had little chance of breaking out of the net that was closing around them. Some in Napoleon's inner circle tried to convince him to make peace, but he would have none of it.[73] The fact that most of the member states of the Confederation of the Rhine deserted him that month, with the exception of Saxony, the Grand Duchy of Frankfurt and the principalities of Leyen and Isenburg, seemed to make no difference.

To make matters worse, a typhoid epidemic was raging through Germany, brought in large part by the remnants of the Grande Armée returning from Moscow.[74] The hospitals of Gumbinnen, Insterburg, Königsberg, Marienburg and Thorn were full of the sick and wounded. Between August and October 1813, more than 90,000 sick and wounded soldiers passed through Leipzig. In Leipzig in the final months of 1813, around 700–800 people fell ill every week. In all, around 13,500 people came down with typhus (that was about a third of the population), of whom 2,700 died.[75] At Mainz, between November 1813 and May 1814, some 10 per cent of the city's population succumbed, around 500 people per day, along with around 30,000 troops.[76] 'The streets of Mainz were framed by two rows of men dying of cold, hunger and the terrible typhus, which had just violently broken out and which promptly ravaged the ranks. One can truthfully say that the city was paved with the dead and the dying.'[77] One of Napoleon's chamberlains confirms the impression, later recalling having to walk through the streets to the palace every day, and seeing nothing but corpses.[78] From Mainz, the epidemic spread to the rest of the Rhine departments. In the Moselle, between October 1813 and the following January, 9,000 people died.[79] About 300 soldiers died each day so that in the last two months of 1813 about 15,000 soldiers (and as many civilians again) eventually succumbed.[80] As with the outbreak of the plague in Egypt and Syria, here too it was naively thought that fear was a factor in the contagion.[81] Many troops, exhausted by malnutrition and the hardships of the campaign they had just endured, succumbed in their weakened state.

Napoleon stayed in Mainz until 7 November 1813, while the army rested and was reorganized. He seems to have clung to the hope that the allies would not undertake a winter campaign – not as far fetched an idea as it might seem – and that if he were given six months' respite he would be able to create another army to defend 'the sacred soil', as he referred to France.[82] That may have been true, but it also gave the allies a chance to rest and regroup. And he was mistaken about his enemies' intentions. A winter campaign is exactly what the allies chose to embark on, throwing his plans for a spring offensive into disarray.

Even under these conditions, Napoleon did not negotiate a settlement. In November 1813, Metternich, with the knowledge of Britain and the consent of Russia, sent a captured French diplomat, Caulaincourt's brother-in-law the

Baron de Saint-Aignan, with a suggestion of peace on the basis of the 'natural borders' of France – the Rhine, the Alps and the Pyrenees, the revolutionary borders of Campo Formio and Lunéville.[83] That meant giving up Spain, Holland, Germany and Italy, although he could keep Belgium, the left bank of the Rhine and Savoy. These were known as the Frankfurt Proposals. Metternich insisted that military operations should continue against Napoleon so that he could not use the cover of negotiations to gain time to reorganize the army, but he also made it clear, by a letter sent to Caulaincourt (10 November), that now was the time to make peace with the allies. Once again, it is highly improbable that Metternich, like Alexander, thought anything would come of these proposals, which is in part why they were offered in the first place.[84] They understood Napoleon well enough to know it was impossible to negotiate with him, under any circumstances.

Metternich's reply (25 November) to Napoleon was adamant – peace talks would not begin until Napoleon accepted the Frankfurt Proposals.[85] Metternich indeed seems to have been playing a double game, as he had throughout 1813 and would continue to do throughout 1814, saying one thing to Napoleon, much of which was meant for public consumption, and something else entirely in his private correspondence. Regardless of Metternich's and the allies' intentions, Napoleon obliged them to continue the struggle. It was only then that the allied monarchs issued a common declaration, on 1 December 1813, that they would not lay down their arms until the balance of power on the Continent had been restored. Note, however, they did not swear to fight on until Napoleon was overthrown. At this stage, they still planned to make a place for Napoleon's France in their concept of Europe. Metternich then drafted a proclamation to the French people which declared that the alliance was directed not against France but against French preponderance, read Napoleon.[86] The allies were attempting to separate Napoleon from the nation.[87]

How do we interpret Napoleon's actions during this period? It is true that Napoleon could not be expected to take too seriously what was, after all, no more than an oral approach on the part of Saint-Aignan with a private letter to Caulaincourt.[88] Besides, the Frankfurt Proposals could not be entirely accepted at face value. Offering them was a move worked out between the Austrians and the Russians. Prussia was not involved in the deal and it did not want to agree to give up the left bank permanently – although of course pressure could have been brought to bear to make Prussia concede – but nor was Britain, and its position on the Rhine was intractable.[89] Nevertheless, even more so than at Dresden, it would have been in Napoleon's interests to negotiate a settlement, and yet he did not. What was it that prevented him from doing so?

When Hegel later reflected on Napoleon's rise and fall he decided that the same reasons that had brought Bonaparte to power had led to his demise. 'The entire mass of mediocrity . . . presses on like lead . . . until it has succeeded in bringing down what is high to the same level as itself or even below.'[90] That view of history is a little abstract; we need look no further than Napoleon's character for an explanation. In June 1814, for example, he opened up to Metternich: 'I would die before I ceded one inch of territory. Your sovereigns born on the throne can be beaten twenty times and still return to their capitals. I cannot do that because I am an upstart soldier. My domination will not be able to survive from the day I cease . . . to be feared.'[91] This was about 'legitimacy' – that is, about whether Napoleon possessed the 'necessary qualities' to call himself emperor. It was a constant source of anxiety for him, a theme he reverted to whenever he felt the need to justify his actions.

That Napoleon believed his power was based on his military triumphs is important in understanding why he always claimed that he could not make peace after defeat. For him, every war was about his very existence as a monarch.[92] Nonetheless, despite underlying currents of royalism and Jacobinism, despite the assassination attempts against him and despite occasional rumblings at court, his power was never seriously threatened from within. The domestic difficulties that had endangered political stability under the Directory and other revolutionary regimes had been largely (if not entirely) resolved by Napoleon during the Consulate. His suggestion that somehow his legitimacy, his authority or even his power would be undermined if not destroyed by a reversal of fortune and a contraction of the Empire's territorial limits does not convince. It is only if one understands that military victories and their corollary, defeat, were intimately tied to his prestige and honour that we can begin to understand his thinking. He did not believe, could not bring himself to believe, that he would continue to reign if he gave up territories that had been conquered by the French armies before he came to power.[93] 'What do they want me to do?' he asked of Metternich. 'Do they want me to degrade myself? Never! I shall know how to die; but I shall not yield one handbreadth of soil.'[94] Exaggeration in the heat of the moment, perhaps, but there was certainly the question of how the regime would look if it were to give up huge tracts that had been conquered and integrated into the Empire. Napoleon believed he would not be able to live it down. Yes, the Bonapartes were not the Hohenzollerns or Habsburgs, but if the Emperor of Austria or the King of Prussia could yield swathes of land and still remain in power, then there is no reason to think Napoleon could not have survived. Metternich reasoned with him in this way, but the 'warning of the oracle' does not doom avert.[95]

Figures tell a different story: Napoleon lost six of the twelve campaigns fought between 1805 and 1815: Egypt in 1798–9, Russia in 1812, Germany in 1813, Spain (even if he were not directly involved), France in 1814 and Waterloo in 1815. To put it another way, at the beginning of 1813 he had only lost two campaigns – Egypt and Russia. Even then Egypt was perceived to be a personal victory for Napoleon and, while the country was ultimately lost to the British, he could always convincingly blame his subordinates. Spain, on the other hand, was not yet lost, and the battles in Germany and France had not yet been fought. The retreat from Russia was a terrible blow to his prestige, and possibly to his self-belief although there is little evidence of that. So, in 1813 and again in 1814, he may have felt compelled to behave in an uncompromising fashion, believing that if he gave up any territory it would be further perceived as a loss of prestige. But Napoleon had never really been capable of compromise, at any level. The only way he could face change was if it were forced upon him. Think back to Corsica when it became evident to everyone but Bonaparte that there could be no arrangement with the leader of the Corsican independence movement, Pasquale Paoli. Whether Napoleon's belief had its foundation in political reality is, in any event, beside the point. He was convinced that he had to keep on producing victories in order to justify his existence because he could not overcome his own inner doubts that he was no more than an upstart.

### The Barbarian Invasions

When Napoleon returned from Mainz on 10 November, the atmosphere at the court was glum, and the prevailing mood in Paris one of anxiety as the imminent invasion of France loomed larger.[96] A few days later, there was an attempt to revive flagging morale when a parade was organized through the streets of Paris, with a military band and the Cavalry of the Guard escorting Austrian and Bavarian flags captured at Hanau. They were taken first to the Tuileries, where they were presented to Marie Louise, and then on to the Invalides. Crowds turned out to see the parade, but the mood was lukewarm at best.[97]

Over the coming weeks and months, the regime had not only to prepare people for the inevitable invasion, but also to galvanize public opinion and raise new troops. Napoleon also had to justify the continuation of the war, no mean feat in the face of the reverses suffered since 1809 and his consequent loss of prestige. He did this by presenting himself as the defender of civilization. His proclamation after the battle of Lützen, for example, referred to Russia as the 'home of slavery, barbarism and corruption where man is reduced to the level of the beast'.[98] Depictions of Russians as a barbaric people oppressed by a despotic political regime, enslaved by the Orthodox Church, appeared in newspaper articles, books, pamphlets and songs, and fed into stereotypes that had existed for centuries.[99] One can find, for example, the *Tableau historique des atrocités commises par les Cosaques en France* (Historical Portrait of the Atrocities Committed by the Cossacks in France), which appeared at the beginning of 1814 and which detailed the supposed outrages carried out by the Cossacks.[100] They were described as 'cannibals' and as the 'barbarians of the North'. In one history of the Cossacks, the author asserted that they had 'always mistreated in the most cruel and ferocious manner the inhabitants of enemy countries'.[101] Charles-Louis Lesur published a so-called *History of the Cossacks* that was commissioned by the ministry of foreign affairs as a propaganda piece. In it, one can find a description of the Cossacks around the River Ob, for example, as having 'a small size and an unpleasant figure: their members tattooed like those of the savages of America . . . their filth disgusting, their idolatry superstitious, announce a race sunk in the worst barbarism'.[102]

It was a taste of what the French public was to be exposed to once the allies crossed the Rhine. They did so in the small hours of the morning of 1 January 1814 at Kaub, halfway between Mainz and Koblenz. Alexander delayed the crossing so that it would coincide with the anniversary of the Russian army crossing the Niemen, one year previously to the day, the beginning of what he saw as the liberation of Europe. There was no master plan to speak of, and no decision had been made to seize Paris. The initial goal was to take the Langre plateau, some 350 kilometres to the south-west. Political developments would then decide further military operations.

For some inexplicable reason, Napoleon seems to have ignored what his generals, as well as the head of his intelligence service, were telling him about a planned allied crossing of the Rhine at the end of 1813 and the beginning of 1814, and maintained from his position in Paris that he knew better.[103] He did not arrive at the front until a month after the allies had entered French territory, by which time it was too late to impede their advance effectively. He had tried to direct the war from Paris, but by remaining there he committed exactly the type of error for which he had criticized the Directory while on his first campaign in Italy: when the orders arrived at the front they were already out of date. Then he had the gall to lambaste his generals for not carrying out his orders. Whenever a general got fed up and wrote to Napoleon giving an accurate picture of what was going on – this was what General Victor, for example, did in the middle of January 1814 – Napoleon did not even bother to answer.[104]

It is possible that Napoleon was surprised by the invasion and believed it could be put off by peace negotiations, but that was wishful thinking. The marshals in place retreated and seemed incapable of taking the initiative, for whatever reason, so that the eastern provinces of France were quickly abandoned to the allies. In these circumstances, discipline started to break down and the front began to collapse. One observer remarked on the similarity between the retreat from Moscow, when small isolated groups of men could be seen wandering aimlessly along the roads, and the conditions in Alsace, Lorraine and Franche-Comté, now in enemy hands, as men returned to their homes.[105]

As the allied armies and especially the Prussians and Russians made inroads into France, their depredations were commensurate with the lack of adequate supplies, and their desire for revenge. The list of atrocities committed by allied troops was detailed in reports compiled during the Restoration.[106] Men were tied up and had to watch while their wives and daughters were violated; others were tortured to reveal supposed hidden riches. In the small town of Nogent, in Champagne, a draper was pulled by his limbs by twelve Prussians, who almost tore him apart, before they put him out of his misery with a shot to the head. All of this was grist to the Napoleonic propaganda mill, a way of arousing popular support for the defence of the *patrie*.

It took a number of weeks, but eventually the peasants most afflicted by the pillaging, rape and murder, and in part encouraged by Napoleon's successes (which we will come to shortly), began to revolt. The imperial government had been urging the peasantry to do so since the end of 1813.[107] Now, the small bands of armed peasants that sought revenge for allied excesses behaved in much the same way as Spanish peasants did, with ferocious brutality. Not far from Essoyes, a widow welcomed sixty Cossacks, got them drunk and then set fire to her own house with the Cossacks still inside. A woman servant at Presles killed with a pitchfork two Cossacks sleeping in a barn. Cossacks were massacred by bands of ten, twenty, fifty, three hundred peasants.[108] These were, nevertheless, isolated incidents limited to north-eastern frontiers, and can be contrasted with the Franche-Comté, further south, where the Austrians were warmly greeted, or with Wellington's campaign in south-west France where the population generally welcomed the allies, largely because Wellington kept a tight rein over his troops and did not allow them to pillage and loot. There was not, however, as had been expected by both the allies and the French imperial authorities a general uprising of citizens against the invader. Marshal Mortier complained of the utter apathy that had overtaken the people of Chaumont.[109] In certain parts of the country, sentiment had turned against the regime and was blatantly pro-royalist.[110] This was true of the south and south-west, disaffected by the economic consequences of the Blockade. Moreover, the depredations of their own army, which was living entirely off the land by this stage, created enormous hostility, damaged Napoleon's reputation and inured others to the fate of the regime.

A good deal of the propaganda from the end of 1812 to the beginning of 1814, well before the enemy had arrived on French soil, was directed against the Cossack. Witnesses' accounts were published in the newspapers of the day, and they all more or less followed the same format: as soon as a town or village was occupied by the enemy, whether there was resistance or not, it was pillaged, its inhabitants molested and sometimes murdered and mutilated, the women gang-raped, regardless of age, entire villages burnt to the ground, the farm animals taken and those not wanted killed.[111] The allied sovereigns were witness to these indescribable atrocities, went the accusation, and never lifted a finger to prevent them.

It is impossible to know the extent to which these reports and the long

Anonymous, *Les cosaques en Champagne* (The Cossacks in Champagne), no date, probably 1814. Caricatures of Cossacks were plastered over the walls of Paris depicting them in postures that were meant to frighten – Cossacks with necklaces made of watches and ears for example.

litany of atrocities were exaggerated, but enough evidence suggests that Russian and Prussian troops in particular exacted a cruel revenge on the inhabitants not only of France but also of central Europe.[112] And this is what Napoleon wanted to hear; he insisted that the atrocities committed by the invading allies be detailed in the press in order to rouse a population overwhelmed by war-weariness.[113] As in 1792, Paris was threatened, at least in the press, with the worst reprisals by the Russians. One can read that the Russians had every intention of burning the city to the ground.[114] The impression the imperial authorities wanted to create was that France was reliving the barbarian invasions all over again.[115] The French of 1814 thus became the Gauls of ancient times opposed to the hordes pouring into the country from the east, a comparison made all the easier because of the parallels between Napoleon's Empire and ancient Rome.

Napoleon was fighting a battle for the hearts and minds of his people, but it is impossible to know how far he succeeded. There is some indication that he was still popular in those frontier regions in the north-east that had been invaded, but information for the rest of France is lacking.[116] Rather than withdraw from the public eye in the face of setback or defeat, he made a point of being seen as often as possible. On 20 November 1813, he moved from Saint-Cloud to the Tuileries, where he remained for the next two months, visiting public works at the Louvre, the Palais du Luxembourg, the Hôtel des Postes and the Palais des Archives. He was present at military parades almost every day, or simply milled with soldiers at the Carrousel. When in public, he often distributed gold coins to the crowds, something that he had not done before, almost as though he now needed to buy their admiration.[117] He thus appeared to be a man of the people while at the same time alleviating any concerns about increased conscription in the capital by continuing a public works programme, although this did not stem the tide of unemployment that had gripped the capital. The fact that more than 20,000 artisans were out of work when the war industry needed to be revved up smacks of a lack of organization on the part of the ministry of the interior.[118] Napoleon's personal popularity nevertheless appears still to have been running high. When he went to have a look at some works being carried out by Fontaine at the Tuileries in November, for example, 'a prodigious crowd' surrounded him, pressing in on him from all sides, cheering him.[119] It was a sure sign of anxiety among his supporters who needed reassurance that all would be well.

Napoleon's popularity in Paris contrasts with the apathy with which the people of France were to meet the collapse of the Empire and the threat of invasion in the course of 1813 and 1814.[120] The messages the regime used to stir the hearts and minds of the people of France failed, on the whole, to find a strong resonance. Part of the problem was that the imperial authorities did not appeal to love of *patrie* in an attempt galvanize the people but rather, and somewhat quizzically, to a sense of 'honour', as though they were afraid of reanimating the political fervour of 1793.[121] Although opposition to the regime rarely went beyond verbal satire, at worst verbal abuse, French elite attachment to Napoleon had reached its limits. There were signs of increasing unrest and discontent with the regime. In Paris, the Legislative Corps convened in December 1813 dared insist on peace.[122] Napoleon, beside himself with fury, ordered it dissolved. In Bordeaux, the uprising that Napoleon attempted to instigate in the face of an invading army in 1814 failed to happen.[123] In some regions, there were riots caused by the burden of conscription, even though in most areas it was carried through without too much difficulty.[124]

Napoleon nevertheless prepared for the onslaught as best he could. Before leaving for the front again, he tried to tidy up a few loose ends, although all of his efforts were quite ineffectual. He withdrew from Switzerland and recognized Swiss neutrality. In the vain hope that the English would now have no reason to continue fighting, he released Fernando whom he had held captive since 1807, and attempted to broker a deal that included a secret marriage pact with his niece, the twelve-year-old Zénaïde, Joseph's daughter.[125] He released the pope from Savona in the hope that Eugène and Murat would receive wider support from the Italian population. A commission of five people was established in order to help influence public opinion.[126] Rather than hide the gravity of the disasters, they were now deliberately used to help mobilize the population. Finally, Napoleon attempted to galvanize the French by dispatching senators as extraordinary commissaries, in imitation of the revolutionary representatives-on-mission that had roused the troops and the civilian population during the early days of the revolutionary wars. They were given sweeping powers to accelerate conscription and mobilize local National Guard, but in reality had little impact on the course of events.[127] The idea was good but the choice of men poor; most of the extraordinary commissaries were senators who had no real ability to get down and dirty, so to speak, to spur people into fighting. Besides, unlike the representatives-on-mission during the revolutionary wars, they did not have the guillotine behind them to help motivate local populations.

None of this could overcome what the French lacked most – apart possibly from a will to fight for a man most no longer loved – matériel, especially muskets and artillery. Russia was producing between 500 and 800 cannon per year after 1808.[128] Napoleon had lost over 1,200 artillery pieces in Russia. He was able to make up for that loss in 1813–14 by stripping field pieces from various arsenals, coastal batteries and his allies so that he mustered about 1,300 cannon, but the bigger problem then became ammunition. At Leipzig, he ran out of cannon shot. During the five days leading up to and including the battle of Leipzig, more than 250,000 shot were used.[129] At the beginning of 1814, it was calculated that the army needed 400,000 cannon balls and charges; 100,000 were in store. The same kinds of figures can be given for the production of muskets. During the campaigns of 1812 and 1813, it was estimated that the French lost around 700,000 muskets.[130] They produced about 125,000 muskets a year, but this fell far short of demand, and became more difficult once the armaments factories at Liège and Namur were occupied at the end of 1813. The British, in contrast, were not only supplying their own needs, but had exported over one million muskets to their allies by 1813, more than the total number of muskets produced by the French for the same period.[131] This type of shortage in matériel applied across the board, from saddles, boots and sabres to cartridge pouches, flints and uniforms. In 1812 and 1813 huge quantities of matériel had been lost in Russia and central Europe where they had been stockpiled in various arsenals and fortresses along the Vistula, Oder and Elbe, which had then been seized by the allies. Even money was in short supply and the attempt to raise more by increasing taxes came to naught. The economy was already strained, so people either could not pay or refused to do so.[132]

Napoleon spent ninety-five million francs of his personal fortune to defend the Empire in 1813 and 1814.[133] His failure to defeat the allies was not simply a question of individual battles or even of campaigns, nor was it only about the regime's ability to conscript men. There were systemic failures in the French military and economic systems.

# 23

# The Naked Emperor

## 'I Shall Know How to Die'

Napoleon left for the army on 25 January 1814 at three in the morning.[1] A proclamation issued by the Paris municipal council a few days beforehand appealed to patriotic sentiment. 'Who would not shed his blood to preserve inviolate the honour we hold from our ancestors to keep France within her natural frontiers?' the proclamation asked.[2] Not many it would seem, since desertion was at an all-time high. The reaction in Paris to a foreign invasion was one of dread – 'Everyone is looking at each other as though they were travellers in danger of sinking. Everyone is packing; hiding what he has of value'[3] – but there was little popular support for the regime, something that can in part be explained by the dire economic straits of the working classes of Paris (in particular).[4]

Things at first did not go well for the allies, despite superior numbers[5] – in the north-east Napoleon had about 70,000 troops facing 200,000 allied troops. Battles were fought at Brienne (29 January), where Blücher was forced to withdraw, and La Rothière (1 February), where Napoleon was outnumbered by two to one. Despite knowing of this disparity, Napoleon was nevertheless forced to engage, hoping to hold off the enemy until he could withdraw under cover of darkness. The bad weather – snow fell during the battle, reducing visibility – helped him mask the extent of his weakness as well as obliging the allies to concentrate their attack on the village of La Rothière. It changed hands three times in the course of the battle, until Napoleon decided to withdraw in good order at the end of the day's fighting with the loss of 5,000–6,000 men, less than the number of allied losses (8,000–9,000 men).[6] Nevertheless, the tactical withdrawal at La Rothière was a moral victory for the eastern powers and a blow to Napoleon's own troops. The second battle of the campaign for France had been lost by Napoleon, and troops deserted in droves in the days that followed. 'The Paris road was covered with soldiers of all arms,' wrote one officer, 'especially of the Young Guard. As an excuse to leave the army, they said they were ill or wounded.'[7] The defeat also shocked Paris when news filtered through. It reignited Alexander's desire to march on the capital, to overthrow Napoleon and to replace him with a king of his own choosing.[8] At this stage, the Tsar seriously contemplated withdrawing Russian troops from Schwarzenberg's Army of Bohemia, combining them with Blücher's Army of

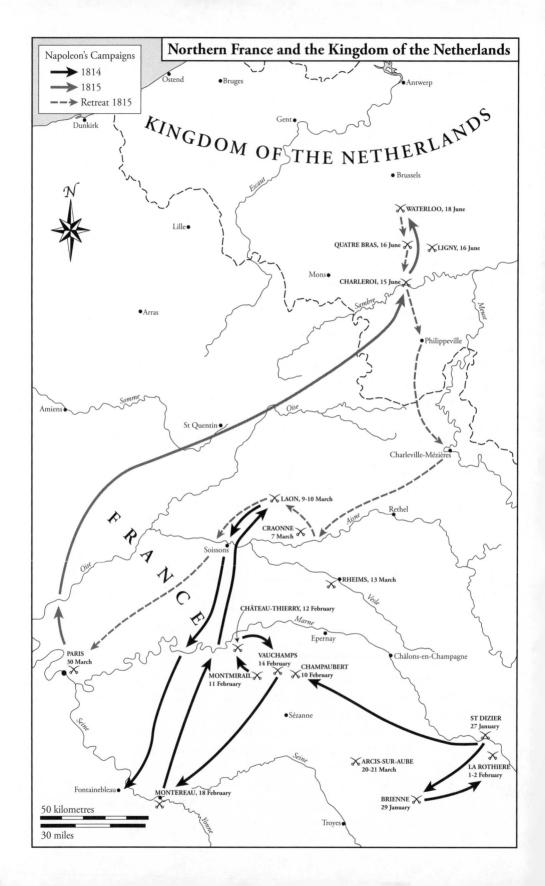

Northern France and the Kingdom of the Netherlands

Napoleon's Campaigns
→ 1814
→ 1815
---→ Retreat 1815

Ostend
Bruges
Antwerp
Gent
Dunkirk

KINGDOM OF THE NETHERLANDS

Brussels

Lille

WATERLOO, 18 June

Mons

QUATRE BRAS, 16 June

LIGNY, 16 June

CHARLEROI, 15 June

Arras

Sambre

Philippeville

Meuse

Somme

Oise

Amiens

St Quentin

Charleville-Mézières

FRANCE

LAON, 9-10 March

Rethel

Soissons

CRAONNE
7 March

Aisne

Oise

RHEIMS, 13 March

Vesle

CHÂTEAU-THIERRY, 12 February

Marne

PARIS
30 March

Epernay

Châlons-en-Champagne

VAUCHAMPS
14 February

MONTMIRAIL
11 February

CHAMPAUBERT
10 February

Seine

Sézanne

ST DIZIER
27 January

ARCIS-SUR-AUBE
20-21 March

Seine

LA ROTHIÈRE
1-2 February

Fontainebleau

MONTEREAU, 18 February

BRIENNE
29 January

50 kilometres

30 miles

Troyes

Yonne

Silesia, where the bulk of Russian troops were anyway, and, together with the Prussians, marching on Paris.[9]

Then news arrived that Murat in Italy had defected to the allies.[10] Incited by the Emperor's own sister, Caroline, Murat betrayed Napoleon by joining the coalition in the hope of saving his own crown, a move Napoleon described as 'without name'.[11] Once again, however, the Emperor's military acumen came to the fore. After Brienne and La Rothière he withdrew to Troyes, where he got a rather sullen reception from the local population, and placed his troops behind the Seine, whence he hoped to muster fresh troops and win a little time before relaunching the offensive. It was while he was at Troyes that he learnt the allies had committed the mistake of splitting their army, with Blücher marching on Châlons and Schwarzenberg on Troyes.

Every battle fought was somehow an opportunity, in Napoleon's mind, for a knockout blow that would end the war. He wrote to Joseph along those lines on 13 February: 'If this operation is successful, we may very well find the whole campaign decided.'[12] It was wishful thinking. His men were mostly raw recruits who had had to live in open country under the rain, who had not eaten properly for days and who were outnumbered by the allies. Even so, he fought and defeated the allies at Champaubert (10 February), Montmirail (11 February), Château-Thierry (12 February) and Vauchamps (14 February), sending the allies into a disorderly retreat. He then turned south and on 17 February attacked an already retreating Schwarzenberg at Nangis and Mormant. It is astonishing under the circumstances just how well Napoleon and his men performed. For the allies, it brought back memories of previous defeats. For Napoleon, it gave him unfounded hope that victory was possible, and made him intractable when the allies offered preliminary peace terms. The outcome of each battle was grossly exaggerated – after Montmirail he wrote Joseph to say that the Army of Silesia was no more.[13] It was hardly the case. Another battle was fought and won against Schwarzenberg at Montereau on 18 February in which the allies lost some 6,000 casualties to the French 2,500. In the space of a week, the Prussian army had lost considerable ground and about 20,000 men.

But this was a different kind of campaign. Napoleon did not have control over its direction, was greatly outnumbered and was sometimes obliged to fight when he did not want to. Even if he had managed to push the allied troops back across the Rhine, as he had hoped, it would only have delayed the inevitable. This was not the first Italian campaign. Napoleon's victories were small affairs that could not decide the outcome of the campaign. Certainly, they deflated Alexander's ego and threw the minor German allies into a panic, even forcing a partial allied withdrawal, but they could not end the war.[14] More importantly, with every victory Napoleon lost men he could ill afford to lose whereas the allies had the vital depth of resources and now the resolve not to admit defeat. After each victory, Napoleon would use the same methods that he had used to celebrate his victories in the past: flags were dispatched to Paris; the regulation thirty cannon salvoes were fired; sometimes prisoners were sent as trophies.

It made little impact. After news of La Rothière had reached Paris, a small panic set in that lasted a good week; people rushed to the banks to get out their money, a great many shops shut, and people started hoarding provisions as if for a siege.[15] Royalists came out of the woodwork and started putting up placards on the walls of towns throughout France either announcing the return of Louis XVIII or issuing proclamations in his name.[16] The general despondency was so obvious that Cambacérès warned Napoleon that the most 'sinister events' would occur if he did not quickly come to the aid of Paris.[17] In the capital, the prefecture of police was receiving up to 1,300 requests a day for passports that would allow their holders to leave the city.[18] Even Letizia, apparently afraid of what would happen if Paris were besieged, asked her daughter-in-law to warn her if ever she decided to leave, so that she could go with her.[19] At the same time, hordes of people from the surrounding countryside were attempting to find refuge in Paris. That is perhaps why, when news of the victories started to come in – this is the bulletin of Champaubert – there was a general sense of relief, not to say of hope. After news of victory at the battle of Château-Thierry on 12 February was announced, a crowd gathered before the Tuileries to acclaim Marie-Louise and the three-year-old King of Rome, who appeared in the uniform of the National Guard.[20] (The previous month, Napoleon had called 900 officers of the National Guard to the Tuileries and entrusted them with the Empress and their son.)[21]

Blücher did not care what his supreme command was doing, or Napoleon for that matter. He was on the march and was heading straight for Paris. Napoleon had to react. He was in Troyes at the time and turned back at the head of the Guard to meet up with troops under Ney and Victor. He finally caught up with Blücher on 7 March at Craonne, about thirty kilometres north-west of Rheims. Once again, despite overwhelming odds – around 85,000 Russian and Prussian troops faced 37,000 French – Napoleon was able to inflict a defeat, although for the loss of about 5,400 men.[22] In terms of the percentages killed and wounded – one in four men involved in the battle – it was one of the bloodiest battles of the campaign.[23] The Prussians blamed the Russian General Wintzingerode for moving too slowly to come to Blücher's assistance, believing that they had missed an opportunity to defeat Napoleon.[24]

Napoleon was obliged to fight them again two days later at Laon, twenty-odd kilometres further north, again against overwhelming odds. Blücher had around 100,000 men and 150 cannon while Napoleon possessed only around

40,000 troops. Napoleon was let down by the lacklustre performance of Marmont, as he had been on a number of occasions during the campaign by his marshals. It was in any event a stroke of good luck for the French Emperor that Blücher fell ill, probably overcome with exhaustion, so that he could not personally direct operations. At the end of the second day's fighting, Napoleon was able to extricate himself and withdraw towards Soissons, but the encounter had cost him another 6,000 casualties (to the allies' 4,000). Soissons was only about a hundred kilometres from Paris. And yet Napoleon fought on. What else could he do? Seeing another chance to defeat the allies at Rheims where they had extended their lines, Napoleon turned east, reaching the outskirts of the town late in the afternoon of 13 March, when darkness had already fallen. He had managed to catch a couple of hours' sleep when the Russians decided on a night attack at around 10 p.m. It was a mistake; Napoleon took the town two hours later with a few thousand allied casualties to 700 French.

The victory went to his head, reinforcing the notion that he was still the man of Austerlitz. He was not, but it was the man of Austerlitz the allies feared. The victory at Rheims, minor as it was, sent them into a tizz and they began to retreat again. This does not mean that Napoleon had a chance of defeating them – on the contrary. When Caulaincourt realized that the allied sovereigns were in a panic, he persuaded Napoleon to accept the 1792 frontiers as terms for negotiations, but his plenipotentiaries were not allowed to pass through the lines. The allies had met at Chaumont, a 'dirty and dull town' about 240 kilometres south-east of Paris, and signed a treaty on 9 March, a twenty-year quadruple alliance, which set out their determination to defeat Napoleon, to return France to its pre-revolutionary borders, to bring about a general peace in Europe and to convene an international congress to discuss any outstanding issues. Castlereagh was crucial in getting the allies to agree to stipulate their common goals.[25] Napoleon's decision to fight on and his refusal to negotiate meant that, some time in the last week of March, the allies resolved to remove him from the throne. There were to be no further negotiations; this was a fight to the finish.

Besides, they did not retreat for long. Schwarzenberg decided to halt and face Napoleon, something that took the Emperor completely by surprise. At Arcis-sur-Aube (20 March), Napoleon again faced far superior forces – about 28,000 French up against 80,000 allied troops – although he was under the mistaken impression that he was dealing only with the allied rearguard. The allies were dispersed around the exposed, low-lying town of Arcis, pounding it with artillery fire. Napoleon threw himself into the thick of it. At one point, he rode his horse over a smoking howitzer shell, which then exploded, disembowelling and killing the horse. 'He disappeared in the dust and smoke. But he got up without a scratch, and mounting a new horse rode off to inspect the positions of the other battalions.'[26] Did he want to impress his troops, to show his men that he was not afraid of death; was he, as one historian has suggested, attempting to place his horse between himself and the explosion; or did he want to end it all? It is, of course, impossible to say.

The first day's fighting petered out when it became dark. The next morning, Napoleon still thought he was fighting the allied rearguard. In fact, Schwarzenberg had fought with only a fraction of the allied army. When Napoleon understood what was before him, there could be no question of continuing the fight; he withdrew during the day, helped by the fact that Schwarzenberg, as cautious as ever, did not attack until three in the afternoon. It is astonishing that the allies did not press home their advantage – a Blücher or a Wellington certainly would have – but such was the quality of allied leadership, and such their fear of Napoleon's military prowess, that an opportunity to end the war there and then was lost. Napoleon retreated with only 12,000 of his men left.

The allies knew what Napoleon was planning to do next. Cossacks had captured a letter from Napoleon to Marie-Louise stating that he intended to draw the allies away from Paris by pushing towards the Marne.[27] The advantage in terms of information gathering and reconnaissance was decidedly in favour of the allies. On 23–24 March, more letters were captured that revealed the poor state of morale of Napoleon's troops, as well as the lack of preparations for a siege in Paris. Most important of all, though, was a letter from Savary to Napoleon declaring that he could not answer for the loyalty of the people of Paris.[28] It coincided with news from Bordeaux, just occupied by Wellington, that the white Bourbon flag had been raised.[29] Castlereagh may have thought this to be 'providential' for the Bourbons,[30] but one should not read too much into this.

As a result of these captured dispatches, as well as other reports, an allied council of war was held on the morning of 24 March. The allies faced two possible courses of action: they could pursue Napoleon or they could march on Paris. It was Alexander who, after consulting with his generals, decided that it would be preferable to ignore Napoleon and to march on Paris as soon as possible, convincing Frederick William and Schwarzenberg in the process (although neither needed too much persuading).[31] It was the sensible thing to do from the allied perspective: supplies were running short after three months' campaigning in Champagne and Napoleon seemed as unyielding as ever. The only means of obtaining a secure peace was through a military solution. Paris thus became the central focus of the allied armies, in the belief that if it fell so too would the regime.

On 28 March, the allied plenipotentiaries who were gathered at Dijon openly drank to the success of the Bourbon cause.[32] The next day, 200,000 troops under Blücher and Schwarzenberg approached Paris, and began their attack on the heights of Belleville and Montmartre at five in the morning.[33]


## 'Everyone Has Lost their Heads'[34]

On a cold, overcast winter's day in March – it was one of the coldest months on record[35] – a mournful line of victims of war wound its way from the Villette towards the Champs-Elysées and the Ecole Militaire.[36] It was made up of the wounded, the sick, prisoners and peasant refugees with their families and whatever they could carry with them. Veterans of the Guard rode by on skinny horses, their white capes covered in mud and blood, their haggard looks revealing what they had just lived through; the wounded were placed on wagons requisitioned for the purpose. The curious came out to see them walk by. Some of the onlookers gave them what little bread and wine they could; some gave money. All the while, the thunder of cannon could be heard in the distance. This was a population used to seeing its soldiers march past in victory parades. It was the first time in living memory that the people of Paris had looked upon a French army in defeat. They were, generally speaking, antagonistic. General Pelleport, wounded in the fighting, wrote that at first no one at Belleville wanted to take care of him but that finally a group of workers from the *faubourg* broke down the door of a hotel to let him in.[37] Colonel Girard, also wounded, was no more successful in getting himself looked after. When his domestics told people that he might succumb, they replied, 'Good' (*Tant mieux*). Nor were the people of Paris happy with Napoleon, whom they blamed for bringing this disaster upon them. 'For the first time,' wrote one British witness who had been a prisoner in France since 1803, 'I heard the people openly dare to venture complaints against the Emperor as the sole cause of the impending calamity.'[38]

Two days previously, on 28 March at 8.30 in the evening, the guns firing on the outskirts of Paris could be heard in the Tuileries Palace where a meeting of the Regency Council was taking place. They had met to decide the fate of the Empire. Everyone, with the exception of Henri Clarke, asserted that Marie-Louise had to stay in the capital and that for her to leave would risk seeing the Empire collapse. It was then that Joseph pulled out two letters he had received from his brother. In the first of these, dated 8 February 1814, Napoleon stated that in the event of his death or the capture of Paris, Marie-Louise and his son should be taken to the Château de Rambouillet, in the Loire Valley, and that under no circumstances should the Empress and his son be allowed to fall into enemy hands.[39] The second letter, dated from Rheims on 16 March, reiterated his desire not to see his wife and son fall into enemy hands. 'I would rather know that he is in the Seine than in the hands of the enemies of France.'[40] Part of the problem here was Napoleon's pride; this was not about protecting his wife and child. They would have been perfectly safe in an occupied city. It was because he could not bear the thought, if ever he were defeated, of having to put himself under the protection of his wife.[41] The letters shook the confidence of the Council, which decided, with some regret, that Napoleon's orders had to be followed and that Marie-Louise should leave for Rambouillet the next day (accompanied by Cambacérès). Talleyrand remarked at the end of the meeting, which finished well after midnight, 'Goodness me, that is to lose a fine game.'[42]

To his credit, Joseph went to the heights of Montmartre the next day to see the fighting for himself, after which he wrote a note to Mortier and Marmont instructing them to negotiate, if they could not hold out. At three or four o'clock in the afternoon, Marmont informed the Russian commander, Barclay, that he was prepared to discuss an armistice.[43] After the two marshals had negotiated with the allies for several hours in a little cabaret just outside the Saint-Denis barrier, they signed the capitulation at two in the morning on 31 March. It was a decision Marmont would spend the rest of his life justifying.[44] During the nineteenth century, the verb *raguser*, a pun on Marmont's title, the Duc de Raguse, became synonymous with betrayal. Napoleon and his followers later needed a scapegoat; Marmont conveniently fitted the bill. In that manner, Napoleon, as we shall see, was always able to argue that he was not defeated but betrayed. It was an idea that was as rife in the France of 1814 as the myth of the 'stab in the back' in Germany at the end of the First World War. The people of Paris were convinced that they had not capitulated, but that Marmont had betrayed them.[45] A similar sentiment was expressed in the towns and villages to the north and east of Paris, such as Craonne, Laon and Soissons. It was a sentiment that pervaded the army as well, and was perpetuated by Napoleon who may have believed it himself.[46] The accusation of betrayal directed at Marmont is, however, excessive.[47] When the 200,000-strong allied army reached the village of Clichy, then a little town not far from Paris, they faced around 38,000 French troops, many of whom were National Guardsmen, ill equipped and ill trained. Under the circumstances, and despite making some mistakes, Marmont and Mortier did remarkably well on 29 March to hold off the allied assaults for as long as they did.[48]

The decision to leave Paris was made against the Empress's better judgement. Marie-Louise had kept in touch with Napoleon by correspondence the whole time he was away, writing to him, for example, on 10 March – it was their child's birthday – to say how much she had been thinking about him.[49] She wrote to her husband immediately after the Regency Council to inform him of the decision. 'I confess that I am quite against the idea, I am sure it will have a terrible effect on the Parisians.'[50] And later that day she wrote again: 'everyone has lost their head, except me, and I hope that in a few days you can tell me that I was right not to want to evacuate the capital.'[51] The next day, the Empress's ladies-in-waiting could be seen through the windows of the palace, running from room to room, some weeping, as they gathered their things.[52]

Marie-Louise set off with her entourage in the evening of 29 March, in about twelve berlines plus a number of baggage wagons that contained the imperial treasury, watched by the people of Paris in the 'most profound silence'.[53] What followed, to paraphrase Marshal Oudinot's wife, was the government, the Empire.[54] They headed for Chartres via Rambouillet, but finally settled on Blois, where they arrived on 2 April. The departure of the court caused a slight panic among some in the Parisian upper classes. The roads to Rouen, Chartres and Dreux were blocked with traffic as the wealthy attempted to get out of the capital and find refuge in quieter country towns.[55] The city itself was relatively calm, if not deserted. Few shops were open, although the Café Tortoni on the Boulevard des Italiens continued to serve ices and punch while French wounded and allied prisoners filed past in front of an indifferent clientele.[56] Those fleeing were joined by Joseph and Jérôme, who had left Paris even before Marmont had officially capitulated, and later by Louis, Letizia and Fesch. Louis was, according to Marie-Louise, 'in such a state of panic . . . and so demented that it was embarrassing'.[57] Hortense received the order to follow Marie-Louise, but before doing so she wrote to her mother to say that she too should flee to Normandy. Josephine wrote to her daughter about how unhappy she was being separated from her children, to the point where she did not care about her own fate. 'I am only worried about you,' she added.[58] She left Malmaison on 29 March with three carriages and travelled about twenty leagues over two days. She reached Navarre in Normandy the next day and was joined by her daughter on the 31st. The trip was 'sad and painful', wrote her chambermaid.

The same morning the capitulation was signed, the 31st, the allies marched into Paris. Not since the days of Joan of Arc had the city fallen to a foreign invader (it would occur twice more, in 1870 and again in 1940). The allied troops marched through Montmartre into the centre of the city and eventually down the Champs-Elysées. It was a stark reminder to the people of Paris that the allies were indeed the stronger of the two forces and that, contrary to Napoleonic propaganda over the past few weeks, they had won the day. It is often said that Frederick William and Alexander (Francis was not there) were greeted by huge enthusiastic crowds, some bearing the white cockades and waving the white flag of the Bourbons, but it was not that clear-cut.[59] The people of the Faubourg Saint-Martin, working class, were sullen (and were later known to harass and even attack small groups of military).[60] As the allies passed through the triumphal arch at Saint-Denis, however, cheers started to be heard. By the time they got to the Tuileries, there was a veritable festival.[61]

That same evening, a conference was held at Talleyrand's house in the rue Saint-Florentin between a number of French politicians and the allied leaders, Alexander, Frederick William and Schwarzenberg (filling in for Francis). They decided to draft a proclamation to the French people announcing that the allies would no longer treat with Napoleon (or any member of his family), that they would respect the integrity of France as it had existed in 1792 and that they would recognize any constitution the French decided to give themselves.[62] The declaration, signed by Alexander and pasted on the walls of Paris, also called on the Senate to elect a provisional government, which it did under Talleyrand's guidance on 1 April. The very next day, the Senate deposed Napoleon and his family.

In the scheme of things, whether Joseph gave up the capital to the allies or held out is neither here nor there; Napoleon's defeat was inevitable. Talleyrand and the Senate played key roles in this. By giving places in the new government to both administrators and the military (especially top-ranking generals and marshals), they made defection all that much easier. If the allies had threatened them with dismissal, there would have been stiff opposition; the French elite would have had nothing to lose. One could paraphrase Louis XIV at the moment of his death in 1715, when he is said to have declared, 'I am going, but the state will always remain.' For Napoleon, however, it was more a case of 'I am going, and so is the imperial regime.'


'Nap the Mighty is – Gone to the Pot!!!'
Napoleon had completely misread the situation, convinced that the allies would never let him out of their sight or allow him to cut off their lines of communication in the rear. He had worked under the impression that a major battle was looming in the days after 24 March.[63] As a consequence, he had lost days in futile marching, exhausting his troops in the process, looking for an enemy that was not there – they were in Paris.

On the night of 27 March news of the allies' march towards Paris started to get back to him. Given the desperate situation in which he now found himself, he decided to push on ahead in the hope of being able to support his commanders in Paris, ordering his army to Troyes, where he arrived in the night of 29 March. Troyes is nevertheless 150 kilometres from Paris, and most of the Guard and the cavalry were still a day behind. Outside Troyes, at the Château de Pouilly, he learnt of the assault on Paris, along with vague rumours of a surrender. He decided to hurry ahead, taking off at a gallop with an escort (the Guard and the rest of the army were to quicken their pace). When his horse gave out beneath him, he climbed into a wicker dogcart (at Villeneuve-l'Archevêque, on the River Vanne), lent to him by a local butcher. At Sens, later in the day, he was able to borrow an open carriage and was at Fontaine-bleau by five that evening.

It was near there, late on the evening of 30 March, that he learnt from General Belliard, leading a group of battle-weary men, that Paris had capitulated. He was at a post-house near Fromenteau-Juvisy (between Essonnes and Villejuif, today the Observatory of Juvisy), and seems to have become disoriented for a short while. He called for his carriage and then, before it could arrive, started down the road towards Paris on foot, 'everyone following sadly after him'.[64] After a while, seeing that his carriage had still not come up, he turned around and went back the way he had come, as though to meet the carriage along the way. Belliard tried to reason with him, although Napoleon seems to have been possessed by the idea of marching on, working himself into a rage as he questioned the hapless Belliard about what had happened in Paris, venting his anger against the minister of war, that incapable Clarke, 'nothing but a head bookkeeper turned vain', and that pig of a brother Joseph. He then turned around again and quickened his pace towards Paris until he came across a column of the Young Guard that had withdrawn from Paris. In the end, he had to face reality, and saw that he really was too far away to make a difference. He kept on walking along the road at a brisk pace for a while, accompanied by Berthier and Caulaincourt, in silence, letting out a deep sigh now and then, intermittently exclaiming, 'Four hours too late, what a mischance!' They walked for over two hours before regaining the post-house, where he went inside, propped his head in his hands and stayed that way for a long time, seemingly lost in thought, sighing heavily and often, exclaiming now and then things like 'Joseph has ruined everything!', or 'All is lost.'

The next day he headed for Fontainebleau where he was to stay for the next three weeks working on plans to renew the fighting, and where some 40,000–60,000 troops had gathered urging him to march on Paris. His response to his powerlessness was to rage at everyone, to cry treason, to concoct schemes to join one army or another in order to fight on. He constantly harped on about how he had been betrayed, 'fourteen times a day', by Talleyrand, by Marmont, by Joseph.[65] On 3 April, after reviewing in the courtyard of Fontainebleau units of the Guard, who shouted, 'To Paris! To Paris!', he came away convinced that he could still march on his former capital. General Boulart and General François Antoine Lallemand passed around a petition asking the Emperor to march on Paris. The common soldier, it seems, was all in favour.[66] Napoleon spent the afternoon with Berthier working on plans to do so, seemingly unaware of or at least not paying attention to those in his entourage who took their leave, one by one, invoking one pretext or another. What Berthier was thinking is impossible to know. Perhaps he too, wrapped up in Napoleon's own delusions, believed that the Emperor could pull it off, or he simply obeyed out of loyalty, out of habit.

The senior military commanders in Napoleon's entourage – Ney, Macdonald, Lefebvre, Oudinot – had other ideas. They met together and then informed him on 4 April that they would no longer continue to fight. Lefebvre told Napoleon that his conscript troops were in no condition to do so, and in any event they wanted peace. It was they who persuaded him to abdicate in favour of his son. Reports vary as to the intensity of the discussions: violent according to some, calm according to others.[67] They were thinking of themselves, yes, but it was also a realistic assessment of the military situation and showed that they felt a certain responsibility towards the general wellbeing of the people. That day, the 4th, Napoleon issued a declaration stating that, in accordance with the oath he had sworn and for the good of the *patrie*, he was prepared to vacate the throne in favour of his son and the regency, and that he was even prepared to leave France.[68] The declaration was taken to Paris by a delegation that comprised Caulaincourt, Ney and Macdonald. In Paris, Alexander demanded an unconditional abdication. The delegation returned to Fontainebleau, and in a moment of defiance Napoleon appealed to his comrades in arms and said, 'Let's march tomorrow and beat them.' It was only in the face of their stony silence that he agreed to draft an act of abdication.[69] After some hesitation, he somewhat petulantly scribbled his name on the act.

It is evident from his contradictory behaviour and language during this period that he did not really know what to do or what he wanted. It is possible he was hoping or expecting the allies to reject the idea of a regency and thus, in his mind at least, oblige his generals to fight on. This is why he held a meeting the next morning to work on plans to march on Paris, again, if the abdication was rejected. It is also possible that Napoleon was, as he had been throughout the campaign for France, playing for time, and using this as a respite while he gathered his forces for another battle. 'The desire to exalt France's renown and prosperity always came into conflict with his best intentions and most peaceful resolve, and he was forever hoping to escape from the necessity of submitting to a peace that ran counter to his lifelong dreams.'[70] In any event, the idea of a regency was illusory, especially after the capitulation of Marmont left Napoleon's military situation untenable. There were too many people working against it; the fact that Napoleon seems to have been blissfully unaware of just how many people wanted him definitively dethroned is an indication of how out of touch with the political reality he was.

*       *       *

As a result of the Treaty of Fontainebleau, which the abdication and the agreement regulating his fate was called, Napoleon was formally granted sovereignty over the island of Elba, off the Tuscan coast, with a pension of six million francs, and he was allowed to keep the title of emperor, despite the fact that Louis XVIII was restored to the French throne. Alexander, it has to be pointed out, made the offer of Elba to Napoleon without consulting his allies (as was his wont). He may have done so to demonstrate to the rest of Europe how generous he was in victory.[71] Talleyrand, in the name of the French provisional government, supported the offer because he was more concerned at this stage with getting Napoleon away from his troops at Fontainebleau and avoiding a possible civil war.[72] The other allied powers, holed up at Dijon, were left out in the cold during these negotiations. So when Metternich, Hardenberg and Castlereagh arrived in Paris on 10 April to find that Alexander had given Elba to Napoleon, they were furious.[73] There was much that could go wrong: Elba's proximity to the Italian shores, the (perceived) popularity of Napoleon in Italy, the popularity of Eugène in Italy and the unpredictability of Murat all made Elba a curious choice. Francis and Metternich objected; Elba was now within Austrian territory. Castlereagh also thought the choice of Elba a poor one and at first refused to sign, but eventually had to waive any objections because Alexander had given his word. When the British cabinet found out about Elba, it was less than impressed. Sir Charles Stewart, envoy extraordinary to the Prussian court, wrote to Lord Bathurst, secretary of state for war and the colonies under Lord Liverpool, to say that 'Very considerable apprehension has arisen . . . as to the mischief and ultimate danger that may accrue.'[74] Some among the English public were calling for blood, arguing that Napoleon should have been either killed in action or put on trial for the murder of the Duc d'Enghien, among others.[75] Other English pamphleteers were urging life imprisonment for the Emperor.[76] No one, in short, was happy with the decision, including Napoleon who at one stage was thinking of asylum in England. Later, in a last face-saving exercise, he would make out that Elba had been his own choice, as though it were somehow a victory carried off by Caulaincourt, with the complicity of Alexander.[77] It was the impression he was trying to create before even setting foot on the island, trying to offset any ideas that he was a prisoner.[78]

When Napoleon's abdication was made public, the reactions were mixed. In the army, among the rank and file, it was one of incredulity. When Marmont's troops realized that their marshal's lack of activity had left Paris open to the enemy and forced Napoleon's abdication, they were furious. A colonel by the name of Ordener refused to carry out his orders and yelled, 'Vive l'Empereur!', a cry that, if he is to be believed, was repeated by the rest of the troops for three hours. This is no doubt an exaggeration, but it did take some time for the generals in Marmont's army to persuade their men not to go to Fontainebleau. It is evident that those in the army still loyal to Napoleon had difficulty resigning themselves to the fact that he had abdicated. At Briare, officers learnt of his abdication in the newspapers, which they tore up in public saying they had been duped.[79] In Versailles, on the morning of 6 April, officers ran through the ranks shouting they had been 'betrayed'.[80] When Jean-Baptiste Barrès and his fellow officers heard the news in Germany, nearly everyone 'shed tears of rage and pain'.[81]

It was a different matter among the highest-ranking officers, and those with royalist sympathies. General Kellermann was one of Napoleon's severest critics.[82] 'A blind man who had recovered his sight would not feel a sweeter sensation,' wrote the artillery colonel Antoine-Augustin-Flavien Pion des Loches. 'I touched myself to make sure it was really me, having survived the battlefields, the snows of Russia.'[83] Even some in Napoleon's entourage, like General Sorbier, were happy to see his fall. 'And this is where that b[ugger] has led us after twenty years of revolution and no one will take a pot shot at him.'[84] These sentiments were shared by a great number of general officers, if Pion des Loches is to be believed. Fontaine remarked that 'those closest to him, those obligated to him, his trusted servants, almost all of them abandoned him as pillagers and as ingrates'. 'I should have expected it,' Napoleon is supposed to have said.[85] It perhaps says as much about him as it does about the men he surrounded himself with.

Among the people, there seems to have been a general sense of relief that the war was at an end and that peace was finally upon them. In the south of France, the French had welcomed the arrival of the British under Wellington. At Toulouse, where the last battle of the war had been fought, the British were offered a banquet by the town.[86] Royalists of course celebrated the return of the monarchy. Volney, the same man who had once been kicked in the stomach by Napoleon, wrote to a friend to say that it was 'a dream for us to find liberty again, I should say civilization, at the hands of foreigners who had been carefully portrayed as ogres'.[87] Once the allies arrived in Paris, and within a very short time, it was as though Napoleon had never lived. He was spoken of as if he had existed in the fourteenth century.[88]

When news of Napoleon's abdication and the end of the war was heard, it was greeted with joy and celebrations throughout Europe. No more so than in Britain where the public celebrated what to all appearances was Napoleon's final defeat. At Yarmouth, 8,000 people feasted at a table more than a kilometre long.[89] Thomas Carlyle, writing to his friend Robert Mitchell, declared that Napoleon had 'gone to the pot'.[90] Only a few months previously, wrote Carlyle, he had been trampling on 'thrones and sceptres, and kings and priests and principalities and powers, and carried ruin and havoc and blood and fire, from Gibraltar to Archangel'.

### 'Napoleon is Always Napoleon'

When Caulaincourt and Macdonald returned from Paris on 2 April to Fontainebleau, they found the place almost empty. A few faithful remained to serve the Emperor, as did some in the imperial household and a few domestics, but many had deserted him. General Pelet remarked that the place was so mournful it seemed as though Napoleon had already been buried. Napoleon's greatest fear during these days was that he would be killed by an angry mob. 'His misgivings on that score', wrote Caulaincourt, 'outran anything that I could imagine.'[91] Napoleon rambled about other great men in history who had taken their lives rather than live in humiliating circumstances, but in this as in all things during this period he appears to have been equivocal. In one breath he could talk about suicide and in the next about how he was 'condemned' to live. 'They say a living gudgeon is better than a dead Emperor.'[92] Given his state of mind, those close to him feared that he might attempt to take his own life.

In the night of 12–13 April, a few hours after going to bed, after a fitful sleep, he got up, placed some poison in a glass of water – a mixture of opium, white hellebore and belladonna that he had been carrying around for the past two years – and drank from it. By now, though, the mixture had lost its potency, or was too weak to take effect, and did nothing more than make him sick. He went back to bed, but when his valet saw that he was restless and showing signs of nausea, he fetched Caulaincourt, who sat by him listening to his gloomy views of the world and his fear that he would never reach Elba alive.

It finally dawned on Caulaincourt, as he watched his imperial master writhe, what had happened. He then called for Dr Yvan. Yvan had been with Bonaparte since Italy; it was he who had seen to Napoleon's wound at Regensburg; he had lived in the Emperor's intimate circle from the very beginning. When Yvan arrived, and Napoleon called out to him to give him a draught so that he could put an end to his suffering, Yvan refused and made him vomit. Once the Emperor was out of danger, Yvan rushed out of the room, found a horse and rode out into the night to Paris, afraid perhaps that he would be implicated in the suicide, since it was he who had given Napoleon the poison in Russia.[93] After vomiting it all back up, Napoleon remained in his apartment, eventually coming around at daybreak, when he began ranting again to the unfortunate Caulaincourt about how he had been mistreated by the sovereigns of Europe, flitting from one subject to another as the morning waxed, about how he would lead a quiet life on Elba, how Louis XVIII would have no need to change anything other than the sheets on his bed, so well run and organized was the administration.

There were a few witnesses to this scene, enough for us to conclude that there was indeed a suicide attempt. Caulaincourt believed that Napoleon had attempted to take his own life because of the humiliation he felt; his honour had been questioned so his life had become unbearable. On Elba, Napoleon denied it. 'What, kill myself? Had I nothing better to do than this – like a miserable bankrupt, who, because he has lost his goods, determines to lose his life? Napoleon is always Napoleon, and always will know how to be content and bear any fortune.'[94] There was of course a certain amount of shame involved not so much in killing oneself as in failing to do so, which is why he would want to deny it.[95] Napoleon's attempt perhaps places him within Mme de Staël's category of the 'repentant criminal', someone who takes his own life in order to redeem himself, out of remorse, as a kind of apology. One may doubt that Napoleon did it for anything other than self-pity, hence the denial. He had forgotten his own injunction, 'that a soldier should know how to conquer pain and the melancholy of passions', that there was as much 'courage in suffering with constance the sorrows of the heart' as there was in standing steady before a battery of cannon. There was part of him that did not want to admit that he was weak (in his own estimation, that is), and that he could have contemplated killing himself. Some historians have since questioned whether in fact he had attempted suicide, but the witnesses all agree that he swallowed a potion that night.[6] In any event, by morning he had come around; it had become obvious that he was not going to die. 'I shall live', he declared, 'since death is no more willing to take me on my bed than on the battlefield.' If death had been given a bit of a helping hand, it might have been able to carry out its job.

## The Struggle for Marie-Louise

Part of the background to his deepening depression was the struggle over Marie-Louise, who was still in Blois. When she learnt that Napoleon had abdicated (Colonel Galbois had been sent to Blois with a letter from Napoleon announcing this), it came as a shock: in her naivety she was unable to believe that the allies would want to overthrow her husband, convinced as she was that her father would never tolerate it.[97] At the time, she reacted like a loyal wife, mother and queen; she wanted to set out immediately to join him at Fontainebleau.[98] When, however, she attempted to leave, on the morning of 9 April, her escape was stymied by her lady-in-waiting, the Duchesse de Montebello, who was able to dissuade her from carrying through her plan (the Duchesse was afraid of ending up on Elba).[99]

Two things had happened the previous day that made her open to persuasion. The first was that she had had to cope with the Bonaparte brothers. When Joseph learnt of Napoleon's abdication, he was deeply afflicted by the news, while Jérôme exploded in anger.[100] Then, when they realized that Marie-Louise might leave they burst into her apartments in travelling clothes on the morning of Good Friday (8 April), told her that the Russian army was close (which was a lie) and that they all had to depart at once.[101] There ensued a shouting match between the two deposed kings, Joseph and Jérôme, and Marie-Louise; the Empress's guard refused to allow her to leave.[102] The second thing that happened was the arrival of the Tsar's aide-de-camp, General Count Shuvalov, and the Baron de Saint-Aignan, the representative of the provisional government. Shuvalov's mission was to escort her to Rambouillet, where her father was to meet her.[103] Halfway along the road to Fontainebleau was Orleans; she naively thought that she could travel on to her husband from there. In any event, the allies and the provisional French government were not yet acting in concert. The provisional French government decided that it had to prevent the imperial couple from meeting up by all possible means. It did not want Napoleon placing himself under the protection of the House of Habsburg, a wish it shared with Napoleon himself.[104] Marie-Louise wrote to her husband on 8 April to say that she was leaving the next day for Orleans, and that she would be in Fontainebleau the day after.[105] Two days later she wrote to say that she had decided to see her father first, and that she believed it her duty to do so, in the interests of Napoleon and her son.[106]

Her departure from Blois (for Orleans) on 9 April in the company of Shuvalov led to a veritable exodus from her entourage. Her decision not to join her husband in exile once led historians to judge her as having a weak, irresolute character.[107] This is undeserved; one has to take into consideration Napoleon's own vacillation on the subject. Shortly before leaving Blois, Marie-Louise wrote to Napoleon at Fontainebleau to say, 'I am awaiting orders from you, and I do beseech you to let me come.'[108] The lack of decisiveness can be seen in a letter he wrote to an exhausted, sickly Marie-Louise at Orleans.[109] His letters during this period show a mind in torment, about his own future and the future of his son. It is easy to conclude from them that he was convinced even at this late stage that Marie-Louise would accompany him to Elba, but anecdotal evidence suggests that he was more than hesitant about obliging her to live in exile.[110] We know that Francis delayed his entrance into Paris so that it did not coincide with the fall of his daughter from the throne.[111] It is likely that, as a result of Napoleon's letters, Marie-Louise now saw her father as her only means of protection.[112] She wrote to Francis on 10 April (twice) to say that she was not going to join Napoleon.[113] It was becoming clear in her letters that she had been swayed by the Austrian lobby, so to speak, and Metternich's assurances that she and her son would have an independent existence.[114] She was apparently turning her back on her husband and putting herself under the protection of her father, but then nothing in the official letters to Napoleon can be taken at face value; they were being read by those who now controlled her movements.

We get a better insight into the workings of her mind from a note to Napoleon scribbled on the way from Orleans to Rambouillet and which was delivered by a Polish officer in her confidence. In it, she exhorts, 'Be on your guard . . . we are being played, I am in mortal anxiety for you, but I will have courage on seeing my father and I will tell him I want absolutely to join you.'[115] But Marie-Louise was a young woman of twenty-two who was torn between loyalty to her husband, ensuring a future for her son, and loyalty to her father. That same day, pressured by the Austrian envoys sent by her father, she left for Rambouillet. 'I thought that I should concede with good grace,' she wrote to her husband, 'but when I have seen him [Francis], I will come and join you; one would have to be barbaric to try and stop me.'[116]

When she arrived at Rambouillet, her father was not yet there. Metternich was trying to draw her even further away from Fontainebleau by persuading her to join her father at Trianon in Versailles where he had decided to set up house while in Paris. She was convinced that they were doing all of that to get her to come to Austria, but she still insisted in her letters to Napoleon that she was going to join him.[117] She used a sore throat as a pretext not to leave Rambouillet, so that Francis and Metternich were obliged to travel to her. We do not know what was said between Francis and his daughter, in the presence of Metternich, when he arrived in there on 14 April, but they persuaded her to leave for Austria.[118] She apparently fell back into the role of the dutiful daughter. It was an easier role than that of an independent, strong-willed woman.[119] She no longer had to think; she simply had to obey, what she had really wanted all along. She wrote to Napoleon to tell him that she was going back to Vienna, 'because my father desires it so strongly, and I see that if I do not go, they will take me by force'. Her plan, she explained, was to travel to Parma during the international congress that was convened in Vienna to discuss the make-up of Europe, and from there to Elba.[120] According to the letter, her father was opposed to the plan, which means she had discussed it with him, but that for the moment she did not want to insist, 'so I beg you not to tell anyone, because that would spoil everything'. 'He has been very good to me,' she wrote of her father, 'but it has not eased the terrible shock he gave me, preventing me from joining you, from seeing you, from travelling with you.' She concluded, 'It is impossible for me to be happy without you.'

## The Long Goodbye

Colonel Sir Neil Campbell, who had fought with Wellington in the Peninsula, and had been at the battle of Bautzen, arrived at Fontainebleau on 16 April ready to escort Napoleon to the south, only to find that the Prussians had already made all the arrangements. The other three allied commissioners who were to accompany Napoleon on the road to Elba were already there: the Russian Count Shuvalov, the Prussian Count Truchsess-Waldburg and the Austrian General Baron Franz Köller. Campbell had his first audience with

Napoleon the next morning, 17 April, after mass. Campbell's left eye was covered in a bandage and his arm was in a sling from wounds received at La-Fère-Champenoise on 26 March, when a party of Cossacks mistook him for a Frenchman. Campbell, who spoke French well, arrived only a few days after the attempted suicide. The meeting must have been a strange one. Napoleon, unshaven, uncombed, with particles of snuff scattered on his upper lip and breast, was 'in the most perturbed and distressed state of mind'. 'I saw before me', wrote Campbell of their first encounter, 'a short active-looking man, who was rapidly pacing the length of his apartment, like some wild animal in his cell.'[121] When he spoke of being separated from his wife and child, 'the tears actually ran down his cheeks. He continued to talk in a wild and excited style, being at times greatly affected.'[122] The Austrian representative, Baron Köller, observed Napoleon unnoticed, while at mass in the palace chapel. The Emperor sometimes rubbed 'his forehead with his hands, then stuffing part of his fingers into his mouth', gnawed 'the ends of them in the most agitated and excited manner'.[123] Over the coming days, he would alternate between these moments of extreme distress and utter calm.

His departure was planned for the morning of 20 April. Napoleon wrote a letter that morning telling Marie-Louise that he intended leaving, and he told Berthier to inform the commissioners that he would indeed be setting off that day. At ten o'clock, however, he informed Köller that he had changed his mind and that he would not be leaving for Elba after all. He insisted that, since the allies had refused to let his wife follow him, they had broken their undertakings; then, vaguely threatening to raise a new army, he repeated that he might seek refuge in England.[124] Köller and the other commissioners were obliged to argue with him for two hours. In the end he was persuaded to leave; what choice did he have?

According to most accounts, Napoleon descended the grand horseshoe staircase in the château's Courtyard of the White Horse, where the Old Guard were waiting in order of battle. The courtyard was also filled with onlookers from the town and the surrounding areas. Maret, whose account of this scene is probably the most accurate, asserts that he came down the stairs 'in an attitude as assured as if he were ascending the steps to the throne'.[125] He then addressed the troops in a farewell that is one of the high points of the legend. 'Officers and soldiers of the Guard, I bid you farewell. I have sacrificed all my rights, and am ready to sacrifice myself, for all my life has been devoted to the happiness and glory of France.'[126] Rather than risk civil war, he had committed the ultimate sacrifice, for the good of France of course. He could not kiss them all goodbye, he said, but he would kiss their general (Charles Lefebvre-Desnouettes), which he then proceeded to do. Next, in a somewhat melodramatic gesture, even for the time, he kissed the Guard's standard three times, and covered his face with it for almost a minute. Raising his left hand he spoke out, 'Farewell, my old companions! My good wishes will always be with you! Keep me in your memories!'[127] – or something to that effect. The message was printed in the newspapers of the day – a sort of press release – and reproduced verbatim in later memoirs.

Napoleon was visibly moved, but one cannot help but wonder how much of this emotion was self-pity, and how much was show put on for his men and for posterity. We have seen how he agonized not over the fate of France, but over his own fate. Of course, it is possible to agonize over both, but Napoleon always put the interests of himself and his family before that of the *patrie*. The message contained in his words and gestures is in any event clear: his main concern had always been the glory of France and the whole of Europe had been armed against him – that is, against France. He presented himself as the sacrificial lamb, the man who could have fought on if he had chosen to, but who decided that it was better to avoid 'civil war'. Of course the logic of the situation seems to have escaped most, that this was a predicament of his own making.

The timing of Napoleon's melodramatic gesture was perfect. According to all the accounts, there was hardly a dry eye in the house; tears streamed down the faces of most of the men present, hardened killers the lot.[128] It even moved the four foreign representatives who wept out of empathy, sharing the moment, realizing possibly that an era had come to an end. That tearful farewell obviously represented different things to different men, but for the faithful this sort of communal mourning was prompted by the loss of the one they had followed and idolized for years. They were losing their father. The Guard then burnt the eagles and, according to some accounts, divided the ashes among themselves. Some took the gesture even further by eating the ashes so that they would not become separated from them.[129] Napoleon then got into a carriage with Bertrand and drove off, or rather fourteen carriages transporting Napoleon and his entourage, escorted by a group of cavalry, drove off.[130] As he passed through the gates he lowered the window, and was seen with tears in his eyes.[131]

If the faithful shed a tear, others were glad to see the back of him, while yet others would try to get a piece of him. At Nevers, some 175 kilometres further south, townspeople cried out, 'Vive l'Empereur!', giving him the mistaken impression that he was not as hated as some of the newspapers made out. When they came to Villeneuve-sur-Allier on Friday evening (22 April), the cavalry escort that had accompanied them up to that point returned home. They were to be replaced by Austrian and Russian cavalry, but Napoleon brashly refused their help asserting, because of the reception he had received till then, that he had no need of them. He soon learnt to regret his decision. By the time he reached Montélimar (25 April), not far from Lyons, he had become aware of a change in

Alfred-Nicolas Normand, *Façade sur la cour des Adieux et l'escalier du Fer à Cheval* (A view of the Farewell Courtyard and the horseshoe staircase). This was built by Francis I, and dubbed the Staircase of the White Horse, at the Château de Fontainebleau, the setting of Napoleon's farewell to the Guard, 1888.

attitude among the people he encountered. Indeed, the cries of 'Vive l'Empereur!' became increasingly scarce after Villeneuve-sur-Allier, replaced with cries of 'Vivent les Bourbons!' and 'Vive Louis XVIII!' At Orange, he was greeted with shouts of 'Vive le Roi!', was jeered at and had stones thrown at his carriage. At Valence he was greeted with silence.[132] At Avignon, a town that had celebrated his fall, the procession passed through at six in the morning. A crowd of two to three hundred people had turned out to see him, and menacingly surrounded his carriage as the horses were being changed. In the end, there was little more than a few boos but it must have put the wind up him.[133] At Orgon, twenty-four kilometres from Avignon, the convoy was met at the entrance to the town by a stuffed dummy hung from a gibbet. A bloody inscription – 'Sooner or later, this will be the fate of the tyrant' – was placed on its stomach; the victim was meant to represent Napoleon. The crowd, 'drunk with hatred', climbed on to the carriage, shook their fists at him and cried (in the local Provençal dialect), 'Open the doors!', 'Drag him out!', 'Hang him!', 'Cut off his head!' Others threw stones at the carriage while some women shouted, 'Give me back my son!' According to one witness, Napoleon hid behind Bertrand: 'he was pale, desperate and speechless'.[134] It was Shuvalov who saved the day by laying into the crowd with his fists, all the while shouting that he was Russian to ensure that they would not turn on him; he managed to quieten them long enough to harangue them into submission.[135]

As a result of this confrontation, Napoleon decided, as a precautionary measure, to change into a shabby blue riding-coat, and to wear a round hat sporting the Bourbon white cockade. He mounted one of the post-horses and rode on ahead of the convoy, accompanied by a courier named Pélart. At Saint-Cannat, Berthier and a courier by the name of Vernet, who had taken Napoleon's place in the carriage, were surrounded by an angry crowd and attacked with stones, which broke the windows of the carriage. When the rest of the party caught up with Napoleon at an inn called La Calade about three leagues out of Aix, they found him in a small room, his elbows on the table, head in his hands, tears streaming down his face, lost in reflection.[136] He had been unsettled by the landlady, who had ranted against Napoleon for causing the deaths of her son and nephew. She did not think that the Emperor would make it away alive, and that he would be justly murdered along the way. Little did she know, of course, that Napoleon was right in front of her while she said this. He had refused to touch the food for fear of being poisoned and sent for some bread and wine from his carriage. When he discovered that there was no back door or window through which he could slip out, he became even more distraught. 'At the least noise,' wrote Truchsess-Waldburg, 'he started up in terror and changed colour.'[137]

It was after this that he decided to put on a mixture of uniforms – an Austrian uniform given to him by Köller, a Prussian forage cap given to him by Truchsess-Waldburg and a cloak donated by Shuvalov, a motley collection of the clothes of the armies that had defeated him. He adopted the name of Lord Burghersh, the British military commissioner to the Allies. To make the subterfuge appear even more authentic, he rode in a carriage with Köller, insisting Köller whistle a tune every time they rode into a town or village, and that the coachman smoke (neither habit would have been allowed normally in the presence of the Emperor).[138] The Emperor was without his clothes, naked before friend and foe. It was quite uncharacteristic of him since he was, as we know, courageous in battle. What he obviously feared above all was the angry mob, a throwback perhaps to the days when he had seen what it was capable of at the Tuileries in 1792. After Aix, he began to feel safer and adopted a more imperious manner, which made his shameful exhibition even more humiliating. What he eventually concluded from this show of hostility was that the Midi had been stirred up by the provisional government, but that on the whole the French were still favourable to him.[139] In other words, he refused to admit that his own government had done wrong.

＊　　＊　　＊

He met his sister Pauline on 26 April in a large country house, the Château du Bouillidou, near the town of Le Luc. They embraced, shed a few tears and spent the next four hours together in private.[140] She was the only sibling to bother trying to see her brother, and perhaps the only one who felt affection for him. Not even his mother made an attempt to see him, although they had passed each other near Auxerre. With the collapse of the Empire, his brothers and sisters now found it prudent to flee and to keep a low profile. Caroline was busy with Murat in Naples intriguing to stay in power. Elisa was obliged to leave Lucca in the Grand Duchy of Tuscany followed by a mob that insulted her along the way. She is reported to have stuck her head out of the carriage, pointed a threatening finger at them and shouted, 'I'll be back, you rabble' (*Je reviendrai, canailles*).[141] She was never to return. Joseph found asylum in Switzerland. Lucien tried to leave for America but was arrested by the English and interned, first on Malta and then in England. While there he wrote an epic poem entitled *Charlemagne ou l'Eglise delivrée* (Charlemagne or the Church delivered). It had little to do with Charlemagne and a great deal more to do with his brother, harking back to the perennial problem of Napoleon's succession. It was a way of criticizing the regime, the last jibe of a brother who had become anti-Napoleon.

Napoleon had in fact stopped in the region fifteen years before, on his return from Egypt, when he had borrowed a carriage from the owner of the Château du Bouillidou, which he subsequently failed to return. Now the mistress of the house apparently barged her way into his presence to remonstrate with him, but refused to believe, at first, that she was before the Emperor, so oddly dressed was he. The next morning, 27 April, they set off again, escorted by two squadrons of Austrian hussars that were stationed at Le Luc. The escort enabled Napoleon to change back into his own clothes; they arrived at Fréjus, a change of itinerary at Napoleon's insistence, early that afternoon. The original destination had been Saint-Tropez, but Napoleon had wanted to spend what might have been his last night in France at the Chapeau Rouge, an inn at Fréjus where, fifteen years earlier, he had stayed the night after landing there from Egypt to launch his remarkable political career. Now he spent a couple of days there, most of which was passed in his room, where he 'walked rapidly up and down', occasionally appearing at the window 'to watch some frigates arriving at anchorage'.[142]

Napoleon does not appear to have been in any great hurry to leave the shores of France. This was perhaps an ultimate controlling moment on his part, a niggling way of letting the British know just who was in charge – Truchsess-Waldburg says that he had 'recovered his imperial dignity' – or it may simply have been hesitation, the realization that he was leaving France once and for all. (It did not prevent him on other occasions talking as though he would be back in a few months' time.) As with the departure from

Fontainebleau, Napoleon procrastinated. On 29 April, the day the commissioners, receiving news that troops loyal to Napoleon were pouring over the border from Italy, decided that it was time to set sail, the Emperor informed Campbell that he was not very well and wanted to delay his departure for a few hours. He may indeed have been ill, it is difficult to say; he had certainly made no mention of it in a letter to Marie-Louise the day before, but that does not mean anything.[143] He seems to have had his hand forced that evening by the captain of the vessel, Captain Sir Thomas Ussher, who, shortly before seven, presented himself to Napoleon and told him that his barge was waiting to take him to the frigate *Undaunted*. Napoleon yielded, fearful once again perhaps that a mob might form and turn against him.[144]

He was escorted to the beach on that moonlit evening by six or seven Hungarian hussars, with the inevitable sound of bugles and the neighing of horses. On the beach, a group of people had assembled, some no doubt loyal supporters wanting to see their Emperor for the last time, others there out of curiosity. Stepping down from the carriage, Napoleon embraced Count Shuvalov, then took Ussher's arm and walked towards the barge. The sea was calm and the only sound that could be heard was the playing of a trumpet march.[145] There had been some discussion about whether he was to receive a twenty-one-gun salute or not. Napoleon insisted, and in the end the captain of the *Undaunted* relented after being shown instructions from Lord Castlereagh (to Campbell), which clearly stated that Napoleon was to be treated as a sovereign.[146] (Ussher thus ignored naval regulations, which prohibited gun salutes after sunset.) At precisely half-past eight in the evening, Napoleon left French soil and boarded the English vessel. Napoleon's Empire had crumbled into the dust of history. After more than twenty years of one of the bloodiest series of wars in European history, Napoleon, France and Europe had little to show for it.

# 24

## Sovereign of Elba

### Napoleon Returns to his Roots

The crossing took place in bad weather so that what normally would have taken two days lasted five. The fact that living conditions were crowded did not make things any easier. Ussher had to find quarters on his already cramped frigate for thirty-six other people. Napoleon took over the captain's quarters.

He was up the next morning at four o'clock with a strong cup of coffee.[1] On the whole, he was in good spirits, admitting that on the journey down to the coast from Fontainebleau he had shown himself at his very worst – *cul-nu* (bare arsed) was the expression he used. In a letter home, an officer on board the *Undaunted*, Lieutenant Hastings, described Napoleon as '5 feet 5 inches, inclining to fatness, which makes him appear inactive and unwieldy. His eyes are grey, extremely penetrating: the expression of his countenance by no means agreeable; and his manners far from dignified or graceful.'[2] It should be remembered that the British had been fed a less than flattering portrait of 'Boney' for the last fifteen years, so some had trouble accepting the affable man who presented himself before them.

On 1 May, the *Undaunted* came within sight of Corsica. Ussher rose to find Napoleon on the bridge, 'very nervous', supposedly worried about the political situation there.[3] Did the sight of Corsica remind him where he had come from, what he had become, and where his fate now lay? We do not know what Napoleon felt about his fall from grace, having gone in the space of months from governing millions of people to ruling over the inhabitants of a small island. We know that Bertrand appeared depressed, although Napoleon managed to maintain his good humour. In some respects, with the appearance of Corsica, Napoleon was forced to confront his origins. Two days later he was on the bridge again, spyglass raised, trying to catch a glimpse of the little black spot on the horizon that was Elba.[4]

The island of Elba is relatively small, about twenty-seven kilometres long and eighteen wide, with a mostly inaccessible shoreline, and a population in 1814 of about 12,000 inhabitants. There were 5,000 troops stationed there as well. The largest town, Portoferraio, contained about 3,000 people, their houses clinging to the hillside between the waterfront and the fort on top of San Rocco. Elbans were very much like their Corsican counterparts no more than fifty-odd kilometres away. Like Corsica, the island had an incredibly chequered history, changing hands so many times that its inhabitants had few allegiances. Like Corsicans, the inhabitants of Elba were fiercely independent and tolerated foreign domination, whether Italian, French or English, with difficulty. And Elbans spoke a similar dialect to Corsicans. Napoleon would have known more or less what to expect for, as usual, he informed himself about where he was going. He had taken a travelogue from his library in Fontainebleau by Arsenne Thiébaut de Berneaud entitled *Voyage à l'isle d'Elbe*. Published in 1808, the account is flattering about the island's inhabitants – a good, hospitable, hard-working people – but is far less so when it comes to describing Portoferraio – 'it has nothing that could interest the mind or the soul'.[5]

What many Elbans did not want was Napoleon. Just as the Empire was collapsing, so too was French authority on the island; it would appear that the inhabitants, including the French officers, were not aware that Napoleon had actually abdicated and that the wars were over. Only weeks before the Emperor arrived, Elbans had risen in revolt against the regime. In principle, the island was commanded by General Dalesme with a force of mostly Italian conscripts. The garrison at Porto Longone had mutinied, killed a number of officers, shot and then hacked to pieces the commanding officer, and deserted to the mainland. The garrison at Portoferraio had been given the option of returning to Italy, and most of them had done so.[6]

The general mood of the Elbans just before Napoleon arrived was, therefore, anti-French to say the least, something the British observed and which understandably worried them a little, while the western part of the island had still not been brought back under French control. At the village of Marciana, an effigy of Napoleon was burnt.[7] Nevertheless, news that the Emperor had been exiled to Elba spread quickly and appears to have been greeted with some enthusiasm as it dawned on people that his presence would mean business, money and trade, a notion helped along by the local bishop who promised his flock that 'wealth will pour into the land'.[8] That night, 3 May, the inhabitants of Portoferraio placed candles in their windows to welcome Napoleon.[9]

The morning of 4 May was spent working out the disembarkation, as well as the religious and military ceremonials that would be used to mark that passage.[10] On landing, Napoleon was received by local military and civil authorities, and was handed the keys to the island by a trembling mayor, Pietro Traditi, so nervous that he could not utter a single word nor find the little speech he had written.[11] The island's inhabitants were so curious to see the great man reduced to the state in which they now found him – they had forgotten how much harm he had caused them – that they pressed in around him so that the troops accompanying the procession through the town had trouble keeping order.[12] The bishop, Joseph-Philippe Arrighi, a distant cousin of

Napoleon's, ended up pushing and shouting at those who blocked the way.[13] Napoleon, under a canopy, accompanied by the music of three violins and two double basses, walked towards the church but was 'uncommonly sombre, and his eyes shifted from one to another of the people surrounding him, trying to make out what they thought, and endeavouring in vain to hide the feelings of distrust and fear which he himself experienced'.[14] A Te Deum was offered in the local church during which Napoleon appears to have shed some tears. One can only imagine what they were for – that this was now his life, on a godforsaken island with a godforsaken people?

The Te Deum was followed by a ceremony in the town hall before Napoleon finally retired to the apartment that had been set up for him on the disused first floor of what was commonly referred to as the 'Biscotteria', the biscuit factory. It had been quickly cleaned while the more prominent members of the town gave furniture so that it resembled some kind of dwelling. 'The accommodation is mediocre,' Napoleon wrote to Marie-Louise that evening, 'but I will arrange for something better in a week or two.'[15] He no doubt realized that these letters would be read, so they possibly lack the intimacy that can usually be found in his more private correspondence. It must also have been a way either of assuaging the allies' fears or of making it clear what he was unhappy about. Marie-Louise, on the other hand, continued to profess her love for him: 'I, tormented, loving you more tenderly than ever, I spend whole days despairing of ever seeing you again.'[16]

### A Dead Man, in Perpetual Movement

What does a man, once the most powerful in Europe, fallen from grace, exiled to a European backwater, do with the rest of his life? Napoleon found solace in habit; he compensated for his loss of power with a frenzy of activity. As much as possible, he imitated court life at the Tuileries.[17] With more than sixty servants, this would have been a relatively easy thing to do. Colonel Campbell remarked that, while those around him sank under the weight of fatigue, Napoleon remained in 'perpetual movement'.[18] The day after he arrived, he woke at four in the morning to go and inspect the town's defences and did not return until ten, six hours later, for breakfast.[19] The defences were better than he had expected. One week after arriving, he went on a trip around the island. He moved into the Villa Mulini – it can still be visited today – and started to renovate and refurbish it with whatever he could get his hands on so that it became a reasonably comfortable but modest thirty-room villa. He added an extra floor, although he himself lived only on the ground floor where there was a bathroom, bedroom, study and library. Upstairs was meant for Marie-Louise and his son. He requisitioned furniture from the Piombino Palace in Tuscany, once the residence of his sister Pauline but now vacant. A ship carrying furniture to Rome was driven to Elba by a storm; Napoleon requisitioned that too. Short of clothes, he bought the cotton cargo of an English ship that had been captured before war's end; he was able to supply his entourage with clean linen and his soldiers with uniforms.

He soon got into a routine.[20] He would invariably wake at four in the morning, go over dispatches, dictate letters and orders, read the newspapers and go for a walk in his garden. He would then have a nap and then sometimes would go riding with Bertrand for a couple of hours, visiting the various constructions that he had ordered carried out on the island. He would eat around ten or eleven o'clock, often alone, sometimes with Bertrand or Antoine Drouot, one of his aides-de-camp. He would then shut himself away, either to work or to nap.[21] It was the time of the day when he would like to take his bath, spending an hour or more reading, dictating letters or conversing. Around four o'clock he would often again go out, this time in a calash, holding audience with just about anyone he met along the way.[22] When he returned to Mulini he would hold a more formal audience with an assortment of French and English tourists wanting to see him, most of whom had an 'intense admiration' for him,[23] Corsicans who had come to solicit favours from Letizia (she arrived in August), officers on half-pay seeking more lucrative commissions, women who had come to throw themselves at him – such as the Prince Regent's mistress, the Countess of Jersey, and Signora Filippi from Lucca who was one of those rare women who had dressed and fought as a man in the Army of Italy – and an assortment of odd characters and charlatans all wanting something. Not that they had direct access to him; court etiquette still applied even if it was not as elaborate as it used to be.[24] Of course they had to be of sufficient rank and standing to be granted an audience or be invited to dinner; otherwise they could hope to talk to Napoleon if they ran into him on the roadside when he was out riding.[25] Some waited five or six hours to see him and then re-embarked as soon as they had done so. Between May 1814 and February 1815 around sixty English visitors made the trip from Leghorn to Elba to see Napoleon; the island had become a destination on the Grand Tour, which was coming back into vogue after its long interruption during the wars.[26] They were mostly young, mostly from educated backgrounds, generally Whigs, and all overwhelmed with a curiosity to see the great man fallen. Napoleon loved to gossip, but there were few on the island who could amuse him for long. He relied on his visitors to keep him informed of what was going on on the Continent. He was often irritable at the end of the day – that is, in the evenings when there was nothing to do. After dinner, which could take place any time between six and eight o'clock, he would play cards or dominoes with his mother for an hour or two, or chess with Drouot, and would retire about nine, sometimes playing the opening lines of Haydn's 'Surprise' symphony on the piano as a cue that he was going to bed where sleep would generally be interrupted.

Part of him wanted, needed to transform his little domain into a model island kingdom, a reflection of his own idealized self-image. Part of him needed to keep his mind occupied, and he did so by turning his attention to the smallest detail, anything from how large an allowance should be given to invalid troops in hospital so that they could buy food, to where horses could be watered, to laws regulating the collection of night soil, to how much the gardener should be paid and for what tasks.[27] Bertrand recalled how Napoleon 'dictated letters about fowls, ducks, meat and all eatables as if he was dealing at Paris with matters of the greatest importance'.[28] One hundred families were sent to the island of Pianosa, about twenty kilometres offshore, to cultivate wheat, the plains of Lacona were to be irrigated, the valleys reforested, olive trees and potatoes planted in every communal plot. Perhaps the most revealing trait though was the extent to which Napoleon would become enthusiastic about a building project, and then, despondent, abandon all interest a short time later. This happened time and again over the few months he was there, indulging what seemed like whims, and then when he became bored, or the novelty wore off, or if the obstacles proved too difficult, or it became too costly, he simply gave up on them.

These swings between a sort of physical agitation and complete inactivity hardly enamoured him to the locals. Within a month of arriving, Campbell noted, there were no longer any cries of 'Vive l'Empereur!' when he went about.[29] We know the inhabitants soon became disillusioned with the amount of taxes they were now being asked to pay. In the town of Capoliveri, in the south of the island, probably egged on by the local priests, they simply refused to pay. Napoleon was obliged to send in 400 Corsican troops along with the fifty-four Polish lancers who had arrived on the island in October, to bend the inhabitants to his will. A couple of priests and a few local notables were arrested and thrown into the dungeons of Fort Falcone, and the townspeople eventually paid up. It was the Empire all over again on a smaller scale, what had happened countless times throughout Europe, as the state increasingly inserted itself into the daily lives of its subjects and citizens. But it is also the kind of thing that must have irked Napoleon.[30] Life on Elba after ruling Europe must have been stultifying.

John Barber Scott, an English tourist, met Napoleon along the roads and described his encounter with him.

> The *first* impression on my mind was – Can this be the great Napoleon? Is that graceless figure, so clumsy and awkward, the figure that awed emperors and kings, has gained victory on victory, and the sight of whom has been equivalent of ten thousand men on the field of battle? Surely, it is impossible? That countenance – it is totally devoid of expression, it appears even to indicate stupidity.

Such were the thoughts that rushed through my mind, and though I soon found reason to change my opinion as far as his countenance was concerned, I still think the figure of Napoleon unmartial, clumsy and awkward.[31]

Scott, as was the case for most Englishmen, could not help but notice that Napoleon was paunchy if not fat by this stage of his life, that he was so addicted to snuff that his clothes were stained with it, that his hair was long and in 'candle-ends', that his complexion was 'doughy', that he looked seedy and that his clothes were dirty and unkempt – a hat that had seen much better times, shabby boots and so on – as though the Emperor, depressed, had completely let himself go.[32]

It was only when these men spoke to him that they were able to overcome their first impressions. He spoke to them with a great deal of ease, appeared to be perfectly frank and, just as importantly for his English visitors, did not appear to hold any resentment at the way in which he had been treated. Of course, he was going out of his way to be polite, thinking that if he were able to influence a few well-placed British they might persuade their government to offer him asylum. But it was also a means of dispelling the idea that he might have been thinking of a return to France. 'I think of nothing outside my little island. I no longer exist for the world,' he told Campbell. 'I am a dead man. I only occupy myself with my family and my retreat, my cows and mules.'[33] Some of the English began to believe him. Even Campbell began to think that Napoleon was 'tolerably happy'.[34] At least one English observer saw this for what it was – a feint. 'The accounts which show him as indifferent, resigned and wanting peace and quiet don't seem to be sincere but are a political front on his part since, all the time the Congress [of Vienna] is in session, he must keep up a pretence that doesn't upset the powers on whom his fate depends.'[35] Nor were a number of French royalist agents convinced that Napoleon had resigned himself to his fate. On the contrary, they were writing back to Paris that he still represented a danger and that he would attempt to regain the Continent at some time in the near future.[36]

A feint it was. The whole time Napoleon was asserting that he was politically dead he was building a network of informants and spies who kept him abreast of the state of play on the mainland. Much of what they told him fed into his own misconceptions about the mood in France, his popularity and the disapproval of the returned Bourbon regime. He had another reason for being so talkative with his British visitors: he was trying to elicit information from them about the situation in England, and the impressions they had formed as they travelled through France and Italy.[37] In this, there was always a bit of projecting going on. In a conversation with Campbell held on 16 September, for example, he claimed that the main failings of the French people were 'pride and love of glory, and it was impossible for them to look forward

*The Sorrows of Boney, or Meditations in the Island of ELBA!!!*, April 1814. This is a reworking of another caricature, *Crocodile's Tears: or, Bonaparte's Lamentation. A New Song*, first printed in 1803. Napoleon weeps on a rock in the sea inscribed 'Elba'. The mushroom on the rock is the emblem of the upstart. Three birds of prey and three bats fly menacingly around his head.

with satisfaction and feelings of tranquillity'.[38] It is difficult not to read 'Napoleon', in place of the 'French people', but if that is too tenuous a connection to make, one need only look to other similar conversations to realize what was going on in his mind in this autumn of 1814. The topics mentioned time and again by Napoleon to his British visitors are: a desire to keep Italian nationalists at play as a distraction; a willingness to let discontent with Bourbons simmer in France; and a desire to see Belgium remain part of France (he played on French glory and the idea of a 'natural frontier'). This might be a 'coherent programme', as one historian put it, but there was yet no indication that Napoleon had anything definite in mind.[39] He was simply getting a feel for things.

In a four-hour conversation Napoleon had in November with a certain John Nicholas Fazakerley and George Venables Vernon, the latter a Whig MP and cousin of Lord Holland, he shrugged off responsibility for anything that had happened in Europe, arguing that Russia had forced his hand, and repeated the phrase, 'I am like a dead man; my role is finished.'[40] The idea seemed to be to flatter the English, to underline how much they had been deceived about him and to point out that he simply wanted to live peacefully. As we have seen, despite this façade, Napoleon kept himself well informed about what was happening on the mainland, receiving pamphlets and newspapers that had been published in Paris since the restoration of the Bourbons.[41] In addition, thousands of letters were secretly delivered to him, and he eagerly questioned any French visitors about conditions in France. Legend has it – it is impossible to verify – that one of these people was an old soldier who supposedly told him, 'They are waiting for you; the present state of affairs cannot last another six months.'[42] When Napoleon said that he was tired, and that in any case he had only one battalion of troops, the veteran is supposed to have assured him that 'Not one soldier will fire on you.' It feeds into the notion that Napoleon abandoned Elba because he was urged to by those loyal to him. He was not, in other words, acting out of self-interest. Urging him to come to the mainland also were Italian patriots who wanted him to put himself at the head of an uprising that would unite Italy. There was little chance of that; he cared little for the idea of a united Italy. Nevertheless, throughout his months on the island, and given the number of visitors who came through with reports of what was happening, he formed an idea of France that would allow him, indeed compel him, to gamble his future.

### Wife, Lover, Sister, Mother

Pauline joined Napoleon on the island at the beginning of June. She had been visiting her sister and brother-in-law in Naples, and stayed but two days before sailing back again. It is possible that she brought Napoleon secret letters from agents loyal to him in France, although this cannot be confirmed. She wrote to her mother and her siblings exhorting them to come and join Napoleon on Elba – 'do not leave the Emperor alone. He is unhappy and we must show him dedication' – but most of them saw no reason to.[43] Eugène had gone to Vienna and was perhaps the only person in the family to be well treated and well considered by both the authorities and the Austrian public.[44] Lucien had left England (where he had been held prisoner, as we have noted) and was living in Rome protected by the pope, accepting from him the title Prince of Canino. He nevertheless sounded out Talleyrand about becoming a member of Louis XVIII's Chamber of Peers. Jérôme, who had fled to Trieste, kept in touch by mail, but dreamt silly dreams of ruling over all of Italy.[45] Louis also took refuge in Rome but was still hurting from having his kingdom occupied and annexed.[46] Elisa was trying to get back her lost property in Italy, confiscated by her 'successor', Ferdinand of Tuscany. She went to Vienna to plead her cause at the Congress, but as soon as she set foot in Tuscany she was detained by Austrian police. Joseph made the best of his life in exile in Switzerland. He managed to pass messages to Napoleon orally through intermediaries but did not visit him on Elba.[47] Pauline was the exception; she returned to Elba in October with the intention of sharing her brother's exile, lending a certain amount of glamour and gaiety to their gatherings in the process.

Nor was there any contact with Josephine. Napoleon's last letter to her was written from Fontainebleau in April 1814 in which he admitted that his 'mind and heart [were] free of an enormous burden'. Josephine died of diphtheria on 29 May that year. Napoleon read about her death in the newspapers and was so overwhelmed with grief that he locked himself away for two days.[48] Her funeral took place on 2 June at Malmaison where the representatives of several foreign sovereigns took part. The allies used Josephine's funeral to make a political statement – namely, that peace was indeed concluded and that the French had nothing to fear.[49] Relations had returned to normal.

After that, Napoleon decided to bring Maria Walewska to the island. He planned to do so, however, in the greatest secrecy so that no rumours would get back to his wife, and so that he would not become the object of ridicule among the courts of Europe. Those, in any event, are the reasons traditionally given, but it is difficult to fathom Napoleon's state of mind and his treatment (or rather mistreatment) of Maria. When he was at Fontainebleau, for example, fretting about his own future, Maria had come to him hoping to share his exile. She spent the night of 4–5 April waiting for him in an antechamber, only to be sent away without so much as seeing him. Admittedly, he had fallen into a 'sort of slump, to the point of seeing nothing of what was around him'.[50] When he finally came around, he is reported as having said, 'The poor woman! She feels humiliated! Constant [his valet], I am really angry about it. If you see her again, tell her as much. But I have so much going on inside here!', and with that he hit his forehead. Still, she was steadfast in her loyalty and contacted Napoleon again of her own accord, offering to come to Elba.[51] He agreed.

The tryst smacks of comic-opera.[52] He had a little hermitage at Marciana restored and renovated for the purpose; it was about as far away as anyone could get on the island. In an attempt to avert prying eyes, he ordered the brig bringing her to the island at the beginning of September 1814 to moor off the coast, which immediately aroused the curiosity of the townspeople of Porto-ferraio; they imagined that Marie-Louise and her son had at last landed. Maria Walewska was obliged to travel to Marciana in the evening. When she got there, she had supper with Napoleon, possibly with Bertrand's wife Fanny acting the hostess. Maria slept at the hermitage while Napoleon slept in a tent outside. On the nights he was there, Napoleon came out of his tent in a dress-ing gown and went to her room where he stayed until daybreak.[53] His behaviour was a tad hypocritical. Those officers who had been lucky enough to come to the island to live with girlfriends or mistresses were not received at the Villa Mulini.[54] Apart from Maria Walewska, Napoleon does not appear to have taken any lovers before the autumn of 1814, after he had given up hope of ever seeing Marie-Louise and his son. Maria had been on the island for almost two weeks before she was again unceremoniously sent away – rumour of her presence had spread throughout the island and he supposedly wanted to avoid any scandal – never again to see Napoleon. She divorced her old husband in 1812 and remarried in 1816. She died one year later of a kidney disease at the age of thirty-one.

Part of the problem was that Napoleon still had no idea whether Marie-Louise would come to join him or not. He wanted to have her by his side, of that there is no doubt, not only because he loved Marie-Louise and his son, but also because it would have been a powerful political gesture. Communications between the two were bad at best, sometimes intercepted by the Austrian secret police and simply not passed on. Napoleon did not receive any letters from her until July; four others that she had written never reached him at all. He complained bitterly to the British about the Austrian Emperor preventing his daughter from joining him.[55] In August he nevertheless wrote to her to say that 'Your accommodation is ready and I am waiting for the month of Septem-ber for the harvest . . . Come then. I am waiting impatiently. You know all the feelings I have for you.'[56] He must have known, however, that the allied powers were not favourably disposed to seeing Marie-Louise leave for the island.[57] Napoleon simply hoped, something that ran counter to past experience, that she would be strong-willed enough to impose herself on her father.

It is true that she still held feelings for Napoleon, and that she wrote to him during her voyage from France to Vienna, letters Napoleon never got.[58] When she arrived in Vienna on 21 May 1814, amid the hurly-burly that was the Congress, she and her son were warmly received. She did not take part in any of the social activities underpinning the Congress, which suited her just fine after the stuffy atmosphere of the French imperial court. It did not even cross her mind that she could have lobbied on behalf of her husband. A simple life is what she hankered after and it is what she was accorded.[59] In July, after being at Vienna for only two months, she was given permission to take the waters at Aix-en-Provence, but she had to leave her son behind. To take him to France, 'one might think I wanted to disturb the peace, which could cause me and my son problems'. In the same letter, however, she wrote that Napoleon should 'reserve a small lodging, because you know I intend to come as soon as I can'.[60] Her plan was to travel to Parma after Aix, and from there to Elba. Along the way to Aix, she made a point of meeting members of the Bonaparte family – Louis in Baden, Jérôme in Payerne in Switzerland and Joseph at the Swiss Château d'Allaman. Is it true that she appeared calm and imperturbable in public but that she cried when alone?[61] All of this gives the impression that as late as August she was still pining for her husband. Her circumstances, however, were about to change.

Waiting for her when she arrived at Aix on 17 July was a young, dashing officer, Adam Adalbert von Neipperg, whom she had met briefly in Paris in 1810 and again in 1812. It has been assumed, usually by French historians, that Metternich deliberately chose Neipperg to escort her so that he could seduce her to help her forget Napoleon, and that he had indeed received secret instructions to that effect, but there is nothing to support this claim.[62] On the contrary, it would appear that the names of other officers were put forward to accompany Marie-Louise in order to keep Vienna informed about her progress and whereabouts, to make sure that she did not head off for Elba. It was General Schwarzenberg who suggested Neipperg.[63] Metternich instructed Neipperg to turn her away, 'by any means whatsoever', from 'all ideas of a journey to Elba', naturally with the greatest tact, and to provide detailed reports on her.[64] Marie-Louise was no doubt of a sensuous nature, but it is unfair to suggest that she could simply be seduced by the first comer. Even if Neipperg had had a reputation for being a rake in his youth, he was now forty years old with a wife and children and perhaps did not cut as dashing a figure as he once had.[65] He had lost an eye in battle, so he always wore a black eye band.

Her first meeting with him did not make a very agreeable impression on her, but that did not last long.[66] A few days later she was writing that he was 'full of attention' and that his manner pleased her very much.[67] Neipperg, who at first seemed a bit of a nuisance, knew how to make himself indispensable so that, very soon, she started to have feelings for him. It naturally tormented her. 'I am', she confided in her secretary, Claude François de Méneval, in August, 'in a very critical and very unhappy position. There are times when my head turns so that I think the best thing to happen would be for me to die.'[68] That is not the confession of a woman entering into an affair lightly; it is a woman attempting to come to grips with conflicting feelings. That is why she was still able to confide in Méneval on Napoleon's birthday (15 August), 'How can I be happy . . . when I am obliged to pass the feast day, so solemn to me, so far from the two people who are dearest to me?'[69]

Aix was amusing, full of balls, garden parties and excursions, but not only did she have to contend with her own feelings, she was also being bombarded with unflattering stories about Napoleon, portrayed as a bad husband who had always been unfaithful. This fell on what was now fertile ground. Napoleon had been sending letters to her directly, through his officers, first a Colonel Laczynski and then a Captain Hurault de Sorbée, whose wife was

Marie-Louise's Austrian reader, saying that a ship was waiting for her at Genoa and that Hurault de Sorbée would arrange everything.[70] Marie-Louise baulked at this. To Napoleon she answered that she had to go to Vienna and that it would be impossible to go to the island without her father's permission. To her father she wrote to say that she 'felt less than ever like wanting to take the trip'.[71] Napoleon's imperious tone, ordering her to set out with Hurault de Sorbée, was the excuse used not to go, unless her father obliged her to. There was little chance of that. It was Metternich, and her father, who wrote to her to say that, at the Congress, the House of Bourbon – that is, Spain and France – did not want a Habsburg princess to reign in Parma. She should, therefore, return to Vienna to defend her interests and the interests of her son. In fact, it is possible that the idea of journeying to Elba inspired more fear in her than either her father or Metternich could instil. If then Marie-Louise was writing to Napoleon to say that she was being obliged to return to Vienna from Aix, she was only half telling the truth. It was on the return voyage from Aix to Vienna (she left on 5 September) that her party, surprised by a storm on the 24th, was obliged to find refuge in the town of Küsnacht at an inn called the Soleil d'Or. It was probably during that night that she consummated her relationship with Neipperg.[72]

In Vienna, her father showed her a letter from Napoleon addressed to her uncle, the Grand Duke of Tuscany, pleading with him to forward letters to his wife. It was the request of a desperate man. Francis then instructed her not to reply to Napoleon's letters. As she told Méneval, she had the choice of bending to her father's will or rebelling against him and her whole family, with what would have been serious consequences.[73] The last letter to him was dated the beginning of January 1815.[74] It is possible that by this stage, with a new lover by her side, she was learning to forget her husband. The change in attitude was spotted by those in Vienna; a secret police report noted that she was still 'attached' to Napoleon, but that she was no longer the same.[75]

Letizia arrived on Elba on 2 August 1814, having embarked from Leghorn amid the jeers of the mob.[76] She was sixty-four years of age, but looked twenty years younger, and had decided to join her son from Rome where she had taken refuge after the collapse of the Empire.[77] Her son was not there to greet her; expecting her to arrive the previous day he had gone to the country. She was a fairly unpretentious woman, but she was nevertheless, like her son, a bit of a stickler for form and refused to go ashore until a guard of honour had been arranged and enough people had been gathered together to give a semblance of a cheering crowd.[78] She settled into the Vantini house, a spacious residence originally destined for Pauline below the Villa Mulini. Napoleon was delighted by her arrival and spent a number of hours with her, visibly happy on his return to the Mulini. Letizia as we know had a formidable character, something that did not fail to impress itself upon those who came into contact with her. Although 'very pleasant and unaffected',[79] more 'eminent people were intimidated in front of her than in front of the Emperor'.[80] Napoleon also treated her with deference, visited her every day, something that he had never been able to do when in Paris, dined once a week at her residence, spent evenings playing cards with her and accorded her a role befitting her former title. When he cheated at cards, which was often, his mother was the only person to pull him up with a brusque, 'Napoleon, you are cheating!'[81]

## The Decision

When he was not keeping himself busy with one building project or another or frittering away his energies on trivial matters, Napoleon had time to mull over the events of the past year. In his inimitable fashion, he proved incapable of anything like self-reflection or self-critique. Instead, he tended to dwell on his own 'feats' during the last campaign, to argue that France had not suffered all that much because the bulk of lives expended were foreign, and to abuse Marmont whose defection he believed had obliged him to give up the struggle.[82] Napoleon was encouraged, it is generally argued, by the stories from France that were filtering back to him about how unpopular Bourbon rule was proving, but one wonders just how much encouragement he needed. Yes, it is obvious that the army was not overly impressed with its new Bourbon masters. Not only had many veterans found themselves out of work or on half-pay – which the government then proceeded to reduce by imposing a number of taxes – and many experienced officers who had campaigned and fought for France had been replaced by men whose only qualification was to have connections at court, but soldiers returning from captivity in Germany, Britain and Russia (the lucky few) now circulated horror stories about their time in captivity. Most of these returning veterans were still loyal to Napoleon; their reinsertion into French society was, therefore, bound to create problems.[83] They fed into the core of loyal supporters who would never accept the return of the Bourbons, creating enormous tensions between royalists and Bonapartists.[84]

Other reasons are put forward to help us understand Napoleon's state of mind around this time. The knowledge that Marie-Louise and his son were not going to join him was a factor. So too was Louis' refusal to pay him the pension he had been promised by the Treaty of Fontainebleau (along with every other member of the Bonaparte family). To be fair to Louis, the new king simply did not feel obliged to conform to a treaty he had no part in elaborating, not to mention the fact that the financial circumstances in which he found France were dire; Napoleon had saddled the Bourbons with an enormous debt. But then Louis was essentially a spiteful man who would have resented having to pay Napoleon at all. Nevertheless, deliberately withholding the funds was a calculated move, not particularly astute as it turned out but calculated none-theless. Louis and his government wanted Napoleon gone and they mistakenly believed that by withholding funds they would oblige him to reduce his staff and his guard, so that he would be more easily moved at a later date.[85]

Of course, this also suited Napoleon, up to a point. Ever willing to play the victim, he made political mileage out of Louis' niggardly behaviour. The more he could point to his own precarious situation, the more people, or so at least he thought, would be inclined to pity him and despise the Bourbons. But the lack of money put him in a difficult situation on several levels. His treasurer, Baron Guillaume Joseph Peyrusse, rescued about 2.5 million francs in gold, and he managed to get another 900,000 out of Marie-Louise, but that appears to have been the extent of Napoleon's personal fortune.[86] If Louis flouted the clauses of the Treaty of Fontainebleau, despite protests from the allies, and let him live in relative poverty, then there was little to stop the king from violating other treaty stipulations, and possibly treating Napoleon as a kind of outlaw.[87] That possibility became even more real after 18 December 1814 when Louis decided to confiscate Napoleon's personal property in France, depriving him of another source of income.

By the beginning of November, it was apparent to Neil Campbell that Napoleon's 'pecuniary difficulties press[ed] upon him', and that if they did so much longer, 'so as to prevent his vanity from being satisfied by the ridiculous establishment of a Court which he has hitherto supported in Elba, and if his doubts are not removed, I think he is capable of crossing over to Piombino with his troops, or of any other eccentricity'.[88] Campbell sent another warning in December along the same lines.[89] By that time too, reports were coming in from the spy that had been placed on Elba by the Chevalier Mariotti (on Talleyrand's payroll). The spy, known mysteriously as the Oil Merchant, was probably Alessandro Forli, an Italian from Lucca who had formerly been a soldier in the Army of Italy. He was now selling olive oil to the imperial house-hold, gathering information in the process, writing reports back to Mariotti which were, on the whole, models of reserve. By the middle of December 1814, Forli was also writing that Napoleon was seriously considering return-ing to France.[90]

The withholding of Napoleon's pension and the confiscation of his prop-erty in France were minor irritations. The rumours flying around about how the allies wanted to assassinate Napoleon, or remove him from Elba, were more concerning.[91] A certain Comte de Chauvigny de Blot wrote to Louis' brother and heir presumptive, the Comte d'Artois, from Toulon in June 1814 offering to have Napoleon assassinated by Corsican officers on the island.[92] It is impossible to know with any certainty how serious were these assassination threats, but the rumours certainly threw the Bonaparte household into a flap.[93] In early September, Napoleon was described as 'very uneasy, very agitated not daring to sleep in the same room for two nights running'.[94] He apparently became so concerned that from the end of 1814, guests were no longer invited to table, and on the rare occasions he left his lodgings, he only went about with an armed escort.[95] As a consequence, the security measures surrounding Napoleon were reinforced. Around 700 Imperial Guard, allowed Napoleon by the Treaty of Fontainebleau, had left Fontainebleau six days before the Emperor (although they did not arrive on the island until 26 May). This was enough for his personal security, but not enough to fend off a sustained attack from the mainland. There had indeed been a few half-hearted, badly organized attempts on his life, some on the part of the minister for the interior, Pierre Louis de Blacas, although to be fair to Louis XVIII he was probably unaware of his minister's intrigues. André Pons de l'Hérault, who managed the iron mines on the island, but who became devoted to Napoleon despite the fact that he was a former Jacobin, wrote of a kind of psychosis that took over the island as rumours, assassination plots and real assassination attempts merged to become indistinguishable.[96]

Much more to the point, however, Napoleon feared above all that Louis would convince the British and Austrians to throw him off Elba. There were rumours floating around at the beginning of November 1814 that he was going to be sent to St Helena.[97] Certainly, in Vienna in October 1814, the allies were considering the Azores, St Lucia and St Helena, 'in all the official mouths'.[98] It was Talleyrand who suggested that Napoleon could be moved to an island in the Azores.[99] The Azores belonged to Portugal and were 500 leagues from land, but Castlereagh seemed to think that the British might be able to buy one of the islands and that the Portuguese would be amenable. They were not, so that by November it was more or less decided: Bonaparte was going to be sent to St Helena.[100]

Napoleon was aware that Talleyrand and Louis were conspiring against him, but what he did not yet know was that so too was Metternich. He had entered into a secret correspondence with Louis, through Blacas, in a bid to oust Napoleon and Murat from Italy.[101] In turn, Louis, through his representative at Vienna, Talleyrand, was pushing to oust not only Murat from Naples, but Napoleon from Elba. The two objectives were linked in the mind of Talleyrand.[102] Realistically, once the Congress of Vienna was concluded, Napoleon would in all probability not be allowed to stay on Elba. By this stage, the European press was openly discussing the possibility of removing him to another location.[103] At most, he might be offered another place of exile, but there was no guarantee that he would not be worse off.

At one point, towards the end of December 1814, Napoleon confronted Campbell with the rumours, declaring that he would never allow himself to be removed and that he would resist with force.[104] It was the last meeting between the two men. Castlereagh would have preferred to move Napoleon (and

Murat) with their agreement, perhaps softening the blow with a financial and territorial sweetener, but he never really attempted to discuss or even persuade his European counterparts. The only person who took the Treaty of Fontaine-bleau seriously was the Tsar, and even he was beginning to lose interest in Napoleon.

Other factors played a role. The situation in France has often been portrayed as dire for the Bourbons and it is true that there were large sections of the population who did not look upon the return of the monarchy with any pleasure. It was not so much that the Bourbons were out of touch with the people – true for some in Louis XVIII's entourage – as that the monarchy had implemented a number of measures that alienated certain elements of the French population: republicans were upset by the return of the white Bourbon flag, the military by the number of redundancies that were made, and the 'granting of a Charter' – the Bourbons could not bear to call it a constitution – flew in the face of more than twenty-five years of political evolution. These measures, combined with the apparent return of the influence of the Church (*demi-soldes*, soldiers on half-pay, were obliged to attend mass on Sunday to receive their money), the return of *ancien régime* etiquette at court (which was nevertheless less elaborate than that formerly used by Napoleon) and the replacement of the tricolour with the fleur de lys all made for a public relations nightmare that haunted sections of the population who believed the Bourbons were determined to overthrow the gains of the Revolution. There were, moreover, a few high-profile incidents that highlighted the regime's reactionary character. Louis XVIII ennobled the father of Georges Cadoudal, who had been killed in the plot to assassinate Napoleon.[105] Former Chouans were decorated with the Croix de Saint-Louis. Returned émigrés upset people with their behaviour, especially when they attempted to retrieve their lands through either coercion or persuasion. Within a year of Louis' coming to power, French political temperament and attitudes towards Napoleon had dramatically changed.

But this is not what brought about Napoleon's return or Louis' demise. Rumours of Napoleon's deportation from Elba were fundamental in deciding him to leave the island, probably as early as December 1814.[106] The newspapers, the conversations he had with visitors and the reports he was receiving from his own spies all confirmed that the allies were resolved to move him from Elba. In Napoleon's mind, the best defence was attack; it was better to tempt fate in France than to wait passively for the allies to remove him. Up to this point he had been under the illusion that his marriage with Marie-Louise would always play in his favour and that Austria would consequently not permit his deportation.[107] It must have been the realization that Marie-Louise was never going to join him that tipped the balance.

On 5 February 1815, Napoleon sent a confidential letter to Pons de l'Hérault. The letter asked Pons to report on how to organize an expeditionary flotilla – that is, how to ship the Guard to France. Napoleon saw Pons the next day, and asked him directly, 'Shall I listen to the wishes of the army and the nation, who hate and mistrust the Bourbons?'[108] This summary of his intentions is a political statement and does not reflect in the slightest what was going on in his mind. There is some speculation that he believed his escape had to be timed with the ending of the Congress of Vienna, and that rumours of Alexander's departure for Russia had already reached Elba.[109] The rumours proved to be false, but speculation about how much better it would have been if Napoleon had indeed waited until the end of the Congress, an idea that he himself maintained later,[110] so that the allies were no longer gathered together in the one place, is really a moot point. At most, it would have delayed Napoleon's inevitable downfall by a few months. Pons was, apparently, the only person in whom Napoleon confided.[111] Not even Bertrand or Drouot were yet aware of what he had in mind.

Napoleon was looking on France from without. What is clear, even if he understood what was going on with French public opinion, is that he did not take into account the international context. Nor did he take into account the veritable outpouring of hatred and venom against him now that people were able to express themselves in books, pamphlets and caricatures unleashed upon the reading public as though a dam had burst. Many of these that appeared immediately after the fall of Napoleon portray him as a tyrant and despot who had been justly overthrown;[112] in others he was used as a sort of moral spectacle whose physical and moral decay was meant to edify. In Charles Malo's *Napoléoniana*, for example, we find a collection of fictive anecdotes that are meant to point to Napoleon's moral bankruptcy. 'Heaven granted Buonaparte great military skill, but no personal bravery; prodigious activity, but to no end; an indomitable will, but without discernment. Not the most incredible favours of fortune, nor the most terrible lessons of misfortune, nor the advice of enlightened men who wanted to show him true glory, nor the devotion of all his warriors, nothing could soften the character of the Corsican soldier, rectify its false spirit, or raise its corrupted soul.'[113] *Le Néron corse*, which portrays him as a criminal, declared that the time of charlatans was over and that the people could no longer be duped.[114] The overriding themes in these works are, first, that Napoleon was not French but a foreigner, and second, that he was driven by an unbounded ambition.[115] The *Précis historique sur Napoléon Bonaparte*, for example, is filled with anecdotes that are meant to illustrate his lack of humanity and his excessive ambition.[116] These kinds of books were enormous publishing successes, going through several editions in a short space of time. Their goal was to 'demythify' his political and military genius, and to set the reader on the right path.

## 'The Die is Cast'

If Napoleon read any of these pamphlets, they do not appear to have weighed heavily in his decision to return. Timing was everything. Campbell was going to be away in Italy, so it was important to carry out the final preparations, which would take about ten days, during that time. It was a question of loading enough supplies for about 1,000 men, as well as getting forty horses and four cannon on board. Napoleon had at his disposal the brig *Inconstant*, a xebec called the *Etoile* and several smaller vessels – in all, seven ships. When the troops received the order to get ready to leave on the afternoon of 26 February, many guessed what their destination was to be.[117] Old soldiers that they were – 'a soldier is not made to be a mason or a gardener' – they were delighted to be going back into action.[118] The sun was setting when the Old Guard left their barracks and marched towards the port through the narrow streets, encumbered now with inhabitants who had come to see them off.

Even then the scheme could have been uncovered if Captain Adye of the British brig the *Partridge* had been a little more observant. He arrived in Portoferraio during the night of 23 February, and weighed anchor not far from the *Inconstant*. Napoleon had ordered his ship to be painted like a British brig to help avoid detection once in open waters. If Captain Adye had seen this, it would naturally have aroused suspicion. Napoleon, therefore, ordered the ship to set sail. The next day, Adye came ashore with half a dozen English tourists, made sure that Napoleon was still on the island and sailed away later that afternoon, oblivious to what was going on around him.

Not all agreed with Napoleon's decision. When the Emperor told Drouot on 25 February that he was leaving – 'the whole of France regrets me and wants me back' – Drouot was 'struck with astonishment'. He nevertheless went along with the plans because, as he later stated at his court martial after Waterloo, he had sworn an oath of loyalty to Napoleon.[119] That evening, Napoleon let his mother and sister, as well as his servants, in on the secret without however telling them where he was headed. His mother was troubled by the news, but was quickly reassured by her son.[120] The rest of the time he spent drafting proclamations to the French people. He left the Villa Mulini around seven or eight o'clock that night. Crowds gathered around his carriage, accompanying him to the same port where he had disembarked ten months previously.[121] Everyone, it seemed, had turned out to see him go. When he finally reached the port, and he turned to address the crowd, there was a prolonged 'Shhh!' A few words were spoken, no doubt from the heart, before he embarked on a boat that was also followed by an array of vessels, some rented by the town's gentry so that they could approach the imperial brig.[122] On board the *Inconstant*, Napoleon is supposed to have said, 'The die is cast.'[123] Indeed, he was like a gambler who had lost everything but his shirt, but who had to have one last throw of the dice. It is what the French call the *maladie du pouvoir*. It is as though Napoleon undertook the journey just to show by his very presence that it was easy to overthrow the old Europe. 'There is no precedent in history for what I am about to do,' Napoleon told Colonel Mallet of the Guard, 'but I can count on popular astonishment, the state of public opinion, the resentment against the Allies, the affection of my soldiers, and the attachment to the Empire which lingers everywhere in France.'[124]

The departure was a bit of an anti-climax. Despite a good wind blowing all day, it had completely died down by evening, so that the convoy lay motionless in the harbour. The only way to get them out to sea within reach of a possible breeze was to row the ships out. It was midnight before they cleared the lighthouse and when dawn broke the next day they were still only about ten kilometres from the island.[125] At one point, as the *Inconstant* approached the island of Capraia, lookouts could see the French royalist frigate the *Melpomène* and the *Partridge* returning from Leghorn.

If Napoleon saw the *Partridge*, the *Partridge* did not see Napoleon. Incredibly, Captain Adye mistook the *Inconstant* for another French brig, the *Zéphir*, a ship that they expected to see in these waters, and so did not pursue it. Besides, Adye and Campbell both expected Napoleon to head for Naples (where he could join Murat) if he ever attempted an escape, not for France. As for the French frigates patrolling the waters, they seemed little interested in what was going on. There was a belief that Captain Collet, commanding the *Melpomène*, would either ignore or even help Napoleon if he ran into trouble, and since he too must have seen the *Inconstant* this appears to have been what happened. As for the *Zéphir*, it actually came so close to the *Inconstant* that the two captains had a shouted conversation. Here too one must presume that, unless Captain Andrieux was completely blind, he must have seen that the *Inconstant* was heavily laden, crowded with men, with other similarly packed ships following. One can only conclude that Andrieux had thus made himself complicit in Napoleon's escape; he was promoted after Napoleon's return to Paris. When the *Partridge* finally got to Elba and Campbell had figured out that Napoleon was heading for France, he lost time searching the islands of Capraia and Gorgona.

It was commonly believed in the south of France and in Piedmont that the English had favoured if not facilitated Napoleon's return, all the better to destroy him.[126] The rumour may have been put around by Napoleon himself in order to create discord among the allies. In fact, he had not been under guard – he had, after all, been granted sovereignty over Elba – and no orders had been issued to the fleet in the Mediterranean to patrol the waters around Elba. Even the English commissioner, Campbell, who initially intended staying on the island, was miffed about Napoleon's behaviour towards him and so spent much of his time in Italy, enjoying the delights and the company of a young lady he had met, and only deigned to visit the island occasionally. The longer Napoleon was on the island, the more bored Campbell became and the more he disliked the Emperor. Consequently he underestimated him: he did not believe Napoleon to be a man of extraordinary abilities. Quite the contrary, he believed Napoleon's talents were no greater than those demanded of a sub-prefect.[127]

If Napoleon was well informed about what was going on in France, Louis XVIII also had his spies on Elba.[128] It should have been obvious to him that Napoleon would not have been able to stay long on the island in relative inactivity. The last police report on Napoleon, made on 3 December 1814, suggested just that.[129] Indeed, there was no concerted policy towards Napoleon on the part of the allied powers; he had more or less been relegated to the margins of great-power politics as more important issues came to the fore. Although agents, prefects and spies were constantly remarking in reports that they simply did not believe Napoleon would stay on Elba, that his show of resignation was a façade and that he would attempt to return to France, they were all dismissed or ignored. The minister of police, Jacques-Claude Beugnot, sarcastically wrote to Louis XVIII, 'As if one could land in France with seven or eight hundred men . . . !'[130] They were about to get a surprise.

# THE SECOND COMING, 1815

# 25

# The Saviour Returns

## 'A Criminal and Impotent Delirium'

At daybreak on the morning of 1 March 1815, a small flotilla of ships came within sight of the French coast. The sky was clear, the sea calm, and a gentle breeze filled the sails. In a few hours they would be on 'sacred soil'. At one point, Napoleon took off the Elban cockade from his hat and replaced it with the tricolour. It took only a moment to accomplish but the reaction was spontaneous, emotional and loud: cheers, clapping, shouting and stamping of feet on the deck.[1] Between one and two o'clock in the afternoon, the anchors were lowered at Golfe Juan, between Cannes and Antibes, where the inhabitants would have been surprised to see the arrival of so many ships in a place that would ordinarily be quiet. The event could not but excite a certain amount of interest among the locals, so Drouot came up with the idea of circulating a rumour that the soldiers being brought ashore were either sick or on leave.[2] The Emperor went ashore around five that evening, helped by his Guard who held up a gangway so that he could walk from the boat without getting his feet wet. He was the ghost of his younger self. Now forty-five years old, he was corpulent, his complexion was dull and pallid, and he walked with a stiff gait.[3] Contemporaries who were to meet him over the next few months were less than impressed with the physique that stood before them. Everyone agreed that he had become 'very fat and browned'.[4]

At first, just a few troops were brought ashore. Captain Antoine Jean-Baptiste Lamouret, in charge of about twenty men, was supposed to take possession of a little coastal fort, but finding that it had been demolished decided to make his way to Antibes, about five kilometres away on another bay. The officer in charge of the local regiment, Major Jean-Léopold-Honoré Dauger, outwitted Lamouret and had him and his men arrested.[5] Napoleon left them there, although he dispatched General Pierre Jacques Etienne Cambronne of the Guard to make sure that no mail made it out of Antibes; it would not do for the rest of the country to learn that Napoleon had arrived and had suffered a setback almost immediately. During the night, he set up camp in an olive grove, in what is today the rue du Bivouac-Napoléon, near the church Notre Dame du Bon Voyage. A cordon of grenadiers was set up around him to keep the curious away. The first objective was to arrive in Paris without inciting a civil war, or without being accused of lighting its fires. To do that Napoleon had to prevent any guns being fired. He made sure his officers knew this, telling Cambronne that he should ride ahead, and that he was forbidden to 'fire a single shot. I do not want to shed one drop of French blood in the recovery of my crown.'[6]

Never one to miss an opportunity to leave his mark on history, Napoleon issued a proclamation, prepared in advance. In fact, there were three proclamations. The first was to the French people in which he declared that the Bourbon government was illegitimate, and that he had been betrayed before Paris (by Marmont). 'Your complaints and your desires have reached me in my exile,' he added. 'I have crossed the seas amid all sorts of perils, and I am here to resume my rights, which are also your own.'[7] The second was addressed to the army, to whom he said, 'We were not defeated.' It was another way of saying he had been betrayed, and many in the army believed it. He implored the troops to rally around him to liberate France, so that one day they could look back on this event and declare that they too had been part of the army that had delivered Paris.[8] The third proclamation was dictated to the Imperial Guard who accompanied him. Those who could made handwritten copies – there was no printing press available – inciting fellow soldiers to 'trample the white cockade, the badge of shame!'[9] These first proclamations mention neither liberty nor a constitution. Instead, Napoleon promised the troops glory and riches, and the people that their enemies would be expelled.[10]

This was a poor attempt to mirror his return from Egypt fifteen years earlier, and to hide his real motives. Napoleon's intense feelings of bitterness at having lost power in the first place come through. He was attempting to present the invasion as a return to power at the behest of the French people. We know, of course, that this was not the case, and that as far as Grenoble at least (see below) there was little popular reaction to his return. Napoleon left Elba not to save France, but to save himself from oblivion. In his declarations to the people of France it was important to present a new face. He adopted the posture of the protector of the poor. He was now a soldier of the Revolution come to liberate France from those who wanted to re-establish old privileges, and he claimed that the Austrians knew in advance and approved of his venture.[11] Interesting, too, is the transformation of his political message as he got nearer to Paris.[12] Napoleon portrayed himself as the reluctant hero who had heard the plaints of his people and now responded by reclaiming the legitimate government.[13] In an article in the *Moniteur* of 23 March, only two days after he had reached Paris, we can read how Napoleon was called to resume his throne at the wishes of the people. The phrase 'le peuple' appears to have replaced the word 'legitimate', as though the people were the foundations on which his legitimacy were built.[14]

At Lyons, Napoleon, perhaps sensing the anti-royalist and pro-Jacobin sentiments among the crowds that welcomed him, began to dismantle the

Bourbon monarchy by reinstating the tricolour flag, by extending an amnesty to military and civilian officers who had worked for the Bourbons (with some exceptions, such as Talleyrand), by confiscating property belonging to the princes of the House of Bourbon, by dismissing officers who had been integrated into the army since their return, and by expelling émigrés who had returned to France since 1 January 1814; in addition, émigré lands that had been restored were now to return to the state, the Chamber of Peers and the Chamber of Deputies were dissolved, and a decree calling for the representatives of the nation to come to Paris (in May) was issued.[15] At Lyons, it looked as though the spirit of 1789 and indeed 1793 was alive and well. The populist, radical reaction took a lot of people by surprise, including Napoleon, who then went about using it to his political advantage. Once in Paris, he issued a number of decrees that were supposed to cement his revolutionary credentials: all 'feudal titles' were suppressed (in fact they no longer existed); the nobility was abolished (it had been done away with in 1791); and all those who had accepted ministerial office under the Bourbons were to be exiled from Paris. Almost a thousand people would be arrested and arbitrarily detained and nearly 3,000 were placed under house arrest.[16] Historians have described these actions of Napoleon as combining the liberal notions of the Revolution, which essentially set out to establish a constitutional monarchy, with the more radical phase of the Revolution of 1793, encapsulated by the Terror, anti-royalism and anti-clericalism.[17]

This is true, but it is an oversimplification. As a child of the Revolution but also as a man wanting to reassert his imperial authority, Napoleon had little choice but to undo the foundations of the returned Bourbon monarchy, and at the same time to promise a more liberal national assembly. Was this going against the grain,[18] or was Napoleon being his most practical, opportunist self? He certainly played to the crowds when he thought it necessary. At Autun, for example, he was heard to talk about hanging priests and nobles from a lantern (*lanterner*).[19] This found an echo with the silk weavers of Lyons, who chanted, 'Down with the priests! Death to royalists!'[20] Napoleon caught on very quickly. He suddenly rediscovered his revolutionary roots, carried away by his own enthusiasm, imitating what he heard around him, pitting the poor against the rich, the peasantry against the local parish priests. He was now a man of the people, democratic, anti-Bourbon.[21] Neo-Jacobins at least liked what they heard; they rallied to him as the legitimate heir of the values of 1789. In the months that followed, anti-Bourbon sentiment was tapped into as Napoleon's new regime churned out caricatures that mocked Louis XVIII's physical appearance and reminded onlookers of the role the allies had played in restoring the Bourbons to the throne.[22]

The revolutionary rhetoric was in complete contrast to the moderate image Napoleon was also cultivating. If it did not inflame old hatreds against priests

Anonymous, *Glorieux règne de 19 ans – Comme il gouverne depuis 15 ans* (The glorious reign of nineteen years – How he has been governing for fifteen years), 1815. In the image on the left we see a corpulent Louis XVIII, who had theoretically reigned since the death of the dauphin in 1795, sitting at a horseshoe table full of food and drink, his responsibilities under his feet marked 'the Charter', 'forgetting the past' and 'freedom of the press', among other things. To the right is Napoleon, working at a table with little food and drink, with a pile of papers whose labels include 'freedom of religion' and 'the abolition of slavery'. He is signing a document releasing from prison the Duc d'Angoulême, the Comte d'Artois' son.

and nobles, the rhetoric opened old wounds that allowed those who had felt oppressed under the Bourbons to vent their frustration and rage. This was especially the case in the provinces where priests and nobles were harassed and sometimes attacked. The revolutionary song, 'La Marseillaise', also revived old animosities. Napoleon had always been very wary of 'La Marseillaise'; it was almost never sung during the Empire, and was deleted from the official list of songs.[23] The troops who rallied to him, however, began to sing it again in the weeks and months leading up to Waterloo.[24]

Napoleon, nevertheless, refused to rely on the people, especially those of Paris, whom he associated with the worst excesses of the Revolution and referred to as the 'dregs of the populace'.[25] His new regime had to be built on more solid foundations if he were to succeed in rallying the notables.

※    ※    ※

What followed has become part of the Napoleonic legend. It took Napoleon nineteen days to journey from the south coast of France to Paris, avoiding those towns and regions where he knew he was likely to get a less than warm welcome. The itinerary had in fact been planned in great detail by two obscure supporters of the Emperor: a glove-maker from Grenoble, Jean-Baptiste Dumoulin, and Napoleon's military surgeon on Elba, Joseph Emery.[26]

We cannot say with certainty that France welcomed Napoleon's return. Certainly, before he landed at Golfe Juan, there had been growing anxiety about the Bourbons and their more extreme supporters, who managed to destroy very quickly what goodwill had existed between the people and the Bourbons.[27] None of this of course explains the rapid collapse of the Restoration government when faced with the landing of Napoleon and a few troops. The reaction of the army was crucial. Just as it had been necessary to Bonaparte in 1799, so too was the army's role fundamental in allowing Napoleon to regain power in 1815.[28] This time, however, it was not so much the superior officers as the subalterns and the rank and file who were decisive. Despite the Restoration paying the army more attention in the first couple of weeks of March than it had done the whole of the previous year, and despite a campaign in the press to rally the army to the Bourbons, the common soldier turned his back on the king and went over to Napoleon.[29] Attempts on the part of high-ranking officers to garner support for Louis with cries of 'Vive le Roi!' were met with stony silence.[30] The 'contagious mutiny' that took place from below was made possible, however, only because the common soldier was pushed along by the people.[31]

In Vienna, things had not been going well. This is not the place to go into the difficulties the allies faced in coming to some sort of post-Napoleonic settlement, but the situation had deteriorated to such an extent over the Polish and Saxon questions that war appeared inevitable. It got to the point where Alexander was reported to have threatened to 'unleash' Napoleon on them.[32] One of Francis I's chamberlains, the Count von Seilern, had the same idea.[33] Frederick William and his generals were so unhappy with the way things were progressing that they talked openly of war.[34] Their inability to obtain the whole of Saxony did not go down at all well in Berlin. The Prussian Chancellor's house in Berlin was attacked by a mob, although nothing more than a few windows were broken.[35] The Prussians it would appear were spoiling for a fight, and not necessarily against France. Many believed it would inevitably come to that at some time in the future. Two days before Napoleon's return, Louis XVIII wrote to Talleyrand with instructions about what to do in the event of war.[36]

And then, on the morning of 7 March, news of the landing of the 'monster' in the south of France arrived. Though the remarks of the Polish Countess

Potocka about sovereigns and ministers sleeping with their hats on and their swords by their sides can be taken with a grain of salt, the initial reaction was nevertheless one of stupefaction mixed with fear.[37] The King of Bavaria 'lost his appetite', Alexander was alarmed and even Metternich was unable to maintain his composure.[38] Frederick William insisted Napoleon should have been treated more harshly.[39] When Marie-Louise heard the news, she remained entirely composed in public, but then burst out crying when she retired to her apartments.[40] The only person not to have been affected appears to have been Talleyrand, who remarked, 'It is a masterstroke.'[41] Later he declared, 'That man is organically mad.'[42] Talleyrand was not the only person to use that expression. Caulaincourt described the 'enterprise of the emperor' as 'mad'.[43] Not everyone, however, was displeased by the news. Some of the minor German princes, but especially the Prussian military, were delighted. The German princes saw it as a chance to reopen negotiations, while Prussia saw it as an opportunity to regain more territory in the inevitable war.[44]

The allies were hoping, in vain, that the French would rally round their king. On the same day that Napoleon was dismantling the Bourbon regime from Lyons, 13 March, the allies issued a declaration in Vienna stating that Napoleon had placed himself beyond the 'pale of civil and social relations' and that the French people would consequently 'annihilate this last attempt of a criminal and impotent delirium'.[45] They argued, hypocritically under the circumstances since they had been contemplating his forced removal from Elba, that as Napoleon had broken the Treaty of Fontainebleau he had 'destroyed the sole legal title by which his existence was bound'. The objective was clear – the allies declared war not against France or the French people, but against Napoleon. It was a well-worn tactic that had been used during the campaigns of 1813 and 1814, and as far back as 1804, when the Russians declared that they were waging war not on the people of France, but on its government, 'as tyrannic for France as for the rest of Europe'.[46] In that way, the coalition would appear to be anti-Napoleonic rather than anti-French.

It was also a call for assassination. Most of the other allied representatives baulked at assassination, but they did agree that Napoleon had placed himself outside the law, which essentially meant that he could be treated as a mad beast and shot on sight by any peasant who wanted to take a crack at him.[47] The idea of killing Napoleon had been around for a long time and had been contemplated by at least some of the allies. During the campaign for Germany in 1813 Bernadotte had declared, 'Bonaparte is a scoundrel. He has to be killed.'[48] In Paris, Louise Cochelet, reader to Hortense de Beauharnais, reported that many royalists were glad that Napoleon had had the idea of leaving his island, and that he would be 'hunted down like a wild beast'.[49] In England, on the other hand, radical writers and thinkers were outraged. An article by William Godwin appeared in the Morning Chronicle dubbing the appeal for assassination counter-productive and ludicrous.[50] More practically, there were some in the allied military camp who thought Napoleon should be captured and shot. The Prussian general, Gneisenau, was one.[51]

## Rumours

The people of Vienna appear quickly to have overcome their consternation.[52] For a brief period, rumours abounded about where Napoleon had landed and what had become of him: he had been defeated in battle and forced to re-embark; he had been victorious in battle and had seized Lyons; he had taken Louis XVIII prisoner; he had been shot by Ney.[53] Reports of his impending return had circulated as early as late spring 1814, that is, almost ten months before he actually did return, often spread by disgruntled demobilized soldiers (more than 300,000 of them), former imperial officers on half-pay (the vast majority fervent Bonapartists) of which there were about 10,000–12,000, schoolteachers and even, in one particular case, a clairvoyant. In the department of the Aisne, north-east of Paris, stories had circulated that Napoleon was about to return at the head of 200,000 troops.[54] At the end of 1814, in the Lower Rhine, 'absurd rumours' were spread about his arrival in Lyons.[55] Often they would be started by the appearance of a poster on a city wall announcing his return, put there by Bonapartists who only half believed what they were writing.[56] News of an impending return could take other forms. In the Lower Rhine, for example, medallions of an eagle with the inscription *Elle dort, elle se reveillera* (It is asleep, it will awaken) were in circulation.[57] Bonapartists meeting each other in the streets would cry out, 'Do you believe in Jesus Christ?', to which the other would reply, 'Yes, and in his resurrection.'[58] By the month of July 1814, reports of Napoleon's imminent return flared up all over the country, repeated by veterans, workers, peasants and habitués of the Paris salons: he had arrived in Leghorn; he had landed somewhere on the Italian coast;[59] he had returned to France at the head of a Turkish, German or Austrian army.[60] The rumours were often accompanied by public demonstrations of support for Napoleon and/or contempt for the Bourbons, especially in the army. It was, for example, difficult to get some regiments to stop shouting out 'Vive l'Empereur!' during assembly.[61] But this pro-Napoleon sentiment could also be found in the civilian population. At Saint-Etienne, for example, a wag posted the following on the church door:

Maison à vendre
Prêtre à pendre
Louis XVIII pour trois jours
Napoléon toujours

(House for sale
Priest to hang
Louis XVIII for three days
Napoleon for ever.)[62]

At Nancy, in the evening of 6 December 1814, four individuals entered the town in a chariot, shouting, 'Long live Bonaparte! Down with the Bourbons!' They were followed by a 'considerable multitude'.[63] At Dole, during the festival of St Louis to celebrate the monarchy, a house was set upon because the inhabitants dared illuminate their windows.[64] Not all demonstrations in favour of Napoleon were so public; the Bourbon regime prosecuted individuals caught expressing anti-Bourbon sentiments. Many displayed their pro-Napoleon tendencies more discreetly, buying and wearing objects that contained effigies of Napoleon.[65]

A number of reasons can be put forward to explain why the Bourbon regime collapsed so quickly, and whether the dangers associated with a landing could have been predicted.[66] First, the royal administration was badly organized. This was especially the case for the ministry of the interior, incapable of dealing with the reports with which it was being flooded from the provinces, not to mention the complete lack of communication between ministries. Then there was the police. Louis' spy network was not as extensive nor as efficient as Napoleon's. It meant that the monarchy was incapable of measuring the extent of the danger it faced. Finally, those in charge of the Bourbon regime were incompetent; there is no other word for it. In retrospect, a general with a couple of thousand loyal troops should have dealt easily with the problem of Napoleon's sudden arrival.

### Marching to Paris with their Hands in their Pockets

The reception Napoleon and his followers received as far as Grenoble had been lukewarm. At Digne, reached after an arduous trek through snow-covered mountain passes, Napoleon harangued the crowd, which acclaimed him, although most of the locals appear to have been less than impressed by his arrival. Only four people rallied to his flag – two soldiers, a gendarme and a shoemaker.[67] Admittedly, this was a sparsely populated region; things started to look up as they got on to the main road to Grenoble. At Sisteron, the mayor came out to greet Napoleon. When asked whether he thought the people of France would welcome him back on the throne, the mayor was forthright enough to tell him that they would, as long as they did not have to put up with conscription that had led to such appalling losses of life.[68] It was not until Gap that a certain amount of enthusiasm greeted Napoleon and his men; they were welcomed by the National Guard, the town was illuminated, and the men danced and drank all night. Fantin des Odoards was in Gap when Napoleon arrived 'like a bomb in the middle of the town'.[69] He was immediately faced with the painful choice between 'honour and duty' on the one hand and feelings of loyalty towards Napoleon on the other.

About the time Napoleon arrived in Sisteron, on Sunday 5 March, shortly after mass, the overweight director of telegraphs, Ignace Chappe, was seen running down one of the corridors of the Tuileries Palace, holding a telegraph message in his hand.[70]* He was heading for the office of the secretary of the King's Council, the Baron de Vitrolles. When he reached Vitrolles, out of breath and quite beside himself, he insisted the message be given to the king immediately. It was hardly correct procedure but Vitrolles understood that the circumstances were exceptional. At this time Louis was suffering terribly from arthritis to the point where he was spending most of his day on a couch with his feet wrapped in sheepskins. He was in that position when the Baron de Vitrolles entered. Louis opened the message and read in silence; his head sank into his hands. It was news that Napoleon had landed on the coast of Provence. 'It is Revolution once more,' the king pronounced; at least it was from his perspective. The monarchy tried to keep it secret as long as it could. A proclamation inserted into the *Moniteur universel* on 7 March referred only obliquely to Napoleon's landing by an order of the king declaring him a traitor and a rebel.[71] Official confirmation did not appear until the next day.[72] By then, news of Napoleon's arrival was already circulating, and some had begun sporting the tricolour cockade, although to do so meant being manhandled if not lynched by royalists.[73]

Reports about how Paris reacted to the news vary according to the political bent of the witnesses. For Germaine de Staël, the reaction was so great that she thought 'the earth was about to open up beneath my feet. For several days . . . the aid of prayer failed me entirely . . . it seemed to me that the Deity had withdrawn from the earth and would no longer communicate with the beings whom he had placed there.'[74] The Duchesse d'Abrantès described the news of Napoleon's return as 'lightning in the middle of a clear day'. She recalled that she and her friends looked at each other with 'an astonishment that was almost stupid'.[75] Antoine Marie Chamans, comte de Lavalette, former minister of posts, confessed that when he heard the news, he was 'half choked by emotion'.[76] Hippolyte Carnot, the son of the minister Lazare Carnot, was still a schoolboy at the time. He recalls the streets of Paris full of people who were sombre and dejected, and that it had 'the characteristic air of a great city on the eve of a catastrophe'.[77] Victor de Broglie, a royalist, asserted that the

---

* In 1794, Claude Chappe (brother of Ignace) invented a semaphore system that he called the 'telegraph'. Lines were established between Brest, Lille, Lyons and Paris, composed of a series of relay towers between ten and fifteen kilometres apart.

news made no discernible impression. The public squares were deserted, the shops closed and the cafés half opened.[78] There were no public outbursts of enthusiasm as there had been fifteen years previously when Bonaparte landed in the south of France on his return from Egypt.[79] But it is possible that royalists either did not comprehend or refused to admit the danger they were facing. The Comte Claude Donatien de Sesmaisons, who rallied to the Bourbons and was part of the Royal Guard, wrote, 'There is no cause for alarm. The man's folly was inconceivable. The situation is being well handled. Everything ought to be over in a week.'[80] He was right on that count at least; everything would be over in a week but not in the way he thought.

Another witness, a young American by the name of James Gallatin, noticed that if people in the streets looked depressed, and all the shops were closed, the cafés were overflowing with people.[81] Jules Michelet, also a schoolboy at this time, had a distinctly different memory. The news of Napoleon's landing exploded in Paris like a 'clap of thunder'.[82] Many Bonapartists appear to have gathered at the Palais Royal, and especially around the Café Montansier. On the evening of 20 March, someone brought along a bust of Napoleon and placed it with a certain amount of pomp on a platform, while the public sang songs in honour of the French army and its commander-in-chief.[83] It was from that café too that the first bouquets of violets, a flower that was going to become a Bonapartist symbol, appeared in Paris.[84]

## From Adventurer to Prince

Laffrey, twenty-odd kilometres south of Grenoble, was the turning point for Napoleon. There, he broke a stand-off between his own troops and nominally royalist forces under the command of General Lessard.[85] Accounts of what occurred vary but, at the head of his Guard, Napoleon stood before the troops sent to arrest him and said something like 'Soldiers! If there is anyone among you who wishes to kill the Emperor, here I am.'[86] He then allowed himself a melodramatic gesture; he opened his greatcoat and bared his chest.[87] Before that, though, it is possible that Lessard's troops dissolved as soon as they saw Napoleon and ran crying, shouting, cheering towards him. The gesture was not as courageous as has sometimes been portrayed, especially by artists in later years. What is often not said is that there had been a considerable coming and going between the two groups of soldiers. Intermediaries would have indicated to Napoleon the mood of the men facing him.

Till then, even those who supported Napoleon had thought that he would be 'shot like a dog'.[88] Napoleon summed it up best on St Helena when he said, 'Before Grenoble I was an adventurer. At Grenoble I became a reigning prince again.'[89] At one point, Louis XVIII relied on Ney to put a stop to Napoleon's journey. Ney, in a fit of zeal, promised to bring Napoleon back in a cage. It was just what the regime wanted to hear; Ney's bon mot quickly did the rounds of Parisian society. When confronted with the reality, though, at Besançon and Lons, where the troops were in no mood to fight for the monarchy, Ney had a change of heart.[90] He went over to Napoleon, and with him went any chance the Bourbons had of remaining in power.

In Grenoble, Napoleon decided to rest his men for thirty-six hours. The number now under his command had increased to 4,000 battle-hardened troops, twenty cannon and a regiment of hussars, hardly enough to wage a standing battle, but an army that was growing all the time as deserters, veterans and Bonapartists from around the region started arriving. That number was to increase, once he entered Lyons, to eleven infantry regiments, two cavalry regiments and fifty cannon, plus about six battalions of individuals who had answered the call. By the time Napoleon reached Avallon on 16 March (fifty kilometres south of Auxerre), 14,000 or so troops had rallied to him, stretched out along the road behind him for at least 160 kilometres.

The 'flight of the eagle', as Napoleon's return is called, is one of the foundational stories of the Napoleonic legend.[91] Even the Emperor's enemies understood that his return was a 'superb' gesture, a 'grandiose spectacle',[92] admired all the more because they also realized the adventure could not possibly succeed. The passage from Grenoble to Paris has been compared to a royal entry, during which time an accord was reached between the Emperor and the people of France who greeted him along the way.[93] At Gap, people prevented the prefect and the commanding general from placing the city in a state of siege.[94] At Grenoble, the cartwrights of the Faubourg Saint-Joseph broke down the gate at the Porte de Bonne to let Napoleon and his men in.[95] At Lyons, the silk workers tore down the barricades on the bridges across the Rhône that had been erected in order to prevent Napoleon from passing. Crowds of people gathered along the bridges and on the quays in such numbers, according to Napoleon's valet, that they risked being crushed, so desperate were they to get a glimpse of the Emperor.[96] At Villefranche, a crowd of 50,000–60,000 people had gathered outside the town hall to see and cheer him, despite the cold weather. Similar crowds gathered at Mâcon, Tournus and Châlons. At Autun, the tanning workers laid siege to the Hôtel de Ville and entered the cathedral with the tricolour flag three days before Napoleon reached the town. There were risings in Nevers, Dijon, Dole, Beaune, Auxonne and many villages throughout Burgundy and the Franche-Comté. In short, Bonapartist urban insurrections preceded Napoleon's arrival and almost always took the same form – the occupation of a central building like the town hall, the prefecture or the church, the suppression of monarchical symbols, the raising of the tricolour flag and often a procession that involved placing Napoleon's bust in a prominent public position. Agricol Perdiguier noted that the first thing that happened in his village after news of Napoleon's return was the hoisting of the tricolour flag on the church steeple.[97]

The *demi-soldes* were often behind these movements,[98] but Napoleon's acolytes were also sent ahead to prepare the way. It is impossible to know of course what motivated people to turn out to see Napoleon, curiosity or fervour. No doubt a core of people in those crowds could be described as Bonapartists, people who desired the return of their hero. It is quite possible that many turned out realizing this was an historic moment they should be a witness to. It does not mean to say they hated the Bourbons, or that they wanted to see Napoleon back in power. It is, however, an indication of the extent of his fame. While some may have welcomed his return, the majority of the French treated the event with either indifference or hostility. Certain regions eventually rose in revolt against Napoleon – the Vendée, the south-west and Provence – while the elite were circumspect to say the least.

Interestingly, few prefects, mayors or municipal councillors came out to support or greet Napoleon when he arrived in towns along the way. The only time he appears to have been officially welcomed was at Auxerre, where republican sentiment in the city was stronger than in other parts of France.[99] Auxerre was the last important city before the dash to Paris so Napoleon spent the day of 16 March, a Saturday, putting some order into his affairs, and writing to Marie-Louise asking her to join him. 'I shall be in Paris by the time you receive this letter. Come and join me with my son,' he pleaded. 'I hope to embrace you before the month is out.'[100]

All the next day, a Sunday, Napoleon was on the road, anxious to get to Paris as quickly as he could. He lunched at Joigny, and was at Sens by five in the afternoon. He left Pont-sur-Yonne at midnight, just as Louis was leaving the Tuileries. He pushed on to Fontainebleau, riding throughout the night, so that he arrived there at ten in the morning. He went straight to his apartments, where a fire had already been lit, and lay half dressed on his bed, exhausted after twenty hours on the road. He awoke after a few hours' sleep to find a number of letters and dispatches, the most important of which was from Lavalette, who had taken over the Post Office in Paris, and who wrote to inform him that Louis had fled and he should make for the Tuileries as soon as possible. That letter decided him to push on to Paris.

That day, 20 March, largely because of the rainy weather, but also because of the crowds of people who lined the road between Fontainebleau and Villejuif,[101] Napoleon made slow progress. It was six o'clock before he reached Essonnes, forty-odd kilometres from the centre of Paris. He arrived before the Tuileries around nine in the evening. By all accounts the crowd awaiting his 'magical arrival' was huge, possibly as many as 20,000, mostly made up of what might loosely be called the popular classes, the very petite bourgeoisie or the working classes.[102] When Napoleon was at last seen, 'the cry rose to such a pitch that you would have thought the ceilings were coming down'.[103] Writing many years later, Captain Léon Routier described how the thought of Napoleon arriving still made his heart palpitate with pleasure. According to some, the Emperor's carriage could barely move for the crowd; it was surrounded by officers 'mad with joy'. 'It was like witnessing the resurrection of Christ,' wrote Thiébault, who prided himself on being able to touch Napoleon or to kiss his clothes.[104]

Accounts of what followed vary. Alexandre de La Borde, an officer in the National Guard, claimed that Napoleon was hoisted on to the shoulders of supporters and carried into the Tuileries.[105] Napoleon is supposed to have confessed to someone close by, 'This is the happiest day of my life.'[106] Caulaincourt was able to shout out to Lavalette to put himself in front of Napoleon so that he could force a path. Lavalette did so, walking backwards for a while, eyes brimming over, exclaiming, 'What! It's you! It's you! It's finally you!',[107] as if he had just seen a ghost. In many respects he had. It was a 'fantastical apparition' that later took on a supernatural or holy character.[108]

## The Passionate and the Afflicted

And that is how it was treated by Napoleon's loyal followers, who were often overcome by the turn of events. The letters of devotion that started to come into Paris from around the country attest to the depth of feelings, some prepared to go so far as to die for him.[109] But there were private declarations of love as well. One officer wrote to his girlfriend, 'I am overwhelmed with happiness. I am mad with love and joy. I have found my Emperor again . . . What more do I need to be happy? . . . I can breathe at last. At the first news of this fortunate event, I pulled off the [fleur de] lys, replaced the white cockade with a red one and raised the eagle which has so often led us to victory.'[110] Jean Bordenave, a teacher, wrote to the ministry of war asking to be employed in the army: 'I found in my heart an emptiness similar to that which a lover has for the object of his passion; all that he sees, all that he hears renews his pain . . . such was my situation for one whole year . . . But now I feel like a lover who has recovered his desire; I offer my body as a bulwark to support His Majesty, and Vive l'Empereur and those who serve him.'[111] Etienne-Maurice Deschamps, who had survived the debacle that was the Russian campaign, described the feeling among his friends at news of Napoleon's return: 'Like children to whom it has been announced that their father, from whom they believed they were forever separated, has returned, they [Napoleon's supporters] could not contain their joy; it was made obvious in a thousand ways. The heart bore all the costs of that scene of general happiness, and if history is able to say that Trajan was loved by the human race, one can add that Napoleon was the idol of the French soldier.'[112]

Nevertheless, Napoleon's return was not without a moral dilemma for those who had sworn an oath of loyalty to Louis XVIII. Commandant de Lauthonnye had been presented by Napoleon with a Legion of Honour. He admitted that when he received the medal, 'I was dizzy with happiness, I cried so much that I could not thank him other than by shouting: "Long live the Emperor."' On Napoleon's return, his family had to make him promise to remain faithful to Louis XVIII. And yet, if Napoleon had personally asked him to follow him, Lauthonnye probably would not have been able to resist the call.[113] Captain Pierre Robinaux reported for duty but explained that he was 'sincerely afflicted' by not being able to keep his oath to Louis.[114] Others bided their time to see how things would play out.[115] Most officers, however, went over to Napoleon.[116] Indeed, many public servants who had served him, and who had yet sworn an oath of loyalty to Louis, reneged on their oaths and re-enlisted under the Emperor. However, some of Napoleon's best generals decided not to throw their lot in with him. Others, like Hippolyte d'Espinchal, came out against him and fought imperial troops on French soil. He reasoned, 'I had served with enthusiasm, zeal and devotion until the last moment, my admiration for him was like the memory of a religious cult, but his abdication had brought his destiny to an end: to abandon him before that time would have been cowardice and to return to him after having sworn an oath of loyalty to the king . . . would have been a breach of all the duties prescribed by honour.'[117]

Although many young men, naive in their assessment of their chances of victory, looked upon Napoleon as the 'avenger' who would rectify the wrongs of the Bourbon regime, the responses among the people varied according to class and region.[118] They were a good deal more muted in royalist strongholds and among the educated classes than in some working-class areas. Napoleon meant war – royalist propaganda worked on that theme – and support for him as a replacement for an unpopular Louis XVIII started to wane as soon as that became clear.[119] If the Tuileries was surrounded by a large group of enthusiasts, mostly workers and veterans, if some of the military were ecstatic about his return, if Napoleon was accompanied by hundreds of peasants, some armed, and if the townspeople warmly greeted him on the way to Paris, these scenes were limited to particular regions. In the rest of France, there appears to have been an extraordinary degree of indifference. Even Napoleon seems to have realized this when he stated, 'They have allowed me to come, just as they have let the others [the Bourbons] go.'[120]

## Napoleon Impotent

There is a difference between holding office and exercising real power. Between the time Napoleon entered Paris on 20 March to the time he fled ninety-eight days later, he was to learn of the chasm that existed between the two. In 1814, his control over the machinery of government was total. He now no longer had that control. Moreover, he left the details of the administration to two close collaborators – Carnot and Fouché. Carnot did not want or was not able to carry out a thorough purge of the administration that would see men loyal to the new regime put in place, while Fouché was playing his own little games, subverting Napoleon, maintaining contact with Louis XVIII in exile in Ghent, with Talleyrand in Vienna and with Wellington in Brussels. Fouché never really believed that Napoleon would prevail, and was only too eager to disrupt the good functioning of government.[121] Even with capable men in place in the provinces, most of the bureaucratic elites were playing a wait-and-see game, failing to pursue directives from Paris with vigour. Some municipalities pandered to both Napoleon and the Bourbons, hedging their bets, as it were.[122] The attitude seems to have been: 'If Napoleon wins, everything will be fine without measures having to be undertaken, and if he is defeated everything that we could have done will not have helped.'[123]

As a consequence, the administration of the country was disjointed, chaotic in places, virtually suspended or on hold in others. Where they could, royalists attempted to maintain their hold on local government; battalions of royalist volunteers, called *verdets*, were formed in the south, ready to rise in revolt when commanded to do so.[124] Royalists in Paris manifested their discontent in discreet ways, in much the same way that Bonapartists had done before the Emperor's return. Female royalists, for example, wore blue flowers (a royal colour and the sign of constancy), shawls were printed with royalist slogans, and royalist pamphlets and songs flooded the city.[125] Napoleon's hold on power was so tenuous – one royalist speaks of the 'decrepitude of power' – that it was enough for a rumour of his arrest to lead to demonstrations of joy in the Haute-Loire.[126] Others urged what today would be called civil disobedience, encouraging people not to pay taxes and to disobey the regime.[127]

All bureaucrats had to swear an oath of loyalty to Napoleon. Many did, some willingly, some reluctantly. This was the case with one of Napoleon's most loyal servitors before 1814, the Comte de Molé.[128] He refused to swear an oath of loyalty to the restored monarchy and was kept out of public office as a result. However, he was no more inclined to resume public office when Napoleon summoned him to the Tuileries and offered him a choice of portfolios, justice or foreign affairs. He turned them down, pleading ill-health, and reluctantly took on a position with less responsibility – Director of the Ponts et Chaussées (Bridges and Roads). The whole time he was there, however, he astutely refused to attend important meetings, signed nothing of significance and even sent a letter to Louis XVIII declaring his loyalty. He was so often absent – supposedly sick, travelling to various spas – it is a wonder Napoleon tolerated him at all.

Etienne-Denis Pasquier is another example. A former prefect of police under Napoleon, and Director of the Ponts et Chaussées under the Bourbons, Pasquier refused to adhere to the new government.[129] Friends intervened on his behalf so that he was not arrested. Napoleon tried to purge the administration, nominating his own men, but many refused to take up their positions, so that, for example, some departments remained without prefects, while others again went through four or five in the space of a few months.[130] There was a similar story in the bureaucracy. Administrators were encouraged to denounce their colleagues who had 'betrayed' Napoleon, but they simply refused to do so.[131] When the Emperor dismissed all the small-town mayors and held new elections to replace them, 80 per cent of those who had been put in place by the royal government were re-elected. If that was not exactly a slap in the face – there were all sorts of reasons why the mayors were returned – it was certainly a setback for Napoleon, who suffered because of it; he was not in complete control of the administration and hence not in complete control of the country.[132]

Among the people of France, the reaction to Napoleon's return was varied and incredibly complex.[133] It is difficult to get an accurate depiction of public opinion, but it is clear the country was divided along ideological lines. In cities such as Metz, Nevers, Grenoble, Lyons and Paris support for Napoleon seems to have been strong.[134] His followers went to considerable lengths to support the regime and the army. At Grenoble, French pupils at the lycée donated 400 francs, pupils from Nancy 500 francs.[135] Old soldiers offered up their pensions; government officials donated their salaries; women sold their jewels; administrative bodies and cultural organizations throughout France donated tens of thousands of francs. Solidarity was one sentiment, revenge was another. Resentment of the Bourbons in some towns and regions in the south, east and south-east of France led to an urban and rural reaction that often resulted in violence and the murder of royalists.

Support for Napoleon was also expressed in the formation of people's militias called the *fédérations*, different from the National Guard.[136] It was a spontaneous, popular movement that began in Brittany in the middle of April and spread quickly to the rest of the country. The *fédérations* brought together up to 100,000 men in various regional centres but especially in Paris where 20,000–25,000 men took part in this movement, predominantly motivated by two sentiments: a rejection of the House of Bourbon, and a patriotism born of the impending allied invasion.[137] In some parts of France, those who volunteered were overwhelmingly middle class. In Paris, however, they were largely working class and were based on the faubourgs Saint-Antoine and Marceau. Napoleon felt obliged to promise that he would arm them, but he did not warm to the idea. He was thinking of the *sans-culottes*, who had committed some of the worst excesses during the dark days of the Revolution. But he was caught in a bind. He could not very well suppress the popular enthusiasm that found expression in the *fédérations*, even as he donned anew the mantle of national reconciliation. In the end, they were never armed, even when Paris was about to be besieged by the allies – as we shall see.[138]

In other regions, however, the initial enthusiasm for Napoleon's return quickly waned, as though the people had collectively woken the morning after a drinking binge, regretting what they had done. In the north of France, Marseilles and the Vendée, support for the Bourbons remained constant.[139] In Poitiers, a bust of Napoleon was smashed. In Toulouse, Rouen, La Rochelle, Bayonne and Versailles, royalist proclamations were put up on the wall of the town overnight. In the town of Agde, in the south of France, violence broke out when a new municipal council was proclaimed. The Vendée rose up against Napoleon and in favour of the monarchy on 15 May, largely as a result of the renewed demands for men for war. In the other major urban centres – Bordeaux, Marseilles, Nîmes – royalists dug in their heels and had to be defeated militarily before control of those regional centres could be gained.[140] The pacification was at best fragile when it did occur. Some regions held out longer than others. The Vendée, for example, tied up 8,000 troops and cavalry, as well as part of the Young Guard. In all, more than 20,000 troops were occupied throughout the country putting down the internal flames of rebellion,[141] all of whom could have been put to better use at Waterloo.

# 26

# A Parody of Empire

## 'Venality Dressed in Ideological Garb'

Once installed in the Tuileries, Napoleon knew he could not simply take up where he had left off. Before Elba, he had been in undisputed command. After the first abdication, the French were given a charter that granted them a constitutional monarchy; anything less than that now would be unacceptable.[1] Napoleon, therefore, had to present the French people with the façade of himself as a liberal, and one way of doing that was to give them a new, more liberal constitution.

The man Napoleon chose to write a new constitution was Benjamin Constant. For most of his career as a writer, Constant had opposed the Napoleonic system, publishing in 1813 *De l'esprit de conquête* (The spirit of conquest), in which he attacked what he considered to be the cornerstone of imperial ideology – Napoleon's love of war and conquest. He insisted that Napoleon had come closer to achieving total control over his subjects than any other previous ruler. The Emperor had, in effect, usurped the Revolution and the principle of popular sovereignty. As late as March 1815, after hearing news of Napoleon's return, he published a vicious personal attack on him in the *Journal des Débats*, describing him as 'more terrible and more odious' than Attila and Genghis Khan.[2] He also pompously declared, 'I am not the man to crawl, a miserable traitor, from one seat of power to another. I am not the man to hide infamy by sophisms, or to mutter profane words with which to purchase a life of which I should feel ashamed.'

In fact, he was. When Constant met Napoleon on 14 April after being summoned to the Tuileries, he wrote in his diary that he thought him 'an astonishing man'. Napoleon had persuaded him to help prepare a new constitution, a fact that is a remarkable testament to his ability to charm even the staunchest opponent (or to Constant's overwhelming egotism and desire for political office). A few days later, Constant was appointed to the Council of State, and over the coming weeks and months became a confidant of the Emperor. During this time he wrote what was to become known as the Additional Act, an amendment to the imperial Constitution which introduced a number of changes: the recognition that sovereignty resided in the nation; greater independence for the judiciary; limited political representation; and freedom of the press. There were to be elections to a lower house, the Chamber of Representatives, but voting rights were limited to men who owned property and who were at least twenty-five years old. Napoleon appointed members to a new Chamber of Peers, much to the disgust of liberals and revolutionaries, who argued that this was a return to the *ancien régime*. Some of Constant's enemies claimed that the amendments were 'venality dressed in ideological garb'.[3] To those in his entourage Napoleon is supposed to have boasted that he would have done with this 'vain chatter' within six weeks.[4] Freedom of the press was a case in point.[5] Although royalists were able to vent their rage against Napoleon, especially in the form of pamphlets, censorship was introduced and the police raided royalist presses, both clandestine and legal, for being 'incendiary'.

There was, moreover, an inherent contradiction between what Napoleon set out to do – that is, introduce a liberal constitution that would win over bourgeois and enlightened opinion – and what the circumstances of the moment required, namely, a firm leader who could bring about a decisive military victory. Rather than consult with those most directly concerned, or have an elected national assembly draw up a new constitution (something that would have taken too long), Napoleon made sure he retained complete control over the whole process. As always, he wanted to be the master, but since no one believed that he would adhere to the Additional Act for long, when it was released to the public on 23 April it was greeted with scepticism.[6] The existence of a hereditary peerage, for example, contradicted the principles of equality demanded by the Revolution. Constant wrote in his journal that 'Never was blame so bitter, never was censure so unanimous.'[7] A cartoon in a liberal newspaper aptly illustrated their concerns. It shows Napoleon undergoing a medical examination by Cambacérès. When Napoleon asks, 'Dear cousin, what do you think of my state?', Cambacérès replies: 'Sire, this cannot last. Your Majesty has a very poor Constitution.'

The Constitution was, in short, badly received in France, unable to please any of the political factions. Even though it was more radical than the Bourbon Charter, liberals disliked being handed a constitution they had no part in shaping; republicans bemoaned the fact that it was not more 'revolutionary' and that it negated the principle of universal suffrage.[8] Bonapartists hardly saw the necessity of an Additional Act and believed Napoleon should govern as a dictator and that he should have dispensed altogether with elected assemblies.[9] Royalists, needless to say, rejected the whole exercise because it excluded any possibility of a return of the Bourbons. Indeed, there was a stream of critical pamphlets, some by those who had initially greeted Napoleon's return, but most by royalists who continued to see him as the 'usurper'.[10] The real problem was that Napoleon did not really believe in the new Constitution, and did not want the elite (certainly not the French public) discussing its terms. There was an evident contradiction in his private and public rhetoric that belied his true intentions. In reality, he did not care for a

Anonymous, *La Consultation* (The consultation), August 1815.

constitution that limited his powers in any way. In this, the accusation often levelled at émigrés is apposite for Napoleon; during his absence, he had neither learnt nor forgotten anything.

## The Last Plebiscite

Given the manner in which Napoleon resumed power and the poor reception accorded the new Constitution, the question of Napoleon's legitimacy was raised once again. He attempted to appease public opinion by adopting a strategy that had worked well at the beginning of his career – asking the people to approve of the new Constitution through a plebiscite. The Council of State reminded Napoleon that the source of all legitimate power was the people. 'The Prince was the first citizen of the State.' Napoleon's response – sovereignty was hereditary only in so far as the interests of the people demanded it.[11]

The polls for the plebiscite remained open from 26 April till the end of May. The relatively poor turnout for the plebiscite has been used to point to the lack of general support for the regime, or at the very least to the indifference most people felt about politics. In fact, it was not as bad as all that. There were around 1.5 million 'yes' votes, a far cry from the 3.2 million votes of 1804 certainly (although the Empire was greatly reduced in size), but comparable to the 1799 figures.[12] A little more than one in five voters turned out, once again a figure comparable to 1799.[13] Only one regiment in the army voted, almost unanimously, against the new Constitution, the 1st Legère. All record of the vote, however, disappeared so that, as in previous referenda, the army's vote appeared unanimous. In any event, the official figures were never published. Napoleon was nevertheless able to use the results to claim that he was legitimate and the Bourbon monarchy was not. He represented the people who had chosen him.[14]

It would be wrong to conclude that turnout demonstrated a lack of support for the regime, or that more people supported the Bourbons than were prepared to support the Additional Act.[15] The turnout can in part be explained by the regime failing to put pressure on people to vote. We know that royalists, on the other hand, threatened those who did with proscription once the king returned. However, neither of those reasons explains the general lack of enthusiasm.[16] It is probably safer to assume that the majority of French people remained indifferent to the new Constitution, not least because it would exclude them from voting in future elections. Besides, these kinds of figures can be deceptive. In Paris, 10,000–15,000 workers demonstrated on 14 May 1815 in favour of Napoleon, and yet we know that only 2,000 bothered to vote.[17] Even bourgeois liberals who fundamentally supported the regime failed to vote.[18] And yet Napoleon was warmly applauded whenever he went to the theatre. Every day people gathered outside the Tuileries to catch a glimpse of him, so that he felt compelled to change residence in order to avoid having to respond to the crowds – he took over the Elysée Palace on 18 April. Once the residence of the Marquise de Pompadour, it now belonged to Joseph, who was ousted to make way for his brother.[19]

If the plebiscite showed that there was at least some support for Napoleon, the results of the elections held in May 1814 positively demonstrated that the elites had turned against him. The electorate, limited to 100,000 people, had to elect 629 members to the lower house, dubbed the Chamber of Representatives. The majority of deputies returned were liberals of various colours (around 500), wary if not hostile towards Napoleon, while the rest were made up of an assortment of monarchists, Jacobins and republicans. Only about sixty deputies were what might be called Bonapartist. A number of prominent personalities, such as Lafayette, were openly hostile to Napoleon. Rather than elect Lucien as its first president, the deputies chose Comte Jean-Denis Lanjuinais, a man who had led the Senate's vote to depose Napoleon in 1814, and who refused to swear an oath of loyalty on Napoleon's return from Elba.[20] Lanjuinais was, in other words, an enemy in a Chamber of Representatives that was hardly compliant. One deputy expressed the mood of both the Chamber of Representatives and the Chamber of Peers by asserting, 'It is the dictatorship of the law that we must establish, and not that of one man.'[21]

### The Champ de Mai

Napoleon faced tremendous problems. What was needed was a man of action. What France got was a man whose inaction paralysed the country. This was not the Napoleon of 1796, or even of 1805. The decisiveness, the vigour and the zeal had gone. Carnot pointed out that Napoleon had become 'vacillating, he hesitates. Instead of acting, he talks . . . he asks for everyone's advice . . . he has become somnolent.'[22] Some even began to doubt his state of mind. Carnot found him staring at a portrait of his son with tears streaming down his face, and stated that he was unable to say the name of former companions in arms without a certain 'sadness'. The 'ungrateful abandonment' of 1814 had, apparently, deeply affected him.[23] He was certainly a good deal more emotional than he once had been, at least when it came to his private life. When he learnt of Berthier's death at the beginning of June – he fell to his death from the third floor of the residence he had retired to in Bamberg – Napoleon gave full vent to his pain.[24] Fontaine confided in his journal that 'his walk, his bearing, his expression, and his speech were characterized by an insensitivity that could be considered to be "an absence of reason". Prestige was destroyed; the extraordinary man was no longer recognizable and regret at seeing such a famous person embarrassingly survive his fall was the only feeling he inspired.'[25] Worried himself by this behaviour, and possibly urged by some in his entourage, Napoleon consulted a doctor, Foureau de Beauregard, whose sole recommendation was to work less and to get more exercise.[26] It was no doubt sound advice, and the symptoms Napoleon displayed were probably the result of nothing more than intense anxiety. Despite his state of mind, Napoleon was still capable of putting in eighteen-hour days, catching up with his sleep in a couple of three-hour slots.

The ceremony held on 1 June 1815 to celebrate the Additional Act was a pale replica of the Festival of the Federation during the Revolution, but Napoleon was also evoking two other traditions: an imperial Roman tradition, that of the Champ de Mai in which the people of Gaul supposedly united to elect their leader; and a Carolingian tradition in which free men bearing arms would renew their oath of loyalty to the regime.[27] In a bloated constitutional demonstration in the middle of the Champ de Mars that was a cross between the coronation and the Distribution of the Eagles, 20,000 troops and National Guard and deputations from various regions of the Empire filed past. The response of the National Guard to Napoleon's request, 'Swear to defend your eagles,' was not particularly keen, but that is hardly surprising when we know the Guard was made up of royalist sympathizers, and that it had refused to be integrated into the Grande Armée.[28] When Napoleon asked the military to swear to protect the eagles, there too the response was less enthusiastic than expected. An officer by the name of Pétiet remarked how disillusioned was the army over the new Constitution.[29]

The 200,000-odd people who turned out to see the ceremony came away disheartened by what they saw, or rather by what they had been unable to see.[30] The people had in fact largely been excluded from the proceedings. The huge pentagonal amphitheatre that was built in front of the Ecole Militaire seated about 20,000 people – invited dignitaries of the Empire – but entirely obscured the view of the people who had gathered in the Champ de Mars. Fontanes devised the ceremony but he was no David. A British witness described it as a 'specimen of imperial *charlatanry*', though he was hardly likely to be an objective observer.[31] Not all the provincial dignitaries managed to get to Paris in time, so tickets were handed out by the court, resulting in what one witness described as a descent into 'plebeian amusements' – drinking and loud behaviour.[32]

Napoleon appeared incredibly late, dressed in Roman garb that was so tight he had difficulty moving. Jules Michelet recalled his 'astonishment' at seeing him in this costume. 'It suited neither his age, nor his Moorish complexion [he was tanned from Elba], nor the circumstances, for he had not come to give us peace.'[33] This was reiterated in a set speech, a dialogue of sorts between one of the 500 electors, speaking in the name of the French people, and Napoleon. The message was clear: if the foreign powers rejected Napoleon's peace offers and left the French people no choice other than war or shame, then the whole nation would rise for war. 'Every Frenchman is a soldier: victory will follow your eagles, and our enemies, which were counting on a divided country, will soon regret having provoked us.'[34] The endless salvoes of artillery, the incredible pomp and the absurd luxury of the costumes worn by Napoleon and his brothers (which most people found bizarre)[35] revealed a complete misreading of what the people of Paris had been expecting and indeed wanted – that is, a return to simpler times, to the beginning of the Consulate when Bonaparte had been renowned for his simplicity. Instead, Napoleon had set out to impress the sovereigns of Europe. He may have uttered the words, 'My will is that of the people,' but the ceremony and the manner in which the people had been physically excluded from the proceedings were vastly at odds with the idea of any kind of political symbiosis.[36]

Napoleon himself appears to have realized this when, halfway through the ceremony, he walked from his throne away from the enclosed semicircle of officials and towards a platform in the middle of the Champ de Mars where, spontaneously, he quickly became surrounded both by the people who had come to see him and by his troops. It was only then, as he handed out eagles to the men who were to defend his regime, that the crowd responded with enthusiasm.

Napoleon knew, as did everyone present at the festival, that war awaited him. Some of the very first measures introduced after he arrived at the Tuileries in March were directed at reorganizing the army.[37] On 3 May, the ministry of war addressed a letter to all prefects, sub-prefects and mayors urging them to defend the national territory.[38] This was a radical departure from 1814 when Napoleon had shown just how reluctant he was to involve the people in the defence of his Empire. Now he was asking for the co-operation of all French people to harass allied convoys, and defend local towns and villages. Felix Le Peletier proposed in the Chamber of Representatives on 7 June 1815 that Napoleon be declared 'Saviour of the *Patrie*'.[39] The war was meant to be 'national'; it was anything but. There was no conscription in 1815. The Chamber refused to allow it. Napoleon was therefore forced to resort to a legislative sleight of hand. He categorized the class of 1815 as discharged soldiers who were therefore obliged to serve.[40] It was a neat trick but did not raise all that many troops – around 46,000 men – none of whom were ever used in the field. The inhabitants of a number of provinces simply refused to comply; the defeat of 1814 was still fresh in people's minds.[41]

### 'Never Did I See Such a Pounding Match'

It was not in Napoleon's make-up, nor for that matter in his interests, to sit and wait. There was every advantage to be gained from going on the offensive and defeating the enemy piecemeal, before the allies had time to amass large numbers of troops and invade France, as they had done in 1814. If that were to happen, Napoleon would once again be obliged to fight a defensive campaign that would almost inevitably lead to defeat. As things stood, it was a difficult situation, but his only hope of survival was to defeat the English and the Prussians in the north, before turning to the Austrians and Russians in Germany.

Napoleon's Army of the North comprised around 124,000 men and 358 cannon. There were almost twice as many men facing him in Belgium – 130,000 Prussians and Saxons under Blücher, and another 112,000 British, German and Dutch troops under Wellington – not to mention the numbers of allied troops converging on France, another 200,000 Austrians and Bavarians, and 250,000 Russians in the vicinity of Frankfurt.[42] As in 1813–14, there is a debate about the quality of the troops at Napoleon's disposal. Then, most contemporary opinions of the troops were negative, but these accounts are coloured by the aftermath of defeat.[43] Later, some historians have gone so far as to assert that, on the contrary, the troops were among the best Napoleon had ever commanded.[44] It is true that of the troops at his disposal, almost all of them had fought in at least one other campaign. There were, however, two overriding problems, not crucial in themselves, but likely to contribute to a collapse in morale if allied pressure were sustained long enough. Many of the veterans did not know each other and were thrown among a high percentage of young recruits who had never seen the face of battle. This does not make for poor troops, but it meant that they had not had time to form the personal bonds that often lead to unshakeable group cohesion.[45] The other problem was the lack of depth in the French army command. Of the twenty-three marshals that had been in the field at the time of the first abdication, only eight had rallied to Napoleon on his return. Berthier, Napoleon's chief of staff since 1796, had been replaced by a not-so-brilliant Soult. Ney and the newly appointed Marshal Emmanuel de Grouchy were competent commanders, but their weaknesses showed through at a time when Napoleon needed them to perform remarkable feats.

Unity of allied command in the north of France was given to Wellington, who rushed back from Vienna to Brussels, arriving on 4 April, as soon as he heard of Napoleon's return. He had his job cut out for him as the few troops to hand were mainly militia who had never seen active service. He set about trying to knock them into shape, but there were few officers he could rely on. He pestered the new prime minister, Lord Liverpool, to send him more over the coming weeks.[46] By the start of the campaign he had managed to cobble together British, Dutch and German contingents of about 112,000 men and 230 cannon. Then there were the Prussians to deal with. An army of about 130,000 men and 304 cannon based in eastern Belgium was centred on Liège. Their conduct throughout the campaign for France in 1814 had been deplorable, but that was perhaps understandable considering how much they had suffered over the years at the hands of the French occupier. In 1815, their behaviour was just as disgraceful. Marching through Holland on their way to Belgium, they behaved as if in enemy territory, looting everything they could along the way and, whenever anyone complained, telling them the British would foot the bill. The Prussian troops' attitude towards the Saxon contingents in Belgium was so bad that in May 1815 the Saxons mutinied and attacked Prussian headquarters. Blücher and Gneisenau were forced to flee.[47] The mutiny was put down – seven officers were shot and 14,000 Saxon troops were sent home – but it was a telling sign of the divisions that rent the allied armies. Given the recent history of relations between Prussia and Saxony, and the fact that the Prussians had occupied part of Saxony even before the Congress of Vienna had come to an end, it is understandable that they hated each other.

The allies under Wellington had briefly considered attacking France but decided to wait until they had overwhelming numerical superiority. As a consequence, Napoleon struck first. His strategy was typical when faced with crushing odds – to drive a wedge between the two armies and to defeat them one after the other. This he would have done if he had managed to defeat Blücher and the Prussians soundly. On 16 June 1815, he met them some forty-five kilometres south of Brussels, at Ligny, 'a village built of stone and thatched with straw, on a small stream which flows through flat meadows'.[48] The French were slightly outnumbered – 76,000 to the Prussians' 83,000 – while the Prussians had managed to dig themselves into the farmhouses, enclosed within walls and gates. Four times the French attacked and were driven back until finally the Prussians withdrew in good order. Napoleon had managed to maul them badly. At Ligny, the French lost 10,000–12,000 men, to the Prussians' 12,000 men killed and and 20,000 wounded.[49] Another 8,000–10,000 Prussians deserted. It was to be Napoleon's last victory. Because he was unable to press home his advantage, the Prussians escaped and would return to the fray at Waterloo on 18 June, turning the tide of battle against him. Grouchy was ordered to pursue Blücher with 33,000 men. That same day, ten kilometres to the north-west, Ney attacked Wellington's forces at Quatre Bras, with casualties of around 4,000 to 5,000 men on each side.

At Waterloo – the battlefield lay in a valley about sixteen kilometres south of Brussels – Napoleon's army slightly outnumbered and significantly outgunned the allies: 72,000 French troops and 246 cannon faced some 68,000 British, German and Dutch troops and 157 cannon.[50] The advantage was virtually negated, however, by the terrain and Wellington's positioning of his troops. They were placed on the reverse side of hills so that cannon fire proved ineffective. Rain before the battle turned much of the field into mud. Commenting on this, Victor Hugo wrote many years later, 'A little rain, and an unseasonable cloud crossing the sky, sufficed for the overthrow of the world.'[51] The battle was one of the most concentrated of the era, nearly 200,000 men fighting over an area of four square kilometres. It perhaps explains the incredibly high casualty rates, even for a Napoleonic battle. Forty-five per cent of the men involved in Waterloo would be either killed or wounded.[52]

The battle of Waterloo is one of the most written about in history, to the point where it has become synonymous with defeat.[53] In the English-language literature, Waterloo is often recounted from a British triumphalist perspective that until recently left little room for the role of the Prussian, Dutch or German contingents.[54] The British contingent made up less than one-quarter of the army facing Napoleon's forces that day. Certainly, Wellington was familiar with the terrain; he had examined the lie of the land on two occasions, in 1814 and again in 1815 when it became apparent that Napoleon was going to attack and that he would have to defend Brussels.[55] Wellington dug in his heels and performed well on the day, but Waterloo was not so much a British as an allied victory. Wellington would not have been able to carry the day had it not been for the Dutch and the Prussians.[56]

No one really knows what time the battle began – some say 10 a.m., others 11.30 – but it soon centred on the large farmhouse called Hougoumont, on the French left flank, defended by British Guards, and attacked relentlessly by the French for most of the afternoon.[57] Hougoumont and another farmhouse, La Haye Sainte, in the centre of the battlefield were key; they lay only a few hundred metres from Wellington's line, meaning that if not taken they would interrupt any advance by the French. There is no need to go into the details of the pounding taken by both sides. Late in the afternoon, the Prussians appeared on Napoleon's right flank. They were held off for some time while Napoleon launched the Guard at Wellington's line, roughly halfway between Hougoumont and La Haye Sainte, at about 7.30 in the evening. The Guard faltered, and retreated. It was the moment Wellington decided to launch a general advance across the line with the consequences that we now know.

Ney and Grouchy bear some of the burden of defeat: Ney for not pressing home his advantage after the battle of Ligny, for squandering his cavalry on useless attacks against British squares, and for pointless and costly attacks against Hougoumont which could easily have been reduced by an astute use of artillery; and Grouchy for letting Blücher slip away, also after Ligny, and for not riding to the sound of the cannon once the battle was engaged.[58] Grouchy actually heard the sound of the Grand Battery opening fire at the beginning of the battle, even though he was about twenty kilometres away to the east, and got into an argument with his commanding generals about whether they should ride to the sound of the guns.[59] Grouchy insisted on pressing after Blücher but never caught up with him, allowing Blücher to join Wellington later in the day.

In subsequent years, Napoleon sought to blame others for the defeat, exaggerating the number of men he faced, pointing to the deficiencies of his generals, and arguing that fate had abandoned him.[60] Ultimately, however, he must assume the responsibility. His efforts remained disappointing. The fact that Berthier, his brilliant former chief of staff, was not around meant that the army was not as numerous, not as well equipped and not as well organized as it could have been, with the consequence that it appears to have performed sluggishly throughout the campaign. So did Napoleon. He may have been looking for what he called a 'coup d'éclat',[61] but his behaviour during the days and weeks leading up to the fateful battle was listless. It is possible that he grossly underestimated the quality of the enemy before him. Wellington's account of the battle in a letter to Lord Beresford is telling: 'Never did I see such a pounding match. Both were what the boxers call gluttons. Napoleon did not manoeuvre at all. He just moved forward in the old style, in columns, and was driven off in the old style. The only difference was, that he mixed cavalry with his infantry, and supported both with an enormous quantity of artillery . . . I had the infantry for some time in squares, and we had the French cavalry walking about us as if they had been our own.'[62]

## Chaos

One of the turning points in the battle was the flight towards the end of the day of the Imperial Guard, which set in motion a general panic in the French ranks. This was not the Imperial Guard of old, decimated in Russia. Of the 50,000 members of the Guard who had entered Russia in 1812, a little over 1,500 returned, 200 of whom were permanently incapacitated. The Young Guard was wiped out entirely.[63] The Guard formed in 1813–14 was made up of experienced soldiers, meeting the minimum requirement of ten years' service and three campaigns, but possibly not as experienced as the Old Guard had once been.

There is an anecdote often told of the Guard's last stand. When asked to surrender Cambronne is famously reputed to have said one of two things: a brief but ballsy 'Merde', or the more prosaic 'Je meurs et je ne me rends pas' ('Shit', or 'I will die but I will not surrender').[64] It lends a romanticism to the end of the battle that conflicts with the harsh reality of a rout. The Guard that had lost the battle was transformed by this heroic, suicidal gesture. The phrase came to represent throughout the nineteenth century the suffering of Bonapartists faced with the fall of their idol.[65] After the battle, Napoleon tried to plunge into the heart of Cambronne's corps and expose himself to enemy fire, but was prevented from doing so by Soult. He was seen riding towards Charleroi with a little group of generals. They reached Quatre-Bras (near Genappe) by one that morning. There they stopped for a while and made a fire; Napoleon was spotted by an officer crying. Colonel Trefcon, who had experienced the retreats in Syria, in Russia and at Leipzig, wrote that he had never seen such a 'horrible disorder'.[66] The officers were unable to overcome the chaos; many of the troops were utterly demoralized, some preferred suicide rather than suffer at the hands of the enemy. Fear gripped the retreating army; small groups of men broke off from the main army and pillaged their way through the towns and villages in their path. Cries of

'Prussians! Prussians!', even when they were nowhere to be seen, were enough to throw men into a panic, tossing their muskets and sacks away, abandoning their colours and making a run for it.[67]

The astonishing thing about Waterloo is not so much that Napoleon lost the battle as his reaction to it. In all, 55,000–60,000 men were killed and wounded during that day in the space of a few square kilometres, along with 10,000 horses. But Napoleon still retained control over about 117,000 men in the north, yet he did not attempt to rally his troops, nor continue the fight and bring the battle to the enemy at another point. Blücher and Wellington did not co-ordinate their advance on France so it is more than possible that, had Napoleon rallied his troops, he could have inflicted defeats on both armies separately in order to be in a stronger position to negotiate. Many of the British troops believed Waterloo was only the first in what would be a series of battles,[68] and in some respects this was true. Other battles ensued in the days and weeks that followed.[69] Between 27 June and 3 July, three of the four Prussian army corps marching into France fought battles in the regions of Picardy and the Île de France.[70] At Rocquencourt, a Prussian brigade was almost completely annihilated. Battles were also fought at Sèvres and Meudon. But none of them involved Napoleon. To be fair, Napoleon was caught between a rock and a hard place. If, as had happened the previous year, he stayed with the army, he was likely to be betrayed in Paris. This time, he reasoned, he would sort out Paris first and return to the army in a few days.

The battle may have been the 'nearest run thing', as many contemporaries will attest,[71] but the fact remains that even if Napoleon had carried the day, it would not have made the slightest difference to his fate. He might have won another battle or two, but he could not possibly have won the campaign. One need only keep in mind the campaigns of 1813 and 1814 when he triumphed in a number of battles but was unable to win the war. This time, not only did he face the combined forces of the coalition but, as we have seen, his position at home was less than assured with little or no support from the elites. A prolonged and sustained campaign would soon have met with opposition if not revolt at home. A striking sign of Napleon's lack of support is that the price of shares in the Paris stock exchange went up on news of Waterloo.[72]

After the battle, Wellington immediately dispatched Major Henry Percy to London with some of the captured French flags and a letter – the now famous Waterloo Dispatch – announcing his victory. This gesture, this act, rewrote the history of the battle by forgetting to mention the role of the Prussians in the victory and by enhancing the Duke's own. It was the start of a romanticized account of the battle that would find its way on to the page of many a British poet and the canvas of many a British painter. When the letter reached London on evening of 21 June, it came as a shock; everybody had expected the renewed war to be protracted, so that news of victory produced a genuine sense of exhilaration among the people.[73]

Shortly after the battle, Walter Scott hurried to visit the field on which Napoleon had been defeated.[74] He was one among thousands of British tourists who now flocked to the Continent, many stopping to see the battlefield on their way to Paris.[75] The excursion to Waterloo was to remain a popular tourist site well into the 1820s and 1830s, and may have attracted up to 5,000 visitors each year.[76] Veterans also made the journey as a sort of pilgrimage. Tourists and veterans were not the only people; enterprising businessmen visited too, not for the relics they might be able to take home, and not out of a sense of history, but for the bones left lying on the ground. In November 1822, the London *Observer* ran a piece estimating that, over the previous year, more than a million bushels (about 36,000 cubic metres) of both human and animal bone had been collected from every battlefield in Europe and shipped back to the port of Hull. From there they were sent to factories in Yorkshire where the bones were ground down and sold as fertilizer.[77]

### 'I Have Received a Mortal Blow'

Napoleon reached Philippeville, a fortified town eighty kilometres south of Brussels, on the morning of 19 June. He stopped long enough to take a room at the Hôtel du Lion d'Or, where he wrote two letters. One was to the Chamber of Representatives, giving a misleading account of the battle and its outcome.[78] The other was to Joseph, almost as misleading, but optimistically, unrealistically defiant.[79] He began it with an ominous 'All is not lost,' and went on to calculate that he could muster up to 400,000 troops to continue the fight. 'The British', he wrote, 'are making slow headway. The Prussians are afraid of the peasantry and dare not advance too far.' Joseph received this letter in the afternoon of 20 June. He read it out to a hastily assembled gathering of ministers, but asked them to keep the news secret for the time being.

Napoleon's letter was part wishful thinking, part propaganda, a desire to hide the truth from the French people. The journey to Paris was not much more than a day's ride, but once there, and faced with the political reality, there was no further question of Napoleon's rejoining the army. Rumours of the defeat followed the army in retreat so that between 19 and 20 June it became general knowledge in Paris.[80] Crowds gathered outside the Chamber of Representatives at the Palais Bourbon trying to pick up news. It is where Emile Labretonnière, a pupil at the Imperial Lycée (today the Lycée Louis-le-Grand), heard of the defeat on 21 June. It is difficult if not impossible to know just what the French people, supporters or otherwise of the regime, thought. There is little in the press of the day and even less in the archives.

Official confirmation more or less came with an account of the battle published in the *Moniteur universel*, which admitted defeat after a fanciful report of what had happened that involved a fictional Middle Guard (*moyenne garde*).[81]

It took Napoleon three days to reach Paris from Waterloo. He arrived, exhausted, on 21 June between six and eight o'clock in the morning. Caulaincourt was there to greet him at the Elysée with the words, 'It would have been preferable for you not to have left the army. The army is your force, your security.'[82] Napoleon reportedly replied, 'The blow I have received is mortal.' He then babbled about calling a special meeting of both Chambers to ask them to give him the power, that is, another army, to 'save the country'. Caulaincourt confronted Napoleon with the reality, telling him that 'deputies seem more hostile to you than ever before . . . the Chamber [of Representatives] will not respond as you hope'. The Comte de Lavalette confirmed that the majority of the Chamber was inclined to demand his abdication. Napoleon's response is said to have been an epileptic laugh that worried those present.

Napoleon met with his ministers as he was taking his bath, receiving his treasurer, Peyrusse, and Davout, minister of war. Peyrusse entered service in 1805 as an employee of the treasury, and had followed Napoleon to Elba. He was devoted to the Emperor but now had to tell him that there was nothing in the treasury, while Davout admitted that few troops were at his disposal. He was possibly playing down the number of effectives available, estimated since then at between 50,000 and 120,000 men, but it might have been a reflection of the poor state of morale, not only among many of the troops but also among their commanders.[83]

During the morning, Napoleon appears to have recovered somewhat from the peripety and started talking about martial law, a temporary dictatorship, moving the government to Tours and fighting it out under the walls of Paris. The ministers, as well as Lucien and Joseph, listened to this ramble with lowered eyes in an embarrassed silence.[84] He then asked for their opinions. The old revolutionary Lazare Carnot, who feared above all another Restoration, fell back on what had once worked but now would no longer, urging Napoleon to declare the *patrie* in danger, just as he had done in 1793.[85] If Paris fell, the army would take up positions behind the Loire. Davout initially thought in terms of a military dictatorship – Brumaire *bis* – and thought that the Chambers should be dissolved (although he later argued against the use of brute force, when he realized that the moment to act had passed).[86] Caulaincourt (along with Cambacérès and Maret) believed on the contrary that the loyalty of the Chambers was paramount; otherwise the occupation of the capital and the end of the Empire would invariably follow. Michel Regnaud de Saint-Jean d'Angély, who had been with Napoleon in one capacity or another since the first Italian campaign, spoke frankly, declaring that the Chambers wanted Napoleon's abdication and that if he did not offer it, they would demand it.[87]

Napoleon was stunned by this admission, but received support for a military dictatorship from both Carnot and Lucien, who declared that if the Chambers were not inclined to join the Emperor, then he would have to save France by himself. At that point, Napoleon went on to describe how he would defend the north from invasion. It was entirely unrealistic. After the meeting had finished, Napoleon kept Carnot and Regnault behind and dictated a message to the deputies. In essence, it said that he had been on the verge of winning a great victory at Waterloo when 'a panic was caused by mischief-makers', but that he was going to take the necessary measures to ensure public safety.[88] The defeat had become a setback.

This kind of message, made of half-truths and exaggerations, might have worked in the past, but no longer. The deputies had already spoken to officers who had taken part in the battle and who had described it as a catastrophe. Besides, it was too late. An hour or so earlier the deputies, fearful that Napoleon was on the verge of carrying out another coup, had acted. Lafayette proposed declaring the Chamber of Representatives in permanent session and adding that any attempt to dissolve it should be considered high treason. While Lafayette may not exactly have 'saved' France, as he later pompously declared in his memoirs,[89] he certainly left Napoleon with far fewer options. The Chamber greeted these suggestions with loud cheering and applause; its members were in fighting mood and had already been considering the idea of Napoleon's dismissal, an idea put about by Fouché and his supporters. The proposal was adopted unanimously. Not only did Napoleon thus lose control of the Chamber, but if he refused to obey it, the deputies threatened, they would declare him an outlaw.[90] A short time later, they summoned Napoleon's ministers to the Chamber to answer their questions. By four o'clock that afternoon, the Elysée was surrounded by elements of the National Guard.[91] Napoleon was effectively a prisoner in his own capital.

Napoleon's rage over this development soon gave way to hesitation and resignation. It was all well and good to declare that he should have dissolved the Chamber of Representatives before leaving on campaign, but it was too late now. This was not Brumaire; there was no military solution to this problem. Faced with the lack of political support, Napoleon abandoned the fight. Rather than act boldly and decisively he dithered, letting the power he had taken on his return from Elba fall from his grasp. He did not challenge the Chamber, nor attempt to overthrow it, but tried to negotiate a political outcome, not for the country, but for himself.

### 'I Want Nothing for Myself'

About five o'clock that evening, Napoleon decided to go for a walk in the grounds of the Elysée Palace with Lucien, amid the echoes of the cries of a pro-Bonapartist crowd at the gates of the palace, possibly as many as 6,000, demanding weapons.[92] Lucien used this demonstration of loyalty to persuade Napoleon that he should take the law into his own hands and act.[93] It was Napoleon who rejected the idea. 'I will attempt everything for France. I want nothing for myself.' At this, Lucien's eyes filled with tears and he literally fell on his knees, 'admiring from the bottom of my heart this father of the *patrie*'. Lucien on his knees before his brother would have been a sight to see, but his account is poppycock, an attempt to create many years after the event the myth of Napoleon's self-sacrificing nature. In reality, Lucien came away from the meeting fuming. 'He is hesitating, he is temporizing,' he complained to a small group of men who included Carnot, Fouché, Caulaincourt and Davout. 'The smoke of Mont Saint-Jean [Waterloo] has gone to his head. He is a lost man.'[94]

He was indeed. Lucien was sent off that evening to the Chamber of Representatives to talk about 'the interests of France', to try to come to terms with them, in part by making menacing noises about a repetition of Brumaire. He entered the Chamber wearing the uniform of the National Guard. It shocked the deputies and seemed to confirm rumours that a coup was imminent.[95] Lucien was, in short, a terrible choice, and his intervention was to little effect.[96] Egged on by Fouché, the deputies openly discussed the possibility of Napoleon's abdication.[97] They did not yet, however, demand it – the motion was set aside – either because they remained wary of Napoleon[98] or because they were afraid of the army's reaction. Instead, they appointed a commission to *invite* Napoleon to abdicate.[99] If he refused, the Chamber would pronounce his deposition.

Later that evening, back at the Elysée, the Bonaparte family, or at least those who were in Paris, started to come together to consult about Napoleon's future. Hortense was the first to arrive, followed by Letizia; Joseph and Lucien joined them in the garden, along with Caulaincourt and Maret. Hortense had already urged Napoleon to write to Alexander or Francis to demand they offer him asylum.[100] He refused; he still felt resentful towards Francis for keeping him from his wife and child, and Alexander, he argued, was but a man. He would rather appeal to a people, like the English. Once more, Lucien tried to persuade Napoleon to dissolve the Chamber of Representatives, and insisted that within twenty-four hours its authority must be ended.[101] Maret and Caulaincourt argued, on the contrary, that he should accede to its demands or risk being deposed; he would lose any chance of his son succeeding him.

Lucien and Joseph left the Elysée around eleven o'clock to attend a meeting of the commission appointed by the Chamber of Representatives at the

Tuileries, presided over by Cambacérès.[102] They did not return until the first light of day; the commission decided that it would negotiate with the enemy, and that the ministers would attempt to obtain Napoleon's abdication. Later, on St Helena, Napoleon portrayed himself as standing alone that night against the world.[103] Two courses were left open to him: to try to save the country (never mind that he was the cause of the dilemma it now faced); or to abdicate, what he referred to as surrendering to the 'general pressure'. All were against him; he was alone; he had to give in. Napoleon thus depicted himself as a tragic figure, betrayed by all those around him, and nobly sacrificing himself after Waterloo for the good of the nation. That kind of self-serving rhetoric is to be expected of a man who had risked all on the throw of a dice. He could have had the most hostile members of the Chamber arrested that night, but he did not, arguing that he had no troops he could rely on. For his enemies and supporters alike, it simply demonstrated his irresolution, a defeatist attitude born of the realization that the powers pitted against France were overwhelming.

What one historian sympathetic to his plight has called the 'decisive battle' between Napoleon and his parliament began on 22 June.[104] He awoke after a night of 'incertitude and anxiety' in which he may have contemplated suicide.[105] At his *lever*, he grumbled something along the lines of 'They think they will save themselves by ruining me, but they will discover how mistaken they are.'[106] He was faced with a dilemma and was not able to come to a decision, whether to reject the Chamber's demands or continue to fight. Perhaps a part of him could not believe that the men he had placed in positions of power dared demand his abdication. Most of them were mediocrities for whom he had little or no respect. He should have known better. Many of these same men had turned on him in 1814. For this to come as a surprise shows the extent to which his hubris had become an impediment to sound politics.

We can spare the reader the painful details of what happened next. Suffice to say that after putting up a show of resistance and indignation, and sulking for a bit, Napoleon, for a second time, abdicated in favour of his son. He had little choice. Nor will we go into the complicated procedures that saw the Chamber proclaim Napoleon II and then shove him aside as a provisional government was named to negotiate with the allies.[107] Rumour had it that the Chamber made the proclamation only in order to placate the army momentarily.[108] Before that, Napoleon dictated an affected 'Declaration to the French People' in which he referred to the recent 'war of national independence'. He stated that his political life was over (for the second time in less than a year) and proclaimed his son emperor of the French under the title 'Napoleon II'. The declaration of abdication is a self-portrait in victimhood. It is the beginning of the progression of Napoleon towards a Christ-like figure who sacrifices himself for the good of the people. He had begun a war to protect the nation's independence (not, in other words, for personal gain), and now that he had failed, he was offering himself as a 'sacrifice to the hatred of France's enemies'.[109] By giving up the throne, even if he had little choice in the matter, he appeared to have committed the ultimate sacrifice for France.[110] 'May they be sincere in their declarations and really only be angry at me.'

The people of France had seen this once before. Napoleon may have convinced himself that he was acting for the greater good. He did not dissolve the assemblies and govern as a military dictator, even though there were crowds of people outside his window in Paris chanting 'Vive l'Empereur!' He did not, Napoleon told Constant, want to see Paris 'drenched in blood'.[111] And this from a man whose wars had cost France and Europe millions of lives.

# Epilogue

On 25 June 1815, around midday, Napoleon left the Elysée Palace for Malmaison where he was received by his stepdaughter, Hortense.[1] If he lingered there for five days it was possibly because, in his inimitable style, he was hoping to turn the situation around. In that eventuality, he drew up a proclamation to the army designed to restore confidence in his troops, in the expectation that his word would somehow spur them into action. The proclamation went something along the lines of 'Soldiers! A few more efforts and the coalition will be dissolved.'[2] The fact that he believed it was enough to issue a proclamation in order to have an impact on the course of events is an indication of how far removed from reality he was.

Napoleon did not do much over the next day or two except await a decision on his fate about whether he was to be allowed to travel with or without safe-conducts. When he was not overcome with torpor, he was fantasizing about possible options, none of them realistic. An anxiety-ridden entourage was forced to wait and watch.[3] The psychological impact of the defeat appears to have been too great for him to overcome the lethargy that now pervaded his mind and body. He plunged into a novel, he reminisced about Josephine with Hortense – 'I cannot get used to this place without her! Every moment I expect to see her come out of the avenues to gather the flowers she loved so much!'[4] – he saw his illegitimate son, Léon, who was now eight years old, taken to Malmaison by the father-in-law of Méneval, who had brought up the child. Léon was the spitting image of Napoleon, who told him that when he got to America, he would send for him.[5] That Napoleon was thinking of America there can be no doubt; he ordered his librarian, Barbier, to bring him some books on America, and started reading Alexander von Humboldt's *Voyages aux régions équinoxiales du Nouveau Continent*.[6] But when his entourage insisted that if he wanted to go to America he had to leave immediately, Napoleon procrastinated.

Reports of the Prussians drawing closer to Malmaison were coming in. A regiment of hussars and two regiments of infantry had supposedly received orders not to take Napoleon alive. Blücher had told Wellington that if he captured Napoleon he had every intention of having him shot on the very spot where the Duc d'Enghien had been executed.[7] It was, however, only once Admiral Decrès arrived at Malmaison early in the morning of 29 June to announce that the provisional government would allow two French frigates, the *Saale* and the *Méduse*, waiting off Rochefort, to sail that Napoleon had a change of heart.

After tearful farewells, after Hortense had generously handed him a diamond necklace worth millions, Napoleon left Malmaison on 29 June at around five in the evening, not through the main gates, where officers and civilians were waiting to acclaim him, but through a small gate at the back of the estate, so that his departure would not be noticed. It is said that before leaving, he spent time alone in the room in which Josephine had died.[8] It was a moment of nostalgia for what had once been, before he set off for a future that remained unclear.

In a calash with four horses, Napoleon was accompanied by Bertrand, Savary and General Nicolas Becker, all in civilian clothes; the valet de chambre, Saint-Denis, rode shotgun.[9] The group was divided into two small

Anonymous, *Le César de 1815* (The Caesar of 1815), July 1815. Napoleon, with winged shoes, is fleeing the battlefield of Waterloo, carrying in one hand a parchment marked 'Swiftly to Paris', and in the other a standard with an upside-down eagle. In a mockery of Caesar's famous dictum, he is made to say, 'Je suis venu, J'ai vu, J'ai fui' (I came, I saw, I fled). The inscription on the placard held by Victory reads, 'He ran from Egypt, Madrid, Moscow, Leipzig, Mont St Jean'.

convoys. Napoleon was fleeing in style. He was incapable of travelling without a retinue, insisting that etiquette be maintained. It was all that existed between Napoleon as great man and Napoleon as commoner. It is worth noting that, as with the flight to Elba, there were no high-ranking figures among the party joining Napoleon, nor indeed any of his family. Of those who did follow him into exile, their motives varied enormously. Some were self-serving. General Charles Tristan, Marquis de Montholon, a former imperial chamberlain, for example, may very well have been motivated by the fact that creditors were knocking on his door. Others again were entirely selfless, wanting simply to serve him as best they could. Loyalty demanded they follow him.

Napoleon reached Rambouillet, the summer residence where he had spent an idyllic time with Marie-Louise in 1810, later on the evening of 29 June. He lingered there a little, delaying his departure until nearly noon the following day. He was hoping, some say, that a courier would arrive recalling him to Paris. He and his party entered Niort on 1 July, stopping at an inn called the Boule d'Or. However, news of his presence spread so quickly, the next day attracting a considerable crowd of people singing patriotic songs to the Emperor, that the prefect insisted on Napoleon transferring his lodgings to the local prefecture.[10] The town was illuminated, and a reception hosted by the prefect was held in Napoleon's honour drawing, once again, a large number of people into the streets. It was at Niort, only about sixty kilometres from Rochefort on the Atlantic coast, that Napoleon received a note from Casimir de Bonnefoux, the prefect of that town, saying that the English blockade of the channels would make it 'extremely dangerous' for anybody trying to break out.

Bonnefoux, a royalist at heart and a man who had had a run-in with Bonaparte in 1800 when he was refused the rank of captain in the navy (largely, it has to be noted, because Bonnefoux refused to put to sea), was deliberately exaggerating. Between 3 and 5 July, although possibly unbeknown to the French, the *Bellerophon* (dubbed 'Billy Ruffian' by its crew because they were unable to pronounce it) was the only British frigate on blockade duty,[11] which made it highly unlikely that the commander could have prevented a determined attempt to break through. It is also highly unlikely that the *Bellerophon*'s commander, the thirty-eight-year-old Frederick Maitland, even knew of Napoleon's presence in Rochefort before 9 July. He was certainly aware that the Emperor had been defeated at Waterloo and that he was heading for the Atlantic coast, but that seems to have been the extent of his information until he received a letter from Rear-Admiral Sir Henry Hotham, in command of the British squadron off Brittany, informing him that Napoleon was indeed making for Rochefort.[12] By that time, Maitland had been joined by two other frigates, the *Myrmidon* and the *Slaney*, increasing his chances of capturing any vessel that attempted to run the blockade.

Napoleon arrived at Rochefort the next day (3 July), at eight in the morning, in front of the maritime prefecture. As he descended from the carriage he appeared, according to the prefect Bonnefoux, 'tired and dejected'.[13] All the witness reports from this period agree. He appears to have lapsed into a deep apathy. Montholon later recalled Napoleon's fits of hesitation, and could not understand why, in retrospect, he dithered so long at Rochefort – five days in all – when he could have made his escape at any time.[14] The procrastination, one can speculate, was probably due to his hope that the provisional government would still call on him to fight,[15] an illusion possibly nurtured by the few hundred demonstrators that had gathered in front of the gates of the prefecture demanding, as they had done in Paris and Niort, that he put himself at their head and continue the struggle. It was all that much more unrealistic since he had no way of knowing what was going on; he could only rely on out-of-date news about the military situation.[16] Later in the day, a crowd of people pushed their way through the garden of the prefecture to get a glimpse of him. They made their voices heard so insistently that Napoleon eventually gave in and appeared before them.[17]

There were a number of options open to Napoleon at this stage, if he truly was determined to try to reach America. Bonnefoux called a meeting on 4 July which involved the maritime authorities and Napoleon's party. The man in charge of the port, Admiral Martin, took control of the discussion. Two options were discussed. The two frigates waiting off Rochefort were the *Saale* and the *Méduse* (later made famous for its shipwreck, in part through the painting by Géricault).[18] At thirty-eight and forty-two guns respectively, with experienced captains, and with the *Saale* being one of the newest and fastest in the French navy, they were probably a match for the British vessels; one could have kept the *Bellerophon* busy while the other made its escape with its valuable cargo. However, Captain Philibert of the *Saale* insisted that they receive safe-conducts from the admiralty before attempting anything. The second, more realistic plan, proposed by Captain Charles Baudin, commander of the corvette *Bayadère*, was to travel further down the coast to Royan, and there board one of the two American vessels, either the *Pike* or the *Ludlow*, at anchor there, both very fast and capable of outrunning the British warships. The two French frigates would create a diversion and allow them to put to sea and escape the British patrols.

And still Napoleon remained undecided.[19] The excuses he gave ranged from not wanting to board a foreign vessel to not wanting to follow Baudin's insistent demands that he escape in great secrecy accompanied by two or three followers at most. That would leave those he left behind – sixty-four people had accompanied him to Rochefort – exposed to the vengeance of the Bourbons. This is possible but unlikely, given Napoleon's past record of caring little about those in his entourage. It is more likely that he was worried about how he would appear to others. What was he without his entourage, his gaggle of courtiers?

Ever since 1812, Napoleon, once resolute and decisive, had appeared invariably to be racked by indecision and inertia. This has something to do with the fact that he was no longer invincible, with the fact that the self-image shaped in his youth no longer coincided with the reality. The end result was depression. We are talking about a still youngish man – he was not yet forty-six – but he was in poor health, overweight and burnt out. Writing some years after the event, Baron Charles Lallemand blamed the delay on members of Napoleon's entourage who wanted him to surrender to the British; but, he also argued, the Emperor had lost any interest in his own personal safety and therefore left everything to others, 'loyal advisers', who were not particularly clear-sighted about what should happen.[20] Napoleon's hesitation may very well be explained by his fear of the consequences if he failed to elude the British blockade. If he had been captured, dressed incognito to boot, it would have been a blot on his reputation, a farce which he would not have been able to live down.

On 7 July, General Becker received a dispatch from the provisional government stating that Napoleon had to embark immediately, 'for the safety and tranquillity of the State are imperilled' by his delays.[21] It was only on 8 July, after repeated representations from Becker and Bonnefoux, that Napoleon agreed to embark for the Île d'Aix at the mouth of the Charente, with his entourage, from the little town of Fouras. There is a tendency on the part of some historians to portray Captain Maitland of the *Bellerophon* as having misled Napoleon or at least having deliberately lulled him into believing that England would welcome him as an exile.[22] It is quite possible that this did indeed happen, that a certain amount of trickery was used to lure him on board the *Bellerophon*. He was, after all, the biggest prize any naval captain could hope to capture. We know that, by Maitland's own admission, at one point in the conversations between the captain and Savary, he asked, rhetorically, 'why not ask asylum in Britain?'[23] The sloop *Falmouth* appeared with new orders from Admiral Hotham emphasizing that, if captured, Napoleon was to be kept in custody and returned to the nearest English port.[24] Maitland, it should be stressed, was never told what would be Napoleon's fate once he had reached port, in part because the British government was still unsure what to do with him. He made it clear on a number of occasions that he could not guarantee what his government's attitude would be once they reached England.[25]

*    *    *

Two days were spent on the island of Aix, 12 and 13 July, during which Napoleon again considered his options: the possibility of escaping with Baudin (General Lallemand was sent to confirm that Baudin was still prepared to risk the blockade); or leaving with Joseph, who arrived on the island on 13 July and who offered, generously under the circumstances, to stay on at Aix and play the part of Napoleon while his brother escaped to America. There appear to have been two cliques at work trying to influence Napoleon's decision: those who were prepared to accept any risk rather than fall into the hands of the English; and those like Bertrand, Savary and Las Cases who, on the contrary, believed that surrender to the English was the best possible course of action.[26] In fact, it would seem that Napoleon had already made up his mind. England appeared to offer him a helping hand, a choice that would enable him to leave France with the dignity by which he held so much store.

At dawn, Napoleon sent Las Cases, this time with Lallemand, back to the *Bellerophon* to negotiate his surrender. The two went away from a discussion with Maitland under the mistaken impression that the Emperor would be free to pursue his voyage to the United States. Even then Lallemand made a last-ditch attempt to persuade Napoleon to escape using Baudin's offer of the *Bayadère*. Had Napoleon been thinking all this time of Paoli, his one-time idol who had found asylum in England when he fled Corsica and French oppression? Napoleon may very well have been under the mistaken impression that because he was seeking asylum he would be granted it automatically, and that he would enjoy the same rights as any Englishman under the law.[27]

Las Cases announced to Maitland that Napoleon would be arriving the next day at four or five in the morning, as a simple citizen, under the name of Colonel Muiron (the young officer who had supposedly sacrificed his life for Bonaparte on the bridge at Arcola), 'to enjoy the protection of your country's laws'. While Maitland often reiterated that he had no authority for granting terms of any kind, Napoleon wanted to believe that his enemy was generous and he, playing the role of some sort of fallen Greek hero, expected the rest of the world to behave magnanimously.

Before coming on board the *Bellerophon*, Napoleon wrote a pretentious letter to an even more pompous man, the Prince Regent, declaring that he had come 'like Themistocles, to throw [himself] upon the hospitality of the British people', putting himself under the protection of British law, which he claimed from the Prince Regent 'as the most powerful, most constant and most generous of my enemies'.[28]* The reference to Themistocles was hardly likely to cut

---

* After defeating the Persians in 483 BC, Themistocles was obliged to flee Greece from the Spartans in 472 or 471 BC. He travelled to Asia Minor, where he entered the service of the Persian king, Artaxerxes I.

it with the English. When the first secretary to the Admiralty, John Wilson Croker, first heard of the reference, he roared with laughter.[29]

Napoleon came on board the *Bellerophon* between six and seven o'clock in the morning (the accounts vary). The act was not without some irony. In Greek mythology, Bellerophon brought upon himself the wrath of the gods by trying to ride the winged horse Pegasus to heaven. Pegasus threw him, and he ended his life as a lonely outcast. The dilemma for Maitland was how to receive Napoleon – as foreign sovereign, or as an enemy general surrendering? In the end he compromised, falling back on custom, which was not to engage in ceremonial honours before eight in the morning or after sunset.[30] Maitland thus decided to order a guard of marines to be drawn up on deck, but stipulated that they were not to present arms. Moreover, although the Emperor was piped aboard, Maitland and the other officers of his crew waited on the quarterdeck, obliging Napoleon to climb up the admittedly short stairway to greet them. He greeted Maitland with the words, necessarily spoken in French, 'I have come to throw myself on the protection of your Prince and your laws.' Maitland virtually treated Napoleon as a royal personage – hats were taken off in his presence, he was addressed as 'Sire' but only after the Emperor had first spoken to his interlocutor – that is, one could not just start a conversation with Napoleon. The attitude of Admiral Hotham, who arrived in the *Superb* the same day, led Napoleon to believe that the British would continue to treat him as a sovereign on reaching English shores. Most of the voyage to the English coast was spent in his cabin, where he would sometimes read or play cards, or fall asleep on the sofa in his cabin. The curiosity he had shown during the first days, enquiring about the workings of the vessel and those who manned it, had given way to lethargy. He did not appear on deck except for a short period after 5 p.m. and before evening meals at six, during which time he appeared distracted and lost in thought.

Seven days later, early in the morning of 23 July, the ship was abreast of the island of Ushant off the coast of Brittany. Midshipman George Home had come on deck and saw Napoleon just about to ascend the ladder to the poop deck. Because the decks had just been washed down, he rushed to offer Napoleon his arm. Napoleon smiled, pointed upwards and said in broken English, 'The poop, the poop.' When they had both climbed up there, he thanked Home, pointed to the island and asked, 'Ushant? Cape Ushant?' He then took out a pocket glass and looked 'eagerly at the land'. It was just after 4 a.m. He stayed on the poop till midday.[31] In the course of the morning, several members of his suite joined him, but he paid no 'attention to what was passing around him' or even addressed his entourage, who stood behind him all this time. It was an unusual posture to hold for such a long period of time and can really only be explained by the deep but no doubt conflicted feelings he was experiencing. After land had entirely disappeared from view, and without having uttered a word the whole time, Napoleon 'tottered down the poop-ladder; his head hung heavily forward, so as to render his countenance scarcely visible'. He would never set eyes on France again.

# NOTES

## REGENERATION, 1799–1802
### 1: The Invention of a Saviour

1. Patrick Gueniffey, *Le Dix-huit Brumaire: l'épilogue de la Révolution française* (Paris, 2008), pp. 307–8.
2. Louis-Antoine Fauvelet de Bourrienne, *Mémoires de M. de Bourrienne, ministre d'Etat: sur Napoléon, le Directoire, le Consulat, l'Empire et la Restauration*, 10 vols (Paris, 1829), iii. p. 108.
3. The hand in a partially unbuttoned waistcoat was an English portrait convention long before Napoleon made it his. See Arline Meyer, 'Re-dressing Classical Statuary: The Eighteenth-Century "Hand-in-Waistcoat" Portrait', *Art Bulletin*, 77(2) (1995), 45–64.
4. Christine Reinhard, *Une femme de diplomate: lettres de Mme Reinhard à sa mere, 1798–1815* (Paris, 1900), pp. 97–8, 99.
5. A[rchives] N[ationales], AFIV 1329, 13 November 1799 (22 brumaire an VIII); François-Alphonse Aulard, 'Le lendemain du dix-huit brumaire', in *Etudes et leçons sur la Révolution française*, seconde série (Paris, 1898), pp. 223–5.
6. See Philip Dwyer, *Napoleon: The Path to Power, 1769–1799* (London, 2007), p. 176.
7. Gilbert Bodinier, 'Que veut l'armée? Soutien et résistance à Bonaparte', in *Terminer la Révolution?: actes du colloque* (Paris, 2003), p. 66.
8. *Moniteur universel*, 24 brumaire an VIII (15 November 1799); Thierry Lentz, *Le 18–Brumaire: les coups d'état de Napoléon Bonaparte* (Paris, 1997), p. 382; Bodinier, 'Que veut l'armée?, in *Terminer la Révolution?*, pp. 65–7.
9. André Masséna, *Mémoires de Masséna*, 7 vols (Paris, 1848–50), iv. p. 6; François Roguet, *Mémoires militaires du lieutenant général Cte Roguet*, 4 vols (Paris, 1862–5), ii. p. 215.
10. Pierre-Bertrand-Louis Brun de Villeret, *Les cahiers du général Brun, baron de Villeret, pair de France: 1773–1845* (Paris, 1953), p. 20; Albert Vandal, *L'avènement de Bonaparte*, 2 vols (Paris, 1903–7), i. pp. 472–5; Thierry Lentz, *Le Grand Consulat, 1799–1804* (Paris, 1999), pp. 161–2; Gueniffey, *Le Dix-huit Brumaire*, pp. 314–16.
11. For oppositional elements within the army see Natalie Petiteau, 'Les fidélités républicaines sous le Consulat et l'Empire', *Annales historiques de la Révolution française*, 346 (2006), 59–74; Walter Bruyère-Ostells, 'Les officiers républicains sous l'Empire: entre tradition républicaine, ralliement et tournant libérale', *Annales historiques de la Révolution française*, 346 (2006), 31–44; Bernard Gainot, 'L'opposition militaire: autour des sociétés secrètes dans l'armée', *Annales historiques de la Révolution française*, 346 (2006), 45–58.
12. Rafe Blaufarb, *The French Army, 1750–1820: Careers, Talent, Merit* (Manchester, 2002), pp. 166–72, who argues that the purge was part of a 'broader push to raise the social standing of the officer corps'.
13. Malcolm Crook, *Napoleon Comes to Power: Democracy and Dictatorship in Revolutionary France, 1795–1804* (Cardiff, 1998), p. 70.
14. Crook, *Napoleon Comes to Power*, p. 66.
15. Natalie Petiteau, *Les Français et l'Empire (1799–1815)* (Paris, 2008), p. 37; Gueniffey, *Le*

*Dix-huit Brumaire*, p. 312. One month after the coup only three departments had not adhered to the new regime, two of them Corsican. The reactions are detailed in Elisabeth Berlioz (ed.), *La situation des départements et l'installation des premiers préfets en l'an VIII* (Paris, 2000); Alphonse Aulard, *L'état de la France en l'an VIII et en l'an IX* (Paris, 1897).

16. See, for example, the letters printed in the *Moniteur universel*, 1 and 19 frimaire an VIII (22 November and 10 December 1799).
17. The most recent and most accessible biography is Peter McPhee's *Robespierre: A Revolutionary Life* (New Haven, 2012).
18. See Howard Brown, 'Echoes of the Terror', *Historical Reflections/Réflexions Historiques*, 29 (2003), 542–50.
19. *Moniteur universel*, 27 brumaire an VIII (18 November 1799).
20. Alphonse Aulard, *Paris sous le Consulat*, 4 vols (Paris, 1903), i. p. 4.
21. Mona Ozouf, *Festivals and the French Revolution*, trans. Alan Sheridan (Cambridge, Mass., 1988), p. 174.
22. Isser Woloch, *Napoleon and his Collaborators: The Making of a Dictatorship* (New York, 2001), p. 27.
23. Vandal, *L'avènement de Bonaparte*, i. pp. 425–7.
24. Alphonse Aulard, *Registre des délibérations du consulat provisoire, 20 brumaire–3 nivôse an VIII (11 novembre–24 décembre 1799)*, 2 vols (Paris, 1894), i. p. 43; Woloch, *Napoleon and his Collaborators*, p. 27.
25. Vandal, *L'avènement de Bonaparte*, i. p. 427.
26. Woloch, *Napoleon and his Collaborators*, pp. 27–8.
27. See, for example, Jonathan Devlin, 'The Army, Politics and Public Order in Directorial Provence, 1795–1800', *Historical Journal*, 32:1 (1989), 87–106.
28. Howard G. Brown, *Ending the French Revolution: Violence, Justice, and Repression from the Terror to Napoleon* (Charlottesville, 2006), pp. 216–21.
29. Napoléon Bonaparte, *Corr[espondance] de Napoléon I publiée par ordre de l'empereur Napoléon III*, 32 vols (Paris, 1858–70), vi. n. 4391 (12 November 1799).
30. *Moniteur universel*, 23 brumaire VIII (13 November 1799).
31. A phrase that, as far as I am aware, Bonaparte never pronounced, but which was adapted from a newspaper article about Consular dress in *Le Diplomate* (6 frimaire an VIII) (Aulard, *Paris sous le Consulat*, i. p. 30). The red bonnets are a reference to the Phrygian caps of the revolutionary *sans-culottes*, and the red heels to aristocratic dress.
32. André-François, comte Miot de Mélito, *Mémoires du comte Miot de Mélito*, 3 vols (Paris, 1873–4), i. p. 265; Natalie Petiteau, 'La Contre-Révolution endiguée? Projets et réalisations sociales impériales', in Jean-Clément Martin (ed.), *La Contre-Revolution en Europe, XVIIIe–XIXe siècles: réalités politiques et sociales, résonances culturelles et idéologiques* (Rennes, 2001), pp. 183–4.
33. *Journal des hommes libres*, 28 December 1799 (6 nivôse an VIII). This was the assertion if not the desire of some notable Brumairians such as Dominique Garat and Pierre-Jean-Georges Cabanis. See Dominique Garat, 'Discours prononcé par Garat dans la séance du 23 frimaire', in Vincent Lombard de Langres, *Le dix-huit brumaire, ou Tableau des événemens qui ont amené cette journée* (Paris, an VIII), pp. 426, 428; and Pierre-Jean-Georges Cabanis, *Quelques Considérations sur l'organisation sociale en général et particulièrement sur la nouvelle constitution, par Cabanis* (Paris, an VIII), pp. 3–4.
34. *Corr.* vi. n. 4468 (27 December 1799).
35. Miot de Mélito, *Mémoires*, i. pp. 266–7.
36. Such as François Barbé-Marbois, deported on 18 fructidor (4 September 1797), called to the Council of State; General Jourdan, who had spoken out against 18 Brumaire, named minister extraordinary in Piedmont; François Antoine de Boissy d'Anglas, a constitutional monarchist condemned to exile by the Directory, named to the Tribunate in March 1801 and who served Napoleon loyally till Waterloo (John R. Ballard, *Continuity during the Storm: Boissy d'Anglas and the Era of the French Revolution* (Westport, Conn., 2000),

pp. 133–7); and Etienne Bernier, a refractory priest who became agent general of the royal and Catholic armies in the Vendée, helped negotiate the Concordat and was made Bishop of Orleans.

37. Comte François Nicolas Mollien, *Mémoires d'un ministre du Trésor public, 1780–1815*, 3 vols (Paris, 1898), i. p. 231. For Bonaparte's views on factions see *Corr.* vi. n. 4385 (9 November 1799); vii. n. 5634 (14 July 1801).

38. Gueniffey, *Le Dix-huit Brumaire*, p. 328.

39. *L'Ami des lois*, 6 December 1799 (16 frimaire an VIII); Aulard, *Paris sous le Consulat*, i. p. 42.

40. Paul Bastid, *Sieyès et sa pensée* (Paris, 1970), pp. 236–7.

41. Henri Gatien Bertrand, *Cahiers de Sainte-Hélène*, ed. Paul Fleuriot de Langle, 3 vols (Paris, 1959), ii. p. 280.

42. *Corr.* xxx. p. 326; Vandal, *L'avènement de Bonaparte*, i. p. 409; Bastid, *Sieyès*, pp. 247–9; Woloch, *Napoleon and his Collaborators*, pp. 26–7.

43. This situation lasted for another six weeks until Bonaparte was officially recognized as First Consul on Christmas Eve 1799. Aulard, *Registre des délibérations du consulat provisoire*, i. p. 5.

44. That is the tenor of the message to the legislative commission announcing his appointment as First Consul (*Corr.* vi. n. 4431 (20 December 1799)).

45. Louis-Alexandre Berthier was named minister of war, replacing Edmond Louis Alexis Dubois-Crancé, who had refused to take part in the coup (Victor-Bernard Derrécagaix, *Le maréchal Berthier, prince de Wagram et de Neuchâtel*, 2 vols (Paris, 1904, reprinted 2002), i. pp. 370–5). Having a faithful ally in this position was a not so subtle means of controlling the army, assuming Bonaparte could purge it of hostile elements, but Berthier was also a competent administrator. The only other new ministers were Martin-Michel-Charles Gaudin in finance (for Jean-Baptiste Robert Lindet, who refused office), and Pierre-Simon, marquis de Laplace, a member of the Institute, who was made minister of the interior as a sop to the Ideologues who had supported the coup (Martin-Michel-Charles Gaudin, *Mémoires, souvenirs, opinions et écrits du Duc de Gaëte*, 2 vols (Paris, 1826), pp. 45–6; Roger Hahn, *Pierre Simon Laplace 1749–1827: A Determined Scientist* (Cambridge, Mass., 2005), pp. 128–30). All the other ministers were, for the moment, kept in place: Jean-Jacques Régis de Cambacérès remained as minister of justice; Charles-Frédéric Reinhard was maintained as minister for foreign affairs; Fouché was maintained as minister of police; while Marc-Antoine Bourdon Vatry was kept in the navy. It was not then a radical departure from the Directory, not at this stage at least.

46. Antoine Boulay de la Meurthe, *Théorie constitutionnelle de Sieyès: Constitution de l'an VIII* (Paris, 1836), pp. 3–4.

47. Boulay de la Meurthe, *Théorie constitutionnelle*, pp. 46, 48; Vandal, *L'avènement de Bonaparte*, i. pp. 493–501. On the various drafts see Jean-Denis Bredin, *Sieyès: la clé de la Révolution française* (Paris, 1988), pp. 466–84. On the Constitution of the Year VIII see Andrew Jainchill, *Reimagining Politics after the Terror: The Republican Origins of French Liberalism* (Ithaca, 2008), pp. 223–42; Paolo Colombo, 'La question du pouvoir exécutif dans l'évolution institutionnelle et le débat politique révolutionnaire', *Annales historiques de la Révolution française*, 319 (2000), 1–26. On the idea of a Grand Elector see Maurice Gauchet, *La révolution des pouvoirs: la souveraineté, le peuple et la représentation, 1789–1799* (Paris, 1995), pp. 219–23.

48. Pierre-Louis Roederer, *Oeuvres du comte de P.-L. Roederer*, 8 vols (Paris, 1853–9), iii. p. 303; Vandal, *L'avènement de Bonaparte*, i. pp. 502–3; Bastid, *Sieyès*, pp. 254–5.

49. See *Corr.* xxx. pp. 344–5; Joseph Fouché, *Mémoires de Joseph Fouché, duc d'Otrant*, 2 vols (Paris, 1824), i. pp. 161–2 (on the reliability of Fouché's memoirs see Jean Tulard, *Joseph Fouché* (Paris, 1998), pp. 429–36); Antoine-Clair Thibaudeau, *Mémoires sur le Consulat, 1799 à 1804* (Paris, 1827), p. 270; Gueniffey, *Le Dix-huit Brumaire*, p. 339; Woloch, *Napoleon and his Collaborators*, pp. 28–31.

50. Vandal, *L'avènement de Bonaparte*, i. p. 504.

51. See Vandal, *L'avènement de Bonaparte*, i. pp. 502–26; Gueniffey, *Le Dix-huit Brumaire*, pp. 334–43; Woloch, *Napoleon and his Collaborators*, pp. 28–35; Lentz, *Grand Consulat*, pp. 103–6.

52. Fouché, *Mémoires*, i. p. 165.

53. For example, Fouché, *Mémoires*, i. pp. 165–6.

54. Jean-Antoine Chaptal, *Mes souvenirs sur Napoléon* (Paris, 1893), p. 333.

55. The phrase was used in Cabanis, *Quelques Considérations*, p. 27.

56. For the Senate see Jean Thiry, *Le Sénat de Napoleon: 1800–1814* (Paris, 1949), pp. 39–50.

57. Jeremy D. Popkin, 'Conservatism under Napoleon: The Political Writings of Joseph Fiévée', *History of European Ideas*, 5 (1984), 387–8.

58. Vandal, *L'avènement de Bonaparte*, i. p. 523. The scene is recounted by Louis-Marie Larevellière-Lépeaux, *Mémoires de Larevellière-Lépeaux, membre du Directoire exécutif de la République française*, 3 vols (Paris, 1895), ii. pp. 420–6. Larevellière-Lépeaux was not present but he was told by Daunou and Cambacérès. Alphonse-Honoré Taillandier, *Documents biographiques sur P.-C.-F. Daunou* (Paris, 1841), pp. 114–15.

59. Aulard, *Paris sous le Consulat*, i. p. 43; Bredin, *Sieyès*, pp. 484–5.

60. The newspapers were consequently able to write that the vote had taken place 'by acclamation, without voting, and unanimously' (Vandal, *L'avènement de Bonaparte*, i. p. 523).

61. Sieyès was named president of the Senate for one year where he could have become the leader of an active opposition movement. Instead, he virtually ceased to count as a political entity. Bonaparte gave Sieyès contested nationalized land near Versailles, which he never occupied but which seems to have damaged his reputation even further.

62. Vandal, *L'avènement de Bonaparte*, i. p. 523.

63. Johann Friedrich Reichardt, *Un hiver à Paris sous le Consulat, 1802–1803* (Paris, 1896), p. 134.

64. Louis-Mathieu Molé, *Le Comte Molé, 1781–1855: sa vie, ses mémoires*, 6 vols (Paris, 1922–30), i. pp. 70, 193.

65. That neglect has in part been rectified by Woloch, *Napolon and his Collaborators*, esp. pp. 120–55; and Laurence Chatel de Brancion, *Cambacérès: maître d'oeuvre de Napoléon* (Paris, 2001).

66. Cited in André Cabanis, *Le sacre de Napoléon* (Paris, 1970), p. 40.

67. Vandal, *L'avènement de Bonaparte*, ii. pp. 46–7; Irene Collins, *Napoleon and his Parliaments: 1800–1815* (London, 1979), pp. 28–46.

68. *Moniteur universel*, 14 nivôse an VIII (5 January 1800); Honoré Duveyrier, *Anecdotes historiques* (Paris, 1907), pp. 312–20, has a different version of events. See Léon de Lanzac de Laborie, *Paris sous Napoléon*, 8 vols (Paris, 1905–13), i. pp. 177–8; Frédéric Masson, *Napoléon et sa famille*, 13 vols (Paris, 1897–1919), i. p. 305.

69. Vandal, *L'avènement de Bonaparte*, ii. pp. 48–55; Kurt Kloocke, *Benjamin Constant: une biographie intellectuelle* (Geneva, 1984), p. 96.

70. Jainchill, *Reimagining Politics*, pp. 198–9.

71. *Gazette de France*, 12 January 1800 (22 nivôse an VIII); *La Décade philosophique, littéraire et politique*, 20 nivôse an VIII (20 January 1800); Aulard, *Paris sous le Consulat*, i. pp. 79–80, 84, 87; Vandal, *L'avènement de Bonaparte*, ii. pp. 54–5; Louis de Villefosse and Janine Bouissounouse, *L'opposition à Napoléon* (Paris, 1969), pp. 116–17.

72. P.M., 'Un document sur l'histoire de la presse: la préparation de l'arrêté du 27 nivôse an VIII', *La Révolution française*, 44 (January–June 1903), 78–82; André Cabanis, *La Presse sous le Consulat et l'Empire* (Paris, 1975), pp. 12–14.

73. P.-J.-B. Buchez and P.-C. Roux, *Histoire parlementaire de la Révolution française, ou Journal des assemblées nationales depuis 1789 jusqu'en 1815*, 40 vols (Paris, 1834–8), xxxviii. pp. 331–2.

74. Cabanis, *La presse*, pp. 11–41, 69–71; 'Introduction', in Hannah Barker and Simon Burrows (eds), *Press, Politics and the Public Sphere in Europe and North America, 1760–1820*

(Cambridge, 2002), p. 16; Henri Welschinger, *La censure sous le Premier Empire, avec documents inédits* (Paris, 1882), p. 119.

75. Michael Marrinan, 'Literal/Literary/"Lexie": History, Text, and Authority in Napoleonic Painting', *Word & Image*, 7:3 (1991), 178–9; Fernand Mitton, *La presse française* (Paris, 1945), ii. pp. 210–11; Simon Burrows, 'The Cosmopolitan Press, 1759–1815', in Barker and Burrows (eds), *Press, Politics and the Public Sphere*, p. 38; Simon Burrows, 'The War of Words: French and British Propaganda in the Napoleonic Era', in David Cannadine (ed.), *Trafalgar in History: A Battle and its Afterlife* (Basingstoke, 2006), p. 48.

76. Jeremy D. Popkin, *Revolutionary News: The Press in France, 1789–1799* (Durham, 1990), pp. 151–62; Michel Biard, *Parlez-vous sans-culotte?: dictionnaire du 'Père Duchesne', 1790–1794* (Paris, 2009), pp. 285–6.

77. Hugh Gough, *The Newspaper Press in the French Revolution* (London, 1988), pp. 141–59; Popkin, *Revolutionary News*, pp. 169–79.

78. P.M., 'Un document sur l'histoire de la presse', 78, 79, 80.

79. Michael Polowetzky, *A Bond Never Broken: The Relations between Napoleon and the Authors of France* (Rutherford, 1993), pp. 71–2.

80. See, for example, Jean-Jacques Régis de Cambacérès, *Mémoires inédits: éclaircissements publiés par Cambacérès sur les principaux événements de sa vie politique*, 2 vols (Paris, 1999), i. p. 480; Cabanis, *La presse*, p. 87.

81. Thibaudeau, *Mémoires sur le Consulat*, p. 267; John Holland Rose, 'The Censorship under Napoleon I', *Journal of Comparative Legislation and International Law*, 18:1 (1918), 62.

82. A. Périvier, *Napoléon journaliste* (Paris, 1918), p. 105, speaks of the 'total enslavement' of the press. See also Geoffrey Ellis, *Napoleon* (Harlow, 1997), pp. 168–9; Felix Markham, *Napoleon* (London, 1963), p. 86; Jeremy D. Popkin, *The Right-Wing Press in France, 1792–1800* (Chapel Hill, 1980), pp. 170–2. The exception is Steven Englund, *Napoleon: A Political Biography* (New York, 2004), pp. 312–13.

83. Jean-Luc Chappey, 'Pierre-Louis Roederer et la presse sous le Directoire et le Consulat: l'opinion publique et les enjeux d'une politique éditoriale', *Annales historiques de la Révolution française*, 334 (2003), 19.

84. See Dennis A. Trinkle, *The Napoleonic Press: The Public Sphere and Oppositionary Journalism* (Lewiston, 2002), pp. 1–4.

85. Jainchill, *Reimagining Politics*, p. 263; Jean Charles Léonard Simonde de Sismondi, *Recherches sur les constitutions des peuples libres*, ed. with an introduction by Marco Minerbi (Geneva, 1965). To cite but one example, in October 1800, after a Jacobin assassination plot against Napoleon had been uncovered, a song circulated that insulted Bonaparte and his whole family. AN F7 3702, 22 vendémiaire an IX (14 October 1800); Aulard, *Paris sous le Consulat*, i. p. 715.

86. *Corr.* vi. n. 4422 (15 December 1799). A second proclamation was issued ten days later, *Corr.* vi. n. 4447 (25 December), and was drawn up by Pierre-Louis Roederer. It states that the new regime's two primary goals were, first, to consolidate the Republic and, second, to make France formidable to its enemies. Roederer, *Oeuvres*, iii. pp. 328–30.

87. Claude Nicolet, *La fabrique d'une nation: la France entre Rome et les Germains* (Paris, 2003), p. 143.

88. *Entretien politique sur la situation actuelle de la France et sur les plans du nouveau gouvernement*. Translation in Marc-Antoine Jullien, *From Jacobin to Liberal: Marc-Antoine Jullien, 1775–1848*, ed. and trans. R. R. Palmer (Princeton, 1993), pp. 94–100 (December 1799), here p. 95.

89. See, for example, the account written one year after Brumaire of a France on the brink of collapse in the opening passages of Pierre-Louis Roederer, *La Première année du Consulat de Bonaparte* (n.p., n.d.).

90. For the following see Jérémie Benoît, 'La peinture allégorique sous le Consulat: structure et politique', *Gazette des Beaux-Arts*, 121 (1993), 78–9; Marc Sandoz, *Antoine-François-Callet: 1741–1823* (Paris, 1985), p. 123.

91. After 1802, when the Consulate for life was proclaimed, there were no longer any references to the people in the paintings commanded by the state.

92. Victor de Broglie (ed.), *Souvenirs, 1785–1870*, 4 vols (Paris, 1886), i. pp. 31–2; Roguet, *Mémoires*, ii. p. 418.

93. The same can be said for the other Napoleonic plebiscites. See Josiane Bourguet-Rouveyre, 'La survivance d'un système électorale sous le Consulat et l'Empire', *Annales historique de la Révolution française*, 346 (2006), 17–29.

94. Malcolm Crook, *Elections in the French Revolution: An Apprenticeship in Democracy, 1789–1799* (Cambridge, 1996), p. 191.

95. For this and the following see Malcolm Crook, 'Les réactions autour de Brumaire à travers le plébiscite de l'an VIII', in Jean-Pierre Jessenne (ed.), *Du Directoire au Consulat*, 3 vols (Villeneuve d'Ascq, 2001), iii. pp. 323–31.

96. Jeff Horn, 'Le plébiscite de l'an VIII et la construction du système préfectoral', in Jessenne (ed.), *Du Directoire au Consulat*, iii. pp. 552–3.

97. Jean Tulard, *Napoléon ou le mythe du sauveur* (Paris, 1977), p. 131.

98. Claude Langlois, 'Le plébiscite de l'an VIII ou le coup d'état du 18 pluviôse an VIII', *Annales historiques de la Révolution française*, 44 (1972), 43–65, 231–6 and 390–415; Claude Langlois, 'Napoléon Bonaparte plébiscité?', in Léo Hamon and Guy Lobrichon (eds), *L'élection du chef de l'état en France de Hugues Capet à nos jours* (Paris, 1988), pp. 90–1; Malcolm Crook, 'Confiance d'en bas, manipulation d'en haut: la pratique plébiscitaire sous Napoléon (1799–1815)', in Philippe Bourdin et al. (eds), *L'incident électoral de la Révolution française à la Ve République* (Clermont-Ferrand, 2002), pp. 77–87.

99. Michel Vovelle, *La Révolution française: 1789–1799* (Paris, 1998), pp. 83–4.

100. Langlois, 'Le plébiscite de l'an VIII', 43–65, 231–46, 390–415, here 241–3. The official figures were 3,011,007 'yes' votes and 1,562 'no' votes.

101. Other meetings took place the following year with Georges Cadoudal, and comtes de Bourmont, Châtillon and d'Autichamp. See *Corr.* vi. n. 4639 (5 March 1800). We shall come across Cadoudal a little further on.

102. According to Jean-Guillaume Hyde de Neuville, *Mémoires et souvenirs du baron Hyde de Neuville*, 3 vols (Paris, 1888), i. pp. 268–75.

103. *Corr.* vi. n. 4473 (28 December 1799).

104. *Corr.* vi. n. 4506 (11 January 1800).

105. Brown, 'Echoes of the Terror', 550; Howard G. Brown, 'Special Tribunals and the Napoleonic Security State', in Philip Dwyer and Alan Forrest (eds), *Napoleon and his Empire: Europe, 1804–1814* (Basingstoke, 2007), pp. 79–95.

106. *Corr.* vi. n. 4603 (18 February 1800); Hyde de Neuville, *Mémoires et souvenirs*, i. pp. 299–302; Léon de La Sicotière, *Louis de Frotté et les insurrections normandes, 1793–1832* (Paris, 1889), pp. 467–542; Villefosse and Bouissounouse, *L'opposition à Napoléon*, pp. 128–30; Brown, *Ending the French Revolution*, pp. 264–5.

107. Cabanis, *Le sacre de Napoléon*, p. 54.

108. *Corr.* vi. n. 4589 (13 February 1800); Hyde de Neuville, *Mémoires et souvenirs*, i. pp. 282–3; Cabanis, *Le sacre de Napoléon*, p. 53.

109. Brown, *Ending the French Revolution*, pp. 325–6, 330–8, 341.

110. *Corr.* vi. n. 4523 (14 January 1800).

111. Charles-Louis Chassin, *Etudes documentaires sur la Révolution française. Les Pacifications de l'Ouest. 1794–1815*, 3 vols (Paris, 1896–9), iii. pp. 545–61; Eric Muraise, *Sainte Anne et la Bretagne* (Paris, 1980), pp. 101–6. Both authors play down the severity of the repression. On the other hand, Brown, *Ending the French Revolution*, pp. 264–5, is much more realistic.

112. *Corr.* vii. n. 5557 (3 May 1801).

113. See, for example, *Corr.* vi. n. 4498 (5 January 1800).

114. Brown, *Ending the French Revolution*, pp. 331–2.

115. Stephen Clay, 'Le brigandage en Provence du Directoire au Consulat (1795–1802)', in Jessenne (ed.), *Du Directoire au Consulat*, iii. pp. 67–89.

116. Brown, *Ending the French Revolution*, pp. 317–20; Brown, 'Special Tribunals and the Napoleonic Security State', pp. 79–95.

117. Brown, *Ending the French Revolution*, p. 323; Brown, 'Echoes of the Terror', 553–5.

118. Brown, *Ending the French Revolution*, pp. 236, 316–24, 330; Brown, 'Echoes of the Terror', 529–58; Howard G. Brown, 'Napoleon Bonaparte, Political Prodigy', *History Compass*, 5 (2007), 1387.

119. Paul R. Hanson, *The Jacobin Republic under Fire: The Federalist Revolt in the French Revolution* (University Park, Pa., 2003), p. 193.

120. Brown, *Ending the French Revolution*, pp. 264–6; Brown, 'Echoes of the Terror', 555.

## 2: 'Perfect Glory and Solid Peace'

1. On this episode see Jacques-Olivier Boudon, 'L'incarnation de l'état de brumaire à floréal', in Jessenne (ed.), *Du Directoire au Consulat*, iii. pp. 334–6.

2. Aulard, *Paris sous le Consulat*, i. p. 156, although one has to wonder to what extent the police may have exaggerated the crowd's reaction in order to please their new masters.

3. Thibaudeau, *Mémoires sur le Consulat*, p. 2.

4. Victorine, comtesse de Chastenay, *Mémoires de Madame de Chastenay, 1771–1815*, 2 vols (Paris, 1896), i. p. 418.

5. Lanzac de Laborie, *Paris sous Napoléon*, i. pp. 77–81.

6. Karl Roider, 'The Habsburg Foreign Ministry and Political Reform, 1801–1805', *Central European History*, 22 (1989), 178. George III was the exception to the rule. The coach he commissioned is still used on state occasions today (Jonathan Marsden and John Hardy, '"O Fair Britannia Hail!" The "Most Superb" State Coach', *Apollo*, 153:468 (2001), 3–12; Jonathan Marsden, 'George III's State Coach in Context', in Jonathan Marsden (ed.), *The Wisdom of George the Third* (London, 2005), pp. 43–59).

7. Jean-Paul Bertaud, 'Napoleon's Officers', *Past & Present*, 112 (1986), 97.

8. Chastenay, *Mémoires*, i. p. 418.

9. Jean-Pierre-Galy Montaglas, *Historique du 12e chasseurs à cheval, depuis le 29 avril 1792 jusqu'au traité de Lunéville (9 février 1801)* (Paris, 1908), p. 78; A. Gautier-Sauzin, *Discours prononcé par le maire de Montauban, le 18 brumaire an X, jour de la fête de la Paix* (Montauban, 1801); Aulard, *Paris sous le Consulat*, i. p. 4; Michael J. Hughes, '"Vive la Republique, Vive l'Empereur!": Military Culture and Motivation in the Armies of Napoleon, 1803–1808', PhD dissertation (University of Illinois at Urbana-Champaign, 2005), p. 65.

10. Lanzac de Laborie, *Paris sous Napoléon*, i. p. 78; Aulard, *Paris sous le Consulat*, i. pp. 158–9, 170.

11. Antoine Boulant, *Les Tuileries, palais de la Révolution (1789–1799)* (Paris, 1989).

12. Cambacérès, *Mémoires inédits*, i. p. 489.

13. See Marie-Cécile Thoral, 'The Limits of Napoleonic Centralization: Notables and Local Government in the Department of the Isère from the Consulate to the Beginning of the July Monarchy', *French History*, 19 (2005), 463–81; John Dunne, 'Les maires de Brumaire, notables ruraux ou "gens des passage"?', in Jessenne (ed.), *Du Directoire au Consulat*, iii. pp. 451–65; John Dunne, 'Napoleon's "Mayoral Problem": Aspects of State–Community Relations in Post-Revolutionary France', *Modern & Contemporary France*, 8 (2000), 479–91; John Dunne, 'Power on the Periphery: Elite–State Relations in the Napoleonic Empire', in Dwyer and Forrest (eds), *Napoleon and his Empire*, pp. 61–78.

14. Lanzac de Laborie, *Paris sous Napoléon*, i. p. 78; Cabanis, *Le sacre de Napoléon*, pp. 44–5.

15. Masson, *Napoléon et sa famille*, ii. pp. 78–9; Lanzac de Laborie, *Paris sous Napoléon*, i. p. 85; iii. pp. 79–83.

16. Thibaudeau, *Mémoires sur le Consulat*, pp. 7–9. For a similar phenomenon in the British army see Scott Hughes Myerly, *British Military Spectacle: From the Napoleonic Wars through the Crimea* (Cambridge, Mass., 1996), pp. 139–50. Myerly argues that dress and discipline moulded the soldier and that the military parade won over the civilian population.

17. On this point see Hughes, 'Vive la République, Vive l'Empereur!', pp. 55–60; Jean Morvan, *Le soldat impérial*, 2 vols (Paris, 1904), ii. pp. 510–17; John R. Elting, *Swords around a Throne: Napoleon's Grande Armée* (New York, 1988), pp. 596–601.

18. J. P. T. Bury and J. C. Barry (eds), *An Englishman in Paris, 1803: The Journal of Bertie Greatheed* (London, 1953), pp. 114–15; Alan Forrest, *Napoleon's Men: The Soldiers of the Revolution and Empire* (London, 2002), pp. 102–3; Hughes, 'Vive la République, Vive l'Empereur!', pp. 57–9.

19. See, for example, the *Moniteur universel*, 23 brumaire an XII (15 November 1803), later printed as *Trait curieux arrivé au Premier Consul en passant l'armée en revue à Boulogne-sur-Mer* (Paris, n.d.).

20. Philip Mansel, *The Eagle in Splendour: Napoleon I and his Court* (London, 1987), p. 14.

21. Francis William Blagdon, *Paris As It Was and As It Is, or a Sketch of the French Capital Illustrative of the Effects of the Revolution*, 2 vols (London, 1803), i. p. 328.

22. On the notion of honour see John A. Lynn, 'Toward an Army of Honor: The Moral Evolution of the French Army, 1789–1815', *French Historical Studies*, 16:1 (1989), 152–73; Julian Pitt-Rivers, 'La maladie de l'honneur', in Marie Gautheron and Jean-Michel Belorgey (eds), *L'honneur: image de soi ou don de soi: un idéal équivoque* (Paris: Autrement, 1991), pp. 20–36.

23. Abraham Raimbach, *Memoirs and Recollections of the late Abraham Raimbach* (London, 1843), p. 102; F. J. Maccunn, *The Contemporary English View of Napoleon* (London, 1914), pp. 50–2.

24. For the following see Marc Belissa, *Repenser l'ordre européen (1795–1802): de la société des rois aux droits des nations* (Paris, 2006), pp. 155–62.

25. *Corr.* vi. nos. 4445 and 4446 (25 December 1799).

26. This is the view of Paul W. Schroeder, *The Transformation of European Politics, 1763–1848* (Oxford, 1994), p. 208; Roider, 'The Habsburg Foreign Ministry', 180.

27. *Corr.* vi. n. 4623 (27 February 1800).

28. See Dwyer, *Napoleon: The Path to Power*, pp. 434–5; Pascal Dupuy, 'Le 18 Brumaire en Grande-Bretagne: le témoignage de la presse et des caricatures', *Annales historiques de la Révolution française*, 318 (1999), 778–9; Stuart Semmel, *Napoleon and the British* (New Haven and London, 2004), pp. 21–4.

29. *Mon dernier mot sur Bonaparte* (London, n.d.), p. 3. The pamphlet was probably written by Francis d'Ivernois.

30. See Semmel, *Napoleon and the British*, pp. 21–3.

31. Hedva Ben-Israel, *English Historians on the French Revolution* (Cambridge, 1968), pp. 25–7; Phillip John Gray, 'Revolutionism as Revisionism: Early British Views of Bonaparte, 1796–1803', MA dissertation (University of Canterbury, 1995), 56–78; Semmel, *Napoleon and the British*, pp. 19–37.

32. Simon Burrows, 'Britain and the Black Legend: The Genesis of the Anti-Napoleonic Myth', in Mark Philp (ed.), *Resisting Napoleon: The British Response to the Threat of Invasion, 1797–1815* (Aldershot, 2006), p. 142.

33. John D. Grainger, *The Amiens Truce: Britain and Bonaparte, 1801–1803* (Woodbridge, 2004), p. 6.

34. Harvey Meyer Bowman, 'Preliminary Stages of the Peace of Amiens: The Diplomatic Relations of Great Britain and France from the Fall of the Directory to the Death of the Emperor Paul of Russia, November 1799–March 1801', *University of Toronto Studies*, 1 (1899), p. 100.

35. A senator/banker by the name of Perregaux made contact with Lord Auckland. See Bowman, 'Preliminary Stages of the Peace of Amiens', pp. 101–2, 152–5.

36. Pitt to Dundas (31 December 1800), in Philip Henry Stanhope, *The Life of the Right Honourable William Pitt*, 4 vols (London, 1861–2), iii. pp. 206–7, 212–13; Piers Mackesy, *War without Victory: The Downfall of Pitt, 1799–1802* (Oxford, 1984), pp. 42–8; John Ehrman, *The Younger Pitt*, 3 vols (London, 1969–96), iii. pp. 332–45; Michael J. Turner, *Pitt the Younger: A Life* (London, 2003), pp. 227–8.

37. The letter was published in *The Annual Register, or, A View of the History, Politics, and Literature for the Year 1800* (London, 1800); Bowman, 'Preliminary Stages of the Peace of Amiens', pp. 104–5.

38. Karl A. Roider, *Baron Thugut and Austria's Response to the French Revolution* (Princeton, 1987), pp. 328–33; Johann Amadeus Franz de Paula, Baron von Thugut, *Vertrauliche Briefe des Freiherrn von Thugut*, 2 vols (Vienna, 1872) ii. nos. 953–64.

39. See Dwyer, *Napoleon: The Path to Power*, pp. 314–17, 319–21.

40. Schroeder, *Transformation of European Politics*, p. 209.

41. Cited in Crook, *Napoleon Comes to Power*, p. 71.

42. *Corr.* xxx. pp. 491–4.

43. *Corr.* vi. n. 4449 (25 December 1799).

44. *Corr.* vi. n. 4552 (25 January 1800).

45. *Moniteur universel*, 5 pluviôse an VIII (4 February 1800).

46. See, for example, the articles entitled 'Observations' and 'Suite des lettres du lord Grenville', published in the *Moniteur universel*, 11–17 ventôse an VIII (2–8 March 1800). Henry Richard, Lord Holland, *Memoirs of the Whig Party during my Time*, 2 vols (London, 1852), i. pp. 154–6.

47. *Moniteur universel*, 18 ventôse an VIII (9 March 1800). The assertion by Antoine-Clair Thibaudeau, councillor of state, that the proclamation caused an 'élan' throughout the country is suspicious (Antoine-Clair Thibaudeau, *Mémoires de A.-C. Thibaudeau, 1799–1815* (Paris, 1913), pp. 24–5).

48. Aulard, *Paris sous le Consulat*, i. pp. 225–6.

49. Edouard Gachot, *Histoire militaire de Masséna: le siège de Gênes (1800)* (Paris, 1908), pp. 213–28.

50. Cited in Ernest Picard, *Bonaparte et Moreau: l'entente initiale, les premiers dissentiments, la rupture* (Paris, 1905), pp. 61, 69.

51. Cited in Gunther E. Rothenberg, *The Art of Warfare in the Age of Napoleon* (Bloomington, 1980), p. 127.

52. David G. Chandler, *The Campaigns of Napoleon* (London, 1966), p. 266; Claus Telp, *The Evolution of Operational Art, 1740–1813: From Frederick the Great to Napoleon* (London, 2005), p. 41.

53. Isser Woloch, *The New Regime: Transformations of the French Civic Order, 1789–1820s* (New York, 1994), pp. 391–7. For a brief overview of conscription see Stuart Woolf, *Napoleon's Integration of Europe* (London, 1991), pp. 156–65.

54. *Corr.* vi. n. 4552 (25 January 1800).

55. *Corr.* vi. n. 4432 (21 December 1799).

56. Picard, *Bonaparte et Moreau*, p. 143.

57. *Corr.* vi. nos. 4432, 4557, 4681, 4695, 4713, 4759 (21 December 1799, 31 January, 19, 22 March, 11 April, 5 May 1800); Jean de Cugnac, *Campagne de l'Armée de Réserve en 1800*, 2 vols (Paris, 1900–1), i. esp. pp. 87–119.

58. Reichardt, *Un hiver à Paris sous le Consulat*, p. 146.

59. See, for example, *Corr.* vi. n. 4433 (21 December 1799).

60. *Corr.* vi. n. 4674 (16 March 1800); Pierre Savinel, *Moreau, rival républicain de Bonaparte* (Paris, 1986), pp. 81–2.

61. Chandler, *Campaigns of Napoleon*, p. 269.

62. See, for example, *Corr.* vi. n. 4713 (11 April), n. 4725 (22 April 1800).

63. Picard, *Bonaparte et Moreau*, pp. 205–12.

64. According to A. B. Rodger, *The War of the Second Coalition, 1798 to 1801: A Strategic Commentary* (Oxford, 1964), p. 231.

65. Miot de Mélito, *Mémoires*, i. p. 273.

66. Cited in Jean Tulard and Louis Garros, *Itinéraire de Napoléon au jour le jour, 1769–1821* (Paris, 1992), p. 154.

67. Lucien Lathion, *Bonaparte et ses soldats au Grand-Saint-Bernard* (Neuchatel, 1978), p. 44.

68. According to Paul Charles François Adrien Henri Dieudonné, baron Thiébault, *Mémoires du général Bon Thiébault*, 5 vols (Paris, 1893–5), iii. p. 73. This is not, however, what Thiébault wrote earlier in his career. In his *Journal des opérations militaires du siège et du blocus de Gênes* (Paris, an IX), pp. 50–1, he credited Bonaparte with the plan. See also *Corr.* vi. n. 4738 (27 April 1800); Lathion, *Bonaparte et ses soldats*, pp. 15, 27.

69. R. J. Knecht, *Francis I* (Cambridge, 1982), pp. 42, 164–5.

70. Jérémie Benoît and Bernard Chevalier (eds), *Marengo: une victoire politique* (Paris, 2000), pp. 110–11.

71. Yuval Noah Harari, *The Ultimate Experience: Battlefield Revelations and the Making of Modern War Culture, 1450–2000* (Basingstoke and New York, 2008), pp. 210–11.

72. *Corr.* vi. n. 4812 (18 May 1800).

73. *Corr.* vi. n. 4811 (18 May 1800); Lathion, *Bonaparte et ses soldats*, pp. 9–10.

74. Chantal de Tourtier-Bonazzi, *Lettres d'amour à Joséphine* (Paris, 1981), p. 150 (18 May 1800). Antoine-Augustin-Flavien Pion des Loches, *Mes campagnes, 1792–1815: notes et correspondance du colonel d'artillerie Pion des Loches* (Paris, 1889), p. 75, described the Saint-Bernard as a 'magnificent horror', but insisted that the crossing was not dangerous.

75. *Corr.* vi. n. 4846 (24 May 1800); Lubin Griois, *Mémoires du général Griois: 1792–1822*, 2 vols (Paris, 1909), i. pp. 120–2.

76. Allain Bernède, 'Autopsie d'une bataille: Marengo, 14 juin 1800', *Revue historique des armées*, 181 (1990), 35. On paper, a demi-brigade would be made up of 2,437 men. The demi-brigade was later replaced by the regiment.

77. Bernède, 'Autopsie d'une bataille', 35; Derrécagaix, *Le maréchal Berthier*, i. pp. 384–400.

78. *Corr.* vi. n. 4836 (24 May 1800).

79. Tourtier-Bonazzi, *Lettres d'amour à Joséphine*, pp. 151–2 (29 May 1800).

80. Joseph Petit, *Marengo, ou Campagne d'Italie, par l'armée de réserve, commandé par le général Bonaparte* (Paris, an IX), pp. 30–3, wrote about 'the hero who commanded us' being enthusiastically received in the main square of the city, the Piazza del Duomo, by a large crowd. The journal of Commandant Brossier, cited in Cugnac, *Campagne de l'Armée de Réserve en 1800*, ii. pp. 42, 85–6, written after the campaign, states that the people of Piedmont, and especially those of Vercelli, about halfway between Turin and Milan, received the French with 'enthusiasm', and that they were received in Milan amid 'general rejoicing'. These accounts are possibly exaggerated. A letter from Pétiet to the municipal officers of Milan (2 June 1800) complains of the 'indifference' and often the 'contempt' (*mépris*) with which the French were received.

81. According to James R. Arnold, *Marengo and Hohenlinden: Napoleon's Rise to Power* (Barnsley, 2005), p. 108.

82. Bourrienne, *Mémoires*, iv. pp. 110–11.

83. *Corr.* vi. n. 4887 (6 June 1800).

84. Frédéric Masson, *Napoléon et les femmes* (Paris, 1894), pp. 84–6.

85. Geoffrey Ellis, 'A Historian's Critique of the Screenplay', in Alison Castle (ed.), *Kubrick's Napoleon: The Greatest Movie Never Made* (Paris, 2011), p. 242.

86. Tourtier-Bonazzi, *Lettres d'amour à Joséphine*, pp. 147, 148 (11 and 13 May 1800).

87. Albert Boime, *Art in an Age of Bonapartism, 1800–1815*, 2 vols (Chicago, 1990), ii. pp. 39–42; Jean-Etienne Delécluze, *Louis David, son école et son temps: souvenirs* (Paris, 1855), p. 233.

88. Antoine Schnapper and Arlette Sérullaz (eds), *Jacques-Louis David 1748–1825* (Paris, 1989), pp. 381–6; Dorothy Johnson, *Jacques-Louis David: Art in Metamorphosis* (Princeton, 1993), pp. 179–83; Alain Pillepich, 'Un tableau célèbre replacé dans son contexte: *Bonaparte franchissant les Alpes au Grand-Saint-Bernard* de David', *Revista Napoleonica*, 1–2 (2000), 77–9.

89. *Journal des arts, des sciences, et de littérature*, 30 fructidor an IX (17 September 1801), x, n. 156, 419–26; Richard Wrigley, *The Origins of French Art Criticism: From the Ancien Régime to the Restoration* (Oxford, 1993), p. 336. Joseph took the painting with him when

he left Spain and later brought it to the United States (Pillepich, 'Un tableau célèbre replacé dans son contexte', 78).

90. See Schnapper and Sérullaz (eds), *Jacques-Louis David 1748–1825*, pp. 381–6. The other versions can today be seen at Versailles, Charlottenburg and Vienna.

91. The *Journal des arts, des sciences, et de littérature* commented that it suffered from excessive abstraction, idealizing Bonaparte out of recognition (Christopher Prendergast, *Napoleon and History Painting: Antoine-Jean Gros's* La Bataille d'Eylau (Oxford, 1997), p. 110).

92. See Dwyer, *Napoleon: The Path to Power*, pp. 133–4.

93. Peter Burke, *Eyewitnessing: The Uses of Images as Historical Evidence* (London, 2001), p. 61.

94. Prendergast, *Napoleon and History Painting*, p. 188.

95. Aulard, *Paris sous le Consulat*, i. p. 397; Vandal, *L'avènement de Bonaparte*, ii. pp. 329, 416–17.

96. Vandal, *L'avènement de Bonaparte*, ii. pp. 417–18.

97. AN F7 3701, Minutes des bulletins quotidiens de police, 21 priairal an VIII (10 June 1800).

## 3: Italy and the Consolidation of Power

1. Bourrienne, *Mémoires*, iv. pp. 85–7.

2. Hermann Hüffer, *Die Schlacht von Marengo und der italienische Feldzug des Jahres 1800*, 3 vols (Leipzig, 1900), ii. pp. 302–3. A good description of the battle of Marengo can be found in Chandler, *Campaigns of Napoleon*, pp. 286–98.

3. Cugnac, *Campagne de l'Armée de Réserve en 1800*, ii. p. 340.

4. Figures in Bruno Ciotti, 'La dernière campagne de Desaix', *Annales historiques de la Révolution française*, 324 (2001), 86–7.

5. Hüffer, *Die Schlacht von Marengo*, ii. pp. 309–12.

6. Cugnac, *Campagne de l'Armée de Réserve en 1800*, ii. pp. 395–6.

7. 'Mémoires du general Danican', in *La bataille de Marengo et ses préliminaires racontés par quatre témoins* (Paris, 1999), p. 139.

8. Benoît and Chevalier (eds), *Marengo*, p. 122. Chandler, *Campaigns of Napoleon*, p. 296, gives 6,000 killed and 8,000 captured.

9. Heinrich Dietrich von Bülow, *Der Feldzug von 1800: militärisch-politisch betrachtet von dem Verfasser des Geistes des neuern Kriegssystems* (Berlin, 1801), p. 531.

10. Cited in David A. Bell, *The First Total War: Napoleon's Europe and the Birth of Warfare as We Know It* (Boston, 2007), p. 225.

11. According to Chandler, *Campaigns of Napoleon*, p. 296. Gachot, *La deuxième campagne d'Italie (1800)*, p. 307 n. 3, gives different figures.

12. There were in all four different accounts of the battle written in 1800, 1803 and 1805 as well as the account told on St Helena. David Chandler, 'Adjusting the Record, Napoleon and Marengo', *History Today*, 17 (1967), 378–85; David Chandler, '"To Lie Like a Bulletin": An Examination of Napoleon's Rewriting of the History of the Battle of Marengo', *Proceedings of the Annual Meeting of the Western Society for French History*, 18 (1991), 37–40.

13. On the first Italian campaign see Dwyer, *Napoleon: The Path to Power*, chs 9–13.

14. Comte de Neipperg, 'Aperçu militaire sur la bataille de Marengo et l'armistice', *Revue de Paris*, 4 (1906), 5–36, here 27. This is the same Count von Neipperg who was later to become the lover of Napoleon's second wife, Marie-Louise.

15. Stanislas Girardin, *Mémoires, journal et souvenirs*, 2 vols (Paris, 1829), i. pp. 175–88; Miot de Mélito, *Mémoires*, i. pp. 275–82.

16. Masson, *Napoléon et sa famille*, i. p. 342.

17. Pierre-Louis Roederer, *Bonaparte me disait: conversations* (Paris, 1942), p. 89; Haegele, *Napoléon et Joseph Bonaparte*, p. 124.

18. Bastid, *Sieyès*, p. 269; Woloch, *Napoleon and his Collaborators*, pp. 96–7.

19. Gilbert Martineau, *Lucien Bonaparte: prince de Canino* (Paris, 1989), pp. 94–5. See also Antonello Pietromarchi, *Lucien Bonaparte: prince romain* (Paris, 1985), pp. 86–90.
20. According to Masson, *Napoléon et sa famille*, i. pp. 339–41.
21. See Vandal, *L'avènement de Bonaparte*, ii. pp. 399–402; Bastid, *Sieyès*, p. 269; Woloch, *Napoleon and his Collaborators*, pp. 96–7.
22. Lazare Carnot, *Mémoires historiques et militaires sur Carnot* (Paris, 1824), p. 111.
23. The scene is described by Fouché, *Mémoires*, i. pp. 183–5. See Henri Gaubert, *Conspirateurs au temps de Napoléon Ier* (Paris, 1962), p. 92; Woloch, *Napoleon and his Collaborators*, p. 97, believes that he 'made a show of fury'.
24. According to Roederer, *Oeuvres*, iii. p. 330.
25. Roederer, *Oeuvres*, iii. p. 333.
26. Woloch, *Napoleon and his Collaborators*, p. 98. After the execution of Louis XVI in 1793, his son was recognized as the titular heir to the throne under the name of Louis XVII. When he died in the Temple prison in June 1795, Louis XVI's brother, the Comte de Provence, took the title Louis XVIII.
27. Roederer, *Oeuvres*, iii. p. 332.
28. Annie Jourdan, 'The Napoleonic Empire in the Age of Revolution: The Contrast of Two National Representations', in Michael Broers, Peter Hicks and Agustin Guimerá (eds), *The Napoleonic Empire and the New European Political Culture* (Basingstoke, 2012), pp. 314–15.
29. *Corr.* vi. n. 4910 (15 June 1800).
30. *Journal des hommes libres*, 5 messidor an VIII (24 June 1800).
31. Raymond Monnier, *Républicanisme, patriotisme et Révolution française* (Paris, 2005), pp. 318–19.
32. Cambacérès, *Mémoires inédits*, i. p. 510.
33. *Journal de Paris*, 3 messidor an VIII (22 June 1800).
34. Laure Junot, duchesse de Abrantès, *Mémoires de Madame la duchesse d'Abrantès, ou Souvenirs historiques sur Napoléon: la Révolution, le Directoire, le Consulat, l'Empire et la Restauration*, 18 vols (Paris, 1831–5), ii. pp. 172–3.
35. Lanzac de Laborie, *Paris sous Napoléon*, i. p. 93. The next day, the papers reported that the 'greatest joy was depicted on all faces' (*Le Publiciste*, 3 messidor an VIII (22 June 1800). See also *La Clef du cabinet des souverains*, 5 messidor an VIII (25 June 1800)).
36. Aulard, *Paris sous le Consulat*, i. pp. 446, 447; Rodney J. Dean, *L'église constitutionnelle: Napoléon et le Concordat de 1801* (Paris, 2004), pp. 83–4.
37. Fouché, *Mémoires*, i. p. 182.
38. Miot de Mélito, *Mémoires*, i. p. 301.
39. According to Anne-Jean-Marie-René Savary, *Mémoires du duc de Rovigo, pour servir à l'histoire de l'empereur Napoléon*, 8 vols (Paris, 1828), i. pp. 185–6.
40. *Corr.* vi. n. 5034 (28 July 1800), in which he urged Spain to declare war on Portugal 'at a time when the Continental war is going to finish'.
41. *Corr.* vi. n. 4955 (29 June 1800).
42. See the bulletin of 24 May 1800 (*Corr.* vi. n. 4846) for allusions to mountains and snow and so on.
43. According to Bourrienne, *Mémoires*, iv. p. 168.
44. *Le Publiciste*, 14 messidor an VIII (3 July 1800).
45. *La Décade philosophique, littéraire et politique*, 10 messidor an VIII (29 June 1800), n. 28, pp. 62–3; *Journal des hommes libres*, 14 messidor an VIII (3 July 1800); *La Clef du cabinet des souverains*, 15 and 18 messidor an VIII (4 and 7 July 1800); Alan Forrest, 'La perspective de la paix dans l'opinion publique et la société militaire', *Bulletin de la Société des Antiquaires de Picardie*, 166 (2002), 252.
46. There is no doubt that the French 'craved' peace at the outset of the Consulate. For the first year see Aulard, *Paris sous le Consulat*, i. pp. 225–6, 227, 241, 270, 333, 341, 500, 535, 540, 562, 566, 569, 579, 591, 666, 768 and 778.
47. Monnier, *Républicanisme, patriotisme et Révolution*, p. 321.

48. *La Décade philosophique, littéraire et politique*, 30 thermidor an VIII (18 August 1800), p. 383.

49. Hyde de Neuville, *Mémoires et souvenirs*, i. p. 328. Monnier, *Républicanisme, patriotisme et Révolution*, p. 305, argues that Marengo placed Bonaparte at the centre of the state and enabled him to appear as the guarantor of stability for the regime.

50. Monnier, *Républicanisme, patriotisme et Révolution*, p. 319.

51. Ozouf, *Festivals and the French Revolution*, esp. ch. 2.

52. Paul Marmottan, 'Lucien, ministre de l'intérieur et les arts', *Revue des études napoléoniennes*, 25 (1925), 26–30; Monnier, *Républicanisme, patriotisme et Révolution*, pp. 315–20; Norbert Savariau, *Louis de Fontanes: belles-lettres et enseignement de la fin de l'Ancien Régime à l'Empire* (Oxford, 2002), pp. 265–7; Jean-Pierre Bois, *Histoire des 14 Juillet, 1789–1919* (Rennes, 1991), pp. 87–90; Petiteau, *Les Français et l'Empire*, pp. 46–7, 48–50, 52. For the festival in the provinces see Christian Pfister, *Les Fêtes à Nancy sous le Consulat et le Premier Empire (1799–1813)* (Nancy, 1914), pp. 20–41.

53. Monnier, *Républicanisme, patriotisme et Révolution*, pp. 319, 320.

54. The programme of the anniversary of 14 July, as well as the speech given that day by Lucien Bonaparte as minister of the interior, can be found in *Anniversaire du 14 juillet, fête de la Concorde: Programme* (Paris, messidor an VIII). Fontanes composed a 'Chant du 14 July' to which Méhul put the music.

55. *Corr.* vi. n. 4938 (21 June 1800), n. 4940 (22 June 1800).

56. Lucien Bonaparte, *Ministère de l'Intérieur. Courses dans le Champ-de-Mars* (Paris, messidor an VIII).

57. *Journal des hommes libres*, 26 messidor an VIII (15 July 1800); *Moniteur universel*, 27 prairial an VIII (16 June 1800).

58. Vandal, *L'avènement de Bonaparte*, ii. pp. 444–9.

59. The project was never carried out (Franck Folliot, 'Des colonnes pour les héros', in *Les architectes de la Liberté: 1789–1799* (Paris, 1989), pp. 305–22; Jean-Marcel Humbert, 'Entre mythe et archéologie: la fortune statuaire égyptisante de Desaix et Kléber', in Jackie Pigeaud and Jean-Paul Barbe (eds), *Le culte des grands hommes au XVIIIe siècle* (Paris, 1998), pp. 219–32). Extracts of Lucien's speech were published in the *Mercure de France*, 1 thermidor an VIII (20 July 1800), pp. 228–36.

60. *Mercure de France*, 1 thermidor an VIII (20 July 1800).

61. *Adresse aux français sur le Quatorze juillet* (n.p., n.d.), p. 6.

62. *Adresse aux français sur le Quatorze juillet*, p. 8.

63. See, for example, *Journal de Paris*, 27 messidor an VIII (16 July 1800).

64. *Journal des Débats*, 28 messidor an VIII (17 July 1800); Aulard, *Paris sous le Consulat*, i. p. 514. And for other descriptions of crowd reactions see *Journal de Paris*, 27 messidor an VIII (16 July 1800); Aulard, *Paris sous le Consulat*, i. pp. 513–14.

65. *La Clef du cabinet des souverains*, 26 messidor an VIII (15 July 1800).

66. According to the marquise de la Tour du Pin, *Journal d'une femme de cinquante ans: 1778–1815*, 2 vols (Paris, 1913), ii. pp. 220–1, the celebrations on the Champ de Mars that 14 July elicited 'very few signs of joy'. That assertion, however, has to be taken with a grain of salt since the marquise was a royalist whose dislike of the Revolution was patent.

67. Lanzac de Laborie, *Paris sous Napoléon*, i. p. 102.

68. *La Clef du cabinet des souverains*, 27 messidor an VIII (16 July 1800); Aulard, *Paris sous le Consulat*, i. pp. 667–8.

69. Monnier, *Républicanisme, patriotisme et Révolution*, p. 305.

70. On the public honours given to revolutionary generals see Joseph Clarke, *Commemorating the Dead in Revolutionary France: Revolution and Remembrance, 1789–1799* (Cambridge, 2007), pp. 243–7, who argues that 'revolutionary culture as a whole had always contained a marked military dimension'; Bernard Gainot, 'Le dernier voyage: rites ambulatoires et rites conjuratoires dans les cérémonies funéraires en l'honneur des généraux révolutionnaires', in Philippe Bourdin, Mathias Bernard and Jean-Claude Caron (eds), *La*

*voix & le geste: une approche culturelle de la violence socio-politique* (Clermont-Ferrand, 2005), pp. 97–113.

71. Monnier, *Républicanisme, patriotisme et Révolution*, pp. 307–8, and on the eulogies to Desaix, pp. 310–15.

72. Marie-Louise Biver, *Le Paris de Napoléon* (Paris, 1963), pp. 151–61.

73. This is in Jean-Roche Coignet, *The Note-Books of Captain Coignet: Soldier of the Empire, 1776–1850* (London, 1998), p. 77. Also Louis-François, baron Lejeune, *Souvenirs d'un officier de l'Empire*, 2 vols (Toulouse, 1851), i. pp. 55–6; Montaglas, *Historique du 12e chasseurs à cheval*, pp. 78–82; Victor-François Perrin, duc de Bellune, 'Mémoires inédits de feu M. le maréchal duc de Bellune: Campagne de l'Armée de Réserve, en l'an VIII', *Spectateur militaire*, xli (1846), 121–204.

74. Thiébault, *Mémoires*, ii. p. 6.

75. According to Monnier, *Républicanisme, patriotisme et Révolution*, p. 305.

76. Albert Soboul, 'Le héro et l'histoire', *Annales historiques de la Révolution française*, 42 (1970), 1–7.

77. Blanning, *Pursuit of Glory*, p. 652. A sentiment echoed by a number of historians, including François Furet, *Revolutionary France, 1770–1880*, trans. Antonia Nevill (Oxford, 1992), p. 218, who describes it as 'the true coronation of his power and his regime'; and Petiteau, *Les Français et l'Empire*, p. 46, who describes Marengo, after Brumaire, as the 'essential moment in the establishment of Bonaparte's power'.

78. Natalie Petiteau, 'Marengo, histoire et mythologie', in Messiez and Sorel (eds), *La deuxième campagne d'Italie*, pp. 209–20; Jacques Garnier, 'Marengo', in Jean Tulard (ed.), *Dictionnaire Napoléon* (Paris, 1989), p. 1137.

79. Lanzac de Laborie, *Paris sous Napoléon*, i. pp. 94–5; Louis-Henry Lecomte, *Napoléon et l'Empire racontés par le théâtre, 1797–1899* (Paris, 1900), pp. 55–6. A number of other plays appeared about the same time, among them: *Bientôt la paix, ou la Voiture cassée* (Soon peace. or The broken carriage) at the Cité-Variétés; *La Pièce curieuse, ou Petit tableau d'un grand evenement* (The curious play, or The small tableau of a great event) at the Vaudeville; and *Paris illuminé, ou le Retour de Marengo* (Paris illuminated, or The return from Marengo) (9 July 1800) at the Gaîté.

80. Gruyer to Berdot, 1 prairial an VIII (18 June 1800), 'Un récit de la bataille de Marengo', *Le carnet historique et littéraire*, ii (1898), 878.

81. According to Chandler, '"To Lie Like a Bulletin"', 38, the bulletin was written by General Pierre Dupont de l'Etang, serving as chief of staff to Berthier, nominally in command of the Army of the Reserve. On the bulletins see Joseph J. Mathews, 'Napoleon's Military Bulletins', *Journal of Modern History*, 22:2 (1950), 137–4; Cabanis, *La presse*, pp. 271–4; Robert B. Holtman, *Napoleonic Propaganda* (Baton Rouge, 1950), pp. 92–6; David P. Jordan, *Napoleon and the Revolution* (Basingstoke, 2012), pp. 144–8.

82. Between 24 May and 15 June 1800, fifteen bulletins were dictated by Bonaparte and sent to Paris. *Corr.* vi. nos 4846, 4848, 4855, 4856, 4858, 4862, 4864, 4865, 4882, 4886, 4893, 4900, 4903, 4905, 4910.

83. *Corr.* vi. n. 4846 (24 May 1800).

84. Chandler, '"To Lie Like a Bulletin"', 33–43; Chandler, 'Adjusting the Record', 326–32 and 378–85; Owen Connelly, *Blundering to Glory: Napoleon's Military Campaigns* (Wilmington, Del., 1987), pp. 66–70.

85. Dwyer, *Napoleon: The Path to Power*, pp. 2, 4, 169.

86. Annie Jourdan, 'Bonaparte et Desaix, une amitié inscrite dans la pierre des monuments?', *Annales historiques de la Révolution française*, 324 (2001), 149–50. Within a week, the legend had become reality. A soldier by the name of Rué des Sagets wrote a long letter to his father on 3 July (that is, after he had had time to absorb the regime's own propaganda on the subject): 'he [Desaix] was carried by four grenadiers who loudly lamented him: "Speak softer my friends, he told them, be careful not to discourage the troops. Tell the First Consul that my regret is to not have done enough to pass into posterity." And he died.' Rué des Sagets to his father, G.M., 'La bataille de

Marengo, d'après un témoin bourbonnais', *Bulletin de la société d'émulation du Bourbonnais*, xix (1911), 3780.

87. Printed in the *Moniteur universel*, 3 messidor VIII (22 June 1800). On the portrayal of the death of Desaix in the press of the day see Raymond Monnier, 'Vertu antique et nouveaux héros: la presse autour de la mort de Desaix et d'une bataille légendaire', *Annales historiques de la Révolution française*, 324 (2001), 118–22.

88. Suzanne Glover Lindsay, 'Mummies and Tombs: Turenne, Napoleon, and Death Ritual', *Art Bulletin*, 82 (2000), 491.

89. Bernard Gainot, 'Les mots et les cendres: l'héroïsme au début du Consulat', *Annales historiques de la Révolution française*, 324 (2001), 129.

90. Jean de Cugnac, 'Mort de Desaix à Marengo', *Revue des études napoléoniennes*, 39 (1934), 14; Gainot, 'Les mots et les cendres', 129.

91. Savary, *Mémoires*, i. pp. 179–80; Auguste Frédéric Louis Wiesse de Marmont, *Mémoires du maréchal Marmont duc de Raguse: de 1792 à 1841*, 9 vols (Paris, 1856–7), ii. p. 140.

92. *Moniteur universel*, 3 messidor VIII (22 June 1800); *Journal de Paris*, 3 messidor an VIII (22 June 1800).

93. Anne Vincent-Buffault, *Histoire des larmes, XVIIIe–XIXe siècles* (Paris, 2001).

94. Jourdan, 'Bonaparte et Desaix', 139–40.

95. See, for example, the letter from Auguste de Colbert, one of Murat's aides-de-camp, to his mother, in Ciotti, 'La dernière campagne de Desaix', 94; Jeanne A. Ojala, *Auguste de Colbert: Aristocratic Survival in an Era of Upheaval, 1793–1809* (Salt Lake City, 1979), pp. 56–7.

96. *Corr.* vi. n. 4909 (15 June 1800).

97. Gainot, 'Le dernier voyage', p. 106; Susan Locke Siegfried, 'Naked History: The Rhetoric of Military Painting in Postrevolutionary France', *Art Bulletin*, 75:2 (1993), 240.

98. For this and the following, Petiteau, 'Marengo, histoire et mythologie', pp. 214–15; Petiteau, *Les Français et l'Empire*, pp. 61–2. In 1805, Napoleon received the official version of the battle written by the Dépôt de la Guerre. He ordered it destroyed and rewritten. The second version is an imagined, idealized battle refought in Napoleon's mind (Pierre Gourmen, 'La second campagne d'Italie', in *Napoléon, de l'histoire à la légende* (Paris, 2000), p. 57).

99. Alexandre Berthier, *Relation de la bataille de Marengo* (Paris, 1805, reprinted 1998); Ciotti, 'La dernière campagne de Desaix', 83–97. See also Petit, *Marengo, ou Campagne d'Italie*, es p. pp. 55–6, which focuses entirely on Bonaparte's sangfroid and only fleetingly mentions Desaix, and Kellerman not at all.

100. Cited in Ciotti, 'La dernière campagne de Desaix', 97; René Reiss, *Kellermann* (Paris, 2009), pp. 344–59.

101. AN F7 3829, rapport de la préfecture de police, 14 prairial an IX (2 June 1801); Picard, *Bonaparte et Moreau*, p. 365.

102. *Moniteur universel*, 3 frimaire an VIII (24 November 1799).

103. Marcel Reinhard, 'L'armée et Bonaparte en 1801', *Annales historiques de la Révolution française*, 25 (1953), 293–5 (letters dated 2 and 21 March 1801); and Aulard, *Paris sous le Consulat*, i. pp. 779–80.

104. Picard, *Bonaparte et Moreau*, p. 375.

105. AN F7 3830, 13 and 22 floréal an IX (3 and 12 May 1801), and 19 nivôse an X (9 January 1802).

106. Jean Tulard, 'La notion de tyrannicide et les complots sous le Consulat', *Revue de l'Institut Napoléon*, 111 (1969), p. 133.

107. See Jens Ivo Engels, 'Furcht und Drohgebärde. Die Denunzianten "falscher Komplotte" gegen den König von Frankreich, 1680–1760', in Michaela Hohkamp and Claudia Ulbrich (eds), *Der Staatsbürger als Spitzel: Denunziation während des 18. und 19. Jahrhunderts aus europäischer Perspektive* (Leipzig, 2001), pp. 323–40.

108. Manuel Eisner, 'Killing Kings: Patterns of Regicide in Europe, AD 600–1800', *British Journal of Criminology*, 51:3 (2011), 556–77.

109. Tulard, 'La notion de tyrannicide', p. 135; Petiteau, *Les Français et l'Empire*, p. 108.

110. M. Bernard, *Le Turc et le militaire français* (n.p., n.d.), pp. 4, 16–17; Aulard, *Paris sous le Consulat*, i. p. 670 (25 September 1800).

111. Silas Titus, *Le Code des tyrannicides, adressé à tous les peuples opprimés* (Lyons, 1800), p. ii. See also Jean Tulard, *Napoléon: Jeudi 12 octobre 1809: le jour où Napoléon faillit être assassiné* (Paris, 1993), pp. 44 and 78; and Bernard Gainot, 'La République contre elle-même: figures et postures de l'opposition à Bonaparte au début du Consulat (novembre 1799–mars 1801)', in Antonino De Francesco (ed.), *Da Brumaio ai cento giorni: cultura di governo e dissenso politico nell'Europa di Bonaparte* (Milan, 2007), pp. 143–55. The quotation is from Bonaparte's address to the Council of Elders on 19 brumaire.

112. Such as *Tuer n'est pas assassiner*, originally a tract written against Cromwell, but reprinted in the *Courrier de Londres*, 55 nos. 2–5 (6–17 January 1804), cited in Simon Burrows, 'The Struggle for European Opinion in the Napoleonic Wars: British Francophone Propaganda, 1803–14', *French History*, 11 (1997), 38.

113. Some of the details are to be found in AN F7 3702, Minutes des bulletins quotidiens de police, 21 vendémiaire an IX (13 October 1800). See also Aulard, *Paris sous le Consulat*, i. pp. 709–11; Gustave Hue, 'Un complot de police sous le Consulat', *Les Contemporains* (10 October 1909), 139–64; Jean Thiry, *La machine infernale* (Paris, 1952), pp. 32–9; Gaubert, *Conspirateurs au temps de Napoléon*, pp. 47–61; Tulard, *Fouché*, pp. 146–49; Elizabeth Sparrow, *Secret Service: British Agents in France, 1792–1815* (Woodbridge, 1999), p. 219; Laurent Boscher, *Histoire de la répression des opposants politiques, 1742–1848: la justice des vainqueurs* (Paris, 2006), pp. 120–5.

114. The Opera, which was then called the Théâtre des Arts, was to be found in the rue de la Loi (rue Richelieu), where the Square Louvois is today, just across from the Bibliothèque nationale, Richelieu.

115. Leo Gershoy, *Bertrand Barère: A Reluctant Terrorist* (Princeton, 1962), pp. 311–13; Michael J. Sydenham, 'The Crime of 3 Nivôse (24 December 1800)', in J. F. Bosher (ed.), *French Government and Society, 1500–1850* (London, 1973), pp. 301–2.

116. Aulard, *Paris sous le Consulat*, i. p. 722; Lanzac de Laborie, *Paris sous Napoléon*, i. p. 121.

117. Aulard, *Paris sous le Consulat*, i. pp. 696, 700–1; Bernard Gainot, 'Un itinéraire démocratique post-thermidorien: Bernard Metge', in Christine Le Bozec and Eric Wauters (eds), *Pour la Révolution française* (Rouen, 1998), pp. 93–106.

118. Cited in Anita Brookner, *Jacques-Louis David* (London, 1980), p. 146.

119. Lentz, *Grand Consulat*, p. 256.

120. Aulard, *Paris sous le Consulat*, i. pp. 729, 730, 732.

121. Pierre-Louis Roederer, *Autour de Bonaparte: journal du Cte P.-L. Roederer, ministre et conseiller d'état, notes intimes et politiques d'un familier des Tuileries* (Paris, 1909), p. 50; Girardin, *Mémoires, journal et souvenirs*, i. p. 197. The pamphlet is reprinted in Iung (ed.), *Lucien Bonaparte*, i. pp. 421–32. On the connections between Fontanes and Lucien see Guy-Edouard Pillard, *Louis Fontanes, 1757–1821: prince de l'esprit* (Maulévrier, 1990), pp. 150–2, 158–9. It is often said that it was distributed to all the prefects and indeed to all public functionaries by the ministry of the interior – some contemporary memoirs say that it was and that it caused a 'grande sensation' (Claude Fauriel, *Les derniers jours du Consulat* (Paris, 1886), p. 10), although there is some doubt as to whether it was distributed at all and whether it was suppressed by Fouché before it got to the public (Miot de Mélito, *Mémoires*, i. p. 317).

122. The military and political leader of the Franks who stopped the western advance of the Arabs at Poitiers in 732.

123. Nicolet, *La fabrique d'une nation*, p. 144.

124. Miot de Mélito, *Mémoires*, i. pp. 318–19; Pierre-Louis Roederer, *Mémoires sur la Révolution, le Consulat et l'Empire* (Paris, 1942), p. 154.

125. According to Lentz, *Grand Consulat*, p. 267, but I have not found any of these complaints in the archives.

126. Savinel, *Moreau*, p. 92; Miot de Mélito, *Mémoires*, i. pp. 338–9.

127. Bourrienne, *Mémoires*, iii. p. 315.

128. Roederer, *Oeuvres*, iii. p. 353.

129. Lentz, *Grand Consulat*, p. 267.

130. Roederer, *Mémoires*, pp. 148–54.

131. Aulard, *Paris sous le Consulat*, i. pp. 770–1, 783; Roederer, *Mémoires*, p. 154; Iung (ed.), *Lucien Bonaparte*, i. p. 432. Girardin, *Mémoires, journal et souvenirs*, i. p. 195, describes how upset Bonaparte looked that evening after a discussion with Lucien.

132. Roederer, *Autour de Bonaparte*, p. 41.

133. Masson, *Napoléon et sa famille*, i. pp. 354–9.

134. Girardin, *Mémoires, journal et souvenirs*, i. p. 192; Iung (ed.), *Lucien Bonaparte*, ii. pp. 50–2.

135. Lentz, *Grand Consulat*, p. 268.

136. Paul Mansfield, 'The Repression of Lyon, 1793–94: Origins, Responsibility and Significance', *French History*, 2 (1988), 74–101.

## 4: Peace

1. *Moniteur universel*, 5 and 6 nivôse an IX (26 and 27 December 1800); Arnaud-Louis-Raoul de Martel, *Etude sur l'affaire de la machine infernale du 3 nivôse an IX* (Paris, 1870); Thibaudeau, *Mémoires sur le Consulat*, pp. 23–63; Gaubert, *Conspirateurs au temps de Napoléon*, pp. 72–121; Thiry, *La machine infernale*, pp. 154–92; Jean Lorédan, *La machine infernale de la rue Nicaise (3 nivôse, an IX)* (Paris, 1924); Villefosse and Bouissounouse, *L'opposition à Napoléon*, pp. 150–9; Sydenham, 'The Crime of 3 Nivôse', pp. 295–320; Sparrow, *Secret Service*, pp. 217–22; Boscher, *Histoire de la repression*, pp. 130–40; Karine Salomé, 'L'attentat de la rue Nicaise en 1800: l'irruption d'une violence inédite?', *Revue d'histoire du XIXe siècle*, 40 (2010), 59–75.

2. Jacques Marquet de Montbreton de Norvins, *Souvenirs d'un historien de Napoléon: mémorial de J. de Norvins*, 3 vols (Paris, 1896), ii. p. 271.

3. Norvins, *Souvenirs*, ii. p. 272; Thibaudeau, *Mémoires sur le Consulat*, p. 24.

4. Hortense de Beauharnais, *The Memoirs of Queen Hortense*, trans. Arthur K. Griggs and F. Mabel Robinson, 2 vols (London, 1928), i. pp. 62–3.

5. Alissan de Chazet, *Mémoires, souvenirs, oeuvres et portraits*, 3 vols (Paris, 1837), iii. p. 70; Lorédan, *La machine infernale*, p. 55; Tulard (ed.), *Dictionnaire Napoléon*, pp. 1107–8; Tulard, *Fouché*, pp. 150–8.

6. *Procès instruit par le tribunal criminel du département de la Seine contre les nommés Saint-Réjant, Carbon, et autres, prévenus de conspiration contre la personne du Premier Consul* (Paris, an IX), i. 31–2. On the iconography surrounding the assassination attempt see Karine Salomé, 'Les représentations iconographiques de l'attentat politique au XIXe siècle: enjeux et usages de la mise en image d'une violence politique', *La Révolution française*, lrf.revues.org/index402, although there is a tendency to confound images and periods.

7. The dream is mentioned in Sigmund Freud, *The Standard Edition of the Complete Psychological Works of Sigmund Freud*, 24 vols (London, 1953–74), iv. pp. 26, 233–4.

8. Woloch, *Napoleon's Collaborators*, pp. 74–5.

9. François-Joseph Boulay de la Meurthe, *Boulay de la Meurthe* (Paris, 1868), pp. 140–5; Roederer, *Mémoires*, p. 164; Charles Durand, *Etudes sur le Conseil d'Etat napoléonien* (Paris, 1949), pp. 632–5; Woloch, *Napoleon and his Collaborators*, pp. 74–5.

10. Thibaudeau, *Mémoires sur le Consulat*, pp. 31, 55.

11. AN AFIV 1302, n. 41, Police générale, affaire du 3 nivôse. Pierre-Marie Desmarets, *Quinze ans de haute police sous le consulat et l'empire* (Paris, 1833), pp. 34–66. According to Desmarets, a blacksmith recognized the horse's hooves, which he had shod. See also Pierre-François Réal, *Les indiscrétions d'un préfet de police de Napoléon*, 2 vols (Paris, 1986), i. pp. 45–7; Marcel Le Clère, 'Comment opérait la police de Fouché', *Revue de criminologie et de police technique*, 1 (1951), 33–6; Lorédan, *La machine infernale*, pp. 68–98.

12. Probably with the backing of the British secret service. See Elizabeth Sparrow, 'The Alien Office, 1792–1806', *Historical Journal*, 33:2 (1990), 378.
13. Thibaudeau, *Mémoires sur le Consulat*, pp. 25–6.
14. Fouché, *Mémoires*, i. pp. 222–3; Woloch, *Napoleon and his Collaborators*, p. 75.
15. Bonaparte had realized in the course of this whole affair that the Senate, made up of men in whose interests it was to maintain the stability of the regime, could be used to impose his will in the face of opposition from the other legislative bodies. Sydenham, 'The Crime of 3 Nivôse', pp. 319–20.
16. Aulard, *Paris sous le Consulat*, ii. pp. 98–103.
17. AN F7 3829, 17 ventôse an IX and ff. (8 March 1801); Lanzac de Laborie, *Paris sous Napoléon*, i. p. 130.
18. Jean Destrem, *Les déportations du Consulat et de l'Empire (d'après des documents inédits)* (Paris, 1885), pp. 7–21; Woloch, *Napoleon and his Collaborators*, pp. 79–80; Sydenham, 'The Crime of 3 Nivose', pp. 309–11; Richard Cobb, 'Note sur la répression contre le personnel sans-culotte de 1795 à 1801', in Richard Cobb, *Terreur et subsistances, 1793–1795* (Paris, 1965), p. 202.
19. Prosper Brugière, baron de Barante, *Souvenirs du baron de Barante, 1782–1866*, 6 vols (Paris, 1890–7), i. p. 73.
20. They were not 'enhanced' by the explosion, as Sydenham, 'The Crime of 3 Nivôse', p. 317, maintains; they were already very much present.
21. Lanzac de Laborie, *Paris sous Napoléon*, i. pp. 123–5; Sydenham, 'The Crime of 3 Nivôse', pp. 300–3.
22. Roederer, *Oeuvres*, iii. pp. 355–7; Lanzac de Laborie, *Paris sous Napoléon*, i. pp. 126–7; Raymonde Monnier, *Le Faubourg Saint-Antoine, 1789–1815* (Paris, 1981), p. 275; Woloch, *Napoleon and his Collaborators*, p. 74.
23. Woloch, *Napoleon and his Collaborators*, pp. 72–3; Petiteau, *Les Français et l'Empire*, pp. 113, 114.
24. Petiteau, 'Les fidélités républicaines', 61, 63, 64.
25. Léon Lecestre, *Lettres inédites de Napoléon Ier (an VIII–1815)*, 2 vols (Paris, 1897), i. p. 269 (12 January 1809).
26. *Corr.* vi. nos. 5014, 5072 (24 July and 24 August 1800).
27. *Corr.* vi. n. 4914 (16 June 1800).
28. Talleyrand was at first consulted by Bonaparte, but he was soon nudged out of the picture and replaced by two other men, both involved in Brumaire, Roederer and Regnaud de Saint-Jean d'Angély. See Paul Bailleu (ed.), *Preußen und Frankreich von 1795 bis 1807: diplomatische Correspondenzen*, 2 vols (Leipzig, 1880–7), i, p. 388 (Sandoz-Rollin to the Prussian court, 31 July 1800); Roider, *Baron Thugut*, pp. 342–5.
29. Charles-Maurice de Talleyrand-Périgord, *Mémoires du prince de Talleyrand*, 5 vols (Paris, 1891–2), i. p. 281.
30. Picard, *Bonaparte et Moreau*, pp. 297–333; Picard, *Hohenlinden* (Paris, 1909); Savinel, *Moreau*, pp. 99–103; James R. Arnold, *Marengo and Hohenlinden: Napoleon's Rise to Power* (Barnsley, 2005), pp. 197–251. The Austrians had around 60,000 men and 214 cannon compared to Moreau's 53,000 men and 99 cannon.
31. According to Bourrienne, *Mémoires*, iv. p. 249.
32. Picard, *Bonaparte et Moreau*, p. 335; Brown, *Ending the French Revolution*, p. 316.
33. *Moniteur universel*, 18, 19 and 20 frimaire an IX (9, 10 and 11 December 1800).
34. Moreau's brother, a member of the Tribunate, was sent at the head of a delegation (*Moniteur*, 14 and 16 nivôse an IX (4 and 6 January 1801); Antoine-Clair Thibaudeau, *Le Consulat et l'Empire, ou Histoire de la France et de Napoléon Bonaparte, de 1799 à 1815*, 10 vols (Paris, 1834–5), ii. pp. 82–3).
35. *Corr.* vi. n. 5250 (2 January 1801).
36. On 16 July 1800 (*Corr.* vi. n. 4993), shortly after the battle of Marengo, Bonaparte ordered paintings of Marengo, and also of Rivoli, Moskirch, the Pyramids, Aboukir and Mount

Thabor (J. Tripier Le Franc, *Histoire de la vie et de la mort du baron Gros* (Paris, 1880), p. 176). They were not completed for many years.

37. Philippe de Ségur, *Histoire et mémoires, par le général comte de Ségur*, 7 vols (Paris, 1873), ii. p. 104.

38. Mathieu Dumas, *Souvenirs du général comte Mathieu Dumas, de 1770 à 1836*, 3 vols (Paris, 1839), iii. p. 217.

39. Charles Decaen, *Mémoires et journaux du général Decaen*, 2 vols (Paris, 1910–11), ii. p. 245; Picard, *Bonaparte et Moreau*, pp. 341–2.

40. *Corr.* vi. n. 5271 (9 January 1801); Picard, *Bonaparte et Moreau*, pp. 342–3.

41. *Moniteur universel*, 12 and 14 germinal an IX (2 and 4 April 1801); Picard, *Bonaparte et Moreau*, pp. 347–51.

42. AN F7 3829, 7 thermidor an IX (26 July 1801).

43. Instructions to Joseph in *Corr.* vi. nos. 5131 (20 October 1800) and 5315 (21 January 1801); Schroeder, *Transformation of European Politics*, pp. 210–13.

44. Paul Marmottan, 'Joseph Bonaparte diplomate (Lunéville, Amiens, 1801, 1802)', *Revue d'histoire diplomatique*, 41 (1927), 276–300; Paul Marmottan, 'Joseph Bonaparte à Mortefontaine, 1800–1803', *Nouvelle Revue*, 100 (1929), 3–16, 113–28, 209–19, 266–73.

45. Haegele, *Napoléon et Joseph Bonaparte*, pp. 131–2; Emmanuel de Waresquiel, *Talleyrand: le prince immobile* (Paris, 2003), pp. 291–2.

46. Hugh Ragsdale, 'Russian Influence at Lunéville', *French Historical Studies*, 5 (1968), 274–84, here 276; Adams, *Napoleon and Russia*, p. 53; Roderick E. McGrew, *Paul I of Russia* (Oxford, 1992), pp. 304–12.

47. Schroeder, *Transformation of European Politics*, p. 212.

48. On Campo Formio see Dwyer, *Napoleon: The Path to Power*, pp. 314–17. On the negotiations see August Fournier, *Napoleon I: A Biography*, trans. Annie Elizabeth Adams, 2 vols (New York, 1911), i. pp. 240–5.

49. Schroeder, *Transformation of European Politics*, p. 213.

50. Thugut, *Vertrauliche Briefe*, ii. pp. 399–400 (9 February 1801), also p. 409 (14 February 1801).

51. 'A one-sided treaty', according to Frederick W. Kagan, *The End of the Old Order: Napoleon and Europe, 1801–1805* (Cambridge, Mass., 2006), pp. 18–19. The exception to the rule is Schroeder, *Transformation of European Politics*, pp. 213–14, who argues that Austria accepted Lunéville as a permanent treaty.

52. *Journal des Débats*, 25 pluviôse an IX (14 February 1801); Aulard, *Paris sous le Consulat*, ii. p. 176.

53. Jean-Nicolas-Auguste Noël, *Souvenirs militaires d'un officier du premier Empire: 1795–1832* (Paris, 1895), p. 31.

54. Masson, *Napoléon et sa famille*, ii. pp. 75–6.

55. Lanzac de Laborie, *Paris sous Napoléon*, i. p. 242.

56. AN AFIV 1449, letter from Pressac des Panche, sub-prefect of the arrondissement of Givray, 29 pluviôse an IX (18 February 1801), f. 42.

57. AN AFIV 1449, letter from Salesse, *curé* of St Colombe, Castillon, 17 vendémiaire an X (9 October 1801), f. 530.

58. AN AFIV 1449, letter from Pieter Pypers from Amsterdam, 22 October 1801, f. 589.

59. Lucien Calvié, '"Le début du siècle nouveau". Guerre, paix, révolution et Europe dans quelques textes allemands de 1795 à 1801', in Marita Gilli (ed.), *Le cheminement de l'idée européenne dans les idéologies de la paix et de la guerre* (Besançon, 1991), pp. 130–1.

60. For a selection of those texts see Belissa, *Repenser l'ordre européen*, pp. 162–9.

61. Philippe Alexandre, 'Le "Hallisches Wochenblatt", un journal de la Franconie wurtembergeoise (1788–1803)', in Pierre Grappin and Jean Moes (eds), *Sçavantes délices: périodiques souabes au siècle des Lumières* (Paris, 1989), pp. 193–217, here p. 208.

62. Douglas Hilt, *The Troubled Trinity: Godoy and the Spanish Monarchs* (Tuscaloosa, 1987), pp. 112–28.

63. Bonaparte undermined Lucien, negotiating in Madrid, by signing a peace treaty with the

Portuguese ambassador in Paris (Schroeder, *Transformation of European Politics*, pp. 224–5).

64. Philip Dwyer, 'Prussia and the Armed Neutrality: The Decision to Invade Hanover in 1801', *International History Review*, 15 (1993), 663.

65. *Corr.* vii. n. 5352 (6 February 1801).

66. McGrew, *Paul I*, p. 315; Schroeder, *Transformation of European Politics*, p. 218. On the French–Russian rapprochement in 1800 see Hugh Ragsdale, 'The Origins of Bonaparte's Russian Policy', *Slavic Review*, 27 (1968), 85–90; Hugh Ragsdale, 'Russia, Prussia, and Europe in the Policy of Paul I', *Jahrbücher für Geschichte Osteuropas*, 31:1 (1983), 81–118; Hugh Ragsdale, 'Was Paul Bonaparte's Fool? The Evidence of Neglected Archives', in Hugh Ragsdale, (ed.), *Paul I: A Reassessment of his Life and Reign* (Pittsburgh, Pa., 1979), pp. 76–90; and Hugh Ragsdale, *Détente in the Napoleonic Era: Bonaparte and the Russians* (Lawrence, Kan., 1980).

67. Alexander DeConde, *The Quasi-War: The Politics and Diplomacy of the Undeclared War with France, 1797–1801* (New York, 1966), pp. 253–8, 316–20; E. Wilson Lyon, 'The Franco-American Convention of 1800', *Journal of Modern History*, 12 (1940), 305–33.

68. See Charles John Fedorak, 'Catholic Emancipation and the Resignation of William Pitt in 1801', *Albion*, 24:1 (1992), 49–64; William Hague, *William Pitt the Younger* (London, 2004), pp. 462–84.

69. On Addington see Philip Ziegler, *Addington: A Life of Henry Addington, First Viscount Sidmouth* (London, 1965); Christopher D. Hall, 'Addington at War: Unspectacular But Not Unsuccessful', *Historical Research*, 61 (1988), 306–15; Charles John Fedorak, *Henry Addington, Prime Minister, 1801–1804: Peace, War, and Parliamentary Politics* (Akron, Ohio, 2002).

70. Marianne Elliott, *Partners in Revolution: The United Irishmen and France* (New Haven, 1982), pp. 282–321.

71. Clive Emsley, *British Society and the French Wars 1793–1815* (London, 1979), pp. 85–9, 94; John Stevenson, 'Popular Radicalism and Popular Protest 1789–1815', in H. T. Dickinson (ed.), *Britain and the French Revolution, 1789–1815* (Basingstoke, 1989), pp. 76–7.

72. B[ritish] L[ibrary], Add Mss 38316, Hawkesbury to Otto (21 March 1801); Charles Ronald Middleton, *The Administration of British Foreign Policy, 1782–1846* (Durham, NC, 1977), pp. 104–5. Otto was a native of Baden.

73. Fedorak, *Henry Addington*, p. 79.

74. AN F7 3830, rapport du préfet de police, 12 vendémiaire an X (4 October 1801); Aulard, *Paris sous le Consulat*, ii. pp. 555–6; Norvins, *Souvenirs*, ii. pp. 278–9.

75. Fedorak, *Henry Addington*, p. 69.

76. Cited in David Johnson, 'Amiens 1802', *History Today*, 52 (2002), 22.

77. For the response of the British to the news see H. F. B. Wheeler and A. M. Broadley, *Napoleon and the Invasion of England: The Story of the Great Terror* (Stroud, 2007, reprint 1908), pp. 211–15.

78. Grainger, *The Amiens Truce*, pp. 50–1.

79. James Harris Malmesbury, *Diaries and Correspondence of James Harris, First Earl of Malmesbury*, 4 vols (London, 1844), iv. pp. 61–2 (29 October 1801); Leonora Nattrass (ed.), *William Cobbett: Selected Writings*, 6 vols (London, 1998), ii. pp. 16–20, 21–30 (14 and 16 October 1801); Semmel, *Napoleon and the British*, pp. 26–7; Grainger, *The Amiens Truce*, p. 52.

80. Fedorak, *Henry Addington*, p. 83.

81. Charles Ross (ed.), *Correspondence of Charles, first Marquis Cornwallis*, 3 vols (London, 1859), iii. p. 395 (20 November 1801).

82. Franklin Wickwire and Mary Wickwire, *Cornwallis: The Imperial Years* (Chapel Hill, 1980), pp. 252–61; Grainger, *The Amiens Truce*, p. 76.

83. Ross (ed.), *Correspondence of Cornwallis*, iii. pp. 435–7 (10 January 1802).

84. Albert Du Casse, *Mémoires et correspondance politique et militaire du roi Joseph*, 10 vols (Paris, 1853–4), i. p. 87.

85. See Fedorak, *Henry Addington*, pp. 79–87; Grainger, *The Amiens Truce*, pp. 49–81.

86. Charles John Fedorak, 'The French Capitulation in Egypt and the Preliminary Anglo-French Treaty of Peace in October 1801: A Note', *International History Review*, 15 (1993), 525–43.

87. William, Lord Auckland, *The Journal and Correspondence of William, Lord Auckland*, 4 vols (London, 1861–2), iv. pp. 136–8, 143–52, 172–3; William Windham, *The Windham Papers: The Life and Correspondence of the Rt. Hon. William Windham, 1750–1810*, 2 vols (London, 1913), ii. p. 173 (1 October 1801). See also Malmesbury, *Diaries and Correspondence*, iv. pp. 59, 60 (29 and 30 September 1801) and 65, 147, 156–7. On 1 October Malmesbury's diary entry reads, 'Lord Bathurst, Lord Pembroke, Lord Camden, and Lord Radnor, all disapprove of it. Lord Grenville and all his family are violent against it.' For other reactions see Ziegler, *Addington*, pp. 125–7.

88. Malmesbury, *Diaries and Correspondence*, iv. p. 61 (29 October 1801); Peter Jupp, *Lord Grenville: 1759–1834* (Oxford, 1985), pp. 309–15.

89. Malmesbury, *Diaries and Correspondence*, iv. p. 60 (1 October 1801).

90. Minto to Paget, *The Paget Papers: Diplomatic and Other Correspondence of Sir Arthur Paget, 1794–1807*, 2 vols (London, 1896), ii. p. 27 (4 January 1802).

91. Malmesbury, *Diaries and Correspondence*, iv. pp. 62–3 (29 October 1801); Hamish Scott, *The Birth of a Great Power System, 1740–1815* (Harlow, 2006), p. 305.

92. Esdaile, *Napoleon's Wars*, p. 107.

93. John Stevenson, 'Food Riots in England', in R. Quinault and John Stevenson (eds), *Popular Protest and Public Order: Six Studies in British History, 1790–1920* (London, 1974), pp. 33–74.

94. Henry Redhead Yorke, *France in Eighteen Hundred and Two Described in a Series of Contemporary Letters* (London, 1906), pp. 10–11.

95. Forrest, 'La perspective de la paix dans l'opinion publique', 254.

96. Elizabeth Mavor (ed.), *The Grand Tours of Katherine Wilmot, France 1801–1803, and Russia 1805–07* (London, 1992), p. 47, writes of witnessing a landlord in the Rhône and Loire sitting at a table composing a letter to Bonaparte, 'and when he had directed his letter "*au premier Consul*", he took us up to a little bedchamber where, in a transport of pride, he told us . . . the "Saviour of his country" had repos'd'.

97. AN AFIV 1449, letter from Vietinghoff, Versailles, 20 brumaire an X (11 November 1801), f. 418.

98. AN AFIV 1449, letter from Rouget, commissioner of police, Bordeaux, 9 brumaire an X (30 October 1801), f. 441. See also Forrest, 'La perspective de la paix dans l'opinion publique', 251–62.

99. Talleyrand, *Mémoires*, i. p. 286.

100. Emile Tersen, *Napoléon* (Paris, 1959), p. 120; Lentz, *Grand Consulat*, p. 296.

101. Gautier-Sauzin, *Discours prononcé par le maire de Montauban*. See also Pierre Crouzet, *La fête de la paix, ou les élèves de Saint-Cyr à Marengo* (Paris, n.d.); and Paul-Henri Marron, *Discours prononcé la veille de la fête de la Paix, 17 brumaire an X, dans le temple des protestans de Paris* (Paris, 1801).

102. Joseph Fiévée, *Lettres sur l'Angleterre et réflexions sur la philosophie du XVIIIe siècle* (Paris, 1802), p. 43. The letter addressed to Bonaparte from a former member of the Constituent Assembly amply illustrates the point (AN AFIV 1449, letter from Brouillet, dated Millau, 16 brumaire an X (7 November 1801), f. 561).

103. Jean-Paul Bertaud, *Quand les enfants parlaient de gloire: l'armée au coeur de la France de Napoléon* (Paris, 2006), pp. 21–2; *Programme de la fête de la paix qui aura lieu le 18 brumaire an X* (Paris, 1801). For other theatrical celebrations of the peace see Patrick Berthier, 'La paix d'Amiens dans la littérature', in Nadine-Josette Chaline (ed.), *La Paix d'Amiens* (Amiens, 2005), pp. 213–15, 221–30.

104. Claire-Elisabeth-Jeanne Gravier de Vergennes, comtesse de Rémusat, *Mémoires de Madame de Rémusat, 1802–1808*, 3 vols (Paris, 1880), i. p. 238.

105. For the reaction in the Parisian press see Berthier, 'La paix d'Amiens dans la littérature', pp. 216–21.

106. *Journal des arts, des sciences, et de littérature*, 25 brumaire an X (16 November 1801); Berthier, 'La paix d'Amiens dans la littérature', p. 219.

107. For this and the following engraving see Bruno Foucart, 'L'accueil de la Paix d'Amiens par les artistes', in Chaline (ed.), *La Paix d'Amiens*, pp. 236, 239.

108. *A Practical Guide during a Journey from London to Paris; with a Correct Description of all the Objects Deserving of Notice in the French Metropolis* (London, 1802), pp. 35–6.

109. Bury and Barry (eds), *An Englishman in Paris*, p. 121.

110. *A Practical Guide during a Journey from London to Paris*, p. 34.

111. Jean Tulard, *Nouvelle histoire de Paris: le Consulat et l'Empire: 1800–1815* (Paris, 1983), pp. 92–3.

112. Henri d'Alméras, *La vie parisienne sous le Consulat et l'Empire* (Paris, 1909), p. 20.

113. Louis Prudhomme, *Miroir historique, politique et critique de l'ancien et du nouveau Paris, et du département de la Seine*, 6 vols (Paris, 1807), i. pp. 303–10; Alméras, *La vie parisienne sous le Consulat et l'Empire*, p. 26. There is a wonderful description of the 'patterns of urban life' in pre-revolutionary Paris in David Garrioch, *The Making of Revolutionary Paris* (Berkeley, 2002), pp. 16–35.

114. Raimbach, *Memoirs*, pp. 95, 101.

115. Mavor (ed.), *The Grand Tours of Katherine Wilmot*, p. 19.

116. Laurent Turcot, 'Entre promenades et jardins publics: les loisirs parisiens et londoniens au XVIIIe siècle', *Revue belge de philologie et d'histoire/Belgisch tijdschrift voor filologie en geschiedenis*, 87 (2009), 645–52.

117. August von Kotzebue, *Souvenirs de Paris en 1804*, 2 vols (Paris, 1805), i. pp. 266–9; Honoré Blanc, *Le Guide des dîneurs, ou Statistique des principaux restaurants de Paris* (Paris, 1814), pp. 15, 94, 194; Rebecca L. Spang, *The Invention of the Restaurant: Paris and Modern Gastronomic Culture* (Cambridge, Mass., 2000), pp. 92, 172–3.

118. Prudhomme, *Miroir historique, politique et critique*, i. pp. 276, 283.

119. Kotzebue, *Souvenirs*, i. pp. 270–1.

120. *A Practical Guide during a Journey from London to Paris*, p. 134; Kotzebue, *Souvenirs*, i. pp. 262–3.

121. Abrantès, *Mémoires*, iii. pp. 34, 53,

122. Steven D. Kale, *French Salons: High Society and Political Sociability from the Old Regime to the Revolution of 1848* (Baltimore, 2004), pp. 77–104.

123. Anne Martin-Fugier, *La vie élégante ou La formation du Tout-Paris, 1815–1848* (Paris, 1990), p. 192; Steven D. Kale, 'Women, Salons, and the State in the Aftermath of the French Revolution', *Journal of Women's History*, 13:4 (2002), 58–9; Steven D. Kale, 'Women, the Public Sphere, and the Persistence of Salons', *French Historical Studies*, 25:1 (2002), 115–48.

124. Aglaé Marie Louise de Choiseul Gouffier, duchesse de Saulx-Tavanes, *Sur les routes de l'émigration: mémoires de la duchesse de Saulx-Tavannes (1791–1806)* (Paris, 1934), pp. 159–60, 174–6.

125. Peter Fritzsche, 'The Historical Actor', in Edward Berenson and Eva Giloi (eds), *Constructing Charisma: Celebrity, Fame, and Power in Nineteenth-Century Europe* (New York, 2010), p. 136. The figures for the number of visitors vary: the British ambassador, Anthony Merry, estimated that in December 1802 there were 5,000 British subjects in Paris (John Goldworth Alger, *Napoleon's British Visitors and Captives 1801–1815* (Edinburgh, 1904), p. 25; Daniel Roche, 'The English in Paris', in Christophe Charle, Julien Vincent and Jay Winter (eds), *Anglo-French Attitudes: Comparisons and Transfers between English and French Intellectuals since the Eighteenth Century* (Manchester, 2007), pp. 78–97; and Renaud Morieux, '"An Inundation from Our Shores": Travelling across the Channel around the Peace of Amiens', in Philp (ed.), *Resisting Napoleon*, pp. 217–40). As for the number of French visitors to Britain, between December 1802 and April 1803 the British embassy in Paris issued over 3,300 passports (Grainger, *The Amiens Truce*, pp. 130–1). The discrepancy came about in part because there was no French tradition of visiting Britain, whereas the British tour of the Continent was a long-established ritual.

126. J. R. Watson, *Romanticism and War: A Study of British Romantic Period Writers and the Napoleonic Wars* (Basingstoke, 2003), p. 85.

127. Thomas U. Sadleir (ed.), *An Irish Peer on the Continent (1801–1803): Being a Narrative of the Tour of Stephen, 2nd Earl Mount Cashell, through France, Italy, etc., as related by Catherine Wilmot* (London, 1920), pp. 1–2.

128. Mavor (ed.), *The Grand Tours of Katherine Wilmot*, p. 10.

129. Blagdon, *Paris As It Was and As It Is*, i. p. 2; Yorke, *France in Eighteen Hundred and Two*, pp. 16–17.

130. Lanzac de Laborie, *Paris sous Napoléon*, ii. pp. 339–40.

131. Yorke, *France in Eighteen Hundred and Two*, pp. 51–5 and 74.

132. Samuel Romilly, *Memoirs of the Life of Sir Samuel Romilly*, 3 vols (London, 1840), ii. p. 90; James Greig (ed.), *The Farington Diary*, 8 vols (London, 1923), ii. p. 28.

133. Raimbach, *Memoirs*, 49; John Carr, *The Stranger in France, or A Tour from Devonshire to Paris* (London, 1803), pp. 101, 106–12; Yorke, *France in Eighteen Hundred and Two*, pp. 123–9, 153–8; *The Manuscripts of the Earl of Westmorland* (London, 1885), p. 56. French tourist guides of Paris date back to the seventeenth century. See Natacha Coquery, *Tenir boutique à Paris au XVIIIe siècle: luxe et demi-luxe* (Paris, 2011), pp. 60–78.

134. Yorke, *France in Eighteen Hundred and Two*, pp. 118–19; Raimbach, *Memoirs*, p. 69.

135. Muriel E. Chamberlain, *Lord Aberdeen: A Political Biography* (London, 1983), p. 32.

136. Greig (ed.), *The Farington Diary*, ii. p. 7. On other English encounters with Bonaparte see: Beata Frances and Eliza Kenny (eds), *The Francis Letters, by Sir Philip Francis and Other Members of the Family*, 2 vols (London, 1908), ii. pp. 502–3 (14 August 1802); Theresa Lewis (ed.), *Extracts of the journals and correspondence of Miss Berry, from the year 1783 to 1852*, 3 vols (London, 1866), ii. pp. 163–5; Anne Plumptre, *A Narrative of a Three Years Residence in France*, 3 vols (London, 1810), i. pp. 109–10.

137. Romilly, *Memoirs*, ii. p. 90.

138. Greig (ed.), *The Farington Diary*, ii. p. 54.

139. On the meeting between the two men see Grainger, *The Amiens Truce*, pp. 94–5; John Bernard Trotter, *Memoirs of the latter years of the Right Honourable Charles James Fox* (London, 1811), pp. 258–74; Earl of Ilchester, *Journal of Elizabeth Lady Holland*, 2 vols (London, 1908), ii. p. 150; Christopher Hobhouse, *Fox* (London, 1947), pp. 279–82; L. G. Mitchell, *Charles James Fox* (Harmondsworth, 1997), pp. 174–6 and 200.

140. Hobhouse, *Fox*, p. 283.

141. Castalia Countess Granville (ed.), *Lord Granville Leveson Gower: Private Correspondence, 1781–1821*, 2 vols (London, 1916), i. pp. 353–4.

142. Mitchell, *Charles James Fox*, p. 175.

143. Cited in Johnson, 'Amiens 1802', p. 25.

144. Cited in Earl of Ilchester, *The Home of the Hollands, 1605–1820* (London, 1937), p. 188.

## 5: The Politics of Fusion

1. François-René de Chateaubriand, *Mémoires d'outre-tombe* (Paris, 1997), i. pp. 755–6.

2. Cited in Cabanis, *Le sacre de Napoléon*, p. 77.

3. The Kaiser said the same thing to Germans on the outbreak of war in 1914 (my thanks to Peter Hempenstall for pointing this out). Cited in Cabanis, *Le sacre de Napoléon*, p. 50. The circular was dated 21 ventôse an VIII (13 March 1800). The sentiment was later echoed by the tribune Nicolas Parent-Réal on 3 September 1800 (in *Archives parlementaires: recueil complet des débats législatifs et politiques des chambres française de 1800 à 1860*, 2e série, 127 vols (Paris, 1862–1913), ii. p. 702).

4. Jean Vidalenc, *Les émigrés français: 1789–1825* (Caen, 1963), pp. 52–5, 115–36; Thierry Lentz, *Nouvelle histoire du Premier Empire*, 4 vols (Paris, 2002–10), iii. p. 623.

5. John Dunne, 'Quantifier l'émigration des nobles pendant la Révolution française:

problèmes et perspectives', in Martin (ed.), *La Contre-Revolution en Europe*, pp. 133–41.

6. Lentz, *Grand Consulat*, p. 331; William Doyle, *Aristocracy and its Enemies in the Age of Revolution* (Oxford, 2009), pp. 311–14.

7. Kale, *French Salons*, p. 78.

8. For this, Louis Madelin, *Fouché, 1759–1820*, 2 vols (Paris, 1903), i. pp. 296–301, 311–13; Vidalenc, *Les émigrés français*, pp. 52–6; Emmanuel de Waresquiel, 'Joseph Fouché et la question de l'amnistie des émigrés (1799–1802)', *Annales historiques de la Révolution française*, 372 (2013); 105–20.

9. *Le Diplomate*, 19 and 24 nivôse an VIII (9 and 14 January 1800). He adopted this line of thinking in a letter to General Beurnonville, French minister plenipotentiary in Berlin, in October 1800 (see Henri Forneron, *Histoire générale des émigrés pendant la Révolution française*, 3 vols (Paris, 1884–90), ii. pp. 386–7).

10. See Madelin, *Fouché*, i. pp. 345–51.

11. Lentz, *Grand Consulat*, p. 334.

12. Ghislain de Diesbach, *Histoire de l'émigration, 1789–1814* (Paris, 1984), pp. 532–42.

13. Ange-Achille-Charles de Brunet, comte de Neuilly, *Dix années d'émigration: souvenirs et correspondance du comte de Neuilly* (Paris, 1863), p. 326.

14. See, for example, Aulard, *Paris sous le Consulat*, i. p. 303; ii. p. 51; Madelin, *Fouché*, i. p. 346; Brown, *Ending the French Revolution*, pp. 344–5.

15. Simon Schama, *Citizens: A Chronicle of the French Revolution* (New York, 1990), pp. 586–8; Doyle, *Aristocracy and its Enemies*, pp. 274–310.

16. Aulard, *Paris sous le Consulat*, ii. pp. 836, 839, 845, 848.

17. Report from the prefecture of police, in Aulard, *Paris sous le Consulat*, iii. p. 17 (27 April 1802).

18. Olivier Paradis, 'De la difficulté à vivre ses choix politiques: les jeunes officiers de l'armée, du service du roi à celui de l'empereur', in Annie Crépin, Jean-Pierre Jessenne and Hervé Leuwers, *Civils, citoyens-soldats et militaires dans l'Etat-Nation* (Paris, 2006), pp. 141–4.

19. Aulard, *Paris sous le Consulat*, ii. pp. 62–3 (13 December 1800).

20. Chastenay, *Mémoires*, i. p. 449; Kale, 'Women, Salons, and the State', 60.

21. Woloch, *Napoleon and his Collaborators*, p. 57. The return of the émigrés and the role the question assumed in domestic politics is a subject that has been entirely neglected. Jean Tulard calculates that the nobility recuperated more than a quarter of their old lands (Jean Tulard, 'Problèmes sociaux de la France napoléonienne', *Annales historiques de la Révolution française*, 199 (1970), 141).

22. A Te Deum is not a mass but rather a hymn to God, one which became increasingly politicized in the course of the eighteenth century, and which was intended to celebrate royal power. The practice of singing a Te Deum to give thanks for a military success dates back to the early sixteenth century (Frédérique Leferme-Falguières, *Les courtisans: une société de spectacle sous l'Ancien Régime* (Paris, 2007), p. 51); Thierry Lentz, 'La proclamation du Concordat à Notre Dame le 18 avril 1802', in Jacques-Olivier Boudon (ed.), *Le Concordat et le retour de la paix religieuse* (Paris, 2008), pp. 101–12.

23. Mavor (ed.), *The Grand Tours of Katherine Wilmot*, p. 33.

24. Aulard, *Paris sous le Consulat*, ii. pp. 802, 808, 814, 820, 833.

25. Bury and Barry (eds), *An Englishman in Paris*, p. 122.

26. Lanzac de Laborie, *Paris sous Napoléon*, i. pp. 370–1.

27. Plumptre, *A Narrative of a Three Years Residence in France*, i. pp. 123–5; Philip Mansel, *Dressed to Rule: Royal and Court Costume from Louis XIV to Elizabeth II* (New Haven, 2005), p. 81.

28. AN F7 3830, rapport du préfet de police, 30 germinal an X (20 April 1802); Aulard, *Paris sous le Consulat*, ii. pp. 844–5; Lanzac de Laborie, *Paris sous Napoléon*, i. pp. 372–4.

29. Cambacérès, *Mémoires inédits*, i. p. 615; Alfred Boulay de la Meurthe, *Documents sur la négociation du Concordat et sur les autres rapports de la France avec le Saint-Siège en 1800 et 1801*, 5 vols (Paris, 1891–7), v. pp. 567, 568.

30. De Staël to Dupont de Nemours (25 April 1802), in James F. Marshall (ed.), *De Staël–Du Pont Letters: Correspondence of Madame de Staël and Pierre Samuel du Pont de Nemours* (Madison, Milwaukee and London, 1968), p. 127.

31. Richard Burton, *Blood in the City: Violence and Revelation in Paris, 1789–1945* (Ithaca, 2001), p. 72.

32. Gaubert, *Conspirateurs au temps de Napoléon*, p. 139.

33. Frédéric Hulot, *Le maréchal Masséna* (Paris, 2005), p. 177.

34. Thiébault, *Mémoires*, iii. pp. 274–5; Hulot, *Masséna*, p. 179.

35. Ferdinand de Bertier, *Souvenirs inédits d'un conspirateur: Révolution, Empire et première Restauration* (Paris, 1990), p. 78.

36. Jean-François Boulart, *Mémoires militaires du général Bon Boulart sur les guerres de la république et de l'empire* (Paris, 1892), pp. 124, 125.

37. Noël, *Souvenirs militaires*, p. 36.

38. Chaptal, *Mes souvenirs*, p. 264; Picard, *Bonaparte et Moreau*, pp. 367–8.

39. Comte Remacle, *Relations secrètes des agents de Louis XVIII à Paris sous le Consulat (1802–1803)* (Paris, 1899), p. 30.

40. Philippe de Ségur, *De 1800 à 1812: un aide de camp de Napoléon: mémoires du général comte de Ségur*, 3 vols (Paris, 1894–5), i. pp. 67–8.

41. Remacle, *Relations secrètes*, p. 31.

42. Soizik Moreau, *Jean-Victor Moreau: l'adversaire de Napoléon* (Paris, 2005), p. 82.

43. Reichardt, *Un hiver à Paris sous le Consulat*, p. 147.

44. Jacques-Olivier Boudon, 'Les fondements religieux du pouvoir impérial', in Natalie Petiteau (ed.), *Voies nouvelles pour l'histoire du Premier Empire: territoires, pouvoirs, identités* (Paris, 2003), pp. 203–6.

45. See Bonaparte's remarks in Roederer, *Oeuvres*, iii. pp. 334–5, 342.

46. As early as December 1800, a journalist writing for the *Mercure de France* compared Bonaparte to Cyrus II of Persia (600 or 576–530 BC), who allowed Jews to return to the Holy Land from exile and to rebuild the Temple of Jerusalem. The bishops of France often used the comparison and not always in a sycophantic manner. See Bernard Plongeron, 'Cyrus ou les lectures d'une figure biblique dans la rhétorique religieuse de l'Ancien Régime à Napoléon', *Revue d'histoire de l'Eglise de France*, 68 (1982), 31–67. For other mentions see *Mercure de France*, 16 frimaire an IX (2 December 1800); Jean-Claude Berchet, 'Le *Mercure de France* et la "Renaissance" des lettres', in Jean-Claude Bonnet (ed.), *L'Empire des muses: Napoléon, les arts et les lettres* (Paris, 2004), p. 36.

47. Eviatar Zerubavel, *The Seven Day Circle: The History and Meaning of the Week* (London, 1985), p. 34.

48. Jacques-Olivier Boudon, *Histoire du Consulat et de l'Empire: 1799–1815* (Paris, 2000), pp. 79–80.

49. *Corr.* vi. n. 4884 (5 June 1800); Roger Dufraisse, *Napoléon: correspondence officielle* (Paris, 1970), i. pp. 93–4.

50. Contrary to what some assert (Antoine Casanova, *Napoléon et la pensée de son temps: une histoire intellectuelle singulière* (Paris, 2000), p. 28). On Napoleon, the Church and religion see Jacques-Olivier Boudon, *Napoléon et les cultes: les religions en Europe à l'aube du XIXe siècle, 1800–1815* (Paris, 2002), pp. 39–46.

51. François G. de Coston, *Biographie des premières années de Napoléon Bonaparte*, 2 vols (Paris, 1840), i. p. 30.

52. As John McManners, *The French Revolution and the Church* (London, 1969), p. 140, pointed out, religion was peripheral to Bonaparte's decision to reconcile with the Church. See also Geoffrey Ellis, 'Religion According to Napoleon: The Limits of Pragmatism', in Nigel Aston (ed.), *Religious Change in Europe, 1650–1914: Essays for John McManners* (Oxford, 1997), p. 244; Marie-Christine de Bouët du Portal, 'A propos de la Saint-Napoléon: la solennité du 15 août sous le Premier et le Second Empire', *Revue de l'Institut Napoléon*, 158–9 (1992), 145.

53. See Dwyer, *Napoleon: The Path to Power*, pp. 274–6.

54. There is a substantial literature on the Concordat. Some of the more important works are: Henry Horace Walsh, *The Concordat of 1801: A Study of the Problem of Nationalism in the Relations of Church and State* (New York, 1933), pp. 39–61; William Roberts, 'Napoleon, the Concordat of 1801, and its Consequences', in Frank J. Coppa (ed.), *Controversial Concordats: The Vatican's Relations with Napoleon, Mussolini, and Hitler* (Washington, DC, 1999), pp. 34–83; Boudon, *Napoléon et les cultes*, pp. 55–67; Jacques-Olivier Boudon (ed.), *Le Concordat et le retour de la paix religieuse* (Paris, 2008); André Latreille, *Napoléon et le Saint-Siège, 1801–1808: l'ambassade du Cardinal Fesch à Rome* (Paris, 1935), pp. 1–21; Jean Leflon, *La crise révolutionnaire 1789–1846*, vol. xx: *Histoire de l'Eglise depuis les origines jusqu'à nos jours* (Paris, 1949), pp. 178–99. The most detailed treatment of this period is Dean, *L'église constitutionnelle*.

55. McManners, *The French Revolution and the Church*, p. 143.

56. François-Désiré Mathieu, *Le Concordat de 1801: ses origines, son histoire* (Paris, 1903), p. 223.

57. According to Adolphe Thiers, *Histoire du Consulat et de l'Empire*, 20 vols (Paris, 1845–62), iii. pp. 255–6. Ercole Consalvi, *Mémoires du cardinal Consalvi*, 2 vols (Paris, 1866), i. p. 351, relates a different version of events. See also John Martin Robinson, *Cardinal Consalvi, 1757–1824* (London, 1987), pp. 66–79.

58. Mathieu, *Le Concordat de 1801*, p. 256.

59. Boudon, 'Les fondements religieux du pouvoir impérial', p. 205.

60. *Corr.* vii. n. 5642 (20 July 1801).

61. They were compiled by the newly appointed director of religious affairs, Jean-Etienne-Marie Portalis. See Jean-Luc A. Chartier, *Portalis, le père du Code civil* (Paris, 2004), pp. 251–7. Roberts, 'Napoleon, the Concordat of 1801', pp. 45–6, explains that the term 'Organic Articles' is inaccurate and describes them as 'administrative regulations'.

62. Ellis, 'Religion According to Napoleon', p. 244.

63. Germaine de Staël, *Considérations sur les principaux événements de la Révolution française*, 2 vols (Paris, 1818), ii. pp. 275–6; Cabanis, *Le sacre de Napoléon*, p. 90.

64. Bernard Plongeron, 'De Napoléon à Metternich: une modernité en état de blocus', in Jean-Marie Mayeur, Charles and Luce Pietri, Andre Vauchez and Marc Venard (eds), *Histoire du christianisme: des origines à nos jours*, 14 vols (Paris, 1997), x. pp. 635–50, highlights the problems that immediately occurred.

65. On this see Bernard Plongeron, 'Face au Concordat (1801), résistances des évêques anciens constitutionnels', *Annales historiques de la Révolution française*, 337 (2004), 85–115.

66. Arno Mayer, *The Furies: Violence and Terror in the French and Russian Revolutions* (Princeton, 2000), p. 572.

67. Martin S. Staum, 'The Class of Moral and Political Sciences, 1795–1803', *French Historical Studies*, 11:3 (1980), 372 n. 3. See also Jean-Luc Chappey, 'Les Idéologues et l'Empire: étude des transformations entre savoirs et pouvoir (1799–1815)', in Antonino De Francesco (ed.), *Da Brumaio ai cento giorni: cultura di governo e dissenso politico nell'Europa di Bonaparte* (Milan, 2007), pp. 211–27.

68. Norman Ravitch, 'Liberalism, Catholicism, and the Abbé Grégoire', *Church History*, 36:4 (1967), 419–39; Alyssa Goldstein Sepinwall, *The Abbé Grégoire and the French Revolution: The Making of Modern Universalism* (Berkeley, 2005), pp. 160–2.

69. Aulard, *Paris sous le Consulat*, ii. pp. 614–15, 642.

70. *Gazette de France*, 16 frimaire an X (7 December 1801). On this episode, Collins, *Napoleon and his Parliaments*, pp. 57–8.

71. Girardin, *Mémoires, journal et souvenirs*, i. p. 233.

72. AN F7 3830, rapport de la préfecture de police, 16 frimaire an X (7 December 1801).

73. Charles Jean Tristan de Montholon, *Récits de la captivité de l'empereur Napoléon à Sainte-Hélène*, 2 vols (Paris, 1847), i. p. 401.

74. Cambacérès presented three projects for a Civil Code, two to the Convention, in 1793 and in 1794, and again in 1796 to the Directory. The 1796 draft would serve as the core to Bonaparte's Code. Jean-Louis Halperin, 'Le codificateur au travail, Cambacérès et ses sources',

in Laurence Chatel de Brancion (ed.), *Cambacérès, fondateur de la justice moderne* (Saint-Rémy-en-l'Eau, 2001), pp. 154–65, questions the extent of Cambacérès' involvement.

75. René Savatier, *L'art de faire les lois: Bonaparte et le Code civil* (Paris, 1927); and Pierre Villeneuve de Janti, *Bonaparte et le Code civil* (Paris, 1934); Jean Carbonnier, 'Le Code Civil', in Pierre Nora (ed.), *Les lieux de mémoire*, 3 vols (Paris, 1984–92), ii. p. 297; Eckhard Maria Theewen, *Napoléons Anteil am Code civil* (Berlin, 1991).

76. Jean-Louis Halpérin, *L'impossible code civil* (Paris, 1992), pp. 263–86.

77. The reported number of sessions over which Bonaparte presided vary from fifty-two to fifty-five (Jean-Pierre Royer, 'Napoléon et l'élaboration du Code civil', in Françoise Bastien-Rabner and Jean-Yves Coppolani (eds), *Napoléon et le Code civil* (Ajaccio, 2009), p. 75 n. 4).

78. Bertrand, *Cahiers de Sainte-Hélène*, i. p. 250.

79. Broglie, *Souvenirs*, i. pp. 65–7.

80. The preponderant role in the preparation of the Code given to Bonaparte in older works like Amédée Madelin, *Le premier Consul législateur, étude sur la part que prit Napoléon aux travaux préparatoires du code* (Paris, 1865), and Honoré Pérouse, *Napoléon Ier et les lois civiles du consulat et de l'empire* (Paris, 1866), written during the reign of Napoleon III, is an exaggeration, one that is repeated in more recent works such as Frank McLynn, *Napoleon: A Biography* (London, 1997), pp. 254–7, and Englund, *Napoleon*, pp. 189–90.

81. Jean-Guillaume Locré, *Esprit du Code Napoléon, tiré de la discussion, ou Conférence... du projet de Code civil, des observations des tribunaux, des procès-verbaux du Conseil d'Etat, des observations du Tribunat, des exposés de motifs*, 5 vols (Paris, 1805–7); and Pierre-Antoine Fenet, *Recueil complet des travaux préparatoires du Code civil*, 15 vols (Paris, 1836).

82. Halpérin, *L'impossible code civil*, pp. 266–9.

83. Jean-Etienne-Marie Portalis, *Discours préliminaire au premier projet de Code civil* (Bordeaux, 1999), p. 15; Chartier, *Portalis*, pp. 165–77. According to Jordan, *Napoleon and the Revolution*, pp. 104–7, the *Discours préliminaire* is a 'superb introduction' to the Code.

84. Natalie Petiteau, 'La Contre-Révolution endiguée? Projets et réalisations sociales impériales', in Martin (ed.), *La Contre-Revolution en Europe*, p. 186.

85. This is the thesis of Xavier Martin, *Mythologie du Code Napoléon: aux soubassements de la France moderne* (Bouère, 2003).

86. Alan Forrest, 'State-Formation and Resistance: The Army and Local Elites in Napoleonic France', in Michael Rowe (ed.), *Collaboration and Resistance in Napoleonic Europe: State-Formation in an Age of Upheaval, c.1800–1815* (Basingstoke, 2003), pp. 44–5.

87. Petiteau, 'Les fidélités républicaines', 65.

88. Collins, *Napoleon and his Parliaments*, pp. 58–62.

89. AN F7 3830, rapport de la préfecture de police, 16 and 26 frimaire an X (7 and 17 December 1801).

90. *Corr.* vii. n. 5907 (2 January 1802).

91. *Corr.* vii. n. 5922 (18 January 1802); Savary, *Mémoires*, i. pp. 282–3; Girardin, *Mémoires, journal et souvenirs*, ii. pp. 247–8; Thibaudeau, *Mémoires sur le Consulat*, pp. 222–3.

92. Halpérin, *L'impossible code civil*, p. 274; Collins, *Napoleon and his Parliaments*, p. 62.

93. Martin Staum, *Minerva's Message: Stabilizing the French Revolution* (Montreal, 1996), p. 222.

94. Lentz, *Grand Consulat*, pp. 320–1; Jacques-Olivier Boudon and Philippe Bourdin, 'Les héritages républicains sous le Consulat et l'Empire', *Annales historiques de la Révolution française*, 346 (2006), 6–7.

95. Mathieu-Augustin Cornet, *Souvenirs sénatoriaux, précédés d'un essai sur la formation de la Cour des Pairs* (Paris, 1824), pp. 5–6, 7.

96. Cornet, *Souvenirs sénatoriaux*, pp. 63–4.

97. Roederer, *Oeuvres*, iii. p. 427.

98. *Corr.* vii. nos. 5922, 5927 and 5931 (18, 21 and 24 January 1802); Jean-Yves Coppolani, *Les élections en France à l'époque napoléonienne* (Paris, 1980), pp. 52–4.

99. According to Chatel de Brancion, 'Napoléon et Cambacérès', in Chatel de Brancion (ed.), *Cambacérès*, p. 133.

100. Cambacérès talks about this, obliquely, in his memoirs, Cambacérès, *Mémoires inédits*, i. p. 601. See also Martin Staum, *Cabanis: Enlightenment and Medical Philosophy in the French Revolution* (Princeton, 1980), p. 293; Lentz, *Nouvelle histoire du Premier Empire*, iii. p. 129; Fauriel, *Les derniers jours du Consulat*, p. 23; Collins, *Napoleon and his Parliaments*, pp. 63–4, 69–71; Fabien Menant, *Les députés de Napoléon, 1799–1815* (Paris, 2012), pp. 328–52. According to Woloch, *Napoleon and his Collaborators*, p. 92, the architect of the purge was François-Denis Tronchet, although Tulard and Lentz believe it was Cambacérès. At least half of the outgoing members of the Tribunate, and at least a third of the Legislative, were dismissed and given official postings within the administration (Collins, *Napoleon and his Parliaments*, pp. 66–7). They thereby became beholden to and supporters of the regime.

101. Extracts from the debates can be found in *Moniteur universel*, 19 and 20 germinal an X (9 and 10 April 1802).

102. Staum, *Cabanis*, pp. 287–97.

103. Woloch, *Napoleon and his Collaborators*, p. 83.

104. AN F7 3830, rapport de la préfecture de police, 17 fructidor an X (4 September 1802); Camille Latreille, *L'opposition religieuse au Concordat, de 1792 à 1803* (Paris, 1910), pp. 219–20; Boudon, *Napoléon et les cultes*, pp. 172–3.

105. Roberts, 'Napoleon, the Concordat of 1801', p. 55; Jean Godel, 'L'Eglise selon Napoléon', *Revue d'histoire moderne et contemporaine*, 17 (1970), 837–45; Englund, *Napoleon*, p. 184.

106. *Corr.* viii. n. 6420 (11 November 1802).

107. Cited in Boudon, 'L'incarnation de l'état de Brumaire', p. 342.

108. Boudon, 'L'incarnation de l'état de Brumaire', pp. 339–40.

109. Boudon, 'L'incarnation de l'état de Brumaire', p. 342.

110. It was a recurring theme throughout the Consulate. See, for example, V.-R. Barbet Du Bertrand, *Les trois hommes illustres, ou Dissertations sur les institutions politiques de César-Auguste, de Charlemagne et de Napoléon Bonaparte* (Paris, 1803), pp. 244–5, in which Bonaparte is lauded as the man who pacified the Vendée and who brought about religious reconciliation and achieved peace through military victories; J.-G.-M.-R. de Montgaillard, *La France sous le gouvernement de Bonaparte* (Paris, 1803), p. 44.

111. Petiteau, *Les Français et l'Empire*, p. 51.

112. On the competition see Foucart, 'L'accueil de la Paix d'Amiens', pp. 232–4. Five of the paintings entered are examined by Guy and Christian Ledoux-Lebard, 'Les tableaux du concours institué par Bonaparte en 1802 pour célébrer le rétablissement du culte', *Archives de l'art français*, 25 (1978), 251–61.

113. Bruno Foucart, 'Les iconographies du Concordat, laboratoire d'une nouvelle politique de l'image', in Boudon (ed.), *Le Concordat et le retour de la paix religieuse*, pp. 151–67; Philippe Bordes and Alain Pougetoux, 'Les portraits de Napoléon en habits impériaux par Jacques-Louis David', *Gazette des Beaux Arts*, 202 (1983), 21; Edward Lilley, 'Consular Portraits of Napoleon Bonaparte', *Gazette des Beaux Arts*, 106 (1985), 143–56.

114. Marc Gerstein, 'Le regard consolateur du grand homme', in Marie-Anne Dupuy (ed.), *Dominique-Vivant Denon: l'oeil de Napoléon* (Paris, 1999), p. 324.

115. Lilley, 'Consular portraits', 144.

116. Bordes and Pougetoux, 'Les portraits de Napoléon', 21.

117. Werner Telesko, *Napoleon Bonaparte: der 'Moderne Held' und die bildende Kunst, 1799–1815* (Vienna, 1998), p. 42.

118. Boime, *Art in an Age of Bonapartism*, ii. pp. 49–50.

119. Peter Burke, *The Fabrication of Louis XIV* (New Haven, 1992), pp. 19, 22; Dimitri Casali and David Chanteranne, *Napoléon par les peintres* (Paris, 2009), p. 61.

120. Mavor (ed.), *The Grand Tours of Katherine Wilmot*, pp. 16–17 (13 December 1801).

121. Boime, *Art in an Age of Bonapartism*, ii. p. 50.

122. Dawson Warren, *The Journal of a British Chaplain in Paris during the Peace Negociations*

*of 1801–2* (London, 1913), p. 208; Yorke, *France in Eighteen Hundred and Two*, pp. 123–6; Kotzebue, *Souvenirs*, i. pp. 140–1.

123. Boudon, 'L'incarnation de l'état de Brumaire', p. 342.
124. Udolpho van de Sandt, 'Le Salon', in Bonnet (ed.), *L'Empire des muses*, pp. 59–78.
125. Udolpho van de Sandt, 'La fréquentation des Salons sous l'Ancien Régime, la Révolution et l'Empire', *Revue de l'Art*, 73 (1986), 46.
126. Frédéric Bluche, *Le Bonapartisme: aux origines de la droite autoritaire (1800–1850)* (Paris, 1980), p. 26.
127. David A. Wisner, *The Cult of the Legislator in France 1750–1830: A Study in the Political Theology of the French Enlightenment* (Oxford, 1997), pp. 125, 129–30.
128. David O'Brien, *After the Revolution: Antoine-Jean Gros, Painting and Propaganda under Napoleon* (University Park, Pa., 2006), p. 84; Dwyer, *Napoleon: The Path to Power*, pp. 1–5, 249–53.

# EMPIRE, 1802–1804

## 6: *The Conservative Turn*

1. Claude-François de Méneval, *Mémoires pour servir à l'histoire de Napoléon Ier depuis 1802 jusqu'à 1815*, 3 vols (Paris, 1893–4), i. p. 173.
2. Pierre-Louis Roederer, *Un citoyen à un sénateur* (n.p., n.d.). It was probably printed too late to make much of an impression (Jean Thiry, *Le Sénat de Napoléon: 1800–1814* (Paris, 1949), pp. 95–6).
3. Girardin, *Mémoires, journal et souvenirs*, ii. pp. 265–6.
4. According to Girardin, *Mémoires, journal et souvenirs*, i. p. 266.
5. *Moniteur universel*, 22 floréal an X (12 May 1802); Thibaudeau, *Mémoires sur le Consulat*, pp. 238–9; Thiers, *Histoire du Consulat et de l'Empire*, iii. p. 501.
6. François-Alphonse Aulard, 'L'établissement du Consulat à vie', in *Etudes et leçons sur la Révolution française*, pp. 255–6.
7. According to Woloch, *Napoleon and his Collaborators*, p. 91.
8. Lentz, *Grand Consulat*, pp. 338–9.
9. Girardin, *Mémoires, journal et souvenirs*, i. pp. 268–9; Cornet, *Souvenirs sénatoriaux*, pp. 18–19, 26–7.
10. *Corr.* vii. n. 6079 (9 May 1802). Thibaudeau, *Mémoires sur le Consulat*, p. 247; Thiry, *Le Sénat de Napoléon*, pp. 98–9; Woloch, *Napoleon and his Collaborators*, p. 92.
11. Thibaudeau, *Mémoires sur le Consulat*, pp. 248–54.
12. Thibaudeau, *Mémoires sur le Consulat*, p. 249.
13. Thibaudeau, *Mémoires sur le Consulat*, pp. 251–2; Roederer, *Oeuvres*, iii. p. 447.
14. Théophile Berlier, *Précis de la vie politique de Théophile Berlier* (Dijon, 1838), p. 88; Woloch, *Napoleon and his Collaborators*, p. 93.
15. Thibaudeau, *Mémoires sur le Consulat*, p. 264.
16. The most complete discussion on the question of an heir is in Thiry, *Le Sénat de Napoléon*, pp. 90–109; Jean Thiry, *Le Concordat et le Consulat à vie: mars 1801–juillet 1802* (Paris, 1956), pp. 195–224.
17. Thiry, *Le Sénat de Napoléon*, pp. 99–100; Lentz, *Grand Consulat*, pp. 340–1.
18. Thibaudeau, *Mémoires sur le Consulat*, p. 282.
19. See also Cornet, *Souvenirs sénatoriaux*, pp. 18–19, 21.
20. In pamphlets such as Louis Pasquier, comte de Franclieu, *Opinion sur la question qui nous est proposée: Napoléon Bonaparte sera-t-il consul à vie?* (Paris, 1801); and Félix Nouvel, *Opinion de Félix Nouvel, du Finistère, sur cette question: Napoléon Bonaparte sera-t-il consul à vie?* (Brest, 1801).
21. Thierry Lentz, 'Contribution à l'étude des plébiscites du Consulat et du Premier Empire: l'exemple de la Moselle', *Revue de l'Institut Napoléon*, 151 (1988), 38.

22. Langlois, 'Napoléon Bonaparte plébiscité', pp. 81–93.
23. Results in AN B II 667, 671. Malcolm Crook, 'Confidence from Below? Collaboration and Resistance in the Napoleonic Plebiscites', in Rowe (ed.), *Collaboration and Resistance in Napoleonic Europe*, p. 23; Philippe Sagnac, 'L'avènement de Bonaparte à l'Empire: le Consulat à vie', *Revue des études napoléoniennes*, 24 (1925), 149.
24. Sagnac, 'L'avènement de Bonaparte', 149–50, 53–4.
25. One can recognize in the phrasing the Roman formula SPQR (Senatus Populusque Romanus) (Valérie Huet, 'Napoleon I: A New Augustus?', in Catherine Edwards (ed.), *Roman Presences: Receptions of Rome in European Culture, 1789–1945* (Cambridge, 1999), pp. 53–69, here p. 55).
26. Valentine Cloncurry, *Personal Recollections of the Life and Times of Valentine, Lord Cloncurry* (Dublin, 1849), p. 157.
27. *Corr.* vii. n. 6320 (3 August 1802).
28. Thibaudeau, *Mémoires sur le Consulat*, p. 263; Sagnac, 'L'avènement de Bonaparte', 195.
29. Aulard, *Paris sous le Consulat*, iii. pp. 206–7; Cambacérès, *Mémoires inédits*, i. p. 633.
30. Roederer, *Oeuvres*, iii. p. 331; Cabanis, *Le sacre de Napoléon*, p. 113.
31. Miot de Mélito, *Mémoires*, i. pp. 296, 297 and 298.
32. Jean Pelet de La Lozère, *Opinions de Napoléon sur divers sujets de politique et d'administration* (Paris, 1833), p. 53; Adrien Dansette, *Napoléon: pensées politiques et sociales* (Paris, 1969), p. 48 (August 1802).
33. Cited in Bluche, *Le Bonapartisme*, p. 30; from Dansette, *Pensées politiques et sociales*, pp. 47–8 (August 1802, to Thibaudeau).
34. Miot de Mélito, *Mémoires*, i. p. 299.
35. Boudon, 'L'incarnation de l'état de Brumaire', p. 340.
36. Staël, *Considérations*, ii. p. 228.
37. Miot de Mélito, *Mémoires*, i. p. 301.
38. Miot de Mélito, *Mémoires*, i. p. 307.
39. Remacle, *Relations secrètes*, pp. 31, 78; Barante, *Souvenirs*, i. pp. 100–1; Etienne-Denis Pasquier, *Histoire de mon temps: mémoires du chancelier Pasquier*, 6 vols (Paris, 1894–6), i. pp. 159–61; Aulard, *Paris sous le Consulat*, ii. p. 492; Petiteau, *Les Français et l'Empire*, pp. 52–3.
40. Petiteau, *Les Français et l'Empire*, p. 108.
41. A good many grumblings were picked up by the secret police. See, for example, AN F7 3829, 7 frimaire an IX (27 November 1800); F7 3830, 19 frimaire, 3 prairial, 3, 17 fructidor, 1er complimentaire, an X (9 January, 22 May, 21 August, 4, 18 September 1802).
42. See Picard, *Bonaparte et Moreau*, pp. 366–7. An insult could be as banal as naming a pet dog after the First Consul (Alfred Hachette, 'Sur un militaire qui, en passant à Sisteron, donnait à son chien le nom de Bonaparte', *Revue des études napoléoniennes*, 12 (1917), 116–18).
43. See, for example, Miot de Mélito, *Mémoires*, p. 313; Haegele, *Napoléon et Joseph Bonaparte*, pp. 136–7.
44. Thibaudeau, *Mémoires sur le Consulat*, p. 152.
45. Lentz, 'La proclamation du Concordat', p. 112.
46. Picard, *Bonaparte et Moreau*, p. 374.
47. Gaubert, *Conspirateurs au temps de Napoléon*, pp. 127–36; Edouard Guillon, *Les complots militaires sous le Consulat et l'Empire: d'après les documents inédits des archives* (Paris, 1894), pp. 16–25; Dunbar Plunket Barton, *Bernadotte and Napoleon, 1763–1810* (London, 1921), pp. 47–52; Gérard Minart, *Les opposants à Napoléon: l'élimination des royalistes et des républicains (1800–1815)* (Paris, 2003), pp. 109–13; Boscher, *Histoire de la repression*, pp. 143–7.
48. Chaptal, *Mes souvenirs*, p. 250; Villefosse and Bouissounouse, *L'opposition à Napoléon*, pp. 224–5.
49. See the police reports in AN F7 3089, 27 July, 16 November, 14 December 1804 and 18 January 1805; Petiteau, *Les Français et l'Empire*, pp. 111–12.

50. Gaubert, *Conspirateurs au temps de Napoléon*, pp. 142–3.
51. Guillon, *Les complots militaires sous le Consulat et l'Empire*, p. 30.
52. AN F7 6315, dossier 6659: Prefect of the Department of Seine et Oise to Fouché, 2 thermidor an X (20 July 1802); Mounier to Fouché, prairial an X (May 1802); report 13 prairial an X (2 June 1802); Gilbert-Augustin Thierry, *Conspirateurs et gens de police: le complot des libelles (1802)* (Paris, 1903); Villefosse and Bouissounouse, *L'opposition à Napoléon*, pp. 225–7; Guillon, *Les complots militaires sous le Consulat et l'Empire*, pp. 26–43; Barton, *Bernadotte and Napoleon*, pp. 59–65; Léonce Pingaud, *Bernadotte et Napoléon (1797–1814)* (Paris, 1933), pp. 68–70; T. T. Höjer, *Bernadotte, maréchal de France*, trans. from the Swedish by Lucien Maury, 2 vols (Paris, 1943), pp. 220–6; Boscher, *Histoire de la repression*, pp. 147–51; Franck Favier, *Bernadotte, un maréchal d'Empire sur le trône de Suède* (Paris, 2010), pp. 112–19.
53. AN F7 6315, dossier 6659, for their files.
54. Höjer, *Bernadotte*, i. p. 225; Emmanuel Cherrier, 'Un itinéraire politique original, l'ascension de Jean-Baptiste Bernadotte', *Nordic Historical Review/Revue d'Histoire Nordique*, 5 (2007), 85–7.
55. Miot de Mélito, *Mémoires*, ii. pp. 41–2.
56. Arthur-Léon Imbert de Saint-Amand, *Les femmes des Tuileries: la femme du Premier consul* (Paris, 1884), pp. 128–34; Kale, 'Women, Salons, and the State', 62.
57. On court life under Louis XIV see Burke, *The Fabrication of Louis XIV*, pp. 87, 89, 90–1; T. C. W. Blanning, *The Culture of Power and the Power of Culture: Old Regime Europe, 1660–1789* (Oxford, 2002), pp. 7, 29–31, 39–41.
58. Louis-Sébastien Mercier, *Tableau de Paris*, 12 vols (Amsterdam, 1788), ix. ch. dcxci, p. 78.
59. See Dwyer, *Napoleon: The Path to Power*, pp. 296–302. Comte Emmanuel de Las Cases, *Le Mémorial de Sainte-Hélène*, ed. and annotated by Marcel Dunan, 2 vols (Paris, 1983), ii. p. 305; Lentz, *Grand Consulat*, p. 373.
60. Eléonore-Adèle d'Osmond, comtesse de Boigne, *Récits d'une tante: mémoires de la comtesse de Boigne*, 4 vols (Paris, 1907–8), i. pp. 395–6; Martin-Fugier, *La vie élégante ou La formation du Tout-Paris*, p. 44; Pierre Branda, *Napoléon et ses hommes: la Maison de l'Empereur, 1804–1815* (Paris, 2011), pp. 322–6. Later, all imperial palaces were reorganized to make access to his person more difficult (Mansel, *The Eagle in Splendour*, pp. 75–8).
61. Blagdon, *Paris As It Was and As It Is*, i. p. 328.
62. Alméras, *La Vie parisienne sous le Consulat et l'Empire*, pp. 285–9; Charles-Otto Zieseniss, *Napoléon et la cour impériale* (Paris, 1980), pp. 74–5; Kale, *French Salons*, p. 83; Branda, *Napoléon et ses hommes*, pp. 307–26.
63. See Kale, *French Salons*, pp. 83–4.
64. AN F7 3831, 3 vendémiaire an XI (25 September 1802); Aulard, *Paris sous le Consulat*, iii. pp. 271–2.
65. Rémusat, *Mémoires*, iii. pp. 233–4, 237, 260.
66. Michael Rowe, *From Reich to State: The Rhineland in the Revolutionary Age, 1780–1830* (Cambridge, 2003), p. 115. On the importance of dress and the uniform, particularly at court, see Mansel, *Dressed to Rule*, esp. pp. 78–88.
67. Boudon, 'L'incarnation de l'état de Brumaire', p. 341; Mansel, *Dressed to Rule*, p. 80.
68. Remacle, *Relations secrètes*, p. 230 (15 January 1803).
69. Rémusat, *Mémoires*, i. pp. 174–5; Raoul Brunon, 'Uniforms in the Napoleonic Era', in Katell le Bourhis (ed.), *The Age of Napoleon: Costume from Revolution to Empire, 1789–1815* (New York, 1989), pp. 180–1. It was a practice that could also be found in, for example, the British army. See Myerly, *British Military Spectacle*, pp. 40–1.
70. Alan Forrest, 'The Napoleonic Armies and their World', *Revista Napoleonica*, 1–2 (2000), 280.
71. Cited in Madeleine Delpierre, 'Une révolution, en trois temps', in *Modes et révolutions, 1780–1804* (Paris, 1989), pp. 11–40; Margaret Waller, 'The Emperor's New Clothes: Display, Cover-Up and Exposure in Modern Masculinity', in Timothy Reeser and Lewis Seifert (eds), *Entre hommes: French and Francophone Masculinities in Literature and Culture* (Newark, 2008), pp. 115–42.

72. Marsha and Linda Frey, '"The Reign of the Charlatans is Over": The French Revolutionary Attack on Diplomatic Practice', *Journal of Modern History*, 65 (1993), 706–44.

73. *Etiquette du palais imperial* (Paris, 1806).

74. A *lever* took place when the sovereign left his apartments and made his appearance in public; only certain people could attend. The *coucher* was the moment when the sovereign retired to his apartments.

75. Waller, 'The Emperor's New Clothes', pp. 115–42.

76. Philippe Séguy, 'Costume in the Age of Napoleon', in le Bourhis (ed.), *The Age of Napoleon*, pp. 84, 110–12. On military uniforms see Brunon, 'Uniforms in the Napoleonic Era', pp. 179–201; and Philip Mansel, 'Monarchy, Uniform, and the Rise of the *Frac*, 1760–1830', *Past & Present*, 96 (1982), 103–32.

77. Mansel, *Dressed to Rule*, pp. 81–2.

78. Figures varied enormously over time, but there were around 1,200 people attached to Louis XIV's household in 1689 and around 2,000 under Louis XVI. See Jeroen Duindam, *Vienna and Versailles: The Courts of Europe's Major Dynastic Rivals, ca. 1550–1780* (Cambridge, 2003), pp. 54–5.

79. Mansel, *The Eagle in Splendour*, pp. 27, 34; Philip Mansel, *The Court of France, 1789–1830* (Cambridge, 1988), p. 188; Kale, *French Salons*, pp. 92–4; Branda, *Napoléon et ses hommes*, pp. 61–2. For an interesting comparative study on the courts of Paris, Vienna and Berlin see, Jeroen Duindam, 'The Dynastic Court in an Age of Change: Frederick II Seen from the Perspective of Habsburg and Bourbon Court Life', in Jürgen Luh and Michael Kaiser (eds), *Friedrich300 – Colloquien, Friedrich der Große und der Hof, 2009*, www.perspectivia.net/content/publikationen/friedrich300-colloquien/friedrich-hof/Duindam_Court?set_language=tr.

80. Oscar Browning (ed.), *England and Napoleon in 1803, being the despatches of Lord Witworth and others* (London, 1887), p. 17; Peter A. Lloyd, *The French Are Coming: The Invasion Scare of 1803–5* (Tunbridge Wells, 1991), p. 16.

81. Browning (ed.), *England and Napoleon in 1803*, p. 190.

82. See, for example, *Corr.* n. 6743 (13 May 1803).

83. On Bonaparte's version of events see *Corr.* viii. nos. 6630 and 6636 (13 and 16 March 1803). See Grainger, *The Amiens Truce*, pp. 174–6.

84. Bury and Barry (eds), *An Englishman in Paris*, pp. 93–4.

85. *Papers Relative to the Discussion with France in 1802 and 1803* (London, 1803), pp. 133–5; Browning (ed.), *England and Napoleon in 1803*, pp. 117–20; Kagan, *The End of the Old Order*, p. 43. It is nonsense, however, to suggest, as does Lentz, *Grand Consulat*, p. 467, that Bonaparte fell into a trap laid for him by the British.

86. Greig (ed.), *The Farington Diary*, ii. pp. 136–7.

87. Petr Ivanovich Bartenev (ed.), *Arkhiv kniazia Vorontsova*, 40 vols (Moscow, 1870–95), xx. pp. 119–21; Morkov, 4/16 March 1803, in *Sbornik Imperatorskogo russkogo istoricheskogo obschestva*, 148 vols (Petersburg, 1867–1916), lxxvii. pp. 63–8. On Morkov's reactions see A. W. Ward and G. P. Gooch, *The Cambridge History of British Foreign Policy, 1783–1919*, 3 vols (Cambridge, 1922–3), i. p. 319.

88. On this point see Stuart Woolf, 'French Civilization and Ethnicity in the Napoleonic Empire', *Past & Present*, 124 (1989), 96–120.

89. There were rumours to that effect in Paris as early as July/August 1802 (AN F7 3830, 13 and 30 thermidor an X (1 and 18 August 1802)).

90. For a summary of the conditions leading to the breakdown of peace in 1802–3 see Conrad Gill, 'The Relations between England and France in 1802', *English Historical Review*, 24 (1909), 61–78; Albert Sorel, *L'Europe et la Révolution française*, 9 vols (Paris, 1885–1991), vi. pp. 266–300; Schroeder, *Transformation of European Politics*, pp. 231–45; Grainger, *The Amiens Truce*.

91. Although it was not until 1803 that Bonaparte became the 'Mediator' of the Swiss Republic. See Gray, 'Revolutionism as Revisionism', pp. 128–9; Georges Andrey, 'L'Acte de médiation du 19 février 1803 porte-il bien son nom?', in Alain-Jacques

Czouz-Tornare (ed.), *Quand Napoléon Bonaparte recréa la Suisse: la genèse et la mise en oeuvre de l'Acte de médiation, aspects des relations franco-suisses autour de 1803* (Paris, 2005), pp. 15–39.

92. Simon Schama, *Patriots and Liberators: Revolution in the Netherlands 1780–1813* (London, 1992), pp. 399–409, 410–19.

93. Browning (ed.), *England and Napoleon in 1803*, pp. 16–19. These fears were fuelled by the departure of Colonel Horace Sébastiani for the Middle East in September 1802 to make sure that the British complied with the Treaty of Amiens and withdrew from Egypt. On his return to Paris, he submitted a report to Bonaparte, made public in the *Moniteur universel*, 10 pluviôse an XI (30 January 1803), in which he claimed that 6,000 troops could easily retake Egypt. On this see *Corr.* viii. nos. 6276 and 6308 (29 August and 5 September 1802); P. Coquelle, 'La mission de Sébastiani à Constantinople', *Revue d'histoire diplomatique*, 17 (1903), 438–55; Jean-Tiburce de Mesmay, *Horace Sébastiani, soldat, diplomate, homme d'Etat, maréchal de France, 1772–1851* (Paris, 1948), pp. 42–50; Simon Burrows, 'Culture and Misperception: The Law and the Press in the Outbreak of War in 1803', *International History Review*, 18 (1996), 811.

94. See Alfred Dufour, 'D'une médiation à l'autre', in Alfred Dufour, Till Hanisch and Victor Monnier (eds), *Bonaparte, la Suisse et l'Europe* (Geneva, 2003), pp. 7–37; and Mario Turchetti (ed.), *La Suisse de la médiation dans l'Europe napoléonienne (1803–1814)* (Fribourg, 2005).

95. Thomas M. Iiams, *Peacemaking from Vergennes to Napoleon: French Foreign Relations in the Revolutionary Era, 1774–1814* (Huntington, NY, 1979), p. 67, asserts that the Foreign Office records show the British were thinking about retaining Malta *before* Bonaparte annexed Piedmont.

96. Browning (ed.), *England and Napoleon*, pp. 52–3, 95–6; Yorke, *France in Eighteen Hundred and Two*, p. 120; Bourrienne, *Mémoires*, iv. pp. 305–7. Bonaparte appointed a secretary by the name of Nettement to translate articles from the English press (cited in Gill, 'The Relations between England and France', 63). On the press and Bonaparte see Simon Burrows, 'The Struggle for European Opinion in the Napoleonic Wars: British Francophone Propaganda, 1803–14', *French History*, 11 (1997), 33–5; and Simon Burrows, 'The French Emigré Press, 1789–1814: A Study in Impotence?', in David W. Lovell (ed.), *Revolution, Politics and Society: Elements in the Making of Modern France* (Canberra, 1994), pp. 31–9; Grainger, *The Amiens Truce*, pp. 146–50.

97. Hélène Maspero-Clerc, *Un journaliste contre-révolutionnaire, Jean-Gabriel Peltier, 1760–1825* (Paris, 1973), p. 148.

98. *Morning Post*, 1 February 1803.

99. Fedorak, *Henry Addington*, p. 113; Burrows, 'Culture and Misperception', 808.

100. Maspero-Clerc, *Un journaliste contre-révolutionnaire*, pp. 159–68; Simon Burrows, *French Exile Journalism and European Politics, 1792–1814* (Woodbridge, 2000), pp. 114–26.

101. Fedorak, *Henry Addington*, p. 114.

102. On the English press during the Revolution see Lucyle Werkmeister, *The London Daily Press, 1772–1792* (Lincoln, 1963), pp. 317–79. On freedom of the press see Arthur Aspinall, *Politics and the Press, c. 1780–1850* (London, 1949), pp. 33–65. On the expulsion of pro-French journalists see Burrow, 'The War of Words', 51.

103. Burrows, *French Exile Journalism*, pp. 107–8; Burrows, 'Culture and Misperception', 818. The sentiment is echoed by Gill, 'The Relations between England and France', 63–5, 66, who suggests that Bonaparte went to war, despite advice from his ministers, because he was irritated by the personal attacks against him in the English press. It prompted Talleyrand to say that if peace failed it was because of the little regard shown for Bonaparte's amour-propre (Browning (ed.), *England and Napoleon*, p. 266).

104. Anglophobia had been rampant in France for a very long time. See Frances Acomb, *Anglophobia in France, 1763–1789: An Essay in the History of Constitutionalism and Nationalism* (Durham, NC, 1950), pp. 89–123; Norman Hampson, *The Perfidy of Albion: French Perceptions of England during the French Revolution* (New York, 1998); Jean-Paul Bertaud,

Alan Forrest and Annie Jourdan, *Napoléon, le monde, et les Anglais: guerre des mots et des images* (Paris, 2004), pp. 13–29; Jean Guiffan, *Histoire de l'anglophobie en France: de Jeanne d'Arc à la vache folle* (Rennes, 2004), pp. 89–104; Bertaud, *Quand les enfants parlaient de gloire*, pp. 203–47. On Anglo-French relations in general see Robert and Isabelle Tombs, *That Sweet Enemy: The French and the British from the Sun King to the Present* (London, 2006), esp. chs 5 and 6.

105. Browning (ed.), *England and Napoleon*, pp. 192–6.

106. Grainger, *The Amiens Truce*, p. 188.

107. Thibaudeau, *Mémoires sur le Consulat*, pp. 405–7; Sorel, *L'Europe et la Révolution française*, vi. p. 217.

108. Throughout the month of April 1803, there were rumours of the inevitability of war. Aulard, *Paris sous le Consulat*, iv. pp. 5, 9, 12, 16, 18–19, 21, 23, 24, 25, 27, 29, 32.

109. *Corr.* viii. n. 6759 (22 May 1803). On this episode see Grainger, *The Amiens Truce*, pp. 200–3; Michael Lewis, *Napoleon and his British Captives* (London, 1962), pp. 22–30; Alger, *Napoleon's British Visitors*, pp. 177–80.

110. [Bertie Greatheed], *A Tour in France, 1802* (London, 1808), p. 86.

111. According to Lewis, *Napoleon and his British Captives*, p. 36; Roy and Lesley Adkins, *War for All the Oceans: From Nelson at the Nile to Napoleon at Waterloo* (London, 2006), p. 116.

112. *Corr.* ix. n. 7273 (12 November 1803).

113. Bell, *Total War*, p. 234.

114. Bertaud, *Quand les enfants parlaient de gloire*, p. 216.

115. Gershoy, *Bertrand Barère*, pp. 317–18.

116. *Mémorial anti-britannique, journal historique et politique*, which went from 26 September 1803 to 30 November 1804. It was then renamed the *Mémorial Européen; journal de politique et de littérature*, until March 1810. See also Barère de Vieuzac's *Les Anglais au XIXe siècle* (Paris, 1804). Barère fell out with Napoleon around the time of the Empire (Jean-Pierre Thomas, *Bertrand Barère: la voix de la Révolution* (Paris, 1989), pp. 263–4).

117. *Mémorial anti-britannique*, 16 November 1804.

118. *Mémorial anti-britannique*, 2 December 1804.

119. Take, for example, Comte de Montlosier's *Le peuple anglais, bouffé d'orgueil, de bière et de thé, jugé au tribunal de la raison* (Paris, 1802). But there were also political pamphlets, like the Comte d'Hauterive's *Observations sur le manifeste du roi d'Angleterre* (Paris, 1802).

120. Examples in Aulard, *Paris sous le Consulat*, iv. pp. 152–3, 635.

121. Lloyd, *The French Are Coming*, pp. 92–4.

122. Lloyd, *The French Are Coming*, pp. 17–23.

123. *Morning Chronicle*, 5 October 1803.

124. For the rumours around the invasion see Wheeler and Broadley, *Napoleon and the Invasion of England*, pp. 281–3, 349–50; Carola Oman, *Britain against Napoleon* (London, 1942), pp. 205–13.

125. John Newman, '"An Insurrection of Loyalty": The London Volunteer Regiments' Response to the Invasion Threat', in Philp (ed.), *Resisting Napoleon*, pp. 75–89; Richard Glover, *Britain at Bay: Defence against Bonaparte, 1803–14* (London, 1973), pp. 30–54; and Charles John Fedorak, 'In Defence of Great Britain: Henry Addington, the Duke of York and Military Preparations against Invasion by Napoléonic France, 1803–1804', in Philp (ed.), *Resisting Napoleon*, pp. 75–89 and 91–110.

126. Norman Longmate, *Island Fortress: The Defence of Great Britain, 1603–1945* (London, 1993), pp. 271–3.

127. See Wheeler and Broadley, *Napoleon and the Invasion of England*, pp. 329–62; Alexandra Franklin and Mark Philp, *Napoleon and the Invasion of Britain* (Oxford, 2003), pp. 60–3.

128. The Martello was a small defensive fort twelve metres high with thick walls built to withstand cannon, garrisoned by fifteen to twenty-five men. It was based on the Genoese tower in Corsica. Frank McLynn, *Invasion: From the Armada to Hitler, 1588–1945* (London, 1987), pp. 100–1; Longmate, *Island Fortress*, pp. 275–9.

129. Longmate, *Island Fortress*, pp. 267–9.
130. Longmate, *Island Fortress*, pp. 279–83.
131. *Spirit of the Public Journals for 1805* (London, 1806), p. 308.

## 7: *The End of the Revolution*

1. AN F7 6391, Signalements de plusieurs individus dont la recherche et l'arrestation sont ordonnées par le Gouvernement, pluviôse an XII; *Moniteur universel*, 7 March 1804.
2. The best biographical description of Cadoudal is Jean-Paul Bertaud, *Bonaparte et le duc d'Enghien, le duel des deux France* (Paris, 1972), pp. 45–54.
3. Forty-six in all, according to Aurélien Lignereux, 'Le moment terroriste de la chouannerie: des atteintes à l'ordre public aux attentats contre le Premier Consul', *La Révolution française*, lrf.revues.org/index390.
4. See Burrows, *French Exile Journalism*, pp. 191–7.
5. Miot de Mélito, *Mémoires*, ii. pp. 135–7.
6. Questions have, nevertheless, been raised about the complicity of Fouché in this affair. Royalists had, it would appear, completely penetrated all branches of the Paris police (Sparrow, 'The Alien Office', 380–81).
7. For the following, Moreau, *Jean-Victor Moreau*, pp. 94–5. On Moreau's involvement in the conspiracy see Maurice Garçot, *Le duel Moreau–Napoléon* (Paris, 1951), pp. 48–52, 55–66.
8. See, for example, the account by Barante, *Souvenirs*, i. pp. 112–13.
9. AN F7 6403, dossier de Jean Louis Picot.
10. AN F7 6391, declaration by and interrogation of Bouvet de Lozier.
11. At least according to his own admission. See Las Cases, *Mémorial*, ii. pp. 622–8; Moreau, *Jean-Victor Moreau*, pp. 95–6.
12. Las Cases, *Mémorial*, i. pp. 656–62; ii. pp. 617–22.
13. Picard, *Bonaparte et Moreau*, pp. 366–76.
14. Moreau's interrogation can be found in AN F7 6391.
15. According to Lentz, *Grand Consulat*, p. 533. In all, 356 conspirators were arrested during this time (Sparrow, *Secret Service*, pp. 291–2).
16. Cambacérès, *Mémoires inédits*, i. p. 706.
17. Aulard, *Paris sous le Consulat*, iv. pp. 679–80, 682 (16 and 17 February 1804); Bertaud, *Bonaparte et le duc d'Enghien*, pp. 96–7.
18. Picard, *Bonaparte et Moreau*, p. 285; Savinel, *Moreau*, p. 91.
19. Ségur, *Un aide de camp de Napoléon*, i. pp. 102–3; Bourrienne, *Mémoires*, vi. pp. 21–2.
20. Jérôme Laugier, *Les cahiers du capitaine Laugier* (Paris, 1893), pp. 257–8. On the other hand, those same officers appear willingly to have signed a letter congratulating Napoleon on his ascension to the thrones of the Empire and the Kingdom of Italy (AN AFIV 1953, no date).
21. Cambacérès, *Mémoires inédits*, i. p. 708.
22. The marquis de Gallo cited in Gaubert, *Conspirateurs au temps de Napoléon*, p. 201.
23. AN F7 6403, interrogation of Pichegru.
24. Aulard, *Paris sous le Consulat*, iv. pp. 720, 721, 722.
25. Aulard, *Paris sous le Consulat*, iv. pp. 330–1, 446 (24 August and 23 October 1803).
26. Alfred Boulay de la Meurthe, *Les dernières années du duc d'Enghien (1801–1804)* (Paris, 1886), pp. 226, 321.
27. Sidney B. Fay, 'The Execution of the Duc d'Enghien I', *American Historical Review*, 3 (1898), 620–1.
28. Cambacérès, *Mémoires inédits*, i. pp. 710–13; Pasquier, *Mémoires*, i. p. 179.
29. Pasquier, *Mémoires*, i. p. 180.
30. Joseph Othenin Bernard de Cléron, comte d'Haussonville, 'L'Eglise Romaine et le premier Empire 1800–1814: le Pape à Savone', *Revue des Deux Mondes*, 67 (1867), 43.

31. Méneval, *Mémoires*, i. pp. 284–5.
32. According to Cambacérès, *Mémoires inédits*, i. pp. 712–13. See also Henri Welschinger, *Le duc d'Enghien, 1772–1804: l'enlèvement d'Ettenheim et l'exécution de Vincennes* (Paris, 1913), pp. 388–5.
33. It is often said that this commando was led by Armand de Caulaincourt, but in fact it was General Ordener who went to Ettenheim to arrest Enghien. Caulaincourt suffered by association all his life, railing against the misconception on his deathbed. See Armand Augustin Louis, marquis de Caulaincourt, duc de Vicence, *Memoirs of General de Caulaincourt, Duke of Vicenza*, ed. Jean Hanoteau, 3 vols (London, 1950), i. pp. 17–20; Jean-Paul Bertaud, *Le duc d'Enghien* (Paris, 2001), pp. 349, 351.
34. Bertaud, *Le duc d'Enghien*, pp. 351–2.
35. Bertaud, *Le duc d'Enghien*, pp. 383–4.
36. Alan Forrest, 'Napoleon as Monarch: A Political Evolution', in Alan Forrest and Peter H. Wilson (eds), *The Bee and the Eagle: Napoleonic France and the End of the Holy Roman Empire, 1806* (Basingstoke, 2009), p. 117.
37. Bertrand, *Cahiers de Sainte-Hélène*, i. p. 58; Las Cases, *Mémorial*, ii. p. 627.
38. On the role of Savary see Thierry Lentz, *Savary: le séide de Napoléon* (Paris, 2001), pp. 113–36.
39. Hortense, *Memoirs*, i. pp. 95–6.
40. Andrew Hilliard Atteridge, *Joachim Murat, Marshal of France and King of Naples* (New York, 1911), p. 108; Jean Tulard, *Murat* (Paris, 1999), pp. 70–2.
41. Eugène de Beauharnais, *Mémoires et correspondance politique et militaire du prince Eugène*, 10 vols (Paris, 1858–60), i. p. 91.
42. Beauharnais, *Mémoires et correspondance politiques*, i. pp. 90–1.
43. Cornet, *Souvenirs sénatoriaux*, pp. 39–41.
44. Translation from William Francis Henry King, *Classical and Foreign Quotations* (London, 1889).
45. François-Joseph-Charles-Marie, comte de Mercy-Argenteau, *Memoirs of the Comte de Mercy-Argenteau: Napoleon's Chamberlain and his Minister Plenipotentiary to the King of Bavaria* (New York, 1917), i. p. 94.
46. Aulard, *Paris sous le Consulat*, iv. p. 730 (20 March 1804); Dalberg to Edelsheim (22 March 1804), Bernhard Erdmannsdörffer and K. Obser (eds), *Politische Correspondenz Karl Friedrichs von Baden, 1783–1806*, 5 vols (Heidelberg, 1888–1901), v. p. 27; Aulard, *Paris sous le Consulat*, iv. pp. 731, 732, 733 (21, 22 and 23 March 1804).
47. Lentz, *Grand Consulat*, p. 550.
48. Pasquier, *Mémoires*, i. p. 210; Welschinger, *Le duc d'Enghien*, pp. 337–83; Henri Welschinger, *L'Europe et l'exécution du duc d'Enghien* (Amiens, 1890).
49. A point underlined by Sorel, *L'Europe et la Révolution française*, vi. p. 359; and Kagan, *The End of the Old Order*, p. 88.
50. Adam Gielgud (ed.), *Memoirs of Prince Adam Czartoryski and his Correspondence with Alexander I*, 2 vols (London, 1888), ii. pp. 14–15; Charles Robert Vasilievitch de Nesselrode, *Lettres et papiers du chancelier comte de Nesselrode, 1760–1850*, 11 vols (Paris, 1908–12), ii. pp. 306–7; Dirk Van Hogendorp, *Mémoires du général Dirk van Hogendorp, comte de l'Empire* (The Hague, 1887), p. 153.
51. Protocol, 5/17 April 1804, in *Sbornik*, lxxvii. pp. 547–63; Joseph de Maistre, *Mémoires politiques et correspondance diplomatique de Joseph de Maistre* (Paris, 1864), pp. 110–11; and Joseph de Maistre, *Oeuvres complètes de J. de Maistre*, 14 vols (Lyons, 1884–6), ix. pp. 156–7.
52. W. H. Zawadzki, 'Prince Adam Czartoryski and Napoleonic France, 1801–1805: A Study in Political Attitudes', *Historical Journal*, 18 (1975), 262; Gielgud (ed.), *Memoirs of Prince Adam Czartoryski*, ii. pp. 16–34.
53. Constantin de Grunwald, *Alexandre Ier, le tsar mystique* (Paris, 1955), p. 99.
54. See the letter from Alexander to Friedrich Wilhelm in Paul Bailleu (ed.), *Briefwechsel König Friedrich Wilhelm III. und der Königin Luise mit Kaiser Alexander I* (Leipzig,

1900), pp. 46–7; Alexander M. Martin, *Romantics, Reformers, Reactionaries: Russian Conservative Thought and Politics in the Reign of Alexander I* (DeKalb, 1997), p. 42.

55. Lombard to Hardenberg (8 May 1804), in Bailleu (ed.), *Preußen und Frankreich*, ii. pp. 261–2; Welschinger, *L'Europe et l'exécution du duc d'Enghien*, pp. 20–3.

56. Welschinger, *Le duc d'Enghien*, pp. 411–14; and Welschinger, *L'Europe et l'exécution du duc d'Enghien*, pp. 25–35.

57. Chandler, *Campaigns of Napoleon*, p. 328; Schroeder, *Transformation of European Politics*, pp. 248–51; Charles Esdaile, *The Wars of Napoleon* (London, 1995), p. 22; Zawadzki, 'Czartoryski and Napoleonic France', 262; David Gates, *The Napoleonic Wars, 1803–1815* (London, 1997), p. 17.

58. Cited in Cabanis, *Le sacre de Napoléon*, p. 79.

59. François-René de Chateaubriand, *Correspondance générale*, 8 vols, vol. i: *1789–1807* (Paris, 1977), p. 183 (13 February 1803); Pawel Matyaszewski, 'Quelques remarques sur l'image de Napoléon chez Chateaubriand', *Annales de lettres et sciences humaines*, 37–8 (1989–90), 26.

60. Cabanis, *Le sacre de Napoléon*, p. 125.

61. Lentz, *Grand Consulat*, pp. 564–5. On the question of the transformation of the Republic into an Empire see Philip Dwyer, 'Napoleon and the Foundation of the Empire', *Historical Journal*, 53 (2010), 339–58.

62. Cited in Gill, 'The Relations between England and France', 62; Morkov to Alexander (1/13 December 1802), in *Sbornik*, lxx. p. 585.

63. Sir George Jackson, *The Diaries and Letters of Sir George Jackson*, 2 vols (London, 1872), i. p. 51.

64. Thibaudeau, *Le Consulat et l'Empire*, iii. pp. 1–2.

65. Thibaudeau, *Mémoires sur le Consulat*, pp. 236, 238–9.

66. Joseph Fiévée, *Correspondance et relations de J. Fiévée avec Bonaparte premier consul et empereur: pendant onze années, 1802 à 1813*, 3 vols (Paris, 1837), i. pp. 11–14, dubbed these people 'royalistes d'intérêt', as distinct from 'royalistes d'opinion'. The latter were pro-Bourbon and would not accept any other form of monarchy; the former were prepared to accept a 'monarchist system' regardless of the sovereign. See Polowetzky, *A Bond Never Broken*, p. 96.

67. Roederer, *Mémoires*, pp. 126–7. The conservative journalist Joseph Fiévée was the first to suggest publicly that Bonaparte be allowed to nominate a successor, and this as early as December 1799. See Popkin, 'Conservatism under Napoleon', 388.

68. Girardin, *Mémoires, Journal et Souvenirs*, i. pp. 268–70; Thierry Lentz, *Roederer, 1754–1835* (Metz, 1989), pp. 142–3.

69. Bailleu (ed.), *Preußen und Frankreich*, ii. pp. 46–8 (25 May 1801).

70. According to Jackson, *The Diaries and Letters*, i. p. 55.

71. Thibaudeau, *Mémoires sur le Consulat*, pp. 455–60; Woloch, *Napoleon and his Collaborators*, pp. 100–1.

72. Berlier, *Précis de la vie politique*, p. 87.

73. Jean Pelet de la Lozère, *Opinions de Napoléon sur divers sujets de politique et d'administration* (Paris, 1833), pp. 61–2.

74. Thibaudeau, *Mémoires sur le Consulat*, p. 461.

75. Berlier, *Précis de la vie politique*, p. 93.

76. Tribunate, 4 May 1804, and proclamation by Senate, 16 May 1804.

77. Annie Jourdan, *L'empire de Napoléon* (Paris, 2000), p. 222.

78. Curée (30 April 1804), in Thierry Lentz and Nathalie Clot (eds), *La proclamation du Premier Empire ou Recueil des pièces et actes relatifs à l'établissement du gouvernement impérial héréditaire* (Paris, 2001), p. 28. This is a reprint of *Recueil des pièces et actes relatifs à l'établissement du gouvernement impérial héréditaire* (Paris, 1804). Some of the speeches surrounding the foundation of the empire can also be found in Joseph-François-Nicolas Dusaulchoy de Bergemont, *Histoire du couronnement, ou Relation des cérémonies religieuses, politiques et militaires qui ont eu lieu pendant les jours mémorables consacrés à*

*célébrer le sacre et le Couronnement et le Sacre de Sa Majesté Impériale Napoléon Ier, Empereur des Français* (Paris, 1805), pp. 3–70.

79. Lazare Carnot in *La proclamation du Premier Empire*, pp. 63–9.

80. On the role of the Senate in the establishment of the Empire see Thiry, *Le Sénat de Napoléon*, pp. 122–45.

81. Woloch, *Napoleon and his Collaborators*, p. 114.

82. See the memoir attached to the Senate's response in *La Proclamation de l'Empire*, pp. 217–21; Annie Jourdan, 'Le sacre ou le pacte social', in *Napoléon le sacre: Musée Fesch, Ville d'Ajaccio, 23 avril–3 octobre 2004* (Ajaccio, 2004), pp. 25–33.

83. *La proclamation du Premier Empire*, p. 143.

84. Cornet, *Souvenirs sénatoriaux*, p. 29.

85. A special commission of ten members, composed of senators, ministers and the three consuls met at Saint-Cloud (11–13 May 1804) to discuss and prepare for the modification of the Constitution.

86. Englund, *Napoleon*, p. 248. The constitution of 1791 modified the king's title from King of France to King of the French.

87. *Moniteur universel*, 19 May 1804.

88. Miot de Mélito, *Mémoires*, ii. pp. 184–5; Louis-Constant Wairy [known as Constant], *Mémoires de Constant, premier valet de l'empereur, sur la vie privée de Napoléon, sa famille et sa cour*, 6 vols (Paris, 1830), i. pp. 230–1.

89. Louis Dubroca, *Les quatre fondateurs des dynasties françaises, ou Histoire de l'établissement de la monarchie française, par Clovis . . . Pépin et Hugues Capet; et . . . Napoléon-le-Grand . . .* (Paris, 1806), p. 327.

90. See, for example, Jean Chas, *Réflexions sur l'hérédité du pouvoir souverain* (Paris, 1804); *Poème à l'occasion du Sénatus-consulte, qui proclame Napoléon Bonaparte, Empereur des Français* (Paris, 1804); Therese Ebbinghaus, *Napoleon, England und die Presse, 1800–1803* (Munich, 1914), p. 148; Jean Tulard, *Joseph Fiévée, conseiller secret de Napoléon* (Paris, 1985), pp. 128–9.

91. *Journal des Débats*, 28 July 1804.

92. *Journal des Débats*, 19 August 1804.

93. *Journal des Débats*, 16, 19 August 1804.

94. Jacques Godechot, 'L'Empire napoléonien', *Recueils de la Société Jean Bodin*, 31 (1973), 433, 434.

95. Lucette Perol, 'Ce qu'évoquait le mot "empire" d'après les dictionnaires de 1690–1771', *Siècles. Cahiers du Centre d'histoire 'Espaces et culture'*, 17 (2003), 25–40, here 29, 31.

96. Jean-Luc Chappey, 'La notion d'empire et la question de légitimité politique', *Siècles. Cahiers du Centre d'histoire 'Espaces et culture'*, 17 (2003), 111–27, here 116–17.

97. Godechot, 'L'Empire napoléonien', 444.

98. *Moniteur universel*, 3 May 1804, p. 1012; Robert Morrissey, 'Charlemagne et la légende impériale', in Bonnet (ed.), *L'empire des muses*, p. 340.

99. Miot de Mélito, *Mémoires*, ii. pp. 152–3.

100. Roederer, *Oeuvres*, iii. p. 461.

101. Fouché, *Mémoires*, i. p. 304.

102. Edouard Driault, *La politique orientale de Napoléon: Sébastiani et Gardane, 1806–1808* (Paris, 1904), pp. 394–5.

103. Miot de Mélito, *Mémoires*, ii. p. 217.

104. Pierre Bertrand (ed.), *Lettres inédites de Talleyrand à Napoléon, 1800–1809* (Paris, 1889), p. 99.

105. Bailleu, *Preußen und Frankreich*, i. p. 330.

106. Take, for example, Mathieu Dumas, *Précis des événemens militaires, ou Essais historiques sur les campagnes de 1799 à 1814*, 19 vols (Paris, 1817–26), viii. p. 454. On the question of heredity see also Natalie Petiteau, 'Les Français et l'empereur', in Hélène Becquet and Bettina Frederking (eds), *La dignité de roi: regards sur la royauté au premier XIXe siècle* (Paris, 2009), pp. 20–2.

107. It led to the rupture of diplomatic relations between the two countries. Christer Jorgensen, *The Anglo-Swedish Alliance against Napoleonic France* (Basingstoke, 2004), pp. 23–5.
108. Zawadzki, 'Czartoryski and Napoleonic France', 264.
109. Paul R. Sweet, *Friedrich von Gentz: Defender of the Old Order* (Madison, 1941), pp. 97–8; Alexander Von Hase, 'Friedrich (v.) Gentz: vom Übergang nach Wien bis zu den "Fragmenten des Gleichgewichts" (1802–1806)', *Historische Zeitschrift*, 211 (1970), 589–615; Schroeder, *Transformation of European Politics*, p. 252.
110. Czartoryski to Razumovsky, 7/19 June 1804, *Vneshniaia Politika Rossii XIX I nachala XX veka*, Series I, 1801–1815, 8 vols (Moscow, 1960–72), ii. n. 31 (19 June 1804).
111. There is a debate about whether Napoleon dissolved a political entity that was already in its death throes or put an end to a thriving state. See Peter H. Wilson, 'The Meaning of Empire in Central Europe around 1800', in Forrest and Wilson (eds), *The Bee and the Eagle*, p. 22.
112. Zawadzki, 'Czartoryski and Napoleonic France', 265.
113. Adolf Beer, 'Österreich und Russland in den Jahren 1804 und 1805', *Archiv fur österreich-ische Geschichte*, 53 (1875), 125–243, here 230 (letter to Stadion, 11 July 1804); Karl A. Roider, 'The Habsburg Foreign Ministry and Political Reform, 1801–1805', *Central European History*, 22:2 (1989), 160–82.
114. August Fournier, *Gentz und Cobenzl: Geschichte der österreichischen Diplomatie in den Jahren 1801–1805* (Vienna, 1880), p. 296 (1 September 1804).
115. Cobenzl's memoir in Gero Walter, *Der Zusammenbruch des heiligen Römischen Reiches deutscher Nation und die Problematik seiner Restauration in den Jahren 1814–15* (Heidelberg, 1980), pp. 132–44; Wilson, 'The Meaning of Empire', pp. 25–6, 30; and Peter H. Wilson, 'Bolstering the Prestige of the Habsburgs: The End of the Holy Roman Empire in 1806', *International History Review*, 28 (2006), 723.
116. Francis retained the title 'elected Roman emperor' but was now also referred to as the 'hereditary Emperor of Austria' (*Erbkaiser von Österreich*).
117. Wilson, 'The Meaning of Empire', p. 26.
118. *Corr.* ix. n. 7900 (3 August 1804); Kaiser Franz Akten, Fasz. 203 neu (4 August 1804), cited in Wilson, 'Bolstering the Prestige of the Habsburgs', 725. The Holy Roman Emperor, Francis II, thereby became Francis I, Emperor of Austria.
119. Haegele, *Napoléon et Joseph Bonaparte*, p. 155.
120. Miot de Mélito, *Mémoires*, ii. p. 180; Haegele, *Napoléon et Joseph Bonaparte*, p. 156. Joseph's position in the succession was eventually embodied in the imperial Constitution. Articles three and four stated that the succession was to be based on Salic law – that is, the crown could be passed only from one male to the next – and that if Napoleon did not have a legitimate or adopted son (and he could adopt only the son or grandson of one of his brothers), the crown would pass to Joseph.
121. Miot de Mélito, *Mémoires*, ii. p. 170.
122. Miot de Mélito, *Mémoires*, ii. p. 171.
123. Miot de Mélito, *Mémoires*, ii. p. 108; Haegele, *Napoléon et Joseph Bonaparte*, pp. 167–8.
124. *Corr.* ix. n. 7693 (18 April 1804); Masson, *Napoléon et sa famille*, ii. pp. 376–80.
125. Recent works on Lucien include: Pietromarchi, *Lucien Bonaparte*; Martineau, *Lucien Bonaparte*; Marcello Simonetta and Noga Arikha, *Napoleon and the Rebel: A Story of Brotherhood, Passion, and Power* (New York, 2011); Maria Teresa Caracciolo (ed.), *Lucien Bonaparte: un homme libre* (Ajaccio, 2010).
126. Pietromarchi, *Lucien Bonaparte*, pp. 79–81.
127. Miot de Mélito, *Mémoires*, ii. p. 110.
128. Miot de Mélito, *Mémoires*, ii. pp. 110–11.
129. On this episode see Glenn J. Lamar, *Jérôme Bonaparte: The War Years, 1800–1815* (Westport, Conn., 2000), pp. 10–20; Jacques-Olivier Boudon, *Le roi Jérôme: frère prodigue de Napoléon, 1784–1860* (Paris, 2008), pp. 82–5, 87–92.
130. *Mémoires et correspondance du roi Jérôme et de la reine Catherine*, 7 vols (Paris, 1861–6), i. p. 271.

131. *Corr.* x. n. 8614 (23 April 1805); *Mémoires et correspondance du roi Jérôme*, i. pp. 295–7.

132. Eugene L. Didier, *The Life and Letters of Madame Bonaparte* (New York, 1879), pp. 46–8; Sidney Mitchell, *A Family Lawsuit: The Story of Elisabeth Patterson and Jérôme Bonaparte* (New York, 1958), pp. 101–7; Claude Bourguignon-Frasseto, *Betsy Bonaparte ou la Belle de Baltimore* (Paris, 1988).

133. Lucien to Napoleon (25 May 1805), in Mitchell, *A Family Lawsuit*, p. 96.

134. *Corr.* x n. 8691 (6 May 1805); Bernardine Melchior-Bonnet, *Jérôme Bonaparte, ou l'envers de l'épopée* (Paris, 1979), p. 58.

135. Chaptal, *Mes souvenirs*, p. 345.

136. Mitchell, *A Family Lawsuit*, p. 116.

137. Roederer, *Mémoires*, p. 206; Gabriel Girod de l'Ain, *Joseph Bonaparte: le roi malgré lui* (Paris, 1970), pp. 109–13.

138. Fouché, *Mémoires*, i. p. 279.

139. Rémusat, *Mémoires*, i. pp. 394–8 (Mme de Rémusat was not present during this scene. Josephine later told her, so Rémusat's account has to be taken with a pinch of salt).

140. Joseph Turquan, *L'impératrice Joséphine, d'après les témoignages des contemporains* (Paris, 1896), pp. 3–4.

141. Hortense, *Memoirs*, i. p. 101; Masson, *Napoléon et sa famille*, ii. pp. 400–2.

142. Iung (ed.), *Lucien Bonaparte*, iii. pp. 4–5.

143. Masson, *Napoléon et sa famille*, ii. pp. 414–18.

144. Henri Gaubert, *Le sacre de Napoléon Ier* (Paris, 1964), p. 149.

145. These sentiments are expressed in the speeches of the Tribunate to Napoleon – see, for example, the speeches by Fabre de l'Aude (reprinted in the *Moniteur*, 1 May); Jaubert (3 May); Faure (4 May) – and indeed in Napoleon's response to the Senate (6 May 1804).

146. Jacques-Barthélemy Salgues, *Mémoire pour servir à l'histoire de France sous le gouvernement de Napoléon Buonaparte et pendant l'absence de la maison de Bourbon (1760–1830)*, 9 vols (Paris, 1814–26), vi. pp. 148–9.

147. David Chanteranne, *Le sacre de Napoléon* (Paris, 2004), pp. 185–7, on which the following is based. See also Dubroca, *Les quatre fondateurs des dynasties françaises*, pp. 247–52, 305–6; Jean Chas, *Coup d'oeil d'un ami de sa patrie, sur les grandes action de l'empereur Napoléon* (Paris, 1804), pp. 1–2.

148. Chas, *Coup d'oeil d'un ami*, p. 1; Joseph-Balthazar Bonnet de Treyches, *Du gouvernement héréditaire et de l'influence de l'autorité d'un seul sur les arts* (Paris, 1804), p. 7.

149. Dubroca, *Les quatre fondateurs des dynasties françaises*, p. 325.

150. Bonnet de Treyches, *Du gouvernement héréditaire*, pp. 7 and 9.

151. Katia Sainson, '"Le Régénérateur de la France": Literary Accounts of Napoleonic Regeneration 1799–1805', *Nineteenth-Century French Studies*, 30 (2001–2), 9–25, here 17.

152. Howard Brown, *Ending the Revolution*, pp. 3–4, argues that the Revolution came to an end in 1802 because it was in that year the regime became 'structurally secure' – that is, it no longer faced a serious domestic threat; the government had become stable and was accepted by the political elite. Blanning, *Pursuit of Glory*, p. 653, argues for 1802 as the year in which the revolutionary wars came to an end.

## 8: 'The First Throne of the Universe'

1. *Recueil des pièces authentiques relatives au suicide de l'ex-général Pichegru* (Paris, 1804).

2. Bertaud, *Bonaparte et le duc d'Enghien*, pp. 101–2.

3. *Vie privée de Georges Cadoudal, son caractère, ses crimes* (Paris, 1804).

4. Claude-Ambroise Régnier, *Liste des brigands chargés, par le Ministère britannique, d'attenter aux jours du Premier Consul* (Paris, an XII); *Pichegru et Moreau* (Paris, 1804); and *Moreau et Pichegru au 18 fructidor an V* (Paris, an XII), probably written by Roederer on Bonaparte's orders. It is interesting to note that the Consular

government always associated Moreau with that of Pichegru whenever he was mentioned in print.

5. *Acte d'accusation de Georges, Pichegru, Moreau, et autres prévenus de conspiration contre la personne du premier consul et contre la sûreté intérieure et extérieure de la république* (Paris, an XII); *Recueil des interrogatoires subis par le général Moreau* (Paris, an XII).

6. See, for example, the *Lettre du général Moreau, au Premier Consul pour se disculper d'avoir pris part à la conspiration de Cadoudal* (Paris, 1804).

7. Chastenay, *Mémoires*, i. p. 336.

8. Moreau, *Jean-Victor Moreau*, p. 104.

9. Cabanis, *Le sacre de Napoléon*, p. 132; Petiteau, *Les Français et l'Empire*, p. 81.

10. Dalberg to Edelsheim (6 June 1804), Erdmannsdörffer and Obser (eds), *Politische Correspondenz Karl Friedrichs von Baden*, v. p. 83.

11. According to AN F7 6403, dossier on Armand and Jules Polignac, Armand was condemned to death but pardoned by Napoleon and sent to the prison of Ham and then, after an attempted escape, back to the Temple in Paris.

12. Lenôtre, *Georges Cadoudal*, pp. 245–51; Bertaud, *Bonaparte et le duc d'Enghien*, pp. 409–13.

13. *Corr.* ix. n. 7804 (9 June 1804).

14. Bourrienne, *Mémoires*, vi. p. 157.

15. Although the official *Correspondance* does not contain a letter from Napoleon to Soult (or any other army commander) with this request, there is an allusion to such a document in a letter from Soult to Napoleon in which the former states, 'You ordered me, general, to report, in the greatest detail, on the opinion of the army . . .' (Soult to Napoleon, AN AFIV 1599, 27 germinal an XII (16 April 1804)). My thanks to Michael J. Hughes for sharing his archival notes and for pointing me in this direction.

16. Soult to Napoleon, AN AFIV 1599, 21 germinal an XII (10 April 1804).

17. Claude-Ambroise Régnier, *Rapport du grand-juge au Premier Consul, et communiqué au Sénat dans sa séance de germinal, contenant toutes les pièces de la conspiration tramée par le gouvernement britannique, contre les jours du Premier Consul!* (Paris, an XII); Woloch, *Napoleon and his Collaborators*, p. 111.

18. At least according to Lentz, *Grand Consulat*, p. 563, but there does not appear to be a great deal of support for this assertion.

19. AN BB/II/850B.

20. AN BB/II/850A, 22 floréal XII. Also cited in Woloch, *Napoleon and his Collaborators*, p. 112.

21. For example, Woloch, *Napoleon and his Collaborators*, p. 114.

22. *Corr.* ix. n. 7683 (14 April 1804); Jourdan, 'Le sacre ou le pacte social', p. 27; and Annie Jourdan, 'Le Premier Empire: un nouveau pacte social', *Cités: philosophie, politique, histoire*, 20 (2004), 51–64.

23. A change came about on 21 March 1804, when the editors announced that the petitions being submitted were so numerous that they were going to abandon publishing them in their entirety and instead print extracts. Many of the letters sent to the authorities and not published can be found in the series AN F/1cIII.

24. AN F/1cIII/Aisne 12, 2 ventôse XII (21 February 1804).

25. AN AFIV 1953, 12 ventôse an XII (2 March 1804). Other examples include a letter from the civil magistrates of Marseilles to Napoleon, F/1cIII/Bouches-du-Rhône 8, 4 ventôse an XII (23 February 1804).

26. For this see Elaine Williamson, 'Denon, la presse et la propagande impériale', in Daniela Gallo (ed.), *Les vies de Dominique-Vivant Denon*, 2 vols (Paris, 2001), i. pp. 154–5.

27. The assertion by Jourdan, 'Le sacre ou le pacte social', p. 27, that the petitions pleaded in favour of heredity or that, more specifically, the electoral colleges of the Var, the Yonne, the Nord, the Hautes-Pyrénées and the Roër (found in the *Moniteur universel*, 14 April 1804) 'begged' Napoleon to accept the crown is not borne out. There is at most a vague hint in

the petition from the Yonne that 'It is time to merge without reserve your [that is, Napoleon's] destiny and that of the state.'

28. For example, *Moniteur universel*, 19 March 1804.

29. *Moniteur universel*, 1 May 1804.

30. AN F/1cIII/Aisne 12, letter from the 'tribunal de commerce' of Soissons (no date but probably end of floréal an XII (May 1804)).

31. AN F/1cIII/Bouches-du-Rhône 8, prefect of the department to the minister of the interior, 9 prairial an XII (28 May 1804).

32. Corinne Legoy, 'Les marges captivantes, de l'histoire: la parole de gloire de la Restauration', in Anne-Emmanuelle Demartini and Dominique Kalifa (eds), *Imaginaire et sensibilités au XIXe siècle: études pour Alain Corbin* (Paris, 2005), pp. 115–24, here pp. 119–20.

33. The quotation is from a letter by Pierre Hartmann Richard, Lyons, no date, in AN AFIV, Fond de la Secrétairerie d'Etat, 1951. Examples from these cartons have also been used by Petiteau, *Les Français et l'Empire*, pp. 160–6; Petiteau, 'Les Français et l'empereur', pp. 24–8.

34. AN AFIV 1951, p. Barrère to the minister of the interior, 25 floréal an XII (14 May 1804).

35. AN AFIV 1953, Paris, 3 ventôse an XII (22 February 1804).

36. AN AFIV 1953, 24 priarial an 12 (14 June 1804).

37. A printed example is *L'avènement de Napoléon à l'empire; stance lyrique par J.B.* (Paris, 1804).

38. Jean Sarrazin, *Le onze frimaire, ou Discours analytique de la vie, des exploits mémorables, et des droits de Napoléon Ier* (Paris, 1804), p. 80.

39. AN BII 850B, letter from the adjutant commandant of the Army of Saint-Domingue, General Henry, Nantes, 13 floréal an XII (2 May 1804).

40. AN AFIV 1953, Lafontaine, 2 May 1804.

41. AN AFIV 1953, the widow Maillet (no date, no place).

42. AN AFIV 1953, Jean-Baptiste Chabrier, Mirmande, 14 ventôse an XII (4 May 1804).

43. Petiteau, *Les Français et l'Empire*, pp. 165, 170, argues that during this period there is a reinvention of relations between monarch and subject and that there is a return to a new kind of sacralization of the monarchy, less superstitious than that which preceded the Revolution.

44. AN AFIV 1953, Pradier, from Castres, Department of Tarn, 30 germinal an XII (19 April 1804).

45. AN AFIV 1953, Jean-Aime Lautour, 7 floréal an XII (26 April 1804); Egron, retired commandant de Place, 11 floréal an XII (30 April 1804); Jean Jacques Nicolas André, 27 floréal an XII (16 May 1804); Jacques Nicolas André, lawyer, Turin, 27 floréal an XII (16 May 1804); and Sarrazin, *Le onze frimaire*, pp. 83–4.

46. AN BII 850B, General Henry, Nantes, 13 floréal an XII (2 May 1804); BII 851A, letter from the camp of Montreuil (no date); F/1cIII/Aisne 12, letter from the sub-prefect of the Aisne, floréal an XII (April 1804).

47. See, for example, the letter from a notary in the Tarn, Pierre Guibert, in AN AFIV 1953, in which he refers to Napoleon as the father of the French people called on to conserve the glory and prosperity of the Empire. Also, F/1cIII/Lot/9, adjunct mayor of the town of Caussade, department of Lot, to Napoleon, 19 floréal an XII (8 May 1804); AFIV, 1953, François Louis Marguet, Besançon, 12 ventôse an XII (2 March 1804); and Lieutenant Boutaud, Paris, 15 floréal an XII (4 May 1804).

48. Jay M. Smith, 'No More Language Games: Words, Beliefs, and Political Culture in Early Modern France', *American Historical Review*, 102 (1997), 1426.

49. Marmont, *Mémoires*, ii. pp. 235–8; Pierre Robinaux, *Journal de route du capitaine Robinaux, 1803–1832* (Paris, 1908), pp. 17–21.

50. Albert Soboul, 'De la Révolution à l'Empire en France: souveraineté populaire et gouvernement autoritaire (1789–1804)', *Recueils de la Société Jean Bodin*, 26 (1965), 16–30; Petiteau, *Les Français et l'Empire*, p. 123.

51. François Arago, *Histoire de ma jeunesse* (Brussels and Leipzig, 1854), pp. 52–3; Remacle, *Relations secrètes*, pp. 53, 74–5.

52. *Souvenirs du général baron Teste* (Paris, 1999), pp. 100–1. He described the swearing of the oath to the imperial regime as a ceremony in which a 'sad and gloomy silence' reigned.

53. Ernest de Hauterive, *La police secrète du premier Empire, bulletins quotidiens adressés par Fouché à l'Empereur*, 5 vols (Paris, 1908–64), i. pp. 22, 94 (27 July and 17 September 1804).

54. Natalie Petiteau, 'Insultes et hostilités politiques sous le Consulat et l'Empire', in Thomas Bouchet, Matthew Legget, Jean Vigreux and Geneviève Verdo (eds), *L'insulte (en) politique: Europe et Amérique latine du XIXe siècle à nos jours* (Dijon, 2005), p. 213.

55. Auxonne-Marie-Théodose de Thiard, *Souvenirs diplomatiques et militaires* (Paris, 2007), pp. 128–9; Gilbert Bodinier, 'Officiers et soldats de l'armée impériale face à Napoléon', in *Napoléon, de l'histoire à la légende: actes du colloque des 30 novembre et 1er décembre 1999* (Paris, 2000), pp. 215–16.

56. Noël, *Souvenirs militaires*, pp. 34–5.

57. Crook, 'Confidence from Below?', p. 24.

58. The minister of the interior, Portalis, reported that the number of 'yes' votes in the army and navy respectively were 120,032 and 16,224. Napoleon simply increased the figures to 400,000 and 50,000. No 'no' votes were recorded (Frédéric Masson, *Le sacre et le couronnement de Napoléon* (Paris, 1978), p. 117).

59. Malcolm Crook, 'The Plebiscite on the Empire', in Dwyer and Forrest (eds), *Napoleon and his Empire*, pp. 19–20.

60. Woloch, *Napoleon and his Collaborators*, p. 119.

61. Cited in Crook, 'Confidence from Below?', p. 31.

62. Isser Woloch, 'From Consulate to Empire: Impetus and Resistance', in Peter Baehr and Melvin Ritcher (eds), *Dictatorship in History and Theory: Bonapartism, Caesarism, and Totalitarianism* (Cambridge, 2004), pp. 29–52, here p. 52.

63. Todd Porterfield and Susan L. Siegfried, *Staging Empire: Napoleon, Ingres, and David* (University Park, Pa., 2006), p. 8. On the creation of monarchical symbolism for later periods see Eric Hobsbawm and Terence Ranger (eds), *The Invention of Tradition* (Cambridge, 1983).

64. It is an argument found in Porterfield and Siegfried, *Staging Empire*.

65. Jean-Pierre Samoyault, 'L'ameublement des salles du Trône dans les palais impériaux sous Napoléon Ier', *Bulletin de la Société de l'histoire de l'art français* (1985), 185–206.

66. Alfred Marquiset, *Napoléon sténographié au Conseil d'Etat, 1804–1805* (Paris, 1913), pp. 29–31 (12 June 1804); Alain Boureau, *L'aigle: chronique politique d'un emblème* (Paris, 1985), pp. 158–74.

67. Jean Tulard, *Le Grand Empire, 1804–1815* (Paris, 1982), pp. 25–6; Annie Duprat, 'Une guerre des images: Louis XVIII, Napoléon et la France en 1815', *Revue d'Histoire moderne et contemporaine*, 47:3 (2000), 488.

68. Masson, *Le sacre et le couronnement de Napoléon*, pp. 75–6.

69. Cited in Chanteranne, *Le sacre de Napoléon*, p. 67.

70. Cited in Cabanis, *Le sacre de Napoléon*, p. 129.

71. On the Legion of Honour see André Fugier, 'La signification sociale et politique des décorations napoléoniennes', *Cahiers d'histoire*, 4 (1959), 339–46; Louis Bonneville de Marsangy, *La Légion d'honneur* (Paris, 1982), pp. 52–120; Michael J. Hughes, 'Making Frenchmen into Warriors: Martial Masculinity in Napoleonic France', in Christopher E. Forth and Bernard Taithe (eds), *French Masculinities: History, Culture and Politics* (Basingstoke, 2007), pp. 58–9; Hughes, 'Vive la République, Vive l'Empereur!', pp. 127–44; Natalie Petiteau, 'Pourquoi Napoléon crée-t-il la Légion d'honneur?', in Jean Tulard, François Monnier and Olivier Echappé (eds), *La Légion d'honneur: deux siècles d'histoire* (Paris, 2004), pp. 35–48; Olivier Ihl, *Le mérite et la République: essai sur la société des émules* (Paris, 2007), pp. 167–92; Natalie Petiteau, 'Légion d'honneur et normes sociales', in Bruno Dumons and Gilles Pollet (eds), *La fabrique de l'honneur: les médailles et les décorations en France, XIXe–XXe siècles* (Rennes, 2009), pp. 17–30.

72. Historians often write that, through a law passed on 20 May 1802, Bonaparte restored slavery. That is one way of seeing it, although it is not entirely accurate. In fact, Bonaparte *maintained* slavery in those colonies that had not abolished it in the first place – namely, Martinique and the Réunion – reintroducing the slave trade in the process (Philippe R. Girard, 'Napoléon Bonaparte and the Emancipation Issue in Saint-Domingue, 1799–1803', *French Historical Studies*, 32 (2009), 611). In other colonies, such as Guadeloupe and Saint-Domingue, he left matters alone. The revolutionaries themselves regretted the haste with which slavery had been abolished and freedom granted, as a result of which there was no opposition or outcry to the decree re-establishing slavery. See Yves Bénot and Marcel Dorigny (eds), *1802, rétablissement de l'esclavage dans les colonies françaises: aux origines d'Haïti: ruptures et continuités de la politique coloniale française, 1800–1830* (Paris, 2003); Thierry Lentz and Pierre Branda, *Napoléon, l'esclavage et les colonies* (Paris, 2006); Philippe R. Girard, *The Slaves Who Defeated Napoleon: Toussaint Louverture and the Haitian War of Independence, 1801–1804* (Tuscaloosa, 2011).

73. Jean-Paul Bertaud, *The Army of the French Revolution: From Citizen-Soldiers to Instrument of Power*, trans. R. R. Palmer (Princeton, 1988), pp. 328–34.

74. According to Petiteau, 'Pourquoi Napoléon crée-t-il la Légion d'honneur?', pp. 41, 42.

75. Rafe Blaufarb, 'The *Ancien Régime* Origins of Napoleonic Social Reconstruction', *French History*, 14:4 (2000), 415.

76. Hughes, 'Vive la République, Vive l'Empereur!', pp. 69–72. Some historians argue that Napoleon was replacing the revolutionary notion of 'virtue' with the monarchical notion of 'honour'. See Lynn, 'Toward an Army of Honor', 153–5; Norman Hampson, 'The French Revolution and the Nationalization of Honour', in M. R. D. Foot (ed.), *War and Society: Historical Essays in Honour and Memory of J. R. Western, 1928–1971* (London, 1973), pp. 211–12.

77. Charles-Hyacinthe His, *Théorie du monde politique, ou de la Science du gouvernement considérée comme science exact* (Paris, 1806), pp. 209–10. This was part of a 'social management technique', a way of channelling energies and passions for the good of the nation. See Olivier Ihl, 'The Market of Honors: On the Bicentenary of the Legion of Honor', *French Politics, Culture & Society*, 24 (2006), 10–11.

78. *Moniteur universel*, 29 floreal an X (19 May 1802); Thibaudeau, *Mémoires sur le Consulat*, pp. 89–90.

79. In fact, very few civilians received the Legion in Napoleon's time – 1,400 out of 48,000 between 1802 and 1814 – that is, only about 3 per cent of recipients. It was largely awarded to the military (Alan Forrest, 'The Military Culture of Napoleonic France', in Philip Dwyer (ed.), *Napoleon and Europe* (London, 2001), p. 52).

80. Remacle, *Relations secrètes*, p. 239 (25 January 1803).

81. Arago, *Histoire de ma jeunesse*, p. 52.

82. According to Abel Hugo, 'Souvenirs et mémoires sur Joseph Napoléon en 1811, 1812 et 1813', *Revue des Deux Mondes*, 1 (1833), 300–24, here 315.

83. Martin van Creveld, 'Napoleon and the Dawn of Operational Warfare', in John Andreas Olsen and Martin van Creveld (eds), *The Evolution of Operational Art: From Napoleon to the Present* (Oxford, 2010), p. 21.

84. On this event see Hughes, 'Vive la République, Vive l'Empereur!', pp. 30–2; Michael J. Hughes, *Forging Napoleon's Grande Armée: Motivation, Military Culture, and Masculinity in the French Army, 1800–1808* (New York, 2012), pp. 51–2.

85. Commandant Giraud, *Le carnet de campagne du commandant Giraud* (Paris, 1899), pp. 67–8 (29 September 1804).

86. Charles François, *Journal du capitaine François: dit le Dromadaire d'Egypte 1792–1830* (Paris, 2003), p. 476 (15 August 1805); Laurence Chatel de Brancion, *Le sacre de Napoléon: le rêve de changer le monde* (Paris, 2004), pp. 102–4.

87. Philippe-Auguste Hennequin, *Un peintre sous la Révolution et le premier Empire: mémoires de Philippe-Auguste Hennequin écrits par lui-même* (Paris, 1933), p. 228; Jérémie Benoît, *Philippe-Auguste Hennequin, 1762–1833* (Paris, 1994), pp. 64–6.

88. Jean-Marguerite Tupinier, *Mémoires du baron Tupinier: directeur des ports et arsenaux, 1779–1850* (Paris, 1994), p. 69; Constant, *Mémoires*, i. pp. 262–5; Louis Béchet de Léocour, *Souvenirs: écrits en 1838–1839* (Paris, 2000), pp. 207–9; Porterfield and Siegfried, *Staging Empire*, pp. 29–30.

89. *Moniteur universel*, 1 fructidor an XII (18 August 1804). 'Et vous soldats, vous jurez de défendre, au péril de votre vie, l'honneur du nom français, votre patrie et votre Empereur?'

90. Tupinier, *Mémoires*, p. 69; Cabanis, *Le sacre de Napoléon*, pp. 129–30.

91. See Dubroca, *Les quatre fondateurs des dynasties françaises*, and Jean-Gabriel-Maurice-Rocque, comte de Montgaillard, *Fondation de la quatrième dynastie, ou la Dynastie impériale* (Paris, 1804), both of which present Napoleon as the fourth dynasty after the Merovingians, the Carolingians and the Capetians. The term 'fourth dynasty' was not used though till 1810 (Jean Tulard, 'Les empires napoléoniens', in Jean Tulard (ed.), *Les empires occidentaux de Rome à Berlin* (Paris, 1997), pp. 363–82, here p. 365).

92. Avner Ben-Amos, *Funerals, Politics and Memory in Modern France, 1789–1996* (Oxford, 2000), p. 4.

93. Tulard, 'Les empires napoléoniens', p. 365; Peter R. Baehr, *Caesar and the Fading of the Roman World: A Study in Republicanism and Caesarism* (New Brunswick, 1998), pp. 92–102.

94. Thomas Biskup, 'Das Schwert Friedrichs des Großen: universalhistorische "Größe" und monarchische Genealogie in der napoleonischen Symbolpolitik nach *Iéna*', in Andreas Klinger, Hans-Werner Hahn and Georg Schmidt (eds), *Das Jahr 1806 im europäischen Kontext: Balance, Hegemonie und politische Kulturen* (Weimar, 2008), p. 197.

95. For this and the following see Masson, *Le sacre et le couronnement de Napoléon*, pp. 60–9; Gaubert, *Le sacre de Napoléon*, pp. 22–32; Robert Morrissey, *La barbe fleuri: Charlemagne dans la mythologie et l'histoire de France* (Paris, 1997), and Morrissey, 'Charlemagne et la légende impériale', pp. 331–47; Jean-Claude Valla, *La nostalgie de l'Empire: une relecture de l'histoire napoléonienne* (Paris, 2004), pp. 41–80; Porterfield and Siegfried, *Staging Empire*, pp. 79–82.

96. Napoleon may have thought of using Charlemagne as a more substantial political symbol, but he was called to the throne by his people, whereas Napoleon presented the imperial title to the French people as a fait accompli. It would not have been prudent or politic to push the analogy too far.

97. *Journal de Paris*, 1 prairial an XII (21 May 1804).

98. *Moniteur universel*, speech by Duveyrier (2 May), Arnould (4 May), and an address from the camp of Montreuil (9 May 1804). See also the extract of C. Théveneau, 'Charlemagne, ou la Caroléide', in *La Décade philosophique, littéraire et politique*, 18 (1804), 543–8; 19 (1804), 27–31; and 23 (1804), 283–92.

99. *Mercure de France*, 1 messidor an VIII (20 June 1800), in the article entitled 'Pièces divers relatives aux opérations militaires'; *Journal des Débats*, 28 thermidor an XII (16 August 1804). A few months later, a book entitled the *Histoire de l'Empereur Charlemagne*, translated from the German, was reviewed in the *Moniteur universel*, 18 December 1804. See also Jacques Mallet du Pan, *Correspondance inédite de Mallet du Pan avec la Cour de Vienne (1794–1798)*, 2 vols (Paris, 1884), ii. pp. 277, 293 (10 May, 17 June 1797); André Cabanis, 'Les courants contre-révolutionnaire sous le Consulat et l'Empire', *Revue des sciences politiques*, 24 (1971), 56; Dean, *L'Eglise constitutionnelle*, pp. 43–6.

100. See Jean Chas, *Parallèle de Bonaparte le Grand avec Charlemagne* (Paris, 1803); Barbet Du Bertrand, *Les trois hommes illustres*; and Dubroca, *Les quatre fondateurs des dynasties françaises*, pp. 39–41.

101. See, for example, his response to the Senate offering him hereditary power, in Lentz and Clot (eds), *La proclamation du Premier Empire*, p. 22 (25 April 1804).

102. Chas, *Coup d'oeil d'un ami*, p. 82; Chanteranne, *Le sacre de Napoléon*, p. 203.

103. Pillard, *Louis Fontanes*, pp. 191, 195–6; Morrissey, *La barbe fleuri*, pp. 247–348; Cabanis, 'Les courants contre-révolutionnaire', 57; Jean Tulard, *Le sacre de l'empereur Napoléon: histoire et légende* (Paris, 2004), p. 14.

104. Alain Ruiz, 'Napoleons Rhein- und Moselreise im Jahre 1804', in Elisabeth Dühr and Christl Lehnert-Leven (eds), *Unter der Trikolore: Trier in Frankreich, Napoleon in Trier, 1794–1814*, 2 vols (Trier, 2004), ii. pp. 649–68; Thomas R. Kraus, 'Napoleon–Aachen–Karl der Große: Betrachtungen zur napoleonischen Herrschaftslegitimation', in Mario Kramp (ed.), *Krönungen: Könige in Aachen, Geschichte und Mythos*, 2 vols (Mainz, 2000), ii. pp. 699–707.

105. J.-B. Poissenot, *Historique et statistique sur la ville d'Aix-la-Chapelle et ses environs, pouvant servir d'itinéraire* (Aix-la-Chapelle, 1808), pp. 113–14; Marie-Jeanne Avrillon, *Mémoires de Mlle Avrillon sur la vie privée de Joséphine, sa famille et sa cour*, 2 vols (Paris, 1833), i. pp. 92–3.

106. Chatel de Brancion, *Le sacre de Napoléon*, pp. 122–4.

107. Alain Ruiz, 'Napoléon vu par les Allemands de son temps', in Françoise Knopper and Jean Mondot (eds), *L'Allemagne face au modèle français de 1789 à 1815* (Toulouse, 2008), pp. 47–9.

108. See Norman Bryson, 'Representing the Real: Gros' Painting of Napoleon', *History of the Human Sciences*, 1 (1988), 75–104; Darcy Grimaldo Grigsby, 'Rumor, Contagion, and Colonization in Gros's *Plague-Stricken of Jaffa* (1804)', *Representations*, 51 (1995), 1–46; Darcy Grimaldo Grigsby, *Extremities: Painting Empire in Post-Revolutionary France* (New Haven, 2002), pp. 65–103; O'Brien, *After the Revolution*, pp. 97–104, 111–16. For a medical/scientific interpretation of the painting see Todd Porterfield, *The Allure of Empire: Art in the Service of French Imperialism, 1798–1836* (Princeton, 1998), pp. 53–61.

109. Hauterive, *La police secrète du premier Empire*, i. p. 115 (29 September 1804); Henri Mollaret and Jacqueline Brossollet, 'A propos des "Pestiférés de Jaffa" de A. J. Gros', *Jaarboek van het Koninklijk Museum voor schoone kunsten* (1968), 273.

110. H. Jouin, *David d'Angers, sa vie, son oeuvre, ses écrits et ses contemporains* (Paris, 1878), i. p. 39; Norman Schlenoff, 'Baron Gros and Napoleon's Egyptian Campaign', in *Essays in Honor of W. Friedlander* (Locust Valley, NY, 1965), p. 162; Mollaret and Brossollet, 'A propos des "Pestiférés de Jaffa"', 270.

111. Delécluze, *Louis David*, pp. 291–2.

112. Mollaret and Brossollet, 'A propos des "Pestiférés de Jaffa"', 271–3.

113. 'L'Hospice de Jaffa', in *Mercure de France* (14 September 1805), 577–80, by J. Camusat, supposedly a student of the Lycée Bonaparte.

114. Grigsby, *Extremities*, pp. 118–19.

115. See Grigsby, *Extremities*, pp. 90–101; Casali and Chanteranne, *Napoléon par les peintres*, p. 37.

116. François, *Journal*, i. p. 335 (26 and 27 May 1798).

117. Robert Thomas Wilson, *History of the British Expedition to Egypt* (London, 1802), esp. pp. xix–xx, 12–23.

118. See Antoine Marie Chamans, comte de Lavalette, *Mémoires et souvenirs du Cte Lavallette, ancien aide-de-camp de Napoléon, directeur des postes sous le premier Empire et pendant les Cent-Jours* (Paris, 1905), p. 215.

119. Grigsby, *Extremities*, p. 100.

120. Walter Friedlaender, 'Napoleon as "Roi Thaumaturge"', *Journal of the Warburg and Courtauld Institutes*, 4 (1941), 139–41; Edgar Munhall, 'Portraits of Napoleon', *Yale French Studies*, 26 (1960), 7.

121. See Marc Bloch, *Les Rois Thaumaturges: étude sur le caractère surnaturel attribué à la puissance royale particulièrement en France et en Angleterre* (Paris, 1983), pp. 399–405; Chantal Grell, 'The *sacre* of Louis XVI: The End of a Myth', in Michael Schaich (ed.), *Monarchy and Religion: The Transformation of Royal Culture in Eighteenth-Century Europe* (Oxford, 2007), pp. 345–66. Charles X reinstated it when he was crowned in 1825, but it was the last time it was used.

122. O'Brien, *After the Revolution*, p. 102.

123. Manfred Heinrich Brunner, *Antoine-Jean Gros: die Napoleonischen Historienbilder* (Bonn, 1979), pp. 152–5, 175–80; Paddy Jill Morse, 'A Revaluation of the Napoleonic

History Paintings of Jean-Antoine Gros', PhD dissertation (Ohio State University, 1993), p. 54.

124. For this see Morse, 'A Revaluation', pp. 74–81, 101–7; Grigsby, 'Rumor, Contagion and Colonization', 36.

125. Grigsby, *Extremities*, pp. 101–2.

126. For a summary of attitudes towards plague in early modern France see Junko Thérèse Takeda, *Between Crown and Commerce: Marseille and the Early Modern Mediterranean* (Baltimore, 2011), ch. 4.

127. Pillard, *Louis Fontanes*, p. 196; Gaubert, *Le sacre de Napoléon*, p. 38; Lentz, *Nouvelle histoire du Premier Empire* (Paris, 2002), i. p. 72.

128. Marquiset, *Napoléon sténographié*, pp. 22–9; Boudon, 'Les fondements religieux du pouvoir impérial', p. 206.

129. Pillard, *Louis Fontanes*, pp. 192–6.

130. Marquiset, *Napoléon sténographié*, p. 25.

131. Lentz, *Nouvelle histoire du Premier Empire*, i. p. 73.

132. *Journal des Débats*, 2 prairial an XII (22 May 1804); Chanteranne, *Le sacre de Napoléon*, p. 62.

133. Fiévée, *Correspondance et relations*, ii. p. 39.

134. Marquiset, *Napoléon sténographié*, pp. 23–4 (12 June 1804).

135. Marquiset, *Napoléon sténographié*, pp. 36–7 (26 June 1804).

136. Gaubert, *Le sacre de Napoléon*, pp. 44–5.

137. Pierre-François Fontaine, *Journal: 1799–1853*, 2 vols (Paris, 1987), i. pp. 84–5 (20 August 1804).

138. Boudon, 'Les fondements religieux du pouvoir impérial', pp. 206–12.

139. Boudon, *Napoléon et les cultes*, p. 127.

140. Porterfield and Siegfried, *Staging Empire*, p. 7.

141. On the negotiations between Napoleon and the pope see Jean Leflon, *Histoire de l'Eglise: depuis les origines jusqu'à nos jours*, vol. xx of *La crise révolutionnaire 1789–1846* (Paris, 1949), pp. 223–6; Gaubert, *Le sacre de Napoléon*, pp. 70–88, 102–12.

142. Leflon, *Histoire de l'Eglise*, p. 223.

143. Jean Leflon, 'Face à Napoléon, Pie VII', *Revue de l'Institut Napoléon*, 131 (1975), 3–19, here 9.

144. Bernardine Melchior-Bonnet, *Napoléon et le Pape* (Paris, 1958), p. 61.

145. Emmanuel Rodocanachi, 'Pie VII à Paris', in Emmanuel Rodocanachi, *Etudes et fantaisies historiques*, 2 vols (Paris, 1912), i. pp. 1–49; Latreille, *Napoléon et le Saint-Siège*, pp. 338–9.

146. Savary, *Mémoires*, ii. pp. 110–11; Chanteranne, *Le sacre de Napoléon*, p. 73.

147. Salgues, *Mémoires*, vi. p. 147.

148. François-Alphonse Aulard, *Paris sous le Premier Empire: recueil de documents pour l'histoire de l'esprit public à Paris*, 3 vols (Paris, 1912–23), i. p. 413 (28 November 1804).

149. Chanteranne, *Le sacre de Napoléon*, p. 234.

150. Rémusat, *Mémoires*, ii. pp. 65–6.

151. Jourdan, 'Le sacre ou le pacte social', p. 28.

152. Consalvi, *Mémoires*, ii. p. 413.

153. Consalvi, *Mémoires*, ii. p. 396.

154. Bourrienne, *Mémoires*, i. p. 211.

155. Henri Welschinger, *Le Divorce de Napoléon* (Paris, 1889), pp. 9–14; Tulard, *Le sacre de l'empereur Napoléon*, p. 20.

156. Miot de Mélito, *Mémoires*, ii. pp. 223–4; Chatel de Brancion, *Le sacre de Napoléon*, pp. 176–7.

157. Cited in Flora Fraser, *Pauline Bonaparte: Venus of Empire* (New York, 2009), p. 122.

158. Roederer, *Mémoires*, pp. 207–10.

159. Miot de Mélito, *Mémoires*, ii. pp. 229–30.

160. Miot de Mélito, *Mémoires*, ii. pp. 225–30.

*9: Citizen Emperor*

1. Miot de Mélito, *Mémoires*, ii. p. 230; Woloch, *Napoleon and his Collaborators*, pp. 116–17. The expression was not used in the official account (*Moniteur universel*, 16 floréal an XII (6 May 1804)).
2. Auguste-Julien Bigarré, *Mémoires du Général Bigarré, 1775–1813* (Paris, 2002), p. 144.
3. Stéphanie de Bade (ed.), 'Souvenirs de Stéphanie de Beauharnais', *Revue des Deux Mondes*, 102 (1932), 80; Avrillon, *Mémoires*, i. p. 114.
4. Abrantès, *Mémoires*, v. p. 120.
5. Siegfried, 'Fashion and the Reinvention of Court Costume', pp. 234–5.
6. Claire-Elisabeth-Jeanne Gravier de Vergennes, comtesse de Rémusat, *Lettres de Mme de Rémusat, 1804–1811*, 2 vols (Paris, 1881), ii. p. 69.
7. Charles Brifaut, *Souvenirs d'un académicien sur la Révolution, le premier Empire et la Restauration*, 2 vols (Paris, 1920–1), i. pp. 1–2.
8. AN F7 3833, 4 frimaire an XIII (25 November 1804); Charles de Rémusat, *Mémoires de ma vie*, 5 vols (Paris, 1958–67), i. p. 51; Alfred Fierro, *La vie des Parisiens sous Napoléon* (Saint-Cloud, 2003), pp. 207–12.
9. Fontaine, *Journal*, i. p. 92 (2 December 1804); Boulart, *Mémoires militaires*, pp. 123–4.
10. Aulard, *Paris sous le Premier Empire*, i. p. 421 (2 December 1804).
11. Fontaine, *Journal*, i. p. 92 (2 December 1804).
12. Savary, *Mémoires*, ii. p. 115.
13. Cornet, *Souvenirs sénatoriaux*, p. 56; Henry d'Ideville, *Le maréchal Bugeaud, d'après sa correspondance intime et des documents inédits, 1784–1849* (Paris, 1885), p. 45; Rodocanachi, 'Pie VII à Paris', pp. 28–9.
14. Lentz, *Le sacre de Napoléon*, p. 84; Masson, *Le sacre et le couronnement de Napoléon*, pp. 152–3.
15. Thiard, *Souvenirs diplomatiques et militaires*, p. 25.
16. Alan Forrest, *The Legacy of the French Revolutionary Wars: The Nation-in-Arms in French Republican Memory* (Cambridge, 2009), p. 59.
17. Linda Colley, 'The Apotheosis of George III: Loyalty, Royalty and the British Nation', *Past & Present*, 102 (1984), 126.
18. Noël, *Souvenirs militaires*, p. 35.
19. H. C. Cheuvreux (ed.), *Journal et correspondance de André-Marie Ampère (de 1793 à 1805)* (Paris, 1872), p. 335.
20. Miot de Melito, *Mémoires*, ii. p. 231; Lentz, *Nouvelle histoire du Premier Empire*, i. pp. 90–2, 94–6; Natalie Petiteau, 'Lecture socio-politique de l'empire: bilan et perspectives', *Annales historiques de la Révolution française*, 359 (2010), 197.
21. Hortense, *Memoirs*, i. p. 115.
22. Rémusat, *Mémoires*, ii. p. 71.
23. Aulard, *Paris sous le Premier Empire*, i. pp. 420–1 (2 December 1804); Gaubert, *Le sacre de Napoléon*, pp. 182–3, asserts that the police reports were fabricated.
24. See, for example, François-Frédéric Billon, *Souvenirs, 1804–1815* (Paris, 2006), pp. 26–7.
25. Elie Krettly, *Souvenirs historiques du capitaine Krettly* (Paris, 2003), pp. 74–5.
26. Thiébault, *Mémoires*, iii. pp. 380–1; Lanzac de Laborie, *Paris sous Napoléon*, iii. p. 29.
27. Rémusat, *Mémoires*, ii. p. 72.
28. Biver, *Le Paris de Napoléon*, p. 65.
29. Biver, *Le Paris de Napoléon*, p. 62.
30. Turquan, *L'impératrice Joséphine*, pp. 40–1.
31. Bigarré, *Mémoires*, p. 147.
32. Cornet, *Souvenirs sénatoriaux*, p. 56; Savary, *Mémoires*, ii. p. 116.
33. This is taken from Cabanis, *Le sacre de Napoléon*, p. 96.

34. Las Cases, *Mémorial*, ii. p. 198.

35. René Boudard, 'Le sacre de Napoléon vu par un figurant', *Revue de l'Institut Napoléon*, 50 (1954), 34.

36. Rémusat, *Mémoires*, ii. p. 71.

37. Waller, 'The Emperor's New Clothes', pp. 121, 122.

38. Marquiset, *Napoléon sténographié*, pp. 49–50 (16 October 1804); Peter Hicks, 'Un sacre sans pareil', in Lentz (ed.), *Le sacre de Napoléon*, pp. 101–39.

39. Bade (ed.), 'Souvenirs de Stéphanie de Beauharnais', p. 81.

40. See Christopher Clark, 'When Culture Meets Power: The Prussian Coronation of 1701', in Hamish Scott and Brendan Simms (eds), *Cultures of Power in Europe* (Cambridge, 2007), p. 19.

41. Lentz (ed.), *Le sacre de Napoléon*, p. 116.

42. The question is raised by Chanteranne, *Le sacre de Napoléon*, p. 153.

43. Rémusat, *Mémoires*, ii. p. 57; Frédéric Masson, *Joséphine, impératrice et reine* (Paris, 1899), p. 225.

44. Abrantès, *Mémoires*, v. p. 129.

45. Chanteranne, *Le sacre de Napoléon*, pp. 158–9; Clark, 'When Culture Meets Power', p. 14.

46. Masson, *Le sacre et le couronnement de Napoléon*, p. 21.

47. Chanteranne, *Le sacre de Napoléon*, p. 157.

48. Bluche, *Le Bonapartisme*, p. 31.

49. See Tulard, *Napoléon ou le mythe du sauveur*, pp. 172–3; Boudon, *Napoléon et les cultes*, p. 128.

50. Chanteranne, *Le sacre de Napoléon*, p. 129.

51. *Corr.* x. n. 8237 (27 December 1804).

52. Dusaulchoy de Bergemont, *Histoire du couronnement*, p. 288. The notion of divine right would gain authority as the Empire progressed.

53. Brookner, *Jacques-Louis David*, p. 150.

54. The following is based on Brookner, *Jacques-Louis David*, pp. 150–6; Prendergast, *Napoleon and History Painting*, pp. 38–48; Boime, *Art in an Age of Bonapartism*, ii. p. 47; Porterfield and Siegfried, *Staging Empire*, pp. 115–69; Todd Porterfield, 'David sans David', in Mark Ledbury (ed.), *David after David: Essays on the Later Work* (Williamstown, Mass., 2007), pp. 39–53; Sylvain Laveissière et al., *Le Sacre de Napoléon peint par David* (Paris, 2004); O'Brien, *After the Revolution*, pp. 145–8.

55. Porterfield and Siegfried, *Staging Empire*, pp. 7–8.

56. Philippe Bordes, *Jacques-Louis David: Empire to Exile* (New Haven, 2005), pp. 19–74, here p. 47.

57. Schnapper and Sérullaz (eds), *Jacques-Louis David*, p. 413.

58. Delécluze, *Louis David*, pp. 312–33; Porterfield, 'David sans David', p. 43.

59. Philippe Bordes, 'La fabrication de l'histoire par Jacques-Louis David', in *Triomphe et mort du héros: la peinture d'histoire en Europe de Rubens à Manet* (London, 1988), p. 116; Porterfield and Siegfried, *Staging Empire*, pp. 10–11.

60. Fanny Cosandey, *La reine de France: symbole et pouvoir: XVe–XVIIIe siècle* (Paris, 2000), pp. 137, 138.

61. Porterfield and Siegfried, *Staging Empire*, p. 7.

62. Pierre Colau, *Couplets adressés à M. David, premier peintre de S.M. l'empereur et roi* (Paris, n.d.); Cabanis, *Le sacre de Napoléon*, p. 22; Chanteranne, *Le sacre de Napoléon*, pp. 195–6; Guillaume Faroult, *David* (Paris, 2003), p. 98; Porterfield and Siegfried, *Staging Empire*, p. 9; Johnson, *Jacques-Louis David*, p. 196.

63. On this point, Porterfield and Siegfried, *Staging Empire*, pp. 158–60.

64. *Moniteur universel*, 16 January 1808; *Description du tableau représentant le couronnement de leurs majestés impériales et royales* (Paris, 1808), p. 5.

65. Delécluze, *Louis David*, pp. 312–14; Prendergast, *Napoleon and History Painting*, p. 38. See also Stefan Germer, 'On marche dans ce tableau: zur Konstituierung des "Realistischen" in den napoleonischen Darstellungen von Jacques-Louis David', in Gudrun

Gersmann and Hubertus Kohle (eds), *Frankreich 1800: Gesellschaft, Kultur, Mentalitäten* (Stuttgart, 1990), pp. 81–103.

66. Johnson, *Jacques-Louis David*, pp. 200, 204.
67. *Nouvelle description du tableau exposé au Musée Napoléon représentant de leurs majestés impériales et royales* (Paris, 1808), p. 3.
68. Hauterive, *La police secrète du premier Empire*, iv. p. 63 (15 February 1808).
69. *Annales de l'architecture et des arts libéraux et mécaniques*, 18 March 1808, pp. 185–90.
70. Antoine Schnapper, *David, témoin de son temps* (Paris, 1980), p. 231.
71. Hauterive, *La police secrète du premier Empire*, iv. pp. 35, 54 and 194 (29 January, 11 February and 24 May 1808); Bernard Chevallier and Christophe Pincemaille, *L'impératrice Joséphine* (Paris, 1996), pp. 332–3.
72. *Arlequin, au Muséum, ou critique en Vaudeville des Tableaux du Salon* (Paris, 1808).
73. Cited in Annie Jourdan, 'Napoleon and his Artists', in Howard Brown and Judith Miller (eds), *Taking Liberties: Problems of a New Order from the French Revolution to Napoleon* (Manchester, 2002), p. 194.
74. Burke, *Eyewitnessing*, pp. 28–9.
75. Burke, *Eyewitnessing*, p. 73.
76. On this painting see Susan Siegfried, 'The Politics of Criticism at the Salon of 1806: Ingres's *Napoleon Enthroned*', *Proceedings of the Consortium on Revolutionary Europe* (Athens, Georgia, 1980), pp. 69–81; Porterfield and Siegfried, *Staging Empire*, pp. 38–60.
77. See Telesko, *Napoleon Bonaparte*, pp. 50–1.
78. Porterfield and Siegfried, *Staging Empire*, p. 50, argue that Ingres had attempted to reinvent the divine body of the king.
79. Porterfield and Siegfried, *Staging Empire*, p. 88.
80. Susan Siegfried suggests that the Legislative Corps was thus attempting to modify its own image as a republican institution by purposefully adopting a particular kind of imperial image (Porterfield and Siegfried, *Staging Empire*, pp. 73–4).
81. Henriette Bessis, 'Ingres et le portrait de l'Empereur', *Archives de l'art français*, 24 (1969), 89–90.
82. According to Pierre-Nolasque Bergeret, *Lettres d'un artiste sur l'état des arts en France* (Paris, 1848), pp. 72–3.
83. Telesko, *Napoleon Bonaparte*, p. 45.
84. Cited in Porterfield and Siegfried, *Staging Empire*, p. 92.
85. Cited in Telesko, *Napoleon Bonaparte*, p. 45.
86. Susan Siegfried, 'The Politicisation of Art Criticism in the Post-Revolutionary Press', in Michael R. Orwicz (ed.), *Art Criticism and its Institutions in Nineteenth-Century France* (Manchester, 1994), pp. 9–28; Adrian Rifkin, 'History, Time and the Morphology of Critical Language, or Publicola's Choice', in ibid., pp. 29–42; Wrigley, *The Origins of French Art Criticism*, pp. 165–349.
87. See the critique by Jean-Baptiste Boutard, 'Salon de l'art 1806', *Journal de l'Empire*, 4 October 1806.
88. Pierre Jean-Baptiste Chaussard, *Le pausanias français* (Paris, 1808); Porterfield and Siegfried, *Staging Empire*, pp. 98, 100.
89. Porterfield and Siegfried, *Staging Empire*, p. 7.
90. Fontaine, *Journal*, i. p. 92 (5 December 1804).
91. Porterfield and Siegfried, *Staging Empire*, pp. 45–6.
92. *Corr.* ix. n. 7876 (27 July 1804). Also Hughes, 'Vive la République, Vive l'Empereur!', p. 56.
93. See, for example, Marcel Baldet, *La vie quotidienne dans les armées de Napoléon* (Paris, 1965), p. 132; Maurice Choury, *Les Grognards et Napoléon* (Paris, 1968), pp. 165–6; Lynn, 'Toward an Army of Honor', 165–6; O'Brien, *After the Revolution*, p. 126.
94. Louis-François Lejeune, *Mémoires du général Lejeune, 1792–1813* (Paris, 2001), p. 160.
95. *Moniteur universel*, 26–27 messidor an IX (14–15 July 1801); Hughes, 'Vive la République, Vive l'Empereur!', p. 41.

96. Fontaine, *Journal*, i. p. 93 (5 December 1804); Boulart, *Mémoires militaires*, pp. 125–6; Masson, *Le sacre et le couronnement de Napoléon*, pp. 220–2.

97. Marrinan, 'Literal/Literary/"Lexie"', 191.

98. Valérie Bajou, 'Painting and Politics under the Empire: David's *Distribution of the Eagles*', in Ledbury (ed.), *David after David*, pp. 55–71.

99. Johnson, *Jacques-Louis David*, p. 207.

100. Johnson, *Jacques-Louis David*, pp. 214–16.

101. Bigarré, *Mémoires*, p. 160.

102. Klemens Wenzel von Metternich, *Mémoires: documents et écrits divers*, 8 vols (Paris, 1881–4), i. p. 283.

103. Katia Malaussena, 'The Birth of Modern Commemoration in France: The Tree and the Text', *French History*, 18 (2004), 154–72, here 159.

104. Bluche, *Le Bonapartisme*, p. 27; Brian Jenkins, *Nationalism in France: Class and Nation since 1789* (Savage, Md, 1990), p. 36.

105. Cited in Keith Michael Baker, *Inventing the French Revolution* (Cambridge, 1990), p. 225.

106. Chanteranne, *Le sacre de Napoléon*, pp. 209, 211. More than 75,000 silver medallions were distributed along the boulevards by heralds in arm during the coronation procession.

107. J.C., *Précis historique-chronologique du voyage du saint-père le pape Pie VII en France* (Brussels, 1804), p. 46; Aulard, *Paris sous le Premier Empire*, i. p. 397 (20 November 1804).

108. Bernard Chevallier, 'Préparatifs des fêtes données par la ville de Paris à l'occasion du sacre', in *Napoléon le sacre*, p. 83.

109. *Corr.* x. n. 8781 (24 May 1805).

110. Chevallier, 'Préparatifs des fêtes', p. 86. Abby Zanger, *Scenes from the Marriage of Louis XIV: Nuptial Fictions and the Making of Absolutist Power* (Stanford, Calif., 1997), pp. 100–12, is, as far as I am aware, the only person to have studied 'the role of fireworks in organizing political culture' in any depth.

111. Dusaulchoy de Bergemont, *Histoire du couronnement*, pp. 282–3.

112. Accounts of the festivities can be found in Pierre-Maurice Saunier, *Tableau historique des cérémonies du sacre et du couronnement de S.M. Napoléon Ier* (Paris, an VIII); Lanzac de Laborie, *Paris sous Napoléon*, iii. pp. 43–4. For a broader discussion of Napoleonic festivities, including the participation of women, see Denise Z. Davidson, 'Women at Napoleonic Festivals: Gender and the Public Sphere during the First Empire', *French History*, 16 (2002), 299–322.

113. Bovet, *Notice sur les solennités célébrées à Strasbourg . . . le jour du couronnement de Napoléon . . .* (Strasbourg, 1804).

114. Rémusat, *Mémoires*, i. p. 80.

115. See Masson, *Le sacre et le couronnement de Napoléon*, pp. 257–60.

116. Chatel de Brancion, *Le sacre de Napoléon*, p. 313.

117. Hauterive, *La police secrète du premier Empire*, i. p. 222 (24 December 1804), and pp. 207, 249; ii. p. 110 (15 December 1804; 16 January; 5 October 1805).

118. Bertaud, *Bonaparte et le duc d'Enghien*, pp. 416–17.

119. Cited in Gaubert, *Le sacre de Napoléon*, p. 184.

120. See the *Moniteur universel*, 3, 4 and 5 December 1804. The pretext used was that 'The magnitude of these solemnities, the order, the brilliance and the pomp with which they were celebrated . . . does not allow the freedom to depict so succinctly such a magnificent spectacle.'

121. Cited in Gaubert, *Le sacre de Napoléon*, p. 235.

## CONQUEST, 1805–1807

### *10: 'The Rage of Conquest and Ambition'*

1. For the following see Edouard Driault, *Napoléon en Italie* (Paris, 1906), pp. 62–81; Albert Pingaud, *La domination française dans l'Italie du Nord (1796–1805): Bonaparte, président de la République italienne*, 2 vols (Paris, 1914), i. pp. 264–381; André Fugier, *Napoléon et l'Italie* (Paris, 1947), pp. 159–64; Desmond Gregory, *Napoleon's Italy* (Madison, 2001), pp. 45–66; Alain Pillepich, *Napoléon et les Italiens: République italienne et Royaume d'Italie, 1802–1814* (Paris, 2003), pp. 51–69.
2. Pillepich, *Napoléon et les Italiens*, p. 58.
3. Driault, *Napoléon en Italie*, pp. 292–339; Pingaud, *La domination française dans l'Italie du Nord*, ii. pp. 392–401; Fugier, *Napoléon et l'Italie*, p. 159.
4. According to Cambacérès, *Mémoires inédites*, ii. pp. 26–7, Napoleon never had any intention of giving the Italian crown to Joseph, or to anyone else for that matter. Historians have mirrored these sentiments: Harold C. Deutsch, 'Napoleonic Policy and the Project of a Descent upon England', *Journal of Modern History*, 2 (1930), 548–9; Schroeder, *Transformation of European Politics*, p. 266; Kagan, *The End of the Old Order*, pp. 169–70. A good general overview of the history of Italy during this period is to be found in Christopher Duggan, *The Force of Destiny: A History of Italy since 1796* (London, 2007), esp. ch. 2.
5. *Corr.* x. n. 8250 (1 January 1805).
6. For this see Roederer, *Oeuvres*, iii. pp. 520–2; Masson, *Napoléon et sa famille*, iii. pp. 4–18; Driault, *Napoléon en Italie*, pp. 307–14; Haegele, *Napoléon et Joseph Bonaparte*, pp. 170–2.
7. Pingaud, *La domination française dans l'Italie du Nord*, ii. pp. 437–8; Masson, *Napoléon et sa famille*, iii. pp. 18–20.
8. Masson, *Napoléon et sa famille*, iii. pp. 31–4.
9. On this episode see Carola Oman, *Napoleon's Viceroy, Eugène de Beauharnais* (London, 1966), pp. 169–79; Françoise de Bernardy, *Eugène de Beauharnais: 1781–1824* (Paris, 1973), pp. 107–28; Alain Pillepich, *Eugène de Beauharnais: honneur et fidélité* (Paris, 1999), pp. 14–18. Napoleon then set about instructing his stepson on how to become a ruler. Much of the correspondence can be found in Albert Du Casse (ed.), *Mémoires et correspondance politique et militaire du prince Eugène*, 10 vols (Paris, 1858–60), i. pp. 110–265.
10. Gregory, *Napoleon's Italy*, pp. 68–9.
11. Asserts Alain Pillepich, 'Napoléon Ier et la couronne de fer', in Graziella Buccellati and Annamaria Ambrosioni (eds), *La corona, il regno e l'impero: un millennio di storia*, 2 vols (Milan, 1995–9), i. p. 202.
12. *Corr.* x. n. 8445 (17 March 1805).
13. Napoleon's interference in Italy was fundamental in pushing Austria into the arms of the Third Coalition (Driault, *Napoléon en Italie*, pp. 313–14).
14. See, for example, Bigarré, *Mémoires*, p. 152.
15. Pingaud, *La domination française dans l'Italie du Nord*, ii. pp. 399–449; Gregory, *Napoleon's Italy*, p. 67.
16. Contends Kagan, *The End of the Old Order*, p. 169. See Pillepich, 'Napoléon Ier et la couronne de fer', pp. 203–4; Valla, *La nostalgie de l'Empire*, pp. 81–104. It was not the same crown used in the coronation of Charlemagne.
17. For the following see Adolf Beer, *Zehn Jahre österreichischer Politik, 1801–1810* (Leipzig, 1877), pp. 82–91; Schroeder, *Transformation of European Politics*, pp. 268–9.

18. Kagan, *The End of the Old Order*, p. 139.
19. On the Franco-Bavarian alliance see Harold C. Deutsch, *The Genesis of Napoleonic Imperialism* (Cambridge, Mass., 1938), pp. 238–53; Marcel Dunan, *Napoléon et l'Allemagne: la Système Continentale et les débuts du Royaume de Bavière, 1806–1810* (Paris, 1943), pp. 8–22; Marcus Junkelmann, *Napoleon und Bayern: von den Anfängen des Königreiches* (Regensburg, 1985), pp. 85–97.
20. *Corr.* x. n. 8282 (22 January 1805).
21. Pitt left the formation of the new coalition to Russia. John M. Sherwig, *Guineas and Gunpowder: British Foreign Aid in the Wars with France, 1793–1815* (Cambridge, 1969), pp. 149–51.
22. Kagan, *The End of the Old Order*, p. 219.
23. Alexander to La Harpe, in Jean Charles Biaudet and Françoise Nicod (eds), *Correspondance de Frédéric-César de La Harpe et Alexandre Ier*, 3 vols (Neuchâtel, 1978–80), ii. pp. 44–5 (7 July 1803).
24. Zawadzki, 'Czartoryski and Napoleonic France', 255.
25. Cited in Zawadzki, 'Czartoryski and Napoleonic France', 252.
26. Zawadzki, 'Czartoryski and Napoleonic France', 248–9; Janet M. Hartley, *Alexander I* (London, 1994), pp. 60, 68, 70–1; Marie-Pierre Rey, *Alexandre Ier* (Paris, 2009), pp. 197–205.
27. Kagan, *The End of the Old Order*, pp. 152–62.
28. Cited in Zawadzki, 'Czartoryski and Napoleonic France', 248.
29. Talleyrand to Oubril, 9 thermidor an XII (28 June 1804), in *Sbornik*, lxxvii. pp. 681–4.
30. *Vneshniaia politika rossi*, ii. n. 104 (17 February 1805).
31. W. H. Zawadzki, *A Man of Honour: Adam Czartoryski as a Statesman of Russia and Poland, 1795–1831* (Oxford, 1993), pp. 92–110; Sparrow, *Secret Service*, p. 329.
32. Prussia decided to continue its policy of neutrality, even if its sympathies lay with the coalition. See Brendan Simms, *The Impact of Napoleon: Prussian High Politics, Foreign Policy and the Crisis of the Executive, 1797–1806* (Cambridge, 1997), pp. 198–201.
33. Mavor (ed.), *The Grand Tours of Katherine Wilmot*, p. 168; A. D. Harvey, 'European Attitudes to Britain during the French Revolutionary and Napoleonic Era', *History*, 63 (1978), 356–65; A. D. Harvey, *Collision of Empires: Britain in Three World Wars, 1793–1945* (London, 1992), pp. 79–90; Schroeder, *Transformation of European Politics*, p. 402.
34. Edouard Driault, *Napoléon et l'Europe*, 5 vols (Paris, 1912), ii. pp. 116–18.
35. Schroeder, *Transformation of European Politics*, p. 274.
36. *Corr.* x. n. 8252 (2 January 1805).
37. Emsley, *British Society and the French Wars*, p. 112; Linda Colley, *Britons: Forging the Nation 1707–1837* (New Haven and London, 1992), pp. 305–6; Tombs and Tombs, *That Sweet Enemy*, p. 248.
38. For Anglo-French rivalry in earlier periods see David A. Bell, 'Jumonville's Death: War Propaganda and National Identity in Eighteenth-Century France', in Colin Jones and Dror Wahrman (eds), *The Age of Cultural Revolutions: Britain and France, 1750–1820* (Berkeley, 2002), p. 49; David A. Bell, *The Cult of the Nation in France: Inventing Nationalism, 1680–1800* (Cambridge, Mass., 2001), pp. 78–106; Hampson, *The Perfidy of Albion*; Bertaud, Forrest and Jourdan, *Napoléon, le monde et les Anglais*, pp. 13–32; Tombs and Tombs, *That Sweet Enemy*, pp. 211–14. Lentz, *Nouvelle histoire du premier Empire*, i. pp. 142–7, 160, argues that public opinion remained 'uncertain' during this time, but he seems to base this assertion on royalist opposition in the military.
39. *Corr.* ix. n. 7333 (29 November 1803).
40. Vivant Denon to Napoleon, 27 July 1803, in Marie-Anne Dupuy, Isabelle Le Masne de Chermont and Elaine Williamson (eds), *Vivant Denon, directeur des musées sous le Consulat et l'Empire: correspondance, 1802–1815*, 2 vols (Paris, 1999), ii. p. 1249; Porterfield and Siegfried, *Staging Empire*, p. 29.
41. Letter from Denon (around 16 December 1803), in Dupuy, Le Masne de Chermont and Williamson (eds), *Vivant Denon*, p. 1253.

42. *Moniteur universel*, 12 November 1803; Staël, *Considérations*, ii. pp. 350–1; Williamson, 'Denon, la presse', pp. 161–2.

43. Letter from Denon (around 16 December 1803), in Dupuy, Le Masne de Chermont and Williamson (eds), *Vivant Denon*, pp. 1253–4; Elaine Williamson, 'A *Vraie-fausse* Statue of William the Conqueror: Representation and Misrepresentation of Anglo-French History', *Franco-British Studies*, 19 (1995), 22–4.

44. Porterfield and Siegfried, *Staging Empire*, pp. 28, 33.

45. *Corr.* xi. n. 9264 (23 September 1805).

46. Cambacérès, *Mémoires inédits*, ii. p. 45.

47. François Crouzet, 'La guerre maritime', in Jean Mistler (ed.), *Napoléon*, 2 vols (Paris, 1969–1970), i. p. 322.

48. See, for example, *Corr.* ix. nos. 7832, 7833 (2 July 1804); Edouard Desbrière, *1793–1805: projets et tentatives de débarquement aux Îles Britanniques*, 4 vols (Paris, 1900–2), iv. pp. 3–8.

49. Deutsch, 'Napoleonic Policy and the Project of a Descent upon England', 541, 550–1; John Holland Rose, 'Napoleon and Sea Power', *Cambridge Historical Journal*, 1 (1924), 146, who believed that a fleet was assembled in 1801 simply as 'a means of intimidating the Addington Ministry'. For a contrary view see Marmont, *Mémoires*, ii. pp. 212–17.

50. Bailleu (ed.), *Preußen und Frankreich*, ii. p. 264 (17 May 1804).

51. Metternich, *Mémoires*, iii. pp. 38–9.

52. Wheeler and Broadley, *Napoleon and the Invasion of England*, pp. 505–6. In Greek mythology, Antaeus was a giant, the son of Poseidon. The reference was, therefore, to Britain. Hercules represented the French people. For the use of Hercules as a symbol during the French Revolution see Lynn Hunt, *Politics, Culture, and Class in the French Revolution* (Berkeley, 1984), pp. 94–116.

53. *Corr.* ix. n. 7801 (3 June 1804).

54. On the former see Marmont, *Mémoires*, ii. pp. 210–12. On the latter see Wheeler and Broadley, *Napoleon and the Invasion of England*, pp. 245–55; David Whittet Thomson, 'Robert Fulton and the French Invasion of England', *Military Affairs*, 18 (1954), 57–63.

55. Desbrière, *Projets et tentatives de débarquement*, iii. pp. 82–113, 381–413. The plans to invade England had a long history that stretched back as far as Louis XIV. For plans proposed in the reigns of Louis XIV–XVI, see P. Coquelle, 'Les projets de descente en Angleterre, d'après les archives des affaires étrangères', *Revue d'histoire diplomatique*, 15 (1901), 433–53; and 16 (1902), 134–57; Michèle Battesti, *Trafalgar: les aléas de la stratégie navale de Napoléon* (Saint-Cloud, 2004), pp. 33–8.

56. See Dwyer, *Napoleon: The Path to Power*, pp. 354–6. Kagan, *The End of the Old Order*, p. 285, considers it to have been 'the most grandiose project Napoleon ever developed'.

57. Deutsch, 'Napoleonic Policy and the Project of a Descent upon England', 562.

58. Fernand Nicolay, *Napoléon Ier au camp de Boulogne, d'après de nombreux documents inédits* (Paris, 1907), pp. 181–213; Constant, *Mémoires*, i. pp. 274–8; Chandler, *Campaigns of Napoleon*, p. 323; Alan Schom, *Trafalgar: Countdown to Battle, 1803–1805* (New York, 1990), pp. 97–9; Lloyd, *The French Are Coming*, pp. 47–8; Battesti, *Trafalgar*, pp. 82–3.

59. Tourtier-Bonazzi, *Lettres d'amour à Joséphine*, pp. 164–5 (21 July 1804).

60. Schom, *Trafalgar*, p. 142.

61. Deutsch, 'Napoleonic Policy and the Project of a Descent upon England', 560–1.

62. Maurice Dupont, *L'amiral Decrès et Napoléon ou La fidélité orageuse d'un ministre* (Paris, 1991), pp. 157–8.

63. Rémi Monaque, *Latouche-Tréville, 1745–1804: l'amiral qui défiait Nelson* (Paris, 2000), pp. 595–6.

64. Deutsch, 'Napoleonic Policy and the Project of a Descent upon England', 551, asserts that he had abandoned the idea in the short term.

65. Outlined with maps in Battesti, *Trafalgar*.

66. Schom, *Trafalgar*, pp. 206–7.

67. See, for example, *Corr.* ix. nos. 7677, 8060 (7 April, 29 September 1804); x. nos. 8206, 8209, 8231, 8232 (12 and 23 December 1804), 8279, 8654 (16 January and 29 April 1805); Deutsch, 'Napoleonic Policy and the Project of a Descent upon England', 553–4; Schom, *Trafalgar*, pp. 173–8.

68. See Schom, *Trafalgar*, pp. 226–7.

69. Schom, *Trafalgar*, pp. 229–36.

70. According to Ségur, *Histoire et mémoires*, ii. pp. 329–37, when later Napoleon found out the details about the engagement, he too went into a fit, under the impression that Villeneuve had wasted an opportunity and had again bottled up the fleet.

71. *Corr.* xi. n. 9066 (11 August 1805).

72. Schom, *Trafalgar*, pp. 240–2.

73. Desbrière, *Projets et tentatives de débarquement*, iv. pt 3, pp. 775–86.

74. *Corr.* xi. n. 9220 (15 September 1805).

75. On the tergiversations surrounding the departure, including at one stage a written refusal on the part of the naval officers to leave port, see Schom, *Trafalgar*, pp. 295–304.

76. John Holland Rose, *The Life of Napoleon I*, 2 vols (London, 1902), ii. pp. 26–8. The literature on the battle is vast. Among the better, more recent works are: Schom, *Trafalgar*, pp. 307–56; Tim Clayton and Phil Craig, *Trafalgar: The Men, the Battle, the Storm* (London, 2004); Roy Adkins, *Trafalgar: The Biography of a Battle* (London, 2004); Adam Nicolson, *Men of Honour: Trafalgar and the Making of the English Hero* (London, 2005).

77. There was, as a result, some speculation among contemporaries about whether he was murdered. See Henry Rollin, 'L'amiral Villeneuve et Napoléon', *Revue des études napoléoniennes*, 3 (1913), 200–34; Dupont, *L'amiral Decrès et Napoléon*, pp. 175–6; Battesti, *Trafalgar*, pp. 308–10.

78. Dupont, *L'amiral Decrès et Napoléon*, pp. 176 and 303–12.

79. Chandler, *Campaigns of Napoleon*, p. 325.

80. Adkins, *Trafalgar*, p. 24; Kagan, *The End of the Old Order*, p. 283.

81. See Samuel Horsley, *The Watchers and the Holy Ones: A Sermon* (London, 1806), pp. 24–7.

82. *Corr.* xi. n. 9069 (13 August 1805).

83. *Corr.* xi. n. 9070 (13 August 1805).

84. *Corr.* xi. n. 9115 (22 August 1805).

85. *Corr.* xi. nos. 9120, and 9117 (23 August 1805).

86. *Corr.* xi. nos. 9038, 9068, 9069 and 9070 (3, 12 and 13 August 1805); Deutsch, 'Napoleonic Policy and the Project of a Descent upon England', 547.

87. See, for example, his letters to Domenico Pino in *Corr.* x. n. 8581 (13 April 1805).

88. Paul-Claude Alombert and Jean Colin, *La campagne de 1805 en Allemagne*, 4 vols (Paris, 1902–8), i. pp. 20, 29–30 and 32–4 (23 January 1805).

89. Kagan, *The End of the Old Order*, p. 285.

90. Kagan, *The End of the Old Order*, pp. 231–54, 255–82.

91. *Corr.* x. n. 8791 (26 May 1805); Kagan, *The End of the Old Order*, pp. 295–6. My thanks to Frederick Kagan for this point on Murat's knowledge of the treaty.

92. *Corr.* x. n. 8790 (26 May 1805).

93. *Corr.* xi. n. 9032 (31 July 1805); and *Campagnes de la grande armée et de l'armée d'Italie en l'an XIV (1805)* (Paris, 1806), pp. 51–9 (the letter is dated 17 thermidor an XIII).

94. Declaration from the court of Vienna to Napoleon, 5 August 1805, in Leopold von Neumann (ed.), *Recueil des traités et conventions conclus par l'Autriche avec les puissances étrangères depuis 1763 jusqu'à nos jours*, 12 vols (Vienna, 1877–88), ii. pp. 162–7.

95. *Corr.* xi. n. 9070 (13 August 1805).

96. See Kagan, *The End of the Old Order*, pp. 307–13; Lentz, *Nouvelle histoire du Premier Empire*, i. p. 154.

97. Kagan, *The End of the Old Order*, p. 362.

98. See Creveld, 'Napoleon and the Dawn of Operational Warfare', pp. 18–24.

99. Englund, *Napoleon*, p. 273.

100. James A. Arnold, 'A Reappraisal of Column versus Line in the Peninsular War', *Journal of Military History*, 68 (2004), 540; Kagan, *The End of the Old Order*, p. 58.

101. Bertaud, *Bonaparte et le duc d'Enghien*, p. 70.

102. Raymond de Montesquiou-Fezensac, *Souvenirs militaires de 1804 à 1814* (Paris, 1870), pp. 31–3.

103. Ideville, *Le maréchal Bugeaud*, p. 71.

104. Kagan, *The End of the Old Order*, p. 377; and on the difficulties of supplying the army see Martin van Creveld, *Supplying War: Logistics from Wallenstein to Patton* (Cambridge, 1977), pp. 42–61.

105. Ideville, *Le maréchal Bugeaud*, pp. 71, 74.

106. Montesquiou-Fezensac, *Souvenirs militaires*, pp. 64–5.

107. For one case of a quartermaster, Jean-Baptiste Charles de Tersac, twenty-one years of age, who died of 'exhaustion' as a direct consequence of the forced marches and the ensuing battle, see J.-J. Hemardinquer, 'Mort d'épuisement après Austerlitz', *Revue de l'Institut Napoléon*, 134 (1978), 115.

108. Kagan, *The End of the Old Order*, p. 343.

109. It is a point raised by Chandler, *Campaigns of Napoleon*, p. 396; Gates, *The Napoleonic Wars*, p. 24. See also Christopher Duffy, *Austerlitz 1805* (London, 1977), p. 48; and Kagan, *The End of the Old Order*, pp. 400, 423, 429.

110. Roger Parkinson, *The Fox of the North: The Life of Kutuzov, General of War and Peace* (New York, 1976), pp. 58–9.

111. Chandler, *The Campaigns of Napoleon*, pp. 148, 390–402.

112. 'Extrait de la relation de la prise d'Ulm, sur le manuscrit original de M . . . , capitaine d'Etat-Major au service de l'Autriche', *Journal des sciences militaires*, 8 (1827), 80.

113. Charles Ingrao, *The Habsburg Monarchy, 1618–1815* (Cambridge, 1994), p. 229.

114. 'Extrait de la relation de la prise d'Ulm', 81; Alfred Krauss, *1805, der Feldzug von Ulm*, 2 vols (Vienna, 1912), i. pp. 468–81.

115. 'Extrait de la relation de la prise d'Ulm', 80; Kagan, *The End of the Old Order*, pp. 430–1.

116. Tourtier-Bonazzi, *Lettres d'amour à Joséphine*, pp. 187–8 (21 October 1805).

117. Henry Reeve, *Journal of a Residence at Vienna and Berlin in the Eventful Winter 1805–6* (London, 1877), p. 37.

118. Frederick William John Hemmings, *Theatre and State in France, 1760–1905* (Cambridge, 1994), p. 130.

119. This is the contention of most military historians (see Chandler, *Campaigns of Napoleon*, pp. 409–10; Gates, *The Napoleonic Wars*, p. 29; Duffy, *Austerlitz*, p. 76), but it is contested by Kagan, *The End of the Old Order*, p. 564.

120. Dunan, *Napoléon et l'Allemagne*, p. 20.

121. Dunan, *Napoléon et l'Allemagne*, p. 17; Adalbert Prinz von Bayern, *Max I. Joseph von Bayern, Pfalzgraf, Kurfürst und König* (Munich, 1957), pp. 481–2.

122. George Jackson, *The Bath Archives: A Further Selection from the Diaries and Letters of Sir George Jackson, K.C.H., from 1809 to 1816*, 2 vols (London, 1873), ii. p. 353; Jean-Gabriel Eynard, *Journal de Jean-Gabriel Eynard: au Congrès de Vienne*, 2 vols (Paris, 1914), i. p. 46; Dunan, *Napoléon et l'Allemagne*, pp. 15–16; Schroeder, *Transformation of European Politics*, pp. 273–4.

123. *Corr.* xi. nos. 9451, 9464 (3 and 8 November 1805).

124. *Corr.* xi. n. 9470 (11 November 1805); Tulard, *Murat*, pp. 81–2; Parkinson, *The Fox of the North*, pp. 67–8; Kagan, *The End of the Old Order*, p. 471.

125. Kagan, *The End of the Old Order*, p. 470.

126. Alistair Horne, *Seven Ages of Paris* (New York, 2004), p. 174.

127. *Journal de l'Empire*, 6 frimaire an XIV (27 November 1805); Lanzac de Laborie, *Paris sous Napoléon*, iii. pp. 46–7.

128. According to Rémusat, *Lettres*, i. pp. 376–7.

129. Lanzac de Laborie, *Paris sous Napoléon*, iii. pp. 47–8.

130. Reeve, *Journal of a Residence at Vienna and Berlin*, pp. 26–7. For the French take on the

Austrian capital see Robert Ouvrard, *1809: les Français à Vienne: chronique d'une occupa-tion* (Paris, 2009), pp. 107–44.

131. Ségur, *Histoire et mémoires,* ii. p. 446; Bailleu (ed.), *Briefwechsel König Friedrich Wilhelm,* n. 83 (28 November 1805). Alexander made a visit to Berlin in October 1805, the crowning moment being a visit to the grave of Frederick the Great in Potsdam, where he supposedly stood some time in meditative reflection, hand in hand with Queen Luise. It led to the Treaty of Potsdam; Prussia was to attempt an 'armed mediation' with Napoleon and if that did not work it would commit 180,000 men to the coalition. Thomas Stamm-Kuhlmann, *König in Preußens großer Zeit: Friedrich Wilhelm III. der Melancholiker auf dem Thron* (Berlin, 1992), pp. 198–200; Kagan, *The End of the Old Order,* pp. 550, 553–4.

132. Thiard, *Souvenirs diplomatiques et militaires,* pp. 200–1.

133. The literature on the battle of Austerlitz is considerable. See Chandler, *Campaigns of Napoleon,* pp. 413–33; Henry Lachouque, *Napoléon à Austerlitz* (Paris, 1961); Duffy, *Austerlitz,* pp. 69–156; Frederick C. Schneid, *Napoleon's Conquest of Europe: The War of the Third Coalition* (Westport, Conn., 2005); Kagan, *The End of the Old Order,* pp. 581–628; Pierre Robin and Christophe Dufourg Burg (eds), *Austerlitz: récits de soldats* (Paris, 2006).

134. Kagan, *The End of the Old Order,* pp. 116, 572, 574.

135. Kagan, *The End of the Old Order,* pp. 568–70, goes over the options open to Napoleon and the allies.

136. Chandler, *The Campaigns of Napoleon,* p. 149.

137. Parkinson, *The Fox of the North,* pp. 82–5; Kagan, *The End of the Old Order,* pp. 576–7.

138. Thiébault, *Mémoires,* iii. pp. 454–5; Lejeune, *Mémoires,* pp. 26–7; Bigarré, *Mémoires,* pp. 170–1; Jean-Baptiste-Antoine-Marcellin, baron de Marbot, *Mémoires du général Bon de Marbot,* 3 vols (Paris, 1897), i. pp. 258–9; Ségur, *Histoire et mémoires,* ii. pp. 461–2; Coignet, *Note-Books,* pp. 122–3.

139. On this event see Jean Baptiste Auguste Barrès, *Souvenirs d'un officier de la Grande Armée* (Paris, 1923), p. 55; Paul-Claude Alombert, 'Le colonel Constant Corbineau', *Carnet de la Sabretache,* 3 (1895), 289–307, here 295; Jean-Pierre Noël Asseré, 'Journal du voltigeur Asseré', *Carnet de la Sabretache,* 14 (1905), 705–31, here 723.

140. Alistair Horne, *How Far from Austerlitz? Napoleon 1805–1815* (New York, 1996), p. 150.

141. Jacques-Olivier Boudon, 'Grand homme ou demi-dieu? La mise en place d'une religion napoléonienne', *Romantisme,* 100 (1998), 139.

142. Barrès, *Souvenirs,* pp. 57–8.

143. *Corr.* xi. nos. 9541, 9544 (3 and 5 December 1805). The idea of firing a howitzer shell into the ice after the cannon balls simply bounced off is supposed to have come from Captain Théodore-Jean-Joseph du Séruzier, *Mémoires militaires du baron Seruzier, colonel d'artillerie légère* (Paris, 1823), pp. 28–9.

144. *Campagnes de la grande armée,* pp. 293–302, here p. 300; Duffy, *Austerlitz,* pp. 148–9; Kagan, *The End of the Old Order,* p. 621.

145. Most historians cite the figure of between 3,000 and 5,000 French killed. A recent examina-tion of the archives reveals that it may have been as low as 1,537 (Lentz, *Nouvelle histoire du Premier Empire,* iii. p. 494). It nevertheless took two weeks to bury the dead (Letter from Toussaint Walthéry, 30 December 1805, in Emile Fairon and Henri Heuse, *Lettres de grognards* (Liège, 1936), pp. 86–7).

146. Theodor von Bernhardi, *Denkwürdigkeiten aus dem Leben des kaiserl. russ. Generals von der Infanterie Carl Friedrich Grafen von Toll,* 5 vols (Leipzig, 1865–6), i. pp. 167–8.

147. According to Rey, *Alexandre Ier,* p. 220.

148. Kagan, *The End of the Old Order,* pp. 626–7. There is no account of this meeting.

149. Even before Austerlitz, Czartoryski and Novosiltsev complained of Alexander's depres-sion and uncertainty. Zawadzki, 'Czartoryski and Napoleonic France', 275–6.

150. Thiard, *Souvenirs diplomatiques et militaires,* pp. 242–5; Victor Bibl, *François II: le beau-père de Napoléon, 1768–1835,* trans. from the German by Adrien F. Vochelle (Paris, 1936), p. 128; Duffy, *Austerlitz,* pp. 152–4.

151. Eynard, *Journal*, i. p. 45.
152. Even then, it was initially reported as a French victory. Burrows, 'The War of Words', p. 51.
153. 'Austerlitz (Lettres de deux témoins de la bataille)', *Carnet de la Sabretache*, 4 (1905), 733.
154. Pierre Glaudes, 'Joseph de Maistre, letter writer', in Carolina Armenteros and Richard A. Lebrun (eds), *The New enfant du siècle: Joseph de Maistre as a Writer* (St Andrews, 2010), pp. 54–5, hdl.handle.net/10023/847.
155. It may be apocryphal. See Ehrman, *The Younger Pitt*, iii. p. 882.
156. Lanzac de Laborie, *Paris sous Napoléon*, iii. pp. 48–9, whose assertion is somewhat contradicted by the police reports in AN F7 3834, 20 and 24, 25 and 29 frimaire an XIV (11 and 15, 16 and 20 December 1804), but police reports often exaggerated positive reactions and played down negative ones.
157. AN F/1cIII/Aisne 12, the prefect of the Aisne to the minister of the interior, 3 January 1806.
158. See, for example, Fiévée, *Correspondance*, ii. pp. 164–7.
159. Lanzac de Laborie, *Paris sous Napoléon*, iii. p. 48.
160. Fiévée, *Correspondance*, ii. p. 166; Lanzac de Laborie, *Paris sous Napoléon*, iii. p. 50. More elaborate plans to celebrate the victory never actually came off. A large concentration of troops was established at Meudon, from where they were supposed to enter Paris, but the troops had to be deployed in eastern Europe (see *Corr.* xii. n. 9832 (17 February 1806); Lanzac de Laborie, *Paris sous Napoléon*, iii. pp. 57–9).
161. M. Siret, *Discours prononcé dans l'église paroissiale de Saint Merry, le dimanche 29 décembre dernier, à l'occasion du Te Deum chanté en actions de graces de la victoire d'Austerlitz* (Paris, 1806), p. 1. For the following theme see also Bertaud, *Quand les enfants parlaient de gloire*, pp. 225–7; Jean-Pierre Bertho, 'Naissance et élaboration d'une théologie de la guerre chez les évêques de Napoléon (1802–1820)', in Jean-René Derré, Jacques Gadille, Xavier de Montclos and Bernard Plongeron (eds), *Civilisation chrétienne: approche historique d'une idéologie, XVIIIe–XXe siècle* (Paris, 1975), pp. 95–103.
162. AN AFIV 1045, Correspondance du ministre des cultes, 1 January 1806.
163. AN AFIV 1452, doss. 2.
164. Rémusat, *Mémoires de ma vie*, i. p. 52.
165. John A. Lynn, *Battle: A History of Combat and Culture from Ancient Greece to Modern America* (Cambridge, Mass., 2003), pp. 180–1.
166. This has been pointed out by Alistair Horne, *How Far from Austerlitz?*, pp. 186–9, who argues that Austerlitz led Napoleon on a grail-like quest for similar victories which almost always eluded him.
167. Peter Paret, 'Napoleon as Enemy', in Peter Paret, *Understanding War: Essays on Clausewitz and the History of Military Power* (Princeton, 1992), p. 77.
168. *Corr.* xi. n. 9069 (13 August 1805).
169. Bertrand (ed.), *Lettres inédites*, pp. 156–65 (17 October 1805).
170. Schroeder, *Transformation of European Politics*, pp. 276–82, 302–4.
171. *Corr.* xi. n. 9561 (13 December 1805).
172. On the treaty see Rudolfine Freiin von Oer, *Der Friede von Pressburg: ein Beitrag zur Diplomatiegeschichte des Napoleonischen Zeitalters* (Münster, 1965), esp. pp. 184–221.
173. Kagan, *The End of the Old Order*, p. 633.
174. *Corr.* xi. nos. 9540, 9542 (3 and 4 December 1805).
175. Jean-Pierre Bois, *De la paix des rois à l'ordre des empereurs, 1714–1815* (Paris, 2003), p. 348.

## *11: The Grand Empire*

1. *Moniteur universel*, 6 January 1806.
2. On the occasion of the plebiscite of 1804 on the acceptance of a hereditary regime, the mayor of Metz, Goussaud d'Antilly, refers to 'the Great Napoleon' (*le Grand*

*Napoléon*) (Thierry Lentz and Denis Imhoff, *La Moselle et Napoléon: étude d'un département sous le Consulat et l'Empire* (Metz, 1986), p. 169).

3. Williamson, 'Denon, la presse', p. 154.

4. *Corr.* x. n. 8821 (1 June 1805).

5. Rowe, *From Reich to State*, p. 151.

6. The expression is from Jean-Paul Bertaud, *Guerre et société en France: de Louis XIV à Napoléon Ier* (Paris, 1998), p. 60.

7. Ellis, 'Religion According to Napoleon', p. 247; Sudhir Hazareesingh, *The Saint-Napoleon: Celebrations of Sovereignty in Nineteenth-Century France* (Cambridge, Mass., 2004), pp. 3–4; Rosemonde Sanson, 'Le 15 août: fête nationale du Second Empire', in Alain Corbin, Noëlle Gérôme and Danielle Tartakowsky (eds), *Les usages politiques des fêtes aux XIXe–XXe siècles* (Paris, 1994), pp. 117–36; and Hippolyte Delehaye, 'La légende de Saint Napoléon', in *Mélanges d'histoire offerts à Henri Pirenne*, 2 vols (Brussels, 1926), i. pp. 81–8.

8. Eugène Hyacinthe Laffillard, *La veille d'une grande fête, hommage en 1 acte et en vers, mêlés de couplets* (Paris, 1808); *Célébration de la fête de Napoléon-Le-Grand* (Besançon, 1809); Fontaine, *Journal*, i. p. 54, for example, refers to this day as the anniversary of the birth of Napoleon. No mention is made of St Napoleon.

9. Diligence and a modest demeanour were the two traits most expected of a French bureaucrat. For the broader context of modesty and French political life see Stéphane Gerson, 'In Praise of Modest Men: Self-Display and Self-Effacement in Nineteenth-Century France', *French History*, 20:2 (2006), 182–203.

10. Bouët du Portal, 'A propos de la Saint-Napoléon', 150–2. There are no scholarly articles on the origins, evolution of and reaction to the feast of St Napoleon.

11. *Détail de la fête du 15 août, pour le double anniversaire de la naissance du Ier Consul et de la signature du Concordat* (Paris, n.d.), p. 2.

12. Bouët du Portal, 'A propos de la Saint-Napoléon', 159.

13. Bouët du Portal, 'A propos de la Saint-Napoléon', 153.

14. Cited in Bouët du Portal, 'A propos de la Saint-Napoléon', 156.

15. Cited in Bouët du Portal, 'A propos de la Saint-Napoléon', 151, 152; Alain Corbin, 'La fête de souveraineté', in Corbin, Gérôme and Tartakowsky (eds), *Les usages politiques des fêtes*, pp. 25–38; Petiteau, *Les Français et l'Empire*, pp. 67–70.

16. Burton, *Blood in the City*, p. 73; Cabanis, *Le sacre de Napoléon*, pp. 97–8.

17. See, for example, Christian Pfister, *Les fêtes à Nancy sous le Consulat et le Premier Empire (1799–1813)* (Nancy, 1914), pp. 89–92.

18. Bouët du Portal, 'A propos de la Saint-Napoléon', 160. In 1804, it was the 'Napoleon Battery' in the harbour of Cherbourg; in 1806, it was the posing of the first stone of the Arc de Triomphe; in 1808, the inauguration of the Arc du Carrousel; in 1809, it was the opening of the Ourcq canal, and the relocation and restitution of the Fontaine des Innocents (today near Les Halles); in 1810, the inauguration of the Vendôme Column; in 1811, the opening of the Port Napoléon at Cherbourg.

19. Such as J. Mayer and Abraham de Cologna, *Odes hébraïques pour la célébration de l'anniversaire de la naissance de S.M. l'Empereur des François et roi d'Italie* (Paris, 1806).

20. Pierre de Joux, *Discours de bénédiction, de reconnaissance et d'actions de grâces pour l'anniversaire de la naissance de l'empereur Napoléon-le-Grand* (Nantes, n.d.), pp. 4–5.

21. See, for example, Melchior-Bonnet, *Napoléon et le Pape*, p. 289.

22. Léon de Lanzac de Laborie, *La Domination française en Belgique: Directoire, Consulat, Empire, 1795–1814*, 2 vols (Paris, 1895), ii. pp. 113–22; Leflon, *Etienne-Alexandre Bernier*, ii. pp. 271–2; Michael Broers, *The Politics of Religion in Napoleonic Italy: The War against God, 1801–1814* (London, 2002), pp. 82–5.

23. André Latreille, *Le Catéchisme Impérial de 1806: études et documents pour servir à l'histoire des rapports de Napoléon et du clergé concordataire* (Paris, 1935), pp. 80–1; Latreille, *L'Eglise catholique et la Révolution française*, ii. pp. 135–9; Melchior-Bonnet, *Napoléon et le Pape*, pp. 86–8.

24. Bernard Plongeron, 'Le catéchisme impérial (1806) et l'irritante leçon VII sur le quatrième commandement', in Marie-Madeleine Fragonard and Michel Peronnet (eds), *Catéchismes et confessions de foi* (Montpellier, 1995), pp. 287–310; Plongeron, 'De Napoléon à Metternich', pp. 652–4.

25. Rowe, *From Reich to State*, p. 147. This was not always the case in the German-speaking departments. Stephan Laux, 'Das Patrozinium "Saint Napoléon" in Neersen (1803–1856): ein Beitrag zur Rezeption der napoleonischen Propaganda im Rheinland', in Jörg Engelbrecht and Stephan Laux (eds), *Landes- und Reichsgeschichte: Festschrift für Hansgeorg Molitor zum 65. Geburtstag* (Bielefeld 2004), pp. 351–81.

26. Hagen Schulze, *States, Nations, and Nationalism: From the Middle Ages to the Present*, trans. from the German by W. E. Yuill (Oxford, 1996), p. 177; Jean-René Aymes, 'Du catéchisme religieux au catéchisme politique (fin du XVIIIe siècle–début du XIXe)', in Jean-René Aymes, *Voir, comparer, comprendre: regards sur l'Espagne des XVIIIe et XIXe siècles* (Paris, 2003), pp. 179–200.

27. Telesko, *Napoleon Bonaparte*, pp. 9–10; Barbara Beßlich, *Der deutsche Napoleon-Mythos: Literatur und Erinnerung 1800–1945* (Darmstadt, 2007), pp. 72–5. The following quotation is from Nancy Nobile, *The School of Days: Heinrich von Kleist and the Traumas of Education* (Detroit, 1999), pp. 121–7, here p. 123.

28. *Corr.* xi. n. 9633 (31 December 1805).

29. Haegele, *Napoléon et Joseph Bonaparte*, p. 192.

30. Jacques Rambaud, *Naples sous Joseph Bonaparte, 1806–1808* (Paris, 1911), pp. 13–14.

31. A good portrait of Maria Carolina is to be had in Jean-Paul Garnier, *Murat, roi de Naples* (Paris, 1959), pp. 110–26.

32. William Henry Flayhart, *Counterpoint to Trafalgar: The Anglo-Russian Invasion of Naples, 1805–1806* (Columbia, SC, 1992), pp. 53–172.

33. On the rise and fall of the Republic see John A. Davis, 'The Neapolitan Revolution of 1799', *Journal of Modern Italian Studies*, 4:3 (1999), 350–8; John A. Davis, *Naples and Napoleon: Southern Italy and the European Revolutions, 1780–1860* (Oxford, 2006), pp. 72–93.

34. Rambaud, *Naples sous Joseph Bonaparte*, pp. 1–2.

35. Davis, *Naples and Napoleon*, pp. 130–2, 147, 249; Jordan, *Napoleon and the Revolution*, pp. 78–80.

36. *Corr.* xi. n. 9625 (27 December 1805).

37. *Corr.* xi. n. 9685 (19 January 1806).

38. According to Miot de Melito, *Mémoires*, ii. pp. 279–80.

39. Haegele, *Napoléon et Joseph Bonaparte*, pp. 206–7.

40. *Moniteur universel*, 1 April 1806.

41. See Martijn van der Burg, 'Transforming the Dutch Republic into the Kingdom of Holland: The Netherlands between Republicanism and Monarchy (1795–1815)', *European Review of History/Revue européenne d'histoire*, 17:2 (2010), 151–70, here 157–60.

42. Rémusat, *Mémoires*, iii. pp. 33–4; Johann Joor, 'Les système continental et sa signification pour le royaume de Hollande', in Annie Jourdan (ed.), *Louis Bonaparte: roi de Hollande, 1806–1810* (Paris, 2010), pp. 132–3.

43. Louis Bonaparte, *Documents historiques et réflexions sur le gouvernement de la Hollande*, 3 vols (Brussels, 1820), iii. p. 260; Schama, *Patriots and Liberators*, p. 609.

44. Burg, 'Transforming the Dutch Republic', 159–62.

45. Napoleon to Louis, 5, 6 and 16 November 1806, in Lecestre (ed.), *Lettres inédites*, i. pp. 77, 79, 80.

46. *Corr.* xii. nos. 9959, 10360, 10400 and 10572 (12 March, 13 and 22 June, 30 July 1806).

47. Las Cases, *Mémorial*, ii. pp. 375–6; Albert Du Casse, *Les rois frères de Napoléon Ier: documents inédits relatifs au premier empire* (Paris, 1883), p. 102.

48. *Corr.* xv. n. 12291 (4 April 1807).

49. Louis Bonaparte, *Documents historiques*, i. pp. 164–5; Schama, *Patriots and Liberators*, p. 547.

50. Masson, *Napoléon et les femmes*, p. 151.

51. Boudon, *Le roi Jérôme*, pp. 155–75.
52. On Louis' reign in Holland see Lentz, *Nouvelle histoire du Premier Empire*, i. pp. 534–40.
53. Ehrmann, *The Younger Pitt*, iii. pp. 819–29; Hague, *William Pitt the Younger*, pp. 569–78, who argues that Pitt probably died of a peptic ulceration of the duodenum.
54. See A. D. Harvey, 'The Ministry of All the Talents: The Whigs in Office, February 1806 to March 1807', *Historical Journal*, 15:4 (1972), 619–48.
55. Fox to Talleyrand, 20 February 1806, in *Papers Relative to the Discussion with France in the Year 1806* (London, 1807), pp. 3–5; Thibaudeau, *Le Consulat et l'Empire*, v. pp. 376–7; Lentz, *Nouvelle histoire du Premier Empire*, i. pp. 224–35.
56. Talleyrand to Fox, 1 April 1806, in *Papers Relative to the Discussion with France in 1806*, pp. 12–17.
57. Schroeder, *Transformation of European Politics*, pp. 296–8.
58. Christopher Clark, *Iron Kingdom: The Rise and Downfall of Prussia, 1600–1947* (London, 2006), p. 300.
59. Adolf Wohlwill, 'Aktenstücke zur Rumboldschen Angelegenheit', *Zeitschrift des Vereins für Hamburgische Geschichte*, 7 (1881), 387–400; Adolf Wohlwill, 'Fernere Aktenstücke zur Rumboldschen Angelegenheit', *Zeitschrift des Vereins für Hamburgische Geschichte*, 8 (1886), 192–207. For the implications of the Rumbold affair see Simms, *The Impact of Napoleon*, pp. 159–68.
60. Simms, *The Impact of Napoleon*, pp. 191–201; Kagan, *The End of the Old Order*, pp. 323–7, 377–8, 535–47.
61. *Corr.* xi. nos. 9316, 9326, 9342 (2, 3 and 5 October 1805); Leopold von Ranke, *Denkwürdigkeiten des Staatskanzlers Fürsten von Hardenberg*, 5 vols (Leipzig, 1877), ii. pp. 279–83; Bailleu (ed.), *Preußen und Frankreich*, ii. pp. 394–6 (9 October 1805).
62. Marbot, *Mémoires*, i. pp. 282–3; Jackson, *The Diaries and Letters*, i. pp. 335–6, 344–5.
63. Simms, *The Impact of Napoleon*, pp. 207–24.
64. The Franco-Prussian alliance, or the Treaty of Schönbrunn, was later transformed into the Treaty of Paris.
65. Haugwitz to Lucchesini, in Bailleu (ed.), *Preußen und Frankreich*, ii. p. 468 (15 June 1806); Brendan Simms, 'The Road to Jena: Prussian High Politics 1804–6', *German History*, 12:3 (1994), 374–94, here 386; and on the political debate around the alliance with France, Simms, *The Impact of Napoleon*, pp. 207–24, 231–40, 280–5.
66. F. M. Kircheisen, 'Pourquoi la guerre éclata en 1806 entre la France et la Prusse?', *Revue d'histoire diplomatique*, 43 (1929), 237–50, far too sympathetic to Napoleon. See Stamm-Kuhlmann, *König in Preußens großer Zeit*, pp. 214–19; Schroeder, *Transformation of European Politics*, pp. 302–10; Simms, *The Impact of Napoleon*, pp. 291–303; Simms, 'The Road to Jena', 390–1.
67. Simms, *The Impact of Napoleon*, pp. 291–6; Simms, 'The Road to Jena', 374–94.
68. Stamm-Kuhlmann, *König in Preußens großer Zeit*, p. 226.
69. Cited in Lothar Kittstein, *Politik im Zeitalter der Revolution: Untersuchungen zur preußischen Staatlichkeit 1792–1807* (Stuttgart, 2003), p. 285 (Lucchesini to Haugwitz, 22 July 1806, Geheimes Staatsarchiv Preußischer Kulturbesitz, I Rep. 11 Nr. 89 Fasc. 409).
70. Lecestre (ed.), *Lettres inédites*, i. pp. 73–6 (12 September 1806).
71. Reference to the 'system' in *Corr.* xiii. n. 10765 (12 September 1805).
72. Lecestre (ed.), *Lettres inédites*, i. p. 74 (12 September 1806).
73. Gunther Rothenberg, 'The Origins, Causes, and Extension of the Wars of the French Revolution and Napoleon', *Journal of Interdisciplinary History*, 18 (1988), 772.
74. The Confederation of the Rhine was created in July 1806, and was composed of sixteen south and west German states. The Holy Roman Empire ceased to exist from that date. See Jean Tulard, 'Napoléon et la Confédération du Rhin', in Eberhard Weis and Elisabeth Müller-Luckner (eds), *Reformen im rheinbündischen Deutschland* (Munich, 1984), pp. 1–4.
75. Peter Paret, 'Jena and Auerstedt', in Paret, *Understanding War*, pp. 85–92.
76. James J. Sheehan, *German History: 1770–1866* (Oxford, 1989), p. 295.

77. Friedrich Carl Ferdinand von Müffling, *The Memoirs of Baron von Müffling: A Prussian Officer in the Napoleonic Wars* (London, 1997), p. 14.
78. Olaf Jessen, *'Preußens Napoleon'? Ernst von Rüchel, 1754–1823: Krieg im Zeitalter der Venunft* (Paderborn, 2007), pp. 263–4.
79. Stamm-Kuhlmann, *König in Preußens großer Zeit*, p. 233.
80. Telp, *The Evolution of Operational Art*, p. 62.
81. Barrès, *Souvenirs*, pp. 69–70; Robert Ouvrard (ed.), *Avec Napoléon à Iéna et Auerstaedt: la campagne de Prusse par ceux qui l'ont vécue: 1806* (Paris, 2006), pp. 124–6, 128; Coignet, *Note-Books*, pp. 131–2.
82. Hegel to Friedrich Immanuel Niethammer, in Johannes Hoffmeister (ed.), *Briefe von und an Hegel*, 4 vols (Hamburg, 1952), i. p. 120 (13 October 1806); Paret, *The Cognitive Challenge of War*, pp. 21–2.
83. *Corr.* xiii. n. 10989 (12 October 1806).
84. On the battle of Jena see Chandler, *Campaigns of Napoleon*, pp. 467–502; Henry Houssaye, *Iéna et la campagne de 1806* (Paris, 1912, reprinted 1991); Henry Lachouque, *Iéna* (Paris, 1962); Paret, *The Cognitive Challenge of War*, pp. 16–32.
85. Alfred-Armand-Robert de Saint-Chamans, *Mémoires du général Cte de Saint-Chamans, ancien aide de camp du maréchal Soult, 1802–1832* (Paris, 1896), p. 39.
86. Esdaile, *Napoleon's Wars*, p. 269. On Davout and Auerstädt see Comte Vigier, *Davout, maréchal d'empire, duc d'Auerstaedt, prince d'Eckmühl (1770–1823)*, 2 vols (Paris, 1898), i. pp. 187–230; John G. Gallaher, *The Iron Marshal: A Biography of Louis N. Davout* (London, 2000), pp. 116–50; Frédéric Hulot, *Le maréchal Davout* (Paris, 2002), pp. 84–104; Pierre Charrier, *Le maréchal Davout* (Paris, 2005), pp. 159–218.
87. Figures necessarily vary between Davout's 66,000 Prussians (Louis Nicolas Davout, *Opérations du 3e corps, 1806–1807: rapport du maréchal Davout, duc d'Auerstaedt* (Paris, 1896), pp. 30–1) and Clausewitz's 45,000 (Carl von Clausewitz, *Notes sur la Prusse dans sa grande catastrophe, 1806*, trans. from the German by A. Niessel (Paris, 1903), p. 148).
88. Stamm-Kuhlmann, *König in Preußens großer Zeit*, pp. 238–9.
89. Ségur, *Un aide de camp de Napoléon*, ii. pp. 310–11. For a different interpretation see Favier, *Bernadotte*, pp. 137–40.
90. Chandler, *Campaigns of Napoleon*, pp. 495–7. It is astonishing that Napoleon left Bernadotte's seeming incompetence unanswered.
91. Marbot, *Mémoires*, i. p. 303.
92. F. Loraine Petre, *Napoleon's Campaign in Poland, 1806–1807* (London, 1907), p. 41; Chandler, *Campaigns of Napoleon*, p. 496.
93. Savary, *Mémoires*, ii. p. 292. On Désirée Clary see Dwyer, *Napoleon: The Path to Power*, pp. 159–63.
94. *Corr.* xiii. n. 11009 (15 October 1806); Paul Foucart, *Campagne de Prusse (1806), d'après les archives de la guerre*, 2 vols (Paris, 1890), i. pp. 614–21.
95. Foucart, *Campagne de Prusse*, p. 614; Thomas Biskup, 'Napoleon's Second Sacre? Iéna and the Ceremonial Translation of Frederick the Great's Insignia in 1807', in Forrest and Wilson (eds), *The Bee and the Eagle*, p. 173.
96. See, for example, *Corr.* xiii. nos. 11011, 11014 (15 and 16 October 1806).
97. Ségur, *Un aide de camp de Napoléon*, ii. p. 311; Savary, *Mémoires*, ii. pp. 292–3; François, *Journal*, p. 502 (13 October 1806).
98. The *Moniteur universel*, 17 November 1806, published a number of poems in honour of Napoleon and his exploits in Germany. Biskup, 'Napoleon's Second Sacre?', pp. 174, 177–86; and Biskup, 'Das Schwert Friedrichs des Großen', pp. 185–203.
99. For the French occupation see Herman Granier', 'Die Franzosen in Berlin 1806–1808', *Hohenzollern-Jahrbuch*, 9 (1905), 1–43.
100. Along with other works of art, the Quadriga was dismantled (between 2 and 8 December), under the supervision of Vivant Denon, and taken back to Paris. It may not have had the same importance as the horses of St Mark in Venice – in fact, its aesthetic value was considered to be insignificant in 1806 – but it was an important symbol in the life of Berliners.

Denon wrote to a friend that he had thereby 'completed his quarrel with the inhabitants of Berlin', even if some of them admitted that under different circumstances they would have acted the same (Dupuy, (ed.), *Dominique-Vivant Denon*, p. 503; Bénédicte Savoy, *Patrimoine annexé: les biens culturels saisis par la France en Allemagne autour de 1800*, 2 vols (Paris, 2003), i. p. 276).

101. Barrès, *Souvenirs*, p. 73.
102. Alfred-Auguste Ernouf, *Les Français en Prusse (1807–1808), d'après des documents contemporains recueillis en Allemagne* (Paris, 1872), pp. 102–3, 105–7.
103. Jérémie Benoît, 'Napoléon à Berlin vu par les peintres', *Revue Napoléon*, 28 (2006), 44–8.
104. Jean-Marie-Félix Girod de l'Ain, *Dix ans de souvenirs militaires de 1805 à 1815* (Paris, 1873), p. 70. On Berlin see Matt Erlin, *Berlin's Forgotten Future: City, History, and Enlightenment in Eighteenth-Century Germany* (Chapel Hill, 2004).
105. Auguste de Sayve, *Souvenirs de Pologne et scènes militaires de la campagne de 1812* (Paris, 1833), p. 6.
106. Denis-Charles Parquin, *Souvenirs, 1803–1814* (Paris, 2003), p. 100.
107. The church was destroyed during a bombing raid in 1945. The sarcophagus is now to be found in the forecourt of Sanssouci Palace, also in Potsdam. On the visit see Ilya Mieck, 'Napoleon in Potsdam', *Francia*, 31:2 (2004), 134–41.
108. Ségur, *Un aide de camp de Napoléon*, i. p. 314.
109. Michel Kerautret, 'Frédéric II et l'opinion française (1800–1870): la compétition posthume avec Napoléon', *Francia*, 28/2 (2001), 65–84.
110. Rémusat, *Mémoires*, iii. pp. 63–4.
111. Hauterive, *La police secrète du premier Empire*, iii. pp. 70 and 99 (29 November and 24 December 1806).
112. Cited in Horne, *Seven Ages of Paris*, pp. 175–6.
113. Laugier, *Les cahiers*, pp. 299–300, 317.
114. According to Metternich, news of Napoleon's victories was greeted in 'bleak silence' (Constantin de Grunwald (ed.), 'Les débuts diplomatiques de Metternich à Paris', *Revue de Paris*, 4 (1936), 513–14, 517). In towns such as Marseilles, Besançon and Bordeaux, on the other hand, the Emperor was still popular enough for the populace to applaud public announcements proclaiming victory or to applaud the bulletins when they were read out in public (Hauterive, *La police secrète du premier Empire*, iii. pp. 49, 51, 53–4 (8, 10 and 12 November 1806)).
115. *Moniteur universel*, 30 November 1806.
116. François, *Journal*, pp. 508–9 (25 October 1806); Savoy, *Patrimoine annexé*, i. p. 137.
117. Some historians – F. Loraine Petre, *Napoleon's Conquest of Prussia, 1806* (London, 1907), p. 229; Michael V. Leggiere, 'From Berlin to Leipzig: Napoleon's Gamble in North Germany, 1813', *Journal of Military History*, 67 (2003), 82 – look upon the gesture as petty and vindictive, but it was part of a long tradition of martial pillaging, one the French armies practised with zeal. For the confiscations of antique armaments as trophies see Stuart W. Pyhrr, 'De la Révolution au romantisme: les origines des collections modernes d'armes et d'armures', in Daniela Gallo (ed.), *Les vies de Dominique-Vivant Denon*, 2 vols (Paris, 2001), ii. pp. 618–50.
118. *Moniteur universel*, 18 May 1807; Cambacérès, *Mémoires inédites*, ii. pp. 147–9. The insignia stayed there until March 1814 when the governor of the Invalides ordered them to be destroyed so that they would not fall back into the hands of the Prussians. According to Alfred Bégis, *Curiosités historiques. Invasion de 1814. Destruction des drapeaux étrangers et de l'épée de Frédéric de Prusse à l'Hôtel des Invalides, d'après des documents inédits* (Paris, 1897); Biskup, 'Das Schwert Friedrichs des Großen', p. 202.
119. Biskup, 'Napoleon's Second Sacre?', p. 180.
120. Biskup, 'Napoleon's Second Sacre?', p. 180; and Biskup, 'Das Schwert Friedrichs des Großen', p. 190.
121. Biskup, 'Napoleon's Second Sacre?', p. 183. A speech given by Fontane is in the *Moniteur universel*, 18 May 1807.

122. Savoy, *Patrimoine annexé*, i. pp. 235–8. For the catalogue of the exhibition see *Statues, bustes, bas reliefs, bronzes et autres antiquités, peintures, dessins et objets curieux, conquis par la Grande Armée, dans les années 1806, 1807* (Paris, 1807).

123. See Dorothy Mackay Quynn, 'The Art Confiscations of the Napoleonic Wars', *American Historical Review*, 50 (1945), 443–5.

124. Blanning, *Pursuit of Glory*, pp. 657–8.

125. On the Pietist movment in Prussia see Richard L. Gawthrop, *Pietism and the Making of Eighteenth-Century Prussia* (Cambridge, 1993); Christopher Clark, 'Piety, Politics and Society: Pietism in Eighteenth-Century Prussia', in Philip Dwyer (ed.), *The Rise of Prussia, 1700–1830* (London, 2000), pp. 68–88.

126. Sir George Jackson, *The Diaries and Letters*, ii. pp. 29–30, accompanied the king on his way east; Frederick William did not return to Berlin until 28 December 1809, and only then at Napoleon's behest.

127. At least according to Karl Friedrich Emil von Suckow, *D'Iéna à Moscou: fragments de ma vie*, trans. Commandant Veling (Paris, 1901), p. 55, a view also held by Heinrich von Bülow.

128. The Declaration of Ortelsburg, 12 December 1806. See Gordon A. Craig, *The Politics of the Prussian Army, 1640–1945* (Oxford, 1964), p. 42; Stamm-Kuhlmann, *König in Preußens großer Zeit*, pp. 245–6; Clark, *Iron Kingdom*, pp. 312–13.

129. Clark, *Iron Kingdom*, p. 312.

130. Mathias Tullner, 'Die preußische Niederlage bei Jena und Auerstedt (Hassenhausen) und die Kapitulation von Magedeburg', in Mathias Tullner and Sascha Möbius (eds), *1806: Jena, Auerstadt und die Kapitulation von Magdeburg: Schande oder Chance?* (Halle, 2007), pp. 130–9; and Wilfried Lübeck, 'November 1806 – die Kapitulation von Magdeburg, die feige Tat des Gouverneurs v. Kleist?', in ibid., pp. 140–52.

131. John G. Gallaher, *Napoleon's Enfant Terrible: General Dominique Vandamme* (Norman, 2008), pp. 176–9.

132. In 1944, Goebbels diverted considerable forces from the eastern front to make a film about the siege in an effort to boost morale. On the making of *Kolberg* see Friedrich Kahlenberg, 'Preußen als Filmsujet in der Propagandasprache der NS-Zeit', in Axel Marquardt and Hans Rathsack (eds), *Preußen im Film* (Hamburg, 1981), pp. 135–63.

133. Metternich, *Mémoires*, i. p. 107.

134. See Katherine Aaslestad, 'Revisiting the Continental System: Exploitation to Self-Destruction in the Napoleonic Empire', in Dwyer and Forrest (eds), *Napoleon and his Empire*, pp. 114–32. On the widespread practice of smuggling see Silvia Marzagalli, *Les boulevards de la fraude: le négoce maritime et le Blocus continental, 1806–1813: Bordeaux, Hambourg, Livourne* (Villeneuve-d'Ascq, 1999); Gavin Daly, 'Napoleon and the "City of Smugglers", 1810–1814', *Historical Journal*, 50:2 (2007), 333–52.

135. Christine Sutherland, *Marie Walewska: Napoleon's Great Love* (London, 1979), pp. 54–5.

136. Savary, *Mémoires*, ii. p. 26.

137. Friedrich Schulz, *Voyage en Pologne et en Allemagne, fait en 1793, par un Livonien*, 2 vols (Brussels, 1807), i. pp. 46–72.

138. Casimir Stryienski (ed.), *Memoirs of the Countess Potocka*, trans. Lionel Strachey (London, 1901), p. 80. The authenticity of the legend is questioned by Andrzej Nieuwazny, 'Marie Walewska, la belle Polonaise de Napoléon', *Napoléon 1er*, 7 (March–April 2001), 6–11; by Gaspard Gourgaud, *Journal de Sainte-Hélène, 1815–1818*, 2 vols (Paris, 1944), i. p. 108, who quotes Napoleon admitting that Talleyrand fixed him up; and by Rémusat, *Mémoires*, i. p. 121, who believed Murat procured Walewska for him.

139. An English translation of her memoirs can be found at www.walewski.org/the_diary_of_marie_walewska.

140. Tourtier-Bonazzi, *Lettres d'amour à Joséphine*, pp. 233–4, 235, 236–7, 237–8, 242 (3, 7, 8, 11 and 23 January 1807); Chevallier and Pincemaille, *L'impératrice Joséphine*, pp. 318–19.

141. Tourtier-Bonazzi, *Lettres d'amour à Joséphine*, pp. 239, 240, 241 (16, 18 and 19 January 1807).

142. Tourtier-Bonazzi, *Lettres d'amour à Joséphine*, pp. 280–1 (10 May 1807).

143. Tourtier-Bonazzi, *Lettres d'amour à Joséphine*, pp. 221, 225, 247, 250 (2, 9 December 1806, 9, 11 February 1807).

144. Max Gallo, *Lettres d'amour: à Désirée, Joséphine, Marie et Marie-Louise* (Paris, 2005), pp. 157, 158 (2 and 12 January 1807); Masson, *Napoléon et les femmes*, pp. 229, 234.

145. Constant, *Mémoires*, iii. pp. 269–70.

146. If Marcel Handelsman, *Napoléon et la Pologne (1806–1807)* (Paris, 1909), pp. 91–2, exaggerates when he states that this was a period in which his 'genius' flourished, there is little doubt that Napoleon was feverishly busy during his stay at Finckenstein.

## 12: Zenith

1. Coignet, *Note-Books*, pp. 137–9.

2. Auguste Thirion, *Souvenirs militaires* (Paris, 1998), pp. 19–20; Morvan, *Le soldat impérial*, ii. pp. 37, 47.

3. François Lavaux, *Mémoires de campagne (1793–1814)* (Paris, 2004), p. 126.

4. Charles-A. Faré, *Lettres d'un jeune officier à sa mère, 1803–1814* (Paris, 1889), p. 133.

5. Stryienski (ed.), *Memoirs of the Countess Potocka*, pp. 62, 63.

6. Iradj Amini, *Napoleon and Persia: Franco-Persian Relations under the First Empire*, trans. Azizeh Azodi (Richmond, 1999), p. 195.

7. On the battle of Eylau see Petre, *Napoleon's Campaign in Poland*, pp. 161–212; Chandler, *Campaigns of Napoleon*, pp. 535–51; Gates, *The Napoleonic Wars*, pp. 71–5; Esdaile, *Napoleon's Wars*, pp. 283–6; Frédéric Naulet, *Eylau, 8 février 1807: la campagne de Pologne, des boues de Pultusk aux neiges d'Eylau* (Paris, 2007).

8. On this point see Chandler, *Campaigns of Napoleon*, pp. 536–7.

9. Chandler, *Campaigns of Napoleon*, p. 538.

10. Bruce McConachy, 'The Roots of Artillery Doctrine: Napoleonic Artillery Tactics Reconsidered', *Journal of Military History*, 65 (2001), 631; Rothenberg, *The Art of Warfare*, p. 143.

11. McConachy, 'The Roots of Artillery Doctrine', p. 631; John A. Lynn, *The Bayonets of the Republic: Motivation and Tactics in the Army of Revolutionary France, 1791–94* (Urbana, 1984), pp. 206–7.

12. Antoine Henri baron de Jomini, *The Art of War*, trans. G. H. Mendell and W. P. Craighill (Philadelphia, 1862), pp. 318–19; Elting, *Swords around a Throne*, p. 533.

13. Pasquier, *Mémoires*, i. p. 301.

14. Pierre-François Percy, *Journal des campagnes du Bon Percy, chirurgien en chef de la Grande-Armée (1754–1825)* (Paris, 1904), p. 165.

15. Saint-Chamans, *Mémoires*, pp. 57–8.

16. Montesquiou-Fezensac, *Souvenirs militaires*, p. 161.

17. Jules-Antoine Paulin, *Les souvenirs du general Bon Paulin (1782–1876)* (Paris, 1895), p. 50.

18. Saint-Chamans, *Mémoires*, pp. 59–60, a reliable source for dissension in the army after Eylau. Robert Herbert, 'Baron Gros's Napoleon and Voltaire's Henri IV', in Francis Haskell and Robert Shackleton (eds), *The Artist and the Writer in France: Essays in Honour of Jean Seznec* (Oxford, 1974), p. 62. These views are countered by Béchet de Léocour, *Souvenirs*, p. 288, who asserts that he never heard a single insult uttered against Napoleon.

19. Victor Dupuy, *Souvenirs militaires de Victor Dupuy, chef d'escadrons de hussards, 1794–1816* (Paris, 1892), p. 79.

20. John Holland Rose, 'A British Agent at Tilsit', *English Historical Review*, 16 (1901), 714.

21. Chandler, *Campaigns of Napoleon*, p. 548; Lentz, *Nouvelle histoire du Premier Empire*, i. p. 275, gives 10,000 French and 12,000 Russian casualties.

22. Jeremy Black, *The Battle of Waterloo* (New York, 2010), pp. 32–3.

23. Jean-Jacques Régis de Cambacérès, *Lettres inédites à Napoléon: 1802–1814*, 2 vols (Paris, 1973), i. p. 455 (1 March 1807); Lanzac de Laborie, *Paris sous Napoléon*, iii. p. 53.

24. Gerstein, 'Le regard consolateur', p. 321.

25. Corr. xiv. nos. 11815, 11819, 11827, 11840, 11907, 11917 and 11988 (14, 17, 18, 20 and 28 February, 2 and 11 March 1807).

26. Corr. xiv. n. 11847 (21 February 1807).

27. Corr. xiv. nos. 11791, 11899, 11990, 12022, 12023 (9 and 28 February, 11 and 13 March 1807). On Napoleon's initial attempts to manipulate public opinion around Eylau see Marrinan, 'Literal/Literary/"Lexie"', 177, 179–80.

28. Corr. xiv. nos. 11789, 11800, 11801, 11813, 11990, 12610 (9, 12 and 14 February, 11 and 25 March 1807).

29. Corr. xiv. n. 11796 (9 February 1797). The Moniteur universel, 2 April 1807, cites the figure of 5,000 killed and wounded. Bell, Total War, p. 256.

30. Found in Bataille de Preussisch-Eylau, gagnée par la grande armée, commandée en personne par S.M. Napoléon Ier (Paris, 1807), pp. 18–23. Napoleon even executed a drawing of the battlefield that he intended to publish, but never did (H. M. A. Berthaut, Les ingénieurs géographes militaires, 1624–1831: étude historique (Paris, 1902), ii. p. 49).

31. Corr. xiv. n. 11853 (21 February 1807); Bataille de Preussisch-Eylau, p. 13; J. M. Thompson, Napoleon Bonaparte: His Rise and Fall (Oxford, 1951), pp. 313–14.

32. O'Brien, After the Revolution, pp. 158–9.

33. Billon, Souvenirs, pp. 68–9; Roger Vaultier, 'La chirurgie militaire sous le Premier Empire', Chroniques (28 March 1951), 415.

34. Gallo, Lettres d'amour, p. 159 (9 February 1807).

35. Tourtier-Bonazzi, Lettres d'amour à Joséphine, p. 252 (14 February 1807).

36. Saint-Chamans, Mémoires, p. 61; Percy, Journal des campagnes, pp. 175, 179–80.

37. John L. H. Keep, Soldiers of the Tsar: Army and Society in Russia, 1462–1874 (Oxford, 1985), p. 195.

38. Chaptal, Mes souvenirs, p. 342.

39. Louis-Florimond Fantin des Odoards, Journal du général Fantin des Odoards, étapes d'un officier de la Grande Armée, 1800–1830 (Paris, 1895), p. 143.

40. Corr. xiv. nos. 11810, 11890 (13 and 26 February 1807); Schroeder, Transformation of European Politics, p. 311.

41. Chandler, Campaigns of Napoleon, pp. 559–60.

42. English-language accounts of the battle of Friedland include: Harold T. Parker, Three Napoleonic Battles (Durham, NC, 1983), pp. 3–26; Petre, Napoleon's Campaign in Poland, pp. 304–29; Chandler, Campaigns of Napoleon, pp. 572–85; Gates, The Napoleonic Wars, pp. 77–80; Laurence Spring (ed.), An Englishman in the Russian Army, 1807: The Journal of Colonel James Bathurst during the East Prussia Campaign, 1807 (Knaphill, 2000).

43. Marbot, Mémoires, i. pp. 364, 370.

44. Savary, Mémoires, iii. p. 91; Emmanuel-Henri de Grouchy, Mémoires du maréchal de Grouchy, 5 vols (Paris, 1873–4), ii. pp. 330–1; Sir Robert Wilson, Brief Remarks on the Character and Composition of the Russian Army and a Sketch of the Campaigns in Poland in the Years 1806 and 1807 (London, 1810), p. 160.

45. Tourtier-Bonazzi, Lettres d'amour à Joséphine, p. 292 (15 June 1807).

46. Fantin des Odoards, Journal, p. 114.

47. Fantin des Odoards, Journal, p. 328.

48. Patricia Kennedy Grimsted, The Foreign Ministers of Alexander I: Political Attitudes and the Conduct of Russian Diplomacy, 1801–1825 (Berkeley and Los Angeles, 1969), p. 165.

49. Granville, Private Correspondence, ii. p. 228.

50. Grimsted, The Foreign Ministers of Alexander I, pp. 152–64.

51. Financially, on the other hand, the campaigns of 1806–8 cost France little. See Tulard, Napoléon ou le mythe du sauveur, pp. 197–8; Pierre Branda, Le prix de la gloire: Napoléon et l'argent (Paris, 2007), pp. 314–19.

52. There are a number of letters from Napoleon to Talleyrand in March 1807 that point in this direction. Corr. xiv. nos. 11918, 11977, 12028 (3, 9 and 14 March 1807).

53. Bertrand (ed.), Lettres inédites, pp. 468–9 (18 June 1807).

54. Cited in Plongeron, 'Cyrus ou les lectures d'une figure biblique dans la rhétorique religieuse', 42, 64.

55. For another period see Jan Hennings, 'The Semiotics of Diplomatic Dialogue: Pomp and Circumstance in Tsar Peter I's Visit to Vienna in 1698', *International History Review*, 30 (2008), 515–44.

56. François, *Journal*, p. 536 (25 June 1807); Johannes Paulmann, *Pomp und Politik: Monarchenbegegnungen in Europa zwischen Ancien Régime und Erstem Weltkrieg* (Paderborn, 2000), p. 46.

57. See Albert Vandal, *Napoléon et Alexandre Ier. L'alliance russe sous le premier Empire*, 3 vols (Paris, 1893–6), i. pp. 57–8; Herbert Butterfield, *The Peace Tactics of Napoleon, 1806–1808* (Cambridge, 1929), pp. 181–276; Jean Thiry, *Eylau, Friedland, Tilsit* (Paris, 1964), pp. 189–218; Gherardo Casaglia, *Le partage du monde: Napoléon et Alexandre à Tilsit, 25 juin 1807* (Paris, 1998), pp. 203–34; Schroeder, *Transformation of European Politics*, pp. 320–3. The Russian perspective is treated in Marie-Pierre Rey, *Alexandre Ier* (Paris, 2009), pp. 235–8.

58. Metternich believed that there was something missing from Alexander, but that it was impossible to put his finger on it (Metternich, *Mémoires*, i. pp. 315–17).

59. Captain Coignet, present during the evening, was a little disgusted to see how the Russian Guard, once they had had their fill of food and drink, stuck fingers down their throats to make themselves vomit and start all over again (Coignet, *Note-Books*, pp. 154–6).

60. Vandal, *Napoléon et Alexandre*, i. p. 108.

61. Vandal, *Napoléon et Alexandre*, i. p. 61; Adams, *Napoleon and Russia*, p. 180.

62. Tourtier-Bonazzi, *Lettres d'amour à Joséphine*, p. 297 (25 June 1807).

63. Cited in Alan Palmer, *Alexander I: Tsar of War and Peace* (New York, 1974), p. 157.

64. According to Abel-François Villemain, *Souvenirs contemporains d'histoire et de literature*, 2 vols (Paris, 1854–5), i. p. 164.

65. Caulaincourt, *Mémoirs*, i. p. 67.

66. Belissa, *Repenser l'ordre européen*, pp. 249–51.

67. Adams, *Napoleon and Russia*, p. 197.

68. Alexander agreed to mediate between France and Britain, an offer that was politely but firmly rejected by London, whose position was intractable. On the mediation efforts see Schroeder, *Transformation of European Politics*, pp. 328–9.

69. Adams, *Napoleon and Russia*, pp. 192–3.

70. Schroeder, *Transformation of European Politics*, pp. 320–1.

71. Frederick William to Luise, 4 July 1807, in Paul Bailleu, 'Die Verhandlungen in Tilsit (1807): Briefwechsel König Friedrich Wilhelm's III. und der Königin Luise', *Deutsche Rundschau*, 110 (1902), 29–45, 199–221, here 216.

72. Stamm-Kuhlmann, *König in Preußens großer Zeit*, pp. 252–4.

73. Las Cases, *Mémorial*, i. pp. 736–8; Paul Bailleu, 'Königin Luise in Tilsit', *Hohenzollern-Jahrbuch. Forschungen und Abbildungen zur Geschichte der Hohenzollern in Brandenburg-Preussen*, 3 (1899), 221–40; Lenz Max, 'Tilsit', *Forschungen zur brandenburgischen und preussischen Geschichte*, 6 (1893), 181–237; Stamm-Kuhlmann, *König in Preußens großer Zeit*, pp. 258–66. On Queen Luise see Günter de Bruyn, *Preußens Luise: vom Entstehen und Vergehen einer Legende* (Berlin, 2001); and for the fascinating cult that developed after her death see Philipp Demandt, *Luisenkult: die Unsterblichkeit der Königin von Preußen* (Cologne, 2003).

74. François, *Journal*, p. 537 (27 June 1807).

75. T. C. W. Blanning, 'The Bonapartes and Germany', in Baehr and Richter (eds), *Dictatorship in History and Theory*, p. 55. The following figures are from: Karl Obermann, 'La situation de la Prusse sous l'occupation française, 1807–1813', in *Occupants Occupés, 1792–1815* (Brussels, 1969), pp. 263–75; Rudolf Ibbeken, *Preussen 1807–1813: Staat und Volk als Idee und in Wirklichkeit: Darstellung und Dokumentation* (Berlin, 1970), pp. 91–5; Bernd von Münchow-Pohl, *Zwischen Reform and Krieg: Untersuchungen zur Bewusstseinslage in Preussen 1809–1812* (Göttingen, 1987), pp. 49–56; Harald Müller, 'Napoleon in der Gruft

der Garnisonkirche', in Bernhard Kroener (ed.), *Potsdam: Staat, Armee, Residenz in der preussisch-deutschen Militärgeschichte* (Frankfurt, 1993), pp. 345–60; Matthew Levinger, *Enlightened Nationalism: The Transformation of Prussian Political Culture, 1806–1848* (Oxford, 2000), p. 44; Karen Hagemann, *'Mannlicher Muth und teutsche Ehre': Nation, Militär und Geschlecht zur Zeit der antinapoleonischen Kriege Preußens* (Paderborn, 2002), pp. 24–8; Karen Hagemann, 'Occupation, Mobilization, and Politics: The Anti-Napoleonic Wars in Prussian Experience, Memory, and Historiography', *Central European History*, 39:4 (2006), 589–94.

76. C. B. A. Behrens, *Society, Government and the Enlightenment: The Experiences of Eighteenth-Century France and Prussia* (London, 1985), pp. 190–1.

77. *Corr.* xiii. n. 10992 (13 October 1806).

78. According to Enno E. Kraehe, *Metternich's German Policy*, 2 vols (Princeton, 1963), i. p. 98.

79. Branda, *Le prix de la gloire*, pp. 332–5.

80. As does, for example, Stamm-Kuhlmann, *König in Preußens großer Zeit*, p. 257, but he repeats what many others before him have asserted.

81. As has been demonstrated by Ilya Mieck, 'Die Rettung Preußens? Napoleon und Alexander I. in Tilsit 1807', in Ilya Mieck and Pierre Guillen (eds), *Deutschland–Frankreich–Rußland: Begegnungen und Konfrontation* (Munich, 2000), pp. 15–35.

82. Alan Palmer, *Metternich: Councillor of Europe* (London, 1972), pp. 56–7.

83. Alexander M. Martin, 'The Russian Empire and the Napoleonic Wars', in Dwyer (ed.), *Napoleon and Europe*, pp. 255–6.

84. Rey, *Alexandre Ier*, p. 225.

85. Roxandra Edling, *Mémoires de la Comtesse Edling (née Stourdza), demoiselle d'honneur de S.M. l'impératrice* (Moscow, 1888), pp. 29–30, 50; Hartley, *Alexander*, pp. 78–9; Martin, 'The Russian Empire', 257; Rey, *Alexandre Ier*, pp. 245–6.

86. See André Ratchinski, *Napoléon et Alexandre Ier: la guerre des idées* (Paris, 2002), pp. 275–84.

87. Hugh Ragsdale, 'Russian Foreign Policy, 1725–1815', in Dominic Lieven (ed.), *The Cambridge History of Russia*, 3 vols (Cambridge, 2006), ii. p. 526.

88. Savary to Talleyrand (23 August 1807), report by Auguste de Saint-Aignan (no date), Savary to Napoleon (9 September 1807), and Savary to Napoleon (23 September 1807), in *Sbornik*, lxxxiii. pp. 33, 41–3, 58–9, 80, 86, 140; Comte de Björnstjerna (ed.), *Mémoires posthumes du Feld-Maréchal comte de Stedingk*, 3 vols (Paris, 1844–7), ii. pp. 354–5 (10 October 1807); Lentz, *Savary*, pp. 165–9.

89. Caulaincourt, in love with the married Mme de Canisy, was promised by Napoleon that if he went away for a year everything would be sorted out when he returned. It was a promise the Emperor did not keep. Caulaincourt, *Memoirs*, i. pp. 53–60.

90. Dominic Lieven, *Russia against Napoleon: The Battle for Europe, 1807 to 1814* (London, 2009), p. 61.

91. Martin, *Romantics, Reformers, Reactionaries*, p. 50.

92. Charles Francis Adams (ed.), *Memoirs of John Quincy Adams*, 12 vols (New York, 1970), ii. p. 69 (16 November 1809).

93. Martin, 'The Russian Empire', p. 256; Martin, *Romantics, Reformers, Reactionaries*, pp. 16–17, 39–56; Tim Blanning, *The Romantic Revolution: A History* (New York, 2011), pp. 146–7.

94. Dimitri Sorokine, *Napoléon dans la littérature russe* (Paris, 1974), pp. 23–6.

95. Marc Raeff, *Michael Speransky: Statesman of Imperial Russia, 1772–1839* (The Hague, 1969), pp. 82–169; David Christian, 'The Political Ideals of Michael Speransky', *Slavonic and East European Review*, 54 (1976), 192–213.

96. The event was offered as a spectacle to the French public in the form of a Panorama of Tilsit the following year. Girod de l'Ain, *Dix ans de souvenirs militaires*, p. 61.

97. Hauterive, *La police secrète du premier Empire*, iii. pp. 302, 314, 316, 318 and 330 (10, 25, 28 and 30 July, and 11 August 1807).

98. Cited in Kôbô Seigan, 'La propagande pour la conscription, l'armée et la guerre dans le département de la Seine-Inférieure, du Directoire à la fin de l'Empire', in Michel Biard, Annie Crépin and Bernard Gainot (eds), *La plume et le sabre: volume d'hommages offerts à Jean-Paul Bertaud* (Paris, 2002), p. 276.

99. Noël, *Souvenirs militaires*, p. 36.

100. Roman Töppel, *Die Sachsen und Napoleon: ein Stimmungsbild 1806–1813* (Cologne, 2008), pp. 93–5.

101. Brendan Simms, 'Britain and Napoleon', *Historical Journal*, 41:3 (1998), 886.

102. See, for example, [Audibert], 'L'accueil des Alpes-Maritimes à la paix de Tilsit', *Revue de l'Institut Napoléon*, 101 (1966), 191–2.

103. Lanzac de Laborie, *Paris sous Napoléon*, iii. pp. 11–12.

104. On the history of the Arc de Triomphe see Isabelle Rouge-Ducos, *L'Arc de Triomphe de l'Etoile: panthéon de la France guerrière: art et histoire* (Dijon, 2008), esp. chs 1–3.

105. Barrès, *Souvenirs*, p. 103.

106. Louis Dubroca, *Discours à la gloire des armées françaises, pour la célébration de la mémorable paix de Tilsit* (Paris, 1807).

107. Lanzac de Laborie, *Paris sous Napoléon*, iii. pp. 55–65; Hughes, *Forging Napoleon's Grande Armée*, pp. 90–8.

108. Barrès, *Souvenirs*, pp. 107–8.

109. Descriptions of the festivities can be found in the *Moniteur universel*, 25, 26 and 29 November 1807; and in Jean-Antoine-Guillaume Bailleul, *Histoire des triomphes militaires, des fêtes guerrières et des honneurs accordés aux braves chez les peuples anciens et modernes; particulièrement aux armées françaises, jusqu'au 1er janvier 1808* (Paris, 1808), pp. 457–64.

110. See, for example, François-Louis Darragon, *Le Bouquet impérial, ou le Tableau Napoléon* (Paris, 1807); Eustache (sons), *Ode à Sa Majesté l'empereur Napoléon, roi d'Italie* (Paris, 1807); J. Leroy, *Epître à Napoléon-le-Grand, poème en trois chants* (Paris, 1807); Jean-Baptiste Rouvier, *Hymne nouveau sur la paix à S.M.I. et R. Napoléon Ier, empereur des Français et roi d'Italie* (n.p., 1807); *Essai sur l'éloge de Napoléon* (Châlons, n.d.).

111. J.-J. Dupont, *Portrait historique de Napoléon le Grand* (Paris, 1807), p. 6.

112. Charles Messiers, *1769: Grande Comète qui a paru à la naissance de Napoléon le Grand, découverte et observée pendant quatre mois* (Paris, n.d.), and in 1801, with the signing of the Treaty of Amiens, the planets were aligned.

113. Pierre-Charles Lecomte, *Les Fastes du génie militaire dirigés par l'héroïsme . . . de Napoléon le Grand* (Paris, 1808).

114. Cited in Bertho, 'Naissance et élaboration d'une théologie de la guerre chez les évêques de Napoléon', p. 90.

115. See, for example, M. Lemoyne, *Discours prononcé dans l'église paroissiale de Saint-Louis de Blois, le premier dimanche du mois de décembre 1808, en mémoire du couronnement de S.M. l'Empereur et de la victoire d'Austerlitz* (Blois, n.d.), pp. 7, 13.

116. Plongeron, 'Cyrus ou les lectures d'une figure biblique dans la rhétorique religieuse', 33–4, 54–66.

117. This included Protestant pastors. See Pierre de Joux, *La Providence et Napoléon, ou les Victoires d'Ulm, d'Austerlitz, de Iéna, de Golymin, de Pultusck, de Dantzick, d'Eylau et de Friedland* (Paris, 1808), p. 206, where one can read, 'It is God who gave this prince . . . the capacity to reign . . .'

118. Gustave de Pontécoulant, *Souvenirs historiques et parlementaires du comte de Pontécoulant, ancien pair de France*, 4 vols (Paris, 1861–5), iii. pp. 105–6.

119. Lentz, *Nouvelle histoire du Premier Empire*, i. pp. 348 and 349.

120. François Piétri, *Napoléon et le Parlement ou la dictature enchaînée* (Paris, 1955), pp. 207–21; Collins, *Napoleon and his Parliaments*, pp. 114–15.

121. Méneval, *Mémoires*, ii. pp. 123–5.

122. Gabriel Vauthier, 'L'épuration de la magistrature en 1808', *Revue des études*

*napoléoniennes*, 15 (1919), 218–23; Jean Bourdon, 'Les sénatus-consulte de 1807: l'épuration de la magistrature en 1807–1808 et ses conséquences', *Revue d'histoire moderne et contemporaine*, 17 (July–September 1970), 829–36.

123. Eugène Hatin, *Histoire politique et littéraire de la presse en France*, 8 vols (Paris, 1859–61), vii. pp. 546–56.

124. See Petiteau, *Les Français et l'Empire*, pp. 76–7.

125. Burrows, *French Exile Journalism*, pp. 181–3; Semmel, *Napoleon and the British*, pp. 44–6. The term 'despot' was widely used in the years preceding the French Revolution, often against the king, and was one of the most important ideas leading to constitutional change in 1789. Yet there is little research into the political use of the term in the eighteenth and nineteenth centuries.

126. Robert Gildea, *The Past in French History* (New Haven, 1994), p. 64.

127. Emile Le Gallo, 'Un témoignage de Bonaparte sur Robespierre en 1797', *Annales Révolutionnaires*, 14 (1922), 60–5. See Casanova, *Napoléon et la pensée de son temps*, pp. 158–73, for an analysis of this document.

128. Bluche, *Le Bonapartisme*, p. 90; Aurélien Lignereux, *Histoire de la France contemporaine*, vol. i: *L'Empire des Français (1799–1815)* (Paris, 2012), pp. 85–6.

129. The comparison is often made, as in John Lukacs, *The Hitler of History* (New York, 1998), pp. 240–51. See R. S. Alexander, *Napoleon* (London, 2001), pp. 90–116; Steven Englund, 'Napoleon and Hitler', *Journal of the Historical Society*, 6 (2006), 151–69; and Michael Rowe, 'Napoleon's France: A Forerunner of Europe's Twentieth-Century Dictators', in Claus-Christian Szejnmann (ed.), *Rethinking History, Dictatorship and War: New Approaches and Interpretations* (London, 2009), pp. 87–106.

130. Godel, 'L'Eglise selon Napoléon', 838.

131. See Vida Azimi, *Les premiers sénateurs français: Consulat et Premier Empire, 1800–1814* (Paris, 2000), pp. 155–6.

132. Pierre Rosanvallon, *Le sacre du citoyen: histoire du suffrage universel en France* (Paris, 1992), p. 197.

133. See, for example, his letter to the government of Genoa in *Corr.* iii. n. 1933 (16 June 1797).

134. For the following see Bluche, *Le Bonapartisme*, p. 29; F. G. Healey, *Rousseau et Napoléon* (Geneva, 1957), pp. 77–9.

## *13: 'The Devil's Business'*

1. Louis de Fontanes, *Oeuvres de M. de Fontanes*, 2 vols (Paris, 1839), i. p. 341 (2 November 1808); Lanzac de Laborie, *Paris sous Napoléon*, iii. p. 126.

2. This idea is more fully elaborated in Philip Dwyer, 'Napoleon and the Drive for Glory: Reflections on the Making of French Foreign Policy', in Dwyer (ed.), *Napoleon and Europe*, pp. 118–35.

3. On Napoleon's relations with the pope see Henri Welschinger, *Le pape et l'empereur, 1804–1815* (Paris, 1905), pp. 1–45; E. E. Y. Hales, *Napoleon and the Pope: The Story of Napoleon and Pius VII* (London, 1962); Margaret M. O'Dwyer, *The Papacy in the Age of Napoleon and the Restoration: Pius VII, 1800–1823* (Lanham, Md, 1985), pp. 83–124; Melchior-Bonnet, *Napoléon et le Pape*; Robin Anderson, *Pope Pius VII, 1800–1823: His Life, Reign and Struggle with Napoleon in the Aftermath of the French Revolution* (Rockford, Ill., 2001); Boudon, *Histoire du Consulat et de l'Empire*, pp. 342–58; Lentz, *Nouvelle histoire du Premier Empire*, i. pp. 349–70, 482–500; ii. pp. 106–34.

4. *Corr.* xi. n. 9655, and xii. n. 9805 (7 January, 13 February 1806).

5. Cited in Melchior-Bonnet, *Napoléon et le Pape*, p. 89.

6. Joseph Othenin Bernard de Cléron, comte d'Haussonville, *L'Eglise romaine et le Premier Empire, 1800–1814*, 5 vols (Paris, 1868–9), ii. pp. 305–9; John Tracy Ellis, *Cardinal Consalvi and Anglo-Papal Relations, 1814–1824* (Washington, DC, 1942), pp. 15–17; Robinson, *Cardinal Consalvi*, pp. 81–5.

7. *Corr.* xv. n. 13093 (31 August 1807).
8. *Corr.* xvi. n. 13441 (10 January 1808).
9. *Corr.* xvi. n. 13536 (7 February 1808).
10. Ellis, 'Religion According to Napoleon', p. 248.
11. Cited in Melchior-Bonnet, *Napoléon et le Pape*, pp. 101 and 102.
12. Lentz, *Nouvelle histoire du Premier Empire*, i. 370; Ellis, 'Religion According to Napoleon', pp. 248–9.
13. On this annexation of the Roman states see Lentz, *Nouvelle histoire du Premier Empire*, i. pp. 526–34.
14. Claude-François André d'Arbelles, *Tableau historique de la politique de la cour de Rome, depuis l'origine de sa puissance temporelle jusqu'à nos jours* (Paris, 1810).
15. For an overview of this complex problem see Esdaile, *Napoleon's Wars*, pp. 301–45; Charles Esdaile, *The Peninsular War: A New History* (London, 2003), pp. 1–36.
16. This is the view of Schroeder, *Transformation of European Politics*, pp. xi, 230, 284, 393; and Paul W. Schroeder, 'Napoleon's Foreign Policy: A Criminal Enterprise', *Journal of Military History*, 54 (1990), 147–61.
17. Shuvalov to Alexander (15 May 1811), in *Sbornik*, xxi. p. 416.
18. Eli F. Heckscher, *The Continental System: An Economic Interpretation* (Oxford, 1922), pp. 92–4. Historians who have recently reiterated this point include Tulard, *Napoléon ou le mythe du sauveur*, pp. 205–6; David Gates, *The Spanish Ulcer: A History of the Peninsular War* (London, 1986), p. 6; Schroeder, *Transformation of European Politics*, pp. 307–10; Jean-Noël Brégeon, *Napoléon et la guerre d'Espagne: 1808–1814* (Paris, 2006), pp. 69–71; Michael V. Leggiere, *The Fall of Napoleon*, vol. i: *The Allied Invasion of France, 1813–1814* (New York, 2007), p. 2. There is necessarily a debate, as with all things Napoleonic, about whether the desire to defeat Britain led to the implementation of the blockade or whether the blockade led to the expansion of the Empire. A concise résumé of the debate can be found in Schroeder, *Transformation of European Politics*, pp. 307–9, along with the assertion that the Continental System was really part of a contest to see which of the three great powers – Britain, France or Russia – would dominate Europe.
19. Heckscher, *The Continental System*, pp. 78, 86, 95; Geoffrey Ellis, *Napoleon's Continental Blockade: The Case of Alsace* (Oxford, 1981), pp. 110–48; Lentz, *Nouvelle histoire du Premier Empire*, i. p. 257.
20. Schroeder, *The Transformation of Europe*, p. 224; Nicole Gotteri, *Napoléon et le Portugal* (Paris, 2004), pp. 115–19.
21. The Directory had considered a number of plans to conquer Portugal between 1796 and 1799 (Gotteri, *Napoléon et le Portugal*, pp. 59–60).
22. *Corr.* xv. n. 12928 (19 July 1807); Schroeder, *Transformation of Europe*, pp. 338–9; Gotteri, *Napoléon et le Portugal*, pp. 137–8.
23. Sorel, *L'Europe et la Révolution française*, vii. p. 217.
24. John Charles Chasteen, *Americanos: Latin America's Struggle for Independence* (Oxford, 2008), p. 42.
25. According to Esdaile, *Napoleon's Wars*, pp. 319–20, 328.
26. *Corr.* xvi. nos. 13181, 13287 and 13300 (25 September, 23 and 27 October 1807).
27. *Corr.* xvi. n. 13257 (16 October 1807). Junot was ordered into Spain *before* a Franco-Spanish accord had been reached.
28. Thiébault, *Mémoires*, iv. p. 139.
29. Gates, *The Spanish Ulcer*, p. 8.
30. Rory Muir, *Britain and the Defeat of Napoleon, 1807–1815* (New Haven, 1996), pp. 29–30. It was the first time that a European monarch had visited a colony; he was to stay in Rio de Janeiro for the next thirteen years. On the Portuguese court in Rio see Kirsten Schultz, *Tropical Versailles: Empire, Monarchy, and the Portuguese Royal Court in Rio de Janeiro, 1808–1821* (London, 2001).
31. Natalie Petiteau, 'Les justifications impériales de l'intervention en Espagne', in Gérard

Dufour and Elisabel Larriba (eds), *L'Espagne en 1808: régénération ou révolution?* (Aix-en-Provence, 2009), p. 12.

32. Gabriel H. Lovett, *Napoleon and the Birth of Modern Spain*, 2 vols (New York, 1965), i. pp. 8–17, 23–6, 90; Hilt, *The Troubled Trinity*, pp. 12–18.

33. Alexandre Tratchevsky, 'L'Espagne à l'époque de la Révolution française', *Revue historique*, 31 (1886), 9.

34. Jacques Chastenet, *Manuel Godoy et l'Espagne de Goya* (Paris, 1961), p. 50; Elizabeth Vassall, Lady Holland, *The Spanish Journal of Elizabeth, Lady Holland* (London, 1910), p. 74; Lovett, *Napoleon and the Birth of Modern Spain*, i. p. 6.

35. AN AFIV 1680 (1), Philippe de Tournon to Napoleon, 20 December 1807; Philippe Loupès, 'De Badajoz à Bayonne, l'irrésistible ascension de Manuel Godoy revisitée', in Josette Pontet, *Napoléon, Bayonne et l'Espagne: actes du colloque* (Paris, 2011), pp. 95–103. On Godoy's ascent see Hilt, *The Troubled Trinity*, pp. 6–9, 22–34.

36. The description is from his own mother, in Hilt, *The Troubled Trinity*, p. 137.

37. José M. Portillo Valdés, 'Imperial Spain', in Broers, Hicks and Guimerá (eds), *The Napoleonic Empire and the New European Political Culture*, pp. 287–8.

38. Hilt, *The Troubled Trinity*, pp. 179–96; Brégeon, *Napoléon et la guerre d'Espagne*, p. 87.

39. André Fugier, *Napoléon et l'Espagne, 1799–1808*, 2 vols (Paris, 1930), ii. pp. 150–4; Hilt, *The Troubled Trinity*, pp. 166–70; Brégeon, *Napoléon et la guerre d'Espagne*, pp. 68–9.

40. Hilt, *The Troubled Trinity*, pp. 210–26.

41. An argument put forward by Emilio La Parra López, 'Méfiance entre les alliés: les relations Napoléon–Godoy (1801–1807)', *Annales historiques de la Révolution française*, 336 (2004), 31–5.

42. Richard Hocquellet, *Résistance et révolution durant l'occupation napoléonienne en Espagne, 1808–1812* (Paris, 2001), pp. 24–5.

43. Lecestre (ed.), *Lettres inédites*, i. p. 184 (26 April 1808).

44. Tulard, *Murat*, p. 118. On the events that lead up to and follow the riot of Aranjuez see Hocquellet, *Résistance et révolution*, pp. 26–41; Esdaile, *The Peninsular War*, pp. 32–4; Brégeon, *Napoléon et la guerre d'Espagne*, pp. 90–2.

45. *Corr.* xvii. nos. 13711 and 13712 (1 April 1808); Tulard, *Murat*, p. 120.

46. Hocquellet, *Résistance et révolution*, pp. 30–1.

47. Tulard, *Napoléon ou le mythe du sauveur*, p. 335.

48. Esdaile, *Napoleon's Wars*, p. 332.

49. *Corr.* xvi. n. 13443 (10 January 1808).

50. Edouard Driault, *Napoléon et l'Europe*, iii. p. 250.

51. Napoleon to Lucien (4 December 1807), cited in Haegele, *Napoléon et Joseph Bonaparte*, pp. 298–9 (from AN 381 AP 1, dossier 1, cahier 1).

52. Albert Du Casse, 'Documents inédits relative au premier Empire. Napoléon et le roi Louis', *Revue historique*, 12 (January–February 1880), 92–3.

53. *Corr.* xvii. n. 13763 (18 April 1808).

54. *Corr.* xvii. n. 13844 (10 May 1808).

55. Girardin, *Mémoires, journal et souvenirs*, i. pp. 68–70.

56. Haegele, *Napoléon et Joseph Bonaparte*, pp. 309–12.

57. Haegele, *Napoléon et Joseph Bonaparte*, pp. 336–7.

58. Gates, *The Spanish Ulcer*, p. 9.

59. Chastenet, *Manuel Godoy*, pp. 172–3. Similar flattering remarks were sent back to Napoleon by Philippe de Tournon, who was dispatched to the Peninsula to study public opinion, as well as to spy on the military installations inside Madrid: 'Spain is in a crisis [and] it awaits its fate from the Emperor, it looks upon Him as its only support and considers Him to be the protector of the Prince of Asturia, who is his only hope' (AN AFIV 1680 (1), 20 December 1807). See also Hilt, *The Troubled Trinity*, pp. 170–3; Lentz, *Savary*, pp. 115–16.

60. Even the otherwise toadying Tournon had changed his mind and could now see the potential difficulties of French involvement in Spain. See, for example, his report in Jacques

Chastenet, *Godoy, Master of Spain 1792–1808*, trans. J. F. Huntington (London, 1953), p. 183.

61. Las Cases, *Mémorial*, i. pp. 385–6, 569–70, 725–34.

62. Hocquellet, *Résistance et révolution*, p. 35; Bell, *Total War*, p. 276.

63. Cited in Robert Hughes, *Goya* (London, 2003), p. 265.

64. Léon-François Hoffmann, *Romantique Espagne: l'image de l'Espagne en France entre 1800 et 1850* (Paris, 1961), pp. 13–15. On Napoleon's low opinion of Spain see Fugier, *Napoléon et l'Espagne*, ii. pp. 452–3.

65. Gérard Dufour, 'Pourquoi les espagnole prirent-ils les armes contre Napoléon?', in *Les Espagnols et Napoléon: actes du colloque international d'Aix-en-Provence* (Aix-en-Provence, 1984), pp. 320–1; Nicole Gotteri, *Napoléon: stratégie politique et moyens de gouvernement: essai* (Paris, 2007), p. 136.

66. Dominique Dufour, baron de Pradt, *Mémoires historiques sur la révolution d'Espagne* (Paris, 1816), p. 109.

67. According to Pradt, *Mémoires historiques*, pp. 109–10.

68. Tulard, *Napoléon ou le mythe du sauveur*, p. 340; Tulard, 'Les responsabilités françaises dans la Guerre d'Espagne', in *Les Espagnols et Napoléon*, pp. 3–4.

69. Lentz, *Nouvelle histoire du Premier Empire*, iii. p. 701. Cambacérès, on the other hand, was against intervention in Spain, while Fouché is supposed to have warned Napoleon that conquest might not be all that easy (Cambacérès, *Mémoires inédites*, ii. pp. 211–12; Fouché, *Mémoires*, i. pp. 364–6). He was for that very reason marginalized from any further discussions on the subject (see Pasquier, *Mémoires*, i. pp. 328–30).

70. Caulaincourt, *Memoirs*, ii. pp. 171, 185. .

71. *Corr.* xvii. n. 13776 (24 April 1808).

72. Esdaile, *Napoleon's Wars*, pp. 333–5, 344; Charles Esdaile, 'Deconstructing the French Wars: Napoleon as Anti-Strategist', *Journal of Strategic Studies*, 31 (2008), 539–40; Esdaile, *The Peninsular War*, 24–36.

73. According to Esdaile, *Napoleon's Wars*, p. 335.

74. *Corr.* xvi. nos. 13737 and 13738 (12 April 1808).

75. *Corr.* xvi. n. 13540 (8 February 1800); Desmond Gregory, *Sicily: The Insecure Base: A History of the British Occupation of Sicily, 1806–1815* (Rutherford, 1988), pp. 71–2; Gregory, *Napoleon's Italy*, pp. 102, 103.

76. The following figures are taken from Richard Glover, 'The French Fleet, 1807–1814: Britain's Problem; and Madison's Opportunity', *Journal of Modern History*, 39 (1967), 233–4.

77. Thomas Munch-Petersen, *Defying Napoleon: How Britain Bombarded Copenhagen and Seized the Danish Fleet in 1807* (London, 2007).

78. Jorgensen, *The Anglo-Swedish Alliance*, pp. 34–40.

79. Glover, 'The French Fleet', pp. 235–6, 238.

80. Glover, 'The French Fleet', p. 235 n. 8.

81. Lentz, *Savary*, pp. 193–200. Savary was also to smooth things over with Murat who was going to be passed over as King of Spain.

82. *Corr.* xvii. n. 13750 (16 April 1808). On the meeting at Bayonne see Lovett, *Napoleon and the Birth of Modern Spain*, i. pp. 110–20; Edouard Ducéré, *Napoléon à Bayonne: d'après les contemporains et des documents inédits* (Paris, 1994), pp. 101–23.

83. Ducéré, *Napoléon à Bayonne*, pp. 50–4.

84. Avrillion, *Mémoires*, pp. 221, 225.

85. *Corr.* xvii. n. 13772 (22 April 1808). For the following see Hilt, *The Troubled Trinity*, pp. 235–42; Jean-François Labourdette, 'Le voyage de Ferdinand VII à Bayonne: la controverse entre Escoïquiz et Cevallos', in Pontet, *Napoléon, Bayonne et l'Espagne*, pp. 119–24.

86. Cited in Lovett, *Napoleon and the Birth of Modern Spain*, i. pp. 114–15.

87. Louis-François-Joseph Bausset, *Mémoires anecdotiques sur l'intérieur du palais et sur quelques évènemens de l'Empire depuis 1805 jusqu'au 1er mai 1814 pour servir à l'histoire de Napoléon*, 2 vols (Paris, 1828), i. p. 229.

88. On this scene see Savary, *Mémoires*, ii. pp. 382–4.

89. Lovett, *Napoleon and the Birth of Modern Spain*, i. p. 118; John Lawrence Tone, *The Fatal Knot: The Guerrilla War in Navarre and the Defeat of Napoleon in Spain* (Chapel Hill, 1994), p. 48.

90. Lecestre (ed.), *Lettres inédites*, i. pp. 192–3 (9 May 1808); Waresquiel, *Talleyrand*, pp. 384–6.

91. Jean-Claude Drouin, 'L'image des Entrevues de Bayonne chez quelques témoins et historiens aux XIXe siècle: de Cevallos à Savine 1808–1908', in Pontet, *Napoléon, Bayonne et l'Espagne*, pp. 144–52.

92. Lecestre (ed.), *Lettres inédites*, i. pp. 188–9 (30 April 1808). Méneval, *Mémoires*, ii. p. 164, thinks that Napoleon was undecided before leaving Paris for Bayonne.

93. Geoffroy de Grandmaison, *L'Espagne et Napoléon*, 3 vols (Paris, 1908–31), i. pp. iii–v; Gotteri, *Napoléon*, p. 135, for example.

94. Suggests Jean-René Aymes, 'Napoléon et Joseph Bonaparte sous le regards des Espagnols', 1 (1998), 28.

95. *Corr.* xvii. n. 13899 (16 May 1808).

96. Bausset, *Mémoires anecdotiques*, i. pp. 232–3; Tone, *The Fatal Knot*, pp. 49–50; Jean-Marc Lafon, 'Occupation, pacification et résistance en Andalousie', *Revue historique des armées*, 210 (1998), 14; and Jean-Marc Lafon, 'Del Dos de Mayo madrileño a los pontones de Cádiz: violencias francesas y españolas a principios de la Guerra de la Independencia', in F. Acosta Ramírez and M. Ruiz Jiménez (eds), *Bailén 1808–2008: Bailén: su impacto en la nueva Europa del XIX y su proyección futura* (Jaén, 2009), pp. 105–28.

97. John Lawrence Tone, 'A Dangerous Amazon: Agustina Zaragoza and the Spanish Revolutionary War, 1808–1814', *European History Quarterly*, 37 (2007), 552; and John Lawrence Tone, 'Spanish Women in the Resistance to Napoleon', in Victoria Lorée Enders and Pamela Beth (eds), *Constructing Spanish Womanhood: Female Identity in Modern Spain* (Albany, NY, 1999), pp. 259–82.

98. For a brief overview see Hocquellet, *Résistance et révolution*, pp. 65–96; Tone, *The Fatal Knot*, pp. 51–7; Charles Esdaile, *Peninsular Eyewitnesses: The Experience of War in Spain and Portugal 1808–1813* (Barnsley, 2008), pp. 1–44. The Spanish reaction to invasion was not 'nationalist', but rather a series of particularistic responses, closely linked to regional structures. For a more detailed study see Ronald Fraser, *Napoleon's Cursed War: Spanish Popular Resistance in the Peninsular War, 1808–1814* (London, 2008).

99. Ordre du Jour, AN 1609 (2), Affaires d'Espagnes (2 May 1808); Lentz, *Nouvelle histoire du Premier Empire*, i. p. 401.

100. Brégeon, *Napoléon et la guerre d'Espagne*, p. 98. Tone, *The Fatal Knot*, pp. 50 and 198 n. 23, places the figure at anywhere between 400 and 1,200.

101. Philippe Gille, *Mémoires d'un conscrit de 1808* (Paris, 1892), pp. 70–2; Bausset, *Mémoires anecdotiques*, i. pp. 234–6; François, *Journal*, pp. 558–61; Jean-Pierre Bois, *Bugeaud* (Paris, 1997), pp. 76–7.

102. Hughes, *Goya*, p. 310.

103. *Moniteur universel*, 11 May 1808; and Napoleon to Fouché, in Lecestre (ed.), *Lettres inédites*, i. p. 194 (21 May 1808).

104. *Moniteur universel*, 14 July 1808 and 5 February 1810.

105. *Jugement sur les affaires d'Espagne tel que le portera lu postérité, par un Espagnol impartial* (n.p., 1808), in AN AFIV 1610 (3), Affaires d'Espagne, Pamphlets sur le changement de dynastie (1808).

106. Metternich reported that the Parisian public was in a sort of stupor over Bayonne (Constantin de Grunwald (ed.), 'La fin d'une ambassade, Metternich', *Revue de Paris*, 19–20 (1937), p. 505 (17 May 1808)). Madelin, *Histoire du Consulat et de l'Empire*, 16 vols (Paris, 1937–54), vii. pp. 142–5.

107. Waresquiel, *Talleyrand*, pp. 378–84.

108. Marbot, *Mémoires*, ii. p. 43.

109. See, for example, *Histoire de Napoléon Buonaparte, depuis sa naissance, en 1769, jusqu'à sa translation à l'île Sainte-Hélène, en 1815*, 4 vols (Paris, 1817–18), iii. pp. 220–1.

110. See, for example, Metternich, *Mémoires*, ii. pp. 202–8 (17 August 1808); and Talleyrand's comments to him in Grunwald (ed.), 'La fin d'une ambassade', 821 (23 August 1808).

111. See, for example, Hauterive, *La police secrète du premier Empire*, iv. p. 228 (11 June 1808).

112. Noël, *Souvenirs militaires*, p. 87.

113. Narcisse Faucheur, *Souvenirs de campagnes du sergent Faucheur* (Paris, 2004), pp. 119–20.

114. Forrest, *Napoleon's Men*, pp. 123–4.

115. Jean-Baptiste Jolyet, 'Episode des guerres de Catalogne (1808–1812)', *Revue des études napoléoniennes*, 16 (July 1919), 182–214.

116. An entry taken from the *Recueil des actions héroïques et civiques des républicains français* (Paris, an II), n. 1, pp. 17–18.

117. Cited in Cabanis, *Le sacre de Napoléon*, p. 229.

118. Jean-Henry Rattier, 'Campagne d'Italie (1796): notes d'un sergent major', *Revue retrospective. Recueil de pièces intéressantes*, xx (1894), pp. 322–3 (26 June 1810). Rattier would later die on the retreat from Moscow.

119. Maurice de Tascher, *Journal de campagne, 1806–1813* (Paris, 2008), pp. 129, 118–19 (13 August and 28 July 1808). On the atrocities committed by imperial troops in Italy and in Spain see Philip Dwyer, '"It Still Makes Me Shudder": Memories of Massacres and Atrocities during the Revolutionary and Napoleonic Wars', *War in History*, 16 (2009), 381–405.

120. The best work in English on the war and the guerrilla in Spain is Charles Esdaile, *Fighting Napoleon: Guerrillas, Bandits and Adventurers in Spain, 1808–1814* (New Haven, 2004). There is a debate about the effectiveness of the guerrilla movement. Esdaile argues that the guerrillas did more harm than good for the allies, while the French historian, Hocquellet, *Résistance et révolution durant l'occupation napoléonienne en Espagne*, argues that without the guerrillas Spain would quickly have succumbed. See also Michael Broers, *Napoleon's Other War: Bandits, Rebels and their Pursuers in the Age of Revolutions* (Oxford, 2010), pp. 105–27.

121. Jean-Philippe Luis, 'Violences politiques et conciliations en Espagne', in Jean-Claude Caron, Frédéric Chauvaud, Emmanuel Fureix and Jean-Noël Luc (eds), *Entre violence et conciliation: la résolution des conflits sociopolitiques en Europe au XIXe siècle* (Rennes, 2008), p. 288.

122. 'Mémoires du capitaine de frégate Pierre Baste', in *Mémoires sur la campagne d'Andalousie et la captivité qui s'en suivit* (Paris, 1998), pp. 92–4.

123. Laforest to Champagny in, Geoffroy de Grandmaison (ed.), *Correspondance du comte de La Forest, ambassadeur de France en Espagne, 1808–1813*, 7 vols (Paris, 1905–13), i. p. 119 (25 June 1808).

124. Caulaincourt, *Mémoirs*, i. p. 273.

125. Georges Lefebvre, *Napoléon* (Paris, 1969), p. 320.

126. *Corr.* xvii. n. 13888 (15 May 1808).

127. Joseph received many other epithets including, 'rey intruso', 'rey errante', 'rey trashumante', 'rey Sin Tierra', 'rey de copas', as well as a number of nicknames that played on the word 'Pepe', such as 'Pepe José', 'Tío Pepe', and 'rey Pepino'. See Gérard Dufour, 'Le roi philosophe', in Emilio La Parra López (ed.), *Actores de la Guerra de la Independencia: dossier des mélanges de la Casa de Velasquez*, nouvelle série, 38:1 (2008), 53–70.

128. Examples of these pamphlets can be found in AN AFIV 1610 (3); Esdaile, *Fighting Napoleon*, pp. 63–4. A selection of this patriotic literature appears in Sabino Delgado (ed.), *Guerra de la Independencia* (Madrid, 1979). See also Emilio La Parra López, 'Les pamphlets dans la guerre d'Espagne: discours des humbles ou discours vers les humbles?', in Jens Ivo Engels, Frédéric Monier and Natalie Petiteau (eds), *La politique vue d'en bas: pratiques privées et débats publics, 19e–20e siècles* (Paris, 2011), pp. 47–61.

129. Aymes, 'Napoléon et Joseph Bonaparte sous le regards des Espagnols', 30–1.

130. Miot de Mélito, *Mémoires*, iii. pp. 12–13; Haegele, *Napoléon et Joseph Bonaparte*, pp. 344–5.

131. Lentz, *Nouvelle histoire du Premier Empire*, i. p. 409.

132. Du Casse, *Mémoires du roi Joseph*, iv. p. 395 (31 July 1808).

133. Jean-Baptiste Nompère Champagny, *Souvenirs de M. de Champagny, duc de Cadore* (Paris, 1846) p. 103.
134. Chandler, *Campaigns of Napoleon*, p. 617, and on Bailén pp. 612–22.
135. On their fate see Gunther E. Rothenberg, 'The Age of Napoleon', in Michael Howard, George J. Andreopoulos and Mark R. Shulman (eds), *The Laws of War: Constraints on Warfare in the Western World* (New Haven, 1994), pp. 90–1; Georges Pariset, 'Les captifs de Bailén', *Revue des études napoléoniennes*, 32 (1931), 209–29; Léonce Bernard, *Les prisonniers de guerre du Premier Empire* (Paris, 2000), pp. 79–83.
136. Tascher, *Journal de campagne*, pp. 122–31; 'Rapport du Capitaine Gerdy', in *Mémoires sur la campagne d'Andalousie*, pp. 139, 145; Lorédan Larchey, *Les Suites d'une capitulation. Relations des captifs de Baylen et de la glorieuse retraite du 116e régiment* (Paris, 1884), pp. 7–8, 26–8, 108; Denis Smith, *The Prisoners of Cabrera: Napoleon's Forgotten Soldiers, 1809–1814* (London, 2001), p. 21.
137. Smith, *The Prisoners of Cabrera*, pp. 61–104.
138. Jean-René Aymes, 'La guerre d'Espagne dans la presse impériale (1808–1814)', *Annales historiques de la Révolution française*, 336 (2004), 131–2.
139. Ibbeken, *Preussen 1807–1813*, pp. 116–45.
140. Martin, *Romantics, Reformers, Reactionaries*, p. 50.
141. Metternich, *Mémoires*, ii. pp. 228–60.
142. Du Casse, *Mémoires du roi Joseph*, iv. p. 389 (28 July 1808).
143. Dumas, *Souvenirs*, iii. pp. 321–2.

## CRUCIBLE, 1808–1811

### *14: The Desolate Father*

1. Talleyrand, *Mémoires*, i. p. 408.
2. *Corr.* xvii. n. 14318 (14 September 1808); Boudon, *Le roi Jérôme*, p. 326.
3. Emile Dard, *Napoléon et Talleyrand* (Paris, 1935), p. 181; Lacour-Gayet, *Talleyrand*, ii. p. 239; Schroeder, *Transformation of Europe*, p. 337.
4. Eugène Forgues (ed.), *Mémoires et relations politiques du baron de Vitrolles*, 3 vols (Paris, 1884), i. pp. 239–40.
5. Louise de Prusse, princesse Antoine Radziwill, *Quarante-cinq années de ma vie (1770 à 1815)* (Paris, 1911), p. 297.
6. Esdaile, *Napoleon's Wars*, p. 386; Werner Greiling, *Napoleon in Thüringen: Wirkung, Wahrnehmung, Erinnerung* (Erfurt, 2006), pp. 109–18.
7. Caulaincourt, *Memoirs*, i. pp. 83–4.
8. Barbe Nikolaévna, comtesse Golovin, *Souvenirs de la comtesse Golovine, née princesse Galitzine, 1766–1821* (Paris, 1910), p. 391; Caulaincourt, *Memoirs*, i. pp. 65–6.
9. Caulaincourt, *Memoirs*, i. pp. 64–5. The Bavarian king was not at first invited either, which greatly worried the court at Munich. It was interpreted, rightly, as a sign that Napoleon was feeling a little cool towards Maximilian Joseph. The king came in the end but against his will. See Matthias Stickler, 'Erfurt als Wende – Bayern und Württemberg und das Scheitern der Pläne Napoleons I. für einen Ausbau der Rheinbundverfassung', in Rudolf Benl (ed.), *Der Erfurter Fürstenkongreß 1808: Hintergründe, Ablauf, Wirkung* (Erfurt, 2008), p. 295.
10. Claus Scharf, 'Rußlands Politik im Bündnis von Tilsit und das Erfurter Gipfeltreffen von 1808', in Benl (ed.), *Der Erfurter Fürstenkongreß*, pp. 181–2.
11. Talleyrand, *Mémoires*, i. p. 414; Vandal, *Napoléon et Alexandre*, i. pp. 411–13; Friedrich von Müller, *Souvenirs des années de guerre: 1806–1813* (Paris, 1992), p. 155; Claudia Ulbrich, 'Die französische Geheimpolizei auf dem Erfurter Fürstenkongreß', in Benl (ed.), *Der Erfurter Fürstenkongreß*, p. 311.
12. Vandal, *Napoléon et Alexandre*, i. pp. 416–18.

13. On the meeting at Erfurt see René Bittard des Portes, 'Les préliminaires de l'entrevue d'Erfurt (1808)', *Revue d'histoire diplomatique*, 4 (1890), 94–144; Vandal, *Napoléon et Alexandre*, i. pp. 397–497; Alexander C. Niven, *Napoleon and Alexander I: A Study in Franco-Russian Relations 1807–1812* (Washington, DC, 1982), pp. 19–24; the essays in Benl (ed.), *Der Erfurter Fürstenkongreß*; and Rey, *Alexandre Ier*, pp. 252–9.

14. Madeleine and Francis Ambrière, *Talma ou L'histoire au théâtre* (Paris, 2007), p. 430.

15. Maistre, *Mémoires politiques et correspondance diplomatique*, pp. 307–8; Golovin, *Souvenirs*, p. 391; Martin, *Romantics, Reformers, Reactionaries*, pp. 50–1; Scharf, 'Rußlands Politik', pp. 218–19; Marie Martin, *Maria Féodorovna en son temps (1759–1828): contribution à l'histoire de la Russie et de l'Europe* (Paris, 2003), p. 164.

16. Catherine to Alexander (25 June 1807), in Nicolaï Mikaïlovich (ed.), *Correspondance de l'empereur Alexandre Ier avec sa soeur la grande-duchesse Catherine, princesse d'Oldenbourg, puis reine de Wurtemberg, 1805–1818* (St Petersburg, 1910), p. 19.

17. Tourtier-Bonazzi, *Lettres d'amour à Joséphine*, p. 313 (October 1808).

18. The following is based on Scharf, 'Rußlands Politik', pp. 211–21.

19. In 1807, Napoleon signed the Convention of Finckenstein with Shah Fath Ali of Persia, giving him a Persian base for an attack on India. General Gardane was sent to Tehran with a large staff to prepare for the operation. See Driault, *La politique orientale de Napoléon*, pp. 392–8; Vernon J. Puryear, *Napoleon and the Dardanelles* (Berkeley, 1951); Schroeder, *Transformation of European Politics*, pp. 335–7.

20. Vandal, *Napoléon et Alexandre*, i. pp. 220–40; Michel Kerautret, 'Frankreich und der Fürstenkongreß', in Benl (ed.), *Der Erfurter Fürstenkongreß*, pp. 149–54.

21. Talleyrand, *Mémoires*, i. p. 424.

22. Metternich, *Mémoires*, ii. p. 248. Waresquiel, *Talleyrand*, p. 390, is one of many who takes the lines at face value.

23. See Quentin Skinner, *Foundations of Modern Political Thought*, 2 vols (Cambridge, 1978), ii. pp. 354–6.

24. Metternich, *Mémoires*, ii. pp. 292, 247–9.

25. Caulaincourt, *Memoirs*, i. p. 88. On Napoleon's hat see Kirstin Buchinger, '*Chapeau!* Napoleons Hut. Ein europäisches imago agens', in Kirstin Buchinger, Claire Gantet and Jakob Vogel (eds), *Europäische Erinnerungsräume: Zirkulationen zwischen Frankreich, Deutschland und Europa* (Frankfurt, 2009), pp. 296–321; and Kirstin Buchinger, '*Chapeau!* – Der Hut als Symbol für Napoleon', in Rüdiger Schmidt and Hans-Ulrich Thamer (eds), *Die Konstruktion von Tradition: Inszenierung und Propaganda napoleonischer Herrschaft (1799–1815)* (Göttingen, 2010), pp. 235–64.

26. Alexander to Catherine (26 September 1808), in Mikaïlovich (ed.), *Correspondance de l'empereur Alexandre Ier avec sa soeur la grande-duchesse Catherine*, p. 20.

27. Martin, *Maria Féodorovna*, pp. 164–5; Rey, *Alexandre Ier*, p. 253.

28. Caulaincourt, *Memoirs*, i. p. 84; Vandal, *Napoléon et Alexandre*, i. pp. 441, 456–7; Herbert F. Collins, *Talma: A Biography of an Actor* (London, 1964), pp. 193–9.

29. Constant, *Mémoires*, iv. pp. 77–8; Georges Mauguin, *Napoléon et la superstition: anecdotes et curiosités* (Rodez, 1946), p. 91.

30. Vandal, *Napoléon et Alexandre*, i. p. 489.

31. Vandal, *Napoléon et Alexandre*, i. pp. 477–97.

32. Nesselrode, *Lettres et papiers*, i. pp. 66 and 69–70.

33. Nesselrode to Alexander, 17 April and 9 May 1811, in Nesselrode, *Lettres et papiers*, iii. pp. 338, 346.

34. Hortense de Beauharnais, *Mémoires de la Reine Hortense, publiés par le prince Napoléon*, 2 vols (Paris, 1927), ii. pp. 28–30; Pasquier, *Mémoires*, i. p. 351; Jacques-Claude Beugnot, *Mémoires du comte Beugnot, ancien ministre (1783–1815)*, 2 vols (Paris, 1866), i. p. 346; Rémusat, *Mémoires*, iii. pp. 331, 362–3; Rémusat, *Mémoires de ma vie*, i. p. 135; Etienne Lamy (ed.), *Mémoires de Aimée de Coigny* (Paris, 1902), pp. 193, 209–12.

35. Lamy (ed.), *Mémoires de Aimée de Coigny*, p. 239.

36. There are numerous expressions of the desire for peace from about 1808 onwards. See Mollien, *Mémoires*, iii. pp. 50–1; Cambacérès, *Lettres inédites à Napoléon*, ii. p. 1131; Caulaincourt, *Memoirs*, iii. pp. 113–14.

37. Metternich, *Mémoires*, ii. pp. 284–5.

38. 'Mandement pour les victoires de Thann, d'Eckmulh et de Ratisbonne', in Etienne Antoine de Boulogne, *Mandemens et instructions pastorales de M. de Boulogne évêque de Troyes. Suivis de divers morceaux oratoires* (Paris, 1827), p. 32.

39. Cited in Bertaud, *Quand les enfants parlaient de gloire*, p. 235.

40. Jean Tulard, 'Le rapprochement de Fouché et de Talleyrand en 1808', in Pontet, *Napoléon, Bayonne et l'Espagne*, pp. 355–7.

41. Pasquier, *Mémoires*, i. pp. 353–4; Metternich, *Mémoires*, ii. pp. 294–5.

42. Alexis-François Artaud de Montor, *Histoire de la vie et des travaux politiques du comte d'Hauterive* (2nd edn, Paris, 1839), pp. 265–70.

43. Cambacérès, *Mémoires inédits*, i. n. 1, p. 533; Tulard, *Fouché*, pp. 127–9; Boudon, *Histoire du Consulat et l'Empire*, p. 63.

44. Nesselrode, *Lettres et papiers*, ii. p. 71.

45. Dard, *Napoléon et Talleyrand*, p. 155; Schroeder, *Transformation of European Politics*, p. 316; Tulard, *Fouché*, pp. 219–28; Waresquiel, *Talleyrand*, p. 398.

46. Madelin, *Fouché*, ii. pp. 80–1; Lentz, *Nouvelle histoire du Premier Empire*, i. pp. 429–30.

47. In the *Moniteur universel*, the *Journal de Paris* and the *Journal de l'Empire*, 2 April 1807. On the competition see Pierre Lelièvre, '*Napoléon sur le champ de bataille d'Eylau* par A.-J. Gros: Précisions sur les conditions de la commande', *Bulletin de la Société de l'histoire de l'art français* (1955), 51–5; Herbert, 'Baron Gros's Napoleon', p. 61; Prendergast, *Napoleon and History Painting*, pp. 152–85.

48. Schlenoff, 'Baron Gros and Napoleon's Egyptian Campaign', p. 154.

49. The following is based on: Gerstein, 'Le regard consolateur', pp. 321–31; John Walker McCoubrey, 'Gros' *Battle of Eylau* and Roman Imperial Art', *Art Bulletin*, 43 (1961), 135–52; Sara Lichtenstein, 'The Baron Gros and Raphael', *Art Bulletin*, 60 (1978), 126–38, here 131 and 133; Morse, 'A Revaluation', pp. 134–50; Jean-Paul Kauffmann, *La chambre noire de Longwood: le voyage à Sainte-Hélène* (Paris, 1997); O'Brien, *After the Revolution*, pp. 154–74.

50. Morse, 'A Revaluation', pp. 134–5.

51. Prendergast, *Napoleon and History Painting*, p. 132.

52. In Dupuy, Le Masne de Chermont and Williamson (eds), *Vivant Denon*, i. 1647.

53. David O'Brien, 'Propaganda and the Republic of the Arts in Antoine-Jean Gros's *Napoleon Visiting the Battlefield of Eylau the Morning after the Battle*', *French Historical Studies*, 26 (2003), 281–314, here 282 and 292.

54. *Observations sur le Salon de l'an 1808* (Paris, 1808), pp. 8 and 9.

55. Norman Bryson, 'Representing the Real: Gros' Paintings of Napoleon', *History of the Human Sciences*, 1 (1988), 98.

56. Porterfield, *The Allure of Empire*, pp. 53–61.

57. For some of the contemporary comments see Irène Perret, 'Réception critique de *Napoléon sur le champ de bataille d'Eylau* d'Antoine-Jean Gros sous le premier empire', *Napoleonica. La Revue*, 4:1 (2009), 50–61.

58. Edgar Munhall, 'Portraits of Napoleon', *Yale French Studies*, 26 (1960), 8, 9.

59. O'Brien, 'Propaganda and the Republic of the Arts', 302.

60. Arsène Alexandre, *Histoire de la peinture militaire en France* (Paris, 1889), pp. 151–2.

61. Prendergast, *Napoleon and History Painting*, p. 181.

62. Prendergast, *Napoleon and History Painting*, p. 163.

63. Charles-Paul Landon, *Salon de 1810. Recueil de pièces choisies parmi les ouvrages exposés au Louvre le 5 novembre 1810* (Paris, 1810), p. 78.

64. *Journal des arts, des sciences, et de littérature*, 18 October 1808, 397.

65. Lindsay, 'Mummies and Tombs', 489–90; Bruno Foucart, 'Les "Salons" sous le Consulat et les diverses représentations de Bonaparte', *Revue de l'Institut Napoléon*, 111 (1969), 118.

66. *Gazette de France*, 30 brumaire an VIII (21 November 1804).

67. For example, the story of Prince Hatzfeld's wife pleading for his life in 1806 in Louis-Guillaume de Puybusque, *Lettres sur la guerre de Russie en 1812, sur la ville de St. Petersbourg, les moeurs et les usages des habitans de la Russie et de Pologne* (Paris, 1816), pp. 18–19 (6 June 1812). See pp. 291–2 in this volume.

68. On the opera see David Chaillou, *Napoléon et l'Opéra: la politique sur la scène, 1810–1815* (Paris, 2004).

69. Yveline Cantarel-Besson, 'Les salons de peintures', in Yveline Cantarel-Besson, Claire Constans and Bruno Foucart (eds), *Napoleon: images et histoire, peintures du château de Versailles, 1789–1815* (Paris, 2001), p. 100; and the series of articles in *Les clémences de Napoléon: l'image au service du mythe* (Paris, 2004); Boime, *Art in an Age of Bonapartism*, ii. pp. 29–30.

70. *Moniteur universel*, 7 November 1806.

71. Bruno Foucart, 'Les clémences de Napoléon et leurs images: art et politique', in *Les clémences de Napoléon*, pp. 26–7.

72. *Corr.* xiii. n. 11191 (6 November 1806); Jean Rapp, *Mémoires du général Rapp, aide-de-camp de Napoléon* (Paris, 1823), pp. 84–9; Savary, *Mémoires*, ii. pp. 314–18; Jacques-Olivier Boudon, 'Les clémences de Napoléon: une arme au service du pouvoir', in *Les clémences de Napoléon*, pp. 14–15.

73. Huet, 'Napoleon I: A New Augustus?', p. 68. The plea of the wife of Prince Hatzfeld was the subject of at least three other paintings, including Louis Lafitte at the Salon of 1808; Pierre Antoine Vafflard at the same Salon; and Charles Boulanger de Boisfremont at the Salon of 1810 (Robert Rosenblum, *Transformations in Late Eighteenth Century Art* (Princeton, 1967), pp. 99–100).

74. *Journal de Paris*, 6 November 1805. The account was reprinted in several other newspapers. Porterfield and Siegfried, *Staging Empire*, pp. 77–8.

75. O'Brien, *After the Revolution*, p. 130.

76. Porterfield, *The Allure of Empire*, p. 76; Huet, 'Napoleon I: A New Augustus?', p. 67.

77. Porterfield, *The Allure of Empire*, pp. 68–74.

78. See Dwyer, *Napoleon: The Path to Power*, pp. 401–7.

79. Gerstein, 'Le regard consolateur du grand homme', pp. 321–31.

80. Cabanis, *La Presse*, pp. 278–81.

81. On Napoleon's intervention in Spain see Chandler, *Campaigns of Napoleon*, pp. 625–58; Gates, *The Spanish Ulcer*, pp. 94–105.

82. Esdaile, *Peninsular Eyewitnesses*, pp. 50–61.

83. Lecestre (ed.), *Lettres inédites*, i. p. 163 (11 March 1808); and pp. 268–9 (12 January 1809).

84. Alphonse-Henri, marquis d'Hautpoul, *Mémoires du général marquis Alphonse d'Hautpoul* (Paris, 1906), pp. 63–4; Marbot, *Mémoires*, ii. p. 69.

85. Hautpoul, *Mémoires*, pp. 63–4.

86. Gaspard de Clermont-Tonnerre, *L'expédition d'Espagne: 1808–1810* (Paris, 1983), pp. 175–6; Nicole Gotteri, *Soult: maréchal d'Empire et homme d'Etat* (Besançon, 2000), p. 274.

87. Miot de Mélito, *Mémoires*, iii. pp. 36–7.

88. Esprit Victor Elisabeth Boniface Castellane, *Journal du maréchal Castellane, 1804–1862*, 5 vols (Paris, 1895–7), i. p. 33.

89. *Corr.* xviii. nos. 14470, 144473, 14499 (13, 14 and 20 November 1808).

90. Cited in Charles Oman, *A History of the Peninsular War*, 7 vols (Oxford, 1902–30), i. p. 467.

91. Oman, *A History of the Peninsular War*, i. pp. 469–70.

92. Jean-François Bourgoing, *Nouveau Voyage en Espagne, ou Tableau de l'état actuel de cette monarchie*, 3 vols (Paris, 1789), i. pp. 209–10, 233–6. For a description of Spain and Madrid in this time see Lovett, *Napoleon and the Birth of Modern Spain*, i. pp. 47–84.

93. Fierro, *La vie des Parisiens sous Napoléon*, p. 32; Jacques Soubeyroux, *Paupérisme et rapports sociaux à Madrid au XVIIIe siècle*, 2 vols (Paris, 1978), i. chs 1–2.

94. *Moniteur universel*, 10 April, and 1 and 8 April 1808; Lejeune, *Mémoires*, p. 77.

95. *Corr.* xviii. nos. 14526, 14527, 14528, 14429, 14554 (4 and 12 December 1808); Oman, *A History of the Peninsular War*, i. pp. 473–80.

96. Ilse Hempel Lipschutz, *Spanish Painting and the French Romantics* (Cambridge, Mass., 1972), pp. 27–56; Jean-Joël Brégeon, 'Les appropriations d'oeuvres d'art par les français au Portugal et en Espagne, de 1807 à 1813; les suites muséales et dans les collections', in Pontet, *Napoléon, Bayonne et l'Espagne*, pp. 377–88.

97. Boulart, *Mémoires militaires*, pp. 193–4.

98. On Soult see Hempel Lipschutz, *Spanish Painting*, pp. 31, 33, 35–9. For other examples see Véronique Gerard-Powell, 'Les prises d'oeuvres d'art en Espagne pendant l'occupation napoléonienne: diversité des responsables, diversité des choix', in Pontet, *Napoléon, Bayonne et l'Espagne*, pp. 392–8.

99. Boudon, 'Les clémences de Napoléon', p. 16, and for what follows. See also Méneval, *Mémoires*, ii. p. 217; Lejeune, *Mémoires*, p. 164.

100. Dumas, *Souvenirs*, iii. p. 335.

101. Aymar-Olivier Le Harivel de Gonneville, *Souvenirs militaires du colonel de Gonneville* (Paris, 1875), p. 106.

102. Tourtier-Bonazzi, *Lettres d'amour à Joséphine*, pp. 323–4 (31 December 1808).

103. *Corr.* xviii. nos. 14716, 14717 (15 January 1809).

104. Cambacérès, *Mémoires inédites*, ii. p. 250; Lentz, *Nouvelle histoire du Premier Empire*, i. pp. 431–2.

105. *Corr.* xviii. n. 14716 (15 January 1809).

106. *Corr.* xviii. n. 14731 (16 January 1809).

107. *Corr.* xviii. n. 14684 (11 January 1809).

108. *Corr.* xviii. n. 14717 (15 January 1809).

109. Dumas, *Souvenirs*, iii. p. 338.

110. Thiébault, *Mémoires*, iv. p. 280.

111. Anonymous letter to Davout in Louis Nicolas Davout, *Correspondance du maréchal Davout, prince d'Eckmühl*, 4 vols (Paris, 1885), ii. pp. 372–4 (20 January 1809).

112. Cambacérès, *Mémoires inédites*, ii. p. 250.

113. Hauterive, *La police secrète du premier Empire*, iv. p. 521; Anatole de Montesquiou, *Souvenirs sur la Révolution, l'Empire, la Restauration et le règne de Louis-Philippe* (Paris, 1961), pp. 154–6, who makes no mention of the insult; Mathieu Couty, 'Quand Napoléon prononça la disgrace de Talleyrand', *Historia*, 506 (February 1989), 68–77; Waresquiel, *Talleyrand*, pp. 400–1.

114. Most of the accounts of this episode are second hand: Pasquier, *Mémoires*, i, pp. 357–8; Mollien, *Mémoires*, ii, pp. 333–43; Forgues (ed.), *Mémoires de Vitrolles*, i. pp. 287–8; Méneval, *Mémoires*, ii. pp. 227–9.

115. See Waresquiel, *Talleyrand*, p. 695 n. 5, for a discussion of the sources on this question.

116. Bourrienne, *Mémoires*, ii. p. 415.

117. Jean-Claude Courtine and Claudine Haroche, *Histoire du visage: exprimer et taire ses émotions: du XVIe au début du XIXe siècle* (Paris, 1994), pp. 238, 243–4; and the preface by Chantal Thomas in Madame de Genlis, *De l'esprit des étiquettes de l'ancienne cour et des usages du monde de ce temps* (Paris, 1996), pp. 8–10, 14.

118. Smith, 'No More Language Games', 1433.

119. The transformation was completed by 1813. See Tour du Pin, *Journal d'une femme de cinquante ans, 1778–1815*, pp. 337–9, in which she speaks of Talleyrand's hatred and bitterness towards Napoleon; and Hortense, *Mémoires*, ii. p. 173.

120. Cambacérès, *Mémoires inédits*, ii. p. 251.

121. Mansel, *The Eagle in Splendour*, pp. 112, 121.

122. Coignet, *Note-Books*, p. 136. See also Rémusat, *Mémoires*, ii. p. 338.

123. François-Yves Besnard, *Souvenirs d'un nonagénaire*, 2 vols (Paris, 1880), ii. pp. 197–8; Remacle, *Relations secrètes*, pp. 44–5.

124. He admitted to Fain that his anger was simulated, 'Otherwise they would come and bite

me in the hand'. C. W. Crawley (ed.), *The New Cambridge Modern History*, vol. ix: *War and Peace in an Age of Upheaval, 1793–1830* (Cambridge, 1965), p. 317; Annie Jourdan, 'La Hollande en tant qu'"objet de désir" et le roi Louis, fondateur d'une monarchie nationale', in Jourdan (ed.), *Louis Bonaparte*, pp. 9–30, here p. 22.

125. Eynard, *Journal*, i. p. 138.

126. Bausset, *Mémoires anecdotiques*, i. p. 14; Agathon-Jean-François, baron Fain, *Mémoires du baron Fain, premier secrétaire du cabinet de l'empereur* (Paris, 1908), pp. 202–3; Branda, *Napoléon et ses hommes*, p. 271.

## *15: The Tide Turns*

1. Oskar Criste, *Erzherzog Karl von Österreich*, 2 vols (Vienna and Leipzig, 1912), ii. p. 436; Ingrao, *The Habsburg Monarchy*, p. 234; and James Allen Vann, 'Habsburg Policy and the Austrian War of 1809', *Central European History*, 7:4 (1974), 305.
2. On how he did this see Vann, 'Habsburg Policy', 300–4.
3. Vann, 'Habsburg Policy', 307.
4. See, for example, Metternich, *Mémoires*, ii. pp. 214–15 (26 August 1808); Grunwald (ed.), 'Les débuts diplomatiques de Metternich à Paris', 503–5, 512, 518–19; Grunwald (ed.), 'La fin d'une ambassade, Metternich', 840–1, 846 (20 January and 10 April 1809); Manfred Botzenhart, *Metternichs Pariser Botschafterzeit* (Münster, 1967), pp. 88–95; Kraehe, *Metternich's German Policy*, i. pp. 85–6; Alan Sked, *Metternich and Austria: An Evaluation* (Basingstoke, 2008), pp. 35–42.
5. Metternich, *Mémoires*, ii. pp. 289–90, 290–2, 292–5, 296–9 (3, 11, 18 and 25 April 1809); Grunwald (ed.), 'Les débuts diplomatiques de Metternich à Paris', 525.
6. Metternich, *Mémoires*, ii. p. 170 (27 April 1808); Kraehe, *Metternich's German Policy*, i. pp. 63–4.
7. Grunwald (ed.), 'La fin d'une ambassade', 839 (11 January 1809).
8. Text in Beer, *Zehn Jahre österreichischer Politik*, pp. 516–35; Botzenhart, *Metternichs Pariser Botschafterzeit*, pp. 279–84; Vann, 'Habsburg Policy', 309. Metternich's role in the preparations for war is unclear. Kraehe, *Metternich's German Policy*, i. p. 65, argues that he was an intimate of the war party; Botzenhart, *Metternichs Pariser Botschafterzeit*, pp. 262–4, 270–84, argues that throughout the autumn of 1808 Metternich was against war with France, but that his reports about the internal divisions at the court of Paris strengthened the hand of the war party.
9. Vann, 'Habsburg Policy', 305.
10. *Corr.* xxvii. n. 14380 (14 October 1808). He supposedly told Jérôme in the spring of 1809 that the Austrian Emperor would cease to reign within two months (Grunwald (ed.), 'La fin d'une ambassade', 485).
11. Vann, 'Habsburg Policy', 305; Gunther E. Rothenberg, *Napoleon's Great Adversary: Archduke Charles and the Austrian Army, 1792–1814* (Staplehurst, 1995), pp. 160–1. It would appear that Charles was not in favour of war when it was declared, on 8 February 1809, on the grounds that the army was not ready. See Moritz von Angeli, *Erzherzog Carl als Feldherr und Heeresorganisator*, 5 vols (Vienna, 1896–8), iv. pp. 9–10; Criste, *Erzherzog Karl von Österreich*, ii. pp. 432–8; John H. Gill, *1809: Thunder on the Danube: Napoleon's Defeat of the Habsburgs*, 3 vols (London, 2008–10), i. pp. 35–6.
12. Ernst Zehetbauer, *Die Landwehr gegen Napoleon: Österreichs erste Miliz und der Nationalkrieg von 1809* (Vienna, 1999).
13. Gunther E. Rothenberg, *The Emperor's Last Victory: Napoleon and the Battle of Wagram* (London, 2005), pp. 43, 60–1.
14. Karl Wagner, 'Die *Wiener Zeitungen* und Zeitschriften der Jahre 1808 und 1809', *Archiv für Österreichische Geschichte*, 104 (1915), 254–348, 383–6; Walter C. Langsam, *The Napoleonic Wars and German Nationalism in Austria* (New York, 1930), p. 60.
15. On Stadion's propaganda campaign see Wagner, 'Die *Wiener Zeitungen* und Zeitschriften der Jahre 1808 und 1809', 197–400. On the pamphlet literature see Langsam, *The*

*Napoleonic Wars*, pp. 56–93; Helmut Hammer, *Oesterreichs Propaganda zum Feldzug 1809: ein Beitrag zur Geschichte der politischen Propaganda* (Munich, 1935); Jörg Echternkamp, *Der Aufstieg des deutschen Nationalismus (1770–1840)* (Frankfurt, 1998), pp. 195–203.

16. Elaborated on by Karen Hagemann, '"Be Proud and Firm, Citizens of Austria!" Patriotism and Masculinity in Texts of the "Political Romantics" Written during Austria's Anti-Napoleonic Wars', *German Studies Review*, 29 (2006), 41–62.

17. For this see Alan Sked, *Radetzky: Imperial Victor and Military Genius* (London, 2011), p. 25.

18. On the battle of Eckmühl see F. Loraine Petre, *Napoleon and the Archduke Charles: A History of the Franco-Austrian Campaign in the Valley of the Danube in 1809* (London, 1909), pp. 167–85.

19. Tourtier-Bonazzi, *Lettres d'amour à Joséphine*, p. 331 (6 May 1809). We do not know, in fact, where exactly on the foot Napoleon was wounded, nor which foot it was. In the large toe of the left foot, according to Ségur, *Histoire et mémoires*, iii. pp. 328–9.

20. Rothenberg, *The Emperor's Last Victory*, pp. 75–6.

21. Peter Csendes and Ferdinand Opll (eds), *Wien: Geschichte einer Stadt*, vol. iii: *Von 1790 bis zur Gegenwart* (Vienna, 2002), pp. 94–5.

22. Ouvrard, *1809: les Français à Vienne*, pp. 42–55.

23. Cited in Ingrao, *The Habsburg Monarchy*, p. 236; Eduard Wertheimer, 'Zur Geschichte Wiens im Jahre 1809. (Ein Beitrag zur Geschichte des Krieges von 1809.)', *Archiv für Österreichische Geschichte*, 74 (1889), 164–94.

24. For the following description of Vienna see John Bramsen, *Letters of a Prussian Traveller*, 2 vols (London, 1818), i. pp. 85–6, 93–9; Stendhal, *Correspondance de Stendhal: 1800–1842*, 3 vols (Paris, 1908), i. p. 343 (18 May 1809);

25. On the battle of Aspern-Essling see Petre, *Napoleon and the Archduke Charles*, pp. 274–98; Chandler, *Campaigns of Napoleon*, pp. 694–707; Parker, *Three Napoleonic Battles*, pp. 27–98; Gill, *1809: Thunder on the Danube*, ii. pp. 129–98.

26. F. Gunther Eyck, *Loyal Rebels: Andreas Hofer and the Tyrolean Uprising of 1809* (Lanham, Md, 1986); Martin p. Schennach, *Revolte in der Region: zur Tiroler Erhebung 1809* (Innsbruck, 2009). The uprising was not so much about hatred of the French as about hatred of Bavaria. Napoleon responded in his habitual manner, ordering General Lefebvre to wipe out six big villages as an example, threatening to put the whole of the Tyrol to fire and blood if the inhabitants did not surrender all their arms (Napoleon to Lefebvre, in Lecestre (ed.), *Lettres inédites*, i. p. 337 (30 July 1809)).

27. Altough both uprisings ended in failure, they were exploited by German nationalists. See Boudon, *Le roi Jérôme*, pp. 283–8; Sam A. Mustafa, *The Long Ride of Major von Schill: A Journey through German History and Memory* (Lanham, Md, 2009).

28. On the Tugendbund see Gérard Hertault and Abel Douay, *Franc-maçonnerie et sociétés secrètes contre Napoléon: naissance de la nation allemande* (Paris, 2005), pp. 109–75.

29. Schama, *Patriots and Liberators*, pp. 595–600. The significance of the expedition has been clearly demonstrated by Schroeder, *Transformation of European Politics*, pp. 360–1.

30. See, for example, Roger Dufraisse, 'La crise économique de 1810–1812 en pays annexé: l'exemple de la rive gauche du Rhin', *Francia*, 6 (1978), 407–40.

31. Chandler, *Campaigns of Napoleon*, p. 699.

32. Ouvrard, *1809: les Français à Vienne*, pp. 99–105.

33. Chandler, *Campaigns of Napoleon*, pp. 699–700; Parker, *Three Napoleonic Battles*, pp. 57–8.

34. Robert M. Epstein, 'Patterns of Change and Continuity in Nineteenth-Century Warfare', *Journal of Military History*, 56:3 (1992), 375–88. Figures in Charles-Gaspard-Louis Saski, *Campagne de 1809 en Allemagne et en Autriche*, 4 vols (Paris, 1899–1902), iii. p. 380 n. 1; Jean Thiry, *Wagram* (Paris, 1966), p. 140; Parker, *Three Napoleonic Battles*, p. 82.

35. Jean-Michel Chevalier, *Souvenirs des guerres napoléoniennes* (Paris, 1970), p. 108, who

claims he let out a long 'cry of pain' (*cri de douleur*); Chaptal, *Mes souvenirs sur Napoléon*, p. 252. See also Brian Joseph Martin, *Napoleonic Friendship: Military Fraternity, Intimacy, and Sexuality in Nineteenth-Century France* (Durham, NH, 2011), pp. 41–7

36. Dominique-Jean Larrey, *Mémoires de chirurgie militaire et campagnes*, 4 vols (Paris, 1812–17), iii. pp. 282–5.
37. Chevalier, *Souvenirs*, p. 108.
38. Cited in Patrick Turnbull, *Napoleon's Second Empress* (London, 1971), p. 26.
39. Stamm-Kuhlmann, *König in Preußens großer Zeit*, pp. 289–90.
40. Kraehe, *Metternich's German Policy*, i. pp. 83–5.
41. Savary, *Mémoires*, iv. p. 147.
42. On this point, Hauterive, *La police secrète du premier Empire*, v. pp. 99–100 (30 June 1809); Petiteau, *Les Français et l'Empire*, p. 202.
43. Chastenay, *Mémoires*, ii. p. 97.
44. Cited in Boudon, *Le roi Jérôme*, pp. 340–1.
45. Boigne, *Récits d'une tante*, i. pp. 291–2.
46. On the battle of Wagram see Petre, *Napoleon and the Archduke Charles*, pp. 351–79; Thiry, *Wagram*; Chandler, *Campaigns of Napoleon*, pp. 677–94; Robert M. Epstein, *Napoleon's Last Victory and the Emergence of Modern War* (Lawrence, Kan., 1994), pp. 129–70; Rothenberg, *Napoleon's Great Adversary*, pp. 208–16; Gill, *1809: Thunder on the Danube*, iii. pp. 185–264.
47. Ouvrard, *1809: les Français à Vienne*, pp. 163–6.
48. Chandler, *Campaigns of Napoleon*, p. 1121.
49. Petre, *Napoleon and the Archduke Charles*, pp. 360–1.
50. *Corr.* xix. n. 15505 (8 July 1809), which states that 1,500 were killed and 3,000 or 4,000 wounded.
51. Thiry, *Wagram*, p. 188.
52. Kraehe, *Metternich's German Policy*, i. p. 89.
53. Angeli, *Erzherzog Carl*, iv. pp. 553–64.
54. On the changing nature of battle see Marie-Cécile Thoral, *From Valmy to Waterloo: France at War, 1792–1815* (Basingstoke, 2011), pp. 14–20.
55. There are two exceptions: one is a painting by Gros, commissioned by Berthier, who was, after all, given the title 'Prince of Wagram' (Brunner, *Antoine-Jean Gros*, pp. 296–302); the other a painting passed to Carle Vernet and never completed (O'Brien, *After the Revolution*, pp. 124, 181–2). Even then, it was a private and not an official commission.
56. One such example was the construction of a panorama in Paris, which one critic described as having been so real that he was 'transported to the scene' (Maurice Samuels, 'Realizing the Past: History and the Spectacle in Balzac's *Adieu*', *Representations*, 79 (2002), 86).
57. *Corr.* xix. n. 15894 (3 October 1809); Nicolet, *La fabrique d'une nation*, p. 147.
58. Serge Tatistcheff, *Alexandre Ier et Napoléon, d'après leur correspondance inédite, 1801–1812* (Paris, 1891), pp. 465–500; Thiry, *Wagram*, pp. 112–14; Kraehe, *Metternich's German Policy*, i. p. 73.
59. Vandal, *Napoléon et Alexandre*, ii. pp. 95–6; Rey, *Alexandre Ier*, pp. 262–3.
60. Domokos Kosáry, *Napoléon et la Hongrie* (Budapest, 1979), pp. 51–3. Schroeder, *Transformation of European Politics*, pp. 282, 366; Ingrao, *The Habsburg Monarchy*, pp. 236–7.
61. *Corr.* xix. n. 15215 (15 May 1809); Kosáry, *Napoléon et la Hongrie*, pp. 53, 67–71, 75. The Hungarian political elite rejected the proposition.
62. Beer, *Zehn Jahre österreichischer Politik*, p. 427; Kraehe, *Metternich's German Policy*, i. p. 91.
63. Scott, *Birth of a Great Power System*, p. 343. According to Sked, *Radetzky*, p. 30, Napoleon attempted to ruin Austrian finances by flooding the country with 300 million Gulden in counterfeit notes, but I have been unable to verify this claim.
64. Kraehe, *Metternich's German Policy*, i. p. 119.
65. Cited in Kraehe, *Metternich's German Policy*, i. p. 119.
66. Dunan, *Napoléon et l'Allemagne*, pp. 260–3; Sked, *Radetzky*, p. 27.

67. Rapp, *Mémoires*, pp. 112–17; Ernst Borkowsky, 'Das Schönbrunner Attentat im Jahr 1809 nach unveröfentlichten Quellen', *Die Grenzboten. Blätter für Deutschland und Belgien*, 57:4 (1898), 293–301; Tulard, *Napoléon: Jeudi 12 octobre 1809*, pp. 85–130; and Jean Tulard, 'Les attentats contre Napoléon', *Revue du Souvenir napoléonien*, 391 (1993), 13–14.

68. Tulard, *Murat*, p. 158.

69. On relations between Napoleon and Pius VII see Lentz, *Nouvelle histoire du Premier Empire*, i. pp. 481–500.

70. *Corr.* xi. n. 9656 (7 January 1805).

71. *Corr.* xii. n. 9806 (13 February 1806).

72. Talleyrand, *Mémoires*, ii. pp. 100–1.

73. *Corr.* nos. 15218 and 15219 (17 May 1809).

74. Victor Bindel, *Un rêve de Napoléon: le Vatican à Paris (1809–1814)* (Paris, 1943), pp. 14, 87, 143.

75. Yves Bercé, 'Rome, 1796–1814', in Bruno Foucart (ed.), *Camille de Tournon: le préfet de la Rome napoléonienne: 1809–1814* (Boulogne-Billancourt, 2001), pp. 25–32, here p. 30.

76. *Corr.* xx. n. 16263 (17 February 1810).

77. Bartolomeo Pacca, *Oeuvres complètes du cardinal B. Pacca*, 2 vols (Paris, 1845), i. p. 113.

78. Sébastien Joseph Comeau de Charry, *Souvenirs des guerres d'Allemagne pendant la Révolution et l'Empire* (Paris, 1900), p. 428.

79. *Corr.* xix. n. 15528 (15 July 1809).

80. Lecestre (ed.), *Lettres inédites*, i. p. 317 (20 June 1809).

81. *Corr.* xix. n. 15383 (19 June 1809).

82. Etienne Radet, *Mémoires du général Radet* (Saint-Cloud, 1892), pp. 169–86.

83. *Corr.* xix. n. 15555 (18 July 1809).

84. *Corr.* xix. n. 15578 (23 July 1809); Cambacérès, *Lettres inédites à Napoléon*, ii. p. 703 (30 July 1809).

85. *Corr.* xix. n. 15634 (10 August 1809).

86. Lecestre (ed.), *Lettres inédites*, i. pp. 362–3 (15 September 1809).

87. Melchior-Bonnet, *Napoléon et le Pape*, pp. 195–7.

88. Chevallier and Pincemaille, *L'impératrice Joséphine*, p. 338.

89. Girardin, *Mémoires, journal et souvenirs*, i. p. 343.

90. On Josephine's expenses see Frédéric Masson, *Joséphine répudiée (1809–1814)* (Paris, 1901), pp. 98–105; Rémusat, *Mémoires*, ii. pp. 342–7; Ernest John Knapton, *Empress Josephine* (Cambridge, Mass., 1964), pp. 264–5.

91. Masson, *Napoléon et sa famille*, i. pp. 327–8.

92. According to Claire de Rémusat, *Mémoires de Mme de Rémusat 1802–1808*, introduction and notes by Charles Kunstler (Paris, 1957), p. 71; McLynn, *Napoleon*, pp. 300–1.

93. See Masson, *Napoléon et les femmes*; Alain Pigeard, *Napoléon amoureux* (Paris, 2007), pp. 81–148; Lilly Marcou, *Napoléon et les femmes* (Paris, 2008), pp. 216–27.

94. Masson, *Joséphine répudiée*, pp. 27–8; Chevallier and Pincemaille, *L'impératrice Joséphine*, p. 331; Lentz, *Nouvelle histoire du Premier Empire*, i. p. 436. Eléonore returned to Paris three husbands and three decades later as the wife of the Bavarian ambassador.

95. *Correspondance inédite de Napoléon Ier, de la famille impériale et de divers personnages avec Pauline Borghèse* (Paris, 1939), pp. 30, 32, 37; Girardin, *Mémoires, journal et souvenirs*, i. p. 339.

96. Berlier, *Précis de la vie politique*, pp. 111–12.

97. Caulaincourt, *Memoirs*, i. p. 89.

98. Vandal, *Napoléon et Alexandre*, i. p. 461.

99. See, for example, the police report dated 11 February 1808, in Hauterive, *La police secrète du premier Empire*, iv. p. 54. They appear to have reached the army on campaign in Germany around the beginning of 1810 (Parquin, *Souvenirs*, p. 207).

100. Roderick Phillips, *Family Breakdown in Late Eighteenth-Century France: Divorces in Rouen, 1792–1803* (Oxford, 1980), pp. 159–65; Roderick Phillips, *Putting Asunder: A*

*History of Divorce in Western Society* (Cambridge, 1988), pp. 405–12; Roderick Phillips, *Untying the Knot: A Short History of Divorce* (Cambridge, 1991), pp. 74–80.

101. Frédéric Masson, *Mme Bonaparte* (Paris, 1920), pp. 336–7; Chevallier and Pincemaille, *L'impératrice Joséphine*, p.6.

102. Bertrand, *Cahiers de Sainte-Hélène*, iii. pp. 98–9.

103. Elie Faure, *Napoléon* (Paris, 1983), pp. 103–11.

104. Masson, *Napoléon et les femmes*; Rémusat, *Mémoires*, ii. pp. 86–95; Caulaincourt, *Memoirs*, ii. pp. 330–1.

105. Caulaincourt, *Memoirs*, ii. pp. 322, 331.

106. For what follows, Bausset, *Mémoires anecdotiques*, i. pp. 369–74; Hortense, *Mémoires*, ii. pp. 44–6; Turquan, *L'Impératrice Joséphine*, pp. 182–5; Chevallier and Pincemaille, *L'impératrice Joséphine*, pp. 338–9.

107. Patricia Mainardi, *Husbands, Wives, and Lovers: Marriage and its Discontents in Nineteenth-Century France* (New Haven, 2003), pp. 12–14. On the divorce see Masson, *Joséphine répudiée*, pp. 1–110; Welschinger, *Le Divorce de Napoléon*; Lentz, *Nouvelle histoire du Premier Empire*, i. pp. 496–9.

108. Chatel de Brancion, *Le sacre de Napoléon*, pp. 139–40.

109. Hauterive, *La police secrète du premier Empire*, iv. p. 54 (11 February 1808).

110. Chatel de Brancion, *Cambacérès*, pp. 496–7.

111. Hortense, *Mémoires*, ii. p. 54.

112. Lavalette, *Mémoires*, p. 263.

113. Lavalette, *Mémoires*, p. 265. Hortense, *Mémoires*, ii. pp. 44–5, describes another occasion on which Napoleon cried at the thought of being 'abandoned'.

114. A similar sentiment is expressed by McLynn, *Napoleon*, p. 465.

115. Chevallier and Pincemaille, *L'impératrice Joséphine*, pp. 345–6.

116. Parquin, *Souvenirs*, p. 207.

117. Berlier, *Précis de la vie politique*, p. 112.

118. Tourtier-Bonazzi, *Lettres d'amour à Joséphine*, pp. 359–70; Chevallier and Pincemaille, *L'impératrice Joséphine*, pp. 343–4.

## *16 : Bourgeois Emperor, Universal Emperor*

1. Lentz, *Nouvelle histoire du Premier Empire*, i. pp. 502–5.

2. The meeting is in Cambacérès, *Mémoires inédites*, ii. pp. 326–9; Talleyrand, *Mémoires*, ii. pp. 7–10; Alfred-Auguste Ernouf, *Maret, duc de Bassano* (Paris, 1878), pp. 275–7.

3. Cambacérès, *Mémoires inédites*, ii. p. 327; Fouché, *Mémoires*, i, pp. 401, 404–9; Beugnot, *Mémoires*, i. pp. 425–6.

4. Hauterive, *La police secrète du premier Empire*, v. p. 326 (21 February 1810).

5. Pillard, *Louis Fontanes*, p. 238.

6. Cambacérès, *Mémoires inédites*, ii. p. 328.

7. Talleyrand, *Mémoires*, i. pp. 447–8.

8. Elisabeth to Alexander (29 August/10 September 1807), Nikolaï Mikhaïlovitch (ed.), *L'impératrice Elisabeth, épouse d'Alexandre Ier*, 3 vols (St Petersburg, 1908–9), ii. p. 253. On Ekaterina see Martin, *Romantics, Reformers, Reactionaries*, pp. 51–2; Maistre, *Oeuvres complètes*, xi. pp. 163–4.

9. Björnstjerna (ed.), *Mémoires du comte de Stedingk*, ii. p. 356 (10 October 1807); J. Merkle, *Katharina Pawlowna, Königin von Württemberg, Beiträge zu einer Lebensbeschreibung der Fürstin* (Stuttgart, 1889), pp. 9–19.

10. Adams (ed.), *Memoirs of John Quincy Adams*, ii. p. 93 (9 January 1810).

11. Björnstjerna (ed.), *Mémoires du comte de Stedingk*, ii. p. 414 (7 December 1807).

12. Mikhaïlovitch (ed.), *L'impératrice Elisabeth*, ii. p. 211; Mikhaïlovitch (ed.), *Correspondance de l'empereur Alexandre Ier avec sa soeur la grande-duchesse Catherine*, pp. xxi, 27; Martin, *Maria Féodorovna*, pp. 166–9.

13. Caulaincourt, *Mémoires*, i. pp. 89–90.

14. Martin, *Romantics, Reformers, Reactionaries*, p. 51.

15. Lecestre (ed.), *Lettres inédites*, ii. pp. 15–16 (26 February 1810).

16. On the theatre see David Chaillou, 'L'annonce du mariage dans les spectacles parisiens', in Thierry Lentz (ed.), *1810: le tournant de l'Empire* (Paris, 2010), pp. 23–35.

17. Arthur-Léon Imbert de Saint-Amand, *Les beaux jours de l'impératrice Marie-Louise: les femmes des Tuileries* (Paris, 1885), pp. 113–15.

18. Jean-Paul Bled, 'Le renversement des alliances', in Lentz (ed.), *1810: le tournant de l'Empire*, p. 19.

19. Michael Rowe, 'France, Prussia, or Germany? The Napoleonic Wars and the Shifting Allegiances in the Rhineland', *Central European History*, 39 (2006), 611–40, here 622.

20. Arthur Chuquet (ed.), *Souvenirs du baron de Frénilly, pair de France (1768–1828)* (Paris, 1908), p. 324.

21. Maistre, *Mémoires politiques et correspondance diplomatique*, pp. 348–9; Geoffroy de Grandmaison, *Napoléon et les cardinaux noirs (1810–1814)* (Paris, 1895), p. 40.

22. Martin, *Romantics, Reformers, Reactionaries*, p. 50.

23. See Caulaincourt, *Memoirs*, i. pp. 112–13; Vandal, *Napoléon et Alexandre*, ii. pp. 288–9; Adam Zamoyski, *1812: Napoleon's Fatal March on Moscow* (London, 2004), p. 58; Rey, *Alexandre Ier*, pp. 264–5.

24. Frédéric Masson, *L'impératrice Marie-Louise: 1809–1815* (Paris, 1902), p. 41. Metternich's assertion that the proposal came as a complete surprise in 1810 and that it was never mentioned either before or after the Peace of Vienna is simply unfounded (Metternich, *Mémoires*, i. pp. 95–7).

25. Pasquier, *Mémoires*, i. pp. 337–9.

26. A theory proposed by Gotteri, *Napoléon*, pp. 144–5.

27. Kraehe, *Metternich's German Policy*, i. p. 124.

28. Kraehe, *Metternich's German Policy*, i. p. 124.

29. See, for example, Cobenzl to Stadion, in Beer, 'Österreich und Russland in den Jahren 1804 und 1805', 214 (1 April 1804).

30. Metternich, *Mémoires*, ii. pp. 376–84.

31. Metternich, *Mémoires*, i. p. 97.

32. Constantin de Grunwald, 'Le mariage de Napoléon et de Marie-Louise', *Revue des Deux Mondes*, 38 (1937), 343–7.

33. Lentz, *Nouvelle histoire du Premier Empire*, i. p. 504.

34. Branda, *Napoléon et ses hommes*, pp. 353–4.

35. Lecestre (ed.), *Lettres inédites*, ii. pp. 15–16 (26 February 1810).

36. Leferme-Falguières, *Les courtisans*, pp. 82–3.

37. On the imperial court see Jean Tulard, 'La cour de Napoléon Ier', in Karl Ferdinand Werner (ed.), *Hof, Kultur und Politik im 19. Jahrhundert* (Bonn, 1985), pp. 55–9. On etiquette Jeroen Duindam, 'Ceremony at Court: Reflections on an Elusive Subject', *Francia*, 26:2 (1999), 131–40.

38. According to Frédéric Masson, *L'impératrice Marie-Louise* (Paris, 1902), pp. 22–3; Françoise Darle, *Au temps de Napoléon Bonaparte* (Paris, 1961), p. 100.

39. Masson, *L'impératrice Marie-Louise*, p. 52; Irmgard Schiel, *Marie-Louise: une Habsbourg pour Napoléon*, trans. from the German by Jacques Dumont (Paris, 1998), p. 98.

40. Claude-François de Méneval, *Napoléon et Marie-Louise: souvenirs historiques de M. le baron Méneval*, 3 vols (Paris, 1844–5), i. pp. 242–3; Schiel, *Marie-Louise*, pp. 27–9.

41. Auguste Fournier, *Marie-Louise et la chute de Napoléon, contribution à la biographie de Marie-Louise* (Paris, 1903), p. 2 n. 1; Schiel, *Marie-Louise*, pp. 29–30.

42. Frédéric Masson, *The Private Diaries of Empress Marie Louise, Wife of Napoleon I* (New York, 1922), pp. 26–7.

43. Leferme-Falguières, *Les courtisans*, pp. 110–14; David Chanteranne, 'Les cérémonies du mariage', in Lentz (ed.), *1810: le tournant de l'Empire*, pp. 37–40.

44. Jean Pierrelongue (ed.), *Napoléon et Marie-Louise: correspondance* (Paris, 2010), pp. 2, 4–5.
45. Douglas Clark Baxter, 'First Encounters: Bourbon Princes Meet their Brides: Ceremony, Gender and Monarchy', *Proceedings of the Annual Meeting of the Western Society for French History*, 22 (1995), 23–31.
46. Turnbull, *Napoleon's Second Empress*, pp. 44–5; Schiel, *Marie-Louise*, pp. 60–1.
47. Joseph Alexander Freiherr von Helfert, *Maria Louise, Erzherzogin von Oesterreich, Kaiserin der Franzosen* (Vienna, 1873), p. 119; Napoleon to Marie-Louise (23 March 1810), in Pierrelongue (ed.), *Napoléon et Marie-Louise*, pp. 9–10.
48. See Garnier, *Murat, roi de Naples*, pp. 17–18, for a portrait of Caroline.
49. Constant, *Mémoires*, iv. pp. 247–8. Napoleon spent over 68,000 francs in 1810 on clothes, mostly associated with the wedding (Colombe Samoyault-Verlet, 'The Emperor's Wardrobe', in le Bourhis (ed.), *The Age of Napoleon*, p. 203).
50. Méneval, *Mémoires*, ii. pp. 333–4; Bausset, *Mémoires anecdotiques*, ii. pp. 7–8, 20–2; Charles de Clary-et-Aldringen, *Souvenirs du prince Charles de Clary-et-Aldringen: trois mois à Paris lors du mariage de l'empereur Napoléon Ier et de l'archiduchesse Marie-Louise* (Paris, 1914), p. 45; Baxter, 'First Encounters', pp. 25–6; Branda, *Napoléon et ses hommes*, pp. 379–82.
51. Geneviève Chastenet, *Marie-Louise: l'otage de Napoléon* (Paris, 2005), p. 69.
52. Gourgaud, *Journal de Sainte-Hélène*, ii. p. 273; Turnbull, *Napoleon's Second Empress*, p. 53.
53. Cited in Masson, *Napoléon et les femmes*, p. 308; James R. Arnold, *Napoleon Conquers Austria: The 1809 Campaign for Vienna* (Westport, Conn., 1995), p. 194.
54. Derrécagaix, *Le maréchal Berthier*, ii. p. 370.
55. Schiel, *Marie-Louise*, p. 16; Eduard Wertheimer, *Die Heirat der Erzherzogin Marie Louise mit Napoleon I: nach ungedruckten Quellen* (Vienna, 1882), pp. 17–18.
56. Chastenet, *Marie-Louise*, pp. 90–1.
57. Masson, *L'impératrice Marie-Louise*, p. 103.
58. Masson, *L'impératrice Marie-Louise*, p. 109.
59. Cornet, *Souvenirs sénatoriaux*, p. 58; André Marié, 'Le mariage civil de Napoléon à Saint-Cloud', *Revue de l'Institut Napoléon*, 72 (1959), 109–14; Chanteranne, 'Les cérémonies du mariage', pp. 37–50.
60. Forrest, 'Napoleon as Monarch', p. 124; Cédric Istasse, 'Les "mariages de la Rosière" dans le département de Sambre-et-Meuse: indices sur la réinsertion sociale des anciens soldats de Napoléon Ier', *Napoleonica. La Revue*, 1:4 (2009), 11–29; Denise Z. Davidson, *France after Revolution: Urban Life, Gender, and the New Social Order* (Cambridge, Mass., 2007), pp. 40–1; Pfister, *Les fêtes à Nancy*, pp. 108–33.
61. There is a sketch of the 'temple' in Clary-et-Aldringen, *Souvenirs*, p. 82.
62. Stryienski (ed.), *Memoirs of the Countess Potocka*, pp. 200–2; Thibaudeau, *Mémoires*, p. 278; Savary, *Mémoires*, iv. pp. 295–6; Clary-et-Aldringen, *Souvenirs*, p. 83.
63. Jacques-Olivier Boudon, 'Napoléon, les catholiques français et le pape', in Lentz (ed.), *1810: le tournant de l'Empire*, pp. 132–3.
64. Pasquier, *Mémoires*, i. p. 381.
65. According to Grandmaison, *Napoléon et les cardinaux noirs*, p. 44.
66. Lecestre (ed.), *Lettres inédites*, ii. pp. 21–3 (3, 4 and 5 April 1810).
67. Chastenet, *Marie-Louise*, p. 98.
68. Clary-et-Aldringen, *Souvenirs*, pp. 78–80.
69. There is a considerable body of work on Royal Entries. For France see: Cosandey, *La reine de France*, pp. 174–81; Pascal Lardellier, *Les miroirs du paon: rites et rhétoriques politiques dans la France de l'Ancien Régime* (Paris, 2003).
70. Arlette Farge, *La vie fragile: violence, pouvoirs et solidarités à Paris au XVIIIe siècle* (Paris, 1992), pp. 26–7.
71. Rowe, *From Reich to State*, p. 155.
72. Mansel, *Court of France*, pp. 56–7.
73. Gotteri, *Napoléon*, pp. 62–3.

74. Woolf, *Napoleon's Integration of Europe*, p. 75.

75. Mansel, *Court of France*, p. 72; Martin-Fugier, *La vie élégante*, p. 82; Branda, *Napoléon et ses hommes*, pp. 101–2.

76. Hélène Meyer, 'De la rencontre à l'idylle sous les ors de Compiègne: à propos de l'exposition du bicentenaire', in Lentz (ed.), *1810: le tournant de l'Empire*, p. 247. On their stay at Compiègne, see also Bernard Chevallier, Anne Dion-Tenenbaum, Marc Desti et al., *1810: la politique de l'amour: Napoléon Ier et Marie-Louise à Compiègne* (Paris, 2010).

77. Hortense, *Mémoires*, ii. p. 72.

78. According to Metternich to Francis (4 April 1810), cited in Schiel, *Marie-Louise*, p. 97.

79. According to Metternich, cited in Schiel, *Marie-Louise*, p. 98.

80. Schiel, *Marie-Louise*, pp. 106–8.

81. Schiel, *Marie-Louise*, p. 101.

82. Schiel, *Marie-Louise*, pp. 108–9.

83. Masson, *L'impératrice Marie-Louise*, pp. 88–9.

84. Palmer, *Metternich*, p. 51.

85. Claude-Philibert, comte de Rambuteau, *Mémoires du comte de Rambuteau* (Paris, 1905), pp. 49–51.

86. Lejeune, *Mémoires*, pp. 286–8; Jacques Jourquin, 'L'incendie de l'ambassade d'Autriche, 1er juillet 1810', *Napoleon Ier*, 8 (May–June 2001), 56–62; Castellane, *Journal*, i. pp. 78–9.

87. Lavalette, *Mémoires*, pp. 266–9.

88. Cambacérès, *Mémoires inédites*, ii. p. 366; Schiel, *Marie-Louise*, p. 116. For a discussion of the birth see June K. Burton, *Napoleon and the Woman Question: Discourses of the Other Sex in French Education, Medicine, and Medical Law 1799–1815* (Lubbock, Tex., 2007), pp.15–25.

89. A slightly different account in Rambuteau, *Mémoires*, p. 56. See Jean Tulard, *Napoléon II* (Paris, 1992), pp. 49–62.

90. Hortense, *Mémoires*, ii. p. 127.

91. Letter from Metternich to Francis (9 May 1810), cited in Schiel, *Marie-Louise*, p. 98.

92. Marie-Louise to Francis (23 April 1811), cited in Schiel, *Marie-Louise*, pp. 119–20.

93. AN F7 3835, Rapports de la préfecture de police, 20 March 1811.

94. Stendhal, *Oeuvres intimes*, i. p. 664; François-Louis Poumiès de la Siboutie, *Souvenirs d'un médecin de Paris* (Paris, 1910), p. 95.

95. Nicole Gotteri (ed.), *La police secrète du Premier Empire*, 7 vols (Paris, 1997–2004), ii. p. 233 (20 March 1811).

96. Boigne, *Récits d'une tante*, i. p. 263.

97. As Frédéric Masson, *Napoléon et son fils* (Paris, 1904), pp. 133–4, argues.

98. AN F7 3835, 21 March 1811.

99. AN F7 3835, 25 March 1811.

100. AN AFIV 1452 contains a number of poems written for the occasion. See also *Hommages poétiques à leurs majestés impériales et royales*, a collection of poems in two volumes. Two plays that met with a 'vif succès' according to the secret police reports were *L'Enfant de Mars et Flore* at the Cirque Olympique, which could hold 2,700 spectators, and *L'Olympe, Vienne, Paris et Rome* at the Odéon (Gotteri (ed.), *La police secrète*, ii. pp. 261 and 271 (28 March and 1 April 1811)). See also John Grand-Carteret, *L'aiglon en images et dans la fiction poétique et dramatique* (Paris, 1901), pp. 33–52, 173–97.

101. *Moniteur universel*, 21, 23 March 1811. Bulletins concerning the state of health of Marie-Louise were published over the following days, but there was no publication of letters of congratulations by the people. See Jean Tulard, *La province au temps de Napoléon* (Paris, 2003), pp. 175–6; Katherine Aaslestad, *Place and Politics: Local Identity, Civic Culture, and German Nationalism in North Germany during the Revolutionary Era* (Leiden, 2005), pp. 251–2.

102. Petiteau, *Les Français et l'Empire*, pp. 183–4.

103. See, for example, Louis Dubroca, *Discours en actions de grâces à l'Eternel pour la fête de la naissance de S.M. le roi de Rome* (Paris, 1811); *La Naissance du roi de Rome. Dithyrambe*

*en prose poétique, par M.N.M. veuve de Rome, membre de l'académie des arcades de Rome* (Paris, 1811).

104. Pierre Lefranc, 'Fêtes et réjouissances dans la Vienne à l'occasion de la naissance du roi de Rome', *Revue de l'Institut Napoléon*, 145 (1985), 59–66; Louis J. Thomas, 'Montpellier et le roi de Rome', *Revue des études napoléoniennes*, 3 (1913), 346–66.

105. Gotteri (ed.), *La police secrète*, ii. p. 389 (14 May 1811).

106. Boudon, *Le roi Jérôme*, pp. 356–7; Branda, *Napoléon et ses hommes*, pp. 384–5.

107. Florence Vidal, *Caroline Bonaparte: soeur de Napoléon Ier* (Paris, 2006), pp. 124–5.

108. Florence Vidal, *Elisa Bonaparte: soeur de Napoléon Ier* (Paris, 2004), pp. 188–9.

109. Cf. Leferme-Falguières, *Les courtisans*, pp. 95–104.

110. Savary, *Mémoires*, v. p. 149.

111. Comeau de Charry, *Souvenirs des guerres*, p. 440.

112. *Corr.* xiv. n. 11800 (12 February 1807).

113. Examples can be found in *Corr.* xi. nos. 9541, 9546 (3 and 5 December 1805).

114. *Corr.* xi. n. 3932 (18 October 1805).

115. On this point see Lynn Hunt, *The Family Romance of the French Revolution* (Berkeley, 1992), pp. 17–52; Hughes, 'Vive la République, Vive l'Empereur!', pp. 60–3. There is an interesting discussion of the 'patriarchal family' and its political implications in Darrin M. McMahon, *Enemies of the Enlightenment: The French Counter-Enlightenment and the Making of Modernity* (New York, 2001), pp. 133–8.

116. See, for example, Georges Bangofsky, 'Les étapes de Georges Bangofsky, officier lorrain. Extraits de son journal de campagnes (1797–1815)', *Mémoires de l'Académie de Stanislas*, ii (1905), 320; Chevalier, *Souvenirs*, p. 99, refers to Napoleon as 'un père de famille au milieu de ses enfants'.

117. *Corr.* x. n. 8705 (9 May 1805); xii. n. 9912 (2 March 1806); xv. n. 12543 (23 April 1807); xx. n. 16540 (9 June 1810); xxii. nos. 17579, 17832 (6 April, 17 June 1811); Lecestre (ed.), *Lettres inédites*, i. pp. 289–90 (6 March 1809).

118. *Moniteur universel*, 8 fructidor an XII (26 August 1804); Robinaux, *Journal de route*, pp. 17–18.

119. Petiteau, *Les Français et l'Empire*, p. 86.

120. Hughes, 'Vive la République, Vive l'Empereur!', pp. 206, 207.

121. Agathon-Jean-François, baron Fain, *Manuscrit de mil huit cent-quatorze, trouvé dans les voitures impériales prises à Waterloo, contenant l'histoire des six derniers mois du règne de Napoléon* (Paris, 1824), pp. 21–3.

122. Cited in Ida Tarbell, *Napoleon's Addresses: Selections from the Proclamations, Speeches and Correspondence of Napoleon Bonaparte* (Boston, 1897), pp. 127–30. By the time he reached Elba in exile Napoleon had completely assumed the role. On landing he is supposed to have said to the people gathered to welcome him, 'I hope that you appreciate my preference for this island, and that you will love me as obedient children [*enfants soumis*]; if so, you will always find me in a mood to treat you with a father's care' (Friedrich Ludwig Truchsess, Graf von Waldbourg, *Nouvelle relation de l'itinéraire de Napoléon, de Fontainebleau à l'Île d'Elbe* (Paris, 1815), p. 52).

123. Schnapper and Sérullaz (eds), *Jacques-Louis David*, pp. 474–7; Johnson, *Jacques-Louis David*, pp. 216, 218–20; Porterfield and Siegfried, *Staging Empire*, p. 17.

124. Burke, *The Fabrication of Louis XIV*, pp. 199–200.

125. Christopher M. S. Johns, *Antonio Canova and the Politics of Patronage in Revolutionary and Napoleonic Europe* (Berkeley, 1998), p. 104.

126. Cited in Johnson, *Jacques-Louis David*, p. 219.

127. Harold T. Parker, 'Napoleon I, Daily Round', in Owen Connelly (ed.), *Historical Dictionary of Napoleonic France, 1799–1815* (Westport, Conn., 1985), pp. 357–8.

128. *Le Publiciste*, 26 nivôse an VIII (16 January 1800).

129. Chaptal, *Mes souvenirs sur Napoléon*, p. 328.

130. Roederer, *Mémoires*, p. 187.

131. Ségur, *Histoire et mémoires*, iii. p. 476; Fain, *Mémoires*, p. 286.

132. Paul de Kock, *Mémoires de Ch.-Paul de Kock, écrits par lui-même* (Paris, 1873), pp. 66–7.
133. Michel Porret, 'Introduction', in Baron de Montesquieu, *Réflexions sur la Monarchie Universelle en Europe* (Geneva, 2000), p. 14. A fuller explanation can be found in Philip Dwyer, 'Napoleon and the Universal Monarchy', *History*, 95 (2010), 293–307.
134. Morkov to Alexander (1/13 December 1802), *Sbornik*, lxx. p. 585.
135. Vorontsov to Morkov (29 May/10 June 1803), in *Sbornik*, lxxvii. p. 190; Zawadzki, 'Czartoryski and Napoleonic France', 252; Hinsley, *Power and the Pursuit of Peace*, pp. 153–85.
136. Both examples cited in Simms, *The Impact of Napoleon*, p. 97.
137. Cited in Simms, *The Impact of Napoleon*, p. 272.
138. Zawadzki, 'Czartoryski and Napoleonic France', 246.
139. Zawadzki, 'Czartoryski and Napoleonic France', 263, 265.
140. Zawadzki, 'Czartoryski and Napoleonic France', 274.
141. Caulaincourt, *Memoirs*, ii. p. 257.
142. Castellane, *Journal*, i. p. 165. René Bourgeois, *Tableau de la campagne de Moscou en 1812* (Paris, 1814), p. 2, initially believed that the army was destined to support the Russians against Turkey or was destined for India rather than an invasion of Russia. See also Puybusque, *Lettres sur la guerre de Russie*, pp. 11–12 (28 May 1812); Castellane, *Journal*, i. p. 165 (5 October 1812); Pierre-Paul Denniée, *Itinéraire de l'empereur Napoléon pendant la campagne de 1812* (Paris, 1842), p. 11; Fantin des Odoards, *Journal*, pp. 321–2; Adrien Bourgogne, *Mémoires du sergent Bourgogne* (Paris, 1898, reprinted 1992), p. 357 n. 8; Eugène Labaume, *Relation circonstanciée de la campagne de Russie* (Paris, 1814), p. 223; Arthur Chuquet (ed.), *1812: la Guerre de Russie: notes et documents* (Paris, 1912), p. 8.
143. Ratchinski, *Napoléon et Alexandre*, pp. 73–4, 291–6. The only other person to argue that Napoleon intended to crown himself in Moscow – in this instance, 'Emperor of the West' – is Alfred Sudre, *Petites causes et grands effets. Le secret de 1812* (Paris, 1887). Ratchinski bases his assertion on the memoranda by Louis Alexandre Andrault, comte de Langeron, found in the Archives des Affaires Etrangères. There is, however, little or nothing to support this claim. It is more likely that they were Russian ornaments and the insignia of the Russian crown that Napoleon had looted from the Kremlin, which he was taking back to France as trophies (Caulaincourt, *Memoirs*, i. p. 314 n. 1; Roguet, *Mémoires militaires*, iv. p. 497).
144. Miot de Melito, *Mémoires*, i. p. 307.
145. *Corr.*, ix. n. 7832 (2 July 1804).
146. Fouché, *Mémoires*, i. p. 354, and ii. p. 114, wrote that 'The idea of destroying the power of England, the sole obstacle to universal monarchy, became his [Napoleon's] fixed obsession.'
147. Fouché, *Mémoires*, ii. p. 114.
148. Cited in Dunan, *Napoléon et l'Allemagne*, p. 409.
149. Dominique Dufour, baron de Pradt, *Histoire de l'ambassade dans le Grand Duché de Varsovie en 1812* (Paris, 1815), pp. 1, 16–17, 22–4, quotation p. 24.
150. Cited in Fournier, *Napoleon*, ii. p. 148.
151. J. Christopher Herold, *The Mind of Napoleon: A Selection from his Written and Spoken Words* (New York, 1955), p. 257.
152. Las Cases, *Mémorial*, i. p. 139.
153. Emil Dard, *Dans l'entourage de l'Empereur* (Paris, 1940), pp. 111–23, here p. 114.
154. Miot de Melito, *Mémoires*, iii. p. 241.
155. Ségur, *Histoire et mémoires*, iv. p. 74.
156. As does Etienne François, 'Das napoleonische Hegemonialsystem auf dem Kontinent', in Klinger, Hahn and Schmidt (eds), *Das Jahr 1806*, pp. 73–83.
157. As does Schroeder, *Transformation of European Politics*, pp. xi, 230, 284, 393; and Schroeder, 'Napoleon's Foreign Policy', 147–61.

## *17:* '*A Very Stormy Year*'

1. Barante, *Souvenirs*, i. pp. 331–2.
2. Lecestre (ed.), *Lettres inédites*, i. pp. 374–6 (November 1809); Félix Rocquain, *Napoléon Ier et le roi Louis, d'après les documents conservés aux Archives nationales* (Paris, 1875), pp. lxxxi–lxxxii, 131–2, 222.
3. Rocquain, *Napoleon I et le roi Louis*, pp. 322–6.
4. Du Casse, 'Napoléon et le roi Louis', 354–79; Owen Connelly, *Napoleon's Satellite Kingdoms* (New York, 1965), p. 127; Schama, *Patriots and Liberators*, pp. 609–10.
5. Du Casse, *Mémoires du roi Joseph*, vii. p. 311 (8 August 1810).
6. Tulard, *Murat*, pp. 156–61, 167–73.
7. *Corr.* xxi. n. 16754 (4 August 1810). Murat was not, for example, given permission to send ambassadors to Vienna or Petersburg.
8. *Corr.* xxi. n. 16806 (18 August 1810).
9. *Mémoires et correspondance du roi Jérôme*, iv. p. 439; Melchior-Bonnet, *Jérôme Bonaparte*, p. 174; Boudon, *Le roi Jérôme*, pp. 347–9.
10. Masson, *Napoléon et sa famille*, vi. pp. 83–4.
11. *Corr.* xxi. n. 17111 (7 November 1810).
12. Although only those who were born in France or of a French father were considered French. See Patrick Weil, *Qu'est-ce qu'un Français?: histoire de la nationalité française depuis la Révolution* (Paris, 2002), pp. 26–42. There was, therefore, no automatic French citizenship for members of the Empire.
13. Harold T. Parker, 'Why Did Napoleon Invade Russia? A Study in Motivation and the Interrelations of Personality and Social Structure', *Journal of Military History*, 54 (1990), 142.
14. Scott, *Birth of a Great Power System*, 332; Woolf, *Napoleon's Integration of Europe*, p. 27. Historians once believed that a federation was Napoleon's original intention, hence the creation of satellite kingdoms. For example, Oscar Browning, 'Hugh Elliot at Naples, 1803–1806', *English Historical Review*, 4 (1889), 218, believed that Napoleon's intention was to form a 'confederation of the Latin races' to oppose the northern European powers. It was a notion first conceived by Rutger Jan Schimmelpennick, head of the Dutch government, in February 1806 (Annie Jourdan, 'La Hollande en tant qu'"objet de désir" et le roi Louis, fondateur d'une monarchie nationale', in Jourdan (ed.), *Louis Bonaparte*, pp. 10 and 435 n. 7).
15. Marie-Louise Biver, 'Rome, second capitale de l'Empire', *Revue de l'Institut Napoléon*, 109 (1968), 145–54.
16. On this point see Hans H. Kohn, *The Prelude to Nation-States: The French and German Experience, 1789–1815* (Princeton, 1967), pp. 102–5.
17. Labaume, *Relation circonstanciée*, p. 13.
18. Vandal, *Napoléon et Alexandre*, i. pp. 1–57. The phrase is cited in Scott, *Birth of a Great Power System*, p. 346.
19. Tolstoy to Rumiantsev (7/19 November 1807), in *Sbornik*, lxxxix. pp. 225–26.
20. Sorel, *L'Europe et la Révolution française*, vii. pp. 306–7.
21. Martin, *Romantics, Reformers, Reactionaries*, p. 49; Grimsted, *The Foreign Ministers of Alexander I*, pp. 151–82.
22. On the Polish question during this period see Abel Mansuy, *Jérôme Napoléon et la Pologne en 1812* (Paris, 1931), pp. 247–93; Zawadzki, 'Russia and the Polish Question', 34–5; Adams, *Napoleon and Russia*, pp. 232–6, 253–7.
23. Caulaincourt to Champagny, in Grand Duc Nicolaï Mikhaïlovitch (ed.), *Les relations de la Russie et de la France d'après les rapports des ambassadeurs d'Alexandre et de Napoléon 1808–1812*, 6 vols (St Petersburg, 1905–8), iv. n. 410 (26 February 1810).
24. *Corr.* xx. n. 16181 (1 July 1810).
25. Adams, *Napoleon and Russia*, pp. 235, 236.

26. For the following see Léonce Pingaud, *Bernadotte, Napoléon et les Bourbons (1797–1844)* (Paris, 1901), pp. 93–110; Favier, *Bernadotte*, pp. 176–83; Cherrier, 'Un itinéraire politique original', 87–90; Jean-François Berdah, 'The Triumph of Neutrality: Bernadotte and European Geopolitics (1810–1844)', *Nordic Historical Review/Revue d'Histoire Nordique*, 6–7 (2008), esp. 32–9.
27. Marzagalli, *Les boulevards de la fraude*, pp. 169–70.
28. Lentz, *Nouvelle histoire du Premier Empire*, ii. p. 218.
29. Kraehe, *Metternich's German Policy*, i. pp. 128–30; Sergei Nikolaivich Iskjul', 'Rußland und die Oldenburger Krise 1810–11', *Oldenburger Jahrbuch*, 85 (1985), 89–110.
30. Tatistcheff, *Alexandre Ier et Napoléon*, pp. 137–8; Rey, *Alexandre Ier*, pp. 266–8.
31. Adams, *Napoleon and Russia*, pp. 258–9.
32. Chernysheva to Alexander (21 April 1811), in *Sbornik*, xxi. p. 62.
33. Friedrich Timme, 'Die geheime Mission des Flügeladjutanten von Wrangel (1812)', *Forschungen zur brandenburgischen und preußischen Geschichte*, 21 (1908), 199–213; Hans A. Schmitt, '1812: Stein, Alexander I and the Crusade against Napoleon', *Journal of Modern History*, 31 (1959), 327.
34. Rey, *Alexandre Ier*, pp. 269, 271. He abandoned this position in the spring of 1811.
35. Martin, *Romantics, Reformers, Reactionaries*, p. 46.
36. Martin, *Romantics, Reformers, Reactionaries*, pp. 42–3.
37. *Corr.* xxi. n. 17514 (24 March 1811).
38. Shuvalov to Alexander (15 May 1811), in *Sbornik*, xxi. pp. 414, 416.
39. Chernysheva to Alexander (1810, and 17 June 1811), in *Sbornik*, xxi. pp. 21, 72.
40. Caulaincourt, *Memoirs*, i. pp. 153–4.
41. *Corr.* xxii. n. 17579 (6 April 1811).
42. Cited in Zamoyski, *1812*, p. 77.
43. Metternich, *Mémoires*, ii. p. 499.
44. Caulaincourt, *Memoirs*, i. pp. 96–115.
45. Vandal, *Napoléon et Alexandre*, iii. pp. 163–91.
46. Including Cambacérès, *Mémoires inédites*, ii. pp. 392–3. It was perhaps the first and only time that the arch-chancellor proffered an opinion on military matters. Zamoyski, *1812*, p. 92; Adams, *Napoleon and Russia*, p. 267.
47. Broglie, *Souvenirs*, i. pp. 246–7; Mansel, *Court of France*, p. 86; Kale, *French Salons*, p. 94.
48. Fantin des Odoards, *Journal*, p. 293.
49. Shuvalov to Alexander (15 May 1811), in *Sbornik*, xxi. p. 418.
50. Caulaincourt, *Memoirs*, i. p. 119.
51. Beugnot, *Mémoires*, i. p. 486.
52. Lentz, *Nouvelle histoire du Premier Empire*, ii. p. 133.
53. *Corr.* xxiii. n. 18710 (21 May 1812).
54. Melchior-Bonnet, *Napoléon et le Pape*, pp. 297, 298–302.
55. Hales, *Napoleon and the Pope*, pp. 163–4; Ellis, 'Religion According to Napoleon', pp. 249–50.
56. *Corr.* xxiii. n. 18447 (19 January 1812).
57. Barton, *Bernadotte and Napoleon*, pp. 265–74; Höjer, *Bernadotte*, i. p. 601; Favier, *Bernadotte*, pp. 206–7.
58. Kraehe, *Metternich's German Policy*, i. pp. 136–9.
59. Kraehe, *Metternich's German Policy*, i. pp. 142–3.
60. L. Naroẑnickij, 'Österreich zwischen Frankreich und Russland 1813', in Anna M. Drabek, Walter Leitsch and Richard G. Plaschka (eds), *Russland und Österreich zur Zeit der Napoleonischen Kriege* (Vienna, 1989), pp. 22–3, 24.
61. Schroeder, *Transformation of European Politics*, pp. 448–9; Adams, *Napoleon and Russia*, p. 272.
62. See, for example, Gotteri (ed.), *La police secrète*, ii. p. 345 (25 April 1811); José Olcina, *L'opinion publique en Belgique entre 1812 et 1814: les Belges face à l'écroulement de l'Empire* (Brussels, 2010), p. 43.

63. See, for example, Poumiès de la Siboutie, *Souvenirs*, pp. 96–7; Hortense, *Mémoires*, ii. p. 147.

64. Chandler, *Campaigns of Napoleon*, p. 734.

65. Gaston Lavalley, *Napoléon et la disette de 1812: à propos d'une émeute aux halles de Caen* (Paris, 1896), pp. 27–8; Lignereux, *L'Empire des Français*, pp. 96–7.

66. Caulaincourt, *Memoirs*, i. p. 171; Charles Corbet, *A l'ère des nationalismes: l'opinion française face à l'inconnue russe (1799–1894)* (Paris, 1967), pp. 63–73.

67. *Corr.* xiv. n. 11722 (29 January 1807).

68. Edward Daniel Clarke, *Travels in Various Countries of Europe, Asia and Africa*, 11 vols (4th edn, London, 1810–23), i. pp. 46–7. It was translated by the Comte d'Hauterive into *Voyages en Russie, en Tartarie et en Turquie* (Paris, 1812). See also Jean-Benoît Schérer, *Anecdotes intéressantes et secrètes de la cour de Russie, tirées de ses archives . . . Publiées par un voyageur qui a séjourné treize ans en Russie*, 6 vols (London and Paris, 1792, 2nd edn 1806).

69. See, for example, the article by V.D.M., 'Recherche et observations générales sur les prisonniers de guerres russes', *La Revue philosophique, littéraire et politique* (1 April 1807), 6–13; and Joux, *La Providence et Napoléon*, pp. 183, 211.

70. Gratien Gilbert Joseph Damaze de Raymond, *Tableau historique, géographique, militaire et moral de l'empire de Russie*, 2 vols (Paris, 1812), i. pp. 273–4. See also Patricia Sorel, 'La campagne de Russie dans la presse quotidienne française et l'almanach du *Messager Boiteux*', in Hans-Jürgen Lüsebrink and Jean-Yves Mollier (eds), *Presse et événement: journaux, gazettes, almanachs (XVIIIe–XIXe siècles)* (Bern, Berlin and Brussels, 2000), pp. 161–2. On French attitudes towards Russians in general see Corbet, *A l'ère des nationalismes*, pp. 77–81; Galina Kabakova, 'Mangeur de chandelles: l'image du cosaque au XIXe siècle', in Katia Dmitrieva and Michel Espagne (eds), *Transferts culturels triangulaires France–Allemagne–Russie* (Paris, 1996), pp. 207–30; Ezequiel Adamovsky, *Euro-Orientalism: Liberal Ideology and the Image of Russia in France (c. 1740–1880)* (Oxford and New York, 2006), pp. 90–3.

71. Charles-Louis Lesur, *Des progrès de la puissance russe: depuis son origine jusqu'au commencement du XIXe siècle* (Paris, 1812). On Peter the Great's 'Testament' see Raymond T. McNalley, 'The Origins of Russophobia in France: 1812–1830', *American Slavic and East European Review*, 17 (1958), 173–4.

72. Iver B. Neumann, *Uses of the Other: 'The East' in European Identity Formation* (Minneapolis, 1999), p. 90.

73. The reference to the 'Army of the twenty nations' has its origins in an imperial proclamation, but it was the expression used by the Russian Orthodox Church to describe the Grande Armée, repeated every Christmas when thanks were given for Russia's deliverance. See Alexander Martin, 'The Response of the Population of Moscow to the Napoleonic Occupation of 1812', in Marshall Poe and Eric Lohr (eds), *The Military and Society in Russia, 1450–1917* (Leiden, 2002), p. 472.

74. *Corr.* xxiii. n. 18348 (19 December 1811).

75. Philippe-Paul, comte de Ségur, *Histoire de Napoléon et de la grande-armée pendant l'année 1812*, 2 vols (Brussels, 1825), i. p. 324.

76. *Corr.* xxiii. n. 18359 (23 December 1811).

77. Peter Simon Pallas, *Nouveau voyage dans les gouvernements méridionaux de l'Empire de Russie, dans les années 1793 et 1794*, trans. from the German, 2 vols (Paris, an X); Jacques Hantraye, *Les cosaques aux Champs-Elysées: l'occupation de la France après la chute de Napoléon* (Paris, 2005), p. 218.

78. Antoine Baudoin Gisbert de Dedem de Gelder, *Un général hollandais sous le premier empire. Mémoires du général Bon de Dedem de Gelder 1774–1825* (Paris, 1900), p. 200. Six hours of training a day according to the grenadier Michel Souchez, in Pierre Charrié, *Lettres de guerres, 1792–1815* (Nantes, 2004), p. 208 (30 March 1812).

79. Heinrich von Roos, *Souvenirs d'un médecin de la Grande Armée* (Paris, 2004), p. 77.

80. If Noël, *Souvenirs militaires*, p. 167, is to be believed.

81. Fantin des Odoards, *Journal*, p. 293.

82. Rowe, *From Reich to State*, p. 158.
83. Castellane, *Journal*, i. p. 146 (4 September 1812).
84. Louis Gardier, *Journal de la campagne de Russie en 1812* (Paris, 1999), p. 18.
85. Montesquiou-Fezensac, *Souvenirs militaires*, p. 219.
86. Craig, *Politics of the Prussian Army*, pp. 58–9; and Gordon A. Craig, 'Problems of Coalition Warfare: The Military Alliance against Napoleon, 1813–14', in Gordon A. Craig, *War, Politics and Diplomacy: Selected Essays* (London, 1966), p. 41.
87. Münchow-Pohl, *Zwischen Reform and Krieg*, pp. 352–84; Obermann, 'La situation de la Prusse sous l'occupation française', pp. 278–83. This is for May and June 1812, before the invasion.
88. *Corr.* xxiii. n. 18622 (30 March 1812).
89. Dedem de Gelder, *Un général hollandais*, pp. 211–12, 203–4; Adams, *Napoleon and Russia*, p. 283.
90. Obermann, 'La situation de la Prusse sous l'occupation française', pp. 257–86, here pp. 278–9.
91. Alexandre Bellot de Kergorre, *Journal d'un commissaire des guerres pendant le Premier Empire (1806–1821)* (Paris, 1997), p. 45; Roman Soltyk, *Napoléon en 1812: souvenirs du général Soltyk* (Paris, 2006), pp. 30–1.
92. Bourgeois, *Tableau de la campagne de Moscou*, p. 17.
93. Armand de Solignac, *La Bérézina. Souvenirs d'un soldat de la Grande Armée* (Limoges, 1881), p. 39 (30 May, 8 June 1812).
94. Caulaincourt, *Memoirs*, i. p. 30.
95. According to Agathon-Jean-François, baron Fain, *Manuscrit de mil huit cent douze*, 2 vols (Paris, 1827), p. 61.
96. Esdaile, *Napoleon's Wars*, p. 452.
97. Fain, *Manuscrit de mil huit cent douze*, i. pp. 66–7.
98. Vandal, *Napoléon et Alexandre*, iii. pp. 402–55; Hermann Freiherrn von Egloffstein, 'Zur Geschichte des Fürstentages in Dresden 1812: Briefe und Aufzeichnungen Carl Augusts', *Historische Zeitschrift*, 121 (1919), 268–82.
99. Schulz, *Voyage en Pologne et en Allemagne*, ii. pp. 53–5.
100. Castellane, *Journal*, i. p. 93 (19 May 1812); Müller, *Souvenirs*, p. 158.
101. There were, for example, no bells or cannon fired on his entry into the city, as required by protocol. Stamm-Kuhlmann, *König in Preußens großer Zeit*, pp. 358–9.
102. Caulaincourt, *Memoirs*, i. p. 155.
103. Caulaincourt, *Memoirs*, i. p. 154; Rambuteau, *Mémoires*, pp. 86–7. Similar reports were passed to Napoleon by his intendant general, Comte Mathieu Dumas. See Michael Josselson and Diana Josselson, *The Commander: A Life of Barclay de Tolly* (Oxford, 1980), pp. 89–90.
104. Castellane, *Journal*, i. p. 96 (26 May 1812); Villemain, *Souvenirs contemporains*, i. pp. 187–8; E. Cazalas, 'La mission de Narbonne à Vilna', *Feuilles d'histoire du XVIIe au XXe siècle*, 3 (1910), 216–30.
105. Cited in Zamoyski, *1812*, p. 130.
106. Zamoyski, *1812*, p. 132.
107. Fain, *Manuscrit de mil huit cent douze*, i. p. 68.
108. Villemain, *Souvenirs contemporains*, i. p. 174; Vandal, *Napoléon et Alexandre*, iii. p. 479.
109. Berthier to Soult, 6 June 1812, cited in Gotteri, *Napoléon*, p. 149.
110. Metternich, *Mémoires*, i. p. 122.
111. Pradt, *Histoire de l'ambassade*, pp. 56–9; Fain, *Manuscrit de mil huit cent douze*, i. p. 75.
112. Esdaile, *Napoleon's Wars*, pp. 461–2.
113. Pasquier, *Mémoires*, i. p. 525.
114. Esdaile, *Napoleon's Wars*, pp. 462, 463.
115. Caulaincourt, *Memoirs*, i. pp. 161, 162.
116. Pierrelongue (ed.), *Napoléon et Marie-Louise*, pp. 22, 24 and 26; Caulaincourt, *Memoirs*, i. p. 163.

# HUBRIS, 1812

## *18: The Second Polish War*

1. The simile is from Comeau de Charry, *Souvenirs des guerres*, p. 443. See also Denniée, *Itinéraire de l'empereur Napoléon*, pp. 14–15; Dupuy, *Souvenirs militaires*, p. 166; François, *Journal*, p. 644 (24 June 1812).
2. Gaspard Ducque, *Journal de marche du sous-lieutenant Ducque* (Paris, 2004), p. 3.
3. Lejeune, *Mémoires*, p. 372.
4. Fantin des Odoards, *Journal*, p. 297.
5. Constantin de Grünwald, *La campagne de Russie* (Paris, 1964), p. 21.
6. Dumas, *Souvenirs*, iii. pp. 417–19; Creveld, *Supplying War*, pp. 65–8.
7. Castellane, *Journal*, i. p. 111 (4 July 1812).
8. Sayve, *Souvenirs de Pologne*, pp. 30–1.
9. Jakob Walter, *The Diary of a Napoleonic Foot Soldier* (Moreton-in-Marsh, 1997), p. 38.
10. According to Ségur, *Histoire de Napoléon et de la grande-armée pendant l'année 1812*, i. pp. 169–70.
11. Pierre Berthezène, *Souvenirs militaires de la République et de l'Empire*, 2 vols (Paris, 1855), i. pp. 323–36; Dedem de Gelder, *Un général hollandais*, pp. 225–7.
12. Caulaincourt, *Memoirs*, i. pp. 202–3.
13. These figures are taken from Zamoyski, *1812*, pp. 142–3. The figures vary enormously from around 400,000 to even over one million men. Esdaile, *Napoleon's Wars*, p. 452, has the army made up of 490,000 with another 121,000 following; Adams, *Napoleon and Russia*, p. 280, cites the figure of 600,000 but states that only 450,000 crossed the Niemen; Chandler, *Campaigns of Napoleon*, p. 756, estimates that 614,000 troops made up the Grande Armée de la Russie, of whom about half were French; Lefebvre, *Napoléon* (Paris, 1969), p. 529, gives 700,000; Albert Meynier, 'Les armées française sous la Révolution et le Premier Empire: la Grande Armée en Russie', *Revue d'études militaires*, 8 (1934), 7–19, cites a figure of 675,000 men, of whom 280,000 were French. Connelly, *Blundering to Glory*, p. 159, suggests there were 611,00 men of whom only one-third were classed as French; Lentz, *Nouvelle histoire du Premier Empire*, ii. p. 259, cites the figure of 680,000 men, but adds that only between 400,000 and 450,000 actually crossed the Niemen, of whom about half were French. See also Jean Delmas (ed.), *Histoire militaire de la France*, 4 vols (Paris, 1992), ii. p. 357, who writes of 578,000 men, including 90,000 cavalry. One contemporary, a survivor of the campaign, cites what appears to be a realistic figure, 460,000 men, including cavalry – but not including the Austrian contingent – with around 1,200 cannon (Labaume, *Relation circonstanciée*, p. 15). For these figures see Claus Scharf, 'Einführung', in Anton Wilhelm Nordhof, *Die Geschichte der Zerstörung Moskaus im Jahre 1812*, Deutsche Geschichtsquellen des 19. und 20. Jahrhunderts, ed. with an introduction by Claus Scharf and Jürgen Kessel (Munich, 2000), p. 16.
14. Anka Muhlstein, *Napoléon à Moscou* (Paris, 2007), pp. 16–17.
15. Adams, *Napoleon and Russia*, pp. 283–5.
16. Pierrelongue (ed.), *Napoléon et Marie-Louise*, pp. 22, 24 and 26; Caulaincourt, *Memoirs*, i. p. 163.
17. Chandler, *Campaigns of Napoleon*, pp. 763, 775; Lentz, *Nouvelle histoire du Premier Empire*, ii. p. 265.
18. Fain, *Manuscrit de mil huit cent douze*, i. p. 75; Soltyk, *Napoléon en 1812*, pp. 27–8. Also, citing Tuchkov, in Serge Nabokov and Sophie de Lastours, *Koutouzov: le vainqueur de Napoléon* (Paris, 1990), p. 156.
19. *Corr.* xxiii. n. 18855 (22 June 1812).

20. Sayve, *Souvenirs de Pologne*, pp. 146–7; Denniée, *Itinéraire de l'empereur Napoléon*, p. 27; Soltyk, *Napoléon en 1812*, pp. 46–8. They were treated even worse on the return leg of the invasion. See, for example, Labaume, *Relation circonstanciée*, pp. 363–4.

21. Cited in Marie-Christiane Torrance, 'Some Russian Attitudes to France in the Period of the Napoleonic Wars as Revealed by Russian Memoirs (1807–14)', *Proceedings of the Royal Irish Academy*, 86c (1986), 293; Josselson and Josselson, *The Commander*, pp. 77, 92–3.

22. Christopher Duffy, *Borodino and the War of 1812* (London, 1972), pp. 53–5; Josselson and Josselson, *The Commander*, p. 77; Lieven, *Russia against Napoleon*, pp. 124–5. It is an exaggeration to claim, however, that Alexander and Barclay de Tolly had outsmarted Napoleon.

23. Bailleu (ed.), *Briefwechsel König Friedrich Wilhelm*, n. 198 (14 May 1811), pp. 219–22.

24. Wilhelm von Oncken, *Österreich und Preußen im Befreiungs-Kriege: urkundliche Aufschlüße über die politische Geschichte des Jahres 1813*, 2 vols (Berlin, 1876–9), ii. pp. 611–14 (13 August 1811).

25. Lieven, *Russia against Napoleon*, pp. 125–32, 149. Lieven believes that this kind of mission was little more than an excuse for intelligence gathering. Balashev was, in fact, accompanied by a young intelligence officer, Mikhail Orlov.

26. Palmer, *Alexander I*, pp. 226–7; Josselson and Josselson, *The Commander*, p. 96.

27. Sayve, *Souvenirs de Pologne*, p. 169; François, *Journal*, p. 645 (28 June 1812); Caulaincourt, *Memoirs*, i. p. 167.

28. For the former, Ségur, *Histoire et mémoires*, iv. p. 148; Denniée, *Itinéraire de l'empereur Napoléon*, p. 24; and for the latter, Caulaincourt, *Memoirs*, i. p. 167.

29. See also Josselson and Josselson, *The Commander*, pp. 86, 93–4, 95–6, 101–3 104; Lieven, *Russia against Napoleon*, p. 150.

30. Josselson and Josselson, *The Commander*, pp. 104–5; Martin, *Romantics, Reformers, Reactionaries*, p. 132.

31. Lieven, *Russia against Napoleon*, p. 151.

32. Caulaincourt, *Memoirs*, i. pp. 168, 173. Napoleon was supposedly helped to believe that the Russians would stand and fight by an agent in Lithuania who passed on disinformation (Lieven, *Russia against Napoleon*, p. 148, and on other 'missions', pp. 149–50).

33. Tatistcheff, *Alexandre Ier et Napoléon*, pp. 588–609; Caulaincourt, *Memoirs*, i. p. 171.

34. Cited in Zamoyski, *1812*, p. 159.

35. Tatistcheff, *Alexandre Ier et Napoléon*, p. 606; Zamoyski, *1812*, p. 160.

36. Emmanuel de Waresquiel (ed.), *Lettres d'un lion: correspondance inédite du général Mouton, comte de Lobau (1812–1815)* (Paris, 2005), p. 59 (30 June 1812).

37. Bellot de Kergorre, *Journal*, p. 47; Coignet, *Note-Books*, p. 207; B. T. Duverger, *Mes Aventures dans la Campagne de Russie* (Paris, 1833), p. 4.

38. Denniée, *Itinéraire de l'empereur Napoléon*, pp. 21–2. Henri-Pierre Everts, 'Campagne et captivité de Russie (1812–1813): extraits des Mémoires inédits du général-major H. p. Everts', in *Carnets et journal sur la campagne de Russie* (Paris, 1997), p. 120, and Caulaincourt, *Memoirs*, i. p. 167, both give a figure of 10,000 dead horses.

39. *Corr*. xxiv. n. 18925 (8 July 1812).

40. Caulaincourt, *Memoirs*, i. p. 186; Curtis Cate, *The War of the Two Emperors: The Duel between Napoleon and Alexander – Russia, 1812* (New York, 1985), p. 255. Half of those again were lost at the battle of Borodino.

41. Alexander M. Martin, 'Lost Arcadia: The 1812 War and the Russian Images of Aristocratic Womanhood', *European History Quarterly*, 37 (2007), 611–14.

42. Aubin Dutheillet de Lamothe, *Mémoires du lieutenant-colonel Aubin Dutheillet de Lamothe* (Brussels, 1899), p. 39.

43. Roos, *Souvenirs*, p. 84; Georges de Chambray, *Histoire de l'expédition de Russie*, 2 vols (Paris, 1823), i. pp. 103–6, 111–13.

44. François, *Journal*, p. 645 (29 June 1812); Antony Brett-James, *1812: Eyewitness Accounts* (New York, 1966), pp. 53–5.

45. Fain, *Manuscrit de mil huit cent douze*, i. pp. 227–8.

46. Roos, *Souvenirs*, p. 84.

47. Coignet, *Note-Books*, p. 215. Similarly, Everts, 'Campagne et captivité de Russie', p. 125.

48. Zamoyski, *1812*, p. 228.

49. These figures vary according to the source. Before the arrival of the army at Vilnius, according to Lentz, *Nouvelle histoire du Premier Empire*, ii. p. 278, more than 30,000 were roaming the countryside.

50. Adams, *Napoleon and Russia*, p. 309.

51. Ducque, *Journal*, p. 11; Roos, *Souvenirs*, p. 81.

52. Gardier, *Journal*, p. 40.

53. Henri Ducor, *Aventures d'un marin de la Garde impériale, prisonnier de guerre sur les pontons espagnols, dans l'île de Cabréra et en Russie*, 2 vols (Paris, 1833), p. 310.

54. See for example Ducque, *Journal*, p. 10.

55. Caulaincourt, *Memoirs*, i. p. 185.

56. Suckow, *D'Iéna à Moscou*, p. 156. Also Walter, *Diary*, p. 40; Everts, 'Campagne et captivité de Russie', p. 127; Paul-Charles-Amable de Bourgoing, *Souvenirs militaires du Bon de Bourgoing, sénateur, ancien ambassadeur en Espagne, ancien pair de France, ministre plénipotentiaire en Russie et en Allemagne, 1791–1815* (Paris, 1897), pp. 88–9. Suicide could lead to veritable epidemics of self-killing in eighteenth-century armies, according to Martin Monestier, *Suicides: histoire, techniques et bizarreries de la mort volontaire des origines à nos jours* (Paris, 1995), pp. 38–9.

57. On Jérôme's performance in Russia see Boudon, *Le roi Jérôme*, pp. 372–82. On his stay in Poland on the way to Russia see Masson, *Napoléon et sa famille*, vii. pp. 297–305; Mansuy, *Jérôme Napoléon et la Pologne en 1812*, pp. 297–531.

58. Cited in Boudon, *Le roi Jérôme*, p. 381.

59. Chevalier, *Souvenirs*, p. 186.

60. Everts, 'Campagne et captivité de Russie', p. 126.

61. Bourgogne, *Mémoires*, p. 62.

62. Fantin des Odoards, *Journal*, p. 324.

63. Detlev von Uexküll (ed.), *Arms and the Woman: The Diaries of Baron Boris Uxkull, 1812–1819*, trans. Joel Carmichael (London, 1966), p. 72 (30 July 1812).

64. Waresquiel (ed.), *Lettres d'un lion*, p. 84 (24 September 1812); Chevalier, *Souvenirs*, pp. 181, 189–90. Chevalier reports that there was even a light fall of snow towards the end of September, *Souvenirs*, p. 83 (20 September 1812).

65. Labaume, *Relation circonstanciée*, pp. 152–3.

66. Thirion, *Souvenirs militaires*, pp. 78–9; François, *Journal*, pp. 646 and 647 (2 and 5 July 1812).

67. Thirion, *Souvenirs militaires*, p. 81; Adrien-Augustin-Amalric, comte de Mailly, *Mon journal pendant la campagne de Russie, écrit de mémoire après mon retour à Paris* (Paris, 1841), pp. 16–17; Walter, *Diary*, p. 44.

68. Chevalier, *Souvenirs*, pp. 181–2.

69. Bellot de Kergorre, *Journal*, p. 48.

70. Gardier, *Journal*, p. 39 (Spain); Duverger, *Mes aventures*, pp. 4–5.

71. Puybusque, *Lettres sur la guerre de Russie*, pp. 32 and 33 (7 July 1812); Gardier, *Journal*, pp. 39–40; Waresquiel (ed.), *Lettres d'un lion*, pp. 53 and 55 (3 and 5 June 1812); Walter, *Diary*, p. 53; Louis-Joseph Vionnet de Maringoné, *Souvenirs d'un ex-commandant des grenadiers de la vieille-garde. Fragments des mémoires inédits du lieutenant-général L.-J. Vionnet de Maringoné* (Paris, 1899), p. 1; Michel Combe, *Mémoires du colonel Combe sur le campagnes de Russie en 1812, de Saxe 1813, de France, 1814 et 1815* (Paris, 1853), p. 78; Brett-James, *1812: Eyewitness*, p. 52.

72. Suckow, *D'Iéna à Moscou*, p. 157.

73. Girod de l'Ain, *Dix ans de souvenirs militaires*, pp. 252–3; Ducor, *Aventures d'un marin de la Garde impériale*, i. pp. 305–6.

74. François, *Journal*, p. 653 (7 August 1812); Suckow, *D'Iéna à Moscou*, p. 157; Franz Joseph Hausmann, *A Soldier for Napoleon: The Campaigns of Lieutenant Franz Joseph*

Hausmann, *7th Bavarian Infantry*, trans. Cynthia Joy Hausmann, ed. John H. Gill (London, 1998), pp. 99, 149.

75. *Corr.* xxiii. and xxiv. nos. 18874 to 18969 (28 June–18 July 1812).

76. Antoine Henri de Jomini, *Précis politique et militaire des campagnes de 1812 à 1814*, 2 vols (Geneva, 1975), i. 72.

77. Duverger, *Mes aventures*, p. 5.

78. Montesquiou-Fezensac, *Souvenirs militaires*, pp. 233–4; Josselson and Josselson, *The Commander*, pp. 110–11.

79. Villemain, *Souvenirs contemporains*, i. p. 198.

80. Constant, *Mémoires*, ii. p. 272; Caulaincourt, *Memoirs*, i. p. 200.

81. Ségur, *Histoire et mémoires*, iv. p. 257.

82. Ducor, *Aventures d'un marin de la Garde impériale*, p. 308.

83. Méneval, *Mémoires*, iii. p. 43; Castellane, *Journal*, i. pp. 126–7 (6 August 1812); Bourgoing, *Souvenirs*, pp. 98–100.

84. *Corr.* xxiv. nos. 19015 to 19093 (29 July–12 August 1812).

85. Ségur, *Histoire de Napoléon*, i. p. 222.

86. Adams, *Napoleon and Russia*, p. 315; Esdaile, *Napoleon's Wars*, p. 472.

87. Lieven, *Russia against Napoleon*, pp. 158–62.

88. On the events leading up to the battle for Smolensk see Lieven, *Russia against Napoleon*, pp. 164–73; Chandler, *Campaigns of Napoleon*, pp. 767–90.

89. According to Philippe-Paul, comte de Ségur, *History of the Expedition to Russia Undertaken by the Emperor Napoleon in the Year 1812*, 2 vols (London, 1826), ii. pp. 263–4, a large ford existed about one kilometre from the city, but that it remained undiscovered for two days.

90. Raymond Faure, *Souvenirs du Nord, ou la Guerre, la Russie et les Russes ou l'esclavage* (Paris, 1821), p. 34.

91. Caulaincourt, *Memoirs*, i. pp. 209–10. In fact, it was probably Charles IX of France (c. 1574).

92. Pierre Paradis to Geneviève Bonnegrâce (20 September 1812), in Léon Hennet and Emmanuel Martin (eds), *Lettres interceptées par les Russes durant la campagne de 1812* (Paris, 1913) (hereafter *Lettres interceptées*), p. 20.

93. Puybusque, *Lettres sur la guerre de Russie*, pp. 52–3 (24 August 1812).

94. Soltyk, *Napoléon en 1812*, pp. 133–6.

95. Chandler, *Campaigns of Napoleon*, pp. 791–2.

96. Caulaincourt, *Memoirs*, i. p. 208.

97. Bourgeois, *Tableau de la campagne de Moscou*, p. 35; Lejeune, *Mémoires*, pp. 385, 386; Denniée, *Itinéraire de l'empereur Napoléon*, pp. 58–9, 62; Rapp, *Mémoires*, p. 157; Boulart, *Mémoires militaires*, p. 250.

98. According to Soltyk, *Napoléon en 1812*, p. 130

99. Caulaincourt, *Memoirs*, i. pp. 216–17.

100. Caulaincourt, *Memoirs*, i. p. 214.

101. Paul Britten Austin, *1812: The March on Moscow* (London, 1993), pp. 157–8.

102. Joseph de Maistre, *Correspondance diplomatique 1811–1817*, 2 vols (Paris, 1860), i. pp. 130–1 (no date but probably July 1812); Nabokov and de Lastours, *Koutouzov*, pp. 143–66.

103. Lieven, *Russia against Napoleon*, p. 189.

104. Esdaile, *Napoleon's Wars*, p. 475.

105. Maurice Paléologue, *Alexandre Ier, un tsar énigmatique* (Paris, 1937), pp. 140–1.

106. Fain, *Manuscrit de mil huit cent douze*, ii. p. 7.

107. Fain, *Manuscrit de mil huit cent douze*, ii. p. 8.

108. Fain, *Manuscrit de mil huit cent douze*, ii. pp. 8–9.

109. Colonel Rodojuzky, cited in Nabokov and de Lastours, *Koutouzov*, p. 172.

110. Ducque, *Journal*, pp. 19–20.

111. On the battle of Borodino see Duffy, *Borodino*; Parkinson, *The Fox of the North*,

pp. 139–57; Zamoyski, *1812*, pp. 252–88; Chandler, *Campaigns of Napoleon*, pp. 790–810; Soltyk, *Napoléon en 1812*, pp. 155–74.

112. Duffy, *Borodino*, pp. 84–5; Adams, *Napoleon and Russia*, p. 340.

113. Vladimir Ivanovitch Löwenstern, *Mémoires du général-major russe baron de Löwenstern*, 2 vols (Paris, 1903), i. p. 273. Although the militia often stole whatever valuables they could find on the wounded (Zamoyski, *1812*, pp. 258–9, 327).

114. On this point see Lieven, *Russia against Napoleon*, pp. 195–6.

115. *Corr.* xxiv. n. 19182 (7 September 1812).

116. Chandler, *Campaigns of Napoleon*, pp. 798–9; Duffy, *Borodino*, p. 85; Lieven, *Russia against Napoleon*, pp. 199–200.

117. Caulaincourt, *Memoirs*, i. p. 245.

118. Lejeune, *Mémoires*, p. 398.

119. Gaspard Gourgaud, *Napoléon et la grande-armée en Russie ou Examen critique de l'ouvrage de M. le comte Ph. de Ségur* (Brussels, 1825), p. 242.

120. Cited in Adams, *Napoleon and Russia*, p. 349. Others (Duffy, *Borodino*, pp. 142–3) have more or less excused both commanders from what appears to be complete lethargy, as though they were paralysed by their responsibilities.

121. Caulaincourt, *Memoirs*, i. pp. 245–6.

122. Lieven, *Russia against Napoleon*, pp. 206–7.

123. Brett-James, *1812: Eyewitness*, p. 48.

124. Esdaile, *Napoleon's Wars*, p. 414.

125. For his health see Constant, *Mémoires*, v. pp. 60–1; Denniée, *Itinéraire de l'empereur Napoléon*, p. 74, who asserts that he was also suffering from a migraine; Marie-Joseph-Thomas Rossetti, *Journal d'un compagnon de Murat: Espagne, Naples, Russie* (Paris, 1998), p. 116, who says that he was 'in pain'; Marie-Elie-Guillaume de Baudus, *Etudes sur Napoléon, par le lieutenant-colonel de Baudus*, 2 vols (Paris, 1841), ii. p. 83.

126. Ducque, *Journal*, p. 22.

127. Ducque, *Journal*, p. 21. Denniée, *Itinéraire de l'empereur Napoléon*, pp. 80–1; Adams, *Napoleon and Russia*, p. 355.

128. Ducque, *Journal*, pp. 21–2.

129. Rostopchin to Vorontsov, 28 April 1814, in Bartenev (ed.), *Archiv kniazia Vorontsova*, viii. p. 319.

130. Adams, *Napoleon and Russia*, p. 355.

131. On Russian losses, Zamoyski, *1812*, pp. 287–8; Nordhof, *Die Geschichte der Zerstörung Moskaus*, p. 164 n. 209; Alexander Mikaberidze, *The Battle of Borodino: Napoleon against Kutuzov* (Barnsley, 2007), pp. 207–18; Lieven, *Russia against Napoleon*, p. 209.

132. On the aftermath of the battle see Faure, *Souvenirs du Nord*, pp. 45–7; Bourgeois, *Tableau de la campagne de Moscou*, pp. 47, 50–2; Dedem de Gelder, *Un général hollandais*, p. 240; François Dumonceau, *Mémoires du général comte François Dumonceau*, 3 vols (Brussels, 1958–63), ii. pp. 142–4; Roos, *Souvenirs*, p. 100; François, *Journal*, p. 666 (7 September 1812); Vionnet de Maringoné, *Souvenirs*, pp. 14–15; La Flize, 'Souvenirs de la Moskowa par un chirurgien de la Garde Impériale', *Feuilles d'histoire du XVIIe au XXe siècle*, 8 (1912), 419–26.

133. Ségur, *Histoire et mémoires*, iv. pp. 411–12.

134. Pierrelongue (ed.), *Napoléon et Marie-Louise*, p. 56 (8 September 1812).

135. Ségur, *Histoire et mémoires*, iv. pp. 411–12.

136. Alphonse Rabbe, *Résumé de l'histoire de Russie depuis l'établissement de Rourik . . . jusqu'à nos jours* (Paris, 1825), pp. 595–6.

## 19: 'The Struggle of Obstinacy'

1. Méneval, *Mémoires*, iii. p. 62. For a description of the city see G. Lecointe de Laveau, *Moscou avant et après l'incendie* (Paris, 1814), pp. 1–13.

2. Labaume, *Relation circonstanciée*, p. 183.

3. Fantin des Odoards, *Journal*, pp. 331–2; Bourgogne, *Mémoires*, p. 13; Faure, *Souvenirs du Nord*, pp. 51–2; Soltyk, *Napoléon en 1812*, pp. 183–6.

4. Bourgogne, *Mémoires*, p. 13; Combe, *Mémoires*, pp. 100–1.

5. Guillaume Peyrusse, *Lettres inédites du baron Guillaume Peyrusse, écrites à son frère André, pendant les campagnes de l'empire, de 1809 à 1814* (Paris, 1894), p. 100 (22 September 1812).

6. Paul Bairoch, 'Une nouvelle distribution des populations: villes et campagnes', in Jean-Pierre Bardet et Jacques Dupâquier (eds), *Histoire des populations de l'Europe*, 3 vols (Paris, 1997), ii. p. 211; Alexander M. Martin, 'Down and Out in 1812: The Impact of the Napoleonic Invasion on Moscow's Middling Strata', in Roger Bartlett and Gabriella Lehmann-Carli (eds), *Eighteenth-Century Russia: Society, Culture, Economy* (Münster, 2008), p. 430.

7. Mavor (ed.), *The Grand Tours of Katherine Wilmot*, pp. 145–6; Constantin de Grunwald, *Société et civilisation russes au XIXe siècle* (Paris, 1975), pp. 41–5; Torrance, 'Some Russian Attitudes to France', 294.

8. Martin, 'Lost Arcadia', 609.

9. Count Ysarn Dunin-Stryzewski to his wife (12 October 1812). Also Prosper to his father-in-law (15 October), in *Lettres interceptées*, pp. 79, 148.

10. Martin, 'The Response of the Population of Moscow', pp. 469–70.

11. On this see Lieven, *Russia against Napoleon*, pp. 210–11.

12. A. A. Orlov, 'Britons in Moscow', *History Today*, 53/7 (2003), 18–19. The figures are from Martin, 'The Response of the Population of Moscow', pp. 473, 474, based on a police report; Nordhof, *Die Geschichte der Zerstörung Moskaus*, p. 166 n. 218; Zamoyski, *1812*, p. 576 n. 5.

13. Ségur, *Histoire et mémoires*, v. p. 57.

14. Ducque, *Journal*, pp. 26–7.

15. Bourgogne, *Mémoires*, pp. 13–16.

16. Martin, 'The Response of the Population of Moscow', p. 479.

17. Fantin des Odoards, *Journal*, p. 332.

18. Fantin des Odoards, *Journal*, p. 241. See also Labaume, *Relation circonstanciée*, pp. 194, 196, 197; Thirion, *Souvenirs militaires*, pp. 103–4; Duverger, *Mes aventures*, p. 8.

19. Caulaincourt, *Memoirs*, i. p. 259; Soltyk, *Napoléon en 1812*, p. 191.

20. Adams, *Napoleon and Russia*, p. 408. About 260,000 men were still operating in various parts of Russia at this point (Ralph Ashby, *Napoleon against Great Odds: The Emperor and the Defenders of France, 1814* (Santa Barbara, Calif., 2010), pp. 12–13). About 100,000 of those had been left to guard the route to Moscow (Marie-Pierre Rey, 'De l'uniforme à l'accoutrement: une métaphore de la retraite? Réalité et symbolique du vêtement dans la campagne de Russie de 1812', in Natalie Petiteau, Jean-Marc Olivier and Sylvie Caucanas (eds), *Les Européens dans les guerre napoléoniennes* (Toulouse, 2012), p. 238).

21. Paradis to Bonnegrâce (20 September 1812), in *Lettres interceptées*, p. 19.

22. Ducque, *Journal*, p. 27.

23. Martin, 'The Response of the Population of Moscow', p. 476.

24. Frédéric List to his wife (22 September 1812), in *Lettres interceptées*, p. 26. Most others had suffered the same conditions (R.S. to Mme Lebrun (13 October 1812), in *Lettres interceptées*, p. 81).

25. Captain Richard to Colonel Borthon (22 September 1812), in *Lettres interceptées*, pp. 333–4.

26. General Baraguay d'Hilliers to his wife (31 October 1812), in *Lettres interceptées*, pp. 343–4.

27. Baron Boulart to his wife (1 November 1812), in *Lettres interceptées*, pp. 184–5.

28. Germaine de Staël-Holstein, *Dix années d'exil* (Paris, 1904), p. 311; Angelica Goodden, *Madame de Staël: The Dangerous Exile* (Oxford, 2008), pp. 204–16.

29. Martin, *Romantics, Reformers, Reactionaries*, pp. 125–36.

30. Nordhof, *Die Geschichte der Zerstörung Moskaus*, pp. 113, 118, 133–5, 143–5, 146.

31. Torrance, 'Some Russian Attitudes to France', 294.

32. For the following, Marina Peltzer, 'Imagerie populaire et caricature: la graphique politique antinapoléonienne en Russie et ses antécédents pétroviens', *Journal of the Warburg and Courtauld Institutes*, 48 (1985), 190; and Marina Peltzer, 'Peasants, Cossacks, "Black Tsar": Russian Caricatures of Napoleon during the Wars of 1812 to 1814', in Alan Forrest, Etienne François and Karen Hagemann (eds), *War Memories: The Revolutionary and Napoleonic Wars in Modern European Culture* (Basingstoke, 2012).

33. Martin, 'Lost Arcadia', 612.

34. Martin, *Romantics, Reformers, Reactionaries*, p. 128.

35. Martin, *Romantics, Reformers, Reactionaries*, p. 135.

36. Adams, *Napoleon and Russia*, p. 320.

37. Zamoyski, *1812*, p. 294.

38. Nordhof, *Die Geschichte der Zerstörung Moskaus*, pp. 154–6; Martin, *Romantics, Reformers, Reactionaries*, pp. 129–30.

39. Torrance, 'Some Russian Attitudes to France', 296.

40. Cited in Torrance, 'Some Russian Attitudes to France', 296–7.

41. Edling, *Mémoires*, pp. 74–6; Lieven, *Russia against Napoleon*, p. 210.

42. Lieven, *Russia against Napoleon*, p. 242.

43. Maistre, *Oeuvres complètes*, xii. p. 180.

44. Edling, *Mémoires*, pp. 79–80.

45. It is impossible to know how many prisoners were released, but we know that around 540 were nevertheless transferred to the prison of Nizhni Novgorod (Nordhof, *Die Geschichte der Zerstörung Moskaus*, pp. 154 n. 172, and 157, 159. Bourgogne, *Mémoires*, p. 17; Adams, *Napoleon and Russia*, pp. 360–1.

46. According to Muhlstein, *Napoléon à Moscou*, p. 162.

47. Boulart, *Mémoires militaires*, p. 261; Denniée, *Itinéraire de l'empereur Napoléon*, pp. 94–5.

48. Bellot de Kergorre, *Journal*, p. 54.

49. Fantin des Odoards, *Journal*, p. 335.

50. Ségur, *Histoire de Napoléon et de la grande-armée pendant l'année 1812*, ii. p. 49. Ancient authors describe the people occupying the region between the north of the Danube and the northern Caucasus, which today would largely incorporate the Ukrainian steppes, as Scythians. In Greek sources, they were archetypal barbarians.

51. Feodor Vasilievitch Rostopchin, *La vérité sur l'incendie de Moscou, par le Cte Rostopchine* (Paris, 1823). For a detailed analysis of this 'controversy', which is nothing of the kind, see Daria Olivier, *The Burning of Moscow, 1812*, trans. M. Heron (London, 1966), pp. 186–97. Rostopchin was dismissed from office in August 1814. Despite his virulent Francophobia during the war, he spent the years 1815–23 in Paris where he was fêted as the man who had burnt Moscow and defeated Napoleon. He died in Moscow in 1826. Even Rostopchin's daughter, in an otherwise exculpatory memoir, wrote of her father setting fire to Moscow. See Natalie Narychkin, *Le comte Rostopchine et son temps: 1812* (St Petersburg, 1912), pp. 151, 158.

52. Torrance, 'Some Russian Attitudes to France', 297.

53. Lieven, *Russia against Napoleon*, p. 213.

54. François-Joseph d'Ysarn Villefort, *Relation du séjour des Français à Moscou et l'incendie de cette ville en 1812, par un habitant de Moscou* (Brussels, 1871), p. 9.

55. On these conflicting views see Torrance, 'Some Russian Attitudes to France', 297.

56. Joseph de Maistre wrote about how the burning of Moscow 'fanaticized' the people and contributed towards the acts of barbarity committed against the invader (Maistre, *Oeuvres complètes*, xii. pp. 295, 307).

57. Grand Duc Nicolas Mikhaïlovitch (ed.), *Perepiska imperatora Aleksandra I so sestroi Velikoi knyaginei Yekaterinoi Pavlovnoi* (St Petersburg, 1910), pp. 83, 84, and 86–93 (3, 6, 7 and 18 September 1812); Daria Olivier, *L'incendie de Moscou* (Paris, 1964), pp. 130–1; Zamoyski, *1812*, pp. 313–14; Rey, *Alexandre Ier*, pp. 325–6.

58. Reported in Adams (ed.), *Memoirs of John Quincy Adams*, ii. p. 409 (30 September 1812).

59. Maret to Berthier, 21 September 1812, in Arthur Chuquet (ed.), *Lettres de 1812: première série* (Paris, 1911), p. 47.

60. Ysarn Villefort, *Relation du séjour des Français à Moscou*, pp. 30–1; (abbé) Adrien Surrugues, *Lettres sur l'incendie de Moscou en 1812* (Paris, 1823), p. 18.

61. Berthezène, *Souvenirs militaires*, ii. pp. 73–4; Adélaïde-Louise d'Eckmühl, marquise de Blocqueville, *Le maréchal Davout, prince d'Eckmühl, raconté par les siens et par lui-même*, 4 vols (Paris, 1879–80), iii. p. 177; Ségur, *Histoire et mémoires*, v. p. 92; Villemain, *Souvenirs contemporains*, i. p. 230.

62. Lieven, *Russia against Napoleon*, p. 246.

63. Labaume, *Relation circonstanciée*, p. 225.

64. Bellot de Kergorre, *Journal*, p. 54; Bourgogne, *Mémoires*, p. 17; Duverger, *Mes aventures*, pp. 11–12; Waresquiel (ed.), *Lettres d'un lion*, p. 89 (27 September 1812); Lecointe de Laveau, *Moscou avant et après l'incendie*, pp. 119–20; Bourgeois, *Tableau de la campagne de Moscou*, pp. 65–6; Puybusque, *Lettres sur la guerre de Russie*, pp. 96–7 (24 October 1812); Dedem de Gelder, *Un général hollandais*, pp. 252–3, 256; Soltyk, *Napoléon en 1812*, pp. 221–3; Maret to Berthier, 21 September 1812, in Chuquet (ed.), *Lettres de 1812*, p. 49, wrote that they had enough supplies for six months.

65. Bourgogne, *Mémoires*, p. 55. On the looting of Moscow in general see Nordhof, *Die Geschichte der Zerstörung Moskaus*, pp. 185–202. On life in Moscow during the French occupation see Muhlstein, *Napoléon à Moscou*, pp. 197–215.

66. Surrugues, *Lettres sur l'incendie de Moscou*, p. 23.

67. Labaume, *Relation circonstanciée*, p. 242 ; Bellot de Kergorre, *Journal*, p. 55; Waresquiel (ed.), *Lettres d'un lion*, p. 58 (20 June 1812); Larrey, *Mémoires*, iv. pp. 77–8.

68. Ségur, *Histoire et mémoires*, v. p. 83.

69. Solignac, *La Bérézina*, p. 161.

70. Peyrusse, *Lettres inédites*, p. 100 (22 September 1812). See, too, Labaume, *Relation circonstanciée*, pp. 109–1.

71. Castellane, *Journal*, i. p. 162 (28 and 30 September 1812).

72. *Corr.* xxiv. n. 19213 (20 September 1812); Caulaincourt, *Memoirs*, i. p. 285.

73. Caulaincourt, *Memoirs*, i. pp. 302–3; Ségur, *Histoire et mémoires*, v. p. 75; Ségur, *Histoire de Napoléon*, ii. pp. 75–7.

74. *Corr.* xxiv. n. 19213 (September 1812); Adams, *Napoleon and Russia*, pp. 366–70; Lieven, *Napoleon against Russia*, pp. 251–2.

75. Caulaincourt, *Memoirs*, i. p. 305.

76. Caulaincourt, *Memoirs*, i. p. 306.

77. Puybusque, *Lettres sur la guerre de Russie*, pp. 142–5 (11 December 1812); Lieven, *Russia against Napoleon*, p. 252.

78. Puybusque, *Lettres sur la guerre de Russie*, pp. 35–6 (19 August 1812).

79. Ségur, *Histoire et mémoires*, v. p. 71.

80. Caulaincourt, *Memoirs*, i. pp. 277.

81. Caulaincourt, *Memoirs*, i. p. 313.

82. François, *Journal*, p. 668 (1–5 October 1812).

83. An employee of the General Intendancy, 19 October 1812, in *Lettres interceptées*, p. 175.

84. Mortier to Berthier, 18 September 1812, in Chuquet (ed.), *Lettres de 1812*, pp. 43–4.

85. Caulaincourt, *Memoirs*, i. p. 310.

86. Caulaincourt, *Memoirs*, i. pp. 297–8, 302, 323; Blocqueville, *Le maréchal Davout*, iii. 181.

87. Waresquiel (ed.), *Lettres d'un lion*, p. 92 (8 October 1812).

88. François, *Journal*, p. 670 (13, 14, 15, 16 and 17 October 1812).

89. Adams, *Napoleon and Russia*, p. 370.

90. Caulaincourt, *Memoirs*, i. pp. 301–3.

91. *Corr.* xxiv. nos. 19238 and 19245 (1 and 4 October 1812).

92. According to Ségur, *Histoire et mémoires*, v. p. 93.

93. Adams, *Napoleon and Russia*, p. 372.

94. Lieven, *Russia against Napoleon*, pp. 251–2.

95. Adams (ed.), *Memoirs of John Quincy Adams*, ii. p. 410 (2 October 1812).

96. *Corr.* xxiv. n. 19237 (no date, but probably 1 October 1812), although, according to

Fain, *Manuscrit de mil huit cent douze*, ii. pp. 93–5, plans were drawn up to threaten Petersburg.

97. For this and the following: Adams, *Napoleon and Russia*, pp. 370–1; Napoleon's options are to be found in a number of documents in *Corr.* xxiv. nos. 19237, 19250, 19258, 19275 (1, 5, 6 and 16 October 1812).

98. Van Boecop to his father (27 September 1812), in *Lettres interceptées*, p. 50.

99. Adams, *Napoleon and Russia*, pp. 371–2, believes that Napoleon had lost confidence and that he was avoiding Kutuzov.

100. Fain, *Manuscrit de mil huit cent douze*, ii. pp. 95–7.

101. Berthier to Dumas, 10 October 1812, in Chuquet (ed.), *Lettres de 1812*, pp. 77–80.

102. *Corr.* xxiv. n. 19273 (14 October 1812); Berthier in Chuquet (ed.), *Lettres de 1812*, pp. 81–2 (14 October 1812).

103. Fain, *Manuscrit de mil huit cent douze*, ii. p. 153.

104. Castellane, *Journal*, i. p. 168; Ernest Picard and Louis Tuetey (eds), *Correspondance inédite de Napoléon Ier, conservée aux Archives de la guerre*, 5 vols (Paris, 1912–25), v. p. 595.

105. Castellane, *Journal*, i. p. 161 (27 September 1812).

106. Caulaincourt, *Memoirs*, i. p. 327.

107. Zamoyski, *1812*, pp. 352–3.

108. *Corr.* xxiv. n. 19285 (18 October 1812); Caulaincourt, *Memoirs*, i. pp. 327–30; Nicolas-Louis Planat de la Faye, *Vie de Planat de la Faye, aide de camp des généraux Lariboisière et Drouot, officier d'ordonnance de Napoléon Ier. Souvenirs, lettres et dictées recueillis et annotés par sa veuve* (Paris, 1895), p. 92.

109. Lieutenant Paradis to Mlle Bonnegrâce (20 September); Frédéric List to his wife (22 September 1812); Marie-François Schaken to his father (29 September); Baron Bacler d'Albe to his wife (14 October), in *Lettres interceptées*, pp. 22, 27, 61, 111.

110. Dauxon to his wife (15 October), in *Lettres interceptées*, p. 155.

111. Bourgogne, *Mémoires*, pp. 55–6.

112. Robert de Vaucorbeil, 'Mémoires inédits d'Alexandre de Cheron sur la campagne de Russie', *Revue de l'Institut Napoléon*, 140 (1983): 27–57, here 35–6.

113. Bourgeois, *Tableau de la campagne de Moscou*, pp. 84–5.

114. Fain, *Manuscrit de mil huit cent douze*, ii. p. 161.

115. Soltyk, *Napoléon en 1812*, pp. 238–9; Montesquiou-Fezensac, *Souvenirs militaires*, pp. 276–8.

116. Baudus, *Etudes sur Napoléon*, ii. pp. 246–7.

117. Zamoyski, *1812*, p. 367.

118. Labaume, *Relation circonstanciée*, pp. 232–3.

119. Denniée, *Itinéraire de l'empereur Napoléon*, pp. 107–8; Castellane, *Journal*, i. p. 173 (19 October 1812). Also Boudon, *Le roi Jérôme*, p. 385.

120. Labaume, *Relation circonstanciée*, p. 249 (several leagues according to Labaume).

121. Bellot de Kergorre, *Journal*, p. 59.

122. Vionnet de Maringoné, *Souvenirs*, p. 61; Louis-Vivant Lagneau, *Journal d'un chirurgien de la Grande Armée, 1803–1815* (Paris, 1913), p. 218.

123. Lejeune, *Mémoires*, p. 408.

124. Mailly, *Mon journal*, pp. 66–7.

125. Mailly, *Mon journal*, p. 71.

126. Duverger, *Mes aventures*, pp. 12, 15.

127. Labaume, *Relation circonstanciée*, p. 229.

128. Lejeune, *Mémoires*, p. 409, asserted that the army took six days to cover 140 kilometres. Bourgogne, *Mémoires*, p. 58; Adams, *Napoleon and Russia*, p. 375.

129. Vaucorbeil, 'Mémoires inédits', 36.

130. Henri-Joseph Paixhans, *Retraite de Moscou, notes écrites au quartier de l'Empereur* (Metz, 1868), pp. 36–7.

131. Labaume, *Relation circonstanciée*, pp. 236–7.

132. Labaume, *Relation circonstanciée*, p. 229.

133. *Corr.* xxiv. nos. 19292, 19304 (20 October and 23 December 1812).

134. Lejeune, *Mémoires*, p. 412; Caulaincourt, *Memoirs*, ii. pp. 21–2; Fain, *Manuscrit de mil huit cent douze*, ii. pp. 250–1; Ségur, *Histoire et mémoires*, v. p. 123.

135. Caulaincourt, *Memoirs*, ii. pp. 16–18; Soltyk, *Napoléon en 1812*, pp. 249–50; Adams, *Napoleon and Russia*, p. 379.

136. Soltyk, *Napoléon en 1812*, pp. 253–5.

137. Adams, *Napoleon and Russia*, p. 379.

138. Adams, *Napoleon and Russia*, p. 380; Lieven, *Russia against Napoleon*, p. 258.

139. Lieven, *Russia against Napoleon*, pp. 261, 262.

140. Caulaincourt, *Memoirs*, ii. pp. 23–8; Rapp, *Mémoires*, pp. 187–8; Ségur, *Histoire de Napoléon*, ii. pp. 140–3.

141. Caulaincourt, *Memoirs*, ii. p. 27; Denniée, *Itinéraire de l'empereur Napoléon*, pp. 114–15.

142. Dwyer, *Napoleon: The Path to Power*, pp. 433–4.

143. Labaume, *Relation circonstanciée*, pp. 271, 274.

144. Caulaincourt, *Memoirs*, ii. pp. 35–8.

145. Ducque, *Journal*, p. 41.

146. Ducque, *Journal*, pp. 41–2.

147. Mailly, *Mon journal*, p. 78.

148. Bourgogne, *Mémoires*, p. 61; Bellot de Kergorre, *Journal*, p. 61; Labaume, *Relation circonstanciée*, pp. 276–8; François, *Journal*, p. 673 (29 October 1812); Vaucorbeil, 'Mémoires inédits', 36; Vionnet de Maringoné, *Souvenirs*, p. 79; 'Extraits du carnets du Général Pelet sur la campagne de Russie de 1812', *Carnet de la Sabretache*, 5 (1906), 519–20.

149. Girod de l'Ain, *Dix ans de souvenirs militaires*, p. 281.

150. Labaume, *Relation circonstanciée*, pp. 274, 302; Vaucorbeil, 'Mémoires inédits', 40; Bourgeois, *Tableau de la campagne de Moscou*, pp. 127–9.

151. Ducque, *Journal*, p. 43.

152. Billiotti to his wife (1 November 1812), in *Lettres interceptées*, p. 182.

153. Billiotti to his wife (1 November 1812), in Chuquet (ed.), *Lettres de 1812*, p. 117.

154. Vionnet de Maringoné, *Souvenirs*, p. 76.

155. Desveaux de Saint-Maurice to his wife (1 November 1812), in *Lettres interceptées*, p. 183.

156. F. de Bausset to Scipion de Nicolaï (11 November 1812), in *Lettres interceptées*, p. 299.

157. Ducque, *Journal*, p. 41.

158. Roos, *Souvenirs*, p. 125.

159. Caulaincourt, *Memoirs*, ii. p. 34.

160. Ducque, *Journal*, p. 42 (around 29 October); Castellane, *Journal*, i. p. 175 (21 October 1812); Paixhans, *Retraite de Moscou*, p. 40; Józef Bonawentura Ignacy Załuski, *Les chevau-légers polonais de la Garde (1812–1814): souvenirs* (Paris, 1997), p. 36; Marie-Henry, comte de Lignières, *Souvenirs de la Grande Armée et de la Vieille Garde impériale: Marie-Henry, comte de Lignières, 1783–1886* (Paris, 1933), p. 116; Walter, *Diary*, pp. 67–8.

161. Roos, *Souvenirs*, pp. 125–6.

162. Léonce Bernard, *Les prisonniers de guerre du Premier Empire* (Paris, 2000), pp. 227–8.

163. Jean-Baptiste Ricome, *Journal d'un grognard de l'Empire* (Paris, 1988), p. 61; Uexküll (ed.), *Arms and the Woman*, p. 105 (21 November–1 December 1812).

164. Rapp, *Mémoires*, p. 199.

165. Adams, *Napoleon and Russia*, p. 403.

166. See, for example, Labaume, *Relation circonstanciée*, p. 368.

167. Bernard Gainot, 'Réflexions sur une forme politique de transition (à propos de la conspiration Malet de 1808)', in Biard, Crépin and Gainot (eds), *La plume et le sabre*, pp. 513–24.

168. There are a number of works on the Malet affair, of varying degrees of interest: Frédéric Masson, *La vie et les conspirations du général Malet, 1754–1812* (Paris, 1921); Comte de Lort de Sérignan, *Un conspirateur militaire sous le premier Empire: le général Malet* (Paris, 1925); Alain Decaux, *La conspiration du général Malet: d'après des documents inédits* (Paris, 1951); Henri Kubnick, *Echec à l'Empereur, la conspiration de Malet* (Geneva, 1959);

Bernardine Melchior-Bonnet, *La conspiration du général Malet* (Paris, 1963); Artom Guido, *Napoleon is Dead in Russia*, trans. Muriel Grindrod (New York, 1970); Thierry Lentz, *La conspiration du général Malet: 23 octobre 1812: premier ébranlement du trône de Napoléon* (Paris, 2011).

169. Lentz, *Nouvelle histoire du Premier Empire*, iii. p. 163.
170. Caulaincourt, *Memoirs*, ii. pp. 48–9.

## 20 : Destiny Forsaken

1. Adrien Guéneau to his father (11 November 1812), in *Lettres interceptées*, p. 283.
2. Domon to Comte Valette (9 November 1812), in *Lettres interceptées*, pp. 220–1.
3. Larrey to his wife (c. November 1812), in *Lettres interceptées*, p. 301.
4. Laurencin to his mother (9 November 1812), in *Lettres interceptées*, pp. 228–9; Bourgogne, *Mémoires*, p. 61.
5. Henri Beyle to Comtesse Daru (9 November 1812), in *Lettres interceptées*, p. 242.
6. Alexandre de Bergognié to Ailhaud de Méouille (9 November 1812), in *Lettres interceptées*, p. 222.
7. Labaume, *Relation circonstanciée*, p. 332; Joachim-Joseph Delmarche, *Les Soirées du grenadier français de la Grande Armée, ou Principaux faits, actions, souffrances et dénuemens du sieur Joachim-Joseph Delmarche* (Rocroy, 1849), p. 41.
8. Labaume, *Relation circonstanciée*, pp. 333–5;, *Mémoires*, ii. pp. 124–5; François, *Journal*, pp. 682–3 (13 November 1812); Lignières, *Souvenirs de la Grande Armée*, pp. 121–2; Planat de la Faye, *Vie de Planat de la Faye*, p. 99.
9. Bellot de Kergorre, *Journal*, p. 63.
10. Auguste Bonet to Bordes the younger (11 November 1812), in *Lettres interceptées*, p. 290; Bellot de Kergorre, *Journal*, p. 64.
11. François Frenel to his mother (11 November 1812), in *Lettres interceptées*, p. 295; Zamoyski, *1812*, p. 439.
12. Gardier, *Journal*, p. 63.
13. *Corr.* xxiv. nos. 19328, 19329, 19331–19336 (9 and 12 November 1812).
14. Zamoyski, *1812*, p. 409. The figure was 50,000 according to Boudon, *Le roi Jérôme*, p. 385.
15. Delmarche, *Les soirées du grenadier français*, p. 30. Although he later managed to find a horse.
16. Zamoyski, *1812*, p. 439.
17. Bourgogne, *Mémoires*, p. 65.
18. François, *Journal*, p. 674 (1 November 1812); Uexküll (ed.), *Arms and the Woman*, pp. 99, 100 (16, 17, 18 and 24 October).
19. Labaume, *Relation circonstanciée*, p. 283. It was something that had been going on for some months. Lejeune recalls that the first time he saw horses being cut up for meat was shortly after the battle of Borodino, at Mozhaisk, in September (Lejeune, *Mémoires*, p. 400).
20. Thirion, *Souvenirs militaires*, p. 124.
21. Thirion, *Souvenirs militaires*, p. 124.
22. Castellane, *Journal*, i. p. 195 (27 November 1812).
23. Bourgeois, *Tableau de la campagne de Moscou*, p. 117.
24. Ducque, *Journal*, p. 45; Bellot de Kergorre, *Journal*, pp. 62–3; Labaume, *Relation circonstanciée*, pp. 300, 305.
25. Bellot de Kergorre, *Journal*, p. 70.
26. Bourgogne, *Mémoires*, p. 63.
27. François, *Journal*, p. 691 (24 November 1812).
28. Bellot de Kergorre, *Journal*, pp. 72, 83; Paixhans, *Retraite de Moscou*, p. 43.
29. Vionnet de Maringoné, *Souvenirs*, pp. 78–9.
30. Lagneau, *Journal*, p. 236; Bourgeois, *Tableau de la campagne de Moscou*, pp. 103–4. Also Denniée, *Itinéraire de l'empereur Napoléon*, pp. 134–5.

31. Lagneau, *Journal*, p. 237.
32. Caulaincourt, *Memoirs*, iii. p. 341 n. 1; Louis Etienne Saint-Denis, *Souvenirs du Mameluck Ali sur l'empereur Napoléon* (Paris, 2000), pp. 62–3.
33. Zamoyski, *1812*, p. 440; Lieven, *Russia against Napoleon*, pp. 267–8.
34. According to Bourgogne, *Mémoires*, pp. 132–3.
35. Robert Thomas Wilson, *Private Diary of Travels, Personal Services, and Public Events, During Mission and Employment with the European Armies in the Campaigns of 1812, 1813, 1814, from the Invasion of Russia to the Capture of Paris*, 2 vols (London, 1861), i. pp. 221, 222, 226.
36. Fantin des Odoards, *Journal*, p. 346.
37. Bourgogne, *Mémoires*, p. 132; Constant, *Mémoires*, v. p. 129; Marie-Théodore Gueilly, comte de Rumigny, *Souvenirs du général comte de Rumigny, aide de camp du roi Louis-Philippe (1789–1860)* (Paris, 1821), p. 64.
38. Caulaincourt, *Memoirs*, ii. p. 90.
39. Roos, *Souvenirs*, pp. 130–1 (around 4–5 November); François, *Journal*, p. 675 (1 November 1812); Vaucorbeil, 'Mémoires inédits', 44.
40. Lieven, *Russia against Napoleon*, pp. 216–17.
41. Wilson, *Private Diary of Travels*, i. p. 215.
42. See Uexküll (ed.), *Arms and the Woman*, p. 89 (7–12 September 1812); and the harrowing account in Marie-Christiane Torrance, 'Les témoignages des mémorialistes russes', *Revue de l'Institut Napoléon*, 135 (1979), 28.
43. Lieven, *Russia against Napoleon*, pp. 245–6.
44. Stephen M. Norris, *A War of Images: Russian Popular Prints, Wartime Culture, and National Identity, 1812–1945* (DeKalb, Ill., 2006), p. 21.
45. See Denis Vasil'evich Davydov, *In the Service of the Tsar against Napoleon: The Memoirs of Denis Davidov, 1806–1814*, trans. and ed. Gregory Troubetzkoy (London, 1999), pp. 134–5; Löwenstern, *Mémoires*, i. pp. 294–5; Wilson, *Private Diary of Travels*, i. pp. 214–15; Faure, *Souvenirs du Nord*, p. 74.
46. Figures are from Janet Hartley, 'Napoleonic Prisoners in Russia', in Natalia Iu. Erpyleva, Maryann E. Gashi-Butler and Jane E. Henderson (eds), *Forging a Common Legal Destiny: Liber Amicorum in Honour of William E. Butler* (London, 2005), pp. 716, 719.
47. Labaume, *Relation circonstanciée*, p. 321.
48. Labaume, *Relation circonstanciée*, pp. 300–1.
49. Rodolphe Vieillot, *Souvenirs d'un prisonnier en Russie pendant les années 1812–1813–1814* (Luneray, 1996), pp. 131–2.
50. Alexander M. Martin, 'Russia and the Legacy of 1812', in Dominic Lieven (ed.), *The Cambridge History of Russia*, 3 vols (Cambridge, 2006), ii. p. 156.
51. Thirion, *Souvenirs militaires*, p. 124.
52. See Stephen M. Norris, 'Images of 1812: Ivan Terebenev and the Russian Wartime *Lubok*', *National Identities*, 7 (2005), 1–21.
53. Caulaincourt, *Memoirs*, ii. pp. 100–1.
54. According to his memoirs, Drujon de Beaulieu, *Souvenirs d'un militaire pendant quelques années du règne de Napoléon Bonaparte* (Belley, 1831), p. 38; Bernard Reinier Frans Van Vlijmen, *Vers la Bérésina (1812), d'après des documents nouveau* (Paris, 1908), p. 322.
55. Edling, *Mémoires*, p. 91.
56. Oleg Sokolov, 'La campagne de Russie', *Napoléon Ier*, 10 (September–October 2001), 46.
57. Bourgogne, *Mémoires*, pp. 132–3, 212; François, *Journal*, p. 691 (24 November 1812); Bourgeois, *Tableau de la campagne de Moscou*, p. 139; Caulaincourt, *Memoirs*, ii. p. 118; Duverger, *Mes aventures*, p. 16; Pion des Loches, *Mes campagnes*, p. 310; Zamoyski, *1812*, p. 465.
58. François Pils, *Journal de marche du Grenadier Pils (1804–1814)* (Paris, 1895), pp. 142–3; Louise Fusil, *Souvenirs d'une actrice. Mémoires de Louise Fusil (1774–1778)* (Paris, n.d.), pp. 283–4.

59. Rossetti, *Journal*, p. 168.

60. Lignières, *Souvenirs de la Grande Armée*, pp. 124–5.

61. Van Vlijmen, *Vers la Bérésina*, pp. 178–228, 322; Heinrich von Brandt, *In the Legions of Napoleon: The Memoirs of a Polish Officer in Spain and Russia, 1808–1813* (London, 1999), pp. 248–9.

62. Adams, *Napoleon and Russia*, p. 393.

63. Bourgogne, *Mémoires*, pp. 210–13; Delmarche, *Les soirées du grenadier français*, pp. 38–40; Thirion, *Souvenirs militaires*, pp. 131–3; Just-Jean-Etienne Roy, *Les Français en Russie, souvenirs de la campagne de 1812 et de deux ans de captivité en Russie* (Tours, 1856), pp. 70–1; Chevalier, *Souvenirs*, pp. 231–7; Suckow, *D'Iéna à Moscou*, pp. 246–64; Planat de la Faye, *Vie de Planat de la Faye*, p. 105; Rossetti, *Journal*, pp. 175–9; Van Vlijmen, *Vers la Bérésina*, pp. 325–6; Marbot, *Mémoires*, iii. pp. 199–200; Griois, *Mémoires*, ii. pp. 155–6.

64. A few examples are: Bellot de Kergorre, *Journal*, pp. 73–7; Labaume, *Relation circonstanciée*, pp. 384–94, from which the River Styx analogy is taken; Vaucorbeil, 'Mémoires inédits', 37–8.

65. Vaucorbeil, 'Mémoires inédits', 37.

66. Coignet, *Note-Books*, p. 235.

67. Bellot de Kergorre, *Journal*, p. 77.

68. Zamoyski, *1812*, pp. 479–80; Adams, *Napoleon and Russia*, p. 397; Lieven, *Russia against Napoleon*, p. 281, puts the number somewhat higher at between 25,000 and 40,000 losses for Napoleon and almost all his artillery and baggage.

69. Caulaincourt, *Memoirs*, ii. p. 115; Arthur Chuquet (ed.), *La campagne de 1812: mémoires du margrave de Bade* (Paris, 1912), p. 145; Fain, *Manuscrit de mil huit cent douze*, ii. pp. 344–7; Lentz, *Nouvelle histoire du Premier Empire*, ii. p. 311.

70. Lieven, *Russia against Napoleon*, p. 282.

71. For a discussion of this see Adams, *Napoleon and Russia*, pp. 398–9.

72. Esdaile, *Napoleon's Wars*, p. 488.

73. According to Drujon de Beaulieu, *Souvenirs d'un militaire*, pp. 46–7.

74. Chevalier, *Souvenirs*, p. 222.

75. Ducque, *Journal*, p. 60.

76. Bangofsky, 'Les étapes', 302.

77. Bourgogne, *Mémoires*, p. 84; Thirion, *Souvenirs militaires*, p. 127; Mailly, *Mon journal*, pp. 112–13; Paixhans, *Retraite de Moscou*, p. 43; Vaucorbeil, 'Mémoires inédits', 38.

78. Bourgogne, *Mémoires*, p. 223.

79. For cannibalism see Labaume, *Relation circonstanciée*, pp. 279, 410; Joseph de Maistre, *Les carnets du comte Joseph de Maistre* (Lyons and Paris, 1923), i. p. 246; Nesselrode, *Lettres et papiers*, iv. p. 120; Wilson, *Private Diary of Travels*, i. p. 214; Torrance, 'Les témoignages des mémorialistes russes', 26–7.

80. See Bourgogne, *Mémoires*, pp. 62, 78.

81. Vionnet de Maringoné, *Souvenirs*, p. 77.

82. Bourgogne, *Mémoires*, pp. 70–1.

83. Bourgogne, *Mémoires*, p. 91.

84. Delmarche, *Les soirées du grenadier français*, pp. 36–7, 40.

85. Bellot de Kergorre, *Journal*, p. 84; Drujon de Beaulieu, *Souvenirs d'un militaire*, p. 47; Castellane, *Journal*, i. p. 183 (7 November 1812).

86. Bourgogne, *Mémoires*, p. 107. Similarly, Chevalier, *Souvenirs*, p. 221.

87. Chevalier, *Souvenirs*, pp. 238–9.

88. Roos, *Souvenirs*, p. 128.

89. Sir Robert Wilson, *Narrative of Events during the Invasion of Russia by Napoleon Bonaparte, and the Retreat of the French Army 1812* (London, 1860), pp. 352–3; and Wilson, *Private Diary of Travels*, i. pp. 242, 243, 267.

90. Chuquet (ed.), *Lettres de 1812*, p. 229.

91. Lentz, *Nouvelle histoire du Premier Empire*, ii. p. 314.

92. Fain, *Manuscrit de mil huit cent douze*, ii. pp. 421–4.

93. Bourgeois, *Tableau de la campagne de Moscou*, pp. 138–9; Thirion, *Souvenirs militaires*, p. 129; François, *Journal*, p. 691 (24 November 1812); Caulaincourt, *Memoirs*, ii. p. 119.

94. Caulaincourt, *Memoirs*, ii. p. 133; Castellane, *Journal*, i. 202 (5 December 1812); Derrécagaix, *Le maréchal Berthier*, ii. pp. 453–5, disputes the assertion that Berthier made a scene.

95. In favour of the decision were Lejeune, *Mémoires*, p. 442; Griois, *Mémoires*, ii. p. 177; Castellane, *Journal*, i. p. 202 n. 1; Dedem de Gelder, *Un général hollandais*, p. 292. Those who felt betrayed included Labaume, *Relation circonstanciée*, pp. 403–5; Denniée, *Itinéraire de l'empereur Napoléon*, p. 168; Bourgeois, *Tableau de la campagne de Moscou*, pp. 170–1; Mailly, *Mon journal*, pp. 105–6; Dumonceau, *Mémoires*, ii. p. 231; Vionnet de Maringoné, *Souvenirs*, p. 76. François, *Journal*, p. 697 (5 December 1812), was implicitly critical.

96. According to Labaume, *Relation circonstanciée*, p. 403.

97. For this see Frederick Schneid, 'The Dynamics of Defeat: French Army Leadership, December 1812–March 1813', *Journal of Military History*, 63 (1999), 7–28.

98. Caulaincourt, *Memoirs*, ii. p. 127.

99. Ségur, *Napoleon's Russian Campaign*, p. 256.

100. Etienne-Jacques-Joseph-Alexandre Macdonald, *Souvenirs du maréchal Macdonald, duc de Tarente* (Paris, 1892), p. 182; Laurent de Gouvion Saint-Cyr, *Mémoires pour servir à l'histoire militaire sous le directoire, le consulat et l'empire*, 4 vols (Paris, 1831), iv. pp. 3–4.

101. Derrécagaix, *Le maréchal Berthier*, ii. pp. 458–60; Jean Thiry, *La campagne de Russie* (Paris, 1969), p. 330.

102. Macdonald, *Souvenirs*, pp. 193–4.

103. See Schneid, 'The Dynamics of Defeat', 18.

104. Jean Lucas-Dubreton, *Murat* (Paris, 1944), pp. 207–8.

105. Beauharnais, *Mémoires et correspondance politique*, viii. pp. 133–4 (17 January 1813).

106. Published later in the *Moniteur universel*, 14 May 1815, in order to embarrass Murat. In that same issue, a letter from Napoleon to Caroline was published in which he stated, 'Your husband is very brave on the battlefield, but he is weaker than a woman or a monk when he does not see the enemy. He has no moral courage.'

107. *Corr.* xxiv. n. 19474 (22 January 1813).

108. Macdonald, *Souvenirs*, p. 193.

109. Beauharnais, *Mémoires et correspondance politique*, viii. pp. 134–6 (17 January 1813).

110. On Vilnius, Griois, *Mémoires*, ii. pp. 181–7.

111. Labaume, *Relation circonstanciée*, pp. 413–15; Bourgogne, *Mémoires*, p. 229.

112. Vionnet de Maringoné, *Souvenirs*, pp. 80–1.

113. Lignières, *Souvenirs de la Grande Armée*, p. 129; Puybusque, *Lettres sur la guerre de Russie*, p. 121 (15 November 1812).

114. Caulaincourt, *Memoirs*, ii. p. 139.

115. Roustam Raza, *Souvenirs de Roustam, mamelouck de Napoléon Ier* (Paris, 1911), p. 220.

116. In France in 1789, the average distance between postal stations, where one could change horses for example, was between 7 and 10.5 kilometres. One could expect to cover about 90 kilometres a day. In 1812 it took around eighteen days for a post-chaise to travel from Paris to Warsaw, and thirty-one days from Paris to Petersburg, assuming of course that the weather permitted. On this see Stuart Woolf, 'The Construction of a European World-View in the Revolutionary-Napoleonic Years', *Past & Present*, 137 (1992), 76 n. 11.

117. Caulaincourt, *Memoirs*, ii. p. 162.

118. Caulaincourt, *Memoirs*, ii. pp. 166, 168.

119. Caulaincourt, *Memoirs*, p. 443. Andrew Roberts, *Napoleon and Wellington: The Battle of Waterloo and the Great Commanders who Fought It* (New York, 2001), p. 96.

120. Fantin des Odoards, *Journal*, p. 354.

121. Friedrich Adami, *Schicksalswende: Preußen 1812/13: nach Aufzeichnungen von Augenzeugen* (Berlin, 1924), pp. 185–7.

122. Jackson, *The Bath Archives*, i. pp. 445–6 (19 December 1812).

123. Eduard Wertheimer, 'Wien und das Kriegsjahr 1813', *Archiv fur österreichische Geschichte*, 79 (1893), 360–1.

124. Lavalette, *Mémoires*, pp. 282–4; Pion des Loches, *Mes campagnes*, p. 357; Petiteau, 'Lecture socio-politique de l'empire', 199–200; Petiteau, *Les Français et l'Empire*, pp. 213–15; Olcina, *L'opinion publique en Belgique*, pp. 50–3.

125. Delécluze, *Louis David*, p. 340.

126. See Gotteri (ed.), *La police secrète*, vi. pp. 12, 15, 47, 59, 92 (1–2, 3–4, 14, 18 and 28 January 1813). For the degradation in public opinion for the period 1813–14 see Petiteau, *Les Français et l'Empire*, pp. 212–21; Olcina, *L'opinion publique en Belgique*, p. 55.

127. It has been estimated, for example, that between 1813 and 1815 more than 1,800 anti-Napoleonic caricatures were printed (Hans Peter Mathis, *Napoleon I im Spiegel der Karikatur* (Zurich, 1998), pp. 38–9).

128. Scharf, 'Einführung', pp. 19–20, who notes that the manner in which the catastrophe was communicated and received throughout Europe has yet to be explored in any great detail.

129. See, for example, Jean-Baptiste-Benoît Barjaud, *La conquête de Moscou* (Paris, 1812); H. Dassier, *Les ruines de Moscou* (Paris, 1812); Auguste Moufle (François-Toussaint-Auguste), *Ode sur l'embrasement de Moscou* (Paris, 1812); and Quaynat, *Ode à Sa Majesté l'Empereur et Roi sur la prise de Moscou* (Paris, 1812).

130. Parkinson, *The Fox of the North*, p. 229.

131. Ute Planert, 'Conscription, Economic Exploitation and Religion in Napoleonic Germany', in Dwyer and Forrest (eds), *Napoleon and his Empire*, p. 141.

132. Clark, *Iron Kingdom*, p. 357; Münchow-Pohl, *Zwischen Reform and Krieg*, p. 377.

133. Fantin des Odoards, *Journal*, p. 349.

134. Girod de l'Ain, *Dix ans de souvenirs militaires*, pp. 288–93.

135. Münchow-Pohl, *Zwischen Reform and Krieg*, pp. 373–4.

136. Jean-Nicolas-Auguste Noël, *With Napoleon's Guns: The Military Memoirs of an Officer of the First Empire*, trans. Rosemary Brindle (London, 2005), pp. 150, 151, 154.

137. Münchow-Pohl, *Zwischen Reform and Krieg*, p. 378.

138. Adams, *Napoleon and Russia*, p. 417; Leggiere, *The Fall of Napoleon*, p. 7, gives a total of 93,000 men and 250 cannon, without citing his source.

139. Sokolov, 'La campagne de Russie', 42–51.

140. Franco Della Peruta, 'War and Society in Napoleonic Italy: The Armies of the Kingdom of Italy at Home and Abroad', in John Davis and Paul Ginsborg (eds), *Society and Politics in the Age of the Risorgimento: Essays in Honour of Denis Mack Smith* (Cambridge, 1991), pp. 26–48, here p. 48.

141. Martin, 'The Russian Empire and the Napoleonic Wars', p. 260.

142. Montesquiou-Fezensac, *Souvenirs militaires*, p. 383.

143. L. Bailly-Maitre, 'La retraite de Russie vue par un artilleur lorrain', *Revue des études napoléoniennes*, 41 (1935), 28–9.

144. Roger Dufraisse, 'L'écroulement de la domination française en Allemagne (1813)', in Jean Tulard (ed.), *L'Europe au temps de Napoléon* (Paris, 1989), p. 477.

145. Ute Planert, *Der Mythos vom Befreiungskrieg: Frankreichs Kriege und der deutsche Süden: Alltag, Wahrnehmung, Deutung 1792–1841* (Paderborn, 2007), pp. 414–15.

146. Robert Bielecki, 'L'effort militaire polonais (1806–1815)', *Revue de l'Institut Napoléon*, 132 (1976), 160.

147. According to Lieven, *Russia against Napoleon*, p. 306, the figure was 175,000. The loss was seriously to hamper Napoleon's ability to defend his Empire in the coming months. Horses were naturally lost as a result of the weather, but one has to say that the enormous losses were also in part due to lack of planning, lack of supplies and negligence. To give but one example, Caulaincourt (*Memoirs*, i. p. 336), in charge of Napoleon's horse, lost only eighty horses out of the 715 belonging to the Imperial Household with which he began the campaign. He showed what could be done with a great deal of care and some foresight.

148. Martin, 'Russia and the Legacy of 1812', ii. pp. 147–8.

149. Gotteri, *Napoléon*, p. 154. On the rebuilding of Moscow see Miliza Korshunova, 'William Hastie in Russia', *Architectural History*, 17 (1974), 14-21, 53-6; Albert J. Schmidt, 'William Hastie, Scottish Planner of Russian Cities', *Proceedings of the American Philosophical Society*, 114:3 (1970), 226-4; Albert J. Schmidt, 'The Restoration of Moscow after 1812', *Slavic Review*, 40:1 (1981), 37-48; Tatiana Ruchinskaya, 'The Scottish Architectural Traditions in the Plan for the Reconstruction of Moscow after the Fire of 1812: A Rare Account of the Influence of Scottish Architect William Hastie on Town Planning in Moscow', *Building Research & Information*, 22:4 (1994), 228-33.

150. Monika Senkowska-Gluck, 'La campagne de 1812', in Tulard (ed.), *L'Europe au temps de Napoléon*, pp. 469-70.

151. Grunwald, *Société et civilisation russes*, p. 44; Lieven, *Russia against Napoleon*, p. 212.

152. Tulard gives the figure of 380,000. Russian losses were not quite as high. Anywhere between 250,000 and 300,000 men were killed or wounded, or deserted, not counting the numbers of Russian civilians, whose numbers we simply do not know. Kutuzov lost around 50,000 men in casualties in the final weeks of the campaign.

153. Here too figures for the number of prisoners taken by the Russians vary but are as high as 150,000 to 190,000, all nationalities confounded. There are numerous accounts of life in Russia as a prisoner of war. See, for example, Vieillot, *Souvenirs*; Everts, 'Campagne et captivité de Russie', pp. 153-72; Jacques Garnier, 'Récits du lieutenant Bressolles sur la campagne de 1813', *Revue de l'Institut Napoléon*, 135 (1979), 57-65; Ducor, *Aventures d'un marin de la Garde impériale*; Vaucorbeil, 'Mémoires inédits', 43-57.

154. Adams, *Napoleon and Russia*, p. 414.

155. Vladilen Sirotkine, 'La campagne de Russie', *Revue de l'Institut Napoléon*, 156 (1991), 64.

156. Bellot de Kergorre, *Journal*, p. 85.

157. *Libération*, 11 December 2002, pp. 34-5; Romain Pigeaud, 'Le charnier des grognards', *Archeologia*, 401 (June 2003), 41-7. Atolija Krulis is one such descendant. His grandmother was a de Courtenay, daughter of Jacques, himself son of Jean-François, a soldier in Napoleon's army, probably an officer. Forty kilometres from Vilnius in the village of Tabariskes, Bogdan Komoliubio, a teacher and peasant, is also convinced that his great-great-grandfather was a soldier in Napoleon's army, although he had an Italian-sounding name, and was from the region of Lyons. In fact, the villagers believe that three men found refuge in the village, completely exhausted, and that, once recuperated, these French-Italians went back home only to return years later with French wives. There is a wood a few kilometres outside the village called 'French forest' in which soldiers of the Grande Armée are said to be buried.

158. Esdaile, *Napoleon's Wars*, p. 487, has called it 'one of the key moments in the international history of the Napoleonic Wars'.

159. Martin, *Romantics, Reformers, Reactionaries*, p. 124; Volker Sellin, *Die geraubte Revolution: der Sturz Napoleons und die Restauration in Europa* (Göttingen, 2001), pp. 42-51.

160. Martin, *Romantics, Reformers, Reactionaries*, pp. 139-40.

161. Rothenberg, *The Art of Warfare*, p. 204. See Kutuzov's remarks to the British liaison officer General Wilson in Wilson, *Narrative of Events*, p. 234.

162. Lieven, *Russia against Napoleon*, pp. 288-9. The idea received support from both Kutuzov and Karl von Toll. Toll submitted a memorandum to Kutuzov espousing this view: Bernhardi, *Denkwürdigkeiten*, iii. pp. 469-70.

163. Cited in Adams, *Napoleon and Russia*, p. 415.

164. See Raeff, *Michael Speransky*, p. 188.

165. There were any number of influential men and women in the Tsar's entourage who saw this as an opportunity to expand Russia's borders to the Vistula and who no doubt brought some influence to bear. Martin, *Romantics, Reformers, Reactionaries*, pp. 141-2. Kraehe, *Metternich's German Policy*, i. p. 149, argues that Alexander's 'political preparations from the very outset had anticipated a campaign beyond the Russian frontier'. Lieven, *Russia against Napoleon*, p. 287.

166. Andrei Zorin, '"Star of the East": The Holy Alliance and European Mysticism', *Kritika: Explorations in Russian and Eurasian History*, 4 (2003), 331.

167. Martin, *Romantics, Reformers, Reactionaries*, pp. 144–5; Rey, *Alexandre Ier*, pp. 328–30.
168. Cited in Adams, *Napoleon and Russia*, p. 415.


THE ADVENTURER, 1813–1814

*21: 'The Enemy of the Human Race'*

1. Caulaincourt, *Memoirs*, ii. pp. 292–3; Bourgoing, *Souvenirs*, pp. 213–14.
2. Caulaincourt, *Memoirs*, ii. p. 318.
3. Chaptal, *Mes souvenirs*, pp. 331–2.
4. Fernand L'Huillier, 'Une crise des subsistances dans le Bas-Rhin (1810–1812), *Annales historiques de la Révolution française*, 14 (1937), 518–36; Pierre Léon, 'La crise des subsistances de 1810–1812 dans le département de l'Isère', *Annales historiques de la Révolution française*, 24 (1952), 289–310; Petiteau, *Les Français et l'Empire*, pp. 206–12; Pascal Chambon, *La Loire et l'aigle: les Foréziens face à l'Etat napoléonien* (Saint-Etienne, 2005), pp. 345–6.
5. Lignereux, *L'Empire des Français*, p. 227.
6. See Eugène Lomier, *Histoire des regiments des Gardes d'Honneur, 1813–1814* (Paris, 1924); Léon Deries, *La conscription des riches: les Gardes d'honneur de Maine-et-Loire de l'année 1813* (Angers, 1929); Chambon, *La Loire et l'aigle*, pp. 361–78; Georges Housset, *La Garde d'honneur de 1813–1814: histoire du corps et de ses soldats* (Paris, 2009), pp. 27–8, 33–41, 141–58. It is true that a little over one-quarter of the overall effectives (around 2,500 out of 9,500 men) would volunteer for these positions, but the majority were there against their better judgement. At the beginning of 1813, letters were addressed to Napoleon by individuals and authorities expressing a desire to form a 'departmental guard' that looks like the precursor to the Guard of Honour (AN AFIV 1453).
7. Lignereux, *L'Empire des Français*, p. 295.
8. Sorel, *L'Europe et la Révolution française*, viii. p. 39.
9. *Corr.* xxiv and xxv. Dozens of letters were sent to the minister of war, General Clarke, and to Berthier as major general of the Grande Armée, at the end of December 1812 and during the months of January, February and March 1813.
10. Léonce de Brotonne (ed.), *Lettres inédites de Napoléon Ier* (Paris, 1898), n. 1026 (7 January 1813).
11. *Corr.* xxiv. n. 19218 (23 September 1812).
12. Leggiere, 'From Berlin to Leipzig', 49.
13. Caulaincourt, *Memoirs*, ii. pp. 346–9; Agathon-Jean-François Fain, *Manuscrit de mil huit cent treize, contenant le précis des événemens de cette année, pour servir à l'histoire de l'empereur Napoléon*, 2 vols (Paris, 1824), i. p. 131.
14. Caulaincourt, *Memoirs*, ii. pp. 61–2.
15. Dard, *Napoléon et Talleyrand*, pp. 301–2.
16. Caulaincourt, *Memoirs*, ii. p. 349.
17. According to Hortense, *Mémoires*, ii. p. 147.
18. Gotteri (ed.), *La police secrète*, vii. p. 384 (13 November 1813).
19. Fouché, *Mémoires*, ii. p. 131.
20. AN F1C I 12, Comptes-résumés des bruits (December 1812–June 1813); Woloch, *The New Regime*, pp. 418–21.
21. See for example the public votes of support by the municipal councils of Paris, Nanterre, Beauvais, Versailles, Dreux, Châteaudun and Seine-Inférieure, January 1813. Note that they are all from the Paris region.
22. See Fontaine, *Journal*, i. p. 382.
23. Hauterive, *La police secrète du premier Empire*, iii. pp. 156, 266, 279, 283, 298, 300, 314 (14 February, 5, 17, 20 June, 7, 8, 25 July 1807).

24. See, for example, Gotteri (ed.), *La police secrète*, vii. p. 385 (13 November 1813), which states that most of those called up in Tuscany had deserted. Other figures can be found in Roger Dufraisse and Michel Kerautret, *La France napoléonienne: aspects extérieurs, 1799–1815* (Paris, 1999), p. 195; Jean Tulard, *La vie quotidienne des Français sous Napoléon* (Paris, 1978), pp. 151–3; Petiteau, *Les Français et l'Empire*, pp. 212–21.

25. Annie Crépin, *La conscription en débats ou le triple apprentissage de la Nation, de la citoyenneté, de la République (1798–1889)* (Artois, 1998), p. 32.

26. Annie Crépin, *Défendre la France: les Français, la guerre et le service militaire, de la guerre de Sept Ans à Verdun* (Rennes, 2005), p. 149.

27. Rowe, 'France, Prussia, or Germany?', 623.

28. Alan Forrest, *Conscripts and Deserters: The Army and French Society during the Revolution and Empire* (Oxford, 1989), p. 41.

29. AN F7 6349, Hambourg. Rapports du directeur général de la police (21, 28 and 31 January 1813); Dufraisse, 'L'écroulement de la domination française en Allemagne', pp. 477, 484–5; Aaslestad, *Place and Politics*, p. 265.

30. AN F7 6349 (13 and 22 January 1813).

31. AN F7 6349 (15 January 1813).

32. Aaslestad, *Place and Politics*, p. 266.

33. Aaslestad, *Place and Politics*, pp. 266–7, and n. 96 for other sources.

34. AN F7 6349 (28 January 1813).

35. Schama, *Patriots and Liberators*, pp. 628–30.

36. Broers, *Napoleon's Other War*, p. 101.

37. Aaslestad, *Place and Politics*, pp. 266–7.

38. Roger Dufraisse, 'A propos des guerres de délivrance allemandes de 1813', *Revue de l'Institut Napoléon*, 148 (1987), 14.

39. Figures cited in Werner K. Blessing, 'Umbruchkrise und "Verstörung": die "Napoleonische" Erschütterung und ihre sozialpsychologische Bedeutung (Bayern als Beispiel)', *Zeitschrift für bayerische Landesgeschichte*, 42 (1979), 78–9 n. 13.

40. Aaslestad, *Place and Politics*, p. 268.

41. Rey, *Alexandre Ier*, pp. 332–4.

42. *Lettres personnelles des souverains à l'empereur Napoléon Ier* (Paris, 1939), p. 387.

43. Fain, *Manuscrit de mil huit cent treize*, i. p. 296.

44. *Corr.* xxv. n. 19664 (5 March 1813).

45. Schroeder, *Transformation of European Politics*, pp. 466–7.

46. Kraehe, *Metternich's German Policy*, i. pp. 154–6; Stamm-Kuhlmann, *König in Preußens großer Zeit*, pp. 362–4.

47. Stamm-Kuhlmann, *König in Preußens großer Zeit*, pp. 370–3; Hagemann, '*Mannlicher Muth*', pp. 406–15; Peter Brandt, 'Einstellungen, Motive und Ziele von Kriegsfreiwilligen 1813/14: das Freikorps Lützow', in Jost Dülffer (ed.), *Kriegsbereitschaft und Friedensordnung in Deutschland 1800–1814* (Münster and Hamburg, 1994), pp. 211–14.

48. See Ernst Friedrich Christian Müsebeck, *Freiwillige Gaben und Opfer des preussischen Volkes in den Jahren 1813–1815* (Leipzig, 1913), p. 132. The Treaty of Kalisch with Russia (28 February) was followed by a formal declaration of war (17 March 1813).

49. Indeed, orders were issued for Yorck's arrest and court martial, although this did not prevent him from inciting garrisons in East Prussia to revolt, arguing that he was acting with the king's secret approval (Peter Paret, *Yorck and the Era of the Prussian Reform, 1807–1815* (Princeton, 1966), pp. 191–6). In fact, it appears that, once again, the Prussian political elite were saying one thing to the French and doing something entirely different behind their backs (Paul R. Sweet, *Wilhelm von Humboldt: A Biography*, 2 vols (Columbus, Ohio, 1978–80), ii. p. 120). The Austrian commander, Schwarzenberg, similarly signed a secret convention with the Russians at Zeycs at the end of January 1813.

50. Stamm-Kuhlmann, *König in Preußens großer Zeit*, pp. 365–9, 370–4; Scott, *Birth of a Great Power System*, p. 350; Clark, *Iron Kingdom*, pp. 362–3.

51. Aaslestad, *Place and Politics*, pp. 292–3; Katherine Aaslestad, 'Republican Traditions: Patriotism, Gender, and War in Hamburg, 1770–1815', *European History Quarterly*, 37 (2007), 592.

52. Hagemann, *'Mannlicher Muth'*, pp. 457–61.

53. Dufraisse, 'A propos des guerres de délivrance allemandes', 16; Dennis Showalter, 'Prussia's Army: Continuity and Change, 1715–1830', in Dwyer (ed.), *The Rise of Prussia*, pp. 231–6; Clark, *Iron Kingdom*, p. 366.

54. Ibbeken, *Preussen 1807–1813*, pp. 393–439.

55. Ibbeken, *Preussen 1807–1813*, pp. 448–9.

56. Cited in Daniel Moran, 'Arms and the Concert: The Nation in Arms and the Dilemmas of German Liberalism', in Daniel Moran and Arthur Waldron (eds), *The People in Arms: Military Myth and National Mobilization since the French Revolution* (Cambridge, 2003), p. 59.

57. On the emergence of 'patriotism' see Hagemann, *'Mannlicher Muth'*, pp. 222–42.

58. Regional influence was the case for Austria. See Hagemann, 'Be Proud and Firm', 51. On the role of religion in the wars against Napoleon see Nigel Aston, *Christianity and Revolutionary Europe, 1750–1830* (Cambridge, 2002), pp. 291–4.

59. Aaslestad, *Place and Politics*, pp. 288–91; Karen Hagemann, '"Deutsche Heldinnen": Patriotisch-nationales Frauenhandeln in der Zeit der antinapoleonischen Kriege', in Ute Planert (ed.), *Nation, Politik und Geschlecht: Frauenbewegungen und Nationalismus in der Moderne* (Frankfurt, 2000), pp. 86–112; Karen Hagemann, 'A Valorous *Volk* Family: The Nation, the Military, and the Gender Order in Prussia in the Time of the Anti-Napoleonic Wars, 1806–15', in Ida Blom, Karen Hagemann and Catherine Hall (eds), *Gendered Nations: Nationalisms and Gender Order in the Long Nineteenth Century* (Oxford, 2000), pp. 179–205; Karen Hagemann, 'Female Patriots: Women, War and the Nation in the Period of the Prussian–German Anti-Napoleonic Wars', *Gender & History*, 16 (2004), 396–424; Dirk Alexander Reder, *Frauenbewegung und Nation: Patriotische Frauenvereine in Deutschland im frühen 19. Jahrhundert (1813–1830)* (Cologne, 1998), pp. 369–84, 423–31; Jean H. Quataert, *Staging Philanthropy: Patriotic Women and the National Imagination in Dynastic Germany, 1813–1916* (Ann Arbor, 2001), pp. 29–39.

60. Aaslestad, 'Republican Traditions', 593.

61. The Austrian women's associations have not yet been studied to the same extent as those of Prussia have been by Karen Hagemann or those of Germany by Reder and Quataert.

62. Adam Zamoyski, *Rites of Peace: The Fall of Napoleon and the Congress of Vienna* (London, 2007), p. 94.

63. Wertheimer, 'Wien und das Kriegsjahr 1813', 370, 393–5.

64. Karen Hagemann, 'Of "Manly Valor" and "German Honor": Nation, War and Masculinity in the Age of the Prussian Uprising against Napoleon', *Central European History*, 30:2 (1997), 187–220; Hagemann, *'Mannlicher Muth'*, pp. 271–349.

65. Historians have managed to document twenty-two cross-dressing women in the Prussian army although there were probably more. On women volunteers see Karen Hagemann, *'Mannlicher Muth'*, pp. 383–93; Karen Hagemann, '"Heroic Virgins" and "Bellicose Amazons": Armed Women, the Gender Order and the German Public during and after the Anti-Napoleonic Wars', *European History Quarterly*, 37 (2007), 507–27.

66. Semmel, *Napoleon and the British*, pp. 83–90; Beßlich, *Der deutsche Napoleon-Mythos*, pp. 92–7.

67. Hasko Zimmer, *Auf dem Altar des Vaterlands: Religion und Patriotismus in der deutschen Kriegslyrik des 19. Jahrhunderts* (Frankfurt, 1971), pp. 11–70; Erich Pelzer, 'Die Wiedergeburt Deutschlands 1813 und die Dämonisierung Napoleon', in Gerd Krumeich und Hartmut Lehmann (eds), *'Gott mit uns': Nation, Religion und Gewalt im 19. und frühen 20. Jahrhundert* (Göttingen, 2000), pp. 135–56; Planert, *Der Mythos vom Befreiungskrieg*, pp. 336–82.

68. Michael Simpson, *Closet Performances: Political Exhibition and Prohibition in the Dramas of Byron and Shelley* (Stanford, Calif., 1998), p. 251; and Leggiere, *The Fall of Napoleon*, p. 33.

69. See Paul Vulliaud, *La fin du monde* (Paris, 1952), pp. 169–76, for a bibliographical sketch. A summary of Napoleon as Antichrist can be found in Bernard McGinn, *Antichrist: Two Thousand Years of the Human Fascination with Evil* (New York, 1996), pp. 242–6. On the English discourse see William Hosking Oliver, *Prophets and Millenialists: The Uses of Biblical Prophecy in England from the 1790s to the 1840s* (Auckland, 1978), pp. 50–9; in Russia, Michael A. Pesenson, 'Napoleon Bonaparte and Apocalyptic Discourse in Early Nineteenth-Century Russia', *Russian Review*, 65 (2006), 373–92; in Germany, Erich Mertens, 'Jung-Stilling und der Kreis um Frau Krudener', in Peter Wörster (ed.), *Zwischen Straßburg und Petersburg* (Siegen, 1992), pp. 41–89; in Guatemala, Robert M. Laughlin, *Beware the Great Horned Serpent!: Chiapas under the Threat of Napoleon* (Albany, NY, 2003).

70. Paul Trensky, 'The Year 1812 in Russian Poetry', *Slavic and East European Journal*, 10 (1966), 283–302. Napoleon was not the first head of state to be dubbed the Antichrist. That distinction goes to Frederick II (Hohenstaufen) who was deposed by Pope Gregory IX, and later excommunicated by Innocent IV, in the 1240s.

71. Semmel, *Napoleon and the British*, p. 76.

72. Cited in Semmel, *Napoleon and the British*, p. 83. Examples include texts such as Lewis Mayer's *Bonaparte, the Emperor of the French, considered as Lucifer and Gog* (London, 1806), and *The prophetic mirror or a hint of England, containing an explanation of the prophesy . . . proving Bonaparte to be the beast* (London, 1806).

73. Pesenson, 'Napoleon Bonaparte and Apocalyptic Discourse', 377; Clarke Garrett, *Respectable Folly: Millenarians and the French Revolution in France and England* (Baltimore, 1975), pp. 211–12.

74. Eliza Gutch and Mabel Peacock, *Examples of Printed Folklore Concerning Lincolnshire*, vol. v of *County Folk-Lore* (London, 1908), pp. 383–4.

75. Peltzer, 'Imagerie populaire et caricature', 205.

76. For the following, Martin, *Romantics, Reformers, Reactionaries*, pp. 47, 48; Michael A. Pesenson, 'Napoleon Bonaparte and Apocalyptic Discourse in Early Nineteenth-Century Russia', *Russian Review*, 65 (2006), 382–92.

77. Martin, 'The Russian Empire and the Napoleonic Wars', pp. 255–6.

78. Lieven, *Russia against Napoleon*, p. 60.

79. Peltzer, 'Imagerie populaire et caricature', 205.

80. Pesenson, 'Napoleon Bonaparte and Apocalyptic Discourse', 374.

81. Pesenson, 'Napoleon Bonaparte and Apocalyptic Discourse', 385.

82. Richard S. Wortman, *Scenarios of Power: Myth and Ceremony in Russian Monarchy*, 2 vols (Princeton, 1995–2000), i. pp. 215–31.

83. Martin, 'The Response of the Population of Moscow', pp. 479–80.

84. Pesenson, 'Napoleon Bonaparte and Apocalyptic Discourse', 381–3, 392.

85. My thanks to Alicia Laspra Rodriguez for allowing me to use her unpublished conference paper, 'The Demonisation of Napoleon in Spain'.

86. An example of the catechism can be found in Joseph-Jacques de Naylies, *Mémoires sur la guerre d'Espagne, pendant les années 1808, 1809, 1810 et 1811* (Paris, 1817), pp. 23–30.

87. Cited in Hughes, *Goya*, p. 267.

88. See Michael Jeismann, *La patrie de l'ennemi: la notion d'ennemi national et la représentation de la nation en Allemagne et en France de 1792 à 1918*, trans. Dominique Lassaigne (Paris, 1997), pp. 70–1. On the German image of Napoleon see Friedrich Stählin, *Napoleons Glanz und Fall im deutschen Urteil: Wandlungen des deutschen Napoleonbildes* (Brunswick, 1952), esp. pp. 40–64.

89. Ernst Moritz Arndt, *Gedichte*, 2 vols (Frankfurt am Rhein, 1818), ii. pp. 31–2.

90. Ernst Moritz Arndt cited in Brendan Simms, *Struggle for Mastery in Germany* (Basingstoke, 1998), pp. 92–3.

91. Hagemann, *'Mannlicher Muth'*, pp. 112–57; Hagemann, 'Occupation, Mobilization, and Politics', 603.

92. Fontaine, *Journal*, i. p. 408 (12 April 1814).

93. Lentz, *Nouvelle histoire du Premier Empire*, ii. pp. 347–51.

94. Fain, *Manuscrit de mil huit cent treize*, i. pp. 24–5.

95. René Tournès, *La campagne de printemps en 1813: Lützen, étude d'une manoeuvre napoléonienne* (Paris, 1931), p. 29.

96. Anderson, *Pope Pius VII*, pp. 127–40.

97. Oncken, *Österreich und Preußen*, ii. pp. 615–25 (26 March 1813).

98. Cited in Henry Kissinger, *A World Restored: Metternich, Castlereagh and the Problems of Peace, 1812–22* (Cambridge, Mass., 1957), pp. 64–5.

99. Kissinger, *A World Restored*, p. 71.

100. Wertheimer, 'Wien und das Kriegsjahr 1813', 365.

101. Guillaume de Bertier de Sauvigny, *Metternich* (Paris, 1986), pp. 147–8.

102. Alexandre-Louis Andrault de Langeron, *Mémoires de Langeron, général d'infanterie dans l'armée russe, campagnes de 1812, 1813, 1814* (Paris, 1902), pp. 200–1; Dominic Lieven, 'Russia and the Defeat of Napoleon (1812–14)', *Kritika: Explorations in Russian and Eurasian History*, 7 (2006), 303–5. As Lieven points out, there are no studies, in Russian or any other language, detailing the enormous effort put into training and supplying the thousands of troops and then transferring them from their camps in central Russia to the battlefields of Germany and France between 1812 and 1814.

103. Gates, *The Napoleonic Wars*, pp. 231–3; Scott, *Birth of a Great Power System*, p. 351, thinks it was poor. It was 'the worst army Napoleon ever commanded', according to Muir, *Britain and the Defeat of Napoleon*, p. 255.

104. Marmont, *Mémoires*, vi. pp. 7–8. Historians differ about the age of these conscripts. Generally in their early twenties, according to Andrew Uffindell, *Napoleon 1814: The Defence of France* (Barnsley, 2009), p. 14. Two-thirds were teenagers, according to Robert M. Epstein, 'Aspects of Military and Operational Efffectiveness of the Armies of France, Austria, Russia and Prussia in 1813', in Frederick C. Schneid (ed.), *The Projection and Limitations of Imperial Powers, 1618–1850* (Leiden, 2012), p. 124.

105. Marmont, *Mémoires*, v. p. 9. On the army's weakness see Paul Foucart, *Bautzen, une bataille de deux jours, 20–21 mai 1813* (Paris, 1897), p. 100; Telp, *The Evolution of Operational Art*, p. 128.

106. *Corr.* xxvi. n. 20504 (2 September 1813).

107. See, for example, *Corr.* xxiv. n. 19602 (21 February 1813).

108. Chandler, *Campaigns of Napoleon*, pp. 874–5; Leggiere, *The Fall of Napoleon*, p. 7.

109. Ernst Otto Innocenz, Freiherr von Odeleben, *Relation circonstanciée de la campagne de 1813 en Saxe*, trans. from the German by M. Aubert de Vitry, 2 vols (Paris, 1817), i. p. 34.

110. Rowe, 'France, Prussia, or Germany?', 622.

111. See, for example, Rowe, *From Reich to State*, p. 218.

112. Lentz, *Nouvelle histoire du Premier Empire*, ii. p. 385.

113. Michael V. Leggiere, *Napoleon and Berlin: The Franco-Prussian War in North Germany, 1813* (Norman, 2002), pp. 49–51.

114. Tournès, *La campagne de printemps en 1813*, pp. 323–69; Chandler, *Campaigns of Napoleon*, pp. 881–98.

115. Marmont, *Mémoires*, v. pp. 17–23; Odeleben, *Relation circonstanciée*, i. pp. 55–9; F. Loraine Petre, *Napoleon's Last Campaign in Germany, 1813* (London, 1912), pp. 66–90.

116. Chandler, *Campaigns of Napoleon*, p. 887.

117. Leggiere, 'From Berlin to Leipzig', 39–40; 120,000, according to Epstein, 'Aspects of Military and Operational Efffectiveness', p. 131.

118. Vionnet de Maringoné, *Souvenirs*, p. 118.

119. Louis-Victor-Léon de Rochechouart, *Souvenirs sur la Révolution, l'Empire et la Restauration, par le général Cte de Rochechouart* (Paris, 1933), pp. 261–4.

120. Vionnet de Maringoné, *Souvenirs*, p. 118.

121. Vionnet de Maringoné, *Souvenirs*, p. 120.

122. Lignereux, *L'Empire des Français*, pp. 211–12.

123. Telp, *The Evolution of Operational Art*, p. 124.

124. Faucheur, *Souvenirs*, p. 174.

125. On the battle of Bautzen see Müffling, *Memoirs*, pp. 35–43; Langeron, *Mémoires*, pp. 177–88; Chandler, *Campaigns of Napoleon*, pp. 893–7; J. p. Riley, *Napoleon and the World War of 1813: Lessons in Coalition Warfighting* (London, 2000), pp. 94–106.

126. Metternich, *Mémoires*, i. p. 284.

127. Marmont, *Mémoires*, v. p. 109. On Duroc see Philip Dwyer, 'Duroc diplomate: un militaire au service de la diplomatie napoléonienne', *Revue du Souvenir napoléonien*, 399 (1995), 21–38; Martin, *Napoleonic Friendship*, pp. 47–9.

128. For the following, Coignet, *Note-Books*, p. 248; Marbot, *Mémoires*, iii. pp. 251–2, 264–81.

129. Odeleben, *Relation circonstanciée*, i. pp. 102–3.

130. Waresquiel (ed.), *Lettres d'un lion*, p. 128 (23 May 1813).

131. Dedem de Gelder, *Un général hollandais*, pp. 323–4.

132. Zamoyski, *Rites of Peace*, pp. 69, 72.

133. Wilson, *Private Diary of Travels*, ii. pp. 45–6; Zamoyski, *Rites of Peace*, p. 69.

134. Fain, *Manuscrit de mil huit cent treize*, i. pp. 430–5, 443–9.

135. Adams, *Napoleon and Russia*, pp. 443–4.

136. See Oskar Regele, *Feldmarschall Radetzky: Leben/Leistung/Erbe* (Vienna, 1957), pp. 121–8; Esdaile, *The Wars of Napoleon*, p. 271.

137. Zamoyski, *Rites of Peace*, p. 94.

138. On the plan see Sked, *Radetzky*, pp. 40–4.

139. Friedrich Luckwaldt, *Österreich und die Anfänge des Befreiungskriege von 1813* (Berlin, 1898), pp. 308–38; and Metternich's somewhat romanticized account of the meeting in Metternich, *Mémoires*, i. pp. 147–53, 185–92; ii. pp. 538–41. For the French perspective see Jean Hanoteau, 'Une nouvelle relation de l'entrevue de Napoléon et de Metternich à Dresde', *Revue d'histoire diplomatique*, 67 (1933), 421–40; Fain, *Manuscrit de mil huit cent treize*, ii. pp. 36–44. A recent reappraisal of the meeting is Munro Price, 'Napoleon and Metternich in 1813: Some New and Some Neglected Evidence', *French History*, 26:4 (2012), 482–503.

140. Montholon, *Récits*, ii. pp. 493–8, here p. 497.

141. Lieven, *Russia against Napoleon*, pp. 357–8.

142. Metternich, *Mémoires*, i. pp. 143–4. At least one historian thinks so: Naro⊠nickij, 'Österreich zwischen Frankreich und Russland 1813', p. 31.

143. *Corr.* xxv. n. 20175 (23 June 1813).

144. Tournès, *La campagne de printemps en 1813*, pp. 47–8.

145. *Corr.* xxv. n. 19820 (7 April 1813). It may have been nothing more than an attempt to reassure his collaborators.

146. Kraehe, *Metternich's German Policy*, i. pp. 180–90; Schroeder, *Transformation of European Politics*, p. 47. Some historians, like Kissinger, *A World Restored*, pp. 64, 70, have doubted Metternich's sincerity, arguing that in the months leading to the Austrian declaration of war he was playing a double game, assuring Russia that Austria would declare war on France, and Napoleon that it would remain loyal, all the while inching closer to the allied camp.

147. Kissinger, *A World Restored*, pp. 75–6.

148. Schroeder, *Transformation of European Politics*, p. 467.

149. Vincent Haegele (ed.), *Napoléon et Joseph Bonaparte: correspondance intégrale 1784–1818* (Paris, 2007), p. 746 (1 July 1813); Muir, *Britain and the Defeat of Napoleon*, pp. 263–6; Esdaile, *The Peninsular War*, pp. 452–3.

150. See Maria Ullrichová (ed.), *Clemens Metternich, Wilhelmine von Sagan: ein Briefwechsel, 1813–1815* (Graz, 1966).

151. Antoine d'Arjuzon, *Caulaincourt: le confident de Napoléon* (Paris, 2012), pp. 244–50.

152. Sorel, *L'Europe et la Révolution française*, viii. pp. 159–60.

153. Charles Webster (ed.), *British Diplomacy, 1813–1815: Select Documents Dealing with the Reconstruction of Europe* (London, 1921), pp. 12–13 (13 July 1813).

154. Pierrelongue (ed.), *Napoléon et Marie-Louise*, p. 126 (15 August 1813).

## 22: The Deliverance of Europe

1. Figures are from Chandler, *Campaigns of Napoleon*, pp. 900–1; Leggiere, 'From Berlin to Leipzig', 64. For the Austrian figures see Sked, *Radetzky*, p. 35, who states that it was able to put 389,000 combat troops into the field by the end of 1813. Gunther E. Rothenberg, *The Napoleonic Wars* (London, 1999), p. 178, gives slightly different figures: 570,000 allied troops against 410,000 French.

2. Gunther E. Rothenberg, 'The Habsburg Army in the Napoleonic Wars', *Military Affairs*, 37 (1973), 1–5, here 4; Craig, 'Problems of Coalition Warfare', p. 28. Archduke Charles was not given the job of commander-in-chief because Metternich feared he would be in the Tsar's pocket.

3. Rothenberg, 'The Habsburg Army', 4.

4. Craig, 'Problems of Coalition Warfare', pp. 29–30.

5. Zamoyski, *Rites of Peace*, pp. 94–5; Llewellyn Cook, 'Schwarzenberg at Dresden: Leadership and Command', *Consortium on Revolutionary Europe 1750–1850: Selected Papers* (Tallahassee, Fla, 1994), p. 644.

6. Craig, 'Problems of Coalition Warfare', p. 30.

7. Cook, 'Schwarzenberg at Dresden', 644.

8. Especially over the best manner in which to invade France at the end of 1813. See Leggiere, *The Fall of Napoleon*, pp. 22, 28–40.

9. Parkinson, *The Fox of the North*, p. 233; Nabokov and de Lastours, *Koutouzov*, pp. 290–1.

10. Gates, *The Napoleonic Wars*, p. 235.

11. Craig, 'Problems of Coalition Warfare', p. 43.

12. Cited in Zamoyski, *Rites of Peace*, p. 75.

13. Cited in Chamberlain, *Lord Aberdeen*, p. 129.

14. Lieven, *Russia against Napoleon*, p. 395.

15. On the battle of Dresden see Petre, *Napoleon's Last Campaign*, pp. 200–26; Riley, *Napoleon and the World War of 1813*, pp. 128–47; Chandler, *Campaigns of Napoleon*, pp. 903–12.

16. Chevalier, *Souvenirs*, p. 269; Bellot de Kergorre, *Journal*, p. 107.

17. Lieven, *Russia against Napoleon*, p. 396.

18. The suggestion of Lieven, *Russia against Napoleon*, pp. 402, 417–18.

19. Oudinot was defeated at Groß Beeren by Bülow and another Prussian general, Friedrich Bogislav von Tauentzien (23 August) just outside Berlin (Leggiere, *Napoleon and Berlin*, pp. 160–76); General Girard's division was defeated at Hagelberg by General-Major von Hirschfeld's Landwehr brigade (27 August); Macdonald was defeated by Blücher while crossing the River Katzbach (26 August), losing 35,000 of 75,000 men; Ney was defeated at Dennewitz by a combined Prussian–Swedish army under Bülow (6 September); General Marie-Nicolas Pécheux was defeated by the allied commander Count Wallmoden in the forest of Göhrde (between Wittenberg and Lüneburg) (16 September); General Charles Lefebvre-Desnouettes was surprised and routed by the Saxon General Johann von Thielmann at Altenburg (28 September); Bertrand was defeated at Wartenburg by Yorck (3 October); and south of Leipzig, at Liebertwolkwitz on 14 October, the greatest cavalry battle up to that time took place, without issue, between Murat on the one hand and Wittgenstein on the other.

20. Löwenstern, *Mémoires*, ii. pp. 100–1.

21. Lieven, *Russia against Napoleon*, p. 425.

22. Lieven, *Russia against Napoleon*, p. 429.

23. Boudon, *Le roi Jérôme*, pp. 392–5.

24. For the situation in southern Germany see Planert, *Der Mythos vom Befreiungskrieg*, pp. 596–613.

25. Kraehe, *Metternich's German Policy*, i. pp. 94–5; Schroeder, *Transformation of European Politics*, pp. 478–85. Michael Klang, 'Bavaria and the War of Liberation, 1813–1814', *French*

*Historical Studies*, 4 (1965), 27, 33–40, suggests that loyalty towards French-inspired reforms among the Bavarian political elite was strong, but that this was not incompatible with an increasing hatred of Napoleon as tyrant. Junkelmann, *Napoleon und Bayern*, pp. 304–31.

26. Odeleben, *Relation circonstanciée*, ii. p. 9.
27. Johan Wolfgang Geothe, *Goethe: The Collected Works*, 11 vols (Princeton, 1987), iv. pp. 187–8. On Leipzig during this period see Robert Beachy, *The Soul of Commerce: Credit, Property, and Politics in Leipzig, 1750–1840* (Leiden, 2005), pp. 137–64. The literature on the battle is extensive. For the following see Petre, *Napoleon's Last Campaign*, pp. 352–72; Riley, *Napoleon and the World War of 1813*, pp. 163–200; Leggiere, *Napoleon and Berlin*, pp. 256–77; Chandler, *Campaigns of Napoleon*, pp. 912–36; Digby Smith, *1813: Leipzig: Napoleon and the Battle of the Nations* (London, 2001).
28. Cited in Smith, *1813*, p. 156.
29. Chevalier, *Souvenirs*, pp. 277–8.
30. Jomini, *Précis politique et militaire*, ii. pp. 183–8.
31. Craig, 'Problems of Coalition Warfare', pp. 33–4.
32. Bellot de Kergorre, *Journal*, p. 116.
33. Odeleben, *Relation circonstanciée*, ii. p. 32.
34. According to Petre, *Napoleon's Last Campaign*, pp. 380–1.
35. Riley, *Napoleon and the World War of 1813*, p. 196.
36. Bellot de Kergorre, *Journal*, p. 117.
37. Lieven, *Russia against Napoleon*, p. 458.
38. Adams, *Napoleon and Russia*, p. 483; Lieven, *Russia against Napoleon*, p. 458; Smith, *1813*, p. 298. Again, figures vary. There were 43,000 dead and wounded according to Leggiere, *The Fall of Napoleon*, p. 12. Riley, *Napoleon and the World War of 1813*, p. 196, writes that Napoleon suffered greater casualties than the allies, around 40,000 dead and wounded on top of which have to be included 15,000 sick, 15,000 prisoners and 5,000 captured deserters.
39. Anna von Sydow (ed.), *Wilhelm und Caroline von Humboldt in ihren Briefen*, 7 vols (Berlin 1906–16), iv. pp. 141–50 (19 and 20 October 1813).
40. Chamberlain, *Lord Aberdeen*, pp. 133–4.
41. Karen Hagemann, '"Unimaginable Horror and Misery": The Battle of Leipzig in October 1813 in Civilian Experience and Perception', in Alan Forrest, Karen Hagemann and Jane Rendall (eds), *Soldiers, Citizens and Civilians: Experiences and Perceptions of the French Wars, 1790–1820* (Basingstoke, 2009), pp. 170–1.
42. Chandler, *Campaigns of Napoleon*, pp. 937–8. Bavaria defected to the allies at the beginning of October.
43. BL Add Mss 20191, 375 (31 October 1813).
44. Priscilla-Ann Wellesley Pole, Lady Burghersh, *The Letters of Lady Burghersh (afterwards countess of Westmorland) from Germany and France during the Campaign of 1813–14* (London, 1893), pp. 66–7.
45. Cited in Zamoyski, *Rites of Peace*, p. 115.
46. Chamberlain, *Lord Aberdeen*, p. 134.
47. Pion des Loches, *Mes campagnes*, p. 357.
48. 'Les deux frères Burnot (1808–1814)', *Carnet de la Sabretache*, 69 (1898), 547 (11 December 1813).
49. *Corr.* xxvi. n. 20645 (27 September 1813).
50. Chandler, *Campaigns of Napoleon*, p. 949.
51. Ashby, *Napoleon against Great Odds*, pp. 3–8, 187. Ashby contends that nearly half of the 930,000 conscripts were either ineligible or not notified. On the attempts to create a new army after Leipzig see his account at pp. 21–42.
52. Roger Dufraisse, 'La fin des départements de la rive gauche du Rhin', in Yves-Marie Bercé (ed.), *La fin de l'Europe napoléonienne, 1814: la vacance du pouvoir* (Paris, 1990), pp. 24–5.

53. Woloch, *The New Regime*, pp. 423–4; Isser Woloch, 'Napoleonic Conscription: State Power and Civil Society', *Past & Present*, 111 (1986), 101–29; Forrest, *Conscripts and Deserters*, pp. 41–2, 52–3; Gavin Daly, *Inside Napoleonic France: State and Society in Rouen, 1800–1815* (Burlington, Vt, 2001), pp. 244–6; Louis Bergès, *Résister à la conscription, 1798–1814: le cas des départements aquitains* (Paris, 2002), pp. 121–52.

54. Bellot de Kergorre, *Journal*, p. 118.

55. This figure is suggested by Lieven, *Russia against Napoleon*, p. 458; Jacques Garnier, 'Campagne de 1813 en Allemagne', in Tulard (ed.), *Dictionnaire Napoléon*, p. 354.

56. Schama, *Patriots and Liberators*, pp. 636–7; Johann Joor, 'Les Pays-Bas contre l'impérialisme napoléonien: les soulèvements anti-Français entre 1806 et 1813', *Annales historiques de la Révolution française*, 326 (2001), 167.

57. Regele, *Feldmarschall Radetzky*, pp. 156–64.

58. Grimsted, *The Foreign Ministers of Alexander*, pp. 205, 208–9; Hartley, *Alexander*, p. 123; Zamoyski, *Rites of Peace*, pp. 125–6.

59. Müffling, *Memoirs*, pp. 93, 395; Leggiere, *The Fall of Napoleon*, pp. 39–40; Sked, *Radetzky*, pp. 51–5.

60. Müffling, *Memoirs*, p. 388; Sked, *Radetzky*, p. 50.

61. Uffindell, *Napoleon 1814*, p. 7.

62. Stamm-Kuhlmann, *König in Preußens großer Zeit*, pp. 383–4; Sked, *Radetzky*, pp. 54–5.

63. Favier, *Bernadotte*, pp. 240–1.

64. Chamberlain, *Lord Aberdeen*, p. 143.

65. For the following see Volker Sellin, 'Restauration et légitimité en 1814', *Francia*, 26/2 (1999), 115–29.

66. Charles William Vane (ed.), *Correspondence, Despatches, and Other Papers of Viscount Castlereagh*, 8 vols (London, 1851–3), ix. p. 247; August Fournier, *Der Congress von Châtillon: die Politik im Kriege von 1814* (Leipzig, 1900), pp. 19–36, for the allies' views on this question.

67. On this question see Pingaud, *Bernadotte, Napoléon et les Bourbons*, pp. 251–312; Franklin D. Scott, 'Bernadotte and the Throne of France, 1814', *Journal of Modern History*, 5 (1933), 465–78; Boudon, *Histoire du Consulat et de l'Empire*, pp. 401–2; Favier, *Bernadotte*, pp. 239–47; Michel Winock, *Madame de Staël* (Paris, 2010), pp. 445–52.

68. Evelyne Lever, *Louis XVIII* (Paris, 1988), p. 292; Philip Mansel, *Louis XVIII* (Stroud, 1999), p. 163.

69. Beugnot, *Mémoires*, ii. p. 96; Noël, *With Napoleon's Guns*, p. 191.

70. Philippe de Ségur, *Du Rhin à Fontainebleau: mémoires du général comte de Ségur* (Paris, n.d.), p. 85.

71. Marmont, *Mémoires*, vi. pp. 8–10.

72. According to what seems a reasonably accurate assessment in a letter from Gneisenau to Alexander published in Leggiere, *The Fall of Napoleon*, p. 558.

73. Marmont, *Mémoires*, vi. pp. 8–9.

74. See Stephan Talty, *The Illustrious Dead: The Terrifying Story of How Typhus Killed Napoleon's Greatest Army* (New York, 2009).

75. Hagemann, '"Unimaginable Horror and Misery"', pp. 168, 170.

76. Rowe, 'France, Prussia, or Germany?', 634; Dufraisse, 'La fin des départements', p. 27. It was the second time that the French had carried typhus to the city. The first occurred in 1795 (Rowe, *From Reich to State*, p. 224).

77. Thirion, *Souvenirs militaires*, p. 169.

78. Mercy-Argenteau, *Memoirs*, i. p. 134.

79. Lentz, *Nouvelle histoire du Premier Empire*, iii. p. 501.

80. Barrès, *Souvenirs*, p. 195; Leggiere, *The Fall of Napoleon*, p. 94.

81. See, for example, the remarks made by Marmont, *Mémoires*, vi. pp. 2, 4–5.

82. Marmont, *Mémoires*, vi. p. 7; Chandler, *Campaigns of Napoleon*, pp. 946–7; Schroeder, *Transformation of European Politics*, pp. 491, 493. There were some in the allied camp who were advocating a spring offensive.

83. Paul W. Schroeder, 'An Unnatural "Natural Alliance": Castlereagh, Metternich, and Aberdeen in 1813', *International History Review*, 10 (1988), 534; Chamberlain, *Lord Aberdeen*, pp. 141–53.

84. At least this is what he later claimed. Metternich, *Mémoires*, i. pp. 173–4.

85. Kraehe, *Metternich*, i. p. 257.

86. Fournier, *Der Congress von Châtillon*, pp. 22–4.

87. Metternich, *Mémoires*, i. pp. 173–4.

88. Sorel, *L'Europe et la Révolution française*, viii. pp. 220–6, argues that Napoleon was justified in responding in a non-committal way to what in all evidence was little more than a diplomatic probe.

89. Charles Webster, *The Foreign Policy of Castlereagh, 1812–1815: Britain and the Reconstruction of Europe*, 2 vols (London, 1931), i. pp. 166–80; Sweet, *Wilhelm von Humboldt*, ii. pp. 151–5.

90. Terry Pinkard, *Hegel: A Biography* (Cambridge, 2000), pp. 310–11.

91. Metternich, *Mémoires*, i. pp. 148–9.

92. There is much to Schroeder's assessment that Napoleon refused to make peace 'because he did not want to, chose not to – and also because he could not; could not make peace because he was no good at it, but also because, by this time, he was probably caught too deeply by his own past to carry it off' (Schroeder, *Transformation of European Politics*, p. 469).

93. Metternich, *Mémoires*, i. p. 182.

94. Metternich, *Mémoires*, i. p. 148.

95. Fournier, *Der Congress von Châtillon*, pp. 193–6; Kissinger, *A World Restored*, p. 130.

96. Pasquier, *Mémoires*, ii. pp. 100–1.

97. Gotteri (ed.), *La police secrète*, vii. p. 395 (16 November 1813).

98. *Corr.* xxv. n. 19952 (3 May 1813).

99. See Marc Belissa, *La Russie mise en Lumières: représentations et débats autour de la Russie dans la France du XVIIIe siècle* (Paris, 2010).

100. See M.P.D., *L'Elan Parisien, chant national, suivi d'un chant guerrier traduit du russe et d'une notice sur diverses peuplades qui fournissent à la Russie les troupes indisciplinées connues sous le nom de Cosaques* (Paris, 1814); Hantraye, *Les cosaques aux Champs-Elysées*, pp. 220–1.

101. L. J. Karr, *Des cosaques, ou Détails historiques sur les moeurs, coutumes, vêtemens, armes . . . recueillis de l'allemand* (Paris, 1814), pp. 84–5.

102. Charles-Louis Lesur, *Histoire des Kosaques*, 2 vols (Paris, 1813), i. pp. 247–8.

103. Leggiere, *The Fall of Napoleon*, pp. 111–12, 117–18.

104. Victor to Napoleon, 15 January 1814, cited in Leggiere, *The Fall of Napoleon*, p. 377.

105. Lefebvre de Behaine, *La campagne de France*, 4 vols (Paris, 1913–35), iii. pp. 144–5; Leggiere, *The Fall of Napoleon*, p. 385.

106. AN AFIV 1668, Campagne de France, Adminstration et police de l'armée, letters dated 24 February 1814; Henry Houssaye, *1814* (Paris, 1937), pp. 48–55; Louis Rogeron, *Les cosaques en Champagne et en Brie, récits de l'invasion de 1814, racontés d'après les contemporains, les auteurs modernes, des documents originaux et des notes inédites de témoins oculaires* (Paris, 1905).

107. Fernand Rude, 'Le réveil du patriotisme révolutionnaire dans la region Rhône-Alpes en 1814', *Cahiers d'histoire*, 16 (1971), 434–8.

108. Houssaye, *1814*, pp. 54–8.

109. Houssaye, *1814*, p. 16.

110. Jean-Paul Bertaud, *Les royalistes et Napoléon* (Paris, 2009), pp. 283–7.

111. Some examples in the *Journal de Paris*, 10 March 1814; the *Journal de l'Empire*, 3, 4, 5, 6, 7, 9, 10, 11, 12, 18 and 20 March 1814; the *Gazette de France*, 10 and 20 March 1814; and the *Journal des Débats*, 4 and 5 March 1814; Jacques Hantraye (ed.), *Le récit d'un civil dans la campagne de France de 1814: les 'Lettres historiques' de Pierre Dardenne (1768–1857)* (Paris, 2008), p. 49; Cabanis, *La Presse*, pp. 302–3.

112. See, for example, Edouard Gachot, '1813: récit d'un témoin', *Revue des études napoléoni-ennes*, 16 (1919), 274, in which Philippe Ballut, as soldier in the Guard Grenadiers, came across the massacre of about one hundred people by Russians in the village of Bischofs-werda, near Bautzen, in May 1813; Ashby, *Napoleon against Great Odds*, pp. 130–42.

113. *Corr.* xxvii. nos. 21328, 21360, 21375 (21, 24 and 26 February 1814).

114. *Journal de Paris*, 22 February 1814; *Journal des Débats*, 26 March 1814.

115. See, for example, Hantraye (ed.), *Le récit d'un civil dans la campagne de France*, p. lvii.

116. Jacques Hantraye, 'Les formes d'information du pouvoir et les représentations de la guerre au cours de la crise de 1813–1814 en France', *Cahiers du GERHICO*, 9 (2006), 97–113.

117. If Alphonse de Beauchamp, *Histoire des campagnes de 1814 et de 1815, comprenant l'histoire politique et militaire des deux invasions de la France*, 4 vols (Paris, 1816–17), i. p. 116, can be believed.

118. *Corr.* xxvi. n. 21015 (17 December 1813).

119. Fontaine, *Journal*, i. pp. 376 and 379 (24 November and 18 December 1813); Houssaye, *1814*, p. 32.

120. Palpable in the letters by Cambacérès, *Lettres inédites à Napoléon*, ii. pp. 1032–3 (26 August 1813); Rémusat, *Mémoires de ma vie*, i. p. 123; Olcina, *L'opinion publique en Belgique*, pp. 93–104.

121. Lignereux, *L'Empire des Français*, pp. 304–5.

122. Collins, *Napoleon and his Parliaments*, pp. 128–39; Menant, *Les députés de Napoléon*, pp. 352–72.

123. Louis Bergès, 'Perception et mise en scène des manifestations d'opposition au pouvoir de la fin du Premier Empire à la Seconde Restauration: analyse du cas girondin', in Bernard Barbiche, Jean-Pierre Poussou and Alain Tallon (eds), *Pouvoirs, contestations et comporte-ments dans l'Europe modern* (Paris, 2005), pp. 787–801.

124. Crépin, *La conscription en débats*, pp. 113–15.

125. Michael Ross, *The Reluctant King: Joseph Bonaparte. King of the Two Sicilies and Spain* (London, 1976), p. 221; Patricia Tyson Stroud, *The Emperor of Nature: Charles-Lucien Bonaparte and his World* (Philadelphia, 2000), p. 27.

126. Cabanis, *La Presse*, pp. 301–2.

127. *Corr.* xxvii. n. 21041 (26 December 1813); Louis Benaerts, *Les commissaires extraordinaires de Napoléon Ier en 1814: d'après leur correspondance inédite* (Paris, 1915), pp. vii–xxiii.

128. For this and the following see Rothenberg, *The Art of Warfare*, pp. 143–4, 202.

129. Bellot de Kergorre, *Journal*, p. 116.

130. Leggiere, *The Fall of Napoleon*, p. 73.

131. Sherwig, *Guineas and Gunpowder*, p. 288; Lignereux, *L'Empire des Français*, p. 203. And were able to do so largely because of their banking system. See Michael Bordo and Eugene White, 'A Tale of Two Currencies: British and French Finances during the Napoleonic Wars', *Journal of Economic History*, 51 (1991), 303–16.

132. Houssaye, *1814*, pp. 24–5.

133. Branda, *Le prix de la gloire*, p. 387.

## 23: *The Naked Emperor*

1. For the following see F. Loraine Petre, *Napoleon at Bay, 1814* (London, 1914); Chandler, *Campaigns of Napoleon*, pp. 945–1004; Uffindell, *Napoleon 1814*; Ashby, *Napoleon against Great Odds*, pp. 87–122.

2. Cited in Maurice Guerrini, *Napoléon et Paris, trente ans d'histoire* (Paris, 1967), p. 435.

3. Fontaine, *Journal*, i. p. 384 (24 January 1814).

4. AN F7 3733, Minutes des bulletins de police, 14 July 1814.

5. Chandler, *Campaigns of Napoleon*, p. 952.

6. Maurice Henri Weil, *La campagne de 1814 d'après les documents des archives impéri-ales et royales de la guerre à Vienne*, 4 vols (Paris, 1891–5), i. p. 493.

7. Charles Nicolas Fabvier, *Journal des opérations du 6e corps pendant la campagne de France en 1814* (Paris, 1819), p. 29; Uffindell, *Napoleon 1814*, pp. 51–2.

8. For this and other motives behind Alexander's decision see Schroeder, *Transformation of European Politics*, p. 497.

9. Kraehe, *Metternich's German Policy*, i. pp. 296–7.

10. Lucas-Dubreton, *Murat*, pp. 222–5.

11. *Corr.* xxvii. n. 21239 (13 February 1814).

12. *Corr.* xxvii. n. 21227 (9 February 1814).

13. *Corr.* xxvii. n. 21231 (11 February 1814).

14. Webster, *The Foreign Policy of Castlereagh*, i. pp. 218–19; John Bew, *Castlereagh: Enlightenment, War and Tyranny* (London, 2011), pp. 343–5.

15. Houssaye, *1814*, pp. 35–6.

16. Gotteri (ed.), *La police secrète*, vii. pp. 678, 700, 727, 801 (5, 12, 21 February and 16 March 1814).

17. Cambacérès, *Lettres inédites à Napoléon*, ii. pp. 1130–1 (11 March 1814).

18. Lentz, *Nouvelle histoire du Premier Empire*, ii. p. 554.

19. Pierrelongue (ed.), *Napoléon et Marie-Louise*, p. 172 (10 February 1814).

20. Houssaye, *1814*, pp. 36–7.

21. Castellane, *Journal*, i. p. 246; Houssaye, *1814*, pp. 32–3; Roger Dupuy, *La Garde nationale, 1789–1872* (Paris, 2010), pp. 336–7.

22. The *Gazette de France*, 10 March 1814, announced that the enemy had been 'repelled' with 'considerable losses' along the whole line.

23. Uffindell, *Napoleon 1814*, p. 90.

24. Sked, *Radetzky*, p. 65.

25. Bew, *Castlereagh*, pp. 345–6, 347.

26. Fain, *Manuscrit de mil huit cent-quatorze*, p. 191; Ségur, *Histoire et mémoires*, vii. pp. 49–50, claims that the horse was only wounded; Chandler, *Campaigns of Napoleon*, p. 997; Uffindell, *Napoleon 1814*, p. 105.

27. Pierrelongue (ed.), *Napoléon et Marie-Louise*, pp. 261–2 (23 March 1814).

28. Savary, *Mémoires*, vi. pp. 329–31.

29. Muir, *Britain and the Defeat of Napoleon*, pp. 304, 322.

30. Webster (ed.), *British Diplomacy*, pp. 173–4 (30 March 1814).

31. Lieven, *Russia against Napoleon*, pp. 507–8.

32. Webster, *The Foreign Policy of Castlereagh*, i. p. 243.

33. Beauchamp, *Histoire des campagnes de 1814 et de 1815*, i. p. 603.

34. On the battle for Paris see Houssaye, *1814*, pp. 487–539; Uffindell, *Napoleon 1814*, pp. 113–19.

35. Uffindell, *Napoleon 1814*, pp. 32–4.

36. The following is based on Rémusat, *Mémoires de ma vie*, i. p. 137; Reinhard, *Une femme de diplomate*, p. 393 (27 March 1814); Marie-Anne de Chateaubriand, comtesse de Marigny, *Paris en 1814: journal inédit de madame de Marigny* (Paris, 1907), p. 48 (28 March 1814).

37. Pierre de Pelleport, *Souvenirs militaires et intimes du général Vte de Pelleport, de 1793 à 1853*, 2 vols (Paris, 1857), ii. pp. 116–17.

38. Thomas Richard Underwood, *A Narrative of Memorable Events in Paris, Preceeding the Capitulation, and During the Occupancy of that City by the Allied Armies, in the Year 1814* (London, 1828), p. 53.

39. *Corr.* xxvii. n. 21210 (8 February 1814).

40. *Corr.* xxvii. n. 21497 (16 March 1814).

41. *Corr.* xxvii. n. 21467 (12 March 1814).

42. Savary, *Mémoires*, vi. p. 378.

43. Lucien Floriet, *Marmont: maréchal d'Empire, 1774–1852* (Marcilly-sur-Tille, 1996), pp. 179–95.

44. Marmont, *Mémoires*, vi. pp. 244–63. Few memoirists, such as Thirion, *Souvenirs militaires*, pp. 173–84, came to his defence.

45. As an English tourist in France in 1814 testifies. See Edward Stanley, *Before and after Waterloo: Letters from Edward Stanley, Sometime Bishop of Norwich (1802, 1814, 1816)* (London, 1907), p. 106.

46. Emmanuel de Waresquiel, *Les Cents Jours: la tentation de l'impossible, mars–juillet 1815* (Paris, 2008), pp. 216–17, 218–19.

47. It is an accusation that can still be found today. See Dominique de Villepin, *La chute ou l'Empire de la solitude, 1807–1814* (Paris, 2008), pp. 465–6.

48. On the people's reaction inside Paris see Emile Labretonnière, *Macédoine: souvenirs du Quartier latin* (Paris, 1863), pp. 109–20.

49. Pierrelongue (ed.), *Napoléon et Marie-Louise*, pp. 236–7 (10 March 1814).

50. Pierrelongue (ed.), *Napoléon et Marie-Louise*, pp. 267–8 (29 March 1814).

51. Carl Frédéric Palmstierna (ed.), *Marie-Louise et Napoléon, 1813–1814: lettres inédites de l'Impératrice avec les réponses déjà connues de Napoléon de la même époque* (Paris, 1955), pp. 176–7 (29 March 1814).

52. Underwood, *A Narrative of Memorable Events in Paris*, p. 49.

53. Underwood, *A Narrative of Memorable Events in Paris*, pp. 49–50; Stendhal, *Oeuvres intimes*, i. pp. 1409–11 (29 March 1814).

54. Gaston Stiegler (ed.), *Le maréchal Oudinot, duc de Reggio: d'après les souvenirs inédits de la maréchale* (Paris, 1894), p. 307.

55. Houssaye, *1814*, pp. 519–20.

56. Philip Mansel, *Paris between Empires: Monarchy and Revolution, 1814–1852* (London, 2001), p. 7.

57. Pierrelongue (ed.), *Napoléon et Marie-Louise*, pp. 271–2 (30 March 1814).

58. Chevallier and Pincemaille, *L'impératrice Joséphine*, pp. 412–13.

59. Forgues (ed.), *Mémoires de Vitrolles*, i. p. 311. Vitrolles was a royalist so his memoirs are somewhat biased. Lieven, *Russia against Napoleon*, pp. 516–17.

60. George Woodberry, *Journal du lieutenant Woodberry, campagnes de Portugal et d'Espagne, de France, de Belgique et de France, 1813–1815*, trans. Georges Hélie (Paris, 1896), pp. 335, 339 (4, 6 July 1815).

61. Louis Véron, *Mémoires d'un bourgeois de Paris* (Paris, 1856), i. pp. 219–20; Pierre-Jean de Béranger, *Ma biographie* (Paris, 1859), pp. 144–5; Houssaye, *1814*, pp. 553–64.

62. *Journal des Débats*, 1 April 1814. Caulaincourt, *Memoirs*, iii. pp. 203–7, believed that Alexander was still toying with the idea of a regency five days later on 5 April, but by this stage a restoration of the Bourbon monarchy had been decided upon and it would have been difficult if not impossible to reverse course. See also Thiry, *Le Sénat de Napoléon*, pp. 302–19; Houssaye, *1814*, p. 567; Lieven, *Russia against Napoleon*, p. 518; Sellin, *Die geraubte Revolution*, pp. 143–71.

63. Caulaincourt, *Memoirs*, iii. pp. 39–40.

64. This account based on Caulaincourt, *Memoirs*, iii. pp. 51–60.

65. Napoleon in a conversation with the mayor of Roanne, 23 April 1814, in J. M. Thompson, 'Napoleon's Journey to Elba in 1814. Part I. By Land', *American Historical Review*, 55 (1949), 10.

66. Pion des Loches, *Mes campagnes*, pp. 389–90.

67. The scene has been reconstructed from the memoirs of Macdonald, *Souvenirs*, pp. 273–4, 275–7; Fain, *Manuscrit de mil huit cent-quatorze*, pp. 246–8, 249–50; Pasquier, *Mémoires*, ii. pp. 322–4; Lentz, *Nouvelle histoire du Premier Empire*, ii. pp. 570–1; Sellin, *Die geraubte Revolution*, pp. 176–83.

68. *Corr.* xxvii. n. 21555 (4 April 1814). The draft was taken to Paris by Caulaincourt. It was to be published only after the signing of a treaty that determined his own fate, as well as that of his wife and son.

69. *Corr.* xxvii. n. 21558 (11 April 1814).

70. Cited in Norman MacKenzie, *Escape from Elba: The Fall and Flight of Napoleon, 1814–1815* (New York, 1982), p. 7.

71. Lieven, *Russia against Napoleon*, pp. 518–19.

72. See Charles Dupuis, *Le ministère de Talleyrand en 1814* (Paris, 1919), pp. 236–85.

73. Ullrichová (ed.), *Clemens Metternich, Wilhelmine von Sagan*, pp. 244, 248.

74. Vane (ed.), *Correspondence, Despatches, and Other Papers of Viscount Castlereagh*, ix. p. 450 (7 April 1814).

75. Ernest de Selincourt (ed.), *The Letters of William and Dorothy Wordsworth*, 6 vols (Oxford, 1935–9), ii. pt 2, pp. 592–3 (24 April 1814).

76. See Semmel, *Napoleon and the British*, pp. 149–52.

77. Las Cases, *Mémorial*, ii. p. 210.

78. Guillaume Peyrusse, *1809–1815. Mémorial et archives de M. le Baron Peyrusse* (Carcassonne, 1869), pp. 223–4.

79. Robinaux, *Journal de route*, p. 191.

80. Chevalier de Jouvencel, 'Les Alliés à Versailles', in *1814: résistance et occupation des villes françaises* (Paris, 2001), p. 263.

81. Barrès, *Souvenirs*, p. 202. See also Paulin, *Les Souvenirs*, p. 277.

82. René Reiss, *Kellermann* (Paris, 2009), esp. pp. 513–56.

83. Pion des Loches, *Mes campagnes*, pp. 395–6.

84. Pion des Loches, *Mes campagnes*, p. 388.

85. Fontaine, *Journal*, i. p. 410 (20 April 1814).

86. Tombs and Tombs, *That Sweet Enemy*, pp. 285–6.

87. Letter dated 16 April 1814, cited in Hantraye, *Les cosaques aux Champs-Elysées*, p. 226.

88. According to Metternich, Ullrichová (ed.), *Clemens Metternich, Wilhelmine von Sagan*, pp. 243, 253.

89. Tombs and Tombs, *That Sweet Enemy*, p. 286.

90. Carlyle to Mitchell, in Charles Richard Sanders (ed.), *The Collected Letters of Thomas and Jane Welsh Carlyle* (Durham, NC, 1970), i. pp. 6–7 (30 April 1814).

91. Cited in MacKenzie, *Escape from Elba*, p. 33.

92. Bausset, *Mémoires anecdotiques*, ii. pp. 188–9.

93. J.-M. des Cilleuls, 'Yvan, chirurgien de Napoléon (1765–1839)', *Archives de médecine et de pharmacie militaires*, 103 (1935), 1024–31; Caulaincourt, *Memoirs*, iii. pp. 308–55; MacKenzie, *Escape from Elba*, p. 35. Apart from Caulaincourt, present were Fain and Saint-Denis. See Fain, *Manuscrit de mil huit cent-quatorze*, pp. 255–8; and Saint-Denis, *Souvenirs du Mameluck Ali*, pp. 62–4.

94. MacKenzie, *Escape from Elba*, p. 189.

95. For a wider context see Emil Szittya, *Selbstmörder: ein Beitrag zur Kulturgeschichte aller Zeiten und Völker* (Vienna, 1985); Georges Minois, *Histoire du suicide: la société occidentale face à la mort volontaire* (Paris, 1995), pp. 318–21, 359–62; Jeffrey Merrick, 'Death and Life in the Archives: Patterns of and Attitudes to Suicide in Eighteenth-Century Paris', in John Weaver and David Wright (eds), *Histories of Suicide: International Perspectives on Self-Destruction in the Modern World* (Toronto, 2009), pp. 73–90.

96. Fournier, *Napoleon*, ii. p. 373, and p. Hillemand, 'Napoleon a-t-il tenté de se suicider à Fontainebleau?', *Revue de l'Institut Napoléon*, 119 (1971), 71–8, doubt whether Napoleon tried to commit suicide.

97. Palmstierna (ed.), *Marie-Louise et Napoléon*, p. 200.

98. She wrote to her father on 8 April to say that she would leave the next day.

99. According to Savary, *Mémoires*, vii. pp. 185–6; Guy Godlewski, *Napoléon à l'île d'Elbe: 300 jours d'exil* (Paris, 2003), pp. 131–2.

100. Bausset, *Mémoires anecdotiques*, i. p. 392, ii. p. 277, although he is less than reliable; Boudon, *Le roi Jérôme*, pp. 407–8.

101. Later, in a letter to her husband, Pierrelongue (ed.), *Napoléon et Marie-Louise*, p. 291 (8 April 1814), Marie-Louise stated that his brothers insisted she hand herself over to an Austrian corps.

102. Bausset, *Mémoires anecdotiques*, ii. pp. 220–4.

103. Masson, *L'impératrice Marie-Louise*, pp. 572–3; Fournier, *Marie-Louise et la chute de Napoléon*, pp. 4–5, says that he was to accompany her to Fontainebleau, but he is wrong.

104. Schiel, *Marie-Louise*, p. 202.
105. Palmstierna (ed.), *Marie-Louise et Napoléon*, pp. 202–3 (8 April 1814).
106. Palmstierna (ed.), *Marie-Louise et Napoléon*, pp. 204–5 (11 April 1814).
107. A judgement that can be found in Masson, *L'impératrice Marie-Louise*, p. 574; Henry Houssaye, *1815*, 3 vols (Paris, 1893), i. p. 161.
108. Pierrelongue (ed.), *Napoléon et Marie-Louise*, pp. 292, 293 (8, 9 April 1814).
109. Palmstierna (ed.), *Marie-Louise et Napoléon*, p. 203 (9 April 1814).
110. Pierrelongue (ed.), *Napoléon et Marie-Louise*, pp. 291, 297, 301 (8, 11, 12 April 1814); Godlewski, *Napoléon à l'île d'Elbe*, pp. 133–5.
111. Metternich to Hudelist, 7 April 1814, cited in Edward de Wertheimer, *The Duke of Reichstadt* (London, 1905), pp. 95–6.
112. According to Fournier, *Marie-Louise et la chute de Napoléon*, p. 4.
113. Cited in Schiel, *Marie-Louise*, p. 204.
114. Palmstierna (ed.), *Marie-Louise et Napoléon*, pp. 212–13 (12 April 1814).
115. Palmstierna (ed.), *Marie-Louise et Napoléon*, p. 216 (12–13 April 1814).
116. Palmstierna (ed.), *Marie-Louise et Napoléon*, p. 214 (12 April 1814).
117. Palmstierna (ed.), *Marie-Louise et Napoléon*, pp. 224–5 (15 April 1814).
118. Méneval, *Napoléon et Marie-Louise*, ii. p. 205.
119. Schiel, *Marie-Louise*, p. 211.
120. Palmstierna (ed.), *Marie-Louise et Napoléon*, pp. 236–7 (20 April 1814).
121. Neil Campbell, *Napoleon at Fontainebleau and Elba: Being a Journal of Occurrences in 1814–1815* (London, 1869), p. 157.
122. Campbell, *Napoleon at Fontainebleau and Elba*, p. 181.
123. For the following account of Napoleon's flight to Elba see Truchsess-Waldbourg, *Nouvelle relation de l'itinéraire de Napoléon*; Jean-Baptiste-Germain Fabry, *Itinéraire de Buonaparte, depuis son départ de Doulevent, le 28 mars, jusqu'à son embarquement à Fréjus, le 29 avril* (Paris, 1815), who appears to have interviewed people along the route; Campbell, *Napoleon at Fontainebleau and Elba*, pp. 178–92; Joseph Alexandre Freiherr von Helfert, *Napoleon I., Fahrt von Fontainebleau nach Elba, April–Mai 1814, mit Benützung der amtlichen Reiseberichte des kaiserlich österreichischen Commissars General Koller* (Vienna, 1874); Thomas Ussher, *Napoleon's last voyages, being the diaries of Admiral Sir Thomas Ussher . . . on board the 'Undaunted', and John R. Glover . . . on board the 'Northumberland'* (2nd edn, London, 1906).
124. Thompson, 'Napoleon's Journey to Elba', 8.
125. Ernouf, *Maret*, p. 642.
126. One can find it, for example, in *Corr.* xxvii. n. 21561 (20 April 1814); A.-D.-B. Monier, *Une année de la vie de l'empereur Napoléon, ou Précis historique de tout ce qui s'est passé depuis le 1er avril 1814 jusqu'au 20 mars 1815* (Paris, 1815), pp. 15–17. Las Cases, *Mémorial*, ii. pp. 559–66. See also, Helfert, *Fahrt von Fontainebleau nach Elba*, pp. 20–2.
127. MacKenzie, *Escape from Elba*, pp. 49–50.
128. Chevalier, *Souvenirs*, p. 305.
129. According to Parquin, *Souvenirs*, p. 365.
130. Lentz, *Nouvelle histoire du Premier Empire*, iv. p. 158, says six carriages and eight *fourgons*.
131. Monier, *Une année de la vie de l'empereur*, p. 18.
132. AN AF7 3733, Minutes des bulletins de police, 2 May 1814.
133. AN AF7 3733, Minutes des bulletins de police, 2 May 1814; 'Passage de l'empereur à Avignon en 1814', in *De l'exil au retour de l'île d'Elbe: récits contemporains* (Paris, 2001), pp. 11–14; Fabry, *Itinéraire de Buonaparte*, pp. 44–6.
134. Truchsess-Waldbourg, *Nouvelle relation de l'itinéraire de Napoléon*, p. 24.
135. Truchsess-Waldbourg, *Nouvelle relation de l'itinéraire de Napoléon*, pp. 24–5.
136. Peyrusse, *Mémorial*, p. 226; Frédéric Schoell, *Recueil de pièces officielles destinées à détromper les François sur les événemens qui se sont passés depuis quelques années*, 12 vols (Paris, 1814–16), vi. pp. 188–93; Fabry, *Itinéraire de Buonaparte*, pp. 47–8; and Truchsess-Waldbourg, *Nouvelle relation de l'itinéraire de Napoléon*, pp. 25–31.

137. Truchsess-Waldbourg, *Nouvelle relation de l'itinéraire de Napoléon*, p. 30.
138. Truchsess-Waldbourg, *Nouvelle relation de l'itinéraire de Napoléon*, p. 34.
139. Campbell, *Napoleon at Fontainebleau and Elba*, pp. 200–1.
140. Truchsess-Waldbourg, *Nouvelle relation de l'itinéraire de Napoléon*, pp. 39–40.
141. Chateaubriand, *Mémoires d'outre-tombe*, ii. p. 3153; Cabanis, *Le sacre de Napoléon*, p. 66.
142. Fabry, *Itinéraire de Buonaparte*, pp. 60–6.
143. Pierrelongue (ed.), *Napoléon et Marie-Louise*, pp. 327, 328 (28 April 1814); Helfert, *Fahrt von Fontainebleau nach Elba*, p. 49.
144. According to Ussher, *Napoleon's last voyages*, p. 46; and Frédéric d'Agay, 'Un témoignage raphaélois sur l'embarquement de Napoléon pour l'île d'Elbe en 1814', *Annales du Sud-Est Varois*, 13 (1988), 19–20.
145. Letter from Lieutenant Hastings cited in Norwood Young, *Napoleon in Exile: Elba* (London, 1914), p. 86.
146. Campbell, *Napoleon at Fontainebleau and Elba*, p. 199; Ussher, *Napoleon's last voyages*, pp. 41–2.

## *24: Sovereign of Elba*

1. Ussher, *Napoleon's last voyages*, p. 49; Truchsess-Waldbourg, *Nouvelle relation de l'itinéraire de Napoléon*, p. 50; Campbell, *Napoleon at Fontainebleau and Elba*, p. 200.
2. Cited in Young, *Napoleon in Exile: Elba*, p. 78.
3. Helfert, *Fahrt von Fontainebleau nach Elba*, pp. 55–6.
4. Peyrusse, *Mémorial*, p. 233.
5. Arsenne Thiébaut de Berneaud, *Voyage à l'isle d'Elbe; suivi d'une notice sur les autres isles de la mer Tyrrhénienne* (Paris, 1808), pp. 44, 126.
6. Louise Laflandre-Lindon, *Napoléon et l'Île d'Elbe* (La Cadière d'Azur, 1989), pp. 80–2.
7. Campbell, *Napoleon at Fontainebleau and Elba*, pp. 214–15.
8. MacKenzie, *Escape from Elba*, p. 71.
9. MacKenzie, *Escape from Elba*, p. 70.
10. Laflandre-Linden, *Napoléon et l'Île d'Elbe*, p. 135.
11. André Pons [dubbed Pons de l'Hérault], *Souvenirs et anecdotes de l'île d'Elbe* (Paris, 1897), p. 39.
12. 'Les cahiers du capitaine Jobit: Napolón à l'île d'Elbe', in *De l'exil au retour de l'île d'Elbe*, p. 27.
13. MacKenzie, *Escape from Elba*, p. 75. Most of the works on Napoleon's stay on Elba are popular histories of no particular interest. Of note are: Godlewski, *Napoléon à l'île d'Elbe*; and Marie-Hélène Baylac, *Napoléon: Empereur de l'île d'Elbe* (Paris, 2011).
14. Fabry, *Itinéraire de Buonaparte*, pp. 72–3.
15. Palmstierna (ed.), *Marie-Louise et Napoléon*, pp. 252–3 (4 May 1814).
16. Palmstierna (ed.), *Marie-Louise et Napoléon*, pp. 254, 256, 260 (24 May, 5 and 24 June 1814).
17. Louis Marchand, *Mémoires de Marchand: premier valet de chambre et exécuteur testamentaire de l'empereur Napoléon* (Paris, 2003), pp. 109–11.
18. Campbell, *Napoleon at Fontainebleau and Elba*, p. 243.
19. Ussher, *Napoleon's last voyages*, p. 72.
20. Monier, *Une année de la vie de l'empereur*, pp. 56–67.
21. Georges Firmin-Didot, *Royauté ou empire. La France en 1814* (Paris, 1897), p. 122.
22. Eugène Welvert, *Napoléon et la police sous la première Restauration d'après les rapports du comte Beugnot au roi Louis XVIII* (Paris, n.d.), p. 48 (9 July 1814).
23. Houssaye, *1815*, i. pp. 154–6.
24. See Baylac, *Napoléon*, pp. 100–3.
25. Peyrusse, *Mémorial*, p. 253; Pons, *Souvenirs et anecdotes*, p. 127.

26. Baylac, *Napoléon*, p. 189.

27. *Corr.* xxvii. n. 21567 (no date but May 1814). All of which can be found in Léon G. Pélissier, *Le registre de l'île d'Elbe: lettres et ordres inédits de Napoléon Ier (28 mai 1814–22 février 1815)* (Paris, 1897).

28. MacKenzie, *Escape from Elba*, pp. 122–4.

29. Campbell, *Napoleon at Fontainebleau and Elba*, pp. 233, 249, 305.

30. Pons, *Souvenirs et anecdotes*, p. 201; Baylac, *Napoléon*, p. 233.

31. John Barber Scott, *An Englishman at Home and Abroad, 1792–1828: With Some Recollections of Napoleon* (Bungay, 1988), pp. 96, 97. A similar description of him is in Peyrusse, *Lettres inédites*, pp. 231–2.

32. Cited in Young, *Napoleon in Exile: Elba*, p. 256.

33. Campbell, *Napoleon at Fontainebleau and Elba*, p. 299 n. 7. Similar sentiments were expressed to Ussher, *Napoleon's last voyages*, p. 84.

34. Arthur Wellesley, Duke of Wellington, *Supplementary Despatches and Memoranda of Field Marshal Arthur Duke of Wellington*, 15 vols (London, 1858–72), ix. pp. 268–72 and 275–6 (17 and 20 September 1814).

35. Chastenay, *Mémoires*, ii. pp. 461–4; Stephen Coote, *Napoleon and the Hundred Days* (London, 2004), p. 114.

36. See, for example, Hyde de Neuville, *Mémoires et souvenirs* (1890), ii. pp. 16–36; Iung (ed.), *Lucien Bonaparte*, iii. pp. 210–12.

37. MacKenzie, *Escape from Elba*, pp. 141–2.

38. Campbell, *Napoleon at Fontainebleau and Elba*, p. 300.

39. MacKenzie, *Escape from Elba*, p. 143.

40. Campbell, *Napoleon at Fontainebleau and Elba*, p. 317; Henry William Edmund Petty-Fitzmaurice, Earl of Kerry (ed.), *The First Napoleon: Some Unpublished Documents from the Bowood Papers* (London, 1925), pp. 80–105. Other British visitors to Elba who left accounts include: George Venables Vernon, *Sketch of a Conversation with Napoleon at Elba* (London, 1863–4); Hugh Fortescue Viscount Ebrington, *Memorandum of Two Conversations between the Emperor Napoleon and Viscount Ebrington at Porto-Ferrajo on the 6th and 8th of December 1814* (London, 1823); Ralph A. Griffiths (ed.), *In Conversation with Napoleon Bonaparte: J. H. Vivian's Visit to the Island of Elba* (Newport, 2008). Others are in John Goldworth Alger, *Napoleon's British Visitors and Captives 1801–1815* (Westminster, 1904); and Katharine MacDonogh, 'A Sympathetic Ear: Napoleon, Elba and the British', *History Today*, 44:2 (1994), 29–35.

41. Saint-Denis, *Souvenirs du Mameluck Ali*, p. 68; Godlewski, *Napoléon à l'île d'Elbe*, pp. 49–51.

42. Cited in MacKenzie, *Escape from Elba*, p. 154. Also Baylac, *Napoléon*, pp. 251–5.

43. Letter from Pauline to Letizia cited in Masson, *Napoléon et sa famille*, x. p. 328 (25 June 1814).

44. Oman, *Napoleon's Viceroy*, pp. 406–21; Bernardy, *Eugène de Beauharnais*, pp. 451–509.

45. Boudon, *Le roi Jérôme*, pp. 417–23.

46. Masson, *Napoléon et sa famille*, x. pp. 292–8.

47. Masson, *Napoléon et sa famille*, x. pp. 221–5; A. Hilliard Atteridge, *Napoleon's Brothers* (London, 1909), p. 420; Godlewski, *Napoléon à l'île d'Elbe*, pp. 72–3.

48. Marchand, *Mémoires*, pp. 124–5.

49. Hantraye, *Les cosaques aux Champs-Elysées*, p. 233.

50. Constant, *Mémoires*, vi. p. 92.

51. Pélissier, *Le registre de l'île d'Elbe*, pp. 64–5 (27 July 1814); Sutherland, *Marie Walewska*, pp. 213–14, 219–22.

52. On this episode see MacKenzie, *Escape from Elba*, pp. 126–30; Baylac, *Napoléon*, pp. 169–72.

53. Saint-Denis, *Souvenirs du Mameluck Ali*, pp. 84–6.

54. MacKenzie, *Escape from Elba*, p. 130; Baylac, *Napoléon*, p. 162.

55. Campbell, *Napoleon at Fontainebleau and Elba*, p. 175.

56. Palmstierna (ed.), *Marie-Louise et Napoléon*, p. 272.

57. Mme de Montesquiou, for one, told him as much in April 1814. See Palmstierna (ed.), *Marie-Louise et Napoléon*, pp. 249–50.

58. Something that she suspected. See Palmstierna (ed.), *Marie-Louise et Napoléon*, pp. 258–9 (5 June 1814).

59. Méneval, *Napoléon et Marie-Louise*, ii. pp. 277–89.

60. Palmstierna (ed.), *Marie-Louise et Napoléon*, pp. 260–1 (22 June 1814).

61. Welvert, *Napoléon et la police*, pp. 116–17 (8 August 1814).

62. Houssaye, *1815*, i. pp. 161–4; Masson, *L'impératrice Marie-Louise*, pp. 602–5.

63. Fournier, *Marie-Louise et la chute de Napoléon*, pp. 10–11.

64. Schiel, *Marie-Louise*, pp. 224–5.

65. Méneval, *Mémoires*, iii. pp. 341–2.

66. Méneval, *Mémoires*, iii. p. 344.

67. Marie-Louise to Francis (July, 3 August 1814), cited in Schiel, *Marie-Louise*, p. 225.

68. Méneval, *Mémoires*, iii. p. 347.

69. Méneval, *Mémoires*, iii. p. 349. Napoleon celebrated the feast of St Napoleon with as much pomp as he could muster (Pons, *Souvenirs et anecdotes*, pp. 231–3; Marchand, *Mémoires*, p. 129.

70. Alan Palmer, *Napoleon & Marie Louise: The Emperor's Second Wife* (London, 2001), pp. 186–7; Godlewski, *Napoléon à l'île d'Elbe*, pp. 154–9.

71. Marie-Louise to Francis, 30 September 1814, Fournier, *Marie-Louise et la chute de Napoléon*, p. 17.

72. It is possible that Napoleon was aware of their liaison. See Godlewski, *Napoléon à l'île d'Elbe*, pp. 171–4.

73. Méneval, *Mémoires*, iii. pp. 421–2.

74. Palmstierna (ed.), *Marie-Louise et Napoléon*, pp. 276–7 (3 January 1815).

75. Maurice-Henri Weil, *Les dessous du Congrès de Vienne: d'après les documents originaux des archives du Ministère impérial et royal de l'intérieur à Vienne*, 2 vols (Paris, 1917), i. p. 634 (3 December 1814); ii. p. 73 (23 January 1815).

76. Campbell, *Napoleon at Fontainebleau and Elba*, pp. 271, 277.

77. See Hippolyte Larrey, *Madame mère: essai historique*, 2 vols (Paris, 1892), ii. pp. 66–76; Scott, *An Englishman at Home and Abroad*, p. 106; Baylac, *Napoléon*, pp. 173–6.

78. Pons, *Souvenirs et anecdotes*, pp. 267–8.

79. Campbell, *Napoleon at Fontainebleau and Elba*, p. 272.

80. Pons, *Souvenirs et anecdotes*, p. 207.

81. Young, *Napoleon in Exile: Elba*, p. 233.

82. According to Campbell, in Wellington, *Supplementary Despatches*, ix. pp. 268–73 (17 September 1814).

83. Chastenay, *Mémoires*, ii. pp. 429–32; Natalie Petiteau, *Lendemains d'Empire: les soldats de Napoléon dans la France du XIXe siècle* (Paris, 2003), pp. 108–14; Natalie Petiteau, 'Le retour de guerre: destins de vétérans après 1815', in Jacques-Olivier Boudon (ed.), *Armée, guerre et société à l'époque napoléonienne* (Paris, 2004), pp. 87–103; Natalie Petiteau, 'La Restauration face aux vétérans de l'Empire', in Martine Reid, Jean-Yves Mollier and Jean-Claude Yon (eds), *Repenser la Restauration* (Paris, 2005), pp. 31–43.

84. See the police reports in AN F7 3783, for accounts of public professions of support for Napoleon among the military (esp. 11, 18, 20 July and 7, 19 October 1814). On the political tensions in Paris see Mansel, *Paris between Empires*, pp. 63–6.

85. Zamoyksi, *Rites of Peace*, p. 450.

86. Branda, *Le prix de la gloire*, p. 62.

87. MacKenzie, *Escape from Elba*, p. 173.

88. Campbell, *Napoleon at Fontainebleau and Elba*, pp. 304, 318–19.

89. Campbell, *Napoleon at Fontainebleau and Elba*, p. 343.

90. Godlewski, *Napoléon à l'île d'Elbe*, pp. 93–9; MacKenzie, *Escape from Elba*, pp. 150–2; David King, *Vienna 1814: How the Conquerors of Napoleon Made Love, War, and Peace at the Congress of Vienna* (New York, 2009), p. 170.

91. Barante, *Souvenirs*, i. p. 120; Weil, *Les dessous du Congrès de Vienne*, i. pp. 404–6 (15 October 1814); Houssaye, *1815*, i. pp. 170–2; Lentz, *Nouvelle histoire du Premier Empire*, iv. pp. 281–3; Baylac, *Napoléon*, pp. 226–30.

92. 'Lettre du Comte de Chauvigny', in *De l'exil au retour de l'île d'Elbe*, pp. 37–42 (12 June 1814); Houssaye, *1815*, i. pp. 171–2 n. 4.

93. Houssaye, *1815*, i. pp. 172–3; Godlewski, *Napoléon à l'île d'Elbe*, pp. 90–8.

94. Cited in MacKenzie, *Escape from Elba*, p. 158.

95. Pélissier, *Le registre de l'île d'Elbe*, pp. 110, 113–14 (9 and 11 September); Young, *Napoleon in Exile: Elba*, pp. 278–81; Baylac, *Napoléon*, pp. 228–9.

96. Pons, *Souvenirs et anecdotes*, pp. 160–3.

97. *Journal des débats politiques et littéraires*, 19 November 1814; Eynard, *Journal*, i. p. 97 (9 November 1814), was told by the King of Bavaria that Napoleon would be taken to St Helena.

98. Bausset, *Mémoires anecdotiques*, iii. p. 66.

99. Georges Pallain (ed.), *Correspondance inédite du Prince de Talleyrand et du roi Louis XVIII pendant le congrès de Vienne* (Paris, 1881), p. 43 (13 October 1814).

100. Baylac, *Napoléon*, p. 221.

101. Louis XVIII's police were reporting on the rapprochement between Napoleon and Murat (Firmin-Didot, *Royauté ou empire*, pp. 75, 87, 139, 158, 234).

102. Pallain (ed.), *Correspondance inédite du Prince de Talleyrand*, pp. 270–91 (15 February 1815); Lentz, *Nouvelle histoire du Premier Empire*, iv. pp. 280–1.

103. See, for example, the *Journal des débats politiques et littéraires*, 19 November 1814. Welvert, *Napoléon et la police*, p. 272 (19 November 1814).

104. Campbell, *Napoleon at Fontainebleau and Elba*, pp. 209–10.

105. See Bettina Frederking, '"Il ne faut pas être le roi de deux peuples": Strategies of National Reconciliation in Restoration France', *French History*, 22:4 (2008), 454, 455.

106. It was also the view of Pons, *Souvenirs et anecdotes*, p. 106.

107. Firmin-Didot, *Royauté ou empire*, pp. 232–3.

108. Cited in MacKenzie, *Escape from Elba*, p. 194.

109. Mollien, *Mémoires*, iii. p. 422; Arthur Chuquet, *Le départ de l'île d'Elbe* (Châtillon-sur-Seine, 1921), pp. 157–9; Lentz, *Nouvelle histoire du Premier Empire*, iv. p. 345.

110. Gourgaud, *Journal de Sainte-Hélène*, ii. p. 7.

111. Pons, *Souvenirs et anecdotes*, pp. 371–2, 374.

112. Such as Charles Louis Alexandre Coriolis d'Espinouse, *Le tyran, les alliés et le roi, par M. le Mis de Coriolis d'Espinouse* (Paris, 1814).

113. Charles Malo, *Napoléoniana, ou Recueil d'anecdotes, saillies, bons mots, réparties, etc. etc, pour servir à l'histoire de la vie de Buonaparte* (Paris, 1814), p. 7. There are dozens if not hundreds of books and pamphlets all directed against Napoleon, not the least of which being Germaine de Staël's *Attila. Le pardon de Napoléon Buonaparte, et le caractère de ce grand homme* (Paris, n.d.); abbé Fugantini Poeteraux, *Confession poétique et véridique de Buonaparte au Révérend Père Boniface, ci-devant capucin d'Ajaccio, suivie de son action de grâce à Louis XVIII* (Paris, 1814); Auguste-Louis Ledrut, *Honneur aux militaires, ou Examen impartial de cette question: Buonaparte est-il un héros?* (Paris, 1814); *Epître du diable à Buonaparte* [signed Lucifer] (n.p., 1814); *Adieux à Buonaparte* (n.p., 1814). Surprisingly, little of this literature is directed at other individuals of the Bonaparte family.

114. L. Verriez, *Le Néron corse* (Gand, 1815), pp. 19, 20. Also F. Chéron, *Napoléon, ou le Corse dévoilé, ode aux Français* (Paris, 1814); *Robespierre et Buonaparte, ou les deux tyrannies* (Paris, 1814); *La queue de Buonaparte, ou les malveillants, les factieux et les agitateurs dévoilés et confondus* (Paris, n.d.). Jean Tulard, *Le mythe de Napoléon* (Paris, 1971), pp. 45–52, outlines a few of the essential texts for 1814 and 1815.

115. Louis-André Pichon, *De l'Etat de la France, sous la domination de Napoléon Bonaparte* (Paris, 1814), pp. 13–23.

116. Charles Doris, *Précis historique sur Napoléon Bonaparte* (Paris, 1814), pp. 17, 82. A similar

format, by the same author, can be found in *Mémoires secrets sur Napoléon Buonaparte, écrits par un homme qui ne l'a pas quitté depuis quinze ans* (Paris, 1815). See also Gabriel de Gaillon, *Règne et chute de Buonaparte, fragment épique* (Paris, 1814); abbé Sébastien-André Sibire, *Le portrait de Buonaparte, suivi d'un discours sur la nature et l'effet des conquêtes* (Paris, 1814).

117. Monier, *Une année de la vie de l'empereur*, pp. 98–9.
118. Pons, *Souvenirs et anecdotes*, p. 382.
119. MacKenzie, *Escape from Elba*, p. 206; Baylac, *Napoléon*, p. 268.
120. Larrey, *Madame mère*, ii. p. 97; Baylac, *Napoléon*, p. 269.
121. Pons, *Souvenirs et anecdotes*, pp. 124–5; Peyrusse, *Mémorial*, p. 274.
122. Pons, *Souvenirs et anecdotes*, p. 126.
123. Pierre-Alexandre-Edouard Fleury de Chaboulon, *Mémoires de Fleury de Chaboulon, ex-secrétaire de l'empereur Napoléon et de son cabinet, pour servir à l'histoire de la privée, du retour et du règne de Napoléon en 1815*, 2 vols (Paris, 1901), i. p. 120.
124. Peyrusse, *Mémorial*, pp. 274–5; MacKenzie, *Escape from Elba*, p. 227; Baylac, *Napoléon*, p. 278.
125. Saint-Denis, *Souvenirs du Mameluck Ali*, p. 90; Peyrusse, *Mémorial*, p. 275.
126. MacKenzie, *Escape from Elba*, p. 237; MacDonogh, 'A Sympathetic Ear', 29–35; Mansel, *Paris between Empires*, p. 69.
127. MacKenzie, *Escape from Elba*, p. 144; Englund, *Napoleon*, p. 421.
128. Welvert, *Napoléon et la police*, p. 21 (21 June 1814); Baylac, *Napoléon*, pp. 203–12.
129. Welvert, *Napoléon et la police*, pp. 300–1 (3 December 1814).
130. Welvert, *Napoléon et la police*, pp. 300–1 (3 December 1814).

# THE SECOND COMING, 1815

## 25: *The Saviour Returns*

1. Marchand, *Mémoires*, p. 126.
2. Antoine Chollier, *La vraie Route Napoléon, de Golfe-Juan à Lyon, histoire de dix jours* (Paris, 1950), p. 19.
3. Auguste-Louis Pétiet, *Souvenirs militaires de l'histoire contemporaine, par le général, baron, Auguste Pétiet* (Paris, 1844), pp. 195–6.
4. Saint-Chamans, *Mémoires*, p. 289; Thiébault, *Mémoires*, v. pp. 341–2; James Gallatin, *The Diary of James Gallatin, Secretary to Albert Gallatin, U.S. Envoy to France and England 1813–1827* (London, 1916), p. 66 (24 March 1815).
5. Arthur Chuquet (ed.), *Lettres de 1815: première série* (Paris, 1911), pp. 11–15.
6. Etienne Laborde, *Napoléon et sa garde, ou relation du voyage de Fontainebleau à l'île d'Elbe en 1814, du séjour de l'empereur dans cette île, et de son retour en France à la tête du petit nombre de troupes qui l'y avaient accompagné* (Paris, 1840), p. 77; Peyrusse, *Mémorial*, p. 280; Houssaye, *1815*, i. p. 209; Coote, *Napoleon and the Hundred Days*, p. 148.
7. *Corr.* xxviii. n. 21681 (1 March 1815); Lentz, *Nouvelle histoire du Premier Empire*, iv. pp. 319–24.
8. *Corr.* xxviii. n. 21682 (1 March 1815).
9. *Corr.* xxviii. n. 21683 (1 March 1815).
10. Benjamin Constant, *Mémoires sur les Cent-Jours* (Tübingen, 1993), p. 250.
11. MacKenzie, *Escape from Elba*, p. 249.
12. For this see Lentz, *Nouvelle histoire du Premier Empire*, iv. pp. 291, 303–5.
13. *Corr.* xxviii. nos. 21681, 21684, 21685 (1, 6 and 9 March 1815).
14. *Moniteur universel*, 23 March 1815; *Corr.* xxviii. n. 21686 (13 March 1815).
15. *Corr.* xxviii. nos. 21686, 21687, 21688, 21689 (13 March 1815).
16. Waresquiel, *Les Cents Jours*, pp. 327–9 and 584 n. 5.

17. Waresquiel, *Les Cents Jours*, pp. 326–7; Lentz, *Nouvelle histoire du Premier Empire*, iv. pp. 303–5.

18. As Emile Le Gallo, *Les Cent-Jours: essai sur l'histoire intérieure de la France depuis le retour de l'île d'Elbe jusqu'à la nouvelle de Waterloo* (Paris, 1923), p. 79, argues.

19. 'Pignot: Napoléon à Autun', in *De l'exil au retour de l'île d'Elbe*, pp. 116, 118.

20. R. S. Alexander, *Bonapartism and Revolutionary Tradition in France: The fédérés of 1815* (Cambridge, 1991), p. 2.

21. Bluche, *Le Bonapartisme*, pp. 99–121; Waresquiel, *Les Cents Jours*, pp. 65–6, 87.

22. See Duprat, 'Une guerre des images', 490–9.

23. Cyril Triolaire, 'Célébrer Napoléon après la République: les héritages commémoratifs révolutionnaire au crible de la fête napoléonienne', *Annales historiques de la Révolution française*, 346 (2006), 75–96, here 90.

24. Michele Vovelle, 'La Marseillaise: War or Peace', in Pierre Nora (ed.), *Realms of Memory: Rethinking the French Past*, trans. Lawrence D. Kritzman and Arthur Goldhammer, 3 vols (New York, 1996–8), iii. pp. 44–6.

25. Caulaincourt, *Memoirs*, ii. p. 250.

26. Le Gallo, *Les Cent-Jours*, pp. 44–5; Godlewski, *Napoléon à l'île d'Elbe*, pp. 42–4; Sudhir Hazareesingh, *The Legend of Napoleon* (London, 2004), p. 22.

27. Ephraïm Harpaz, *L'école libérale sous la Restauration: le 'Mercure' et la 'Minerve', 1817–1820* (Geneva, 1968), p. 231.

28. Le Gallo, *Les Cent-Jours*, pp. 26–9.

29. See, for example, Chuquet (ed.), *Lettres de 1815*, pp. 400–4. On this point see Waresquiel, *Les Cents Jours*, pp. 214–19.

30. See, for example, AN F7 3733 (25 March 1815), in which General Antoine Rigau attempted to rally the troops at Chalon-sur-Saône. Witness the accounts in Gaston Stiegler (ed.), *Le maréchal Oudinot, duc de Reggio: d'après les souvenirs inédits de la maréchale* (Paris, 1894), pp. 360–1; Macdonald, *Souvenirs*, p. 337.

31. Pierre Lévêque, 'La "revolution de 1815": le movement populaire pendant les Cent-Jours', in Léo Hamon (ed.), *Les Cent-Jours dans l'Yonne: aux origines d'un bonapartisme libéral* (Paris, 1988), pp. 53–4.

32. Sorel, *L'Europe et la Révolution française*, viii. p. 403.

33. Weil, *Les dessous du Congrès de Vienne*, ii. p. 57 (16 January 1815).

34. Weil, *Les dessous du Congrès de Vienne*, ii. p. 127 (3 February 1815).

35. Zamoyski, *Rites of Peace*, pp. 440–1.

36. Pallain (ed.), *Correspondance inédite du Prince de Talleyrand*, pp. 314–15 (5 March 1815).

37. Stryienski (ed.), *Memoirs of the Countess Potocka*, p. 373; Henry Vallotton, *Metternich* (Paris, 1965), p. 136.

38. Charles Vane (ed.), *Memoirs and Correspondence of Viscount Castlereagh, Second Marquess of Londonderry*, 12 vols (London, 1848–53), x. pp. 264–5; Elise von Bernstorff, *Ein Bild aus der Zeit von 1789 bis 1835*, 2 vols (Berlin, 1899), i. p. 178; Zamoyski, *Rites of Peace*, p. 443.

39. Weil, *Les dessous du Congrès de Vienne*, ii. pp. 297, 316 (8 and 11 March 1815).

40. Méneval, *Mémoires*, iii. p. 412.

41. Weil, *Les dessous du Congrès de Vienne*, ii. p. 312 (9 March 1815).

42. Alexandrine Prévost de La Boutetière de Saint-Mars de Fisson Du Montet, *Souvenirs de la baronne Du Montet, 1785–1866* (Paris, 1914), pp. 137–8.

43. Pasquier, *Mémoires*, iii. p. 177.

44. According to Zamoyski, *Rites of Peace*, p. 444.

45. Semmel, *Napoleon and the British*, p. 164.

46. In secret instructions to Novosiltsev, *Vneshniaia Politika Rossii*, ii. pp. 140, 141 (23 September 1804); Zawadzki, 'Czartoryski and Napoleonic France,' 268–9.

47. Pallain (ed.), *Correspondance inédite du Prince de Talleyrand*, p. 326; Comte d'Angeberg [pseudonym for Léonard Chodzko], *Le Congrès de Vienne et les traités de 1815*, 2 vols (Paris, 1863–4), ii. p. 912; Sydow (ed.), *Wilhelm und Caroline von*

*Humboldt in ihren Briefen*, iv. p. 494 (14 March 1815); Kraehe, *Metternich's German Policy*, ii. pp. 330–1.

48. Rochechouart, *Souvenirs*, p. 293.
49. Louise Cochelet, *Mémoires sur la reine Hortense et la famille imperial*, 4 vols (Paris, 1836–8), ii. p. 347; Edouard Bonnal, *Les royalistes contre l'armée (1815–1820) d'après les archives du ministère de la guerre*, 2 vols (Paris, 1906), i. pp. 47–65.
50. Semmel, *Napoleon and the British*, pp. 164–5.
51. Müffling, *Memoirs*, pp. 272–3 (27 June 1815).
52. Weil, *Les dessous du Congrès de Vienne*, ii. pp. 297–8, 316 (8, 11 March 1815).
53. Firmin-Didot, *Royauté ou empire*, pp. 82, 93 (31 July, 9 August 1814); Méneval, *Mémoires*, iii. p. 415; Weil, *Les dessous du Congrès de Vienne*, ii. p. 354 (18 March 1815). For this and most of the following on rumours see Welvert, *Napoléon et la police*, pp. 72, 100–1, 153–4 (19 and 31 July, 23 August 1814); François Ploux, *De bouche à l'oreille: naissance et propagation des rumeurs dans la France du XIXe siècle* (Paris, 2003), pp. 130–3; Baylac, *Napoléon*, pp. 199–201.
54. Houssaye, *1815*, i. pp. 43–60; Ploux, *De bouche à l'oreille*, p. 130.
55. Paul Leuilliot, *La Première Restauration et les Cent Jours en Alsace* (Paris, 1958), pp. 117–18.
56. Welvert, *Napoléon et la police*, p. 11 (16 June 1814).
57. Ploux, *De bouche à l'oreille*, p. 131.
58. Cited in Armand Dayot, *Napoléon raconté par l'image, d'après les sculpteurs, les graveurs et les peintres* (Paris, 1902), p. 121, from police reports dated 16 July and 6 September 1814.
59. Welvert, *Napoléon et la police*, p. 101.
60. See Welvert, *Napoléon et la police*, pp. 53, 58–9, 70, 74, 107, 153–4 (11, 14, 19 and 20 July, 2 and 23 August 1814). Also Jean Vidalenc, *Le département de l'Eure sous la monarchie constitutionnelle, 1814–1848* (Paris, 1952), p. 48; Bernard Ménager, *Les Napoléon du peuple* (Paris, 1988), pp. 20–1; Ploux, *De bouche à l'oreille*, p. 141.
61. According to Houssaye, *1815*, i. pp. 47–54.
62. Firmin-Didot, *Royauté ou empire*, p. 60 (11 July 1814).
63. Firmin-Didot, *Royauté ou empire*, p. 185 (20 December 1814).
64. Houssaye, *1815*, i. p. 49.
65. Firmin-Didot, *Royauté ou empire*, pp. 177, 199–200 (7 December 1814, 7 January 1815).
66. On this question see Pierre Karila-Cohen, *L'état des esprits: l'invention de l'enquête politique en France, 1814–1848* (Rennes, 2008), pp. 151–3.
67. According to Coote, *Napoleon and the Hundred Days*, p. 129. See also Paul Britten Austin, *1815: The Return of Napoleon* (London, 2002), pp. 93–4.
68. 'De Gombert: Napoléon à Sisteron', in *De l'exil au retour de l'île d'Elbe*, pp. 71–85.
69. Fantin des Odoards, *Journal*, pp. 422–3.
70. Forgues (ed.), *Mémoires de Vitrolles*, ii. pp. 283–6.
71. *Moniteur universel*, 7 March 1815.
72. *Moniteur universel*, 7, 8, 9, 10, 11, 13, 14, 15, 16, 17 18, 19 March 1814. The *Moniteur* underplayed Napoleon's progress through France, exaggerating the support for the monarchy, never suggesting Napoleon was about to arrive in Paris.
73. Firmin-Didot, *Royauté ou empire*, p. 273 (5 and 6 March 1815); Waresquiel, *Les Cents Jours*, pp. 35, 184.
74. Staël, *Considérations*, iii. p. 128; Peter Fritzsche, 'How Nostalgia Narrates Modernity', in Alon Confino and Peter Fritzsche (eds), *The Work of Memory: New Directions in the Study of German Society and Culture* (Urbana, 2002), p. 70.
75. Abrantès, *Mémoires*, xviii. p. 306.
76. Lavalette, *Mémoires*, p. 332.
77. Hippolyte Carnot, *Mémoires sur Carnot par son fils*, 2 vols (Paris, 1861–3), ii. pp. 404–5.
78. Broglie, *Souvenirs*, i. pp. 296–7.
79. Duchesse de Maillé, *Souvenirs des deux Restaurations: journal inédit* (Paris, 1984), pp. 29–30.

80. Cited in Coote, *Napoleon and the Hundred Days*, p. 131.

81. Gallatin, *Diary*, pp. 65–6 (19 and 20 March 1815).

82. Jules Michelet, *Ma jeunesse* (Paris, 1884), pp. 133.

83. *Gazette de France*, 22 April 1815; Auguste Jal, *Souvenirs d'un homme de lettres (1795–1873)* (Paris, 1877), p. 255.

84. Waresquiel, *Les Cents Jours*, p. 53.

85. On this episode see Jacques Berriat-Saint-Prix, *Napoléon Ier à Grenoble, histoire du 7 mars 1815* (Grenoble, 1861), pp. 66–79; Chuquet (ed.), *Lettres de 1815*, pp. 89–93, 109–18; MacKenzie, *Escape from Elba*, pp. 245–6.

86. Peyrusse, *Mémorial*, pp. 286–7. There is a detailed account of this episode in General Randon, 'Retour de l'Île d'Elbe', *Revue de l'Empire*, v (1847), 329–41.

87. This gesture was also recorded in letters of the day. See, for example, Sophie et Anthelme Troussier, *La Chevauchée héroïque du retour de l'île d'Elbe* (Lausanne, 1964), p. 143; Austin, *1815*, pp. 142–8.

88. Bernstorff, *Ein Bild aus der Zeit*, i. p. 178.

89. Cited in MacKenzie, *Escape from Elba*, p. 248.

90. Raymond Horricks, *Military Politics from Bonaparte to the Bourbons: The Life and Death of Michel Ney, 1769–1815* (New Brunswick, 1995), pp. 188–99; Frédéric Hulot, *Le maréchal Ney* (Paris, 2000), pp. 193–207. Ney was later tried and executed. On his trial and rehabilitation see Michel Désiré Pierre, *Ney, du procès politique à la réhabilitation du 'Brave des braves': 1815–1991* (Paris, 2003).

91. Now a popular tourist itinerary, the National 85 corresponds imperfectly with the route taken to reach Paris, but it has been known as the 'Route Napoléon' since 1932. See Chollier, *La vraie Route Napoléon*; René Reymond, *La route Napoléon: de l'Île d'Elbe aux Tuileries* (Lyons, 1985); Régis Bertrand, 'De "l'itinéraire de Buonaparte" à la "Route Napoléon": mémoire écrite et monuments commémoratifs', *Recherches régionales*, 185 (2007), 83–90.

92. Jal, *Souvenirs d'un homme de lettres*, pp. 253–4; Rémusat, *Mémoires de ma vie*, i. p. 191.

93. Jean-Marie Roulin, 'Le Retour des Cendres de Napoléon: une cérémonie palimpseste', in Corinne and Eric Perrin-Saminadayar (eds), *Imaginaire et représentations des entrées royales au XIXe siècle: une sémiologie du pouvoir politique* (Saint-Etienne, 2006), p. 83.

94. Waresquiel, *Les Cents Jours*, p. 90.

95. Léon G. Palissier, 'Les Cent-Jours. Passage de l'Empereur à Grenoble (mars 1815). Journal du colonel de gendarmerie Jubé', *Nouvelle Revue rétrospective*, 3 (July–December 1895), 73–100.

96. Marchand, *Mémoires*, pp. 182.

97. Agricol Perdiguier, *Mémoires d'un compagnon* (Paris, 2002), p. 76.

98. Waresquiel, *Les Cents Jours*, pp. 90–1.

99. J.-B. Robineau-Desvoidy, *Le 17 mars 1815* (Auxerre, 1829). On the republicanism of many of Napoleon's supporters see Georges Weil, 'L'idée républicaine en France pendant la Restauration', *Revue d'histoire moderne*, 2 (1927), 321–48.

100. Alan Schom, *One Hundred Days: Napoleon's Road to Waterloo* (New York, 1992), p. 50. She had no intention of doing so, however. On 18 March, she wrote to her father reaffirming her commitment to stay under his protection. Fournier, *Marie-Louise et la chute de Napoléon*, pp. 23–4. A little later, once in Paris, Napoleon would write to Francis asking Marie-Louise to be allowed to travel to Strasbourg (*Corr.* xxviii. n. 21753 (1 April 1815)).

101. Lavalette, *Mémoires*, p. 344.

102. Michel Fleury (ed.), *Souvenirs inédits de M. le comte Chabrol de Volvic* (Paris, 2002), pp. 23–4.

103. Léon-Michel Routier, *Récits d'un soldat: de la République et de l'Empire* (Paris, 2004), p. 176; Gallatin, *Diary*, p. 66 (20 March 1815); Lavalette, *Mémoires*, p. 345; Planat de la Faye, *Vie de Planat de la Faye*, pp. 199–200; Thiébault, *Mémoires*, v. p. 295; baron Hennet de Goutel, 'Les derniers jours de l'Empire racontés par un Cent-Suisse, d'après le journal inédit de M. de Marsilly (1811–1816)', *Revue des études napoléoniennes*, 13 (1918), 278–9 (20 March 1815).

104. Thiébault, *Mémoires*, v. p. 295.

105. Alexandre-Louis-Joseph, comte de La Borde, *Quarante-huit heures de garde au château des Tuileries pendant les journées des 19 et 20 mars 1815, par un grenadier de la Garde Nationale* (Paris, 1816), p. 20; Fontaine, *Journal*, i. pp. 447–8 (20 March 1815).

106. Eynard, *Journal*, ii. pp. 264–5 (8 August 1815).

107. Lavalette, *Mémoires*, pp. 343–5.

108. Thiébault, *Mémoires*, v. p. 295.

109. Some examples can be found in Chuquet (ed.), *Lettres de 1815*, pp. 319–27.

110. (Lieutenant) Anciaume, 'Lettres d'un vélite', *La curiosité historique et militaire*, 25 (1895), 30.

111. Cited in Bodinier, 'Officiers et soldats de l'armée impériale', in *Napoléon de l'histoire à la légende*, p. 220.

112. Etienne-Maurice Deschamps, *Souvenirs militaires, persécutions sous la Restauration, songe, etc.* (Pontarlier, 1835), p. 139.

113. Frédéric-Charles-Louis-François de Paule, commandant de Lauthonnye, 'Ma vie militaire (1789–1860)', *Carnet de la Sabretache*, 10 (1911), 295.

114. Robinaux, *Journal de route*, p. 203.

115. Alexandre de Puymaigre, *Souvenirs sur l'émigration, l'Empire et la Restauration* (Paris, 1884), pp. 198–9.

116. Waresquiel, *Les Cents Jours*, p. 70.

117. Hippolyte d'Espinchal, *Souvenirs militaires, 1792–1814*, 2 vols (Paris, 1901), ii. pp. 337–8.

118. Poumiès de la Siboutie, *Souvenirs*, pp. 157–8; 'Waterloo – Lettre d'un officier genevois du 45e', *Carnet de la Sabretache*, 3 (1895), 495–6.

119. See, for example, John Cam Hobhouse, *The Substance of Some Letters Written by an Englishman Resident at Paris During the Last Reign of the Emperor Napoleon*, 2 vols (London, 1816), i. pp. 178–9; Helen Maria Williams, *A Narrative of the Events which Have Taken Place in France From the Landing of Napoleon Bonaparte on the First of March, 1815, Till the Restoration of Louis XVIII* (Cleveland, 1815), pp. 63–4.

120. Barante, *Souvenirs*, ii. p. 123.

121. Madelin, *Fouché*, ii. pp. 369–79; Jean-Paul Bertaud, *L'abdication: 21–23 juin 1815* (Paris, 2011), pp. 42–3.

122. See, for example, the letters from the municipality of Elbeuf, in Normandy, to Napoleon and Louis XVIII in Jeffry Kaplow, *Elbeuf during the Revolutionary Period: History and Social Structure* (Baltimore, 1964), pp. 254–5.

123. AN AFIV 1935, Séance de la commission du gouvernement: finances, police, intérieur, rapport du commissaire Résigny à l'Empereur, 6 May 1815, cited in Pascal Cyr, 'L'opposition des fonctionnaires pendant les cent-jours', *Napoleonica. La Revue*, 3 (2008), 9.

124. Brian Fitzpatrick, 'The *Royaume du Midi* of 1815', in David Laven and Lucy Riall (eds), *Napoleon's Legacy: Problems of Government in Restoration Europe* (Oxford, 2000), pp. 172–3.

125. Williams, *A Narrative of the Events which Have Taken Place in France*, p. 69; Marquise de Montcalm, *Mon journal, 1815–1818* (Paris, 1935), p. 42 (21 May 1815); Mansel, *Paris between Empires*, p. 79.

126. Le Gallo, *Les Cent-Jours*, pp. 329–78, here p. 363.

127. This was the case for the Somme (Bertaud, *L'abdication*, p. 95).

128. Molé, *Le Comte Molé*, i. pp. 203–18; Jacques-Alain de Sédouy, *Le comte Molé ou La séduction du pouvoir* (Paris, 1994), pp. 105–8.

129. Pasquier, *Mémoires*, iii. pp. 168–9; Frédéric Guillaume de Vaudoncourt, *Quinze années d'un proscrit* (Paris, 1835), ii. pp. 47–8.

130. On 6 April 1815, sixty of the eighty-seven prefects were dismissed. On this see Jean Vidalenc, 'Note sur les épurations de 1814 et de 1815', in *Les Epurations administratives: XIXe et XXe siècles* (Geneva, 1977), pp. 63–8; Jean Tulard, 'Les épurations en 1814 et 1815', *Revue du Souvenir napoléonien*, 396 (1994), 5–21; Jacques-Olivier Boudon, 'Le corps

préfectoral entre dux pouvoirs (1814–1815)', in Maurice Vaisse (ed.), *Les préfets, leur rôle, leur action dans le domaine de la défense de 1800 à nos jours* (Brussels, 2001), pp. 17–19; Cyr, 'L'opposition des fonctionnaires pendant les cent-jours'.

131. Ralph Kingston, *Bureaucrats and Bourgeois Society: Office Politics and Individual Credit in France, 1789–1848* (Basingstoke, 2012), pp. 69–71.

132. Waresquiel, *Les Cents Jours*, p. 416.

133. A selection of regional studies includes: Leuilliot, *La Première Restauration*, esp. pp. 179–269; Charles Alleaume, *Les Cent Jours dans le Var* (Draguignan, 1938). More needs to be done.

134. For Lyons see Georges Ribe, *L'opinion publique et la vie politique à Lyon lors des premières années de la seconde Restauration* (Paris, 1957), pp. 37–44.

135. Houssaye, *1815*, i. pp. 630–1.

136. See Alexander, *Bonapartism and Revolutionary Tradition in France*, esp. pp. 21–46.

137. Historians have suggested that most of the *fédérés* marched not out of loyalty to Napoleon but out of hatred for the Bourbons. See Le Gallo, *Les Cent-Jours*, p. 290; Bluche, *Le Bonapartisme*, p. 102; Lentz, *Nouvelle histoire du Premier Empire*, iv. p. 426.

138. Kare D. Tønneson, 'Les Fédérés de Paris pendant les Cent Jours', *Annales historiques de la Révolution française*, 249 (1982), 393–415; Bertaud, *L'abdication*, pp. 142–4.

139. For Marseilles see Granville, *Private Correspondence*, ii. p. 526 (16 March 1814).

140. On the regional unrest caused by Napoleon's return see Houssaye, *1815*, i. pp. 509–18; Roger Grand, *La Chouannerie de 1815* (Paris, 1942); Petiteau, *Les Français et l'Empire*, pp. 242–5.

141. Francis Démier, *La France de la Restauration: 1814–1830: l'impossible retour du passé* (Paris, 2012), p. 106.

## 26: A Parody of Empire

1. The literature on the Restoration is considerable. Among more recent works relevant to an understanding of the problems facing the regime are: Robert Alexander, *Re-Writing the French Revolutionary Tradition* (Cambridge, 2003), esp. pp. 1–29; Munro Price, *The Perilous Crown: France between Revolutions* (London, 2008), pp. 50–88; Démier, *La France de la Restauration*, pp. 86–152.

2. Constant, *Mémoires sur les Cent-Jours*, pp. 11–12, and his justification, pp. 205–6; Benjamin Constant, 'De l'esprit de conquête', in *Oeuvres: Benjamin Constant* (Paris, 1979), pp. 1031–2; *Journal des Débats*, 19 March 1815, in Ephraïm Harpaz (ed.), *Recueil d'articles, 1795–1817* (Geneva, 1978), pp. 149–51. See also Stéphane Rials, 'La question constitutionelle en 1814–1815: dispersion des légitimités et convergence des techniques', *Révolution et contre-révolution au XIXe siècle* (Paris, 1987), pp. 133–5; Dennis Michael Wood, *Benjamin Constant: A Biography* (London and New York, 1993), pp. 205–9, 213.

3. Wood, *Benjamin Constant*, pp. 214–15; Hazareesingh, *The Legend of Napoleon*, pp. 160–4, for this and the following.

4. Gourgaud, *Journal de Sainte-Hélène*, ii. pp. 241–2.

5. On the press see Alexander, *Bonapartism and Revolutionary Tradition in France*, pp. 7–8.

6. Pasquier, *Mémoires*, iii. pp. 218–19; Hortense, *Mémoires*, ii. p. 354; Poumiès de la Siboutie, *Souvenirs*, p. 158.

7. Constant, *Mémoires sur les Cent-Jours*, p. 241.

8. Frédéric Bluche, *Le plébiscite des Cent-Jours: avril–mai 1815* (Geneva, 1974), p. 9.

9. See, for example, Marie-Victorine Perrier, *Adresse de Marie-Victorine aux Français* (Paris, 1815), pp. 1–7.

10. Examples include: J.-F. Mayeux, *A l'Empereur, sur l'impossibilité de concilier l'Acte additionnel aux Constitutions, avec la majesté, l'indépendance et le bonheur du peuple* (Paris, 1815); *Motif du vote négatif d'Adolphe de Montaigu … sur l'Acte additionnel aux*

*Constitutions de l'Empire, en date du 22 avril 1815* (Paris, n.d.). There were, of course, pamphleteers who defended Napoleon and the Constitution: Louis Dubroca, *Un vieux républicain à Napoléon, sur la puissance de l'opinion publique dans le gouvernement des Etats* (Paris, 1815). See also Le Gallo, *Les Cent-Jours*, pp. 229–40; Frédéric Bluche, 'Les pamphlets royalistes des Cent Jours', *Revue de l'Institut Napoleon*, 131 (1975), 148; Bertaud, *L'abdication*, pp. 75–7.

11. Léon Radiguet, *L'acte additionnel aux Constitutions de l'Empire du 22 avril 1815* (Caen, 1911), pp. 90–1.

12. On this and for what follows see Malcolm Crook, '"Ma volonté est celle du peuple": Voting in the Plebiscite and Parliamentary Elections during Napoléon's Hundred Days, April–May 1815', *French Historical Studies*, 32 (2009), 628–31. Also Bluche, *Le plébiscite des Cent-Jours*, pp. 36–51; Petiteau, *Les Français et l'Empire*, pp. 246–7.

13. Bluche, *Le plébiscite des Cent-Jours*, p. 38; Crook, '"Ma volonté est celle du people"', 628.

14. Melvin Richter, 'Toward a Concept of Political Illegitimacy: Bonapartist Dictatorship and Democratic Legitimacy', *Political Theory*, 10 (1982), 190.

15. Gregor Dallas, *The Final Act: The Roads to Waterloo* (New York, 1997), pp. 320–1. Cf. Bluche, *Le plébiscite des Cent-Jours*, pp. 125–6; Englund, *Napoleon*, pp. 434–5; Warsquiel, *Les Cent Jours*, pp. 435–6; Alexander, *Bonapartism and Revolutionary Tradition in France*, pp. 6–7.

16. Bertaud, *L'abdication*, pp. 82–5.

17. Monnier, *Le Faubourg Saint-Antoine*, p. 289; Petiteau, *Les Français et l'Empire*, p. 247.

18. Bluche, *Le plébiscite des Cent-Jours*, pp. 123–4.

19. According to Houssaye, *1815*, i. p. 524.

20. On Lanjuinais see Woloch, *Napoleon and his Collaborators*, pp. 220, 230; Collins, *Napoleon and his Parliaments*, p. 169; Bertaud, *L'abdication*, pp. 36–8.

21. Le Gallo, *Les Cent-Jours*, p. 475.

22. Carnot, *Mémoires sur Carnot par son fils*, ii. p. 423.

23. Carnot, *Mémoires sur Carnot par son fils*, ii. p. 453.

24. Thiébault, *Mémoires*, v. pp. 320–1; Derrécagaix, *Le maréchal Berthier*, ii. pp. 597–606; Frédéric Hulot, *Le maréchal Berthier* (Paris, 2007), pp. 284–6; Jérôme Zieseniss, *Berthier: frère d'armes de Napoléon* (Paris, 1985), pp. 283–4.

25. Fontaine, *Journal*, i. p. 460 (21 June 1815).

26. Marchand, *Mémoires*, p. 201.

27. Jean Favier, *Charlemagne* (Paris, 1999), pp. 293–300; Morrissey, 'Charlemagne et la légende impériale', p. 343.

28. Coignet, *Note-Books*, pp. 272–3; Louis Girard, *La Garde nationale* (Paris, 1964), pp. 42–57; Dupuy, *La Garde nationale*, pp. 341–4.

29. Pétiet, *Souvenirs militaires*, pp. 182–3; Noël, *With Napoleon's Guns*, pp. 215–16.

30. Houssaye, *1815*, i. pp. 594–606.

31. Hobhouse, *The Substance of Some Letters*, i. p. 198. See also Marie-Joseph Gilbert du Motier, marquis de Lafayette, *Mémoires, correspondance et manuscrits du général La Fayette*, 6 vols (Paris, 1837–8), v. pp. 404–5.

32. Hobhouse, *The Substance of Some Letters*, i. pp. 401, 408–25.

33. Michelet, *Ma jeunesse*, p. 134.

34. Pierre-Alexandre-Edouard Fleury de Chaboulon, *Les cent jours, mémoires pour servir à l'histoire de la vie privée, du retour et du règne de Napoléon en 1815*, 2 vols (London, 1820), ii. pp. 96–9.

35. Lavalette, *Mémoires*, p. 348; Hortense, *Mémoires*, iii. p. 11.

36. Crook, '"Ma volonté est celle du people"', 619.

37. *Corr.* xxviii. nos. 21692, 21700, 21701, 2172, 21703 (21 and 23 March 1815).

38. Hantraye, *Les cosaques aux Champs-Elysées*, p. 47.

39. Lentz, *Nouvelle histoire du Premier Empire*, iv. pp. 435–6.

40. Black, *Waterloo*, p. 71.

41. Le Gallo, *Les Cent-Jours*, pp. 329–78; Bertaud, *L'abdication*, pp. 67–9, 71–3.

42. Walter Haweis James, *The Campaign of 1815, Chiefly in Flanders* (Edinburgh, 1908), pp. 10–30.
43. Alessandro Barbero, *The Battle: A New History of Waterloo*, trans. John Cullen (New York, 2005), p. 28.
44. Englund, *Napoleon*, p. 440.
45. Camille Lévi (ed.), *Mémoires du capitaine Duthilt* (Lille, 1909), p. 308.
46. Muir, *Britain and the Defeat of Napoleon*, pp. 352–5.
47. Müffling, *Memoirs*, pp. 208–11; Kraehe, *Metternich's German Policy*, ii. p. 354; Lawrence J. Flockerzie, 'Saxony, Austria, and the German Question after the Congress of Vienna, 1815–1816', *International History Review*, 12:4 (1990), 667–8.
48. Extract of a letter from a German officer in *The Battle of Waterloo: Containing the Accounts Published by Authority, British and Foreign, and Other Relative Documents* (London, 1815), p. lxxi (16 July 1815).
49. Charles Oman, 'The French Losses in the Waterloo Campaign', *English Historical Review*, 19 (1904), 681–93. Slightly different figures are given in Houssaye, *1815*, ii. pp. 184, 213.
50. Chandler, *Campaigns of Napoleon*, p. 1066; Black, *Waterloo*, p. 28. Another 17,000 allied troops under Prince Frederick of Orange were stationed in a defensive position south of the village of Hal, fourteen kilometres to the west. Inexplicably, they were not used during the battle.
51. Victor Hugo, *Les misérables*, trans. Charles E. Wilbour (New York, 1992), p. 271.
52. Bertaud, *Guerre et société en France*, p. 74.
53. For the campaign and the battle itself see Parker, *Three Napoleonic Battles*, pp. 102–209; Chandler, *Campaigns of Napoleon*, pp. 1008–93; Andrew Roberts, *Waterloo: Napoleon's Last Gamble* (London, 2005); Barbero, *The Battle*; Black, *Waterloo*; Pascal Cyr, *Waterloo: origines et enjeux* (Paris, 2011).
54. Lieven, 'Russia and the Defeat of Napoleon', 289.
55. Barbero, *The Battle*, p. 13.
56. The theme of Peter Hofschröer's *1815: The Waterloo Campaign: The German Victory, from Waterloo to the Fall of Napoleon* (London, 1999).
57. Roberts, *Waterloo*, pp. 55–6.
58. Lagneau, *Journal*, pp. 301–3.
59. Black, *Waterloo*, p. 136.
60. Las Cases, *Mémorial*, ii. pp. 244–58.
61. Carnot, *Mémoires sur Carnot par son fils*, ii. p. 503.
62. Arthur Wellesley, Duke of Wellington, *The Dispatches of Field Marshal the Duke of Wellington during his Various Campaigns in India, Denmark, Portugal, Spain, the Low Countries and France, from 1799 to 1818*, 13 vols (London, 1837–9), xii. p. 529 (2 July 1815).
63. Figures quoted in Gates, *The Napoleonic Wars*, p. 221.
64. Attributed to Cambronne but probably pronounced by a simple soldier (*Moniteur universel*, 29 June 1815).
65. Jean-Marc Largeaud, 'Waterloo dans la culture française (1815–1914)', *Revista Napoleonica*, 1–2 (2000), 120.
66. Toussaint-Jean Trefcon, *Carnet de campagne du colonel Trefcon, 1793–1815* (Paris, 1914), p. 193.
67. Jean-Baptiste Lemonnier-Delafosse, *Souvenirs militaires du capitaine Jean-Baptiste Lemonnier-Delafosse* (Paris, 2002), p. 229; Joseph Tyrbas de Chamberet, *Mémoires d'un médecin militaire: aux XVIIIe et XIXe siècles* (Paris, 2001), pp. 167, 168; Silvain Larreguy de Civrieux, *Souvenirs d'un cadet (1812–1823)* (Paris, 1912), pp. 172–3; Fantin des Odoards, *Journal*, p. 439.
68. An officer in Picton's division.
69. See Black, *Waterloo*, pp. 159–66.
70. Hantraye, *Les cosaques aux Champs-Elysées*, p. 23.
71. Barbero, *The Battle*, pp. 309–10.

72. Montcalm, *Mon journal*, pp. 82–3 (4 July 1815).
73. Although when John Quincy Adams, in London at the time, read the dispatch he was convinced that Wellington had been annihilated. Wellington's dispatches were notoriously understated (Philip Henry, fifth Earl of Stanhope, *Notes of Conversations with the Duke of Wellington, 1831–1851* (London, n.d.), p. 145).
74. Scott published a poem, *The Field of Waterloo*, in October of the same year.
75. Many returned home to publish their impressions in travelogues. See the list of travel accounts published in Jules Deschamps, 'En Belgique avec les anglais après Waterloo', *Revue des études napoléoniennes*, 31 (1930), 225–6.
76. Stuart Semmel, 'Reading the Tangible Past: British Tourism, Collecting, and Memory after Waterloo', *Representations*, 69 (Winter 2000), 9–37, here 26.
77. Cited in Samuel Hynes, *The Soldier's Tale: Bearing Witness to Modern War* (New York, 1997), p. 17.
78. *Corr.* xxviii. n. 22062 (21 June 1815).
79. Lecestre (ed.), *Lettres inédites*, ii. pp. 357–8.
80. Jean-Marc Largeaud, 'Les temps retrouvés de Waterloo', *Revue d'histoire du XIXe siècle*, 25 (2002), 145; Jean-Marc Largeaud, *Napoléon et Waterloo: la défaite glorieuse de 1815 à nos jours* (Paris, 2006), pp. 32–3.
81. *Moniteur universel*, 21 June 1815.
82. Claude Etienne Guyot, *Carnets de campagnes (1792–1815)* (Paris, 1999), p. 367.
83. Bertaud, *L'abdication*, pp. 56–7.
84. According to Villemain, *Souvenirs contemporains*, ii. p. 262.
85. Carnot, *Mémoires sur Carnot par son fils*, ii. pp. 510–11.
86. Houssaye, *1815*, iii. p. 15; John G. Gallaher, 'Marshal Davout and the Second Bourbon Restoration', *French Historical Studies*, 6:3 (1970), 351.
87. Fleury de Chaboulon, *Mémoires*, ii. pp. 211–14.
88. *Corr.* xxviii. n. 22061 (20 June 1815).
89. Lafayette, *Mémoires*, v. pp. 455, 459–62; Paul Chanson, *Lafayette et Napoléon* (Lyons, 1958), pp. 281–338; Harlow Giles Unger, *Lafayette* (Hoboken, NJ, 2002), p. 345.
90. *Moniteur universel*, 22 June 1815; Thibaudeau, *Mémoires*, p. 510.
91. *Moniteur universel*, 22 June 1815; Bertaud, *L'abdication*, pp. 126–8.
92. Bertaud, *L'abdication*, p. 144.
93. Lucien Bonaparte, *La vérité sur les Cent-Jours* (Paris, 1835), pp. 56–61.
94. Cited in Gilbert Martineau, *Napoleon Surrenders*, trans. Frances Partridge (London, 1971), p. 22.
95. *Esquisse historique sur les Cent Jours* (Paris, 1819), pp. 39–40.
96. Bertaud, *L'abdication*, pp. 136–8.
97. On the political machinations of the Chamber during these days and hours see Martineau, *Napoleon Surrenders*, pp. 17–30; Bertaud, *L'abdication*, esp. here pp. 145–51.
98. Norman MacKenzie, *Fallen Eagle: How the Royal Navy Captured Napoleon* (London, 2009), p. 52.
99. *Esquisse historique sur les Cent-Jours*, p. 44.
100. Houssaye, *1815*, iii. p. 46.
101. Bertaud, *L'abdication*, pp. 155–7.
102. Bertaud, *L'abdication*, pp. 163–6.
103. Montholon, *Récits*, i. pp. 2–25.
104. Martineau, *Napoleon Surrenders*, p. 31.
105. Bertaud, *L'abdication*, pp. 166–9.
106. Martineau, *Napoleon Surrenders*, p. 31.
107. See Bertaud, *L'abdication*, pp. 198–208, 233–43, 259–79, 283–92.
108. Wellington to Bathurst (2 July 1815), in Wellington, *The Dispatches*, xii. p. 535.
109. *Corr.* xxviii. n. 22063 (22 June 1815).
110. For an interesting reflection on abdication in an earlier period see Jacques Le Brun, *Le pouvoir d'abdiquer: essai sur la déchéance volontaire* (Paris, 2009), pp. 7–13, 247–67.
111. Constant, *Mémoires sur les Cent-Jours*, pp. 285–91.

## Epilogue

1. Hortense, *Memoirs*, ii. pp. 186–7.
2. *Corr.* xxviii. n. 22065 (25 June 1815).
3. Albine de Montholon, *Souvenirs de Sainte-Hélène par la comtesse de Montholon, 1815–1816* (Paris, 1901), p. 19.
4. Hortense, *Memoirs*, ii. p. 187.
5. Hortense, *Memoirs*, ii. p. 191.
6. *Corr.* xxviii. n. 22064 (25 June 1815).
7. Muffling, *Memoirs*, p. 274 (29 June 1815).
8. Frances Mossiker, *Napoleon and Josephine: The Biography of a Marriage* (New York, 1964), p. 402.
9. Marchand, *Mémoires*, pp. 246–7.
10. Henri Gatien Bertrand, *Lettres à Fanny: 1808–1815*, annotated by Suzanne de La Vaissière-Orfila (Paris, 1979), p. 451.
11. MacKenzie, *Fallen Eagle*, p. 126; David Cordingly, *The Billy Ruffian: The Bellerophon and the Downfall of Napoleon: The Biography of a Ship of the Line, 1782–1836* (London, 2004), p. 1.
12. Frederick Lewis Maitland, *Narrative of the surrender of Buonaparte and of his residence on H.M.S. Bellerophon* (London, 1826), pp. 12–16; Cordingly, *The Billy Ruffian*, pp. 3, 232–3.
13. Paul Ganière, *Napoléon à Sainte-Hélène* (Paris, 1998), p. 11.
14. Montholon, *Récits*, i. pp. 70–1.
15. MacKenzie, *Fallen Eagle*, pp. 100, 104.
16. MacKenzie, *Fallen Eagle*, p. 105.
17. According to the *Relation de la mission du Lieutenant-général comte Becker auprès de l'empereur Napoléon depuis la seconde abdication jusqu'au passage à bord du Béllérophon* (Clermont-Ferrand, 1841); Houssaye, *1815*, iii. pp. 364, 367–8.
18. Jonathan Miles, *The Wreck of the Medusa: The Most Famous Sea Disaster of the Nineteenth Century* (New York, 2007); Alexander McKee, *Wreck of the Medusa: Mutiny, Murder, and Survival on the High Seas* (New York, 2007).
19. For the following, Ganière, *Napoléon à Sainte-Hélène*, pp. 20–1. A French Captain Besson, commanding the Danish sloop *Magdaline*, also offered his services at Rochefort, but was similarly rebuffed.
20. François-Antoine Lallemand, 'Embarquement de l'Empereur à Rochefort. Notes du général baron Charles Lallemand', *Nouvelle Revue rétrospective*, 11 (July–December 1899), 1–14.
21. Michael John Thornton, *Napoleon after Waterloo: England and the St. Helena Decision* (Stanford, Calif., 1968), p. 15.
22. One of those minor controversies that appear to have raged as soon as Maitland's book appeared. It was refuted by Félix Barthe, *Refutation de la relation du Capitaine Maitland, touchant l'embarquement de Napoléon à son bord* (Paris, 1827).
23. Maitland, *Narrative of the surrender*, p. 35.
24. Thornton, *Napoleon after Waterloo*, pp. 21–2.
25. See his letter to Bertrand in Maitland, *Narrative of the surrender*, pp. 30–2.
26. Ganière, *Napoléon à Sainte-Hélène*, pp. 31–5.
27. MacKenzie, *Fallen Eagle*, pp. 143–4.
28. Themistocles was an Athenian statesman and general who, in 464 BC, after being tried on a charge of treason and condemned to death, sought asylum from the Persian king, Artaxerxes I.
29. John Wilson Croker, *The Croker Papers: The Correspondence and Diaries of the Late Right Honourable John Wilson Croker*, ed. L. J. Jennings, 3 vols (London, 1884), i. p. 68.
30. These details from Cordingly, *The Billy Ruffian*, pp. 248–9.
31. George Home, *Memoirs of an Aristocrat and Reminiscences of the Emperor Napoleon, by a Midshipman of the 'Bellerophon'* (London, 1838), pp. 233–5.

# Bibliography

Aaslestad, Katherine. *Place and Politics: Local Identity, Civic Culture, and German Nationalism in North Germany during the Revolutionary Era*. Leiden: Brill, 2005.

Aaslestad, Katherine, 'Republican Traditions: Patriotism, Gender, and War in Hamburg, 1770–1815', *European History Quarterly*, 37 (2007): 582–602.

Aaslestad, Katherine, 'Revisiting the Continental System: Exploitation to Self-Destruction in the Napoleonic Empire', in Dwyer and Forrest (eds), *Napoleon and his Empire*, pp. 114–32.

Abrantès, Laure Junot, duchesse de. *Mémoires de Madame la duchesse d'Abrantès, ou Souvenirs historiques sur Napoléon: la Révolution, le Directoire, le Consulat, l'Empire et la Restauration*, 18 vols. Paris: Ladvocat, 1831–5.

Acomb, Frances. *Anglophobia in France, 1763–1789: An Essay in the History of Constitutionalism and Nationalism*. Durham, NC: Duke University Press, 1950.

*Acte d'accusation de Georges, Pichegru, Moreau, et autres prévenus de conspiration contre la personne du premier consul et contre la sûreté intérieure et extérieure de la république*. Paris: C.-F. Patris, an XII.

Adami, Friedrich. *Schicksalswende: Preuß en 1812/13: nach Aufzeichnungen von Augenzeugen*. Berlin: Falken, 1924.

Adamovsky, Ezequiel. *Euro-Orientalism: Liberal Ideology and the Image of Russia in France (c. 1740–1880)*. Oxford and New York: Peter Lang, 2006.

Adams, Charles Francis (ed.). *Memoirs of John Quincy Adams*, 12 vols. New York: AMS Press, 1970.

Adams, Michael. *Napoleon and Russia*. London and New York: Hambledon Continuum, 2006.

*Adieux à Buonaparte*. N.p., 1814.

Adkins, Roy. *Trafalgar: The Biography of a Battle*. London: Little, Brown, 2004.

Adkins, Roy and Lesley. *War for All the Oceans: From Nelson at the Nile to Napoleon at Waterloo*. London: Little, Brown, 2006.

*Adresse aux français sur le Quatorze juillet*. N.p., n.d.

Agay, Frédéric d', 'Un témoignage raphaëlois sur l'embarquement de Napoléon pour l'île d'Elbe en 1814', *Annales du Sud-Est Varois*, 13 (1988): 19–20.

Alexander, R. S. *Bonapartism and Revolutionary Tradition in France: The fédérés of 1815*. Cambridge: Cambridge University Press, 1991.

Alexander, R. S. *Napoleon*. London: Arnold, 2001.

Alexander, R. S. *Re-Writing the French Revolutionary Tradition*. Cambridge: Cambridge University Press, 2003.

Alexandre, Arsène. *Histoire de la peinture militaire en France*. Paris: H. Laurens, 1889.

Alexandre, Philippe, 'Le "Hallisches Wochenblatt", un journal de la Franconie wurtembergeoise (1788–1803)', in Pierre Grappin and Jean Moes (eds), *Sçavantes délices: périodiques souabes au siècle des Lumières* (Paris: Didier-Erudition, 1989), pp. 193–216.

Alger, John Goldworth. *Napoleon's British Visitors and Captives 1801–1815*. Edinburgh: Constable, 1904.

Alleaume, Charles. *Les Cent Jours dans le Var*. Draguignan: Société d'études scientifiques et archéologiques, 1938.

Alméras, Henri d'. *La vie parisienne sous le Consulat et l'Empire*. Paris: Albin Michel, 1909.

Alombert, Paul-Claude, 'Le colonel Constant Corbineau', *Carnet de la Sabretache*, 3 (1895): 289–307.

Alombert, Paul-Claude and Colin, Jean. *La campagne de 1805 en Allemagne*. 4 vols. Paris: Chapelot, 1902–8.

Ambrière, Madeleine and Francis. *Talma ou L'histoire au théâtre*. Paris: Fallois, 2007.

Amini, Iradj. *Napoleon and Persia: Franco-Persian Relations under the First Empire*. Trans. Azizeh Azodi. Richmond: Curzon, 1999.

Anderson, Robin. *Pope Pius VII, 1800–1823: His Life, Reign and Struggle with Napoleon in the Aftermath of the French Revolution*. Rockford, Ill.: Tan Books, 2001.

Andrey, Georges, 'L'Acte de médiation du 19 février 1803 porte-il bien son nom?', in Czouz-Tornare (ed.), *Quand Napoléon Bonaparte recréa la Suisse*, pp. 15–39.

Angeberg, Comte de [pseudonym for Léonard Chodzko]. *Le Congrès de Vienne et les traités de 1815*. 2 vols. Paris: Lahure, 1863–4.

Angeli, Moritz von. *Erzherzog Carl als Feldherr und Heeresorganisator*. 5 vols. Vienna: W. Braumüller, 1896–8.

Anonymous [Bertie Greatheed]. *A Tour in France, 1802*. London: J. Barfield, 1808.

Arago, François. *Histoire de ma jeunesse*. Brussels and Leipzig: Kiessling, Schnée, 1854.

Arbelles, Claude-François André d'. *Tableau historique de la politique de la cour de Rome, depuis l'origine de sa puissance temporelle jusqu'à nos jours*. Paris: A. Galland, 1810.

*Archives parlementaires; recueil complet des débats législatifs et politiques des chambres françaises de 1800 à 1860*. 2e série. 127 vols. Paris: Librairie administrative de Paul Dupont, 1862–1913.

*Arlequin, au Muséum, ou critique en Vaudeville des Tableaux du Salon*. Paris: Delaunay, 1808.

Armenteros, Carolina and Lebrun, Richard A. (eds). *The New enfant du siècle: Joseph de Maistre as a Writer*. St Andrews: Centre for French History and Culture at the University of St Andrews, 2010. hdl.handle.net/10023/847.

Arndt, Ernst Moritz. *Gedichte*. 2 vols. Frankfurt am Rhein: Eichenberg, 1818.

Arnold, James R. *Napoleon Conquers Austria: The 1809 Campaign for Vienna*. Westport, Conn.: Praeger, 1995.

Arnold, James R., 'A Reappraisal of Column versus Line in the Peninsular War', *Journal of Military History*, 68 (2004): 535–52.

Arnold, James R. *Marengo and Hohenlinden: Napoleon's Rise to Power*. Barnsley: Pen & Sword, 2005.

Artaud de Montor, Alexis-François. *Histoire de la vie et des travaux politiques du comte d'Hauterive, comprenant une grande partie des actes de la diplomatie française, depuis 1784, jusqu'en 1830*. 2nd edn. Paris: A. Le Clère, 1839.

Ashby, Ralph. *Napoleon against Great Odds: The Emperor and the Defenders of France, 1814*. Santa Barbara, Calif.: Praeger, 2010.

Askenazy, Simon. *Napoléon et la Pologne*. Trans. from the Polish by Henri Grégoire. Brussels and Paris: Editions du 'Flambeau', 1925.

Aspinall, Arthur. *Politics and the Press, c.1780–1850*. London: Home & Van Thal, 1949.

Asseré, Jean-Pierre Noël, 'Journal du voltigeur Asseré', *Carnet de la Sabretache*, 14 (1905): 705–31.

Aston, Nigel (ed.). *Religious Change in Europe, 1650–1914: Essays for John McManners*. Oxford: Clarendon Press, 1997.

Aston, Nigel. *Christianity and Revolutionary Europe, 1750–1830*. Cambridge: Cambridge University Press, 2002.

*L'Attaque de Paris par les troupes alliées, le 18 mars 1814*. Paris: J. B. Tardieu, 1814.

Atteridge, A. Hilliard. *Napoleon's Brothers*. London: Methuen, 1909.

Atteridge, A. Hilliard. *Joachim Murat, Marshal of France and King of Naples*. New York: Brentano's, 1911.

Auckland, William, Lord. *The Journal and Correspondence of William, Lord Auckland*. 4 vols. London: R. Bentley, 1861–2.

[Audibert], 'L'accueil des Alpes-Maritimes à la paix de Tilsit', *Revue de l'Institut Napoléon*, 101 (1966): 191–2.

Aulard, Alphonse. *Registre des délibérations du consulat provisoire, 20 brumaire–3 nivôse an VIII (11 novembre–24 décembre 1799)*. 2 vols. Paris: Au siège de la société, 1894.

Aulard, François-Alphonse. *L'état de la France en l'an VIII et en l'an IX*. Paris: Au siège de la société, 1897.

Aulard, François-Alphonse. *Etudes et leçons sur la Révolution française*, 2e série. Paris: Félix Alcan, 1898.

Aulard, François-Alphonse, 'L'établissement du Consulat à vie', in *Etudes et leçons sur la Révolution française*, pp. 253–83.

Aulard, François-Alphonse, 'Le lendemain du dix-huit brumaire', in *Etudes et leçons sur la Révolution française*, pp. 213–52.

Aulard, François-Alphonse. *Paris sous le Consulat: recueil de documents pour l'histoire de l'esprit public à Paris*. 4 vols. Paris: Cerf, Noblet, Quantin, 1903–9.

Aulard, François-Alphonse. *Paris sous le Premier Empire: recueil de documents pour l'histoire de l'esprit public à Paris*. 3 vols. Paris: Cerf, Noblet, Quantin, 1912–23.

'Austerlitz (Lettres de deux témoins de la bataille)', *Carnet de la Sabretache*, 4 (1905): 732–4.

Austin, Paul Britten. *1812: The March on Moscow*. London: Greenhill Books, 1993.

Austin, Paul Britten. *1815: The Return of Napoleon*. London: Greenhill Books, 2002.

*L'avènement de Napoléon à l'empire; stances lyriques par J. B*. Paris: Imp. de Brosselard, 1804.

Avrillon, Marie-Jeanne. *Mémoires de Mlle Avrillon sur la vie privée de Joséphine, sa famille et sa cour*. 2 vols. Paris: Ladvocat, 1833.

Aymes, Jean-René, 'Napoléon et Joseph Bonaparte sous le regards des Espagnols', *Clefs pour l'Histoire. Culture & Nation*, 1 (1998): 26–32.

Aymes, Jean-René, 'Du catéchisme religieux au catéchisme politique (fin du XVIIIe siècle–début du XIXe)', in *Voir, comparer, comprendre: regards sur l'Espagne des XVIIIe et XIXe siècles* (Paris: Presses Sorbonne Nouvelle, 2003), pp. 179–200.

Aymes, Jean-René, 'La guerre d'Espagne dans la presse impériale (1808–1814)', *Annales historiques de la Révolution française*, 336 (2004): 129–45.

Azimi, Vida. *Les premiers sénateurs français: Consulat et Premier Empire, 1800–1814*. Paris: Picard, 2000.

Bade, Stéphanie de (ed.), 'Souvenirs de Stéphanie de Beauharnais', *Revue des Deux Mondes*, 102 (1932): 61–104.

Baehr, Peter R. *Caesar and the Fading of the Roman World: A Study in Republicanism and Caesarism*. New Brunswick: Transaction Publishers, 1998.

Baehr, Peter and Richter, Melvin (eds). *Dictatorship in History and Theory: Bonapartism, Caesarism, and Totalitarianism*. Cambridge: Cambridge University Press, 2004.

Bailleu, Paul (ed.). *Preußen und Frankreich von 1795 bis 1807: diplomatische Correspondenzen*. 2 vols. Leipzig: Hirzel, 1880–7.

Bailleu, Paul, 'Königin Luise in Tilsit', *Hohenzollern-Jahrbuch. Forschungen und Abbildungen zur Geschichte der Hohenzollern in Brandenburg-Preussen*, 3 (1899): 221–40.

Bailleu, Paul (ed.). *Briefwechsel König Friedrich Wilhelm III. und der Königin Luise mit Kaiser Alexander I*. Leipzig: Hirzel, 1900.

Bailleu, Paul, 'Die Verhandlungen in Tilsit (1807): Briefwechsel König Friedrich Wilhelm's III. und der Königin Luise', *Deutsche Rundschau*, 110 (1902): 29–45, 199–221.

Bailleul, Jean-Antoine-Guillaume. *Histoire des triomphes militaires, des fêtes guerrières et des honneurs accordés aux braves chez les peuples anciens et modernes; particulièrement aux armées françaises, jusqu'au 1er janvier 1808*. Paris: A. Bailleul, 1808.

Bairoch, Paul, 'Une nouvelle distribution des populations: villes et campagnes', in Jean-Pierre Bardet et Jacques Dupâquier (eds), *Histoire des populations de l'Europe*, 3 vols (Paris: Fayard, 1997), pp. 195–229.

Bajou, Valérie, 'Painting and Politics under the Empire: David's *Distribution of the Eagles*', in Ledbury (ed.), *David after David*, pp. 55–71.

Baker, Keith Michael. *Inventing the French Revolution*. Cambridge: Cambridge University Press, 1990.

Baldet, Marcel. *La vie quotidienne dans les armées de Napoléon*. Paris: Hachette, 1965.

Ballard, John R. *Continuity during the Storm: Boissy d'Anglas and the Era of the French Revolution*. Westport, Conn.: Greenwood Press, 2000.

Bangofsky, Georges, 'Les étapes de Georges Bangofsky, officier lorrain. Extraits de son journal de campagnes (1797–1815)', *Mémoires de l'Académie de Stanislas*, ii (1905): 241–340.

Barante, Prosper Brugière, baron de. *Souvenirs du baron de Barante, 1782–1866.* 6 vols. Paris: Calmann-Lévy, 1890–7.

Barbero, Alessandro. *The Battle: A New History of Waterloo.* Trans. John Cullen. New York: Walker, 2005.

Barbet du Bertrand, V.-R. *Les trois hommes illustres, ou Dissertations sur les institutions politiques de César-Auguste, de Charlemagne et de Napoléon Bonaparte.* Paris: Michelet, 1803.

Barère de Vieuzac, Bertrand. *Les Anglais au XIXe siècle.* Paris: P. Mongie, Delaunay, 1804.

Barjaud, Jean-Baptiste-Benoît. *La conquête de Moscou.* Paris: Brasseur, 1812.

Barker, Hannah and Burrows, Simon (eds). *Press, Politics and the Public Sphere in Europe and North America, 1760–1820.* Cambridge: Cambridge University Press, 2002.

Barrès, Jean Baptiste Auguste. *Souvenirs d'un officier de la Grande Armée.* Paris: Plon-Nourrit, 1923.

Bartenev, Petr Ivanovich (ed.). *Arkhiv kniazia Vorontsova.* 40 vols. Moscow: A. I. Mamontova, 1870–95.

Barthe, Félix. *Refutation de la relation du Capitaine Maitland, touchant l'embarquement de Napoleon à son bord.* Paris: A. Dupont, 1827.

Barton, Dunbar Plunket. *Bernadotte and Napoleon, 1763–1810.* London: J. Murray, 1921.

Bastid, Paul. *Sieyès et sa pensée.* Paris: Hachette, 1970.

Bastien-Rabner, Françoise and Coppolani, Jean-Yves (eds). *Napoléon et le Code civil.* Ajaccio: Alain Piazzola, 2009.

*Bataille de Preussisch-Eylau, gagnée par la grande armée, commandée en personne par S.M. Napoléon Ier.* Paris: n.p., 1807.

Battesti, Michèle. *Trafalgar: les aléas de la stratégie navale de Napoléon.* Saint-Cloud: Napoléon 1er éd., 2004.

*The Battle of Waterloo: Containing the Accounts Published by Authority British and Foreign and Other Relative Documents.* London: J. Bother, T. Gerton, 1815.

Baudus, Marie-Elie-Guillaume de. *Etudes sur Napoléon, par le lieutenant-colonel de Baudus.* 2 vols. Paris: Debrécourt, 1841.

Bausset, Louis-François-Joseph, baron de. *Mémoires anecdotiques sur l'intérieur du palais de Napoléon, sur celui de Marie-Louise et sur quelques événemens de l'Empire, depuis 1805 jusqu'en 1816.* 4 vols. Paris: A. Levasseur, 1829.

Baxter, Douglas Clark, 'First Encounters: Bourbon Princes Meet their Brides: Ceremony, Gender and Monarchy', *Proceedings of the Annual Meeting of the Western Society for French History*, 22 (1995): 23–31.

Bayern, Adalbert Prinz von. *Max I. Joseph von Bayern, Pfalzgraf, Kurfürst und König.* Munich: F. Bruckmann, 1957.

Baylac, Marie-Hélène. *Napoléon. Empereur de l'île d'Elbe.* Paris: Tallandier, 2011.

Beachy, Robert. *The Soul of Commerce: Credit, Property, and Politics in Leipzig, 1750–1840.* Leiden: Brill, 2005.

Beauchamp, Alphonse de. *Histoire des campagnes de 1814 et de 1815, comprenant l'histoire politique et militaire des deux invasions de la France.* 4 vols. Paris: Le Normant, 1816–17.

Beauharnais, Eugène de. *Mémoires et correspondance politique et militaire du prince Eugène.* 10 vols. Paris: Michel Lévy frères, 1858–60.

Beauharnais, Hortense de. *Mémoires de la Reine Hortense, publiés par le prince Napoléon.* 3 vols. Paris: Plon, 1927.

Beauharnais, Hortense de. *The Memoirs of Queen Hortense.* Trans. Arthur K. Griggs and F. Mabel Robinson. 2 vols. London: Thornton Butterworth, 1928.

Béchet de Léocour, Louis. *Souvenirs: écrits en 1838–1839.* Paris: Teissèdre, 2000.

Becquet, Hélène and Frederking, Bettina (eds). *La dignité de roi: regards sur la royauté au premier XIXe siècle.* Paris: Presses Universitaires de Rennes, 2009.

Beer, Adolf, 'Österreich und Russland in den Jahren 1804 und 1805', *Archiv fur Österreichische Geschichte*, 53 (1875): 125–243.

Beer, Adolf. *Zehn Jahre österreichischer Politik, 1801–1810.* Leipzig: F. A. Brockhaus, 1877.

Bégis, Alfred. *Curiosités historiques. Invasion de 1814. Destruction des drapeaux étrangers et de l'épée de Frédéric de Prusse à l'Hôtel des Invalides, d'après des documents inédits.* Paris: Imp. pour les Amis des Livres, 1897.

Behaine, Lefebvre de. *La campagne de France.* 4 vols. Paris: Perrin, 1913–35.

Behrens, C. B. A. *Society, Government and the Enlightenment: The Experiences of Eighteenth-Century France and Prussia.* London: Thames & Hudson, 1985.

Belissa, Marc. *Repenser l'ordre européen (1795–1802): de la société des rois aux droits des nations.* Paris: Kimé, 2006.

Belissa, Marc. *La Russie mise en Lumières: représentations et débats autour de la Russie dans la France du XVIIIe siècle.* Paris: Kimé, 2010.

Bell, David A. *The Cult of the Nation in France: Inventing Nationalism, 1680–1800.* Cambridge, Mass.: Harvard University Press, 2001.

Bell, David A., 'Jumonville's Death. War Propaganda and National Identity in Eighteenth-Century France', in Colin Jones and Dror Wahrman (eds), *The Age of Cultural Revolutions: Britain and France, 1750–1820* (Berkeley: University of California Press, 2002), pp. 33–61.

Bell, David A. *The First Total War: Napoleon's Europe and the Birth of Warfare as We Know It.* Boston, Mass. and New York: Houghton Mifflin, 2007.

Bellot de Kergorre, Alexandre. *Journal d'un commissaire des guerres pendant le Premier Empire (1806–1821).* Paris: La Vouivre, 1997.

Bellune, Victor-François Perrin, duc de, 'Mémoires inédits de feu M. le maréchal duc de Bellune. Campagne de l'Armée de Réserve, en l'an VIII', *Spectateur militaire*, xli (1846): 121–204.

Ben-Amos, Avner. *Funerals, Politics and Memory in Modern France, 1789–1996.* Oxford: Oxford University Press, 2000.

Ben-Israel, Hedva. *English Historians on the French Revolution.* Cambridge: Cambridge University Press, 1968.

Benaerts, Louis. *Les Commissaires extraordinaires de Napoléon 1er en 1814: d'après leur correspondance inédite.* Paris: F. Rieder, 1915.

Benl, Rudolf (ed.). *Der Erfurter Fürstenkongreß 1808: Hintergründe, Ablauf, Wirkung.* Erfurt: Stadtarchiv Erfurt, 2008.

Benoît, Jérémie, 'La peinture allégorique sous le Consulat: structure et politique', *Gazette des Beaux Arts*, 121 (1993): 77–92.

Benoît, Jérémie. *Philippe-Auguste Hennequin, 1762–1833.* Paris: Arthéna, 1994.

Benoît, Jérémie, 'Napoléon à Berlin vu par les peintres', *La Revue Napoléon*, 28 (2006): 44–8.

Benoît, Jérémie and Chevallier, Bernard (eds). *Marengo: une victoire politique.* Paris: Réunion des musées nationaux, 2000.

Bénot, Yves and Dorigny, Marcel (eds). *1802, rétablissement de l'esclavage dans les colonies françaises: aux origines d'Haïti: ruptures et continuités de la politique coloniale française, 1800–1830.* Paris: Maisonneuve et Larose, 2003.

Béranger, Pierre-Jean de. *Ma biographie.* Paris: Perrotin, 1858.

Bercé, Yves, 'Rome, 1796–1814', in Bruno Foucart (ed.), *Camille de Tournon: le préfet de la Rome napoléonienne: 1809–1814* (Boulogne-Billancourt: Bibliothèque Marmottan, 2001), pp. 25–32.

Bercé, Yves-Marie (ed.). *La fin de l'Europe napoléonienne, 1814: la vacance du pouvoir.* Paris: Kronos, 1990.

Berchet, Jean-Claude, 'Le *Mercure de France* et la "Renaissance" des lettres', in Bonnet (ed.), *L'empire des muses*, pp. 21–58.

Berdah, Jean-François, 'The Triumph of Neutrality: Bernadotte and European Geopolitics (1810–1844)', *Nordic Historical Review/Revue d'Histoire Nordique*, 6–7 (2008): 31–94.

Bergeret, Pierre-Nolasque. *Lettres d'un artiste sur l'état des arts en France.* Paris: the author, 1848.

Bergès, Louis. *Résister à la conscription, 1798–1814: le cas des départements aquitains.* Paris: CTHS, 2002.

Bergès, Louis, 'Perception et mise en scène des manifestations d'opposition au pouvoir de la fin
    du Premier Empire à la Seconde Restauration: analyse du cas girondin', in Bernard Barbiche,
    Jean-Pierre Poussou and Alain Tallon (eds), *Pouvoirs, contestations et comportements dans
    l'Europe moderne: mélanges en l'honneur du professeur Yves-Marie Bercé* (Paris: Presses de
    l'Université Paris-Sorbonne, 2005), pp. 787–801.
Berlier, Théophile. *Précis de la vie politique de Théophile Berlier*. Dijon: A. Douillier, 1838.
Berlioz, Elisabeth (ed.). *La situation des départements et l'installation des premiers préfets en
    l'an VIII (23 septembre 1799–22 septembre 1800)*. Paris: Documentation française, 2000.
Bernard, Léonce. *Les prisonniers de guerre du Premier Empire*. Paris: Christian, 2000.
Bernard, M. *Le Turc et le militaire français*. N.p., n.d.
Bernardy, Françoise de. *Eugène de Beauharnais: 1781–1824*. Paris: Perrin, 1973.
Bernède, Allain, 'Autopsie d'une bataille: Marengo, 14 juin 1800', *Revue historique des armées*,
    181 (1990): 33–47.
Bernhardi, Theodor von. *Denkwürdigkeiten aus dem Leben des kaiserl. russ. Generals von der
    Infanterie Carl Friedrich Grafen von Toll*. 5 vols. Leipzig: O. Wigand, 1865–6.
Bernstorff, Elise von. *Ein Bild aus der Zeit von 1789 bis 1835*. 2 vols. Berlin: Ernst Siegfried,
    1899.
Berriat-Saint-Prix, Jacques. *Napoléon Ier à Grenoble, histoire du 7 mars 1815*. Grenoble:
    Maisonville et fils et Jourdan, 1861.
Bertaud, Jean-Paul. *Bonaparte et le duc d'Enghien, le duel des deux France*. Paris: R. Laffont,
    1972.
Bertaud, Jean-Paul, 'Napoleon's Officers', *Past & Present*, 112 (1986): 91–111.
Bertaud, Jean-Paul. *The Army of the French Revolution: From Citizen-Soldiers to Instrument of
    Power*. Trans. R. R. Palmer. Princeton: Princeton University Press, 1988.
Bertaud, Jean-Paul. *Guerre et société en France: de Louis XIV à Napoléon Ier*. Paris: Armand
    Colin, 1998.
Bertaud, Jean-Paul. *Le duc d'Enghien*. Paris: Fayard, 2001.
Bertaud, Jean-Paul. *Quand les enfants parlaient de gloire: l'armée au coeur de la France de
    Napoléon*. Paris: Aubier, 2006.
Bertaud, Jean-Paul. *Les royalistes et Napoléon, 1799–1816*. Paris: Flammarion, 2009.
Bertaud, Jean-Paul. *L'abdication: 21–23 juin 1815*. Paris: Flammarion, 2011.
Bertaud, Jean-Paul, Forrest, Alan and Jourdan, Annie. *Napoléon, le monde et les Anglais: guerre
    des mots et des images*. Paris: Editions Autrement, 2004.
Berthaut, H. M. A. *Les ingénieurs géographes militaires, 1624–1831: étude historique*. Paris:
    Imprimerie du Service géographique, 1902.
Berthezène, Pierre. *Souvenirs militaires de la République et de l'Empire*. 2 vols. Paris: J.
    Dumaine, 1855.
Berthier, Alexandre. *Relation de la bataille de Marengo*. Paris: Impr. impériale, 1805, reprinted
    1998.
Berthier, Patrick, 'La paix d'Amiens dans la littérature', in Nadine-Josette Chaline (ed.), *La Paix
    d'Amiens* (Amiens: Enrage, 2005), pp. 213–30.
Bertho, Jean-Pierre, 'Naissance et élaboration d'une théologie de la guerre chez les évêques de
    Napoléon (1802–1820)', in Jean-René Derré, Jacques Gadille, Xavier de Montclos and
    Bernard Plongeron (eds), *Civilisation chrétienne: approche historique d'une idéologie,
    XVIIIe–XXe siècle* (Paris: Beauchesne, 1975), pp. 89–104.
Bertier, Ferdinand de. *Souvenirs inédits d'un conspirateur: Révolution, Empire et première
    Restauration*. Paris: Tallandier, 1990.
Bertier de Sauvigny, Guillaume de. *Metternich*. Paris: Fayard, 1986.
Bertrand, Henri Gatien. *Cahiers de Sainte-Hélène*. Ed. Paul Fleuriot de Langle. 3 vols. Paris:
    Albin Michel, 1949–59.
Bertrand, Henri Gatien. *Lettres à Fanny: 1808–1815*. Annotated by Suzanne de La Vaissière-
    Orfila. Paris: Albin Michel, 1979.
Bertrand, Pierre (ed.). *Lettres inédites de Talleyrand à Napoléon, 1800–1809*. Paris: Perrin,
    1889.

Bertrand, Régis, 'De "l'itinéraire de Buonaparte" à la "Route Napoléon": mémoire écrite et monuments commémoratifs', *Recherches régionales*, 185 (2007): 83–90.

Besnard, François-Yves. *Souvenirs d'un nonagénaire*. 2 vols. Paris: H. Champion, 1880.

Bessis, Henriette, 'Ingres et le portrait de l'Empereur', *Archives de l'art français*, 24 (1969): 89–90.

Beßlich, Barbara. *Der deutsche Napoleon-Mythos: Literatur und Erinnerung 1800–1945*. Darmstadt: Wissenschaftliche Buchgesellschaft, 2007.

Beugnot, Jacques-Claude. *Mémoires du comte Beugnot, ancien ministre (1783–1815)*. 2 vols. Paris: Dentu, 1866.

Bew, John. *Castlereagh: Enlightenment, War and Tyranny*. London: Quercus, 2011.

Biard, Michel. *Parlez-vous sans-culotte?: dictionnaire du 'Père Duchesne', 1790–1794*. Paris: Tallandier, 2009.

Biard, Michel, Crépin, Annie and Gainot, Bernard (eds). *La plume et le sabre: volume d'hommages offerts à Jean-Paul Bertaud*. Paris: Publications de la Sorbonne, 2002.

Biaudet, Jean Charles and Nicod, Françoise (eds). *Correspondance de Frédéric-César de La Harpe et Alexandre Ier*. 3 vols. Neuchatel: A la Baconnière, 1978–80.

Bibl, Victor. *François II: le beau-père de Napoléon, 1768–1835*. Trans. from the German by Adrien F. Vochelle. Paris: Payot, 1936.

Bielecki, Robert, 'L'effort militaire polonais (1806–1815)', *Revue de l'Institut Napoléon*, 132 (1976): 147–64.

Bigarré, Auguste. *Mémoires du Général Bigarré, 1775–1813*. Paris: Editions du Grenadier, 2002.

Billon, François-Frédéric. *Souvenirs, 1804–1815*. Paris: La Boutique de l'Histoire, 2006.

Bindel, Victor. *Un rêve de Napoléon: le Vatican à Paris (1809–1814)*. Paris: Alsatia, 1943.

Biskup, Thomas, 'Das Schwert Friedrichs des Großen: universalhistorische "Größe" und monarchische Genealogie in der napoleonischen Symbolpolitik nach *Iéna*', in Klinger, Hahn and Schmidt (eds), *Das Jahr 1806*, pp. 185–203.

Biskup, Thomas, 'Napoleon's Second Sacre? Iéna and the Ceremonial Translation of Frederick the Great's Insignia in 1807', in Forrest and Wilson (eds), *The Bee and the Eagle*, pp. 172–90.

Bittard des Portes, René, 'Les préliminaires de l'entrevue d'Erfurt (1808)', *Revue d'histoire diplomatique*, 4 (1890): 94–144.

Biver, Marie-Louise. *Le Paris de Napoléon*. Paris: Plon, 1963.

Biver, Marie-Louise, 'Rome, second capitale de l'Empire', *Revue de l'Institut Napoléon*, 109 (1968): 145–54.

Björnstjerna, Comte de (ed.). *Mémoires posthumes du Feld-Maréchal comte de Stedingk*, 3 vols. Paris: Arthus-Bertrand, 1844–7.

Black, Jeremy. *The Battle of Waterloo*. New York: Random House, 2010.

Blagdon, Francis William. *Paris As It Was and As It Is, or a Sketch of the French Capital illustrative of the Effects of the Revolution*. 2 vols. London: C. A. Baldwin, 1803.

Blanc, Honoré. *Le Guide des dîneurs, ou Statistique des principaux restaurants de Paris*. Paris: Chez les Marchands de Nouveautés, 1814.

Blanning, T. C. W. *The Culture of Power and the Power of Culture: Old Regime Europe, 1660–1789*. Oxford: Oxford University Press, 2002.

Blanning, T. C. W., 'The Bonapartes and Germany', in Baehr and Richter (eds), *Dictatorship in History and Theory*, pp.53–66.

Blanning, T. C. W. *The Pursuit of Glory: Europe 1648–1815*. London: Allen Lane, 2007.

Blanning, Tim. *The Romantic Revolution: A History*. New York: Modern Library, 2011.

Blaufarb, Rafe, 'The *Ancien Régime* Origins of Napoleonic Social Reconstruction', *French History*, 14:4 (2000): 408–23.

Blaufarb, Rafe. *The French Army, 1750–1820: Careers, Talent, Merit*. Manchester: Manchester University Press, 2002.

Bled, Jean-Paul, 'Le renversement des alliances', in Lentz (ed.), *1810: le tournant de l'Empire*, pp. 15–21.

Blessing, Werner K., 'Umbruchkrise und "Verstörung": die "Napoleonische" Erschütterung und ihre sozialpsychologische Bedeutung (Bayern als Beispiel)', *Zeitschrift für bayerische Landesgeschichte*, 42 (1979): 75–106.

Bloch, Marc. *Les Rois Thaumaturges: étude sur le caractère surnaturel attribué à la puissance royale particulièrement en France et en Angleterre.* Paris: Gallimard, 1983.

Blocqueville, Adélaïde-Louise d'Eckmühl, marquise de. *Le maréchal Davout, prince d'Eckmühl, raconté par les siens et par lui-même.* 4 vols. Paris: Didier, 1879–80.

Bluche, Frédéric. *Le plébiscite des Cent-Jours: avril–mai 1815.* Geneva: Droz, 1974.

Bluche, Frédéric, 'Les pamphlets royalistes des Cent-Jours', *Revue de l'Institut Napoleon*, 131 (1975): 145–56.

Bluche, Frédéric. *Le Bonapartisme: aux origines de la droite autoritaire (1800–1850).* Paris: Nouvelles Editions Latines, 1980.

Bodinier, Gilbert, 'Officiers et soldats de l'armée impériale face à Napoléon', in *Napoléon, de l'histoire à la légende*, pp. 211–32.

Bodinier, Gilbert, 'Que veut l'armée? Soutien et résistance à Bonaparte', in *Terminer la Révolution?*, pp. 65–87.

Boigne, Eléonore-Adèle d'Osmond, comtesse de. *Récits d'une tante: mémoires de la Ctesse de Boigne.* 4 vols. Paris: Plon-Nourrit, 1907–8.

Boime, Albert. *Art in an Age of Bonapartism, 1800–1815.* 2 vols. Chicago: University of Chicago Press, 1990.

Bois, Jean-Pierre. *Histoire des 14 Juillet, 1789–1919.* Rennes: Ouest-France, 1991.

Bois, Jean-Pierre. *Bugeaud.* Paris: Fayard, 1997.

Bois, Jean-Pierre. *De la paix des rois à l'ordre des empereurs, 1714–1815.* Paris: Seuil, 2003.

Bonaparte, Louis. *Documents historiques et réflexions sur le gouvernement de la Hollande.* 3 vols. Brussels: H. Rémy, 1820.

Bonaparte, Lucien. *Ministère de l'Intérieur. Courses dans le Champ-de-Mars.* Paris: Impr. de la République, messidor an VIII.

Bonaparte, Napoléon. *Correspondance de Napoléon I publiée par ordre de l'empereur Napoléon III.* 32 vols. Paris: Plon, 1858–70.

Bonaparte, Napoléon. *Napoléon Bonaparte. Correspondance Générale* Ed. Thierry Lentz. 12 vols. Paris: Fayard, 2004–.

Bonnal, Edouard. *Les royalistes contre l'armée (1815–1820) d'après les archives du ministère de la guerre.* 2 vols. Paris, R. Chapelot, 1906.

Bonnet, Jean-Claude (ed.). *L'empire des muses: Napoléon, les Arts et les Lettres.* Paris: Belin, 2004.

Bonnet de Treyches, Joseph-Balthazar. *Du gouvernement héréditaire et de l'influence de l'autorité d'un seul sur les arts.* Paris: Ballard, 1804.

Bonneville de Marsangy, Louis. *La Légion d'honneur.* Paris: H. Charles-Lavauzelle, 1982.

Bordes, Philippe, 'La fabrication de l'histoire par Jacques-Louis David', in *Triomphe et mort du héros: la peinture d'histoire en Europe de Rubens à Manet* (London: Nelson Press, 1988), pp. 110–19.

Bordes, Philippe and Pougetoux, Alain, 'Les portraits de *Napoléon en habits impériaux* par Jacques-Louis David', *Gazette des Beaux Arts*, 202 (1983): 21–34.

Bordo, Michael and White, Eugene, 'A Tale of Two Currencies: British and French Finances during the Napoleonic Wars', *Journal of Economic History*, 51 (1991): 303–16.

Borkowsky, Ernst, 'Das Schönbrunner Attentat im Jahr 1809 nach unveröffentlichten Quellen', *Die Grenzboten. Blätter für Deutschland und Belgien*, 57:4 (1898): 293–301.

Boscher, Laurent. *Histoire de la répression des opposants politiques, 1742–1848: la justice des vainqueurs.* Paris: L'Harmattan, 2006.

Botzenhart, Manfred. *Metternichs Pariser Botschafterzeit.* Münster: Aschendorff, 1967.

Boudard, René, 'Le sacre de Napoléon vu par un figurant', *Revue de l'Institut Napoléon*, 50 (1954): 33–4.

Boudon, Jacques-Olivier, 'Grand homme ou demi-dieu? La mise en place d'une religion napoléonienne', *Romantisme*, 100 (1998): 131–41.

Boudon, Jacques-Olivier. *Histoire du Consulat et de l'Empire: 1799–1815*. Paris: Perrin, 2000.

Boudon, Jacques-Olivier, 'Le corps préfectoral entre dux pouvoirs (1814–1815)', in Maurice Vaisse (ed.), *Les préfets, leur rôle, leur action dans le domaine de la défense de 1800 à nos jours* (Brussels: Bruylant, 2001), pp. 13–25.

Boudon, Jacques-Olivier, 'L'incarnation de l'Etat de brumaire à floréal', in Jessenne (ed.), *Du Directoire au Consulat*, iii. pp. 333–45.

Boudon, Jacques-Olivier. *Napoléon et les cultes: les religions en Europe à l'aube du XIXe siècle, 1800–1815*. Paris: Fayard, 2002.

Boudon, Jacques-Olivier, 'Les fondements religieux du pouvoir impérial', in Petiteau (ed.), *Voies nouvelles pour l'histoire du Premier Empire*, pp. 194–212.

Boudon, Jacques-Olivier, 'Les clémences de Napoléon: une arme au service du pouvoir', in *Les clémences de Napoléon*, pp. 13–21.

Boudon, Jacques-Olivier (ed.). *Armée, guerre et société à l'époque napoléonienne*. Paris: SPM, 2004.

Boudon, Jacques-Olivier, 'La Restauration face aux vétérans de l'Empire', in Martine Reid, Jean-Yves Mollier and Jean-Claude Yon (eds), *Repenser la Restauration* (Paris: Nouveau Monde éditions, 2005), pp. 31–43.

Boudon, Jacques-Olivier. *Le roi Jérôme: frère prodigue de Napoléon, 1784–1860*. Paris: Fayard, 2008.

Boudon, Jacques-Olivier (ed.). *Le Concordat et le retour de la paix religieuse*. Paris: SPM, 2008.

Boudon, Jacques-Olivier, 'Napoléon, les catholiques français et le pape', in Lentz (ed.), *1810: le tournant de l'Empire*, pp. 131–48.

Boudon, Jacques-Olivier and Bourdin, Philippe, 'Les héritages républicains sous le Consulat et l'Empire', *Annales historiques de la Révolution française*, 346 (2006): 3–15.

Bouët du Portal, Marie-Christine de, 'A propos de la Saint-Napoléon: la solennité du 15 août sous le Premier et le Second Empire', *Revue de l'Institut Napoléon*, 158–9 (1992): 145–68.

Boulant, Antoine. *Les Tuileries, palais de la Révolution (1789–1799)*. Paris: A. Boulant, 1989.

Boulart, Jean-François. *Mémoires militaires du général Bon Boulart sur les guerres de la république et de l'empire*. Paris: librairie illustrée, 1892.

Boulay de la Meurthe, Alfred. *Les dernières années du duc d'Enghien (1801–1804)*. Paris: Hachette, 1886.

Boulay de la Meurthe, Alfred. *Documents sur la négociation du Concordat et sur les autres rapports de la France avec le Saint-Siège en 1800 et 1801*. 5 vols. Paris: E. Leroux, 1891–7.

Boulay de la Meurthe, Antoine. *Théorie constitutionnelle de Sieyès. Constitution de l'an VIII*. Paris: P. Renouard, 1836.

Boulay de la Meurthe, François-Joseph. *Boulay de la Meurthe*. Paris: Lahure, 1868.

Boulogne, Etienne Antoine de. *Mandemens et instructions pastorales de M. de Boulogne évêque de Troyes. Suivis de divers morceaux oratoires*. Paris: A. Le Clère, 1827.

Bourdin, Philippe, Bernard, Mathias and Caron, Jean-Claude (eds). *La voix et le geste: une approche culturelle de la violence socio-politique*. Clermont-Ferrand: Presses Universitaires Blaise-Pascal, 2005.

Bourdon, Jean, 'Les sénatus-consulte de 1807: l'épuration de la magistrature en 1807–1808 et ses conséquences', *Revue d'histoire moderne et contemporaine*, 17 (July–September 1970): 829–36.

Boureau, Alain. *L'aigle: chronique politique d'un emblème*. Paris: Cerf, 1985.

Bourgeois, René. *Tableau de la campagne de Moscou en 1812*. Paris: J. G. Dentu, 1814.

Bourgogne, Adrien. *Mémoires du sergent Bourgogne*. Paris: Hachette, 1898, reprinted 1992.

Bourgoing, Jean-François. *Nouveau Voyage en Espagne, ou Tableau de l'état actuel de cette monarchie*. 3 vols. Paris: Regnault, 1789.

Bourgoing, Paul-Charles-Amable de. *Souvenirs militaires du Bon de Bourgoing, sénateur, ancien ambassadeur en Espagne, ancien pair de France, ministre plénipotentiaire en Russie et en Allemagne, 1791–1815*. Paris: E. Plon, Nourrit, 1897.

Bourguet-Rouveyre, Josiane, 'La survivance d'un système électorale sous le Consulat et l'Empire', *Annales historique de la Révolution française*, 346 (2006): 17–29.

Bourguignon-Frasseto, Claude. *Betsy Bonaparte ou la Belle de Baltimore*. Paris: J.-C. Lattès, 1988.

Bourrienne, Louis-Antoine Fauvelet de. *Mémoires de M. de Bourrienne, ministre d'Etat: sur Napoléon, le Directoire, le Consulat, l'Empire et la Restauration*. 10 vols. Paris: Ladvocat, 1829.

Bovet. *Notice sur les solennités célébrées à Strasbourg, pour le département du Bas-Rhin, le jour du couronnement de Napoléon Premier, Empereur des Français*. Strasbourg: Levrault, 1804.

Bowman, Hervey Meyer, 'Preliminary Stages of the Peace of Amiens: The Diplomatic Relations of Great Britain and France from the Fall of the Directory to the Death of the Emperor Paul of Russia, November 1799–March 1801', *University of Toronto Studies*, 1 (1899): 75–155.

Bramsen, John. *Letters of a Prussian Traveller*. 2 vols. London: H. Colburn, 1818.

Branda, Pierre. *Le prix de la gloire: Napoléon et l'argent*. Paris: Fayard, 2007.

Branda, Pierre. *Napoléon et ses hommes: la Maison de l'Empereur, 1804–1815*. Paris: Fayard, 2011.

Brandt, Heinrich von. *In the Legions of Napoleon: The Memoirs of a Polish Officer in Spain and Russia, 1808–1813*. London: Greenhill Books, 1999.

Brandt, Peter, 'Einstellungen, Motive und Ziele von Kriegsfreiwilligen 1813/14: das Freikorps Lützow', in Jost Dülffer (ed.), *Kriegsbereitschaft und Friedensordnung in Deutschland 1800–1814* (Münster and Hamburg: Lit, 1994), pp. 211–33.

Bredin, Jean-Denis. *Sieyès: la clé de la Révolution française*. Paris: Fallois, 1988.

Brégeon, Jean-Joël. *Napoléon et la guerre d'Espagne: 1808–1814*. Paris: Perrin, 2006.

Brégeon, Jean-Joël, 'Les appropriations d'oeuvres d'art par les français au Portugal et en Espagne, de 1807 à 1813; les suites muséales et dans les collections', in Pontet, *Napoléon, Bayonne et l'Espagne*, pp. 377–88.

Brett-James, Antony. *1812: Eyewitness Accounts*. London: Macmillan, 1966.

Brifaut, Charles. *Souvenirs d'un académicien sur la Révolution, le premier Empire et la Restauration*. 2 vols. Paris: Albin Michel, 1920–1.

Broers, Michael. *The Politics of Religion in Napoleonic Italy: The War against God, 1801–1814*. London: Routledge, 2002.

Broers, Michael. *Napoleon's Other War: Bandits, Rebels and their Pursuers in the Age of Revolutions*. Oxford: Peter Lang, 2010.

Broglie, Victor de (ed.). *Souvenirs, 1785–1870, du feu duc de Broglie*. 4 vols. Paris: Calmann-Lévy, 1886.

Brookner, Anita. *Jacques-Louis David*. London: Chatto & Windus, 1980.

Brotonne, Léonce de (ed.). *Lettres inédites de Napoléon Ier*. Paris: H. Champion, 1898.

Brown, Howard G., 'Echoes of the Terror', *Historical Reflections/Réflexions historiques*, 29 (2003): 529–58.

Brown, Howard G. *Ending the French Revolution: Violence, Justice, and Repression from the Terror to Napoleon*. Charlottesville: University of Virginia Press, 2006.

Brown, Howard G., 'Napoleon Bonaparte, Political Prodigy', *History Compass*, 5 (2007): 1382–98.

Brown, Howard G., 'Special Tribunals and the Napoleonic Security State', in Dwyer and Forrest (eds), *Napoleon and his Empire*, pp. 79–95.

Browning, Oscar (ed.). *England and Napoleon in 1803, Being the Despatches of Lord Witworth and Others*. London: Longmans, Green, 1887.

Browning, Oscar, 'Hugh Elliot at Naples, 1803–1806', *English Historical Review*, 4 (1889): 209–28.

Brun de Villeret, Pierre-Bertrand-Louis. *Les cahiers du général Brun, baron de Villeret, pair de France: 1773–1845*. Paris: Plon, 1953.

Brunner, Manfred Heinrich. *Antoine-Jean Gros: die Napoleonischen Historienbilder*. Bonn: Rheinische Friedrich-Wilhelms-Universität, 1979.

Brunon, Raoul, 'Uniforms in the Napoleonic Era', in le Bourhis (ed.), *The Age of Napoleon*, pp. 179–201.

Bruyère-Ostells, Walter, 'Les officiers républicains sous l'Empire: entre tradition républicaine, ralliement et tournant libérale', *Annales historiques de la Révolution française*, 346 (2006): 31–44.

Bruyn, Günter de. *Preußens Luise: vom Entstehen und Vergehen einer Legende*. Berlin: Siedler, 2001.

Bryson, Norman, 'Representing the Real: Gros' Paintings of Napoleon', *History of the Human Sciences*, 1 (1988): 74–104.

Buchez, P.-J.-B. and Roux, P.-C. *Histoire parlementaire de la Révolution française, ou Journal des assemblées nationales depuis 1789 jusqu'en 1815*. 40 vols. Paris: Paulin, 1834–8.

Buchinger, Kirstin, '*Chapeau!* Napoleons Hut. Ein europäisches imago agens', in Kirstin Buchinger, Claire Gantet and Jakob Vogel (eds), *Europäische Erinnerungsräume: Zirkulationen zwischen Frankreich, Deutschland und Europa* (Frankfurt: Campus, 2009), pp. 296–321.

Buchinger, Kirstin, '*Chapeau!* – Der Hut als Symbol für Napoleon', in Rüdiger Schmidt and Hans-Ulrich Thamer (eds), *Die Konstruktion von Tradition: Inszenierung und Propaganda napoleonischer Herrschaft (1799–1815)* (Göttingen: Rhema Verlag, 2010), pp. 235–64.

Bülow, Heinrich Dietrich von. *Der Feldzug von 1800; militärisch-politisch betrachtet von dem Verfasser des Geistes des neuern Kriegssystems*. Berlin: H. Frölich, 1801.

Burg, Martijn van der, 'Transforming the Dutch Republic into the Kingdom of Holland: The Netherlands between Republicanism and Monarchy (1795–1815)', *European Review of History/Revue européenne d'histoire*, 17:2 (2010): 151–70.

Burghersh, Priscilla-Ann Wellesley Pole, Lady. *The Letters of Lady Burghersh (afterwards countess of Westmorland) from Germany and France during the Campaign of 1813–14*. London: J. Murray, 1893.

Burke, Peter. *The Fabrication of Louis XIV*. New Haven and London: Yale University Press, 1992.

Burke, Peter. *Eyewitnessing: The Uses of Images as Historical Evidence*. London: Reaktion, 2001.

Burrows, Simon, 'The French Emigré Press, 1789–1814: A Study in Impotence?', in David W. Lovell (ed.), *Revolution, Politics and Society: Elements in the Making of Modern France* (Canberra: Politics Dept, University College, Australian Defence Force Academy, 1994), pp. 31–9.

Burrows, Simon, 'Culture and Misperception: The Law and the Press in the Outbreak of War in 1803', *International History Review*, 18 (1996): 793–818.

Burrows, Simon, 'The Struggle for European Opinion in the Napoleonic Wars: British Francophone Propaganda, 1803–14', *French History*, 11 (1997): 29–53.

Burrows, Simon. *French Exile Journalism and European Politics, 1792–1814*. Woodbridge: Boydell Press, 2000.

Burrows, Simon, 'The Cosmopolitan Press, 1759–1815', in Barker and Burrows (eds), *Press, Politics and the Public Sphere*, pp. 23–47.

Burrows, Simon, 'Britain and the Black Legend: The Genesis of the Anti-Napoleonic Myth', in Philp (ed.), *Resisting Napoleon*, pp. 141–57.

Burrows, Simon, 'The War of Words: French and British Propaganda in the Napoleonic Era', in Cannadine (ed.), *Trafalgar in History*, pp. 44–60.

Burton, June K. *Napoleon and the Woman Question: Discourses of the Other Sex in French Education, Medicine, and Medical Law 1799–1815*. Lubbock, Tex.: Texas Tech University Press, 2007.

Burton, Richard D. E. *Blood in the City: Violence and Revelation in Paris, 1789–1945*. Ithaca: Cornell University Press, 2001.

Bury, J. P. T. and Barry, J. C. (eds). *An Englishman in Paris, 1803: The Journal of Bertie Greatheed*. London: Geoffrey Bles, 1953.

Butterfield, Herbert. *The Peace Tactics of Napoleon, 1806–1808*. Cambridge: Cambridge University Press, 1929.

Cabanis, André. *Le sacre de Napoléon*. Paris: Gallimard, 1970.

Cabanis, André, 'Les courants contre-révolutionnaire sous le Consulat et l'Empire', *Revue des sciences politiques*, 24 (1971): 9–87.

Cabanis, André. *La presse sous le Consulat et l'Empire*. Paris: Société des Etudes Robespierristes, 1975.

Cabanis, Pierre-Jean-Georges. *Quelques Considérations sur l'organisation sociale en général et particulièrement sur la nouvelle constitution, par Cabanis*. Paris: Impr. nationale, frimaire an VIII.

Calvié, Lucien, '"Le début du siècle nouveau": guerre, paix, révolution et Europe dans quelques textes allemands de 1795 à 1801', in Marita Gilli (ed.), *Le cheminement de l'idée européenne dans les idéologies de la paix et de la guerre* (Besançon: Annales Littéraires de l'Université de Franche-Comté, 1991), pp. 129–38.

Cambacérès, Jean-Jacques Régis de. *Lettres inédites à Napoléon: 1802–1814*. Presentation and notes by Jean Tulard. 2 vols. Paris: Klincksieck, 1973.

Cambacérès, Jean-Jacques Régis de. *Mémoires inédits: éclaircissements publiés par Cambacérès sur les principaux événements de sa vie politique*. 2 vols. Paris: Perrin, 1999.

*Campagnes de la grande armée et de l'armée d'Italie en l'an XIV (1805)*. Paris: rue de la Harpe, 1806.

Campbell, Neil. *Napoleon at Fontainebleau and Elba: Being a Journal of Occurrences in 1814–1815*. London: J. Murray, 1869.

Campbell, Peter R., 'Louis XVI, King of the French', in Colin Lucas (ed.), *The French Revolution and the Creation of Modern Political Culture*, vol. ii: *The Political Culture of the French Revolution* (Oxford: Pergamon Press, 1988), pp. 161–82.

Cannadine, David (ed.). *Trafalgar in History: A Battle and its Afterlife*. Basingstoke: Palgrave Macmillan, 2006.

Cantarel-Besson, Yveline, Constans, Claire and Foucart, Bruno (eds). *Napoleon: images et histoire, peintures du château de Versailles, 1789–1815*. Paris: Réunion des musées nationaux, 2001.

Cantarel-Besson, Yveline, 'Les salons de peintures', in Cantarel-Besson, Constans and Foucart (eds), *Napoleon : images et histoire*, pp. 99–109.

Caracciolo, Maria Teresa (ed.). *Lucien Bonaparte: un homme libre, 1775–1840*. Ajaccio: Palais Fesch-Musée des beaux-arts, 2010.

Carbonnier, Jean, 'Le Code Civil', in Nora (ed.), *Les lieux de mémoire*, ii. pp. 293–315.

Carnot, Hippolyte. *Mémoires sur Carnot par son fils*. 2 vols. Paris: Pagnerre, 1861–3.

Carnot, Lazare. *Mémoires historiques et militaires sur Carnot*. Paris: Baudoin, 1824.

Carr, John. *The Stranger in France, or a Tour from Devonshire to Paris*. London: J. Johnson, 1803.

Casaglia, Gherardo. *Le partage du monde: Napoléon et Alexandre à Tilsit, 25 juin 1807*. Paris: SPM, 1998.

Casali, Dimitri and Chanteranne, David. *Napoléon par les peintres*. Paris: Seuil, 2009.

Casanova, Antoine. *Napoléon et la pensée de son temps: une histoire intellectuelle singulière*. Paris: La Boutique de l'Histoire, 2000.

Castellane, Esprit Victor Elisabeth Boniface. *Journal du maréchal Castellane, 1804–1862*. 5 vols. Paris: E. Plon, Nourrit, 1895–7.

Castle, Alison (ed.). *Kubrick's* Napoleon: *The Greatest Movie Never Made*. Paris: Taschen, 2011.

Cate, Curtis. *The War of the Two Emperors: The Duel between Napoleon and Alexander – Russia, 1812*. New York: Random House, 1985.

Caulaincourt, Armand Augustin Louis, marquis de, duc de Vicence. *Memoirs of General de Caulaincourt, Duke of Vicenza*. Ed. Jean Hanoteau. 3 vols. London: Cassell, 1950.

Cazalas, E., 'La mission de Narbonne à Vilna', *Feuilles d'histoire du XVIIe au XXe siècle*, 3 (1910): 216–30.

*Célébration de la fête de Napoléon-Le-Grand*. Besançon: Cl.-Fr. Mourgeon, 1809.

Chaillou, David. *Napoléon et l'Opéra: la politique sur la scène, 1810–1815*. Paris: Fayard, 2004.

Chaillou, David, 'L'annonce du mariage dans les spectacles parisiens', in Lentz, (ed.), *1810: le tournant de l'Empire*, pp. 23–35.

Chaline, Nadine-Josette (ed.). *La Paix d'Amiens*. Amiens: Encrage, 2005.

Chamberlain, Muriel E. *Lord Aberdeen: A Political Biography*. London: Longman, 1983.

Chambon, Pascal. *La Loire et l'Aigle: les Foréziens face à l'Etat napoléonien*. Saint-Etienne: Publications de l'Université de Saint-Etienne, 2005.

Chambray, Georges de. *Histoire de l'expédition de Russie*. 2 vols. Paris: Pillet, 1823.

Champagny, Jean-Baptiste Nompère. *Souvenirs de M. de Champagny, duc de Cadore*. Paris: Paul Renouard, 1846.

Chandler, David. *The Campaigns of Napoleon*. London: Weidenfeld & Nicolson, 1966.

Chandler, David, 'Adjusting the Record: Napoleon and Marengo', *History Today*, 17 (1967): 326–32, 378–85.

Chandler, David, '"To Lie Like a Bulletin": An Examination of Napoleon's Rewriting of the History of the Battle of Marengo', *Proceedings of the Annual Meeting of the Western Society for French History*, 18 (1991): 33–44.

Chanson, Paul. *Lafayette et Napoléon*. Lyons: Les Editions de Lyon, 1958.

Chanteranne, David. *Le sacre de Napoléon*. Paris: Tallandier, 2004.

Chanteranne, David, 'Les cérémonies du mariage', in Lentz, (ed.), *1810: le tournant de l'Empire*, pp. 37–50.

Chappey, Jean-Luc, 'La notion d'empire et la question de légitimité politique', *Siècles. Cahiers du Centre d'histoire 'Espaces et culture'*, 17 (2003): 111–27.

Chappey, Jean-Luc, 'Pierre-Louis Roederer et la presse sous le Directoire et le Consulat: l'opinion publique et les enjeux d'une politique éditoriale', *Annales historiques de la Révolution française*, 334 (2003): 1–21.

Chappey, Jean-Luc, 'Les Idéologues et l'Empire: étude des transformations entre savoirs et pouvoir (1799–1815)', in De Francesco (ed.), *Da Brumaio ai cento giorni*, pp. 211–27.

Chaptal, Jean-Antoine. *Mes souvenirs sur Napoléon*. Paris: E. Plon, Nourrit, 1893.

Charrié, Pierre. *Lettres de guerres, 1792–1815*. Nantes: Editions du Canonnier, 2004.

Charrier, Pierre. *Le maréchal Davout*. Paris: Nouveau Monde éditions: 2005.

Chartier, Jean-Luc A. *Portalis, le père du Code civil*. Paris: Fayard, 2004.

Chas, Jean. *Parallèle de Bonaparte le Grand avec Charlemagne*. Paris: Everat, 1803.

Chas, Jean. *Coup d'oeil d'un ami de sa patrie, sur les grandes action de l'empereur Napoléon, depuis ses opérations militaires à Toulon jusqu'à son avènement au Trône*. Paris: Brochot, 1804.

Chas, Jean. *Réflexions sur l'hérédité du pouvoir souverain*. Paris: Chez les Marchands de Nouveautés, 1804.

Chassin, Charles-Louis. *Etudes documentaires sur la Révolution française. Les Pacifications de l'Ouest. 1794–1815*. 3 vols. Paris: P. Dupont, 1896–9.

Chasteen, John Charles. *Americanos: Latin America's Struggle for Independence*. Oxford: Oxford University Press, 2008.

Chastenay, Victorine, comtesse de. *Mémoires de Madame de Chastenay, 1771–1815*. 2 vols. Paris: E. Plon, Nourrit, 1896–7.

Chastenet, Geneviève. *Marie-Louise: l'otage de Napoléon*. Paris: Perrin, 2005.

Chastenet, Jacques. *Godoy, Master of Spain 1792–1808*. Trans. J. F. Huntington. London: Batchworth Press, 1953.

Chastenet, Jacques. *Manuel Godoy et l'Espagne de Goya*. Paris: Hachette, 1961.

Chateaubriand, François-René de. *Correspondance générale*. 8 vols. Paris: Gallimard, 1977.

Chateaubriand, François-René de. *Mémoires d'outre-tombe*. Paris: Flammarion, 1997.

Chatel de Brancion, Laurence (ed.). *Cambacérès, fondateur de la justice moderne*. Saint-Rémy-en-l'Eau: Monelle Hayot, 2001.

Chatel de Brancion, Laurence. *Cambacérès: maître d'oeuvre de Napoléon*. Paris: Perrin, 2001.

Chatel de Brancion, Laurence, 'Napoléon et Cambacérès, maître d'ouvrage et maître d'oeuvre', in Chatel de Brancion (ed.), *Cambacérès, fondateur de la justice moderne*, pp. 131–9.

Chatel de Brancion, Laurence. *Le sacre de Napoléon: le rêve de changer le monde*. Paris: Perrin, 2004.

Chaussard, Pierre Jean-Baptiste. *Le pausanias français*. Paris: F. Buisson, 1808.

Chazet, Alissan de. *Mémoires, souvenirs, oeuvres et portraits*. 3 vols. Paris: Postel, 1837.

Chéron, F. *Napoléon, ou le Corse dévoilé, ode aux Français*. Paris: Le Normant, 1814.

Cherrier, Emmanuel, 'Un itinéraire politique original, l'ascension de Jean-Baptiste Bernadotte', *Nordic Historical Review/Revue d'Histoire Nordique*, 5 (2007): 65–99.

Cheuvreux, H. C. (ed.). *Journal et correspondance de André-Marie Ampère (de 1793 à 1805)*. Paris: J. Hetzel, 1872.

Chevalier, Jean-Michel. *Souvenirs des guerres napoléoniennes*. Paris: Hachette, 1970.

Chevallier, Bernard, 'Préparatifs des fêtes données par la ville de Paris à l'occasion du Sacre', in *Napoléon le sacre*, pp. 83–90.

Chevallier, Bernard, Dion-Tenenbaum, Anne and Desti, Marc et al. *1810: la politique de l'amour: Napoléon Ier et Marie-Louise à Compiègne*. Paris: RMN, 2010.

Chevallier, Bernard and Pincemaille, Christophe. *L'impératrice Joséphine*. Paris: Payot & Rivages, 1996.

Chollier, Antoine. *La vraie Route Napoléon, de Golfe-Juan à Lyon, histoire de dix jours*. Paris: Editions Alpina, 1950.

Choury, Maurice. *Les Grognards et Napoléon*. Paris: Perrin, 1968.

Christian, David, 'The Political Ideals of Michael Speransky', *Slavonic and East European Review*, 54 (1976): 192–213.

Chuquet, Arthur (ed.). *Souvenirs du baron de Frénilly, pair de France (1768–1828)*. Paris: Plon-Nourrit, 1908.

Chuquet, Arthur (ed.). *Lettres de 1812: première série*. Paris: H. Champion, 1911.

Chuquet, Arthur (ed.). *Lettres de 1815: première série*. Paris: H. Champion, 1911.

Chuquet, Arthur. *1812: la Guerre de Russie: notes et documents*. Paris: Fontemoing, 1912.

Chuquet, Arthur (ed.). *La campagne de 1812: mémoires du margrave de Bade*. Paris: Fontemoing, 1912.

Chuquet, Arthur. *Le départ de l'île d'Elbe*. Châtillon-sur-Seine: Euvrard-Pichat, 1921.

Cilleuls, J.-M. des, 'Yvan, chirurgien de Napoleon (1765–1839)', *Archives de médecine et de pharmacie militaires*, 103 (1935): 1017–39.

Ciotti, Bruno, 'La dernière campagne de Desaix', *Annales historiques de la Révolution française*, 324 (2001): 83–97.

Clark, Christopher, 'Piety, Politics and Society: Pietism in Eighteenth-Century Prussia', in Dwyer (ed.), *The Rise of Prussia*, pp. 68–88.

Clark, Christopher. *Iron Kingdom: The Rise and Downfall of Prussia, 1600–1947*. London: Allen Lane, 2006.

Clark, Christopher, 'When Culture Meets Power: The Prussian Coronation of 1701', in Scott and Simms (eds), *Cultures of Power in Europe*, pp. 14–35.

Clarke, Edward Daniel. *Travels in Various Countries of Europe, Asia and Africa*. 11 vols. 4th edn, London: Cadell and Davies, 1810–23.

Clarke, Joseph. *Commemorating the Dead in Revolutionary France: Revolution and Remembrance, 1789–1799*. Cambridge: Cambridge University Press, 2007.

Clary-et-Aldringen, Charles de. *Souvenirs du prince Charles de Clary-et-Aldringen: trois mois à Paris lors du mariage de l'empereur Napoléon Ier et de l'archiduchesse Marie-Louise*. Paris: Plon-Nourrit, 1914.

Clausewitz, Carl von. *Notes sur la Prusse dans sa grande catastrophe, 1806*. Trans. from the German by A. Niessel. Paris: R. Chapelot, 1903.

Clay, Stephen, 'Le brigandage en Provence du Directoire au Consulat (1795–1802)', in Jessenne (ed.), *Du Directoire au Consulat*, iii. pp. 67–89.

Clayton, Tim and Craig, Phil. *Trafalgar: The Men, the Battle, the Storm*. London: Hodder & Stoughton, 2004.

*Les clémences de Napoléon: l'image au service du mythe*. Paris: Somogy; Boulogne-Billancourt: Bibliothèque Marmottan, 2004.

Clermont-Tonnerre, Gaspard de. *L'expédition d'Espagne: 1808–1810*. Paris: Perrin, 1983.

Cloncurry, Valentine. *Personal Recollections of the Life and Times of Valentine, Lord Cloncurry*. Dublin: James McGlashan, 1849.

Cobb, Richard, 'Note sur la répression contre le personnel sans-culotte de 1795 à 1801', in *Terreur et subsistances, 1793–1795* (Paris: Clavreuil, 1965), pp. 179–210.

Cochelet, Louise. *Mémoires sur la reine Hortense et la famille imperial*. 4 vols. Paris: Ladvocat, 1836–8.

Coignet, Jean-Roch. *The Note-Books of Captain Coignet: Soldier of the Empire, 1776–1850*. London: Greenhill Books, 1998.

Colau, Pierre. *Couplets adressés à M. David, premier peintre de S.M. l'empereur et roi*. Paris: Aubry, n.d.

Colombo, Paolo, 'La question du pouvoir exécutif dans l'évolution institutionnelle et le débat politique révolutionnaire', *Annales historiques de la Révolution française*, 319 (2000): 1–26.

Colley, Linda, 'The Apotheosis of George III: Loyalty, Royalty and the British Nation', *Past & Present*, 102 (1984): 94–129.

Colley, Linda. *Britons: Forging the Nation 1707–1837*. New Haven and London: Yale University Press, 1992.

Collins, Herbert F. *Talma: A Biography of an Actor*. London: Faber & Faber, 1964.

Collins, Irene. *Napoleon and his Parliaments: 1800–1815*. London: E. Arnold, 1979.

Combe, Michel. *Mémoires du colonel Combe sur le campagnes de Russie en 1812, de Saxe 1813, de France, 1814 et 1815*. Paris: Blot, 1853.

Comeau de Charry, Sébastien-Joseph. *Souvenirs des guerres d'Allemagne pendant la Révolution et l'Empire*. Paris: Plon-Nourrit, 1900.

Connelly, Owen. *Napoleon's Satellite Kingdoms*. New York: Free Press, 1965.

Connelly, Owen (ed.). *Historical Dictionary of Napoleonic France, 1799–1815*. Westport, Conn.: Greenwood Press, 1985.

Connelly, Owen. *Blundering to Glory: Napoleon's Military Campaigns*. Wilmington, Del.: Scholarly Resources, 1987.

Consalvi, Ercole. *Mémoires du cardinal Consalvi*. 2 vols. Paris: Henri Plon, 1866.

Constant, Benjamin. *Oeuvres: Benjamin Constant*. Paris: Gallimard, 1979.

Constant, Benjamin. *Mémoires sur les Cent-Jours*. Tübingen: Max Niemeyer, 1993.

Cook, Llewellyn, 'Schwarzenberg at Dresden: Leadership and Command', *Consortium on Revolutionary Europe 1750–1850: Selected Papers* (Tallahassee, Fla: Institute on Napoleon and the French Revolution, 1994), pp. 642–51.

Coote, Stephen. *Napoleon and the Hundred Days*. London: Simon & Schuster, 2004.

Coppolani, Jean-Yves. *Les élections en France à l'époque napoléonienne*. Paris: Editions Albatros, 1980.

Coquelle, P., 'Les projets de descente en Angleterre, d'après les archives des affaires étrangères', *Revue d'histoire diplomatique*, 15 (1901): 433–53, 16 (1902): 134–57.

Coquelle, P., 'La mission de Sébastiani à Constantinople', *Revue d'histoire diplomatique*, 17 (1903), 438–55.

Coquery, Natacha. *Tenir boutique à Paris au XVIIIe siècle: luxe et demi-luxe*. Paris: Editions du Comité des travaux historiques et scientifiques, 2011.

Corbet, Charles. *A l'ère des nationalismes: l'opinion française face à l'inconnue russe (1799–1894)*. Paris: Didier, 1967.

Corbin, Alain, 'La fête de souveraineté', in Corbin, Gérôme and Tartakowsky (eds), *Les usages politiques des fêtes*, pp. 25–38.

Corbin, Alain, Gérôme, Noëlle and Tartakowsky, Danielle (eds). *Les usages politiques des fêtes aux XIXe–XXe siècles*. Paris: Publications de la Sorbonne, 1994.

Cordingly, David. *The Billy Ruffian: The Bellerophon and the Downfall of Napoleon: The Biography of a Ship of the Line, 1782–1836*. London: Bloomsbury, 2004.

Coriolis d'Espinouse, Charles Louis Alexandre. *Le tyran, les alliés et le roi, par M. le Mis de Coriolis d'Espinouse*. Paris: Le Normant, 1814.

Cornet, Mathieu-Augustin. *Souvenirs sénatoriaux, précédés d'un essai sur la formation de la Cour des Pairs*. Paris: Baudouin, 1824.

*Correspondance inédite de Napoléon Ier, de la famille impériale et de divers personnages avec Pauline Borghèse*. Paris: P. Cornuau, 1939.

Cosandey, Fanny. *La reine de France: symbole et pouvoir: XVe–XVIIIe siècle*. Paris: Gallimard, 2000.

Coston, François G. de. *Biographie des premières années de Napoléon Bonaparte*. 2 vols. Paris: Marc Aurel frères, 1840.

Courtine, Jean-Claude and Haroche, Claudine. *Histoire du visage: exprimer et taire ses émotions: du XVIe au début du XIXe siècle*. Paris: Payot & Rivages, 1994.

Couty, Mathieu, 'Quand Napoléon prononça la disgrace de Talleyrand', *Historia*, 506 (February 1989): 68–77.

Craig, Gordon A. *The Politics of the Prussian Army, 1640–1945*. Oxford: Oxford University Press, 1964.

Craig, Gordon A., 'Problems of Coalition Warfare: The Military Alliance against Napoleon, 1813–14', in *War, Politics and Diplomacy: Selected Essays* (Oxford: Weidenfeld & Nicolson, 1966), pp. 22–45.

Crawley, C. W. (ed.). *The New Cambridge Modern History*, vol. ix: *War and Peace in an Age of Upheaval, 1793–1830*. Cambridge: Cambridge University Press, 1965.

Crépin, Annie. *La conscription en débats ou le triple apprentissage de la Nation, de la citoyenneté, de la République (1798–1889)*. Artois: Artois Presses Université, 1998.

Crépin, Annie. *Défendre la France: les Français, la guerre et les service militaire, de la guerre de Sept Ans à Verdun*. Rennes: Presses Universitaires de Rennes, 2005.

Crépin, Annie, Jessenne, Jean-Pierre and Leuwers, Hervé (eds). *Civils, citoyens-soldats et militaires dans l'état-nation*. Paris: Société des études robespierristes, 2006.

Creveld, Martin van. *Supplying War: Logistics from Wallenstein to Patton*. Cambridge: Cambridge University Press, 1977.

Creveld, Martin van, 'Napoleon and the Dawn of Operational Warfare', in John Andreas Olsen and Martin van Creveld (eds), *The Evolution of Operational Art: From Napoleon to the Present* (Oxford, 2010), pp. 9–32.

Criste, Oskar. *Erzherzog Karl von Österreich*. 2 vols. Vienna and Leipzig: Wilhelm Braumüller, 1912.

Croker, John Wilson. *The Croker Papers: The Correspondence and Diaries of the Late Right Honourable John Wilson Croker, LL.D., F.R.S., Secretary to the Admiralty from 1809 to 1830*. Ed. L. J. Jennings. 3 vols. London: J. Murray, 1884.

Crook, Malcolm. *Elections in the French Revolution: An Apprenticeship in Democracy, 1789–1799*. Cambridge: Cambridge University Press, 1996.

Crook, Malcolm. *Napoleon Comes to Power: Democracy and Dictatorship in Revolutionary France, 1795–1804*. Cardiff: University of Wales Press, 1998.

Crook, Malcolm, 'The Uses of Democracy. Elections and Plebiscites in Napoleonic France', in Máire F. Cross and David Williams (eds), *The French Experience from Republic to Monarchy, 1792–1824: New Dawns in Politics, Knowledge and Culture* (Basingstoke, 2000), pp. 58–71.

Crook, Malcolm, 'Les réactions autour de Brumaire à travers le plébiscite de l'an VIII', in Jessenne (ed.), *Du Directoire au Consulat*, iii. pp. 323–31.

Crook, Malcolm, 'Confiance d'en bas, manipulation d'en haut: la pratique plébiscitaire sous Napoléon (1799–1815)', in Philippe Bourdin et al. (eds), *L'incident électoral de la Révolution française à la Ve République* (Clermont-Ferrand: Presses Universitaires Blaise-Pascal, 2002), pp. 77–87.

Crook, Malcolm, 'Confidence from Below? Collaboration and Resistance in the Napoleonic Plebiscites', in Rowe (ed.), *Collaboration and Resistance in Napoleonic Europe*, pp. 19–36.

Crook, Malcolm, 'The Plebiscite on the Empire', in Dwyer and Forrest (eds), *Napoleon and his Empire*, pp. 16–28.

Crook, Malcolm, '"Ma volonté est celle du people": Voting in the Plebiscite and Parliamentary Elections during Napoléon's Hundred Days, April–May 1815', *French Historical Studies*, 32 (2009): 619–45.

Crouzet, Pierre. *La fête de la paix, ou les élèves de Saint-Cyr à Marengo*. Paris: Impr. de Gillé, n.d.

Crouzet, François, 'La guerre maritime', in Jean Mistler (ed.), *Napoléon*, 2 vols (Paris, 1969–70), i. pp. 317–32.

Csendes, Peter and Opll, Ferdinand (eds). *Wien: Geschichte einer Stadt*, vol. iii: *Von 1790 bis zur Gegenwart*. Vienna: Böhlau, 2002.

Cugnac, Jean de. *Campagne de l'Armée de Réserve en 1800*. 2 vols. Paris: Chapelot, 1900–1.

Cugnac, Jean de, 'Mort de Desaix à Marengo', *Revue des études napoléoniennes*, 39 (1934): 5–32.

Cyr, Pascal, 'L'opposition des fonctionnaires pendant les cent-jours', *Napoleonica. La Revue*, 3 (2008): 16–40.

Cyr, Pascal. *Waterloo: origines et enjeux*. Paris: L'Harmattan, 2011.

Czouz-Tornare, Alain-Jacques (ed.). *Quand Napoléon Bonaparte recréa la Suisse: la genèse et la mise en oeuvre de l'Acte de médiation, aspects des relations franco-suisses autour de 1803*. Paris: Société des études robespierristes, 2005.

Dallas, Gregor. *The Final Act: The Roads to Waterloo*. New York: Henry Holt, 1997.

Daly, Gavin. *Inside Napoleonic France: State and Society in Rouen, 1800–1815*. Burlington, Vt: Ashgate, 2001.

Daly, Gavin, 'Napoleon and the "City of Smugglers", 1810–1814', *Historical Journal*, 50:2 (2007): 333–52.

Damaze de Raymond, Gratien Gilbert Joseph. *Tableau historique, géographique, militaire et moral de l'empire de Russie*. 2 vols. Paris: Le Normant, 1812.

Dansette, Adrien. *Napoléon: pensées politiques et sociales*. Paris: Flammarion, 1969.

Dard, Emile. *Napoléon et Talleyrand*. Paris: Plon, 1935.

Dard, Emile. *Dans l'entourage de l'Empereur*. Paris: Plon, 1940.

Darle, Françoise. *Au temps de Napoléon Bonaparte*. Paris: F. Lanore, 1961.

Darragon, François-Louis. *Le Bouquet impérial, ou le Tableau Napoléon*. Paris: Hénée et Dumas, 1807.

Dassier, H. *Les ruines de Moscou*. Paris: Didot, 1812.

Davidson, Denise Z., 'Women at Napoleonic Festivals: Gender and the Public Sphere during the First Empire', *French History*, 16 (2002): 299–322.

Davidson, Denise Z. *France after Revolution: Urban Life, Gender, and the New Social Order*. Cambridge, Mass.: Harvard University Press, 2007.

Davis, John A., 'The Neapolitan Revolution of 1799', *Journal of Modern Italian Studies*, 4:3 (1999): 350–8.

Davis, John A. *Naples and Napoleon: Southern Italy and the European Revolutions, 1780–1860*. Oxford: Oxford University Press, 2006.

Davout, Louis Nicolas. *Correspondance du maréchal Davout, prince d'Eckmühl*. 4 vols. Paris: E. Plon, Nourrit, 1885.

Davout, Louis Nicolas. *Opérations du 3e corps, 1806–1807. Rapport du maréchal Davout, duc d'Auerstaedt*. Paris: Calmann-Lévy, 1896.

Davydov, Denis Vasil'evich. *In the Service of the Tsar against Napoleon: The Memoirs of Denis Davidov, 1806–1814*. Trans. and ed. Gregory Troubetzkoy. London: Greenhill Books, 1999.

Dayot, Armand. *Napoléon raconté par l'image, d'après les sculpteurs, les graveurs et les peintres*. Paris: Hachette, 1902.

Dean, Rodney J. *L'Eglise constitutionnelle: Napoléon et le Concordat de 1801*. Paris: R. J. Dean, 2004.

Decaen, Charles. *Mémoires et journaux du général Decaen*. 2 vols. Paris: Plon-Nourrit, 1910–11.

Decaux, Alain. *La conspiration du général Malet: d'après des documents inédits*. Paris: A. Bonne, 1951.

DeConde, Alexander. *The Quasi-War: The Politics and Diplomacy of the Undeclared War with France, 1797–1801*. New York: C. Scribner's Sons, 1966.

Dedem de Gelder, Antoine Baudoin Gisbert de. *Un général hollandais sous le premier empire. Mémoires du général Bon de Dedem de Gelder 1774–1825*. Paris: E. Plon, Nourrit,1900.

De Francesco, Antonino (ed.). *Da Brumaio ai cento giorni: cultura di governo e dissenso politico nell'Europa di Bonaparte*. Milan: Guerini, 2007.

Delécluze, Jean-Etienne. *Louis David, son école et son temps. Souvenirs*. Paris: Didier, 1855.

Delehaye, Hippolyte. 'La légende de Saint Napoléon', in *Mélanges d'histoire offerts à Henri Pirenne*. 2 vols. Brussels: Vromant, 1926.

*De l'exil au retour de l'île d'Elbe: récits contemporains*. Paris: Teissèdre, 2001.

Delgado, Sabino (ed.). *Guerra de la Independencia*. Madrid: Editora nacional, 1979.

Della Peruta, Franco, 'War and Society in Napoleonic Italy: The Armies of the Kingdom of Italy at Home and Abroad', in John Davis and Paul Ginsborg (eds), *Society and Politics in the Age of the Risorgimento: Essays in Honour of Denis Mack Smith* (Cambridge: Cambridge University Press, 1991), pp. 26–48.

Delmarche, Joachim-Joseph. *Les Soirées du grenadier français de la Grande Armée, ou Principaux faits, actions, souffrances et dénuemens du sieur Joachim-Joseph Delmarche*. Rocroy: De Gamaches-Colson, 1849.

Delmas, Jean (ed.). *Histoire militaire de la France*. 4 vols. Paris: Presses Universitaires de France, 1992.

Delpierre, Madeleine, 'Une révolution, en trois temps', in *Modes et révolutions, 1780–1804* (Paris: Paris-Musées, 1989), pp. 11–40.

Demandt, Philipp. *Luisenkult: die Unsterblichkeit der Königin von Preußen*. Cologne: Böhlau, 2003.

Démier, Francis. *La France de la Restauration: 1814–1830: l'impossible retour du passé*. Paris: Gallimard, 2012.

Denniée, Pierre-Paul. *Itinéraire de l'empereur Napoléon pendant la campagne de 1812*. Paris: Paulin, 1842.

Deries, Léon. *La conscription des riches: les Gardes d'honneur de Maine-et-Loire de l'année 1813*. Angers: Grassin, 1929.

Derrécagaix, Victor-Bernard. *Le maréchal Berthier, prince de Wagram et de Neuchâtel*. 2 vols. Paris: Teissèdre, 1904, reprinted 2002.

Desbrière, Edouard. *1793–1805: projets et tentatives de débarquement aux Îles Britanniques*. 4 vols. Paris: R. Chapelot, 1900–2.

Deschamps, Etienne-Maurice. *Souvenirs militaires, persécutions sous la Restauration, songe, etc.* Pontarlier: Veuve Faivre, 1835.

Deschamps, Jules, 'En Belgique avec les anglais après Waterloo', *Revue des études napoléoniennes*, 31 (1930): 224–49, 276–304.

*Description du tableau représentant le couronnement de leurs majestés impériales et royales*. Paris: Aubry, 1808.

Desmarets, Pierre-Marie. *Quinze ans de haute police sous le consulat et l'empire*. Paris: A. Levavasseur, 1833.

Destrem, Jean. *Les déportations du Consulat et de l'Empire (d'après des documents inédits)*. Paris: Jeanmaire, 1885.

*Détail de la fête du 15 août, pour le double anniversaire de la naissance du Ier Consul et de la signature du Concordat*. Paris: Duchon, n.d.

'Les deux frères Burnot (1808–1814)', *Carnet de la Sabretache*, 69 (1898): 530–57.

Deutsch, Harold C., 'Napoleonic Policy and the Project of a Descent upon England', *Journal of Modern History* 2 (1930): 541–68.

Deutsch, Harold C. *The Genesis of Napoleonic Imperialism*. Cambridge, Mass.: Harvard University Press, 1938.

Devlin, Jonathan D., 'The Army, Politics and Public Order in Directorial Provence, 1795–1800', *Historical Journal*, 32:1 (1989): 87–106.

Dickens, A. G. (ed.). *The Courts of Europe: Politics, Patronage and Royalty 1400–1800*. London: Thames & Hudson, 1977.

Dickinson, H. T. (ed.). *Britain and the French Revolution, 1789–1815*. Basingstoke: Macmillan, 1989.

Didier, Eugene L. *The Life and Letters of Madame Bonaparte*. New York: C. Scribner, 1879.

Diesbach, Ghislain de. *Histoire de l'émigration, 1789–1814*. Paris: Perrin, 1984.

Doris, Charles. *Précis historique sur Napoléon Bonaparte*. Paris: G. Mathiot, 1814.

Doris, Charles. *Mémoires secrets sur Napoléon Buonaparte, écrits par un homme qui ne l'a pas quitté depuis quinze ans*. Paris: G. Mathiot, 1815.

Doyle, William. *Aristocracy and its Enemies in the Age of Revolution*. Oxford: Oxford University Press, 2009.

Drabek, Anna M., Leitsch, Walter and Plaschka, Richard G. (eds). *Russland und Österreich zur Zeit der Napoleonischen Kriege*. Vienna: Verlag der österreichischen Akademie der Wissenschaften, 1989.

Driault, Edouard. *La politique orientale de Napoléon: Sébastiani et Gardane, 1806–1808*. Paris: Félix Alcan, 1904.

Driault, Edouard. *Napoléon en Italie*. Paris: Félix Alcan, 1906.

Driault, Edouard. *Napoléon et l'Europe*. 5 vols. Paris: Félix Alcan, 1912.

Drouin, Jean-Claude, 'L'image des Entrevues de Bayonne chez quelques témoins et historiens aux XIXe siècle: de Cevallos à Savine 1808–1908', in Pontet, *Napoléon, Bayonne et l'Espagne*, pp. 144–52.

Drujon de Beaulieu. *Souvenirs d'un militaire pendant quelques années du règne de Napoléon Bonaparte*. Belley: J.-B. Verpillon, 1831.

Dubroca, Louis. *Les quatre fondateurs des dynasties françaises, ou Histoire de l'établissement de la monarchie française, par Clovis . . . Pépin et Hugues Capet; et . . . Napoléon-le-Grand . . .* Paris: Dubroca, 1806.

Dubroca, Louis. *Discours à la gloire des armées françaises, pour la célébration de la mémorable paix de Tilsit*. Paris: Dubroca, 1807.

Dubroca, Louis. *Discours en actions de grâces à l'Eternel pour la fête de la naissance de S.M. le roi de Rome*. Paris: Dubroca, 1811.

Dubroca, Louis. *Un vieux républicain à Napoléon, sur la puissance de l'opinion publique dans le gouvernement des Etats*. Paris: Delaunay, 1815.

Du Casse, Albert (ed.). *Mémoires et correspondance politique et militaire du roi Joseph*. 10 vols. Paris: Perrotin, 1853–4.

Du Casse, Albert (ed.). *Mémoires et correspondance politique et militaire du prince Eugène*. 10 vols. Paris: Michel Lévy frères, 1858–60.

Du Casse, Albert, 'Documents inédits relative au premier Empire. Napoléon et le roi Louis', *Revue historique*, 12 (January–February 1880): 70–95, 354–79.

Du Casse, Albert. *Les rois frères de Napoléon Ier: documents inédits relatifs au premier empire*. Paris: Germer Baillière, 1883.

Ducéré, Edouard. *Napoléon à Bayonne: d'après les contemporains et des documents inédits*. Paris: Editions de la Couronne, 1994.

Ducor, Henri. *Aventures d'un marin de la Garde impériale, prisonnier de guerre sur les pontons espagnols, dans l'île de Cabréra et en Russie*. 2 vols. Paris: Ambroise Dupont, 1833.

Ducque, Gaspard. *Journal de marche du sous-lieutenant Ducque*. Paris: La Vouivre, 2004.

Duffy, Christopher. *Borodino and the War of 1812*. London: Cassell, 1972.

Duffy, Christopher. *Austerlitz 1805*. London: Seeley Service, 1977.

Dufour, Alfred, 'D'une médiation à l'autre', in Alfred Dufour, Till Hanisch and Victor Monnier (eds), *Bonaparte, la Suisse et l'Europe* (Geneva: Schulthess, 2003), pp. 7–37.

Dufour, Gérard, 'Pourquoi les espagnoles prirent-ils les armes contre Napoléon?', in *Les Espagnols et Napoléon*, pp. 317–25.

Dufour, Gérard, 'Le roi philosophe', in Emilio La Parra López (ed.), *Actores de la Guerra de la Independencia. Dossier des Mélanges de la Casa de Velázquez*, nouvelle série, 38:1 (2008): 53–70.

Dufour, Gérard and Larriba, Elisabel (eds). *L'Espagne en 1808: régénération ou révolution?* Aix-en-Provence: Publications de l'Université de Provence, 2009.

Dufraisse, Roger. *Napoléon: correspondence officielle*. Paris: Club du livre, 1970.

Dufraisse, Roger, 'La crise économique de 1810–1812 en pays annexé: l'exemple de la rive gauche du Rhin', *Francia*, 6 (1978): 407–40.

Dufraisse, Roger, 'L'intégration "hégémoniale" de l'Europe sous Napoléon Ier', *Revue de l'Institut Napoléon* 142 (1984): 11–42.

Dufraisse, Roger, 'A propos des guerres de délivrance allemandes de 1813', *Revue de l'Institut Napoléon*, 148 (1987): 11–44.

Dufraisse, Roger, 'La fin des départements de la rive gauche du Rhin', in Bercé (ed.), *La fin de l'Europe napoléonienne*, pp. 11–61.

Dufraisse, Roger, 'L'écroulement de la domination française en Allemagne (1813)', in Tulard (ed.), *L'Europe de Napoléon*, pp. 473–510.

Dufraisse, Roger and Kerautret, Michel. *La France napoléonienne: aspects extérieurs, 1799–1815*. Paris: Seuil, 1999.

Duggan, Christopher. *The Force of Destiny: A History of Italy since 1796*. London: Allen Lane, 2007.

Dühr, Elisabeth and Lehnert-Leven, Christl (eds). *Unter der Trikolore: Trier in Frankreich, Napoleon in Trier, 1794–1814*. 2 vols. Trier: Stadtisches Museum Simeonstift Trier, 2004.

Duindam, Jeroen, 'Ceremony at Court: Reflections on an Elusive Subject', *Francia*, 26:2 (1999): 131–40.

Duindam, Jeroen. *Vienna and Versailles: The Courts of Europe's Major Dynastic Rivals, ca. 1550–1780*. Cambridge: Cambridge University Press, 2003.

Duindam, Jeroen. 'The Dynastic Court in an Age of Change: Frederick II Seen from the Perspective of Habsburg and Bourbon Court Life', in Jürgen Luh and Michael Kaiser (eds), *Friedrich300 – Colloquien, Friedrich der Große und der Hof, 2009*, www.perspectivia.net/content/publikationen/friedrich300-colloquien/friedrich-hof/Duindam_Court?set_language=tr.

Dumas, Mathieu. *Précis des événemens militaires, ou Essais historiques sur les campagnes de 1799 à 1814*. 19 vols. Paris: Treuttel et Würtz, 1817–26.

Dumas, Mathieu. *Souvenirs du général comte Mathieu Dumas, de 1770 à 1836*. 3 vols. Paris: Gosselin, 1839.

Dumonceau, François. *Mémoires du général comte François Dumonceau*. 3 vols. Brussels: Brépols, 1958–63.

Du Montet, Alexandrine Prévost de La Boutetière de Saint-Mars de Fisson. *Souvenirs de la baronne Du Montet, 1785–1866*. Paris: Plon-Nourrit, 1914.

Dunan, Marcel. *Napoléon et l'Allemagne: la Système Continentale et les débuts du Royaume de Bavière, 1806–1810*. Paris: Plon, 1943.

Dunne, John, 'Les maires de Brumaire, notables ruraux ou "gens des passage"?', in Jessenne (ed.), *Du Directoire au Consulat*, iii. pp. 451–65.

Dunne, John, 'Quantifier l'émigration des nobles pendant la Révolution française: problèmes et perspectives', in Martin (ed.), *La Contre-Revolution en Europe*, pp. 133–41.

Dunne, John, 'Napoleon's "Mayoral Problem": Aspects of State–Community Relations in Post-Revolutionary France', *Modern & Contemporary France*, 8 (2000): 479–91.

Dunne, John, 'Power on the Periphery: Elite–State Relations in the Napoleonic Empire', in Dwyer and Forrest (eds), *Napoleon and his Empire*, pp. 61–78.

Dupont, J.-J. *Portrait historique de Napoléon le Grand*. Paris: Poulet, 1807.

Dupont, Maurice. *L'amiral Decrès et Napoléon ou La fidélité orageuse d'un ministre*. Paris: Economica, 1991.

Duprat, Annie, 'Une guerre des images: Louis XVIII, Napoléon et la France en 1815', *Revue d'Histoire moderne et contemporaine*, 47:3 (2000): 487–504.

Dupuis, Charles. *Le ministère de Talleyrand en 1814*. Paris: Plon-Nourrit, 1919.

Dupuy, Marie-Anne (ed.). *Dominique-Vivant Denon: l'oeil de Napoléon*. Paris: Musée du Louvre, 1999.

Dupuy, Marie-Anne, Le Masne de Chermont, Isabelle and Williamson, Elaine (eds). *Vivant Denon, directeur des musées sous le Consulat et l'Empire: correspondance, 1802–1815*. 2 vols. Paris: Editions de la Réunion des musées nationaux, 1999.

Dupuy, Pascal, 'Le 18 Brumaire en Grande-Bretagne: le témoignage de la presse et des caricatures', *Annales historiques de la Révolution française*, 318 (1999): 773–87.

Dupuy, Roger. *La Garde nationale, 1789–1872*. Paris: Gallimard, 2010.

Dupuy, Victor. *Souvenirs militaires de Victor Dupuy, chef d'escadrons de hussards, 1794–1816*. Paris: Calmann-Lévy, 1892.

Durand, Charles. *Etudes sur le Conseil d'Etat napoléonien*. Paris: Presses Universitaires de France, 1949.

Dusaulchoy de Bergemont, Joseph-François-Nicolas. *Histoire du couronnement, ou Relation des cérémonies religieuses, politiques et militaires, qui ont eu lieu pendant les jours mémorables consacrés à célébrer le Couronnement et le Sacre de Sa Majesté Impériale Napoléon Ier, Empereur des Français*. Paris: Dubray, 1805.

Dutheillet de Lamothe, Aubin. *Mémoires du lieutenant-colonel Aubin Dutheillet de Lamothe*. Brussels: Lamertin, 1899.

Duverger, B. T. *Mes Aventures dans la Campagne de Russie*. Paris: Crapelet, 1833.

Duveyrier, Honoré. *Anecdotes historiques*. Paris: Picard, 1907.

Dwyer, Philip, 'Prussia and the Armed Neutrality: The Decision to Invade Hanover in 1801', *International History Review*, 15 (1993): 661–87.

Dwyer, Philip, 'Duroc diplomate: un militaire au service de la diplomatie napoléonienne', *Revue du Souvenir napoléonien*, 399 (1995): 21–38.

Dwyer, Philip (ed.). *The Rise of Prussia, 1700–1830*. London: Longman, 2000.

Dwyer, Philip, 'Napoleon and the Drive for Glory: Reflections on the Making of French Foreign Policy', in Dwyer (ed.), *Napoleon and Europe*, pp. 118–35.

Dwyer, Philip (ed.). *Napoleon and Europe*. London: Longman, 2001.

Dwyer, Philip. *Napoleon: The Path to Power, 1769–1799*. London: Bloomsbury, 2007.

Dwyer, Philip, '"It Still Makes Me Shudder": Memories of Massacres and Atrocities during the Revolutionary and Napoleonic Wars', *War in History*, 16 (2009): 381–405.

Dwyer, Philip, 'Napoleon and the Foundation of the Empire', *Historical Journal*, 53 (2010): 339–58.

Dwyer, Philip, 'Napoleon and the Universal Monarchy', *History*, 95 (2010): 293–307.

Dwyer, Philip and Forrest, Alan (eds). *Napoleon and his Empire: Europe, 1804–1814*. Basingstoke: Palgrave Macmillan, 2007.

Ebbinghaus, Therese. *Napoleon, England und die Presse, 1800–1803*. Munich: R. Oldenbourg, 1914.

Ebrington, Hugh Fortescue, Viscount. *Memorandum of Two Conversations between the Emperor Napoleon and Viscount Ebrington at Porto-Ferrajo on the 6th and 8th of December 1814*. London: J. Ridgway, 1823.

Echternkamp, Jörg. *Der Aufstieg des deutschen Nationalismus (1770–1840)*. Frankfurt: Campus, 1998.

Edling, Roxandra. *Mémoires de la comtesse Edling (née Stourdza), demoiselle d'honneur de S.M. l'impératrice*. Moscow: St Synode, 1888.

Egloffstein, Hermann Freiherrn von, 'Zur Geschichte des Fürstentages in Dresden 1812: Briefe und Aufzeichnungen Carl Augusts', *Historische Zeitschrift*, 121 (1919): 268–82.

Ehrman, John. *The Younger Pitt*. 3 vols. London: Constable, 1969–96.

Eisner, Manuel, 'Killing Kings: Patterns of Regicide in Europe, AD 600–1800', *British Journal of Criminology*, 51:3 (2011): 556–77.

Elliott, Marianne. *Partners in Revolution: The United Irishmen and France*. New Haven: Yale University Press, 1982.

Ellis, Geoffrey. *Napoleon's Continental Blockade: The Case of Alsace*. Oxford: Clarendon Press, 1981.

Ellis, Geoffrey. *Napoleon*. Harlow: Longmans, 1997.

Ellis, Geoffrey, 'Religion According to Napoleon: The Limits of Pragmatism', in Nigel Aston (ed.), *Religious Change in Europe, 1650–1914: Essays for John McManners* (Oxford: Clarendon Press, 1997), pp. 235–55.

Ellis, Geoffrey, 'A Historian's Critique of the Screenplay', in Castle (ed.), *Kubrick's Napoleon: The Greatest Movie Never Made*, pp. 237–49.

Ellis, John Tracy. *Cardinal Consalvi and Anglo-Papal Relations, 1814–1824*. Washington, DC: Catholic University of America Press, 1942.

Emsley, Clive. *British Society and the French Wars 1793–1815*. London: Macmillan, 1979.

Elting, John R. *Swords around a Throne: Napoleon's Grande Armée*. New York: Free Press, 1988.

Engels, Jens Ivo, 'Furcht und Drohgebärde: die Denunzianten "falscher Komplotte" gegen den König von Frankreich, 1680–1760', in Michaela Hohkamp and Claudia Ulbrich (eds), *Der Staatsbürger als Spitzel: Denunziation während des 18. und 19. Jahrhunderts aus europäischer Perspektive* (Leipzig: Leipziger Universitätsverlag, 2001), pp. 323–40.

Englund, Steven. *Napoleon: A Political Biography*. New York: Scribner, 2004.

Englund, Steven, 'Napoleon and Hitler', *Journal of the Historical Society*, 6 (2006): 151–69.

*Epître du diable à Buonaparte* [signed Lucifer]. N.p., 1814.

Epstein, Robert M., 'Patterns of Change and Continuity in Nineteenth-Century Warfare', *Journal of Military History*, 56:3 (1992): 375–88.

Epstein, Robert M. *Napoleon's Last Victory and the Emergence of Modern War*. Lawrence, Kan.: Kansas University Press, 1994.

Epstein, Robert M., 'Aspects of Military and Operational Efffectiveness of the Armies of France, Austria, Russia and Prussia in 1813', in Schneid (ed.), *The Projection and Limitations of Imperial Powers*, pp. 122–48.

Erdmannsdorffer, Bernhard (ed.). *Politische Correspondenz Karl Friedrichs von Baden, 1783–1806*. 5 vols. Heidelberg: C. Winter, 1888–1901.

Erlin, Matt. *Berlin's Forgotten Future: City, History, and Enlightenment in Eighteenth-Century Germany*. Chapel Hill: University of North Carolina Press, 2004.

Ernouf, Alfred-Auguste. *Les Français en Prusse (1807–1808), d'après des documents contemporains recueillis en Allemagne*. Paris: Didier, 1872.

Ernouf, Alfred-Auguste. *Maret, duc de Bassano*. Paris: Charpentier, 1878.

Esdaile, Charles. *The Wars of Napoleon*. London: Longman, 1995.

Esdaile, Charles. *The Peninsular War: A New History*. London: Penguin, 2003.

Esdaile, Charles. *Fighting Napoleon: Guerrillas, Bandits and Adventurers in Spain, 1808:1814*. New Haven: Yale University Press, 2004.

Esdaile, Charles. *Napoleon's Wars: An International History, 1803–1815*. London: Allen Lane, 2007.

Esdaile, Charles. *Peninsular Eyewitnesses: The Experience of War in Spain and Portugal 1808–1813*. Barnsley: Pen & Sword, 2008.

Esdaile, Charles, 'Deconstructing the French Wars: Napoleon as Anti-strategist', *Journal of Strategic Studies*, 31 (2008): 515–52.

*Les Espagnols et Napoléon: Actes du colloque international d'Aix-en-Provence, 13, 14, 15 octobre 1893*. Aix-en-Provence: Université de Provence, 1984.

Espinchal, Hippolyte d'. *Souvenirs militaires, 1792–1814*. 2 vols. Paris: Ollendorff, 1901.

Espinouse, Coriolis de. *Le tyran, les alliés et le roi*. Paris: Le Normant, 1814.

*Esquisse historique sur les Cent Jours*. Paris: Baudouin, 1819.

*Essai sur l'éloge de Napoléon*. Châlons: Vve Boniez, n.d.

*Etiquette du palais imperial*. Paris: Impr. impériale, 1806.

Eustache (sons). *Ode à Sa Majesté l'empereur Napoléon, roi d'Italie*. Paris: Henri et Dumas, 1807.

Everts, Henri-Pierre, 'Campagne et captivité de Russie (1812–1813): extraits des Mémoires inédits du général-major H. P. Everts', in *Carnets et journal sur la campagne de Russie: extraits du 'Carnet de la Sabretache', années 1901–1902–1906–1912*. Paris: Teissèdre, 1997.

'Extrait de la relation de la prise d'Ulm, sur le manuscrit original de M..., capitaine d'Etat-Major au service de l'Autriche', *Journal des sciences militaires*, 8 (1827): 74–84.

'Extraits du carnets du Général Pelet sur la campagne de Russie de 1812', *Carnet de la Sabretache*, 5 (1906): 519–52, 626–40, 682–702.

Eyck, F. Gunther. *Loyal Rebels: Andreas Hofer and the Tyrolean Uprising of 1809*. Lanham, Md: University Press of America, 1986.

Eynard, Jean-Gabriel. *Journal de Jean-Gabriel Eynard: au Congrès de Vienne*. 2 vols. Paris: Plon-Nourrit, 1914.

Fabry, Jean-Baptiste-Germain. *Itinéraire de Buonaparte, depuis son départ de Doulevent, le 28 mars, jusqu'à son embarquement à Fréjus, le 29 avril*. Paris: Le Normant, 1815.

Fabvier, Charles-Nicolas. *Journal des opérations du 6e corps pendant la campagne de France en 1814*. Paris: Carez, Thomine, 1819.

Fain, Agathon-Jean-François, Baron. *Manuscrit de mil huit cent-quatorze, trouvé dans les voitures impériales prises à Waterloo, contenant l'histoire des six derniers mois du règne de Napoléon*. Paris: Bossange, 1824.

Fain, Agathon-Jean-François, Baron. *Manuscrit de mil huit cent treize, contenant le précis des événemens de cette année, pour servir à l'histoire de l'empereur Napoléon*. 2 vols. Paris: Delaunay, 1824.

Fain, Agathon-Jean-François, Baron. *Manuscrit de mil huit cent douze*. 2 vols. Paris: Delaunay, 1827.

Fain, Agathon-Jean-François, Baron. *Mémoires du baron Fain, premier secrétaire du cabinet de l'empereur*. Paris: Plon-Nourrit, 1908.

Fairon, Emile and Heuse, Henri. *Lettres de grognards*. Liège: Imprimerie Bénard; Paris: Librairie Georges Courville, 1936.

Fantin des Odoards, Louis-Florimond. *Journal du général Fantin des Odoards, étapes d'un officier de la Grande Armée, 1800–1830*. Paris: E. Plon, Nourrit, 1895.

Faré, Charles-A. *Lettres d'un jeune officier à sa mère, 1803–1814*. Paris: C. Delagrave, 1889.

Farge, Arlette. *La vie fragile: violence, pouvoirs et solidarités à Paris au XVIIIe siècle*. Paris: Seuil, 1992.

Faroult, Guillaume. *David*. Paris: J.-P. Gisserot, 2003.

Faucheur, Narcisse. *Souvenirs de campagnes du sergent Faucheur*. Paris: Tallandier, 2004.

Faure, Raymond. *Souvenirs du Nord, ou la Guerre, la Russie et les Russes ou l'esclavage*. Paris: Pelicier, 1821.

Fauriel, Claude, *Les derniers jours du Consulat, manuscrit inédit de Claude Fauriel*. Paris: Calmann-Lévy, 1886.

Favier, Jean. *Charlemagne*. Paris: Fayard, 1999.

Favier, Franck. *Bernadotte, un maréchal d'Empire sur le trône de Suède*. Paris: Ellipses, 2010.

Fay, Sidney B., 'The Execution of the Duc d'Enghien I', *American Historical Review*, 3 (1898): 620–40; and 'The Execution of the Duc d'Enghien II', 4 (1898): 21–37.

Fedorak, Charles John, 'Catholic Emancipation and the Resignation of William Pitt in 1801', *Albion*, 24:1 (1992): 49–64.

Fedorak, Charles John, 'The French Capitulation in Egypt and the Preliminary Anglo-French Treaty of Peace in October 1801', *International History Review*, 15 (1993): 525–34.

Fedorak, Charles John. *Henry Addington, Prime Minister, 1801–1804: Peace, War, and Parliamentary Politics*. Akron, Ohio: University of Akron Press, 2002.

Fedorak, Charles John, 'In Defence of Great Britain: Henry Addington, the Duke of York and Military Preparations against Invasion by Napoleonic France, 1803–1804', in Philp (ed.), *Resisting Napoleon*, pp. 91–110.

Fenet, Pierre-Antoine. *Recueil complet des travaux préparatoires du Code civil*. 15 vols. Paris: Videcoq, 1836.

Fierro, Alfred. *La vie des Parisiens sous Napoléon*. Saint-Cloud: Fayard, 2003.

Fiévée, Joseph. *Lettres sur l'Angleterre et réflexions sur la philosophie du XVIIIe siècle*. Paris: Perlet, 1802.

Fiévée, Joseph. *Correspondance et relations de J. Fiévée avec Bonaparte premier consul et empereur: pendant onze années (1802 à 1813)*. 3 vols. Paris: A. Desrez, Beauvais, 1836.

Firmin-Didot, Georges. *Royauté ou empire. La France en 1814, d'après les rapports inédits du Cte Anglès*. Paris: Firmin-Didot, 1897.

Fitzpatrick, Brian, 'The *Royaume du Midi* of 1815', in Laven and Riall (eds), *Napoleon's Legacy*, pp. 167–82.

Flayhart III, William Henry. *Counterpoint to Trafalgar: The Anglo-Russian Invasion of Naples, 1805–1806*. Columbia, SC: University of South Carolina Press, 1992.

Fleury, Michel (ed.). *Souvenirs inédits de M. le comte Chabrol de Volvic*. Paris: Commission des travaux historiques, Ville de Paris, 2002.

Fleury de Chaboulon, Pierre-Alexandre-Edouard. *Les cent jours, mémoires pour servir à l'histoire de la vie privée, du retour et du règne de Napoléon en 1815.* 2 vols. London: C. Roworth, 1820.

Fleury de Chaboulon, Pierre-Alexandre-Edouard, *Mémoires de Fleury de Chaboulon, ex-secrétaire de l'empereur Napoléon et de son cabinet, pour servir à l'histoire de la privée, du retour et du règne de Napoléon en 1815.* 2 vols. Paris: E. Rouveyre, 1901.

Flockerzie, Lawrence J., 'Saxony, Austria, and the German Question after the Congress of Vienna, 1815–1816', *International History Review*, 12:4 (1990): 661–87.

Floriet, Lucien. *Marmont: maréchal d'Empire, 1774–1852.* Marcilly-sur-Tille: L. Floriet, 1996.

Folliot, Franck, 'Des colonnes pour les héros', in *Les architectes de la Liberté, 1789–1799* (Paris: Ecole nationale supérieure des beaux-arts, 1989), pp. 305–22.

Fontaine, Pierre-François. *Journal: 1799–1853.* 2 vols. Paris: Ecole nationale supérieure des beaux-arts, 1987.

Fontanes, Louis de. *Parallèle entre César, Cromwell, Monck et Bonaparte, fragment traduit de l'anglais.* N.p., n.d.

Fontanes, Louis de. *Oeuvres de M. de Fontanes.* 2 vols. Paris: Hachette, 1839.

Forgues, Eugène (ed.). *Mémoires et relations politiques du Baron de Vitrolles.* 3 vols. Paris: G. Charpentier, 1884.

Forneron, Henri. *Histoire générale des émigrés pendant la Révolution française.* 3 vols. Paris: E. Plon, Nourrit, 1884–90.

Forrest, Alan. *Conscripts and Deserters: The Army and French Society during the Revolution and Empire.* Oxford: Oxford University Press, 1989.

Forrest, Alan, 'The Napoleonic Armies and their World', *Revista Napoleonica*, 1–2 (2000): 277–84.

Forrest, Alan, 'The Military Culture of Napoleonic France', in Dwyer (ed.), *Napoleon and Europe*, pp. 43–59.

Forrest, Alan. *Napoleon's Men: The Soldiers of the Revolution and Empire.* London: Hambledon, 2002.

Forrest, Alan, 'La perspective de la paix dans l'opinion publique et la société militaire', *Bulletin de la Société des Antiquaires de Picardie*, 166 (2002): 251–62.

Forrest, Alan, 'State-Formation and Resistance: The Army and Local Elites in Napoleonic France', in Rowe (ed.), *Collaboration and Resistance in Napoleonic Europe*, pp. 37–54.

Forrest, Alan, 'Napoleon as Monarch: A Political Evolution', in Forrest and Wilson (eds), *The Bee and the Eagle*, pp. 112–30.

Forrest, Alan. *The Legacy of the French Revolutionary Wars: The Nation-in-Arms in French Republican Memory.* Cambridge: Cambridge University Press, 2009.

Forrest, Alan, Hagemann, Karen and Rendall, Jane (eds). *Soldiers, Citizens and Civilians: Experiences and Perceptions of the French Wars, 1790–1820.* Basingstoke: Palgrave Macmillan, 2009.

Forrest, Alan and Wilson, Peter H. (eds). *The Bee and the Eagle: Napoleonic France and the End of the Holy Roman Empire, 1806.* Basingstoke: Palgrave Macmillan, 2009.

Foucart, Bruno, 'Les "Salons" sous le Consulat et les diverses représentations de Bonaparte', *Revue de l'Institut Napoléon*, 111 (1969): 113–19.

Foucart, Bruno, 'Les clémences de Napoléon et leurs images: art et politique', in *Les clémences de Napoléon*, pp. 23–9.

Foucart, Bruno, 'L'accueil de la Paix d'Amiens par les artistes', in Chaline (ed.), *La Paix d'Amiens.* pp. 231–43.

Foucart, Bruno, 'Les iconographies du Concordat, laboratoire d'une nouvelle politique de l'image', in Boudon (ed.), *Le Concordat et le retour de la paix religieuse*, pp. 151–67.

Foucart, Paul-Jean. *Bautzen, une bataille de deux jours, 20–21 mai 1813.* Paris: Berger-Levrault, 1897.

Foucart, Paul-Jean. *Campagne de Prusse (1806), d'après les archives de la guerre.* 2 vols. Paris: Berger-Levrault, 1890.

Fouché, Joseph. *Mémoires de Joseph Fouché, duc d'Otrante, ministre de la police générale.* 2 vols. Paris: chez Le Rouge, 1824.

Fournier, August. *Gentz und Cobenzl: Geschichte der österreichischen Diplomatie in den Jahren 1801–1805*. Vienna: Wilhelm Braumüller, 1880.

Fournier, August. *Der Congress von Châtillon: die Politik im Kriege von 1814*. Leipzig: Freytag, 1900.

Fournier, August. *Marie-Louise et la chute de Napoléon, contribution à la biographie de Marie-Louise*. Paris: Daupeley-Gouverneur, 1903.

Fournier, August. *Napoleon I: A Biography*. Trans. Annie Elizabeth Adams. 2 vols. New York: Henry Holt, 1911.

Frances, Beata and Kenny, Eliza (eds). *The Francis Letters, by Sir Philip Francis and Other Members of the Family*. 2 vols. London: Hutchinson, 1908.

Franclieu, Louis Pasquier, comte de. *Opinion sur la question qui nous est proposée: Napoléon Bonaparte sera-t-il consul à vie?* Paris: Chez les Marchands de Nouveautés, 1801.

François, Charles. *Journal du capitaine François: dit le Dromadaire d'Egypte 1792–1830*. Paris: Tallandier, 2003.

François, Etienne, 'Das napoleonische Hegemonialsystem auf dem Kontinent', in Klinger, Hahn and Schmidt (eds), *Das Jahr 1806*, pp. 73–83.

Franklin, Alexandra and Philp, Mark. *Napoleon and the Invasion of Britain*. Oxford: Bodleian Library, 2003.

Fraser, Flora. *Pauline Bonaparte: Venus of Empire*. New York: Alfred A. Knopf, 2009.

Frederking, Bettina, '"Il ne faut pas être le roi de deux peuples": Strategies of National Reconciliation in Restoration France', *French History*, 22:4 (2008): 446–68.

Freud, Sigmund. *The Standard Edition of the Complete Psychological Works of Sigmund Freud*. 24 vols. London: Hogarth Press, 1953–75.

Frey, Marsha and Linda, '"The Reign of the Charlatans is Over": The French Revolutionary Attack on Diplomatic Practice', *Journal of Modern History*, 65 (1993): 706–44.

Friedlaender, Walter, 'Napoleon as Roi Thaumaturge', *Journal of the Warburg and Courtauld Institutes*, 4 (1941): 139–41.

Fritzsche, Peter, 'Specters of History: On Nostalgia, Exile and Modernity', *American Historical Review*, 106 (2001): 1587–1618.

Fritzsche, Peter, 'How Nostalgia Narrates Modernity', in Alon Confino and Peter Fritzsche (eds), *The Work of Memory: New Directions in the Study of German Society and Culture* (Urbana: University of Illinois Press, 2002), pp. 62–85.

Fritzsche, Peter, 'The Historical Actor', in Edward Berenson and Eva Giloi (eds), *Constructing Charisma: Celebrity, Fame, and Power in Nineteenth-Century Europe* (New York: Berghahn, 2010), pp. 134–44.

Fugier, André. *Napoléon et l'Espagne, 1799–1808*. 2 vols. Paris: Félix Alcan, 1930.

Fugier, André. *Napoléon et l'Italie*. Paris: Janin, 1947.

Fugier, André, 'La signification sociale et politique des décorations napoléoniennes', *Cahiers d'histoire*, 4 (1959): 339–46.

Furet, François. *Revolutionary France, 1770–1880*. Trans. Antonia Nevill. Oxford: Oxford University Press, 1992.

Fusil, Louise. *Souvenirs d'une actrice. Mémoires de Louise Fusil (1774–1778)*. Paris: Schmid, n.d.

G.M., 'La bataille de Marengo, d'après un témoin bourbonnais', *Bulletin de la société d'émulation du Bourbonnais*, xix (1911): 377–81.

Gachot, Edouard. *La deuxième Campagne d'Italie (1800)*. Paris: Perrin, 1899.

Gachot, Edouard. *Histoire militaire de Masséna: le siège de Gênes (1800); la guerre dans l'Apennin; journal du blocus; les opérations de Suchet*. Paris: Plon-Nourrit, 1908.

Gachot, Edouard, '1813: récit d'un témoin', *Revue des études napoléoniennes*, 16 (1919): 264–81.

Gaillon, Gabriel de. *Règne et chute de Buonaparte, fragment épique*. Paris: Delaunay, 1814.

Gainot, Bernard, 'Un itinéraire démocratique post-thermidorien: Bernard Metge', in Christine Le Bozec and Eric Wauters (eds), *Pour la Révolution française* (Rouen: Publications de l'Université de Rouen, 1998), pp. 93–106.

Gainot, Bernard, 'Les mots et les cendres; l'héroïsme au début du Consulat', *Annales historiques de la Révolution française*, 324 (2001): 127–38.

Gainot, Bernard, 'Réflexions sur une forme politique de transition (à propos de la conspiration Malet de 1808)', in Biard, Crépin and Gainot (eds), *La plume et le sabre*, pp. 513–24.

Gainot, Bernard, 'Le dernier voyage: rites ambulatoires et rites conjuratoires dans les cérémonies funéraires en l'honneur des généraux révolutionnaires', in Bourdin, Bernard and Caron (eds), *La voix et le geste*, pp. 97–113.

Gainot, Bernard, 'L'opposition militaire: autour des sociétés secrètes dans l'armée', *Annales historiques de la Révolution française*, 346 (2006): 45–58.

Gainot, Bernard, 'La République contre elle-même: figures et postures de l'opposition à Bonaparte au début du Consulat (novembre 1799–mars 1801)', in De Francesco (ed.), *Da Brumaio ai cento giorni*, pp. 143–55.

Gallaher, John G., 'Marshal Davout and the Second Bourbon Restoration', *French Historical Studies*, 6:3 (1970): 350–64.

Gallaher, John G. *The Iron Marshal: A Biography of Louis N. Davout*. London: Greenhill Books, 2000.

Gallaher, John G. *Napoleon's Enfant Terrible: General Dominique Vandamme*. Norman: University of Oklahoma Press, 2008.

Gallatin, James. *The Diary of James Gallatin, Secretary to Albert Gallatin, U.S. Envoy to France and England 1813–1827*. London: William Heinemann, 1916.

Gallo, Daniela (ed.). *Les vies de Dominique-Vivant Denon*. 2 vols. Paris: Musée du Louvre, 2001.

Gallo, Max. *Lettres d'amour: à Désirée, Joséphine, Marie et Marie-Louise*. Paris: l'Archipel, 2005.

Ganière, Paul. *Napoléon à Sainte-Hélène*. Paris: Perrin, 1998.

Garat, Dominique, 'Discours prononcé par Garat dans la séance du 23 frimaire', in Lombard de Langres, *Le dix-huit brumaire*, pp. 425–31.

Garçot, Maurice. *Le duel Moreau–Napoléon*. Paris: Nouvelles Editions Latines, 1951.

Gardier, Louis. *Journal de la campagne de Russie en 1812*. Paris: Teissèdre, 1999.

Garnier, Jacques, 'Récits du lieutenant Bressolles sur la campagne de 1813', *Revue de l'Institut Napoléon*, 135 (1979): 57–65.

Garnier, Jacques, 'Campagne de 1813 en Allemagne', in Tulard (ed.), *Dictionnaire Napoléon*, pp. 350–5.

Garnier, Jacques, 'Marengo', in Tulard (ed.), *Dictionnaire Napoléon*, pp. 1135–7.

Garnier, Jean-Paul. *Murat, roi de Naples*. Paris: Plon, 1959.

Garrett, Clarke. *Respectable Folly: Millenarians and the French Revolution in France and England*. Baltimore: Johns Hopkins University Press, 1975.

Garrioch, David. *The Making of Revolutionary Paris*. Berkeley: University of California Press, 2002.

Gates, David. *The Spanish Ulcer: A History of the Peninsular War*. London: Allen & Unwin, 1986.

Gates, David. *The Napoleonic Wars, 1803–1815*. London: Arnold, 1997.

Gaubert, Henri. *Conspirateurs au temps de Napoléon Ier*. Paris: Flammarion, 1962.

Gaubert, Henri. *Le sacre de Napoléon Ier*. Paris: Flammarion, 1964.

Gauchet, Marcel. *La révolution des pouvoirs: la souveraineté, le peuple et la représentation, 1789–1799*. Paris: Gallimard, 1995.

Gaudin, Martin-Michel-Charles. *Mémoires, souvenirs, opinions et écrits du Duc de Gaëte*. 2 vols. Paris: Baudoin, 1826.

Gautier-Sauzin, A. *Discours prononcé par le maire de Montauban, le 18 brumaire an X, jour de la fête de la Paix*. Montauban: Impr. de C. Crosilhes, an X.

Gawthrop, Richard L. *Pietism and the Making of Eighteenth-Century Prussia*. Cambridge: Cambridge University Press, 1993.

Genlis, Madame de. *De l'esprit des étiquettes de l'ancienne cour et des usages du monde de ce temps*. Paris: Mercure de France, 1996.

Gerard-Powell, Véronique, 'Les prises d'œuvres d'art en Espagne pendant l'occupation napoléonienne: diversité des responsables, diversité des choix', in Pontet, *Napoléon, Bayonne et l'Espagne*, pp. 389–98.

Germer, Stefan, 'On marche dans ce tableau: zur Konstituierung des "Realistischen" in den napoleonischen Darstellungen von Jacques-Louis David', in Gersmann and Kohle (eds), *Frankreich 1800*, pp. 81–103.

Gershoy, Leo. *Bertrand Barère: A Reluctant Terrorist*. Princeton: Princeton University Press, 1962.

Gersmann, Gudrun and Kohle, Hubertus (eds). *Frankreich 1800: Gesellschaft, Kultur, Mentalitäten*. Stuttgart: Franz Steiner, 1990.

Gerson, Stéphane, 'In Praise of Modest Men: Self-Display and Self-Effacement in Nineteenth-Century France', *French History*, 20:2 (2006): 182–203.

Gerstein, Marc, 'Le regard consolateur du grand homme', in Dupuy (ed.), *Dominique-Vivant Denon*, pp. 321–31.

Gielgud, Adam (ed.). *Memoirs of Prince Adam Czartoryski and his Correspondence with Alexander I*. 2 vols. London: Remington, 1888.

Gildea, Robert. *The Past in French History*. New Haven: Yale University Press, 1994.

Gill, Conrad, 'The Relations between England and France in 1802', *English Historical Review*, 24 (1909): 61–78.

Gill, John H. *1809: Thunder on the Danube: Napoleon's Defeat of the Habsburgs*. 3 vols. Barnsley: Frontline, 2008–10.

Gille, Philippe. *Mémoires d'un conscrit de 1808*. Paris: Victor-Havard, 1892.

Girard, Louis. *La Garde nationale*. Paris: Plon, 1964.

Girard, Philippe R., 'Napoléon Bonaparte and the Emancipation Issue in Saint-Domingue, 1799–1803', *French Historical Studies*, 32 (2009): 587–618.

Girard, Philippe R. *The Slaves Who Defeated Napoleon: Toussaint Louverture and the Haitian War of Independence, 1801–1804*. Tuscaloosa: University of Alabama Press, 2011.

Girardin, Stanislas. *Mémoires, Journal et Souvenirs*. 2 vols. Paris: Moutardier, 1829.

Giraud, Commandant. *Le carnet de campagne du commandant Giraud*. Paris: Téqui, 1899.

Girod de l'Ain, Jean-Marie-Félix. *Dix ans de souvenirs militaires de 1805 à 1815*. Paris: J. Dumaine, 1873.

Girod de l'Ain, Gabriel. *Joseph Bonaparte: le roi malgré lui*. Paris: Perrin, 1970.

Giroud, Frédéric, 'Bonaparte franchissant le Grand-Saint-Bernard ou la construction d'une légende confrontée à la réalité du passage', in Messiez and Sorrel (eds), *La deuxième campagne d'Italie*, pp. 101–12.

Glaudes, Pierre, 'Joseph de Maistre, letter writer', in Carolina Armenteros and Richard A. Lebrun (eds), *The New enfant du siècle: Joseph de Maistre as a Writer* (St Andrews: Centre for French History and Culture, 2010), pp. 47–74.

Glover, Richard, 'The French Fleet, 1807–1814: Britain's Problem; and Madison's Opportunity', *Journal of Modern History*, 39 (1967): 233–52.

Glover, Richard. *Britain at Bay: Defence against Bonaparte, 1803–14*. London: Allen & Unwin, 1973.

Godechot, Jacques, 'L'Empire napoléonien', *Recueils de la Société Jean Bodin*, 31 (1973): 433–55.

Godel, Jean, 'L'Eglise selon Napoléon', *Revue d'histoire moderne et contemporaine*, 17 (1970): 837–45.

Godlewski, Guy. *Napoléon à l'île d'Elbe: 300 jours d'exil*. Paris: Nouveau Monde éditions, 2003.

Goethe, Johann Wolfgang. *Goethe: The Collected Works*. 11 vols. Princeton: Princeton University Press, 1987.

Golovin, Barbe Nikolaévna, comtesse. *Souvenirs de la comtesse Golovine, née princesse Galitzine, 1766–1821*. Paris: Plon-Nourrit, 1910.

Gonneville, Aymar-Olivier Le Harivel de. *Souvenirs militaires du colonel de Gonneville*. Paris: Didier, 1875.

Goodden, Angelica. *Madame de Staël: The Dangerous Exile*. Oxford: Oxford University Press, 2008.

Gotteri, Nicole (ed.). *La police secrète du Premier Empire*. 7 vols. Paris: H. Champion, 1997–2004.

Gotteri, Nicole. *Soult: maréchal d'Empire et homme d'Etat*. Charenton: B. Giovanangeli, 2000.

Gotteri, Nicole. *Napoléon et le Portugal*. Paris: B. Giovanangeli, 2004.

Gotteri, Nicole. *Napoléon: stratégie politique et moyens de gouvernement: essai*. Paris: SPM, 2007.

Gough, Hugh. *The Newspaper Press in the French Revolution*. London: Routledge, 1988.

Gourgaud, Gaspard. *Napoléon et la grande-armée en Russie ou Examen critique de l'ouvrage de M. le comte Ph. de Ségur*. Brussels: H. Tarlier, 1825.

Gourgaud, Gaspard. *Journal de Sainte-Hélène, 1815–1818*. 2 vols. Paris: Flammarion, 1944.

Gourmen, Pierre, 'La second campagne d'Italie', in *Napoléon, de l'histoire à la légende*, pp. 47–57.

Gouvion Saint-Cyr, Laurent de. *Mémoires pour servir à l'histoire militaire sous le Directoire, le Consulat et l'Empire*. 4 vols. Paris: Anselin, 1831.

Grainger, John D. *The Amiens Truce: Britain and Bonaparte, 1801–1803*. Woodbridge: Boydell Press, 2004.

Grand, Roger. *La Chouannerie de 1815*. Paris: Perrin, 1942.

Grand-Carteret, John. *L'aiglon en images et dans la fiction poétique et dramatique*. Paris: Charpentier et Fasquelle, 1901.

Grandmaison, Geoffroy de. *Napoléon et les cardinaux noirs (1810–1814)*. Paris: Perrin, 1895.

Grandmaison, Geoffroy de (ed.). *Correspondance du comte de La Forest, ambassadeur de France en Espagne, 1808–1813*. 7 vols. Paris: A. Picard et fils, 1905–13.

Grandmaison, Geoffroy de. *L'Espagne et Napoléon*. 3 vols. Paris: Plon-Nourrit, 1908–31.

Granier, Herman, 'Die Franzosen in Berlin 1806–1808', *Hohenzollern-Jahrbuch*, 9 (1905): 1–43.

Granville, Castalia Countess (ed.). *Lord Granville Leveson Gower: Private Correspondence, 1781–1821*. 2 vols. London: J. Murray, 1916.

Gray, Phillip John, 'Revolutionism as Revisionism: Early British Views of Bonaparte, 1796–1803', MA dissertation, University of Canterbury, 1995.

Gregory, Desmond. *Sicily: The Insecure Base: A History of the British Occupation of Sicily, 1806–1815*. Madison: Fairleigh Dickinson University Press, 1988.

Gregory, Desmond. *Napoleon's Italy*. Madison: Fairleigh Dickinson University Press, 2001.

Greig, James (ed.). *The Farington Diary*. 8 vols. London: Hutchinson, 1923.

Greiling, Werner. *Napoleon in Thüringen: Wirkung, Wahrnehmung, Erinnerung*. Erfurt: Landeszentrale für politische Bildung Thüringen, 2006.

Grell, Chantal, 'The *sacre* of Louis XVI: The End of a Myth', in Michael Schaich (ed.), *Monarchy and Religion: The Transformation of Royal Culture in Eighteenth-Century Europe* (Oxford: Oxford University Press, 2007), pp. 345–66.

Griffiths, Ralph A. (ed.). *In Conversation with Napoleon Bonaparte: J. H. Vivian's Visit to the Island of Elba*. Newport: South Wales Record Society, 2008.

Grigsby, Darcy Grimaldo, 'Rumor, Contagion, and Colonization in Gros's *Plague-Stricken of Jaffa* (1804)', *Representations*, 51 (1995): 1–46.

Grigsby, Darcy Grimaldo. *Extremities: Painting Empire in Post-Revolutionary France*. New Haven: Yale University Press, 2002.

Grimsted, Patricia Kennedy. *The Foreign Ministers of Alexander I: Political Attitudes and the Conduct of Russian Diplomacy, 1801–1825*. Berkeley and Los Angeles: University of California Press, 1969.

Griois, Lubin. *Mémoires du général Griois (1792–1822)*. 2 vols. Paris: Plon-Nourrit, 1909.

Grouchy, Emmanuel-Henri de. *Mémoires du maréchal de Grouchy*. 5 vols. Paris: E. Dentu, 1873–4.

Grunwald, Constantin de (ed.), 'Les débuts diplomatiques de Metternich à Paris', *Revue de Paris*, 4 (1936): 492–537.

Grunwald, Constantin de (ed.), 'La fin d'une ambassade, Metternich', *Revue de Paris*, 19–20 (1937): 481–513, 819–46.

Grunwald, Constantin de, 'Le mariage de Napoléon et de Marie-Louise', *Revue des Deux Mondes*, 38 (1937): 320–52.

Grunwald, Constantin de. *Alexandre Ier, le tsar mystique*. Paris: Amiot-Dumont, 1955.

Grunwald, Constantin de. *La campagne de Russie*. Paris: Julliard, 1964.

Grunwald, Constantin de. *Société et civilisation russes au XIXe siècle*. Paris: Seuil, 1975.

Gueniffey, Patrick. *Le Dix-huit Brumaire: l'épilogue de la Révolution française, 9–10 novembre 1799*. Paris: Gallimard, 2008.

Guerrini, Maurice. *Napoléon et Paris, trente ans d'histoire*. Paris: Téqui, 1967.

Guido, Artom. *Napoleon is Dead in Russia*. Trans. Muriel Grindrod. New York: Atheneum, 1970.

Guiffan, Jean. *Histoire de l'anglophobie en France: de Jeanne d'Arc à la vache folle*. Rennes: Terre de Brume, 2004.

Guillon, Edouard. *Les complots militaires sous le Consulat et l'Empire: d'après les documents inédits des archives*. Paris: E. Plon, Nourrit, 1894.

Gutch, Eliza and Peacock, Mabel. *Examples of Printed Folklore Concerning Lincolnshire*, vol. v of *County Folk-Lore*. London: David Nutt, 1908.

Guyot, Claude Etienne. *Carnets de campagnes (1792–1815)*. Paris: Teissèdre, 1999.

Hachette, Alfred, 'Sur un militaire qui, en passant à Sisteron, donnait à son chien le nom de Bonaparte', *Revue des études napoléoniennes*, 12 (1917): 116–18.

Haegele, Vincent (ed.). *Napoléon et Joseph Bonaparte: correspondance intégrale 1784–1818*. Paris: Tallandier, 2007.

Haegele, Vincent. *Napoléon et Joseph Bonaparte: le pouvoir et l'ambition*. Paris: Tallandier, 2010.

Hagemann, Karen, 'Of "Manly Valor" and "German Honor": Nation, War and Masculinity in the Age of the Prussian Uprising against Napoleon', *Central European History*, 30:2 (1997): 187–220.

Hagemann, Karen, '"Deutsche Heldinnen": Patriotisch-nationales Frauenhandeln in der Zeit der antinapoleonischen Kriege', in Ute Planert (ed.), *Nation, Politik und Geschlecht: Frauen-bewegungen und Nationalismus in der Moderne* (Frankfurt: Campus, 2000), pp. 86–112.

Hagemann, Karen, 'A Valorous *Volk* Family: The Nation, the Military, and the Gender Order in Prussia in the Time of the Anti-Napoleonic Wars, 1806–15', in Ida Blom, Karen Hagemann and Catherine Hall (eds), *Gendered Nations: Nationalisms and Gender Order in the Long Nineteenth Century* (Oxford: Berg, 2000), pp. 179–205.

Hagemann, Karen. *'Mannlicher Muth und Teutsche Ehre': Nation, Militär und Geschlecht zur Zeit der Antinapoleonischen Kriege Preußens*. Paderborn: Verlag Ferdinand Schöningh, 2002.

Hagemann, Karen, 'Female Patriots: Women, War and the Nation in the Period of the Prussian–German Anti-Napoleonic Wars', *Gender & History*, 16 (2004): 396–424.

Hagemann, Karen, '"Be Proud and Firm, Citizens of Austria!" Patriotism and Masculinity in Texts of the "Political Romantics" Written during Austria's Anti-Napoleonic Wars', *German Studies Review*, 29 (2006): 41–62.

Hagemann, Karen, 'Occupation, Mobilization, and Politics: The Anti-Napoleonic Wars in Prussian Experience, Memory, and Historiography', *Central European History*, 39:4 (2006): 589–94.

Hagemann, Karen, '"Heroic Virgins" and "Bellicose Amazons": Armed Women, the Gender Order and the German Public during and after the Anti-Napoleonic Wars', *European History Quarterly*, 37 (2007): 507–27.

Hagemann, Karen, '"Unimaginable Horror and Misery": The Battle of Leipzig in October 1813 in Civilian Experience and Perception', in Forrest, Hagemann and Rendall (eds), *Soldiers, Citizens and Civilians*, pp. 157–78.

Hague, William. *William Pitt the Younger*. London: HarperCollins, 2004.

Hahn, Roger. *Pierre Simon Laplace 1749–1827: A Determined Scientist*. Cambridge, Mass.: Harvard University Press, 2005.

Hales, E. E. Y. *Napoleon and the Pope: The Story of Napoleon and Pius VII*. London: Eyre & Spottiswoode, 1962.

Hall, Christopher D., 'Addington at War: Unspectacular But Not Unsuccessful', *Historical Research*, 61 (1988): 306–15.

Halpérin, Jean-Louis. *L'impossible code civil*. Paris: Presses Universitaires de France, 1992.

Halpérin, Jean-Louis, 'Le codificateur au travail, Cambacérès et ses sources', in Chatel de Brancion (ed.), *Cambacérès, fondateur de la justice*, pp. 154–65.

Hammer, Helmut. *Oesterreichs Propaganda zum Feldzug 1809: ein Beitrag zur Geschichte der politischen Propaganda*. Munich: Zeitungswissenschaftliche Vereinigung, 1935.

Hampson, Norman, 'The French Revolution and the Nationalization of Honour', in M. R. D. Foot (ed.), *War and Society: Historical Essays in Honour and Memory of J. R. Western, 1928–1971* (London: Elek, 1973), pp. 199–213.

Hampson, Norman. *The Perfidy of Albion: French Perceptions of England during the French Revolution*. Basingstoke: Macmillan, 1998.

Handelsman, Marcel. *Napoléon et la Pologne, 1806–1807*. Paris: Félix Alcan, 1909.

Hanoteau, Jean, 'Une nouvelle relation de l'entrevue de Napoléon et de Metternich à Dresde', *Revue d'histoire diplomatique*, 67 (1933): 421–40.

Hanoteau, Jean (ed.). *Memoirs of General de Caulaincourt, Duke of Vicenza*. 3 vols. London: Cassell, 1950.

Hanson, Paul R. *The Jacobin Republic under Fire: The Federalist Revolt in the French Revolution*. University Park, Pa.: Pennsylvania State University Press, 2003.

Hantraye, Jacques. *Les cosaques aux Champs-Elysées: l'occupation de la France après la chute de Napoléon*. Paris: Belin, 2005.

Hantraye, Jacques, 'Les formes d'information du pouvoir et les représentations de la guerre au cours de la crise de 1813–1814 en France', *Cahiers du GERHICO*, 9 (2006): 97–113.

Hantraye, Jacques (ed.). *Le récit d'un civil dans la campagne de France de 1814: les 'Lettres historiques' de Pierre Dardenne (1768–1857)*. Paris: CTHS, 2008.

Harari, Yuval Noah. *The Ultimate Experience: Battlefield Revelations and the Making of Modern War Culture, 1450–2000*. Basingstoke and New York: Palgrave Macmillan, 2008.

Harpaz, Ephraïm. *L'école libérale sous la Restauration: le 'Mercure' et la 'Minerve', 1817–1820*. Geneva: Droz, 1968.

Harpaz, Ephraïm (ed.). *Recueil d'articles, 1795–1817*. Geneva: Droz, 1978.

Hartley, Janet M., 'Is Russia Part of Europe? Russian Perceptions of Europe in the Reign of Alexander I', *Cahiers du monde russe et soviétique*, xxxiii (1992): 369–85.

Hartley, Janet M. *Alexander I*. London: Longman, 1994.

Hartley, Janet M., 'Napoleonic Prisoners in Russia', in Natalia Iu. Erpyleva, Maryann E. Gashi-Butler and Jane E. Henderson (eds), *Forging a Common Legal Destiny: Liber Amicorum in Honour of William E. Butler* (London: Simmonds & Hill, 2005), pp. 714–23.

Harvey, A. D., 'The Ministry of All the Talents: The Whigs in Office, February 1806 to March 1807', *Historical Journal*, 15:4 (1972): 619–48.

Harvey, A. D., 'European Attitudes to Britain during the French Revolutionary and Napoleonic Era', *History*, 63 (1978): 356–65.

Harvey, A. D. *Collision of Empires: Britain in Three World Wars, 1793–1945*. London: Hambledon Press, 1992.

Hase, Alexander von, 'Friedrich (v.) Gentz: vom Übergang nach Wien bis zu den "Fragmenten des Gleichgewichts" (1802–1806)', *Historische Zeitschrift*, 211 (1970): 589–615.

Hatin, Eugène. *Histoire politique et littéraire de la presse en France*. 8 vols. Paris: Poulet-Malassis et de Broise, 1859–61.

Hausmann, Franz Joseph. *A Soldier for Napoleon: The Campaigns of Lieutenant Franz Joseph Hausmann, 7th Bavarian Infantry*. Trans. Cynthia Joy Hausmann and ed. John H. Gill. London: Greenhill Books, 1998.

Haussonville, Joseph Othenin Bernard de Cléron, comte d', 'L'Eglise Romaine et le premier Empire 1800–1814: le Pape à Savone', *Revue des Deux Mondes*, 67 (1867): 32–66.

Haussonville, Joseph Othenin Bernard de Cléron, comte de. *L'Eglise romaine et le Premier Empire, 1800–1814*. 5 vols. Paris: Michel Lévy frères, 1868–9.

Hauterive, Alexandre-Maurice, comte d'. *Observations sur le manifeste du roi d'Angleterre*. Paris: Chez les Marchands de Nouveautés, 1802.

Hauterive, Ernest de. *La police secrète du premier Empire, bulletins quotidiens adressés par Fouché à l'Empereur*. 5 vols. Paris: Clavreuil, 1908–64.

Hautpoul, Alphonse-Henri, marquis d'. *Mémoires du général marquis Alphonse d'Hautpoul*. Paris: Perrin, 1906.

Hazareesingh, Sudhir. *The Legend of Napoleon*. London: Granta, 2004.

Hazareesingh, Sudhir. *The Saint-Napoleon: Celebrations of Sovereignty in Nineteenth-Century France*. Cambridge, Mass.: Harvard University Press, 2004.

Healey, F. G. *Rousseau et Napoléon*. Geneva: Droz, 1957.

Heckscher, Eli F. *The Continental System: An Economic Interpretation*. Oxford: Clarendon Press, 1922.

Helfert, Joseph Alexander Freiherr von. *Maria Louise, Erzherzogin von Oesterreich, Kaiserin der Franzosen*. Vienna: W. Braumüller, 1873.

Helfert, Joseph Alexandre Freiherr von. *Napoleon I., Fahrt von Fontainebleau nach Elba, April– Mai 1814, mit Benützung der amtlichen Reiseberichte des kaiserlich österreichischen Commissars General Koller*. Vienna: W. Braumüller, 1874.

Hemardinquer, J.-J., 'Mort d'épuisement après Austerlitz', *Revue de l'Institut Napoléon*, 134 (1978): 115.

Hemmings, Frederick William John. *Theatre and State in France, 1760–1905*. Cambridge: Cambridge University Press, 1994.

Hempel Lipschutz, Ilse. *Spanish Painting and the French Romantics*. Cambridge, Mass.: Harvard University Press, 1972.

Hennequin, Philippe-Auguste. *Un peintre sous la Révolution et le premier Empire: mémoires de Philippe-Auguste Hennequin écrits par lui-même*. Paris: Calmann-Lévy, 1933.

Hennet, Léon and Martin, Emmanuel (eds). *Lettres interceptées par les Russes durant la campagne de 1812*. Paris: La Sabretache, 1913.

Hennet de Goutel, baron, 'Les derniers jours de l'Empire racontés par un Cent-Suisse, d'après le journal inédit de M. de Marsilly (1811–1816)', *Revue des études napoléoniennes*, 13 (1918): 271–95.

Hennings, Jan, 'The Semiotics of Diplomatic Dialogue: Pomp and Circumstance in Tsar Peter I's Visit to Vienna in 1698', *International History Review*, 30 (2008): 515–44.

Herbert, Robert, 'Baron Gros's Napoleon and Voltaire's Henri IV', in Francis Haskell and Robert Shackleton (eds), *The Artist and the Writer in France: Essays in Honour of Jean Seznec* (Oxford: Clarendon Press, 1974), pp. 52–75.

Herold, J. Christopher. *The Mind of Napoleon: A Selection from his Written and Spoken Words*. New York: Columbia University Press, 1955.

Hertault, Gérard and Douay, Abel. *Franc-maçonnerie et sociétés secrètes contre Napoléon: naissance de la nation allemande*. Paris: Nouveau Monde éditions, 2005.

Hicks, Peter, 'Un sacre sans pareil', in Lentz (ed.), *Le sacre de Napoléon*, pp. 101–39.

Hillemand, P., 'Napoleon a-t-il tenté de se suicider à Fontainebleau?', *Revue de l'Institut Napoléon*, 119 (1971): 71–8.

Hilt, Douglas. *The Troubled Trinity: Godoy and the Spanish Monarchs*. Tuscaloosa: University of Alabama Press, 1987.

His, Charles-Hyacinthe. *Théorie du monde politique, ou de la Science du gouvernement considérée comme science exact*. Paris: Schoell, 1806.

*Histoire de Napoléon Buonaparte, depuis sa naissance, en 1769, jusqu'à sa translation à l'île Sainte-Hélène, en 1815*. 4 vols. Paris: L.-G. Michaud, 1817–18.

Hobhouse, Christopher. *Fox*. London: Constable, 1947.

Hobhouse, John Cam. *The Substance of Some Letters Written by an Englishman Resident at Paris During the Last Reign of the Emperor Napoleon*, 2 vols. London: Ridgways, 1816.

Hobsbawm, Eric and Ranger, Terence (eds). *The Invention of Tradition*. Cambridge: Cambridge University Press, 1983.

Hocquellet, Richard. *Résistance et révolution durant l'occupation napoléonienne en Espagne, 1808–1812*. Paris: La Boutique de l'Histoire, 2001.

Hoffmann, Léon-François. *Romantique Espagne: l'image de l'Espagne en France entre 1800 et 1850* Paris: Presses Universitaires de France, 1961.

Hoffmeister, Johannes (ed.). *Briefe von und an Hegel*. 4 vols. Hamburg: Felix Meiner Verlag, 1952.

Hofschröer, Peter. *1815: The Waterloo Campaign: The German Victory, from Waterloo to the Fall of Napoleon*. London: Greenhill Books, 1999.

Höjer, T. T. *Bernadotte, maréchal de France*. Trans. from the Swedish by Lucien Maury. 2 vols. Paris: Plon, 1943.

Holland, Elizabeth Vassall, Lady. *The Spanish Journal of Elizabeth, Lady Holland*. London: Longmans, 1910.

Holland, Henry Richard, Lord. *Memoirs of the Whig Party during my Time*. 2 vols. London: Longman, 1852.

Holmes, Stephen, 'Two Concepts of Legitimacy: France after the Revolution', *Political Theory*, 10 (1982): 165–83.

Holtman, Robert B. *Napoleonic Propaganda*. Baton Rouge: Louisiana State University Press, 1950. Reprint New York: Greenwood Press, 1969.

Home, George. *Memoirs of an Aristocrat and Reminiscences of the Emperor Napoleon, by a Midshipman of the 'Bellerophon'*. London: Whittaker, 1838.

*Hommages poétiques à leurs majestés impériales et royales sur la naissance de S.M. le roi de Rome*. 2 vols. Paris: n.p., 1811.

Horn, Jeff, 'Le plébiscite de l'an VIII et la construction du système préfectoral', in Jessenne (ed.), *Du Directoire au Consulat*, iii. pp. 547–59.

Horne, Alistair. *How Far from Austerlitz? Napoleon 1805–1815*. New York: Macmillan, 1996.

Horne, Alistair. *Seven Ages of Paris*. New York: Vintage, 2004.

Horricks, Raymond. *Military Politics from Bonaparte to the Bourbons: The Life and Death of Michel Ney, 1769–1815*. New Brunswick: Transaction Publishers, 1995.

Horsley, Samuel. *The Watchers and the Holy Ones: A Sermon*. London: J. Hatchard, 1806.

Houssaye, Henry. *1815*. 3 vols. Paris: Perrin, 1893.

Houssaye, Henry. *Iéna et la campagne de 1806*. Paris: Bernard Giovanangelli, 1991, reprinted 1912.

Houssaye, Henry. *1814*. Paris: Perrin, 1937.

Housset, Georges. *La Garde d'honneur de 1813–1814: histoire du corps et de ses soldats*. Paris: B. Giovanangeli, 2009.

Hue, Gustave, 'Un complot de police sous le Consulat', *Les Contemporains* (10 October 1909): 139–64.

Huet, Valérie, 'Napoleon I: A New Augustus?', in Catherine Edwards (ed.), *Roman Presences: Receptions of Rome in European Culture, 1789–1945* (Cambridge: Cambridge University Press, 1999), pp. 53–69.

Hüffer, Hermann (ed.). *Die Schlacht von Marengo und der italienische Feldzug des Jahres 1800*. 3 vols. Leipzig: B. G. Teubner, 1900.

Hughes, Michael J., '"Vive la Republique, Vive l'Empereur!": Military Culture and Motivation in the Armies of Napoleon, 1803–1808', PhD dissertation, University of Illinois at Urbana-Champaign, 2005.

Hughes, Michael J., 'Making Frenchmen into Warriors: Martial Masculinity in Napoleonic France', in Christopher E. Forth and Bernard Taithe (eds), *French Masculinities: History, Culture and Politics* (Basingstoke: Palgrave Macmillan, 2007), pp. 51–66.

Hughes, Michael J. *Forging Napoleon's Grande Armée: Motivation, Military Culture, and Masculinity in the French Army, 1800–1808*. New York: New York University Press, 2012.

Hughes, Robert. *Goya*. London: Harvill Press, 2003.

Hugo, Abel, 'Souvenirs et mémoires sur Joseph Napoléon en 1811, 1812 et 1813', *Revue des Deux Mondes*, 1 (1833): 300–24.

Hugo, Victor. *Les misérables*. Trans. Charles E. Wilbour. New York: Random House, 1992.

Hulot, Frédéric. *Le maréchal Ney*. Paris: Pygmalion, 2000.

Hulot, Frédéric. *Le maréchal Davout*. Paris: Pygmalion, 2002.

Hulot, Frédéric. *Le maréchal Masséna*. Paris: Pygmalion, 2005.

Hulot, Frédéric. *Le maréchal Berthier*. Paris: Pygmalion, 2007.

Humbert, Jean-Marcel, 'Entre mythe et archéologie: la fortune statuaire égyptisante de Desaix et Kléber', in Jackie Pigeaud et Jean-Paul Barbe (eds), *Le culte des grands hommes au XVIIIe siècle* (Paris: Institut universitaire de France, 1998), pp. 219–32.

Hunt, Lynn. *Politics, Culture, and Class in the French Revolution*. Berkeley: University of California Press, 1984.

Hunt, Lynn. *The Family Romance of the French Revolution*. Berkeley: University of California Press, 1993.

Hyde de Neuville, Jean-Guillaume. *Mémoires et souvenirs du baron Hyde de Neuville*. Paris: E. Plon, Nourrit, 1892.

Hynes, Samuel. *The Soldier's Tale: Bearing Witness to Modern War*. New York: Allen Lane, 1997.

Ibbeken, Rudolf. *Preussen 1807–1813: Staat und Volk als Idee und in Wirklichkeit: Darstellung und Dokumentation*. Berlin: G. Grote, 1970.

Ideville, Henry d'. *Le maréchal Bugeaud, d'après sa correspondance intime et des documents inédits. 1784–1849*. Paris: Firmin-Didot, 1885.

Ihl, Olivier, 'The Market of Honors: On the Bicentenary of the Legion of Honor', *French Politics, Culture & Society*, 24 (2006): 8–26.

Ihl, Olivier. *Le mérite et la République: essai sur la société des émules*. Paris: Gallimard, 2007.

Iiams, Thomas M. *Peacemaking from Vergennes to Napoleon: French Foreign Relations in the Revolutionary Era, 1774–1814*. Huntington, NY: R. E. Krieger, 1979.

Ilchester, Earl of. *Journal of Elizabeth Lady Holland*. 2 vols. London: Longmans, Green, 1908.

Ilchester, Earl of. *The Home of the Hollands, 1605–1820*. London: J. Murray, 1937.

Imbert de Saint-Amand, Arthur-Léon. *Les femmes des Tuileries: la femme du Premier consul*. Paris: E. Dentu, 1884.

Imbert de Saint-Amand, Arthur-Léon. *Les beaux jours de l'impératrice Marie-Louise: les femmes des Tuileries*. Paris: E. Dentu, 1885.

Ingrao, Charles. *The Habsburg Monarchy, 1618–1815*. Cambridge: Cambridge University Press, 1994.

Iskjul', Sergei Nikolaivich, 'Rußland und die Oldenburger Krise 1810–11', *Oldenburger Jahrbuch*, 85 (1985): 89–110.

Istasse, Cédric, 'Les "mariages de la Rosière" dans le département de Sambre-et-Meuse: indices sur la réinsertion sociale des anciens soldats de Napoléon Ier', *Napoleonica. La Revue*, 1:4 (2009): 11–29.

Iung, Théodore (ed.). *Lucien Bonaparte et ses mémoires, 1775–1840: d'après les papiers déposés aux Archives étrangères et d'autres documents inédits*. 3 vols. Paris: Charpentier, 1882–3.

J.C. *Précis historique-chronologique du voyage du saint-père le pape Pie VII en France*. Brussels: Pauwels, 1804.

Jackson, Sir George. *The Diaries and Letters of Sir George Jackson*. 2 vols. London: R. Bentley & son, 1872.

Jackson, George. *The Bath Archives. A Further Selection from the Diaries and Letters of Sir George Jackson, K.C.H., from 1809 to 1816*. 2 vols. London: Bentley, 1873.

Jainchill, Andrew. *Reimagining Politics after the Terror: The Republican Origins of French Liberalism*. Ithaca: Cornell University Press, 2008.

Jal, Auguste. *Souvenirs d'un homme de lettres (1795–1873)*. Paris: L. Techener, 1877.

James, Walter Haweis. *The Campaign of 1815, Chiefly in Flanders*. Edinburgh: W. Blackwood, 1908.

Jeismann, Michael. *La patrie de l'ennemi: la notion d'ennemi national et la représentation de la nation en Allemagne et en France de 1792 à 1918*. Trans. Dominique Lassaigne. Paris: CNRS Editions, 1997.

Jenkins, Brian. *Nationalism in France: Class and Nation since 1789*. Savage, Md: Barnes & Noble, 1990.

Jessen, Olaf. *'Preußens Napoleon'? Ernst von Rüchel, 1754–1823: Krieg im Zeitalter der Venunft*. Paderborn: Verlag Ferdinand Schöningh, 2007.

Jessenne, Jean-Pierre (ed.). *Du Directoire au Consulat*, vol. iii: *Brumaire dans l'histoire du lien politique et de l'Etat-nation*. Villeneuve d'Ascq: Centre de Recherche sur l'Histoire de l'Europe du Nord-Ouest, 2001.

Johns, Christopher M. S. *Antonio Canova and the Politics of Patronage in Revolutionary and Napoleonic Europe*. Berkeley: University of California Press, 1998.

Johnson, David, 'Amiens 1802: The Phoney Peace', *History Today*, 52 (2002): 20–6.

Johnson, Dorothy. *Jacques-Louis David: Art in Metamorphosis*. Princeton: Princeton University Press, 1993.

Jolyet, Jean-Baptiste, 'Episodes des guerres en Catalogne (1808–1812)', *Revue des études napoléoniennes*, 16 (1919): 182–214, 312–30.

Jomini, Antoine Henri baron de. *The Art of War*. Trans. G. H. Mendell and W. P. Craighill. Philadelphia: Lippincott, 1862.

Jomini, Antoine Henri baron de. *Précis politique et militaire des campagnes de 1812 à 1814*. 2 vols. Geneva: Slatkine, 1975.

Joor, Johann, 'Les Pays-Bas contre l'impérialisme napoléonien: les soulèvements anti-Français entre 1806 et 1813', *Annales historiques de la Révolution française*, 326 (2001): 161–71.

Joor, Johann, 'Le système continental et sa signification pour le royaume de Hollande', in Jourdan (ed.), *Louis Bonaparte*, pp. 131–44.

Jordan, David P. *Napoleon and the Revolution*. Basingstoke: Palgrave Macmillan, 2012.

Jorgensen, Christer. *The Anglo-Swedish Alliance against Napoleonic France*. Basingstoke: Palgrave Macmillan, 2004.

Josselson, Michael and Josselson, Diana. *The Commander: A Life of Barclay de Tolly*. Oxford: Oxford University Press, 1980.

Jouin, Henry. *David d'Angers, sa vie, son oeuvre, ses écrits et ses contemporains*. Paris: E. Plon, 1878.

Jourdan, Annie, 'Le sacre ou le pacte social', in *Napoléon le sacre*, pp. 25–33.

Jourdan, Annie. *L'empire de Napoléon*. Paris: Flammarion, 2000.

Jourdan, Annie, 'Bonaparte et Desaix, une amitié inscrite dans la pierre des monuments?', *Annales historiques de la Révolution française*, 324 (2001): 139–50.

Jourdan, Annie, 'Napoleon and his Artists', in Howard Brown and Judith Miller (eds), *Taking Liberties: Problems of a New Order from the French Revolution to Napoleon* (Manchester: Manchester University Press, 2002), pp. 185–204.

Jourdan, Annie, 'Le Premier Empire: un nouveau pacte social', *Cités: philosophie, politique, histoire*, 20 (2004): 51–64.

Jourdan, Annie (ed.). *Louis Bonaparte: roi de Hollande, 1806–1810*. Paris: Nouveau Monde éditions/Fondation Napoléon, 2010.

Jourdan, Annie, 'La Hollande en tant qu'"objet de désir" et le roi Louis, fondateur d'une monarchie nationale', in Annie Jourdan (ed.), *Louis Bonaparte*, pp. 9–30.

Jourdan, Annie, 'The Napoleonic Empire in the Age of Revolution: The Contrast of Two National Representations', in Michael Broers, Peter Hicks and Agustin Guimerá (eds), *The Napoleonic Empire and the New European Political Culture* (Basingstoke: Palgrave Macmillan, 2012), pp. 313–26.

Jourquin, Jacques, 'L'incendie de l'ambassade d'Autriche, 1er juillet 1810', *Napoleon Ier*, 8 (May–June 2001): 56–62.

Joux, Pierre de. *Discours de bénédiction, de reconnaissance et d'actions de grâces pour l'anniversaire de la naissance de l'empereur Napoléon-le-Grand*. Nantes: Busseuil jeune, n.d.

Joux, Pierre de. *La Providence et Napoléon, ou les victoires d'Ulm, d'Austerlitz, de Jena, de Golymin, du Pultusck, de Dantzick, d'Eylau et de Friedland, ainsi que les fêtes du Sacre*. Paris: Gautier et Bretin, 1808.

*Jugement sur les affaires d'Espagne tel que le portera lu postérité, par un Espagnol impartial*. N.p., 1808.

Jullien, Marc-Antoine. *From Jacobin to Liberal: Marc-Antoine Jullien, 1775–1848*. Ed. and trans. R. R. Palmer. Princeton: Princeton University Press, 1993.

Junkelmann, Marcus. *Napoleon und Bayern: von den Anfängen des Königreiches.* Regensburg: Verlag Friedrich Pustet, 1985.

Jupp, Peter. *Lord Grenville: 1759–1834.* Oxford: Clarendon Press, 1985.

Kabakova, Galina, 'Mangeur de chandelles: l'image du cosaque au XIXe siècle', in Katia Dmitrieva and Michel Espagne (eds), *Transferts culturels triangulaires France–Allemagne–Russie* (Paris: Editions de la Maison des sciences de l'homme, 1996), pp. 207–30.

Kagan, Frederick W. *The End of the Old Order: Napoleon and Europe, 1801–1805.* Cambridge, Mass.: Da Capo Press, 2006.

Kahlenberg, Friedrich, 'Preußen als Filmsujet in der Propagandasprache der NS-Zeit', in Axel Marquardt and Hans Rathsack (eds), *Preußen im Film* (Hamburg: Rowohlt, 1981), pp. 135–63.

Kale, Steven D., 'Women, the Public Sphere, and the Persistence of Salons', *French Historical Studies*, 25:1 (2002): 115–48.

Kale, Steven D., 'Women, Salons, and the State in the Aftermath of the French Revolution', *Journal of Women's History*, 13:4 (2002): 54–80.

Kale, Steven D. *French Salons: High Society and Political Sociability from the Old Regime to the Revolution of 1848.* Baltimore: Johns Hopkins University Press, 2004.

Kaplow, Jeffry. *Elbeuf during the Revolutionary Period: History and Social Structure.* Baltimore: Johns Hopkins University Press, 1964.

Karila-Cohen, Pierre. *L'état des esprits: l'invention de l'enquête politique en France, 1814–1848.* Rennes: Presses Universitaires de Rennes, 2008.

Karr, L. J. *Des cosaques, ou Détails historiques sur les moeurs, coutumes, vêtemens, armes . . . recueillis de l'allemand.* Paris: Lebègue, 1814.

Kauffmann, Jean-Paul. *La chambre noire de Longwood: le voyage à Sainte-Hélène.* Paris: Le Table ronde, 1997.

Keep, John L. H. *Soldiers of the Tsar: Army and Society in Russia, 1462–1874.* Oxford: Clarendon Press, 1985.

Kerautret, Michel, 'Frédéric II et l'opinion française (1800–1870): la compétition posthume avec Napoléon', *Francia*, 28/2 (2001): 65–84.

Kerautret, Michel, 'Frankreich und der Fürstenkongreß', in Benl (ed.), *Der Erfurter Fürstenkongreß*, pp. 141–66.

Kerry, Henry William Edmund Petty-Fitzmaurice, Earl of (ed.). *The First Napoleon: Some Unpublished Documents from the Bowood Papers.* London: Constable, 1925.

King, David. *Vienna 1814: How the Conquerors of Napoleon Made Love, War, and Peace at the Congress of Vienna.* New York: Random House, 2009.

Kingston, Ralph. *Bureaucrats and Bourgeois Society: Office Politics and Individual Credit in France, 1789–1848.* Basingstoke: Palgrave Macmillan, 2012.

Kircheisen, Friedrich M., 'Pourquoi la guerre éclata en 1806 entre la France et la Prusse?', *Revue d'histoire diplomatique*, 43 (1929): 237–50.

Kissinger, Henry. *A World Restored: Metternich, Castlereagh and the Problems of Peace, 1812–22.* Cambridge, Mass.: Houghton Mifflin, 1957.

Kittstein, Lothar. *Politik im Zeitlater der Revolution: Untersuchungen zur preußischen Staatlichkeit 1792–1807.* Stuttgart: Franz Steiner Verlag, 2003.

Klang, Michael, 'Bavaria and the War of Liberation, 1813–1814', *French Historical Studies*, 4 (1965): 22–41.

Klinger, Andreas, Hahn, Hans-Werner and Schmidt, Georg (eds). *Das Jahr 1806 im europäischen Kontext: Balance, Hegemonie und politische Kulturen.* Weimar: Böhlau, 2008.

Kloocke, Kurt. *Benjamin Constant: une biographie intellectuelle.* Geneva: Droz, 1984.

Knapton, Ernest John. *Empress Josephine.* Cambridge, Mass.: Harvard University Press, 1964.

Knecht, R. J. *Francis I.* Cambridge: Cambridge University Press, 1982.

Knopper, Françoise and Mondot, Jean (eds). *L'Allemagne face au modèle français de 1789 à 1815.* Toulouse: Presses Universitaires du Mirail, 2008.

Kock, Paul de. *Mémoires de Ch.-Paul de Kock, écrits par lui-même.* Paris: E. Dentu, 1873.

Kohn, Hans H. *The Prelude to Nation-States: The French and German Experience, 1789–1815*. Princeton: D. van Nostrand, 1967.

Korshunova, Miliza, 'William Hastie in Russia', *Architectural History*, 17 (1974): 14–21, 53–6.

Kosáry, Domokos. *Napoléon et la Hongrie*. Budapest: Akadémiai kiadó, 1979.

Kotzebue, August von. *Souvenirs de Paris en 1804*. 2 vols. Paris: Barba, 1805.

Kraehe, Enno E. *Metternich's German Policy*. 2 vols. Princeton: Princeton University Press, 1963.

Kraus, Thomas R., 'Napoleon – Aachen – Karl der Große: Betrachtungen zur napoleonischen Herrschaftslegitimation', in Mario Kramp (ed.), *Krönungen: Könige in Aachen, Geschichte und Mythos*, 2 vols (Mainz: von Zabern, 2000), pp. 699–707.

Krauss, Alfred. *1805, der Feldzug von Ulm*. 2 vols. Vienna: L. W. Seidel, 1912.

Krettly, Elie. *Souvenirs historiques du capitaine Krettly: première réédition intégrale de l'édition de 1839*. Paris: Nouveau Monde éditions, 2003.

Kubnick, Henri. *Echec à l'Empereur, la conspiration de Malet*. Geneva: La Palatine, 1959.

*La bataille de Marengo et ses préliminaires racontés par quatre témoins*. Paris: Teissèdre, 1999.

La Borde, Alexandre-Louis-Joseph, comte de. *Quarante-huit heures de garde au château des Tuileries pendant les journées des 19 et 20 mars 1815, par un grenadier de la Garde Nationale*. Paris: Nicole et Le Normant, 1816.

Labaume, Eugène. *Relation circonstanciée de la campagne de Russie*. Paris: Pancoucke, 1815.

Laborde, Etienne. *Napoléon sa garde, ou relation du voyage de Fontainebleau à l'île d'Elbe en 1814, du séjour de l'empereur dans cette île, et de son retour en France à la tête du petit nombre de troupes qui l'y avaient accompagné*. Paris: A. Desrez, 1840.

Labretonnière, Emile. *Macédoine. Souvenirs du Quartier latin*. Paris: L. Marpon, 1863.

Lachouque, Henry. *Napoléon à Austerlitz*. Paris: G. Victor, 1961.

Lachouque, Henry. *Iéna*. Paris: G. Victor, 1962.

Lafayette, Marie-Joseph Gilbert du Motier, marquis de. *Mémoires, correspondance et manuscrits du général La Fayette*. 6 vols. Paris: H. Fournier, 1837–8.

Laffillard, Eugène Hyacinthe. *La veille d'une grande fête, hommage en 1 acte et en vers, mêlés de couplets*. Paris: Hénée, 1808.

Laflandre-Linden, Louise. *Napoléon et l'Île d'Elbe*. La Cadière d'Azur: Castel, 1989.

La Flize, 'Souvenirs de la Moskowa par un chirurgien de la Garde Impériale', *Feuilles d'histoire du XVIIe au XXe siècle*, 8 (1912): 419–26.

Lafon, Jean-Marc, 'Occupation, pacification et résistance en Andalousie', *Revue historique des armées*, 210 (1998): 13–26.

Lafon, Jean-Marc, 'Del Dos de Mayo madrileño a los pontones de Cádiz: violencias francesas y españolas a principios de la Guerra de la Independencia', in Ramírez and Jiménez (eds), *Baylen 1808–2008*, pp. 105–28.

Lagneau, Louis-Vincent. *Journal d'un chirurgien de la Grande Armée, 1803–1815*. Paris: Emile-Paul, 1913.

Lallemand, François-Antoine, 'Embarquement de l'Empereur à Rochefort. Notes du général baron Charles Lallemand', *Nouvelle Revue rétrospective*, 11 (1899): 1–14.

Lamar, Glenn J. *Jérôme Bonaparte: The War Years, 1800–1815*. Westport, Conn.: Greenwood Press, 2000.

Lamy, Etienne (ed.). *Mémoires de Aimée de Coigny*. Paris: Calmann-Lévy, 1902.

Landon, Charles-Paul. *Salon de 1810. Recueil de pièces choisies parmi les ouvrages exposés au Louvre le 5 novembre 1810*. Paris: chez l'auteur, 1810.

Landon, Charles-Paul. *Salon de 1812. Recueil de pièces choisies parmi les ouvrages exposés au Louvre le premier novembre 1812*. Paris: chez l'auteur, 1812.

Langeron, Alexandre-Louis Andrault de. *Mémoires de Langeron, général d'infanterie dans l'armée russe, campagnes de 1812, 1813, 1814*. Paris: Picard, 1902.

Langlois, Claude, 'Le plébiscite de l'an VIII ou le coup d'Etat du 18 pluviôse an VIII', *Annales historiques de la Révolution française*, 44 (1972): 43–65, 231–46, 390–415.

Langlois, Claude, 'Napoléon Bonaparte plébiscité?', in Léo Hamon and Guy Lobrichon (eds), *L'élection du chef de l'Etat en France de Hugues Capet à nos jours* (Paris: Beauchesne, 1988), pp. 81–93.

Langsam, Walter C. *The Napoleonic Wars and German Nationalism in Austria.* New York: Columbia University Press, 1930.

Lanzac de Laborie, Léon de. *La Domination française en Belgique: Directoire, Consulat, Empire, 1795–1814.* 2 vols. Paris: E. Plon, Nourrit, 1895.

Lanzac de Laborie, Léon de. *Paris sous Napoléon.* 8 vols. Paris: Plon-Nourrit, 1905–13.

La Parra López, Emilio, 'Méfiance entre les alliés: les relations Napoléon–Godoy (1801–1807)', *Annales historiques de la Révolution française*, 336 (2004): 19–35.

La Parra López, Emilio (ed.). *Actores de la Guerra de la Independencia. Dossier des Mélanges de la Casa de Velázquez,* nouvelle série, 38:1 (2008).

La Parra López, Emilio, 'Les pamphlets dans la guerre d'Espagne: discours des humbles ou discours vers les humbles?', in Jens Ivo Engels, Frédéric Monier and Natalie Petiteau (eds), *La politique vue d'en bas: pratiques privées et débats publics, 19e–20e siècles* (Paris: Armand Colin, 2011), pp. 47–61.

Larchey, Lorédan. *Les Suites d'une capitulation. Relations des captifs de Baylen et de la glorieuse retraite du 116e régiment.* Paris: Lombaerts, 1884.

Lardellier, Pascal. *Les miroirs du paon: rites et rhétoriques politiques dans la France de l'Ancien Régime.* Paris: H. Champion, 2003.

Larevellière-Lépeaux, Louis-Marie. *Mémoires de Larevellière-Lépeaux, membre du Directoire exécutif de la République française.* 3 vols. Paris: E. Plon, Nourrit, 1895.

Largeaud, Jean-Marc, 'Waterloo dans la culture française (1815–1914)', *Revista Napoleonica,* 1–2 (2000): 119–27.

Largeaud, Jean-Marc, 'Les temps retrouvés de Waterloo', *Revue d'histoire du XIXe siècle,* 25 (2002): 145–52.

Largeaud, Jean-Marc. *Napoléon et Waterloo: la défaite glorieuse de 1815 à nos jours.* Paris: La Boutique de l'Histoire, 2006.

Larreguy de Civrieux, Silvain. *Souvenirs d'un cadet (1812–1823).* Paris: Hachette, 1912.

Larrey, Dominique-Jean. *Mémoires de chirurgie militaire et campagnes.* 4 vols. Paris: J. Smith, 1812–17.

Larrey, Hippolyte. *Madame mère: essai historique,* 2 vols. Paris: E. Dentu, 1892.

La Sicotière, Léon de. *Louis de Frotté et les insurrections normandes, 1793–1832.* 3 vols. Paris: E. Plon, Nourrit, 1889.

Las Cases, Comte Emmanuel de. *Le Mémorial de Sainte-Hélène.* Ed. and annotated by Marcel Dunan. 2 vols. Paris: Flammarion, 1983.

Lathion, Lucien. *Bonaparte et ses soldats au Grand-Saint-Bernard.* Neuchatel: Victor Attinger, 1978.

Latreille, André. *Le Catéchisme Impériale de 1806: études et documents pour servir à l'histoire des rapports de Napoléon et du clergé concordataire.* Paris: Les Belles Lettres, 1935.

Latreille, André. *Napoléon et le Saint-Siège, 1801–1808: l'ambassade du Cardinal Fesch à Rome.* Paris: Félix Alcan, 1935.

Latreille, André. *L'Eglise catholique et la Révolution française.* 2 vols. Paris: Hachette, 1946–50.

Latreille, Camille. *L'opposition religieuse au Concordat, de 1792 à 1803.* Paris: Hachette, 1910.

Laughlin, Robert M. *Beware the Great Horned Serpent!: Chiapas under the Threat of Napoleon.* Albany, NY: Institute for Mesoamerican Studies, University at Albany, 2003.

Laugier, Jérôme-Roland. *Les cahiers du capitaine Laugier. De la guerre et de l'anarchie, ou Mémoires historiques des campagnes et aventures du 27e Régiment d'Infanterie légère.* Aix: J. Remondet-Aubin, 1893.

Lauthonnye, Frédéric-Charles-Louis-François de Paule, commandant de, 'Ma vie militaire (1789–1860)', *Carnet de la Sabretache,* 10 (1911): 320–52.

Laux, Stephan, 'Das Patrozinium "Saint Napoléon" in Neersen (1803–1856): ein Beitrag zur Rezeption der napoleonischen Propaganda im Rheinland', in Jörg Engelbrecht and Stephan Laux (eds), *Landes- und Reichsgeschichte: Festschrift für Hansgeorg Molitor zum 65. Geburtstag* (Bielefeld: Verlag für Regionalgeschichte, 2004), pp. 351–81.

Lavalette, Antoine Marie Chamans, comte de. *Mémoires et souvenirs du Cte Lavallette, ancien aide-de-camp de Napoléon, directeur des postes sous le premier Empire et pendant les Cent-Jours*. Paris: Société parisienne d'éditions, 1905.

Lavalley, Gaston. *Napoléon et la disette de 1812: à propos d'une émeute aux halles de Caen*. Paris: A. Picard, 1896.

Lavaux, François. *Mémoires de campagne (1793–1814)*. Paris: Arléa, 2004.

Laveissière, Sylvain et al. *Le Sacre de Napoléon peint par David*. Paris: Musée du Louvre, 2004.

Laven, David and Riall, Lucy (eds). *Napoleon's Legacy: Problems of Government in Restoration Europe*. Oxford: Berg, 2000.

Le Bourhis, Katell (ed.). *The Age of Napoleon: Costume from Revolution to Empire, 1789–1815*. New York: Metropolitan Museum of Art, 1989.

Le Brun, Jacques. *Le pouvoir d'abdiquer: essai sur la déchéance volontaire*. Paris: Gallimard, 2009.

Lecestre, Léon. *Lettres inédites de Napoléon Ier (an VIII–1815)*. 2 vols. Paris: E. Plon, Nourrit, 1897.

Le Clère, Marcel, 'Comment opérait la police de Fouché', *Revue de criminologie et de police technique*, 1 (1951): 33–6.

Lecointe de Laveau, G. *Moscou avant et après l'incendie, notice contenant une description de cette capitale, des moeurs de ses habitans, des événemens qui se passèrent pendant l'incendie et des malheurs qui accablèrent l'armée française pendant la retraite de 1812*. Paris: Gide fils, 1814.

Lecomte, Louis-Henry. *Napoléon et l'Empire racontés par le théâtre, 1797–1899*. Paris: J. Raux, 1900.

Lecomte, Pierre-Charles. *Les Fastes du génie militaire dirigés par l'héroïsme . . . de Napoléon le Grand*. Paris: the author, 1808.

Ledbury, Mark (ed.). *David after David: Essays on the Later Work*. Williamstown, Mass.: Sterling and Francine Clark Art Institute, 2007.

Ledoux-Lebard, Guy and Christian, 'Les tableaux du concours institué par Bonaparte en 1802 pour célébrer le rétablissement du culte', *Archives de l'art français*, 25 (1978): 251–61.

Ledrut, Auguste-Louis. *Honneur aux militaires, ou Examen impartial de cette question: Buonaparte est-il un héros?* Paris: Chez les Marchands de Nouveautés, 1814.

Lefebvre, Georges. *Napoléon*. Paris: Presses Universitaires de France, 1969.

Leferme-Falguières, Frédérique. *Les courtisans: une société de spectacle sous l'Ancien Régime*. Paris: Presses Universitaires de France, 2007.

Leflon, Jean. *Etienne-Alexandre Bernier, évêque d'Orléans (1762–1806)*. 2 vols. Paris: Plon, 1938.

Leflon, Jean. *La crise révolutionnaire 1789–1846*, vol. xx: *Histoire de l'Eglise depuis les origines jusqu'à nos jours*. Paris: Bloud et Gay, 1949.

Leflon, Jean, 'Face à Napoléon, Pie VII', *Revue de l'Institut Napoléon*, 131 (1975): 3–19.

Lefranc, Pierre, 'Fêtes et réjouissances dans la Vienne à l'occasion de la naissance du roi de Rome', *Revue de l'Institut Napoléon*, 145 (1985): 59–66.

Le Gallo, Emile, 'Un témoignage de Bonaparte sur Robespierre', *Annales Révolutionnaires*, 14 (1922): 60–5.

Le Gallo, Emile. *Les Cent-Jours: essai sur l'histoire intérieure de la France depuis le retour de l'île d'Elbe jusqu'à la nouvelle de Waterloo*. Paris: Félix Alcan, 1923.

Leggiere, Michael V. *Napoleon and Berlin: The Franco-Prussian War in North Germany, 1813*. Norman: University of Oklahoma Press, 2002.

Leggiere, Michael V., 'From Berlin to Leipzig: Napoleon's Gamble in North Germany, 1813', *Journal of Military History*, 67 (2003): 39–84.

Leggiere, Michael V. *The Fall of Napoleon*, vol. i: *The Allied Invasion of France, 1813–1814*. New York: Cambridge University Press, 2007.

Legoy, Corinne, 'Les marges captivantes, de l'histoire: la parole de gloire de la Restauration', in Anne-Emmanuelle Demartini and Dominique Kalifa (eds), *Imaginaire et sensibilités au XIXe siècle: études pour Alain Corbin* (Paris: Créaphis, 2005), pp. 115–24.

Lejeune, Louis-François, baron. *Souvenirs d'un officier de l'Empire*. 2 vols. Toulouse: Viguier, 1851.

Lejeune, Louis-François. *Mémoires du général Lejeune, 1792–1813*. Paris: Editions du Grenadier, 2001.

Lelièvre, Pierre, '*Napoléon sur le champ de bataille d'Eylau* par A.-J. Gros: précisions sur les conditions de la commande', *Bulletin de la société de l'histoire de l'art français* (1955): 51–5.

Lemonnier-Delafosse, Jean-Baptiste. *Souvenirs militaires du capitaine Jean-Baptiste Lemonnier-Delafosse*. Paris: Le Livre chez Vous, 2002.

Lemoyne, abbé. *Discours prononcé dans l'église paroissiale de Saint-Louis de Blois, le premier dimanche du mois de décembre 1808, en mémoire du couronnement de S.M. l'Empereur et de la victoire d'Austerlitz*. Blois: Impr. de P.-D. Verdier, n.d.

Lenôtre, G. *Georges Cadoudal*. Paris: Grasset, 1929.

Lentz, Thierry, 'Contribution à l'étude des plébiscites du Consulat et du Premier Empire: l'exemple de la Moselle', *Revue de l'Institut Napoléon*, 151 (1988): 29–46.

Lentz, Thierry. *Roederer, 1754–1835*. Metz: Serpenoise, 1989.

Lentz, Thierry. *Le 18-Brumaire: les coups d'état de Napoléon Bonaparte*. Paris: Jean Picollec, 1997.

Lentz, Thierry. *Le Grand Consulat, 1799–1804*. Paris: Fayard, 1999.

Lentz, Thierry. *Savary: le séide de Napoléon*. Paris: Fayard, 2001.

Lentz, Thierry. *Nouvelle histoire du premier Empire*, vol. i: *Napoléon et la conquête de l'Europe, 1804–1810*. Paris: Fayard, 2002.

Lentz, Thierry (ed.). *Le sacre de Napoléon*. Paris: Nouveau Monde éditions, 2003.

Lentz, Thierry. *Nouvelle histoire du premier Empire*, vol. ii: *L'effondrement de l'Empire, 1810–1814*. Paris: Fayard, 2004.

Lentz, Thierry. *Nouvelle histoire du Premier Empire*, vol. iii: *La France et l'Europe de Napoléon, 1804–1814*. Paris: Fayard, 2007.

Lentz, Thierry, 'La proclamation du Concordat à Notre Dame le 18 avril 1802', in Jacques-Olivier Boudon (ed.), *Le Concordat et le retour de la paix religieuse* (Paris, 2008), pp. 95–12.

Lentz, Thierry. *Nouvelle histoire du Premier Empire*, vol. iv: *Les Cents-Jours, 1815*. Paris: Fayard, 2010.

Lentz, Thierry (ed.). *1810: Le tournant de l'Empire*. Paris: Nouveau Monde éditions, 2010.

Lentz, Thierry. *La conspiration du général Malet: 23 octobre 1812: premier ébranlement du trône de Napoléon*. Paris: Perrin, 2011.

Lentz, Thierry and Branda, Pierre, *Napoléon, l'esclavage et les colonies*. Paris: Fayard, 2006

Lentz, Thierry and Imhoff, Denis. *La Moselle et Napoléon: étude d'un département sous le Consulat et l'Empire*. Metz: Serpenoise, 1986.

Léon, Pierre, 'La crise des subsistances de 1810–1812 dans le département de l'Isère', *Annales historiques de la Révolution française*, 24 (1952): 289–310.

Leroy, J. *Epître à Napoléon-le-Grand, poème en trois chants*. Paris: the author, 1807.

Lesur, Charles-Louis. *Des progrès de la puissance russe: depuis son origine jusqu'au commencement du XIXe siècle*. Paris: Chez Fantin, 1812.

Lesur, Charles-Louis. *Histoire des Kosaques*. 2 vols. Paris: Impr. impériale, 1813.

*Lettre du général Moreau, au Premier Consul pour se disculper d'avoir pris part à la conspiration de Cadoudal*. Paris: Impr. de Clermont, 1804.

Leuilliot, Paul. *La Première Restauration et les Cent Jours en Alsace*. Paris: SEVPEN, 1958.

Lévêque, Pierre, 'La "revolution de 1815": le movement populaire pendant les Cent-Jours', in Léo Hamon (ed.), *Les Cent-Jours dans l'Yonne: aux origines d'un bonapartisme libéral* (Paris, 1988), pp. 51–73.

Lever, Evelyne. *Louis XVIII*. Paris: Fayard, 1988.

Lévi, Camille (ed.). *Mémoires du capitaine Duthilt*. Lille: Tallandier, 1909.

Levinger, Matthew. *Enlightened Nationalism: The Transformation of Prussian Political Culture, 1806–1848*. Oxford: Oxford University Press, 2000.

Lewis, Michael. *Napoleon and his British Captives*. London: Allen & Unwin, 1962.

Lewis, Theresa (ed.). *Extracts of the journals and correspondence of Miss Berry, from the year 1783 to 1852.* 3 vols. London: Longmans, Green, 1866.

L'Huillier, Fernand, 'Une crise des subsistances dans le Bas-Rhin (1810–1812), *Annales historiques de la Révolution française,* 14 (1937): 518–36.

L'Huillier, Fernand, 'Note sur Napoléon et les peoples de l'Europe d'après la Correspondance de l'Empereur', *Francia: Forschungen zur westeuropäischen Geschichte,* 1 (1973): 369–73.

Lichtenstein, Sara, 'The Baron Gros and Raphael', *Art Bulletin,* 60 (1978): 126–38.

Lieven, Dominic (ed.). *The Cambridge History of Russia.* 3 vols. Cambridge: Cambridge University Press, 2006.

Lieven, Dominic, 'Russia and the Defeat of Napoleon (1812–14)', *Kritika: Explorations in Russian and Eurasian History,* 7 (2006): 283–308.

Lieven, Dominic. *Russia against Napoleon: The Battle for Europe, 1807 to 1814.* London: Allen Lane, 2009.

Lignereux, Aurélien. *Histoire de la France contemporaine,* vol. i: *L'Empire des Français (1799– 1815).* Paris: Seuil, 2012.

Lignereux, Aurélien, 'Le moment terroriste de la chouannerie: des atteintes à l'ordre public aux attentats contre le Premier Consul', *La Révolution française,* L'attentat, objet d'histoire, mis en ligne le 18 mars 2012, consulted 8 April 2012: lrf.revues.org/index390.

Lignières, Marie-Henry, comte de. *Souvenirs de la Grande Armée et de la Vieille Garde impériale: Marie-Henry, comte de Lignières, 1783–1886.* Paris: Pierre Roger, 1933.

Lilley, Edward, 'Consular Portraits of Napoleon Bonaparte', *Gazette des Beaux Arts,* 106 (1985): 143–56.

Lindsay, Suzanne Glover, 'Mummies and Tombs: Turenne, Napoleon, and Death Ritual', *Art Bulletin,* 82 (2000): 476–502.

Lloyd, Peter A. *The French Are Coming: The Invasion Scare of 1803–5.* Tunbridge Wells: Spellmount, 1991.

Locré, Jean-Guillaume. *Esprit du Code Napoléon, tiré de la discussion, ou Conférence . . . du projet de Code civil, des observations des tribunaux, des procès-verbaux du Conseil d'Etat, des observations du Tribunat, des exposés de motifs.* 5 vols. Paris: Impr. impériale, 1805–7.

Lombard de Langres, Vincent. *Le dix-huit brumaire, ou Tableau des événements qui ont amené cette journée, des moyens secrets par lesquels elle a été préparée, des faits qui l'ont accompagnée et des résultats qu'elle doit avoir, auquel on a ajouté des anecdotes sur les principaux personnages qui étaient en place et les pièces justificatives.* Paris: Garnery, an VIII.

Lomier, Eugène. *Histoire des regiments des Gardes d'Honneur, 1813–1814.* Paris: E. Champion, 1924.

Longmate, Norman. *Island Fortress: The Defence of Great Britain, 1603–1945.* London: Grafton Books, 1993.

Lorédan, Jean. *La machine infernale de la rue Nicaise (3 nivôse, an IX).* Paris: Perrin, 1924.

Lort de Sérignan, Comte de. *Un conspirateur militaire sous le premier Empire: le général Malet.* Paris, Payot, 1925.

Loupès, Philippe, 'De Badajoz à Bayonne, l'irrésistible ascension de Manuel Godoy revisitée', in Pontet, *Napoléon, Bayonne et l'Espagne,* pp. 81–103.

Lovett, Gabriel H. *Napoleon and the Birth of Modern Spain.* 2 vols. New York: New York University Press, 1965.

Löwenstern, Vladimir Ivanovitch. *Mémoires du général-major russe baron de Löwenstern.* 2 vols. Paris: A. Fontemoing, 1903.

Lübeck, Wilfried, 'November 1806 – die Kapitulation von Magdeburg, die feige Tat des Gouverneurs v. Kleist?', in Tullner and Möbius (eds), *1806,* pp. 140–52.

Lucas-Dubreton, Jean. *Murat.* Paris: Fayard, 1944.

Luckwaldt, Friedrich. *Österreich und die Anfänge des Befreiungskriege von 1813.* Berlin: E. Ebering, 1898.

Luis, Jean-Philippe, 'Violences politiques et conciliations en Espagne', in Jean-Claude Caron, Frédéric Chauvaud, Emmanuel Fureix and Jean-Noël Luc (eds), *Entre violence et conciliation: la résolution des conflits sociopolitiques en Europe au XIXe siècle* (Rennes: Presses Universitaires de Rennes, 2008), pp. 287–97.

Lukacs, John. *The Hitler of History*. New York: Vintage Books, 1998.

Lynn, John A. *The Bayonets of the Republic: Motivation and Tactics in the Army of Revolutionary France, 1791–94*. Urbana: University of Illinois Press, 1984.

Lynn, John A., 'Toward an Army of Honor: The Moral Evolution of the French Army, 1789–1815', *French Historical Studies*, 16:1 (1989): 152–73.

Lynn, John A. *Battle: A History of Combat and Culture from Ancient Greece to Modern America*. Boulder, Col.: Westview Press, 2003.

Lyon, E. Wilson, 'The Franco-American Convention of 1800', *Journal of Modern History*, 12 (1940): 305–33.

M.P.D. *L'Elan Parisien, chant national, suivi d'un chant guerrier traduit du russe et d'une notice sur diverses peuplades qui fournissent à la Russie les troupes indisciplinées connues sous le nom de* Cosaques. Paris: the author, 1814.

McConachy, Bruce, 'The Roots of Artillery Doctrine: Napoleonic Artillery Tactics Reconsidered', *Journal of Military History*, 65 (2001): 617–40.

McCoubrey, John Walker, 'Gros' *Battle of Eylau* and Roman Imperial Art', *Art Bulletin*, 43 (1961): 135–52.

Maccunn, F. J. *The Contemporary English View of Napoleon*. London: G. Bell, 1914.

Macdonald, Etienne-Jacques-Joseph-Alexandre. *Souvenirs du maréchal Macdonald, duc de Tarente*. Paris: E. Plon, Nourrit, 1892.

MacDonogh, Katharine, 'A Sympathetic Ear: Napoleon, Elba and the British', *History Today*, 44:2 (1994): 29–35.

McGinn, Bernard. *Antichrist: Two Thousand Years of the Human Fascination with Evil*. New York: Columbia University Press, 1996.

McGrew, Roderick E. *Paul I of Russia*. Oxford: Clarendon Press, 1992.

McKee, Alexander. *Wreck of the Medusa: Mutiny, Murder, and Survival on the High Seas*. New York: Skyhorse, 2007.

MacKenzie, Norman. *Escape from Elba: The Fall and Flight of Napoleon, 1814–1815*. New York: Oxford University Press, 1982.

MacKenzie, Norman. *Fallen Eagle: How the Royal Navy Captured Napoleon*. London: Bellerophon Books, 2009.

Mackesy, Piers. *War without Victory: The Downfall of Pitt, 1799–1802*. Oxford: Clarendon Press, 1984.

McLynn, Frank. *Invasion: From the Armada to Hitler, 1588–1945*. London: Routledge & Kegan Paul, 1987.

McLynn, Frank. *Napoleon: A Biography*. London: Jonathan Cape, 1997.

McMahon, Darrin M. *Enemies of the Enlightenment: The French Counter-Enlightenment and the Making of Modernity*. Oxford: Oxford University Press, 2001.

McManners, John. *The French Revolution and the Church*. London: SPCK for the Church Historical Society, 1969.

McNalley, Raymond T., 'The Origins of Russophobia in France: 1812–1830', *American Slavic and East European Review*, 17 (1958): 173–89.

McPhee, Peter. *Robespierre: A Revolutionary Life*. New Haven: Yale University Press, 2012.

Madelin, Amédée. *Le premier Consul législateur, étude sur la part que prit Napoléon aux travaux préparatoires du code*. Paris: Durand, 1865.

Madelin, Louis. *Fouché, 1759–1820*. 2 vols. Paris: Plon-Nourrit, 1903.

Madelin, Louis. *Histoire du Consulat et de l'Empire*. 16 vols. Paris: Hachette, 1937–54.

Maitland, Frederick Lewis. *Narrative of the surrender of Buonaparte and of his residence on H.M.S. Bellerophon*. London: H. Colburn, 1826.

Maillé, Duchesse de. *Souvenirs des deux Restaurations: journal inédit*. Paris: Perrin, 1984.

Mailly, Adrien-Augustin-Amalric, Comte de [marquis de Nesle, pseudonym Turki]. *Mon journal pendant la campagne de Russie, écrit de mémoire après mon retour à Paris*. Paris: J.-B. Gros, 1841.

Mainardi, Patricia. *Husbands, Wives, and Lovers: Marriage and its Discontents in Nineteenth-Century France*. New Haven: Yale University Press, 2003.

Maistre, Joseph de. *Correspondance diplomatique 1811–1817*. 2 vols. Paris: Michel Lévy frères, 1860.

Maistre, Joseph de. *Mémoires politiques et correspondance diplomatique de Joseph de Maistre*. Paris: Michel Lévy frères, 1864.

Maistre, Joseph de. *Oeuvres complètes de J. de Maistre*. 14 vols. Lyons: Vitte et Perrussel, 1884–6.

Maistre, Joseph de. *Les carnets du comte Joseph de Maistre*. Lyons and Paris: Vitte, 1923.

Malaussena, Katia, 'The Birth of Modern Commemoration in France: The Tree and the Text', *French History*, 18 (2004): 154–72.

Mallet du Pan, Jacques. *Correspondance inédite de Mallet du Pan avec la Cour de Vienne (1794–1798)*. 2 vols. Paris: E. Plon, Nourrit, 1884.

Malmesbury, James Harris. *Diaries and Correspondence of James Harris, First Earl of Malmesbury*, 4 vols. London: R. Bentley, 1844.

Malo, Charles. *Napoléoniana, ou Recueil d'anecdotes, saillies, bons mots, réparties, etc. etc, pour servir à l'histoire de la vie de Buonaparte*. Paris: J. Moronval, 1814.

'Mandement pour les victoires de Thann, d'Eckmulh et de Ratisbonne', in Boulogne, *Mandemens et instructions pastorales*, pp. 30–4.

Mansel, Philip, 'Monarchy, Uniform, and the Rise of the *Frac*, 1760–1830', *Past & Present*, 96 (1982): 103–32.

Mansel, Philip. *The Eagle in Splendour: Napoleon I and his Court*. London: George Philip, 1987.

Mansel, Philip. *The Court of France, 1789–1830*. Cambridge: Cambridge University Press, 1988.

Mansel, Philip. *Louis XVIII*. Stroud: Sutton, 1999.

Mansel, Philip. *Paris between Empires: Monarchy and Revolution, 1814–1852*. London: Phoenix, 2001.

Mansel, Philip. *Dressed to Rule: Royal and Court Costume from Louis XIV to Elizabeth II*. New Haven: Yale University Press, 2005.

Mansfield, Paul, 'The Repression of Lyon, 1793–94: Origins, Responsibility and Significance', *French History*, 2 (1988): 74–101.

Mansuy, Abel. *Jérôme Napoléon et la Pologne en 1812*. Paris: Félix Alcan, 1931.

*The Manuscripts of the Earl of Westmorland, and others*. London: Eyre & Spottiswoode, 1885.

Marbot, Jean-Baptiste-Antoine-Marcellin, baron de. *Mémoires du général Bon de Marbot*. 3 vols. Paris: E. Plon, Nourrit, 1897.

Marchand, Louis. *Mémoires de Marchand: premier valet de chambre et exécuteur testamentaire de l'empereur Napoléon*. Paris: Tallandier, 2003.

Marcou, Lilly. *Napoléon et les femmes*. Paris: La Martinière, 2008.

Marié, André, 'Le mariage civil de Napoléon à Saint-Cloud', *Revue de l'Institut Napoléon*, 72 (1959): 109–14.

Marigny, Marie-Anne de Châteaubriand, Comtesse de. *Paris en 1814: journal inédit de madame de Marigny*. Paris, Emile-Paul, 1907.

Markham, Felix. *Napoleon*. London: Weidenfeld & Nicolson, 1963.

Marmottan, Paul, 'Lucien, ministre de l'intérieur et les arts', *Revue des études napoléoniennes*, 25 (1925): 3–40.

Marmottan, Paul, 'Joseph Bonaparte diplomate (Lunéville, Amiens, 1801, 1802)', *Revue d'histoire diplomatique*, 41 (1927): 276–300.

Marmottan, Paul, 'Joseph Bonaparte à Mortefontaine, 1800–1803', *Nouvelle Revue*, 100 (1929): 3–16, 113–28, 209–19, 266–73.

Marquiset, Alfred. *Napoléon sténographié au Conseil d'Etat, 1804–1805*. Paris: H. Champion, 1913.

Marrinan, Michael, 'Literal/Literary/"Lexie": History, Text, and Authority in Napoleonic Painting', *Word & Image*, 7:3 (1991): 177–200.

Marron, Paul-Henri. *Discours prononcé la veille de la fête de la Paix, 17 brumaire an X, dans le temple des protestans de Paris*. Paris: Impr. de H.-J. Jansen, 1801.

Marsden, Jonathan, 'George III's State Coach in Context', in Jonathan Marsden (ed.), *The Wisdom of George the Third* (London: Royal Collection Publications, 2005), pp. 43–59.

Marsden, Jonathan and Hardy, John, '"O Fair Britannia Hail!" The "Most Superb" State Coach', *Apollo*, 153:468 (2001): 3–12.

Marshall, James F. (ed.). *De Staël–Du Pont Letters: Correspondence of Madame de Staël and Pierre Samuel du Pont de Nemours.* Madison, Milwaukee and London: University of Wisconsin Press, 1968.

Martel, Arnaud-Louis-Raoul de. *Etude sur l'affaire de la machine infernale du 3 nivôse an IX.* Paris: E. Lachaud, 1870.

Martin, Alexander M. *Romantics, Reformers, Reactionaries: Russian Conservative Thought and Politics in the Reign of Alexander I.* DeKalb: Northern Illinois University Press, 1997.

Martin, Alexander M., 'The Russian Empire and the Napoleonic Wars', in Dwyer, *Napoleon and Europe*, pp. 243–63.

Martin, Alexander M., 'The Response of the Population of Moscow to the Napoleonic Occupation of 1812', in Poe and Lohr, *The Military and Society in Russia*, pp. 469–89.

Martin, Alexander M., 'Russia and the Legacy of 1812', in Dominic Lieven (ed.), *The Cambridge History of Russia*, 3 vols (Cambridge: Cambridge University Press, 2006), ii. pp. 145–61.

Martin, Alexander M., 'Down and Out in 1812: The Impact of the Napoleonic Invasion on Moscow's Middling Strata', in Roger Bartlett and Gabriela Lehmann-Carli (eds), *Eighteenth-Century Russia: Society, Culture, Economy* (Münster: Lit, cop., 2008), pp. 429–44.

Martin, Alexander M., 'Lost Arcadia: The 1812 War and the Russian Images of Aristocratic Womanhood', *European History Quarterly*, 37 (2007): 603–21.

Martin, Brian Joseph. *Napoleonic Friendship: Military Fraternity, Intimacy, and Sexuality in Nineteenth-Century France.* Durham, NH: University of New Hampshire Press, 2011.

Martin, Jean-Clément (ed.). *La Contre-Revolution en Europe, XVIIIe–XIXe siècles: réalités politiques et sociales, résonances culturelles et idéologiques.* Rennes: Presses Universitaires de Rennes, 2001.

Martin, Marie. *Maria Féodorovna en son temps (1759–1828): contribution à l'histoire de la Russie et de l'Europe.* Paris: L'Harmattan, 2003.

Martin, Xavier. *Mythologie du Code Napoléon: aux soubassements de la France moderne.* Bouère: DMM, 2003.

Martin-Fugier, Anne. *La vie élégante ou La formation du Tout-Paris, 1815–1848.* Paris: Fayard, 1990.

Martineau, Gilbert. *Napoleon Surrenders.* Trans. Frances Partridge. London: J. Murray, 1971.

Martineau, Gilbert. *Lucien Bonaparte: prince de Canino.* Paris: Editions France-Empire, 1989.

Marzagalli, Silvia. *Les boulevards de la fraude: le négoce maritime et le Blocus continental, 1806–1813: Bordeaux, Hambourg, Livourne.* Villeneuve-d'Ascq: Presses Universitaires du Septentrion, 1999.

Maspero-Clerc, Hélène. *Un journaliste contre-révolutionnaire, Jean-Gabriel Peltier, 1760–1825.* Paris: Société des études robespierristes, 1973.

Masséna, André. *Mémoires de Masséna.* 7 vols. Paris: Paulin et Lechevalier, 1848–50.

Masson, Frédéric. *Napoléon et les femmes.* Paris: Ollendorff, 1894.

Masson, Frédéric. *Napoléon et sa famille.* 13 vols. Paris: Ollendorff, 1897–1919.

Masson, Frédéric. *Joséphine, impératrice et reine.* Paris: Ollendorff, 1899.

Masson, Frédéric. *Joséphine répudiée (1809–1814).* Paris: Ollendorff, 1901.

Masson, Frédéric. *L'impératrice Marie-Louise: 1809–1815.* Paris: Ollendorff, 1902.

Masson, Frédéric. *Napoléon et son fils.* Paris: Ollendorff, 1904.

Masson, Frédéric. *Le sacre et le couronnement de Napoléon.* Paris: Tallandier, 1908 (reprinted 1978).

Masson, Frédéric. *Napoléon à Sainte-Hélène, 1815–1822.* Paris: Ollendorff, 1912.

Masson, Frédéric. *Mme Bonaparte.* Paris: Ollendorff, 1920.

Masson, Frédéric. *La vie et les conspirations du général Malet, 1754–1812.* Paris: Ollendorff, 1921.

Masson, Frédéric. *The Private Diaries of Empress Marie Louise, Wife of Napoleon I*. New York: Appleton, 1922.

Mathews, Joseph J., 'Napoleon's Military Bulletins', *Journal of Modern History*, 22:2 (1950): 137–44.

Mathis, Hans Peter. *Napoleon I im Spiegel der Karikatur*. Zurich: Neue Zürcher Zeitung, 1998.

Matyaszewski, Pawel, 'Quelques remarques sur l'image de Napoléon chez Chateaubriand', *Annales de lettres et sciences humaines*, 37–8 (1989–90): 21–39.

Mauguin, Georges. *Napoléon et la superstition: anecdotes et curiosités*. Rodez: Carrère, 1946.

Mavor, Elizabeth (ed.). *The Grand Tours of Katherine Wilmot, France 1801–1803, and Russia 1805–07*. London: Weidenfeld & Nicolson, 1992.

Max, Lenz, 'Tilsit', *Forschungen zur brandenburgischen und preussischen Geschichte*, 6 (1893): 181–237.

Mayer, Arno. *The Furies: Violence and Terror in the French and Russian Revolutions*. Princeton: Princeton University Press, 2000.

Mayer, J. and Cologna, Abraham de. *Odes hébraïques pour la célébration de l'anniversaire de la naissance de S.M. l'Empereur des François et roi d'Italie*. Paris: Impr. impériale, 1806.

Mayer, Lewis. *Bonaparte, the Emperor of the French, considered as Lucifer and Gog* (London: n.p., 1806), and *The prophetic mirror or a hint of England, containing an explanation of the prophesy . . . proving Bonaparte to be the beast*. London: Williams and Smith, J. Pearmain and Sumner, 1806.

Mayer-Michalon, Isabelle. *Charles Meynier (1763–1832)*. Paris: Arthena, 2008.

Mayeur, Jean-Marie, Pietri, Charles and Luce, Vauchez, André and Venard, Marc (eds). *Histoire du christianisme: des origines à nos jours*. 14 vols. Paris: Desclée, 1990–2001.

Mayeux, J.-F. *A l'Empereur, sur l'impossibilité de concilier l'Acte additionnel aux Constitutions, avec la majesté, l'indépendance et le bonheur du people*. Paris: chez Babeuf, 1815.

Melchior-Bonnet, Bernardine. *Napoléon et le Pape*. Paris: Amiot-Dumont, 1958.

Melchior-Bonnet, Bernardine. *La conspiration du général Malet*. Paris: Del Duca, 1963.

Melchior-Bonnet, Bernardine. *Jérôme Bonaparte, ou l'envers de l'épopée*. Paris: Perrin, 1979.

*Mémoires et correspondance du roi Jérôme et de la reine Catherine*. 7 vols. Paris: E. Dentu, 1861–6.

*Mémoires sur la campagne d'Andalousie et la captivité qui s'en suivit*. Paris: Teissèdre, 1998.

Ménager, Bernard. *Les Napoléon du peuple*. Paris: Aubier, 1988.

Menant, Fabien. *Les députés de Napoléon, 1799–1815*. Paris: Nouveau Monde éditions, 2012.

Méneval, Claude-François de. *Mémoires pour servir à l'histoire de Napoléon Ier depuis 1802 jusqu'à 1815*. 3 vols. Paris: E. Dentu, 1893–4.

Méneval, Claude-François de. *Napoléon et Marie-Louise: souvenirs historiques de M. le baron Méneval*. 3 vols. Paris: Amyot, 1844–5.

Mercier, Louis-Sébastien. *Tableau de Paris*. 12 vols. Amsterdam: Société typographique, 1788.

Mercy-Argenteau, François-Joseph-Charles-Marie, Comte de. *Memoirs of the Cte de Mercy-Argenteau: Napoleon's Chamberlain and his Minister Plenipotentiary to the King of Bavaria*. 2 vols. New York: Putnam's Sons, 1917.

Merkle, J. *Katharina Pawlowna, Königin von Württemberg, Beiträge zu einer Lebensbeschreibung der Fürstin*. Stuttgart: W. Kohlhammer, 1889.

Merrick, Jeffrey, 'Death and Life in the Archives: Patterns of and Attitudes to Suicide in Eighteenth-Century Paris', in John Weaver and David Wright (eds), *Histories of Suicide: International Perspectives on Self-Destruction in the Modern World* (Toronto: University of Toronto Press, 2009), pp. 73–90.

Mertens, Erich, 'Jung-Stilling und der Kreis um Frau Krudener', in Peter Wörster (ed.), *Zwischen Straßburg und Petersburg* (Siegen: J. G. Herder, 1992), pp. 41–96.

Mesmay, Jean-Tiburce de. *Horace Sébastiani, soldat, diplomate, homme d'Etat, maréchal de France, 1772–1851*. Paris: H. Champion, 1948.

Messiers, Charles. *1769. Grande Comète qui a paru à la naissance de Napoléon le Grand, découverte et observée pendant quatre mois*. Paris: Delance, n.d.

Messiez, Maurice and Sorrel, Christian (eds). *La deuxième campagne d'Italie et les conséquences de la Bataille de Marengo*. Chambéry: Société Savoisienne d'Histoire et d'Archéologie, 2001.

Metternich, Klemens Wenzel von. *Mémoires: documents et écrits divers*. 8 vols. Paris: E. Plon, Nourrit, 1881–4.

Meyer, Arline, 'Re-dressing Classical Statuary: The Eighteenth-Century "Hand-in-Waistcoat" Portrait', *Art Bulletin*, 77(2) (1995): 45–64.

Meyer, Hélène, 'De la rencontre à l'idylle sous les ors de Compiègne: à propos de l'exposition du bicentenaire', in Lentz (ed.), *1810: le tournant de l'Empire*, pp. 247–55.

Meynier, Albert, 'Les armées française sous la Révolution et le Premier Empire: la Grande Armée en Russie', *Revue d'études militaires*, 8 (1934): 7–19.

Michelet, Jules. *Ma Jeunesse*. Paris: Calmann-Lévy, 1884.

Middleton, Charles Ronald. *The Administration of British Foreign Policy, 1782–1846*. Durham, NC: Duke University Press, 1977.

Mieck, Ilya, 'Die Rettung Preußens? Napoleon und Alexander I. in Tilsit 1807', in Ilya Mieck and Pierre Guillen (eds), *Deutschland–Frankreich–Rußland: Begegnungen und Konfrontation* (Munich: R. Oldenbourg, 2000), pp. 15–35.

Mieck, Ilya, 'Napoleon in Potsdam', *Francia*, 31:2 (2004): 121–46.

Mikaberidze, Alexander. *The Battle of Borodino: Napoleon against Kutuzov*. Barnsley: Pen & Sword, 2007.

Mikhaïlovitch, Nikolaï. *L'impératrice Elisabeth, épouse d'Alexandre Ier*. 3 vols. St Petersburg: Manufacture des papiers de l'Etat, 1908–9.

Mikhaïlovich, Nikolaï (ed.). *Les relations de la Russie et de la France d'après les rapports des ambassadeurs d'Alexandre et de Napoléon 1808–1812*. 6 vols. St Petersburg: Manufacture des papiers de l'Etat, 1905–8.

Mikhaïlovich, Nikolaï (ed.). *Correspondance de l'empereur Alexandre Ier avec sa soeur la grande-duchesse Catherine, princesse d'Oldenbourg, puis reine de Wurtemberg, 1805–1818*. St Petersburg: Manufacture des papiers de l'Etat, 1910.

Miles, Jonathan. *The Wreck of the Medusa: The Most Famous Sea Disaster of the Nineteenth Century*. New York: Grove Press, 2007.

Minart, Gérard. *Les opposants à Napoléon: l'élimination des royalistes et des républicains (1800–1815)*. Paris: Privat, 2003.

Minois, Georges. *Histoire du suicide: la société occidentale face à la mort volontaire*. Paris: Fayard, 1995.

Miot de Mélito, André-François, comte. *Mémoires du comte de Miot de Mélito*. 3 vols. Paris: Michel Lévy frères, 1858.

Mitchell, L. G. *Charles James Fox*. Harmondsworth: Penguin, 1997.

Mitchell, Sidney. *A Family Lawsuit: The Story of Elisabeth Patterson and Jérôme Bonaparte*. New York: Farrar, Straus & Cudahy, 1958.

Mitton, Fernand. *La presse française*. Paris: Guy Le Prat, 1945.

Molé, Louis-Mathieu. *Le Comte Molé, 1781–1855: sa vie, ses memoires*. 6 vols. Paris: Impr. Philippe Renouard, 1922–30.

Mollaret, Henri and Brossollet, Jacqueline, 'A propos des "Pestiférés de Jaffa" de A. J. Gros', *Jaarboek van het Koninklijk Museum voor schoone kunsten* (1968): 263–308.

Mollien, François-Nicolas. *Mémoires d'un ancien ministre du Trésor public de 1800 à 1814*. 3 vols. Paris: Guillaumin, 1898.

Monaque, Rémi. *Latouche-Tréville, 1745–1804: l'amiral qui défiait Nelson*. Paris: SPM, 2000.

*Mon dernier mot sur Bonaparte*. London: W. and C. Sphibury, n.d.

Monestier, Martin. *Suicides: histoire, techniques et bizarreries de la mort volontaire des origines à nos jours*. Paris: Le Cherche Midi, 1995.

Monier, A.-D.-B. *Une année de la vie de l'empereur Napoléon, ou Précis historique de tout ce qui s'est passé depuis le 1er avril 1814 jusqu'au 20 mars 1815*. Paris: Alexis Eymery, 1815.

Monnier, Raymond. *Le Faubourg Saint-Antoine, 1789–1815*. Paris: Société des études robespierristes, 1981.

Monnier, Raymond, 'Vertu antique et nouveaux héros: la presse autour de la mort de Desaix et d'une bataille légendaire', *Annales historiques de la Révolution française*, 324 (2001): 113–25.

Monnier, Raymond. *Républicanisme, patriotisme et Révolution française*. Paris: L'Harmattan, 2005.

Montaglas, Jean-Pierre-Galy. *Historique du 12e chasseurs à cheval, depuis le 29 avril 1792 jusqu'au traité de Lunéville (9 février 1801): mémoires inédits du chef d'escadrons Galy Montaglas*. Paris: R. Chapelot, 1908.

Montaigu, Adolphe de. *Motif du vote négatif d'Adolphe de Montaigu . . . sur l'Acte additionnel aux Constitutions de l'Empire, en date du 22 avril 1815*. Paris: Le Normant, n.d.

Montcalm, Marquise de. *Mon journal, 1815–1818*. Paris: Grasset, 1935.

Montesquieu, Baron de. *Réflexions sur la Monarchie Universelle en Europe*. Geneva: Droz, 2000.

Montesquiou, Anatole de. *Souvenirs sur la Révolution, l'Empire, la Restauration et le règne de Louis-Philippe*. Paris: Plon, 1961.

Montesquiou-Fezensac, Raymond de. *Souvenirs militaires de 1804 à 1814*. Paris: J. Dumaine, 1863.

Montgaillard, Jean-Gabriel-Maurice-Rocque, comte de. *La France sous le gouvernement de Bonaparte*. Paris: Cussac, 1803.

Montgaillard, Jean-Gabriel-Maurice-Rocque, comte de. *Fondation de la quatrième dynastie, ou la Dynastie impériale*. Paris: n.p., 1804.

Montgaillard, Jean-Gabriel-Maurice-Rocque, comte de (attributed to Roederer). *Moreau et Pichegru au 18 fructidor an V*. Paris: Bertrand-Pottier, an XII.

Montholon, Albine de. *Souvenirs de Sainte-Hélène par la comtesse de Montholon, 1815–1816*. Paris: E. Paul, 1901.

Montholon, Charles Jean Tristan de. *Récits de la captivité de l'empereur Napoléon à Sainte-Hélène*. 2 vols. Paris: Paulin, 1847.

Montlosier, François-Dominique de Reynaud, comte de. *Le peuple anglais, bouffé d'orgueil, de bière et de thé, jugé au tribunal de la raison*. Paris: Surosne, 1802.

Moran, Daniel, 'Arms and the Concert: The Nation in Arms and the Dilemmas of German Liberalism', in Daneil Moran and Arthur Waldron (eds), *The People in Arms: Military Myth and National Mobilization since the French Revolution* (Cambridge: Cambridge University Press, 2003), pp. 49–74.

Morvan, Jean. *Le soldat imperial*. 2 vols. Paris: Teissèdre, 1904.

Moreau, Jean-Victor. *Discours prononcé par le général Moreau, au Tribunal criminel spécial du département de la Seine*. Paris: Lebour, 1804.

Moreau, Soizik. *Jean-Victor Moreau: l'adversaire de Napoléon*. Paris: Punctum, 2005.

Morieux, Renaud, '"An Inundation from Our Shores": Travelling across the Channel around the Peace of Amiens', in Philp (ed.), *Resisting Napoleon*, pp. 217–40.

Morrissey, Robert. *La barbe fleuri: Charlemagne dans la mythologie et l'histoire de France*. Paris: Gallimard, 1997.

Morrissey, Robert, 'Charlemagne et la légende impériale', in Bonnet (ed.), *L'empire des muses*, pp. 331–47.

Morse, Paddy Jill, 'A Revaluation of the Napoleonic History Paintings of Jean-Antoine Gros', PhD dissertation, Ohio State University, 1993.

Mossiker, Frances. *Napoleon and Josephine: The Biography of a Marriage*. New York: Simon & Schuster, 1964.

Moufle, Auguste (François-Toussaint-Auguste). *Ode sur l'embrasement de Moscou*. Paris: Martinet, 1812.

Müffling, Friedrich Carl Ferdinand, Baron von. *The Memoirs of Baron von Müffling: A Prussian Officer in the Napoleonic Wars*. London: Greenhill Books, 1997.

Muhlstein, Anka. *Napoléon à Moscou*. Paris: Odile Jacob, 2007.

Muir, Rory. *Britain and the Defeat of Napoleon, 1807–1815*. New Haven: Yale University Press, 1996.

Müller, Friedrich von. *Souvenirs des années de guerre: 1806–1813*. Paris: Fondation Napoléon, 1992.

Müller, Harald, 'Napoleon in der Gruft der Garnisonkirche', in Bernhard Kroener (ed.), *Potsdam: Staat, Armee, Residenz in der preussisch-deutschen Militärgeschichte* (Frankfurt: Propyläen, 1993), pp. 345–60.

Munch-Petersen, Thomas. *Defying Napoleon: How Britain Bombarded Copenhagen and Seized the Danish Fleet in 1807*. London: Sutton, 2007.

Münchow-Pohl, Bernd von. *Zwischen Reform and Krieg: Untersuchungen zur Bewusstseinslage in Preussen 1809–1812*. Göttingen: Vandenhoeck und Ruprecht, 1987.

Munhall, Edgar, 'Portraits of Napoleon', *Yale French Studies*, 26 (1960): 3–20.

Muraise, Eric. *Sainte Anne et la Bretagne*. Paris: F. Lanore, 1980.

Müsebeck, Ernst Friedrich Christian. *Freiwillige Gaben und Opfer des preussischen Volkes in den Jahren 1813–1815*. Leipzig, 1913.

Mustafa, Sam A. *The Long Ride of Major von Schill: A Journey through German History and Memory*. Lanham, Md: Rowman & Littlefield, 2009.

Myerly, Scott Hughes. *British Military Spectacle: From the Napoleonic Wars through the Crimea*. Cambridge, Mass.: Harvard University Press, 1996.

Nabokov, Serge and Lastours, Sophie de. *Koutouzov: le vainqueur de Napoléon*. Paris: Albin Michel, 1990.

Nafziger, George. *Napoleon's Invasion of Russia*. Novato, Calif.: Presidio Press, 1988.

*La Naissance du roi de Rome. Dithyrambe en prose poétique, par M.N.M. veuve de Rome, membre de l'académie des arcades de Rome*. Paris: Lefebvre, 1811.

*Napoléon, de l'histoire à la légende. Actes du colloque des 30 novembre et le 1er décembre 1999*. Paris: In Forma, 2000.

*Napoléon le sacre: Musée Fesch, Ville d'Ajaccio, 23 avril–3 octobre 2004*. Ajaccio: Musée Fesch, 2004.

Naročnickij, A. L., 'Österreich zwischen Frankreich und Russland 1813', in Drabek, Leitsch and Plaschka (eds), *Russland und Österreich zur Zeit der Napoleonischen Kriege*, pp. 15–32.

Narychkin, Natalie. *Le comte Rostopchine et son temps: 1812*. St Petersburg: R. Golicke and A. Willborg, 1912.

Nattrass, Leonora (ed.). *William Cobbett: Selected Writings*. 6 vols. London: Pickering & Chatto, 1998.

Naulet, Frédéric. *Eylau, 8 février 1807: la campagne de Pologne, des boues de Pultusk aux neiges d'Eylau*. Paris: Economica, 2007.

Naylies, Joseph-Jacques de. *Mémoires sur la guerre d'Espagne, pendant les années 1808, 1809, 1810 et 1811*. Paris: Magimel, Anselm et Pochard, 1817.

Neipperg, comte de, 'Aperçu militaire sur la bataille de Marengo et l'armistice', *Revue de Paris*, 4 (1906): 5–36.

Nesselrode, Charles Robert Vasilievitch de. *Lettres et papiers du chancelier comte de Nesselrode, 1760–1850*. 11 vols. Paris: A. Lahure, 1908–12.

Neuilly, Ange-Achille-Charles de Brunet, Cte de. *Dix années d'émigration. Souvenirs et correspondance du comte de Neuilly*. Paris: C. Douniol, 1863.

Neumann, Iver B. *Uses of the Other: 'The East' in European Identity Formation*. Minneapolis: University of Minneapolis Press, 1999.

Neumann, Leopold von (ed.). *Recueil des traités et conventions conclus par l'Autriche avec les puissances étrangères depuis 1763 jusqu'à nos jours*. 12 vols. Vienna: Imprimerie I. et R. de la Cour et de l'Etat, 1877–88.

Newman, John, '"An Insurrection of Loyalty": The London Volunteer Regiments' Response to the Invasion Threat', in Philp (ed.), *Resisting Napoleon*, pp. 75–89.

Nicolay, Fernand. *Napoléon Ier au camp de Boulogne, d'après de nombreux documents inédits*. Paris: Perrin, 1907.

Nicolet, Claude. *La fabrique d'une nation: la France entre Rome et les Germains*. Paris: Perrin, 2003.

Nicolson, Adam. *Men of Honour: Trafalgar and the Making of the English Hero*. London: HarperCollins, 2005.

Nieuwazny, Andrzej, 'Marie Walewska, la belle Polonaise de Napoléon', *Napoléon 1er*, 7 (March–April 2001): 6–11.

Niven, Alexander C. *Napoleon and Alexander I: A Study in Franco-Russian Relations 1807–1812*. Washington, DC: University Press of America, 1982.

Nobile, Nancy. *The School of Days: Heinrich von Kleist and the Traumas of Education*. Detroit: Wayne State University Press, 1999.

Noël, Jean-Nicolas-Auguste. *Souvenirs militaires d'un officier du premier Empire: 1795–1832*. Paris: Berger-Levrault, 1895.

Noël, Jean-Nicolas-Auguste. *With Napoleon's Guns: The Military Memoirs of an Officer of the First Empire*. Trans. Rosemary Brindle. London: Greenhill Books, 2005.

Nora, Pierre (ed.). *Les lieux de mémoire*. 3 vols. Paris: Gallimard, 1984–92.

Nora, Pierre (ed.). *Realms of Memory: Rethinking the French Past*. Trans. Lawrence D. Kritzman and Arthur Goldhammer. 3 vols. New York: Columbia University Press, 1996–8.

Nordhof, Anton Wilhelm. *Die Geschichte der Zerstörung Moskaus im Jahre 1812*, Deutsche Geschichtsquellen des 19. und 20. Jahrhunderts. Ed. with an introduction by Claus Scharf and Jürgen Kessel. Munich: R. Oldenbourg, 2000.

Norris, Stephen M., 'Images of 1812: Ivan Terebenev and the Russian Wartime *Lubok*', *National Identities*, 7 (2005): 1–21.

Norris, Stephen M. *A War of Images: Russian Popular Prints, Wartime Culture, and National Identity, 1812–1945*. DeKalb: Northern Illinois University Press, 2006.

Norvins, Jacques Marquet de Montbreton de. *Souvenirs d'un historien de Napoléon. Mémorial de J. de Norvins*. 3 vols. Paris: E. Plon, Nourrit, 1896.

Nouvel, Félix. *Opinion de Félix Nouvel, du Finistère, sur cette question: Napoléon Bonaparte sera-t-il consul à vie?* Brest: Michel, 1801.

*Nouvelle description du tableau exposé au Musée Napoléon représentant de leurs majestés impériales et royales*. Paris: Gauthier, 1808.

Obermann, Karl, 'La situation de la Prusse sous l'occupation française, 1807–1813', in *Occupants occupés*, pp. 257–86.

O'Brien, David, 'Propaganda and the Republic of the Arts in Antoine-Jean Gros's *Napoleon Visiting the Battlefield of Eylau the Morning after the Battle*', *French Historical Studies*, 26 (2003): 281–314.

O'Brien, David. *After the Revolution: Antoine-Jean Gros, Painting and Propaganda under Napoleon*. University Park, Pa.: Pennsylvania State University Press, 2006.

*Observations sur le Salon de l'an 1808*. Paris: Vve Gueffier, 1808.

*Occupants occupés, 1792–1815: Colloque de Bruxelles, 29 et 30 janvier 1968*. Brussels: Université libre, 1969.

Odeleben, Ernst Otto Innocenz, Freiherr von. *Relation circonstanciée de la campagne de 1813 en Saxe*. Trans. from the German by M. Aubert de Vitry. 2 vols. Paris: Plancher, 1817.

O'Dwyer, Margaret M. *The Papacy in the Age of Napoleon and the Restoration: Pius VII, 1800–1823*. Lanham, Md: University Press of America, 1985.

Oer, Rudolfine Freiin von. *Der Friede von Pressburg: ein Beitrag zur Diplomatiegeschichte des Napoleonischen Zeitalters*. Münster: Aschendorffsche Verlagsbuchhandlung, 1965.

Ojala, Jeanne A. *Auguste de Colbert: Aristocratic Survival in an Era of Upheaval, 1793–1809*. Salt Lake City: University of Utah Press, 1979.

Olcina, José. *L'opinion publique en Belgique entre 1812 et 1814: les Belges face à l'écroulement de l'Empire*. Brussels: Académie royale de Belgique, 2010.

Oliver, William Hosking. *Prophets and Millenialists: The Uses of Biblical Prophecy in England from the 1790s to the 1840s*. Auckland: Auckland University Press, 1978.

Olivier, Daria. *L'incendie de Moscou*. Paris: R. Laffont, 1964.

Olivier, Daria. *The Burning Of Moscow, 1812*. London: Allen & Unwin, 1966.

Olsen, John Andreas and Creveld, Martin van. *The Evolution of Operational Art: From Napoleon to the Present*. Oxford: Oxford University Press, 2011.

Oman, Carola. *Britain against Napoleon*. London: Faber & Faber, 1942.

Oman, Carola. *Napoleon's Viceroy, Eugène de Beauharnais*. London: Hodder & Stoughton, 1966.

Oman, Charles. *A History of the Peninsular War*. 7 vols. Oxford: Clarendon Press, 1902–30.

Oman, Charles, 'The French Losses in the Waterloo Campaign', *English Historical Review*, 19 (1904): 681–93.

Oncken, Wilhelm von. *Österreich und Preußen im Befreiungs-Kriege: urkundliche Aufschlüße über die politische Geschichte des Jahres 1813*. 2 vols. Berlin: Grote, 1876–9.

Orlov, A. A., 'Britons in Moscow', *History Today*, 53/7 (2003): 17–23.

Orwicz, Michael R. (ed.). *Art Criticism and its Institutions in Nineteenth-Century France*. Manchester: Manchester University Press, 1994.

Ouvrard, Robert (ed.). *Avec Napoléon à Iéna et Auerstaedt: la campagne de Prusse par ceux qui l'ont vécue: 1806*. Paris: Cosmopole, 2006.

Ouvrard, Robert. *1809: les Français à Vienne: chronique d'une occupation*. Paris: Nouveau Monde éditions, 2009.

Ozouf, Mona. *Festivals and the French Revolution* Trans. Alan Sheridan. Cambridge, Mass.: Harvard University Press, 1988.

P.M., 'Un document sur l'histoire de la presse: la préparation de l'arrêté du 27 nivôse an VIII', *La Révolution française*, 44 (January–June 1903): 78–82.

Pacca, Bartolomeo. *Oeuvres complètes du cardinal B. Pacca*. 2 vols. Paris: Pradel et Goujon, 1845.

*The Paget Papers: Diplomatic and Other Correspondence of Sir Arthur Paget, 1794–1807*. 2 vols. London: William Heinemann, 1896.

Paixhans, Henri-Joseph. *Retraite de Moscou, notes écrites au quartier de l'Empereur*. Metz: V. Maline, 1868.

Paléologue, Maurice. *Alexandre Ier, un tsar énigmatique*. Paris: Plon, 1937.

Palissier, Léon G., 'Les Cent-Jours. Passage de l'Empereur à Grenoble (mars 1815): journal du colonel de gendarmerie Jubé', *Nouvelle Revue rétrospective* (July–December 1895): 73–100.

Pallain, Georges (ed.). *Correspondance inédite du Prince de Talleyrand et du roi Louis XVIII pendant le congrès de Vienne*. Paris: E. Plon, 1881.

Pallas, Peter Simon. *Nouveau voyage dans les gouvernements méridionaux de l'Empire de Russie, dans les années 1793 et 1794*. Trans. from the German. 2 vols. Paris: A. Koenig, an X.

Palmer, Alan. *Metternich: Councillor of Europe*. London: Weidenfeld & Nicolson, 1972.

Palmer, Alan. *Alexander I: Tsar of War and Peace*. New York: Harper & Row, 1974.

Palmer, Alan. *Napoleon & Marie Louise: The Emperor's Second Wife*. London: Constable, 2001.

Palmstierna, Carl Frédéric. *Marie-Louise et Napoléon, 1813–1814: lettres inédites de l'Impératrice avec les réponses déjà connues de Napoléon de la même époque*. Paris: Stock, 1955.

*Papers Relative to the Discussion with France in 1802 and 1803*. London: Strahan, 1803.

*Papers Relative to the Discussion with France in the Year 1806*. London: Strahan, 1807.

Paradis, Olivier, 'De la difficulté à vivre ses choix politiques: les jeunes officiers de l'armée, du service du roi à celui de l'empereur', in Crépin, Jessenne and Leuwers (eds), *Civils, citoyens-soldats et militaires*, pp. 135–47.

Paret, Peter. *Yorck and the Era of the Prussian Reform, 1807–1815*. Princeton: Princeton University Press, 1966.

Paret, Peter, 'Jena and Auerstedt', in *Understanding War*, pp. 85–94.

Paret, Peter, 'Napoleon as Enemy', in *Understanding War*, pp. 75–84.

Paret, Peter. *Understanding War: Essays on Clausewitz and the History of Military Power*. Princeton: Princeton University Press, 1992.

Paret, Peter. *The Cognitive Challenge of War: Prussia 1806*. Princeton and Oxford: Princeton University Press, 2009.

Pariset, Georges, 'Les captifs de Bailén', *Revue des études napoléoniennes*, 32 (1931): 209–29.

Parker, Harold T. *Three Napoleonic Battles*. Durham, NC: Duke University Press, 1983.

Parker, Harold T., 'Napoleon I, Daily Round', in Owen Connelly (ed.), *Historical Dictionary of Napoleonic France, 1799–1815* (Westport, Conn.: Greenwood Press, 1985), pp. 357–8.

Parker, Harold T., 'Why Did Napoleon Invade Russia? A Study in Motivation and the Interrelations of Personality and Social Structure', *Journal of Military History*, 54 (1990): 131–46.

Parkinson, Roger. *The Fox of the North: The Life of Kutuzov, General of War and Peace*. New York: David McKay, 1976.

Parquin, Denis-Charles. *Souvenirs de commandant Parquin*. Paris: Tallandier, 2003.

Pasquier, Etienne-Denis. *Histoire de mon temps. Mémoires du chancelier Pasquier*. 6 vols. Paris: E. Plon, Nourrit, 1894–6.

Paulin, Jules-Antoine. *Les Souvenirs du general Bon Paulin (1782–1876)*. Paris: E. Plon, Nourrit, 1895.

Paulmann, Johannes. *Pomp und Politik: Monarchenbegegnungen in Europa zwischen Ancien Régime und Erstem Weltkrieg*. Paderborn: Verlag Ferdinand Schöningh, 2000.

Pelet, Jean-Jacques-Germain, baron. *Mémoires sur la guerre de 1809, en Allemagne*. 4 vols. Paris: Roret, 1824–6.

Pelet, Jean-Jacques-Germain, baron, 'Carnets du général Pelet sur la campagne de Russie de 1812', *Carnet de La Sabretache*, 5 (1906): 519–52, 626–40, 682–702.

Pelet de La Lozère, Jean. *Opinions de Napoléon sur divers sujets de politique et d'administration, recueillies par un membre de son conseil d'Etat, et récit de quelques événements de l'époque*. Paris: Firmin-Didot, 1833.

Pélissier, Léon G. *Le registre de l'île d'Elbe: lettres et ordres inédits de Napoléon Ier (28 mai 1814–22 février 1815)*. Paris: A. Fontemoing, 1897.

Peltzer, Marina, 'Imagerie populaire et caricature: la graphique politique antinapoléonienne en Russie et ses antécédents pétroviens', *Journal of the Warburg and Courtauld Institutes*, 48 (1985): 189–221.

Peltzer, Marina, 'Peasants, Cossacks, "Black Tsar": Russian Caricatures of Napoleon during the Wars of 1812 to 1814', in Alan Forrest, Etienne François and Karen Hagemann (eds), *War Memories: The Revolutionary and Napoleonic Wars in Modern European Culture* (Basingstoke: Palgrave Macmillan, 2012).

Pelzer, Erich, 'Die Widergeburt Deutschlands 1813 und die Dämonisierung Napoleon', in Gerd Krumeich und Hartmut Lehmann (eds), *'Gott mit uns': Nation, Religion und Gewalt im 19. und frühen 20. Jahrhundert* (Göttingen: Vandenhoeck & Ruprecht, 2000), pp. 135–56.

Percy, Pierre-François. *Journal des campagnes du Bon Percy, chirurgien en chef de la Grande-Armée (1754–1825)*. Paris: Plon-Nourrit, 1904.

Perdiguier, Agricol. *Mémoires d'un compagnon*. Paris: La Découverte, 2002.

Périvier, A. *Napoléon journaliste*. Paris: Plon-Nourrit, 1918.

Perol, Lucette, 'Ce qu'évoquait le mot "empire" d'après les dictionnaires de 1690–1771', *Siècles. Cahiers du Centre d'histoire 'Espaces et culture'*, 17 (2003): 25–40.

Pérouse, Honoré. *Napoléon Ier et les lois civiles du consulat et de l'empire*. Paris: Durand, 1866.

Perret, Irène, 'Réception critique de Napoléon sur le champ de bataille d'Eylau d'Antoine-Jean Gros sous le premier empire', *Napoleonica. La Revue*, 4:1 (2009): 50–61.

Perrier, Marie-Victorine. *Adresse de Marie-Victorine aux Français*. Paris: Pelzin, 1815.

Pesenson, Michael A., 'Napoleon Bonaparte and Apocalyptic Discourse in Early Nineteenth-Century Russia', *Russian Review*, 65 (2006): 373–92.

Pétiet, Auguste-Louis. *Souvenirs militaires de l'histoire contemporaine, par le général, baron, Auguste Pétiet*. Paris: Dumaine, 1844.

Petit, Joseph. *Marengo, ou Campagne d'Italie, par l'armée de réserve, commandé par le général Bonaparte*. Paris: Chez les Marchands de Nouveautés, an IX.

Petiteau, Natalie, 'Marengo, histoire et mythologie', in Messiez and Sorrel (eds), *La deuxième campagnes d'Italie*, pp. 209–20.

Petiteau, Natalie. *Napoléon, de la mythologie à l'histoire*. Paris: Seuil, 1999.

Petiteau, Natalie, 'La Contre-Révolution endiguée? Projets et réalisations sociales impériales', in Martin (ed.), *La Contre-Revolution en Europe*, pp. 183–92.

Petiteau, Natalie, 'Le retour de guerre: destins de vétérans après 1815', in Boudon (ed.), *Armée, guerre et société à l'époque napoléonienne*, pp. 87–103.

Petiteau, Natalie (ed.). *Voies nouvelles pour l'histoire du Premier Empire: territoires, pouvoirs, identités*. Paris: La Boutique de l'Histoire, 2003.

Petiteau, Natalie. *Lendemains d'Empire: les soldats de Napoléon dans la France du XIXe siècle*. Paris: La Boutique de l'Histoire, 2003.

Petiteau, Natalie, 'Pourquoi Napoléon crée-t-il la Légion d'honneur?', in Jean Tulard, François Monnier and Olivier Echappé (eds), *La Légion d'honneur: deux siècles d'histoire* (Paris: Perrin, 2004), pp. 35–48.

Petiteau, Natalie, 'Insultes et hostilités politiques sous le Consulat et l'Empire', in Thomas Bouchet, Matthew Legget, Jean Vigreux and Geneviève Verdo (eds), *L'Insulte (en) politique: Europe et Amérique latine du XIXe siècle à nos jours* (Dijon: Editions Universitaires de Dijon, 2005), pp. 209–16.

Petiteau, Natalie, 'La Restauration face aux vétérans de l'Empire', in Martine Reid, Jean-Yves Mollier and Jean-Claude Yon (eds), *Repenser la Restauration* (Paris: Nouveau Monde éditions, 2005), pp. 31–43.

Petiteau, Natalie, 'Les fidélités républicaines sous le Consulat et l'Empire', *Annales historiques de la Révolution française*, 346 (2006): 59–74.

Petiteau, Natalie. *Les Français et l'Empire (1799–1815)*. Paris: La Boutique de l'Histoire, 2008.

Petiteau, Natalie, 'Les Français et l'empereur', in Hélène Becquet and Bettina Frederking (eds), *La dignité de roi: regards sur la royauté au premier XIXe siècle* (Paris: Presses Universitaires de Rennes, 2009), pp. 19–34.

Petiteau, Natalie, 'Légion d'honneur et normes sociales', in Bruno Dumons et Gilles Pollet (eds), *La fabrique de l'honneur: les médailles et les décorations en France, XIXe–XXe siècles* (Rennes: Presses Universitaires de Rennes, 2009), pp. 17–30.

Petiteau, Natalie, 'Les justifications impériales de l'intervention en Espagne', in Dufour and Larriba (eds), *L'Espagne en 1808*, pp. 9–24.

Petiteau, Natalie, 'Lecture socio-politique de l'empire: bilan et perspectives', *Annales historiques de la Révolution française*, 359 (2010): 181–202.

Petiteau, Natalie, Olivier, Jean-Marc and Caucanas, Sylvie (eds). *Les Européens dans les guerre napoléoniennes*. Toulouse: Privat, 2012.

Petre, F. Loraine. *Napoleon's Campaign in Poland, 1806–1807*. London: Bodley Head, 1907.

Petre, F. Loraine. *Napoleon's Conquest of Prussia (1806)*. London: John Lane, 1907.

Petre, F. Loraine. *Napoleon and the Archduke Charles: A History of the Franco-Austrian Campaign in the Valley of the Danube in 1809*. London: John Lane, 1909.

Petre, F. Loraine. *Napoleon's Last Campaign in Germany, 1813*. London: John Lane, 1912.

Petre, F. Loraine. *Napoleon at Bay, 1814*. London: John Lane, 1914.

Peyrusse, Guillaume. *1809–1815. Mémorial et archives de M. le Baron Peyrusse*. Carcassonne: La Bau, 1869.

Peyrusse, Guillaume. *Lettres inédites du baron Guillaume Peyrusse, écrites à son frère André, pendant les campagnes de l'empire, de 1809 à 1814*. Paris: Perrin, 1894.

Pfister, Christian. *Les fêtes à Nancy sous le Consulat et le Premier Empire (1799–1813)*. Nancy: Berger-Levrault, 1914.

Phillips, Roderick. *Family Breakdown in Late Eighteenth-Century France: Divorces in Rouen, 1792–1803*. Oxford: Clarendon Press, 1980.

Phillips, Roderick. *Putting Asunder: A History of Divorce in Western Society*. Cambridge: Cambridge University Press, 1988.

Phillips, Roderick. *Untying the Knot: A Short History of Divorce*. Cambridge: Cambridge University Press, 1991.

Philp, Mark (ed.). *Resisting Napoleon: The British Response to the Threat of Invasion, 1797–1815*. Aldershot: Ashgate, 2006.

Picard, Ernest. *Bonaparte et Moreau: l'entente initiale, les premiers dissentiments, la rupture*. Paris: Plon-Nourrit, 1905.

Picard, Ernest. *Hohenlinden*. Paris: H. Charles-Lavauzelle, 1909.

Picard, Ernest and Tuetey, Louis (eds). *Correspondance inédite de Napoléon Ier, conservée aux Archives de la guerre*. 5 vols. Paris: H. Charles-Lavauzelle, 1912–25.

*Pichegru et Moreau*. Paris: Chez les Marchands de Nouveautés, 1804.

Pichon, Louis-André. *De l'Etat de la France, sous la domination de Napoléon Bonaparte*. Paris: J.-G. Dentu, 1814.

Pierre, Michel Désiré. *Ney, du procès politique à la réhabilitation du 'Brave des braves': 1815–1991*. Paris: SPM, 2003.

Pierrelongue, Jean (ed.). *Napoléon et Marie-Louise: correspondance*. Paris: SPM, 2010.

Piétri, François. *Napoléon et le Parlement ou la dictature enchaînée*. Paris: Fayard, 1955.

Pietromarchi, Antonello. *Lucien Bonaparte: prince romain*. Paris: Perrin, 1985.

Pigeard, Alain. *Napoléon amoureux*. Paris: Tallandier, 2007.

Pigeaud, Romain, 'Le charnier des grognards', *Archeologia*, 401 (June 2003): 41–7.

Pillard, Guy-Edouard. *Louis Fontanes, 1757–1821: prince de l'esprit*. Maulévrier: Hérault, 1990.

Pillepich, Alain, 'Napoléon Ier et la couronne de fer', in Graziella Buccellati and Annamaria Ambrosioni (eds), *La corona, il regno e l'impero: un millennio di storia*. 2 vols. Milan: G. Mondadori, 1995–9, i. pp. 197–212.

Pillepich, Alain. *Eugène de Beauharnais: honneur et fidélité*. Paris: Réunion des musées nationaux, 1999.

Pillepich, Alain, 'Un tableau célèbre replacé dans son contexte: *Bonaparte franchissant les Alpes au Grand-Saint-Bernard* de David', *Revista Napoleonica*, 1–2 (2000): 75–81.

Pillepich, Alain. *Napoléon et les Italiens: République italienne et Royaume d'Italie, 1802–1814*. Paris: Nouveau Monde éditions, 2003.

Pils, François. *Journal de marche du Grenadier Pils (1804–1814)*. Paris: Ollendorff, 1895.

Pingaud, Albert. *La domination française dans l'Italie du Nord (1796–1805): Bonaparte, président de la République italienne*. 2 vols. Paris: Perrin, 1914.

Pingaud, Léonce. *Bernadotte, Napoléon et les Bourbons (1797–1844)*. Paris: Plon-Nourrit, 1901.

Pingaud, Léonce. *Bernadotte et Napoléon (1797–1814)*. Paris: Plon, 1933.

Pinkard, Terry. *Hegel: A Biography*. Cambridge: Cambridge University Press, 2000.

Pion des Loches, Antoine-Augustin-Flavien. *Mes campagnes, 1792–1815: notes et correspondance du colonel d'artillerie Pion des Loches*. Paris: Firmin-Didot, 1889.

Pitt-Rivers, Julian, 'La maladie de l'honneur', in Marie Gautheron and Jean-Michel Belorgey (eds), *L'honneur: image de soi ou don de soi: un idéal équivoque* (Paris: Autrement, 1991), pp. 20–36.

Planat de La Faye, Nicolas Louis. *Vie de Planat de La Faye, aide de camp des généraux Lariboisière et Drouot, officier d'ordonnance de Napoléon Ier. Souvenirs, lettres et dictées recueillis et annotés par sa veuve*. Paris: Ollendorff, 1895.

Planert, Ute (ed.). *Nation, Politik und Geschlecht: Frauenbewegungen und Nationalismus in der Moderne*. Frankfurt: Campus, 2000.

Planert, Ute. *Der Mythos vom Befreiungskrieg: Frankreichs Kriege und der deutsche Süden: Alltag, Wahrnehmung, Deutung 1792–1841*. Paderborn: Verlag Ferdinand Schöningh, 2007.

Planert, Ute, 'Conscription, Economic Exploitation and Religion in Napoleonic Germany', in Dwyer and Forrest (eds), *Napoleon and his Empire*, pp. 133–48.

Plongeron, Bernard, 'Cyrus ou les lectures d'une figure biblique dans la rhetorique religieuse, de l'ancien Regime à Napoleon', *Revue d'histoire de l'Eglise de France*, 68 (1982): 31–67.

Plongeron, Bernard, 'Le catéchisme impérial (1806) et l'irritante leçon VII sur le quatrième commandement', in Marie-Madeleine Fragonard and Michel Peronnet (eds), *Catéchismes et confessions de foi* (Montpellier: Université Paul Valéry, 1995), pp. 287–310.

Plongeron, Bernard, 'De Napoléon à Metternich: une modernité en état de blocus', in Mayeur et al. (eds), *Histoire du christianisme*, vol. x: *Les défis de la modernité (1750–1840)*, pp. 627–738.

Plongeron, Bernard, 'Face au Concordat (1801), résistances des évêques anciens constitutionnels', *Annales historiques de la Révolution française*, 337 (2004): 85–115.

Plongeron, Bernard. *Des résistances religieuses à Napoléon, 1799–1813*. Paris: Letouzey & Ané, 2006.

Ploux, François. *De bouche à l'oreille: naissance et propagation des rumeurs dans la France du XIXe siècle*. Paris: Aubier, 2003.

Plumptre, Anne. *A Narrative of a Three Years Residence in France.* 3 vols. London: R. Taylor, 1810.

Poe, Marshall and Lohr, Eric (eds). *The Military and Society in Russia, 1450–1917.* Leiden: Brill, 2002.

*Poëme à l'occasion du Sénatus-consulte, qui proclame Napoléon Bonaparte, Empereur des Français.* Paris: Maradan, 1804.

Poeteraux, abbé Fugantini. *Confession poétique et véridique de Buonaparte au Révérend Père Boniface, ci-devant capucin d'Ajaccio, suivie de son action de grâce à Louis XVIII.* Paris: Impr. de L.-P. Sétier fils, 1814.

Poissenot, J.-B. *Historique et statistique sur la ville d'Aix-la-Chapelle et ses environs, pouvant servir d'itinéraire.* Aix-la-Chapelle: D.-P. La Ruelle, 1808.

Polowetzky, Michael. *A Bond Never Broken: The Relations between Napoleon and the Authors of France.* Rutherford: Fairleigh Dickinson University Press, 1993.

Pons, André [dubbed Pons de l'Hérault]. *Souvenirs et anecdotes de l'île d'Elbe.* Paris: E. Plon, Nourrit, 1897.

Pontécoulant, Gustave de. *Souvenirs historiques et parlementaires du comte de Pontécoulant, ancien pair de France.* 4 vols. Paris: Michel Lévy frères, 1861–5.

Pontet, Josette (ed.). *Napoléon, Bayonne et l'Espagne: actes du colloque.* Paris: H. Champion, 2011.

Popkin, Jeremy D. *The Right-Wing Press in France, 1792–1800.* Chapel Hill: University of North Carolina Press, 1980.

Popkin, Jeremy D., 'Conservatism under Napoleon: The Political Writings of Joseph Fiévée', *History of European Ideas,* 5 (1984): 385–400.

Popkin, Jeremy D. *Revolutionary News: The Press in France, 1789–1799.* Durham, NC: Duke University Press, 1990.

Portalis, Jean-Etienne-Marie. *Discours préliminaire au premier projet de Code civil.* Bordeaux: Editions Confluences, 1999.

Porterfield, Todd. *The Allure of Empire: Art in the Service of French Imperialism, 1798–1836.* Princeton: Princeton University Press, 1998.

Porterfield, Todd and Siegfried, Susan L. *Staging Empire: Napoleon, Ingres, and David.* University Park, Pa.: Pennsylvania State University Press, 2006.

Porterfield, Todd, 'David sans David', in Ledbury (ed.), *David after David,* pp. 39–53.

Poumiès de la Siboutie, François-Louis. *Souvenirs d'un médecin de Paris.* Paris: Plon-Nourrit, 1910.

*A Practical Guide during a Journey from London to Paris; with a Correct Description of all the Objects Deserving of Notice in the French Metropolis.* London: R. Phillips, 1802.

Pradt, Dominique Dufour, baron de. *Histoire de l'ambassade dans le Grand Duché de Varsovie en 1812.* Paris: Pillet, 1815.

Pradt, Dominique Dufour, baron de. *Mémoires historiques sur la révolution d'Espagne.* Paris: Rosa, 1816.

Prendergast, Christopher. *Napoleon and History Painting: Antoine-Jean Gros's La Bataille d'Eylau.* Oxford: Oxford University Press, 1997.

Price, Munro. *The Perilous Crown: France between Revolutions.* London: Macmillan, 2008.

Price, Munro, 'Napoleon and Metternich in 1813: Some New and Some Neglected Evidence', *French History,* 26:4 (2012): 482–503.

*Procès instruit par le tribunal criminel du département de la Seine contre les nommés Saint-Réjant, Carbon, et autres, prévenus de conspiration contre la personne du Premier Consul.* Paris: Imprimerie de la République, an IX.

*La proclamation du Premier Empire ou Recueil des pièces et actes relatifs à l'établissement du gouvernement impérial héréditaire, imprimé par ordre du Sénat conservateur.* Introduction by Thierry Lentz. Paris: Nouveau Monde éditions, 2001.

*Programme de la fête de la paix qui aura lieu le 18 brumaire an X.* Paris: Gauthier, 1801.

Prudhomme, Louis-Marie. *Miroir historique, politique et critique de l'ancien et du nouveau Paris, et du département de la Seine.* 6 vols. Paris: Prudhomme fils, 1807.

Puryear, Vernon J. *Napoleon and the Dardanelles*. Berkeley: University of California Press, 1951.

Puybusque, Louis-Guillaume de. *Lettres sur la guerre de Russie en 1812, sur la ville de St. Petersbourg, les moeurs et les usages des habitans de la Russie et de Pologne*. Paris: Magimel, Anselin et Pochard, 1816.

Puymaigre, Alexandre de. *Souvenirs sur l'émigration, l'Empire et la Restauration*. Paris: E. Plon, Nourrit, 1884.

Pyhrr, Stuart W., 'De la Révolution au romantisme: les origines des collections modernes d'armes et d'armures', in Gallo (ed.), *Les vies de Dominique-Vivant Denon*, ii. pp. 618–50.

Quataert, Jean H. *Staging Philanthropy: Patriotic Women and the National Imagination in Dynastic Germany, 1813–1916*. Ann Arbor: University of Michigan Press, 2001.

Quaynat. *Ode à Sa Majesté l'Empereur et Roi sur la prise de Moscou*. Paris: chez tous les libraires, 1812.

*La queue de Buonaparte, ou les malveillants, les factieux et les agitateurs dévoilés et confondus*. Paris: Impr. de J. Moronval, n.d.

Quinault, Roland E. and Stevenson, John (eds). *Popular Protest and Public Order: Six Studies in British History, 1790–1920*. London: Allen & Unwin, 1974.

Quynn, Dorothy Mackay, 'The Art Confiscations of the Napoleonic Wars', *American Historical Review*, 50 (1945): 437–60.

Rabbe, Alphonse. *Résumé de l'histoire de Russie depuis l'établissement de Rourik . . . jusqu'à nos jours*. Paris: Lecointe et Durey, 1825.

Radet, Etienne. *Mémoires du général Radet*. Saint-Cloud: Belin frères, 1892.

Radiguet, Léon. *L'acte additionnel aux Constitutions de l'Empire du 22 avril 1815*. Caen: E. Domin, 1911.

Radziwill, Louise de Prusse, princesse Antoine. *Quarante-cinq années de ma vie (1770 à 1815)*. Paris: Plon-Nourrit, 1911.

Raeff, Marc. *Michael Speransky: Statesman of Imperial Russia, 1772–1839*. The Hague: M. Nijhoff, 1969.

Ragsdale, Hugh, 'The Origins of Bonaparte's Russian Policy', *Slavic Review*, 27 (1968): 85–90.

Ragsdale, Hugh, 'Russian Influence at Lunéville', *French Historical Studies*, 5 (1968): 274–84.

Ragsdale, Hugh, 'Was Paul Bonaparte's Fool? The Evidence of Neglected Archives', in Hugh Ragsdale (ed.), *Paul I*, pp. 76–90.

Ragsdale, Hugh (ed.). *Paul I: A Reassessment of his Life and Reign*. Pittsburgh, Pa.: University Center for International Studies, University of Pittsburgh, 1979.

Ragsdale, Hugh. *Détente in the Napoleonic Era: Bonaparte and the Russians*. Lawrence, Kan.: Regents Press of Kansas, 1980.

Ragsdale, Hugh, 'Russia, Prussia, and Europe in the Policy of Paul I', *Jahrbücher für Geschichte Osteuropas*, 31:1 (1983): 81–118.

Ragsdale, Hugh, 'Russian Foreign Policy, 1725–1815', in Dominic Lieven (ed.), *The Cambridge History of Russia*, 3 vols (Cambridge, 2006), ii. pp. 504–29.

Raimbach, Abraham. *Memoirs and Recollections of the late Abraham Raimbach*. London: Frederick Shoberl, 1843.

Rambaud, Alfred, 'La Grande Armée à Moscou d'après les témoignages Moscovites', *Revue des Deux Mondes*, 106 (1873): 194–228.

Rambaud, Jacques. *Naples sous Joseph Bonaparte, 1806–1808*. Paris: Plon-Nourrit, 1911.

Rambuteau, Claude-Philibert, comte de. *Mémoires du comte de Rambuteau*. Paris: Calmann-Lévy, 1905.

Ramírez, F. Acosta and Jiménez, M. Ruiz (eds). *Baylen 1808–2008: Bailén: su impacto en la nueva Europa del XIX y su proyección futura*. Jaén: Universidad de Jaén, 2009.

Randon, General, 'Retour de l'Île d'Elbe', *Revue de l'Empire*, v (1847): 329–41.

Ranke, Leopold von. *Denkwürdigkeiten des Staatskanzlers Fürsten von Hardenberg*. 5 vols. Leipzig: Duncker und Humbolt, 1877.

Rapp, Jean. *Mémoires du général Rapp, aide-de-camp de Napoléon*. Paris: Bossange, 1823.

Ratchinski, André. *Napoléon et Alexandre Ier: la guerre des idées*. Paris: B. Giovanangeli, 2002.

Rattier, Jean-Henry, 'Campagne d'Italie (1796): notes d'un sergent major', *Revue retrospective. Recueil de pièces intéressantes*, xx (1894): 217–88, 322–41.

Ravitch, Norman, 'Liberalism, Catholicism, and the Abbé Grégoire', *Church History*, 36:4 (1967): 419–39.

Réal, Pierre-François. *Les indiscrétions d'un préfet de police de Napoléon*. 2 vols. Paris: Tallandier, 1986.

'Un récit de la bataille de Marengo', *Le carnet historique et littéraire*, ii (1898): 877–80.

*Recueil des actions héroïques et civiques des républicans français*. Paris: l'imprimerie nationale, an II.

*Recueil des interrogatoires subis par le général Moreau, des interrogatoires de quelques-uns de ses coaccusés, des procès-verbaux de confrontation et autres pièces produites au soutien de l'accusation dirigée contre ce général*. Paris: Impr. impériale, an XII.

*Recueil des pièces authentiques relatives au suicide de l'ex-général Pichegru*. Paris: Impr. de Patris, 1804.

*Recueil précieux pour les historiens de ce temps, ou choix de brochures et de pamphlets sur les personnages et les événements de la Révolution à dater de la première abdication de Buonaparte jusqu'au moment present*. 4 vols. Paris: Chez les Marchands de Nouveautés, 1815.

Reder, Dirk Alexander. *Frauenbewegung und Nation: Patriotische Frauenvereine in Deutschland im frühen 19. Jahrhundert (1813–1830)*. Cologne: SH-Verlag, 1998.

Reeve, Henry. *Journal of a Residence at Vienna and Berlin in the Eventful Winter 1805–6*. London: Longmans, Green, 1877.

*Réflexions philosophiques et critiques sur les couronnes et les couronnemens*. Paris: Chez Tous les Marchands de Nouveautés, 1804.

Regele, Oskar. *Feldmarschall Radetzky: Leben/Leistung/Erbe*. Vienna: Verlagherold, 1957.

Régnier, Claude-Ambroise. *Liste des brigands chargés, par le Ministère britannique, d'attenter aux jours du Premier Consul*. Paris: Impr. de la République, an XII.

Régnier, Claude-Ambroise. *Rapport du grand-juge au Premier Consul, et communiqué au Sénat dans sa séance de germinal, contenant toutes les pièces de la conspiration tramée par le gouvernement britannique, contre les jours du Premier Consul!* Paris: Impr. de Clermont, an XII.

Reichardt, Johann Friedrich. *Un hiver à Paris sous le Consulat, 1802–1803*. Paris: E. Plon, Nourrit, 1896.

Reinhard, Christine. *Une femme de diplomate: lettres de Mme Reinhard à sa mere, 1798–1815*. Paris: Picard, 1900.

Reinhard, Marcel, 'L'armée et Bonaparte en 1801', *Annales historiques de la Révolution française*, 25 (1953): 292–6.

Reiss, René. *Kellermann*. Paris: Tallandier, 2009.

*Relation de la mission du Lieutenant-général comte Becker auprès de l'empereur Napoléon depuis la seconde abdication jusqu'au passage à bord du 'Béllérophon'*. Clermont-Ferrand: Perol, 1841.

Remacle, Comte. *Relations secrètes des agents de Louis XVIII à Paris sous le Consulat (1802–1803)*. Paris: E. Plon, Nourrit, 1899.

Rémusat, Charles de. *Mémoires de ma vie*. 5 vols. Paris: Plon, 1958–67.

Rémusat, Claire-Elisabeth-Jeanne Gravier de Vergennes, comtesse de. *Mémoires de Madame de Rémusat, 1802–1808*. 3 vols. Paris: Calmann-Lévy, 1880.

Rémusat, Claire-Elisabeth-Jeanne Gravier de Vergennes, comtesse de. *Lettres de Mme de Rémusat, 1804–1811*. 2 vols. Paris: Calmann-Lévy, 1881.

Rémusat, Claire-Elisabeth-Jeanne Gravier de Vergennes, comtesse de. *Mémoires de Mme de Rémusat 1802–1808*. Introduction and notes by Charles Kunstler. Paris: Hachette, 1957.

Rey, Marie-Pierre. *Alexandre Ier*. Paris: Flammarion, 2009.

Rey, Marie-Pierre, 'De l'uniforme à l'accoutrement: une métaphore de la retraite? Réalité et symbolique du vêtement dans la campagne de Russie de 1812', in Petiteau, Olivier and Caucanas (eds), *Les Européens dans les guerre napoléoniennes*, pp. 237–50.

Reymond, René. *La route Napoléon: de l'Île d'Elbe aux Tuileries.* Lyons: La Manufacture, 1985.

Rials, Stéphane. *Révolution et contre-révolution au XIXe siècle.* Paris: Albatros, 1987.

Ribe, Georges. *L'opinion publique et la vie politique à Lyon lors des premières années de la seconde Restauration.* Paris: Librairie du Recueil Sirey, 1957.

Richter, Melvin, 'Toward a Concept of Political Illegitimacy: Bonapartist Dictatorship and Democratic Legitimacy', *Political Theory*, 10 (1982): 185–214.

Ricome, Jean-Baptiste. *Journal d'un grognard de l'Empire.* Paris: Presses du CNRS, 1988.

Rifkin, Adrian, 'History, Time and the Morphology of Critical Language, or Publicola's Choice', in Orwicz (ed.), *Art Criticism and its Institutions in Nineteenth-Century France*, pp. 29–42.

Riley, J. P. *Napoleon and the World War of 1813: Lessons in Coalition Warfighting.* London: Frank Cass, 2000.

Robert, André. *L'idée nationale autrichienne et les guerres de Napoléon: l'apostolat du baron de Hormayr et le salon de Caroline Pichler.* Paris: Félix Alcan, 1933.

Roberts, Andrew. *Napoleon and Wellington: The Battle of Waterloo and the Great Commanders who Fought It.* New York: Simon & Schuster, 2001.

Roberts, Andrew. *Waterloo: Napoleon's Last Gamble.* London: HarperCollins, 2005.

Roberts, William, 'Napoleon, the Concordat of 1801, and its Consequences', in Frank J. Coppa (ed.), *Controversial Concordats: The Vatican's Relations with Napoleon, Mussolini, and Hitler* (Washington, DC: The Catholic University of America Press, 1999), pp. 34–83.

*Robespierre et Buonaparte, ou les deux tyrannies.* Paris: Chez Tous les Marchands de Nouveautés, 1814.

Robin, Pierre and Dufourg Burg, Christophe (eds). *Austerlitz: récits de soldats.* Paris: B. Giovanangeli, 2006.

Robinaux, Pierre. *Journal de route du capitaine Robinaux, 1803–1832.* Paris: Plon-Nourrit, 1908.

Robineau-Desvoidy, J.-B. *Le 17 mars 1815.* Auxerre: Mme Robert, 1829.

Robinson, John Martin. *Cardinal Consalvi, 1757–1824.* London: Bodley Head, 1987.

Roche, Daniel, 'The English in Paris', in Christophe Charle, Julien Vincent and Jay Winter (eds), *Anglo-French Attitudes: Comparisons and Transfers between English and French Intellectuals since the Eighteenth Century* (Manchester: Manchester University Press, 2007), pp. 78–97.

Rochechouart, Louis-Victor-Léon de. *Souvenirs sur la Révolution, l'Empire et la Restauration, par le général Cte de Rochechouart.* Paris: Plon, 1933.

Rocquain, Félix. *Napoléon Ier et le roi Louis, d'après les documents conservés aux Archives nationales.* Paris: Firmin-Didot, 1875.

Rodger, A. B. *The War of the Second Coalition, 1798 to 1801: A Strategic Commentary.* Oxford: Clarendon Press, 1964.

Rodocanachi, Emmanuel. *Etudes et fantaisies historiques.* 2 vols. Paris: Hachette, 1912–19.

Rodocanachi, Emmanuel, 'Pie VII à Paris', in *Etudes et fantaisies historiques*, i. pp. 1–49.

Roederer, Pierre-Louis. *Un Citoyen à un sénateur. 18 floréal an X.* N.p., n.d.

Roederer, Pierre-Louis. *La Première année du Consulat de Bonaparte.* N.p., n.d.

Roederer, Pierre-Louis. *Oeuvres du comte Pierre-Louis Roederer.* 8 vols. Paris: Firmin-Didot, 1853–9.

Roederer, Pierre-Louis. *Autour de Bonaparte: journal du Cte P.-L. Roederer, ministre et conseiller d'Etat, notes intimes et politiques d'un familier des Tuileries.* Paris: H. Daragon, 1909.

Roederer, Pierre-Louis. *Bonaparte me disait: conversations.* Paris: Horizons de France, 1942.

Roederer, Pierre-Louis. *Mémoires sur la Révolution, le Consulat et l'Empire.* Paris: Plon, 1942.

Rogeron, Louis. *Les cosaques en Champagne et en Brie, récits de l'invasion de 1814, racontés d'après les contemporains, les auteurs modernes, des documents originaux et des notes inédites de témoins oculaires.* Paris: E. Gaillard, 1905.

Roguet, François. *Mémoires militaires du lieutenant général Cte Roguet (François), colonel en second des grenadiers à pied de la vieille garde, pair de France.* 4 vols. Paris: J. Dumaine, 1862–5.

Roider, Karl A. *Baron Thugut and Austria's Response to the French Revolution.* Princeton: Princeton University Press, 1987.

Roider, Karl, 'The Habsburg Foreign Ministry and Political Reform, 1801–1805', *Central European History*, 22:2 (1989): 160–82.

Rollin, Henry, 'L'amiral Villeneuve et Napoléon', *Revue des études napoléoniennes*, 3 (1913): 200–34.

Romilly, Samuel. *Memoirs of the life of Sir Samuel Romilly.* 3 vols. London: J. Murray, 1840.

Roos, Heinrich von. *Souvenirs d'un médecin de la Grande Armée.* Paris: La Vouivre, 2004.

Rosanvallon, Pierre. *Le sacre du citoyen: histoire du suffrage universel en France.* Paris: Gallimard, 1992.

Rose, John Holland, 'A British Agent at Tilsit', *English Historical Review*, 16 (1901): 712–18.

Rose, John Holland. *The Life of Napoleon I.* 2 vols. London: G. Bell, 1902.

Rose, John Holland, 'The Censorship under Napoleon I', *Journal of Comparative Legislation and International Law*, 18:1 (1918): 58–65.

Rose, John Holland, 'Napoleon and Sea Power', *Cambridge Historical Journal*, 1 (1924): 138–57.

Rosenberg, Martin, 'Raphael's Transfiguration and Napoleon's Cultural Politics', *Eighteenth Century Studies*, 19 (1985–6): 180–205.

Rosenblum, Robert. *Transformations in Late Eighteenth Century Art.* Princeton: Princeton University Press, 1967.

Ross, Charles (ed.). *Correspondence of Charles, first Marquis Cornwallis.* 3 vols. London: J. Murray, 1859.

Ross, Michael. *The Reluctant King: Joseph Bonaparte. King of the Two Sicilies and Spain.* London: Sidgwick & Jackson, 1976.

Rossetti, Marie-Joseph-Thomas. *Journal d'un compagnon de Murat: Espagne, Naples, Russie.* Paris: Teissèdre, 1998.

Rostopchin, Feodor Vasilievitch. *La Vérité sur l'incendie de Moscou, par le Cte Rostopchine.* Paris: Ponthieu, 1823.

Rothenberg, Gunther E., 'The Habsburg Army in the Napoleonic Wars', *Military Affairs*, 37 (1973): 1–5.

Rothenberg, Gunther E. *The Art of Warfare in the Age of Napoleon.* Bloomington: Indiana University Press, 1980.

Rothenberg, Gunther E. *Napoleon's Great Adversary: Archduke Charles and the Austrian Army 1792–1814.* Staplehurst: Spellmount, 1982.

Rothenberg, Gunther E., 'The Origins, Causes, and Extension of the Wars of the French Revolution and Napoleon', *Journal of Interdisciplinary History*, 18 (1988): 771–93.

Rothenberg, Gunther E., 'The Age of Napoleon', in Michael Howard, George J. Andreopoulos and Mark R. Shulman (eds), *The Laws of War: Constraints on Warfare in the Western World* (New Haven: Yale University Press, 1994), pp. 86–97.

Rothenberg, Gunther E. *The Napoleonic Wars.* London: Cassell, 1999.

Rothenberg, Gunther E. *The Emperor's Last Victory: Napoleon and the Battle of Wagram.* London: Cassell, 2005.

Rouge-Ducos, Isabelle. *L'Arc de Triomphe de l'Etoile: panthéon de la France guerrière: art et histoire.* Dijon: Ed. Faton, impr. 2008.

Roulin, Jean-Marie, 'Le Retour des Cendres de Napoléon: une cérémonie palimpseste', in Corinne and Eric Perrin-Saminadayar (eds), *Imaginaire et représentations des entrées royales au XIXe siècle: une sémiologie du pouvoir politique* (Saint-Etienne: Publications de l'Université de Saint-Etienne, 2006), pp. 83–105.

Roustam Raza, *Souvenirs de Roustam, mamelouck de Napoléon Ier.* Paris: Ollendorff, 1911.

Routier, Léon-Michel. *Récits d'un soldat: de la République et de l'Empire.* Paris: B. Giovanangeli, 2004.

Rouvier, Jean-Baptiste. *Hymne nouveau sur la paix à S.M.I. et R. Napoléon Ier, empereur des Français et roi d'Italie.* N.p., 1807.

Rowe, Michael, 'Debate: Napoleon and the Post-Revolutionary Management of Sovereignty', *Modern & Contemporary France*, 8:4 (2000): 510–13.

Rowe, Michael (ed.). *Collaboration and Resistance in Napoleonic Europe: State-Formation in an Age of Upheaval, c.1800–1815*. Basingstoke: Palgrave Macmillan, 2003.

Rowe, Michael. *From Reich to State: The Rhineland in the Revolutionary Age, 1780–1830*. Cambridge: Cambridge University Press, 2003.

Rowe, Michael, 'France, Prussia, or Germany? The Napoleonic Wars and the Shifting Allegiances in the Rhineland', *Central European History*, 39 (2006): 611–40.

Rowe, Michael, 'Napoleon's France: A Forerunner of Europe's Twentieth-Century Dictatorships?', in Claus-Christian Szejnmann (ed.), *Rethinking History, Dictatorship and War: New Approaches and Interpretations* (London: Continuum, 2009), pp. 87–106.

Roy, Just-Jean-Etienne. *Les Français en Russie, souvenirs de la campagne de 1812 et de deux ans de captivité en Russie*. Tours: Mame, 1856.

Royer, Jean-Pierre, 'Napoléon et l'élaboration du Code civil', in Bastien-Rabner and Coppolani (eds), *Napoléon et le Code civil*, pp. 73–82.

Ruchinskaya, Tatiana, 'The Scottish Architectural Traditions in the Plan for the Reconstruction of Moscow after the Fire of 1812: A Rare Account of the Influence of Scottish Architect William Hastie on Town Planning in Moscow', *Building Research & Information*, 22:4 (1994): 228–33.

Rude, Fernand, 'Le réveil du patriotisme révolutionnaire dans la region Rhône-Alpes en 1814', *Cahiers d'histoire*, 16 (1971): 433–55.

Ruiz, Alain, 'Napoleons Rhein- und Moselreise im Jahre 1804', in Dühr and Lehnert-Leven (eds), *Unter der Trikolore*, ii. pp. 649–68.

Ruiz, Alain, 'Napoléon vu par les Allemands de son temps', in Knopper and Mondot (eds), *L'Allemagne face au modèle français de 1789 à 1815*, pp. 43–63.

Rumigny, Marie-Théodore Gueilly, comte de. *Souvenirs du général comte de Rumigny, aide de camp du roi Louis-Philippe (1789–1860)*. Paris: Emile-Paul, 1821.

Sadleir, Thomas U. (ed.). *An Irish Peer on the Continent (1801–1803). Being a Narrative of the Tour of Stephen, 2nd Earl Mount Cashell, through France, Italy, etc., as related by Catherine Wilmot*. London: Williams & Norgate, 1920.

Sagnac, Philippe, 'L'avènement de Bonaparte à l'Empire: le Consulat à vie', *Revue des études napoléoniennes*, 24 (1925): 133–54, 193–211.

Sainson, Katia, '"Le Régénérateur de la France": Literary Accounts of Napoleonic Regeneration 1799–1805', *Nineteenth-Century French Studies*, 30 (2001–2): 9–25.

Saint-Chamans, Alfred-Armand-Robert de. *Mémoires du général Cte de Saint-Chamans, ancien aide de camp du maréchal Soult, 1802–1832*. Paris: E. Plon, Nourrit, 1896.

Saint-Cyr, Laurent de Gouvion. *Mémoires pour servir à l'histoire militaire sous le directoire, le consulat et l'empire*. 4 vols. Paris: Anselin, 1831.

Saint-Denis, Louis Etienne. *Souvenirs du Mameluck Ali sur l'empereur Napoléon*. Paris: Arléa, 2000.

Salgues, Jacques-Barthélemy. *Mémoire pour servir à l'histoire de France sous le gouvernement de Napoléon Buonaparte et pendant l'absence de la maison de Bourbon (1760–1830)*. 9 vols. Paris: L. Fayolle, 1814–26.

Salomé, Karine, 'L'attentat de la rue Nicaise en 1800: l'irruption d'une violence inédite?', *Revue d'histoire du XIXe siècle*, 40 (2010): 59–75.

Salomé, Karine, 'Les représentations iconographiques de l'attentat politique au XIXe siècle', *La Révolution française*, L'attentat, objet d'histoire, mis en ligne le 19 mars 2012, consulted 8 April 2012: lrf.revues.org/index402.

Samoyault, Jean-Pierre, 'L'ameublement des salles du Trône dans les palais impériaux sous Napoléon Ier', *Bulletin de la Société de l'histoire de l'art français* (1985): 185–206.

Samoyault-Verlet, Colombe, 'The Emperor's Wardrobe', in le Bourhis (ed.), *The Age of Napoleon*, pp. 203–15.

Samuels, Maurice, 'Realizing the Past: History and the Spectacle in Balzac's *Adieu*', *Representations*, 79 (2002): 82–99.

Sand, Georges. *Oeuvre autobiographiques*. 2 vols. Paris: Gallimard, 1970–1.

Sanders, Charles Richard (ed.). *The Collected Letters of Thomas and Jane Welsh Carlyle*. Durham, NC: Duke University Press, 1970.

Sandoz, Marc. *Antoine-François Callet: 1741–1823*. Paris: Editart-les Quatre chemins, 1985.

Sandt, Udolpho van de, 'La fréquentation des Salons sous l'Ancien Régime, la Révolution et l'Empire', *Revue de l'Art*, 73 (1986): 43–8.

Sandt, Udolpho van de, 'Le Salon', in Bonnet (ed.), *L'empire des muses*, pp. 59–78.

Sanson, Rosemonde, 'Le 15 août: fête nationale du Second Empire', in Corbin, Gérôme and Tartakowsky (eds), *Les usages politiques des fêtes*, pp. 117–36.

Sarrazin, Jean. *Le onze frimaire, ou Discours analytique de la vie, des exploits mémorables, et des droits de Napoléon Ier*. Paris: Dubroca, 1804.

Saski, Charles-Gaspard-Louis. *Campagne de 1809 en Allemagne et en Autriche*. 4 vols. Paris: Berger-Levrault, 1899–1902.

Saulx-Tavanes, Aglaé Marie Louise de Choiseul Gouffier, Duchesse de. *Sur les routes de l'émigration: mémoires de la duchesse de Saulx-Tavannes (1791–1806)*. Paris: Calmann-Lévy, 1934.

Saunier, Pierre-Maurice. *Tableau historique des cérémonies du sacre et du couronnement de S.M. Napoléon Ier*. Paris: Rochette, an XIII.

Savariau, Norbert. *Louis de Fontanes: belles-lettres et enseignement de la fin de l'Ancien Régime à l'Empire*. Oxford: Voltaire Foundation, 2002.

Savary, Anne-Jean-Marie-René. *Mémoires du duc de Rovigo, pour servir à l'histoire de l'empereur Napoléon*. 8 vols. Paris: Bossange, 1828.

Savatier, René. *L'art de faire les lois: Bonaparte et le Code civil*. Paris: Dalloz, 1927.

Savinel, Pierre. *Moreau, rival républicain de Bonaparte*. Paris: Ouest-France, 1986.

Savoy, Bénédicte. *Patrimoine annexé: les biens culturels saisis par la France en Allemagne autour de 1800*. 2 vols. Paris: Ed. de la Maison des sciences de l'homme, 2003.

Sayve, Auguste de. *Souvenirs de Pologne et scènes militaires de la campagne de 1812*. Paris: Dufart, 1833.

*Sbornik Imperatorskogo Russkogo istoricheskogo obshchestva*. 148 vols. St Petersburg: Russkoe istoricheskoe obshchestvo, 1867–1916.

Schama, Simon. *Citizens: A Chronicle of the French Revolution*. New York: Vintage Books, 1990.

Schama, Simon. *Patriots and Liberators: Revolution in the Netherlands 1780–1813*. London: Fontana, 1992.

Scharf, Claus, 'Rußlands Politik im Bündnis von Tilsit und das Erfurter Gipfeltreffen von 1808', in Benl (ed.), *Der Erfurter Fürstenkongreß*, pp. 167–221.

Schennach, Martin P. *Revolte in der Region: zur Tiroler Erhebung 1809*. Innsbruck: Universitätsverlag Wagner, 2009.

Schérer, Jean-Benoît. *Anecdotes intéressantes et secrètes de la cour de Russie, tirées de ses archives . . . Publiées par un voyageur qui a séjourné treize ans en Russie*. 6 vols. London and Paris: Buisson, 1792, 2nd edn 1806.

Schiel, Irmgard. *Marie-Louise: une Habsbourg pour Napoléon*. Trans. from the German by Jacques Dumont. Paris: Racine, 1998.

Schlenoff, Norman, 'Baron Gros and Napoleon's Egyptian Campaign', in *Essays in Honor of W. Friedlander* (Locust Valley, NY: NYU Institute of Fine Arts, 1965), pp. 152–64.

Schmidt, Albert J., 'William Hastie, Scottish Planner of Russian Cities', *Proceedings of the American Philosophical Society*, 114:3 (1970), 226–4.

Schmidt, Albert J., 'The Restoration of Moscow after 1812', *Slavic Review*, 40:1 (1981): 37–48.

Schmitt, Hans A., '1812: Stein, Alexander I and the Crusade against Napoleon', *Journal of Modern History*, 31 (1959): 325–8.

Schnapper, Antoine. *David, témoin de son temps*. Paris: Bibliothèque des Arts, 1980.

Schnapper, Antoine and Sérullaz, Arlette (eds). *Jacques-Louis David: 1748–1825*. Paris: Ed. de la Réunion des musées nationaux, 1989.

Schneid, Frederick C., 'The Dynamics of Defeat: French Army Leadership, December 1812–March 1813', *Journal of Military History*, 63 (1999): 7–28.

Schneid, Frederick C. *Napoleon's Conquest of Europe: The War of the Third Coalition*. Westport, Conn.: Greenwood Press, 2005.

Schneid, Frederick C. (ed.). *The Projection and Limitations of Imperial Powers, 1618–1850*. Leiden: Brill, 2012.

Schoell, Frédéric. *Recueil de pièces officielles destinées à détromper les François sur les événemens qui se sont passés depuis quelques années*. 12 vols. Paris: Librairie grecque-latine-allemande, 1814–16.

Schom, Alan. *Trafalgar: Countdown to Battle, 1803–1805*. New York: Atheneum, 1990.

Schom, Alan. *One Hundred Days: Napoleon's Road to Waterloo*. New York: Atheneum, 1992.

Schroeder, Paul W., 'An Unnatural "Natural Alliance": Castlereagh, Metternich, and Aberdeen in 1813', *International History Review*, 10 (1988): 517–688.

Schroeder, Paul W., 'Napoleon's Foreign Policy: A Criminal Enterprise', *Journal of Military History*, 54 (1990): 147–61.

Schroeder, Paul W. *The Transformation of European Politics, 1763–1848*. Oxford: Oxford University Press, 1994.

Schultz, Kirsten. *Tropical Versailles: Empire, Monarchy, and the Portuguese Royal Court in Rio de Janeiro, 1808–1821*. London: Routledge, 2001.

Schulz, Friedrich. *Voyage en Pologne et en Allemagne, fait en 1793, par un Livonien, où l'on trouve des détails très étendus sur la révolution de Pologne, en 1791 et en 1794, ainsi que la description de Varsovie, Dresde, Nuremberg, Vienne, Munich*. Brussels: Weissenbruch, 1807.

Schulze, Hagen. *States, Nations, and Nationalism: From the Middle Ages to the Present*. Trans. from the German by W. E. Yuill. Oxford: Basil Blackwell, 1996.

Scott, Franklin D., 'Bernadotte and the Throne of France, 1814', *Journal of Modern History*, 5 (1933): 465–78.

Scott, Hamish. *The Birth of a Great Power System, 1740–1815*. Harlow: Pearson/Longman, 2006.

Scott, Hamish and Simms, Brendan (eds). *Cultures of Power in Europe during the Long Eighteenth Century*. Cambridge: Cambridge University Press, 2007.

Scott, John Barber. *An Englishman at Home and Abroad, 1792–1828: With Some Recollections of Napoleon*. Bungay: Morrow, 1988.

Ségur, Philippe de. *Histoire de Napoléon et de la grande-armée pendant l'année 1812*. 2 vols. Brussels: A. Lacrosse, 1825.

Ségur, Philippe de. *Histoire et Mémoires, par le général comte de Ségur*. 7 vols. Paris: Firmin-Didot, 1873.

Ségur, Philippe de. *De 1800 à 1812. Un aide de camp de Napoléon. Mémoires du général comte de Ségur*. 3 vols. Paris: Firmin-Didot, 1894–5.

Ségur, Philippe de. *Du Rhin à Fontainebleau: mémoires du général comte de Ségur*. Paris: Nelson, n.d.

Ségur, Philippe-Paul, comte de. *History of the Expedition to Russia Undertaken by the Emperor Napoleon in the Year 1812*. 2 vols. London: Treuttel and Würtz, 1825.

Ségur, Philippe-Paul, comte de. *Napoleon's Russian Campaign*. Trans. J. David Townsend. New York: Time, 1965.

Séguy, Philippe, 'Costume in the Age of Napoleon', in le Bourhis (ed.), *The Age of Napoleon*, pp. 23–117.

Seigan, Kôbô, 'La propagande pour la conscription, l'armée et la guerre dans le département de la Seine-Inférieure, du Directoire à la fin de l'Empire', in Biard, Crépin and Gainot (eds), *La plume et le sabre*, pp. 271–81.

Selincourt, Ernest de (ed.). *The Letters of William and Dorothy Wordsworth*. 6 vols. Oxford: Clarendon Press, 1935–9.

Sellin, Volker, 'Restauration et légitimité en 1814', *Francia*, 26/2 (1999): 115–29.

Sellin, Volker. *Die geraubte Revolution: der Sturz Napoleons und die Restauration in Europa*. Göttingen: Vandenhoeck & Ruprecht, 2001.

Semmel, Stuart, 'Reading the Tangible Past: British Tourism, Collecting, and Memory after Waterloo', *Representations*, 69 (Winter 2000): 9–37.

Semmel, Stuart. *Napoleon and the British*. New Haven and London: Yale University Press, 2004.

Senkowska-Gluck, Monika, 'La campagne de 1812', in Tulard (ed.), *L'Europe au temps de Napoléon*, pp. 445–70.

Sepinwall, Alyssa Goldstein. *The Abbé Grégoire and the French Revolution: The Making of Modern Universalism*. Berkeley: University of California Press, 2005.

Séruzier, Théodore-Jean-Joseph, Baron du. *Mémoires militaires du Baron Seruzier, colonel d'artillerie légère*. Paris: Anselin et Pochard, 1823.

Sheehan, James J. *German History: 1770–1866*. Oxford: Clarendon Press, 1989.

Sherwig, John M. *Guineas and Gunpowder; British Foreign Aid in the Wars with France, 1793–1815*. Cambridge, Mass.: Harvard University Press, 1969.

Showalter, Dennis, 'Prussia's Army: Continuity and Change, 1713–1830', in Dwyer (ed.), *The Rise of Prussia*, pp. 220–36.

Sibire, abbé Sébastien-André. *Le portrait de Buonaparte, suivi d'un discours sur la nature et l'effet des conquêtes*. Paris: Lenormant, 1814.

Siegfried, Susan Locke, 'The Politics of Criticism at the Salon of 1806: Ingres's *Napoleon Enthroned*', *Proceedings of the Consortium on Revolutionary Europe* (Athens, Georgia: Institute on Napoleon and the French Revolution, 1980), pp. 69–81.

Siegfried, Susan Locke, 'Naked History: The Rhetoric of Military Painting in Postrevolutionary France', *Art Bulletin*, 75:2 (1993): 235–58.

Siegfried, Susan Locke, 'The Politicisation of Art Criticism in the Post-Revolutionary Press', in Orwicz (ed.), *Art Criticism and its Institutions in Nineteenth-Century France*, pp. 9–28.

Siegfried, Susan Locke. *The Art of Louis-Leopold Boilly: Modern Life in Napoleonic France*. New Haven: Yale University Press, 1995.

Siegfried, Susan Locke, 'Fashion and the Reinvention of Court Costume in Portrayals of Josephine de Beauharnais (1794–1809)', in Isabelle Paresys and Natacha Coquery (eds), *Se vêtir à la cour en Europe (1400–1815)* (Villeneuve d'Ascq and Versailles: IRHiS-CEGES-CRCV, 2011), pp. 229–53.

Simms, Brendan, 'The Road to Jena: Prussian High Politics 1804–6', *German History*, 12:3 (1994): 374–94.

Simms, Brendan. *The Impact of Napoleon: Prussian High Politics, Foreign Policy and the Crisis of the Executive, 1797–1806*. Cambridge: Cambridge University Press, 1997.

Simms, Brendan. *Struggle for Mastery in Germany*. Basingstoke: Macmillan, 1998.

Simms, Brendan, 'Britain and Napoleon', *Historical Journal*, 41:3 (1998): 885–94.

Simonetta, Marcello and Arikha, Noga. *Napoleon and the Rebel: A Story of Brotherhood, Passion, and Power*. New York: Palgrave Macmillan, 2011.

Simpson, Michael. *Closet Performances: Political Exhibition and Prohibition in the Dramas of Byron and Shelley*. Stanford, Calif.: Stanford University Press, 1998.

Siret, M. *Discours prononcé dans l'église paroissiale de Saint Merry, le dimanche 29 décembre dernier, à l'occasion du Te Deum chanté en actions de graces de la victoire d'Austerlitz*. Paris: Impr. de Hacquart, 1806.

Sirotkine, Vladilen, 'La campagne de Russie', *Revue de l'Institut Napoléon*, 156 (1991): 57–65.

Sismondi, Jean Charles Léonard Simonde de. *Recherches sur les constitutions des peuples libres*. Ed. with an introduction by Marco Minerbi. Geneva: Droz, 1965.

Sked, Alan. *Metternich and Austria: An Evaluation*. Basingstoke: Palgrave Macmillan, 2008.

Sked, Alan. *Radetzky: Imperial Victor and Military Genius*. London: I. B. Tauris, 2011.

Skinner, Quentin. *Foundations of Modern Political Thought*. 2 vols. Cambridge: Cambridge University Press, 1978.

Smith, Denis. *The Prisoners of Cabrera: Napoleon's Forgotten Soldiers, 1809–1814*. London: Four Walls Eight Windows, 2001.

Smith, Digby. *1813: Leipzig: Napoleon and the Battle of the Nations*. London: Greenhill Books, 2001.

Smith, Jay M., 'No More Language Games: Words, Beliefs, and Political Culture in Early Modern France', *American Historical Review*, 102 (1997): 1413–40.

Soboul, Albert. 'De la Révolution à l'Empire en France: souveraineté populaire et gouvernement autoritaire (1789–1804)', *Recueils de la Société Jean Bodin*, 26 (1965): 9–46.

Soboul, Albert, 'Le héro et l'histoire', *Annales historiques de la Révolution française*, 42 (1970): 1–7.

Sokolov, Oleg, 'La campagne de Russie', *Napoleon Ier*, 10 (September–October 2001): 42–51.

Solignac, Armand de. *La Bérézina. Souvenirs d'un soldat de la Grande Armée.* Limoges: Eugène Ardent, 1881.

Soltyk, Roman. *Napoleon en 1812: souvenirs du général Soltyk.* Paris: Le Livre chez Vous, 2006.

Sorel, Albert. *L'Europe et la Révolution française.* 9 vols. Paris: E. Plon, Nourrit, 1885–1991.

Sorel, Patricia, 'La campagne de Russie dans la presse quotidienne française et l'almanach du *Messager Boiteux*', in Hans-Jürgen Lüsebrink and Jean-Yves Mollier (eds), *Presse et événement: journaux, gazettes, almanachs (XVIIIe–XIXe siècles)* (Bern, Berlin and Brussels: Peter Lang, 2000), pp. 149–67.

Sorokine, Dimitri. *Napoléon dans la littérature russe.* Paris: Publications orientalistes de France, 1974.

Soubeyroux, Jacques. *Paupérisme et rapports sociaux à Madrid au XVIIIe siècle.* 2 vols. Paris: H. Champion, 1978.

*Souvenirs du général baron Teste.* Paris: Teissèdre, 1999.

Spang, Rebecca L. *The Invention of the Restaurant: Paris and Modern Gastronomic Culture.* Cambridge, Mass.: Harvard University Press, 2000.

Sparrow, Elizabeth, 'The Alien Office, 1792–1806', *Historical Journal*, 33:2 (1990): 361–84.

Sparrow, Elizabeth. *Secret Service: British Agents in France, 1792–1815.* Woodbridge: Boydell Press, 1999.

*Spirit of the Public Journals for 1805.* London: James Ridgeway, 1806.

Spring, Laurence (ed.). *An Englishman in the Russian Army, 1807: The Journal of Colonel James Bathurst during the East Prussia Campaign, 1807.* Knaphill: Spring Offensive, 2000.

Staël, Germaine de. *Considérations sur les principaux événements de la Révolution française.* 2 vols. Paris: Leclerc, 1818.

Staël, Germaine de. *Attila. Le pardon de Napoléon Buonaparte, et le caractère de ce grand homme.* Paris: n.p., n.d.

Staël-Holstein, Germaine de. *Dix années d'exil.* Paris: Plon-Nourrit, 1904.

Stählin, Friedrich. *Napoleons Glanz und Fall im deutschen Urteil: Wandlungen des deutschen Napoleonbildes.* Brunswick: Georg Westermann Verlag, 1952.

Stamm-Kuhlmann, Thomas. *König in Preußens großer Zeit: Friedrich Wilhelm III. der Melancholiker auf dem Thron.* Berlin: Siedler, 1992.

Stanhope, Philip Henry, fifth Earl of. *The Life of the Right Honourable William Pitt.* 4 vols. London: J. Murray, 1861–2.

Stanhope, Philip Henry. *Notes of Conversations with the Duke of Wellington, 1831–1851.* London: J. Murray, 1889.

Stanley, Edward. *Before and after Waterloo: Letters from Edward Stanley, Sometime bishop of Norwich (1802, 1814, 1816).* London: Jane H. Adeane and Maud Grenfell, 1907.

*Statues, bustes, bas reliefs, bronzes et autres antiquités, peintures, dessins et objets curieux, conquis par la Grande Armée, dans les années 1806, 1807.* Paris: Dubray 1807.

Staum, Martin S. *Cabanis: Enlightenment and Medical Philosophy in the French Revolution.* Princeton: Princeton University Press, 1980.

Staum, Martin S., 'The Class of Moral and Political Sciences, 1795–1803', *French Historical Studies*, 11:3 (1980): 371–97.

Staum, Martin S. *Minerva's Message: Stabilizing the French Revolution.* Montreal: McGill-Queen's University Press, 1996.

Stendhal. *Correspondance de Stendal: 1800–1842.* 3 vols. Paris: C. Bosse, 1908.

Stendhal. *Oeuvres intimes.* 2 vols. Paris: Gallimard, 1981–2.

Stevenson, John, 'Food Riots in England', in Quinault and Stevenson (eds), *Popular Protest and Public Order*, pp. 33–74.

Stevenson, John, 'Popular Radicalism and Popular Protest 1789–1815', in Dickinson (ed.), *Britain and the French Revolution*, pp. 61–82.

Stickler, Matthias, 'Erfurt als Wende – Bayern und Württemberg und das Scheitern der Pläne Napoleons I. für einen Ausbau der Rheinbundverfassung', in Benl (ed.), *Der Erfurter Fürstenkongreß*, pp. 265–300.

Stiegler, Gaston (ed.). *Le maréchal Oudinot, duc de Reggio: d'après les souvenirs inédits de la maréchale*. Paris: E. Plon, Nourrit, 1894.

Stroud, Patricia Tyson. *The Emperor of Nature: Charles-Lucien Bonaparte and his World*. Philadelphia: University of Pennsylvania Press, 2000.

Stryienski, Casimir (ed.). *Memoirs of the Countess Potocka*. Trans. Lionel Strachey. London: Grant Richards, 1901.

Suckow, Karl Friedrich Emil von. *D'Iéna à Moscow: fragments de ma vie, par le colonel Suckow de l'armée wurtembergeoise*. Trans. commandant Veling. Paris: Plon-Nourrit, 1901.

Sudre, Alfred. *Petites causes et grands effets. Le secret de 1812*. Paris: Spectateur Militaire, 1887.

Surrugues, (abbé) Adrien. *Lettres sur l'incendie de Moscou*. Paris: Plancher, 1823.

Sutherland, Christine. *Marie Walewska: Napoleon's Great Love*. London: Weidenfeld & Nicolson, 1979.

Sweet, Paul R. *Friedrich von Gentz: Defender of the Old Order*. Madison: University of Wisconsin Press, 1941.

Sweet, Paul R. *Wilhelm von Humboldt: A Biography*. 2 vols. Columbus: Ohio State University Press, 1978–80.

Sydenham, Michael J., 'The Crime of 3 Nivôse (24 December 1800)', in J. F. Bosher (ed.), *French Government and Society, 1500–1850* (London: Athlone Press, 1973), pp. 295–320.

Sydow, Anna von (ed.). *Wilhelm und Caroline von Humboldt in ihren Briefen*. 7 vols. Berlin: Mittler, 1906–16.

Szittya, Emil. *Selbstmörder: ein Beitrag zur Kulturgeschichte aller Zeiten und Völker*. Vienna: Löcker, 1985.

Taillandier, Alphonse-Honoré. *Documents biographiques sur P.-C.-F. Daunou*. Paris: Firmin-Didot, 1841.

Takeda, Junko Thérèse. *Between Crown and Commerce: Marseille and the Early Modern Mediterranean*. Baltimore: Johns Hopkins University Press, 2011.

Talleyrand-Périgord, Charles-Maurice de. *Mémoires du prince de Talleyrand*. 5 vols. Paris: Calmann-Lévy, 1891–2.

Talty, Stephan. *The Illustrious Dead: The Terrifying Story of How Typhus Killed Napoleon's Greatest Army*. New York: Crown Publishers, 2009.

Tarbell, Ida. *Napoleon's Addresses: Selections from the Proclamations, Speeches and Correspondence of Napoleon Bonaparte*. Boston: Joseph Knight, 1897.

Tascher, Maurice de. *Journal de campagne, 1806–1813*. Paris: Giovanangeli, 2008.

Tatistcheff, Serge (ed.). *Alexandre Ier et Napoléon, d'après leur correspondance inedite, 1801–1812*. Paris: Perrin, 1891.

Telesko, Werner. *Napoleon Bonaparte: der 'Moderne Held' und die bildende Kunst, 1799–1815*. Vienna: Böhlau, 1998.

Telp, Claus. *The Evolution of the Operational Art, 1740–1813: From Frederick the Great to Napoleon*. London: Frank Cass, 2005.

*Terminer la Révolution?: actes du colloque . . . 4 et 5 décembre 2001*. Paris: Economica, 2003.

Tersen, Emile. *Napoléon*. Paris: Le Club français du livre, 1959.

Theewen, Eckhard Maria. *Napoléons Anteil am Code civil*. Berlin: Duncker und Humbolt, 1991.

Thiard, Auxonne-Marie-Théodose de. *Souvenirs diplomatiques et militaires*. Paris: Napoléon Ier éditions, 2007.

Thibaudeau, Antoine-Clair. *Mémoires sur le Consulat, 1799 à 1804*. Paris: Ponthieu, 1827.

Thibaudeau, Antoine-Clair. *Le Consulat et l'Empire, ou Histoire de la France et Napoléon Bonaparte, de 1799 à 1815*. 10 vols. Paris: J. Renouard, 1834–5.

Thibaudeau, Antoine-Clair. *Mémoires de A.-C. Thibaudeau, 1799–1815*. Paris: Plon-Nourrit, 1913.

Thiébaut de Berneaud, Arsenne. *Voyage à l'isle d'Elbe; suivi d'une notice sur les autres isles de la mer Tyrrhénienne*. Paris: D. Colas, 1808.

Thiébault, Paul Charles François Adrien Henri Dieudonné, baron. *Journal des opérations militaires du siège et du blocus de Gênes*. Paris: Magimel, an IX.

Thiébault, Paul Charles François Adrien Henri Dieudonné, baron. *Mémoires du général Bon Thiébault*. 5 vols. Paris: E. Plon, Nourrit, 1893–5.

Thierry, Augustin. *Conspirateurs et gens de police: le complot des libelles (1802)*. Paris: Armand Colin, 1903.

Thiers, Adolphe. *Histoire du Consulat et de l'Empire*. 20 vols. Paris: Paulin, 1845–62.

Thirion, Auguste. *Souvenirs militaires*. Paris: Librairie des Deux Empires, 1998.

Thiry, Jean. *Les Cent Jours*. Paris: Berger-Levrault, 1943.

Thiry, Jean. *Le Sénat de Napoléon: 1800–1814*. Paris: Berger-Levrault, 1949.

Thiry, Jean. *La machine infernale*. Paris: Berger-Levrault, 1952.

Thiry, Jean. *Le Concordat et le Consulat à vie: mars 1801–juillet 1802*. Paris: Berger-Levrault, 1956.

Thiry, Jean. *L'avènement de Napoléon*. Paris: Berger-Levrault, 1959.

Thiry, Jean. *Eylau, Friedland, Tilsit*. Paris: Berger-Levrault, 1964.

Thiry, Jean. *La Guerre d'Espagne*. Paris: Berger-Levrault, 1965.

Thiry, Jean. *Wagram*. Paris: Berger-Levrault, 1966.

Thomas, Jean-Pierre. *Bertrand Barère: la voix de la Révolution*. Paris: Editions Desjonquères, 1989.

Thomas, Louis J., 'Montpellier et le roi de Rome', *Revue des études napoléoniennes*, 3 (1913): 346–66.

Thompson, J. M., 'Napoleon's Journey to Elba in 1814. Part I. By Land', *American Historical Review*, 55 (1949): 1–21.

Thompson, J. M., 'Napoleon's Journey to Elba in 1814. Part II. By Sea', *American Historical Review*, 55 (1950): 301–20.

Thompson, J. M. *Napoleon Bonaparte: His Rise and Fall*. Oxford: Basil Blackwell, 1951.

Thomson, David Whittet, 'Robert Fulton and the French Invasion of England', *Military Affairs*, 18 (1954): 57–63.

Thoral, Marie-Cécile, 'The Limits of Napoleonic Centralization: Notables and Local Government in the Department of the Isère from the Consulate to the Beginning of the July Monarchy', *French History*, 19 (2005): 463–81.

Thoral, Marie-Cécile. *From Valmy to Waterloo: France at War, 1792–1815*. Basingstoke: Palgrave Macmillan, 2011.

Thornton, Michael John. *Napoleon after Waterloo: England and the St. Helena Decision*. Stanford, Calif.: Stanford University Press, 1968.

Thugut, Johann Amadeus Franz de Paula, Bon von. *Vertrauliche Briefe des Freiherrn von Thugut, österr. Ministers des Äussern. Beiträge zur Beurtheilung der politischen Verhältnisse Europa's in den Jahren 1792–1801*. 2 vols. Vienna: W. Braumüller, 1872.

Timme, Friedrich, 'Die geheime Mission des Flügeladjutanten von Wrangel (1812)', *Forschungen zur brandenburgischen und preußischen Geschichte*, 21 (1908): 199–213.

Titus, Silas [pseudonym for Colonel William Allen]. *Le Code des tyrannicides, adressé à tous les peuples opprimés*. Lyons: Lefranc, 1800.

Tombs, Robert and Isabelle. *That Sweet Enemy: The French and the British from the Sun King to the Present*. London: William Heinemann, 2006.

Tone, John Lawrence. *The Fatal Knot: The Guerrilla War in Navarre and the Defeat of Napoleon in Spain*. Chapel Hill: University of North Carolina Press, 1994.

Tone, John Lawrence, 'Spanish Women in the Resistance to Napoleon', in Victoria Lorée Enders and Pamela Beth (eds), *Constructing Spanish Womanhood: Female Identity in Modern Spain* (Albany, NY, 1999), pp. 259–82.

Tone, John Lawrence, 'A Dangerous Amazon: Agustina Zaragoza and the Spanish Revolutionary War, 1808–1814', *European History Quarterly*, 37 (2007): 548–61.

Tønneson, Kare D., 'Les Fédérés de Paris pendant les Cent Jours', *Annales historiques de la Révolution française*, 249 (1982): 393–415.

Töppel, Roman. *Die Sachsen und Napoleon: ein Stimmungsbild 1806–1813*. Cologne: Böhlau, 2008.

Torrance, Marie-Christiane, 'Les témoignages des mémorialistes russes', *Revue de l'Institut Napoléon*, 135 (1979): 3–30.

Torrance, Marie-Christiane, 'Some Russian Attitudes to France in the Period of the Napoleonic Wars as Revealed by Russian Memoirs (1807–14)', *Proceedings of the Royal Irish Academy*, 86c (1986): 289–303.

Tour du Pin, marquise de la. *Journal d'une femme de cinquante ans: 1778–1815*. 2 vols. Paris: M. Imhaus and R. Chapelot, 1913.

Tournès, René. *La campagne de printemps en 1813: Lützen, étude d'une manoeuvre napoléonienne*. Paris, Limoges and Nancy: H. Charles-Lavauzelle, 1931.

Tourtier-Bonazzi, Chantal de. *Lettres d'amour à Joséphine*. Paris: Fayard, 1981.

Traer, James F. *Marriage and the Family in Eighteenth-Century France*. Ithaca: Cornell University Press, 1980.

Tratchevsky, Alexandre, 'L'Espagne à l'époque de la Révolution française', *Revue historique*, 31 (1886): 1–55.

Trefcon, Toussaint-Jean. *Carnets de campagne du colonel Trefcon, 1793–1815*. Paris: Edmond Dubois, 1914.

Trensky, Paul, 'The Year 1812 in Russian Poetry', *Slavic and East European Journal*, 10 (1966): 283–302.

Trinkle, Dennis A. *The Napoleonic Press: The Public Sphere and Oppositionary Journalism*. Lewiston: Edwin Mellen Press, 2002.

Triolaire, Cyril, 'Célébrer Napoléon après la République: les héritages commémoratifs révolutionnaire au crible de la fête napoléonienne', *Annales historiques de la Révolution française*, 346 (2006): 75–96.

Tripier Le Franc, J. *Histoire de la vie et de la mort du baron Gros*. Paris: Jules Martin, 1880.

Trotter, John Bernard. *Memoirs of the latter years of the Right Honourable Charles James Fox*. London: Richard Phillips, 1811.

Troussier, Sophie and Anthelme. *La Chevauchée héroïque du retour de l'île d'Elbe*. Lausanne: Editions du Grand chêne, 1964.

Tulard, Jean, 'La notion de tyrannicide et les complots sous le Consulat', *Revue de l'Institut Napoléon*, 111 (1969): 133–9.

Tulard, Jean, 'Problèmes sociaux de la France napoléonienne', *Annales historiques de la Révolution française*, 199 (1970): 135–60.

Tulard, Jean. *Le mythe de Napoléon*. Paris: Armand Colin, 1971.

Tulard, Jean. *Napoléon ou le mythe du sauveur*. Paris: Fayard, 1977.

Tulard, Jean. *La vie quotidienne des Français sous Napoléon*. Paris: Hachette, 1978.

Tulard, Jean. *Le Grand Empire, 1804–1815*. Paris: Albin Michel, 1982.

Tulard, Jean. *Nouvelle histoire de Paris: le Consulat et l'Empire: 1800–1815*. Paris: Bibliothèque historique de la ville de Paris, 1983.

Tulard, Jean, 'Napoléon et la Confédération du Rhin', in Eberhard Weis and Elisabeth Müller-Luckner (eds), *Reformen im rheinbündischen Deutschland* (Munich: R. Oldenbourg, 1984), pp. 1–4.

Tulard, Jean, 'Les responsabilités françaises dans la Guerre d'Espagne', in *Les Espagnols et Napoléon*, pp. 1–5.

Tulard, Jean, 'La Cour de Napoléon Ier', in Werner (ed.), *Hof, Kultur und Politik im 19. Jahrhundert*, pp. 55–9.

Tulard, Jean. *Joseph Fiévée, conseiller secret de Napoléon*. Paris: Fayard, 1985.

Tulard, Jean (ed.). *Dictionnaire Napoléon*. Paris: Fayard, 1989.

Tulard, Jean (ed.). *L'Europe au temps de Napoléon*. Le Coteau: Horvath, 1989.

Tulard, Jean. *Napoléon II*. Paris: Fayard, 1992.

Tulard, Jean, 'Les attentats contre Napoléon', *Revue du Souvenir napoléonien*, 391 (1993): 2–19.

Tulard, Jean. *Napoléon, jeudi 12 octobre 1809: le jour où Napoléon faillit être assassiné*. Paris: J.-C. Lattès, 1993.

Tulard, Jean, 'Les épurations en 1814 et 1815', *Revue du Souvenir napoléonien*, 396 (1994): 5–21.

Tulard, Jean, 'Les empires napoléoniens', in Jean Tulard (ed.), *Les empires occidentaux de Rome à Berlin* (Paris: Presses Universitaires de France, 1997), pp. 363–82.

Tulard, Jean. *Joseph Fouché*. Paris: Fayard, 1998.

Tulard, Jean. *Murat*. Paris: Fayard, 1999.

Tulard, Jean (ed.). *Napoléon Bonaparte: oeuvres littéraires et écrits militaires*. 3 vols. Paris: Bibliothèque des Introuvables, 2001.

Tulard, Jean. *La province au temps de Napoléon*. Paris: SPM, 2003.

Tulard, Jean. *Le sacre de l'empereur Napoléon: histoire et légende*. Paris: Fayard, 2004.

Tulard, Jean, 'Le rapprochement de Fouché et de Talleyrand en 1808', in Pontet, *Napoléon, Bayonne et l'Espagne*, pp. 355–7.

Tulard, Jean and Garros, Louis. *Itinéraire de Napoléon au jour le jour, 1769–1821*. Paris: Talandier, 1992.

Tullner, Mathias, 'Die preußische Niederlage bei Jena und Auerstedt (Hassenhausen) und die Kapitulation von Magedeburg', in Tullner and Möbius (eds), *1806*, pp. 130–9.

Tullner, Mathias and Möbius, Sascha (eds). *1806: Jena, Auerstadt und die Kapitulation von Magdeburg: Schande oder Chance?* Halle: Landesheimatbund Sachsen-Anhalt, 2007.

Tupinier, Jean-Marguerite. *Mémoires du baron Tupinier: directeur des ports et arsenaux, 1779–1850*. Paris: Editions Desjonquères, 1994.

Turchetti, Mario (ed.). *La Suisse de la médiation dans l'Europe napoléonienne (1803–1814)*. Fribourg: Academic Press Fribourg, 2005.

Turcot, Laurent, 'Entre promenades et jardins publics: les loisirs parisiens et londoniens au XVIIIe siècle', *Revue belge de philologie et d'histoire/Belgisch tijdschrift voor filologie en geschiedenis*, 87 (2009): 645–63.

Turnbull, Patrick. *Napoleon's Second Empress*. London: Michael Joseph, 1971.

Turner, Michael J. *Pitt the Younger: A Life*. London: Hambledon & London, 2003.

Turquan, Joseph. *L'impératrice Joséphine, d'après les témoignages des contemporains*. Paris: Tallandier, 1896.

Tyrbas de Chamberet, Joseph. *Mémoires d'un médecin militaire: aux XVIIIe et XIXe siècles*. Paris: Christian, 2001.

Ubersfeld, Annie and Rosa, Guy (eds). *Victor Hugo raconté par Adèle Hugo*. Paris: Plon, 1985.

Uexküll, Detlev von (ed.). *Arms and the Woman: The Diaries of Baron Boris Uxkull, 1812–1819*. Trans. Joel Carmichael. London: Secker & Warburg, 1966.

Uffindell, Andrew. *Napoleon 1814: The Defence of France*. Barnsley: Pen & Sword, 2009.

Ulbrich, Claudia, 'Die französische Geheimpolizei auf dem Erfurter Fürstenkongreß', in Benl (ed.), *Der Erfurter Fürstenkongreß*, pp. 301–20.

Ullrichová, Maria (ed.). *Clemens Metternich, Wilhelmine von Sagan: ein Briefwechsel, 1813–1815*. Graz: Hermann Böhlaus, 1966.

Underwood, Thomas Richard. *A Narrative of Memorable Events in Paris, Preceeding the Capitulation, and During the Occupancy of that City by the Allied Armies, in the Year 1814*. London: Longman, 1828.

Unger, Harlow Giles. *Lafayette*. Hoboken, NJ: John Wiley, 2002.

Ussher, Thomas. *Napoleon's last voyages, being the diaries of Admiral Sir Thomas Ussher . . . on board the 'Undaunted', and John R. Glover . . . on board the 'Northumberland'*. 2nd edn, London: T. Fisher Unwin, 1906.

V.D.M., 'Recherche et observations générales sur les prisonniers de guerres russes', *Revue philosophique, littéraire et politique* (1 April 1807): 6–13.

Valla, Jean-Claude. *La nostalgie de l'Empire: une relecture de l'histoire napoléonienne*. Paris: Ed. de la Librairie nationale, 2004.

Van Hogendorp, Dirk. *Mémoires du général Dirk van Hogendorp, comte de l'Empire*. The Hague: M. Nijhoff, 1887.

Vandal, Albert. *Napoléon et Alexandre Ier. L'alliance russe sous le premier empire*. 3 vols. Paris: E. Plon, Nourrit, 1893–6.

Vandal, Albert. *L'avènement de Bonaparte*. 2 vols. Paris: Plon-Nourrit, 1903–7.

Vane, Charles (ed.). *Memoirs and Correspondence of Viscount Castlereagh, Second Marquess of Londonderry*. 12 vols. London: H. Colburn, 1848–53.

Vane, Charles William (ed.). *Correspondence, Despatches and Other Papers of Viscount Castlereagh*. 8 vols. London: J. Murray, 1851–3.

Vann, James Allen, 'Habsburg Policy and the Austrian War of 1809', *Central European History*, 7:4 (1974): 291–310.

Vanssay, Auguste de. *Fragments de mémoires inédits, écrits en 1817 sous le titre de Souvenirs militaires d'un officier de Dragons pendant les campagnes de la Grande Armée des années 1804 à 1811*. Mortagne: Dauplay frères, 1864.

Van Vlijmen, Bernard Reinier Frans. *Vers la Bérésina (1812), d'après des documents nouveau*. Paris: Plon-Nourrit, 1908.

Vaucorbeil, Robert de, 'Mémoires inédits d'Alexandre de Cheron sur la campagne de Russie', *Revue de l'Institut Napoléon*, 140 (1983): 27–57.

Vaudoncourt, Frédéric Guillaume de. *Quinze années d'un proscrit*. Paris: Dufey, 1835.

Vauthier, Gabriel, 'L'épuration de la magistrature en 1808', *Revue des études napoléoniennes*, 15 (1919): 218–23.

Vaultier, Roger, 'La chirurgie militaire sous le Premier Empire', *Chroniques* (28 March 1951): 414–16.

Vernon, George Venables. *Sketch of a Conversation with Napoleon at Elba*. London: Whittingham & Wilkins, 1863–4.

Véron, Louis. *Mémoires d'un bourgeois de Paris*. Paris: Librairie nouvelle, 1856.

Verriez, L. *Le Néron corse*. Gand: Chez Tous les Marchands de Nouveautés, 1815.

Vidal, Florence. *Elisa Bonaparte: soeur de Napoléon Ier*. Paris: Pygmalion, 2004.

Vidal, Florence. *Caroline Bonaparte: soeur de Napoléon Ier*. Paris: Pygmalion, 2006.

Vidalenc, Jean. *Le département de l'Eure sous la monarchie constitutionnelle, 1814–1848*. Paris: M. Rivière, 1952.

Vidalenc, Jean. *Les émigrés français: 1789–1825*. Caen: Association des publications de la Faculté des lettres et sciences humaines de l'Université de Caen, 1963.

Vidalenc, Jean, 'Note sur les épurations de 1814 et de 1815', in *Les Epurations administratives: XIXe et XXe siècles* (Geneva: Droz, 1977), pp. 63–8.

*Vie privée de Georges Cadoudal, son caractère, ses crimes*. Paris: Impr. de Clermont, 1804.

Vieillot, Rodolphe. *Souvenirs d'un prisonnier en Russie pendant les années 1812–1813–1814*. Luneray: Bertout, 1996.

Vigier, Comte. *Davout, maréchal d'empire, duc d'Auerstaedt, prince d'Eckmühl (1770–1823)*. 2 vols. Paris: Ollendorff, 1898.

Villefort, François-Joseph d'Ysarn. *Relation du séjour des Français à Moscou et l'incendie de cette ville en 1812, par un habitant de Moscou*. Brussels: F. J. Olivier, 1871.

Villefosse, Louis de and Bouissounouse, Janine. *L'opposition à Napoléon*. Paris: Flammarion, 1969.

Villemain, Abel-François. *Souvenirs contemporains d'histoire et de littérature*. 2 vols. Paris: Didier, 1854–5.

Villeneuve de Janti, Pierre. *Bonaparte et le Code civil*. Paris: F. Loviton, 1934.

Villepin, Dominique de. *La chute ou l'Empire de la solitude, 1807–1814*. Paris: Perrin, 2008.

Vincent-Buffault, Anne. *Histoire des larmes, XVIIIe–XIXe siècles*. Paris: Payot, 2001.

Vionnet de Maringoné, Louis-Joseph. *Souvenirs d'un ex-commandant des grenadiers de la vieille-garde. Fragments des mémoires inédits du lieutenant-général L.-J. Vionnet de Maringoné*. Paris: Dubois, 1899.

*Vneshniaia Politika Rossii XIX I nachala XX veka*. Series I, 1801–15, 8 vols. Moscow: Politizdat, 1960–72.

Vovelle, Michel, 'La Marseillaise: War or Peace', in Nora (ed.), *Realms of Memory*, iii. pp. 29–74.

Vovelle, Michel. *La Révolution française: 1789–1799*. Paris: Armand Colin, 1998.

Vulliaud, Paul. *La fin du monde*. Paris: Bussière, 1952.

Wagner, Karl, 'Die *Wiener Zeitungen* und Zeitschriften der Jahre 1808 und 1809', *Archiv für Österreichische Geschichte*, 104 (1915): 197–400.

Wairy, Louis-Constant [known as Constant]. *Mémoires de Constant, premier valet de l'empereur, sur la vie privée de Napoléon, sa famille et sa cour*. 6 vols. Paris: Ladvocat, 1830.

Waldbourg, Friedrich Ludwig Truchsess, Graf von. *Nouvelle relation de l'itinéraire de Napoléon, de Fontainebleau à l'Île d'Elbe*. Paris: C.-L.-F. Panckoucke, 1815.

Waller, Margaret, 'The Emperor's New Clothes: Display, Cover-Up and Exposure in Modern Masculinity', in Timothy Reeser and Lewis Seifert (eds), *Entre hommes: French and Francophone Masculinities in Literature and Culture* (Newark: University of Delaware Press, 2008), pp. 115–42.

Walsh, Henry Horace. *The Concordat of 1801: A Study of the Problem of Nationalism in the Relations of Church and State*. New York: Columbia University Press, 1933.

Walter, Gero. *Der Zusammenbruch des heilgen Römischen Reiches deutscher Nation und die Problematik seiner Restauration in den Jahren 1814–15*. Heidelberg: C. F. Müller, 1980.

Walter, Jakob. *The Diary of a Napoleonic Foot Soldier*. Moreton-in-Marsh: Windrush Press, 1997.

Ward, A. W. and Gooch, G. P. *The Cambridge History of British Foreign Policy, 1783–1919*. 3 vols. Cambridge: Cambridge University Press, 1922–3.

Ward, A. W., Prothero, G. W. and Leathes, Stanley (eds). *The Cambridge Modern History*. 13 vols. Cambridge: Cambridge University Press, 1902–11.

Waresquiel, Emmanuel de. *Talleyrand: le prince immobile*. Paris: Fayard, 2003.

Waresquiel, Emmanuel de (ed.). *Lettres d'un lion: correspondance inédite du général Mouton, comte de Lobau (1812–1815)*. Paris: Nouveau Monde éditions, 2005.

Waresquiel, Emmanuel de. *Les Cents Jours: la tentation de l'impossible, mars–juillet 1815*. Paris: Fayard, 2008.

Waresquiel, Emmanuel de. 'Joseph Fouché et la question de l'amnistie des émigrés (1799–1802)', *Annales historiques de la Révolution française*, 372 (2013): 105–20.

Warren, Dawson. *The Journal of a British Chaplain in Paris during the Peace Negociations of 1801–2*. London: Chapman & Hall, 1913.

Watson, J. R. *Romanticism and War: A Study of British Romantic Period Writers and the Napoleonic Wars*. Basingstoke: Palgrave Macmillan, 2003.

Webster, Charles (ed.). *British Diplomacy, 1813–1815: Select Documents Dealing with the Reconstruction of Europe*. London: G. Bell, 1921.

Webster, Charles. *The Foreign Policy of Castlereagh, 1812–1815: Britain and the Reconstruction of Europe*. 2 vols. London: G. Bell, 1931.

Weil, Georges, 'L'idée républicaine en France pendant la Restauration', *Revue d'histoire moderne*, 2 (1927): 321–48.

Weil, Maurice Henri (ed.). *La campagne de 1814 d'après les documents des archives impériales et royales de la guerre à Vienne*. 4 vols. Paris: Baudoin, 1891–5.

Weil, Maurice Henri (ed.). *Les dessous du Congrès de Vienne: d'après les documents originaux des archives du Ministère impérial et royal de l'intérieur à Vienne*. 2 vols. Paris: Payot, 1917.

Weil, Patrick. *Qu'est-ce qu'un Français?: histoire de la nationalité française depuis la Révolution*. Paris: Grasset, 2002.

Wellington, Arthur Wellesley, Duke of. *The Dispatches of Field Marshal the Duke of Wellington During his Various Campaigns in India, Denmark, Portugal, Spain, the Low Countries and France, from 1799 to 1818*. 13 vols. London: J. Murray, 1837–9.

Wellington, Arthur Wellesley, Duke of. *Supplementary Despatches and Memoranda of Field Marshal Arthur Duke of Wellington*. 15 vols. London: J. Murray, 1858–72.

Welschinger, Henri. *La censure sous le premier empire, avec documents inédits*. Paris: Charavay frères, 1882.

Welschinger, Henri. *Le Divorce de Napoléon*. Paris: E. Plon, Nourrit, 1889.

Welschinger, Henri. *L'Europe et l'exécution du duc d'Enghien*. Amiens: Delattre-Lenoël, 1890.

Welschinger, Henri. *Le pape et l'empereur, 1804–1815*. Paris: Plon-Nourrit, 1905.

Welschinger, Henri. *Le duc d'Enghien, 1772–1804: l'enlèvement d'Ettenheim et l'exécution de Vincennes*. Paris: Plon-Nourrit, 1913.

Welvert, Eugène (ed.). *Napoléon et la police sous la première Restauration d'après les rapports du comte Beugnot au roi Louis XVIII*. Paris: R. Roger et F. Chernoviz, n.d.

Werkmeister, Lucyle. *The London Daily Press, 1772–1792*. Lincoln: University of Nebraska, 1963.

Werner, Karl Ferdinand (ed.). *Hof, Kultur und Politik im 19. Jahrhundert*. Bonn: Ludwig Röhrscheid Verlag, 1985.

Wertheimer, Eduard. *Die Heirat der Erzherzogin Marie Louise mit Napoleon I: nach ungedruckten Quellen*. Vienna: C. Gerold, 1882.

Wertheimer, Eduard, 'Zur Geschichte Wiens im Jahre 1809. (Ein Beitrag zur Geschichte des Krieges von 1809.)', *Archiv für Österreichische Geschichte*, 74 (1889): 161–202.

Wertheimer, Eduard, 'Wien und das Kriegsjahr 1813', *Archiv für Österreichische Geschichte*, 79 (1893): 355–400.

Wertheimer, Edward de. *The Duke of Reichstadt*. London: John Lane, 1905.

Wheeler, H. F. B. and Broadley, A. M. *Napoleon and the Invasion of England: The Story of the Great Terror*. Stroud: Nonesuch, 2007, orig. 1908.

Wickwire, Franklin and Wickwire, Mary. *Cornwallis: The Imperial Years*. Chapel Hill: University of North Carolina Press, 1980.

Wiesse de Marmont, Auguste-Frédéric-Louis. *Mémoires du maréchal Marmont, duc de Raguse, de 1792 à 1841*. 9 vols. Paris: Perrotin, 1856–7.

Williams, Helen Maria. *A Narrative of the Events which Have Taken Place in France From the Landing of Napoleon Bonaparte on the First of March, 1815, Till the Restoration of Louis XVIII*. Cleveland: Burrows Brothers, 1815.

Williamson, Elaine, 'A *Vraie-fausse* Statue of William the Conqueror: Representation and Misrepresentation of Anglo-French History', *Franco-British Studies*, 19 (1995): 21–5.

Williamson, Elaine, 'Denon, la presse et la propagande impériale', in Gallo (ed.), *Les vies de Dominique-Vivant Denon* (Paris, 2001), i. pp. 151–73.

Wilson, Peter H., 'Bolstering the Prestige of the Habsburgs: The End of the Holy Roman Empire in 1806', *International History Review*, 28 (2006): 709–36.

Wilson, Peter H., 'The Meaning of Empire in Central Europe around 1800', in Forrest and Wilson (eds), *The Bee and the Eagle*, pp. 22–41.

Wilson, Sir Robert. *Brief Remarks on the Character and Composition of the Russian Army and a Sketch of the Campaigns in Poland in the Years 1806 and 1807*. London: T. Egerton, 1810.

Wilson, Sir Robert. *Narrative of Events during the Invasion of Russia by Napoleon Bonaparte, and the Retreat of the French Army 1812*. London: J. Murray, 1860.

Wilson, Sir Robert. *Private Diary of Travels, Personal Services, and Public Events, During Mission and Employment with the European Armies in the Campaigns of 1812, 1813, 1814, from the Invasion of Russia to the Capture of Paris*. 2 vols. London: J. Murray, 1861.

Wilson, Robert Thomas. *History of the British Expedition to Egypt*. London: T. Egerton, 1802.

Windham, William. *The Windham Papers: The Life and Correspondence of the Rt. Hon. William Windham, 1750–1810*, 2 vols. London: H. Jenkins, 1913.

Winock, Michel. *Madame de Staël*. Paris: Fayard, 2010.

Wisner, David A. *The Cult of the Legislator in France 1750–1830: A Study in the Political Theology of the French Enlightenment*. Oxford: Voltaire Foundation, 1997.

Wohlwill, Adolf, 'Aktenstücke zur Rumboldschen Angelegenheit', *Zeitschrift des Vereins für Hamburgische Geschichte*, 7 (1881): 387–400.

Wohlwill, Adolf, 'Fernere Aktenstücke zur Rumboldschen Angelegenheit', *Zeitschrift des Vereins für Hamburgische Geschichte*, 8 (1886): 192–207.

Woloch, Isser, 'Napoleonic Conscription: State Power and Civil Society', *Past & Present*, 111 (1986): 101–29.

Woloch, Isser. *The New Regime: Transformations of the French Civic Order, 1789–1820s*. New York: W. W. Norton, 1994.

Woloch, Isser. *Napoleon and his Collaborators: The Making of a Dictatorship*. New York: W. W. Norton, 2001.

Woloch, Isser, 'From Consulate to Empire: Impetus and Resistance', in Baehr and Ritcher (eds), *Dictatorship in History and Theory*, pp. 29–52.

Wood, Dennis Michael. *Benjamin Constant: A Biography*. London and New York: Routledge, 1993.

Woodberry, George. *Journal du lieutenant Woodberry, campagnes de Portugal et d'Espagne, de France, de Belgique et de France, 1813–1815*. Trans. Georges Hélie. Paris: E. Plon, Nourrit, 1896.

Woolf, Stuart, 'French Civilization and Ethnicity in the Napoleonic Empire', *Past & Present*, 124 (1989): 96–120.

Woolf, Stuart, 'The Construction of a European World-View in the Revolutionary-Napoleonic Years', *Past & Present*, 137 (1992): 72–101.

Woolf, Stuart. *Napoleon's Integration of Europe*. London: Routledge, 1991.

Wortman, Richard S. *Scenarios of Power: Myth and Ceremony in Russian Monarchy*. 2 vols. Princeton: Princeton University Press, 1995–2000.

Wrigley, Richard. *The Origins of French Art Criticism: From the Ancien Régime to the Restoration*. Oxford: Clarendon Press, 1993.

Yorke, Henry Redhead. *France in Eighteen Hundred and Two Described in a Series of Contemporary Letters*. London: William Heinemann, 1906.

Young, Norwood. *Napoleon in Exile: Elba*. London: Stanley Paul, 1914.

Załuski, Józef Bonawentura Ignacy. *Les chevau-légers polonais de la Garde (1812–1814): souvenirs*. Paris: Teissèdre, 1997.

Zamoyski, Adam. *1812: Napoleon's Fatal March on Moscow*. London: HarperCollins, 2004.

Zamoyski, Adam. *Rites of Peace: The Fall of Napoleon and the Congress of Vienna*. London: HarperCollins, 2007.

Zanger, Abby. *Scenes from the Marriage of Louis XIV: Nuptial Fictions and the Making of Absolutist Power*. Stanford, Calif.: Stanford University Press, 1997.

Zawadzki, W. H., 'Prince Adam Czartoryski and Napoleonic France, 1801–1805: A Study in Political Attitudes', *Historical Journal*, 18 (1975): 245–77.

Zawadzki, W. H., 'Russia and the Re-opening of the Polish Question, 1801–1804', *International History Review*, 7 (1985): 19–44.

Zawadzki, W. H. *A Man of Honour: Adam Czartoryski as a Statesman of Russia and Poland, 1795–1831*. Oxford: Clarendon Press, 1993.

Zehetbauer, Ernst. *Die Landwehr gegen Napoleon: Österreichs erste Miliz und der Nationalkrieg von 1809*. Vienna: ÖBV & HPT, 1999.

Zerubavel, Eviatar. *The Seven Day Circle: The History and Meaning of the Week*. London: Collier Macmillan, 1985.

Ziegler, Philip. *Addington: A Life of Henry Addington, First Viscount Sidmouth*. London: Collins, 1965.

Zieseniss, Charles-Otto. *Napoléon et la cour impériale*. Paris: Tallandier, 1980.

Zieseniss, Jérôme. *Berthier: frère d'armes de Napoléon*. Paris: P. Belfond, 1985.

Zimmer, Hasko. *Auf dem Altar des Vaterlands: Religion und Patriotismus in der deutschen Kriegslyrik des 19. Jahrhunderts*. Frankfurt: Thesen, 1971.

Zorin, Andrei, '"Star of the East": The Holy Alliance and European Mysticism', *Kritika: Explorations in Russian and Eurasian History*, 4 (2003): 313–42.

# Acknowledgements

For this, as in the previous volume, I have relied heavily on works old and new to develop what I hope is a different and more thorough interpretation of a man who, although written about many times before, has often escaped the biographer's critical gaze. To all those who gave of their time and ideas in the course of writing this book by answering my questions, my sincerest thanks: Thomas Biskup, Kirsty Carpenter, Malcolm Crook, Charles Esdaile, Alan Forrest, Alexander Grab, Jacques Hantraye, Michael J. Hughes, Frederick Kagan, Michael Rapport, Michael Rowe, Michael Sibalis, Margaret Waller and Peter Wilson. To those who took the time to read the manuscript in its entirety, Ed Wright, my friend and colleague Peter Hempenstall, the copyeditor Peter James and proofreader Catherine Best, their collective input has made this a vastly improved work and I thank them all from the bottom of my heart. Anna Simpson at Bloomsbury and Christina Tucker at Yale helped me through the editorial process. My thanks to Michael Fishwick at Bloomsbury for allowing me the luxury to write a book of this length, and to my agent, Bill Hamilton, for his support.

This project has been assisted by the Australian Government through the Australia Council for the Arts, its arts funding and advisory body. It enabled me to spend two months writing a draft of the book in Ledig House in upstate New York in 2010. My thanks to D. W. Gibson for making my stay there a welcome one. Over the years the University of Newcastle has generously assisted me with travel to research in Paris. I would like to thank the university and also my colleagues in the School of Humanities who make working as a teacher and scholar an incredibly rewarding experience, especially (but not only) Lyndall Ryan, Michael Ondaatje, Camilla Russell, Lisa Featherstone, Julie McIntyre and Trisha Pender. The Newcastle University library has provided much needed assistance in sourcing some of the more obscure books for me when I could not get them at the Bibliothèque nationale in Paris. In Paris, my dear friends Cyril and Marie-Noël Malapert, Marie-Françoise Dufief and Laurent Peyron have been an enormous support over the years. Paris would not be the same without them. And to my darling Andrea who has had to endure long absences over the years. You are the best thing that has ever happened to me.

# Index

INDEX

# A NOTE ON THE AUTHOR

Philip Dwyer studied in Perth (Australia), Berlin and Paris, where he was a student of France's pre-eminent Napoleonic scholar, Jean Tulard. He has published widely on the Revolutionary and Napoleonic eras, and is Director of the Centre for the History of Violence at the University of Newcastle, Australia.